THE
PUBLIC GENERAL ACTS
AND GENERAL SYNOD MEASURES
1980

[IN FOUR PARTS]

PART I

(Chapters 1–43)

with

Lists of the Public General Acts,
Local Acts and General Synod Measures and an Index

LONDON
HER MAJESTY'S STATIONERY OFFICE
£105·00 net

H.M.S.O
£55
6.82

ISBN 0 11 840200 5*

c

THIS PUBLICATION
relates to
the Public General Acts
and General Synod Measures
which received the Royal Assent in 1980
in which year ended the TWENTY-EIGHTH
and began the TWENTY-NINTH YEAR
of the Reign of HER MAJESTY
QUEEN ELIZABETH THE SECOND
and
ended the First Session
and began the Second Session
of the Forty-Eighth Parliament of the
United Kingdom of Great Britain
and Northern Ireland.

d

Produced in England by W. J. SHARP
Controller and Chief Executive of Her Majesty's Stationery Office
and Queen's Printer of Acts of Parliament

e

CONTENTS

TABLE I

Alphabetical List of
the Public General Acts of 1980

TABLE II

Chronological List of
the Public General Acts of 1980

* Consolidation Act.

---

* **Consolidation Act.**

TABLE II

Chronological List of
the Public General Acts of 1980

* Consolidation Act.

---

* **Consolidation Act.**

TABLE III

Alphabetical List of
the Local and Personal Acts of 1980

TABLE IV

Chronological List of
the General Synod Measures of 1980

*Measures passed by the General Synod of the Church of England
which received the Royal Assent during the year* 1980

Petroleum Revenue Tax Act 1980

1980 CHAPTER 1

An Act to make new provision in respect of petroleum revenue tax so as to require payments on account of tax to be made in advance of the making of an assessment, to bring forward the date from which interest is payable on unpaid and overpaid tax and to provide for altering the rate at which such interest is payable.

[31st January 1980]

Most Gracious Sovereign,

WE, Your Majesty's most dutiful and loyal subjects, the Commons of the United Kingdom in Parliament assembled, towards raising the necessary supplies to defray Your Majesty's public expenses, and making an addition to the public revenue, have freely and voluntarily resolved to make the provision hereinafter mentioned; and do therefore most humbly beseech Your Majesty that it may be enacted, and be it enacted by the Queen's most Excellent Majesty, by and with the advice and consent of the Lords Spiritual and Temporal, and Commons, in this present Parliament assembled, and by the authority of the same, as follows:—

1.—(1) Every participator in an oil field shall, at the time when he delivers to the Board the return for a chargeable period required by paragraph 2 of Schedule 2 to the Oil Taxation Act 1975— *Payments on account of tax. 1975 c. 22.*

    (a) deliver to the Board a statement showing whether any, and if so what, amount of tax is payable by him in accordance with the Schedule to this Act for that period in respect of the field; and

    (b) pay to the Board a sum equal to the amount of tax, if any, shown in the statement.

Part I   A

(2) The statement under subsection (1)(*a*) above shall be in such form as the Board may prescribe.

(3) The sum paid under subsection (1)(*b*) above shall constitute a payment on account of the tax charged in any assessment made on the participator in respect of the assessable profit accruing to him for the chargeable period from the oil field; and if the payment on account exceeds the tax so charged the excess shall be repaid to the participator.

(4) In paragraph 13 of Schedule 2 to the said Act of 1975 (time for payment of tax charged in an assessment) after the words " the tax charged in an assessment made on a participator for any chargeable period " there shall be inserted the words " so far as not paid on account ".

(5) Where a participator gives notice of appeal under paragraph 14 of the said Schedule 2 against an assessment charging tax in respect of which he has made a payment on account, the amount, if any, to be repaid under subsection (3) above shall be calculated as if the tax charged in the assessment were limited to the tax which he would not be entitled to withhold under sub-paragraph (3) of that paragraph.

1968 c. 13.

(6) Certificates of tax deposit issued by the Treasury under section 12 of the National Loans Act 1968 on terms published on or before 14th May 1979 may be used for making payments on account under this section; and for that purpose those terms shall have effect with the necessary modifications and as if the tax in or towards the payment of which a certificate is used were due two months after the end of the chargeable period to which it relates.

Interest on tax and on repayments. 1975 c. 22.

2.—(1) In paragraph 15(1) of Schedule 2 to the Oil Taxation Act 1975 and paragraph 8(4) of Schedule 5 to that Act (interest on unpaid tax to run from four months after the end of the chargeable period) for the words " four months " there shall be substituted the words " two months ".

(2) In paragraph 16 of the said Schedule 2 (interest on repayments of tax charged by an assessment to run from four months after the end of the chargeable period) after the words " tax charged by an assessment to tax " there shall be inserted the words " or paid on account of tax so charged " and for the words from " from four months " onwards there shall be substituted the words " from—

(*a*) two months after the end of the chargeable period for which the assessment was made; or

(*b*) the date on which it was paid,

whichever is the later, until repayment.".

(3) Any alteration made under section 89(2) of the Taxes 1970 c. 9. Management Act 1970 in the rate of interest mentioned in the said paragraph 15(1) shall apply also to the rate of interest mentioned in the said paragraphs 8(4) and 16.

3.—(1) This Act may be cited as the Petroleum Revenue Tax Short title, Act 1980. construction and com-

(2) This Act shall be construed as one with Part I of the Oil mencement. Taxation Act 1975. 1975 c. 22.

(3) Section 1 above has effect in relation to chargeable periods ending on or after 31st December 1979, section 2(1) and (2) above have effect in relation to tax charged for any such period and section 2(3) above has effect from 1st January 1980.

A 2

SCHEDULE
COMPUTATION OF PAYMENT ON ACCOUNT

1. For the purposes of section 1(1)(*a*) of this Act the tax payable by a participator for any chargeable period in respect of an oil field shall be determined as provided in the following provisions of this Schedule; and references in those provisions to any section or Schedule is a reference to that section or Schedule in the Oil Taxation Act 1975.

1975 c. 22.

2.—(1) There shall first be determined whether a computation made in accordance with section 2 as modified by the following provisions of this paragraph would result in an assessable profit, an allowable loss or neither an assessable profit or allowable loss and, if it would result in an assessable profit or allowable loss, the amount of that profit or loss.

(2) The market value, price and amounts referred to in section 2(5), (6)(*b*)(ii) and (7)(*b*) and (*c*) shall be taken from the particulars included in the return in pursuance of paragraph 2(2) and (3) of Schedule 2.

(3) The amount referred to in section 2(8)(*b*) shall be treated as nil and section 2(9)(*a*), (10) and (11) shall be omitted.

(4) Any expenditure in respect of which a claim has been made under Schedule 5, 6 or 7 and in respect of which the Board have not notified their decision under that Schedule may be treated for the purposes of section 2(9)(*b*), (*c*) or (*d*)—

    (*a*) as having been allowed; and

    (*b*) in the case of expenditure claimed as qualifying for supplement under section 2(9)(*b*)(ii) or (*c*)(ii), as having been allowed as so qualifying.

(5) The participator's share of any expenditure which by virtue of sub-paragraph (4) above is treated as having been allowed on a claim under Schedule 5 shall be the share proposed in the claim in pursuance of paragraph 2(4)(*b*) of that Schedule.

(6) Any loss in respect of which a claim has been made under Schedule 8 and in respect of which the Board have not notified their decision under that Schedule may be treated for the purposes of section 2(9)(*e*) as having been allowed.

(7) No expenditure or loss shall be taken into account under sub-paragraph (4), (5) or (6) above in relation to more than one chargeable period or more than one oil field.

3. The amount of any assessable profit resulting from the computation under paragraph 2 above may be reduced by any allowable loss in accordance with section 7(1) and shall be reduced in accordance with section 8 by reference to the participator's share, if any, of the oil allowance for the chargeable period.

4.—(1) The tax payable shall be arrived at by—

    (*a*) calculating the tax on the amount of assessable profit resulting from the computation under paragraph 2 above as reduced under paragraph 3 above; and

    (*b*) applying the limit imposed by section 9.

(2) In applying section 9 under this paragraph in relation to the later (or only) chargeable period comprised in a calendar year—

    (*a*) the assessable profit or allowable loss referred to in subsection (2)(*a*)(i) of that section shall be computed as provided in paragraph 2 above; and

    (*b*) the expenditure to be excluded under subsection (2)(*a*)(ii) and (3) of that section from the expenditure taken into account in computing the assessable profit or allowable loss for that period shall not include any expenditure treated under paragraph 2(4)(*b*) above as having been allowed as qualifying for supplement.

Papua New Guinea, Western Samoa and Nauru (Miscellaneous Provisions) Act 1980

1980 CHAPTER 2

An Act to make provision in connection with the attainment by Papua New Guinea of independence within the Commonwealth and with the membership of the Commonwealth of Western Samoa and Nauru.

[31st January 1980]

BE IT ENACTED by the Queen's most Excellent Majesty, by and with the advice and consent of the Lords Spiritual and Temporal, and Commons, in this present Parliament assembled, and by the authority of the same, as follows:—

Commonwealth citizenship. 1948 c. 56.

1.—(1) The British Nationality Act 1948 shall have effect as if in section 1(3) (Commonwealth countries having separate citizenship) there were added at the end the words "Papua New Guinea, Western Samoa and Nauru".

(2) It is hereby declared that Papua New Guinea has never been a colony within the meaning of the British Nationality Act 1948.

1967 c. 4.

(3) In accordance with section 3(3) of the West Indies Act 1967 it is hereby declared that this section and section 3(2) below extend to all associated states.

Registration of births and deaths. 1958 c. 10.

2. For the purposes of section 4 of the British Nationality Act 1958 (registration of births and deaths by High Commissioner in countries mentioned in section 1(3) of the British Nationality

Act 1948) section 1(1) above in its application to Papua New Guinea shall be deemed to have come into force on 16th September 1975.

3.—(1) The enactments specified in the Schedule to this Act shall have effect subject to the provisions of that Schedule, being provisions consequential on the attainment of independence by and the entry into the Commonwealth of Papua New Guinea, Western Samoa and Nauru. Miscellaneous amendments and repeals.

(2) In section 32(1) of the British Nationality Act 1948 (interpretation), in the definition of " Australia ", the words " the territories of Papua and " are hereby repealed. 1948 c. 56.

(3) Paragraphs 1, 3 and 5 of the Schedule to this Act shall be deemed to have come into force on 16th September 1975.

4. This Act may be cited as the Papua New Guinea, Western Samoa and Nauru (Miscellaneous Provisions) Act 1980. Short title.

Section 3.

SCHEDULE
ENACTMENTS AMENDED
COLONIAL LAWS VALIDITY ACT 1865 (c. 63)

1. The Colonial Laws Validity Act 1865 shall not apply in relation to Papua New Guinea.

COLONIAL STOCK ACT 1877 (c. 59)

2. The Colonial Stock Act 1877 shall not apply in relation to Papua New Guinea.

COLONIAL COURTS OF ADMIRALTY ACT 1890 (c. 27)

3. The Colonial Courts of Admiralty Act 1890 shall not apply in relation to Papua New Guinea.

MERCHANT SHIPPING ACT 1894 (c. 60)

1949 c. 43.

4. In section 427(2) of the Merchant Shipping Act 1894, as set out in section 2 of the Merchant Shipping (Safety Convention) Act 1949, before the words " or in any " there are inserted the words " Papua New Guinea, Western Samoa or Nauru ".

5. Sections 735 and 736 of the Act of 1894 shall not apply in relation to Papua New Guinea.

IMPERIAL INSTITUTE ACT 1925 (Ch. xvii)

1958 c. 16.

6. In section 8(2) of the Imperial Institute Act 1925, as amended by the Commonwealth Institute Act 1958, at the end there are added the words " Papua New Guinea, Western Samoa and Nauru ".

VISITING FORCES (BRITISH COMMONWEALTH) ACT 1933 (c. 6)

7. Section 4 of the Visiting Forces (British Commonwealth) Act 1933 shall apply in relation to forces raised in Papua New Guinea, Western Samoa or Nauru as it applies to forces raised in Dominions within the meaning of the Statute of Westminster 1931.

1931 c. 4.
(22 & 23 Geo. 5).

WHALING INDUSTRY (REGULATION) ACT 1934 (c. 49)

8. In the Whaling Industry (Regulation) Act 1934 the expression " British ship to which this Act applies " shall not include a British ship registered in Papua New Guinea, Western Samoa or Nauru.

VISITING FORCES ACT 1952 (c. 67)

9. In section 1(1)(*a*) of the Visiting Forces Act 1952 at the end there are added the words " Papua New Guinea, Western Samoa or Nauru, or " ; and any Order in Council under section 8 of that Act for the time being in force shall be deemed to apply to the visiting forces of Papua New Guinea, Western Samoa and Nauru until express provision with respect to those countries is made under that section.

ARMY ACT 1955 (c. 18)

10. In the definition of " Commonwealth force " in section 225(1) of the Army Act 1955 at the end there are added the words " Papua New Guinea, Western Samoa or Nauru ".

AIR FORCE ACT 1955 (c. 19)

11. In the definition of "Commonwealth force" in section 223(1) of the Air Force Act 1955 at the end there are added the words "Papua New Guinea, Western Samoa or Nauru".

NAVAL DISCIPLINE ACT 1957 (c. 53)

12. In the definition of "Commonwealth country" in section 135(1) of the Naval Discipline Act 1957 at the end there are added the words "Papua New Guinea, Western Samoa or Nauru".

OFFICES, SHOPS AND RAILWAY PREMISES ACT 1963 (c. 41)

13. In section 84(2) of the Offices, Shops and Railway Premises Act 1963 before the words "and any country" there are inserted the words "Western Samoa, Nauru".

OFFICE AND SHOP PREMISES ACT (NORTHERN IRELAND) 1966

14. In section 78(2) of the Office and Shop Premises Act (Northern Ireland) 1966 before the words "and any country" there are inserted the words "Western Samoa, Nauru".

Representation of the People Act 1980

1980 CHAPTER 3

An Act to make further provision with respect to the registration for electoral purposes of persons having a service qualification and the correction of registers of electors; and for purposes connected with those matters. [31st January 1980]

BE IT ENACTED by the Queen's most Excellent Majesty, by and with the advice and consent of the Lords Spiritual and Temporal, and Commons, in this present Parliament assembled, and by the authority of the same, as follows:—

Registration of persons having a service qualification.
1949 c. 68.

1.—(1) In section 8 of the Representation of the People Act 1949 (right to be registered) there shall be inserted after subsection (2) the following subsections—

" (2A) A person who on the qualifying date has a service qualification shall not be entitled to be registered as mentioned in subsection (1) or (2) above except in pursuance of an appropriate service declaration; and in this subsection and subsection (2B) below " appropriate service declaration " means—

    (a) in the case of a person who on the qualifying date is a member of the forces or the wife or husband of such a member, a service declaration made in accordance with section 10 of this Act and in force on that date; and

    (b) in any other case, a service declaration made in accordance with that section with reference to that date.

(2B) Subsection (2A) above does not apply to any person who on the qualifying date is the wife or husband of a member of the forces if on that date—

(a) that person has no other service qualification;

(b) that person is resident in the United Kingdom; and

(c) no appropriate service declaration is in force in respect of that person."

(2) In section 10 of the said Act of 1949 (service qualification)—

(a) in subsection (5) there shall be inserted immediately before the words " shall be attested " the words " , except where the declarant is a member of the forces or the wife or husband of such a member," ; and

(b) in subsection (7) there shall be inserted immediately before the word " attested " the words " (where required) ".

(3) In the said section 8—

(a) the provisos to subsections (1) and (2); and

(b) subsection (3) as inserted by section 3(3) of the Representation of the People (Armed Forces) Act 1976,   1976 c. 29.

(which are superseded by subsection (1) above) shall cease to have effect.

2.—(1) In section 9 of the Representation of the People Act 1949 (preparation of registers) there shall be inserted at the end the following subsections—   Correction of registers of electors.

1949 c. 68.

" (3) Where a register of electors as published does not carry out the intention of the registration officer—

(a) to include the name of any person shown in the electors lists as a person entitled to be registered; or

(b) to give or not to give in a person's entry a date as that on which he will attain voting age, or as to the date to be given; or

(c) to give effect to a decision on a claim or objection made with respect to the electors lists,

then (subject to the decision on any appeal from a decision on a claim or objection) the registration officer on becoming aware of the fact shall make the necessary correction in the register.

(4) Where subsection (3)(a) above does not apply but the registration officer is satisfied by such evidence as he may require that any person whose name is not included in a register of electors as published is entitled to be registered in that register, he shall make the necessary correction in the register.

(5) An alteration made in a register of electors under subsection (3) or (4) above on or after the date on which notice of an election is given shall not have effect for the purposes of that election.

(6) No alteration shall be made in a register of electors as published otherwise than under subsection (3) or (4) above or the provisions of section 45 of this Act relating to appeals."

(2) In section 45(1) of the said Act of 1949 (registration appeals) there shall be inserted after paragraph (*c*) the following paragraph—

" (*d*) from any decision under this Act of the registration officer to make or not to make an alteration in a register as published; ".

1969 c. 15.

(3) Subsection (2) of section 7 of the Representation of the People Act 1969 (which is superseded by subsection (1) above) shall cease to have effect.

Citation, repeals and commencement.

3.—(1) This Act may be cited as the Representation of the People Act 1980, and shall be included among the Acts which may be cited as the Representation of the People Acts.

(2) The enactments mentioned in the Schedule to this Act are hereby repealed to the extent specified in the third column of that Schedule.

(3) The provisions of this Act shall come into force on such day as the Secretary of State may by order made by statutory instrument appoint, and different days may be appointed for different provisions or different purposes.

SCHEDULE

Enactments Repealed

Chapter	Short title	Extent of repeal
12 & 13 Geo. 6. c. 68.	The Representation of the People Act 1949.	In section 8, the provisos to subsections (1) and (2) and subsection (3).
1969 c. 15.	The Representation of the People Act 1969.	Section 7(2). In Schedule 4, the entry relating to section 7(2).
1976 c. 29.	The Representation of the People (Armed Forces) Act 1976.	Section 3(2) and (3).

Bail etc. (Scotland) Act 1980

1980 CHAPTER 4

An Act to amend the law of Scotland relating to bail and the interim liberation of persons who have been arrested and to make provision in respect of the sittings of the sheriff and district courts.   [31st January 1980]

BE IT ENACTED by the Queen's most Excellent Majesty, by and with the advice and consent of the Lords Spiritual and Temporal, and Commons, in this present Parliament assembled, and by the authority of the same, as follows:—

1.—(1) After the commencement of this Act, it shall not be lawful to grant bail or release for a pledge or deposit of money, and— *(Release on conditions.)*

    (a) release on bail may be granted only on conditions which, subject to subsection (3) below, shall not include a pledge or deposit of money ;

    (b) liberation may be granted by the police under section 18, 294, 295 or 296 of the 1975 Act as amended by sections 7 to 9 of this Act.

(2) The conditions which the court or, as the case may be, the Lord Advocate imposes in granting bail shall be such as the court or the Lord Advocate considers necessary to secure that the accused—

    (a) appears at the appointed time at every diet relating to the offence with which he is charged of which he is given due notice ;

    (b) does not commit an offence while on bail ;

(c) does not interfere with witnesses or otherwise obstruct the course of justice whether in relation to himself or any other person ; and

(d) makes himself available for the purposes of enabling inquiries or a report to be made to assist the court in dealing with him for the offence with which he is charged.

(3) The court or, as the case may be, the Lord Advocate may impose as one of the conditions of release on bail a requirement that the accused or a cautioner on his behalf deposits a sum of money in court, but only where the court or, as the case may be, the Lord Advocate is satisfied that the imposition of such condition is appropriate to the special circumstances of the case.

(4) In any enactment, including the following provisions of this Act and any enactment passed after this Act—

(a) any reference to bail shall be construed as a reference to release on conditions in accordance with this Act or to conditions imposed on bail, as the context requires ;

(b) any reference to an amount of bail fixed shall be construed as a reference to conditions, including a sum required to be deposited under subsection (3) above ;

(c) any reference to finding bail or finding sufficient bail shall be construed as a reference to acceptance of conditions imposed or the finding of a sum required to be deposited under subsection (3) above.

(5) In this section and sections 2 to 4 of this Act, references to an accused and to appearance at a diet shall include references respectively to an appellant and to appearance at the court on the day fixed for the hearing of an appeal.

Provisions supplementary to s. 1.   **2.**—(1) The court shall specify in the order granting bail, a copy of which shall be given to the accused—

(a) the conditions imposed ; and

(b) an address, within the United Kingdom (being the accused's normal place of residence or such other place as the court may, on cause shown, direct) which, subject to subsection (2) below, shall be his proper domicile of citation.

(2) The court may on application in writing by the accused while he is on bail alter the address specified in the order granting bail, and this new address shall, as from such date as the court

may direct, become his proper domicile of citation ; and the court shall notify the accused of its decision on any application under this subsection.

(3) In this section " proper domicile of citation " means the address at which the accused may be cited to appear at any diet relating to the offence with which he is charged or an offence charged in the same proceedings as that offence or to which any other intimation or document may be sent ; and any citation at or the sending of an intimation or document to the proper domicile of citation shall be presumed to have been duly carried out.

3.—(1) Subject to subsection (3) below, an accused who Breach of having been granted bail fails without reasonable excuse— conditions.

    (*a*) to appear at the time and place appointed for any diet of which he has been given due notice ; or

    (*b*) to comply with any other condition imposed on bail ;

shall be guilty of an offence and liable on conviction to the penalties specified in subsection (2) below.

(2) The penalties mentioned in subsection (1) above are—

    (*a*) a fine not exceeding £200 ; and

    (*b*) imprisonment for a period—

        (i) where conviction is in the district court, not exceeding 60 days ; or

        (ii) where conviction is in the sheriff court or in the High Court, not exceeding 3 months.

(3) An accused who having been granted bail in relation to solemn proceedings fails without reasonable excuse to appear at the time and place appointed for any diet of which he has been given due notice (where such diet is in respect of solemn proceedings) shall be guilty of an offence and liable on conviction on indictment to the following penalties—

    (*a*) a fine ; and

    (*b*) imprisonment for a period not exceeding 2 years.

(4) At any time before the trial of an accused under solemn procedure for the original offence, it shall be competent—

    (*a*) to amend the indictment to include an additional charge of an offence under this section ;

    (*b*) to include in the list of witnesses or productions relating to the original offence, witnesses or productions relating to the offence under this section.

(5) The penalties provided for in subsection (2) above may be imposed in addition to any other penalty which it is competent for the court to impose, notwithstanding that the total of penal-

ties imposed may exceed the maximum penalty which it is competent to impose in respect of the original offence.

(6) A court which finds an accused guilty of an offence under this section may remit the accused for sentence in respect of that offence to any court which is considering the original offence.

(7) A constable may arrest without warrant an accused who has been released on bail where the constable has reasonable grounds for suspecting that the accused has broken, is breaking, or is likely to break any condition imposed on his bail.

(8) An accused who is arrested under this section shall wherever practicable be brought before the court to which his application for bail was first made not later than in the course of the first day after his arrest, such day not being a Saturday, a Sunday or a court holiday prescribed for that court under section 10 of this Act:

Provided that nothing in this subsection shall prevent such person being brought before a court on a Saturday, a Sunday or such a court holiday where the court is, in pursuance of the said section 10, sitting on such day for the disposal of criminal business.

(9) Where an accused is brought before a court under subsection (8) above, the court, after hearing the parties, may—

    (a) recall the order granting bail ;

    (b) release the accused under the original order granting bail ; or

    (c) vary the order granting bail so as to contain such conditions as the court thinks it necessary to impose to secure that the accused complies with the requirements of paragraphs (a) to (d) of section 1(2) of this Act.

(10) The same rights of appeal shall be available against any decision of the court under subsection (9) above as were available against the original order of the court relating to bail.

(11) For the purposes of this section, an extract from the minute of proceedings, containing the order granting bail and bearing to be signed by the clerk of court, shall be sufficient evidence of the making of that order and of its terms and of the acceptance by the accused of the conditions imposed under section 1 of this Act.

(12) In this section " the original offence " means the offence with which the accused was charged when he was granted bail or an offence charged in the same proceedings as that offence.

4.—(1) Without prejudice to section 3 of this Act, where the accused or a cautioner on his behalf has deposited a sum of money in court under section 1(3) of this Act, then—

Provisions relating to monetary conditions.

(*a*) if the accused fails to appear at the time and place appointed for any diet of which he has been given due notice, the court may, on the motion of the prosecutor, immediately order forfeiture of the sum deposited:

Provided that the court, if it is satisfied that it is reasonable in all the circumstances to do so, may recall the order and direct that the money forfeited shall be refunded, and any decision of the court under this proviso shall be final and not subject to review ;

(*b*) if the accused fails to comply with any other condition imposed on bail, the court may, on conviction of an offence under section 3(1)(*b*) of this Act and on the motion of the prosecutor, order forfeiture of the sum deposited.

(2) A cautioner, who has deposited a sum of money in court under section 1(3) of this Act, shall be entitled to recover the sum deposited at any diet of the court at which the accused appears personally:

Provided that, where the accused has been charged with an offence under section 3(1)(*b*) of this Act, nothing in this subsection shall entitle a cautioner to recover the sum deposited unless and until—

(*a*) the charge is not proceeded with ; or

(*b*) the accused is acquitted of the charge ; or

(*c*) on the accused's conviction of the offence, the court has determined not to order forfeiture of the sum deposited.

(3) The references in subsection (1)(*b*) above and in paragraph (*c*) of the proviso to subsection (2) above to conviction of an offence shall include references to the making of an order in respect of the offence under section 383 (absolute discharge) or 384 (probation) of the 1975 Act.

5. In each of sections 179 and 380 of the 1975 Act (power of court to adjourn case before sentence)—

Bail on adjournment before sentence.

(*a*) there shall be inserted before the proviso the words— "and where the court so adjourns the case it shall remand the accused in custody or on bail " ;

(*b*) at the end there shall be added the following subsection—

" (2) An accused who is remanded under this section may appeal against the refusal of bail or against the conditions imposed within 24 hours of

his remand, by note of appeal presented to the High
Court, and the High Court, either in court or in
chambers, may, after hearing parties—

(a) review the order and grant bail on such
conditions as it thinks fit ; or

(b) confirm the order.".

Remand or
inquiry into
physical or
mental
condition.

6. In each of sections 180 and 381 of the 1975 Act (remand
for inquiry into physical or mental condition)—

(a) in subsection (2), the words " bail shall be found by bail
bond, and ", and subsection (3) shall cease to have
effect ;

(b) at the end there shall be added the following subsection—

" (5) A person remanded under this section may
appeal against the refusal of bail or against the
conditions imposed within 24 hours of his remand,
by note of appeal presented to the High Court, and
the High Court, either in court or in chambers, may
after hearing parties—

(a) review the order and grant bail on such
conditions as it thinks fit ; or

(b) confirm the order."

Interim
liberation by
constable of
person charged
with offence
against a
person under
17 years.

7.—(1) In section 18 of the 1975 Act (power of constables to
take offenders into custody), for subsection (2) there shall be
substituted the following subsections—

" (2) Where a person has been arrested under this
section, the officer in charge of a police station may—

(a) liberate him upon a written undertaking, signed by
him and certified by the said officer, in terms of
which that person undertakes to appear at a
specified court at a specified time ; or

(b) liberate him without any such undertaking ; or

(c) refuse to liberate him ; and such refusal and the
detention of that person until his case is tried in the
usual form shall not subject the officer to any claim
whatsoever.

(3) A person in breach of an undertaking given by him
under subsection (2)(a) above without reasonable excuse
shall be guilty of an offence and liable to the following
penalties—

(a) a fine not exceeding £200 ; and

(b) imprisonment for a period not exceeding 3 months.

(4) The penalties provided for in subsection (3) above may be imposed in addition to any other penalty which it is competent for the court to impose, notwithstanding that the total of penalties imposed may exceed the maximum penalty which it is competent to impose in respect of the original offence.

(5) In any proceedings relating to an offence under this section, a writing, purporting to be such an undertaking as is mentioned in subsection (2)(*a*) above and bearing to be signed and certified, shall be sufficient evidence of the terms of the undertaking given by the arrested person.".

(2) In section 294 of the 1975 Act (power of constables to take offenders into custody), for subsection (2) there shall be substituted the following subsections—

" (2) Where a person has been arrested under this section, the officer in charge of a police station may—

(*a*) liberate him upon a written undertaking, signed by him and certified by the said officer, in terms of which that person undertakes to appear at a specified court at a specified time ; or

(*b*) liberate him without any such undertaking ; or

(*c*) refuse to liberate him ; and such refusal and the detention of that person until his case is tried in the usual form shall not subject the officer to any claim whatsoever.

(3) A person in breach of an undertaking given by him under subsection (2)(*a*) above without reasonable excuse shall be guilty of an offence and liable to the following penalties—

(*a*) a fine not exceeding £200 ; and

(*b*) imprisonment for a period—

(i) where conviction is in the district court, not exceeding 60 days ; or

(ii) where conviction is in the sheriff court, not exceeding 3 months.

(4) The penalties provided for in subsection (3) above may be imposed in addition to any other penalty which it is competent for the court to impose, notwithstanding that the total of penalties imposed may exceed the maximum penalty which it is competent to impose in respect of the original offence.

(5) In any proceedings relating to an offence under this section, a writing, purporting to be such an undertaking as is

mentioned in subsection (2)(*a*) above and bearing to be signed and certified, shall be sufficient evidence of the terms of the undertaking given by the arrested person.".

Interim
liberation by
officer in
charge of
police station.

8. For section 295 of the 1975 Act (chief constable may in certain circumstances accept bail) there shall be substituted the following section—

"Interim
liberation by
officer in
charge of
police
station.

295.—(1) Where a person has been arrested and charged with an offence which may be tried summarily, the officer in charge of a police station may—

(*a*) liberate him upon a written undertaking, signed by him and certified by the said officer, in terms of which that person undertakes to appear at a specified court at a specified time ; or

(*b*) liberate him without any such undertaking ; or

(*c*) refuse to liberate him, and such refusal and the detention of that person until his case is tried in the usual form shall not subject the officer to any claim whatsoever.

(2) A person in breach of an undertaking given by him under subsection (1) above without reasonable excuse shall be guilty of an offence and liable on summary conviction to the following penalties—

(*a*) a fine not exceeding £200 ; and

(*b*) imprisonment for a period—

(i) where conviction is in the district court, not exceeding 60 days ; or

(ii) where conviction is in the sheriff court, not exceeding 3 months.

(3) Subsections (4) and (5) of section 294 of this Act shall, subject to any necessary modifications, apply for the purposes of this section as they apply for the purposes of that section.".

Police
liberation
or detention
of children
arrested.

9. In section 296 of the 1975 Act (police liberation or detention of children arrested)—

(*a*) in subsection (1), for the word "obligation" there shall be substituted the word "undertaking" and for the words from "or on bail" to "unless" there shall be substituted "; and such undertaking shall be in writing, signed by the child or the parent or guardian as the case may be, and certified by the said officer ; and the said officer shall so liberate the child unless—" ;

(b) at the end there shall be added the following subsections—

" (5) Any person, who without reasonable excuse is in breach of an undertaking entered into by him under subsection (1) above after having been given due notice of the time and place of the diet (including any continuation of the diet), shall be guilty of an offence, and liable on summary conviction in addition to any other penalty which it is competent for the court to impose on him, to a fine not exceeding £200.

(6) In any proceedings relating to an offence under this section, a writing, purporting to be such an undertaking as is mentioned in subsection (1) above and bearing to be signed and certified, shall be sufficient evidence of the undertaking given by the accused.".

10.—(1) Notwithstanding any enactment or rule of law, a sheriff court or a district court—

(a) shall not be required to sit on any Saturday or Sunday or on a day which by virtue of subsection (2) or (3) below is a court holiday ; but

(b) may sit on any day for the disposal of criminal business.

(2) A sheriff principal may in an order made under section 17(1)(b) of the Sheriff Courts (Scotland) Act 1971 prescribe in respect of criminal business not more than 10 days (other than Saturdays and Sundays) in a calendar year as court holidays in the sheriff courts within his jurisdiction.

(3) Notwithstanding section 2(1) of the District Courts (Scotland) Act 1975, a sheriff principal may, after consultation with the appropriate district or islands council, prescribe not more than 10 days (other than Saturdays and Sundays) in a calendar year as court holidays in the district courts within his jurisdiction.

(4) A sheriff principal may in pursuance of subsection (2) or (3) above prescribe different days as court holidays in relation to different sheriff or district courts.

11.—(1) In this Act—

" the 1975 Act " means the Criminal Procedure (Scotland) Act 1975 ;

" constable " means a constable within the meaning of the Police (Scotland) Act 1967 acting in the course of his duties ;

" diet " includes any continuation of a diet.

[margin notes]

Sittings of sheriff and district courts.

1971 c. 58.

1975 c. 20.

Interpretation.

1975 c. 21.

1967 c. 77.

(2) Except where the context otherwise requires, expressions used in this Act and in the 1975 Act shall have the same meanings in this Act as in that Act.

Transitional provision, consequential amendments and repeals.

12.—(1) A provision contained in any of sections 1 to 9 of this Act, and any related amendment or repeal provided for in Schedule 1 or 2 to this Act, shall not apply in relation to bail granted or release authorised before the coming into force of that provision.

(2) The enactments specified in Schedule 1 to this Act shall have effect subject to the amendments there specified, being amendments consequential on the provisions of this Act.

(3) The enactments specified in Schedule 2 to this Act are hereby repealed to the extent specified in the third column of that Schedule.

Short title, commencement and extent.

13.—(1) This Act may be cited as the Bail etc. (Scotland) Act 1980.

(2) This Act (except this section) shall come into force on such day as the Secretary of State may appoint by order made by statutory instrument.

(3) Any order under subsection (2) above may make such transitional provision as appears to the Secretary of State to be expedient in connection with the provisions thereby brought into force.

(4) This Act extends to Scotland only.

SCHEDULES

SCHEDULE 1

CONSEQUENTIAL AMENDMENTS

The Licensing (Scotland) Act 1903 (c.25)

1. In section 70(1) (penalties for drunkenness, riotous behaviour and other offences involving drunkenness)—

    (*a*) in the first paragraph after " custody " where it occurs for the second time insert ", such day not being a Saturday, a Sunday or a court holiday prescribed for that court under section 10 of the Bail etc. (Scotland) Act 1980," ;

    (*b*) at the end of the first paragraph insert—

        " Provided that nothing in this paragraph of this sub-section shall prevent such person being brought before the court on a Saturday, a Sunday or a court holiday prescribed for that court under the said section 10 where the court is in pursuance of that enactment sitting on such day for the disposal of criminal business.".

The District Courts (Scotland) Act 1975 (c.20)

2. In section 2(1) (district of, and exercise of jurisdiction by, district court), after " sits, and " insert—
    " subject to section 10 of the Bail etc. (Scotland) Act 1980 (sittings of sheriff and district courts) ".

The Criminal Procedure (Scotland) Act 1975 (c.21)

3. In section 26(2) (bail competent before committal), for the words from " liberation " to " him " substitute " bail ".

4. In section 30(2) (application for review), for " at a lower amount " substitute " on different conditions ".

5. In section 180(2) (remand for inquiry into physical or mental condition), for " bond " wherever it occurs substitute " order granting bail ".

6. In section 299(2) (application for review), for " at a lower amount " substitute " on different conditions ".

7. In section 321(3) (warrants of apprehension and search), for " public or local holiday " substitute " Saturday, a Sunday or a court holiday prescribed for that court under section 10 of the Bail etc. (Scotland) Act 1980:

    Provided that nothing in this subsection shall prevent such person being brought before the court on a Saturday, a Sunday or such a court holiday where the court is, in pursuance of the said section 10, sitting on such day for the disposal of criminal business.".

8. In section 337(*d*) (plea of not guilty), for " without " to the end substitute " if he is not granted bail or until the accused or a cautioner on his behalf has deposited a sum of money in court where such deposit has been required as a condition of release on bail under section 1(3) of the Bail etc. (Scotland) Act 1980 ;".

9. In section 381(2) (remand for inquiry into physical or mental condition), for " bond " wherever it occurs substitute " order granting bail ".

10. In section 444(5) (manner and time of appeal), for " interim liberation " substitute " bail ".

11. In section 446 (procedure where appellant in custody)—

    (*a*) for " interim liberation " and " liberation " wherever they occur substitute " bail " ;

    (*b*) in each of subsections (2) and (3), for " amount of caution fixed " substitute " conditions imposed ".

12. In section 448(8) (adjustment and signature of case), for " interim liberation " substitute " bail ".

13. In section 452(5) (hearing of appeal), for " interim liberation " substitute " bail ".

14. In section 462(1) (interpretation), for the definition of " bail " substitute " ' bail ' means release of an accused or an appellant on conditions, or conditions imposed on bail, as the context requires ; ".

15. In paragraph 4 of Schedule 3, after " day " wherever it occurs insert ", not including a Saturday, a Sunday or a court holiday prescribed for that court under section 10 of the Bail etc. (Scotland) Act 1980.".

SCHEDULE 2

REPEALS

Chapter	Short Title	Extent of Repeal
3 Edw. 7. c. 25.	The Licensing (Scotland) Act 1903.	In section 70(1), in the first paragraph, the word " lawful ".
1975 c. 21.	The Criminal Procedure (Scotland) Act 1975.	Section 29. Section 30(5). Section 34. Section 36. In section 180, in subsection (2) the words " bail shall be found by bail bond, and," and subsection (3). In section 296(1) the words from " or on bail " to the second " hearing of the charge ". Section 299(5). Section 301. Section 302. Section 303(2) and (3). In section 321(3) the word " lawful ". In section 337(a) the word "or". Section 337(*e*). Section 338(*d*). In section 381, in subsection (2) the words " bail shall be found by bail bond, and ", and subsection (3). In section 446, in subsection (1) the words " as to caution or otherwise " and " or may dispense with further consignation or caution ". In paragraph 4 of Schedule 3 the word " lawful " wherever it occurs.

Child Care Act 1980

1980 CHAPTER 5

An Act to consolidate certain enactments relating to the care of children by local authorities or voluntary organisations and certain other enactments relating to the care of children.   [31st January 1980]

BE IT ENACTED by the Queen's most Excellent Majesty, by and with the advice and consent of the Lords Spiritual and Temporal, and Commons, in this present Parliament assembled, and by the authority of the same, as follows:—

PART I

POWERS AND DUTIES OF LOCAL AUTHORITIES IN RELATION TO THE WELFARE AND CARE OF CHILDREN

General duty of local authorities to promote welfare of children

1.—(1) It shall be the duty of every local authority to make available such advice, guidance and assistance as may promote the welfare of children by diminishing the need to receive children into or keep them in care under this Act or to bring children before a juvenile court ; and any provisions made by a local authority under this subsection may, if the local authority think fit, include provision for giving assistance in kind or, in exceptional circumstances, in cash.

Duty of local authorities to promote welfare of children.

(2) In carrying out their duty under subsection (1) above, a local authority may make arrangements with voluntary organisations or other persons for the provision by those organisations or other persons of such advice, guidance or assistance as is mentioned in that subsection.

(3) Where any provision which may be made by a local authority under section (1) above is made (whether by that or any other authority) under any other enactment, the local authority shall not be required to make the provision under this section but shall have power to do so.

(4) In this section " child " means a person under the age of eighteen.

Duty of local authorities to assume care of orphans and deserted children etc.

Duty of local
authority to
provide for
orphans,
deserted
children etc.

2.—(1) Where it appears to a local authority with respect to a child in their area appearing to them to be under the age of seventeen—

(*a*) that he has neither parent nor guardian or has been and remains abandoned by his parents or guardian or is lost ; or

(*b*) that his parents or guardian are, for the time being or permanently, prevented by reason of mental or bodily disease or infirmity or other incapacity or any other circumstances from providing for his proper accommodation, maintenance and upbringing ; and

(*c*) in either case, that the intervention of the local authority under this section is necessary in the interests of the welfare of the child,

it shall be the duty of the local authority to receive the child into their care under this section.

(2) Where a local authority have received a child into their care under this section, it shall, subject to the provisions of this Part of this Act, be their duty to keep the child in their care so long as the welfare of the child appears to them to require it and the child has not attained the age of eighteen.

(3) Nothing in this section shall authorise a local authority to keep a child in their care under this section if any parent or guardian desires to take over the care of the child, and the local authority shall, in all cases where it appears to them consistent with the welfare of the child so to do, endeavour to secure that the care of the child is taken over either—

(*a*) by a parent or guardian of his, or

(*b*) by a relative or friend of his, being, where possible, a person of the same religious persuasion as the child or who gives an undertaking that the child will be brought up in that religious persuasion.

(4) Where a local authority receive into their care under this section a child who is then ordinarily resident in the area of another local authority—

(*a*) that other local authority may at any time not later than three months after the determination (whether

(6) On hearing a complaint made under subsection (5) above the court may if it is satisfied—

(a) that the grounds mentioned in subsection (1) above on which the local authority purported to pass the resolution were made out, and

(b) that at the time of the hearing there continue to be grounds on which a resolution under that subsection could be founded, and

(c) that it is in the interests of the child to do so,

order that the resolution shall not lapse by reason of the service of the counter-notice.

(7) Any notice under this section (including a counter-notice) may be served by post, so however that a notice served by a local authority under subsection (2) above shall not be duly served by post unless it is sent by registered post or recorded delivery service.

(8) Where, after a child has been received into the care of a local authority under section 2 of this Act, the whereabouts of any parent of his have remained unknown for twelve months, then, for the purposes of this section, the parent shall be deemed to have abandoned the child.

(9) The Secretary of State may by order a draft of which has been approved by each House of Parliament amend subsection (1)(d) above by substituting a different period for the period mentioned in that paragraph (or the period which, by a previous order under this subsection, was substituted for that period).

(10) In this section—

" parent ", except in subsection (1)(a), includes a guardian or custodian ;

" parental rights and duties ", in relation to a particular child, does not include—

(a) the right to consent or refuse to consent to the making of an application under section 18 of the Adoption Act 1976 (orders freeing a child for adoption in England and Wales) or section 18 of the Adoption (Scotland) Act 1978 (orders freeing a child for adoption in Scotland), and 1976 c. 36. 1978 c. 28.

(b) the right to agree or refuse to agree to the making of an adoption order or an order under section 55 of the Adoption Act 1976 (orders in England and Wales authorising adoption abroad) or section 49 of the Adoption (Scotland) Act 1978 (orders in Scotland authorising adoption abroad).

B

6. An appeal shall lie to the High Court from the making by PART I Appeal to the High Court. a juvenile court of an order under section 3(6) or 5(4) of this Act or from the refusal by a juvenile court to make such an order.

7.—(1) In any proceedings under section 3(6) or 5(4) or 6 of Guardians ad litem and reports in care proceedings. this Act a juvenile court or the High Court may, where it considers it necessary in order to safeguard the interests of the child to whom the proceedings relate, by order make the child a party to the proceedings and appoint, subject to rules of court, a guardian ad litem of the child for the purposes of the proceedings.

(2) A guardian ad litem appointed in pursuance of this section shall be under a duty to safeguard the interests of the child in the manner prescribed by rules of court.

(3) Section 6 of the Guardianship Act 1973 shall apply in 1973 c. 29. relation to complaints under section 3(6) or 5(4) of this Act as it applies in relation to applications under section 3(3) of the said Act of 1973.

8.—(1) The reception of a child into their care by a local Application of Part I in relation to children subject to orders of court. authority under section 2 of this Act, and the passing of a resolution with respect to him under section 3 of this Act, shall not affect any supervision order or probation order previously made with respect to him by any court.

(2) Where an order of any court is in force giving the custody of a child to any person, the foregoing provisions of this Part of this Act shall have effect in relation to the child as if for references to the parents or guardian of the child or to a parent or guardian of his there were substituted references to that person.

9.—(1) The parent of a child who is in the care of a local Duty of parents to maintain contact with local authorities having their children in care. authority under section 2 of this Act shall secure that the appropriate local authority are informed of the parent's address for the time being.

(2) Where under section 2(4) of this Act a local authority take over the care of a child from another local authority, that other authority shall where possible inform the parent of the child that the care of the child has been so taken over.

(3) For the purposes of subsection (1) above, the appropriate local authority shall be the authority in whose care the child is for the time being; but where under section 2(4) of this Act a local authority have taken over the care of a child from another authority, then unless and until a parent is informed that the care of a child has been so taken over the appropriate local

authority shall in relation to that parent continue to be the authority from whom the care of the child was taken over.

(4) Any parent who knowingly fails to comply with subsection (1) above shall be guilty of an offence and liable on summary conviction to a fine not exceeding £10.

(5) It shall be a defence in any proceeding under subsection (4) above to prove that the defendant was residing at the same address as the other parent of the child and had reasonable cause to believe that the other parent had informed the appropriate authority that both parents were residing at that address.

Provisions as to children subject to care order etc.

10.—(1) It shall be the duty of a local authority to whose care a child is committed by a care order or by a warrant under section 23(1) of the Children and Young Persons Act 1969 (which relates to remands in the care of local authorities) to receive the child into their care and, notwithstanding any claim by his parent or guardian, to keep him in their care while the order or warrant is in force.

(2) A local authority shall, subject to the following provisions of this section, have the same powers and duties with respect to a person in their care by virtue of a care order or such a warrant as his parent or guardian would have apart from the order or warrant and may (without prejudice to the foregoing provisions of this subsection but subject to regulations made in pursuance of section 39 of this Act) restrict his liberty to such extent as the authority consider appropriate.

(3) A local authority shall not cause a child in their care by virtue of a care order to be brought up in any religious creed other than that in which he would have been brought up apart from the order.

(4) It shall be the duty of a local authority to comply with any provision included in an interim order in pursuance of section 22(2) of the Children and Young Persons Act 1969 and, in the case of a person in their care by virtue of section 23 of that Act, to permit him to be removed from their care in due course of law.

11.—(1) If a child who is subject to a care order and has attained the age of five is accommodated in a community home or other establishment which he has not been allowed to leave during the preceding three months for the purpose of ordinary attendance at an educational institution or at work and it appears to the local authority to whose care he is committed by the order that—

    (a) communication between him and his parent or guardian has been so infrequent that it is appropriate to appoint a visitor for him ; or (*b*) he has not lived with or visited or been visited by either of his parents or his guardian during the preceding twelve months,

it shall be the duty of the authority to appoint an independent person to be his visitor for the purposes of this subsection ; and a person so appointed shall—

(i) have the duty of visiting, advising and befriending the child to whom the care order relates ; and

(ii) be entitled to exercise on behalf of that child his powers under section 21(2) of the Children and Young Persons 1969 c. 54. Act 1969 (which relates to the discharge of care orders) ; and

(iii) be entitled to recover from the authority who appointed him any expenses reasonably incurred by him for the purposes of his functions under this subsection.

(2) A person's appointment as a visitor in pursuance of subsection (1) above shall be determined if the care order in question ceases to be in force or he gives notice in writing to the authority who appointed him that he resigns the appointment or the authority give him notice in writing that they terminate it ; but the determination of such an appointment shall not prejudice any duty under subsection (1) above to make a further appointment.

(3) In this section " independent person " means a person satisfying such conditions as may be prescribed by regulations made by the Secretary of State with a view to securing that he is independent of the local authority in question and unconnected with any community home.

12.—(1) While a care order other than an interim order is in force in respect of a child who has not attained the age of eighteen, it shall be the duty of his parent to keep the local authority to whose care he is committed by the order informed of the parent's address ; and if the parent knows of the order and fails to perform his duty under this subsection, the parent shall be guilty of an offence and liable on summary conviction to a fine not exceeding £10 unless he shows that at the material time he was residing at the address of the other parent and had reasonable cause to believe that the other parent had kept the authority informed of their address. Supplementary provisions relating to children subject to care order etc.

(2) The functions conferred on a local authority by sections 10 and 11 of this Act in respect of any child are additional to the functions which are conferred on the authority in respect of the child by Part III of this Act.

PART II

ABSENCE FROM CARE

Provisions relating to children in care of local authorities under section 2

Penalty for assisting children in care under s. 2 to run away etc.

13.—(1) Any person who—

(a) knowingly assists or induces or persistently attempts to induce a child to whom this subsection applies to run away, or

(b) without lawful authority takes away such a child, or

(c) knowingly harbours or conceals such a child who has run away or who has been taken away or prevents him from returning,

shall be guilty of an offence and liable on summary conviction to a fine not exceeding £400 or to imprisonment for a term not exceeding three months or to both.

This subsection applies to any child in the care of a local authority under section 2 of this Act with respect to whom a resolution is in force under section 3 of this Act and for whom accommodation (whether in a home or otherwise) is being provided by the local authority in pursuance of Part III of this Act.

(2) Except in relation to an act done—

(a) with the consent of the local authority or

(b) by a parent or guardian of the child who has given the local authority not less than twenty-eight days' notice of his intention to do it,

subsection (1) above shall apply to a child in the care of a local authority under section 2 of this Act (notwithstanding that no resolution is in force under section 3 of this Act with respect to the child) if he has been in the care of that local authority throughout the preceding six months ; and for the purposes of the application of paragraph (b) of that subsection in such a case a parent or guardian of the child shall not be taken to have lawful authority to take him away.

(3) References in subsection (1) above to running away or taking away or to returning are references to running away or taking away from, or to returning to, a place where accommodation is or was being provided in pursuance of Part III of this Act by the local authority in whose care the child is.

(4) Where an order of any court is in force giving custody of a child to any person, this section shall have effect in relation to that child as if for references to a parent or guardian of the child there were substituted references to that person.

(5) The Secretary of State may by order a draft of which has been approved by each House of Parliament amend subsection (2) above by substituting a different period for the period of twenty-eight days or of six months mentioned in that subsection, or by substituting a different period for any period substituted by a previous order under this subsection.

14. Where a local authority have, in accordance with section 21(2) of this Act, allowed any person to take charge of a child with respect to whom a resolution under section 3 of this Act is in force and have by notice in writing required that person to return the child at a time specified in the notice (which, if that person has been allowed to take charge of the child for a fixed period, shall not be earlier than the end of that period) any person who harbours or conceals the child after that time or prevents him from returning as required by the notice shall be guilty of an offence and liable on summary conviction to a fine not exceeding £100 or to imprisonment for a term not exceeding two months or to both.

15.—(1) This section applies to a child—

    (*a*) who is in the care of a local authority under section 2 of this Act ; and

    (*b*) with respect to whom there is in force a resolution under section 3 of this Act ; and

    (*c*) who—

        (i) has run away from accommodation provided for him by the local authority under Part III of this Act ; or

        (ii) has been taken away from such accommodation contrary to section 13(1) of this Act ; or

        (iii) has not been returned to the local authority as required by a notice served under section 14 of this Act on a person under whose charge and control the child was, in accordance with section 21(2) of this Act, allowed to be.

(2) If a justice of the peace is satisfied by information on oath that there are reasonable grounds for believing that a person specified in the information can produce a child to whom this section applies, he may issue a summons directed to the person

B 4

so specified and requiring him to attend and produce the child before a magistrates' court acting for the same petty sessions area as the justice.

(3) Without prejudice to the powers under subsection (2) above, if a justice of the peace is satisfied by information on oath that there are reasonable grounds for believing that a child to whom this section applies is in premises specified in the information, he may issue a search warrant authorising a person named in the warrant, being an officer of the local authority in whose care the child is, to search the premises for the child ; and if the child is found, he shall be placed in such accommodation as the local authority may provide for him under Part III of this Act.

(4) A person who, without reasonable excuse, fails to comply with a summons under subsection (2) above shall, without prejudice to any liability apart from this subsection, be guilty of an offence and liable on summary conviction to a fine not exceeding £100.

Provisions relating to children in care of local authorities by virtue of care order etc.

Recovery
of children
subject to care
order etc.
1969 c. 54.

16.—(1) If any child—

(a) who is committed to the care of a local authority by a care order or by a warrant under section 23(1) of the Children and Young Persons Act 1969 (which relates to remands to the care of local authorities) ; or

(b) who is in the care of a local authority in pursuance of arrangements under section 29(3) of that Act (which relates to the detention of arrested children),

is absent from the premises at which he is required by the local authority to live at a time when he is not permitted by the local authority to be absent from the premises, he may be arrested by a constable anywhere in the United Kingdom or the Channel Islands without a warrant and shall if so arrested be conducted, at the expense of the authority, to those premises or such other premises as the authority may direct.

(2) If a magistrates' court is satisfied by information on oath that there are reasonable grounds for believing that a person specified in the information can produce a child who is absent as mentioned in subsection (1) above, the court may issue a summons directed to the person so specified and requiring him to attend and produce the absent child before the court; and a person who without reasonable excuse fails to comply with any such requirement shall, without prejudice to any liability apart from this subsection, be guilty of an offence and liable on summary conviction to a fine not exceeding £100.

(3) Without prejudice to its powers under subsection (2) PART II
above a magistrates' court may, if it is satisfied by information on oath that there are reasonable grounds for believing
that a child who is absent as mentioned in subsection (1) above
is in premises specified in the information, issue a search warrant
authorising a constable to search the premises for that child.

(4) A person who knowingly compels, persuades, incites or
assists a child to become or continue to be absent as mentioned
in subsection (1) above shall be guilty of an offence and liable
on summary conviction to imprisonment for a term not exceeding six months or to a fine not exceeding £400 or to both.

(5) The reference to a constable in subsections (1) and (3)
above includes a reference to a person who is a constable
under the law of any part of the United Kingdom, to a member of the police in Jersey and to an officer of police within
the meaning of section 43 of the Larceny (Guernsey) Law 1958
or any corresponding law for the time being in force.

(6) In the application of subsections (2) and (3) above to
Northern Ireland, " magistrates' court " means a magistrates'
court within the meaning of the Magistrates' Courts Act 1964 c. 21.
(Northern Ireland) 1964. (N.I.).

PART III

TREATMENT OF CHILDREN WHO ARE OR HAVE BEEN IN CARE OF LOCAL AUTHORITIES

17. Except where the contrary intention appears, any refer- Children to
ence in this Part of this Act to a child who is or was in the whom Part III
care of a local authority is a reference to a child who is or applies.
was in the care of the authority under section 2 of this Act
or by virtue of a care order or a warrant under section 23(1)
of the Children and Young Persons Act 1969 (which relates 1969 c. 54.
to remands to the care of local authorities).

18.—(1) In reaching any decision relating to a child in their General duty
care, a local authority shall give first consideration to the need of local
to safeguard and promote the welfare of the child throughout authority in
his childhood ; and shall so far as practicable ascertain the children in
wishes and feelings of the child regarding the decision and give their care.
due consideration to them, having regard to his age and understanding.

(2) In providing for a child in their care a local authority shall
make such use of facilities and services available for children
in the care of their own parents as appears to the local authority
reasonable in his case.

(3) If it appears to the local authority that it is necessary, for the purpose of protecting members of the public, to exercise their powers in relation to a particular child in their care in a manner which may not be consistent with their duty under subsection (1) above, the authority may, notwithstanding that duty, act in that manner.

Power of Secretary of State to give directions to local authority for protection of public.

19. If the Secretary of State considers it necessary, for the purpose of protecting members of the public, to give directions to a local authority with respect to the exercise of their powers in relation to a particular child in their care, he may give such directions to the authority; and it shall be the duty of the authority, notwithstanding their general duty under section 18(1) of this Act, to comply with any such directions.

Review of care cases.

20.—(1) Without prejudice to their general duty under section 18(1) of this Act, it shall be the duty of a local authority to review the case of each child in their care in accordance with regulations made under subsection (2) below.

(2) The Secretary of State may by regulations make provision as to—

(a) the manner in which cases are to be reviewed under this section;

(b) the considerations to which the local authority are to have regard in reviewing cases under this section; and

(c) the time when a child's case is first to be reviewed and the frequency of subsequent reviews under this section.

Provision of accommoda- tion and maintenance for children in care.

21.—(1) A local authority shall discharge their duty to provide accommodation and maintenance for a child in their care in such one of the following ways as they think fit, namely,—

(a) by boarding him out on such terms as to payment by the authority and otherwise as the authority may, subject to the provisions of this Act and regulations thereunder, determine; or

(b) by maintaining him in a community home or in any such home as is referred to in section 80 of this Act; or

(c) by maintaining him in a voluntary home (other than a community home) the managers of which are willing to receive him;

or by making such other arrangements as seem appropriate to the local authority.

(2) Without prejudice to the generality of subsection (1) above, a local authority may allow a child in their care, either for a fixed period or until the local authority otherwise determine, to

be under the charge and control of a parent, guardian, relative or friend.

(3) The terms, as to payment and other matters, on which a child may be accommodated and maintained in any such home as is referred to in section 80 of this Act shall be such as the Secretary of State may from time to time determine.

22.—(1) The Secretary of State may by regulations make provision for the welfare of children boarded out by local authorities under section 21(1)(*a*) of this Act. Regulations as to boarding out.

(2) Without prejudice to the generality of subsection (1) above, regulations under this section may provide—

(*a*) for the recording by local authorities of information relating to persons with whom children are boarded out under section 21(1)(*a*) of this Act and persons who are willing to have children so boarded out with them ;

(*b*) for securing that children shall not be boarded out in any household unless that household is for the time being approved by such local authority as may be prescribed by the regulations ;

(*c*) for securing that where possible the person with whom any child is to be boarded out is either of the same religious persuasion as the child or gives an undertaking that the child will be brought up in that religious persuasion ;

(*d*) for securing that children boarded out under section 21(1)(*a*) of this Act, and the premises in which they are boarded out, will be supervised and inspected by a local authority and that the children will be removed from those premises if their welfare appears to require it.

23. While a child is in the care of a local authority under section 2 of this Act, the local authority may undertake any obligation by way of guarantee under any deed of apprenticeship or articles of clerkship entered into by that child ; and where the local authority have undertaken any such obligation under any deed or articles they may at any time (whether or not the person concerned is still in their care) undertake the like obligation under any deed or articles supplemental thereto. Power of local authority to guarantee apprenticeship deeds etc. of children in their care.

24.—(1) A local authority may, with the consent of the Secretary of State, procure or assist in procuring the emigration of any child in their care. Power of local authorities to arrange for emigration of children.

PART III

(2) Subject to subsection (3) below, the Secretary of State shall not give his consent under this section unless he is satisfied that emigration would benefit the child and that suitable arrangements have been or will be made for the child's reception and welfare in the country to which he is going, that the parents or guardians of the child have been consulted or that it is not practicable to consult them, and that the child consents.

(3) Where a child is too young to form or express a proper opinion on the matter, the Secretary of State may consent to his emigration notwithstanding that the child is unable to consent thereto in any case where the child is to emigrate in company with a parent, guardian or relative of his, or is to emigrate for the purpose of joining a parent, guardian, relative or friend.

(4) In subsection (2) above the reference to the parents or guardians of a child shall be construed as a reference to all the persons who are parents of the child or who are guardians of the child.

1976 c. 36.

1978 c. 28.

(5) Section 56 of the Adoption Act 1976 (which requires the authority of an order under section 55 of that Act or section 49 of the Adoption (Scotland) Act 1978 for the taking or sending abroad for adoption of a child who is a British subject) shall not apply in the case of any child emigrating with the consent of the Secretary of State given under this section.

Burial or cremation of deceased children.

25.—(1) A local authority may cause to be buried or cremated the body of any deceased child who immediately before his death was in the care of the authority; but the authority shall not cause the body to be cremated where cremation is not in accordance with the practice of the child's religious persuasion.

1975 c. 18.

(2) Where a local authority exercise the power referred to in subsection (1) above, they may if at the time of his death the child had not attained the age of sixteen years recover from any parent of the child any expenses incurred by them under that subsection less any amount received by the authority by way of death grant in respect of that death under section 32 of the Social Security Act 1975.

(3) Any sums recoverable by a local authority under subsection (2) above shall, without prejudice to any other method for the recovery thereof, be recoverable summarily as a civil debt.

(4) Nothing in this section shall affect any enactment regulating or authorising the burial, cremation or anatomical examination of the body of a deceased person.

26. A local authority may make payments to any parent or guardian of, or other person connected with, a child in their care in respect of travelling, subsistence or other expenses incurred by the parent, guardian or other person in visiting the child or attending his funeral, if it appears to the authority that the parent, guardian or other person would not otherwise be able to visit the child or attend the funeral without undue hardship and that the circumstances warrant the making of the payments.

PART III
Power of local authority to defray expenses of parents etc. visiting children or attending funerals.

27.—(1) A local authority may make contributions to the cost of the accommodation and maintenance of any person to whom this subsection applies in any place near the place where he may be employed, or seeking employment, or in receipt of education or training.

Financial assistance towards expenses of maintenance, education or training of persons over seventeen.

This subsection applies to any person over compulsory school age but under the age of twenty-one who is, or has at any time after ceasing to be of compulsory school age been, in the care of a local authority being either—

(a) a person who has attained the age of seventeen but has not attained the age of eighteen and who has ceased to be in the care of a local authority ; or

(b) a person who has attained the age of eighteen.

(2) A local authority may make grants to any person to whom this subsection applies to enable him to meet expenses connected with his receiving suitable education or training.

This subsection applies to any person who has attained the age of seventeen but has not attained the age of twenty-one and who at or after the time when he attained the age of seventeen was in the care of a local authority.

(3) Where a person—

(a) is engaged in a course of education or training at the time when he attains the age of twenty-one ; or

(b) having previously been engaged in a course of education or training which has been interrupted by any circumstances, resumes the course as soon as practicable,

then, if a local authority are at that time, or were at the time when the course was interrupted, as the case may be, making any contributions or grants in respect of him under subsection (1) or (2) above, their powers under those subsections shall continue with respect to him until the completion of the course.

28.—(1) Where it comes to the knowledge of a local authority that there is in their area any child over compulsory school age who at the time when he ceased to be of that age or at any subsequent time was, but is no longer, in the care of a local authority under section 2 of this Act, then, unless the authority

After-care of children formerly in care of local authorities under s. 2.

PART III　are satisfied that the welfare of the child does not require it, they shall be under a duty so long as he has not attained the age of eighteen to advise and befriend him.

(2) Where a child over compulsory school age ceases to be in the care of a local authority under section 2 of this Act and proposes to reside in the area of another local authority, the first mentioned local authority shall inform that other local authority.

(3) Where it comes to the knowledge of a local authority that a child whom they have been befriending in pursuance of this section proposes to transfer or has transferred his residence to the area of another local authority, the first mentioned local authority shall inform that other local authority.

Power of local authority to visit and assist persons formerly in their care.

29. Where a person was at or after the time when he attained the age of seventeen in the care of a local authority under section 2 of this Act but has ceased to be in their care, then, while he is under the age of twenty-one, the local authority, if so requested by him, may cause him to be visited, advised and befriended and, in exceptional circumstances, to be given financial assistance.

Allocation of functions as between local authority and local education authority.

30. The Secretary of State for Social Services, the Secretary of State for Education and Science and the Secretary of State for Wales acting jointly may make regulations for providing, where a local authority under this Part of this Act and a local education authority as such have concurrent functions, by which authority the functions are to be exercised, and for determining as respects any functions of a local education authority specified in the regulations whether a child in the care of a local authority is to be treated as a child of parents of sufficient resources or a child of parents without resources.

PART IV

Community Homes

Regional planning of accommodation for children in care.

31.—(1) With a view to the preparation, in pursuance of the provisions of this Part of this Act, of regional plans for the provision of accommodation for children in the care of local authorities and for the equipment and maintenance of the accommodation, the Secretary of State may by order provide that any area specified in the order shall be a separate area (in this Act referred to as a " planning area ") for the purposes of those provisions.

(2) Before making an order under subsection (1) above, the Secretary of State shall consult each local authority whose area or any part of whose area is included in the planning area which

he proposes should be specified in the order and such other local authorities, if any, as he thinks fit.

(3) It shall be the duty of the local authorities whose areas are wholly or partly included in a planning area (in this Act referred to, in relation to such an area, as " the relevant authorities ") to establish for the area, within such period as may be provided by the order specifying the planning area or such longer period as the Secretary of State may allow, a body to be called the children's regional planning committee.

(4) The provisions of Schedule 1 to this Act shall have effect in relation to children's regional planning committees.

(5) In the case of an order under subsection (1) above which varies or revokes a previous order under that subsection—

(a) the reference in subsection (2) above to the planning area which the Secretary of State proposes should be specified in the order shall be construed as a reference to the planning area as it would be if the variation were made or, as the case may be, to the planning area as it is before the revocation ; and

(b) the order may contain such transitional provisions (including provisions as to the expenses and membership of any existing or former children's regional planning committee for a planning area) as the Secretary of State thinks fit.

32.—(1) The children's regional planning committee for a planning area (in this and section 33 of this Act referred to as " the committee ") shall prepare and submit to the Secretary of State, in accordance with the following provisions of this section, a plan (in this Act referred to as a " regional plan ") for the provision and maintenance of homes, to be known as community homes, for the accommodation and maintenance of children in the care of the relevant authorities. *Regional plans for community homes.*

(2) The community homes for which provision may be made by a regional plan shall be—

(a) community homes provided by the relevant authorities ; and

(b) voluntary homes provided by voluntary organisations but in the management of each of which the plan proposes that a relevant authority should participate in accordance with an instrument of management.

(3) Where a regional plan makes provision for any such voluntary home as is referred to in paragraph (b) of subsection

(2) above, the plan shall designate the home as either a controlled community home or an assisted community home, according as it is proposed in the plan that the management, equipment and maintenance of the home should be the responsibility of one of the relevant authorities or of the voluntary organisation by which the home is provided.

(4) Every regional plan shall contain proposals—

    (a) with regard to the nature and purpose of each of the community homes for which the plan makes provision ; and

    (b) for the provision of facilities for the observation of the physical and mental condition of children in the care of the relevant authorities and for the assessment of the most suitable accommodation and treatment for those children.

(5) Before including provision in a regional plan that a community home should be provided by any of the relevant authorities or that a voluntary home provided by a voluntary organisation should be designated as a controlled or assisted community home, the committee shall obtain the consent of the authority or voluntary organisation by which the home is or is to be provided and, in the case of a home which is to be designated as a controlled or assisted community home, the consent of the local authority which it is proposed should be specified in the instrument of management for the home.

(6) A regional plan shall be prepared in such form and shall contain such information as the Secretary of State may direct, either generally or in relation to a particular planning area or particular kinds of plans ; and the Secretary of State may direct that the regional plan for a particular planning area shall be submitted to him within such period as may be specified in the direction or such longer period as he may allow.

Approval and variation of regional plans.

33.—(1) After considering any regional plan submitted to him under section 32 of this Act and after making in the plan such modifications (if any) as he may agree with the committee by which the plan was submitted and as he may consider appropriate for securing that the plan makes proper provision for the accommodation and maintenance of children in the care of the relevant authorities, the Secretary of State may approve the plan.

(2) Where the Secretary of State considers that, either with or without such modifications as are referred to in subsection (1) above, part but not the whole of a plan submitted to him under section 32 of this Act makes proper provision for the accommodation and maintenance of the children to whom

that part of the plan relates, the Secretary of State may approve that part of the plan.

(3) Where the Secretary of State has approved part only of a regional plan, the committee for the planning area concerned shall prepare and submit to him under section 32 of this Act a further regional plan containing proposals to supplement that part of the previous plan which was approved by the Secretary of State.

(4) If, at any time after the approval of the whole or part of a regional plan by the Secretary of State, the committee for the planning area concerned consider that the plan, or such part of it as was approved, should be varied or replaced, they shall prepare and submit to the Secretary of State under section 32 of this Act a further regional plan for that purpose ; and any such further regional plan may—

> (a) take the form of a replacement for the regional plan or part thereof which was previously approved by the Secretary of State ; or
>
> (b) contain proposals for the amendment of that regional plan or part thereof.

(5) In relation to a further regional plan which contains proposals for supplementing or amending a regional plan or part of a regional plan which has been previously approved by the Secretary of State (in this subsection referred to as " the approved plan ")—

> (a) section 32(4) of this Act shall have effect as if references to a regional plan were references to the approved plan as it would have effect if supplemented or amended in accordance with the proposals contained in the further regional plan ; and
>
> (b) subsection (1) above shall have effect as if the reference therein to children in the care of the relevant authorities were a reference to the children to whom the proposals in the plan relate ; and
>
> (c) in so far as the further regional plan contains proposals under which a home would cease to be a community home, or would become a community home of a different description, or would be used for a purpose different from that provided for in the approved plan, the committee preparing the further plan shall, before submitting it to the Secretary of State, obtain the consent of the local authority or voluntary organisation by which the home is provided and, if the proposal is for a home to become or to cease to be a controlled or assisted community home, the consent of the local authority which it is proposed should be, or which is, specified in the instrument of management for the home.

(6) Where the Secretary of State approves a regional plan, in whole or in part, he shall give notice in writing of his approval to the committee for the planning area concerned specifying the date on which the plan is to come into operation, and the committee shall send a copy of the notice to each of the relevant authorities and to any voluntary organisation whose consent was required to any provision of the plan.

Provision of community homes by local authorities.

34. Where a regional plan for a planning area includes provision for a community home to be provided by one of the relevant authorities, it shall be the duty of the local authority concerned to provide, manage, equip and maintain that home.

Instruments of management for assisted and controlled community homes.

35.—(1) The Secretary of State may by order make an instrument of management providing for the constitution of a body of managers for any voluntary home which, in accordance with a regional plan approved by him, is designated as a controlled or assisted community home.

(2) Where, in accordance with a regional plan approved by the Secretary of State, two or more voluntary homes are designated as controlled community homes or as assisted community homes, then if—

(a) those homes are, or are to be, provided by the same voluntary organisation ; and

(b) the same local authority is to be represented on the body of managers for those homes,

a single instrument of management may be made by the Secretary of State under this section constituting one body of managers for those homes or for any two or more of them.

(3) The number of persons who, in accordance with an instrument of management under this section, constitute the body of managers for a voluntary home shall be such number, being a multiple of three, as may be specified in the instrument of management, but the instrument shall provide that a proportion of the managers shall be appointed by such local authority as may be so specified and—

(a) in the case of a voluntary home which is designated in a regional plan as a controlled community home, the proportion shall be two-thirds ; and

(b) in the case of a voluntary home which is so designated as an assisted community home, the proportion shall be one-third.

(4) An instrument of management shall provide that the " foundation managers ", that is to say, those of the managers of the voluntary home to which the instrument relates who are not appointed by a local authority in accordance with subsection

(3) above, shall be appointed, in such manner and by such persons as may be specified in the instrument,—

    (*a*) so as to represent the interests of the voluntary organisation by which the home is, or is to be, provided ; and

    (*b*) for the purpose of securing that, as far as practicable, the character of the home as a voluntary home will be preserved and that, subject to section 36(3) of this Act, the terms of any trust deed relating to the home are observed.

(5) An instrument of management under this section shall come into force on such date as may be specified in the instrument, and if such an instrument is in force in relation to a voluntary home the home shall be and be known as a controlled community home or an assisted community home, according to its designation in the regional plan.

36.—(1) An instrument of management for a controlled or assisted community home shall contain such provisions as the Secretary of State considers appropriate for giving effect to the provisions of the regional plan by which the home is designated as a controlled or assisted community home, but nothing in the instrument of management for such a home shall affect the purposes for which the premises comprising the home are held.

Supplementary provisions as to instruments of management and trust deeds.

(2) Without prejudice to the generality of subsection (1) above, an instrument of management may contain—

    (*a*) provisions specifying the nature and purpose of the home or each of the homes to which it relates ;

    (*b*) provisions requiring a specified number or proportion of the places in that home or those homes to be made available to local authorities and to any other body specified in the instrument ; and

    (*c*) provisions relating to the management of that home or those homes and the charging of fees in respect of children placed therein or places made available to any local authority or other body.

(3) Subject to subsection (1) above, in the event of any inconsistency between the provisions of any trust deed and the instrument of management relating to a controlled or assisted community home, the instrument of management shall prevail over the provisions of the trust deed in so far as they relate to that home.

(4) After consultation with the voluntary organisation by which a controlled or assisted community home is provided and with the local authority specified in the instrument of management for the time being in force for that home, the Secretary of State may vary or revoke any provisions of that instrument of management by a further instrument of management.

(5) In this Act the expression " trust deed ", in relation to a voluntary home, means any instrument (other than an instrument of management) regulating the maintenance, management or conduct of the home or the constitution of a body of managers or trustees of the home.

37.—(1) The management, equipment and maintenance of a controlled community home shall be the responsibility of the local authority specified in the instrument of management for that home, and in the following provisions of this section " the responsible authority ", in relation to such a home, means the local authority responsible for its management, equipment and maintenance.

(2) Subject to the following provisions of this section, the responsible authority shall exercise their functions in relation to a controlled community home through the body of managers constituted by the instrument of management for the home, and anything done, liability incurred or property acquired by the managers shall be done, incurred or acquired by the managers as agents of the responsible authority.

(3) In so far as any matter is reserved for the decision of the responsible authority, either by subsection (4) below or by the instrument of management for the controlled community home in question or by the service by the responsible authority on the managers or any of them of a notice reserving any matter, that matter shall be dealt with by the responsible authority themselves and not by the managers, but in dealing with any matter so reserved the responsible authority shall have regard to any representations made to them by the managers.

(4) The employment of persons at a controlled community home shall be a matter reserved for the decision of the responsible authority, but where the instrument of management so provides the responsible authority may enter into arrangements with the voluntary organisation by which the home is provided whereby, in accordance with such terms as may be agreed between the responsible authority and the voluntary organisation, persons who are not in the employment of the responsible authority shall undertake duties at the home.

(5) The accounting year of the managers of a controlled community home shall be such as may be specified by the responsible authority and, before such date in each accounting year as may be so specified, the managers of a controlled community home shall submit to the responsible authority estimates, in such form as the authority may require, of expenditure and receipts in respect of the next accounting year ; and any expenses incurred by the managers of a controlled community home with the approval of the responsible authority shall be defrayed by that authority.

(6) The managers of a controlled community home shall keep proper accounts in respect of that home and proper records in relation to the accounts, but where an instrument of management relates to more than one controlled community home, one set of accounts and records may be kept in respect of all the homes to which the instrument relates.

38.—(1) The management, equipment and maintenance of an assisted community home shall be the responsibility of the voluntary organisation by which the home is provided, and in the following provisions of this section " the responsible organisation ", in relation to such a home, means the voluntary organisation responsible for its management, equipment and maintenance.

(2) Subject to the following provisions of this section, the responsible organisation shall exercise its functions in relation to the home through the body of managers constituted by the instrument of management for the home, and any thing done, liability incurred or property acquired by the managers shall be done, incurred or acquired by the managers as agents of the responsible organisation.

(3) In so far as any matter is reserved for the decision of the responsible organisation, either by subsection (4) below or by the instrument of management for the assisted community home in question or by the service by the responsible organisation on the managers or any of them of a notice reserving any matter, that matter shall be dealt with by the responsible organisation itself and not by the managers, but in dealing with any matter so reserved the responsible organisation shall have regard to any representations made to the organisation by the managers.

(4) The employment of persons at an assisted community home shall be a matter reserved for the decision of the responsible organisation but, subject to subsection (5) below—

   (a) where the responsible organisation proposes to engage any person to work at the home or to terminate without notice the employment of any person at the home, the responsible organisation shall consult the local authority specified in the instrument of management and, if the local authority so directs, the responsible organisation shall not carry out its proposal without the consent of the local authority ; and

   (b) the local authority may, after consultation with the responsible organisation, require the organisation to terminate the employment of any person at the home.

(5) Paragraphs (a) and (b) of subsection (4) above shall not apply—

> (a) in such cases or circumstances as may be specified by notice in writing given by the local authority to the responsible organisation ; and

> (b) in relation to the employment of any persons or class of persons specified in the instrument of management.

(6) The accounting year of the managers of an assisted community home shall be such as may be specified by the responsible organisation and, before such date in each accounting year as may be so specified, the managers of an assisted community home shall submit to the responsible organisation estimates, in such form as the organisation may require, of expenditure and receipts in respect of the next accounting year ; and all expenses incurred by the managers of an assisted community home with the approval of the responsible organisation shall be defrayed by the organisation.

(7) The managers of an assisted community home shall keep proper accounts in respect of that home and proper records in relation to those accounts, but where an instrument of management relates to more than one assisted community home, one set of accounts and records may be kept in respect of all the homes to which the instrument relates.

Regulations as to conduct of community homes etc.

39.—(1) The Secretary of State may make regulations with respect to the conduct of community homes and for securing the welfare of the children in community homes.

(2) Without prejudice to the generality of subsection (1) above, regulations under this section may—

> (a) impose requirements as to the accommodation and equipment to be provided in community homes and as to the medical arrangements to be made for protecting the health of the children in the homes ;

> (b) impose requirements as to the facilities which are to be provided for giving religious instruction to children in community homes ;

> (c) require the approval of the Secretary of State for the provision and use of accommodation for the purpose of restricting the liberty of children in community homes and impose other requirements as to the placing of a child in accommodation provided for that purpose, including a requirement to obtain the permission of the local authority or voluntary organisation in whose care the child is ;

(*d*) authorise the Secretary of State to give and revoke directions requiring—

(i) the local authority by whom a community home is provided or who are specified in the instrument of management for a controlled community home, or

(ii) the voluntary organisation by which an assisted community home is provided,

to accommodate in the home a child in the care of a local authority for whom no places are made available in that home or to take such action in relation to a child accommodated in the home as may be specified in the directions ;

(*e*) require reviews of any permission given in pursuance of paragraph (*c*) above and provide for such a review to be conducted in a manner approved by the Secretary of State by a committee of persons representing the local authority or voluntary organisation in question but including at least one person satisfying such conditions as may be prescribed by the regulations with a view to securing that he is independent of the authority or organisation and unconnected with any community home containing such accommodation as is mentioned in the said paragraph (*c*) ;

(*f*) prescribe standards to which premises used for community homes are to conform ;

(*g*) require the approval of the Secretary of State to the use of buildings for the purpose of community homes and to the doing of anything (whether by way of addition, diminution or alteration) which materially affects the buildings or grounds or other facilities or amenities available for children in community homes ;

(*h*) provide that, to such extent as may be provided for in the regulations, the Secretary of State may direct that any provision of regulations under this section which is specified in the direction and makes any such provision as is referred to in paragraph (*a*), (*f*) or (*g*) above shall not apply in relation to a particular community home or the premises used for it, and may provide for the variation or revocation of any such direction by the Secretary of State.

(3) Without prejudice to the power to make regulations under this section conferring functions on the local authority or voluntary organisation by which a community home is provided or on the managers of a controlled or assisted community home, regulations under this section may confer functions in relation

to a controlled or assisted community home on the local authority named in the instrument of management for the home.

Directions
that premises
no longer to
be used for
community
home.

40.—(1) Where it appears to the Secretary of State that any premises used for the purposes of a community home are unsuitable for those purposes, or that the conduct of a community home is not in accordance with regulations made by him under section 39 of this Act or is otherwise unsatisfactory, he may by notice in writing served on the responsible body, direct that as from such date as may be specified in the notice the premises shall not be used for the purposes of a community home.

(2) Where the Secretary of State has given a direction in relation to a controlled or assisted community home under subsection (1) above and the direction has not been revoked, the Secretary of State may at any time by order revoke the instrument of management for that home.

(3) For the purposes of subsection (1) above the responsible body—

(a) in relation to a community home provided by a local authority, is that local authority ;

(b) in relation to a controlled community home, is the local authority specified in the instrument of management for that home ; and

(c) in relation to an assisted community home, is the voluntary organisation by which the home is provided.

Controlled
and assisted
community
homes
exempted
from certain
provisions of
Part VI.

41. While a voluntary home is a controlled or assisted community home, sections 57 to 60 of this Act shall not apply in relation to it.

Determination
of disputes
relating to
controlled
and assisted
community
homes.

42.—(1) Subject to subsection (5) below, where any dispute relating to a controlled community home arises between the local authority specified in the instrument of management and either the voluntary organisation by which the home is provided or any other local authority who have placed, or desire or are required to place, a child in their care in the home, the dispute may be referred by either party to the Secretary of State for his determination.

(2) Subject to subsection (5) below, where any dispute relating to an assisted community home arises between the voluntary organisation by which the home is provided and any local authority who have placed, or desire to place, a child

in their care in the home, the dispute may be referred by either party to the Secretary of State for his determination.

(3) Where a dispute is referred to the Secretary of State under this section he may, in order to give effect to his determination of the dispute, give such directions as he thinks fit to the local authority or voluntary organisation concerned.

(4) The provisions of this section shall apply notwithstanding that the matter in dispute may be one which, under or by virtue of the preceding provisions of this Part of this Act, is reserved for the decision, or is the responsibility, of the local authority specified in the instrument of management or, as the case may be, the voluntary organisation by which the home is provided.

(5) Where any trust deed relating to a controlled or assisted community home contains provision whereby a bishop or any other ecclesiastical or denominational authority has power to decide questions relating to religious instruction given in the home, no dispute which is capable of being dealt with in accordance with that provision shall be referred to the Secretary of State under this section.

43.—(1) The voluntary organisation by which a controlled or assisted community home is provided shall not cease to provide the home except after giving to the Secretary of State and the local authority specified in the instrument of management not less than two years' notice in writing of their intention to do so.

Discontinuance by voluntary organisation of controlled or assisted community home.

(2) A notice under subsection (1) above shall specify the date from which the voluntary organisation intends to cease to provide the home as a community home ; and where such a notice is given and is not withdrawn before the date specified in it, then, subject to subsection (4) below, the instrument of management for the home shall cease to have effect on that date and accordingly the home shall then cease to be a controlled or assisted community home.

(3) Where a notice is given under subsection (1) above, the local authority to whom the notice is given shall inform the children's regional planning committee responsible for the regional plan under which the voluntary home in question was designated as a controlled or assisted community home of the receipt and content of the notice.

(4) Where a notice is given under subsection (1) above and the body of managers for the home to which the notice relates give notice in writing to the Secretary of State that they are unable or unwilling to continue as managers of the home until the date specified in the first-mentioned notice, the Secretary of State may by order—

   (*a*) revoke the instrument of management ; and

(b) require the local authority who were specified in that instrument to conduct the home, until the date specified in the notice under subsection (1) above or such earlier date (if any) as may be specified for the purposes of this paragraph in the order, as if it were a community home provided by the local authority.

(5) Where the Secretary of State makes such a requirement as is specified in subsection (4)(b) above—

(a) nothing in the trust deed for the home in question shall affect the conduct of the home by the local authority; and

(b) the Secretary of State may by order direct that for the purposes of any provision specified in the direction and made by or under any enactment relating to community homes (other than this section) the home shall, until the date or earlier date specified as mentioned in subsection (4)(b) above, be treated as an assisted community home or as a controlled community home, but except in so far as the Secretary of State so directs, the home shall until that date be treated for the purposes of any such enactment as a community home provided by the local authority; and

(c) on the date or earlier date specified as mentioned in subsection (4)(b) above the home shall cease to be a community home.

Financial provisions applicable on cessation of controlled or assisted community home.

44.—(1) Where the instrument of management for a controlled or assisted community home ceases to have effect by virtue either of an order under subsection (2) of section 40 of this Act or of subsection (2) or subsection (4)(a) of section 43 of this Act, the voluntary organisation by which the home was provided or, if the premises used for the purposes of the home are not vested in that organisation, the persons in whom those premises are vested (in this section referred to as "the trustees of the home"), shall become liable, in accordance with the following provisions of this section, to make repayment in respect of any increase in the value of the premises and other property belonging to the voluntary organisation or the trustees of the home which is attributable to the expenditure of public money thereon.

(2) Where an instrument of management has ceased to have effect as mentioned in subsection (1) above and the instrument related—

(a) to a controlled community home; or

      (*b*) to an assisted community home which, at any time before that instrument of management came into force, was a controlled community home,

then, on the home ceasing to be a community home, the voluntary organisation by which the home was provided or, as the case may be, the trustees of the home, shall pay to the local authority specified in that instrument of management a sum equal to that part of the value of any relevant premises which is attributable to expenditure by the local authority who at the time the expenditure was incurred had responsibility for the management, equipment and maintenance of the home by virtue of section 37(1) of this Act.

(3) For the purposes of subsection (2) above, " relevant premises ", in relation to a controlled or assisted community home, means premises used for the purposes of the home and belonging to the voluntary organisation or the trustees of the home but erected, extended or improved, at any time while the home was a controlled community home, by the local authority having, at that time, such responsibility in relation to the home as is mentioned in that subsection.

(4) Where an instrument of management has ceased to have effect as mentioned in subsection (1) above and the instrument related—

      (*a*) to an assisted community home ; or

      (*b*) to a controlled community home which, at any time before the instrument of management came into force, was an assisted community home,

then, on the home ceasing to be a community home, the voluntary organisation by which the home was provided or, as the case may be, the trustees of the home, shall pay to the Secretary of State a sum equal to that part of the value of the premises and any other property used for the purposes of the home which is attributable to the expenditure of money provided by way of grant under section 82 of this Act.

(5) Where an instrument of management has ceased to have effect as mentioned in subsection (1) above and the controlled or assisted community home to which it related was conducted in premises which formerly were used as an approved school or were an approved probation hostel or home but which were designated as a community home in a regional plan approved by the Secretary of State, then, on the home ceasing to be a community home, the voluntary organisation by which the home was provided or, as the case may be, the trustees of the home, shall pay to the Secretary of State a sum equal to that part of the value of the premises concerned and of any other property

used for the purposes of the home and belonging to the voluntary organisation or the trustees of the home which is attributable to the expenditure—

    (*a*) of sums paid towards the expenses of the managers of an approved school under section 104 of the Children and Young Persons Act 1933 ; or

    (*b*) of sums paid under section 51(3)(*c*) of the Powers of Criminal Courts Act 1973 in relation to expenditure on approved probation hostels or homes.

(6) The amount of any sum payable under this section by the voluntary organisation by which a controlled or assisted community home was provided or by the trustees of the home shall be determined in accordance with such arrangements—

    (*a*) as may be agreed between the voluntary organisation by which the home was provided and the local authority concerned or, as the case may be, the Secretary of State ; or

    (*b*) in default of agreement, as may be determined by the Secretary of State ;

and with the agreement of the local authority concerned or the Secretary of State, as the case may be, the liability to pay any sum under this section may be discharged, in whole or in part, by the transfer of any premises or other property used for the purposes of the home in question.

(7) The provisions of this section shall have effect notwithstanding anything in any trust deed for a controlled or assisted community home and notwithstanding the provisions of any enactment or instrument governing the disposition of the property of a voluntary organisation.

(8) Any sums received by the Secretary of State under this section shall be paid into the Consolidated Fund.

PART V

CONTRIBUTIONS TOWARDS MAINTENANCE OF CHILDREN IN CARE OF LOCAL AUTHORITIES

Liability for contributions in respect of children in care.

45.—(1) Where—

    (*a*) a child is in the care of a local authority under section 2 of this Act, or

    (*b*) a child is in the care of a local authority by virtue of a care order (other than an interim order),

the following persons (and no others) shall be liable to make contributions in respect of the child, that is to say—

    (i) if the child has not attained the age of sixteen, the father or mother of the child, and

(ii) if the child has attained the age of sixteen and is engaged in remunerative full-time work, the child himself.

(2) Any contribution which any person is required to make under subsection (1) above shall be payable to the local authority for the area in which that person is for the time being residing.

(3) Whether or not a contribution order has been made under section 47 of this Act in respect of any child in the care of a local authority, no contribution shall be payable in respect of him for any period during which he is allowed by the local authority to be under the charge and control of a parent, guardian, relative or friend, although remaining in the care of the local authority.

(4) Where a contribution order is made under section 47 of this Act requiring the father or mother of the child to make contributions in respect of the child, no payments shall be required to be made under the order in respect of any period after the child has attained the age of sixteen.

46.—(1) Where a person is liable under section 45 of this Act to make a contribution in respect of a child in the care of a local authority then, subject to the provisions of this section, the amount of his contribution shall be such as may be proposed by the local authority and agreed by that person or, in default of agreement, as may be determined by a court under section 47 or 48 of this Act in proceedings for, or for the variation of, a contribution order.

Amount of contributions.

(2) The maximum contribution which may be proposed by a local authority in respect of a child in their care shall be a weekly amount equal to the weekly amount which, in the opinion of the local authority, they would normally be prepared to pay if a child of the same age were boarded out by them (whether or not the child in respect of whom the contribution is proposed is in fact so boarded out and, if he is, whether or not the local authority are in fact paying that amount).

47.—(1) Where—

Contribution orders.

    (*a*) the local authority in whose care a child is have, by notice in writing given to a person liable to make a contribution in respect of the child under section 45 of this Act (in this section and section 48 of this Act referred to as a " contributor "), proposed an amount as the amount of his contribution ; and

    (*b*) either the contributor and the local authority have not, within the period of one month beginning with the day on which the notice was given to the contributor, agreed on the amount of his contribution or the contributor has defaulted in making one or more contributions of an amount which has been agreed,

the local authority entitled under section 45(2) of this Act to receive contributions in respect of the child may apply to a magistrates' court appointed for the commission area where the contributor is for the time being residing for an order under this section.

(2) On an application under subsection (1) above, the court may make an order (in this Act referred to as a " contribution order ") requiring the contributor to contribute such weekly sum as the court having regard to his means thinks fit, not being greater than the amount proposed in the notice given to the contributor under subsection (1)(a) above.

(3) Subject to the provisions of this Act, a contribution order in respect of a child in the care of a local authority under section 2 of this Act shall remain in force so long as the child remains in the care of a local authority under that section and a contribution order in respect of a child who is in the care of a local authority by virtue of a care order shall remain in force so long as the child to whom it relates is in the care of the local authority to whose care he is committed by the care order.

(4) A contribution order may be enforced in like manner as an affiliation order and the enactments relating to the enforcement of affiliation orders shall, with any necessary modifications, apply accordingly, except that any powers conferred on a magistrates' court by any such enactment shall as respects a contribution order be exercisable, and exercisable only, by a magistrates' court appointed for the commission area where the contributor is for the time being residing.

Variation of contribution orders.
1952 c. 55.

48.—(1) Any powers conferred on a magistrates' court by section 53 of the Magistrates' Courts Act 1952 (which confers power to revoke, vary or revive orders for periodical payments) shall as respects a contribution order be exercisable, and exercisable only, by a magistrates' court appointed for the commission area where the contributor is for the time being residing.

(2) In proceedings for the variation of a contribution order, the local authority concerned shall specify the weekly amount which, having regard to section 46(2) of this Act, they propose should be the amount of the contribution payable under the order and the court shall not vary the contribution order so as to require the contributor to pay a contribution greater than that proposed by the local authority.

49.—(1) Where a child who is in the care of a local authority under section 2 of this Act is illegitimate and an affiliation order for his maintenance is in force, any magistrates' court appointed for the commission area where the putative father is for the time being residing may at any time order the payments under the affiliation order to be paid to the local authority who are from time to time entitled under section 45(2) of this Act to receive contributions in respect of the child.

(2) Where a child who is in the care of a local authority by virtue of a care order (other than an interim order) is illegitimate and an affiliation order for his maintenance is in force, the court which makes the order may at the same time, and any magistrates' court appointed for the commission area where the putative father is for the time being residing may subsequently at any time, order the payments under the affiliation order to be paid to the local authority who are from time to time entitled under section 45(2) of this Act to receive contributions in respect of the child.

(3) Applications for orders under subsection (1) or (2) above may be made by the local authority by whom applications for contribution orders may be made.

(4) Where an order made under subsection (1) or (2) above with respect to an affiliation order is in force—

(a) any powers conferred on a magistrates' court by the enactments relating to the enforcement of affiliation orders or by section 53 of the Magistrates' Courts Act 1952 (which confers power to revoke, vary or revive orders for periodical payments) shall as respects the affiliation order in question be exercisable, and exercisable only, by a magistrates' court appointed for the commission area where the person liable is for the time being residing ;

1952 c. 55.

(b) any sums received under the affiliation order shall be applied in like manner as if they were contributions received under a contribution order ;

(c) if the putative father changes his address he shall forthwith give notice thereof to the local authority who were immediately before the change entitled to receive payments under the order and, if he fails to do so, he shall be guilty of an offence and liable on summary conviction to a fine not exceeding £50.

(5) The making of an order under subsection (1) or (2) above with respect to an affiliation order shall not extend the duration of the affiliation order.

(6) Where an order is made under this section with respect to an affiliation order, the affiliation order shall not remain in force (except for the purpose of the recovery of arrears)—

> (a) in the case of an order made by virtue of subsection (1) above, after the child has ceased to be in the care of the local authority under section 2 of this Act, or
>
> (b) in the case of an order made by virtue of subsection (2) above, after the child has ceased to be the subject of the care order ; or
>
> (c) in either case, if the child is allowed by the local authority to be under the charge and control of a parent, guardian, relative or friend, although remaining in the care of the local authority.

(7) Where an affiliation order would, but for the provisions of subsection (6) above, have continued in force, the mother, or any person entitled to make an application for an order under 1957 c. 55. section 5 of the Affiliation Proceedings Act 1957, may apply to a magistrates' court appointed for the commission area where she or he is for the time being residing for an order that the affiliation order may be revived and that payments thereunder may until the expiration thereof be made to the applicant at such a rate as may be proper, and the court may make such an order accordingly, and where such an order is so made, any power to vary, revoke or again revive the affiliation order or any part thereof, being a power which would but for the provisions of this subsection be vested in the court which originally made the affiliation order, shall be exercisable, and exercisable only, by the court which made the order under this subsection.

Application by local authority for affiliation order. **50.**—(1) Subject to the provisions of subsection (2) below, where—

> (a) an illegitimate child is in the care of a local authority under section 2 of this Act, or
>
> (b) an illegitimate child is in the care of a local authority by virtue of a care order (other than an interim order),

and no affiliation order has been made in respect of the child, the local authority whose area includes the place where the mother of the child resides may apply to a magistrates' court appointed for the commission area which includes that place for a summons to be served under section 1 of the Affiliation Proceedings Act 1957.

(2) No application shall be made under subsection (1) above—

> (a) in a case falling within paragraph (a) of that subsection, after the expiration of three years from the time when the child was received or last received into the care of the local authority or of another local authority

from whom the care of the child was taken over by the first mentioned authority ;

(b) in a case falling within paragraph (b) of that subsection, after the expiration of three years from the coming into force of the care order.

(3) In any proceedings on an application under subsection (1) above the court shall hear such evidence as the local authority may produce, and shall in all other respects, but subject to the provisions of subsection (4) below, proceed as on an application made by the mother under section 1 of the Affiliation Proceedings Act 1957.

1957 c. 55.

(4) An order made under section 4 of the Affiliation Proceedings Act 1957 on an application under subsection (1) above shall provide that the payments to be made under the order shall, in lieu of being made to the mother or a person appointed to have the custody of the child, be made to the local authority who are from time to time entitled under section 45 (2) of this Act to receive contributions in respect of the child.

(5) Where in accordance with section 49(6) of this Act an affiliation order has ceased to be in force, and but for that subsection the order would still be in force, then if the condition specified in paragraph (a) or (b) of subsection (1) above is fulfilled, the local authority whose area includes the place where the putative father of the child resides may make application to a magistrates' court appointed for the commission area which includes that place—

(a) for the affiliation order to be revived, and

(b) for payments thereunder to be made to the local authority who are from time to time entitled under section 45(2) of this Act to receive contributions in respect of the child,

and the court may make an order accordingly.

(6) Subsections (4) to (7) of section 49 of this Act shall apply in relation to an order made on an application under subsection (1) above or to an affiliation order revived under subsection (5) above as if it were an affiliation order in respect of which an order had been made under subsection (1) or (2) of that section.

51.—(1) Where during any period (in this section referred to as " the period of default ")—

Recovery of arrears of contributions.

(a) a person was liable to make contributions in respect of a child ; but

(b) no order was in force requiring him to make the contributions ;

Part 1   C

a magistrates' court having jurisdiction in the place where he is for the time being residing may, on the application of the local authority who would have been entitled to receive payments under such an order, make an order (in this Act referred to as an " arrears order ") requiring him to pay such weekly sum, for such period, as the court, having regard to his means, thinks fit ; but the aggregate of the payments required to be made by any person under an arrears order shall not exceed the aggregate that, in the opinion of the court, would have been payable by him under a contribution order in respect of the period of the default or, if it exceeded three months, the last part thereof, less the aggregate of the payments (if any) made by him in respect of his liability during that period or, as the case may be, the last part thereof.

For the purposes of this subsection the last part of the period of default shall be taken to be the last three months thereof and such time, if any, preceding the last three months as is equal to the time during which it continued after the making of the application for the arrears order.

(2) No application for an arrears order shall be made later than three months after the end of the period of default.

(3) An arrears order shall be treated as a contribution order, and payments under it as contributions, for the purposes of sections 45(2) and (3), 47(4), 48 and 53 of this Act.

(4) A person liable to make payments under an arrears order shall, except at a time when he is under a duty to give information of his address under section 12 of this Act, keep the local authority to whom the payments are to be made informed of his address ; and if he fails to do so he shall guilty of an offence and liable on summary conviction to a fine not exceeding £10.

Appeals from orders made under Part V.

52.—(1) An appeal to the Crown Court from an order made by a magistrates' court under this Part of this Act may be brought in the following cases and by the following persons, that is to say—

(a) in the case of an order requiring a person to contribute in respect of himself or any other person (whether a contribution order or an arrears order), by the person required to contribute ;

(b) in the case of an order requiring all or any part of the payments accruing due under an affiliation order to be paid to some other person, by the person who would but for the order be entitled to the payments.

(2) Nothing in this section shall be construed as affecting any other right of appeal conferred by this or any other Act.

53.—(1) Where contributions payable under section 45 of this
Act in respect of a child in the care of a local authority are
payable, by the person liable to make the contributions, to an
authority other than the authority responsible for maintenance,
the authority receiving the contributions from that person shall
pay them over to the authority responsible for maintenance, subject, however, to such deductions in respect of services rendered
by the authority paying the contributions over as may be agreed
between the two authorities or as in default of agreement may
be determined by the Secretary of State.

(2) In this section references to the authority responsible for
maintenance—

    (*a*) in relation to a child who is in the care of a local
           authority by virtue of a care order, are references to that
           authority ;

    (*b*) in relation to a child who is received into the care of
           a local authority under section 2 of this Act, are refer-
           ences to the local authority into whose care the child
           has been received, except that where the authority to
           whom the contributions are payable by the person liable
           to make them has been notified that under section 2(4)
           of this Act expenses are being recovered from another
           authority, the said references shall be construed as
           references to that other authority.

54.—(1) Where by virtue of an order made under section 47,
49, 50 or 51 of this Act any sum is payable to a local authority,
the local authority within whose area the person liable under the
order is for the time being residing shall be entitled to receive and
give a discharge for, and, if necessary, enforce payment of, any
arrears accrued due under the order, notwithstanding that those
arrears may have accrued at a time when he was not resident
in the area of that authority.

(2) In any proceedings under section 47, 49, 50 or 51 of this
Act a certificate purporting to be signed by the clerk to an
authority for the time being entitled to receive contributions, or
by some other officer of the authority duly authorised in that
behalf, and stating that any sum due to the authority under an
order is overdue and unpaid shall be evidence of the facts stated
therein.

55.—(1) A magistrates' court shall have jurisdiction in proceedings against a person residing in Scotland or Northern
Ireland for a contribution order under section 47 of this Act
or for an arrears order under section 51 of this Act.

(2) A magistrates' court by which an order has been made under section 47 or 51 of this Act shall have jurisdiction in proceedings by or against a person residing in Scotland or Northern Ireland for the revocation, revival or variation of that order.

(3) A magistrates' court shall have jurisdiction in proceedings against a man residing in Scotland or Northern Ireland for an affiliation order under section 50 of this Act if the act of intercourse resulting in the birth of the child or any act of intercourse between the parties which may have resulted therein took place in England or Wales.

(4) The provisions of this Part of this Act shall, in the cases mentioned in Schedule 2 to this Act, have effect subject to the modifications set out in that Schedule, being modifications consequential on the foregoing provisions of this section.

(5) Nothing in this section shall be construed as derogating from any jurisdiction exercisable, apart from the provisions of this section, by any court in England or Wales ; and it is hereby declared that any jurisdiction conferred by this section is exercisable notwithstanding that any party to the proceedings is not domiciled in England and Wales and any jurisdiction conferred by this section in affiliation proceedings shall be exercisable notwithstanding that the child to whom the proceedings relate was not born in England or Wales.

PART VI

VOLUNTARY HOMES AND VOLUNTARY ORGANISATIONS

Definition of voluntary home

Definition of voluntary home.

56. In this Act, except where otherwise indicated, the expression " voluntary home " means any home or other institution for the boarding, care and maintenance of poor children, being either—

> (a) a home or other institution supported wholly or partly by voluntary contributions, or
>
> (b) a home or other institution supported wholly or partly by endowments, not being a school within the meaning of the Education Act 1944,

1944 c. 31.

but does not in either case include a mental nursing home within the meaning of the Nursing Homes Act 1975 or a residential home for mentally disordered persons within the meaning of the Residential Homes Act 1980.

1975 c. 37.

Registration etc. of voluntary homes

Registration of voluntary homes.

57.—(1) No voluntary home shall be carried on unless it is for the time being registered in a register to be kept for the purposes of this section by the Secretary of State.

(2) Application for registration under this section shall be made by the persons intending to carry on the home to which the application relates, and shall be made in such manner, and accompanied by such particulars, as the Secretary of State may by regulations prescribe.

(3) On an application duly made under subsection (2) above the Secretary of State may either grant or refuse the application, as he thinks fit, but where he refuses the application he shall give the applicant notice in writing of the refusal.

(4) Where at any time it appears to the Secretary of State that the conduct of any voluntary home is not in accordance with regulations made or directions given under section 60 of this Act or is otherwise unsatisfactory, he may, after giving to the persons carrying on the home not less than twenty-eight days' notice in writing of his proposal to do so, remove the home from the register.

(5) Any person who carries on a voluntary home in contravention of the provisions of subsection (1) above shall be guilty of an offence and liable on summary conviction to a fine not exceeding £500.

(6) Where—

    (a) a voluntary home is carried on in contravention of the provisions of subsection (1) above, or

    (b) notice of a proposal to remove a voluntary home from the register is given under subsection (4) above,

the Secretary of State may, notwithstanding that the time for any appeal under section 58 of this Act has not expired or that such an appeal is pending, notify the local authority in whose area the home is situated and require them forthwith to remove from the home and receive into their care under section 2 of this Act all or any of the children for whom accommodation is being provided in the home ; and the local authority shall comply with the requirement whether or not the circumstances of the children are such that they fall within paragraphs (a) to (c) of subsection (1) of that section and notwithstanding that any of the children may appear to the local authority to be over the age of seventeen.

For the purposes of carrying out the duty of the local authority under this subsection, any person authorised in that behalf by the local authority may enter any premises in which the home in question is being carried on.

(7) Where the Secretary of State registers a home under this section or removes a home from the register he shall notify the local authority in whose area the home is situated.

(8) Any notice under this section required to be given by the Secretary of State to the persons carrying on, or intending to

PART VI

1978 c. 30.

Appeals.

carry on, a voluntary home may be given to those persons by being delivered personally to any one of them, or being sent by post in a registered letter to them or any one of them.

For the purposes of section 7 of the Interpretation Act 1978 (which defines " service by post ") a letter enclosing a notice under this section to the persons carrying on a voluntary home or anyone of them shall be deemed to be properly addressed if it is addressed to them or him at the home.

58.—(1) Where under section 57 of this Act application for the registration of a voluntary home is refused, or it is proposed to remove a voluntary home from the register, the persons intending to carry on or carrying on the home, as the case may be, may within fourteen days from the giving of the notice under subsection (3) or subsection (4) of that section appeal against the refusal or proposal ; and where the appeal is brought against a proposal to remove a home from the register, the home shall not be removed therefrom before the determination of the appeal.

(2) An appeal under this section shall be brought by notice in writing addressed to the Secretary of State requiring him to refer the refusal or proposal to an appeal tribunal constituted in accordance with the provisions of Schedule 3 to this Act.

(3) On an appeal under this section the appeal tribunal may confirm the refusal or proposal of the Secretary of State or may direct that the home shall be registered or, as the case may be, shall not be removed from the register, and the Secretary of State shall comply with the direction.

(4) The Lord Chancellor may with the concurrence of the Lord President of the Council make rules as to the practice and procedure to be followed with respect to the constitution of appeal tribunals for the purposes of this section, as to the manner of making appeals to such tribunals, and as to proceedings before such tribunals and matters incidental or consequential on such proceedings ; and without prejudice to the generality of the foregoing provisions of this subsection such rules may make provision as to the particulars to be supplied by or to the Secretary of State of matters relevant to the determination of the appeal and as to representation before such tribunals, whether by counsel or solicitor or otherwise.

(5) The Secretary of State may out of moneys provided by Parliament—

    (a) pay to members of tribunals constituted for the purposes of this section such fees and allowances as he may with the consent of the Minister for the Civil Service determine ;

(*b*) defray the expenses of such tribunals up to such amount as he may with the like consent determine.

(6) The provisions of the Arbitration Act 1950 shall not apply to any proceedings before a tribunal constituted for the purposes of this section except so far as any provisions thereof may be applied thereto with or without modifications by rules made under this section.

59.—(1) It shall be the duty of the person in charge of any voluntary home established after the commencement of this Act to send to the Secretary of State within three months from the establishment of the home such particulars with respect to the home as the Secretary of State may by regulations prescribe.

(2) It shall be the duty of the person in charge of any voluntary home (whether established before or after the commencement of this Act) to send to the Secretary of State—

(*a*) in the case of a home established before the commencement of this Act, in every year, or

(*b*) in the case of a home established after the commencement of this Act, in every year subsequent to the year in which particulars are sent under subsection (1) above,

by such date as the Secretary of State may by regulations prescribe, such particulars with respect to the home as may be so prescribed.

(3) Where the Secretary of State by regulations varies the particulars which are to be sent to him under subsection (1) or (2) above by the person in charge of a voluntary home—

(*a*) the person in charge of such a home shall send to the Secretary of State the prescribed particulars within three months from the date of the making of the regulations ;

(*b*) where any such home was established before, but not more than three months before, the making of the regulations, compliance with paragraph (*a*) above shall be sufficient compliance with the requirement of subsection (1) above to send the prescribed particulars within three months from the establishment of the home ;

(*c*) in the year in which the particulars are varied, compliance with paragraph (*a*) above by the person in charge of any voluntary home shall be sufficient compliance with the requirement of subsection (2) above to send the prescribed particulars before the prescribed date in that year.

C 4

(4) If default is made in sending the prescribed particulars with respect to any voluntary home in accordance with the requirements of this section, the person in charge of the home shall be guilty of an offence and liable on summary conviction to a fine not exceeding £25 and to a further fine not exceeding £1 in respect of each day during which the default continues after conviction.

Regulations as to voluntary homes and organisations

Regulations as
to conduct
of voluntary
homes.

60.—(1) The Secretary of State may make regulations as to the conduct of voluntary homes and for securing the welfare of the children therein, and regulations under this section may in particular—

(*a*) impose requirements as to the accommodation and equipment to be provided in homes, authorise the Secretary of State to give directions prohibiting the provision for the children in any home of clothing of any description specified in the directions, and impose requirements as to the medical arrangements to be made for protecting the health of the children in the homes ;

(*b*) require the furnishing to the Secretary of State of information as to the facilities provided for the parents and guardians of children in the homes to visit and communicate with the children and authorise the Secretary of State to give directions as to the provision of such facilities ;

(*c*) authorise the Secretary of State to give directions limiting the number of children who may at any one time be accommodated in any particular home ;

(*d*) provide for consultation with the Secretary of State as to applicants for appointment to the charge of a home and empower the Secretary of State to prohibit the appointment of any particular applicant therefor except in the cases (if any) in which the regulations dispense with such consultation by reason that the person to be appointed possesses such qualifications as may be prescribed by the regulations ;

(*e*) require notice to be given to the Secretary of State of any change of the person in charge of a home ; and

(*f*) impose requirements as to the facilities which are to be given for children to receive a religious upbringing appropriate to the persuasion to which they belong ;

and may contain different provisions for different descriptions of cases and as respects different descriptions of homes.

(2) Where any regulation under this section provides that this subsection shall have effect in relation thereto, any person who contravenes or fails to comply with the regulation or any requirement or direction thereunder shall be guilty of an offence and liable on summary conviction to a fine not exceeding £500.

61.—(1) The power conferred by Part III of this Act on the Regulations Secretary of State to make regulations as to the boarding out as to the of children by local authorities shall extend also to the boarding boarding out of children out of children by voluntary organisations, subject to the modi- by voluntary fication that in the provisions of the said Part III conferring organisations. that power any reference to the supervision and inspection by a local authority of boarded out children and the premises in which they are boarded out shall, in relation to children boarded out by voluntary organisations, be deemed to be a reference to supervision and inspection either by a local authority or, where it is so provided by or under the regulations, by a voluntary organisation.

(2) Where any regulation under this section provides that this subsection shall have effect in relation thereto, any person who contravenes or fails to comply with the regulation shall be guilty of an offence and liable on summary conviction to a fine not exceeding £50.

62.—(1) The Secretary of State may by regulations control Regulations the making and carrying out by voluntary organisations of as to arrange-arrangements for the emigration of children. ments by voluntary organisations (2) Any regulations made under this section may contain for emigration such consequential and incidental provisions as appear to the of children. Secretary of State to be necessary or expedient, including, in particular, provisions for requiring information to be given to the Secretary of State as to the operations or intended operations of the organisation and for enabling the Secretary of State to be satisfied that suitable arrangements have been or will be made for the children's reception and welfare in the country to which they are going.

(3) Where any regulation under this section provides that this subsection shall have effect in relation thereto, any person who contravenes or fails to comply with the regulation shall be guilty of an offence and liable on summary conviction to a fine not exceeding £50.

Restriction on removal of child from care of voluntary organisation

Restriction
on removal
of child from
care of
voluntary
organisation.

63.—(1) Section 13(1) of this Act shall apply in relation to children who are not in the care of local authorities under section 2 of this Act but who are in voluntary homes or are boarded out, as it applies by virtue of subsection (2) of that section to children in the care of the local authority, except that in the case of a child who is not in the care of a local authority the references in subsection (2) of that section to a local authority shall be construed as references to the voluntary organisation in whose care the child is.

(2) For the purposes of this section a child is boarded out if he is boarded out, by the voluntary organisation in whose care he is, with foster parents to live in their home as a member of their family.

Transfer of parental rights and duties in relation to children in care of voluntary organisations

Transfer of
parental
rights and
duties to
voluntary
organisations.

64.—(1) Where it appears to a local authority as respects a child in the care of a voluntary organisation which is an incorporated body—

   (a) that the child is not in the care of any local authority ; and

   (b) that a condition specified in section 3(1) of this Act is satisfied ; and

   (c) that it is necessary in the interests of the welfare of the child for the parental rights and duties to be vested in the organisation,

the authority may, subject to subsections (5) and (6) below, resolve that there shall vest in the organisation the parental rights and duties with respect to that child.

(2) While a resolution under this section is in force the parental rights and duties shall vest in the organisation in whose care the child is when the resolution is passed.

(3) If, immediately before the resolution is passed, the parental rights and duties are vested in the parent in relation to whom the resolution is passed jointly with any other person, then on the passing of the resolution the parental rights and duties shall vest jointly in that other person and the organisation in whose care the child is.

(4) In determining for the purposes of subsection (1) above whether the condition specified in section 3(1)(b)(i) of this Act is satisfied if the whereabouts of any parent of the child have

remained unknown for twelve months, that parent shall be deemed to have abandoned the child.

(5) A resolution under subsection (1) above may not be passed by a local authority in respect of any child unless—

    (a) the child is living in the area of the authority either in a voluntary home or with foster parents with whom he has been boarded by the organisation in whose care he is ; and

    (b) that organisation has requested the authority to pass the resolution.

(6) The parental rights and duties which may vest in an organisation by virtue of this section do not include—

    (a) the right to consent or refuse to consent to the making of an application under section 18 of the Adoption Act 1976 (orders freeing a child for adoption in England and Wales) or section 18 of the Adoption (Scotland) Act 1978 (orders freeing a child for adoption in Scotland) and

    (b) the right to agree or refuse to agree to the making of an adoption order or an order under section 55 of the Adoption Act 1976 (orders in England and Wales authorising adoption abroad) or section 49 of the Adoption (Scotland) Act 1978 (orders in Scotland authorising adoption abroad),

and regulations made under section 62 of this Act shall apply to the emigration of a child notwithstanding that the parental rights and duties relating to the child are vested in the voluntary organisation.

(7) Section 5(2) of this Act shall apply in relation to a resolution under subsection (1) above as if it were a resolution under section 3 of this Act.

65.—(1) Where the parental rights and duties with respect to a child are by virtue of a resolution under section 64 of this Act vested in a voluntary organisation, then, if it appears to the local authority for the area in which the child is living that, having regard to the interests of the welfare of the child, it is necessary that the parental rights and duties should no longer be vested in the organisation, the local authority shall resolve that there shall vest in them the parental rights and duties relating to the child.

(2) The local authority shall within seven days of passing a resolution under subsection (1) above by notice in writing inform the organisation and each parent, guardian or custodian of the child whose whereabouts are known to them that the resolution has been passed.

Marginal notes:

1976 c. 36.

1978 c. 28.

Duty of local authority to assume parental rights and duties.

66.—(1) A resolution under subsection (1) of section 64 of this Act shall cease to have effect on the passing of a resolution under subsection (1) of section 65 of this Act.

(2) Section 8 of this Act shall have effect in relation to a resolution under subsection (1) of section 64 of this Act as it has effect in relation to a resolution under section 3 of this Act.

(3) A resolution under subsection (1) of section 65 of this Act shall be deemed to be a resolution under section 3 of this Act except that sections 3(2) to (7), 4(1) and 5(4) of this Act shall not apply.

Appeals by
parents etc.

67.—(1) Subsections (2) to (7) of section 3 of this Act shall apply to a resolution under section 64 of this Act as they apply to a resolution under the said section 3, with the substitution for the reference in subsection (2) to the vesting of parental rights and duties in the local authority of a reference to the vesting of parental rights and duties in the voluntary organisation.

(2) An appeal may be made—

(a) where the complaint relates to a resolution under section 64 of this Act, by a person deprived of parental rights and duties by the resolution, or

(b) where the complaint relates to a resolution under section 65 of this Act, by a person who but for that resolution and an earlier resolution under section 64 would have parental rights and duties,

to a juvenile court having jurisdiction in the area of the authority which passed the resolution, on the ground that—

(i) there was no ground for the making of the resolution, or

(ii) that the resolution should in the interests of the child be determined.

(3) An appeal shall lie to the High Court against the decision of a juvenile court under this section.

(4) Section 7 of this Act shall apply in relation to proceedings under this section.

Visiting of children in voluntary homes

Visiting of
children in
voluntary
homes.

68.—(1) It shall be the duty of local authorities from time to time to cause children in voluntary homes in their area, other than community homes, to be visited in the interests of the well-being of the children, and any person authorised in that behalf by a local authority may enter any such voluntary home in the area of the authority for the purpose of visiting the children in the home.

(2) Any person authorised in that behalf by a local authority may enter any voluntary home outside the area of the authority for the purpose of visiting children in the home who are in the care of the authority under section 2 of this Act or are for the time being committed to the care of the authority by a care order or by a warrant under section 23(1) of the Children and 1969 c. 54. Young Persons Act 1969 (which relates to remands in the care of local authorities).

(3) Nothing in subsection (1) or (2) above shall apply to a voluntary home which, otherwise than by virtue of section 74 of this Act, is as a whole subject to inspection by or under the authority of a government department.

(4) A person who proposes to exercise any power of entry or inspection conferred by this section shall if so required produce some duly authenticated document showing his authority to exercise the power.

(5) Any person who obstructs the exercise of any power of entry or inspection conferred by this section shall be guilty of an offence and liable on summary conviction to a fine not exceeding £25 or, in the case of a second or subsequent conviction, to a fine not exceeding £50

After-care of children formerly in care of voluntary organisations

69.—(1) Where it comes to the knowledge of a local authority After-care that there is in their area any child over compulsory school of children age who at the time when he ceased to be of that age or at any formerly in subsequent time was, but is no longer, in the care of a voluntary care of voluntary organisation, then, unless the authority are satisfied that the organisations. welfare of the child does not require it, they shall be under a duty so long as he has not attained the age of eighteen to advise and befriend him ; but if the local authority are satisfied that the voluntary organisation have the necessary facilities for advising and befriending the child, the local authority may make arrangements whereby, while the arrangements continue in force, he shall be advised and befriended by the voluntary organisation instead of by the local authority.

(2) Where a child over compulsory school age ceases to be in the care of a voluntary organisation, the organisation shall inform the local authority for the area in which the child proposes to reside.

(3) Where it comes to the knowledge of a local authority or a voluntary organisation that a child whom they have been advising and befriending in pursuance of this section proposes to transfer or has transferred his residence to the area of another local authority, the first mentioned local authority or, as the case may be, the voluntary organisation shall inform that other local authority.

Returns of information

70. Every voluntary organisation shall, at such times and in such form as the Secretary of State may direct, transmit to him such particulars as he may require with respect to the children who are accommodated and maintained in voluntary homes provided by the organisation or who have been boarded out by the organisation.

PART VII

MISCELLANEOUS AND SUPPLEMENTARY PROVISIONS

Advisory Council on Child Care

Advisory
Council on
Child Care.

71.—(1) There shall continue to be a council, to be known as the Advisory Council on Child Care, for the purpose of advising the Secretary of State on matters connected with the discharge of his functions in England and Wales under—

(a) this Act,

(b) the Children and Young Persons Acts 1933 to 1969,

1975 c. 72.   (c) the Children Act 1975, and

1976 c. 36.   (d) the Adoption Act 1976.

(2) The Advisory Council on Child Care shall consist of such persons, to be appointed by the Secretary of State, as the Secretary of State may think fit, being persons specially qualified to deal with matters affecting the welfare of children and persons having such other qualifications as the Secretary of State considers requisite.

Among the persons appointed under this subsection there shall be persons having experience in local government.

(3) The Secretary of State shall appoint a person to be chairman, and a person to be the secretary, of the Advisory Council on Child Care.

(4) It shall be the duty of the Advisory Council on Child Care to advise the Secretary of State on any matter which the Secretary of State may refer to them, being such a matter as is mentioned in subsection (1) above, and they may also, of their own motion, make representations to the Secretary of State as respects any such matter as is mentioned in that subsection.

(5) The Secretary of State may make out of moneys provided by Parliament such payments to the members of the Advisory Council on Child Care in respect of travelling, subsistence and other expenses as he may with the consent of the Minister for the Civil Service determine.

Powers and duties of local authorities

72. A local authority may provide accommodation in a community home for any person who is over compulsory school age but has not attained the age of twenty-one if the community home is provided for children who are over compulsory school age and is near the place where that person is employed or seeking employment or receiving education or training.

73.—(1) Local authorities shall make provision in community homes provided by them or in controlled community homes for the reception and maintenance of—

(*a*) children removed to a place of safety under the Children and Young Persons Act 1933, sections 2(5), 16(3) or 28 of the Children and Young Persons Act 1969, section 34 of the Adoption Act 1976, or section 12 of the Foster Children Act 1980, and

(*b*) children detained by them in pursuance of arrangements under section 29(3) of the Children and Young Persons Act 1969.

(2) Where under any of the enactments mentioned in subsection (1) above a child is removed to a place of safety, not being a community home provided by a local authority or a controlled community home and not being a hospital vested in the Secretary of State, the expenses of the child's maintenance there shall be recoverable from the local authority within whose area the child was immediately before his removal.

Inspection and Inquiries

74.—(1) Subject to subsection (2) below, the Secretary of State may cause to be inspected from time to time—

(*a*) any community home provided by a local authority under section 34 of this Act;

(*b*) any voluntary home (whether a community home or not);

(*c*) any premises in which a child is living with a person (other than his parent, guardian, relative or custodian) with whom he has been placed by an adoption agency within the meaning of section 1 of the Adoption Act 1976;

(*d*) any other premises at which one or more children in the care of a local authority are being accommodated and maintained;

(*e*) any other premises at which one or more children are being boarded out by a voluntary organisation, and

PART VII
1976 c. 36.
1980 c. 6.

(*f*) any other premises where a protected child within the meaning of Part III of the Adoption Act 1976 or a foster child within the meaning of the Foster Children Act 1980, or a child to whom any of the provisions of the said Act of 1980 are extended by section 17 or 18 thereof, is being accommodated or maintained.

(2) Subsection (1) above does not apply to any home or other premises which is as a whole subject to inspection by or under the authority of a government department.

(3) An inspection under this section shall be conducted by a person authorised in that behalf by the Secretary of State, but an officer of a local authority shall not be so authorised except with the consent of that authority.

(4) Any person inspecting a home or other premises under this section may inspect the children therein and make such examination into the state and management of the home or other premises and the treatment of children therein as he thinks fit.

Powers of entry supplemental to s. 74.

75.—(1) A person authorised to inspect any home or other premises under section 74 of this Act shall have a right to enter the home or other premises for that purpose and for any other purpose specified in subsection (4) of that section, but shall if so required produce some duly authenticated document showing his authority to exercise the power of entry conferred by this subsection.

(2) A person who obstructs the exercise by a person authorised as mentioned in subsection (1) above of a power of entry conferred thereby shall be guilty of an offence and liable on summary conviction to a fine not exceeding £5 or, in the case of a second or subsequent conviction, to a fine not exceeding £20.

1933 c. 12.

(3) A refusal to allow any such person as is mentioned in subsection (1) above to enter any such home or other premises as are mentioned in section 74(1) of this Act shall be deemed, for the purposes of section 40 of the Children and Young Persons Act 1933 (which relates to search warrants), to be a reasonable cause to suspect that a child in the home or other premises is being neglected in a manner likely to cause him unnecessary suffering or injury to health.

Inquiries.

76.—(1) The Secretary of State may cause an inquiry to be held into any matter relating to—

(*a*) the functions of the social services committee of a local authority, in so far as those functions relate to children;

(*b*) the functions of an adoption agency within the meaning of section 1 of the Adoption Act 1976;

(*c*) the functions of a voluntary organisation in so far as those functions relate to voluntary homes;

(d) a home maintained by the Secretary of State for the PART VII
accommodation of children who are in the care of local
authorities and are in need of the particular facilities
and services provided in the home ;

(e) the detention of a child under section 53 of the Children
and Young Persons Act 1933. 1933 c. 12.

(2) The Secretary of State may, before an inquiry is commenced, direct that it shall be held in private, but where no such
direction has been given, the person holding the inquiry may if
he thinks fit hold it or any part of it in private.

(3) Subsections (2) to (5) of section 250 of the Local Govern- 1972 c. 70.
ment Act 1972 (powers in relation to local inquiries) shall apply
in relation to an inquiry under this section as they apply in relation to a local inquiry under that section.

(4) In this section—

" functions " includes powers and duties which a person has
otherwise than by virtue of any enactment ;

" voluntary home " means a home or other institution for
the boarding, care and maintenance of poor children
which is supported wholly or partly by voluntary contributions, but does not include a mental nursing home
within the meaning of the Nursing Homes Act 1975 1975 c. 37.
or a residential home for mentally disordered persons
within the meaning of the Residential Homes Act 1980.

Research and training

Research.

77.—(1) The Secretary of State may conduct or assist other
persons in conducting research into any matter connected with
his functions or the functions of local authorities under—

(a) this Act,

(b) the Children and Young Persons Acts 1933 to 1969, or

(c) the Foster Children Act 1980, 1980 c. 6.

or any matter connected with the adoption of children.

(2) Any local authority may conduct or assist other persons
in conducting research into any matter connected with their
functions under the enactments mentioned in subsection (1) above
or their functions connected with the adoption of children.

(3) Any expenses incurred by the Secretary of State under this
section shall be defrayed out of moneys provided by Parliament.

78.—(1) The Secretary of State with the consent of the Grants for
Treasury may out of moneys provided by Parliament defray or training in
contribute towards any fees or expenses incurred by persons child care.

undergoing training approved by the Secretary of State with a view to, or in the course of, their employment for the purposes of any of the enactments specified in subsection (2) below, or their employment by a voluntary organisation for similar purposes, and may defray or contribute towards the cost of maintenance of persons undergoing such training.

(2) The enactments referred to in subsection (1) above are—

(a) this Act,

1933 c. 12. (b) Parts III and IV of the Children and Young Persons Act 1933,

1963 c. 37. (c) the Children and Young Persons Act 1963, except Part II and section 56,

1969 c. 54. (d) the Children and Young Persons Act 1969,

1969 c. 46. (e) section 7(4) of the Family Law Reform Act 1969,
1973 c. 18. section 44 of the Matrimonial Causes Act 1973 and
1978 c. 22. section 9 of the Domestic Proceedings and Magistrates' Courts Act 1978,

1976 c. 36. (f) the Adoption Act 1976,

1980 c. 6. (g) the Foster Children Act 1980.

Returns of information and presentation of reports etc.
to Parliament

Returns of information and presentation of reports etc. to Parliament.
79.—(1) Every local authority shall, at such times and in such form as the Secretary of State may direct, transmit to the Secretary of State such particulars as he may require—

(a) with respect to the performance by the local authority of all or any of their functions under the enactments mentioned in subsection (5) below ; and

(b) with respect to the children in relation to whom the authority have exercised those functions.

(2) The clerk of each juvenile court shall, at such times and in such form as the Secretary of State may direct, transmit to him such particulars as he may require with respect to the proceedings of the court.

(3) The Secretary of State shall in each year lay before Parliament a consolidated and classified abstract of the information transmitted to him under subsection (1) and (2) above and under section 70 of this Act.

(4) The Secretary of State shall lay before Parliament in 1982 and in every third subsequent year a report with respect to the exercise by local authorities of their functions under the enactments mentioned in subsection (5) below, the provision by voluntary organisations of facilities for children and such other matters relating to children as he thinks fit.

(5) The enactments referred to in subsections (1) and (4) PART VII
above are—

(a) this Act,

(b) Parts III and IV of the Children and Young Persons 1933 c. 12.
Act 1933,

(c) section 9 of the Mental Health Act 1959 and section 10 1959 c. 72.
of that Act so far as it relates to children and young
persons in respect of whom the rights and powers of a
parent are vested in a local authority as mentioned in
subsection (1)(a) of that section,

(d) section 10 of the Mental Health (Scotland) Act 1960 so 1960 c. 61.
far as it relates to children and young persons in
respect of whom the rights and powers of a parent are
vested in a local authority as mentioned in subsection
(1)(a) of that section,

(e) the Children and Young Persons Act 1963, except Part 1963 c. 37.
II and section 56,

(f) the Children and Young Persons Act 1969, 1969 c. 54.

(g) section 7(4) of the Family Law Reform Act 1969, 1969 c. 46.
section 44 of the Matrimonial Causes Act 1973 and 1973 c. 18.
section 9 of the Domestic Proceedings and Magistrates' 1978 c. 22.
Courts Act 1978,

(h) the Adoption Act 1976, 1976 c. 36.

(i) the Foster Children Act 1980. 1980 c. 6.

Financial Provisions

80. There shall be defrayed out of moneys provided by Expenses of
Parliament any expenses incurred by the Secretary of State in Secretary of
providing, equipping and maintaining homes for the accommoda- State in
tion of children who are in the care of local authorities and are homes offering
in need of particular facilities and services which are provided specialised
in those homes and are, in the opinion of the Secretary of State, facilities.
unlikely to be readily available in community homes.

81.—(1) The Secretary of State may make to local authorities Grants in
out of moneys provided by Parliament grants of such amount and respect of
subject to such conditions as he may with the consent of the secure
Treasury determine in respect of expenditure incurred by the accommo-
authorities in providing secure accommodation in community dation.
homes other than assisted community homes.

(2) The Secretary of State may with the consent of the
Treasury require the local authority to repay the grant, in whole
or in part, if the secure accommodation in respect of which the
grant was made (including such accommodation in a controlled
community home) ceases to be used as such.

(3) In this section " secure accommodation " means accommodation provided for the purposes of restricting the liberty
of children in a community home.

PART VII
Grants in
respect of
voluntary
homes which
are assisted
community
homes.
82. The Secretary of State may make to voluntary organisations out of moneys provided by Parliament grants of such amounts and subject to such conditions as he may with the consent of the Treasury determine towards expenditure incurred by them in connection with the establishment, maintenance or improvement of voluntary homes which at the time the expenditure was incurred were assisted community homes or were designated as such in a regional plan which was then in operation, including expenses incurred by them in respect of the borrowing of money to defray any such expenditure.

83. Any administrative expenses incurred by the Secretary of State under this Act shall be defrayed out of moneys provided by Parliament.

Supplementary provisions

84. A local authority may institute proceedings for any offence under section 9(4) or 13(1) of this Act and any offence under Part VI of this Act.

85.—(1) Any power conferred on the Secretary of State by this Act to make an order or regulations, except an order under section 35(1) or 40(2) of this Act, shall be exercisable by statutory instrument.

(2) Any statutory instrument made in exercise of any power to make regulations or orders conferred by this Act, except an instrument containing only an order under section 43 of this Act, shall be subject to annulment in pursuance of a resolution of either House of Parliament.

(3) Any directions given by the Secretary of State under any provision of this Act may be revoked or varied by subsequent directions under that provision.

(4) Any regulations made by the Secretary of State under section 11 or 39 of this Act or any order made by the Secretary of State under this Act may—

(a) make different provision for different circumstances ;

(b) provide for exemptions from any provisions of the regulations or order ; and

(c) contain such incidental and supplemental provisions as the Secretary of State considers expedient for the purposes of the regulations or order.

86. A document purporting to be a copy—

(a) of an order made by a court under or by virtue of any of the provisions contained in sections 47, 48 and 49 of this Act, or

(*b*) of an affiliation order referred to in an order under
section 49 of this Act,

shall, if it purports to be certified as a true copy by the clerk
of the court, be evidence of the order.

87.—(1) In this Act, unless the context otherwise requires— Interpretation.
" arrears order " has the meaning assigned to it by section
51 of this Act ;
" care order " has the meaning assigned to it by section 20
of the Children and Young Persons Act 1969 ; 1969 c. 54.
" child " means a person under the age of eighteen years
and any person who has attained that age and is the
subject of a care order ;
" commission area " has the same meaning as in section 1
of the Justices of the Peace Act 1979 ; 1979 c. 55.
" compulsory school age " has the same meaning as in the
Education Act 1944 ; 1944 c. 31.
" contribution order " has the meaning assigned to it by
section 47 of this Act ;
" functions " includes powers and duties ;
" guardian " means a person appointed by deed or will or
by order of a court of competent jurisdiction to be the
guardian of a child ;
" hospital " has the meaning assigned to it by section 128(1)
of the National Health Service Act 1977 ; 1977 c. 49.
" instrument of management " means an instrument of
management made under section 35 of this Act ;
" interim order ", in relation to a care order, has the meaning assigned to it by section 20 of the Children and
Young Persons Act 1969 ;
" local authority " means the council of a county (other
than a metropolitan county), of a metropolitan district
or of a London borough or the Common Council of the
City of London ;
" local education authority " means a local education
authority for the purposes of the Education Act 1944 ;
" parent ", in relation to a child who is illegitimate, means
his mother, to the exclusion of his father ;
" planning area " has the meaning assigned to it by section
31(1) of this Act ;
" regional plan " has the meaning assigned to it by section
32(1) of this Act ;
" relative ", in relation to a child, means a grand-parent,
brother, sister, uncle or aunt, whether of the full blood,
of the half blood, or by affinity, and includes, where

PART VII

the child is illegitimate, the father of the child and any person who would be a relative of the child within the meaning of this definition if the child were the legitimate child of his mother and father ;

" the relevant authorities ", in relation to a planning area, has the meaning assigned to it by section 31(3) of this Act ;

1968 c. 49.

" supervision requirement " has the same meaning as in the Social Work (Scotland) Act 1968 ;

" trust deed " has the meaning assigned to it by section 36 of this Act ;

" voluntary home " has the meaning assigned to it by section 56 of this Act ;

" voluntary organisation " means a body the activities of which are carried on otherwise than for profit, but does not include any public or local authority.

(2) Any reference in this Act to an enactment of the Parliament of Northern Ireland shall be construed as a reference to that enactment as amended by any Act of that Parliament or by any Measure of the Northern Ireland Assembly, whether passed before or after this Act, and to any enactment of that Parliament or Assembly for the time being in force which re-enacts the said enactment with or without modifications.

Application to Isles of Scilly.

88. This Act shall, in its application to the Isles of Scilly, have effect subject to such exceptions, adaptations and modifications as the Secretary of State may by order prescribe.

Transitional provisions, consequential amendments and repeals.

89.—(1) This Act shall have effect subject to the transitional provisions and savings set out in Schedule 4 to this Act.

(2) The enactments specified in Schedule 5 to this Act shall have effect subject to the amendments specified in that Schedule, being amendments consequential on the provisions of this Act.

(3) The enactments specified in Schedule 6 to this Act are repealed to the extent specified in the third column of that Schedule.

1978 c. 30.

(4) The inclusion in this Act of any express saving or amendment shall not be taken as prejudicing the operation of section 16 or 17 of the Interpretation Act 1978 (which relate to the effect of repeals).

90.—(1) Subject to the provisions of subsections (2), (3) and (4) below, this Act shall come into force on such date as the Secretary of State may by order appoint. PART VII Commencement.

(2) If, on the date appointed under subsection (1) above, the provision of section 58 of the Children Act 1975 which provides 1975 c. 72. for the insertion into the Children Act 1948 of section 4B (guardians ad litem and reports in care proceedings) is not in force, then section 7 of this Act (and the repeal by this Act of section 58 of the Act of 1975 and section 4B of the Act of 1948) shall not come into force until the date appointed under section 108(2) of the Act of 1975 for the coming into force of that provision.

(3) If, on the date appointed under subsection (1) above, paragraph 71(*b*) of Schedule 3 to the Children Act 1975 is not in force, then section 20 of this Act (and the repeal by this Act of the said paragraph 71 and section 27(4) of the Children and Young Persons Act 1969) shall not come into force until the date appointed under section 108(2) of the Act of 1975 for the coming into force of that paragraph ; and, until that paragraph is in force, section 20 of this Act shall have effect as if in subsection (1) of that section for the words from " to review the case " to the end of the section there were substituted the words—

" who have at any time had a child in their care throughout the preceding six months and have not during that period held a review of his case in pursuance of this section to review his case as soon as is practicable after the expiration of that period and, if a care order is in force with respect to him, to consider in the course of the review whether to make an application for the discharge of the order ".

(4) If, on the date appointed under subsection (1) above, sections 60 to 63 of the Children Act 1975 (which relate to the transfer of parental rights and duties to voluntary organisations) are not in force, then sections 64 to 67 of this Act (and the repeal by this Act of the said sections 60 to 63) shall not come into force until the date appointed under section 108(2) of the Act of 1975 for the coming into force of those sections.

91.—(1) This Act may be cited as the Child Care Act 1980. Short title, and extent.

(2) Except for the following provisions, that is to say—

(*a*) section 2(4) and (5),

(*b*) section 16(1), (4) and (5),

(*c*) section 89(2) and paragraphs 2 to 4, 9 to 11, 13, 15, 16, 21 and 22 of Schedule 5,

(d) section 89(3) and Schedule 6 so far as they relate to—
the Adoption of Children Act 1949,
the Maintenance Orders Act 1950,
paragraph 38 of Schedule 3 to the Children and Young Persons Act 1963,
the entry relating to the Children Act 1948 in Schedule 3 to the Criminal Justice Act 1967,
the Social Work (Scotland) Act 1968, and
section 32(1) of the Children and Young Persons Act 1969,

(e) section 90(1), and

(f) this section,

this Act does not extend to Scotland.

(3) Except for the following provisions, that is to say—

(a) section 16,

(b) section 89(2) and paragraphs 2 and 3 of Schedule 5,

(c) section 89(3) and Schedule 6 so far as they relate to—
the Maintenance Orders Act 1950, and
section 32(1) of the Children and Young Persons Act 1969,

(d) section 90(1), and

(e) this section,

this Act does not extend to Northern Ireland.

(4) Section 16(1) and (5) of this Act and this section extend to the Channel Islands.

(5) It is hereby declared that the provisions of section 87 of this Act extend to each of the countries aforesaid so far as appropriate for the purposes of any other provision of this Act which extends to the country in question.

SCHEDULES

SCHEDULE 1

Section 31(4).

CHILDREN'S REGIONAL PLANNING COMMITTEES

1.—(1) Subject to the following provisions of this Schedule, the children's regional planning committee for a planning area (in this Schedule referred to as "the committee") shall consist of such number of persons selected and appointed in such manner and holding office on such terms as the relevant authorities may from time to time approve.

(2) No person who is disqualified by virtue of section 80 of the Local Government Act 1972 from being a member of any local 1972 c. 70. authority which is one of the relevant authorities for a planning area may be a member of the committee for that area.

2.—(1) Subject to sub-paragraph (2) of this paragraph, the relevant authorities for a planning area shall so exercise their powers under paragraph 1(1) of this Schedule as to secure that each authority nominates as a member of the committee for the area at least one person who is not so nominated by any other of the relevant authorities.

(2) If the Secretary of State considers that owing to special circumstances the requirement imposed by sub-paragraph (1) of this paragraph should be dispensed with in the case of a particular authority he may direct accordingly.

(3) The members of the committee for a planning area who are nominated by the relevant authorities are in the following provisions of this Schedule referred to as "the nominated members".

3.—(1) Without prejudice to any power of co-option conferred on the committee for a planning area under paragraph 1(1) of this Schedule, but subject to paragraph 4 of this Schedule, the nominated members of the committee may co-opt other persons to serve as members of the committee, either generally or in relation only to such matters as may be specified by the nominated members.

(2) Where any persons are co-opted to serve as members of the committee for a planning area in relation only to such matters as are specified by the nominated members then, subject to any directions given by the relevant authorities, the extent to which those persons shall be entitled to attend, speak and vote at meetings of the committee shall be such as may be determined by the nominated members.

4. The relevant authorities for a planning area shall so exercise their powers under paragraph 1(1) of this Schedule, and the nominated members of the committee for a planning area shall so limit any exercise of their power under paragraph 3 of this Schedule, as to secure that at all times a majority of the members of the committee for the planning area are members of the relevant authorities.

SCH. 1

5. Subject to any directions given by the relevant authorities, the procedure and quorum of the committee for a planning area shall be such as may be determined by the nominated members.

1972 c. 70.

6. Section 103 of the Local Government Act 1972 (which relates to the expenses of joint committees of local authorities) shall apply to the committee for a planning area as it applies to such a joint committee as is mentioned in that section, but as if—

(*a*) for references to the local authorities by whom the committee is appointed there were substituted references to the relevant authorities ; and

(*b*) for paragraphs (*a*) and (*b*) of that section there were substituted the words " by the Secretary of State " ;

and Part VIII of the Local Government Act 1972 (which relates to accounts and audit) shall apply to the accounts of the committee for a planning area as it applies to the accounts of such a joint committee as is mentioned in section 154(1) of that Act.

Section 55(4).

SCHEDULE 2

MODIFICATION OF PROVISIONS OF PART V OF THIS ACT IN RELATION TO PERSONS RESIDING IN SCOTLAND OR NORTHERN IRELAND

1. Where the person liable to make contributions in respect of a child is for the time being residing in Scotland or Northern Ireland, section 45(2) of this Act shall have effect as if for the reference to the local authority for the area in which that person is for the time being residing there were substituted a reference to the local authority having the care of the child.

2.—(1) Where the person to be charged under a contribution order resides in Scotland or Northern Ireland, section 47(1) of this Act shall have effect as if for the reference to a magistrates' court appointed for the commission area where that person is for the time being residing there were substituted a reference to a magistrates' court having jurisdiction within the area of the authority entitled to receive the contributions.

(2) Where the person on whom a contribution order has been made is for the time being residing in Scotland or Northern Ireland, section 47(4) of this Act shall have effect as if the words from " except that " to the end of the subsection were omitted.

3. Where the person on whom a contribution order or arrears order has been made is for the time being residing in Scotland or Northern Ireland, section 48(1) of this Act shall not apply.

4.—(1) Where the putative father of an illegitimate child resides in Scotland or Northern Ireland, subsections (1) and (2) of section 49 of this Act shall have effect as if for the reference in each subsection to the commission area where the putative father is for the time being residing there were substituted a reference to the place where the mother of the child is for the time being residing.

(2) Where the person liable under an affiliation order in respect of which an order under section 49(1) or (2) of this Act is in force is for the time being residing in Scotland or Northern Ireland, paragraph (*a*) of section 49(4) of this Act shall not apply.

5. Where the putative father of a child in respect of whom an order has been made under section 49 of this Act is for the time being residing in Scotland or Northern Ireland, section 50(5) of this Act shall have effect as if for references to the local authority whose area includes the place where the putative father of the child resides, and to the magistrates' court appointed for the commission area which includes that place, there were substituted references to the local authority who, if the affiliation order were still in force, would be entitled to payments thereunder, and to a magistrates' court having jurisdiction within the area of that authority.

6. Where the person who was liable to make contributions in respect of a child resides in Scotland or Northern Ireland, section 51(1) of this Act shall have effect as if for the reference to the magistrates' court therein mentioned there were substituted a reference to a magistrates' court having jurisdiction in the area or part of the area of the local authority which is applying for an arrears order.

7. Where the person liable to make payments under an order made under section 47, 49, 50 or 51 of this Act is for the time being residing in Scotland or Northern Ireland, section 54(1) of this Act shall have effect as if for the reference to the local authority within whose area the person liable under the order is for the time being residing there were substituted a reference to the local authority to whom sums are payable under the order and as if for the words " when he was not resident in the area of that authority " there were substituted the words " when that authority were not entitled to sums payable under the order ".

SCHEDULE 3

Constitution of Appeal Tribunals

1. For the purpose of enabling appeal tribunals to be constituted as occasion may require, there shall be appointed two panels, that is to say—

(*a*) a panel (hereinafter referred to as the " legal panel ") appointed by the Lord Chancellor, of persons who will be available to act when required as chairman of any such tribunal ; and

(*b*) a panel (hereinafter referred to as the " welfare panel ") appointed by the Lord President of the Council, of persons who will be available to act when required as members of any such tribunal.

2.—(1) No person shall be qualified to be appointed to the legal panel unless he possesses such legal qualifications as the Lord Chancellor considers suitable, and no person shall be qualified to be appointed to the welfare panel unless he has had such experience

SCH. 3 in children's welfare work as the Lord President of the Council considers suitable.

(2) An officer of any government department shall be disqualified from being appointed to either of the said panels.

3. Any person appointed to be a member of either of the said panels shall hold office as such subject to such conditions as to the period of his membership and otherwise as may be determined by the Lord Chancellor or the Lord President of the Council, as the case may be.

4. Where any appeal is required to be determined by a tribunal constituted in accordance with this Schedule, the tribunal shall consist of a chairman being a member of the legal panel and two other members being members of the welfare panel, and the chairman and other members of the tribunal shall be impartial persons appointed from those panels by the Lord Chancellor and the Lord President of the Council respectively.

Section 89.

SCHEDULE 4

Transitional Provisions and Savings.

Children in care under Children Act 1948

1. Any reference in this Act to a child in the care of a local authority under section 2 of this Act shall be construed as including a reference to a child received into the care of the authority under section 1 of the Children Act 1948.

1948 c. 43.

Children in care by virtue of an order which is deemed to be a care order

2. Any reference in this Act to a care order committing a child to the care of a local authority shall be construed as including an order made under the Children and Young Persons Act 1933 which is deemed, by virtue of Schedule 4 to the Children and Young Persons Act 1969, to be a care order committing the child to the care of that authority.

1933 c. 12.
1969 c. 54.

3. Sections 23 and 29 of this Act shall apply in relation to a child who is or has been in the care of a local authority by virtue of an order made under the Children and Young Persons Act 1933 which is deemed by virtue of paragraph 8 of Schedule 4 to the Children and Young Persons Act 1969 to be a care order as they apply in relation to a child who is or has been in the care of a local authority under section 2 of this Act.

Periods of time

4. Where a period of time specified in an enactment repealed by this Act is current at the commencement of this Act, this Act shall have effect as if the corresponding provision thereof had been in force when that period began to run.

Custodians

1975 c. 72.

5. If at the commencement of this Act section 33 of the Children Act 1975 (which relates to custodianship orders) is not in force, then, until that section is in force,—

    (*a*) section 3 of this Act shall have effect as if in subsections (1) and (10) the words " or custodian " were omitted ; and (*b*) section 5 of this Act shall have effect as if in subsection (1)(*a*) for the words " parent, guardian or custodian " there were substituted the words " parent or guardian ". SCH. 4

Children in care by virtue of order under Matrimonial Proceedings (Magistrates' Courts) Act 1960

6. Sections 23 and 29 of this Act shall apply in relation to a child who is or has been in the care of a local authority by virtue of an order made under the Matrimonial Proceedings (Magistrates' Courts) 1960 c. 48. Act 1960 as they apply in relation to a child who is or has been in the care of a local authority under section 2 of this Act.

References to section 9 of the Domestic Proceedings and Magistrates' Courts Act 1978

7. If at the commencement of this Act section 9 of the Domestic 1978 c. 72. Proceedings and Magistrates' Courts Act 1978 (which relates to supervision orders) is not in force then, until that section is in force, the references in sections 78 and 79 of this Act to that section shall be construed as references to section 2(1)(*f*) of the Matrimonial Proceedings (Magistrates' Courts) Act 1960.

References to provisions of Adoption Act 1976 and Adoption (Scotland) Act 1978

8. If at the commencement of this Act any provision of the Adop- 1976 c. 36. tion Act 1976 or the Adoption (Scotland) Act 1978 referred to in 1978 c. 28. this Act is not in force, then any reference in this Act to that provision shall, until that provision is in force, be construed as a reference to the enactment for which that provision, when it is in force, will be substituted.

Saving of amendments

9. Notwithstanding the repeal by this Act of section 60 of and Schedule 3 to the Children Act 1948, the amendments made by that Schedule to the Children and Young Persons Act 1933 shall continue to have the same effect as they had immediately before the commencement of this Act.

SCHEDULE 5

Section 89.

CONSEQUENTIAL AMENDMENTS

Children and Young Persons Act 1933 (c.12)

1. In section 96 of the Children and Young Persons Act 1933 after subsection (1) there shall be inserted the following subsection—

" (1A) The local authorities for the purposes of Parts III and IV of this Act shall be the councils of counties (other than metropolitan counties), of metropolitan districts and of London boroughs and the Common Council of the City of London.".

Maintenance Orders Act 1950 (c.37)

2. In section 15(1) of the Maintenance Orders Act 1950 after the words " Children Act 1975 " there shall be inserted the words " or section 55 of the Child Care Act 1980 ".

3. In section 16(2)(*a*) of the said Act of 1950, in sub-paragraph (iv) for the words " section 26 of the Children Act 1948 " there shall be substituted the words " section 50 of the Child Care Act 1980 " and in sub-paragraph (v) for the words " section 87 of the Children and Young Persons Act 1933 " there shall be substituted the words " section 47 of the Child Care Act 1980 ".

The Affiliation Orders Act 1952 (c.41)

4. In section 3 of the Affiliation Orders Act 1952—

   (*a*) in subsection (3)(*a*)(ii) for the words " section 1 of the Children Act 1948 " there shall be substituted the words " section 2 of the Child Care Act 1980 " ;

   (*b*) in subsection (6) for the words " section 1 of the Children Act 1948 " there shall be substituted the words " section 2 of the Child Care Act 1980 ".

The Magistrates' Courts Act 1952 (c.55)

5. In section 56(1) of the Magistrates' Courts Act 1952 after paragraph (*m*) there shall be added the following paragraph—

   " (*n*) section 47, 49 or 50 of the Child Care Act 1980 ; ".

Affiliation Proceedings Act 1957 (c.55)

6. In section 5(2) of the Affiliation Proceedings Act 1957—

   (*a*) for paragraph (*a*) there shall be substituted the following paragraph—
   " (*a*) section 49 of the Child Care Act 1980 (which provides that, where an illegitimate child is in the care of a local authority, the authority entitled to receive contributions in respect of the child under section 45(2) of that Act may be given the benefit of payments under an affiliation order in respect of the child) ; " ;

   (*b*) paragraph (*b*) shall be omitted ;

   (*c*) in paragraph (*d*) for the words " section 26 of the Children Act 1948 " there shall be substituted the words " section 50 of the Child Care Act 1980 ".

7. In section 6A(3) of the said Act of 1957 for the words " section 1 of the Children Act 1948 " there shall be substituted the words " section 2 of the Child Care Act 1980 ".

8. In section 7 of the said Act of 1957—

   (*a*) in subsection (4)(*a*) for the words " section 1 of the Children Act 1948 " there shall be substituted the words " section 2 of the Child Care Act 1980 " ;

   (*b*) in subsection (6) for the words " section 1 of the Children Act 1948 " there shall be substituted the words " section 2 of the Child Care Act 1980 ".

Children Act 1958 (c. 65)

9. In section 2(3)(*b*) of the Children Act 1958 for the words " Part V of the Children and Young Persons Act 1933 " there shall be substituted the words " Part VI of the Child Care Act 1980 ".

10. In section 6(1)(*d*) of the said Act of 1958 after the words
" Children Act 1948 " there shall be inserted the words " or under
section 3 of the Child Care Act 1980 ".

11. In section 7(4) of the said Act of 1958 for the words " section
1 of the Children Act 1948 " there shall be substituted the words
" section 2 of the Child Care Act 1980 " and for the words " the
said section 1 " there shall be substituted the words " the said section
2 ".

Mental Health Act 1959 (*c.72*)

12. In section 9 of the Mental Health Act 1959—

(*a*) in subsection (1) for the words " section 38 of the Children
and Young Persons Act 1969 " there shall be substituted
the words " section 34 of the Child Care Act 1980 " and
for the words " Part II of the Children Act 1948 " there
shall be substituted the words " Part III of that Act " ;

(*b*) in subsection (3) for the words " section 1 of the Children
Act 1948 " there shall be substituted the words " section
2 of the Child Care Act 1980 " ;

(*c*) in subsection (4) for the words " Children Act 1948 " there
shall be substituted the words " Child Care Act 1980 ".

13. In section 10(1)(*a*) of the said Act of 1959—

(*a*) for sub-paragraph (i) there shall be substituted the following sub-paragraph—

" (i) section 10 of the Child Care Act 1980 (which
relates to the powers and duties of local authorities with
respect to persons committed to their care under the
Children and Young Persons Act 1969) ; " ;

(*b*) for sub-paragraph (iii) there shall be substituted the following sub-paragraph—

" (iii) section 3 of the Child Care Act 1980 (which
relates to the assumption by a local authority of parental
rights and duties in relation to a child in their care) ; ".

14. In section 50 of the said Act of 1959—

(*a*) for paragraph (*a*) there shall be substituted the following
paragraph—

" (*a*) section 10 of the Child Care Act 1980 (which
relates to the powers and duties of local authorities with
respect to persons committed to their care under the
Children and Young Persons Act 1969) ; " ;

(*b*) for paragraph (*c*) there shall be substituted the following
paragraph—

" (*c*) section 3 of the Child Care Act 1980 (which
relates to the assumption by a local authority of parental
rights and duties in relation to a child in their care) ; " ;

(c) for the words " subsection (2) of the said section 3 " there
shall be substituted the words " subsection (1) of the said
section 3 ".

Mental Health (Scotland) Act 1960 (c. 61)

15. In section 10(1)(*a*) of the Mental Health (Scotland) Act 1960—

(*a*) in sub-paragraph (ii) for the words " section 24 of the Children and Young Persons Act 1969 " there shall be substituted the words " section 10 of the Child Care Act 1980 ; "

(*b*) for sub-paragraph (iii) there shall be substituted the following sub-paragraph—

" (iii) section 3 of the Child Care Act 1980 (which relates to the assumption by a local authority of parental rights and duties in relation to a child in their care) ; ".

16. In section 46 of the said Act of 1960—

(*a*) in paragraph (*b*) for the words " section 24 of the Children and Young Persons Act 1969 " there shall be substituted the words " section 10 of the Child Care Act 1980 " ;

(*b*) in paragraph (*d*) for the words " Children Act 1948 " there shall be substituted the words " Child Care Act 1980 " ;

(*c*) for the words " subsection (2) of the said section 3 " there shall be substituted the words " subsection (1) of the said section 3 ".

London Government Act 1963 (c. 33)

17. In section 47(4) of the London Government Act 1963 for the words " Children Act 1948 or the Children and Young Persons Act 1933 " there shall be substituted the words " Child Care Act 1980 ".

Children and Young Persons Act 1963 (c.37)

18. In section 63 of the Children and Young Persons Act 1963 after subsection (1) there shall be inserted the following subsection—

" (1A) The local authorities for the purposes of Parts I and III of this Act shall be the councils of counties (other than metropolitan counties), of metropolitan districts and of London boroughs and the Common Council of the City of London. ".

Health Services and Public Health Act 1968 (c.46)

19. In section 64(3)(*a*) of the Health Services and Public Health Act 1968 there shall be added at the end the following paragraph—

" (xix) the Child Care Act 1980 except so far as it relates to any voluntary home designated as mentioned in section 35(1) of that Act as a controlled or assisted community home ".

20. In section 65(3)(*b*) of the said Act of 1968 there shall be added at the end the following paragraph—

" (xx) the Child Care Act 1980 ".

Social Work (Scotland) Act 1968 (c.49)

21. In section 21(3) of the Social Work (Scotland) Act 1968 for the words " section 13 of the Children Act 1948 " there shall be substituted the words " section 21 of the Child Care Act 1980 ".

22. In section 86(3) of the said Act of 1968 for the words " Children Act 1948, the Children and Young Persons Act 1933 " there shall be substituted the words " Child Care Act 1980 ".

Family Law Reform Act 1969 (*c*.46)

23. In section 7 of the Family Law Reform Act 1969—

(*a*) in subsection (2) for the words " Part II of the Children Act 1948 " there shall be substituted the words " Part III of the Child Care Act 1980 " and for the words " section 1 " there shall be inserted the words " section 2 " ; and

(*b*) in subsection (3) there shall be added at the end the words " and as if, in relation to a ward of court, the reference in subsection (5)(*b*) to sections 24 and 28 of the Child Care Act 1980 included a reference to section 23 of that Act (guarantee of apprenticeship deeds) and section 29 of that Act (visiting and assistance of persons formerly in care)."

Children and Young Persons Act 1969 (*c*.54)

24. In section 22(4) of the Children and Young Persons Act 1969 for the words " section 13(2) of the Children Act 1948 " there shall be substituted the words " section 21(2) of the Child Care Act 1980 ".

25. In section 26(3) of the said Act of 1969 the words " and in section 27(4) the words from ' and if ' onwards " shall be omitted and for the words " section 13(2) of the Children Act 1948 " there shall be substituted the words " section 21(2) of the Child Care Act 1980 ".

26. In paragraph 11 of Schedule 5 to the said Act of 1969 for the words from " for the words " to the end of the paragraph there shall be substituted the words " for the words from ' section fifty-six ' to ' Schedule to ' there shall be substituted the words ' section fifty-six of '."

Administration of Justice Act 1970 (*c*.31)

27. In Schedule 1 to the Administration of Justice Act 1970 at the end there shall be added the following paragraph—

" Proceedings on appeal under section 6 of the Child Care Act 1980 ".

28. In Schedule 8 to the said Act of 1970—

(*a*) in paragraph 5 for the words " section 26 of the Children Act 1948 " there shall be substituted the words " section 50 of the Child Care Act 1980 " ;

(*b*) in paragraph 6 for the words " section 87 of the Children and Young Persons Act 1933, section 30 of the Children and Young Persons Act 1963 " there shall be substituted the words " section 47 or 51 of the Child Care Act 1980 ".

Local Authority Social Services Act 1970 (*c*.42)

29. In Schedule 1 to the Local Authority Social Services Act 1970 there shall be added at the end the following entry—

" Child Care Act 1980 (c.5)   Promotion of welfare of children ; provision for orphans, deserted children, children suffering from mental disorder etc. ; assumption by local authority of parental rights ; children in care ;

financing of children's maintenance and education etc; assistance of persons formerly in care ;
accommodation for children in
care ; registration of voluntary
children's homes and use of voluntary organisations ; research
into matters connected with functions under enactments relating
to children and young persons.".

Guardianship of Minors Act 1971 (c.3)

30. In section 5(2) of the Guardianship of Minors Act 1971 for
the words " section 2 of the Children Act 1948 " there shall be substituted the words " section 3 of the Child Care Act 1980 ".

31. In section 14A(4) of the said Act of 1971 for the words " Part
II of the Children Act 1948 " there shall be substituted the words
" Part III of the Child Care Act 1980 ".

Attachment of Earnings Act 1971 (c.32)

32. In Schedule 1 to the Attachment of Earnings Act 1971—
   (a) in paragraph 6 for the words " section 26 of the Children
       Act 1948 " there shall be substituted the words " section 50
       of the Child Care Act 1980 " ; and
   (b) in paragraph 7 for the words " section 87 of the Children
       and young Persons Act 1933, section 30 of the Children
       and Young Persons Act 1963 " there shall be substituted
       the words " section 47 or 51 of the Child Care Act 1980 ".

Tribunals and Inquiries Act 1971 (c.62)

33. In paragraph 4 of Schedule 1 to the Tribunals and Inquiries
Act 1971 for the words " section 30 of, and Part I of Schedule 1 to,
the Children Act 1948 " there shall be substituted the words " section
58 of, and Schedule 3 to, the Child Care Act 1980 ".

Matrimonial Causes Act 1973 (c.18)

34. In section 43 of the Matrimonial Causes Act 1973—
   (a) in subsection (1) for the words " Part II of the Children
       Act 1948 " there shall be substituted the words " Part III
       of the Child Care Act 1980 " and for the words " section 1
       of that Act " there shall be substituted the words " section 2
       of that Act " ; and
   (b) for subsection (5) there shall be substituted the following
       subsection—
         " (5) In the application of Part III of the Child Care
       Act 1980 by virtue of this section—
            (a) the exercise by the local authority of their powers
                under sections 18, 21 and 22 of that Act (which
                among other things relate to the accommodation
                and welfare of a child in the care of a local
                authority) shall be subject to any directions given
                by the court ; and

(*b*) section 24 of that Act (which relates to arrange- SCH. 5
ments for the emigration of such a child) and
section 28 of that Act (which relates to the after-
care of a child in the care of a local authority
under section 2 of that Act) shall not apply.".

Guardianship Act 1973 (c.29)

35. In section 4 of the Guardianship Act 1973 for subsection (4)
there shall be substituted the following subsection—

" (4) On the making of an order under section 2(2)(*b*) above
with respect to a minor, Parts III and V of the Child Care Act
1980 (which relate to the treatment of children in the care of a
local authority and to contributions towards their maintenance)
shall apply as if the minor had been received by the local authority into their care under section 2 of that Act except that—

(*a*) the exercise by the local authority of their powers under
sections 18 and 21 of that Act shall, where the order is
made by the High Court, be subject to any directions given
by the court ;

(*b*) section 24 of that Act (which relates to arrangements for
emigration) shall not apply ;

(*c*) section 28 of that Act (which relates to the after-care of a
child in the care of a local authority under section 2 of
that Act) shall not apply ; and

(*d*) section 45(1) of that Act so far as it requires a child's
father or mother to make contributions in respect of him
shall not apply, but so that references to the local authority
who are entitled to receive contributions shall be construed
as if section 45(1) did so apply.".

Legal Aid Act 1974 (c.4)

36. In Schedule 1 to the Legal Aid Act 1974 for paragraph 3(*g*)
there shall be substituted the following sub-paragraph—

" (*g*) proceedings under section 3, 5 or 67(2) of the Child Care
Act 1980 ".

Children Act 1975 (c.72)

37. In section 103(1)(*a*) of the Children Act 1975 for paragraph
(iii) there shall be substituted the following paragraph—
" (iii) section 7 of the Child Care Act 1980 ".

Adoption Act 1976 (c.36)

38. In section 31(3) of the Adoption Act 1976 for the words
" section 86 of the Children and Young Persons Act 1933 " there
shall be substituted the words " section 45 of the Child Care Act
1980 ".

39. In section 34(3) of the said Act of 1976 for the words " section
1 of the Children Act 1948 " there shall be substituted the words
" section 2 of the Child Care Act 1980 ".

    Domestic Proceedings and Magistrates' Courts Act 1978 (c.22)

40. In section 8(7) of the Domestic Proceedings and Magistrates' Courts Act 1978 for the words " Part II of the Children Act 1948 " there shall be substituted the words " Part III of the Child Care Act 1980 ".

41. In section 9(4) of the said Act of 1978 for the words " Part II of the Children Act 1948 " there shall be substituted the words " Part III of the Child Care Act 1980 ".

42. In section 10 of the said Act of 1978—
  (a) for subsection (4) there shall be substituted the following subsection—

  " (4) On the making of an order under this section—
    (a) Part III of the Child Care Act 1980 (which relates to the treatment of children in the care of a local authority), except section 24 (which relates to arrangements for the emigration of such children) and section 28 (which relates to the after-care of children who have been in the care of a local authority under section 2 of that Act) ; and
    (b) for the purposes only of contributions by the child himself at a time when he has attained the age of 16 and is engaged in remunerative full-time work, Part V of that Act (which relates to contributions towards the maintenance of children in the care of a local authority),

  shall apply as if the child had been received by the local authority into their care under section 2 of that Act." ;

  (b) in subsection (8) for the words " Part II of the Children Act 1948 " there shall be substituted the words " Part III of the Child Care Act 1980 ".

Section 89.

SCHEDULE 6

REPEALS

Chapter	Short Title	Extent of Repeal
1933 c. 12.	The Children and Young Persons Act 1933.	Sections 86 to 89. Sections 92 and 93. In section 102(1), paragraphs (c) and (d). In section 106(2), paragraph (c). In section 107(1) the definition of " commission area ".
1948 c. 43.	The Children Act 1948.	The whole Act.
1949 c. 98.	The Adoption of Children Act 1949.	In section 13(2) the words " subsection (1) of section fifty-nine of the Children Act 1948 and ".

Chapter	Short Title	Extent of Repeal
1950 c. 37.	The Maintenance Orders Act 1950.	In section 3(1) the words " section twenty-six of the Children Act 1948 ". In section 4(1), paragraph (*a*) and in section 4(2) the words " the said section eighty-seven." Section 14. Schedule 1.
1952 c. 55.	The Magistrates' Courts Act 1952.	In section 56(1), paragraphs (*b*) and (*d*).
1958 c. 55.	The Local Government Act 1958.	In Schedule 8, paragraph 2.
1958 c. 65.	The Children Act 1958.	In Schedule 2, the entry relating to section 38 of the Children Act 1948.
1963 c. 37.	The Children and Young Persons Act 1963.	Sections 1, 30, 45, 46, 47, 49, 55 and 58. In Schedule 3, paragraphs 38 and 40.
1967 c. 80.	Criminal Justice Act 1967.	In Part I of Schedule 3, the entries relating to section 88(2)(*c*) of the Children and Young Persons Act 1933, section 10(4) of the Children Act 1948 and section 30(5) of the Children and Young Persons Act 1963.
1968 c. 46.	The Health Services and Public Health Act 1968.	In section 64(3)(*a*), sub-paragraph (iv) and in sub-paragraph (xiv) the words from " except so far as " to the end of the sub-paragraph. In section 65(3)(*b*), sub-paragraph (iv).
1968 c. 49.	The Social Work (Scotland) Act 1968.	In Schedule 8, paragraphs 17 and 19.
1969 c. 54.	The Children and Young Persons Act 1969.	Sections 24 and 27. In section 32(1), paragraphs (*a*) and (*c*), the words " the local authority or " in the first place where those words occur, the words " the local authority or the managers of the home or ", and the words " or managers " in both places where those words occur. Sections 35 to 45. Sections 47 to 50. Sections 58 and 59. Sections 62 to 64A. Section 65(1). In section 69(1) the words " 39 or 43(5) " and " 47 ". In section 70(1) the definition of " instrument of management ", "planning area ",

Chapter	Short Title	Extent of Repeal
1969 c. 54—*cont.*	The Children and Young Persons Act 1969—*cont.*	" regional plan ", " the relevant authorities ", " trust deed ", " voluntary home " and " voluntary organisation ". Schedule 2. In Schedule 5, paragraphs 8 to 10, 14 to 17, 19 to 22, 50 to 52 and 73.
1970 c. 31.	The Administration of Justice Act 1970.	In Schedule 1, the words " Proceedings on appeal under section 4A of the Children Act 1948 ".
1970 c. 42.	The Local Authority Social Services Act 1970.	In Schedule 1, the entries relating to the Children Act 1948 and Part III of the Children and Young Persons Act 1963, in the entry relating to Part I of the said Act of 1963 the words " Promotion of welfare of children " and " recovery of contributions in respect of child " and in the entry relating to the Children and Young Persons Act 1969 the words " accommodation for children in care ". In Schedule 2, paragraphs 5 and 11.
1972 c. 70.	The Local Government Act 1972.	In Schedule 23, paragraph 3.
1973 c. 18.	The Matrimonial Causes Act 1973.	In section 43, subsection (8). In Schedule 2, paragraph 9.
1974 c. 4.	The Legal Aid Act 1974.	In Schedule 1, in paragraph 3(*c*) the words " section 2 or 4 of the Children Act 1948."
1975 c. 18.	The Social Security (Consequential Provisions) Act 1975.	In Schedule 2, paragraph 9.
1975 c. 37.	The Nursing Homes Act 1975.	In Schedule 1, paragraph 5.
1975 c. 72.	The Children Act 1975.	Sections 56 to 63. Sections 67, 71 and 98. In Schedule 3, paragraphs 4 to 6, 42, 71, 72 and 73(1)(*a*).
1976 c. 36.	The Adoption Act 1976.	In Schedule 3, paragraphs 1, 2, 3, 12, 13 and 20.
1977 c. 45.	The Criminal Law Act 1977.	In Schedule 6 the entry relating to the Children Act 1948.
1978 c. 22.	The Domestic Proceedings and Magistrates' Courts Act 1978.	In Schedule 2, paragraphs 3, 4, 5, 8, 20 and 24.

Foster Children Act 1980

1980 CHAPTER 6

An Act to consolidate certain enactments relating to foster children as they have effect in England and Wales.
[31st January 1980]

BE IT ENACTED by the Queen's most Excellent Majesty, by and with the advice and consent of the Lords Spiritual and Temporal, and Commons, in this present Parliament assembled, and by the authority of the same, as follows:—

Foster children for purposes of the Act

1. Subject to section 2 below, a child is a foster child for the purposes of this Act if he is below the upper limit of the compulsory school age and his care and maintenance are undertaken by a person who is not a relative, guardian or custodian of his.

Foster children.

2.—(1) A child is not a foster child while he is in the care of a local authority or a voluntary organisation or is boarded out by a local authority or a local education authority.

Exceptions to section 1.

(2) A child is not a foster child while he is in the care of any person—

    (*a*) in premises in which any parent, adult relative or guardian of his is for the time being residing;

    (*b*) in any voluntary home within the meaning of Part VI of the Child Care Act 1980 ;

1980 c. 5.

    (*c*) in any school within the meaning of the Education Act 1944 in which he is receiving full-time education ;

1944 c. 31.

D 4

1975 c. 37.

(d) in any hospital, or in any nursing home registered or
exempted from registration under the Nursing Homes
Act 1975 ; or

(e) in any home or institution not specified in this subsection or subsection (5) below but maintained by a
public or local authority.

(3) A child is not a foster child at any time while his care
and maintenance are undertaken by any person—

(a) who is not a regular foster parent and at that time does
not intend to, and does not in fact, undertake his care
and maintenance for a continuous period of more than
27 days ; or

(b) who is a regular foster parent but at that time does not
intend to, and does not in fact, undertake his care
and maintenance for a continuous period of more than
six days.

In this subsection " regular foster parent " means a person
who—

(i) during the period of 12 months immediately preceding
the date on which he begins to undertake the care
and maintenance of the child in question, and

(ii) otherwise than as a relative or guardian,

had the care and maintenance of one or more children either
for a period of, or periods amounting in the aggregate to, not
less than three months or for at least three continuous periods
each of which was of more than six days.

(4) A child is not a foster child while he is in the care of
any person in compliance with a supervision order within the
1969 c. 54.
1968 c. 49.
meaning of the Children and Young Persons Act 1969 or a
supervision requirement within the meaning of the Social Work
(Scotland) Act 1968.

(5) A child is not a foster child while he is liable to be detained
1959 c. 72.
or subject to guardianship under the Mental Health Act 1959, or
is resident in a residential home for mentally disordered persons
within the meaning of the Residential Homes Act 1980.

(6) A child is not a foster child—

(a) while he is placed in the care and possession of a
person who proposes to adopt him under arrangements
made by an adoption agency within the meaning of
1976 c. 36.
1978 c. 28.
section 1 of the Adoption Act 1976 or section 1 of the
Adoption (Scotland) Act 1978 ; or

(b) while he is a protected child within the meaning of Part
III of the Adoption Act 1976.

Duties of local authorities

3.—(1) Subject to subsection (3) below, it shall be the duty of every local authority to satisfy themselves as to the well-being of foster children within their area and, for that purpose, to secure— Local authorities to ensure well-being of, and to visit, foster children.

    (*a*) that the children are visited by officers of the authority in accordance with regulations made under subsection (2) below ; and

    (*b*) that such advice is given as to the care and maintenance of the children as appears to be needed.

(2) The Secretary of State may make regulations requiring foster children in a local authority's area to be visited by an officer of the local authority on specified occasions or within specified periods of time.

(3) Until such time as the Secretary of State may by order made by statutory instrument appoint, subsection (1) above shall have effect with the substitution for paragraph (*a*) of the following paragraph—

    " (*a*) that, so far as appears to the authority to be appropriate, the children are visited from time to time by officers of the authority ; and ".

Notification of fostering to local authorities

4.—(1) The Secretary of State may by regulations make provision for requiring parents whose children are, or are going to be, maintained as foster children to give to the local authority for the area where the children are, or are going to be, living as foster children such information about the fostering as may be specified in the regulations. Notification by parents.

(2) Regulations under this section may include such incidental and supplementary provisions as the Secretary of State thinks fit.

5.—(1) A person who proposes to maintain as a foster child a child not already in his care shall give written notice thereof to the local authority in whose area the premises in which the child is to be kept are situated, not less than two weeks and not more than four weeks before he receives the child, unless he receives him in an emergency. Notification by persons maintaining, or proposing to maintain, foster children.

(2) A person who maintains a foster child—

    (*a*) whom he received in an emergency, or

    (*b*) who became a foster child while in his care,

shall give written notice thereof to the local authority in whose area the premises in which the child is being kept are situated, not later than 48 hours after he receives the child or, as the case may be, after the child becomes a foster child.

(3) A notice under subsection (1) or (2) above shall specify—

    (a) the date on which it is intended that the child should be received or (as the case may be) on which the child was in fact received or became a foster child, and

    (b) the premises in which the child is to be or is being kept.

(4) Where a person who is maintaining one or more foster children changes his permanent address or the premises in which the child is, or the children are, kept, he shall give written notice to the local authority—

    (a) not less than two weeks and not more than four weeks before the change, or

    (b) if the change is made in an emergency, not later than 48 hours after the change,

specifying the new address or premises ; and if the new premises are in the area of another local authority, or of a local authority in Scotland, the authority to whom the notice is given shall inform that other authority and give them such of the particulars mentioned in subsection (5) below as are known to them.

(5) At the request of the local authority, a person maintaining or proposing to maintain a foster child shall give them, so far as known to him, the following particulars—

    (a) the name, sex and date and place of birth of the child ; and

    (b) the name and address of every person who is a parent or guardian or acts as a guardian of the child or from whom the child was or is to be received.

Notification by persons ceasing to maintain foster children.
    6.—(1) If a foster child dies, the person who was maintaining him shall give, not later than 48 hours after the death, written notice of the death to the local authority and to the person from whom the child was received.

(2) Subject to subsection (3) below, where a person who has been maintaining a foster child at any premises—

    (a) ceases to maintain that foster child at those premises, and

    (b) the circumstances are such that no notice is required to be given under section 5(4) or subsection (1) above,

that person shall give written notice thereof to the local authority not later than 48 hours after he ceases to maintain that foster child at those premises.

(3) A person need not give the notice required by subsection (2) above in consequence of his ceasing to maintain a foster child

at any premises if, at the time he so ceases, he intends within 27 days again to maintain that foster child at those premises; but if—

(a) he subsequently abandons that intention, or

(b) that period expires without his having given effect to it,

he shall give the said notice within 48 hours of that event.

(4) Where a foster child is removed or removes himself from the care of the person maintaining him, that person shall give the local authority at their request the name and address, if known, of the person (if any) into whose care the child has been removed.

Disqualification for fostering

7.—(1) A person shall not maintain a foster child if—

(a) an order removing a child from his care has been made against him under this Act or (whether before or after the commencement of this Act) under Part I of the Children Act 1958;

(b) an order has been made under the Children and Young Persons Act 1933, the Children and Young Persons Act 1969, or the Children and Young Persons (Scotland) Act 1937, or a supervision requirement has been made under the Social Work (Scotland) Act 1968, and by virtue of the order or requirement a child was removed from his care;

(c) he has been convicted of any offence specified in Schedule 1 to the said Act of 1933 or Schedule 1 to the Criminal Procedure (Scotland) Act 1975, or has been placed on probation or discharged absolutely or conditionally for any such offence;

(d) his rights and powers with respect to a child have been vested under section 2 of the Children Act 1948 or section 3 of the Child Care Act 1980 in a local authority or under section 2 of the Children Act 1948 or section 16 of the Social Work (Scotland) Act 1968 in a local authority in Scotland;

(e) an order under section 1(3) or (4) of the Nurseries and Child-Minders Regulation Act 1948 has been made against him refusing, or an order has been made under section 5 of that Act cancelling, the registration of any premises occupied by him or his registration; or

(f) an order has been made under section 43 of the Adoption Act 1958, section 34 of the Adoption Act 1976 or section 34 of the Adoption (Scotland) Act 1978 for the removal of a protected child who was being kept or was about to be received by him,

unless he has disclosed that fact to the local authority and obtained their written consent.

Persons disqualified from keeping foster children.
1958 c. 65.
1933 c. 12.
1969 c. 54.
1937 c. 37.
1968 c. 49.
1975 c. 21.
1948 c. 43.
1980 c. 5.
1948 c. 53.
1958 c. 5.
(7 & 8 Eliz. 2)
1976 c. 36.
1978 c. 28.

(2) Where subsection (1) above applies to any person, otherwise than by virtue of this subsection, it shall apply also to any other person who lives in the same premises as he does or who lives in premises at which he is employed.

Control by local authorities of fostering

Power to
inspect
premises.

8. Any officer of a local authority authorised to visit foster children may, after producing, if asked to do so, some duly authenticated document showing that he is so authorised, inspect any premises in the area of the authority in the whole or any part of which foster children are to be or are being kept.

Power to
impose
requirements
as to
the keeping
of foster
children.

9.—(1) Where a person is keeping or proposes to keep foster children in premises used (while foster children are kept in them) wholly or partly for that purpose, the local authority may impose on him requirements as to—

(a) the number, age and sex of the foster children who may be kept at any one time in the premises or any part of them ;

(b) the accommodation and equipment to be provided for the children ;

(c) the medical arrangements to be made for protecting the health of the children ;

(d) the giving of particulars of the person for the time being in charge of the children ;

(e) the number, qualifications or experience of persons employed in looking after the children ;

(f) the keeping of records ;

(g) the fire precautions to be taken in the premises ;

(h) the giving of particulars of any foster child received in the premises and of any change in the number or identity of the foster children kept in them.

(2) A requirement imposed under this section may be limited to a particular class of foster children kept in the premises ; and a requirement imposed under paragraphs (b) to (h) above may be limited by the authority so as to apply only when the number of foster children kept in the premises exceeds a specified number.

(3) A person shall, after such time as the local authority may specify, comply with any requirement imposed on him under this section whenever a foster child is kept in the premises in question.

(4) A requirement imposed under this section shall be imposed by notice in writing addressed to the person on whom it is imposed and informing him of his right under section 11(1) below to appeal against the requirement and of the time within which he may do so.

10.—(1) Where a person proposes to keep a foster child in any premises and the local authority are of the opinion that—

(a) the premises are not suitable premises in which to keep foster children, or

(b) that person is not a suitable person to have the care and maintenance of foster children, or

(c) it would be detrimental to that child to be kept by that person in those premises,

the local authority may impose a prohibition on that person under subsection (2) below.

(2) A prohibition imposed on any person under this subsection may—

(a) prohibit him from keeping any foster child in premises specified in the prohibition ; or

(b) prohibit him from keeping any foster child in any premises in the area of the local authority ; or

(c) prohibit him from keeping a particular child specified in the prohibition in premises so specified.

(3) A local authority who have imposed a prohibition on any person under subsection (2) above, may, if they think fit, cancel the prohibition, either of their own motion or on an application made by that person on the ground of a change in the circumstances in which a foster child would be kept by him.

(4) Where a local authority impose a requirement on any person under section 9 above as respects any premises, they may prohibit him from keeping foster children in the premises after the time specified for compliance with the requirement unless the requirement is complied with.

(5) A prohibition imposed under this section shall be imposed by notice in writing addressed to the person on whom it is imposed and informing him of his right under section 11(1) below to appeal against the prohibition and of the time within which he may do so.

Power to prohibit the keeping of foster children.

Proceedings

11.—(1) A person aggrieved by a requirement imposed under section 9 above or by a prohibition imposed under section 10 above may appeal to a juvenile court—

(a) within 14 days from the date on which he is notified of the requirement or prohibition ; or

Appeal to juvenile court against requirement or prohibition imposed under s. 9 or 10.

(*b*) in the case of a prohibition imposed under section 10(2) above, within 14 days from the refusal by the local authority to accede to an application by him for the cancellation of the prohibition ;

and where the appeal is against a requirement imposed under section 9, the requirement shall not have effect while the appeal is pending.

(2) Where the court allows an appeal under subsection (1) above, the court, instead of cancelling the requirement or prohibition—

(*a*) may vary the requirement, or allow more time for compliance with it ; or

(*b*) if an absolute prohibition has been imposed, may substitute for it a prohibition on using the premises after such time as the court may specify unless such specified requirements as the local authority had power to impose under section 9 above are complied with.

(3) Any requirement or prohibition specified or substituted under this section by the court shall be deemed for the purposes of this Act, other than this section, to have been imposed by the local authority under section 9 or (as the case may be) section 10 above.

Removal of foster children kept in unsuitable surroundings.

12.—(1) If a juvenile court is satisfied, on the complaint of a local authority, that a foster child is being kept or is about to be received—

(*a*) by any person who is unfit to have his care, or

(*b*) in contravention of section 7 above or of any prohibition imposed by a local authority under section 10 above, or

(*c*) in any premises or any environment detrimental or likely to be detrimental to him,

the court may make an order for his removal to a place of safety until he can be restored to a parent, relative or guardian of his, or until other arrangements can be made with respect to him.

(2) On proof that there is imminent danger to the health or well-being of the child, the power to make an order under this section may be exercised by a justice of the peace acting on the application of a person authorised to visit foster children.

(3) An order under this section made on the ground that a prohibition of a local authority under section 10 above has been contravened may require the removal from the premises of all the foster children kept there.

(4) An order under this section may be executed by any person authorised to visit foster children or by any constable.

(5) A local authority may receive into their care under section 2 of the Child Care Act 1980 any child removed under this section, whether or not the circumstances of the child are such that they fall within paragraphs (*a*) to (*c*) of subsection (1) of the said section 2 and notwithstanding that he may appear to the local authority to be over the age of 17. 1980 c. 5.

(6) Where a child is removed under this section, the local authority shall, if practicable, inform a parent or guardian of the child, or any person who acts as his guardian.

13.—(1) If it is shown to the satisfaction of a justice of the peace on sworn information in writing— Search warrants.

> (*a*) that there is reasonable cause to believe that a foster child is being kept in any premises or in any part of any premises, and

> (*b*) that admission to those premises or that part has been refused to a duly authorised officer of the local authority or that such a refusal is apprehended or that the occupier is temporarily absent,

the justice may by warrant under his hand authorise an officer of the local authority to enter the premises, if need be by force, at any reasonable time within 48 hours of the issue of the warrant, for the purpose of inspecting the premises.

(2) Without prejudice to the provisions of subsection (1) above, a refusal to allow the visiting of a foster child or the inspection of any premises by a person authorised to do so under this Act shall be treated, for the purposes of section 40 of the Children and Young Persons Act 1933 (under which a warrant authorising the search for and removal of a child may be issued on suspicion of unnecessary suffering caused to, or certain offences committed against, the child), as giving reasonable cause for such suspicion. 1933 c. 12.

14.—(1) Section 47(2) of the Children and Young Persons Act 1933 (which restricts the time and place at which a sitting of a juvenile court may be held and the persons who may be present at such a sitting) shall not apply to any sitting of a juvenile court in any proceedings under section 11 or 12 above. Sittings of juvenile courts, and appeals to Crown Court.

(2) An appeal shall lie to the Crown Court from any order made under section 11 or 12 above by a juvenile court or a justice of the peace.

Advertisements

Prohibition of
advertisements
relating to
the fostering
of children.

15.—(1) No advertisement indicating that a person will under-take, or will arrange for, the care and maintenance of a child shall be published, unless it truly states that person's name and address.

(2) The Secretary of State may by regulations prohibit the parent or guardian of any child from publishing or causing to be published any advertisement indicating that foster parents are sought for the child.

(3) The Secretary of State may by regulations prohibit—

> (*a*) a member of a class of persons specified in the regula-tions, or
>
> (*b*) a person other than a person specified in the regulations, or other than a member of a class of persons so specified,

from publishing or causing to be published any advertisement indicating that he is willing to undertake, or to arrange for, the care and maintenance of a child.

(4) Regulations made under this section—

> (*a*) may make different provision for different cases or classes of cases ; and
>
> (*b*) may exclude specified cases or classes of cases.

Offences

Offences
relating
to foster
children.

16.—(1) A person shall be guilty of an offence if—

> (*a*) being required, under any provision of this Act or of regulations made under section 4 above, to give any notice or information, he—
>
>> (i) fails to give the notice within the time specified in that provision, or
>>
>> (ii) fails to give the information within a reason-able time, or
>>
>> (iii) knowingly makes, or causes or procures another person to make, any false or misleading statement in the notice or information ;
>
> (*b*) he refuses to allow—
>
>> (i) the visiting of any foster child by a duly authorised officer of a local authority, or
>>
>> (ii) the inspection under section 8 above of any premises ;
>
> (*c*) he maintains a foster child in contravention of section 7 above ;
>
> (*d*) he fails to comply with any requirement imposed by a local authority under this Act or keeps any foster child in any premises in contravention of a prohibition so imposed ;

    (*e*) he refuses to comply with an order under this Act for the removal of any child or obstructs any person in the execution of such an order ; or

    (*f*) he wilfully obstructs a person entitled to enter any premises by virtue of a warrant under section 13(1) above ;

    (*g*) he causes to be published or knowingly publishes an advertisement in contravention of section 15 above or of regulations made under that section.

(2) Where subsection (1) of section 7 above applies to any person by virtue only of subsection (2) of that section he shall not be guilty of an offence under subsection (1)(*c*) above if he proves that he did not know, and had no reasonable ground for believing, that a person living or employed in the premises in which he lives was a person to whom subsection (1) of that section applies.

(3) A person guilty of an offence under this section shall be liable on summary conviction to imprisonment for a term not exceeding six months, or a fine not exceeding £400, or both.

(4) If any person who is required, under any provision of this Act, to give a notice fails to give the notice within the time specified in that provision, then, notwithstanding anything in section 104 of the Magistrates' Courts Act 1952 (time limit for 1952 c. 55. proceedings), proceedings for the offence may be brought at any time within six months from the date when evidence of the offence came to the knowledge of the local authority.

(5) A local authority may institute proceedings for an offence under this section.

Extension of provisions of the Act to other children

17.—(1) Where a child below the upper limit of the com- Extension of pulsory school age resides during school holidays in a school to Act to certain which this section applies, then, if he so resides for a period school children exceeding two weeks, the provisions of this Act shall apply in holidays. relation to him as if section 2(2)(*c*) above were omitted, but subject to the modifications specified in subsection (2) below.

(2) Where this Act applies to a child by virtue of subsection (1) above—

    (*a*) subsections (1) to (4) of section 5, sections 6, 9 and 10 above and section 18 below shall not apply ; but

    (*b*) the person undertaking the care and maintenance of children in the school during the school holidays shall, not less than two weeks before this Act first applies to a child in that school during those holidays, give written notice to the local authority that children to whom this Act applies will reside in the school during those holidays, and any such notice shall state the estimated number of the children.

(3) A local authority may exempt any person from the duty of giving notices under this section; and any such exemption may be granted for a specified period or indefinitely, and may be revoked at any time by notice in writing given to that person.

1944 c. 31.

(4) This section applies to any school within the meaning of the Education Act 1944 which is not a school maintained by a local education authority.

Extension of Act to certain children above compulsory school age.

18. Where a child is a foster child on attaining the upper limit of the compulsory school age, this Act shall apply in relation to him as it applies in relation to a foster child, until—

　　(a) he would, apart from that limit, have ceased to be a foster child, or

　　(b) he reaches the age of 18, or

　　(c) he lives elsewhere than with the person with whom he was living when he attained the said limit,

whichever first occurs.

Miscellaneous and supplementary

Avoidance of insurances on lives of foster children. 1774 c. 48.

19. A person who maintains a foster child for reward shall be deemed for the purposes of the Life Assurance Act 1774 to have no interest in the life of the child.

Service of notices by post.

20. Any notice or information required to be given under this Act may be given by post.

Regulations.

21. Any power to make regulations conferred on the Secretary of State by this Act shall be exercisable by statutory instrument, which shall be subject to annulment in pursuance of a resolution of either House of Parliament.

Interpretation.

22. In this Act—

　　" child " means a person under the age of 18 ;

　　" compulsory school age " has the same meaning as in the Education Act 1944 ;

　　" local authority " means the council of a non-metropolitan county, metropolitan district or London borough, or the Common Council of the City of London ;

" local authority in Scotland " means a regional or islands council ;

" place of safety " means a community home provided by a local authority, a controlled community home, a police station, or any hospital, surgery or other suitable place whose occupier is willing temporarily to receive a child ;

" relative ", in relation to a child, means a granaparent, brother, sister, uncle or aunt (whether of the full blood or half-blood or by affinity) and includes, where the child is illegitimate, the father of the child and any person who would be a relative within the meaning of this definition if the child were the legitimate child of his mother and father ;

" voluntary organisation " means a body the activities of which are carried on otherwise than for profit.

23.—(1) This Act shall have effect subject to the transitional provisions set out in Schedule 1 to this Act.

(2) The enactments mentioned in Schedule 2 to this Act shall have effect subject to the amendments specified in that Schedule, being amendments consequential on the provisions of this Act.

(3) The enactments specified in Schedule 3 to this Act are hereby repealed to the extent specified in the third column of that Schedule.

(4) The inclusion in this Act of any express saving or amendment shall not be taken as prejudicing the operation of section 16 or 17 of the Interpretation Act 1978 (which relate to the effect of repeals).

Transitional provisions, consequential amendments and repeals.

1978 c. 30.

24.—(1) This Act may be cited as the Foster Children Act 1980.

(2) This Act shall come into force on the date appointed under section 90(1) of the Child Care Act 1980 for the coming into force of that Act.

(3) This Act (except Part II of Schedule 2 which extends only to Scotland) extends to England and Wales only.

Citation, etc.

1980 c. 5.

Section 23(1).

SCHEDULES

SCHEDULE 1

TRANSITIONAL PROVISIONS

Custodians

1975 c. 72.
1. If at the commencement of this Act section 33 of the Children Act 1975 (custodianship orders) is not in force, then, until that section is in force, section 1 above shall have effect as if for the words " relative, guardian or custodian " there were substituted the words " relative or guardian ".

Children subject to subsisting fit person orders

2. Without prejudice to the provisions of paragraph 9 of Schedule
1969 c. 54.
4 to the Children and Young Persons Act 1969, a child is not a foster child for the purposes of this Act if he is subject to such an order as is mentioned in sub-paragraph (*a*) of that paragraph (orders under
1933 c. 12.
Children and Young Persons Act 1933 committing a person under 17 to the care of a person other than a local authority and in force on 1st January 1971).

Periods of time

3. Where a period of time specified in an enactment repealed by this Act is current at the commencement of this Act, this Act shall have effect as if the corresponding provision thereof had been in force when that period began to run.

Notification under s.5

4.—(1) In this paragraph " the relevant date " means the date on which regulations made under section 3(2) above come into force.

(2) A person shall not at any time before the relevant date be required to give notice under subsection (1) or (2) of section 5 above in relation to a child if—

(*a*) he has on a previous occasion given notice under subsection (1) of that section in respect of that or any other child, specifying the premises at which he proposes to keep the child in question ; and

(*b*) he has not, at any time since that notice was given, ceased to maintain at least one foster child at those premises and been required to give notice under section 6(2) above in respect of those premises.

(3) Every person who is maintaining a foster child within the area of a local authority on the relevant date and who before that date has not given notice in respect of the child to the local authority under subsection (1) or (2) of section 5 above shall within eight weeks of that date give written notice to the local authority that he is maintaining the child.

Children above compulsory school age

SCH. 1

5. Where immediately before the commencement of this Act Part I of the Children Act 1958 applied in relation to a child by virtue only of section 13 of that Act, this Act shall apply in relation to him as it applies in relation to a foster child, until— 1958 c. 65.

   (a) he would, apart from the upper limit of the compulsory school age, have ceased to be a foster child, or

   (b) he reaches the age of 18, or

   (c) he lives elsewhere than with the person with whom he was living when he attained the said limit,

whichever first occurs.

References to provisions of Adoption Act 1976 and Adoption (Scotland) Act 1978

6.—(1) If at the commencement of this Act section 1 of the Adoption Act 1976 or section 1 of the Adoption (Scotland) Act 1978 is not in force, then, until that section is in force, section 2(6)(a) above shall have effect as if for the reference to arrangements made by an adoption agency within the meaning of that section there were substituted a reference to arrangements made by a local authority or a local authority in Scotland, or by any adoption society within the meaning of the Adoption Act 1958 for the time being registered under Part II of that Act or approved under Part I of the Children Act 1975. 1976 c. 36.
1978 c. 28.

1958 c. 5
(7 & 8 Eliz. 2).
1975 c.72.

(2) If at the commencement of this Act section 32 of the Adoption Act 1976 is not in force, then, until that section is in force, section 2(6)(b) above shall have effect as if for the reference to Part III of that Act there were substituted a reference to Part IV of the Adoption Act 1958.

SCHEDULE 2

Section 23(2).

CONSEQUENTIAL AMENDMENTS

PART I

AMENDMENTS EXTENDING ONLY TO ENGLAND AND WALES

NURSERIES AND CHILD-MINDERS REGULATION ACT 1948 (c.53)

1. In section 8(1) (exemption of certain institutions from provisions of Act), for " section two of the Children Act 1958 " substitute " section 2 of the Foster Children Act 1980 ".

2. In section 13(2) (interpretation), for " of Part I of the Children Act 1958 " substitute " of the Foster Children Act 1980 ".

CHILDREN AND YOUNG PERSONS ACT 1963 (c.37)

In section 23(1)(c) (children and young persons detained in places of safety), or " section 7 of the Children Act 1958 " substitute " section 12 of the Foster Children Act 1980 ".

HEALTH SERVICES AND PUBLIC HEALTH ACT 1968 (*c*.46)

1. In section 60(7)(*a*) (amendments of Nurseries and Child-Minders Regulation Act 1948), for " section 6 of the Children Act 1958 " substitute " section 7 of the Foster Children Act 1980 ".

2. In section 64(3)(*a*) (financial assistance by Secretary of State to certain voluntary organisations), for sub-paragraph (vi) substitute—

" (vii) the Foster Children Act 1980,".

3. In section 65(3)(*b*) (financial and other assistance by local authorities to certain voluntary organisations), for sub-paragraph (vii) substitute—

" (vii) the Foster Children Act 1980,".

LOCAL AUTHORITY SOCIAL SERVICES ACT 1970 (*c*.42)

In Schedule 1 (enactments conferring functions assigned to Social Services Committee)—

(*a*) omit the entry relating to the Children Act 1958 ; and

(*b*) at the end add—

"Foster Children Act 1980 (c.6)	Protection of children living away from their parents; prosecution of offences."

ADOPTION ACT 1976 (*c*.36)

1. In section 2(*c*) (local authorities' social services), for " the Children Act 1958 " substitute " the Foster Children Act 1980 ".

2. In section 32(3)(*a*) (meaning of protected child), for " subsection (3) or (5) of section 2 of the Children Act 1958 " substitute " section 2(2) of the Foster Children Act 1980 ".

PART II

AMENDMENT EXTENDING ONLY TO SCOTLAND

CHILDREN ACT 1958 (c.65)

In section 6(1)(*a*) (disqualification for keeping foster children), after " this Act " insert " or under section 12 of the Foster Children Act 1980 ".

SCHEDULE 3

Section 23(3).

REPEALS

Chapter	Short Title	Extent of Repeal
6 & 7 Eliz. 2. c. 65.	Children Act 1958.	The whole Act, so far as unrepealed, except the entry in Schedule 2 relating to section 38 of the Children Act 1948.
7 & 8 Eliz. 2. c. 72.	Mental Health Act 1959.	In Schedule 7, in Part II, the entry relating to the Children Act 1958.
8 & 9 Eliz. 2. c. 61.	Mental Health (Scotland) Act 1960.	In Schedule 4, the entry relating to the Children Act 1958.
1968 c. 49.	Social Work (Scotland) Act 1968.	In Schedule 8, paragraphs 44 to 47.
1969 c. 54.	Children and Young Persons Act 1969.	Section 51. In section 52, subsections (1) to (3) and (5). Sections 53 to 57. Section 72(5). In Schedule 4, paragraphs 10 and 16. In Schedule 5, paragraphs 29 to 32 and paragraph 82. Schedule 7.
1970 c. 42.	Local Authority Social Services Act 1970.	In Schedule 1, the entry relating to the Children Act 1958.
1971 c. 23.	The Courts Act 1971.	In Schedule 9, in Part I, the entry relating to the Children Act 1958.
1972 c. 70.	Local Government Act 1972.	In Schedule 23, paragraph 7.
1975 c. 72.	Children Act 1975.	Sections 95 to 97. In Schedule 3, paragraphs 16(*a*) and 18 to 20.
1976 c. 36.	Adoption Act 1976.	In Schedule 3, paragraphs 5 and 6.

Residential Homes Act 1980

1980 CHAPTER 7

An Act to consolidate certain enactments relating to the registration, inspection and conduct of residential homes for disabled, old or mentally disordered persons and to the provision by district councils of meals and recreation for old people.   [20th March 1980]

BE IT ENACTED by the Queen's most Excellent Majesty, by and with the advice and consent of the Lords Spiritual and Temporal, and Commons, in this present Parliament assembled, and by the authority of the same, as follows:—

Registration etc. of residential homes

1.—(1) The homes to which this Act applies are disabled persons' or old persons' homes and residential homes for mentally disordered persons. Homes to which Act applies.

(2) In this Act " disabled persons' or old persons' home " means any establishment the sole or main object of which is, or is held out to be, the provision of accommodation, whether for reward or not, for disabled persons or old persons oɪ both, but does not include—

   (a) any hospital within the meaning of section 128(1) of the National Health Service Act 1977 which is maintained in pursuance of an Act of Parliament; 1977 c. 49.

   (b) any nursing home or mental nursing home within the meaning of the Nursing Homes Act 1975; 1975 c. 37.

   (c) any voluntary home within the meaning of the Child Care Act 1980; 1980 c. 5.

(*d*) any other premises being premises managed by a government department or local authority, or any other authority or body constituted by special Act of Parliament or incorporated by Royal Charter ; or

(*e*) any pre-1948 Act establishment exempted from the operation of this Act by or under regulations of the Secretary of State made after consultation with the Charity Commissioners ;

1948 c. 29.

and in paragraph (*e*) above " pre-1948 Act establishment " means an establishment which was being carried on immediately before the coming into operation of section 37 of the National Assistance Act 1948, but no establishment so carried on shall be exempted under that paragraph as respects any premises in which it was not being carried on immediately before the coming into operation of that section.

(3) In this Act " residential home for mentally disordered persons " means any establishment the sole or main object of which is, or is held out to be, the provision of accommodation, whether for reward or not, for mentally disordered persons, but does not include—

1959 c. 72.

(*a*) any hospital within the meaning of section 147(1) of the Mental Health Act 1959 ;

1975 c. 37.

(*b*) any mental nursing home within the meaning of the Nursing Homes Act 1975 ; or

(*c*) any other premises managed by a government department or provided by a local authority.

Registration of homes.

2.—(1) If any person carries on a home to which this Act applies without being registered under this Act in respect of that home, he shall be liable on summary conviction to a fine not exceeding £500 or, in the case of a second or subsequent offence, to imprisonment for a term not exceeding three months or a fine not exceeding £500 or both.

(2) An application for registration under this Act shall be made to the registration authority and shall be accompanied by a fee of £1.

(3) Subject to the provisions of this section and section 3 below, the registration authority shall, on receipt of an application under subsection (2) above, register the applicant in respect of the home named in the application and issue to him a certificate of registration.

(4) It shall be a condition of the registration of any person in respect of a residential home for mentally disordered persons

that the number of persons kept at any one time in the home (excluding persons carrying on or employed in the home and their families) does not exceed such number as may be specified in the certificate of registration ; and without prejudice to the foregoing provision, the registration may be effected subject to such conditions (to be specified in the certificate) as the registration authority consider appropriate for regulating the age, sex or other category of persons who may be received in the home.

(5) If any condition imposed by or under subsection (4) above is not complied with, the person carrying on the home shall be liable on summary conviction to a fine not exceeding £500.

(6) The certificate of registration under this Act issued in respect of any home shall be kept affixed in a conspicuous place in the home ; and if default is made in complying with this subsection the person carrying on the home shall be liable on summary conviction to a fine not exceeding £25 and to a further fine not exceeding £2 for each day on which the offence continues after conviction.

(7) Notwithstanding anything in subsection (1) above, where the person registered under this Act in respect of a home dies, his executor or his widow or any other member of his family may for a period not exceeding four weeks from his death, or such longer period as the registration authority may sanction, carry on the home without being registered in respect of the home.

(8) The registers kept for the purposes of this Act shall be available for inspection at all reasonable times, and the person inspecting any such register shall be entitled to make copies of entries in the register on payment of such fee (if any), not exceeding 5p for each entry, as the registration authority may determine.

(9) In this Act " registration authority ", in relation to any home to which this Act applies, means the council which for the purposes of the Local Authority Social Services Act 1970 is 1970 c. 42. the local authority for the area in which the home is situated ; and the local authorities for the purposes of that Act are, at the passing of this Act, the councils of non-metropolitan counties, metropolitan districts and London boroughs and the Common Council of the City of London.

3.—(1) The registration authority may by order refuse to Refusal or register an applicant if they are satisfied— cancellation of registration.

(a) that he or any person employed or proposed to be employed by him in the management of the home or any part of the home is not a fit person, whether by reason of age or otherwise, to carry on or to be so employed at a home of such a description as the home named in the application ;

(b) that for reasons connected with the situation, construction, state of repair, accommodation, staffing or equipment, the home or any premises used in connection with the home are not fit to be used for a home of such a description as aforesaid ; or

(c) that the way in which it is proposed to conduct the home is such as not to provide services or facilities reasonably required by persons resorting to such a home.

(2) The registration authority may by order at any time cancel the registration of a person in respect of a home—

(a) on any ground which would entitle them to refuse an application for the registration of that person in respect of that home ;

(b) in the case of a disabled persons' or old persons' home, on the ground that that person has been convicted of an offence against this Act or against any regulations made under it in respect of that or any other disabled persons' or old persons' home or that any other person has been convicted of such an offence in respect of that home ; or

(c) in the case of a residential home for mentally disordered persons, on the ground that that person has been convicted of an offence against this Act or against any regulations made under it in respect of that or any other residential home for mentally disordered persons, that any other person has been convicted of such an offence in respect of that home or that any condition imposed by or under section 2(4) above in respect of that home has not been complied with.

(3) Not less than 14 days before making an order refusing an application for registration or an order cancelling any registration, the registration authority shall send by post to the applicant or to the person registered, as the case may be, notice of their intention to make such an order.

(4) Every such notice shall state the grounds on which the authority intend to make the order and shall contain an intimation that if within 14 days after the receipt of the notice the applicant or person registered, as the case may be, informs the authority in writing of his desire to show cause in person or by a representative, why the order should not be made, the authority will before making the order afford him an opportunity to do so.

(5) If the registration authority after giving the applicant or person registered, as the case may be, an opportunity of being

heard by them, decide to refuse the application for registration, or to cancel the registration, they shall make an order to that effect and send by post to the applicant or person registered, as the case may be,—

(*a*) a copy of the order ; and

(*b*) a statement of the right of appeal to a magistrates' court for which provision is made by section 4(1) below and the time within which such an appeal may be brought.

4.—(1) A person aggrieved by an order under section 3 above refusing an application for registration or cancelling any registration may appeal to a magistrates' court having jurisdiction in the place where the home in question is situated ; and the cancellation of any registration shall not take effect until the expiration of the time within which an appeal may be brought under this subsection or, where such an appeal is brought, before the determination of the appeal. Appeals against refusal or cancellation.

(2) The procedure on an appeal to a magistrates' court under subsection (1) above shall be by way of complaint for an order, and the Magistrates' Courts Act 1952 shall apply to the proceedings. 1952 c. 55.

(3) The time within which any such appeal may be brought shall be 21 days from the date on which the copy of the registration authority's order was served upon the person desiring to appeal, and for the purpose of this subsection the making of the complaint shall be deemed to be the bringing of the appeal.

(4) A person aggrieved by an order, determination or other decision of a magistrates' court under subsection (1) above may appeal to the Crown Court.

(5) Where on an appeal under this section a court reverses any decision of a registration authority, it shall be the duty of the authority to give effect to the order of the court and, in particular, to issue any certificate and to make any necessary entry in any register.

5.—(1) The Secretary of State may make regulations as to the conduct of homes to which this Act applies, and in particular— Conduct of homes.

(*a*) as to the facilities and services to be provided in such homes ;

(*b*) for empowering the registration authority to limit the number of persons or persons of any description who may be received into any disabled persons' or old persons' home and for enabling registration of any such home to be made subject to the condition that persons shall not be received in the home in excess of the number fixed for the home in accordance with the regulations ; and

(*c*) as to the records to be kept and notices to be given in respect of persons received in residential homes for mentally disordered persons.

(2) The registers to be kept by registration authorities for the purposes of this Act shall be in such form, and contain such particulars, as may be provided by regulations under this section, and such regulations may make provision as to the information to be supplied on any application for registration under this Act.

(3) Regulations under this section may provide that a contravention of or failure to comply with any specified provision of the regulations shall be an offence against the regulations ; and any person guilty of an offence against the regulations shall be liable on summary conviction to a fine not exceeding £500.

Inspection of homes.

6.—(1) Any person authorised in that behalf by the Secretary of State may at all reasonable times enter and inspect any premises which are used, or which that person has reasonable cause to believe to be used, for the purposes of a home to which this Act applies.

(2) Any person authorised in that behalf by the registration authority may at all reasonable times enter and inspect any premises in the area of the authority which are used, or which that person has reasonable cause to believe to be used, for those purposes.

(3) The powers of inspection conferred by subsections (1) and (2) above, in their application to residential homes for mentally disordered persons, shall include power to inspect any records required to be kept in accordance with regulations made under section 5(1)(*c*) above.

(4) A person who proposes to exercise any power of entry or inspection conferred by this section shall if so required produce some duly authenticated document showing his authority to exercise the power.

(5) Any person who obstructs the exercise of any such power shall be liable on summary conviction to a fine not exceeding £500.

Prosecutions etc.

7.—(1) Offences against this Act or any regulations made under it may be prosecuted by the registration authority.

(2) Where an offence against this Act or any regulations made under it has been committed by a body corporate, every person who at the time of the commission of the offence was a director, general manager, secretary or other similar officer of

the body corporate, or was purporting to act in any such capacity, shall also be guilty of the offence unless he proves—

(a) that it was committed without his consent or connivance; and

(b) that he exercised all such diligence to prevent its commission as he ought to have exercised having regard to the nature of his functions in that capacity and to all the circumstances.

Provision of meals and recreation for old people

8.—(1) A district council shall have power to make such arrangements as they may from time to time determine for providing meals and recreation for old people in their homes or elsewhere, and may employ as their agent for the purposes of this subsection any voluntary organisation whose activities consist in or include the provision of meals or recreation for old people.

Provision of meals and recreation.

(2) A district council may recover from persons availing themselves of any service provided under subsection (1) above such charges (if any) as, having regard to the cost of the service, the council may determine, whether generally or in the circumstances of any particular case.

(3) A district council may assist any such organisation as is referred to in subsection (1) above to provide meals or recreation for old people by contributing to the funds of the organisation, by permitting them to use premises belonging to the council on such terms as may be agreed, and by making available furniture, vehicles or equipment (whether by way of gift or loan or otherwise) and the services of any staff who are employed by the council in connection with the premises or other things which they permit the organisation to use.

(4) District councils shall exercise their functions under this section (including any discretion conferred on them under this section) in accordance with the provisions of any regulations of the Secretary of State made for the purposes of this subsection; and without prejudice to the generality of the foregoing provision, regulations under this subsection—

(a) may provide for conferring on officers of the Secretary of State authorised under the regulations such powers of inspection as may be prescribed in relation to the exercise of functions under this section by or by arrangement with or on behalf of district councils; and

(b) may make provision with respect to the qualifications of officers employed by district councils for the purposes of this section or by voluntary organisations acting under arrangements with or on behalf of district councils for those purposes.

(5) In this section " voluntary organisation " means a body the activities of which are carried on otherwise than for profit, but does not include any public or local authority.

Supplemental

Regulations.

9. Any power of the Secretary of State to make regulations under this Act shall be exercisable by statutory instrument; and any statutory instrument containing regulations under this Act shall be subject to annulment in pursuance of a resolution of either House of Parliament.

Interpretation etc.

10.—(1) In this Act, unless the context otherwise requires,—

" blind person " means a person so blind as to be unable to perform any work for which eyesight is essential;

" disabled person " means a person who is blind, deaf or dumb or who is substantially and permanently handicapped by illness, injury or congenital deformity or any other disability for the time being prescribed for the purposes of section 29(1) of the National Assistance Act 1948;

1948 c. 29.

" disabled persons' or old persons' home " has the meaning assigned to it by section 1(2) above;

" functions " includes powers and duties;

" mentally disordered person " means a person who is suffering from any mental disorder within the meaning of the Mental Health Act 1959;

1959 c. 72.

" prescribed " means prescribed by regulations under this Act;

" registration authority " has the meaning assigned to it by section 2(9) above;

" residential home for mentally disordered persons " has the meaning assigned to it by section 1(3) above.

(2) This Act shall, in its application to the Isles of Scilly, have effect subject to such exceptions, adaptations and modifications as the Secretary of State may by order made by statutory instrument direct.

Transitional provisions, consequential amendments and repeals.

11.—(1) Where a period of time specified in an enactment repealed by this Act is current at the commencement of this Act, this Act shall have effect as if the corresponding provision of this Act had been in force when that period began to run.

(2) For the purposes of determining the punishment which may be imposed on a person in respect of the commission by him of an offence under any provision of this Act, an offence

committed by that person under the corresponding enactment repealed by this Act shall be deemed to have been committed under that provision.

(3) Where an offence, for the continuance of which a penalty was provided, has been committed under any enactment repealed by this Act, proceedings may be taken under this Act in respect of the continuance of the offence after the commencement of this Act, in the same manner as if the offence had been committed under the corresponding provision of this Act.

(4) The enactments mentioned in Schedule 1 to this Act shall have effect subject to the amendments specified in that Schedule, being amendments consequential on the provisions of this Act.

(5) The enactments mentioned in Schedule 2 to this Act are hereby repealed to the extent specified in the third column of that Schedule.

(6) Nothing in this section shall be taken as prejudicing the operation of sections 16 and 17 of the Interpretation Act 1978 1978 c. 30. (effect of repeals).

12.—(1) This Act may be cited as the Residential Homes Short title, Act 1980. commencement and

(2) This Act shall come into force on such day as the Secretary extent. of State may by order made by statutory instrument appoint.

(3) This Act does not extend to Scotland or Northern Ireland.

SCHEDULES

SCHEDULE 1

Consequential Amendments

The National Assistance Act 1948

1. In section 41(2) of the National Assistance Act 1948 (registration of charities for disabled persons) for the words " section 37 of this Act " there shall be substituted the words " the Residential Homes Act 1980 ".

The Mental Health Act 1959

2.—(1) In section 8(3) of the Mental Health Act 1959 (functions of welfare authorities) for the words from " disabled persons' homes " onwards there shall be substituted the words " charities for disabled persons ".

(2) In section 128(1) of that Act (sexual intercourse with patients) for the words " Part III of this Act " there shall be substituted the words " the Residential Homes Act 1980 ".

The Local Government Act 1966

3. In Part II of Schedule 3 to the Local Government Act 1966 (variation of fees for licences, registration etc.), for paragraph 31 there shall be substituted the following paragraph—
" 31. Section 2(2) of the Residential Homes Act 1980 ".

The Local Authority Social Services Act 1970

4.—(1) In Schedule 1 to the Local Authority Social Services Act 1970 (which specifies the enactments conferring functions assigned to the social services committee of a local authority), for the entry relating to sections 37 to 41 of the National Assistance Act 1948 there shall be substituted the following entry—

" Section 41   Charities for disabled."

(2) At the end of that Schedule there shall be inserted the following entry—

" Residential Homes Act 1980   Registration of disabled or old
    (c. 7) Sections 1 to 7   persons' homes and residen-
                                        tial homes for mentally dis-
                                        ordered persons."

The Adoption Act 1976

5. In section 32(3) of the Adoption Act 1976 (meaning of " protected child ") for the words " section 19 of the Mental Health Act 1959 " there shall be substituted the words " section 1(3) of the Residential Homes Act 1980 ".

SCHEDULE 2

ENACTMENTS REPEALED

Chapter	Short title	Extent of repeal
11 & 12 Geo. 6. c. 29.	The National Assistance Act 1948.	Section 31. In section 33(1), the proviso. Sections 37 to 40.
7 & 8 Eliz. 2. c. 72.	The Mental Health Act 1959.	Sections 19 to 21. Section 23(1). In Schedule 7, in Part II, the entry relating to section 37 of the National Assistance Act 1948.
8 & 9 Eliz. 2. c. 61.	The Mental Health (Scotland) Act 1960.	In Schedule 4, the entry relating to section 37 of the National Assistance Act 1948.
10 & 11 Eliz. 2. c. 24.	The National Assistance Act 1948 (Amendment) Act 1962.	Section 1(1).
1968 c. 46.	The Health Services and Public Health Act 1968.	Section 45(10).
1972 c. 70.	The Local Government Act 1972.	In Schedule 23, paragraph 2(8).
1975 c. 37.	The Nursing Homes Act 1975.	In Schedule 1, paragraph 6.
1977 c. 45.	The Criminal Law Act 1977.	In Schedule 6, the entries relating to sections 37(1) and 40(3) of the National Assistance Act 1948 and the entry relating to section 20(2) of the Mental Health Act 1959.

Gaming (Amendment) Act 1980

1980 CHAPTER 8

An Act to amend subsection (3) of section 20 of the
Gaming Act 1968 to enable the Secretary of State, by
order, to amend the limit of £1,000 therein.

[20th March 1980]

BE IT ENACTED by the Queen's most Excellent Majesty, by and
with the advice and consent of the Lords Spiritual and
Temporal, and Commons, in this present Parliament
assembled, and by the authority of the same, as follows:—

Amendment
of s. 20 of
Gaming
Act 1968.

1968 c. 65.

1.—(1) Subsection (3) of section 20 of the Gaming Act 1968
(which specifies the maximum permitted aggregate amount of
the winnings in respect of games of bingo played in one week
simultaneously on different bingo club premises) shall be amended
in accordance with subsection (2) below.

(2) At the end of subsection (3) there shall be added the
following proviso:—

"Provided that the Secretary of State may by order
provide that this subsection shall have effect with the substitution, for the reference to £1,000, of a reference to such
other sum as may be specified in the order."

Short title.

2. This Act may be cited as the Gaming (Amendment) Act
1980.

Reserve Forces Act 1980

1980 CHAPTER 9

An Act to consolidate certain enactments relating to the reserve and auxiliary forces, and the lieutenancies, with amendments to give effect to a recommendation of the Law Commission; and to repeal certain obsolete enactments relating to those forces.

[20th March 1980]

BE IT ENACTED by the Queen's most Excellent Majesty, by and with the advice and consent of the Lords Spiritual and Temporal, and Commons, in this present Parliament assembled, and by the authority of the same, as follows:—

PART I

THE RESERVE AND AUXILIARY FORCES

Naval and marine reserves

1.—(1) The Secretary of State may as provided by Part III of this Act maintain the force known as the Royal Naval Reserve. Royal Naval Reserve.

(2) The Royal Naval Reserve (together with its division, the Royal Fleet Reserve, mentioned in section 2 below) shall consist of seafaring men and others deemed suitable, entering voluntarily—

    (*a*) in such manner as the Secretary of State shall direct, **and**

    (*b*) in such number as he may determine.

2.—(1) The Secretary of State may, in addition to the persons of the Royal Naval Reserve, and as provided by Part III of this Act, maintain the division of the Royal Naval Reserve known as the Royal Fleet Reserve, consisting of such number of persons as he may determine. Royal Fleet Reserve and its special class.

PART I

(2) The Royal Fleet Reserve shall consist of—

(a) persons—

(i) who are in receipt of pensions in respect of service in the navy or marines, and

(ii) who are entitled to their pensions subject to a condition of service in the Royal Fleet Reserve, and

(b) persons—

(i) who have served in the navy or marines, and

(ii) who have enlisted in the Royal Fleet Reserve.

(3) The special class of the Royal Fleet Reserve (consisting of such number of men as the Secretary of State may determine) shall continue in being as provided by Part III.

Royal
Marines
Reserve.

3. The Secretary of State may as provided by Part III of this Act maintain the reserve volunteer force of marines known as the Royal Marines Reserve.

Army reserves and auxiliaries

Army
Reserve.

4.—(1) Her Majesty may as provided by Part IV of this Act maintain the force in the United Kingdom known as the Army Reserve.

(2) That reserve shall consist of such number of men as may from time to time be determined by Parliament being—

(a) men transferred (whether before or after the commencement of this Act) to the Army Reserve in pursuance of the Army Act 1955 ; or

1955 c. 18.

(b) men enlisted or re-engaged in the Army Reserve in pursuance of Part IV.

Territorial
Army.

5.—(1) Her Majesty may as provided by Part V of this Act maintain the Territorial and Army Volunteer Reserve (the force in this Act called the Territorial Army).

(2) The Territorial Army shall consist of such number of officers, warrant officers, non-commissioned officers and men as may from time to time be determined by Parliament.

Home Service
Force of the
Territorial
Army.

6.—(1) The Home Service Force shall continue in being—

(a) as part of the Territorial Army ; and

(b) as a force for home service.

(2) That force shall consist of—

(a) persons who on 2nd April 1967 were members of any unit of the Territorial Army designated by warrant of Her Majesty as a unit of the Home Service Force ;

(*b*) persons who become officers of, or enlist or re-engage in, the Territorial Army for service with the Home Service Force ;

(*c*) members of the Territorial Army—

> (i) who are not members of the Home Service Force by virtue of paragraphs (*a*) and (*b*) above ; and

> (ii) who are transferred to the Home Service Force with their consent.

(3) Notwithstanding anything in this Act or any other enactment, a member of the Home Service Force shall not—

(*a*) be required to serve, either on permanent service or otherwise, outside the United Kingdom, the Channel Islands and the Isle of Man, or

(*b*) except in the case of the holder of a land forces commission (including one entitled to the issue of such a commission), be transferred to any other part of the military forces without his consent,

but a member of the Home Service Force who is transferred to another part of the military forces shall cease to be a member of that force.

7.—(1) Her Majesty may as provided by Part VII of this Act maintain the force known as the Ulster Defence Regiment. Ulster Defence Regiment.

(2) The Ulster Defence Regiment shall consist of the number from time to time determined by Parliament of those persons—

(*a*) who voluntarily undertake to serve in that force, and

(*b*) who may be accepted for such service.

Air force reserves and auxiliaries

8.—(1) Her Majesty may as provided by Part IV of this Act maintain the force known as the Air Force Reserve. Air Force Reserve.

(2) That reserve shall consist of such number of officers as may from time to time be determined by Parliament, and of such number of men as may be so determined.

(3) Those men shall be either—

(*a*) men transferred (whether before or after the commencement of this Act) to the Air Force Reserve in pursuance of the Air Force Act 1955 ; or 1955 c. 19.

(*b*) men enlisted or re-engaged in the Air Force Reserve in pursuance of Part IV.

PART I
Royal
Auxiliary
Air Force.

9.—(1) Her Majesty may as provided by Part V of this Act maintain the force known as the Royal Auxiliary Air Force.

(2) The Royal Auxiliary Air Force shall consist of such number of officers, warrant officers, non-commissioned officers and men as may from time to time be determined by Parliament.

PART II

CALL OUT AND RECALL

General provisions as to call out for permanent service

Call out for
national
danger.

10.—(1) If it appears to Her Majesty that national danger is imminent or that a great emergency has arisen She may by order signified under the hand of the Secretary of State authorise the calling out of any reserve force for permanent service in any part of the world.

(2) The occasion of the making of any order under subsection (1) above shall forthwith be communicated to Parliament; and if Parliament is then separated by such adjournment or prorogation as will not expire within 5 days—

(a) a proclamation shall be issued for the meeting of Parliament within 5 days; and

(b) Parliament shall accordingly meet and sit upon the day appointed by the proclamation; and

(c) Parliament shall continue to sit and act in like manner as if it had stood adjourned or prorogued to the same day.

(3) An order in force under subsection (1) may be revoked by an order of Her Majesty signified as there mentioned, but the revocation shall not affect the liability for service of any person called out for service by virtue of the order at the time of its revocation.

(4) In this section " reserve force " means any of the following bodies—

(a) the Army Reserve;

(b) the Territorial Army;

(c) the Air Force Reserve;

(d) the Royal Auxiliary Air Force;

(e) the Royal Naval Reserve including the Royal Fleet Reserve and the special class of the Royal Fleet Reserve; and

(f) the Royal Marines Reserve.

(5) An order under subsection (1) may authorise the calling out of the Ulster Defence Regiment for permanent service in Northern Ireland, and section 26 below applies for the purposes of this subsection as if the Ulster Defence Regiment were a reserve force within the meaning of subsection (4) above.

(6) In relation to a man of the Royal Auxiliary Air Force in whose case it was agreed at the time of his enlistment that he was accepted for home service only, subsection (1) has effect as if for the reference to any part of the world there were a reference to the United Kingdom, the Channel Islands and the Isle of Man.

11.—(1) A person to whom this section applies shall be liable Call out for to be called out for permanent service in any part of the world warlike when warlike operations are in preparation or progress, subject operations. to sections 12 and 13(1) below.

(2) The persons to whom this section applies are—

(a) any member of the Army Reserve or the Air Force Reserve who became such a member on or after 1st April 1967 otherwise than in consequence of his having enlisted in the regular army or the regular air force before that day ;

(b) any member of the Territorial Army who became such a member on or after 1st April 1967 by enlisting or re-engaging in the Territorial Army or by becoming an officer of the Territorial Army ;

(c) any member of the special class of the Royal Fleet Reserve who became such a member on or after 1st April 1967 otherwise than in consequence of his having, before that day, been entered for non-continuous service in the naval service of Her Majesty or enlisted to serve in the royal marine forces ; and

(d) any other member of a reserve or class mentioned in paragraphs (a) to (c) above who has elected in pursuance of subsections (4) and (5) below to be a person to whom this section applies and has been notified in the prescribed manner that he has been accepted as such a person.

(3) In subsection (2) above—

(a) the references in paragraphs (a) and (c) to becoming a member of a reserve or class include references to remaining a member of it by virtue of a new engagement or other agreement ; and

(b) a notification in pursuance of paragraph (d) may be made to take effect on a day determined by the notification.

(4) A member of a reserve or class mentioned in subsection (2) who is not a person to whom this section applies may (subject to section 13(1) below) elect irrevocably in the prescribed manner to be such a person.

(5) A person who immediately before 1st April 1967—

(*a*) was a man of the regular army or the regular air force, or

(*b*) was serving by reason of his having been entered or enlisted as mentioned in paragraph (*c*) of subsection (2),

may (subject to section 13(1)) elect irrevocably in the prescribed manner that, on his becoming a member of such a reserve or class, he shall be a person to whom this section applies.

(6) In relation to the calling out of persons by virtue of this section—

(*a*) any such calling out shall be reported to Parliament forthwith ;

(*b*) the number of persons for the time being called out shall not be reckoned in the numbers for the time being authorised by Parliament for the regular army and the regular air force.

Call out for
Territorial
Army under
s. 11.
12.—(1) A member of the Territorial Army shall not be liable to be called out under section 11(1) above unless there is in force an order of Her Majesty, signified under the hand of the Secretary of State, authorising the calling out under that section of members of the Territorial Army.

(2) An order in force under subsection (1) above may be revoked by an order of Her Majesty signified as there mentioned, but the revocation shall not affect the liability for service of any person called out for service by virtue of the order at the time of its revocation.

Provisions
supplemental
to ss. 10 to 12.
13.—(1) A member of the Home Service Force shall not be a person to whom section 11 above applies, and the Secretary of State may by regulations provide—

(*a*) for securing that persons of such descriptions as may be prescribed who but for the regulations would be persons to whom that section applies shall not be such persons ;

(*b*) for relaxing, in such cases as may be prescribed, the liability imposed by subsection (1) of that section on persons to whom that section applies.

(2) A man of the Territorial Army or the Royal Auxiliary Air Force who is called out for permanent service shall, subject to subsections (3) and (4) below, be liable to serve—

(*a*) until Her Majesty no longer requires his services, or

(b) until the expiry of his term of service in that reserve or force,

whichever first occurs, and a member of the special class of the Royal Fleet Reserve who is called out for permanent service by virtue of section 11(1) shall be under a like liability to serve.

(3) The period or aggregate of the periods during which a man is called out for service by virtue of section 11(1) during the term of his current engagement shall not without his consent exceed 12 months.

(4) Where the time at which (apart from this subsection)—

(a) the term of service in the special class of the Royal Fleet Reserve of a man of that class would expire, or

(b) a man of the Territorial Army would be entitled to discharge,

occurs while he is called out for service by virtue of section 11(1), he may be required to continue in service under that subsection for such further period as may be ordered by—

(i) the Defence Council, or

(ii) an officer designated for the purposes of this subsection by the Defence Council,

but the period so ordered (together with the period or aggregate of the periods of the man's service under section 11(1) apart from this subsection during the term of his current engagement) shall not exceed 12 months.

Call out under special agreement

14.—(1) Where any person who is a member of—

(a) any reserve of army officers,

(b) the Army Reserve, or

(c) the Territorial Army,

has entered into a written agreement to that effect, the Secretary of State may, at any time during the period specified in the agreement, by written notice call out that person for army service.

(2) Schedule 1 to this Act (additional provisions in relation to call out under special agreement) has effect for the purposes of this section.

(3) Where any person has been called out by such a notice as is mentioned in subsection (1) above, then at all times during the period beginning with the date and time specified in the notice and ending with the completion of his service by virtue of that notice—

(a) he shall be liable to serve in any place whether in the United Kingdom or elsewhere ; and

Call out under special agreement.

(b) the Army Act 1955 shall (subject to paragraph 10 of Schedule 1) apply to him as if he were an officer holding a land forces commission, warrant officer, non-commissioned officer or soldier, as the case may be, of the regular forces, and not a member of the Territorial Army, the Army Reserve or a reserve of officers, as the case may be.

(4) The number of persons who for the time being are—

    (a) liable to be called out by agreements made in pursuance of this section, shall not in aggregate exceed such number as may from time to time be provided by Parliament ;

    (b) called out as mentioned in paragraph (a), shall not be reckoned in the numbers for the time being authorised by Parliament for the regular forces.

(5) The Secretary of State shall from time to time report to Parliament with respect to the exercise of his powers to call out persons under this section, and any such report may be made, as the Secretary of State thinks fit, either with respect to any use made, or with respect to any use proposed to be made, of those powers.

Regular army
agreements
under s. 14.

15. An officer or soldier of the regular army may enter into such an agreement as is mentioned in section 14 above, and where he does so—

    (a) the agreement shall not come into force until he becomes a member of a reserve of army officers or the Army Reserve or until such later date, if any, during his membership of that reserve as is provided by the agreement ; and

    (b) the power conferred by paragraph 1(2) of Schedule 1 to this Act to give notice of revocation of the agreement shall be exercisable both before and after the agreement comes into force ; and

    (c) when the agreement comes into force it shall be deemed to have been made in pursuance of section 14.

Other provisions as to call out for service

Permanent
service call
out of
naval and
marine
reserves.

16.—(1) Every officer and man serving in—

    (a) the Royal Naval Reserve and the Royal Fleet Reserve, except a man of the special class of the Royal Fleet Reserve to whom section 11 above applies,

    (b) the Royal Marines Reserve,

is liable, during the whole of that service, to be called out for permanent service in the event of actual or apprehended attack on the United Kingdom.

The reference in this subsection to the United Kingdom shall
be construed as if that expression included the Channel Islands
and the Isle of Man.

(2) The provisions of subsection (1) above are in addition to,
and not in substitution for, the provisions of any other enactment under which officers or men of the reserves mentioned in
that subsection are liable to be called into permanent service.

17.—(1) Every officer and man of the Royal Naval Reserve, Naval and
the Royal Fleet Reserve and the Royal Marines Reserve called marine
out for permanent service by virtue of section 10 or section 16 reserve
above shall be— service under
ss. 10 and 16.

    (a) liable to that service for a term of 3 years from the time
        of his coming into such service ;

    (b) entitled to be discharged from that service at the expiry
        of that term.

(2) If in any emergency Her Majesty sees fit She may, by
order signified under the hand of the Secretary of State, provide
that at the date of the order the officers and men of the Royal
Naval Reserve and the Royal Fleet Reserve in permanent service
by virtue of section 10 or section 16 shall continue in that service
for a period of 5 years from the date of their respectively coming
into that service, if their services be so long required.

(3) The officers and men mentioned in subsection (2) above
shall at the date of the order—

    (a) be liable to such permanent service accordingly ; and

    (b) not be entitled to claim their discharge during that
        period.

(4) Where any officer or man of the Royal Naval Reserve
and the Royal Fleet Reserve—

    (a) is called into permanent service by virtue of section 10
        or section 16, and

    (b) is detained in that service for a period of less than 5
        years,

he shall, during the period of 5 years from the date of his
joining the reserve be liable from time to time to be again
called into that service, and to serve accordingly for such period
as with his former such service will make up a period of 5 years
in that service.

18.—(1) Any man of the Army Reserve (whether he entered Permanent
the reserve on transfer or re-engagement or on being enlisted or service call
on being deemed to be enlisted) shall during the whole of his out of Army
service in that reserve be liable to be called out for permanent Reserve.
service on home defence service.

PART II

(2) Where a man of the Army Reserve is called out for permanent service—

(a) he may be appointed to any corps ;

1955 c. 18.

(b) subsection (3) of section 3 of the Army Act 1955 shall apply to him as it applies to a soldier of the regular forces.

(3) The number of men for the time being called out under this section shall not be reckoned in the numbers for the time being authorised by Parliament for the regular forces.

Duration of Army Reserve permanent service.

19.—(1) Subject to this section and section 13(3) above, a man of the Army Reserve when called out for permanent service shall be liable to serve until Her Majesty no longer requires his services.

(2) No man called out for permanent service shall be required to serve for a period exceeding in the whole the remainder unexpired of his term of service in the Army Reserve.

(3) Sections 9 and 13 of the Army Act 1955, so far as they relate to discharge, shall apply to men of the Army Reserve called out for permanent service as they apply to soldiers of the regular forces, and nothing in subsection (2) above shall prejudice the operation of sections 9 and 13 as applied by this subsection.

Permanent service call out of Air Force Reserve.

20.—(1) Any man of the Air Force Reserve (whether he entered the reserve on transfer or re-engagement or on being enlisted or on being deemed to be enlisted) shall during the whole of his service in that reserve be liable to be called out for permanent service on home defence service.

(2) The number of men for the time being called out under this section shall not be reckoned in the numbers for the time being authorised by Parliament for the regular air force.

Duration of Air Force Reserve permanent service.

21.—(1) Subject to this section and section 13(3) above, a man of the Air Force Reserve when called out for permanent service shall be liable to serve until Her Majesty no longer requires his services.

(2) No man called out for permanent service shall be required to serve for a period exceeding in the whole the remainder unexpired of his term of service in the Air Force Reserve, subject to section 69 below.

1955 c. 19.

(3) Sections 9 and 13 of the Air Force Act 1955, so far as they relate to discharge, shall apply to men of the Air Force Reserve called out for permanent service as they apply to airmen of the regular air force, and nothing in subsection (2) above and section

69 shall prejudice the operation of sections 9 and 13 as applied by this subsection.

22. Every officer and man of the Territorial Army and of the Royal Auxiliary Air Force is liable to be called out for home defence service notwithstanding that—

    (*a*) the Territorial Army or that part to which he belongs has not been called out for permanent service by virtue of section 10(1) or section 11(1) above, or

    (*b*) the Royal Auxiliary Air Force or that part to which he belongs has not been called out for permanent service by virtue of section 10(1).

23.—(1) The Secretary of State may, at any time when occasion appears to require, call out the whole or so many as he thinks necessary of the men of the Army Reserve or the Air Force Reserve to aid the civil power in the preservation of the public peace.

(2) For the purpose mentioned in subsection (1) above, and on the requisition in writing of any justice of the peace—

    (*a*) any officer commanding Her Majesty's forces in any town or district may call out the men of the Army Reserve who are resident in the town or district, or so many of them as he thinks necessary ; or

    (*b*) any officer commanding the regular air force in any town or district may call out the men of the Air Force Reserve who are resident in the town or district, or so many of them as he thinks necessary.

24. The Ulster Defence Regiment is liable to be called out for permanent service in Northern Ireland in defence of the United Kingdom against actual or apprehended attack.

25.—(1) Any officer authorised in accordance with this section to exercise the powers conferred by this subsection may (subject to that authority) call out the Ulster Defence Regiment or any part of it for emergency service in Northern Ireland if, and for so long as, it appears to that officer to be necessary or expedient for the defence of life or property in Northern Ireland against armed attack or sabotage, whether actual or apprehended.

(2) The Secretary of State may—

    (*a*) grant authority in writing to any designated officer of the regular forces within the meaning of the Army Act 1955 of a rank not lower than major to exercise the powers conferred by subsection (1) above, and

(b) by that authority authorise that officer in turn to authorise any other officer designated by him (being an officer of the regular forces within the meaning of that Act of 1955 of a rank not lower than major) to exercise those powers,

and any authorisation in pursuance of this subsection may be given either in general terms or subject to specified limitations.

Call-out notices under certain enactments

Call-out
notices under
s. 10(1) and
other
enactments.

26.—(1) In any case where—

(a) an order is in force under section 10(1) above authorising the calling out of a reserve force within the meaning of that section, or

(b) persons are liable to be called into service by virtue of any of the enactments mentioned below,

any person who is a member of that force or any person so liable may be called into service by the Secretary of State by notice in writing.

The enactments referred to in paragraph (b) above are—

      (i) section 10(1) ;

      (ii) section 11(1) above ;

      (iii) section 16(1) above ;

      (iv) section 18(1) above ;

      (v) section 20(1) above ;

      (vi) section 22 above ;

      (vii) section 24 above ;

      (viii) section 30 below ;

      (ix) paragraph 15(1) of Schedule 8 to this Act ; and

      (x) sub-paragraphs (1) to (6) of paragraph 16 of that Schedule.

(2) A call-out notice under subsection (1) above shall—

(a) specify the time and place at which the person is to present himself for service, and

(b) specify under which of the enactments mentioned in subsection (1) the person is called into service,

and a call-out notice shall be deemed to be served on the person if it is delivered to him personally or sent by registered post or the recorded delivery service to him at his latest address known to the appropriate service authorities.

(3) A call-out notice under subsection (1) may be revoked or varied by the Secretary of State by a subsequent notice in writing, and subsection (2) above applies to the service of such a notice as it applies to the service of a call-out notice under subsection (1).

(4) Subject to section 28 below, a person shall be deemed to be called into service by virtue of the enactment specified in a call-out notice served on him in pursuance of this section during the period— PART II

   (*a*) beginning with the time so specified, and

   (*b*) ending with—

      (i) the date on which he is released from service in pursuance of section 29 below ; or

      (ii) any earlier date on which his service is terminated by the appropriate service authorities.

27. Where a person who is liable to be called into service by a call-out notice under section 26(1) above— Call-out notices deemed on personal attendance.

   (*a*) attends in person at such place as may be prescribed, and

   (*b*) presents himself for service to such authority as may be prescribed, and

   (*c*) is informed by that authority that by virtue of this section he is accepted for service,

he shall be deemed to have been served with a call-out notice specifying as the time, place and enactment mentioned in section 26(2)—

      (i) the time at which he is informed and the place at which he attends, and

      (ii) such of the enactments mentioned in section 26(1) as is determined in the prescribed manner,

and any call-out notice under section 26(1) previously issued for him shall cease to have effect, without prejudice to any liability arising from his failure to comply with the notice before he attends as described above.

28.—(1) Where a person— Differing service liabilities of those called out.

   (*a*) is in service in pursuance of a notice under section 14(1) above or in pursuance of a call-out notice under section 26(1) above specifying an enactment mentioned in section 26(1), and

   (*b*) if he were not in service he would be liable to be called into service by a call-out notice under section 26(1) or, as the case may be, by such a call-out notice specifying a different enactment so mentioned,

the Secretary of State may direct that, on the date of the direction or a later date specified in the direction, that person shall be deemed to be called into service by a call-out notice under section 26(1) specifying such of those enactments applicable to him as is specified in the direction.

(2) Where a person is deemed in pursuance of subsection (1) above to be called into service by virtue of an enactment specified in a direction under that subsection, his service under any other enactment by virtue of which he was previously serving shall cease.

(3) The power to give a direction under this section includes power—

    (a) to make provision for persons of such descriptions as are specified in the direction or in respect of an individual ; and

    (b) to make different provision for different circumstances.

29.—(1) In any case where—

    (a) the services of a person called into service by a call-out notice under section 26(1) above are no longer required, or

    (b) a person is in service in pursuance of such a call-out notice at the expiry of the period of his liability for service in pursuance of the enactment specified by the notice,

he shall be entitled to be released from whole-time service in the prescribed manner with all convenient speed.

(2) The reference in paragraph (b) of subsection (1) above to a period of liability for service in pursuance of a particular enactment includes a reference to such a period as extended under any other enactment.

Recall of service pensioners and former soldiers

30.—(1) Whenever any emergency arises which in the Secretary of State's opinion renders it advisable to require the services in the Royal Navy of any persons who—

    (a) have served as petty officers or seamen in the navy, and

    (b) are in receipt of pensions in respect of such service,

he may order any of those persons to join the navy, and those so ordered shall serve in the navy during such time as the emergency in the Secretary of State's opinion continues, and while so serving they shall continue to receive their pensions.

(2) The enactments concerning the discharge of seamen serving in the Royal Navy and becoming entitled to be discharged shall be applicable to and for the discharge of any of those serving under subsection (1) above, and becoming entitled to be discharged.

(3) Subsection (1) above applies to persons who—

(*a*) have served as non-commissioned officers and men of the Royal Marines, and

(*b*) are in receipt of pensions in respect of such service,

as it applies to petty officers or seamen of the Royal Navy, but those required to serve under this subsection shall serve as non-commissioned officers and marines in the Royal Marines, and not as petty officers and seamen.

(4) If any person who—

(*a*) has served as a non-commissioned officer or marine of the Royal Marines, and

(*b*) is one to whom subsection (1) above applies by virtue of subsection (3) above, and

(*c*) has been required to serve in the Royal Navy under subsection (1) at the time and place specified in a call-out notice—

(i) which is served on him in pursuance of section 26(1) above, and

(ii) which specifies subsection (1) as the enactment by virtue of which he is called into service,

does not appear for the purpose of entering into permanent service (or join any of Her Majesty's ships or vessels which he may be required to join for that purpose) he shall be liable to be apprehended and punished in the same manner as any person belonging to the Royal Navy and deserting or improperly absenting himself from duty.

31.—(1) An army or air force pensioner to whom this section applies shall be liable under this section to be recalled for service in such circumstances and for such period as are specified in this section and in sections 32 and 33 below.   Liability of army and air force pensioners to recall.

(2) This section applies to army and air force pensioners whose service pensions have been assessed or re-assessed in accordance with pension provisions made on or after 16th December 1948, other than—

(*a*) pensioners whose service pensions were originally granted before 3rd September 1939 ;

(*b*) pensioners being those of any description mentioned in Schedule 2 to this Act.

(3) In subsection (2) above the expression " pension provisions made on or after 16th December 1948 " means—

(*a*) in the case of army pensioners, the provisions of a Royal Warrant issued on or after 16th December 1948, (*b*) in the case of air force pensioners, the provisions of an Order by Her Majesty so issued,

not being provisions as to which the Warrant or Order directs that they shall be disregarded for the purposes of this section.

(4) A person shall cease to be liable under this section to be recalled for service when he attains the age of 60 years.

(5) A person recalled for service under this section shall not suffer—

(*a*) any reduction in pay or other emoluments in respect of his service while recalled by reason of being in receipt of a service pension ; or

(*b*) the withholding or reduction of his service pension by reason of his being in receipt of any such pay or emoluments.

(6) In this section—

" army pensioner " and " air force pensioner " mean persons who have been discharged from service as soldiers and as airmen respectively and are in receipt of service pensions,

" service pension " means a pension granted in respect of service as a soldier of the regular forces or an airman of the regular air force or in respect of that service and other service, but does not include a pension awarded in respect of disablement,

and other expressions used in this section and in sections 32 and 33 below have in relation to army pensioners the same meanings as in the Army Act 1955, and in relation to air force pensioners the same meanings as in the Air Force Act 1955.

1955 c. 18.
1955 c. 19.

(7) For the purposes of those sections, a person shall be deemed to be in receipt of a pension if the pension has been granted to him and has not been wholly forfeited, notwithstanding—

(*a*) that any part of the pension has been commuted for a sum of money in lieu of the pension ; or

(*b*) that the pension or any part of it is for the time being administered or otherwise applied for any purpose or paid to some other person ; or

(*c*) that the pension or any part of it has not been paid for any period.

For the purposes of this subsection the forfeiture of a pension shall be disregarded if the whole or any part of the pension has been restored since the forfeiture was incurred.

32.—(1) An army pensioner liable under section 31 above to be recalled for service may be recalled at any time when persons of the Army Reserve are called out for permanent service.

In this subsection the expression " called out for permanent service " means called out for permanent service under section 10 above, or under section 18(1) above.

PART II
Occasion for and period of recall under s. 31.

(2) An air force pensioner liable under section 31 to be recalled for service may be recalled at any time when persons of the Air Force Reserve are called out for permanent service.

In this subsection the expression " called out for permanent service " means called out for permanent service under section 10, or under section 20(1) above.

(3) A person recalled for service under section 31—

(a) shall be deemed to be enlisted in the regular forces or the regular air force, according as he was an army pensioner or an air force pensioner, for the period mentioned in subsection (4) below, unless

(b) on his recall he requires to be enlisted for that period in accordance with section 2 of the Army Act 1955, or section 2 of the Air Force Act 1955, as the case may require, and upon such enlistment he shall not be deemed to have been enlisted by virtue of paragraph (a) above.

1955 c. 18.
1955 c. 19.

(4) The period referred to in subsection (3) above is one—

(a) beginning with the time as from which a person is recalled for service under section 31, and

(b) ending with such date as Her Majesty may by Order in Council declare to be the end of the emergency which was the occasion of the calling out for permanent service of persons of the reserve in question.

(5) Nothing in the following provisions shall prejudice the operation of the provisions of this section—

(a) the provisions of the Army Act 1955 or the Air Force Act 1955 as to the term for which a person may be enlisted ;

(b) the provisions of the Army and Air Force Act 1961 corresponding to the provisions mentioned in paragraph (a) above ; and

1961 c. 52.

(c) the provisions of section 2 of the Armed Forces Act 1966 and regulations made under that section corresponding to the provisions mentioned in paragraph (a).

1966 c. 45.

33.—(1) The Defence Council may cause to be served on any person liable to be recalled for service under section 31 above a notice stating that he is recalled for service and requiring him to present himself—

> (a) at such place and at such time (not earlier than the third day after the service of the notice), and
>
> (b) to such authority,

as may be specified in the notice, and that person shall be deemed to be so recalled as from that time (in this section referred to as " the time of recall ").

(2) A notice under this section may, before the time of recall, be—

> (a) cancelled by a subsequent notice under this section ; or
>
> (b) varied by altering the place at which or authority to whom the person is by a notice under this section required to present himself at the time of recall.

(3) A notice under this section shall cease to have effect if before the time of recall the person on whom it is served ceases to be liable under section 31 to be recalled for service.

(4) Any notice under this section shall be deemed to be duly served on a person if it is sent to him by post addressed to his last known address.

(5) No steps shall be taken against a person in respect of failure to comply with a notice under this section unless either—

> (a) it is proved that the notice was received by him, or
>
> (b) the notice was sent addressed to his last known address by registered post or the recorded delivery service,

and where in the case of a notice not so sent it appears to the Defence Council that the person to whom the notice relates may not have received the notice the Defence Council may serve on him by registered post or the recorded delivery service a subsequent notice superseding the original notice.

34.—(1) Any former soldier to whom this section applies may be recalled for service by the Secretary of State by notice in writing at any time when men of the Army Reserve are called out for permanent service under section 10 or section 18(1) above.

(2) This section applies to any person who is not a woman and who is for the time being under the age of 45, and—

> (a) who is not—
>
>> (i) a member of the armed forces of the Crown apart from this section ;
>>
>> (ii) liable to be recalled to service under section 31 above ;

(iii) such a person as is mentioned in Schedule 2 to this Act ;

(b) who enlisted in pursuance of regulations made under section 2 of the Armed Forces Act 1966 ;

(c) who has not been discharged in respect of that enlistment under section 14 of the Army Act 1955, or under any regulations made by virtue of section 2 of the Armed Forces Act 1966 conferring a right to discharge by purchase ;

(d) who has not been granted a commission.

(3) A person recalled for service by such a notice as is referred to in subsection (1) shall be deemed to be enlisted in the regular forces within the meaning of the Army Act 1955 for the period—

(a) beginning with the time specified in the notice, and

(b) ending (unless he is previously discharged) with such date as Her Majesty may by Order in Council declare to be the end of the emergency which was the occasion of the calling out of the Army Reserve.

(4) To enable service of any notice under subsection (1) above, every person to whom this section applies shall from time to time furnish such information in such manner and within such period as the Secretary of State may by regulations made by statutory instrument require, and—

(a) any person who without reasonable excuse fails to comply with any such regulations shall be liable on summary conviction to a fine not exceeding £10,

(b) any person who, in giving any information required by any such regulations, knowingly or recklessly makes a statement false in any material particular shall be liable on summary conviction to imprisonment for a term not exceeding 3 months or to a fine not exceeding £50 or to both,

and proceedings against any person for an offence under paragraph (a) or (b) above may be taken at any place at which he is for the time being.

(5) A person who on 27th February 1964 was—

(a) a warrant officer, non-commissioned officer or man of the regular forces within the meaning of the Army Act 1955 (not being a person serving in the Royal Marines), or

(b) a member of the first class of the army reserve in consequence of his transfer to that reserve under the Army Act 1955 or the Army and Air Force Act 1961,

may consent in writing to be subject to this section, and that consent may be revoked at any time by 3 months' written notice but shall not cease to be in force until the expiry of that notice.

(6) While that consent remains in force this section shall have effect in relation to that person as if—

    (a) paragraphs (b) and (c) of subsection (2) above did not apply to him ; and

    (b) he were subject (instead of by virtue of those paragraphs) to this section by his consent under subsection (5) above.

Recall notices under s. 34.

35.—(1) A notice to any person under section 34(1) above shall specify the time and place at which that person is to present himself for service in accordance with the notice, and the notice may be revoked or varied by a subsequent notice under that section.

(2) Any such notice shall be deemed to have been duly served on the person to whom it is directed if—

    (a) it is delivered to him personally, or

    (b) it is sent by registered post or the recorded delivery service addressed to him at his latest address known to the military authorities,

but any such notice shall cease to have effect if before the time so specified he ceases to be a person to whom this section applies.

Recall notices deemed served on personal attendance.

36.—(1) Where a person who is liable to be recalled into service under section 31 or section 34 above—

    (a) attends in person at such place as may be prescribed, and

    (b) presents himself for service to such authority as may be prescribed, and

    (c) is informed by that authority that by virtue of this subsection he is accepted for service,

he shall be deemed to have been served with a notice under section 33 above or section 35 above, as the case may be, specifying the time at which he is informed and the place at which he attends.

(2) Where subsection (1) above takes effect—

    (a) so much of section 33(1) above as—

        (i) provides for a notice under that section to specify the authority to whom a person is to present himself, and

        (ii) requires the time of recall specified by such a notice to be not earlier than the third day after the service of the notice,

    shall not apply to a notice which is deemed to be served on that person under subsection (1) ; and

    (b) any notice previously issued for that person under section 33 or 35, as the case may be, shall cease to have effect, but without prejudice to any liability arising from

his failure to comply with the notice before he attends
as described in subsection (1).

Call out for training

37.—(1) The Defence Council may cause all or any of the
men of the Royal Naval Reserve and the Royal Fleet Reserve to
be trained on shore or on board any ships or vessels, or partly on
shore and partly on board any ships or vessels.   *Training and exercise of Royal Naval Reserve and Royal Fleet Reserve.*

(2) All or any of the men of the Royal Naval Reserve and the
Royal Fleet Reserve may be called out for the purpose of such
training, and may be required to attend at such times and places,
and may be placed under the command of such officers, as the
Defence Council think fit.

(3) No man of the Royal Naval Reserve or the Royal Fleet
Reserve shall under this section be required to attend training
more than 92 days in the whole in any one year.

(4) The Secretary of State may make regulations as to the
manner in which notices may be given of the times and places
at which men of the Royal Naval Reserve and the Royal Fleet
Reserve may be required to attend training.

38. A person to whom this section applies by virtue of section
39 below may, in accordance with regulations made by the
Secretary of State, be called out in any year for training in the
United Kingdom or elsewhere—   *Army Reserve, Air Force Reserve and Territorial Army training.*
> (a) for one period not exceeding 15 days, and
> (b) for such other periods as may be prescribed, none of
> which shall exceed 36 hours without the consent of the
> person in question,

and may while so called out be attached to and trained with any
body of Her Majesty's forces.

39.—(1) The persons to whom section 38 above applies are
(subject to subsection (3) below)—   *Application of s. 38.*
> (a) any member of the Army Reserve or the Air Force
> Reserve who became such a member on or after 1st
> April 1967 otherwise than in consequence of his having
> enlisted in the regular army or the regular air force be-
> fore that day ;
> (b) any member of the Territorial Army who became such a
> member on or after 1st April 1967 by enlistment or re-
> engagement or by becoming an officer ; and
> (c) any other person—
>> (i) who has elected in pursuance of subsection (2)
>> below to be a person to whom section 38 applies, and
>> (ii) who has been notified in the prescribed manner
>> that he has been accepted as such a person.

(2) A member of—

   (a) the Army Reserve,

   (b) the Air Force Reserve, or

   (c) the Territorial Army,

who is not a person to whom section 38 applies may (subject to subsection (3) below) elect irrevocably in the prescribed manner to be such a person.

(3) The Secretary of State may by regulations provide—

   (a) for securing that persons of such descriptions as may be prescribed who but for the regulations would be persons to whom section 38 applies shall not be such persons;

   (b) for relaxing, in such cases as may be prescribed, the liability imposed by section 38 on persons to whom that section applies.

Preliminary training of Royal Auxiliary Air Force.

40.—(1) Every man of the Royal Auxiliary Air Force shall, by way of preliminary training during the first year of his original enlistment—

   (a) if so provided by Order in Council, and

   (b) for such periods not exceeding in the whole the number of days specified by the Order in Council,

be trained at such places within the United Kingdom and at such times as may be prescribed, and for that purpose may be called out once or more often.

(2) Whether or not such an Order in Council has been made he shall attend the number of drills and instructional parades and fulfil the other conditions prescribed for a recruit in the Royal Auxiliary Air Force.

(3) The requirements of this section are in addition to the requirements of this Act relating to annual training.

Annual training of Royal Auxiliary Air Force.

41.—(1) Every man of the Royal Auxiliary Air Force shall by way of annual training be trained for not less than 8 or more than 15 days in every year at such times and at such places within the United Kingdom as may be prescribed, and may for that purpose be called out once or more often in every year.

(2) Every such man shall attend the number of drills and instructional parades and fulfil the other conditions relating to training prescribed for the Royal Auxiliary Air Force.

(3) The requirements of this section may be dispensed with in whole or in part—

   (a) as respects any unit of the Royal Auxiliary Air Force by the prescribed air officer, and

   (b) as respects an individual man of the Royal Auxiliary Air Force, by his commanding officer subject to any general directions of the prescribed air officer.

42. Her Majesty may by Order in Council made in relation to all or any part of the Royal Auxiliary Air Force direct—

(a) that the period of annual training in any year shall be extended to such period not exceeding 30 days as may be specified in the Order ; or

(b) that the period of annual training in any year shall be reduced to such period as to Her Majesty may seem fit ; or

(c) that the annual training in any year shall be dispensed with.

PART II
Variation and cancellation of training periods for Royal Auxiliary Air Force.

43. Nothing in sections 38 to 42 above shall be construed as preventing a man with his own consent, in addition to any other training, being called out for the purpose of duty or instruction in accordance with orders and regulations under the provisions of this Act relating to the Territorial Army and the Royal Auxiliary Air Force.

Voluntary training.

44.—(1) Any member of the Ulster Defence Regiment may, in accordance with regulations under Part VII of this Act, be required to undergo training in Northern Ireland in any year—

(a) for one or more periods which shall not exceed 12 days in the aggregate and of which—

    (i) none shall exceed 8 consecutive days, and

    (ii) except with his consent, not more than 2 shall exceed 36 consecutive hours, and

(b) for such other periods as may be prescribed, none of which shall except with his consent exceed 2 hours,

and may while so undergoing training be attached to and trained with any body of Her Majesty's forces which is for the time being in Northern Ireland.

(2) Regulations under that Part may provide—

(a) for securing that subsection (1) above shall not apply to persons of such descriptions as may be prescribed to whom but for the regulations that subsection would apply ; and

(b) for relaxing, in such cases as may be prescribed, the liability imposed by subsection (1) on members of the force.

Requirement as to training of Ulster Defence Regiment in Northern Ireland.

PART III

NAVAL AND MARINE RESERVES

Officers of reserve to the Royal Navy

45. Her Majesty may, upon such terms and conditions as She thinks fit, accept the offers to serve as officers of reserve to the Royal Navy of—

(a) any persons who have been or are masters, mates, or engineers of ships in the merchant service of the

Offers to serve as officers of reserve.

PART III

United Kingdom, or of other British ships not belonging to Her Majesty ; and

(b) any other persons whom the Secretary of State may recommend.

Enrolment of officers.

46.—(1) The Secretary of State may enrol as officers of reserve to the Royal Navy so many of such persons as are referred to in section 45 above as he thinks fit, under such rules, orders and regulations as he may from time to time make.

(2) The persons so enrolled shall have such rank as respects the officers of the Royal Navy as the Secretary of State shall direct.

General provisions as to the naval and marine reserves

False answers on enlistment.

47. If a person offering himself to be entered for service in any of the naval reserve forces—

(a) knowingly makes a false answer in connection with his entry into such service, and

(b) that answer is to a question put to him in that connection by, or by the direction of, any officer or other person authorised by regulations made by the Defence Council to enter persons for such service,

he shall be guilty of an offence and liable on summary conviction to imprisonment for a term not exceeding 3 months or to a fine not exceeding £20.

Void enlistment in regular forces.

48. Where any officer or other person enlists a man to serve in Her Majesty's regular forces who at the time of such enlisting is entered to serve as a man of the Royal Naval Reserve, Royal Fleet Reserve or Royal Marines Reserve that enlisting shall be null and void.

Enlistment outside British Islands.

49. The powers under this Act to enter men to serve in the Royal Naval Reserve, the Royal Fleet Reserve and the Royal Marines Reserve may, subject to the Secretary of State's regulations, be exercised outside the British Islands, but only in the case of a Commonwealth citizen or a citizen of the Republic of Ireland.

Term of service in Royal Naval Reserve and Royal Fleet Reserve.

50.—(1) Every man joining the Royal Naval Reserve shall be entered for a term of 5 years, and shall continue subject to this Act as a man of that reserve during and for no longer than that term, except as otherwise provided by this Act.

(2) A man entitled to claim his discharge under subsection (1) above shall continue subject to the provisions of this Act as

a man of the Royal Naval Reserve until actually discharged from that reserve by the Defence Council, or by some officer duly appointed by the Defence Council to give such discharges.

(3) The term of service of a man joining the Royal Fleet Reserve shall be regulated—

> (a) in the case of a pensioner entitled to his pension subject to a condition of service in the Royal Fleet Reserve, by the conditions attached to the pension; and
>
> (b) in any other case, by the terms of his enlistment.

51. Every man of the Royal Naval Reserve, the Royal Fleet Reserve and the Royal Marines Reserve called out for permanent service— *Naval and marine reserves called into permanent service.*

> (a) Shall be placed under the command of such officers as the Defence Council may direct;
>
> (b) shall be liable to serve on shore or on board any ship or vessel, or partly on shore and partly on board any ship or vessel, as the Defence Council may direct.

52. Men who have served in the Royal Marines and who have enlisted in the Royal Fleet Reserve shall— *Marines serving in Royal Fleet Reserve.*

> (a) when called out for permanent service, and
>
> (b) when being trained or exercised,

be liable to serve, subject to the same conditions, as other non-commissioned officers and men of the marines and not as petty officers and seamen.

53.—(1) All provisions for the time being in force in relation to the billeting of the Royal Marines shall be applicable to the men of the Royal Naval Reserve, the Royal Fleet Reserve and the Royal Marines Reserve during such time as they attend training, or be in permanent service. *Billeting.*

(2) All powers and authorities in relation to the billeting of the Royal Marines which may be exercised by any colonel, commandant, or commanding officer of any division of Royal Marines, may, for the purpose of billeting the men of the Royal Naval Reserve, the Royal Fleet Reserve or the Royal Marines Reserve, be exercised by any officer in the Royal Navy holding the rank of commander, or any higher rank authorised in this behalf by the regulations made under section 56 below.

54.—(1) The Defence Council may in their discretion at any time discharge any man of the Royal Naval Reserve, the Royal Fleet Reserve and the Royal Marines Reserve. *Discharge.*

PART III   (2) The enactments concerning the discharge of ratings (which in this subsection means a member of the Royal Navy of or below the rank of warrant officer) becoming entitled to be discharged shall be applicable to and for the discharge of men of the Royal Naval Reserve, the Royal Fleet Reserve and the Royal Marines Reserve where those men are in permanent service.

Admission to Greenwich Hospital.

55.—(1) Every man of the Royal Naval Reserve, the Royal Fleet Reserve and the Royal Marines Reserve, under such regulations as may be made by the Secretary of State, shall be—

(a) eligible for admission to the Royal Hospital at Greenwich ; and

(b) thereupon entitled to the same privileges and advantages as those who are or have been in Her Majesty's navy.

(2) The Greenwich Hospital Acts 1865 to 1967 have effect as if references in those Acts to any naval reserve force included references to the Royal Marines Reserve.

Regulations for naval and marine reserves.

56. The Secretary of State may—

(a) in relation to the Royal Marines Reserve, make regulations for the purpose of carrying section 3 above into effect, and

(b) in relation to the Royal Naval Reserve and the Royal Fleet Reserve, and (without prejudice to the power conferred by paragraph (a) above) the Royal Marines Reserve, make regulations—

(i) as to the manner or form in which men of those reserves shall be entered to serve, and generally as to the entry and re-entry of such persons ;

(ii) as to the arms, clothing and accoutrements with which such men are to be provided ;

(iii) for forming such men into divisions or classes, or other bodies, and assigning numbers to them ;

(iv) for the purpose of calling out such men for permanent service under this Act ;

(v) for securing and enforcing the attendance, good conduct and discipline of and among such men ;

(vi) for imposing fines or forfeitures of pay, allowances or pensions for misconduct and breach of discipline or of any of the regulations made under this section and section 37(4) above ; and

(vii) generally as to all other matters and proceedings.

Special class of Royal Fleet Reserve

57.—(1) The special class of the Royal Fleet Reserve shall consist of—

(a) men who, on engaging or re-engaging in the Royal Fleet Reserve or during a term of engagement or re-engagement in that reserve agree in writing—

(i) to be entered in or transferred to that class, and

(ii) to undertake the liability for service in that class specified in this Act ; or

(b) men who, having before 16th December 1949 been entered for non-continuous service in the naval service of Her Majesty or enlisted to serve in the royal marine forces, on transfer to the Royal Fleet Reserve or during their service in that reserve pursuant to such transfer agree in writing—

(i) to be entered in or transferred to that class, and

(ii) to undertake the liability for service in that class specified in this Act ; or

(c) men entered in that class in accordance with the following provisions of this section.

(2) Any man who—

(a) having been entered for non-continuous service in the naval service of Her Majesty on or after 16th December 1949, or

(b) having been enlisted to serve in the royal marine forces on or after that date,

is transferred to the Royal Fleet Reserve shall, if on his transfer he was designated by the Defence Council or an officer designated by the Defence Council as a man to whom this subsection applies, be entered in that class of the reserve and shall be liable to serve in that class as specified by this Act.

(3) The following provisions shall have effect as to the duration of service in the special class of the Royal Fleet Reserve—

(a) a man entered in that class or transferred to it in pursuance of an agreement under paragraph (a) of subsection (1) above shall be liable to serve in that class until the end of his term of engagement or re-engagement referred to in that paragraph ;

(b) a man entered in or transferred to the special class in pursuance of an agreement under paragraph (b) of subsection (1) shall be liable to serve in the special class until the end of his term of service in the Royal

Fleet Reserve in pursuance of his transfer to that reserve referred to in that paragraph (*b*) ; and

(*c*) a man entered in the special class by virtue of the provisions of subsection (2) above shall be liable to serve in that class until the expiry of the first 12 months of his service in the Royal Fleet Reserve and shall then be transferred from the special class to the general body of the reserve.

(4) If a man to whom paragraph (*c*) of subsection (3) above applies agrees in writing to continue to serve in the special class during the residue of the term for which he is transferred to the Royal Fleet Reserve, he shall be liable to serve in that class in accordance with the agreement.

(5) An agreement made for the purposes of subsection (1) or subsection (4) above may be revoked by 3 months' written notice.

Transfers to Royal Fleet Reserve.

58. References in section 57 above to transfer to the Royal Fleet Reserve shall be construed—

(*a*) in relation to a man entered for non-continuous service in the naval service of Her Majesty, as references to being entered in the Royal Fleet Reserve in pursuance of a liability incurred under the terms of his engagement, in accordance with regulations made by the Defence Council under section 2 of the

1966 c. 45.

Armed Forces Act 1966 to serve in the Royal Fleet Reserve after the completion of his term of service in the navy ; and

(*b*) in relation to a man enlisted to serve in the royal marine forces, as references to being entered in the Royal Fleet Reserve in pursuance of a liability incurred under the terms of his engagement to serve in the Royal Fleet Reserve after the completion of his term of service in the Royal Marines.

Pay, pensions and other payments in respect of naval and marine reserves

Rates of pay and allowances.

59.—(1) Her Majesty may by Order in Council fix the rates of pay, bounty and allowances payable to the persons described in subsection (2) below, and in relation to Orders in Council under this section—

1865 c. 73.

(*a*) section 12 of the Naval and Marine Pay and Pensions Act 1865 (which provides for the publication and laying before Parliament of Orders in Council under that Act) shall apply ; and

1946 c. 36.

(*b*) the Statutory Instruments Act 1946 shall not apply.

(2) The persons referred to in subsection (1) above are—   PART III

  (*a*) Officers of reserve to the Royal Navy ;

  (*b*) men of the Royal Naval Reserve including the Royal Fleet Reserve ;

  (*c*) Officers and men of the Royal Marines Reserve ;

  (*d*) persons in receipt of pensions in respect of service as men in the Royal Navy or the Royal Marines, being persons called out for permanent service or undergoing training.

(3) Sections 3 and 5 of the Naval and Marine Pay and Pensions Act 1865 (which respectively provide for regulating the payment of naval and marine pay, pensions, bounty and other allowances, and prohibit their assignment) apply in relation to pay, bounty and allowances payable to any person described in subsection (2) above as they apply in relation to pay, bounty and allowances payable in respect of services in Her Majesty's naval or marine force to a person being an officer or subordinate officer, seaman or marine.   1865 c. 73.

(4) The Naval Forces (Enforcement of Maintenance Liabilities) Act 1947 has effect as if any reference in that Act to an officer, seaman or marine included a reference to any person so described.   1947 c. 24.

60.—(1) Where any officer of reserve to the Royal Navy sustains any disability of mind or body which is attributable to the conditions of naval service he may be granted an allowance or pension in respect of that disability at such rate and subject to such conditions as the Secretary of State with the consent of Her Majesty in Council may appoint.   Allowances and pensions for officers of reserve.

(2) Where any such officer is killed or dies as the result of any wound, accident, injury or disease attributable to the conditions of naval service, his widow, children or other dependent relatives may be granted such pension, allowances or gratuity as the Secretary of State with the like consent may appoint.

61.—(1) The Secretary of State, with the consent of the Minister for the Civil Service, may grant pensions to men of the Royal Naval Reserve and the Royal Fleet Reserve.   Pensions for persons of Royal Naval Reserve and Royal Fleet Reserve.

(2) The Secretary of State may, in relation to any such pension, make regulations as to—

  (*a*) the amount ;

  (*b*) the time or respective times and the manner of payment ; and

  (*c*) the ages at which it shall be payable.

PART III   (3) Any pension conferred under this section shall be paid to the pensioner himself only, and not to his agent, attorney or assignee.

PART IV

ARMY RESERVE AND AIR FORCE RESERVE

Army Reserve

Government, discipline and pay of Army Reserve.
62.—(1) Orders or regulations under this Act may provide with respect to the government, discipline and pay of the Army Reserve, and with respect to other matters and things relating to the Army Reserve.

(2) No such order or regulation shall render a man who entered the Army Reserve before the date of the order or regulation liable without his consent to be appointed, transferred or attached to any military body to which he could not, without his consent, have been appointed, transferred or attached if the order or regulation had not been made.

Exercise of powers vested in military office holder.
63.—(1) Any power or jurisdiction given to, and any act or thing to be done by, to, or before, any person holding any military office may, in relation to the Army Reserve, be exercised by or done by, to, or before any other person for the time being authorised in that behalf according to the custom of the service.

(2) Where by this Act, or by any order or regulation under this Act, any order is authorised to be made by any military authority, the order may be signified by an order, instruction or letter under the hand of any officer authorised to issue orders on behalf of that military authority, and an order, instruction or letter purporting to be signed by any officer who appears from it to be so authorised shall be evidence of his being so authorised.

Payment and management of Army Reserve pensions.
64. Where (either before or after the passing of this Act) a man of the Army Reserve—

(a) has been called out for permanent service and continued as a man of the Army Reserve after the termination of that service, and

(b) has become entitled to pension under any order or regulation under this Act,

all powers exercisable for the award and payment of the pension and otherwise in relation to the pension shall be exercisable by the like authority as if he were a man discharged from the army on reduction.

65.—(1) A man of the Army Reserve may, with the consent of the prescribed authority, enlist in the Territorial Army and Transfer to shall on so enlisting cease to be a man of the Army Reserve. Territorial Army.

(2) If a man who has enlisted into the Territorial Army in pursuance of subsection (1) above—

(*a*) ceases to be a member of that reserve before the date on which his term of service in the Army Reserve would have expired if he had not so enlisted, then,

(*b*) he shall, unless the prescribed authority otherwise directs (and that power of direction includes power to make different provision for different circumstances), again be a man of the Army Reserve by virtue of this sub-section for the residue of that term, without prejudice to the operation of any enactment under which that term may be extended.

Air Force Reserve

66. Orders or regulations under this Act may provide with Government, respect to the government, discipline and pay of the Air Force discipline and Reserve, and with respect to other matters and things relating pay of Air Force to the Air Force Reserve. Reserve.

67.—(1) Any power or jurisdiction given to, and any act or Exercise of thing to be done by, to, or before, any person holding any air powers vested force office may, in relation to the Air Force Reserve, be exer- in air force cised by or done by, to, or before any other person for the time office holder. being authorised in that behalf according to the custom of the service.

(2) Where by this Act, or by any order or regulation under this Act, any order is authorised to be made by any air force authority, the order may be signified by an order, instruction or letter under the hand of any officer authorised to issue orders on behalf of that air force authority, and an order, instruction or letter purporting to be signed by any officer who appears from it to be so authorised shall be evidence of his being so authorised.

68.—(1) A man enlisted into the Air Force Reserve may, Service in whether or not he has previously served in the regular air force, Air Force be enlisted in the Air Force Reserve for service as a special Reserve as special reservist. reservist.

(2) A special reservist may be re-engaged, and when re-engaged shall continue subject to the terms of service applicable to special reservists.

(3) A man may be enlisted in the Air Force Reserve for service as a special reservist with a liability to serve only within the limits of the United Kingdom, the Channel Islands and the Isle of Man.

(4) Orders and regulations under this Act may provide—

> (a) for the formation of special reservists into squadrons or other air force units, and for the formation of such squadrons or other air force units into wings, groups or other formations, either alone or jointly with any other part of Her Majesty's air force ; and

> (b) for appointing, transferring or attaching special reservists to such units or formations ; and

> (c) for posting, attaching or otherwise dealing with special reservists within such units or formations.

(5) A special reservist who enlists into the regular air force shall upon such enlistment be deemed to be discharged from the Air Force Reserve.

Special reservist called out for permanent service.

69.—(1) The Secretary of State may, by regulations under this Act, authorise any special reservist having the qualifications prescribed by those regulations to agree in writing that—

> (a) if the time at which he would otherwise be entitled to be discharged from the Air Force Reserve occurs when he is called out for permanent service, then

> (b) he will continue to serve in the Air Force Reserve until the expiry of such period, whether definite or indefinite, as may be specified in the agreement.

(2) If any man who enters into such an agreement is called out for permanent service, he shall be liable to be detained in service for the period specified in his agreement in the same manner in all respects as if his term of service were still unexpired.

Special reservist called out for special courses, etc.

70.—(1) A special reservist may, in addition to being called out for annual training, be called out for a special course or special courses of training—

> (a) at such place or places in the United Kingdom or the Isle of Man,

> (b) at such time or times, and

> (c) for such period or periods, not exceeding in the whole 6 months,

as may be prescribed, in like manner and subject to the like conditions as if he were called out for annual training.

(2) Where one of the conditions on which a special reservist
was enlisted or re-engaged is that he shall not be called out for
training, whether special or annual, for a longer period than the
period specified in his attestation paper, he shall not be liable
under this section to be called out for any longer period.

Enlistment in Army Reserve and Air Force Reserve

71.—(1) Every man who becomes a man of the Army Reserve   Procedure
or of the Air Force Reserve by being enlisted or re-engaged   and term of
in pursuance of this Act shall be enlisted or re-engaged, as the   service on
case may be, in such manner, and for a term of such length and   enlistment
to begin on such date, as may be prescribed.   or re-
engagement.

(2) Where a man enlists in the Army Reserve or the Air
Force Reserve—

   (a) he shall be attested in the same manner as a recruit in
       the regular forces or the regular air force, as the case
       may be, subject to the provisions of this Part of this
       Act, and save as is otherwise prescribed ; and

   (b) the provisions of Schedule 3 to this Act shall apply in
       relation to enlistment in the Army Reserve or the Air
       Force Reserve, as the case may be.

(3) A man enlisting in the Army Reserve or the Air Force
Reserve may be attested by a regular officer, and the provisions
of Schedule 3 shall in their application to the Army Reserve or
to the Air Force Reserve, as the case may be, be construed as if
the expression " recruiting officer " included any regular officer.

72.—(1) Men may be enlisted into the Army Reserve or   Enlistment
the Air Force Reserve in any part of Her Majesty's dominions   and residence
outside the United Kingdom and in any British protectorate—   outside
United
   (a) not being territories specified in Schedule 4 to this Act,   Kingdom.
       and

   (b) subject to such conditions as may be prescribed by
       regulations under this Act,

and the power conferred by this subsection to enlist men into
the Army Reserve or the Air Force Reserve includes power to
enlist or re-engage British subjects and British protected persons
into either of those reserves in any country or territory outside
the United Kingdom.

(2) A man of the Army Reserve or the Air Force Reserve
may reside outside the United Kingdom—

   (a) if so authorised by or under the directions of the
       Secretary of State, and

   (b) subject to such conditions as may be prescribed under
       subsection (1) above.

F 3

(3) This Part of this Act applies—

(*a*) to any enlistment under subsection (1) above, and

(*b*) to a man of the Army Reserve or the Air Force Reserve during such time as he resides outside the United Kingdom in pursuance of an authorisation of the Secretary of State under subsection (2) above,

subject to such adaptations as may be prescribed.

(4) Her Majesty may by Order in Council provide for the inclusion among the territories specified in Schedule 4 any part of Her dominions outside the United Kingdom, the Channel Islands and the Isle of Man, being a part of Her dominions to which responsible government has been granted since 20th July 1906 and not being a Dominion other than Sri Lanka.

(5) The provisions of this section corresponding to enactments repealed and re-enacted by this Act have in relation to Her Majesty's dominions and any British protectorate the same effect as those enactments had immediately before their repeal and re-enactment.

Offences

Failure to attend for permanent service, training etc.

73.—(1) Any man of the Army Reserve or of the Air Force Reserve who—

(*a*) being called out for permanent service or in aid of the civil power,

(*b*) fails—

(i) without leave lawfully granted, or

(ii) without such reasonable excuse (including sickness) as may be allowed in the prescribed manner,

to appear at any time and place at which he is required on being so called out to attend,

shall be guilty, according to the circumstances, of desertion or absence without leave, and on conviction by court-martial shall be punishable as provided by subsection (2) below.

(2) On conviction under subsection (1) above a man—

(*a*) of the Army Reserve shall be punishable as for an offence under section 37 (desertion) or, as the case may be, section 38 (absence without leave) of the Army Act 1955,

(*b*) of the Air Force Reserve shall be punishable as for an offence under section 37 (desertion) or, as the case may be, section 38 (absence without leave) of the Air Force Act 1955,

1955 c. 18.

1955 c. 19.

but without prejudice to his liability apart from this subsection and subsection (1) in respect of such an offence.

(3) Any man of the Army Reserve or of the Air Force Reserve who, being called out for training, fails without such

leave or excuse as is referred to in subsection (1) to appear at any time and place at which he is required on being so called out to attend, shall be guilty of absence without leave, and on conviction by court-martial that person—

  (a) being a man of the Army Reserve, shall be punishable as for an offence under section 38 of the Army Act 1955; 1955 c. 18.

  (b) being a man of the Air Force Reserve, shall be punishable as for an offence under section 38 of the Air Force 1955 c. 19. Act 1955.

(4) Any man—

  (a) being a man of the Army Reserve who commits an offence under section 37 or section 38 of the Army Act 1955 may be tried, convicted and punished under that Act whether or not otherwise subject to military law;

  (b) being a man of the Air Force Reserve who commits an offence under section 37 or section 38 of the Air Force Act 1955 may be tried, convicted and punished under that Act whether or not otherwise subject to air-force law.

(5) Without prejudice to subsections (1) to (4) above, any man—

  (a) of the Army Reserve who commits an offence contrary to subsection (1) or subsection (3) above, or section 37 or section 38 of the Army Act 1955,

  (b) of the Air Force Reserve who commits an offence contrary to subsection (1) or subsection (3) above, or section 37 or section 38 of the Air Force Act 1955,

shall be liable on summary conviction to a fine of not less than £2 and not more than £50, and in default of payment of the fine to imprisonment for any term not less than 7 days and not more than the maximum term allowed by law for non-payment of the fine, and may in any case be taken into military custody or into air-force custody, as the case may be.

(6) The provisions of Schedule 5 to this Act, in relation to the Army Reserve or the Air Force Reserve, as the case may be, shall apply to a deserter or absentee without leave.

(7) The delivery under those provisions of a man—

  (a) of the Army Reserve into military custody, or

  (b) of the Air Force Reserve into air-force custody,

or the committal of any such man for the purpose of being so delivered, shall not prevent his subsequently being tried as provided by subsection (5) above.

PART IV
Inducing a
person to
desert or
absent
himself.

74.—(1) Any person who, in the United Kingdom or else-where, by any means whatsoever—

    (a) procures or persuades any man of the Army Reserve or of the Air Force Reserve to commit an offence of desertion or attempts to procure or persuade any man of those reserves to commit such an offence, or

    (b) knowing that any man of those reserves is about to commit such an offence aids or assists him in so doing, or

    (c) knowing any man of those reserves to be a deserter, procures or persuades or assists him to remain a deserter, or assists in his rescue from custody,

shall be liable on summary conviction to a fine not exceeding £50 or to imprisonment for a term not exceeding 6 months.

(2) Subsection (1) above shall apply to absence without leave and absentees without leave as it applies to desertion and deserters, but with the substitution for the reference to such fine or imprisonment as is mentioned in that subsection of a reference to a fine not exceeding £50.

False
pretence of
desertion or
absence
without leave.

75. Any person who falsely represents himself to be a deserter or absentee without leave from the Army Reserve or the Air Force Reserve shall be liable on summary conviction to imprisonment for a term not exceeding 3 months.

Offences
against
orders and
regulations.

76.—(1) Any man of the Army Reserve or of the Air Force Reserve is guilty of an offence under this section if he—

    (a) fails without reasonable excuse on two consecutive occasions to comply with the orders or regulations made under this Act respecting the payment of the Army Reserve or the Air Force Reserve, as the case may be ; or

    (b) when required by or in pursuance of the orders or regulations made under this Act or by a call-out notice served on him in pursuance of this Act to attend at any place, fails without reasonable excuse to attend in accordance with the requirement ; or

    (c) uses threatening or insulting language or behaves in an insubordinate manner to any officer or warrant officer or non-commissioned officer who in pursuance of the orders or regulations made under this Act is acting in the execution of his office, and who would be the superior officer of the offender if he were subject to military law or air-force law, as the case may be ; or

    (d) by any fraudulent means obtains or is an accessory to the obtaining of any pay or other sum contrary to the orders or regulations made under this Act ; or (*e*) fails without reasonable excuse to comply with the orders and regulations made under this Act.

(2) Any man of the Army Reserve or the Air Force Reserve who commits an offence under this section, whether otherwise subject to military law or air-force law, as the case may be, or not, shall be liable—

(*a*) on conviction by court-martial to suffer imprisonment, or such less punishment as is mentioned in the Army Act 1955 or the Air Force Act 1955, as the case may be, or 1955 c. 18.
1955 c. 19.

(*b*) on summary conviction to a fine of not less than £2 and not more than £50, and in default of payment of the fine to imprisonment for any term not less than 7 days and not more than the maximum term allowed by law for non-payment of the fine,

and may in any case be taken into military custody or air-force custody, as the case may be.

(3) A certificate—

(*a*) purporting to be signed by an officer who is mentioned in it as an officer appointed to pay a man of the Army Reserve or the Air Force Reserve, and

(*b*) stating that the man has failed on two consecutive occasions to comply with the orders or regulations made under this Act respecting the payment of the Army Reserve or the Air Force Reserve, as the case may be,

shall without proof of the signature or appointment of the officer be evidence of the failure.

Where a person other than an officer is appointed to pay men of the Army Reserve or the Air Force Reserve, as the case may be, this subsection shall apply to certificates purporting to be signed by him as it applies to certificates purporting to be signed by an officer in the like behalf.

(4) Where a man of the Army Reserve or the Air Force Reserve is required—

(*a*) by or in pursuance of the orders or regulations made under this Act, or

(*b*) by a call-out notice served on him in pursuance of this Act,

to attend at any place, a certificate purporting to be signed by any officer or person who is mentioned in it as being appointed to be present at that place for the purpose of inspecting men of the Army Reserve or the Air Force Reserve, as the case may be, or for any other purpose connected with the Army Reserve or the Air Force Reserve, and stating that the man failed to attend in accordance with that requirement shall without proof of the signature or appointment of the officer or person be evidence of the failure.

(5) Where a man of the Army Reserve or of the Air Force Reserve, as the case may be, commits in the presence of an officer of that reserve an offence under this section, that officer may, if he thinks fit, order the offender, in lieu of being taken into military custody or air-force custody, as the case may be, to be taken into custody by any constable and to be brought before a magistrates' court for the purpose of being dealt with by that court.

Trial of
offences.

1955 c. 18.
1955 c. 19.

77.—(1) Any offence which under this Part of this Act is punishable on conviction by court-martial shall for all purposes of and incidental to the arrest, trial and punishment of the offender, including the summary disposal of the case by his commanding officer, be deemed to be an offence under the Army Act 1955 or the Air Force Act 1955, as the case may be.

References in those Acts to forfeitures and stoppages shall be construed in relation to any such offence as references to such forfeitures and stoppages as may be prescribed.

(2) For all purposes in relation to the arrest, trial and punishment of a person for any offence punishable under this Part, including the summary disposal of the case by the commanding officer, this Part shall extend to the Channel Islands.

Jurisdiction
of courts.

78.—(1) In the United Kingdom or any colony, a civil court of any description having jurisdiction in the place where an offender is for the time being shall have jurisdiction to try him for any offence under this Part of this Act which is triable by a court of that description.

(2) Subsection (1) above applies notwithstanding that the offence was committed outside the jurisdiction of the court, except that where the offence was committed in any part of the United Kingdom it shall not be triable outside that part of the United Kingdom.

(3) Notwithstanding anything contained in any other Act—

    (a) the minimum fixed by this Part for the amount of any fine or the term of any imprisonment shall be duly observed by a magistrates' court and shall not be reduced by way of mitigation or otherwise, but

    (b) where that minimum exceeds the maximum which such a court has power to inflict (whether by reason of its constitution or by reason of the place where it is sitting) that maximum shall be deemed in proceedings

before that court to be substituted for the minimum   PART IV
fixed by this Part.

79. The following provisions shall have effect as respects   Offences
the trial and punishment of men charged with offences which   triable by
in pursuance of this Part of this Act are cognisable both by a   court-martial
court-martial and by a magistrates' court—   or magistrates' court.

   (a) a man so charged shall not be liable to be tried in both of the following ways, that is to say, on the one hand by court-martial or by the case being disposed of summarily by his commanding officer and on the other hand by a magistrates' court, but shall be proceeded against in one or other of those ways according as may be prescribed ;

   (b) proceedings against a man so charged, before either a court-martial, or his commanding officer or a magistrates' court may be instituted whether or not the term of the man's service in the Army Reserve or the Air Force Reserve, as the case may be, has expired ;

   (c) any such proceedings may, notwithstanding anything in any other Act, be instituted within 2 months after whichever of the following times is the later—

      (i) the time at which the offence becomes known to an officer who by orders or regulations under this Act has power to direct the way in which the offender is to be tried ; or

      (ii) the time at which the offender is apprehended, whether by a civil or a military or an air force authority, as the case may be ;

   (d) nothing in any other Act which provides for a period of limitation respecting the time for hearing and determining offences shall apply in the case of any proceedings so instituted.

80.—(1) Where a man of the Army Reserve is subject to   Record of
military law, or a man of the Air Force Reserve is subject   illegal
to air-force law, as the case may be, and is unlawfully absent   absence.
from his duty—

   (a) a board of inquiry under section 135 of the Army Act   1955 c. 18.
1955, or under section 135 of the Air Force Act 1955,   1955 c. 19.
as the case may be, may be assembled after the expiry of 21 days from the date of the man's absence, notwithstanding that the period during which the man was subject to military law or air-force law is less than 21 days, or has expired before the expiry of 21 days ; and

(b) the record mentioned in section 136 of the Army Act 1955, or in section 136 of the Air Force Act 1955, as the case may be, may be entered in the manner there provided, or in such regimental or service books and by such officer as may be prescribed.

(2) Where a man of the Army Reserve or the Air Force Reserve, as the case may be—

(a) fails to appear at the time and place at which he is required upon being called out for training or on permanent service to attend, and

(b) his absence continues for not less than 14 days,

an entry of the man's absence shall be made by the prescribed officer in the prescribed manner and in the prescribed regimental or service books and the entry shall be conclusive evidence of the fact of the man's absence.

Evidence generally under Part IV.

81.—(1) Paragraph 1 of Schedule 6 to this Act has effect in relation to all proceedings under this Part of this Act.

(2) Paragraph 2 of Schedule 6 shall have effect in the case of a man of the Army Reserve or the Air Force Reserve, as the case may be, who is tried by a civil court, whether or not he is at the time of the trial subject to military law or air-force law.

(3) Where by virtue of this Part a document is admissible in evidence or is evidence of any matter stated in it in proceedings before a civil court in England, it shall be sufficient evidence of the matter so stated in such proceedings in Scotland.

Miscellaneous

Transfer outside United Kingdom.

82.—(1) Where in pursuance of—

(a) the proviso to subsection (2) of section 12 of the Army Act 1955, a soldier of the regular forces, or

(b) the proviso to subsection (2) of section 12 of the Air Force Act 1955, an airman of the regular air force,

is transferred to the reserve outside the United Kingdom he shall serve in that reserve subject to such conditions as to residence, as to liability to be called out for training or for permanent service or in aid of the civil power, or as to any other matters, as may be prescribed by regulations under this Act.

(2) The provisions of this Act relating to the Army Reserve or to the Air Force Reserve shall apply to a man transferred in pursuance of this section subject to such adaptations as may be so prescribed.

83.—(1) In the application to a man to whom this subsection applies of—

    (*a*) section 9 of the Army Act 1955, and

    (*b*) section 9 of the Air Force Act 1955,

Postponement
of discharge
or transfer
to reserve.
1955 c. 18.
1955 c. 19.

(which among other things provide for postponement of discharge or transfer to the reserve when men of the reserve
are called out for permanent service), the references to men of
the reserve being called out for permanent service shall (notwithstanding anything in section 225(2) of the Army Act 1955
or section 223(2) of the Air Force Act 1955) include references
to such men being called out under section 11 above or paragraph 16(1) to (6) of Schedule 8 to this Act.

(2) Subsection (1) above applies to a man of the regular
army, the Army Reserve, the regular air force or the Air Force
Reserve who—

    (*a*) is such a man in consequence of his having enlisted
        or re-engaged in one of those forces on or after 1st April
        1967 ; or

    (*b*) has elected irrevocably in the prescribed manner that
        subsection (1) shall apply to him.

(3) In section 9 of the Army Act 1955, in its application to a
man who enters into an agreement on or after 1st January 1967
in pursuance of section 14(1) above and is called into service
in pursuance of the agreement the references to men of the
reserve being called out for permanent service shall (notwithstanding anything in section 225(2) of that Act of 1955) include
references to such men being called out under section 11 or paragraph 16 (1) to (3) of Schedule 8.

84. For the purposes of—

    (*a*) section 184 of the Army Act 1955,

    (*b*) section 184 of the Air Force Act 1955, and

    (*c*) all other enactments relating to the duties, tolls and
        ferries which are mentioned in those sections,

officers and men of the Army Reserve or the Air Force Reserve,
when going to or returning from any place at which they are
required to attend, and for non-attendance at which they are
liable to be punished, shall be deemed to be officers and soldiers
of the regular military forces on duty, or officers and airmen
of the regular air force on duty, as the case may be.

PART IV
Service of
notices for
Army
Reserve and
Air Force
Reserve.
85. The following provisions have effect with respect to notices required in pursuance of orders or regulations made under this Act to be given to men of the Army Reserve or the Air Force Reserve—

(a) a notice may be served on any such man either by being sent by post to his last registered place of abode or by being served in the prescribed manner;

(b) evidence of the delivery at the last registered place of abode of a man of the Army Reserve or of the Air Force Reserve, as the case may be, of a notice, or of a letter addressed to the man containing a notice, shall be evidence that the notice was brought to his knowledge;

(c) the publication of a notice in the prescribed manner in the parish in which the last registered place of abode of a man of the Army Reserve, or of the Air Force Reserve, as the case may be, is situate shall be sufficient notice to him, notwithstanding that a copy of the notice is not served on him.

Orders and
regulations
for Army
Reserve and
Air Force
Reserve.
86.—(1) Where by this Part of this Act or paragraph 17 of Schedule 8 to this Act, power is conferred to provide for any matter relating to the Army Reserve or the Air Force Reserve by orders or regulations under this Act—

(a) Her Majesty may, by order signified under the hand of the Secretary of State, make orders, and

(b) subject to the provisions of any such order, the Secretary of State may make general or special regulations,

with respect to the matter in question.

(2) Where by those provisions power is conferred to provide for any matter by regulations under this Act, the Secretary of State may make general or special regulations with respect to that matter.

(3) All orders and general regulations made under this section shall be laid before Parliament after being made.

87. In this Part of this Act, except where the context otherwise requires—

" absence without leave " and " desertion " mean respectively absence without leave contrary to subsection (1) or (3) of section 73 above and desertion contrary to subsection (1) of that section, and " absentee without leave " and " deserter " shall be construed accordingly;

" airman " includes a warrant officer and a non-commissioned officer ;

" soldier " includes a warrant officer and a non-commissioned officer ; and

" special reservist " means a man of the Air Force Reserve who is serving in that reserve as a special reservist pursuant to section 68 above.

PART V

TERRITORIAL ARMY AND ROYAL AUXILIARY AIR FORCE

Government, discipline and pay of Territorial Army and Royal Auxiliary Air Force

88. Her Majesty may by order signified under the hand of the Secretary of State, make orders—

(a) with respect to the government, discipline, and pay and allowances of the Territorial Army and of the Royal Auxiliary Air Force, and

(b) with respect to all other matters and things relating to the Territorial Army or to the Royal Auxiliary Air Force,

and including any matter authorised to be prescribed or expressed to be subject to orders or regulations by—

(i) sections 40, 41 and 43 above ;

(ii) the following provisions of this Part of this Act ;

(iii) paragraph 18 of Schedule 8 to this Act.

All orders under this section shall be laid before Parliament after being made.

Her Majesty's orders as to Territorial Army and Royal Auxiliary Air Force.

89. Orders made under section 88 above as respects the Territorial Army may—

(a) provide for the formation of men of the Territorial Army into regiments, battalions, or other military bodies ;

(b) provide for appointing, transferring or attaching men of the Territorial Army to corps and for posting, attaching, or otherwise dealing with such men within the corps ;

(c) provide for the constitution of a permanent staff, including adjutants and staff sergeants who shall, except in special circumstances certified by the general officer commanding, be members of Her Majesty's regular military forces ; and

(d) regulate the appointment, rank, duties and numbers of the officers, warrant officers and non-commissioned officers of the Territorial Army.

Her Majesty's orders as to Territorial Army.

PART V
Her Majesty's
orders as to
Royal
Auxiliary Air
Force.

90. Orders made under section 88 above as respects the Royal Auxiliary Air Force may—

   (a) provide for the formation of men of the Royal Auxiliary Air Force into wings, squadrons or other air force bodies and for the formation of such wings, squadrons or other air force bodies into higher formations, either alone or jointly with any other part of Her Majesty's air forces ;

   (b) provide for posting, transferring, or attaching men of the Royal Auxiliary Air Force to units ;

   (c) provide for the constitution of a permanent staff, including adjutants and non-commissioned officers who shall, except in special circumstances certified by the air officer commanding, be members of Her Majesty's regular air force ; and

   (d) regulate the appointment, rank, duties and numbers of the officers, warrant officers and non-commissioned officers of the Royal Auxiliary Air Force.

91. Subject to sections 88 to 90 above, and to any order made under them, the Defence Council may make general or special regulations—

   (a) with respect to any matters relating to the Territorial Army, and

   (b) with respect to any matters relating to the Royal Auxiliary Air Force,

being matters with respect to which Her Majesty may make orders under those sections.

All regulations under this section shall be laid before Parliament after being made.

Matters not
to be within
orders or
regulations
under ss. 88
to 91.

92. Orders or regulations made under sections 88 to 91 shall not affect or extend the term for which, or the area within which, a man of the Territorial Army or the Royal Auxiliary Air Force is liable to serve or, except as expressly provided by this Part of this Act—

   (a) authorise a man of the Territorial Army when belonging to one corps to be transferred, without his consent, to another corps ; or

   (b) where the corps of a man of the Territorial Army includes more than one unit, authorise him when not called out for permanent service by virtue of section 10(1) or section 11(1) above to be posted, without his consent, to any unit other than that to which he was posted on enlistment ; or

(c) where the corps of a man of the Territorial Army includes any battalion or other body of the regular forces, authorise him to be posted, without his consent, to that battalion or body ; or

(d) authorise a man of the Royal Auxiliary Air Force when not called out for permanent service by virtue of section 10(1) above to be posted, without his consent, to any unit other than that to which he was posted on enlistment ; or

(e) authorise a man of the Royal Auxiliary Air Force to be posted, without his consent, to a unit of the regular air force.

93.—(1) Any power or jurisdiction given to, and act or thing to be done by, to or before any person holding any military or air force office, may—

Exercise of powers of military and air force office holders.

(a) in relation to the Territorial Army, or

(b) in relation to the Royal Auxiliary Air Force,

as the case may be, be exercised by or done by, to or before any other person for the time being authorised in that behalf according to the custom of the service.

(2) Where by this Part of this Act, or by any order or regulation in force under it, any order is authorised to be made by any military or air force authority—

(a) the order may be signified by an order, instruction or letter under the hand of any officer authorised to issue orders on behalf of that authority ; and

(b) an order, instruction or letter purporting to be signed by any officer who appears from it to be so authorised shall be evidence of his being so authorised.

Enlistment

94.—(1) Where a man enlists in the Territorial Army or the Royal Auxiliary Air Force—

Procedure for enlistment.

(a) he shall be enlisted by such persons and in such manner and subject to such regulations as may be prescribed ; and

(b) the provisions of Schedule 3 to this Act shall apply.

(2) A recruit may be attested by a lord-lieutenant or deputy lieutenant of any county or, in Scotland, of any area, or—

(a) in the case of a recruit to the Territorial Army, by an officer of the regular military forces or of the Territorial Army, or

PART V

(*b*) in the case of a recruit to the Royal Auxiliary Air Force, by an officer of the regular air force or of the Royal Auxiliary Air Force,

and the provisions of Schedule 3, as applied to the Territorial Army or the Royal Auxiliary Air Force, as the case may be, shall be construed as if references in those provisions to a recruiting officer included references to any such lord-lieutenant, deputy lieutenant or officer.

(3) The attestation paper to be used for the purpose of attesting recruits to the Territorial Army shall be in such form as may be prescribed.

Conditions of enlistment.

95.—(1) British subjects and British protected persons may enlist or re-engage as men of the Territorial Army or the Royal Auxiliary Air Force in any country or territory outside the United Kingdom as well as in the United Kingdom.

(2) Every man enlisted under this Part of this Act shall—

(*a*) if enlisted into the Territorial Army be enlisted for service in such corps and be posted to such unit in that corps as he may select ; or

(*b*) if enlisted into the Royal Auxiliary Air Force be enlisted for service in such unit as he may select.

Term and area of service.

96.—(1) Every man enlisted under this Part of this Act shall be enlisted to serve for such a period as may be prescribed, not exceeding 4 years, reckoned from the date of his attestation.

(2) A man of the Territorial Army or the Royal Auxiliary Air Force shall, until duly discharged in the prescribed manner, remain subject to this Part as a man of that reserve or that force, as the case may be.

(3) Officers and men of the Territorial Army and of the Royal Auxiliary Air Force are liable to serve in any part of the United Kingdom, the Channel Islands, the Isle of Man and, subject to section 6 above and in so far as is provided in this Part, elsewhere.

Re-engagement for service.

97. A man enlisted under this Part of this Act in the Territorial Army or in the Royal Auxiliary Air Force—

(*a*) may be re-engaged within the period of 12 months expiring with the end of his current term of service for such a period as may be prescribed, not exceeding 4 years from the end of that term, and

(*b*) on that re-engagement shall make the prescribed declaration before a justice of the peace or an officer,

and so from time to time.

Discharge

98.—(1) A man of the Territorial Army or of the Royal Auxiliary Air Force shall (save as is provided in this Act) be entitled to be discharged before the end of his current term of service on complying with the following conditions—

> (a) giving to his commanding officer 3 months' notice in writing, or such less notice as may be prescribed, of his desire to be discharged ; and
>
> (b) paying for the use of the association administering the unit in which he is serving, or, if the unit is administered by more than one association, the association administering the part of that unit in which he is serving, such sum as may be prescribed not exceeding £5 ; and
>
> (c) delivering up in good order, fair wear and tear only excepted, all arms, clothing and appointments, being public property issued to him, or, in cases where for any good or sufficient cause the delivery of that property is impossible, paying its value.

(2) The association, or any officer authorised by the association may, in any case in which it appears that the reasons for which the discharge is claimed are of sufficient urgency or weight, dispense either wholly or in part with all or any of the above conditions.

99.—(1) A man of the Territorial Army or of the Royal Auxiliary Air Force may be discharged by his commanding officer—

> (a) for disobedience to orders by him while doing any military or air force duty, as the case may be ; or
>
> (b) for neglect of such duty, or for misconduct by him as a man of the Territorial Army or of the Royal Auxiliary Air Force, as the case may be ; or
>
> (c) for other sufficient cause, the existence and sufficiency of such cause to be judged by the commanding officer.

(2) A man so discharged shall be entitled to appeal to the Defence Council, who may give such directions in any such case as they may think just and proper.

100.—(1) Where the time at which a man of the Territorial Army or the Royal Auxiliary Air Force would otherwise be entitled to be discharged occurs during a period of emergency, he may be required to prolong his service for such further term, not exceeding 12 months, as the Defence Council or an officer designated by them may order.

(2) A man shall not during a period of emergency be entitled to be discharged under section 98 above.

(3) In this section the expression " period of emergency " means—

> (a) in relation to a man of the Territorial Army, any period while an order under section 10(1) above is in force ordering the Army Reserve to be called out for permanent service ;

> (b) in relation to a man of the Royal Auxiliary Air Force, any period—

>> (i) while an order under section 10(1) is in force ordering the Air Force Reserve to be called out for permanent service ; or

>> (ii) while the man in question is called out for home defence service.

101.—(1) A man of the Territorial Army who is a person to whom section 11 above applies shall not be entitled to be discharged under section 98 above during any period while an order is in force under section 12(1) above.

(2) Subsections (1) and (2) of section 100 above shall have effect, in relation to a man who enlists or re-engages in the Territorial Army on or after 1st April 1967, as if the period of emergency within the meaning of that section included any period while he is called out for home defence service.

102. If a man—

> (a) of the Territorial Army enlists into the Army Reserve without being discharged from the Territorial Army, or

> (b) of the Royal Auxiliary Air Force enlists into the Air Force Reserve without being discharged from the Royal Auxiliary Air Force,

the terms and conditions of service applicable to men of the Territorial Army or of the Royal Auxiliary Air Force shall cease to apply to him while he remains in the Army Reserve or in the Air Force Reserve, as the case may be.

Additional provisions as to call-out

103. A man of the Territorial Army may, by order of the Defence Council or an officer designated by them—

> (a) at any time while the part of the Territorial Army to which he belongs is called out for permanent service by virtue of section 10(1) or section 11(1) above, be

posted without his consent to any unit within his corps
or be transferred without his consent to any corps, and

(*b*) at any time while he is serving under section 22 above,
be posted without his consent to any unit within his
corps.

104. A man of the Royal Auxiliary Air Force may, by
order of the Defence Council or an officer designated by them—

(*a*) at any time while the part of the Royal Auxiliary Air
Force to which he belongs is called out for permanent
service by virtue of section 10(1) above, or

(*b*) at any time while he is serving under section 22 above,

be posted without his consent to any unit of Her Majesty's air
forces.

Transfer and
posting on
call-out of
Royal
Auxiliary
Air Force.

105. Where a man—

(*a*) has been transferred or posted by virtue of section 103
or section 104 above, and

(*b*) continues in Territorial Army or Royal Auxiliary Air
Force service, as the case may be,

then, if he so desires there shall, as soon as may be convenient
after the end of the period of call-out or, as the case may be, of
the period of his service under section 22 above, be taken all
such steps as are necessary to enable him to serve again—

> (i) in the case of the Territorial Army, in the
> corps or unit, or

> (ii) in the case of the Royal Auxiliary Air Force,
> in the unit,

in which he was serving at the time when he was first so transferred or posted.

Offences

106.—(1) Any man of the Territorial Army or of the Royal
Auxiliary Air Force who without leave lawfully granted, or
without such reasonable excuse (including sickness) as may be
allowed in the prescribed manner, fails to appear at the time
and place specified by a call-out notice served on him in pursuance of this Act, specifying—

(*a*) in any case, section 10(1) above or section 22 above,

(*b*) in the case of a man of the Territorial Army to whom
section 11 above applies, section 11(1),

as the enactment by virtue of which he is called into service, shall
be guilty, according to the circumstances, of desertion or absence
without leave, and on conviction by court-martial shall be punishable as provided by subsection (2) below.

(2) On conviction under subsection (1) above a man shall be punishable—

    (*a*) as for an offence under section 37 or, as the case may be, section 38, of the Army Act 1955, or

    (*b*) as for an offence under section 37, or, as the case may be, section 38, of the Air Force Act 1955,

without prejudice to his liability apart from this section in respect of such an offence, and he may be taken into military or air-force custody, as the case may be.

(3) Where a man of the Territorial Army or of the Royal Auxiliary Air Force deserts contrary to this section the time which elapsed between the time of his desertion and the time of his apprehension or voluntary surrender shall not be taken into account in reckoning his service for the purpose of discharge.

(4) The provisions of Schedule 5 to this Act, in relation to the Territorial Army or the Royal Auxiliary Air Force, as the case may be, shall apply to a deserter or absentee without leave.

107. Any person who, in the United Kingdom or elsewhere, by any means whatsoever—

    (*a*) procures or persuades any man of the Territorial Army or of the Royal Auxiliary Air Force to commit an offence of desertion contrary to section 106 above, or attempts to procure or persuade any such man to commit such an offence, or

    (*b*) knowing that any such man is about to commit such an offence aids or assists him in so doing, or

    (*c*) knowing any such man to be a deserter contrary to section 106 above, procures or persuades or assists him to remain such a deserter, or assists in his rescue from custody,

shall be liable on summary conviction to a fine not exceeding £50 or to imprisonment for a term not exceeding 6 months.

108. Where a man of the Territorial Army or of the Royal Auxiliary Air Force, without leave lawfully granted, or such reasonable excuse (including sickness) as may be allowed in the prescribed manner—

    (*a*) fails to appear at the time and place appointed for training, or

    (*b*) fails to attend the number of drills or instructional parades or to fulfil the other conditions relating to training which may be prescribed,

he shall be liable on summary conviction to a fine not exceeding
£25, except for Northern Ireland, where the fine shall not exceed
£5.

109. Where any person— Wrongful
sale, etc., of
public
property.

   (*a*) designedly makes away with, sells, or pawns, or wrong-
      fully destroys or damages, or negligently loses, anything
      issued to him as an officer or man of the Territorial
      Army or of the Royal Auxiliary Air Force, or

   (*b*) wrongfully refuses or neglects to deliver upon demand
      anything issued to him as an officer or man of the
      Territorial Army or of the Royal Auxiliary Air
      Force,

the value of that thing shall be recoverable from him on complaint to a magistrates' court (or, in Scotland, on proceedings in
any competent court) by such authority as may be prescribed.

110.—(1) Any offence to which this subsection applies which Trial of
offences by
magistrates'
court. is cognisable by a court-martial shall also be cognisable by a magistrates' court and on conviction by such court shall be punishable with imprisonment for a term not exceeding 3 months, or with a fine not exceeding £50, or with both such imprisonment and fine.

(2) Subsection (1) above applies—

   (*a*) to any offence under the Army Act 1955 if committed 1955 c. 18.
      by a man of the Territorial Army when not called
      out for permanent service by virtue of section 10(1) or
      section 11(1) above;

   (*b*) to any offence under the Air Force Act 1955 if com- 1955 c. 19.
      mitted by a man of the Royal Auxiliary Air Force
      when not called out for home defence service and when
      not called out for permanent service by virtue of sec-
      tion 10(1); and

   (*c*) to any offence under this Part of this Act.

(3) Nothing in subsection (1) affects the liability of a person
charged with any offence to which that subsection applies to
be taken into military or air-force custody.

111. Any offence which under this Part of this Act is punish- Offences
punishable by
court-martial. able on conviction by court-martial shall for all purposes of and incidental to the arrest, trial and punishment of the offender, including the summary dealing with the case by any officer having power so to deal with the case—

   (*a*) be deemed to be an offence under the Army Act 1955,
      if the offence relates to a man of the Territorial Army,
   or

(*b*) be deemed to be an offence under the Air Force Act 1955, if the offence relates to a man of the Royal Auxiliary Air Force,

but those Acts in their application for the purposes of this section shall have effect with the substitution for any reference to forfeiture and stoppages of a reference to such forfeitures and stoppages as may be prescribed.

Jurisdiction
of courts.

112.—(1) In the United Kingdom or any colony, a civil court of any description having jurisdiction in the place where an offender is for the time being shall have jurisdiction to try an officer or man of the Territorial Army or the Royal Auxiliary Air Force for any offence under this Part of this Act which is triable by a court of that description.

(2) Subsection (1) above applies notwithstanding that the offence was committed outside the jurisdiction of the court, except that where the offence was committed in any part of the United Kingdom it shall not be triable outside that part of the United Kingdom.

(3) Every fine—

(*a*) imposed under this Part on a man of the Territorial Army or the Royal Auxiliary Air Force otherwise than by a court in England or Wales, and

(*b*) recovered on a prosecution instituted under this Part otherwise than in such a court,

shall, notwithstanding anything in any Act or charter to the contrary, be paid to the prescribed authority, except that all fines imposed in proceedings taken before a magistrates' court in Northern Ireland shall, notwithstanding anything in para-
1954 c. 9 (N.I.). graph (ii) of subsection (5) of section 20 of the Administration of Justice Act (Northern Ireland) 1954, be dealt with in the manner provided by that section.

Time for
institution of
proceedings.

113. Proceedings against an offender before either—

(*a*) a court-martial, or

(*b*) an officer having power to deal with the case summarily, or

(*c*) a magistrates' court,

in respect of an offence punishable under this Part of this Act and alleged to have been committed by him during his period of service in the Territorial Army or the Royal Auxiliary Air Force may be instituted whether the term of his service has or

has not expired, and may, notwithstanding anything in any
other Act, be instituted—

> (i) at any time within 2 months after the time at
> which the offence becomes known to his command-
> ing officer, if the alleged offender is then appre-
> hended, or,
>
> (ii) if he is not then apprehended, then within 2
> months after the time at which he is apprehended.

114. Where a man of the Territorial Army or of the Royal Courts of
Auxiliary Air Force— inquiry.

> (*a*) is subject to military law or air-force law, as the case
> may be, and
>
> (*b*) is illegally absent from his duty,

a board of inquiry under section 135 of the Army Act 1955, 1955 c. 18.
or section 135 of the Air Force Act 1955, as the case may be, 1955 c. 19.
may be assembled after the expiry of 21 days from the date
of his absence, notwithstanding that the period during which
the man was subject to military law or air-force law is less
than 21 days or has expired before the expiry of 21 days.

115.—(1) A person charged with an offence which under this Offences
Part of this Act is cognisable both by a court-martial and by triable both by
a magistrates' court shall not be liable to be tried both by a court-martial
court-martial and by a magistrates' court, but may be tried by summarily.
either of them, as may be prescribed.

(2) For the purposes of subsection (1) above a man who has
been dealt with summarily by any officer having power so to deal
with the case shall be deemed to have been tried by court-
martial.

116.—(1) Paragraph 1 of Schedule 6 to this Act has effect in Evidence
relation to all proceedings under this Part of this Act. generally
under Part V.

(2) Paragraph 2 of that Schedule shall have effect in the case
of a man of the Territorial Army or the Royal Auxiliary Air
Force, as the case may be, who is tried by a civil court, whether
or not he is at the time of the trial subject to military law or to
air-force law.

(3) Where by virtue of this Part a document is admissible in
evidence or is evidence of any matter stated in it in proceedings
before a civil court in England, it shall be sufficient evidence of
the matter so stated in such proceedings in Scotland.

Miscellaneous

Certain
provisions as
to commissions
in Territorial
Army.

117.—(1) All officers in the Territorial Army shall hold commissions from Her Majesty, and such commissions shall be prepared, authenticated and issued in the manner in which commissions of officers in Her Majesty's land forces are prepared, authenticated and issued, according to any law or custom for the time being in force.

(2) The holder of a land forces commission (including a person entitled to the issue of one) may be placed on the active list of officers of the Territorial Army, and while on that list shall be an officer of that reserve.

For the purposes of this subsection " active list " has such meaning as may be prescribed.

(3) Any reference—

1955 c. 18.

(*a*) in the Army Act 1955, and

(*b*) in such other enactment (if any) as may be prescribed for the purposes of this subsection,

to an officer holding a commission in the Territorial Army shall be construed as including a reference to a person who is an officer of that reserve by virtue of subsection (2) above.

The power to make regulations under this subsection shall be exercisable by statutory instrument.

Civil rights
and
exemptions.

118.—(1) An officer or man of the Territorial Army or the Royal Auxiliary Air Force shall not be liable to any penalty or punishment for or on account of his absence—

(*a*) during the time he is voting at any election of a member to serve in Parliament ; or

(*b*) during the time he is going to or returning from such voting.

(2) While a sheriff—

(*a*) is an officer of the Territorial Army and is called out for permanent service under section 10(1) or section 11(1) above, or

(*b*) is an officer of the Royal Auxiliary Air Force and is called out for permanent service under section 10(1) above or called out for home defence service,

he shall be discharged from personally performing the office of sheriff, and the under-sheriff shall be answerable for the execution of that office in the name of the high sheriff, and the security given by the under-sheriff and his pledges to the high sheriff shall stand as a security to the Queen and to all persons whomsoever for the due performance of the office of sheriff during that time.

(3) A field officer of the Territorial Army or an officer of the Royal Auxiliary Air Force not below the rank of squadron leader shall not be required to serve in the office of high sheriff.

(4) Subsections (2) and (3) above do not apply to Scotland.

119. For the purposes of—

   (*a*) section 184 of the Army Act 1955,

   (*b*) section 184 of the Air Force Act 1955, and

   (*c*) other enactments relating to the duties, tolls and ferries as are mentioned in those sections,

officers and men belonging to the Territorial Army or the Royal Auxiliary Air Force, when going to or returning from any place at which they are required to attend, and for non-attendance at which they are liable to be punished, shall be deemed to be officers and soldiers of the regular military forces on duty, or officers and airmen of the regular air force on duty, as the case may be.

Exemption from tolls, etc.
1955 c. 18.
1955 c. 19.

120. Notices required in pursuance of—

   (*a*) this Part of this Act, or

   (*b*) the orders and regulations in force under this Part,

to be given to men of the Territorial Army or of the Royal Auxiliary Air Force shall be served or published in such manner as may be prescribed and, if so served or published, shall be deemed to be sufficient notice.

Service of notices for Territorial Army and Royal Auxiliary Air Force.

PART VI

TERRITORIAL, AUXILIARY AND VOLUNTEER RESERVE ASSOCIATIONS, AND THE LIEUTENANCIES

Army and air force associations

121.—(1) In this Part of this Act—

the expression " joint association " means an association established for any area in the United Kingdom, being an area determined by the Defence Council, for the purposes of the organisation and administration of Her Majesty's military and air forces other than the regulars and their reserves and for such other purposes of the establishment of associations as are mentioned in this Part ;

the expression " territorial and army volunteer reserve association " means an association established for any such area for the like purposes in relation to Her Majesty's military forces ;

Associations.

the expression "auxiliary air force association" means an association established for any such area for the like purposes in relation to Her Majesty's air forces.

(2) An association of any of the kinds mentioned in subsection (1) above—

(a) may be established for any such area as is mentioned in that subsection for which an association of that kind is not for the time being in existence, but

(b) in the case of an auxiliary air force association the area shall be one which in the opinion of the Defence Council cannot be suitably administered through a joint association.

Constitution of associations.
122.—(1) Such an association as is mentioned in section 121 above shall be constituted, and the members of that association shall be appointed and hold office, in accordance with a scheme—

(a) made by the Defence Council, and

(b) as to which the provisions of Schedule 7 to this Act shall have effect.

(2) The scheme under subsection (1) above by which a joint association is established for any area shall provide—

(a) for the winding-up, as from the date of the establishment of the joint association, of any territorial and army volunteer reserve association or auxiliary air force association previously established for that area, and

(b) for any matter incidental to or consequential on the winding-up, whether as respects the transfer of property, rights and liabilities, financial adjustment or otherwise, as the Defence Council may think necessary.

(3) The Secretary of State may by order make such changes in the provisions of Schedule 7 as he considers appropriate, and the order may contain such supplemental, incidental and transitional provisions as the Secretary of State considers expedient.

(4) The Defence Council may make an order for the winding-up of any such association as is mentioned in section 121 and the order shall provide for any matter incidental to or consequential on the winding-up, whether as respects the transfer of property, rights and liabilities, financial adjustment or otherwise, as the Defence Council may think necessary.

(5) The power to make an order under subsection (3) above shall be exercisable by statutory instrument, and any such order shall be subject to annulment in pursuance of a resolution of either House of Parliament.

123.—(1) It shall be the duty of each association—

    (*a*) to make itself acquainted with and conform to the plan of the Defence Council—

        (i) for the organisation of all Her Majesty's military forces within the area for which the association is established, and

        (ii) for the organisation of all Her Majesty's air forces within that area ;

    (*b*) to ascertain the military and air force resources and capabilities of the area for which the association is established and to render advice and assistance to the Defence Council and to such officers as the Defence Council may direct ;

    (*c*) to make itself acquainted with and conform to the plan of the Defence Council for the organisation within the area for which the association is established of the reserves of the Royal Navy and of the reserves of the Royal Marines in so far as that plan relates to matters with respect to which functions are conferred on the association under subsection (1) of section 124 below.

(2) The provisions of this section and sections 124 to 127 below apply (save as they otherwise expressly provide) to all such associations as are mentioned in section 121 above, but with the following modifications in their application to an association other than a joint association—

    (*a*) in their application to a territorial and army volunteer reserve association they shall be read with the omission of all references to Her Majesty's air forces, and also of references to the Royal Auxiliary Air Force, air force authorities, air force resources and capabilities, actual air force service, the Air Training Corps, aviation clubs and aerodromes, landing grounds and hangars ;

    (*b*) in their application to an auxiliary air force association they shall be read with the omission of all references to Her Majesty's military forces, and also of references to the Territorial Army, military authorities, military resources and capabilities, actual military service, and the Army Cadet Force.

124.—(1) An association shall have, exercise and discharge such powers and duties connected with the organisation and administration of Her Majesty's military and air forces as may for the time being be transferred or assigned to it by order of Her Majesty signified under the hand of the Secretary of State or, subject to such an order, by regulations under this Part of this Act, and also such powers and duties as may be transferred or assigned to it as mentioned above connected with the organisation and administration of—

> (a) the reserves of the Royal Navy and the reserves of the Royal Marines, or
>
> (b) the Army Cadet Force, the Air Training Corps, the Combined Cadet Force and the Sea Cadet Corps,

but an association shall not have any powers of command or training over any part of Her Majesty's forces.

(2) The powers and duties so transferred or assigned to an association may include any powers conferred on or vested in Her Majesty, and any powers or duties conferred or imposed on the Defence Council or the Secretary of State, by statute or otherwise, and in particular respecting the following matters—

> (a) the organisation of the units of the Territorial Army and the Royal Auxiliary Air Force and their administration (including maintenance) at all times other than when they are called out for training or permanent military or air force service, or other than when—
>
>> (i) the Territorial Army is called out for permanent service by virtue of section 10(1) or 11(1) above, or
>>
>> (ii) the Royal Auxiliary Air Force is called out for permanent service by virtue of section 10(1);
>
> (b) the recruiting for the Territorial Army and the Royal Auxiliary Air Force both in peace and in war, and defining the limits of recruiting areas;
>
> (c) the provision and maintenance of rifle ranges, buildings, magazines, sites of camps, aerodromes, landing grounds and hangars for the Territorial Army and the Royal Auxiliary Air Force;
>
> (d) facilitating the provision of areas to be used for manoeuvres;
>
> (e) arranging with employers of labour as to holidays for training, and ascertaining, after consultation with the representatives of employers in and of persons employed in the principal industries of the area for which the association is established, the times of training which having regard to those industries are best suited to the circumstances of civil life;
>
> (f) establishing or assisting cadet units and also rifle and aviation clubs;
>
> (g) the provision of mechanical transport and horses for the peace requirements of the Territorial Army and the Royal Auxiliary Air Force;

(*h*) providing accommodation for the safe custody of arms and equipment;

(*i*) the supply of the requirements on mobilisation of the units of the Territorial Army and the Royal Auxiliary Air Force within the area for which the association is established in so far as those requirements are directed by the Defence Council to be met locally;

(*j*) the registration in conjunction with the military and air force authorities of vehicles, horses, stores and equipment for any of Her Majesty's military or air forces (or, in the case of a territorial and army volunteer reserve association, any of Her Majesty's forces);

(*k*) the welfare of members and former members of Her Majesty's military and air forces and of members and former members of the reserves of the Royal Navy and of the reserves of the Royal Marines;

(*l*) in the case of a joint association and of an auxiliary air force association, the undertaking in relation to the Air Force Reserve of any functions undertaken in relation to the Royal Auxiliary Air Force.

For the purposes of paragraph (i) of this subsection the Defence Council shall from time to time make and issue to associations regulations specifying, so far as practicable, the requirements mentioned in that paragraph which are to be met locally.

(3) The members of an association shall not be under any pecuniary liability for any act done by them in their capacity as members of the association in carrying out the provisions of this Part of this Act.

125.—(1) The Defence Council shall pay to an association, out of money provided by Parliament, such sums as in the opinion of the Defence Council are required to meet the necessary expenditure incurred by the association.

Expenses of associations.

(2) An association—

(*a*) shall annually at the prescribed time, and

(*b*) may at any other time for any special purpose,

submit in the prescribed form and manner a statement of its necessary requirements to the Defence Council; and all payments under this section to an association shall be made upon the basis of such a statement, so far as approved by the Defence Council.

(3) Subject to regulations under this Part of this Act, any money paid to an association by the Defence Council shall be applicable to any of the purposes specified in the approved

statements in accordance with which money has been granted and, except with the written consent of the Defence Council shall not be applicable otherwise.

(4) Nothing in this section shall be construed as enabling the Defence Council to give their consent to the application of money to any purpose to which, apart from this section, it could not lawfully be applied, or to give their consent without the authority of the Treasury in any case in which, apart from this section, the authority of the Treasury would be required.

(5) All money received by an association otherwise than from the Defence Council (except such money, if any, as may be received by the association for specified purposes) shall be available for the purposes of any of the powers and duties of the association.

(6) In the case of a joint association, the income from investments representing money originally received for the purpose of the Territorial Army or of the Royal Auxiliary Air Force shall be applied only to that purpose, unless the Defence Council otherwise direct.

Accounts of associations.

126.—(1) An association shall cause its accounts to be made up annually and audited in such a manner as may be prescribed.

(2) An association shall send copies of its accounts, together with any report of the auditors on them, to—

    (a) the Defence Council, or

    (b) such authority or person as may be directed by regulations under this Part of this Act.

Joint committees of associations.

127.—(1) Associations may from time to time join in appointing out of their respective bodies a joint committee for any purpose in respect of which they are jointly interested.

(2) An association joining in appointing a joint committee under this section may delegate to it any power which such an association may exercise for the purpose for which the committee is appointed.

(3) Subject to the terms of delegation a joint committee appointed under this section shall in respect of any matter delegated to it have the same power in all respects as the associations appointing it.

(4) The costs of such joint committee shall be defrayed by the associations by whom it has been appointed in such proportion as may be agreed between them, and the accounts of such joint committees and their officers shall for the purposes of the provisions of this Part of this Act be deemed to be accounts of the associations appointing them and of their officers.

128.—(1) Regulations for carrying into effect the foregoing provisions of this Part of this Act as respects joint associations may be made by the Defence Council and such regulations may, among other things, provide for the following matters—

(a) for regulating the manner in which powers are to be exercised and duties performed by such associations, and for specifying the services to which money paid by the Defence Council is to be applicable ;

(b) for authorising and regulating the acquisition by or on behalf of such an association of land for the purposes of this Part and the disposal of any land so acquired ;

(c) for authorising and regulating the borrowing of money by such an association ;

(d) for authorising the acceptance of any money or other property, and the taking over of any liability, by such an association, and for regulating the administration of any money or property so acquired and the discharge of any liability so taken over ;

(e) for facilitating the co-operation of such an association with any other association such as is mentioned in section 121 above or with any local authority or other body, and for providing by the constitution of joint committees or otherwise for co-operative action in the organisation and administration of divisions, brigades and other military bodies and of groups, wings, squadrons and other air force bodies, and for the provision of assistance by one association to another ;

(f) for affiliating cadet units, rifle and aviation clubs and other bodies to the Territorial Army or to the Royal Auxiliary Air Force or to any part of them ;

(g) for or in respect of anything by the foregoing provisions of this Part directed or authorised to be done or provided for by regulations or to be done in the prescribed manner ;

(h) for the application for the purposes of the foregoing provisions of this Part, as respects any matters to be dealt with by regulations, of any provision in any Act of Parliament dealing with the like matters, with the necessary modifications or adaptations, and in particular of any provisions as to the acquisition of land by or on behalf of volunteer corps.

(2) Regulations for carrying into effect the foregoing provisions of this Part as respects territorial and army volunteer reserve associations and auxiliary air force associations respectively may be made by the Defence Council, and such regulations may among other things, provide for the matters mentioned in

paragraphs (*a*) to (*h*) of subsection (1) above read with the following modifications—

> (*a*) for references to joint associations there shall be substituted references to territorial and army volunteer reserve associations or to auxiliary air force associations, as the case may be;
>
> (*b*) as respects territorial and army volunteer reserve associations there shall be omitted the references to the Royal Auxiliary Air Force, to groups, wings, squadrons, and other air force bodies, and to aviation clubs;
>
> (*c*) as respects auxiliary air force associations there shall be omitted the references to the Territorial Army, to divisions, brigades and other military bodies.

(3) All regulations under this section as respects joint, territorial and army volunteer reserve and auxiliary air force associations respectively shall be applicable to all joint, territorial and army volunteer reserve and auxiliary air force associations respectively, except in so far as may be otherwise provided by the regulations or by any scheme made under this Part.

(4) In relation to this section—

> (*a*) regulations made for the purposes of section 125 or of section 126 above shall be subject to the Treasury's consent; and
>
> (*b*) all regulations shall be laid before Parliament after being made.

Compensation of displaced employees.   **129.**—(1) The Secretary of State may, with the consent of the Minister for the Civil Service, make regulations providing for the payment by the Secretary of State, out of moneys provided by Parliament, of compensation to or in respect of any person who in the Secretary of State's opinion—

> (*a*) has ceased to be employed by an association established for the purposes of this Part of this Act, or has suffered a diminution in the emoluments of his employment by such an association, in consequence of the winding-up of the association or any change in its activities or of any proposal to wind up the association or change its activities; or
>
> (*b*) has ceased to be employed by the body commonly known as the Council of Territorial, Auxiliary and Volunteer Reserve Associations (formerly the Council of Territorial and Auxiliary Forces Associations), or has suffered a diminution in the emoluments of his employment by that body, in consequence of the winding-up of associations so established or of changes in their activities.

(2) The power to make regulations under subsection (1) above shall be exercisable by statutory instrument, and any such regulation shall be subject to annulment in pursuance of a resolution of either House of Parliament.

The lieutenancies

130.—(1) Her Majesty—

  Lieutenancies in England and Wales.

(a) shall appoint a lord-lieutenant for each county in England and Wales and for Greater London ; and

(b) may appoint lieutenants for each county and for Greater London.

(2) For the purposes of the provisions of this Act relating to the lieutenancies—

(a) " Greater London " in subsection (1) above does not include the City of London, or the Inner Temple and the Middle Temple, but otherwise shall be treated as a county ; and

(b) the Isles of Scilly shall be deemed to form part of the county of Cornwall.

(3) Paragraph (a) of subsection (2) above—

(a) so far as it provides that Greater London other than the City shall be treated as a county, and

(b) so far as it relates to Schedule 7 to this Act,

has effect subject to any order made by virtue of section 84(3) of the London Government Act 1963. 1963 c. 33.

131.—(1) Her Majesty—

  Lieutenancies in Scotland.

(a) shall appoint for each region of Scotland such number of lord-lieutenants as She thinks fit ;

(b) shall appoint a lord-lieutenant for each islands area of Scotland ; and

(c) may appoint lieutenants for each region and islands area.

(2) The Lord Provost of the cities of Aberdeen, Dundee, Edinburgh and Glasgow shall by virtue of his office be lord-lieutenant for the district of the city concerned and Her Majesty may appoint lieutenants for each such district.

(3) The lord-lieutenants and lieutenants appointed for a region under subsection (1) above shall discharge their functions in such parts of the region as may be determined by Order in Council made by Her Majesty.

(4) Where an Order in Council is made in pursuance of subsection (3) above, any deputy lieutenant holding office immediately before the date on which the Order in Council is made

G 2

PART VI   shall (without prejudice to any power of removal or of directing removal from any office) continue to hold office on and after the date as deputy lieutenant of the part of the region in which he resides or of such other part as may be specified in the Order in Council.

(5) In this section " region " does not include the districts of the cities of Aberdeen, Dundee, Edinburgh and Glasgow.

Lieutenancies in Northern Ireland.
S.I. 1975/156.
1973 c. 36.

132. The provisions of this Part of this Act relating to the lieutenancies do not affect the provisions of the Northern Ireland (Lieutenancy) Order 1975, made under section 36(5) of the Northern Ireland Constitution Act 1973.

Deputy lieutenants.

133.—(1) A lord-lieutenant appointed under section 130 or section 131 above shall from time to time appoint such persons as he thinks fit to be his deputy lieutenants.

(2) A person may be appointed to be a deputy lieutenant for a county in England and Wales, or for an area in Scotland, if—

(a) he has a place of residence in the county or area, or within 7 miles from the boundary of the county or area ; and

(b) he is shown to the satisfaction of the Secretary of State to have rendered either—

(i) worthy service as a member of, or in a civil capacity in connection with, Her Majesty's naval, military or air forces, or

(ii) such other service as, in the Secretary of State's opinion, makes him suitable for appointment as a deputy lieutenant.

(3) The lord-lieutenant—

(a) shall certify to Her Majesty the name of every person whom he proposes to appoint deputy lieutenant ; and

(b) shall not grant a commission as deputy lieutenant to any person until informed by the Secretary of State that Her Majesty does not disapprove of the granting of such a commission.

(4) The commission of a deputy lieutenant shall not be vacated by the lord-lieutenant who granted it ceasing to be a lord-lieutenant.

(5) The clerk of the lieutenancy shall (at the cost of the county rate, or, in Scotland, the regional or general rate) arrange for the publication in the London Gazette of the names of the persons appointed deputy lieutenants, with the dates of their commissions, in like manner as commissions of officers of Her Majesty's land forces are published.

134. Where—

(a) the lord-lieutenant of a county or, in Scotland, an area, is absent from the United Kingdom, or by reason of sickness or otherwise is unable to act, or

(b) there is no lord-lieutenant of a county or an area,

Her Majesty may authorise any three deputy lieutenants, or lieutenants appointed under section 130(1) or section 131(1) above, of that county or area to act as its lord-lieutenant, and such deputy lieutenants or lieutenants while so authorised—

> (i) may do all acts which might be done by the lord-lieutenant ; and

> (ii) shall for all purposes stand in the lord-lieutenant's place.

135.—(1) The lord-lieutenant of a county, or, in Scotland, an area, with Her Majesty's approbation, may appoint any deputy lieutenant, or any lieutenant appointed under section 130(1) or section 131(1) above, of that county or area as vice lord-lieutenant to act for him during his absence from the county or area, sickness or other inability to act.

(2) Every such vice lord-lieutenant, until his appointment is revoked or he is removed by Her Majesty (and without prejudice to Her Majesty's authority to make other provision under section 134 above)—

(a) may from time to time, whenever such absence, sickness or inability occurs, do all acts which might be done by the lord-lieutenant ; and

(b) shall for all purposes stand in his place.

136. Whenever Her Majesty may think fit to signify her pleasure to the lord-lieutenant of any county, or, in Scotland, of any area, that any vice lord-lieutenant or deputy lieutenants of the county or area be removed, that lord-lieutenant shall—

(a) forthwith remove them ; and

(b) appoint others in their place, subject to the provisions of this Part of this Act.

137.—(1) The lord-lieutenant and deputy lieutenants appointed under this Part of this Act for any county, or, in Scotland, for any area, shall respectively have such jurisdiction, duties, powers, and privileges as are vested in the lord-lieutenant and the deputy lieutenants respectively for that county or area under any Act for the time being in force.

(2) The lord-lieutenant of every county, or, in Scotland, of every area, shall appoint a clerk of the lieutenancy, and he may

PART VI

remove that clerk if he thinks fit, and appoint another in his place.

Commissioners of lieutenancy for City of London.

138.—(1) Her Majesty may issue commissions of lieutenancy in respect of the City of London to such persons as She thinks fit to be such lieutenants.

(2) The City of London continues to be a separate county for the purposes of the lieutenancies and the militia, and so far as is consistent with the special enactments relating to the City the provisions of this Part of this Act relating to the lieutenancies apply accordingly.

(3) Her Majesty's Commissioners of Lieutenancy for the City of London are for the purposes of those special enactments and those provisions the lieutenant of the county, but the provisions of this Part with respect to deputy lieutenants do not apply to the City.

(4) Nothing in this Part affects the raising and levying of the Trophy Tax in the City.

(5) The proceeds of that tax may be applied by the Commissioners of Lieutenancy for the City of London (if in their discretion they see fit) for the purposes of any of the powers and duties of an association established under this Part for the City.

PART VII

ULSTER DEFENCE REGIMENT

Membership of Ulster Defence Regiment

Enrolment, re-engagement and resignation.

139.—(1) The provisions as to the enrolment, re-engagement and resignation of members of the Ulster Defence Regiment (otherwise than as officers) are—

 (a) a person volunteering and accepted for service in that force shall be enrolled for a prescribed period not exceeding 3 years;

 (b) a member of that force may, if he so desires and is accepted for re-engagement, re-engage from time to time for a further such period;

 (c) a member of that force may if he so desires cease to be a member of it upon the expiry of one month's notice of his desire so to cease given in writing to his commanding officer.

(2) A person shall not cease to be a member of the Ulster Defence Regiment by virtue of paragraph (a), (b) or (c) of subsection (1) above if immediately before the expiry—

 (a) of the period for which he was enrolled, or

 (b) of the period for which he was re-engaged, or

(c) of the period of his notice,

as the case may be, he is on permanent service in pursuance of
section 10 or section 24 above.

140.—(1) The conditions for the acceptance of persons as
members of the Ulster Defence Regiment and the conditions
of service of members of that force (including conditions as
to pay, allowances and pensions or other grants in respect of
death or disablement) shall be such as may be prescribed.

Orders and
regulations
as to
acceptance
and service.

(2) Orders or regulations shall provide for the organisation,
administration, government and duties of the Ulster Defence
Regiment, but shall not require members of that force to give
whole-time service except—

(a) during any period in which that force or the part of
it to which they belong is called out under section 10, or
section 24 or section 25 above, or

(b) while they are undergoing training under paragraph (a)
of section 44(1) above,

and those orders or regulations shall not require members of
that force to serve or train outside Northern Ireland.

(3) In this Part of this Act—

(a) references to orders are to orders of Her Majesty signified
under the hand of the Secretary of State, and

(b) references to regulations are to regulations made by the
Secretary of State,

and any orders or regulations under this Part shall be laid before
Parliament after being made.

Military status of members of Ulster Defence Regiment

141. Persons of the Ulster Defence Regiment shall be members
of the armed forces of the Crown, and—

Membership
of armed
forces and
application
of military
law.

(a) any holder of a land forces commission who is for the
time being assigned for duty with the Ulster Defence
Regiment, and any other member of that force when
serving on its permanent staff, shall be subject to
military law ;

(b) any member of the Ulster Defence Regiment to whom
paragraph (a) above does not apply shall be subject to
military law—

(i) at all times when called out for service under
sections 10, 24, 25 and 44 above or when undergoing training whether in pursuance of an obligation
under those sections or not ; and

(ii) at any other time when he is in possession, or
when, in pursuance of any order given or permission
granted by a superior officer of his, he is required or
authorised to be in possession, of any arms or

ammunition or of any prescribed description of equipment, being arms, ammunition or equipment belonging to Her Majesty.

Application of Army Act 1955 c. 18.
142. References in Parts II to V of the Army Act 1955 to the regular forces shall include references to persons of the Ulster Defence Regiment while subject to military law, but any other references in that Act to the regular forces shall not include references to the Ulster Defence Regiment.

Offences

Failure to attend or comply.
143.—(1) Any member of the Ulster Defence Regiment who—

(a) when required by or in pursuance of regulations making any such provision as is mentioned in section 44 above to attend at any place fails without reasonable excuse to attend in accordance with the requirement, or

(b) fails without reasonable excuse to comply with orders or regulations under this Part of this Act,

shall, whether otherwise subject to military law or not, be guilty of an offence and liable on conviction by court-martial to a fine not exceeding £5.

(2) That offence shall, for all purposes of and incidental to the trial of the offender, including the summary disposal of the case otherwise than by court-martial, be deemed to be an offence under the Army Act 1955.

Assistance in desertion, etc.
144.—(1) Any person who, in Northern Ireland or elsewhere—

(a) procures or persuades any member of the Ulster Defence Regiment to desert within the meaning of section 37 of the Army Act 1955 or to absent himself without leave, or

(b) knowing that any member of that force is about to desert as mentioned in paragraph (a) above or to absent himself without leave, assists him in so doing, or

(c) knowing any person to be a deserter within the meaning of that section 37 or an absentee without leave from that force, procures or persuades or assists him to remain such a deserter or absentee, or assists in his rescue from custody,

shall be liable—

(i) on summary conviction to a fine not exceeding the statutory maximum or to imprisonment for a term not exceeding 3 months or to both;

(ii) on conviction on indictment in Northern Ireland to a fine not exceeding £500 or to imprisonment for a term not exceeding 2 years or to both;

(iii) on conviction on indictment elsewhere in the United Kingdom to a fine or to imprisonment for a term not exceeding 2 years or to both.

(2) In subsection (1) above "the statutory maximum", in relation to a fine on summary conviction, means—

(a) in England and Wales, the prescribed sum within the meaning of section 28 of the Criminal Law Act 1977 (at the passing of this Act £1,000) ; 1977 c. 45.

(b) in Scotland, the prescribed sum within the meaning of section 289B of the Criminal Procedure (Scotland) Act 1975 (at the passing of this Act £1,000) ; and 1975 c. 21.

(c) in Northern Ireland, £50.

PART VIII

MISCELLANEOUS AND SUPPLEMENTAL

Reinstatement in civil employment, and protection of other civil interests

145.—(1) Where any person is, or is liable to be—

(a) called out under section 14(1) above, or

(b) recalled under section 34 above,

the provisions of the Reinstatement in Civil Employment Act 1950 shall apply to that person as they apply to a person who has entered, or, (as the case may be), may be required to enter, upon a period of whole-time service in the armed forces of the Crown in the circumstances mentioned in paragraph (a) of section 1 of that Act.

Reinstatement in civil employment.

1950 c. 10.

(2) Where any person is, or is liable to be, called out under—

(a) section 10(5) above, or

(b) section 24 above, or

(c) section 25(1) above,

the provisions of that Act of 1950 applicable to Northern Ireland shall apply to that person as they apply to a person who has entered, or, (as the case may be), may be required to enter, upon a period of whole-time service in the armed forces of the Crown in the circumstances mentioned in paragraph (a) of section 1 of that Act of 1950.

(3) It is declared—

(a) that for the purposes of that Act of 1950 service for which a person is accepted—

(i) by virtue of section 27 above is service in pursuance of a call-out notice under section 26(1) above,

(ii) by virtue of section 36 above is service in pursuance of a notice under section 33 above or section 35 above, as the case may be ; and

(b) that nothing in this Act shall be taken as prejudicing the application of that Act of 1950.

Protection of other civil interests.

146.—(1) Any service rendered by virtue of—

(a) section 14(1) above, or

(b) section 34 above,

1951 c. 65.

shall be relevant service within the meaning of the Reserve and Auxiliary Forces (Protection of Civil Interests) Act 1951.

(2) Any service rendered by virtue of—

(a) section 10(5) above, or

(b) section 24 above, or

(c) section 25(1) above, or

(d) any continuous period of training of 7 days or longer performed as a member of the Ulster Defence Regiment, whether in pursuance of an obligation under section 44(1) above or under voluntary arrangements,

shall be relevant service within the meaning of the provisions of that Act of 1951 applicable to Northern Ireland.

(3) It is declared—

(a) that for the purposes of that Act of 1951 service for which a person is accepted—

(i) by virtue of section 27 above is service in pursuance of a call-out notice under section 26(1) above,

(ii) by virtue of section 36 above is service in pursuance of a notice under section 33 above or section 35 above, as the case may be ; and

(b) that nothing in this Act shall be taken as prejudicing the application of that Act of 1951.

Charitable property on disbanding of units

Charities in England and Wales on disbanding of units.

147.—(1) Where by warrant of Her Majesty—

(a) a unit of the Territorial Army or the Army Reserve is designated as the successor of a body of either of those reserves which has been or is to be disbanded, or

(b) a unit of the Royal Auxiliary Air Force is designated as the successor of a body of that force which has been or is to be disbanded,

any charitable property held for the purposes of the body in question shall (subject to the provisions of this section), as from the time at which the warrant comes into force, be held for the corresponding purposes of the unit so designated.

(2) The Secretary of State shall, as soon as may be after it is made, deliver a copy of any such warrant by post or otherwise to the Charity Commissioners and to a trustee of the charity in question.

(3) If the Commissioners consider that subsection (1) above should not apply to all or part of the property affected by the warrant they may at any time within the period—

(a) beginning with the date on which the warrant is made, and

(b) ending with the expiry of 6 months beginning with the date on which the warrant comes into force,

make an order providing that that subsection shall not apply or shall cease to apply to the property or part.

(4) If—

(a) a charity affected by such a warrant as is mentioned in subsection (1), or

(b) any trustee of or person interested in such a charity,

considers that subsection (1) should not apply to all or part of any property which belongs to the charity and is affected by the warrant, then the charity, trustee or person interested, as the case may be, may, at any time within the period of 6 months beginning with the date on which the warrant comes into force, apply to the court for an order providing that subsection (1) shall cease to apply to the property or part.

An application under this subsection is subject to subsections (2) to (5) of section 28 of the Charities Act 1960 (which provide that charity proceedings may not be begun without the consent of the Charity Commissioners or leave of a judge of the High Court). 1960 c. 58.

(5) For the purposes of section 28(5) of that Act of 1960 in its application to proceedings under subsection (4) above an application for an order of the Charity Commissioners authorising such proceedings shall be deemed to be refused if it is not granted during the period of one month beginning with the day on which the application is received by the Commissioners.

(6) No such warrant or order as mentioned above shall affect the validity of anything done or omitted with respect to any property affected by the warrant or order before a copy of it is served on a trustee of the charity in question.

(7) In any case where—

(a) an order is made under the foregoing provisions of this section, or

(b) the Secretary of State requests the Commissioners to make provision with respect to any charitable property held for the purposes of a body of the Territorial Army, the Army Reserve or the Royal Auxiliary Air Force which has been or is to be disbanded,

the Commissioners may, notwithstanding anything in subsection (4) of section 18 of the Charities Act 1960, exercise their jurisdiction under that section with respect to the property to which the order or request relates.

(8) The foregoing provisions of this section shall not apply to any charitable property held for the purposes of such a body as is mentioned in subsection (1) if, under the terms on which the property is so held—

(a) any interest of the charity in question in the property is determined on the disbanding of that body, and

(b) any person or charity other than the charity in question has an interest in the property contingent upon the determination of the interest of the charity in question.

(9) Where subsection (1) applies to any charitable property, the same jurisdiction and powers shall be exercisable in relation to the charity in question as would be exercisable if that subsection were not a provision of an Act of Parliament regulating the charity.

(10) In this section—

(a) " charitable property " means property belonging to a charity, and

(b) " the court " and " charity " mean the same as in the Charities Act 1960,

1960 c. 58.

and references to disbandment of a body include references to its amalgamation with another body.

148.—(1) Where by warrant of Her Majesty—

(a) a unit of the Territorial Army or the Army Reserve is designated as the successor of a body of either of those reserves which has been or is to be disbanded, or

(b) a unit of the Royal Auxiliary Air Force is designated as the successor of a body of that force which has been or is to be disbanded,

any property which is held for charitable purposes for the body in question and which is administered for those purposes according to the law of Scotland shall (subject to the provisions of this section), as from the time at which the warrant comes into force, be held for the corresponding purposes of the unit so designated.

(2) The Secretary of State shall, as soon as may be after it is made, deliver a copy of any such warrant by post or otherwise to a trustee of the trust in question.

(3) Where the Secretary of State considers that subsection (1) above should not apply to all or part of the property affected by the warrant he may at any time within the period—

(a) beginning with the date on which the warrant is made, and

(b) ending with the expiry of 6 months beginning with the date on which the warrant comes into force,

make a direction that that subsection shall not apply or shall cease to apply to the property or part.

(4) If any trustee of or person interested in any property held for charitable purposes affected by such a warrant as is mentioned in subsection (1) considers that that subsection should not apply to all or part of such property, that person may, at any time within the period of 6 months beginning with the date on which the warrant comes into force, apply by petition to the Court of Session—

(a) for the court to make such a direction as is mentioned in subsection (3) above in relation to that property or part, and

(b) to exercise, with respect to that property or part, any of the court's powers relating to a charitable or other permanent endowment,

and the court, if it is satisfied that on the making of such a direction it would be entitled to exercise its powers in the manner craved and that it is necessary for these purposes to make that direction, may itself make such a direction.

(5) No such warrant or direction as mentioned above shall affect the validity of anything done or omitted with respect to any property affected by the warrant or direction before a copy of the warrant or direction is seved on a tustee of the trust in question.

(6) The foregoing provisions of this section shall not apply to any property held for charitable purposes for such a body as is mentioned in subsection (1) if, under the terms on which the property is so held, any person has an interest charitable or otherwise in the property contingent upon the determination of the charitable interest therein of that body.

(7) Where a body of the Territorial Army, the Army Reserve or the Royal Auxiliary Air Force has been or is to be disbanded, the Secretary of State may apply by petition to the Court of Session for the court to exercise, with respect to any property held for charitable purposes for the body in question, any of the court's powers relating to a charitable or other permanent endowment.

(8) In this section—

   (a) references to disbandment of a body include references to its amalgamation with another body ; and

   (b) the power to give directions includes power to make different provision for different circumstances.

149.—(1) Where by warrant of Her Majesty—

   (a) a unit of the Territorial Army or the Army Reserve is designated as the successor of a body of either of those reserves which has been or is to be disbanded, or

   (b) a unit of the Royal Auxiliary Air Force is designated as the successor of a body of that force which has been or is to be disbanded,

any charitable property held for the purposes of the body in question and which is administered for those purposes according to the law of Northern Ireland shall (subject to the provisions of this section), as from the time at which the warrant comes into force, be held for the corresponding purposes of the unit so designated.

(2) The Secretary of State shall, as soon as may be after it is made, deliver a copy of any such warrant by post or otherwise to the Department of Finance for Northern Ireland and to a trustee of the charity in question.

(3) If the Department considers that subsection (1) above should not apply to all or part of the property affected by the warrant it may at any time within the period—

   (a) beginning with the date on which the warrant is made, and

   (b) ending with the expiry of 6 months beginning with the date on which the warrant comes into force,

make an order providing that that subsection shall not apply or shall cease to apply to the property or part.

(4) If—

   (a) a charity affected by such a warrant as is mentioned in subsection (1), or

   (b) any trustee of or person interested in such a charity,

considers that subsection (1) should not apply to all or part of any property which belongs to the charity and is affected by the warrant, then the charity, trustee or person interested, as the case may be, may, at any time within the period of 6 months beginning with the date on which the warrant comes into force, apply to the court for an order providing that subsection (1) shall cease to apply to the property or part.

An application under this subsection is subject to section PART VIII
29(3) of the Charities Act (Northern Ireland) 1964 (under which 1964 c. 33
an application for an order of the court in connection with the (N.I.).
administration of a charity may not be made without the consent
of the Attorney General for Northern Ireland).

(5) No such warrant or order as mentioned above shall affect
the validity of anything done or omitted with respect to any
property affected by the warrant or order before a copy of it
is served on a trustee of the charity in question.

(6) In any case where—

    (a) an order is made under the foregoing provisions of this
section, or

    (b) the Secretary of State requests the Department of
Finance for Northern Ireland to make provision with
respect to any charitable property held for the purposes
of a body of the Territorial Army, the Army Reserve
or the Royal Auxiliary Air Force which has been or
is to be disbanded,

the Department may, notwithstanding anything in subsection (1)
of section 13 of the Charities Act (Northern Ireland) 1964 and 1964 c. 33
irrespective of the value of the property in question exercise its (N.I.).
jurisdiction under that section with respect to the property to
which the order or request relates.

(7) The foregoing provisions of this section shall not apply to
any charitable property held for the purposes of such a body
as is mentioned in subsection (1) if, under the terms on which
the property is so held—

    (a) any interest of the charity in question in the property
is determined on the disbanding of that body, and

    (b) any person or charity other than the charity in question
has an interest in the property contingent upon the
determination of the interest of the charity in question.

(8) Where subsection (1) applies to any charitable property,
the same jurisdiction and powers shall be exercisable in relation
to the charity in question as would be exercisable if that subsection were not a provision of an Act of Parliament regulating
the charity.

(9) In this section—

    (a) " charitable property " means property belonging to a
charity,

    (b) " the court " and " charity " mean the same as in the
Charities Act (Northern Ireland) 1964,

and references to disbandment of a body include references to
its amalgamation with another body.

PART VIII

Further power for Secretary of State to make regulations.

Further powers as to orders and regulations

150.—(1) The Secretary of State may make regulations for prescribing anything falling to be prescribed under the following provisions of this Act—

(a) subsections (2), (4) and (5) of section 11,

(b) section 13(1),

(c) section 27,

(d) section 29(1),

(e) section 38,

(f) section 39,

(g) section 65,

(h) section 83(2),

(i) subsections (2) and (3) of section 117, and

(j) paragraph 19 of Schedule 8,

and any regulations under this subsection shall be laid before Parliament after being made.

(2) The power to make regulations—

(a) under subsection (1) above, and

(b) under section 129(1) above,

includes power (without prejudice to any other power in this Act to make regulations) to make different provision for different circumstances.

Pensions and other grants under Home Guard Act 1951 c. 8.

151. The conditions as to pensions and other grants in respect of death or disablement from service in the Home Guard under the Home Guard Act 1951 shall be such as may be prescribed—

(a) by orders of Her Majesty signified under the hand of the Secretary of State, or

(b) by regulations made by the Defence Council,

and any such orders or regulations shall be laid before Parliament as soon as may be after they are made.

Application and modification of enactments.

152.—(1) Her Majesty may by Order in Council apply, with the necessary adaptations—

(a) to the Territorial Army or the Royal Auxiliary Air Force, or

(b) to the officers or men of that reserve or that force,

any enactment passed before 2nd August 1907 and in force at that date relating to the Militia or Volunteers, or officers or men of the Militia or Volunteers, other than enactments with respect to the raising, service, pay, discipline or government of the Militia or Volunteers.

An Order in Council under this subsection shall be laid before Parliament after being made.

(2) Her Majesty may by Order in Council make such modifications of any enactment relating to any of the armed forces of the Crown as She considers expedient in consequence of the

passing of the Reserve Forces Act 1966, including any enactment as amended by that Act.

PART VIII
1966 c. 30.

A draft of any Order in Council proposed to be made under this subsection shall be laid before Parliament.

Other provisions as to orders, schemes and regulations

153. For the purposes of the Statutory Instruments Act 1946 the provisions of this Act—

Provisions as to Statutory Instruments Act 1946 c. 36.

   (a) relating to the Army Reserve, in sections 4, 18, 19 and 23, in Part IV and in paragraphs 16 and 17 of Schedule 8,

   (b) relating to the Air Force Reserve, in sections 8, 20, 21 and 23, in Part IV and in paragraphs 16 and 17 of Schedule 8,

   (c) relating to the Territorial Army and the Royal Auxiliary Air Force, as the case may be, in sections 5, 9, 22, 40 to 43, in Part V, in section 152(1), and in paragraph 18 of Schedule 8,

   (d) relating to territorial, auxiliary and volunteer reserve associations, in sections 121 to 129,

shall be deemed to be provisions of an Act passed before the commencement of that Act of 1946, and any reference in regulations under section 8(1) of that Act of 1946 to—

1946 c. 36.

   (i) any provision of the Reserve Forces Act 1882,

   (ii) any provision of that Act of 1882 as applied to the Air Force Reserve by the Air Force Reserve Order 1924,

45 & 46 Vict. c. 48.

SRO 1924/1213

   (iii) any provision of the Territorial and Reserve Forces Act 1907,

7 Edw. 7. c. 9.

shall, without prejudice to any power to vary the regulations under that Act of 1946, be construed as a reference to the corresponding provision of this Act.

154.—(1) In relation to any Order in Council under section 40 above, or paragraph (a) of section 42 above, or paragraph 18(4)(a) of Schedule 8 to this Act—

Additional provisions as to Orders in Council and schemes.

   (a) before any such Order is made the draft of the Order shall be laid before each House of Parliament for a period of not less than 40 days during the session of Parliament, and

   (b) if either of those Houses before the expiry of those 40 days presents an address to Her Majesty against the draft Order or any part of it, no further proceedings shall be taken in respect of the Order, without prejudice to the laying of a new draft Order.

(2) In relation to any scheme under section 122(1) above or any Order in Council under section 152(1) above—

   (a) every such scheme or Order in Council shall be laid before Parliament within 40 days after it is made, or, if

PART VIII

Parliament is not then sitting, within 40 days after the beginning of the next session of Parliament, and

(b) if an address is presented to Her Majesty by either House of Parliament within the next following 40 days, praying that any such scheme or Order may be annulled, Her Majesty may thereupon by Order in Council annul it, and the scheme or Order so annulled shall thenceforth become void and of no effect, but without prejudice to the validity of any proceedings which may in the meantime have been taken under it.

Amendment of subordinate legislation.
1978 c. 30.

155. Section 14 of the Interpretation Act 1978 applies to this Act as if in paragraph (b) of that section there were no requirement that Orders in Council, orders or other subordinate legislation should be made by statutory instrument.

Other supplemental provisions

Interpretation.

156.—(1) In this Act, except where the context otherwise requires—

" home defence service " means military or air force service in any place in the United Kingdom, the Channel Islands or the Isle of Man in defence of the United Kingdom or those islands against actual or apprehended attack ;

" man ", in relation to—

(a) the naval forces, means a person of or below the rate of warrant officer ;

(b) the military or air forces, includes a warrant officer and non-commissioned officer ;

" permanent service " includes actual service ;

" prescribed " means prescribed by orders or regulations made under this Act ;

" regular air force " has the same meaning as in the Air Force Act 1955 ;

1955 c. 19.

" regular army " means the regular forces within the meaning of the Army Act 1955, but in sections 11(4) and

1955 c. 18.

(5), 15, 39(2), 83(1) and (2) above, and paragraph 19 of Schedule 8 to this Act, does not include the Royal Marines ;

" Territorial Army " means the Territorial and Army Volunteer Reserve.

(2) Except where the context otherwise requires, other expressions in this Act—

(a) relating to the Army Reserve and the Territorial Army, have the same meanings as in the Army Act 1955 ;

(b) relating to the Air Force Reserve and the Royal Auxiliary Air Force, have the same meanings as in the Air Force Act 1955.

(3) This Act, so far as it relates to the military and air forces, PART VIII applies to women as it applies to men.

(4) In this Act—

    (*a*) in relation to the definition of " home defence service " in subsection (1) above, and

    (*b*) for the purposes of sections 10(6), 68(3) and 96(3) above,

service on any flight of which the points of departure and intended return are within the boundaries of the United Kingdom, the Channel Islands, and the Isle of Man, or of the territorial waters of the United Kingdom and those islands, shall be deemed to be service within the United Kingdom notwithstanding that the flight may in its course extend beyond those boundaries.

(5) The expression " magistrates' court ", in the application of this Act—

    (*a*) to Scotland, shall be construed as a reference to the sheriff sitting as a court of summary jurisdiction ;

    (*b*) to Northern Ireland, shall be construed as a reference to a court of summary jurisdiction.

157.—(1) Subject to the saving and transitional provisions Saving and contained in Schedule 8 to this Act— transitional provisions,

    (*a*) the enactments specified in Schedule 9 to this Act have consequential effect subject to the amendments (being amendments amendments consequent on this Act) specified in that Schedule, and repeals. and

    (*b*) the enactments specified in Part I of Schedule 10 to this Act (repeal of obsolete enactments) and those specified in Part II of that Schedule (consequential repeals) are repealed to the extent specified in the third column of that Schedule,

but nothing in Schedule 8 or in Schedule 9 shall be taken as prejudicing the operation of sections 15 to 17 of the Inter- 1978 c. 30. pretation Act 1978 (which relate to the effect of repeals).

(2) Paragraphs 15 to 19 of Schedule 8 contain provisions made transitory by operation of the Reserve Forces Act 1966. 1966 c. 30.

158.—(1) This Act may be cited as the Reserve Forces Act Citation, 1980. extent and

(2) This Act extends to Northern Ireland. commence-
ment.

(3) Her Majesty may by Order in Council direct that any of the provisions of this Act shall extend to the Isle of Man, subject to such exceptions and modifications, if any, as may be specified in the Order.

(4) This Act shall commence on the expiry of the period of one month beginning on the date of its passing.

SCHEDULES

Section 14.

SCHEDULE 1

ADDITIONAL PROVISIONS IN RELATION TO CALL OUT UNDER SPECIAL AGREEMENT

Special agreements

1.—(1) Any agreement for the purposes of section 14 above shall be made with respect to such period of 12 months as may be specified in that agreement and, without prejudice to the making of a further agreement, shall cease to be in force at the expiry of that period.

(2) An agreement for the purposes of section 14 may be revoked at any time by 3 months' notice in writing, but shall not cease to be in force until the expiry of that notice.

Notices

2.—(1) A notice to any person under section 14(1) above shall specify the time and place at which he is to present himself for service in accordance with the notice and may be revoked or varied by a subsequent notice under that subsection.

(2) Any such notice shall be deemed to have been duly served on the person to whom it is directed if—

    (*a*) it is delivered to him personally ; or

    (*b*) it is sent by registered post or the recorded delivery service addressed to him at his latest address known to the military authorities.

Length of call out

3.—(1) The term for which a person may be called out under section 14(1) above shall be such a term (consistent with sub-paragraph (2) below) beginning on such date falling within the period specified in the agreement as may be specified in the notice, whether or not any of that term falls after the date when the agreement ceases to be in force.

(2) Subject to paragraphs 4 to 6 below, the term, or, if more than one, the aggregate of the terms, for which any person is called out for service under section 14(1) in pursuance of any one agreement shall not exceed 6 months.

Calculation of length of service

4. If, in the case of any person, at the time when the term of any service by him under section 14 above would otherwise be completed, that person has become liable to be proceeded against for an offence against the Naval Discipline Act 1957, military law or air-force law, that term shall not be completed until he has been tried or otherwise dealt with for that offence and has undergone any punishment awarded for that offence, or, if at that time punishment for such an offence as is mentioned above has already been awarded, until he has undergone that punishment.

1957 c. 53.

5. In determining in the case of any person the end of any such term as is mentioned in paragraph 4 above no account shall be taken—

> (*a*) in relation to any service under section 14 above, of any day before the day on which that person presented himself in pursuance of the notice to him under section 14(1);
>
> (*b*) of any continuous period exceeding 14 days during which that person was absent as a deserter or absent without leave;
>
> (*c*) of any continuous period exceeding 14 days during which that person—
>
>> (i) was serving, or would if he had not been unlawfully at large have been serving, a term of imprisonment, detention, or detention in a detention centre, or
>>
>> (ii) was detained, or would if he had not been unlawfully at large have been detained, in a borstal institution,
>
> in pursuance of a sentence of a court or an award by his commanding officer or in default of payment of any sum of money or for doing or failing to do or abstain from doing anything required to be done or left undone.

6. If, in the case of any such term as is mentioned in paragraph 4 above, leave of absence is granted to the person in question for a period comprising or immediately following the date on which that term would otherwise be completed, the Defence Council may postpone the completion of that term until a date not later than the expiry of his leave.

Special agreements and the Territorial Army

7. Any notice given by any person under section 98(1) above of his desire to be discharged from the Territorial Army shall be deemed to include notice of revocation of any agreement entered into by that person for the purposes of section 14 above.

8. If the term of any person's enlistment in the Territorial Army expires during the period specified in any agreement entered into by that person for the purposes of section 14 above or during the term of any service by him by virtue of that section, he shall not be entitled to be discharged from the Territorial Army before the expiry of that period or term.

9. Where a member of the Territorial Army has been called out for army service under section 14 above, and if he so desires, there shall be taken, as soon as may be convenient after the end of the term of his service by virtue of that section, all such steps as are necessary to enable him to serve again in the corps and unit of the Territorial Army in which he was serving at the time when he was so called out.

Application of the Army Act 1955

10. In the case of a person who does not for the time being hold a commission—

> (*a*) the provisions of the Army Act 1955 applied by paragraph

(*b*) of section 14(3) above shall not include the proviso to section 3(3) and sections 13, 15, 17, or 18(2) ; and

(*b*) section 9(1) of that Act shall not apply by reason only that the person is serving outside the United Kingdom.

SCHEDULE 2

ARMY AND AIR FORCE PENSIONERS AND OTHER FORMER SOLDIERS NOT LIABLE TO BE RECALLED FOR SERVICE

1. A man in holy orders or a regular minister of any religious denomination.

2. A person who is receiving treatment for mental disorder as an in-patient—

(*a*) in a hospital within the meaning of the Mental Health Act 1959, or

(*b*) in a hospital (other than a private hospital) within the meaning of the Mental Health (Scotland) Act 1960, or

(*c*) in a hospital within the meaning of the Mental Health Act (Northern Ireland) 1961,

or is receiving such treatment as an in-patient in any other place at the expense of a Regional Health Authority, of an Area Health Authority of which the area is in Wales, of a special health authority, or of a Health Board, or, as the case may be, of a Health and Social Services Board in Northern Ireland.

3. A person certified to be registered as a blind person—

(*a*) by a local authority, as defined for the purposes of Part III of the National Assistance Act 1948, under arrangements made by the authority under section 29 of that Act ;

(*b*) by a Health and Social Services Board in Northern Ireland under arrangements made under Article 15(1) of the Health and Personal Social Services (Northern Ireland) Order 1972.

SCHEDULE 3

ENLISTMENT UNDER PART IV OR PART V

Enlistment

1.—(1) A person offering to enlist shall be given a notice in the prescribed form setting out the questions to be answered on attestation and stating the general conditions of the engagement to be entered into by him ; and a recruiting officer shall not enlist any person unless satisfied by that person that he has been given such a notice, understands it and wishes to be enlisted.

(2) The procedure for enlisting a person shall be that set out in paragraph 2 below.

(3) A recruiting officer shall not enlist a person under the appropriate minimum age unless consent to the enlistment has been given in writing—

 (a) if the person offering to enlist is living with both or one of his parents, by the parents or parent ;

 (b) if he is not living with both or one of his parents, but any person (whether a parent or not) whose whereabouts are known or can after reasonable enquiry be ascertained has parental rights and powers in respect of him, by that person ;

 (c) if there is no such person as is mentioned in paragraph (b) of this sub-paragraph or if after reasonable enquiry it cannot be ascertained whether there is any such person, by any person in whose care (whether in law or in fact) the person offering to enlist may be.

(4) Where the recruiting officer is satisfied, by the production of a certified copy of an entry in the register of births or by any other evidence appearing to him to be sufficient, that a person offering to enlist has or has not attained the appropriate minimum age, that person shall be deemed for the purposes of this Act to have attained, or as the case may be, not to have attained, that age.

A document purporting to be a certificate signed by the recruiting officer, stating that he is satisfied as aforesaid, shall be sufficient evidence, until the contrary is proved, that he is so satisfied.

Procedure on attestation

2.—(1) The recruiting officer shall warn the person to be enlisted that if he makes any false answers to the questions to be read out to him he will be liable to be punished as provided by this Act.

(2) He shall then read, or cause to be read, to that person the questions set out in the attestation paper and satisfy himself that he understands each of those questions and that his answers thereto have been duly recorded in the attestation paper.

(3) He shall then ask that person to make and sign the declaration set out in the attestation paper as to the truth of the answers and shall administer to him the oath of allegiance as set out in the attestation paper.

(4) Upon signing the declaration and taking the oath the said person shall become a man of the Army Reserve, the Air Force Reserve, the Territorial Army or the Royal Auxiliary Air Force, as the case may be.

(5) The recruiting officer shall by signature attest, in the manner required by the attestation paper, that the requirements of this Act as to the attestation of the recruit have been carried out and deliver the attestation paper duly dated to such person as may be prescribed by regulations of the Defence Council.

(6) When in accordance with the regulations the recruit is finally approved for service, the officer by whom he is approved shall at his request furnish him with a certified copy of the attestation paper.

Validity of attestation and enlistment

3.—(1) Where a person has signed the declaration required by paragraph 2 above (and in the case of either the Army Reserve or the Air Force Reserve has thereafter received pay as a person of one of those reserves)—

(a) the validity of his enlistment shall not be called in question on the ground of any error or omission in his attestation paper ;

(b) if within 3 months from the date on which he signed the declaration he claims that his enlistment is invalid by reason of any non-compliance with the requirements of this Act as to enlistment or attestation, or any other ground whatsoever (not being an error or omission in his attestation paper) on which apart from this sub-paragraph the validity of his enlistment could have been called in question, the claim shall be submitted as soon as may be to the Defence Council, and if the claim is well founded the Defence Council shall cause him to be discharged with all convenient speed ;

(c) if—

(i) when he signed the declaration he had not attained the appropriate minimum age, and

(ii) within 3 months from the date on which he signed the declaration he, or any person whose consent to the enlistment was required under paragraph 1(3) above but who did not duly consent, claims that his enlistment is invalid by reason of any non-compliance with the requirements of this Act as to enlistment or attestation, or any other ground whatsoever (not being an error or omission in his attestation paper) on which apart from this sub-paragraph the validity of his enlistment could have been called in question,

the claim shall be submitted as soon as may be to the Defence Council, and if the claim is well founded the Defence Council shall cause him to be discharged with all convenient speed ;

(d) subject to the provisions of paragraphs (b) and (c) above, he shall be deemed as from the expiry of the said 3 months to have been validly enlisted notwithstanding any such non-compliance or other grounds as aforesaid ;

(e) notwithstanding any such non-compliance or other grounds as aforesaid, or the making of a claim in pursuance of paragraph (b) or paragraph (c) above, he shall be deemed to be a man of the Army Reserve, the Air Force Reserve, the Territorial Army, or the Royal Auxiliary Air Force, as the case may be, until his discharge.

(2) Where a person has received pay as a man of the Army Reserve or the Air Force Reserve, as the case may be, without having previously signed the declaration required by paragraph 2, then—

(a) he shall be deemed to be a man of the Army Reserve or the Air Force Reserve, as the case may be, until discharged;

(b) he may claim his discharge at any time, and if he does so the claim shall be submitted as soon as may be to the

Defence Council, who shall cause him to be discharged with all convenient speed.

(3) Nothing in this paragraph shall be construed as prejudicing the determination of any question as to the term for which a person was enlisted or as preventing the discharge of a person who has not claimed his discharge.

False answers in attestation papers

4.—(1) If a person appearing before a recruiting officer for the purpose of being attested, knowingly makes a false answer to any question contained in the attestation paper and put to him by or by the direction of the recruiting officer, he shall be liable on summary conviction to imprisonment for a term not exceeding 3 months or to a fine not exceeding £20.

(2) A person may be proceeded against under sub-paragraph (1) above notwithstanding that he has since become subject to military law or to air-force law, as the case may be.

(3) Any person who—

(a) when before a recruiting officer for the purpose of being attested in pursuance of this Act,

(b) knowingly makes a false answer to any question contained in the attestation paper and put to him by or by the direction of the recruiting officer,

shall be, if he has since become and remains subject to military law or to air-force law, as the case may be, liable on conviction by court-martial to the like imprisonment as on summary conviction of an offence against sub-paragraph (1) above or to any less punishment provided by the Army Act 1955 or by the Air Force Act 1955, as the case may be.

Evidence as to attestation papers

5. With respect to evidence in proceedings under Part IV or Part V of this Act, whether before a court-martial, a civil court or otherwise—

(a) a document purporting to be a copy of the attestation paper signed by any person and to be certified to be a true copy by a person stated in the certificate to have the custody of the attestation paper shall be evidence of the enlistment of the person attested ;

(b) the attestation paper purporting to be signed by a person on his enlistment shall be evidence of his having given the answers to questions which he is recorded in that paper as having given.

Interpretation of Schedule 3

6. In this Schedule—

" appropriate minimum age " means the age of 17 years and 6 months, except that in such classes of case as may be prescribed it means the age of 17 years ;

" prescribed " means precribed by regulations made under Part I of the Army Act 1955 or Part I of the Air Force Act 1955, as the case may be.

Section 72.

SCHEDULE 4

TERRITORIES IN WHICH PERSONS MAY NOT BE ENLISTED INTO THE ARMY RESERVE OR THE AIR FORCE RESERVE

Canada

Australia

New Zealand

Sections 73 and 106.

SCHEDULE 5

DESERTERS AND ABSENTEES WITHOUT LEAVE UNDER PART IV OR PART V

Arrest of deserters and absentees without leave

1.—(1) A constable may arrest any person whom he has reasonable cause to suspect of being an officer or man of the reserve forces (that is, in this Schedule, an officer or man of the Army Reserve, Air Force Reserve, Territorial Army and Royal Auxiliary Air Force) who has deserted or is absent without leave.

(2) Where no constable is available, any officer, warrant officer, non-commissioned officer or soldier of the regular forces, or airman of the regular air force, or any other person, may arrest any person whom he has reasonable cause to suspect of having deserted or being absent without leave as mentioned in sub-paragraph (1) above.

(3) Any person having authority to issue a warrant for the arrest of a person charged with crime, if satisfied by evidence on oath that there is, or is reasonably suspected of being, within his jurisdiction an officer or man of the reserve forces who has deserted or is absent without leave or is reasonably suspected of having deserted or being absent without leave, may issue a warrant authorising his arrest.

(4) Any person in custody in pursuance of this paragraph shall as soon as practicable be brought before a magistrates' court.

(5) This paragraph shall have effect in the United Kingdom and in any colony.

Proceedings before a civil court where persons suspected of illegal absence

2.—(1) Where a person who is brought before a magistrates' court is alleged to be an officer or man of the reserve forces who has deserted or is absent without leave, the following provisions shall have effect.

(2) If he admits that he is illegally absent from the reserve forces and the court is satisfied of the truth of the admission, then—

    (*a*) unless he is in custody for some other cause the court shall, and

    (*b*) notwithstanding that he is in custody for some other cause, the court may, forthwith either cause him to be delivered into military or air-force custody, as the case may be, in such manner as the court may think fit or commit him to some prison, police station or other place provided for the confinement of persons in custody, to be kept there for such reasonable time as the court may specify (not exceeding such time as appears to the court reasonably necessary for the purpose of enabling him to be delivered into military or air-force custody, as the case may be) or until sooner delivered into such custody.

Any time specified by the court may be extended by the court from time to time if it appears to the court reasonably necessary so to do for the purpose aforesaid.

(3) If he does not admit that he is illegally absent as aforesaid, or the court is not satisfied of the truth of the admission, the court shall consider the evidence and any statement of the accused, and if satisfied that he is subject to military law or air-force law, as the case may be, and if of opinion that there is sufficient evidence to justify his being tried under this Act for an offence of desertion or absence without leave then, unless he is in custody for some other cause, the court shall cause him to be delivered into military or air-force custody, as the case may be, or commit him as aforesaid, but otherwise shall discharge him:

Provided that if he is in custody for some other cause the court shall have power, but shall not be required, to act in accordance with this sub-paragraph.

(4) The following provisions of the Magistrates' Courts Act 1952 1952 c. 55. or any corresponding enactment in force as respects the court in question, that is to say the provisions relating to the constitution and procedure of magistrates' courts acting as examining justices and conferring powers of adjournment and remand on such courts so acting, and the provisions as to evidence and the issue and enforcement of summonses or warrants to secure the attendance of witnesses, shall apply to any proceedings under this paragraph.

(5) This paragraph shall have effect in the United Kingdom and in any colony.

Deserters and absentees without leave surrendering to police

3.—(1) Where in the United Kingdom or any colony a person surrenders himself to a constable as being illegally absent from the reserve forces, the constable shall (unless he surrenders himself at a police station) bring him to a police station.

(2) The officer of police in charge of a police station at which a person has surrendered himself as aforesaid, or to which a person who has so surrendered himself is brought, shall forthwith inquire into the case and if it appears to that officer that the said person is illegally absent as aforesaid he may cause him to be delivered into military or air-force custody, as the case may be, without bringing him before a magistrates' court or may bring him before such a court.

Certificates of arrest or surrender of deserters and absentees

4.—(1) Where a magistrates' court in pursuance of paragraph 2 above deals with a person as illegally absent, then when that person is delivered into military or air-force custody, as the case may be, there shall be handed over with him a certificate in the prescribed form, signed by a justice of the peace, containing the prescribed particulars as to his arrest or surrender and the proceedings before the court ; and for any such certificate there shall be payable to the clerk of the court, by such person as the Defence Council may direct, such fee (if any) as may be prescribed.

(2) Where under sub-paragraph (1) above, a person is delivered into military or air-force custody without being brought before a court, there shall be handed over with him a certificate in the prescribed form, signed by the officer of police who causes him to be delivered into custody, containing the prescribed particulars relating to his surrender.

(3) In any proceedings for an offence under section 73(1) above or section 106(1) above—

(a) a document purporting to be a certificate under either sub-paragraph (1) or (2) above and to be signed as thereby required, shall be evidence of the matters stated in the document ;

(b) where the proceedings are against a person who has been taken into military, naval or air-force custody on arrest or surrender, a certificate purporting to be signed by a provost officer, or any corresponding officer of a Commonwealth force or a force raised under the law of a colony, or by any other officer in charge of the guardroom or other place where that person was confined on being taken into custody, stating the fact, date, time and place of arrest or surrender shall be evidence of the matters stated in the certificate.

(4) In this paragraph the expression " prescribed " means prescribed by regulations made by the Secretary of State by statutory instrument under section 189 of the Army Act 1955 or section 189 of the Air Force Act 1955, as the case may be.

1955 c. 18.
1955 c. 19.

Duties of governors of prisons and others to receive
deserters and absentees

5.—(1) It shall be the duty of the governor of a civil prison in the United Kingdom or the superintendent or other person in charge of a civil prison in a colony to receive any person duly committed to that prison by a magistrates' court as illegally absent from the reserve forces and to detain him until in accordance with the directions of the court he is delivered into military or air-force custody, as the case may be.

(2) Sub-paragraph (1) above shall apply to the person having charge of any police station or other place (not being a prison) provided for the confinement of persons in custody, whether in the United Kingdom or in a colony, as it applies to the governor or superintendent of a prison.

SCHEDULE 6

EVIDENCE UNDER PART IV OR PART V

General provisions as to evidence

1.—(1) The following provisions of this paragraph shall have effect with respect to evidence in proceedings under Part IV or Part V of this Act, whether before a court-martial, a civil court or otherwise.

(2) A letter, return or other document stating that any person—

(a) was or was not serving at any specified time or during any specified period in any part of Her Majesty's forces or was discharged from any part of those forces at or before any specified time, or

(b) held or did not hold at any specified time any specified rank or appointment in any of those forces, or had at or before any specified time been attached, posted or transferred to any part of those forces, or at any specified time or during any specified period was or was not serving or held or did not hold any rank or appointment in any particular country or place, or

(c) was or was not at any specified time authorised to use or wear any decoration, badge, wound stripe or emblem,

shall, if purporting to be issued by or on behalf of the Defence Council or by a person authorised by them, be evidence of the matters stated in the document.

(3) A record made in any service book or other document prescribed by Queen's Regulations for the purposes of this sub-paragraph, being a record made in pursuance of any Act or of Queen's Regulations, or otherwise in pursuance of military or air-force duty, as the case may be, and purporting to be signed by the commanding officer or by any person whose duty it was to make the record, shall be evidence of the facts stated therein.

(4) A copy of a record (including the signature thereto) in any such book or other document as aforesaid, purporting to be certified to be a true copy by a person stated in the certificate to have the custody of the book or other document, shall be evidence of the record.

(5) A document purporting to be issued by order of the Defence Council and to contain instructions or regulations given or made by the Defence Council shall be evidence of the giving of the instructions or making of the regulations and of their contents.

(6) A certificate purporting to be issued by or on behalf of the Defence Council or by a person authorised by them, and stating—

(a) that a decoration of a description specified in or annexed to the certificate is a military, naval or air force decoration, or

(b) that a badge, wound stripe or emblem of a description specified in or annexed to the certificate is one supplied or authorised by the Defence Council,

shall be evidence of the matters stated in the certificate.

(7) A certificate purporting to be signed by a person's commanding officer or any officer authorised by him to give the certificate, and stating the contents of, or of any part of, standing orders or other routine orders of a continuing nature made for—

(a) any formation or unit or body of troops, or

(b) any formation or unit or body of the air force, or

(c) any command or other area, garrison or place, or

(d) any ship, train or aircraft,

shall in proceedings against the said person be evidence of the matters stated in the certificate.

(8) Where, in relation to one of the Army Reserve, the Air Force Reserve, the Territorial Army or the Royal Auxiliary Air Force, any document would be evidence in any proceedings under Part IV or Part V of this Act by virtue of this paragraph, or paragraph 5 of Schedule 3 to this Act, that document shall—

(a) in like manner,

(b) subject to the same conditions, and

(c) for the like purpose,

be evidence in the like proceedings in relation to any other of the Army Reserve, Air Force Reserve, Territorial Army or the Royal Auxiliary Air Force.

Proof of outcome of civil trial

2.—(1) Where a person subject to military law or to air-force law has been tried before a civil court (whether at the time of the trial he was or was not subject to military law or air-force law, as the case may be), a certificate signed by the clerk of the court and stating all or any of the following matters—

(a) that the said person has been tried before the court for an offence specified in the certificate,

(b) the result of the trial,

(c) what judgment or order was given or made by the court,

(d) that other offences specified in the certificate were taken into consideration at the trial,

shall for the purposes of Part IV or Part V of this Act be evidence of the matters stated in the certificate.

(2) The clerk of the court shall, if required by the commanding officer of the person in question or any other officer, furnish a certificate under this paragraph and shall be paid such fee as may be prescribed by regulations made by the Secretary of State under

1955 c. 18.   section 199 of the Army Act 1955 or section 199 of the Air Force
1955 c. 19.   Act 1955, as the case may be.

(3) A document purporting to be a certificate under this paragraph and to be signed by the clerk of the court shall, unless the contrary is shown, be deemed to be such a certificate.

(4) References in this paragraph to the clerk of the court include references to his deputy and to any other person having the custody of the records of the court.

SCHEDULE 7

PROVISIONS OF SCHEMES FOR THE CONSTITUTION OF ASSOCIATIONS

1. A scheme for the constitution of an association shall provide—

   (a) for the date of the establishment of the association ;

   (b) for the incorporation of the association by an appropriate name ;

   (c) for appointment as members of the association of military members and air force members the aggregate number of such members to be not less than half of the whole number of members of the association ;

   (d) for the appointment as members of the association by the Defence Council, after consultation with, and on the recommendation of, the bodies to be represented, of representatives of such of the local authorities wholly or partly within the area for which the association is established as the Defence Council may from time to time determine ;

   (e) for the mode of appointment, dismissal, term of office and rotation of members of the association and the filling of casual vacancies ;

   (f) for the election of a chairman and a vice-chairman or vice-chairmen by the association and for defining their powers and duties ;

   (g) for the appointment by the association, subject to the approval of the Defence Council, of a secretary and other officers and members of the staff of the association provided that a secretary or other officer or member of the staff who is in the employment of the association by virtue of the provisions of an order made by the Defence Council in exercise of the powers conferred upon the Defence Council by subsection (4) of section 122 above shall be deemed for the purpose of this provision in the scheme to have been appointed by the association ;

   (h) for the procedure to be adopted, including the appointment of committees and the delegation to committees of any of the powers or duties of the association ;

   (i) for enabling general or air officers of any part of Her Majesty's forces, or officers deputed by them, to attend the meetings of the association, and to speak but not to vote.

2. A scheme for the constitution of an association other than an association established for an area including Greater London shall provide—

   (a) for constituting as president of the association the lord-lieutenant of one of the counties or parts of counties for which the association is established, as the Defence Council may from time to time think fit, or, failing any of those lord-lieutenants, such other person as the Defence Council may think fit, and

(b) for constituting as vice-presidents of the association the lord-lieutenants of any of those counties or parts of counties in any case where they are not president of the association and are willing to act as vice presidents.

3. A scheme for the establishment of an association in Scotland shall provide—

(a) in the case where an association area coincides with a region or where a region contains two or more association areas, for the selection by the Defence Council of the president and vice-presidents of the association from the lord-lieutenants residing in the region or from such other persons as the Defence Council may think fit ; or

(b) in the case where an association area falls within two or more regions, for the selection by the Defence Council of the president and vice-presidents of the association from the lord-lieutenants residing in those regions or from such other persons as the Defence Council may think fit.

4. A scheme for the constitution of an association established for an area including Greater London shall provide for constituting the lord-lieutenant of Greater London or, failing him, such other person as the Defence Council may think fit, president of the association.

5. A scheme for the constitution of an association may provide—

(a) for the appointment as members of the association by the Defence Council, of representatives of universities whose activities are carried on wholly or partly within the area for which the association is established ;

(b) for the appointment as members of the association by the Defence Council, of persons representing the Army Cadet Force, the Air Training Corps, the Combined Cadet Force and the Sea Cadet Corps ;

(c) for the appointment as members of the association by the Defence Council, of persons representing employers in and persons employed in the area for which the association is established ;

(d) for the appointment of co-opted members ;

(e) for dividing the area for which the association is established into two or more parts and for establishing sub-associations for any of the parts and for delegating to a sub-association such of the powers and duties of the association as may be approved by the Defence Council and regulating the relations of a sub-association to the association and, where any association has established more than one sub-association, regulating the relations of one sub-association to another.

6. A scheme shall provide that of the chairman and the vice-chairman or vice-chairman at least one shall be a military member

of the association and at least one an air force member of **the** association.

7. A scheme may contain any consequential, supplemental, or transitory provisions which may appear to be necessary or proper for the purposes of the scheme, and also as respects any matter for which provision may be made by regulations under this Act and for which it appears desirable to make special provision affecting the association established by the scheme.

8.—(1) A scheme for the constitution of an association established for an area including or including any part of the counties of Kent and Sussex may provide that the Lord Warden of the Cinque Ports shall ex-officio be a member of the association.

(2) A scheme for the constitution of an association established for an area including or including any part of the counties of Devon and Cornwall may provide that the Warden of the Stannaries shall ex-officio be a member of the association.

(3) The Governor or Deputy Governor of the Isle of Wight shall ex-officio be a member of an association established for an area including the Isle of Wight.

(4) The Lord Mayor of the City of London shall ex-officio be president of a sub-association establishment for the City of London.

(5) In this Schedule—

" air force member " means one who is a member or former member of Her Majesty's air forces or who is specially qualified by his interest in and knowledge of matters relating to aviation ;

" military member " means one who is a member or former member of Her Majesty's military forces.

SCHEDULE 8

Section 157.

SAVING AND TRANSITIONAL PROVISIONS

General

1. References in paragraph (*b*) of section 17(2) of the Interpretation Act 1978 to subordinate legislation made or other thing done under enactments repealed and re-enacted by this Act shall be construed as including references to subordinate legislation or other thing having effect as if made or done by virtue of— *1978 c. 30.*

   (*a*) the Army Reserve Act 1950 section 29(4) ;   *1950 c. 32.*
   (*b*) the Air Force Reserve Act 1950 section 30(4) ;   *1950 c. 33.*
   (*c*) the Auxiliary Forces Act 1953 section 46(2).   *1953 c. 50.*

2. Where any period of time specified in an enactment repealed by this Act is current at the commencement of this Act, this Act has effect as if the corresponding provision of the Act had been in force when that period began to run.

Part I   H

SCH. 8   3. The repeal of an enactment by this Act does not affect the operation of that enactment in relation to any offence committed before the commencement of the Act.

4. A conviction for an offence under an enactment repealed by this Act shall be treated for the purposes of the Act as a conviction for an offence under the corresponding provision of the Act.

Saving of amendments

5.—(1) The amendments made—

1966 c. 30.   (a) by section 23(6) of, and paragraph 32 of Schedule 1 to, the Reserve Forces Act 1966, and

1973 c. 34.   (b) by section 1(3) of the Ulster Defence Regiment Act 1973, shall continue in force, notwithstanding the repeal by this Act of the amending provisions.

(2) The Territorial Army and the Royal Marine Forces Volunteer Reserve shall continue to be known respectively as the Territorial and Army Volunteer Reserve and the Royal Marines Reserve, and references to that army or marine volunteer reserve in any enactment or instrument shall continue to be construed accordingly.

1955 c. 18.   (3) In section 210(2)(b) of the Army Act 1955 the reference to actual service shall continue to be construed as including a reference to permanent service in the marine forces in pursuance of section 11(1) above.

Permanent service in naval and marine reserves

1859 c. 40.   6. Any reference in any enactment to actual service under section 4 of the Royal Naval Reserve (Volunteer) Act 1859 shall be construed as a reference to permanent service in the naval or marine forces by virtue of section 10(1) above.

Militia storehouses

1921 c. 37.   7.—(1) Notwithstanding the repeal by this Act of section 4 of the Territorial Army and Militia Act 1921, any enactment repealed by that Act which related to militia storehouses shall continue to apply in relation to militia storehouses provided before the commencement of that Act as though that Act and this Act had not been passed.

In this sub-paragraph " militia storehouses " means any building or premises provided for keeping in them the arms, accoutrements, clothing and other stores belonging to any regiment, battalion or corps of militia, when not embodied.

(2) Any moneys—

(a) which have been paid to and invested by or shall be paid to the proper officer of a county council on account of the proceeds of the sale of any place provided for keeping militia stores, and

1854 c. 105.   (b) which are not required for the purposes of the Militia Law Amendment Act 1854, may be applied to any of the purposes to which money raised on the security of the county rate or stock is applicable or it may be invested in any security in which trustees may by law invest trust moneys, and the interest applied in aid of the county rate or stock, as shall be directed by the county council.

Enlistment in the Territorial Army or Royal Auxiliary Air Force prior to order or regulation under Auxiliary Forces Act 1953   1953 c. 50.

8. Where a man—

(a) is a member of the Territorial Army or the Royal Auxiliary Air Force, and

(b) was enlisted before the date of any order or regulation under the Auxiliary Forces Act 1953,

nothing in any order or regulation made under any provision of that Act or made or having effect under a corresponding provision of this Act shall render him liable without his consent to be appointed, transferred or attached to any military or air force body to which he could not without his consent have been appointed, transferred or attached if that order or regulation had not been made.

Reserve of officers maintained under section 11(4) of Auxiliary Forces Act 1953

9. In relation to the Reserve Forces Act 1966—   1966 c. 30

(a) the provisions of section 3(2) of that Act (which abolished reserve divisions of the Territorial Army Reserve), and

(b) the repeal by that Act of section 11(7) of the Auxiliary Forces Act 1953,

do not affect any reserve of officers maintained in pursuance of that section 11(7) immediately before 9th August 1966, but any such reserve may be abolished by order of Her Majesty signified under the hand of the Secretary of State.

Transfers to reserve under Army Act and Air Force Act

10. In this Act—

(a) references to the Army Act 1955 in connection with transfers 1955 c. 18. to the reserve include such transfers under the Army Act ;

(b) references to the Air Force Act 1955 in connection with 1955 c. 19. transfers to the reserve include such transfers under the Air Force Act.

Modifications of other enactments

11. Without prejudice to section 152(2) above—

(a) any reference in any enactment to, or to provisions which include, section 5 of the Army Reserve Act 1950 or section 1950 c. 32. 5 of the Air Force Reserve Act 1950 or to a proclamation 1950 c. 33. ordering the calling out of the Army Reserve or the Air Force Reserve under those sections shall be construed respectively as, or as including, a reference to section 10 above or to an order authorising the calling out of the Army Reserve or the Air Force Reserve under that section 10 ;

(*b*) any reference in any enactment to the embodying or dis-embodying of the Territorial Army or the Royal Auxiliary Air Force or any part or member of that reserve or force shall be construed—

(i) in relation to a member of the Territorial Army, as a reference to his being called into, or released from, service by virtue of section 10(1) or section 11(1) above;

(ii) in relation to a member of the Royal Auxiliary Air Force, as a reference to his being called into, or released from, service by virtue of section 10(1).

Naval and Marine Reserves Pay Act 1957

12. Notwithstanding the repeal by this Act of the references to—

(*a*) officers and men of the Royal Naval Volunteer Reserve, and

(*b*) officers and men of the Royal Naval Special Reserve,

1957 c. 32.

in Schedule 1 to the Naval and Marine Reserves Pay Act 1957, those officers and men described in paragraphs (*a*) and (*b*) above shall be deemed to be among those described in subsection (2) of section 59 above for the purposes of that section.

The lieutenancies in England and Wales

13.—(1) Any reference to a lieutenant of a county or of Greater London—

(*a*) in any enactment passed before the end of the session in which the Local Government Act 1972 was passed, or

1972 c. 70.

(*b*) in any instrument made before the passing of that Act,

shall be construed as a reference to the lord-lieutenant of a county or of Greater London, as the case may be.

(2) Where immediately before 1st April 1974—

(*a*) any lieutenant held office, Her Majesty may by Order in Council provide that he shall continue to hold office on and after that date as a lord-lieutenant or as a lieutenant of a new county or Greater London, according as may be specified in the Order;

(*b*) any deputy lieutenant held office outside Greater London, he shall continue to hold office on and after that date as deputy lieutenant of the new county in which he resides or such other new county as may be specified in an order made by the Secretary of State.

In this sub-paragraph—

(i) nothing prejudices any power of removal or of directing removal from any office; and

(ii) "Greater London" does not include the City of London or the Inner Temple and the Middle Temple; and

(iii) "new county" has the meaning given by the Local Government Act 1972.

The lieutenancies in Scotland

14.—(1) Any reference to a lieutenant of a county in Scotland—

(*a*) in any enactment passed before the end of the session in which the Local Government (Scotland) Act 1973 was 1973 c. 65. passed, or

(*b*) in any instrument made before the passing of that Act,

shall be construed as a reference to the lord-lieutenant holding office for an area by virtue of section 131 above.

(2) Where immediately before 16th May 1975—

(*a*) any lieutenant held office in Scotland, Her Majesty may by Order in Council provide that he shall continue to hold office on and after that date as lord-lieutenant for such part of a region as may be specified in the Order or for an islands area ;

(*b*) any deputy lieutenant held office in Scotland, he shall continue to hold office on and after that date as deputy lieutenant of the part of the region, islands area or district of the city in which he resides or of such other area as may be specified in an order made by the Secretary of State.

Nothing in this sub-paragraph prejudices any power of removal or of directing removal from any office.

Permanent service call out of special class of Royal Fleet Reserve otherwise than under section 11

15.—(1) Where section 11 above does not apply to a man of the special class of the Royal Fleet Reserve he is liable during the whole of his service in that class of the reserve to be called out for permanent service at any time when warlike operations are in preparation or in progress outside the United Kingdom (including the Channel Islands and the Isle of Man), but this sub-paragraph—

(*a*) does not make the man liable to serve for a period or periods exceeding 12 months in all without his written consent,

(*b*) is without prejudice to any liability imposed on the man by section 16(1) above,

and any exercise of the power under this sub-paragraph to call men out for permanent service shall be reported to Parliament forthwith.

(2) The provisions of sub-paragraph (1) above are in addition to, and not in substitution for, the provisions of any other enactment under which officers or men of—

(*a*) the Royal Naval Reserve and the Royal Fleet Reserve, and

(*b*) the Royal Marines Reserve,

are liable to be called out for permanent service.

Permanent service call out of Army Reserve and Air Force Reserve otherwise than under section 11

16.—(1) Where section 11 above does not apply to a man—

(*a*) who enlisted in the regular forces within the meaning of the Army Act 1955 before 27th February 1964, and   1955 c. 18.

H 3

Sch. 8
1955 c. 18.
1961 c. 52.
1966 c. 45.

(*b*) who was transferred to the Army Reserve in pursuance of—

   (i) the Army Act 1955, or

   (ii) the Army and Air Force Act 1961, or

   (iii) regulations under section 2 of the Armed Forces Act 1966, and

(*c*) who on his transfer was designated by the competent military authority as a man to whom this provision applies,

he is liable to be called out for permanent service on overseas service at any time during the first year of his service in the Army Reserve.

(2) Where section 11 does not apply to a man—

(*a*) who enlisted in the regular forces within the meaning of the Army Act 1955 after 26th February 1964, and

(*b*) who was transferred to the Army Reserve in pursuance of—

   (i) the Army Act 1955, or

   (ii) the Army and Air Force Act 1961, or

   (iii) regulations under section 2 of the Armed Forces Act 1966, and

(*c*) who on his transfer was designated by the competent military authority as subject to this provision for a specified period not exceeding 3 years beginning with the beginning of his service in the Army Reserve,

he is liable to be called out for permanent service on overseas service at any time during that period.

(3) Where section 11 does not apply to a man of the Army Reserve, that man, whether he entered the reserve—

(*a*) on transfer, or

(*b*) on re-engagement, or

(*c*) on being enlisted or on being deemed to be enlisted,

shall, if he has entered into a written agreement (which may be revoked by 3 months' written notice) to be so liable at the time in question, be liable at any time during his service in that reserve to be called out for permanent service on overseas service.

This sub-paragraph is without prejudice to sub-paragraphs (1) and (2) above.

(4) Where section 11 does not apply to a man—

1955 c. 19.

(*a*) who enlisted in the regular air force within the meaning of the Air Force Act 1955 before 27th February 1964, and

(*b*) who was transferred to the Air Force Reserve in pursuance of—

   (i) the Air Force Act 1955, or

   (ii) the Army and Air Force Act 1961, or

   (iii) regulations under section 2 of the Armed Forces Act 1966, and (*c*) who on his transfer was designated by the competent air force authority as a man to whom this provision applies,

he is liable to be called out for permanent service on overseas service at any time during the first year of his service in the Air Force Reserve.

(5) Where section 11 does not apply to a man—

(*a*) who enlisted in the regular air force within the meaning of the Air Force Act 1955 after 26th February 1964, and

(*b*) who was transferred to the Air Force Reserve in pursuance of—

(i) the Air Force Act 1955, or 1955 c. 19.

(ii) the Army and Air Force Act 1961, or 1961 c. 52.

(iii) regulations under section 2 of the Armed Forces 1966 c. 45. Act 1966, and

(*c*) who on his transfer was designated by the competent air force authority as subject to this provision for a specified period not exceeding 3 years beginning with the beginning of his service in the Air Force Reserve,

he is liable to be called out for permanent service on overseas service at any time during that period.

(6) Where section 11 does not apply to a man of the Air Force Reserve, that man, whether he entered the reserve—

(*a*) on transfer, or

(*b*) on re-engagement, or

(*c*) on being enlisted or on being deemed to be enlisted,

shall, if he has entered into a written agreement (which may be revoked by 3 months' written notice) to be so liable at the time in question, be liable at any time during his service in that reserve to be called out for permanent service on overseas service.

This sub-paragraph is without prejudice to sub-paragraphs (1) and (2) above.

(7) A man shall not without his written consent be liable to serve under sub-paragraphs (1) to (6) above for a period which, together with any previous period for which he was called out under any of those sub-paragraphs, exceeds 12 months.

(8) Any exercise of the power of calling out men under this paragraph shall be reported to Parliament forthwith.

(9) The number of men for the time being called out under any of the provisions of this paragraph shall not be reckoned in the numbers for the time being authorised by Parliament for the regular forces or for the regular air force.

(10) In this paragraph " overseas service " means service when the men in question are required for service outside the United Kingdom when warlike operations are in preparation or progress ; and the reference to the United Kingdom in this sub-paragraph shall be construed as if that expression included the Channel Islands and the Isle of Man.

Call out for training of Army Reserve and Air Force Reserve otherwise than under section 38

17.—(1) Where section 38 above does not apply to a man of the Army Reserve he may be called out for annual training—

(*a*) at such time or times, and

(*b*) at such place or places within the United Kingdom, and

(*c*) for such period or periods,

as may be prescribed, but he is not liable to be called out under this sub-paragraph in any one year for more than 12 days or 20 drills.

(2) Such a man may, during any period of training for which he may be called out, be attached to and trained with any body of the regular or auxiliary forces.

(3) Where section 38 does not apply to a man of the Air Force Reserve he may be called out for annual training—

(*a*) at such time or times, and

(*b*) at such place or places within the United Kingdom, and

(*c*) for such period or periods,

as may be prescribed.

(4) The period or periods so prescribed shall not exceed in any one year—

(*a*) 24 days in the case of a man who is serving as a qualified pilot or as a qualified navigator ;

(*b*) 6 months in the case of a man who is undergoing instruction with a view to his qualifying for service as a pilot or navigator ;

(*c*) 12 days or 20 drills or instructional parades in the case of any other man.

In this sub-paragraph " navigator " includes " observer ", and " qualified " means qualified in accordance with orders or regulations made under the provisions of this Act relating to the Air Force Reserve.

(5) A man of the Air Force Reserve may, during any period of training for which he may be called out or which he may be required to undergo, be attached to and trained with any body of the regular or auxiliary air force.

(6) Sub-paragraphs (3) to (5) above are subject to the provisions of this Act relating to special reservists.

Call out for training of Territorial Army otherwise than under section 38

18.—(1) Where section 38 above does not apply to a man of the Territorial Army—

(*a*) he shall during the first year of his original enlistment be subject to any requirements as to preliminary training provided for under section 40 above in the same way as a man of the Royal Auxiliary Air Force and he shall attend the number of drills and fulfil the other conditions prescribed for a recruit of his arm or branch of the Territorial Army accordingly ;

(*b*) he shall by way of annual training be trained for not less than 8 or more than 15 days (or, for the mounted branch,

18 days) in every year at such times and at such places within the United Kingdom as may be prescribed, and may for that purpose be called out once or more often in every year. Sch. 8

(2) A man mentioned in sub-paragraph (1)(*b*) above shall (subject to the provisions of this paragraph) attend the number of drills and fulfil the other conditions relating to training prescribed for his arm or branch of the Territorial Army.

(3) The requirements of this paragraph as to annual training may be dispensed with in whole or in part—

(*a*) as respects any unit of the Territorial Army, by the prescribed general officer, and

(*b*) as respects an individual man of the Territorial Army, by his commanding officer subject to any general directions of the prescribed general officer.

(4) Her Majesty may by Order in Council made in relation to any man of the Territorial Army to whom this paragraph applies direct—

(*a*) that the period of annual training in any year shall be extended to such period not exceeding 30 days as may be specified in the Order ; or

(*b*) that the period of annual training in any year shall be reduced to such period as to Her Majesty may seem fit, or

(*c*) that the annual training in any year shall be dispensed with.

(5) Nothing in this paragraph shall be construed as preventing a man with his own consent, in addition to any other training, being called up for the purpose of duty or instruction in accordance with orders and regulations under this Act relating to the Territorial Army.

Election for section 38 to apply

19. A person who immediately before 1st January 1967 was a man of the regular army or the regular air force may elect irrevocably in the prescribed manner that, on his becoming a member of the Army Reserve or the Air Force Reserve, he shall be a person to whom section 38 above applies.

Section 12 of Social Security (Miscellaneous Provisions) Act 1977 — 1977 c. 5.

20. Where section 12 of the Social Security (Miscellaneous Provisions) Act 1977 applied immediately before the commencement of this Act to any provision which is repealed and re-enacted by this Act that section continues to apply to that provision as so re-enacted as it applied immediately before that commencement.

SCHEDULE 9

Section 157.

CONSEQUENTIAL AMENDMENTS
ACTS

Home Guard Act 1951

1951 c. 8.

1. In section 2 of the Home Guard Act 1951 for " section 5(1) or the Reserve Forces Act 1966 " substitute " section 10(1) of the Reserve Forces Act 1980 ".

Army Act 1955

2. In section 211 of the Army Act 1955—

(*a*) in subsection (4), for " the Army Reserve Act 1950, or the Auxiliary Forces Act, 1953," substitute " the Reserve Forces Act 1980 " ; and

(*b*) in subsection (5), for " section 5(1) or section 6(1) of the Reserve Forces Act 1966 " substitute " section 10(1) or section 11(1) of the Reserve Forces Act 1980 ".

3. In section 225(2) of the Army Act 1955—

(*a*) for " section 5 of the Reserve Forces Act 1966 " substitute " section 10 of the Reserve Forces Act 1980 " ; and

(*b*) for " section 6(1)(*b*) or (*c*) of the Army Reserve Act 1950 or section 6 of the Reserve Forces Act 1966 " substitute " section 11 of or paragraph 16(1) or (2) or (3) of Schedule 8 to the Reserve Forces Act 1980 ".

4. In paragraph 4A(8) of Schedule 7 to the Army Act 1955 for " section 10(1) of the Auxiliary and Reserve Forces Act 1949 " substitute " section 16(1) of the Reserve Forces Act 1980 ".

Air Force Act 1955

5. In section 210 of the Air Force Act 1955—

(*a*) in subsection (4) for " the Air Force Reserve Act, 1950, or the Auxiliary Forces Act, 1953," substitute " the Reserve Forces Act 1980 " ; and

(*b*) in subsection (5), for " section 5(1) of the Reserve Forces Act 1966 " substitute " section 10(1) of the Reserve Forces Act 1980 ".

6. In section 223(2) of the Air Force Act 1955—

(*a*) for " section 5 of the Reserve Forces Act 1966 " substitute " section 10 of the Reserve Forces Act 1980 " ; and

(*b*) for " section 6(1)(*b*) or (*c*) of the Air Force Reserve Act 1950 or section 6 of the Reserve Forces Act 1966 " substitute " section 11 of or paragraph 16(4) or (5) or (6) of Schedule 8 to the Reserve Forces Act 1980 "

Naval Discipline Act 1957

7. In section 111(4) of the Naval Discipline Act 1957, for " section sixteen of the Naval Volunteers Act 1853," substitute " section 30(1) of the Reserve Forces Act 1980 ".

London Government Act 1963

8. In section 84(3) of the London Government Act 1963—

(*a*) for " section 2 of the Auxiliary Forces Act 1953," substitute " section 121 of the Reserve Forces Act 1980 " ; and

(*b*) for " said Act of 1953 " substitute " said Act of 1980 ".

Contracts of Employment and Redundancy Payments Act   SCH. 9
(Northern Ireland) 1965

9. In paragraph 11A(3) of Schedule 1 to the Contracts of Employ- ment and Redundancy Payments Act (Northern Ireland) 1965 for " the Auxiliary Forces Act 1953 " substitute " Part VI of the Reserve Forces Act 1980 ".

1965 c. 19.
(N.I.)

Armed Forces Act 1966   1966 c. 45.

10. In section 4(9) of the Armed Forces Act 1966 for " section 10(1) of the Auxiliary and Reserve Forces Act 1949 " substitute " section 16(1) of the Reserve Forces Act 1980 ".

Pensions (Increase) Act 1971   1971 c. 56.

11. In paragraph 37 of Part I of Schedule 2 to the Pensions (Increase) Act 1971 for " section 17(5) of the Reserve Forces Act 1966 " substitute " section 129 of the Reserve Forces Act 1980 ".

Housing (Financial Provisions) (Scotland) Act 1972   1972 c. 46.

12. In paragraph 9(4) of Schedule 2 to the Housing (Financial Provisions) (Scotland) Act 1972, in paragraph (a) of the definition of " special widow's pension ", for " the Home Guard Act 1951 or the Ulster Defence Regiment Act 1969 " substitute " Part VII of the Reserve Forces Act 1980 or section 151 of that Act of 1980 ".

Housing Finance Act 1972   1972 c. 47.

13. In paragraph 9(5) of Schedule 3 to the Housing Finance Act 1972, in paragraph (a) of the definition of "special widow's pension ", for " the Home Guard Act 1951 or the Ulster Defence Regiment Act 1969 " substitute " Part VII of the Reserve Forces Act 1980 or section 151 of that Act of 1980 "

Local Government (Scotland) Act 1973   1973 c. 65.

14. In section 114(7), in paragraph (a) of the definition of " special widow's pension ", for " the Home Guard Act 1951 or the Ulster Defence Regiment Act 1969 " substitute " Part VII of the Reserve Forces Act 1980 or section 151 of that Act of 1980 ".

Trade Union and Labour Relations Act 1974   1974 c. 52.

15. In paragraph 33(4) of Part IV of Schedule 1 to the Trade Union and Labour Relations Act 1974 for "Auxiliary Forces Act 1953 " substitute " Part VI of the Reserve Forces Act 1980 ".

Supplementary Benefits Act 1976   1976 c. 71.

16. In paragraph 23(6)(a) of Part III of Schedule 1 to the Supplementary Benefits Act 1976, for " the Home Guard Act 1951 and the Ulster Defence Regiment Act 1969 " substitute " Part VII of the Reserve Forces Act 1980 and section 151 of that Act of 1980 ".

Employment Protection (Consolidation) Act 1978   1978 c. 44.

17. In the Employment Protection (Consolidation) Act 1978—

    (a) in section 138(3), and

      (*b*) in paragraph 19(3) of Schedule 13,
for " the Auxiliary Forces Act 1953 " substitute " Part VI of the
Reserve Forces Act 1980 ".

1979 c. 48.   *Pensioners' Payments and Social Security Act 1979*

18. In section 2(2) of the Pensioners' Payments and Social Security
Act 1979, in paragraph (*a*) of the definition of " war disablement
pension ", for " the Home Guard Act 1951 or the Ulster Defence
Regiment Act 1969 " substitute " Part VII of the Reserve Forces Act
1980 or section 151 of that Act of 1980 ".

ORDERS

S.I. 1976/1043   *Industrial Relations (Northern Ireland) Order 1976*
(N.I. 16).

19. In article 79(4) of the Industrial Relations (Northern Ireland)
Order 1976 for " the Auxiliary Forces Act 1953 " substitute " Part
VI of the Reserve Forces Act 1980 ".

S.I. 1976/2147   *Industrial Relations (No. 2) (Northern Ireland) Order 1976*
(N.I. 28).

20. In article 62(3) of the Industrial Relations (No. 2) (Northern
Ireland) Order 1976 for " the Auxiliary Forces Act 1953 " substitute
" Part VI of the Reserve Forces Act 1980.".

S.I. 1977/2156   *Supplementary Benefits (Northern Ireland) Order 1977*
(N.I. 27).

21. In paragraph 23(6)(*a*) of Schedule 1 to the Supplementary
Benefits (Northern Ireland) Order 1977 for " the Home Guard Act
1951 and the Ulster Defence Regiment Act 1969 " substitute " Part
VII of the Reserve Forces Act 1980 and section 151 of that Act of
1980 ".

Section 157.   **SCHEDULE 10**

REPEALS

PART I

REPEAL OF OBSOLETE ENACTMENTS

Chapter	Short title	Extent of repeal
14 Geo. 6. c. 32.	The Army Reserve Act 1950.	Section 22(2).
14 Geo. 6. c. 33.	The Air Force Reserve Act 1950.	Section 22(2).

Chapter	Short title	Extent of repeal
1 & 2 Eliz. 2. c. 50.	The Auxiliary Forces Act 1953.	In section 2(1), the words " area consisting of one or more counties or any other ", so far as unrepealed. In section 39(3), the words " An officer or man of the Territorial Army or the Royal Auxiliary Air Force shall not be compelled to serve as a peace officer or parish officer and ". In section 43(1), the definition of " county ". Schedule 3, so far as unrepealed.
1966 c. 30.	The Reserve Forces Act 1966.	Section 14(4).

Part II

Consequential Repeals

Chapter	Short title	Extent of repeal
14 Chas. 2. c. 3.	City of London Militia Act 1662.	Section 1.
42 Geo. 3. c. 90.	The Militia Act 1802.	The whole Act.
42 Geo. 3. c. 91.	The Militia (Scotland) Act 1802.	The whole Act.
16 & 17 Vict. c. 73.	The Naval Volunteers Act 1853.	The whole Act.
22 & 23 Vict. c. 40.	The Royal Naval Reserve (Volunteer) Act 1859.	The whole Act.
26 & 27 Vict. c. 69.	The Officers of Royal Naval Reserve Act 1863.	The whole Act.
34 & 35 Vict. c. 86.	The Regulation of the Forces Act 1871.	The whole Act.
35 & 36 Vict. c. 73.	The Merchant Shipping Act 1872.	The whole Act.
45 & 46 Vict. c. 12.	The Militia Storehouses Act 1882.	The whole Act.
45 & 46 Vict. c. 49.	The Militia Act 1882.	The whole Act.
47 & 48 Vict. c. 46.	The Naval Enlistment Act 1884.	The whole Act.
59 & 60 Vict. c. 33.	The Royal Naval Reserve Volunteer Act 1896.	The whole Act.
63 & 64 Vict. c. 52.	The Naval Reserve Act 1900.	The whole Act.

Chapter	Short title	Extent of repeal
2 Edw. 7. c. 5.	The Royal Naval Reserve Act 1902.	The whole Act.
3 Edw. 7. c. 6.	The Naval Forces Act 1903.	The whole Act.
6 Edw. 7. c. 5.	The Seamen's and Soldiers' False Characters Act 1906.	Section 3.
11 & 12 Geo. 5. c. 37.	The Territorial Army and Militia Act 1921.	The whole Act.
16 & 17 Geo. 5. c. 41.	The Naval Reserve (Officers) Act 1926.	The whole Act.
17 & 18 Geo. 5. c. 18.	The Royal Naval Reserve Act 1927.	The whole Act.
11 & 12 Geo. 6. c. 25.	The Royal Marines Act 1948.	The whole Act.
12, 13 & 14 Geo. 6. c. 8.	The Recall of Army and Air Force Pensioners Act 1948.	The whole Act.
12, 13 & 14 Geo. 6. c. 96.	The Auxiliary and Reserve Forces Act 1949.	The whole Act.
14 Geo. 6. c. 32.	The Army Reserve Act 1950.	The whole Act, so far as unrepealed.
14 Geo. 6. c. 33.	The Air Force Reserve Act 1950.	The whole Act, so far as unrepealed.
15 & 16 Geo. 6 & 1 Eliz. 2. c. 8.	The Home Guard Act 1951.	In section 1(4), the words " and as to pensions and other grants in respect of death or disablement ".
1 & 2 Eliz. 2. c. 50.	The Auxiliary Forces Act 1953.	The whole Act, so far as unrepealed.
3 & 4 Eliz. 2. c. 20.	The Revision of the Army and Air Force Acts (Transitional Provisions) Act 1955.	In Schedule 2, paragraphs 11 to 14 and 18.
5 & 6 Eliz. 2. c. 32.	The Naval and Marine Reserves Pay Act 1957.	The whole Act.
9 & 10 Eliz. 2. c. 52.	The Army and Air Force Act 1961.	In Schedule 2, the entries relating to the Recall of Army and Air Force Pensioners Act 1948, the Army Reserve Act 1950, and the Air Force Reserve Act 1950.
10 & 11 Eliz. 2. c. 10.	The Army Reserve Act 1962.	The whole Act.
1964 c. 11.	The Navy, Army and Air Force Reserves Act 1964.	The whole Act.
1964 c. 42.	The Administration of Justice Act 1964.	Section 18(1) and (2).
1966 c. 30.	The Reserve Forces Act 1966.	The whole Act, so far as unrepealed.
1966 c. 45.	The Armed Forces Act 1966.	In Schedule 4, the entries relating to— (a) the Seamen's and Soldiers' False Characters Act 1906; (b) the Recall of Army and Air Force Pensioners Act 1948;

Chapter	Short title	Extent of repeal
1966 c. 45— *cont.*	The Armed Forces Act 1966—*cont.*	(c) the Auxiliary and Reserve Forces Act 1949; (d) the Army Reserve Act 1950; (e) the Air Force Reserve Act 1950; and (f) the Navy, Army and Air Force Reserves Act 1964.
1967 c. 80.	The Criminal Justice Act 1967.	In Schedule 3, Parts I and IV, the entries relating to the Army Reserve Act 1950, the Air Force Reserve Act 1950, and the Auxiliary Forces Act 1953.
1969 c. 65.	The Ulster Defence Regiment Act 1969.	The whole Act.
1971 c. 33.	The Armed Forces Act 1971.	Section 64(2). Section 69(1) and (2). In section 76, the words from " in section 21 of the Army Reserve Act 1950 " to end. In Schedule 3, paragraph 6.
1972 c. 70.	The Local Government Act 1972.	Section 218.
1973 c. 34.	The Ulster Defence Regiment Act 1973.	The whole Act.
1973 c. 65.	The Local Government (Scotland) Act 1973.	Section 205. In Schedule 27, Part II, paragraphs 114 and 163.
1977 c. 18.	The Statute Law (Repeals) Act 1977.	In Schedule 2, the entry relating to the Army Reserve Act 1962.
1977 c. 49.	The National Health Service Act 1977.	In Schedule 14, in paragraph 13(1)(b), the reference to paragraph 49 of Schedule 4 to the National Health Service Reorganisation Act 1973.
1978 c. 29.	The National Health Service (Scotland) Act 1978.	In Schedule 15, in paragraph 10(c), the reference to paragraph 49 of Schedule 4 to the National Health Service Reorganisation Act 1973.

Police Negotiating Board Act 1980

1980 CHAPTER 10

An Act to provide for a Police Negotiating Board for the United Kingdom in place of the Police Council for the United Kingdom.

[20th March 1980]

BE IT ENACTED by the Queen's most Excellent Majesty, by and with the advice and consent of the Lords Spiritual and Temporal, and Commons, in this present Parliament assembled, and by the authority of the same, as follows:—

The Police Negotiating Board for the United Kingdom.

1.—(1) There shall be a Board, to be known as the Police Negotiating Board for the United Kingdom, for the consideration by persons representing the interests of—

(*a*) the authorities who between them maintain the police forces in Great Britain and the Royal Ulster Constabulary, and

(*b*) the persons who are members of those police forces or of that Constabulary or are police cadets,

of questions relating to hours of duty, leave, pay and allowances, pensions or the issue, use and return of police clothing, personal equipment and accoutrements.

(2) The Chairman and any deputy chairman or chairmen of the Board shall be appointed by the Prime Minister.

(3) Subject to subsection (2), the Board shall be established in accordance with such arrangements made after consultations

between the Secretary of State and organisations representing the interests referred to in subsection (1) as appear to him to be satisfactory.

(4) The Secretary of State may—

(*a*) pay to the Chairman and to any deputy chairman or chairmen of the Board such fees as the Secretary of State may determine with the approval of the Minister for the Civil Service; and

(*b*) defray any expenses incurred by the Board;

and expenses incurred by the Secretary of State under paragraph (*a*) or (*b*), and any other administrative expenses incurred by him in connection with the Board, shall be defrayed out of money provided by Parliament.

(5) The Police Council for the United Kingdom shall cease to exist.

2.—(1) Before making, with respect to any of the matters mentioned in section 1(1) (other than pensions)— Functions of the Board with respect to regulations.

(*a*) regulations under section 33 or 35 of the Police Act 1964; 1964 c. 48.

(*b*) regulations under section 26 or 27 of the Police (Scotland) Act 1967 (other than regulations relating to special constables); or 1967 c. 77.

(*c*) regulations under section 10(4) or 25 of the Police Act (Northern Ireland) 1970, 1970 c. 9 (N.I.).

the Secretary of State shall take into consideration any recommendation made by the Police Negotiating Board for the United Kingdom and shall furnish the Board with a draft of the regulations.

(2) The arrangements referred to in section 1(3) shall regulate the procedure for reaching agreement on a recommendation to be made by the Board for the purposes of subsection (1) of this section and shall include provision for arriving at such a recommendation by arbitration in such circumstances as may be determined by or under the arrangements.

(3) In section 1(1) of the Police Pensions Act 1976 for the reference to the Police Council for the United Kingdom there shall be substituted a reference to the Police Negotiating Board for the United Kingdom; and no regulations relating to pensions shall be made under section 35 of the Police Act 1964, section 27 of the Police (Scotland) Act 1967 or section 10(4) or 25 of the Police Act (Northern Ireland) 1970 except after consultation with the Board. 1976 c. 35.

1964 c. 48.
1967 c. 77.

(4) In section 46(3) of the Police Act 1964 and section 26(9) of the Police (Scotland) Act 1967 (which provide for consultation on certain matters with Police Advisory Boards or other bodies) for the words " other than regulations with respect to any of the matters mentioned in section 4(1) of the Police Act 1969 " there shall be substituted the words " other than regulations with respect to any of the matters mentioned in section 1(1) of the Police Negotiating Board Act 1980 ".

Short title, commencement, repeals and extent.

3.—(1) This Act may be cited as the Police Negotiating Board Act 1980.

(2) This Act shall come into force at the end of the period of two months beginning with the day on which it is passed.

(3) The following enactments are repealed—

1969 c. 63.
    (*a*) section 4 of the Police Act 1969;

1970 c. 9 (N.I.).
    (*b*) section 22 of the Police Act (Northern Ireland) 1970;

1976 c. 35.
    (*c*) paragraph 7 of Schedule 2 to the Police Pensions Act 1976.

(4) This Act extends to Northern Ireland.

Protection of Trading Interests Act 1980

1980 CHAPTER 11

An Act to provide protection from requirements, prohibitions and judgments imposed or given under the laws of countries outside the United Kingdom and affecting the trading or other interests of persons in the United Kingdom. [20th March 1980]

BE IT ENACTED by the Queen's most Excellent Majesty, by and with the advice and consent of the Lords Spiritual and Temporal, and Commons, in this present Parliament assembled, and by the authority of the same, as follows:—

1.—(1) If it appears to the Secretary of State— *Overseas measures affecting United Kingdom trading interests.*

  (a) that measures have been or are proposed to be taken by or under the law of any overseas country for regulating or controlling international trade ; and

  (b) that those measures, in so far as they apply or would apply to things done or to be done outside the territorial jurisdiction of that country by persons carrying on business in the United Kingdom, are damaging or threaten to damage the trading interests of the United Kingdom,

the Secretary of State may by order direct that this section shall apply to those measures either generally or in their application to such cases as may be specified in the order.

(2) The Secretary of State may by order make provision for requiring, or enabling the Secretary of State to require, a person in the United Kingdom who carries on business there

to give notice to the Secretary of State of any requirement or prohibition imposed or threatened to be imposed on that person pursuant to any measures in so far as this section applies to them by virtue of an order under subsection (1) above.

(3) The Secretary of State may give to any person in the United Kingdom who carries on business there such directions for prohibiting compliance with any such requirement or prohibition as aforesaid as he considers appropriate for avoiding damage to the trading interests of the United Kingdom.

(4) The power of the Secretary of State to make orders under subsection (1) or (2) above shall be exercisable by statutory instrument subject to annulment in pursuance of a resolution of either House of Parliament.

(5) Directions under subsection (3) above may be either general or special and may prohibit compliance with any requirement or prohibition either absolutely or in such cases or subject to such conditions as to consent or otherwise as may be specified in the directions; and general directions under that subsection shall be published in such manner as appears to the Secretary of State to be appropriate.

(6) In this section " trade " includes any activity carried on in the course of a business of any description and " trading interests " shall be construed accordingly.

Documents and information required by overseas courts and authorities.

2.—(1) If it appears to the Secretary of State—

(*a*) that a requirement has been or may be imposed on a person or persons in the United Kingdom to produce to any court, tribunal or authority of an overseas country any commercial document which is not within the territorial jurisdiction of that country or to furnish any commercial information to any such court, tribunal or authority; or

(*b*) that any such authority has imposed or may impose a requirement on a person or persons in the United Kingdom to publish any such document or information,

the Secretary of State may, if it appears to him that the requirement is inadmissible by virtue of subsection (2) or (3) below, give directions for prohibiting compliance with the requirement.

(2) A requirement such as is mentioned in subsection (1)(*a*) or (*b*) above is inadmissible—

(*a*) if it infringes the jurisdiction of the United Kingdom or is otherwise prejudicial to the sovereignty of the United Kingdom; or (*b*) if compliance with the requirement would be prejudicial to the security of the United Kingdom or to the relations of the government of the United Kingdom with the government of any other country.

(3) A requirement such as is mentioned in subsection (1)(*a*) above is also inadmissible—

    (*a*) if it is made otherwise than for the purposes of civil or criminal proceedings which have been instituted in the overseas country ; or

    (*b*) if it requires a person to state what documents relevant to any such proceedings are or have been in his possession, custody or power or to produce for the purposes of any such proceedings any documents other than particular documents specified in the requirement.

(4) Directions under subsection (1) above may be either general or special and may prohibit compliance with any requirement either absolutely or in such cases or subject to such conditions as to consent or otherwise as may be specified in the directions ; and general directions under that subsection shall be published in such manner as appears to the Secretary of State to be appropriate.

(5) For the purposes of this section the making of a request or demand shall be treated as the imposition of a requirement if it is made in circumstances in which a requirement to the same effect could be or could have been imposed ; and

    (*a*) any request or demand for the supply of a document or information which, pursuant to the requirement of any court, tribunal or authority of an overseas country, is addressed to a person in the United Kingdom ; or

    (*b*) any requirement imposed by such a court, tribunal or authority to produce or furnish any document or information to a person specified in the requirement,

shall be treated as a requirement to produce or furnish that document or information to that court, tribunal or authority.

(6) In this section " commercial document " and " commercial information " mean respectively a document or information relating to a business of any description and " document " includes any record or device by means of which material is recorded or stored.

3.—(1) Subject to subsection (2) below, any person who without reasonable excuse fails to comply with any requirement imposed under subsection (2) of section 1 above or knowingly contravenes any directions given under subsection (3) of that section or section 2(1) above shall be guilty of an offence and liable— Offences under ss. 1 and 2.

    (*a*) on conviction on indictment, to a fine ;

(*b*) on summary conviction, to a fine not exceeding the statutory maximum.

(2) A person who is neither a citizen of the United Kingdom and Colonies nor a body corporate incorporated in the United Kingdom shall not be guilty of an offence under subsection (1) above by reason of anything done or omitted outside the United Kingdom in contravention of directions under section 1(3) or 2(1) above.

(3) No proceedings for an offence under subsection (1) above shall be instituted in England, Wales or Northern Ireland except by the Secretary of State or with the consent of the Attorney General or, as the case may be, the Attorney General for Northern Ireland.

(4) Proceedings against any person for an offence under this section may be taken before the appropriate court in the United Kingdom having jurisdiction in the place where that person is for the time being.

(5) In subsection (1) above "the statutory maximum" means—

(*a*) in England and Wales and Northern Ireland, the prescribed sum within the meaning of section 28 of the Criminal Law Act 1977 (at the passing of this Act £1,000);

1977 c. 45.

(*b*) in Scotland, the prescribed sum within the meaning of section 289B of the Criminal Procedure (Scotland) Act 1975 (at the passing of this Act £1,000);

1975 c. 21.

and for the purposes of the application of this subsection in Northern Ireland the provisions of the said Act of 1977 relating to the sum mentioned in paragraph (*a*) shall extend to Northern Ireland.

Restriction of Evidence (Proceedings in Other Jurisdictions) Act 1975.

1975 c. 34.

4. A court in the United Kingdom shall not make an order under section 2 of the Evidence (Proceedings in Other Jurisdictions) Act 1975 for giving effect to a request issued by or on behalf of a court or tribunal of an overseas country if it is shown that the request infringes the jurisdiction of the United Kingdom or is otherwise prejudicial to the sovereignty of the United Kingdom; and a certificate signed by or on behalf of the Secretary of State to the effect that it infringes that jurisdiction or is so prejudicial shall be conclusive evidence of that fact.

Restriction on enforcement of certain overseas judgments.

1920 c. 81.

1933 c. 13.

5.—(1) A judgment to which this section applies shall not be registered under Part II of the Administration of Justice Act 1920 or Part I of the Foreign Judgments (Reciprocal Enforcement) Act 1933 and no court in the United Kingdom shall entertain proceedings at common law for the recovery of any sum payable under such a judgment.

(2) This section applies to any judgment given by a court of an overseas country, being—

    (*a*) a judgment for multiple damages within the meaning of subsection (3) below ;

    (*b*) a judgment based on a provision or rule of law specified or described in an order under subsection (4) below and given after the coming into force of the order ; or

    (*c*) a judgment on a claim for contribution in respect of damages awarded by a judgment falling within paragraph (*a*) or (*b*) above.

(3) In subsection (2)(*a*) above a judgment for multiple damages means a judgment for an amount arrived at by doubling, trebling or otherwise multiplying a sum assessed as compensation for the loss or damage sustained by the person in whose favour the judgment is given.

(4) The Secretary of State may for the purposes of subsection (2)(*b*) above make an order in respect of any provision or rule of law which appears to him to be concerned with the prohibition or regulation of agreements, arrangements or practices designed to restrain, distort or restrict competition in the carrying on of business of any description or to be otherwise concerned with the promotion of such competition as aforesaid.

(5) The power of the Secretary of State to make orders under subsection (4) above shall be exercisable by statutory instrument subject to annulment in pursuance of a resolution of either House of Parliament.

(6) Subsection (2)(*a*) above applies to a judgment given before the date of the passing of this Act as well as to a judgment given on or after that date but this section does not affect any judgment which has been registered before that date under the provisions mentioned in subsection (1) above or in respect of which such proceedings as are there mentioned have been finally determined before that date.

6.—(1) This section applies where a court of an overseas country has given a judgment for multiple damages within the meaning of section 5(3) above against— Recovery of awards of multiple damages.

    (*a*) a citizen of the United Kingdom and Colonies ; or

    (*b*) a body corporate incorporated in the United Kingdom or in a territory outside the United Kingdom for whose international relations Her Majesty's Government in the United Kingdom are responsible ; or

    (*c*) a person carrying on business in the United Kingdom,

(in this section referred to as a " qualifying defendant ") and an amount on account of the damages has been paid by the qualifying defendant either to the party in whose favour the judgment was given or to another party who is entitled as against the qualifying defendant to contribution in respect of the damages.

(2) Subject to subsections (3) and (4) below, the qualifying defendant shall be entitled to recover from the party in whose favour the judgment was given so much of the amount referred to in subsection (1) above as exceeds the part attributable to compensation ; and that part shall be taken to be such part of the amount as bears to the whole of it the same proportion as the sum assessed by the court that gave the judgment as compensation for the loss or damage sustained by that party bears to the whole of the damages awarded to that party.

(3) Subsection (2) above does not apply where the qualifying defendant is an individual who was ordinarily resident in the overseas country at the time when the proceedings in which the judgment was given were instituted or a body corporate which had its principal place of business there at that time.

(4) Subsection (2) above does not apply where the qualifying defendant carried on business in the overseas country and the proceedings in which the judgment was given were concerned with activities exclusively carried on in that country.

(5) A court in the United Kingdom may entertain proceedings on a claim under this section notwithstanding that the person against whom the proceedings are brought is not within the jurisdiction of the court.

(6) The reference in subsection (1) above to an amount paid by the qualifying defendant includes a reference to an amount obtained by execution against his property or against the property of a company which (directly or indirectly) is wholly owned by him ; and references in that subsection and subsection (2) above to the party in whose favour the judgment was given or to a party entitled to contribution include references to any person in whom the rights of any such party have become vested by succession or assignment or otherwise.

(7) This section shall, with the necessary modifications, apply also in relation to any order which is made by a tribunal or authority of an overseas country and would, if that tribunal or authority were a court, be a judgment for multiple damages within the meaning of section 5(3) above.

(8) This section does not apply to any judgment given or order made before the passing of this Act.

7.—(1) If it appears to Her Majesty that the law of an over- Enforcement
seas country provides or will provide for the enforcement in of overseas
that country of judgments given under section 6 above, Her judgment
Majesty may by Order in Council provide for the enforcement provision
in the United Kingdom of judgments given under any provision corresponding
of the law of that country corresponding to that section.   to s. 6.

(2) An Order under this section may apply, with or without
modification, any of the provisions of the Foreign Judgments 1933 c. 13.
(Reciprocal Enforcement) Act 1933.

8.—(1) This Act may be cited as the Protection of Trading Short title,
Interests Act 1980.   interpretation,
repeals and

(2) In this Act " overseas country " means any country or extent.
territory outside the United Kingdom other than one for whose
international relations Her Majesty's Government in the United
Kingdom are responsible.

(3) References in this Act to the law or a court, tribunal or
authority of an overseas country include, in the case of a federal
state, references to the law or a court, tribunal or authority
of any constituent part of that country.

(4) References in this Act to a claim for, or to entitlement
to, contribution are references to a claim or entitlement based
on an enactment or rule of law.

(5) The Shipping Contracts and Commercial Documents Act 1964 c. 87.
1964 (which is superseded by this Act) is hereby repealed, together with paragraph 18 of Schedule 2 and paragraph 24 of
Schedule 3 to the Criminal Law Act 1977 (which contain amend- 1977 c. 45.
ments of that Act).

(6) Subsection (5) above shall not affect the operation of
the said Act of 1964 in relation to any directions given under
that Act before the passing of this Act.

(7) This Act extends to Northern Ireland.

(8) Her Majesty may by Order in Council direct that this Act
shall extend with such exceptions, adaptations and modifications, if any, as may be specified in the Order to any territory
outside the United Kingdom, being a territory for the international relations of which Her Majesty's Government in the
United Kingdom are responsible.

Bees Act 1980

1980 CHAPTER 12

An Act to make new provision for the control of pests and diseases affecting bees. [20th March 1980]

BE IT ENACTED by the Queen's most Excellent Majesty, by and with the advice and consent of the Lords Spiritual and Temporal, and Commons, in this present Parliament assembled, and by the authority of the same, as follows:—

1.—(1) The Minister of Agriculture, Fisheries and Food, the Secretary of State for Scotland and the Secretary of State for Wales, acting jointly, may by order make such provision as they think fit for the purpose of preventing the introduction into or spreading within Great Britain of pests or diseases affecting bees.

Control of pests and diseases affecting bees.

(2) Without prejudice to the generality of subsection (1) above, for the purpose there mentioned an order under this section—

    (*a*) may prohibit or regulate the importation into or movement within Great Britain of bees and combs, bee products, hives, containers and other appliances used in connection with keeping or transporting bees, and of any other thing which has or may have been exposed to infection with any pest or disease to which the order applies ;

    (*b*) may make provision with respect to any of the matters specified in the Schedule to this Act ; and

(c) may make different provision for different cases or different areas.

(3) Any authorised person may examine any bees or other things subject to control under an order under this section, and may take samples of them, in order to see if they are free from infection.

(4) Where any bees or other things subject to control under any such order are found to be infected, or to have been exposed to infection, with any pest or disease to which the order applies, any authorised person may destroy them by such means as he thinks fit, or cause them to be so destroyed.

(5) Without prejudice to subsection (4) above, where any bees or other things are imported into Great Britain in contravention of an order under this section, any authorised person may destroy them by such means as he thinks fit, or cause them to be so destroyed, and may do so with or without first allowing an opportunity for them to be re-exported.

(6) No compensation shall be payable in respect of any exercise of the powers conferred by subsections (3) and (5) above.

(7) Any person who—

   (a) imports any bees or other things into Great Britain in contravention of an order under this section ;

   (b) moves any bees or other things within Great Britain in contravention of any such order ; or

   (c) otherwise contravenes or fails to comply with the provisions of any such order or with any condition imposed by any licence issued under any such order ;

shall be liable on summary conviction to a fine not exceeding £1,000.

(8) Any expenses incurred by any of the Ministers mentioned in subsection (1) above under this section (or under any order made under this section) shall be defrayed out of moneys provided by Parliament.

(9) The power to make an order under this section shall be exercisable by statutory instrument, which shall be subject to annulment by resolution of either House of Parliament.

Power of entry.

   2.—(1) For the purpose of exercising any power conferred on him by or under section 1 of this Act an authorised person may at any time enter—

   (a) any premises or other place ; or

   (b) any vessel, boat, hovercraft, aircraft or vehicle of any other description ;

on or in which he has reasonable grounds for supposing there are or have been any bees or other things subject to control under an order under that section.

(2) A person seeking to enter any premises or other place, or any vessel, boat, hovercraft, aircraft or other vehicle in exercise of the power of entry under this section, shall, if so required by or on behalf of the owner or occupier or person in charge, produce evidence of his authority before entering.

(3) Any person who intentionally obstructs a person acting in exercise of the power of entry under this section shall be liable on summary conviction, or, in Scotland, on conviction by a court of summary jurisdiction, to a fine not exceeding £200.

3. In this Act—   Interpretation.
" authorised person " means a person generally or specially authorised in writing by the responsible Minister ;
" bees " includes bees in any stage of their life cycle ;
" bee product " means any natural product of the activities of bees (such as, for example, honey or beeswax) in its natural state ; and
" the responsible Minister " means—
    (a) in relation to England, the Minister of Agriculture, Fisheries and Food ; and
    (b) in relation to Scotland and Wales, the Secretary of State.

4. An Order in Council under paragraph 1(1)(b) of Schedule 1 to the Northern Ireland Act 1974 (legislation for Northern Ireland in the interim period) which contains a statement that it operates only so as to make for Northern Ireland provision corresponding to this Act—   Enactment of same provisions for Northern Ireland. 1974 c. 28.
(a) shall not be subject to paragraph 1(4) and (5) of that Schedule (affirmative resolution by both Houses of Parliament) ; but
(b) shall be subject to annulment by resolution of either House.

5.—(1) This Act may be cited as the Bees Act 1980.   Short title, commencement, repeals, transitional provision and extent.
(2) This Act shall come into force on such day as the Minister of Agriculture, Fisheries and Food, the Secretary of State for Scotland and the Secretary of State for Wales, acting jointly, may by order made by statutory instrument appoint.
(3) The following enactments shall cease to have effect—
sections 11 and 12(8) of the Agriculture (Miscellaneous Provisions) Act 1941 ;   1941 c. 50.

1954 c. 39.   section 10 of the Agriculture (Miscellaneous Provisions) Act 1954.

1978 c. 30.   (4) Without prejudice to section 17(2)(*b*) of the Interpretation Act 1978 (effect of repeal and re-enactment in relation to subordinate legislation), any order made under section 11 of the 1941 c. 50. Agriculture (Miscellaneous Provisions) Act 1941 which is in force at the commencement of this Act shall have effect as if made under section 1 of this Act (and may be revoked or amended by an order made under section 1 accordingly).

(5) This Act, with the exception of section 4, does not extend to Northern Ireland.

SCHEDULE

Section 1(2).

SPECIFIC MATTERS WITH RESPECT TO WHICH PROVISION MAY BE
MADE BY ORDERS UNDER SECTION 1

1. The conditions to be observed before, during and after importation.

2. Exemptions from prohibitions on importation in the order by means of licences, whether general or specific and whether conditional or unconditional, issued in accordance with the order (whether on or before importation) by the responsible Minister or (where the order so provides) by any authorised person.

3. The revocation of any licence issued in accordance with the order and the variation of any conditions attached to a licence so issued.

4. Securing information with respect to—
   (a) the persons who keep bees ;
   (b) the occurrence of any pest or disease to which the order applies ;
   (c) the country or place of origin or consignment, contacts in transit and destination of any bees or other things subject to control under the order (whether the information is required on, before or following their importation into or transportation within Great Britain) ;
   (d) any other matter relevant to determining whether any bees or other things subject to control under the order have been exposed to infection with any pest or disease to which the order applies.

5. The circumstances in which and the time when any bees or other things brought into Great Britain are to be regarded for the purposes of this Act as being imported into Great Britain.

6. Treatment of any bees found to be infected or to have been exposed to infection with any pest or disease to which the order applies.

7. Cleansing and disinfection.

8. Marking of hives or other containers for identification.

9. Recovery of costs.

10. Payment of compensation for bees or other things subject to control destroyed in accordance with section 1(4).

11. Any matter incidental or supplementary to any of the matters mentioned above.

Slaughter of Animals (Scotland) Act 1980

1980 CHAPTER 13

An Act to consolidate certain enactments relating to slaughterhouses, knackers' yards and the slaughter of animals in Scotland. [20th March 1980]

BE IT ENACTED by the Queen's most Excellent Majesty, by and with the advice and consent of the Lords Spiritual and Temporal, and Commons, in this present Parliament assembled, and by the authority of the same, as follows:—

1. Subject to sections 3 and 8 of this Act, a local authority may provide and, if they think fit, operate a slaughterhouse and may dispose of any slaughterhouse belonging to them by feu, sale, lease or excambion ; and any slaughterhouse so disposed of shall be deemed to be disposed of under Part VI of the Local Government (Scotland) Act 1973.

[margin: Power of local authorities to provide public slaughter-houses. 1973 c. 65.]

2.—(1) A local authority may be authorised by the Secretary of State to purchase compulsorily any land, whether situated within or outside its area, for the purpose of any of their functions under section 1, 3, 4, 5 or 8 of this Act.

(2) In relation to the compulsory purchase of land under this section, the Acquisition of Land (Authorisation Procedure) (Scotland) Act 1947 shall apply as if subsection (1) above had been in force immediately before the commencement of that Act.

[margin: Acquisition of land for purposes relating to slaughter-houses. 1947 c. 42.]

3.—(1) A local authority by whom a slaughterhouse has been provided under section 1 of this Act or under any other enactment—

(a) may make charges in respect of the use of the slaughterhouse and in respect of any services provided by them in connection therewith ; and

[margin: Management of public slaughter-houses.]

Part I   I

(*b*) may provide plant or apparatus for disposing of or treating waste matter or refuse, or processing by-products resulting from the slaughter of animals in such a slaughterhouse.

(2) In fixing or varying any such charges as aforesaid a local authority shall consult with such persons or organisations as appear to them to be representative of interests substantially affected by such charges.

Registration
in respect
of private
slaughter-
houses.

4.—(1) Subject to the provisions of this section and section 5 of this Act, no person other than a local authority shall use any premises as a slaughterhouse for the slaughter of any kind of animal unless he is registered in respect of the premises for that purpose by the local authority.

(2) Any person who contravenes the provisions of subsection (1) above shall be guilty of an offence and shall be liable on summary conviction to a fine not exceeding one hundred pounds or to imprisonment for a term not exceeding three months, or to both such fine and imprisonment.

(3) An application for registration under this section in respect of any premises shall be made by the person who proposes to use the premises; and in the case of an application in respect of premises not yet erected, or of premises to be reconstructed, shall be accompanied by plans showing the proposed works.

(4) Subject to the provisions of this section and section 5 of this Act the local authority shall, on an application for registration under this section being duly made by a person in respect of any premises, register that person in respect of the premises; and they shall, upon so registering him, issue to him a certificate to that effect.

(5) A local authority may for the protection of the public health prohibit the slaughter, on any premises in respect of which a person is to be registered in pursuance of this section, of any kind of animal other than that specified in the certificate, relating to those premises, to be issued under subsection (4) above.

Refusal and
cancellation of
registration
in respect
of private
slaughter-
houses.

5.—(1) Subject to the provisions of this section, if it appears to the local authority in the case of—

(*a*) an application for registration under section 4 of this Act that in connection with the premises specified in the application;

(*b*) a registration under that section that in connection with the premises specified, or business carried on in the premises specified, in the registration, the requirements of any enactment relating to slaughterhouses are not, and are not likely within a reasonable time to be, complied with, the authority shall refuse or as the case may be cancel the registration.

(2) A local authority may for the protection of the public health vary any registration under section 4 of this Act by prohibiting the slaughter on any premises to which the registration relates of any kind of animal other than that which may be specified by the authority.

(3) If the local authority refuse, cancel or vary a registration they shall forthwith give the applicant or the person registered in respect of the premises notice of their decision in the matter ; and any such notice shall state the grounds on which the decision is based and the time within which an appeal may be brought in accordance with the provisions of subsection (5) of this section.

(4) An application for registration shall, if not already determined by the local authority, be deemed to have been refused by the authority at the expiry of three months from the date upon which the application was made.

(5) A person aggrieved by a local authority's decision under this section to refuse, cancel or vary any registration under section 4 of this Act may appeal to the sheriff ; and any such appeal shall be disposed of in a summary manner and shall be made within one month from the date on which notice of the said decision was served upon the person desiring to appeal or from the date on which a refusal is, under subsection (4) above, deemed to have been made.

(6) For the purposes of subsection (5) above, any—

(a) prohibition under subsection (5) of section 4 of this Act ;

(b) refusal of express authorisation under subsection (1) of section 7 of this Act,

shall be treated as a refusal of a registration under the said section 4.

6.—(1) A person carrying on the business of slaughterman or knacker shall not use any premises as a knacker's yard without a licence from the local authority ; and if he does he shall be guilty of an offence and shall be liable on summary conviction to a fine not exceeding twenty-five pounds and the fact that animals (other than asses or mules) have been taken into unlicensed premises shall be *prima facie* evidence that an offence under this section has been committed. Licensing of knackers' yards,

(2) A licence under this section shall expire on such day in every year as the local authority fix and when a licence is first

granted shall expire on the day so fixed which secondly occurs after the grant of the licence ; and a fee not exceeding twenty-five pence may be charged for the licence or any renewal thereof.

(3) Not less than twenty-one days before a new licence for any premises is granted under this section, notice of the intention to apply for it shall be advertised as provided in section 32(2) of the Public Health (Scotland) Act 1897 by the local authority in whose area the premises are situated ; and any person interested may show cause against the grant or renewal of the licence.

1897 c. 38.

(4) An objection shall not be entertained to the renewal of a licence under this section unless seven days previous notice of the objection has been served on the applicant:

Provided that, on an objection being made of which notice has not been given, the local authority may, if they think it just to do so, direct notice thereof to be served on the applicant, adjourn the question of the renewal to a future date, require the attendance of the applicant on that day, then hear the case and consider the objection as if the said notice had been duly given.

(5) For the purposes of this section a licence shall be deemed to be renewed where a further licence is granted in immediate succession to a prior licence for the same premises.

(6) Where any person has been refused a renewal of a licence under this section, such person may appeal to the Secretary of State against such refusal ; and the decision of the Secretary of State shall be final.

Further provisions in relation to registration in respect of slaughter-houses and to licensing of knackers' yards.

7.—(1) In relation to the use of any premises for or in connection with the slaughter of horses—

(a) a licence granted under section 6 of this Act ;

(b) a registration under section 4 of this Act,

shall be of no effect unless expressly authorising the use of the premises for that purpose.

(2) Where any premises used or to be used for the confinement of animals awaiting slaughter in a slaughterhouse or knacker's yard are situated outside the curtilage of the premises used or to be used for the slaughter—

(a) separate licences may be granted under the said section 6 ; or

(b) there may, as the case may be, be separate registration under the said section 4,

authorising the use of those premises for those purposes respectively.

(3) A licence under the said section 6 shall not be granted in respect of any premises unless the local authority are satisfied that the requirements of any regulations in force under sections 9 and 20 of this Act with respect to the construction, lay-out and equipment of premises are complied with or will be complied with before the date on which the licence or renewed licence comes into force in respect of those premises; but nothing in this subsection shall be taken as affecting so much of the said section 6 as confers a right of appeal on a person aggrieved by the refusal of a local authority to renew a licence under that section.

8.—(1) A local authority may, and if required by the Secretary of State shall, make byelaws for securing that slaughterhouses are kept in a clean and sanitary condition and are properly managed and conducted. Byelaws as to slaughterhouses.

(2) The Secretary of State shall be the confirming authority as respects byelaws made under subsection (1) above.

(3) If and in so far as a byelaw made under this section is inconsistent with any regulations relating to slaughterhouses or the slaughter of animals therein, the regulations shall prevail.

(4) The repeal by this Act of section 18(1) of the Slaughterhouses Act 1954 (savings) shall not invalidate any byelaw made under any enactment repealed by that Act; and any such byelaw in force at the commencement of this Act shall have effect as if made under this section, and may be amended, varied, revoked or enforced accordingly. 1954 c. 42.

9.—(1) The Secretary of State may make such regulations as appear to him to be expedient for securing humane conditions and practices in connection with the slaughter of animals at slaughterhouses and knackers' yards and for securing the proper management of such premises for those purposes; and such regulations may in particular prescribe— Securing humane conditions in slaughterhouses and knackers' yards.

    (a) requirements as to the construction, lay-out and equipment of premises used as slaughterhouses or knackers' yards;

    (b) conditions to be observed in connection with the confinement and treatment of animals while awaiting slaughter in such premises, and in connection with the slaughter of animals therein.

(2) Regulations made under this section may make different provision in relation to different kinds of animals and in relation to premises used for different purposes in connection with the

slaughter of animals and may, so far as they are made for the purposes mentioned in paragraph (*a*) of subsection (1) above, be made to apply subject to exceptions or modifications in relation to premises constructed or adapted for use before the date on which the regulations come into force.

(3) Regulations made under this section may prescribe penalties for offences against the regulations, not exceeding those specified in section 18 of this Act, and may impose on the occupiers of premises to which the regulations apply responsibility for compliance with any of the provisions of the regulations.

Method of slaughtering animals in slaughter-houses and knackers' yards.

10.—(1) Subject to the provisions of this section and section 11 of this Act, no animal shall, in a slaughterhouse or knacker's yard, be slaughtered otherwise than instantaneously by means of a mechanically-operated instrument in proper repair unless—

(*a*) by stunning, effected by means of a mechanically-operated instrument or an instument for stunning by means of electricity, being in either case an instrument in proper repair, it is instantaneously rendered insensible to pain until death supervenes ; or

(*b*) by such other means as may be prescribed, it is rendered insensible to pain until death supervenes, and there are complied with such conditions (if any) as respects the use of those means as may be prescribed.

(2) In subsection (1) above " prescribed " means prescribed by regulations made by the Secretary of State after consultation with such organisations as appear to him to represent the interests concerned.

(3) Regulations under this section may make—

(*a*) provision as respects all animals or any class of animals ;

(*b*) different provision as respects different classes of animals and as respects different classes of slaughterhouses or knackers' yards ; and

(*c*) such incidental or consequential provisions as may appear to the Secretary of State to be necessary or expedient for the purposes of the regulations, including, in particular, in a case where a condition as respects the use of any means of rendering an animal insensible to pain consists in the giving of approval to any matter by a local authority, provision for securing a right of appeal to the sheriff against a withholding or withdrawal of approval.

11. Section 10 of this Act shall not apply where an animal is slaughtered for the food of— Saving for Jewish and Muslim method of slaughter.

   (*a*) Jews by a Jew appropriately licensed by the Chief Rabbi and holding a licence granted under section 15 of this Act by the local authority ; or

   (*b*) Muslims by a Muslim holding a licence granted under section 15 of this Act by the local authority,

if such slaughter is carried out according to the Jewish or the Muslim method of slaughter, as the case may be, and no unnecessary suffering is inflicted.

12. No swine exceeding twelve weeks in age shall be slaughtered in any place other than a slaughterhouse or knacker's yard otherwise than instantaneously by means of a mechanically-operated instrument in proper repair unless by stunning, effected by means of a mechanically-operated instrument or an instrument for stunning by means of electricity, being in either case an instrument in proper repair, it is instantaneously rendered insensible to pain until death supervenes: Method of slaughtering swine otherwise than in slaughter-house or knacker's yard.

   Provided that this section shall not apply if the swine is, at any laboratory, research station or similar institution, slaughtered for the purposes of—

   (i) the diagnosis of disease ; or

   (ii) research in connection with the arts of veterinary surgery or medicine.

13.—(1) Subject to the provisions of this section, any officer of a local authority shall, if he is authorised for the purpose, have a right, on producing if so required some duly authenticated document showing his authority, to enter any premises at all reasonable hours— Power of local authority to enter premises.

   (*a*) for the purpose of ascertaining whether there is or has been on, or in connection with, the premises any contravention of the provisions of section 4, or this section, of this Act or of any byelaws made under section 8 of this Act ; and

   (*b*) generally for the purpose of the performance by the authority of their functions under sections 4 and 5 of this Act or under such byelaws.

   (2) If, by written evidence on oath, a sheriff or justice of the peace is satisfied that there is reasonable ground for entry into any premises for any such purpose as is mentioned in subsection (1) above and that—

   (*a*) admission to the premises has been refused ;

   (*b*) such refusal is apprehended ;

I 4

(c) an application for admission would defeat the object of the entry ;

(d) the premises are unoccupied ;

(e) the occupier is temporarily absent ; or

(f) the case is one of urgency,

the sheriff, or justice of the peace as the case may be, may grant a warrant, which shall continue in force for a period of one month, authorising the local authority by any authorised officer to enter the premises, if need be by force :

Provided that such warrant shall not be granted on any ground mentioned in paragraphs (a) to (c) of this subsection unless the sheriff, or justice of the peace as the case may be, is satisfied either that notice of the intention to apply for a warrant has been given to the occupier or that the giving of such notice would defeat the object of the entry.

(3) An authorised officer entering any premises by virtue of this section, or of a warrant issued thereunder, may take with him such other persons as may be necessary ; and on leaving any unoccupied premises which he has entered by virtue of such a warrant he shall leave them as effectively secured against unauthorised entry as he found them.

(4) Nothing in this section or in section 14 of this Act shall authorise any person, except with the permission of the local authority under the Diseases of Animals Act 1950, to enter any premises which for the time being are, or are comprised in, an infected place within the meaning of that Act.

1950 c. 36.

Further powers of entry.

14.—(1) Subject to section 13(4) of this Act, an empowered officer shall have a right to enter any slaughterhouse or knacker's yard, at any time when business is or appears to be in progress or is usually carried on therein, for the purpose of ascertaining whether there is or has been any contravention of the provisions of section 10, 11 or 15 of this Act or of any regulations made under section 9 of, or by virtue of section 10(1) of, this Act.

(2) Any person who refuses to permit an empowered officer to enter any premises which the officer is entitled to enter under subsection (1) above or who obstructs or impedes the officer in the exercise of the officer's duties under that subsection, shall be guilty of an offence and shall be liable on summary conviction to a fine not exceeding twenty pounds.

(3) In subsections (1) and (2) above, " empowered officer " means—

(a) any constable ;

(b) any officer of the Secretary of State ;

(c) any person authorised in writing, or appointed as a veterinary surgeon, by the local authority within whose area the slaughterhouse or knacker's yard is situated.

(4) The local authority shall have a right to enter any knacker's yard at any hour between nine o'clock in the morning and six o'clock in the evening, or at any hour when business is in progress or is usually carried on therein, for the purpose of examining whether there is any contravention of—

    (i) section 6 of this Act ;

    (ii) the Public Health (Scotland) Act 1897 ; or   1897 c. 38.

    (iii) any byelaw made under that Act.

15.—(1) No animal shall be slaughtered or stunned in a Licensing of slaughterhouse or knacker's yard by any person except in slaughtermen accordance with a licence granted by a local authority and in and knackers. force under this section:

Provided that this subsection shall not apply with respect to the slaughter, under the Diseases of Animals Act 1950, of an 1950 c. 36. animal by an officer of, or person employed by, the Minister of Agriculture, Fisheries and Food or the Secretary of State.

(2) A licence under this section shall not be granted except to a male person of the age of eighteen years or upwards who is, in the opinion of the local authority, a fit and proper person to hold such a licence.

(3) A licence under this section—

    (a) shall be valid only in the area of the local authority granting the licence and for a period not exceeding twelve months ;

    (b) may be renewed from time to time at the discretion of the local authority ;

    (c) may be suspended at any time by the local authority for such period as they may determine ; and

    (d) may be revoked by the local authority where they are satisfied that the person is no longer a fit and proper person to hold such a licence.

(4) Any person aggrieved by the refusal of the local authority to grant a licence under this section or by the suspension or revocation by the local authority of such a licence may appeal to the sheriff against such refusal, suspension, or revocation, within one month of the intimation thereof, and the decision of the sheriff shall be final.

(5) A fee may be charged by the local authority for each such licence and a fee for every renewal thereof.

(6) In any application for a licence under this section the person making the application shall state whether—

(a) he holds any such licence in any area or areas other than that to which his application relates and the names of any such areas ;

(b) he has been refused, or has had suspended or revoked, any such licence in any other area and, if so, the name of that area ; and

(c) he has any similar application pending in any other area and, if so, the name of that area.

Further provisions in relation to the licensing of slaughtermen and knackers.

16.—(1) Subject to the provisions of this section, any licence granted under section 15 of this Act shall specify—

(a) the kinds of animals which may be slaughtered or stunned by the holder of the licence ; and

(b) the types of instrument which may be used by him for slaughtering or stunning any such animals,

and may, in such cases as may be prescribed by regulations under this section, be granted subject to a condition prohibiting the slaughter of any animal in pursuance of the licence except under the supervision of a person who is the holder of a licence, in force under the said section 15, which is not subject to a like condition.

(2) In relation to the slaughter of animals by the Jewish method for the food of Jews or by the Muslim method for the food of Muslims, so much of subsection (1) above as requires a licence under the said section 15 to specify the matters referred to in paragraphs (a) and (b) of that subsection shall not apply.

(3) The Secretary of State may make regulations for prescribing qualifications for holding licences, or licences of any class, under the said section 15 and for prohibiting the grant of such licences to persons not having the prescribed qualifications.

(4) Without prejudice to the provisions of the said section 15, a local authority may refuse an application for the grant of a licence under that section, or revoke or suspend the operation of such a licence, if the applicant or holder has failed to comply with any condition of his licence granted by that or any other local authority under the said section 15, or has been convicted of an offence under—

1933 c. 39.
1953 c. 27.
1954 c. 59.
1958 c. 8.

(a) the Slaughter of Animals Acts 1933 to 1954 or—

(i) the Slaughter of Animals Act 1958 in so far as re-enacting (with or without modifications) provisions of the said Acts of 1933 to 1954 ; or

(ii) the Slaughterhouses Act 1974 in so far as 1974 c. 3.
re-enacting (with or without modifications) provisions
of so much of the said Act of 1958 as is mentioned in
subparagraph (i) of this paragraph ;

(*b*) section 14 or 18 of this Act ;

(*c*) the Protection of Animals Act 1911 or the Protection 1911 c. 27.
of Animals (Scotland) Act 1912 ;   1912 c. 14.

(*d*) any regulations made under section 9 or 16 of this
Act ; or

(*e*) any order, made under section 20 of the Diseases of 1950 c. 36.
Animals Act 1950, regulating the transport of animals.

17. Any local authority who have provided or established a Employment of
slaughterhouse may, if they think fit, employ persons to slaughter slaughtermen
or stun animals in accordance with the provisions of section 10, by local
11 and 15 of this Act and may make such charges as they con- authority.
sider reasonable for the services of the persons so employed.

18.—(1) Subject to the provisions of this section, any person Offences and
who slaughters or stuns, or attempts to slaughter or stun, any penalties.
animal in contravention of section 10, 12 or 15 of this Act or
who knowingly makes any false statement for the purposes of
obtaining a licence under the said section 15 shall be guilty of
an offence and liable on summary conviction to a fine not
exceeding one hundred pounds or to imprisonment for a term
not exceeding six months or to both.

(2) A person shall not be guilty of an offence in respect of
any such contravention as aforesaid if he proves that by reason of
an accident or other emergency the contravention was necessary
for preventing physical injury or suffering to any person or
animal.

(3) Where a person convicted of an offence in respect of any
such contravention as aforesaid or of an offence against regulations made under section 9 of this Act is registered in respect of
premises under section 4 of, or is the holder of a licence granted
under section 6 of, this Act the court may, where such registration or licence relates to premises where the offence was committed, in addition to any other penalty cancel the registration
or the licence as the case may be.

19.—(1) It shall be the duty of every local authority to execute Enforcement.
and enforce within their area the provisions of—

(i) sections 7, 10 to 12, 14 to 16 and 18 ; and

(ii) any regulations made under section 9 or 16 or by virtue
of section 10,

of this Act ; but this subsection shall not be construed as
authorising a local authority to institute proceedings for any
offence.

1956 c. 30. (2) For the purposes of any regulations made under section 13 of the Food and Drugs (Scotland) Act 1956 (regulations as to food hygiene) in respect of any premises to which the provisions mentioned in subsection (1)(i) above apply, the provisions of section 36 of the said Act of 1956 (power to enter premises) shall apply in relation to an authorised officer of the Secretary of State as they apply in relation to an authorised officer of the local authority who are empowered to enforce those regulations so far as they apply to such premises.

Regulations.   **20.** Any power to make regulations under section 9, 10 or 16 of this Act shall be exercisable by statutory instrument which shall be subject to annulment in pursuance of a resolution of either House of Parliament.

Defraying of certain expenses.   **21.** A local authority owning a slaughterhouse may, if they so determine, defray out of the funds from which such slaughterhouse is maintained any expenses incurred by them in the exercise of their powers under section 14, 15 or 17 of this Act.

Interpretation.   **22.** In this Act, unless the context otherwise requires—

" animal " means any description of cattle, sheep, goat, swine or horse ;

1967 c. 77. " constable " has the same meaning as in the Police (Scotland) Act 1967 ;

" enactment " includes an enactment contained in a local Act and any order, regulation or other instrument having effect by virtue of an Act ;

" grant ", in relation to a licence, includes renew or, as the case may be, renewal ;

" horse " includes ass and mule ;

" knacker's yard " means any building or place used for the killing of animals the flesh of which is not intended for sale for human consumption ; and " knacker " means a person whose business it is to carry out such killing ;

" local authority " means an islands or district council ;

" premises ", except in section 6, means a building or any part thereof and any forecourts, yards and places of storage used in connection therewith ; and in section 6 1897 c. 38. has the same meaning as in the Public Health (Scotland) Act 1897 ;

" slaughterhouse " means any building or place used for the killing of animals the flesh of which is intended for sale for human consumption ; and " slaughterman " means a person whose business it is to carry out such killing.

23. The enactments specified in Schedule 1 to this Act shall have effect subject to the amendments there specified, being amendments consequential upon the provisions of this Act.

Consequential amendments.

24.—(1) The transitional provisions and savings contained in Schedule 2 to this Act shall have effect.

(2) Subject to the provisions of the said Schedule 2, the enactments specified in Schedule 3 to this Act are hereby repealed to the extent specified in the third column of the said Schedule 3.

(3) Nothing in this Act shall be taken as prejudicing the operation of sections 16 and 17 of the Interpretation Act 1978 (which relate to the effect of repeals).

Transitional provisions, savings and repeals.

1978 c. 30.

25.—(1) This Act may be cited as the Slaughter of Animals (Scotland) Act 1980.

(2) This Act extends to Scotland only.

Citation and extent.

SCHEDULES

Section 23.

SCHEDULE 1

CONSEQUENTIAL AMENDMENTS OF ENACTMENTS

1956 c. 30.

1.—In section 12(4) of the Food and Drugs (Scotland) Act 1956, for paragraph (*a*) there shall be substituted the following paragraph—

"(*a*) in subsection (1) the expression—

"animal" means cattle, sheep, goats, swine and horses; and in this definition "horses" includes asses and mules;

"slaughterhouse" means any premises used for slaughtering animals the flesh of which is intended for sale for human consumption and includes any place other than premises used in connection therewith; and".

1957 c. 57.

2.—In section 25(6) of the Agriculture Act 1957, for the words "Part II of the Slaughterhouses Act, 1954," there shall be substituted the words "section 1 of the Slaughter of Animals (Scotland) Act 1980.".

1968 c. 27.

3.—In section 10(1) of the Firearms Act 1968, for the words "section 2 of the Slaughter of Animals (Scotland) Act 1928" there shall be substituted the words "section 15 of the Slaughter of Animals (Scotland) Act 1980".".

Section 24(1).

SCHEDULE 2

TRANSITIONAL PROVISIONS AND SAVINGS.

1.—(1) Without prejudice to section 8(4) of this Act and subject to paragraph 4 of this Schedule, in so far as anything done or having effect as if done under or in pursuance of any of the enactments repealed by this Act (in this Schedule referred to as "the repealed enactments") could have been done under or in pursuance of a corresponding provision of this Act, it shall not be invalidated by reason only of the repeal but shall have effect as if done under or in pursuance of that provision; and anything begun under any of the repealed enactments may be continued under the corresponding provision of this Act as if begun under that provision.

(2) Subparagraph (1) above applies in particular to any regulation, byelaw, determination, decision, authorisation, application, licence, renewal, suspension, revocation, notice, purchase, disposal, charge, certificate, prohibition, registration, refusal, cancellation, variation, appeal, objection, advertisement, specification, condition or penalty prescribed, responsibility imposed or warrant granted.

2.—Without prejudice to any express amendment made by this Act, where any enactment or document refers, either expressly or by implication, to any of the repealed enactments, the reference shall, except where the context otherwise requires, be construed as, or as including, a reference to the corresponding provision of this Act.

3.—Where any period of time specified in any of the repealed SCH. 2
enactments is current at the commencement of this Act, this Act
shall have effect as if the corresponding provision of this Act had
been in force when that period began to run.

4.—(1) Nothing in this Act shall affect the repealed enactments in
their operation in relation to offences committed before the commencement of this Act.

(2) Where an offence, for the continuance of which a penalty was
provided, has been committed under any of the repealed enactments
proceedings may, in the same manner as if the offence had been
committed under the corresponding provision of this Act, be taken
under this Act in respect of the continuance, after the commencement
of this Act, of the offence.

5. Without prejudice to paragraph 1 or 4 above, any reference in
this Act (whether express or implied) to a thing done or required or
authorised to be done, or omitted to be done, or to any event which
has occurred, under or for the purposes of or by reference to or in
contravention of any of the provisions of this Act shall, except where
the context otherwise requires, be construed as including a reference
to the corresponding thing done or required or authorised to be done,
or omitted, or to the corresponding event which occurred as the case
may be, under or for the purposes of or by reference to or in contravention of the corresponding provisions of the repealed enactments and of the enactments repealed by those enactments.

SCHEDULE 3

Section 24(2).

REPEALS

Chapter	Short Title	Extent of Repeal
60 & 61 Vict. c. 38.	The Public Health (Scotland) Act 1897.	Section 33.
18 & 19 Geo. 5. c. 29.	The Slaughter of Animals (Scotland) Act 1928.	The whole Act.
1 & 2 Eliz. 2. c. 27.	The Slaughter of Animals (Pigs) Act 1953.	The whole Act.
2 & 3 Eliz. 2. c. 42.	The Slaughterhouses Act 1954.	The whole Act.
2 & 3 Eliz. 2. c. 59.	The Slaughter of Animals (Amendment) Act 1954.	The whole Act.
1972 c. 62.	The Agriculture (Miscellaneous Provisions) Act 1972.	Sections 6 and 7. Schedules 1 and 2.

Consolidated Fund Act 1980

1980 CHAPTER 14

An Act to apply certain sums out of the Consolidated Fund to the service of the years ending on 31st March 1979 and 1980.

[20th March 1980]

Most Gracious Sovereign,

WE, Your Majesty's most dutiful and loyal subjects, the Commons of the United Kingdom in Parliament assembled, towards making good the supply which we have cheerfully granted to Your Majesty in this Session of Parliament, have resolved to grant unto Your Majesty the sums hereinafter mentioned; and do therefore most humbly beseech Your Majesty that it may be enacted, and be it enacted by the Queen's most Excellent Majesty, by and with the advice and consent of the Lords Spiritual and Temporal, and Commons, in this present Parliament assembled, and by the authority of the same, as follows:—

Issue out of the Consolidated Fund for the year ending 31st March 1979.
1. The Treasury may issue out of the Consolidated Fund of the United Kingdom and apply towards making good the supply granted to Her Majesty for the service of the year ending on 31st March 1979 the sum of £60,375,250·04.

Issue out of the Consolidated Fund for the year ending 31st March 1980.
2. The Treasury may issue out of the Consolidated Fund of the United Kingdom and apply towards making good the supply granted to Her Majesty for the service of the year ending on 31st March 1980 the sum of £837,997,000.

Short title.
3. This Act may be cited as the Consolidated Fund Act 1980.

National Health Service (Invalid Direction) Act 1980

1980 CHAPTER 15

An Act to give temporary effect to an instrument purporting to be a direction given by the Secretary of State for Social Services. [20th March 1980]

BE IT ENACTED by the Queen's most Excellent Majesty, by and with the advice and consent of the Lords Spiritual and Temporal, and Commons, in this present Parliament assembled, and by the authority of the same, as follows:—

1. The instrument dated 1st August 1979 and purporting to be a direction given by the Secretary of State for Social Services with respect to the functions of the Lambeth, Southwark and Lewisham Area Health Authority (Teaching) shall have effect and be deemed to have had effect as if it had been a valid direction under section 86 of the National Health Service Act 1977 specifying as the period during which those functions were to be performed by others the period beginning on 1st August 1979 and ending on 31st March 1980. Effect of Secretary of State's instrument. 1977 c. 49.

2. This Act may be cited as the National Health Service (Invalid Direction) Act 1980. Short title.

New Hebrides Act 1980

1980 CHAPTER 16

An Act to make provision in connection with the attainment by the New Hebrides of independence within the Commonwealth.   [20th March 1980]

B E IT ENACTED by the Queen's most Excellent Majesty, by and with the advice and consent of the Lords Spiritual and Temporal, and Commons, in this present Parliament assembled, and by the authority of the same, as follows:—

Common-wealth citizenship.
1948 c. 56.

1.—(1) On and after such day as Her Majesty may by Order in Council appoint (in this Act referred to as the " appointed day ") the British Nationality Act 1948 shall have effect as if in section 1(3) (Commonwealth countries having separate citizenship) there were added at the end the words " and the New Hebrides ".

(2) Section 30(2) of that Act (power to apply Act to the New Hebrides) shall cease to have effect.

1967 c. 4.

(3) In accordance with section 3(3) of the West Indies Act 1967 it is hereby declared that this section extends to all associated states.

(4) An Order in Council under this section shall be laid before Parliament after being made.

Consequential amendments and repeals.

2.—(1) The provisions specified in Schedule 1 to this Act shall have effect subject to the amendments there specified, being amendments consequential on the attainment of independence within the Commonwealth by the New Hebrides.

(2) The enactments and instruments mentioned in Schedule 2 to this Act are hereby repealed to the extent specified in column 3 of that Schedule.

3.—(1) Her Majesty may by Order in Council make such provision as appears to Her to be expedient in relation to—

Pending appeals to Privy Council.

(a) appeals from any court having jurisdiction for the New Hebrides in respect of proceedings originating in any court in the New Hebrides in which records have been registered in the Office of the Judicial Committee of the Privy Council before the appointed day; and

(b) petitions for leave to appeal from such a court in respect of such proceedings filed in that Office before that day.

(2) An Order in Council under this section shall be laid before Parliament after being made.

4.—(1) This Act may be cited as the New Hebrides Act 1980.

Short title and commencement.

(2) Sections 1(2) and 2 and Schedules 1 and 2 shall come into force on the appointed day.

SCHEDULES

SCHEDULE 1

CONSEQUENTIAL AMENDMENTS

Diplomatic immunities

1961 c. 11.

1. In section 1(5) of the Diplomatic Immunities (Conferences with Commonwealth Countries and Republic of Ireland) Act 1961 (countries to which the Act applies), before the word " and " in the last place where it occurs there shall be inserted the words " the New Hebrides ".

The Services

2. In the definitions of " Commonwealth force " in section 225(1)
1955 c. 18.   and 223(1) respectively of the Army Act 1955 and the Air Force Act
1955 c. 19.   1955, and in the definition of " Commonwealth country " in section
1957 c. 53.   135(1) of the Naval Discipline Act 1957, at the end there shall be added the words " or the New Hebrides ".

Visiting forces

1933 c. 6.

3. In the Visiting Forces (British Commonwealth) Act 1933, section 4 (attachment and mutual powers of command) shall apply in relation to forces raised in the New Hebrides as it applies to forces raised in
1931 c. 4.   Dominions within the meaning of the Statute of Westminster 1931.
(22 & 23 Geo. 5).
1952 c. 67.   4. In the Visiting Forces Act 1952 in section 1(1)(*a*) (countries to which the Act applies), at the end there shall be added the words " the New Hebrides or "; and, until express provision with respect to the New Hebrides is made by an Order in Council under section 8 of that Act (application to visiting forces of law relating to home forces), any such Order for the time being in force shall be deemed to apply to visiting forces of the New Hebrides.

Shipping

1894 c. 60.   5. In section 427(2) of the Merchant Shipping Act 1894, as set out
1949 c. 43.   in section 2 of the Merchant Shipping (Safety Convention) Act 1949 (ships to which section 427 does not apply), before the words " or in any " there shall be inserted the words " or the New Hebrides ".

1934 c. 49.   6. In the Whaling Industry (Regulation) Act 1934, the expression " British ship to which this Act applies " shall not include a British ship registered in the New Hebrides.

Commonwealth Institute

1925 ch. xvii.   7. In section 8(2) of the Imperial Institute Act 1925, as amended
1958 c. 16.   by the Commonwealth Institute Act 1958 (power to vary the provisions of the said Act of 1925 if an agreement for the purpose is made with the governments of certain territories which for the time being are contributing towards the expenses of the Commonwealth Institute), at the end there shall be added the words " and the New Hebrides ".

Offices, shops and railway premises   SCH. 1

8. In section 84(2) of the Offices, Shops and Railway Premises Act 1963 c. 41.
1963 (exclusion of visiting forces from Act) before the words " and
any country " there are inserted the words " the New Hebrides ".

9. In section 78(2) of the Office and Shop Premises Act (Northern 1966 c. 26 (N.I.).
Ireland) 1966 (exclusion of visiting forces from Act) before the words
" and any country " there are inserted the words " the New Hebrides ".

Section 2(2).

SCHEDULE 2

REPEALS

Chapter or Number	Short title	Extent of repeal
1948 c. 56.	British Nationality Act 1948.	Section 30(2).
1962 c. 41.	Colonial Loans Act 1962.	Section 1(3).
1978 c. 2.	Commonwealth Development Corporation Act 1978.	Section 17(3).
S.R. & O. 1922/717.	New Hebrides Order 1922.	The whole Order.
S.R. & O. 1923/356.	New Hebrides Order 1923.	The whole Order.
S.I. 1961/1831.	New Hebrides Order 1961.	The whole Order.
S.I. 1963/1324.	New Hebrides Order 1963.	The whole Order.
S.I. 1968/2033.	Fugitive Offenders (United Kingdom Dependencies) Order 1968.	The whole Order.
S.I. 1970/950.	New Hebrides Order 1970.	The whole Order.
S.I. 1973/1758.	New Hebrides Order 1973.	The whole Order.
S.I. 1975/1505.	New Hebrides (Appeals to Privy Council) Order 1975.	The whole Order.
S.I. 1975/1514.	New Hebrides Order 1975.	The whole Order.
S.I. 1976/2142.	Fugitive Offenders (United Kingdom Dependencies) (Amendment) Order 1976.	The whole Order.
S.I. 1977/49.	New Hebrides Order 1977.	The whole Order.

National Heritage Act 1980

1980 CHAPTER 17

An Act to establish a National Heritage Memorial Fund for providing financial assistance for the acquisition, maintenance and preservation of land, buildings and objects of outstanding historic and other interest; to make new provision in relation to the arrangements for accepting property in satisfaction of capital transfer tax and estate duty; to provide for payments out of public funds in respect of the loss of or damage to objects loaned to or displayed in local museums and other institutions; and for purposes connected with those matters.

[31st March 1980]

BE IT ENACTED by the Queen's most Excellent Majesty, by and with the advice and consent of the Lords Spiritual and Temporal, and Commons, in this present Parliament assembled, and by the authority of the same, as follows:—

PART I

THE NATIONAL HERITAGE MEMORIAL FUND

1.—(1) There shall be a fund known as the National Heritage Memorial Fund, to be a memorial to those who have died for the United Kingdom, established in succession to the National Land Fund, which shall be applicable for the purposes specified in this Part of this Act.

Establishment of National Heritage Memorial Fund.

(2) The Fund shall be vested in and administered by a body corporate known as the Trustees of the National Heritage Mem-

PART I

orial Fund and consisting of a chairman and not more than ten other members appointed by the Prime Minister.

(3) The persons appointed under this section shall include persons who have knowledge, experience or interests relevant to the purposes for which the Fund may be applied and who are connected by residence or otherwise with England, Wales, Scotland and Northern Ireland respectively.

(4) References in this Part of this Act to the Trustees are to the body constituted by subsection (2) above; and Schedule 1 to this Act shall have effect with respect to the Trustees and the discharge of their functions.

Payments into the Fund.

2.—(1) The Secretary of State and the Chancellor of the Duchy of Lancaster (in this Act referred to as " the Ministers ") shall pay into the Fund in the first month of each financial year a sum determined by them before the beginning of the year; and the Ministers may at any time pay into the Fund such further sum or sums as they may from time to time determine.

(2) There shall also be paid into the Fund any other sums received by the Trustees in consequence of the discharge of their functions.

Grants and loans from the fund.

3.—(1) Subject to the provisions of this section, the Trustees may make grants and loans out of the Fund to eligible recipients for the purpose of assisting them to acquire, maintain or preserve—

(a) any land, building or structure which in the opinion of the Trustees is of outstanding scenic, historic, aesthetic, architectural or scientific interest;

(b) any object which in their opinion is of outstanding historic, artistic or scientific interest;

(c) any collection or group of objects, being a collection or group which taken as a whole is in their opinion of outstanding historic, artistic or scientific interest;

(d) any land or object not falling within paragraph (a), (b) or (c) above the acquisition, maintenance or preservation of which is in their opinion desirable by reason of its connection with land or a building or structure falling within paragraph (a) above; or

(e) any rights in or over land the acquisition of which is in their opinion desirable for the benefit of land or a building or structure falling within paragraph (a) or (d) above.

(2) The Trustees shall not make a grant or loan under this section in respect of any property unless they are of opinion, after obtaining such expert advice as appears to them to be

appropriate, that the property (or, in the case of land or an PART I
object falling within paragraph (*d*) of subsection (1) above, the
land, building or structure with which it is connected or, in the
case of rights falling within paragraph (*e*) of that subsection, the
land, building or structure for whose benefit they are acquired) is
of importance to the national heritage.

(3) In determining whether and on what terms to make a grant
or loan under this section in respect of any property the Trustees shall have regard to the desirability of securing, improving
or controlling public access to, or the public display of, the
property.

(4) In making a grant or loan under this section in respect of
any property the Trustees may impose such conditions as they
think fit, including—

    (*a*) conditions with respect to—

        (i) public access to, or the public display of, the
        property;

        (ii) the maintenance, repair, insurance and safe
        keeping of the property;

        (iii) the disposal or lending of the property; and

    (*b*) conditions requiring the amount of a grant and the out-
    standing amount of a loan to be repaid forthwith on
    breach of any condition.

(5) A grant under this section for the purpose of assisting in
the maintenance or preservation of any property may take the
form of a contribution to a trust established or to be established
for that purpose.

(6) Subject to subsection (7) below, the eligible recipients for
the purposes of this section are—

    (*a*) any museum, art gallery, library or other similar institu-
    tion having as its purpose or one of its purposes the
    preservation for the public benefit of a collection of
    historic, artistic or scientific interest;

    (*b*) any body having as its purpose or one of its purposes
    the provision, improvement or preservation of ameni-
    ties enjoyed or to be enjoyed by the public or the
    acquisition of land to be used by the public;

    (*c*) any body having nature conservation as its purpose or
    one of its purposes;

    (*d*) the Secretary of State acting in the discharge of his
    functions under section 5 of the Historic Buildings and 1953 c. 49.
    Ancient Monuments Act 1953 or section 11(1) or 13
    of the Ancient Monuments and Archaeological Areas 1979 c. 46
    Act 1979; and

(e) the Department of the Environment for Northern Ireland acting in the discharge of its functions under so much of section 1(1) of the Historic Monuments Act (Northern Ireland) 1971 as relates to the acquisition of historic monuments by agreement, section 4 of that Act or Article 84 of the Planning (Northern Ireland) Order 1972.

(7) The institutions referred to in paragraph (a) of subsection (6) above include any institution maintained by a Minister or Northern Ireland department; but neither that paragraph nor paragraph (b) or (c) of that subsection applies to any institution or body established outside the United Kingdom or established or conducted for profit.

Other
expenditure
out of the
Fund.

4.—(1) Subject to the provisions of this section, the Trustees may apply the Fund for any purpose other than making grants or loans, being a purpose connected with the acquisition, maintenance or preservation of property falling within section 3(1) above, including its acquisition, maintenance or preservation by the Trustees.

(2) Subsections (2) and (3) of section 3 above shall have effect in relation to the application of any sums out of the Fund under this section as they have effect in relation to the making of a grant or loan under that section.

(3) The Trustees shall not retain any property acquired by them under this section except in such cases and for such period as either of the Ministers may allow.

Acceptance
of gifts.

5.—(1) Subject to the provisions of this section, the Trustees may accept gifts of money or other property.

(2) The Trustees shall not accept a gift unless it is either unconditional or on conditions which enable the subject of the gift (and any income or proceeds of sale arising from it) to be applied for a purpose for which the Fund may be applied under this Part of this Act and which enable the Trustees to comply with subsection (3) below and section 2(2) above.

(3) The Trustees shall not retain any property (other than money) accepted by them by way of gift except in such cases and for such period as either of the Ministers may allow.

(4) References in this section to gifts include references to bequests and devises.

Powers of
investment.

6.—(1) Any sums in the Fund which are not immediately required for any other purpose may be invested by the Trustees in accordance with this section.

(2) Sums directly or indirectly representing money paid into PART I
the Fund under section 2(1) above may be invested in any manner
approved by the Treasury ; and the Trustees—

(a) shall not invest any amount available for investment
which represents such money except with the consent of
the Treasury ; and

(b) shall, if the Treasury so require, invest any such amount
specified by the Treasury in such manner as the
Treasury may direct.

(3) Any sums to which subsection (2) above does not apply
may be invested in accordance with the Trustee Investments Act 1961 c. 62.
1961 ; and sections 1, 2, 5, 6, 12 and 13 of that Act shall have
effect in relation to such sums, and in relation to any investments for the time being representing such sums, as if they
constituted a trust fund and the Trustees were the trustees of
that trust fund.

7.—(1) As soon as practicable after the end of each financial Annual
year the Trustees shall make a report to the Ministers on the reports and
activities of the Trustees during that year ; and the Ministers accounts.
shall cause the report to be published and lay copies of it before
Parliament.

(2) It shall be the duty of the Trustees—

(a) to keep proper accounts and proper records in relation
to the accounts ;

(b) to prepare in respect of each financial year a statement
of account in such form as the Ministers may with
the approval of the Treasury direct ; and

(c) to send copies of the statement to the Ministers and the
Comptroller and Auditor General before the end of
the month of November next following the end of the
financial year to which the statement relates.

(3) The Comptroller and Auditor General shall examine,
certify and report on each statement received by him in pursuance
of this section and lay copies of it and of his report before
Parliament.

PART II

PROPERTY ACCEPTED IN SATISFACTION OF TAX

8.—(1) Where under paragraph 17 of Schedule 4 to the Payments by
Finance Act 1975 the Commissioners of Inland Revenue have Ministers to
accepted any property in satisfaction of any amount of capital Commissioners
transfer tax, the Ministers may pay to the Commissioners a sum of Inland
equal to that amount. Revenue.

1975 c. 7.

(2) Any sums paid to the Commissioners under this section shall be dealt with by them as if they were payments on account of capital transfer tax.

(3) Subsections (1) and (2) above shall apply in relation to estate duty chargeable on a death occurring before the passing of the said Act of 1975 as they apply in relation to capital transfer tax ; and for that purpose the reference in subsection (1) to paragraph 17 of Schedule 4 to that Act shall be construed as a reference to—

(*a*) section 56 of the Finance (1909-1910) Act 1910 ;

(*b*) section 30 of the Finance Act 1953 and section 1 of the Finance (Miscellaneous Provisions) Act (Northern Ireland) 1954 ; and

(*c*) section 34(1) of the Finance Act 1956, section 46 of the Finance Act 1973, Article 10 of the Finance (Northern Ireland) Order 1972 and Article 5 of the Finance (Miscellaneous Provisions) (Northern Ireland) Order 1973.

(4) References in this Part of this Act to property accepted in satisfaction of tax are to property accepted by the Commissioners under the provisions mentioned in this section.

9.—(1) Any property accepted in satisfaction of tax shall be disposed of in such manner as either of the Ministers may direct.

(2) Without prejudice to the generality of subsection (1) above, either Minister may in particular direct that any such property shall, on such conditions as he may direct, be transferred to any institution or body falling within section 3(6)(*a*), (*b*) or (*c*) above which is willing to accept it, to the National Art Collections Fund or the Friends of the National Libraries if they are willing to accept it, to the Secretary of State or to the Department of the Environment for Northern Ireland.

(3) Where either of the Ministers has determined that any property accepted in satisfaction of tax is to be disposed of under this section to any such institution or body as is mentioned in subsection (2) above or to any other person who is willing to accept it, he may direct that the disposal shall be effected by means of a transfer direct to that institution or body or direct to that other person instead of being transferred to the Commissioners.

(4) Either of the Ministers may in any case direct that any property accepted in satisfaction of tax shall, instead of being transferred to the Commissioners, be transferred to a person nominated by the Ministers ; and where property is so transferred

the person to whom it is transferred shall, subject to any directions subsequently given under subsection (1) or (2) above, hold the property and manage it in accordance with such directions as may be given by the Minister.

(5) In exercising their powers under this section in respect of an object or collection or group of objects having a significant association with a particular place, the Ministers shall consider whether it is appropriate for the object, collection or group to be, or continue to be, kept in that place, and for that purpose the Ministers shall obtain such expert advice as appears to them to be appropriate.

(6) The Ministers shall lay before Parliament as soon as may be after the end of each financial year a statement giving particulars of any disposal or transfer made in that year in pursuance of directions given under this section.

(7) References in this section to the disposal or transfer of any property include references to leasing, sub-leasing or lending it for any period and on any terms.

10.—(1) This section applies where property is accepted in Receipts and satisfaction of tax and the Ministers have made a payment in expenses in respect of the property under section 8 above. respect of property

(2) Any sums received on the disposal of, or of any part of, accepted by the property (including any premium, rent or other consideration Commisarising from the leasing, sub-leasing or lending of the property) sioners. and any sums otherwise received in connection with the property shall be paid to the Ministers.

(3) Any expenses incurred in connection with the property so far as not disposed of under section 9 above, including in the case of leasehold property any rent payable in respect of it, shall be defrayed by the Ministers.

11. No stamp duty shall be payable on any conveyance or Exemption transfer of property made under section 9 above to any such from stamp institution or body as is mentioned in subsection (2) of that section duty. or on any conveyance or transfer made under subsection (4) of that section.

12.—(1) In paragraph 17 of Schedule 4 to the Finance Act Approval of 1975— property for

    (*a*) in sub-paragraph (1) (power of Commissioners of Inland acceptance in
        Revenue, if they think fit, to accept property in satis- of tax.
        faction of capital transfer tax) after the words " if they 1975 c. 7.
        think fit " there shall be inserted the words " and the
        Ministers agree " ;

    (*b*) in sub-paragraphs (3) and (4) (approval by Treasury of objects to be accepted) for the words " the Treasury ", in each place where they occur, there shall be substituted the words " the Ministers " ;

    (*c*) in sub-paragraph (5) (interpretation) after the words " In this paragraph " there shall be inserted the words " ' the Ministers ' means the Secretary of State and the Chancellor of the Duchy of Lancaster and " ;

    (*d*) at the end of sub-paragraph (5) there shall be inserted the words " and, in determining under sub-paragraph (4) above whether an object or collection or group of objects is pre-eminent, regard shall be had to any significant association of the object, collection or group with a particular place."

(2) The power of the Commissioners of Inland Revenue to accept property in satisfaction of estate duty under the provisions mentioned in subsection (3) of section 8 above shall not be exercisable except with the agreement of the Ministers ; and the Ministers shall exercise the functions conferred on the Treasury by the provisions mentioned in paragraphs (*b*) and (*c*) of that subsection (which correspond to paragraph 17(3) and (4) of Schedule 4 to the said Act of 1975).

(3) Any question whether an object or collection or group of objects is pre-eminent shall be determined under the provisions mentioned in section 8(3)(*b*) or (*c*) above in the same way as under the said paragraph 17(4).

Acceptance of property in satisfaction of interest on tax.

13.—(1) In paragraph 19 of Schedule 4 to the Finance Act 1975 (interest on capital transfer tax) after sub-paragraph (5) there shall be inserted—

    " (6) In paragraphs 17(1) and 18(1) above references to tax include references to interest payable under sub-paragraph (1) above."

(2) References to estate duty in—

    (*a*) the provisions mentioned in section 8(3) above ; and

1958 c. 56.
1958 c. 56.
(N.I.).

    (*b*) section 32 of the Finance Act 1958 and section 5 of the Finance Act (Northern Ireland) 1958,

1896 c. 28.

shall include references to interest payable under section 18 of the Finance Act 1896.

(3) Section 8 above shall have effect where by virtue of this section property is accepted in satisfaction of interest as it has effect where property is accepted in satisfaction of capital transfer tax or estate duty and references in this Part of this Act to property accepted in satisfaction of tax shall be construed accordingly.

14.—(1) Her Majesty may by Order in Council provide for the transfer to the Trustees of the National Heritage Memorial Fund of any functions exercisable by the Ministers or either of them under any of the provisions of this Part of this Act or of the provisions amended by section 12 above.

(2) An Order under this section may contain such incidental, consequential and supplemental provisions as may be necessary or expedient for the purpose of giving effect to the Order, including provisions adapting any of the provisions referred to in subsection (1) above.

(3) No Order shall be made under this section unless a draft of the Order has been laid before, and approved by a resolution of, each House of Parliament.

15.—(1) Sections 48, 50 and 51 of the Finance Act 1946 (which establish the National Land Fund for the purpose of making such payments as are mentioned in section 8 above and contain other provisions superseded by this Part of this Act) and section 7 of the Historic Buildings and Ancient Monuments Act 1953 (which enables payments to be made out of that Fund for various other purposes) shall cease to have effect.

(2) Subsection (1) above does not affect subsection (4) of the said section 48 (accounts) in relation to any receipts into or payments out of the National Land Fund at any time before that section ceases to have effect.

(3) The Treasury shall, within six months of the date on which the said section 48 ceases to have effect, cancel all investments of the National Land Fund in debt charged on the National Loans Fund.

PART III

MISCELLANEOUS AND SUPPLEMENTARY

16.—(1) Subject to subsections (3) and (4) below, either of the Ministers may, in such cases and to such extent as he may determine, undertake to indemnify any institution, body or person falling within subsection (2) below for the loss of, or damage to, any object belonging to that institution, body or person while on loan to any other institution, body or person falling within that subsection.

(2) The institutions, bodies and persons referred to above are—

(a) a museum, art gallery or other similar institution in the United Kingdom which has as its purpose or one of its purposes the preservation for the public benefit of a collection of historic, artistic or scientific interest and which is maintained—

    (i) wholly or mainly out of moneys provided by Parliament or out of moneys appropriated by Measure ; or

    (ii) by a local authority or university in the United Kingdom ;

  (*b*) a library which is maintained—

    (i) wholly or mainly out of moneys provided by Parliament or out of moneys appropriated by Measure ; or

    (ii) by a library authority ;

or the main function of which is to serve the needs of teaching and research at a university in the United Kingdom ;

  (*c*) the National Trust for Places of Historic Interest or Natural Beauty ;

  (*d*) the National Trust for Scotland for Places of Historic Interest or Natural Beauty ; and

  (*e*) any other body or person for the time being approved for the purposes of this section by either of the Ministers with the consent of the Treasury.

(3) Neither Minister shall give an undertaking under this section unless he considers that the loan will facilitate public access to the object in question or contribute materially to public understanding or appreciation of it.

(4) Neither Minister shall give an undertaking under this section unless the loan of the object in question is made in accordance with conditions approved by him and the Treasury and the Minister is satisfied that appropriate arrangements have been made for the safety of the object while it is on loan.

(5) Subsections (1) to (4) above shall apply in relation to the loan of an object belonging to an institution, body or person established or resident in Northern Ireland with the substitution for references to either of the Ministers and the Treasury of references to the Department of Education for Northern Ireland and the Department of Finance for Northern Ireland respectively.

1964 c. 75.

1955 c. 75.
S.I. 1972/1263.

(6) In subsection (2) above " library authority " means a library authority within the meaning of the Public Libraries and Museums Act 1964, a statutory library authority within the meaning of the Public Libraries (Scotland) Act 1955 or an Education and Library Board within the meaning of the Education and Libraries (Northern Ireland) Order 1972 and " university " includes a university college and a college, school or hall of a university.

(7) References in this section to the loss of or damage to, or to the safety of, an object while on loan include references to the loss of or damage to, or the safety of, the object while being taken to or returned from the place where it is to be or has been kept while on loan.

17. Any sums required by any Minister for making payments Expenses under this Act shall be defrayed out of moneys provided by and receipts. Parliament, and any sums received by any Minister under this Act shall be paid into the Consolidated Fund.

18.—(1) This Act may be cited as the National Heritage Act Short title, 1980.
interpretation, repeals and

(2) In this Act— extent.

" financial year " means the twelve months ending with 31st March ;

" the Ministers " means the Secretary of State and the Chancellor of the Duchy of Lancaster.

(3) References in this Act and in the provisions amended by section 12(1) above to the Chancellor of the Duchy of Lancaster are references to the Chancellor in his capacity as a Minister of the Crown with responsibility for the Arts.

(4) References in this Act to the making of a grant or loan or the transfer or conveyance of any property to any institution or body include references to the making of a grant or loan or the transfer or conveyance of property to trustees for that institution or body.

(5) The enactments mentioned in Schedule 2 to this Act are hereby repealed to the extent specified in the third column of that Schedule.

(6) This Act extends to Northern Ireland.

SCHEDULES

SCHEDULE 1

THE TRUSTEES OF THE NATIONAL HERITAGE MEMORIAL FUND

Status

1. The Trustees shall not be regarded as acting on behalf of the Crown and neither they nor their officers or servants shall be regarded as Crown servants.

1967 c. 9.
1962 c. 9.

S.I. 1977/2157.

2. Section 40 of the General Rate Act 1967 (relief for charities and other organisations), section 4 of the Local Government (Financial Provisions etc.) (Scotland) Act 1962 (corresponding provisions for Scotland) and Article 41 of the Rates (Northern Ireland) Order 1977 (corresponding provisions for Northern Ireland) shall apply to any hereditament, lands and heritages occupied by the Trustees for the purposes of this Act as they apply to a hereditament, lands and heritages occupied by trustees for a charity.

Tenure of office of trustee

3.—(1) Subject to the provisions of this paragraph, a member of the body constituted by section 1 (2) of this Act (in this Schedule referred to as " a trustee ") shall hold and vacate his office in accordance with the terms of his appointment.

(2) A person shall not be appointed a trustee for more than three years.

(3) A trustee may resign by notice in writing to the Prime Minister.

(4) The Prime Minister may terminate the appointment of a trustee if he is satisfied that—

    (*a*) for a period of six months beginning not more than nine months previously he has, without the consent of the other trustees, failed to attend the meetings of the trustees ;

    (*b*) he is an undischarged bankrupt or has made an arrangement with his creditors or is insolvent within the meaning of paragraph 9(2)(*a*) of Schedule 3 to the Conveyancing and Feudal Reform (Scotland) Act 1970 ;

1970 c. 35.

    (*c*) he is by reason of physical or mental illness, or for any other reason, incapable of carrying out his duties ; or

    (*d*) he has been convicted of such a criminal offence, or his conduct has been such, that it is not in the Prime Minister's opinion fitting that he should remain a trustee.

(5) A person who ceases or has ceased to be a trustee may be re-appointed.

(d) conditions to be complied with by participating schools with respect to the selection of pupils for assisted places, the admission of pupils, the fees to be charged, the keeping and auditing of accounts and the furnishing of information to the Secretary of State ; and

(e) such other matters as appear to him to be requisite for the purposes of the scheme.

(7) Regulations under subsection (6) above may authorise the Secretary of State to make provision for any purpose specified in the regulations.

(8) Before making regulations under subsection (6) above the Secretary of State shall consult such bodies as appear to him to be appropriate and to be representative of participating schools or, in the case of regulations made within twelve months of the coming into force of this section, of schools eligible to participate in the scheme.

(9) Regulations made under subsection (6)(b) above shall be reviewed by the Secretary of State in consultation with such bodies as appear to him to be appropriate and to be representative of participating schools—

(a) not later than two years after the date on which the first such regulations are made ; and

(b) thereafter at intervals not exceeding two years.

(10) Except where the context otherwise requires, references in this section and section 18 below to a school include references to the proprietors of the school and persons acting with their authority ; and references in this section to an independent school are references to an independent school that is finally registered and conducted for charitable purposes only.

18.—(1) The Secretary of State may make regulations requiring or enabling schools participating in the scheme referred to in section 17 above to make grants in respect of such expenses, and to remit such charges, as may be specified in the regulations, being expenses or charges in respect of matters incidental to or arising out of the attendance at the schools of pupils holding assisted places under the scheme. *Incidental expenses of pupils holding assisted places.*

(2) Any such regulations shall require any amounts granted or remitted by a school in accordance with the regulations to be reimbursed to the school by the Secretary of State.

(3) Regulations under this section may in particular prescribe—

(a) the conditions subject to which, the extent to which, and the arrangements in accordance with which, grants and remissions are to be made :

(*b*) the time and manner in which schools are to claim and receive reimbursements from the Secretary of State.

(4) Regulations under this section may authorise the Secretary of State to make provision for any purpose specified in the regulations.

Awards for further and higher education.
1962 c. 12.

19. For sections 1 to 4 of the Education Act 1962 and Schedule 1 to that Act (awards for further and higher education) there shall be substituted the provisions set out in Schedule 5 to this Act which—

(*a*) extend the courses capable of designation under section 1 to include certain courses provided in conjunction with overseas institutions ;

1973 c. 16.
1975 c. 2.
1976 c. 81.

(*b*) incorporate the effect of amendments made by the Education Act 1973, the Education Act 1975 and the Education Act 1976 ; and

(*c*) omit provisions that are spent or no longer required.

Industrial scholarships.

20.—(1) The Secretary of State may award industrial scholarships or make payments to any other person in respect of the award of such scholarships by that person.

(2) In this section " industrial scholarships " means scholarships (however described) tenable by persons undertaking full-time courses of higher education provided by a university, college or other institution in the United Kingdom, being courses which appear to the Secretary of State or, as the case may be, the person awarding the scholarships to be relevant to a career in industry.

(3) In subsection (2) above the reference to a full-time course includes a reference to a course consisting of alternate periods of—

(*a*) full-time study in the university, college or institution in question ; and

(*b*) associated industrial, professional or commercial experience ;

and the reference in that subsection to a course provided by a university, college or institution in the United Kingdom includes a reference to a course provided by such a university, college or institution in conjunction with a university, college or other institution in another country.

Grants for education in Welsh.

21.—(1) The Secretary of State shall by regulations make provision for the payment by him to local education authorities and other persons of grants in respect of expenditure incurred or to be incurred in, or in connection with, the teaching of the Welsh language or the teaching in that language of other subjects.

(2) Any regulations made by the Secretary of State under this section may make provision whereby the making of payments by him in pursuance of the regulations is dependent on the fulfilment of such conditions as may be determined by or in accordance with the regulations, and may also make provision for requiring local education authorities and other persons to whom payments have been made in pursuance of the regulations to comply with such requirements as may be so determined.

School meals

22.—(1) A local education authority— School meals: England and Wales.

   (*a*) may provide registered pupils at any school maintained by them with milk, meals or other refreshment ; and

   (*b*) shall provide such facilities as the authority consider appropriate for the consumption of any meals or other refreshment brought to the school by such pupils.

(2) A local education authority shall exercise their power under subsection (1)(*a*) above in relation to any pupil whose parents are in receipt of supplementary benefit or family income supplement so as to ensure that such provision is made for him in the middle of the day as appears to the authority to be requisite.

(3) A local education authority—

   (*a*) may make such charges as they think fit for anything provided by them under subsection (1)(*a*) above, except where it is provided by virtue of subsection (2) above ; but

   (*b*) shall remit the whole or part of any charge that would otherwise be made if, having regard to the particular circumstances of any pupil or class or description of pupils, they consider it appropriate to do so.

(4) The governors of a school maintained by a local education authority shall—

   (*a*) afford the authority such facilities as they require to enable them to exercise their functions under this section ; and

   (*b*) allow the authority to make such use of the premises and equipment of the school and such alterations to the school buildings as the authority consider necessary for that purpose ;

but nothing in this subsection shall require the governors of a voluntary school to incur any expenditure.

(5) The power under section 78(2)(*a*) of the Education Act 1944 to make arrangements as to the provision of milk for pupils in attendance at non-maintained schools shall apply in relation to all such pupils ; and accordingly section 1(3) of the 1944 c. 31.

1971 c. 74. Education (Milk) Act 1971 (which restricts the power to provision for children under the age of eight and children at special schools) shall cease to have effect.

School meals: Scotland. **23.**—(1) An education authority—

    (*a*) may provide milk, meals or other refreshment for pupils in attendance at public schools and other educational establishments under their management ; and

    (*b*) shall provide such facilities as the authority consider appropriate for the consumption of any meals or other refreshment brought to the school or other educational establishment by such pupils.

(2) An education authority shall exercise their power under subsection (1)(*a*) above in relation to any pupil whose parents are in receipt of supplementary benefit or family income supplement so as to ensure that such provision is made for him in the middle of the day as appears to the authority to be requisite.

(3) An education authority—

    (*a*) may make such charges as they think fit for anything provided by them under subsection (1)(*a*) above, except where it is provided by virtue of subsection (2) above ; but

    (*b*) shall remit the whole or any part of any charge that would otherwise be made, if having regard to the particular circumstances of any pupil or class or description of pupils, they consider it appropriate to do so.

(4) For the purposes of this section, a pupil for whom an education authority have made special arrangements under section 14 of the Education (Scotland) Act 1962 may, at the discretion of the authority, be deemed to be in attendance at a public school under their management.

1962 c. 47.

(5) The power under section 55 of the Education (Scotland) Act 1962 to make arrangements as to the provision of milk for pupils in attendance at schools other than public schools shall apply in relation to all such pupils ; and accordingly section 2(4) of the Education (Milk) Act 1971 (which restricts the power to provision for pupils under the age of eight and pupils receiving special education) shall cease to have effect.

(6) In section 24(1) of the Education (Scotland) Act 1962 (provision by education authority for education of pupils belonging to areas of other authorities) after the word " Act " there shall be inserted the words " or the Education Act 1980 ".

(7) This section applies to Scotland only.

Nursery education

24.—(1) A local education authority shall have power to establish nursery schools, to maintain such schools established by them or a former authority and to assist any such school which is not so established. Nursery education: England and Wales.

(2) A local education authority shall not by virtue of section 8(1)(*a*) of the Education Act 1944 be under any duty in respect of junior pupils who have not attained the age of five years but this subsection shall not affect the power of an authority under section 9(1) of that Act to establish, maintain or assist a school at which education is provided both for such pupils and older pupils, including a school at which there is a nursery class for such junior pupils as aforesaid. 1944 c. 31.

(3) In the definition of " pupil " in section 114(1) of the said Act of 1944 (which defines pupils as those for whom education is required to be provided under that Act) there shall be added at the end the words " but includes a junior pupil who has not attained the age of five years.".

25.—(1) An education authority shall have power to provide for their area school education in nursery schools and nursery classes. Nursery education: Scotland.

(2) The duties of an education authority under section 1 of the Education (Scotland) Act 1962 shall not apply in relation to the provision of school education in nursery schools and nursery classes. 1962 c. 47.

(3) This section applies to Scotland only.

26.—(1) Subject to subsection (3) below, a local education authority may, in accordance with arrangements made by them in that behalf, make available to any day nursery the services of any teacher who— Day nurseries.

(*a*) is employed by them in a nursery school or in a primary school having one or more nursery classes ; and

(*b*) has agreed to provide his services for the purposes of the arrangements.

(2) Subject to subsection (3) below, the governors of any county or voluntary primary school having one or more nursery classes may, in accordance with arrangements made by them in that behalf, make available to any day nursery the services of any teacher who is employed by them in the school and has agreed to provide his services for the purposes of the arrangements.

(3) Arrangements made under subsection (1) above in respect of a teacher in a voluntary school shall require the concurrence of the governors of the school; and no arrangements shall be made under subsection (2) above except at the request of the local education authority and on terms approved by them.

(4) Arrangements under this section may make provision—

  (a) for the supply of equipment for use in connection with the teaching services made available under the arrangements;

  (b) for regulating the respective functions of any teacher whose services are made available under the arrangements, the head teacher of his school and the person in charge of the day nursery;

  (c) for any supplementary or incidental matters connected with the arrangements, including, where the teacher's school and the day nursery are in the areas of different local education authorities, financial adjustments between those authorities.

1977 c. 49.   (5) In this section " day nursery " means a day nursery provided under the National Health Service Act 1977 by a local social services authority.

(6) A teacher shall not be regarded as ceasing to be a member of the teaching staff of his school and subject to the general directions of his head teacher by reason only of his services being made available in pursuance of arrangements under this section.

Miscellaneous

School and further education regulations.

27.—(1) The Secretary of State may by regulations make provision—

  (a) for requiring teachers at schools and further education establishments to which this section applies to possess such qualifications as may be determined by or under the regulations and for requiring such teachers to serve probationary periods;

  (b) with respect to the teaching staff to be provided in such schools and establishments;

  (c) for requiring the approval of the Secretary of State to be obtained for the use in such schools and establishments of such materials or apparatus as may be specified in the regulations, being materials or apparatus which could or might involve a serious risk to health;

  (d) with respect to the keeping, disclosure and transfer of educational records about pupils at such schools and establishments;

(*e*) with respect to the duration of the school day and school year at, and the granting of leave of absence from, any such schools.

(2) The Secretary of State may by regulations make provision for imposing requirements as to the health and physical capacity of—

(*a*) teachers at schools and further education establishments to which this section applies;

(*b*) teachers employed by local education authorities otherwise than at such schools or establishments; and

(*c*) persons employed by local education authorities in work otherwise than as teachers which brings them regularly into contact with persons who have not attained the age of nineteen years.

(3) The Secretary of State may by regulations make provision for prohibiting or restricting the employment or further employment of persons—

(*a*) as teachers at schools and further education establishments to which this section applies;

(*b*) by local education authorities as teachers otherwise than at such schools or establishments; or

(*c*) by local education authorities in such work as is mentioned in subsection (2)(*c*) above,

on medical grounds, in cases of misconduct and, as respects employment or further employment as a teacher, on educational grounds.

(4) The Secretary of State may by regulations make provision requiring his approval to be obtained for the provision of new premises for, or the alteration of the premises of, any school or further educational establishment to which this section applies or any boarding hostel provided by a local education authority for pupils attending any such school or establishment and for the inspection of any such hostel.

(5) In section 71(*a*) of the Public Health Act 1936 and section 63(2) of the Education Act 1944 (exemption from building regulations etc.) references to plans approved by the Secretary of State shall include references to any particulars submitted to and approved by him under regulations made by virtue of subsection (4) above.   1936 c. 49.   1944 c. 31.

(6) The Secretary of State may make regulations with respect to the provision of, and the fees to be charged for, courses of further education at further education establishments to which this section applies, including provision for requiring his approval to be obtained for the provision at such establishments of courses

designated by or under the regulations as courses of advanced further education and for enabling him to give directions for the discontinuance of any such course at such an establishment or as to the number and categories of students to be admitted to such courses at such establishments.

(7) This section applies to any school maintained by a local education authority, any special school not so maintained, any further education establishment provided by a local education authority and any further education establishment designated by or under the regulations as an establishment substantially dependent for its maintenance on assistance from local education authorities or on grants under section 100(1)(*b*) of the said Act of 1944.

Provision of education at non-maintained schools.
1944 c. 31.
1953 c. 33.

28.—(1) So much of section 9(1) of the Education Act 1944 and section 6(1) of the Education (Miscellaneous Provisions) Act 1953 (arrangements with non-maintained schools) as makes the exercise of the powers of local education authorities under those provisions subject to the approval of the Secretary of State shall cease to have effect.

(2) In the said section 6(1) the words " For the purpose of fulfilling their duties under the principal Act " shall be omitted.

1976 c. 81.

(3) Section 5(2) of the Education Act 1976 (under which regulations empowering local education authorities to pay fees and expenses in respect of children attending fee-paying schools may include provision requiring authorities to exercise their powers in accordance with arrangements approved by the Secretary of State) shall cease to have effect.

Provision of clothing for physical training etc.
1948. c. 40.

29.—(1) In subsection (3) of section 5 of the Education (Miscellaneous Provisions) Act 1948 (provision of clothing for physical training) for the words " The Minister may make regulations empowering a local education authority to provide " there shall be substituted the words " A local education authority may provide " and for the words " as may be prescribed " there shall be substituted the words " as may be determined by the authority ".

(2) After subsection (6) of that section (under which the parent of a person provided with clothing under that section may be required to make a payment to the local education authority) there shall be inserted—

" (6A) Where a person who has attained the age of eighteen years (other than a registered pupil at a school) is provided with clothing under this section any reference in subsection (6) above to his parent shall be construed as a reference to that person."

30.—(1) So much of the provisions of the Education Act 1944 mentioned in subsection (2) below as makes the exercise of any power by a local education authority subject to the approval or consent of the Secretary of State or subject to the provisions of regulations made by him shall cease to have effect.

(2) The provisions referred to above are—

    (*a*) section 53(1) (recreation facilities) ;

    (*b*) section 61(2) (boarding fees) ;

    (*c*) section 82 (educational research) ;

    (*d*) section 83 (education conferences) ; and

    (*e*) section 84 (assistance for universities etc.).

(3) Section 12 of the said Act of 1944 (duty to make local education orders) shall cease to have effect.

31.—(1) Subject to subsection (2) below, where any provision for primary or secondary education is made by a local education authority in respect of a pupil who belongs to the area of another local education authority, the providing authority shall, on making a claim within the prescribed period, be entitled to recoupment of an amount equal to the cost to them of the provision from the other authority and the amount of the recoupment shall be determined by agreement between the authorities or, in default of agreement, by the Secretary of State.

(2) Subsection (1) above does not apply to any provision for primary education made in respect of a pupil who has not attained the age of five years unless it is made with the consent of the authority from whom recoupment is claimed.

(3) Where any provision for further education is made by a local education authority in respect of a pupil who belongs to the area of another local education authority, and that other authority have consented to the making of the provision, the providing authority shall, on making a claim within the prescribed period, be entitled to recoupment of the amount of the cost to them of the provision from the other authority and the amount of the recoupment shall be determined by agreement between the authorities or, in default of agreement, by the Secretary of State.

(4) A local education authority may make a payment by way of recoupment to another such authority of the cost incurred by the other authority in making any provision for primary, secondary or further education in respect of a pupil belonging to the area of the paying authority notwithstanding that no claim in respect of the cost has been made by the other authority in accordance with subsection (1) or (3) above.

(5) The Secretary of State may make regulations requiring or authorising payments of amounts determined by or under the regulations to be made by one authority to another where—

    (a) the authority receiving the payment makes, in such cases or circumstances as may be specified in the regulations, provision for education in respect of a pupil having such connection with the area of the paying authority as may be so specified ; and

    (b) one of the authorities is a local education authority and the other an education authority in Scotland.

(6) References in this section to provision for education include references to provision of any benefits or services for which provision is made by or under the enactments relating to education.

(7) References in subsections (3) and (4) above to further education do not include references to further education of a kind such that expenditure on its provision would fall within paragraph 3A of Schedule 2 to the Local Government Act 1974 as amended by section 32 below.

1974 c. 7.

(8) In section 31(8) of the London Government Act 1963 for the words " section 7(1) of the Education (Miscellaneous Provisions) Act 1953 " there shall be substituted the words " section 31(3) of the Education Act 1980 ".

1963 c. 33.

Education expenditure and rate support grant.

32.—(1) Part I of Schedule 2 to the Local Government Act 1974 (adjustment of needs element of rate support grant by reference to education and other expenditure) shall be amended in accordance with Schedule 6 to this Act.

(2) Regulations under sub-paragraph (4)(a) of paragraph 3 of the said Schedule 2 as amended by this section shall apply that paragraph to—

    (a) expenditure incurred by local education authorities in the making of provision for primary and secondary education in respect of pupils not belonging to the area of any local education authority or to the area of any education authority in Scotland ; and

    (b) expenditure, other than that to which paragraph 3A of that Schedule applies, incurred by local education authorities in the making of provision for further education in respect of such pupils.

(3) Regulations under sub-paragraph (4)(a) of paragraph 3 of the said Schedule 2 as amended by this section may be made with retrospective effect to 1st April 1977 insofar as they

apply that paragraph to expenditure in making payments to persons who, in consequence of a direction given by the Secretary of State under regulation 3(2) of the Further Education S.I. 1975/1054. Regulations 1975, have ceased to be employed in colleges for the training of teachers or in institutions having a department for the training of teachers, being—

(a) payments made by an authority as compensating authority under the Colleges of Education (Compen- S.I. 1975/1092. sation) Regulations 1975 ; or

(b) the amount by which the salary to which such a person is entitled under a document such as is mentioned in section 5(2) of the Remuneration of Teachers Act 1965 1965 c. 3. exceeds the salary which would normally be appropriate to the post held by him.

(4) Without prejudice to subsection (3) above, regulations made by virtue of this section under the said Schedule 2 may be made so as to have effect from 1st April 1980 and in relation to regulations made as respects the year beginning on that date under paragraph 3A(2)(*a*) of that Schedule that paragraph shall have effect as if the words " in advance for each year " were omitted.

33.—(1) In section 23(1) of the Sex Discrimination Act 1975 Discrimination and section 18(1) of the Race Relations Act 1976 (discrimina- by local tion by local education authorities) for the words " the Education education Acts 1944 to 1975 " there shall be substituted the words " the authorities. Education Acts 1944 to 1980 ". 1975 c. 65. 1976 c. 74.

(2) In section 23(2) of the said Act of 1975 and section 18(2) of the said Act of 1976 (discrimination by education authorities) for the words " the Education (Scotland) Acts 1939 to 1974 " and " the Education (Scotland) Acts 1939 to 1975 " respectively there shall be substituted the words " the Education (Scotland) Acts 1939 to 1980 ".

(3) In Schedule 2 to the said Act of 1975, paragraph 2 shall be omitted and for paragraph 4 there shall be substituted—

" 4. Regulations under section 27 of the Education Act 1980 may provide for the submission to the Secretary of State of an application for the making by him of a transitional exemption order in relation to any school or further education establishment to which that section applies and not falling within paragraph 3 above, and for the making by him of the order."

34.—(1) In the definition of "independent school" and "school" in section 114(1) of the Education Act 1944 for the words "a school in respect of which grants are made by the Minister to the proprietor of the school" there shall be substituted the words "a special school not maintained by a local education authority".

(2) Subsection (2) of section 70 of the said Act of 1944 (order exempting schools from registration) shall cease to have effect.

(3) The Registrar of Independent Schools shall, without any application in that behalf, enter in the register kept by him under subsection (1) of the said section 70—

(a) any school which by virtue of subsection (1) above becomes an independent school ; and

(b) any school which was exempt from registration by virtue of subsection (2) of the said section 70 immediately before the coming into force of this section.

(4) Proviso (b) to subsection (1) of the said section 70 (registration of school to be provisional until it has been inspected) shall not apply to the registration of a school under subsection (3) above unless the Registrar has before the coming into force of this section given written notice to the proprietor of the school that the registration will be provisional.

(5) In this section "the Registrar of Independent Schools" means, in relation to any school in England, the Registrar of Independent Schools for England and, in relation to any school in Wales, the Registrar of Independent Schools for Wales.

(6) After subsection (3) of the said section 70 (offences) there shall be inserted—

" (3A) A person shall not be guilty of an offence under subsection (3)(a) above by reason of conducting a school at any time within the period of one month from the date on which it was first conducted (whether by that person or another) if an application for the registration of the school has been duly made within that period."

(7) For subsection (4) of the said section 70 (furnishing of particulars about independent schools) there shall be substituted—

" (4) The Secretary of State may by regulations make provision for requiring the proprietor of a registered or provisionally registered school to furnish the Registrar from time to time with such particulars relating to the school as may be prescribed and for enabling the Secretary of State to order the deletion from the register of the name of any school in respect of which any requirement imposed by or under the regulations is not complied with.

(5) The power to make regulations under this section shall be exercisable by the Secretary of State for Education and Science in relation to schools in England and by the Secretary of State for Wales in relation to schools in Wales.".

Supplementary

35.—(1) Any power of the Secretary of State to make orders Orders and or regulations under this Act (other than orders under section regulations. 2(11)(*b*)) shall be exercisable by statutory instrument.

(2) No regulations shall be made under section 17(6) above unless a draft of the regulations has been laid before and approved by a resolution of each House of Parliament.

(3) Any statutory instrument containing regulations under any provision of this Act other than section 17(6), or an order under section 15(8) above, shall be subject to annulment in pursuance of a resolution of either House of Parliament.

(4) Regulations under this Act may make different provision for different cases or different circumstances and may contain such incidental, supplementary or transitional provisions as the Secretary of State thinks fit.

(5) Without prejudice to subsection (4) above, regulations under any provision of this Act other than section 27(1)(*a*), (2) or (3) or section 38(5) may make in relation to Wales provision different from that made in relation to England.

36. There shall be defrayed out of moneys provided by Parlia- Expenses. ment—

(*a*) any expenses incurred by the Secretary of State under this Act ; and

(*b*) any increase attributable to this Act in the sums payable out of such moneys under any other Act.

37.—(1) This Act shall come into force on such date as the Commence-Secretary of State may by order appoint, and different dates ment. may be appointed for different provisions or different purposes.

(2) Any order under this section may make such transitional provision as appears to the Secretary of State to be necessary or expedient in connection with the provisions thereby brought into force, including such adaptations of those provisions, or of any other provisions of this Act then in force, as appear to

him to be necessary or expedient for the purpose or in consequence of the operation of any provision of this Act before the coming into force of any other provision.

Citation,
construction,
repeals and
extent.

38.—(1) This Act may be cited as the Education Act 1980.

(2) This Act and the Education Acts 1944 to 1979 may be cited as the Education Acts 1944 to 1980 and this Act and the Education (Scotland) Acts 1939 to 1976 may be cited as the Education (Scotland) Acts 1939 to 1980.

1944 c. 31.

(3) Subject to subsection (4) below, this Act shall, in its application to England and Wales, be construed as one with the Education Act 1944 and, in its application to Scotland, with the Education (Scotland) Acts 1939 to 1976.

(4) In the provisions of this Act relating to admissions to schools " child " includes any person who has not attained the age of nineteen years.

(5) For the purposes of this Act an individual shall be treated as belonging to the area of a particular local education authority or education authority or as not belonging to the area of any such authority in accordance with regulations made by the Secretary of State and any question under the regulations shall, in case of dispute, be determined by the Secretary of State.

(6) The enactments mentioned in Schedule 7 to this Act (which include spent provisions) are hereby repealed to the extent specified in the third column of that Schedule.

(7) In this Act—

(a) sections 20, 23, 25, 31(5) and (6), 33, 35 and 37, this section and so much of Schedule 7 as relates to enactments extending to Scotland, extend to Scotland ;

(b) sections 20, 35 and 37 and this section extend to Northern Ireland ;

but save as aforesaid this Act extends to England and Wales only.

SCHEDULES

SCHEDULE 1

SCHOOL GOVERNMENT: CONSEQUENTIAL AMENDMENTS

The Education Act 1944

1.—(1) In the provisions of the Education Act 1944 mentioned in sub-paragraph (2) below the words " managers or ", wherever they occur, shall be omitted.

(2) The provisions referred to above are sections 14(1), (3) and (4), 15(2), (3), (4) and (5), 16(3), 25(1) and (7), 31(3), 65, 67(1), 68, 80(1), 90(1), 95(2)(*b*), 99, 102, 105, 114(2)(*a*), paragraphs 1, 3, 5, 6 and 7 of Schedule 2, paragraphs 8, 9 and 10 of Schedule 3 and Schedule 4.

2.—(1) In subsection (1) of section 17 of that Act for the words from " managers or governors " onwards there shall be substituted the words " governors of the school in accordance with the provisions of this Act, and the instrument providing for the constitution of the body of governors is in this Act referred to as an instrument of government."

(2) In subsection (2) of that section for the words " The instrument of management or the instrument of government, as the case may be," there shall be substituted the words " The instrument of government ".

(3) In subsection (3)(*a*) of that section for the words " rules of management " there shall be substituted the words " articles of government ".

(4) In subsection (4) of that section the words " instrument of management, rules of management " shall be omitted.

(5) In subsection (5) of that section the words " management or " shall be omitted.

3. In section 18 of that Act for the words " instrument of management " and " managers ", wherever they occur, there shall be substituted respectively the words " instrument of government " and " governors ".

4. In subsections (1) and (3) of section 20 of that Act the words " managers or " shall be omitted and in subsection (6) of that section the words " managers or ", in both places, and " manager or " shall be omitted.

5. In section 21 of that Act the words " manager or " and " managers or ", wherever they occur, shall be omitted.

6. In section 22 of that Act the words " managers or " and " foundation managers or ", wherever they occur, shall be omitted.

7. In section 23(1) and (3) of that Act the words " rules of management or " shall be omitted.

8. In section 24(1) and (2) of that Act the words " rules of man-agement or " and " managers or ", wherever they occur, shall be omitted.

9. In sections 27 and 28 of that Act the words " managers or " and " foundation managers or ", wherever they occur, shall be omitted.

10. In section 39(5) of that Act the word " managers " shall be omitted.

11. In section 77(5) of that Act the words " managers or " and " foundation managers or " shall be omitted.

12. In subsection (1) of section 103 of that Act the words " man-agers or ", in both places, shall be omitted and in subsection (3) of that section the word " managers " shall be omitted.

13. In section 114(1) of that Act—

(*a*) in the definition of " Foundation managers " and " foundation governors " for the words from the beginning to " appointed " there shall be substituted the words " ' Found-ation governors ' means, in relation to any voluntary school, governors appointed " and the words " ' managers ' or ", " foundation managers or " and " managers or " shall be omitted ;

(*b*) in the definition of " Trust deed " the words " instrument of management ", " rules of management " and " managers or " shall be omitted.

14. In section 120(1)(*c*) of that Act the word " secondary ", in both places, shall be omitted.

The Education Act 1946

15. In sections 2(1)(*b*), (3), (4) and (6) and 6 of the Education Act 1946 the words " managers or ", wherever they occur, shall be omitted.

16. In section 3(1) of that Act the words " managers and " shall be omitted.

17. In section 4(1) of that Act the word " managers " shall be omitted.

18. In section 7(2) of that Act the words " managers or " and " managers and " shall be omitted.

The Education (Miscellaneous Provisions) Act 1948

19. In sections 4(3) and 10(3) of the Education (Miscellaneous Provisions) Act 1948 the words " managers or ", wherever they occur, shall be omitted.

The Reserve and Auxiliary Forces (Protection of Civil Interests) Act 1951   Sch. 1

1951 c. 65.

20. In paragraph 10 of Schedule 2 to the Reserve and Auxiliary Forces (Protection of Civil Interests) Act 1951 the words " managers or " shall be omitted.

The Education (Miscellaneous Provisions) Act 1953   1953 c. 33.

21. In section 8(1) and (3) of the Education (Miscellaneous Provisions) Act 1953 the words " managers or " shall be omitted.

The Education Act 1959   1959 c. 60.

22. In section 1(4) of the Education Act 1959 the words " managers or " shall be omitted.

The Education Act 1967   1967 c. 3.

23. In section 1(2) and (4) of the Education Act 1967 the words " managers or ", wherever they occur, shall be omitted.

The Education Act 1968   1968 c. 17.

24. In section 3(4) of the Education Act 1968 the words " managers or ", in both places, shall be omitted.

The Education (No. 2) Act 1968   1968 c. 37.

25. In section 3(3) the words " managers or ", wherever they occur, shall be omitted.

The Education Act 1973   1973 c. 16.

26. In section 1(2)(*a*) of the Education Act 1973 the word " managers " shall be omitted.

The Sex Discrimination Act 1975   1975 c. 65.

27. In paragraph 1 of the Table in section 22 of the Sex Discrimination Act 1975 the words " managers or " shall be omitted.

The Race Relations Act 1976   1976 c. 74.

28. In paragraph 1 of the Table in section 17 of the Race Relations Act 1976 the words " managers or " shall be omitted.

The National Health Service Act 1977   1977 c. 49.

29. In paragraph 3 of Schedule 1 to the National Health Service Act 1977 the words " managers or " shall be omitted.

The Employment Protection (Consolidation) Act 1978   1978 c. 44.

30. In section 80(1) of the Employment Protection (Consolidation) Act 1978 the words " or managers " shall be omitted.

The Education Act 1979   1979 c. 49.

31. In subsection (2) of section 1 of the Education Act 1979 the words " managers or " shall be omitted and in subsections (3) and (4) of that section the word " managers " shall be omitted.

SCHEDULE 2

SCHOOL ADMISSION APPEALS

PART I

CONSTITUTION OF APPEAL COMMITTEES

1.—(1) An appeal pursuant to arrangements made by a local education authority under section 7(1) of this Act shall be to an appeal committee constituted in accordance with this paragraph.

(2) An appeal committee shall consist of three, five or seven members nominated by the authority from among persons appointed by the authority under this paragraph ; and sufficient persons may be appointed to enable two or more appeal committees to sit at the same time.

(3) The persons appointed shall comprise—

    (a) members of the authority or of any education committee of the authority ; and

    (b) persons who are not members of the authority or of any education committee of the authority but who have experience in education, are acquainted with the educational conditions in the area of the authority or are parents of registered pupils at a school ;

but shall not include any person employed by the authority otherwise than as a teacher.

(4) The members of an appeal committee who are members of the authority or of any education committee of the authority shall not outnumber the others by more than one.

(5) A person who is a member of an education committee of the authority shall not be chairman of an appeal committee.

(6) A person shall not be a member of an appeal committee for the consideration of any appeal against a decision if he was among those who made the decision or took part in discussions as to whether the decision should be made.

(7) A person who is a teacher at a school shall not be a member of an appeal committee for the consideration of an appeal involving a question whether a child is to be admitted to that school.

2.—(1) An appeal pursuant to arrangements made by the governors of an aided or special agreement school under section 7(2) of this Act shall be to an appeal committee constituted in accordance with this paragraph.

(2) An appeal committee shall consist of three, five or seven members nominated by the governors from among persons appointed by them under this paragraph ; and sufficient persons may be appointed to enable two or more appeal committees to sit at the same time.

(3) The persons appointed—

(a) may include one or more of the governors ;

(b) shall include persons appointed from a list drawn up by the local education authority by whom the school is maintained ; and

(c) shall not include any person employed by the authority otherwise than as a teacher.

(4) Half the members of an appeal committee (excluding the chairman) shall be nominated from among such persons as are mentioned in sub-paragraph (3)(b) above.

(5) None of the governors shall be chairman of an appeal committee.

(6) A person shall not be a member of an appeal committee for the consideration of any appeal against a decision if he was among those who made the decision or took part in discussions as to whether the decision should be made.

(7) A person who is a teacher at a school shall not be a member of an appeal committee for the consideration of an appeal involving a question whether a child is to be admitted to that school.

3. An appeal pursuant to joint arrangements made by virtue of section 7(3) of this Act by the governors of two or more schools shall be to an appeal committee constituted as provided in paragraph 2 above, taking references to the governors as references to the governors of both or all the schools.

4. An appeal committee constituted in accordance with paragraph 2 or 3 above shall be included in the bodies to which sections 173(4) and 174 of the Local Government Act 1972 (allowances) 1972 c. 70. apply.

Part II

Procedure

5. An appeal shall be by notice in writing setting out the grounds on which it is made.

6. An appeal committee shall afford the appellant an opportunity of appearing and making oral representations and may allow the appellant to be accompanied by a friend or to be represented.

7. The matters to be taken into account by an appeal committee in considering an appeal shall include—

(a) any preference expressed by the appellant in respect of the child as mentioned in section 6 of this Act ; and

(b) the arrangements for the admission of pupils published by the local education authority or the governors under section 8 of this Act.

8. In the event of disagreement between the members of an appeal committee the appeal under consideration shall be decided by a simple majority of the votes cast and in the case of an equality of votes the chairman of the committee shall have a second or casting vote.

9. The decision of an appeal committee and the grounds on which it is made shall be communicated by the committee in writing to—

    (*a*) the appellant and the local education authority ; and

    (*b*) in the case of an appeal to an appeal committee constituted in accordance with paragraph 2 or 3 above, to the governors by or on whose behalf the decision appealed against was made.

10. Appeals pursuant to arrangements made under section 7 of this Act shall be heard in private except when otherwise directed by the authority or governors by whom the arrangements are made but, without prejudice to paragraph 6 above, a member of the local education authority may attend as an observer any hearing of an appeal by an appeal committee constituted in accordance with paragraph 1 above and a member of the Council on Tribunals may attend as an observer any meeting of any appeal committee at which an appeal is considered.

11. Subject to paragraphs 5 to 10 above, all matters relating to the procedure on appeals pursuant to arrangements made under section 7 of this Act, including the time within which they are to be brought, shall be determined by the authority or governors by whom the arrangements are made ; and neither section 106 of the Local
1972 c. 70.   Government Act 1972 nor paragraph 44 of Schedule 12 to that Act (procedure of committees of local authorities) shall apply to an appeal committee constituted in accordance with paragraph 1 above.

SCHEDULE 3

Section 16(4).   ESTABLISHMENT ETC. OF SCHOOLS: CONSEQUENTIAL AMENDMENTS

The Education Act 1944

1944 c. 31.   1. In section 16(2) of the Education Act 1944 for the words " subsection (2) of section thirteen of this Act " there shall be substituted the words " section 13 of the Education Act 1980 ".

2. In section 17(6) of that Act for the words " section 13 of this Act " there shall be substituted the words " section 13 of the Education Act 1980 ".

3. In section 85 of that Act for subsections (2) and (3) there shall be substituted—

    " (2) Any intention on the part of a local education authority that a school for providing primary or secondary education (other than a nursery school or a special school) should be vested in the authority as trustees shall be treated for the purposes of subsection (1) of section 12 of the Education Act 1980 as an intention on the part of the authority to maintain the school as a county school ; and accordingly proposals for that purpose shall be published and submitted as required by that section, and the other provisions of that section and of sections 14 and 16 of that Act shall apply as in a case where a local education authority intend to maintain a school as a county school.

(3) Any school for providing primary or secondary education   Sch. 3
which in accordance with subsection (2) above is vested in a
local education authority as trustees shall be a county school."

4. In section 102 of that Act for the words " section 13 of this
Act " there shall be substituted the words " section 13 of the Education Act 1980 ".

5. In paragraph 5 of Schedule 3 to that Act for the words " subsection (7) of section thirteen of this Act " there shall be substituted
the words " section 13(6) of the Education Act 1980 ".

The Education Act 1946   1946 c. 50.

6. In section 1(1) of the Education Act 1946 for the words " section
thirteen of the Education Act 1944 " there shall be substituted the
words " section 13 of the Education Act 1980 ".

7. In section 2(2) of that Act for the words " section thirteen of
the principal Act " there shall be substituted the words " section 12
or 13 of the Education Act 1980 ".

8. In paragraph 1(*a*) of Schedule 1 to that Act for the words
" section thirteen of the principal Act " there shall be substituted the
words " section 13 of the Education Act 1980 ".

The Education (Miscellaneous Provisions) Act 1953   1953 c. 33.

9. In section 2(*a*) of the Education (Miscellaneous Provisions) Act
1953 for the words " subsection (2) of section thirteen of the principal
Act " there shall be substituted the words " section 13 of the Education Act 1980 ".

The London Government Act 1963   1963 c. 33.

10. In subsection (5) of section 31 of the London Government Act
1963 for the words " the Education Acts 1944 to 1968 " there shall
be substituted the words " the Education Acts 1944 to 1980 " and
in subsection (10) of that section for the words " section 13 of the
said Act of 1944 " there shall be substituted the words " section 12,
13 or 15 of the Education Act 1980 ".

The Education Act 1964   1964 c. 82.

11. In section 1(1) of the Education Act 1964 for the words
" section 13 of the Education Act 1944 " there shall be substituted
the words " section 12 or 13 of the Education Act 1980 ".

12. For section 1(2) of that Act there shall be substituted—

" (2) The Secretary of State shall make regulations for determining, or enabling him to determine, whether a school in
respect of which proposals making such provision as is mentioned in the preceding subsection are implemented is to be
deemed for the purposes of the Education Act 1944 and the
other enactments relating to education to be a primary or a
secondary school."

SCH. 3
1967 c. 3.

The Education Act 1967

13. In section 1(2)(*a*) of the Education Act 1967 for the words " section 13(2) of the Education Act 1944 " there shall be substituted the words " section 13 of the Education Act 1980 ".

14. In section 3 of that Act for the words " persons other than a local education authority submit proposals to the Secretary of State under section 13 of the Education Act 1944 " there shall be substituted the words " persons submit proposals to the Secretary of State under section 13 of the Education Act 1980 ".

1968 c. 17.

The Education Act 1968

15. In section 1(1) of the Education Act 1968 after the words " section 13 of the Education Act 1944 " there shall be inserted the words " or section 12 of the Education Act 1980 ".

16. In section 3(4) of that Act for the words " section 13 of the Education Act 1944 " there shall be substituted the words " section 13 of the Education Act 1980 ".

1973 c. 16.

The Education Act 1973

17. In section 1(2)(*a*) of the Education Act 1973 for the words " proposals approved or order made by him under section 13 or 16 of the Education Act 1944 " there shall be substituted the words " order made by him under section 16 of the Education Act 1944 or proposals falling to be implemented under section 12 or 13 of the Education Act 1980 ".

1975 c. 65.

The Sex Discrimination Act 1975

18. In paragraph 1 of Schedule 2 to the Sex Discrimination Act 1975 for the words " under section 13 of the Education Act 1944 (as set out in Schedule 3 to the Education Act 1968) a responsible body submits to the Secretary of State, in accordance with subsection (1) or (2) of that section " there shall be substituted the words " under the provisions of section 12 or 13 of the Education Act 1980 a responsible body submits to the Secretary of State ".

Section 17(5).

SCHEDULE 4

TERMINATION OF PARTICIPATION AGREEMENTS

1.—(1) Every participation agreement shall provide that it may be terminated in accordance with this Schedule.

(2) A participation agreement shall not be capable of being terminated by either party otherwise than as aforesaid.

2. The proprietors of the school may terminate a participation agreement by giving three years written notice to the Secretary of State or such shorter notice as he may in any particular case accept.

3. Subject to paragraph 4 below, the Secretary of State may terminate a participation agreement by giving three years written notice to the proprietors of the school.

4.—(1) If the Secretary of State—

(*a*) is not satisfied that appropriate educational standards are being maintained at the school; or

(*b*) is satisfied that any condition applying to the school under the agreement or by virtue of regulations made under section 17 of this Act has been contravened,

he may at any time terminate the agreement by written notice to the proprietors of the school.

(2) A notice of termination given under this paragraph may provide that it shall be treated as of no effect if the proprietors of the school satisfy the Secretary of State within such time as may be specified in the notice that they have complied with any condition specified therein.

5. Any notice of termination given under paragraph 3 or 4 above shall contain a statement of the reason for which it is given.

6. The termination of a participation agreement shall not affect the operation of the agreement or of the scheme referred to in section 17 of this Act (including any regulations made under that section) in relation to any pupil holding an assisted place at the school on the date of the termination.

SCHEDULE 5

Section 19.

Provisions Substituted in the Education Act 1962

1.—(1) It shall be the duty of every local education authority, subject to and in accordance with regulations made under this Act, to bestow on persons who are ordinarily resident in the area of the authority awards in respect of their attendance at courses to which this section applies. *Local education authority awards for designated courses.*

(2) This section applies to any course which—

(*a*) is provided by a university, college or other institution in the United Kingdom or by such a university, college or institution in conjunction with a university, college or other institution in another country; and

(*b*) is designated by or under the regulations for the purposes of this section as being such a course as is mentioned in subsection (3) of this section.

(3) The courses referred to in subsection (2)(*b*) of this section are—

(*a*) full-time courses which are either first degree courses or comparable to first degree courses;

(*b*) full-time courses for the diploma of higher education;

(*c*) courses for the initial training of teachers;

(*d*) full-time courses for the higher national diploma, for the higher diploma of the Technician Education Council or for the higher national diploma of the Business Education Council.

(4) A local education authority shall not be under a duty under subsection (1) above to bestow an award on a person in respect of a course designated as comparable to a first degree course unless he possesses such educational qualifications as may be prescribed by or under the regulations, either generally or with respect to that course or a class of courses which includes that course.

(5) Regulations made for the purposes of subsection (1) of this section shall prescribe the conditions and exceptions subject to which the duty imposed by that subsection is to have effect, and the descriptions of payments to be made in pursuance of awards bestowed thereunder, and, with respect to each description of payments, shall—

(*a*) prescribe the circumstances in which it is to be payable, and the amount of the payment or the scales or other provisions by reference to which that amount is to be determined, and

(*b*) indicate whether the payment is to be obligatory or is to be at the discretion of the authority bestowing the award ;

and, subject to the exercise of any power conferred by the regulations to suspend or terminate awards, a local education authority by whom an award has been bestowed under subsection (1) of this section shall be under a duty, or shall have power, as the case may be, to make such payments as they are required or authorised to make in accordance with the regulations.

(6) Without prejudice to the duty imposed by subsection (1) of this section, a local education authority shall have power to bestow an award on any person in respect of his attendance at a course to which this section applies, where he is not eligible for an award under subsection (1) of this section in respect of that course.

(7) The provisions of subsection (5) of this section and of the regulations made in accordance with that subsection (except so much of those provisions as relates to the conditions and exceptions subject to which the duty imposed by subsection (1) of this section is to have effect) shall apply in relation to awards under the last preceding subsection as they apply in relation to awards under subsection (1) of this section.

(8) The reference in subsection (1) of this section to persons who are ordinarily resident in the area of a local education authority is a reference to persons who, in accordance with the provisions of Schedule 1 to this Act, are to be treated as being so resident.

Local education authority awards for other courses.

2.—(1) A local education authority shall have power to bestow awards on persons over compulsory school age (including persons undergoing training as teachers) in respect of their attendance at courses to which this section applies and to make such payments as are payable in pursuance of such awards.

(2) Subject to subsection (3) of this section, this section applies to any course of full-time or part-time education (whether held in Great Britain or elsewhere) which is not a course of primary or secondary education, or (in the case of a course held outside Great

Britain) is not a course of education comparable to primary or secondary education in Great Britain, and is not a course to which section 1 of this Act applies.

(3) Except in the case of a person undergoing training as a teacher who attends the course as such training, this section does not apply to any course provided by a university, college or other institution which is for the time being designated by or under regulations made for the purposes of this section as being a postgraduate course or comparable to a postgraduate course.

3. Provision may be made by regulations under this Act for authorising the Secretary of State— *Awards by Secretary of State.*

   (a) to pay grants to or in respect of persons undergoing training as teachers;

   (b) to bestow awards on persons in respect of their attendance at such courses provided by universities, colleges or other institutions (whether in Great Britain or elsewhere) as may for the time being be designated by or under the regulations for the purposes of this section as being postgraduate courses or comparable to postgraduate courses;

   (c) to bestow awards on persons who, at such time as may be prescribed by the regulations, have attained such age as may be so prescribed, being awards in respect of their attendance at courses provided by any institution which—

   (i) is in receipt of payments under section 100 of the Education Act 1944 or section 75 of the Education (Scotland) Act 1962; and *1944 c. 31. 1962 c. 47.*

   (ii) is designated by or under the regulations as a college providing long-term residential courses of full-time education for adults;

and in the case of awards bestowed in accordance with paragraph (b) or (c) of this section, for authorising the Secretary of State to make such payments as are payable in pursuance of the awards.

4.—(1) For the purposes of the exercise of any power or the performance of any duty conferred or imposed by or under any of the provisions of sections 1 to 3 of this Act, it is immaterial— *Provisions supplementary to ss. 1 to 3.*

   (a) whether an award is designated by that name or as a scholarship, studentship, exhibition or bursary or by any similar description, or

   (b) in what terms the bestowal of an award is expressed.

(2) Any enactment contained in those sections which requires or authorises the making of regulations shall be construed as requiring or authorising regulations to be made by the Secretary of State; and regulations made for the purposes of any such enactment may make different provision for different cases to which that enactment is applicable.

(3) Without prejudice to subsection (2) above, regulations under section 3(a) or (c) above may make in relation to persons ordinarily resident in Wales provision different from that made in relation to persons so resident in England.

SCH. 5

(4) Any power to make regulations under those sections shall be exercisable by statutory instrument; and any statutory instrument containing any such regulations shall be subject to annulment in pursuance of a resolution of either House of Parliament.

(5) In sections 2 and 3 of this Act "training" (in relation to training as a teacher) includes further training, whether the person undergoing the further training is already qualified as a teacher or not; and any reference to a person undergoing training includes a person admitted or accepted by the appropriate university, college or other authorities for undergoing that training.

SCHEDULE 1

ORDINARY RESIDENCE

1. The provisions of this Schedule shall have effect for the purposes of section 1 of this Act.

2. Subject to the following provisions of this Schedule, a person shall be treated for those purposes as ordinarily resident in the area of a local education authority if he would fall to be treated as belonging to that area for the purposes of section 31(3) of the Education Act 1980.

3. Regulations made under this Act may modify the operation of the last preceding paragraph in relation to cases where a person applies for an award under section 1 of this Act in respect of a course and, at any time within the period of twelve months ending with the date on which that course is due to begin, a change occurs or has occurred in the circumstances by reference to which (apart from this paragraph) his place of ordinary residence would fall to be determined.

4. Regulations made under this Act may make provision whereby a person who under paragraph 2 of this Schedule would fall to be treated for the purposes of section 1 of this Act as not being ordinarily resident in any area is to be treated for those purposes as being ordinarily resident in the area of such local education authority as may be specified by or under the regulations.

5. Subsections (1), (2) and (4) of section 4 of this Act shall have effect in relation to paragraphs 3 and 4 of this Schedule as they have effect in relation to section 1 of this Act.

Section 32.

1974 c. 7.

SCHEDULE 6

AMENDMENTS OF SCHEDULE 2 TO THE LOCAL GOVERNMENT ACT 1974

1. In paragraph 1 for the words "Subject to paragraph 3 below" there shall be substituted the words "Subject to paragraphs 3 and 3A below".

2. In paragraph 3 for sub-paragraphs (4) and (5) there shall be substituted—

"(4) Subject to sub-paragraph (5) below, this paragraph applies to such expenditure as may be specified by regulations made by the Secretary of State, being—

 (a) expenditure, other than that to which paragraph 3A below applies, incurred by local authorities in the exercise of their functions as local education authorities ;

 (b) expenditure incurred by local authorities on research into any of their functions, in the training of persons in matters connected with the functions of local authorities or in respect of persons to whom the training is given.

(5) Regulations specifying expenditure of any description under sub-paragraph (4) above may provide that only a specified proportion of that expenditure shall be expenditure to which this paragraph applies."

3. After paragraph 3 there shall be inserted—

"3A.—(1) The needs element shall also be subject to adjustment, in accordance with the following provisions of this paragraph, in respect of expenditure to which this paragraph applies.

(2) The Secretary of State may by regulations provide—

 (a) for the determination by the Secretary of State, in advance for each year, of the amount of expenditure to which this paragraph applies which is to be taken into account for the purposes of the regulations in relation to that year ;

 (b) for enabling the Secretary of State to determine additional amounts of such expenditure which are to be so taken into account ;

 (c) for apportioning among local authorities, under or in accordance with the regulations, either the whole or a part specified by or in accordance with the regulations of—

   (i) the amount determined for any year as mentioned in paragraph (a) above ;

   (ii) any additional amounts determined for that year as mentioned in paragraph (b) above ;

 and for informing local authorities of the shares apportioned to them respectively ;

 (d) for the determination, under or in accordance with the regulations, of the appropriate contribution of each local authority to the expenditure apportioned as mentioned in paragraph (c) above ;

 (e) for ascertaining the amount by which the needs element payable to each authority ought to be increased or decreased by reference to the share apportioned to it as compared with its appropriate contribution.

(3) Regulations under sub-paragraph (2) above shall provide for any determination as mentioned in paragraph (*a*) or (*b*) of that sub-paragraph to be made by the Secretary of State after consultation with such associations of local authorities as appear to him to be concerned and with any local authority with whom consultation appears to him to be desirable.

(4) Regulations under this paragraph may make provision requiring local authorities to furnish the Secretary of State, at such times and in such manner and form as may be specified in the regulations, with such estimates of their expenditure and with such other information required by him for the purposes of the regulations as may be so specified.

(5) The Secretary of State shall in paying the needs element for any year adjust the amount of that element (in addition to any adjustment under paragraph 3 above) in accordance with the amount ascertained as mentioned in sub-paragraph (2)(*e*) above.

(6) This paragraph applies to such expenditure incurred by local authorities in connection with further education of an advanced character, including the training of teachers, as may be specified for the purposes of this paragraph by or under regulations made by the Secretary of State."

SCHEDULE 7

REPEALS

Chapter	Short title	Extent of repeal
7 & 8 Geo. 6. c. 31.	The Education Act 1944.	Section 8 (2) (*b*). In section 9(1) the words " so far as may be authorised by arrangements approved by the Minister ". Sections 11, 12 and 13. Section 21(2). Section 31(1). Section 32. Section 49. In section 53(1) the words " with the approval of the Minister ". In section 61(2) the words " not exceeding such amounts as may be determined in accordance with scales approved by the Minister ". Section 66. In section 82 the words " with the approval of the Minister ". In section 83 the words " Subject to any regulations made by the Minister ". In section 84 the words " with the consent of the Minister ". Section 90(2) and (3). Section 97. Section 100(1)(*a*)(i) and (ii). In section 114, in subsection (1) the definition of " local education order ", in the definition of " primary school " the words " subject to the provisions of subsection (3) of this section ", and subsection (3). In Part I of Schedule 1, in paragraph 3(*a*) the words from " without prejudice " to " joint boards) ". In Schedule 3, paragraph 3. Schedule 4.
9 & 10 Geo. 6. c. 50.	The Education Act 1946.	In Part II of Schedule 2 the entry relating to section 13 of the Education Act 1944.
11 & 12 Geo. 6. c. 40	The Education (Miscellaneous Provisions) Act 1948.	Section 6. In section 7, subsections (2) and (2A) and in subsection (3) the words "except subsection (2A) ".

Chapter	Short title	Extent of repeal
11 & 12 Geo. 6. c. 40—*cont.*	The Education (Miscellaneous Provisions) Act 1948—*cont.*	In Part I of Schedule 1, the entry relating to Schedule 4 to the Education Act 1944.
1 & 2 Eliz. 2. c. 33.	The Education (Miscellaneous Provisions) Act 1953.	In section 6(1) the words " For the purpose of fulfilling their duties under the principal Act " and " with the approval of the Minister ". Section 7. Section 9. Section 16. In Schedule 1 the entry relating to section 13 of the Education Act 1944.
6 & 7 Eliz. 2. c. 55.	The Local Government Act 1958.	In Schedule 8, paragraph 16(2)(i) and (ii).
10 & 11 Eliz. 2. c. 47.	The Education (Scotland) Act 1962.	Section 53. In section 55 the proviso.
1963 c. 33.	The London Government Act 1963.	Section 31(1)(*a*) and (*b*), (2), (3) and (9). Section 33.
1966 c. 42.	The Local Government Act 1966.	Section 14.
1968 c. 17.	The Education Act 1968.	Section 1(2). Section 3(1) and (2). Section 5(1) and (2) so far as relating to section 13 of the Education Act 1944. In Schedule 1 paragraph 7. In Schedule 3 Part A.
1971 c. 74.	The Education (Milk) Act 1971.	The whole Act so far as unrepealed.
1973 c. 16.	The Education Act 1973.	Section 4.
1975 c. 2.	The Education Act 1975.	Sections 1 and 2. Section 5(4).
1975 c. 65.	The Sex Discrimination Act 1975.	In Schedule 2, paragraph 2.
1976 c. 20.	The Education (Scotland) Act 1976.	Section 3.
1976 c. 81.	The Education Act 1976.	Sections 4 and 5. Sections 7 to 9.

Competition Act 1980

1980 CHAPTER 21

An Act to abolish the Price Commission; to make provision for the control of anti-competitive practices in the supply and acquisition of goods and the supply and securing of services; to provide for references of certain public bodies and other persons to the Monopolies and Mergers Commission; to provide for the investigation of prices and charges by the Director General of Fair Trading; to provide for the making of grants to certain bodies; to amend and provide for the amendment of the Fair Trading Act 1973; to make amendments with respect to the Restrictive Trade Practices Act 1976; to repeal the remaining provisions of the Counter-Inflation Act 1973; and for purposes connected therewith. [3rd April 1980]

BE IT ENACTED by the Queen's most Excellent Majesty, by and with the advice and consent of the Lords Spiritual and Temporal, and Commons, in this present Parliament assembled, and by the authority of the same, as follows:—

Abolition of Price Commission

1.—(1) At the expiry of the winding-up period specified in subsection (2) below the Price Commission shall cease to exist and, during that period, the Commission shall exercise their functions solely in accordance with directions given to them by the Secretary of State with a view to bringing the activities of the Commission to an end at or before the expiry of that period.
Abolition of Price Commission.

(2) In this Act "the winding-up period" means the period beginning on the appointed day and ending on the thirtieth day after the appointed day or on such later date as the Secretary of State may specify by order.

(3) The provisions of Schedule 1 to this Act shall have effect in connection with the dissolution of the Price Commission and, subject to the provisions of that Schedule—

 (*a*) any rights or obligations of the Price Commission which remain in existence immediately before the expiry of the winding-up period and any property held by the Commission at that time shall, on the expiry of that period, become rights, obligations and property of the Secretary of State ; and

 (*b*) after the expiry of the winding-up period, anything which, apart from subsection (1) above, would be required or permitted to be done by or to the Price Commission shall or may be done by or to the Secretary of State.

Control of anti-competitive practices

Anti-
competitive
practices.

2.—(1) The provisions of sections 3 to 10 below have effect with a view to the control of anti-competitive practices, and for the purposes of this Act a person engages in an anti-competitive practice if, in the course of business, that person pursues a course of conduct which, of itself or when taken together with a course of conduct pursued by persons associated with him, has or is intended to have or is likely to have the effect of restricting, distorting or preventing competition in connection with the production, supply or acquisition of goods in the United Kingdom or any part of it or the supply or securing of services in the United Kingdom or any part of it.

(2) To the extent that a course of conduct is required or envisaged by a material provision of, or a material recommendation in, an agreement which is registered or subject to registra-

1976 c. 34.

tion under the Restrictive Trade Practices Act 1976, that course of conduct shall not be regarded as constituting an anti-competitive practice for the purposes of this Act ; and for the purposes of this subsection—

 (*a*) a provision of an agreement is a material provision if, by virtue of the existence of the provision (taken alone or together with other provisions) the agreement is one to which that Act applies ; and

 (*b*) a recommendation is a material recommendation in an agreement if it is one to which a term implied into the agreement by any provision of section 8 or section 16 of that Act (terms implied into trade association agreements and services supply association agreements) applies.

(3) For the purposes of this Act, a course of conduct does not constitute an anti-competitive practice if it is excluded for those purposes by an order made by the Secretary of State ; and any

such order may limit the exclusion conferred by it by reference to a particular class of persons or to particular circumstances.

(4) Without prejudice to the generality of subsection (3) above, an order under that subsection may exclude the conduct of any person by reference to the size of his business, whether expressed by reference to turnover, as defined in the order, or to his share of a market, as so defined, or in any other manner.

(5) For the purpose only of enabling the Director General of Fair Trading (in this Act referred to as " the Director ") to establish whether any person's course of conduct is excluded by virtue of any such provision of an order under subsection (3) above as is referred to in subsection (4) above, the order may provide for the application, with appropriate modifications, of any provisions of sections 44 and 46 of the Fair Trading Act 1973 c. 41. 1973 (power of Director to require information).

(6) For the purposes of this section any two persons are to be treated as associated—

(*a*) if one is a body corporate of which the other directly or indirectly has control either alone or with other members of a group of interconnected bodies corporate of which he is a member, or

(*b*) if both are bodies corporate of which one and the same person or group of persons directly or indirectly has control ;

and for the purposes of this subsection a person or group of persons able directly or indirectly to control or materially to influence the policy of a body corporate, but without having a controlling interest in that body corporate, may be treated as having control of it.

(7) In this section " the supply or securing of services " includes providing a place or securing that a place is provided other than on a highway, or in Scotland a public right of way, for the parking of a motor vehicle (within the meaning of the Road Traffic Act 1972). 1972 c. 20.

(8) For the purposes of this Act any question whether, by pursuing any course of conduct in connection with the acquisition of goods or the securing of services by it, a local authority is engaging in an anti-competitive practice shall be determined as if the words " in the course of business " were omitted from subsection (1) above ; and in this subsection " local authority " means—

(*a*) in England and Wales, a local authority within the meaning of the Local Government Act 1972, the 1972 c. 70. Common Council of the City of London or the Council of the Isles of Scilly,

1973 c. 65.

(b) in Scotland, a local authority within the meaning of the Local Government (Scotland) Act 1973, and

1972 c. 9.
(N.I.).

(c) in Northern Ireland, a district council established under the Local Government Act (Northern Ireland) 1972.

Preliminary
investigation
by Director of
possible
anti-
competitive
practice.

3.—(1) If it appears to the Director that any person has been or is pursuing a course of conduct which may amount to an anti-competitive practice, the Director may in accordance with this section carry out an investigation with a view to establishing whether that person has been or is pursuing a course of conduct which does amount to such a practice.

(2) Before carrying out an investigation under this section, the Director shall—

(a) give to the Secretary of State and the person or persons whose conduct is to be investigated notice of the proposed investigation, together with an indication of the matters to be investigated, the person or persons concerned and the goods or services to which the investigation is to relate ; and

(b) arrange for notice of the proposed investigation, together with an indication of the matters to be investigated, the person or persons concerned and the goods or services to which the investigation is to relate, to be published in such manner as the Director considers most suitable for bringing the proposed investigation to the attention of any other persons who, in the opinion of the Director, would be affected by or be likely to have an interest in the investigation.

(3) The Secretary of State may by regulations prescribe the manner in which any notice is to be given under subsection (2) above, and the evidence which is to be sufficient evidence of its having been given, and of its contents and authenticity.

(4) Subject to the following provisions of this section, where notice of a proposed investigation has been given in accordance with paragraph (a) and published in accordance with paragraph (b) of subsection (2) above, the Director shall proceed with the investigation as expeditiously as possible.

(5) If, before the end of the period of two weeks beginning with the day on which the Secretary of State receives notice of a proposed investigation under paragraph (a) of subsection (2) above, the Secretary of State directs the Director not to proceed with the investigation the Director shall take no further action under this section with respect to the matters referred to in the notice ; but nothing in this subsection shall prevent the Director from proceeding with a subsequent investigation, notwithstanding that it relates wholly or partly to the same matters.

(6) Where the Secretary of State gives a direction under sub-section (5) above, he shall—

    (*a*) give notice of the direction to the person or persons whose conduct was to be investigated ; and

    (*b*) arrange for the direction to be published in such manner as he considers most suitable for bringing it to the attention of any other person who, in his opinion, would have been affected by, or likely to have had an interest in, the direction.

(7) For the purposes of an investigation under this section the Director may, by notice in writing signed by him—

    (*a*) require any person to produce, at a time and place specified in the notice, to the Director or to any person appointed by him for the purpose, any documents which are specified or described in the notice and which are documents in his custody or under his control and relating to any matter relevant to the investigation ; or

    (*b*) require any person carrying on any business to furnish to the Director such estimates, returns or other information as may be specified or described in the notice, and specify the time, the manner and the form in which any such estimates, returns or information are to be furnished ;

but no person shall be compelled for the purpose of any such investigation to produce any document which he could not be compelled to produce in civil proceedings before the High Court or, in Scotland, the Court of Session or, in complying with any requirement for the furnishing of information, to give any information which he could not be compelled to give in evidence in such proceedings.

(8) Subsections (5) to (8) of section 85 of the Fair Trading Act 1973 (enforcement provisions relating to notices under sub-section (1) of that section requiring production of documents etc.) shall apply in relation to a notice under subsection (7) above as they apply in relation to a notice under subsection (1) of that section. 1973 c. 41.

(9) At any time before the completion of an investigation under this section the Director may, with the consent of the Secretary of State, determine not to proceed with the investigation and, in that event, he shall—

    (*a*) give notice of his determination to the person or persons whose conduct was being investigated ; and (*b*) arrange for the determination to be published in such manner as he considers most suitable for bringing it to the attention of any other person who, in his opinion, would have been affected by, or likely to have had an interest in, the investigation.

(10) As soon as practicable after the completion of an investigation under this section the Director shall, in such manner as he considers appropriate, publish a report stating, with reasons, whether in his opinion any course of conduct described in the report constituted or constitutes an anti-competitive practice and, if so—

(*a*) specifying the person or persons concerned and the goods or services in question ; and

(*b*) stating, with reasons, whether he considers that it is appropriate for him to make a reference under section 5 below.

Undertakings in consequence of Director's reports.

4.—(1) Where a report is published under section 3 above stating, in accordance with subsection (10)(*b*) of that section, that it is appropriate for the Director to make a reference under section 5 below, the Director shall consider any representations in writing which are made to him by a person specified in the report as a person who was or is engaged in an anti-competitive practice and which contain proposals as to what should be done in consequence of the conclusions of the report so far as they relate to that person.

(2) Any such representations may include an undertaking by which the person who makes the representations agrees to be bound, if the undertaking is accepted by the Director, for a period specified in the representations.

(3) At any time before the Director makes a reference under section 5 below in relation to a report under section 3 above, the Director may, by notice given to the person concerned, accept an undertaking which is offered by that person by reference to that report.

(4) It shall be the duty of the Director—

(*a*) to arrange for any undertaking accepted by him under this section to be published in such manner as appears to him to be appropriate,

(*b*) to keep under review the carrying out of any such undertaking and from time to time to consider whether, by reason of any change of circumstances, the undertaking is no longer appropriate and either the person concerned can be released from the undertaking or the undertaking needs to be varied or superseded by a new undertaking, and

(c) if it appears to him that the person by whom an undertaking was given has failed to carry it out, to give that person notice of that fact.

(5) If at any time the Director concludes under subsection (4)(*b*) above—

(a) that any person can be released from an undertaking, or

(b) that an undertaking needs to be varied or superseded by a new undertaking,

he shall give notice to that person stating that he is so released, or specifying the variation or, as the case may be, the new undertaking which in his opinion is required.

(6) Where a notice is served on any person under subsection (5) above specifying a variation or new undertaking, the notice shall state the change of circumstances by virtue of which the notice is served.

(7) Subject to subsection (8) below, the Director may at any time, by notice given to the person concerned—

(a) agree to the continuation of an undertaking in relation to which he has given notice under subsection (5) above specifying a variation or new undertaking, or

(b) accept a new or varied undertaking which is offered by that person as a result of such a notice.

(8) If the Director makes a reference under section 5 below in relation to a notice under subsection (5) above, he shall not, after the reference has been made, agree to the continuation of the undertaking in relation to which that notice was given or accept a new or varied undertaking which is offered as a result of that notice.

(9) The Secretary of State may by regulations prescribe the manner in which any notice is to be given under this section, and the evidence which is to be sufficient evidence of its having been given, and of its contents and authenticity.

5.—(1) In any case where—

(a) a report has been published under section 3 above stating, in accordance with subsection (10)(*b*) of that section, that it is appropriate for the Director to make a reference under this section and the Director has not accepted from each of the persons specified in the relevant report such undertaking or undertakings as, in his opinion, covers or cover every course of conduct which is described in the report as constituting an anti-competitive practice, or

Competition references.

(*b*) the Director has given notice to any person under section 4(4)(*c*) above with respect to an undertaking given by that person, or

(*c*) the Director has given notice to any person under section 4(5) above specifying either a variation of an undertaking or a new undertaking which is required and has neither accepted a new or varied undertaking from that person nor agreed upon the continuation of the original undertaking,

then, subject to the following provisions of this section, the Director may make a reference under this section to the Monopolies and Mergers Commission (in the following provisions of this Act referred to as a " competition reference ").

(2) In this section a competition reference is referred to—

(*a*) as a " report reference " if it is made by virtue of subsection (1)(*a*) above ; and

(*b*) as a " notice reference " if it is made by virtue of subsection (1)(*b*) or subsection (1)(*c*) above.

(3) No competition reference may be made within the period of four weeks beginning with the relevant date nor, subject to subsection (4) below, may such a reference be made after the expiry of the period of eight weeks beginning on that date ; and in this subsection " the relevant date " means—

(*a*) in the case of a report reference, the date on which was first published, in accordance with section 3(10) above, the report of the Director to which the reference relates ; and

(*b*) in the case of a notice reference, the date on which notice was given as mentioned in subsection (1)(*b*) or, as the case may be, subsection (1)(*c*) above.

(4) If the Secretary of State so directs, subsection (3) above shall have effect in relation to a competition reference of a description specified in the direction as if for the period of eight weeks specified in that subsection there were substituted such longer period not exceeding twelve weeks as may be specified in the direction ; but the Secretary of State shall not give a direction under this subsection unless, upon representations made to him by the Director, it appears to the Secretary of State that it would be appropriate in the case in question to allow the Director a longer period in which to negotiate one or more undertakings under section 4 above.

(5) In this section and section 6 below " the relevant report " means—

(*a*) in the case of a report reference, the report referred to in subsection (1)(*a*) above ;

(b) in the case of a notice reference made by virtue of subsection (1)(*b*) above, the report by reference to which the person to whom the notice was given under section 4(4)(*c*) above gave the undertaking to which that notice refers; and

(c) in the case of a notice reference made by virtue of subsection (1)(*c*) above, the report by reference to which the person to whom the notice was given under section 4(5) above gave the undertaking which the Director proposes should be varied or superseded.

6.—(1) In a competition reference the Director shall specify— Scope of competition references.

(a) the person or persons whose activities are to be investigated by the Commission (in this section referred to as the person or persons " subject to the reference "),

(b) the goods or services to which the investigation is to extend, and

(c) the course or courses of conduct to be investigated.

(2) The Director may not under subsection (1) above specify in a competition reference any person who is not specified in the relevant report nor any goods or services which are not so specified nor any course of conduct which is not described in that report but, subject to that and subsection (3) below, the Director may under subsection (1) above specify such person or persons, such goods or services and such course or courses of conduct as he considers appropriate.

(3) To the extent that the Director is of the opinion that an undertaking accepted by him under section 4 above covers the activities of any person specified in the relevant report, or any goods or services so specified, or any course of conduct described in that report, the Director shall exclude that person, those goods or services or, as the case may require, that course of conduct from the reference.

(4) In subsection (3) above the reference to an undertaking accepted by the Director under section 4 above does not include—

(a) an undertaking in respect of which notice has been served under subsection (4)(*c*) of that section, or

(b) an undertaking in respect of which the Director has given notice under subsection (5)(*b*) of that section specifying a new or varied undertaking, unless he has agreed upon its continuation with or without variation.

(5) Subject to subsection (6) below, on a competition reference the Commission shall investigate and report on the following questions, namely—

(*a*) whether any person subject to the reference was at any time during the period of twelve months ending on the date of the reference pursuing, in relation to goods or services specified in the reference, a course of conduct so specified or any other course of conduct which appears to be similar in form and effect to the one so specified ; and

(*b*) whether, by pursuing any such course of conduct, a person subject to the reference was at any time during that period engaging in an anti-competitive practice ; and

(*c*) whether, if any person was so engaging in an anti-competitive practice, the practice operated or might be expected to operate against the public interest.

(6) The Director may at any time, by notice given to the Commission, restrict the scope of a competition reference by excluding from the reference—

(*a*) some or all of the activities of any person subject to the reference,

(*b*) any goods or services specified in the reference, or

(*c*) any course of conduct so specified,

and, subject to section 7 below, on the receipt of such notice the Commission shall discontinue their investigation so far as it relates to any matter so excluded and shall make no reference to any such matter in their report.

Supplementary provisions as to competition references.

7.—(1) On making a competition reference or on varying such a reference under section 6(6) above the Director shall send a copy of the reference or, as the case may be, the variation to the Secretary of State.

(2) If, before the end of the period of two weeks beginning with the day on which the Secretary of State receives a copy of a competition reference under subsection (1) above, the Secretary of State directs the Commission not to proceed with the reference—

(*a*) the Commission shall not proceed with that reference, but

(*b*) nothing in paragraph (*a*) above shall prevent the Commission from proceeding with a subsequent competition reference, notwithstanding that it relates wholly or partly to the same matters.

(3) If, before the end of the period of two weeks beginning with the day on which the Secretary of State receives a copy of a variation of a competition reference under subsection (1) above, the Secretary of State directs the Commission not to give effect to the variation—

(a) the Commission shall proceed with the reference as if that variation had not been made, but

(b) nothing in paragraph (a) above shall prevent the Commission from giving effect to any subsequent variation, notwithstanding that it relates wholly or partly to the matters to which that variation related.

(4) On making a competition reference or on varying such a reference under section 6(6) above the Director shall arrange for the reference or, as the case may be, the variation to be published in such manner as he considers most suitable for bringing it to the attention of persons who, in his opinion, would be affected by it or be likely to have an interest in it.

(5) Where the Secretary of State gives a direction under subsection (2) or subsection (3) above, the Secretary of State shall arrange for the direction to be published in such manner as he considers most suitable for bringing it to the attention of persons who, in his opinion, would have been affected by, or likely to have had an interest in, the reference or variation to which the direction relates.

(6) Sections 70 (time limit for report on merger reference), 84 (public interest) and 85 (attendance of witnesses and production of documents) of the Fair Trading Act 1973 and Part II of Schedule 3 to that Act (performance of functions of Commission) shall apply in relation to competition references as if— 1973 c. 41.

(a) the functions of the Commission in relation to those references were functions under that Act;

(b) the expression "merger reference" included a competition reference;

(c) in paragraph 11 of that Schedule the reference to section 71 of that Act were a reference to section 6(6) above; and

(d) in paragraph 16(2) of that Schedule the reference to section 56 of that Act were a reference to sections 9 and 10 below.

8.—(1) A report of the Commission on a competition reference shall be made to the Secretary of State. Conclusions and reports of the Commission.

(2) Subject to section 6(6) above and subsection (3) below, a report on a competition reference shall state, with reasons, the conclusions of the Commission with respect to the following matters—

(*a*) whether any person whose activities were investigated was at any time during the period of twelve months referred to in paragraph (*a*) of subsection (5) of section 6 above pursuing any such course of conduct as is referred to in that paragraph ; and

(*b*) if so, whether by pursuing such a course of conduct any such person was at any time during that period engaging in an anti-competitive practice ; and

(*c*) if so, whether that anti-competitive practice operated or might be expected to operate against the public interest ; and

(*d*) if so, what are, or are likely to be, the effects adverse to the public interest.

(3) If, on a competition reference, the Commission conclude that any person was pursuing such a course of conduct as is referred to in section 6(5)(*a*) above but that, by virtue of section 2(2) above, that course of conduct does not, in whole or in part, constitute an anti-competitive practice, the Commission shall state their conclusion in their report and shall not make any recommendation under subsection (4) below with respect to things done as mentioned in section 2(2) above.

(4) If, on a competition reference, the Commission conclude that any person was at any time during the period of twelve months referred to in section 6(5)(*a*) above engaging in an anti-competitive practice which operated or might be expected to operate against the public interest, the Commission—

(*a*) shall, as part of their investigations, consider what action (if any) should be taken for the purpose of remedying or preventing the adverse effects of that practice ; and

(*b*) may, if they think fit, include in their report recommendations as to such action including, where appropriate, action by one or more Ministers (including Northern Ireland departments) or other public authorities.

(5) A copy of every report of the Commission on a competition reference shall be transmitted by the Commission to the Director ; and the Secretary of State shall take account of any advice given to him by the Director with respect to any such report.

Undertakings
following
report on
competition
reference.

9.—(1) In any case where—

(*a*) the report of the Commission on a competition reference concludes that any person specified in the report was engaging in an anti-competitive practice which operated or might be expected to operate against the public interest, and (*b*) it appears to the Secretary of State that the effects of that practice which are adverse to the public interest might be remedied or prevented if that person or any other person specified in the report took or refrained from taking any action,

the Secretary of State may by notice in writing request the Director to seek to obtain from the person or, as the case may be, each of the persons specified in the notice an undertaking to take or refrain from taking any action with a view to remedying or preventing those adverse effects.

(2) Where the Secretary of State makes a request under subsection (1) above—

(*a*) he shall at the same time send a copy of the notice by which the request is made to the person or, as the case may be, each of the persons from whom an undertaking is to be sought ; and

(*b*) it shall be the duty of the Director to seek to obtain an undertaking or undertakings of the description requested.

(3) In any case where—

(*a*) the Director is satisfied that a person from whom he has been requested to seek to obtain an undertaking is unlikely to give a suitable undertaking within a reasonable time, or

(*b*) having allowed such time as in his opinion is reasonable for the purpose, he is satisfied that a suitable undertaking has not been given by the person in question,

the Director shall give such advice to the Secretary of State as he may think proper in the circumstances.

(4) Where, following a request under subsection (1) above, an undertaking has been accepted by the Director, it shall be his duty—

(*a*) to give a copy of the undertaking to the Secretary of State ;

(*b*) to arrange for the undertaking to be published in such manner as appears to him to be appropriate ;

(*c*) to keep under review the carrying out of the undertaking and from time to time to consider whether, by reason of any change of circumstances, the undertaking is no longer appropriate and either the person concerned can be released from the undertaking or the undertaking needs to be varied or to be superseded by a new undertaking ; and (*d*) if it appears to him that any person can be so released or that an undertaking has not been or is not being fulfilled, or needs to be varied or superseded, to give such advice to the Secretary of State as he may think proper in the circumstances.

(5) If, following advice from the Director that a person can be released from an undertaking, the Secretary of State considers that it is appropriate for the Director to release him from it—

(*a*) the Secretary of State shall request the Director to do so, and

(*b*) the Director shall give the person concerned notice that he is released from the undertaking ;

and regulations under subsection (9) of section 4 above shall apply in relation to such a notice as they apply to a notice under subsection (5) of that section.

(6) The Secretary of State shall take account of any advice given to him by the Director under this section (including advice as to the exercise by the Secretary of State of any of his powers under this Act).

Orders
following
report on
competition
reference.

10.—(1) If, in any case where the report of the Commission on a competition reference concludes that any person specified in the report was engaged in an anti-competitive practice which operated or might be expected to operate against the public interest—

(*a*) the Secretary of State has not under section 9(1) above requested the Director to seek to obtain undertakings from one or more of the persons so specified, or

(*b*) following a request under subsection (1) of section 9 above, the Director has informed the Secretary of State that he is satisfied as mentioned in paragraph (*a*) or paragraph (*b*) of subsection (3) of that section, or

(*c*) the Director has informed the Secretary of State that an undertaking accepted by him under section 9 above from a person specified in the report has not been or is not being fulfilled,

the Secretary of State may, if he thinks fit, make an order under this section.

(2) Subject to the following provisions of this section, an order under this section may do either or both of the following, that is to say—

(*a*) prohibit a person named in the order from engaging in any anti-competitive practice which was specified in the report or from pursuing any other course of conduct which is similar in form and effect to that practice ; and (*b*) for the purpose of remedying or preventing any adverse effects which are specified in the report as mentioned in section 8(2)(*d*) above, exercise one or more of the powers specified in Part I of Schedule 8 to the Fair 1973 c. 41. Trading Act 1973 to such extent and in such manner as the Secretary of State considers necessary for that purpose.

(3) No order may be made by virtue of paragraph (*a*) of subsection (2) above in respect of any person unless he is a person specified in the Commission's report and either—

(*a*) he has not given an undertaking which the Director sought to obtain from him in pursuance of a request under section 9(1) above ; or

(*b*) the Director was not requested under section 9(1) above to seek to obtain an undertaking from him ; or

(*c*) the Director has informed the Secretary of State that an undertaking given by him and accepted by the Director under section 9 above has not been or is not being fulfilled.

(4) In the Fair Trading Act 1973—

(*a*) section 90 (general provisions as to orders under section 56 etc.) except subsection (2),

(*b*) section 91(2) (publication of proposals to make an order),

(*c*) section 93 (enforcement of certain orders), and

(*d*) Part I of Schedule 8 (powers exercisable by orders under section 56 etc.),

shall have effect as if any reference in those provisions to an order under section 56 of that Act included a reference to an order under this section.

Further references and investigations

11.—(1) The Secretary of State may at any time refer to the References of Commission any question relating to— public bodies and certain

(*a*) the efficiency and costs of, other persons

(*b*) the service provided by, or to the Commission.

(*c*) possible abuse of a monopoly situation by,

a person falling within subsection (3) below and specified in the reference, including any question whether, in relation to a matter falling within paragraph (*a*), (*b*) or (*c*) above, the person is pursuing a course of conduct which operates against the public interest.

(2) For the purposes of subsection (1)(c) above "monopoly situation" includes a monopoly situation which is limited to a part of the United Kingdom and, accordingly, for those purposes references to the United Kingdom in sections 6 and 7 of the Fair Trading Act 1973 shall be taken to include references to a part of the United Kingdom.

1973 c. 41.

(3) The persons referred to in subsection (1) above are—

(a) any body corporate—

(i) which supplies goods or services by way of business,

(ii) the affairs of which are managed by its members, and

(iii) the members of which hold office as such by virtue of their appointment to that or another office by a Minister under any enactment ; or

1968 c. 73.
1966 c. 21.
(N.I.).
1969 c. 35.

(b) any person (not falling within paragraph (a) above) who provides a bus service, within the meaning of the Transport Act 1968 or the Finance Act (Northern Ireland) 1966, or a London bus service, within the meaning of the Transport (London) Act 1969 ; or

1973 c. 37.

(c) any statutory water undertaker, within the meaning of the Water Act 1973 ; or

1958 c. 47.
1964 c. 13.
(N.I.).

(d) any board administering a scheme under the Agricultural Marketing Act 1958 or the Agricultural Marketing Act (Northern Ireland) 1964 ; or

(e) any body corporate with a statutory duty to promote and assist the maintenance and development of the efficient supply of any goods or services by a body falling within paragraphs (a) to (d) above ; or

1948 c. 38.

(f) any subsidiary, within the meaning of the Companies Act 1948, of a body falling within paragraphs (a) to (e) above.

(4) The Secretary of State may by order exclude from subsection (3)(b) above persons of such descriptions as may be specified in the order.

(5) No question concerning a person falling within subsection (3)(b) above or a subsidiary of a body falling within that subsection may be referred to the Commission under this section unless it relates to the carriage of passengers by the person or, as the case may be, the subsidiary.

(6) The Secretary of State may at any time by notice given to the Commission vary a reference under this section.

(7) On making a reference under this section or on varying such a reference under subsection (6) above the Secretary of

State shall arrange for the reference or, as the case may be, the variation to be published in such manner as he considers most suitable for bringing it to the attention of persons who in his opinion would be affected by it or be likely to have an interest in it.

(8) On a reference under this section the Commission shall investigate and report on any question referred to them but shall exclude from their investigation and report consideration of—

  (a) any question relating to the appropriateness of any financial obligations or guidance as to financial objectives (however expressed) imposed on or given to the person in question by or under any enactment, or otherwise by a Minister ; and

  (b) the question whether any course of conduct required or envisaged as mentioned in section 2(2) above operates against the public interest.

(9) Sections 70 (time limit for report on merger reference), 84 (public interest) and 85 (attendance of witnesses and production of documents) of the Fair Trading Act 1973 and Part II of 1973 c. 41. Schedule 3 to that Act (performance of functions of Commission) shall apply in relation to a reference under this section as if—

  (a) the functions of the Commission under this section were functions under that Act ;

  (b) the expression " merger reference " included a reference to the Commission under this section ;

  (c) in paragraph 11 of that Schedule, the reference to section 71 of that Act were a reference to subsection (6) above ; and

  (d) in paragraph 16(2) of that Schedule, the reference to section 56 of that Act were a reference to section 12 below.

(10) A report of the Commission on a reference under this section shall be made to the Secretary of State and shall state, with reasons, the conclusions of the Commission with respect to any question referred to them and, where the Commission conclude that the person specified in the reference is pursuing a course of conduct which operates against the public interest, the report may include recommendations as to what action (if any) should be taken by the person for the purpose of remedying or preventing what the Commission consider are the adverse effects of that course of conduct.

(11) In this section " Minister " includes a Northern Ireland department and the head of such a department.

12.—(1) This section applies where a report of the Commis- Orders sion on a reference under section 11 above concludes that the following person specified in the reference is pursuing a course of conduct report under which operates against the public interest. section 11.

(2) If it appears to the Secretary of State that any other Minister has functions directly relating to the person specified in the reference or, in the case of a reference only concerning the activities of the person in a part of the United Kingdom, functions directly relating to the person in respect of his activities in that part, he shall send a copy of the report of the Commission on the reference to that Minister; and in subsection (3) below " the relevant Minister " means—

    (*a*) in a case where it appears to the Secretary of State that any Minister (including himself) has such functions, that Minister, and

    (*b*) in a case where it appears to the Secretary of State that no Minister has such functions, the Secretary of State.

(3) If—

    (*a*) the relevant Minister considers it appropriate for the purpose of remedying or preventing what he considers are the adverse effects of the course of conduct specified in the report of the Commission as operating against the public interest, and

    (*b*) the person specified in the reference does not fall within paragraph (*d*) of section 11(3) above and is not a subsidiary of a body falling within that paragraph,

he may by order direct the person to prepare within such time, if any, as may be specified in the order a plan for remedying or preventing such of those effects as are so specified; but where there is more than one relevant Minister no such order shall be made except by all the relevant Ministers acting jointly and where none of the relevant Ministers is the Secretary of State no such order shall be made except after consultation with him.

(4) It shall be the duty of a person to whom a direction is given under subsection (3) above to prepare such a plan as is mentioned in that subsection and to send a copy of that plan to the Minister or Ministers by whom the order containing the direction was made who shall lay it before Parliament; and, in a case where the plan involves the use by a body of its powers in relation to any subsidiary within the meaning of the Companies Act 1948, the plan shall specify the manner in which the body proposes using those powers.

1948 c. 38.

(5) Whether or not an order has been or may be made under subsection (3) above, the Secretary of State may, if he considers it appropriate for the purpose of remedying or preventing what he considers are the adverse effects of the course of conduct specified in the report of the Commission as operating against the public interest, by order exercise one or more of the powers

specified in Part I, excluding paragraph 10, of Schedule 8 to the Fair Trading Act 1973, to such extent and in such manner 1973 c. 41. as he considers apropriate.

(6) In the Fair Trading Act 1973—

(a) section 90 (general provisions as to orders under section 56 etc.) except subsections (2) and (3),

(b) section 91(2) (publication of proposals to make an order),

(c) section 93 (enforcement of certain orders), and

(d) Part I (except paragraph 10) of Schedule 8 (powers exercisable by orders under section 56 etc.),

shall have effect as if any reference in those provisions to an order under section 56 of that Act included a reference to an order under subsection (5) above.

13.—(1) If so directed by the Secretary of State, the Director shall carry out an investigation into any price specified in the direction with a view to providing the Secretary of State with information of a description so specified relating to that price: but the giving of a direction under this section shall not affect the power of the Director to initiate an investigation under section 3 above (subject to subsection (5) of that section) into a course of conduct pursued by any person by or to whom the price specified in the direction is charged. *Investigations of prices directed by Secretary of State.*

(2) The Secretary of State shall not give a direction under this section unless he is satisfied that the price in question is one of major public concern and, in this connection, he shall have regard to whether—

(a) the provision or acquisition of the goods or services in question is of general economic importance ; or

(b) consumers are significantly affected, whether directly or indirectly, by the price.

(3) The Secretary of State may at any time vary or revoke a direction given under this section, but he shall not exercise his power to vary such a direction unless he is satisfied that the direction as proposed to be varied would be such as he could have given, having regard to subsection (2) above.

(4) On giving a direction under this section or on varying or revoking such a direction, the Secretary of State shall arrange for the direction, variation or revocation to be published in such manner as he considers most suitable for bringing it to the attention of persons who, in his opinion, would be affected by, or be likely to have an interest in, the investigation to which the direction, variation or revocation relates.

(5) A direction under this section shall specify a period within which the Director is to report on his investigation to the Secretary of State, and, before the expiry of the period specified in the direction (whether as originally given or as varied under subsection (3) above), the Director shall make a report on the investigation to the Secretary of State—

　(*a*) stating his findings of fact which are material to the information which he is required to provide in accordance with the direction ; and

　(*b*) containing such additional observations (if any) as the Director considers should be brought to the attention of the Secretary of State as a result of the investigation.

(6) Subsections (7) and (8) of section 3 above shall have effect in relation to an investigation under this section as they have effect in relation to an investigation under that section.

Patents and agricultural schemes

Applications by Crown concerning patents.
1977 c. 37.

14.—(1) After subsection (2) of section 51 of the Patents Act 1977 (application by Crown in cases of monopoly or merger) there shall be inserted the following subsection : —

　" (2A) Where—

　(*a*) on a reference under section 5 of the Competition Act 1980, a report of the Commission, as laid before Parliament, contains conclusions to the effect that—

　　(i) any person was engaged in an anti-competitive practice in relation to a description of goods which consist of or include patented products or in relation to a description of services in which a patented product or process is used, and

　　(ii) that practice operated or might be expected to operate against the public interest ; or

　(*b*) on a reference under section 11 of that Act, such a report contains conclusions to the effect that—

　　(i) any person is pursuing a course of conduct in relation to such a description of goods or services, and

　　(ii) that course of conduct operates against the public interest,

the appropriate Minister or Ministers may, subject to subsection (3) below, apply to the comptroller for relief under subsection (5A) below in respect of the patent.".

(2) In subsection (3) of that section (publication of details of proposed applications under subsection (1) or (2) of that section)

for the words " subsection (1) or (2) " there shall be substituted the words " subsection (1), (2) or (2A) ".

(3) After subsection (5) of that section there shall be inserted the following subsection: —

" (5A) If on an application under subsection (2A) above it appears to the comptroller that the practice or course of conduct in question involved or involves the imposition of any such condition as is mentioned in paragraph (*a*) of subsection (4) above or such a refusal as is mentioned in paragraph (*b*) of that subsection, the comptroller may by order cancel or modify any such condition or may, instead or in addition, make an entry in the register to the effect that licences under the patent are to be available as of right.".

15.—(1) In subsection (1) of section 19A of the Agricultural Marketing Act 1958 (power of Minister to make orders under section 19 of that Act where report of Commission on monopoly reference contains certain conclusions) after the words " Fair Trading Act 1973 " there shall be inserted the words " or section 8 or 11 of the Competition Act 1980 ". Agricultural schemes: special provisions. 1958 c. 47.

(2) The Secretary of State shall not—

   (*a*) give a direction under subsection (5) of section 3 above or a consent under subsection (9) of that section in relation to an investigation under that section, or

   (*b*) give a direction under section 7(2) or (3) above in relation to a competition reference, or

   (*c*) make or vary a reference under section 11 above,

in a case where the person to whom or to whose conduct or activities the investigation or reference relates falls within section 11(3)(*d*) above unless he has first consulted the relevant Minister.

(3) Where the report of the Commission on a competition reference concludes that a board administering a scheme under the said Act of 1958 or the Agricultural Marketing Act (Northern Ireland) 1964 was engaging in an anti-competitive practice which operated or might be expected to operate against the public interest, the Secretary of State shall not exercise any function under section 9 above except acting jointly with the relevant Minister and, in its application in such a case, section 9 above shall have effect as if the references in it to the Secretary of State (except the second reference in subsection (6)) were references to both the Secretary of State and the relevant Minister. 1964 c. 13. (N.I.).

(4) Before carrying out an investigation under section 3 above into any course of conduct being pursued by a person falling within section 11(3)(*d*) above the Director shall give

notice as required by section 3(2)(*a*) above also to the relevant Minister and on making any competition reference arising from that investigation or varying such a reference under section 6(6) above the Director shall send a copy of the reference or, as the case may be, the variation to the relevant Minister.

(5) In this section " the relevant Minister " means—

(*a*) in the case of a board administering a scheme under the said Act of 1958, the Minister who would have power to make an order under section 19 of that Act in relation to that board or the board administering that scheme, and

(*b*) in the case of a board administering a scheme under the said Act of 1964, the Department of Agriculture for Northern Ireland.

General provisions about references and investigations

General provisions as to reports. **16.**—(1) In making any report under this Act the Commission or the Director shall have regard to the need for excluding, so far as that is practicable—

(*a*) any matter which relates to the private affairs of an individual, where the publication of that matter would or might, in the opinion of the Commission or the Director, as the case may be, seriously and prejudicially affect the interests of that individual, and

(*b*) any matter which relates specifically to the affairs of a body of persons, whether corporate or unincorporate, where publication of that matter would or might, in the opinion of the Commission or the Director, as the case may be, seriously and prejudicially affect the interests of that body, unless in the opinion of the Commission or the Director, as the case may be, the inclusion of that matter relating specifically to that body is necessary for the purposes of the report.

(2) For the purposes of the law relating to defamation, absolute privilege shall attach to any report of the Commission or of the Director under this Act.

Laying before Parliament and publication of reports. **17.**—(1) Subject to subsection (2) below, the Secretary of State shall lay a copy of any report made to him under section 8(1), 11(10) or 13(5) above before each House of Parliament and shall arrange for the report to be published in such manner as appears to him appropriate.

(2) The Secretary of State shall not lay a copy of a report made to him under section 8(1) or 11(10) above before either House of Parliament unless at least twenty-four hours before doing so he has transmitted to every person specified in the

reference a copy of the report in the form in which it is laid (or by virtue of subsection (3) below is treated as being laid) before each House of Parliament.

(3) If a report made to him under section 8(1), 11(10) or 13(5) above is presented by command of Her Majesty to either House of Parliament otherwise than at or during the time of a sitting of that House, the presentation of the report shall for the purposes of this section be treated as the laying of a copy of it before that House by the Secretary of State.

(4) If it appears to the Secretary of State that the publication of any matter in a report made to him under section 8(1), 11(10) or 13(5) above would be against the public interest, he shall exclude that matter from the copies of the report as laid before Parliament and from the report as published under this section.

(5) Without prejudice to subsection (4) above, if the Secretary of State considers that it would not be in the public interest to disclose—

(a) any matter contained in a report made to him under section 8(1), 11(10) or 13(5) above relating to the private affairs of an individual whose interests would, in the opinion of the Secretary of State, be seriously and prejudicially affected by the publication of that matter, or

(b) any matter contained in such a report relating specifically to the affairs of a particular person whose interests would, in the opinion of the Secretary of State, be seriously and prejudicially affected by the publication of that matter,

the Secretary of State shall exclude that matter from the copies of the report as laid before Parliament and from the report as published by virtue of subsection (1) above.

(6) Any reference in sections 9, 10 or 12 above to a report of the Commission shall be construed as a reference to the report in the form in which copies of it are laid (or by virtue of subsection (3) of this section are treated as having been laid) before each House of Parliament under this section.

18. The Director shall arrange for the dissemination in such form and manner as he considers appropriate of such information and advice as it may appear to him expedient to give the public in the United Kingdom about the operation of this Act.

Information and advice about operation of Act.

19.—(1) Subject to subsection (2) below, no information obtained under or by virtue of the preceding provisions of this Act about any business shall, so long as the business continues to be carried on, be disclosed without the consent of the person for the time being carrying it on.

Restriction on disclosure of information.

(2) Subsection (1) above does not apply to any disclosure of information made—

(a) for the purpose of facilitating the performance of any functions under this Act or any of the enactments specified in subsection (3) below of any Minister, any Northern Ireland department, the head of any such department, the Director, the Commission or a local weights and measures authority in Great Britain; or

(b) in connection with the investigation of any criminal offence or for the purposes of any criminal proceedings; or

(c) for the purposes of any civil proceedings brought under or by virtue of this Act or any of the enactments specified in subsection (3) below; or

(d) in pursuance of a Community obligation.

(3) The enactments referred to in subsection (2) above are—

1968 c. 29.   (a) the Trade Descriptions Act 1968;

1973 c. 41.   (b) the Fair Trading Act 1973;

1974 c. 39.   (c) the Consumer Credit Act 1974;

1976 c. 34.   (d) the Restrictive Trade Practices Act 1976;

1976 c. 53.   (e) the Resale Prices Act 1976; and

1979 c. 38.   (f) the Estate Agents Act 1979.

(4) For the purpose of enabling information obtained under certain other enactments to be used for facilitating the performance of functions under this Act, the following amendments shall be made in provisions respecting disclosure of information, namely—

1958 c. 47.   (a) at the end of paragraph (aa) of the proviso to section 47(2) of the Agricultural Marketing Act 1958 there shall be added the words " or the Competition Act 1980 ";

1964 c. 13.   (b) at the end of paragraph (aaa) of section 23(2) of the
(N.I.).   Agricultural Marketing Act (Northern Ireland) 1964 there shall be added the words " or the Competition Act 1980 ";

(c) at the end of paragraph (a) of subsection (2) of section 133 of the Fair Trading Act 1973 there shall be added the words " the Competition Act 1980, or ";

(d) in paragraph (a) of subsection (3) of section 174 of the Consumer Credit Act 1974 after the words " Estate Agents Act 1979 " there shall be added the words " or the Competition Act 1980 ";

(e) at the end of paragraph (a) of subsection (1) of section 41 of the Restrictive Trade Practices Act 1976 there shall be added the words " or the Competition Act 1980 " ; and

(f) in paragraph (a) of subsection (3) of section 10 of the Estate Agents Act 1979 after the words " Restrictive 1979 c. 38. Trade Practices Act 1976 " there shall be added the words " or the Competition Act 1980 ".

(5) Nothing in subsection (1) above shall be construed—

(a) as limiting the matters which may be included in any report of the Director or of the Commission made under this Act ; or

(b) as applying to any information which has been made public as part of such a report or as part of the register kept for the purposes of the Act of 1976.

(6) Any person who discloses information in contravention of this section shall be liable on summary conviction to a fine not exceeding the statutory maximum and, on conviction on indictment, to imprisonment for a term not exceeding two years or to a fine or both.

(7) In subsection (6) above " the statutory maximum ", in relation to a fine on summary conviction, means—

(a) in England and Wales and Northern Ireland, the prescribed sum within the meaning of section 28 of the Criminal Law Act 1977 (at the passing of this Act 1977 c. 45. £1,000) ; and

(b) in Scotland, the prescribed sum within the meaning of section 289B of the Criminal Procedure (Scotland) 1975 c. 21. Act 1975 (at the passing of this Act £1,000) ;

and for the purposes of the application of this definition in Northern Ireland, the provisions of the Criminal Law Act 1977 which relate to the sum mentioned in paragraph (a) above shall extend to Northern Ireland.

Grants

20. If the Secretary of State is satisfied that—   Power to
make grants
(a) the general advice of any body on matters of interest to certain
to users of goods and services would be useful to him bodies.
in the formulation of policy concerning those matters
and

(b) the body disseminates information of such interest,
he may make a grant to the body on such terms as he thinks fit.

Amendments of Fair Trading Act 1973

Monopoly
references by
Secretary
of State alone.
1973 c. 41.

21. It is hereby declared that where it appears to the Secretary of State that—

(a) a monopoly situation exists or may exist as mentioned in subsection (1) of section 51 of the Fair Trading Act 1973 (monopoly references by Ministers), and

(b) the goods or services in question are of a description mentioned in subsection (2) of that section, and

(c) none of the Ministers mentioned in subsection (3) of that section has such functions as are mentioned in subsection (2) of that section in relation to goods or services of that description,

the Secretary of State may make a monopoly reference with respect to the existence or possible existence of that situation acting alone; and accordingly any reference which has been made in such circumstances by the Secretary of State acting alone has been made in compliance with that section.

Disclosure
of reports on
monopoly
references
to persons
named.

22.—In section 83 of the Fair Trading Act 1973 (laying before Parliament of reports under that Act)—

(a) at the beginning of subsection (1) there shall be inserted the words " Subject to subsection (1A) below "; and

(b) after subsection (1) there shall be inserted the following subsection:—

" (1A) The Minister or Ministers to whom a report of the Commission on a monopoly reference is made shall not lay a copy of the report before either House of Parliament unless at least twenty-four hours before doing so he transmits or they transmit to every person named in the report as a person in whose favour a monopoly situation exists a copy of the report in the form in which it is laid (or by virtue of subsection (2) below is treated as being laid) before each House of Parliament.".

Amendment
of s. 137(3) of
Fair Trading
Act 1973.

23. In section 137(3) of the Fair Trading Act 1973 (definition of " the supply of services ") there shall be inserted after paragraph (b) the following words:—

" and

(c) includes the making of arrangements for a person to put or keep on land a caravan (within the meaning of Part I of the Caravan Sites and Control of Development Act 1960) other than arrangements by virtue of which the person may occupy the caravan as his only or main residence ".

24.—(1) The Secretary of State may by order make such modifications in Part II of Schedule 3 to the Fair Trading Act 1973 (performance of functions of Commission) as appear to him to be appropriate for improving the performance by the Commission of their functions.

Modification of provisions about performance of Commission's functions.
1973 c. 41.

(2) An order under this section may contain such transitional, incidental or supplementary provisions as the Secretary of State thinks fit.

Amendments of Restrictive Trade Practices Act 1976

25. Where on an application under section 1(3) of the Restrictive Trade Practices Act 1976 the Court declares at any time after the coming into force of this section that any restrictions or information provisions are contrary to the public interest, that declaration shall not have effect—

Suspension of declarations under section 1(3) of Restrictive Trade Practices Act 1976 pending appeals.
1976 c. 34.

(a) until the expiration of the period of 21 days beginning with the expiration of the period within which any party to that application may appeal against the declaration, and

(b) in a case where such an appeal is brought, until the expiration of the period of 21 days after the date on which the appeal has been finally determined or withdrawn.

26.—(1) Where the Court has declared under section 1(3) of the Restrictive Trade Practices Act 1976 that any restrictions or information provisions in an agreement are contrary to the public interest, any party to the agreement or to the proceedings in which the declaration was made may, at any time before the declaration comes into effect, submit a revised agreement or a draft of a revised agreement to the Court and the Court may declare that any restrictions or information provisions contained in the revised agreement by virtue of which the said Act of 1976 applies or would apply to that agreement are not contrary to the public interest.

Suspension of declarations under section 1(3) of Restrictive Trade Practices Act 1976 pending revision of agreements.

(2) Variations of the agreement in relation to which the declaration under section 1(3) of the said Act of 1976 was made may not be submitted to the Court under subsection (1) above unless particulars of them have been furnished to the Director under section 24(2) of that Act and a new agreement may not be so submitted unless it has been registered under that Act and particulars of any variation of it have been so furnished.

(3) The duty of taking proceedings before the Court imposed on the Director by section 1(2)(c) of the said Act of 1976 shall not apply in respect of an agreement if the Court has declared under subsection (1) above that all the restrictions or information

provisions by virtue of which that Act applies to the agreement are not contrary to the public interest.

(4) Where any person who may make an application under subsection (1) above in relation to a declaration applies to the Court at any time before the declaration comes into effect for an extension of the period after which it will come into effect to enable an application to be made to the Court under subsection (1) above and it appears to the Court reasonable to do so, it may extend that period by such period (not exceeding six months on a first application under this subsection or three months on a second such application) as it thinks fit, but no more than two extensions may be made in respect of any declaration.

(5) Where, following a declaration under section 1(3) of the said Act of 1976, an application is made under subsection (1) or (4), above, the declaration shall not come into effect until the application has been determined.

(6) The Court may, if it thinks fit, grant an extension under subsection (4) above in relation to some but not all of the restrictions and information provisions in question and in that event—

(*a*) the period within which an application under subsection (1) above or a second application under subsection (4) above may be made shall not expire until the declaration has come into effect in relation to all the restrictions or information provisions, and

(*b*) subsection (5) above shall not prevent a declaration coming into effect in relation to any restriction or information provision in relation to which no extension was granted.

(7) Notice of an application made under subsection (1) or (4) above shall be served on the Director in accordance with rules of court and the Director shall be entitled in accordance with such rules to appear and to be heard on the application.

(8) Where a declaration is made under subsection (1) above the Director shall cause notice of it to be entered in the register kept by him under section 23 of the said Act of 1976—

(*a*) in the case of a declaration in relation to restrictions or information provisions contained in an agreement registered under the Act, on the making of the declaration, and

(*b*) in the case of a declaration in relation to restrictions or information provisions contained in a draft agreement, on the registration of an agreement in the form of the draft.

(9) Sections 10 and 19 of the said Act of 1976 (public interest) shall apply to proceedings under this section as they apply to proceedings under Part I of that Act.

27.—(1) An order under section 11 of the Restrictive Trade Practices Act 1976 (restrictive agreements as to services) may provide that section 16(3) of that Act (recommendations by services supply associations to members about services) shall not apply to recommendations of such descriptions as may be specified in the order and an order under section 12 of that Act (information agreements as to services) may make similar provision in relation to section 16(5) of that Act (recommendations by services supply associations to members about furnishing information). Recommendations by services supply associations. 1976 c. 34.

(2) Where—

   (*a*) section 16 of that Act would (apart from this subsection) apply in relation to a recommendation by a services supply association, and

   (*b*) if the sole term of the agreement for the constitution of the association were a term by which each member of it agreed to comply with that recommendation, the agreement would be excluded by the terms of the order from the operation of an order made, or having effect as if made, under section 11 of that Act which came into force after 21st March 1976 and before the coming into force of this section

subsection (3) of the said section 16 shall not apply and shall be deemed never to have applied in relation to that recommendation during the continuance in force of the order.

(3) Subsection (2) above shall have effect in relation to a recommendation made before the repeal of section 112(3) of the Fair Trading Act 1973 as if each reference to section 16(3) of the 1976 Act included a reference to that section. 1973 c. 41.

(4) In the Table in paragraph 5 of Schedule 2 to the said Act of 1976 (time within which particulars of agreements and variations to be furnished under that Act)—

   (*a*) there shall be added at the end of the first column of paragraph (*f*) the words " not being a variation which becomes subject to registration by virtue of an order under section 11 or 12 above " ; and

   (*b*) there shall be added at the end of the first column of paragraph (*i*) the words " other than a variation to which (*ii*) below applies " ; and

(c) after paragraph (i) there shall be added the following paragraph:—

" (ii) Variation of an agreement being a variation which extends or adds to the restrictions accepted or information provisions made under the agreement and which becomes subject to registration by virtue of the revocation or variation of an order made under section 11 or 12 above.	Within 1 month from the day on which the variation becomes so subject."

Amendments to s. 19 of Restrictive Trade Practices Act 1976.

1976 c. 34.

28.—(1) In section 19(1) of the Restrictive Trade Practices Act 1976 (which provides amongst other things that there is a presumption that a restriction or information provision is against the public interest unless the Court is satisfied the removal of it would deny benefits to the public as purchasers, consumers or users of any goods)—

(a) the word " vendors " shall be inserted before the word " purchasers " in both places where it occurs, and

(b) the words " or other property " shall be inserted—

(i) after the words " users of any goods " in paragraph (b), and

(ii) after the words " users of goods " in the words following paragraph (h).

(2) In subsection (2) of that section (" purchasers ", " consumers " and " users " to include persons purchasing, consuming and using for trade, business and public purposes) the word " ' vendors ' " shall be inserted before the word " ' purchasers ' " and the word " selling " shall be inserted before the word " purchasing ".

Exemption of certain undertakings from Restrictive Trade Practices Acts.

1973 c. 41.

29.—(1) The Restrictive Trade Practices Act 1976 shall not apply in relation to any agreement by virtue only of restrictions being accepted or information provisions being made under it which are comprised in undertakings which have been—

(a) given pursuant to section 88 of the Fair Trading Act 1973, or

(b) certified by the Secretary of State under paragraph 9 of Schedule 11 to the said Act of 1973, or

(c) accepted under section 4 or 9 above.

1956 c. 74.

(2) The said Act of 1976 and Part I of the Restrictive Trade Practices Act 1956 shall be deemed never to have applied in relation to any agreement by virtue only of restrictions being accepted or information provisions being made under it which are comprised in undertakings falling within paragraph (a) or (b) of subsection (1) above.

30.—(1) The following paragraph shall be inserted in Schedule Exemption
3 of the Restrictive Trade Practices Act 1976 (excepted agree- of copyright agreements
ments) after paragraph 5 :— from Restrictive Trade

" Copyrights

Practices Acts.

5A.—(1) This Act does not apply to—
  (a) a licence granted by the owner or a licensee of any 1976 c. 34.
      copyright ;
  (b) an assignment of any copyright ; or
  (c) an agreement for such a licence or assignment ;

being a licence, assignment or agreement such as is
described in sub-paragraph (2) or sub-paragraph (3) below.

(2) The licence, assignment or agreement referred to in
sub-paragraph (1) above is in relation to Part II of this Act
one under which no such restrictions as are described in
section 6(1) above are accepted or no such information
provisions as are described in section 7(1) above are made
except in respect of the work or other subject-matter in
which the copyright subsists or will subsist.

(3) The licence, assignment or agreement referred to in
sub-paragraph (1) above is in relation to Part III of this
Act one under which—
  (a) in the case of an order under section 11 above, no
      restrictions in respect of matters specified in the
      order for the purposes of subsection (1)(b) of that
      section are accepted except in respect of the work
      or other subject-matter in which the copyright
      subsists or will subsist ; or
  (b) in the case of an order under section 12 above, no
      information provision with respect to matters
      specified in the order for the purposes of subsec-
      tion (1)(b) of that section is made except in respect
      of that work or other subject-matter.

(4) In relation to Scotland references in this paragraph
to an assignment mean an assignation."

(2) The said Act of 1976 and Part I of the Restrictive Trade
Practices Act 1956 shall be deemed never to have applied in 1956 c. 74.
relation to—
  (a) a licence granted by the owner or a licensee of any copy-
      right,
  (b) an assignment or assignation of any copyright, or
  (c) an agreement for such a licence, assignment or
      assignation,
by virtue only of restrictions being accepted or information
provisions being made under it in respect of the work or other
subject-matter in which the copyright subsists or will subsist.

Supplementary

Orders and
regulations.

31.—(1) Any power of the Secretary of State to make orders or regulations under this Act shall be exercisable by statutory instrument.

(2) An order under section 2(3) above shall be laid before Parliament and shall cease to have effect (but without prejudice to the making of a new statutory instrument) unless, within forty days of the making of the order, it is approved by a resolution of each House of Parliament; and in reckoning any period of forty days for the purposes of this subsection, no account shall be taken of any period during which Parliament is dissolved or prorogued or during which both Houses are adjourned for more than four days.

(3) Any statutory instrument containing regulations under this Act or an order under section 10, 11(4) or 12(3) or (5) above shall be subject to annulment in pursuance of a resolution of either House of Parliament.

(4) No order shall be made under section 24(1) above unless a draft of the order has been laid before, and approved by a resolution of, each House of Parliament.

Financial
provisions.

32.—(1) There shall be defrayed out of moneys provided by Parliament—

    (*a*) any expenses incurred by the Secretary of State in consequence of the provisions of this Act; and

    (*b*) any increase attributable to this Act in the sums payable out of moneys so provided under any other Act.

1973 c. 41.

(2) In section 135(2)(*c*) of the Fair Trading Act 1973 (which provides for any expenses duly incurred by the Director or his staff in consequence of the provisions of that Act to be defrayed out of moneys provided by Parliament) for the words " of this Act " there shall be substituted the words " of this or any other Act ".

Short title,
interpretation,
repeals,
commence-
ment and
extent.

33.—(1) This Act may be cited as the Competition Act 1980.

(2) Except in so far as any provision of this Act otherwise provides, section 137 of the Fair Trading Act 1973 (general interpretation provisions) shall have effect in relation to sections 2 to 24 above as if those sections were contained in that Act; and for ease of reference the expressions which are used in those

sections and have meanings assigned to them by the said section
137 are—

" the Act of 1976 "
" agreement "
" business "
" the Commission "
" consumer "
" the Director "
" enactment '
" goods "
" group "
" group of inter-connected bodies corporate "
" inter-connected bodies corporate "
" Minister "
" monopoly situation "
" practice "
" price "
" services "
" supply "
" the supply of services ".

(3) Section 43 of the Restrictive Trade Practices Act 1976 1976 c. 34.
(interpretation and construction) shall have effect in relation to
sections 25 to 30 above as if those sections were contained in
that Act; and for ease of reference the expressions which are
used in those sections and have meanings assigned to them by
the said section 43 are—

" agreement "
" the Court "
" the Director "
" goods "
" information provision "
" restriction "
" services supply association "
" supply ".

(4) So much of the Counter-Inflation Act 1973 as remains 1973 c. 9.
in force immediately before the passing of this Act shall cease
to have effect and, in consequence of that and of the preceding
provisions of this Act, the enactments specified in Schedule 2 to
this Act are hereby repealed to the extent specified in the third
column of that Schedule.

(5) This Act shall come into operation on such day as the
Secretary of State may by order appoint, and different days may
be so appointed for different provisions and for different
purposes.

(6) An order under this section appointing a day for the coming into operation of any provision of Schedule 2 to this Act may contain such savings with respect to the operation of that provision and such incidental and transitional provisions as appear to the Secretary of State to be appropriate.

(7) Any reference in any provision of this Act to the appointed day shall be construed as a reference to the day appointed or, as the case may require, first appointed under this section for the coming into operation of that provision.

(8) This Act extends to Northern Ireland.

SCHEDULES

SCHEDULE 1

SUPPLEMENTARY PROVISIONS
IN CONNECTION WITH DISSOLUTION OF PRICE COMMISSION

1. Any liability in respect of pensions, allowances or gratuities which after the end of the winding-up period would, but for the dissolution of the Price Commission, have arisen or existed as a liability of the Commission to any of their officers or servants, or former officers or servants, shall instead be a liability of the Paymaster General.

2. Any legal proceedings to which the Price Commission are a party may be continued after the end of the winding-up period by or in relation to the Secretary of State.

3. A certificate signed by or on behalf of the Secretary of State that any instrument purporting to be made or issued by or on behalf of the Price Commission was so made or issued shall be conclusive evidence of that fact ; and any document purporting to be such a certificate shall be deemed to be such a certificate unless the contrary is shown.

4. Every contract, agreement, licence and authority, whether written or not, and every deed, bond, instrument and document made before the expiry of the winding-up period and still in effect at that time which relates to property, rights or obligations of the Price Commission which are vested in the Secretary of State by section 1(3) of this Act shall continue in effect but subject to the following modifications, so far as they are applicable—

(a) if the Price Commission are a party thereto, the Secretary of State shall be substituted as that party ;

(b) for a reference (however worded and whether express or implied) to the Price Commission there shall, as respects anything falling to be done or occurring after the expiry of the winding-up period, be substituted a reference to the Secretary of State ;

(c) for a reference (however worded and whether express or implied) to the members or any member, or to any officer or officers of the Price Commission there shall be substituted, as respects anything done or falling to be done or occurring after the expiry of the winding-up period, a reference to such officer or officers as the Secretary of State shall appoint for the purpose ; and

(d) for a reference to the office or place of business of the Price Commission there shall be substituted a reference to the principal offices of the Department of Trade.

Competition Act 1980

Section 33(4).

SCHEDULE 2
ENACTMENTS REPEALED

Chapter	Short Title	Extent of Repeal
1973 c. 9.	The Counter-Inflation Act 1973.	Parts I, II and V, so far as unrepealed.
1974 c. 24.	The Prices Act 1974.	In the Schedule, in paragraph 11, the words " or of the Price Commission ".
1975 c. 24.	The House of Commons Disqualification Act 1975.	In Part II of Schedule 1, the words " The Price Commission ".
1975 c. 25.	The Northern Ireland Assembly Disqualification Act 1975.	In Part II of Schedule 1, the words " The Price Commission ".
1975 c. 57.	The Remuneration, Charges and Grants Act 1975.	In section 2, subsection (4), in subsection (5) paragraph (b) and the word " or " immediately preceding it. Section 3.
1977 c. 33.	The Price Commission Act 1977.	The whole Act, except sections 16 and 17.
1978 c. 54.	The Dividends Act 1978.	The whole Act.
1979 c. 1.	The Price Commission (Amendment) Act 1979.	The whole Act.

Companies Act 1980

1980 CHAPTER 22

An Act to amend the law relating to companies.
[1st May 1980]

BE IT ENACTED by the Queen's most Excellent Majesty, by and with the advice and consent of the Lords Spiritual and Temporal, and Commons, in this present Parliament assembled, and by the authority of the same, as follows:—

PART I

CLASSIFICATION AND REGISTRATION OF COMPANIES, ETC.

Classification of companies

1.—(1) Subject to section 8(2) below, in this Act and in the Companies Acts 1948 to 1976— *(Classification of companies.)*

" public company " means a company limited by shares or limited by guarantee and having a share capital, being a company—

    (*a*) the memorandum of which states that the company is to be a public company ; and

    (*b*) in relation to which the provisions of the Companies Acts as to the registration or re-registration of a company as a public company have been complied with on or after the appointed day ; and

" private company ", unless the context otherwise requires, means a company that is not a public company.

PART I

(2) On or after the appointed day, no company may be formed as, or become, a company limited by guarantee with a share capital.

(3) Section 21(2) of the 1948 Act (meaning of provision for share capital in relation to a company limited by guarantee) shall apply for the purposes of this section as it applies for the purposes of that section.

Membership and name of a public company.

2.—(1) The minimum number of persons who may form a public company under section 1 of the 1948 Act (mode of forming an incorporated company) shall be two instead of seven.

(2) The name of a public company must end with the words " public limited company " or, in the case of a company the memorandum of which states that its registered office is to be situated in Wales, those words or their equivalent in Welsh; and those words or that equivalent may not be preceded by the word " limited " or its equivalent in Welsh.

(3) Subject to subsection (2) above, a resolution that a company be re-registered as a public company or, in the case of a company applying to be registered in accordance with section 13 below, that it be a public company may change the name of the company by deleting—

(a) the word " company " or the words " and company "; or

(b) its or their equivalent in Welsh ;

including any abbreviation of them.

(4) The memorandum of a public company shall be in the form set out in Part I of Schedule 1 to this Act or, if it is a company limited by guarantee and having a share capital, in the form set out in Part II of that Schedule or, in either case, as near thereto as circumstances admit ; and those forms supersede in the case of a public company the forms of memorandum set out respectively in Tables B and D in Schedule 1 to the 1948 Act.

Registration and re-registration of companies, etc.

Registration of companies.

3.—(1) Where any memorandum is delivered for registration under section 12 of the 1948 Act (registration of memorandum and articles), the registrar shall not register the memorandum unless he is satisfied that all the requirements of the Companies Acts in respect of registration and of matters precedent and incidental thereto have been complied with.

(2) Where a memorandum which is so delivered states that the association to be registered is to be a public company, the amount of the share capital stated in the memorandum to be

that with which the company proposes to be registered must not be less than the authorised minimum.

(3) Where the registrar registers an association's memorandum which states that the association is to be a public company, the certificate of incorporation given in respect of that association under section 13 of the 1948 Act (effect of registration) shall contain a statement that the company is a public company.

(4) A certificate of incorporation given under that section in respect of any association shall be conclusive evidence—

  (a) that the requirements mentioned in subsection (1) above have been complied with, and that the association is a company authorised to be registered and is duly registered under the 1948 Act ; and

  (b) if the certificate contains a statement that the company is a public company, that the company is such a company.

(5) A statutory declaration in the prescribed form by a solicitor engaged in the formation of a company, or by a person named as a director or secretary of the company in the statement delivered under section 21 of the 1976 Act (statement of first directors and secretary), that the requirements mentioned in subsection (1) above have been complied with shall be delivered to the registrar, and the registrar may accept such a declaration as sufficient evidence of compliance.

4.—(1) A company registered as a public company on its original incorporation shall not do business or exercise any borrowing powers unless the registrar of companies has issued it with a certificate under this section or the company is re-registered as a private company. *Public company not to do business unless requirements as to share capital complied with.*

(2) The registrar shall issue a company with a certificate under this section if, on an application made to him in the prescribed form by the company, he is satisfied that the nominal value of the company's allotted share capital is not less than the authorised minimum, and there is delivered to him a statutory declaration complying with subsection (3) below.

(3) The statutory declaration shall be in the prescribed form and signed by a director or secretary of the company and shall state—

  (a) the nominal value of the company's allotted share capital is not less than the authorised minimum ;

  (b) the amount paid up, at the time of the application, on the allotted share capital of the company ;

(c) the amount, or estimated amount, of the preliminary expenses of the company and the persons by whom any of those expenses have been paid or are payable ; and

(d) any amount or benefit paid or given or intended to be paid or given to any promoter of the company, and the consideration for the payment or benefit.

(4) For the purposes of subsection (2) above, a share allotted in pursuance of an employees' share scheme may not be taken into account in determining the nominal value of the company's allotted share capital unless it is paid up at least as to one-quarter of the nominal value of the share and the whole of any premium on the share.

(5) The registrar may accept a statutory declaration delivered to him under subsection (2) above as sufficient evidence of the matters stated therein.

(6) A certificate under this section in respect of any company is conclusive evidence that the company is entitled to do business and exercise any borrowing powers.

(7) If a company does business or exercises borrowing powers in contravention of this section, the company and any officer of the company who is in default shall be liable on conviction on indictment to a fine and on summary conviction to a fine not exceeding the statutory maximum.

(8) The provisions of this section are without prejudice to the validity of any transaction entered into by a company ; but, if a company enters into a transaction in contravention of those provisions and fails to comply with its obligations in connection therewith within 21 days from being called upon to do so, the directors of the company shall be jointly and severally liable to indemnify the other party to the transaction in respect of any loss or damage suffered by him by reason of the failure of the company to comply with those obligations.

Re-registration of private companies as public companies.

5.—(1) Subject to section 7 below, a private company, other than a company not having a share capital or an old public company, may be re-registered as a public company if—

(a) a special resolution, complying with subsection (2) below, that it should be so re-registered is passed ; and

(b) an application for the purpose, in the prescribed form and signed by a director or secretary of the company, is delivered to the registrar, together with the documents mentioned in subsection (3) below ; and

(c) the conditions specified in subsection (5)(a) and (b) below (where applicable) and section 6(1)(a) to (d) below are satisfied in relation to the company.

(2) The special resolution must—

(a) alter the company's memorandum so that it states that the company is to be a public company ;

(b) make such other alterations in the memorandum as are necessary to bring it in substance and in form into conformity with the requirements of this Act with respect to the memorandum of a public company ; and

(c) make such alterations in the company's articles as are requisite in the circumstances.

(3) The documents referred to in subsection (1) above are—

(a) a printed copy of the memorandum and articles as altered in pursuance of the resolution ;

(b) a copy of a written statement by the auditors of the company that in their opinion the relevant balance sheet shows that at the balance sheet date the amount of the company's net assets was not less than the aggregate of its called-up share capital and undistributable reserves ;

(c) a copy of the relevant balance sheet, together with a copy of an unqualified report by the company's auditors in relation to that balance sheet ;

(d) a copy of any report prepared under subsection (5)(b) below ; and

(e) a statutory declaration in the prescribed form by a director or secretary of the Company—

(i) that the special resolution mentioned in subsection (1)(a) above has been passed and that the conditions specified in subsection (1)(c) above have been satisfied ; and

(ii) that, between the balance sheet date and the application of the company for re-registration, there has been no change in the financial position of the company that has resulted in the amount of the company's net assets becoming less than the aggregate of its called-up share capital and undistributable reserves.

(4) The registrar may accept a declaration under subsection (3)(e) above as sufficient evidence that the special resolution has been passed and the said conditions have been satisfied.

(5) Where shares are allotted by the company between the balance sheet date and the passing of the special resolution as fully or partly paid up as to their nominal value or any premium on them otherwise than in cash, the company shall not make an

application for re-registration under this section unless before the making of the application—

    (a) the consideration for that allotment has been valued in accordance with the provisions of section 24 below applied by this subsection ; and

    (b) a report with respect to its value has been made to the company in accordance with those provisions during the six months immediately preceding the allotment of the shares ;

and subsections (2) to (7) and (11) and (12) of that section shall apply for the purposes of this subsection as they apply for the purposes of that section and as if the references to subsection (1) of that section were references to this subsection.

(6) If the registrar is satisfied on an application made under subsection (1) above that a company may be re-registered under this section as a public company, he shall—

    (a) retain the application and other documents delivered to him under that subsection ; and

    (b) issue the company with a certificate of incorporation stating that the company is a public company.

(7) The registrar shall not issue a certificate of incorporation under subsection (6) above if it appears to him that the court has made an order confirming a reduction of the company's capital which has the effect of bringing the nominal value of the company's allotted share capital below the authorised minimum.

(8) Upon the issue to a company of a certificate of incorporation under subsection (6) above—

    (a) the company shall by virtue of the issue of that certificate become a public company ; and

    (b) any alterations in the memorandum and articles set out in the resolution shall take effect accordingly.

(9) A certificate of incorporation issued to a company under subsection (6) above shall be conclusive evidence—

    (a) that the requirements of this Act in respect of re-registration and of matters precedent and incidental thereto have been complied with ; and

    (b) that the company is a public company.

(10) In this section—

    " undistributable reserves " has the same meaning as in section 40 below ;

    " relevant balance sheet " means, in relation to a company, a balance sheet prepared as at a date not more than seven months before the company's application for re-registration under this section ; and

" unqualified report " means, in relation to a balance sheet of a company—

    (*a*) if the balance sheet was prepared in respect of an accounting reference period of the company, a report made in pursuance of section 14(3)(*a*) or (*b*) of the 1967 Act (auditor's report) and stating without material qualification—

        (i) that, in the opinion of the person making the report, the balance sheet has been properly prepared in accordance with the provisions of the Companies Acts ; and

        (ii) where the report is made in pursuance of the said section 14(3)(*a*), that, in the opinion of that person, the balance sheet gives a true and fair view of the state of the company's affairs as at the balance sheet date ; and

    (*b*) in any other case, a report stating without material qualification—

        (i) that, in the opinion of the person making the report, the balance sheet complies with the requirements of sections 149 and 155 of the 1948 Act (contents, form and signing of accounts) ; and

        (ii) without prejudice to sub-paragraph (i) above, that, except where the company is entitled to avail itself, and has availed itself, of the benefit of any of the provisions of Part III of Schedule 8 to the 1948 Act (exemptions from requirements as to accounts), in the opinion of that person, the balance sheet gives a true and fair view of the state of the company's affairs as at the balance sheet date.

(11) A qualification shall be treated for the purposes of the definition of an unqualified report in subsection (10) above as being not material in relation to any balance sheet if, but only if, the person making the report states in writing that the thing giving rise to the qualification is not material for the purpose of determining, by reference to that balance sheet, whether at the balance sheet date the amount of the company's net assets was not less than the aggregate of its called up share capital and undistributable reserves.

(12) For the purposes of the making, in relation to the balance sheet of a company, of a report falling within paragraph (*b*) of the definition in subsection (10) above of an unqualified report, section 149 of and Schedule 8 to the 1948 Act shall be deemed

PART I

to have effect in relation to that balance sheet with such modifications as are necessary by reason of the fact that that balance sheet is prepared otherwise than in respect of an accounting reference period.

Requirements as to share capital of private company applying to re-register as public.

6.—(1) Subject to subsection (2) below, a private company shall not be re-registered under section 5 above as a public company unless, at the time the special resolution referred to in that section is passed—

   (a) the nominal value of the company's allotted share capital is not less than the authorised minimum ;

   (b) each of its allotted shares is paid up at least as to one-quarter of the nominal value of that share and the whole of any premium on it ;

   (c) where any share in the company or any premium payable on it has been fully or partly paid up by an undertaking given by any person that he or another should do work or perform services for the company or another, the undertaking has been performed or otherwise discharged ; and

   (d) where shares have been allotted as fully or partly paid up as to their nominal value or any premium payable on them otherwise than in cash and the consideration for the allotment consists of or includes an undertaking (other than one to which paragraph (c) above applies) to the company, either—

      (i) that undertaking has been performed or otherwise discharged ; or

      (ii) there is a contract between the company and any person pursuant to which that undertaking must be performed within five years from that time.

(2) Subject to subsection (3) below, any share allotted by the company—

   (a) which was allotted before the end of the transitional period, or

   (b) which was allotted in pursuance of an employees' share scheme and by reason of which the company would, but for this subsection, be precluded under subsection (1)(b) above, but not otherwise, from being re-registered as a public company,

may be disregarded for the purpose of determining whether subsection (1)(b) to (d) above is complied with in relation to the company, and a share so disregarded shall be treated for the purposes of subsection (1)(a) above as if it were not part of the allotted share capital of the company.

(3) A share shall not be disregarded by virtue of subsection (2)(*a*) above if the aggregate in nominal value of that share and the other shares which it is proposed so to disregard is more than one-tenth of the nominal value of the company's allotted share capital (not including any share disregarded by virtue of subsection (2)(*b*) above).

7.—(1) In its application to unlimited companies section 5 above shall have effect subject to the modifications contained in the following provisions of this section.

(2) The special resolution required by section 5(1) must, in addition to the matters mentioned in section 5(2)—

> (*a*) state that the liability of the members is to be limited by shares and what the share capital of the company is to be ; and
>
> (*b*) make such alterations in the company's memorandum as are necessary to bring it in substance and in form into conformity with the requirements of the Companies Acts with respect to the memorandum of a company limited by shares.

(3) The certificate of incorporation issued under section 5(6) shall, in addition to containing the statement required by paragraph (*b*) of that subsection, state that the company has been incorporated as a company limited by shares and—

> (*a*) the company shall by virtue of the issue of that certificate become a public company so limited ; and
>
> (*b*) the certificate shall be conclusive evidence of the fact that it is such a public company.

(4) Section 44(6) and (7) of the 1967 Act (provisions supplementary to re-registration of an unlimited company as a limited company) shall have effect as if any reference to the re-registration of a company in pursuance of that section included a reference to the re-registration of an unlimited company as a public company under section 5 above, but except as aforesaid the said section 44 shall not apply in relation to the re-registration of an unlimited company as a public company under section 5 above.

8.—(1) In this Act " old public company " means a company limited by shares or a company limited by guarantee and having a share capital in respect of which the following conditions are satisfied, that is to say—

> (*a*) the company either existed on the appointed day or was incorporated after that day pursuant to an application made before that day ;

Marginal notes:

PART I

Re-registration of unlimited company as public company.

Old public companies.

N3

(b) on that day, or, if later, on the day of the company's incorporation, the company was not, or, as the case may be, would not have been, a private company within the meaning of section 28 of the 1948 Act (meaning of private company) ; and

(c) the company has not since the appointed day or the day of the company's incorporation, as the case may be, either been re-registered as a public company or become a private company.

(2) The references in the Companies Acts 1948 to 1976 and, after the end of the transitional period, in this Act other than this Part to a public company or a company other than a private company shall, unless the context otherwise requires, include references to an old public company; and references in the Companies Acts to a private company shall be construed accordingly.

(3) An old public company may (either before or after the end of the transitional period) be re-registered as a public company if—

(a) the directors pass a resolution, complying with subsection (4) below, that it should be so re-registered ; and

(b) an application for the purpose in the prescribed form and signed by a director or secretary of the company is delivered to the registrar, together with the documents mentioned in subsection (5) below ; and

(c) at the time of the resolution, the conditions specified in subsection (11) below are satisfied.

(4) The resolution referred to in subsection (3) above must alter the company's memorandum so that it states that the company is to be a public company and make such other alterations in it as are necessary to bring it in substance and in form into conformity with the requirements of this Act with respect to the memorandum of a public company.

(5) The documents referred to in subsection (3) above are—

(a) a printed copy of the memorandum as altered in pursuance of the resolution ; and

(b) a statutory declaration in the prescribed form by a director or secretary of the company that the resolution mentioned in subsection (3)(a) above has been passed and that the conditions specified in subsection (11) below were satisfied at the time of the resolution.

(6) The registrar may accept a declaration under subsection (5)(b) above as sufficient evidence that the said resolution has been passed and the said conditions were so satisfied.

(7) Subsections (6) to (9) of section 5 above shall apply on an application for re-registration under this section as they apply on an application for re-registration under that and as if the reference to subsection (1) of that section were a reference to subsection (3) of this.

(8) An old public company may pass a special resolution not to be re-registered under this section as a public company and if either—

(a) 28 days from the passing of the resolution expire without an application being made under section 11(2) below for the cancellation of the resolution ; or

(b) such an application is made under that subsection and proceedings are concluded thereon without the court making an order for the cancellation of the resolution ;

the registrar shall issue the company with a certificate stating that it is a private company and the company shall become a private company by virtue of the issue of that certificate.

(9) If an old public company delivers to the registrar a statutory declaration in the prescribed form by a director or secretary of the company that the company does not at the time of the declaration satisfy the conditions specified in subsection (11) below, the registrar shall issue the company with a certificate stating that it is a private company and the company shall become a private company by virtue of the issue of that certificate.

(10) A certificate issued to a company under subsection (8) or (9) above shall be conclusive evidence that the requirements of that subsection have been complied with and that the company is a private company.

(11) The conditions referred to in subsections (3)(c) and (9) above are that, at the time concerned, the nominal value of the company's allotted share capital is not less than the authorised minimum and that in the case of all the shares of the company or all those of its shares which are comprised in a portion of that capital which satisfies that condition—

(a) each share is paid up at least as to one-quarter of the nominal value of that share and the whole of any premium on it ;

(b) where any of the shares in question or any premium payable on them has been fully or partly paid up by an undertaking given by any person that he or another should do work or perform services for the company or another, the undertaking has been performed or otherwise discharged ; and

(c) where any of the shares in question has been allotted as fully or partly paid up as to its nominal value or any premium payable on it otherwise than in cash and the consideration for the allotment consists of or includes an undertaking (other than one to which paragraph (b) above applies) to the company, either—

> (i) that undertaking has been performed or otherwise discharged ; or

> (ii) there is a contract between the company and any person pursuant to which that undertaking must be performed within five years from that time.

(12) For the purposes of subsection (8) above proceedings on an application under section 11(2) below are concluded—

(a) except in a case falling within paragraph (b) below, when the period mentioned in section 11(5)(b) below for delivering an office copy of the order to the registrar expires ; or

(b) when the company is notified that the application has been withdrawn.

Failure by old public company to obtain new classification.

9.—(1) If, at any time after the end of the period of fifteen months from the appointed day (in this Act referred to as the " re-registration period "), a company which is an old public company has not delivered to the registrar a declaration under section 8(9) above, the company and any officer of the company who is in default shall be guilty of an offence unless at that time the company—

(a) has applied to be re-registered under section 8 above, and the application has not been refused or withdrawn ; or

(b) has passed a special resolution not to be re-registered under that section, and the resolution has not been revoked and has not been cancelled under section 11 below.

(2) A person guilty of an offence under subsection (1) above shall be liable on summary conviction to a fine not exceeding one-fifth of the statutory maximum or, on conviction after continued contravention, to a default fine not exceeding one-fiftieth of the statutory maximum for every day on which that subsection is contravened.

Re-registration of public company as private company.

10.—(1) A public company may be re-registered as a private company if—

(a) a special resolution complying with subsection (2) below that it should be so re-registered is passed and has not been cancelled bv the court under section 11(6) below ;

(*b*) an application for the purpose in the prescribed form and signed by a director or secretary of the company is delivered to the registrar, together with a printed copy of the memorandum and articles of the company as altered by the resolution ; and

(*c*) the period during which an application for the cancellation of the resolution under section 11(2) below may be made has expired without any such application having been made ; or

(*d*) where such an application has been made, the application has been withdrawn or an order has been made under section 11(6) below confirming the resolution and a copy of that order has been delivered to the registrar.

(2) The resolution must alter the company's memorandum so that it no longer states that the company is to be a public company and must make such other alterations in the company's memorandum and articles as are requisite in the circumstances.

(3) If the registrar is satisfied that a company may be re-registered under subsection (1) above, he shall—

(*a*) retain the application and other documents delivered to him under that subsection ; and

(*b*) issue the company with a certificate of incorporation appropriate to a company that is not a public company.

(4) Upon the issue of a certificate of incorporation under subsection (3) above—

(*a*) the company shall by virtue of the issue of that certificate become a private company ; and

(*b*) the alterations in the memorandum and articles set out in the resolution shall take effect accordingly.

(5) A certificate of incorporation issued to a company under subsection (3) above shall be conclusive evidence—

(*a*) that the requirements of this section in respect of re-registration and of matters precedent and incidental thereto have been complied with ; and

(*b*) that the company is a private company.

11.—(1) This section applies to the following special resolutions, namely—

(*a*) a special resolution by an old public company not to be re-registered under section 8 above as a public company ;

(*b*) a special resolution by a public company to be re-registered under section 10 above as a private company.

Special resolutions resulting in company becoming private company.

(2) Where a special resolution to which this section applies has been passed, an application may be made to the court for the cancellation of that resolution.

(3) An application under subsection (2) above may be made—

(a) by the holders of not less in the aggregate than five per cent. in nominal value of the company's issued share capital or any class thereof;

(b) if the company is not limited by shares, by not less than five per cent. of the company's members; or

(c) by not less than 50 of the company's members;

but any such application shall not be made by any person who has consented to or voted in favour of the resolution.

(4) Any such application must be made within 28 days after the passing of the resolution and may be made on behalf of the persons entitled to make the application by such one or more of their number as they may appoint in writing for the purpose.

(5) If an application is made under subsection (2) above, the company—

(a) shall forthwith give notice in the prescribed form of that fact to the registrar; and

(b) where on the hearing of that application an order cancelling or confirming the resolution is made under subsection (6) below, shall, within 15 days from the making of that order, or within such longer period as the court may at any time by order direct, deliver an office copy of the order to the registrar.

(6) On the hearing of an application under subsection (2) above the court shall make an order either cancelling or confirming the resolution and—

(a) may make that order on such terms and conditions as it thinks fit, and may, if it thinks fit, adjourn the proceedings in order that an arrangement may be made to the satisfaction of the court for the purchase of the interests of dissentient members; and

(b) may give such directions and make such orders as it thinks expedient for facilitating or carrying into effect any such arrangement.

(7) An order under this section may, if the court thinks fit, provide for the purchase by the company of the shares of any members of the company and for the reduction accordingly of the company's capital and may make such alterations in the memorandum and articles of the company as may be required in consequence of that provision.

(8) Where an order under this section requires the company not to make any, or any specified, alteration in its memorandum or articles, then, notwithstanding anything in the Companies Acts, the company shall not have power without the leave of the court to make any such alteration in breach of that requirement.

(9) Any alteration in the memorandum or articles of the company made by virtue of an order under this section, other than one made by resolution of the company, shall be of the same effect as if duly made by resolution of the company, and the provisions of the Companies Acts shall apply to the memorandum or articles as so altered accordingly.

(10) A company which fails to comply with subsection (5) above and any officer of the company who is in default shall be liable on summary conviction to a fine not exceeding one-fifth of the statutory maximum or, on conviction after continued contravention, a default fine not exceeding one-fiftieth of the statutory maximum for each day until the notice or, as the case may be, the copy required to be given or delivered by that subsection is given or delivered.

12.—(1) Where the court makes an order confirming a reduction of a public company's capital which has the effect of bringing the nominal value of the company's allotted share capital below the authorised minimum, the registrar shall not register the order under section 69(1) of the 1948 Act (registration of order of reduction of capital) unless the court otherwise directs or the company is first re-registered as a private company.

(2) A court making any such order in respect of a company may authorise the company to be re-registered as a private company under section 10 above without its having passed a special resolution and, where the court so authorises a company, the court shall specify in the order the alterations in the company's memorandum and articles to be made in connection with that re-registration.

(3) In its application to a company that applies to be re-registered as a private company in pursuance of an authority given under subsection (2) above, section 10 above shall have effect with the following modifications—

   (*a*) references to the special resolution of the company shall have effect as references to the order of the court under that subsection ;

   (*b*) section 10(1)(*a*), (*c*) and (*d*) and (2) shall not apply ; and

   (*c*) in section 10(3), for the words from " If " to " shall " there shall be substituted the words " On receipt of an application for re-registration under this section made in pursuance of an order of the court under section 12(2) below, the registrar shall ".

PART I
Registration
of joint stock
companies
as public
companies.

13.—(1) A joint stock company (within the meaning of section 383 of the 1948 Act) applying to be registered in pursuance of Part VIII of that Act as a company limited by shares may, subject to satisfying the conditions specified in section 5(5)(*a*) and (*b*) above (where applicable) and section 6(1)(*a*) to (*d*) above, as applied by this section, and to complying with the requirements of subsection (4) below, apply to be so registered as a public company.

(2) The said sections 5(5) and 6 shall apply to a joint stock company applying to register under the said Part VIII as they apply to a private company applying to be re-registered under section 5 above, but as if any reference to the special resolution mentioned in section 5 were a reference to the resolution mentioned in subsection (4)(*a*) below.

(3) In the following provisions of this section an application by a company made in pursuance of the said Part VIII to register as a public company limited by shares is referred to as a relevant application.

(4) A relevant application shall be made in the form prescribed for the purpose and shall be delivered to the registrar together with the following documents (as well as with the documents referred to in section 384 of the 1948 Act), namely—

(*a*) a copy of the resolution that the company be a public company;

(*b*) a copy of a written statement by a person, who would be qualified under section 161 of the 1948 Act for appointment as auditor of the company if it were a company registered under that Act, that in his opinion a relevant balance sheet shows that at the balance sheet date the amount of the company's net assets was not less than the aggregate of the called-up share capital of the company and its undistributable reserves;

(*c*) a copy of the relevant balance sheet, together with a copy of an unqualified report by such a person in relation to that balance sheet;

(*d*) a copy of any report prepared under section 5(5)(*b*) above, as applied by this section; and

(*e*) a statutory declaration in the prescribed form by a director or secretary of the company—

(i) that the conditions specified in section 5(5)(*a*) and (*b*) above (where applicable) and section 6(1)(*a*) to (*d*) above have been satisfied; and

(ii) that, between the balance sheet date referred to in paragraph (*b*) above and the relevant application, there has been no change in the financial position of the company that has resulted in the amount

of the company's net assets becoming less than the
aggregate of its called-up share capital and undistributable reserves.

(5) The registrar may accept a declaration under subsection (4)(*e*) above as sufficient evidence that the conditions referred to in sub-paragraph (i) of that paragraph have been satisfied.

(6) Where on a relevant application the registrar is satisfied that the company may be registered as a public company limited by shares, the certificate of incorporation given by him under section 390 of the 1948 Act (certificate of registration of existing company) shall state that the company is a public company ; and such a statement shall be conclusive evidence that the requirements of this section have been complied with and that the company is a public company so limited.

(7) In this section—

" relevant balance sheet " means, in relation to a company, a balance sheet prepared as at a date not more than seven months before the relevant application ;

" undistributable reserves " has the same meaning as in section 40 below ; and

" unqualified report " has the same meaning as in section 5 above ;

and section 5(11) above applies to the making in pursuance of this section of an unqualified report such as is mentioned in that subsection, as it applies to the making of such a report in pursuance of the said section 5.

PART II

THE CAPITAL OF A COMPANY

The issue of share capital

14.—(1) The directors of a company shall not exercise any Authority of power of the company to allot relevant securities, unless the company directors are, in accordance with this section, authorised to do required for allotment of so by— certain securities by
    (*a*) the company in general meeting ; or directors.
    (*b*) the articles of the company.

(2) Authority for the purposes of this section may be given for a particular exercise of that power or for the exercise of that power generally, and may be unconditional or subject to conditions.

(3) Any such authority shall state the maximum amount of relevant securities that may be allotted thereunder and the date

on which the authority will expire, which shall be not more than five years from whichever is relevant of the following dates—

(*a*) in the case of an authority contained at the time of the original incorporation of the company in the articles of the company, the date of that incorporation ; and

(*b*) in any other case, the date on which the resolution is passed by virtue of which that authority is given ;

but any such authority (including an authority contained in the articles of the company) may be previously revoked or varied by the company in general meeting.

(4) Any such authority (whether or not it has been previously renewed under this subsection) may be renewed by the company in general meeting for a further period not exceeding five years ; but the resolution must state (or restate) the amount of relevant securities which may be allotted under the authority or, as the case may be, the amount remaining to be allotted thereunder, and must specify the date on which the renewed authority will expire.

(5) The directors may allot relevant securities, notwithstanding that any authority for the purposes of this section has expired, if the relevant securities are allotted in pursuance of an offer or agreement made by the company before the authority expired and the authority allowed it to make an offer or agreement which would or might require relevant securities to be allotted after the authority expired.

(6) A resolution of a company to give, vary, revoke or renew such an authority may, notwithstanding that it alters the articles of the company, be an ordinary resolution, but section 143 of the 1948 Act (registration of copies of certain resolutions and agreements) shall apply to it.

(7) Any director who knowingly and wilfully contravenes, or permits or authorises a contravention of, this section shall be liable on conviction on indictment to a fine and on summary conviction to a fine not exceeding the statutory maximum.

(8) Nothing in this section shall affect the validity of any allotment of relevant securities.

(9) This section does not apply to any allotment of relevant securities by a company, other than a public company registered as such on its original incorporation, if it is made in pursuance of an offer or agreement made before the date on which the earlier of the following events occurs, that is to say, the holding of the first general meeting of the company after its re-registration or registration as a public company and the end of the transitional period ; but any resolution to give, vary or revoke

an authority for the purposes of this section shall have effect for those purposes if it is passed at any time after the passing of this Act.

(10) In this section " relevant securities " means, in relation to a company,—

    (*a*) shares in the company other than shares shown in the memorandum to have been taken by the subscribers thereto or shares allotted in pursuance of an employees' share scheme ; and

    (*b*) any right to subscribe for, or to convert any security into, shares in the company other than shares so allotted ;

and any reference to the allotment of relevant securities shall include a reference to the grant of such a right but shall not include any reference to the allotment of shares pursuant to such a right.

15.—(1) A private limited company (other than a company limited by guarantee and not having a share capital) shall be guilty of an offence if it— *Shares and debentures of private company not to be offered to public.*

    (*a*) offers to the public (whether for cash or otherwise) any shares in or debentures of the company ; or

    (*b*) allots, or agrees to allot, (whether for cash or otherwise) any shares in or debentures of the company with a view to all or any of those shares or debentures being offered for sale to the public.

(2) Sections 45(2) of the 1948 Act (circumstances in which it is presumed that an allotment or agreement to allot shares or debentures was made with a view to their being offered to the public) and 55 of that Act (construction of references to offering shares or debentures to the public) shall apply for the purposes of this section as they apply for the purposes of that Act.

(3) A company guilty of an offence under subsection (1) above and any officer of the company who is in default shall be liable on conviction on indictment to a fine and on summary conviction to a fine not exceeding the statutory maximum.

(4) Nothing in this section shall affect the validity of any allotment or sale of shares or debentures or of any agreement to allot or sell shares or debentures.

(5) This section shall not apply during the transitional period to an old public company, but after the end of that period shall apply to such a company as if it were a private company such as is mentioned in subsection (1) above.

PART II
Prospectus,
etc., to state
if shares to
be allotted
where issue
not fully
subscribed.

16.—(1) Without prejudice to section 47 of the 1948 Act (prohibition of allotment unless minimum subscription received), no allotment shall be made of any share capital of a public company offered for subscription unless—

    (a) that capital is subscribed for in full ; or

    (b) the offer states that, even if the capital is not subscribed for in full, the amount of that capital subscribed for may be allotted in any event or in the event of the conditions specified in the offer being satisfied ;

and, where conditions are so specified, no allotment of the capital shall be made by virtue of paragraph (b) above unless those conditions are satisfied.

(2) Section 47(4) (repayment of money paid by applicants) and section 49 (effect of irregular allotment) of the 1948 Act shall apply where shares are prohibited from being allotted by subsection (1) above as they apply where the conditions mentioned in subsection (1) of the said section 47 are not complied with ; and subsection (5) of the said section 47 (prohibition on waiver of compliance with requirements of that section) shall apply to this section as it applies to that section.

(3) The provisions of this section shall apply in the case of shares offered as wholly or partly payable otherwise than in cash as they apply in the case of shares offered for subscription ; and—

    (a) in subsection (1) above, the word " subscribed " shall be construed accordingly: and

    (b) in the said section 47(4), as it applies by virtue of subsection (2) above to the former case, references to the repayment of money received from applicants for shares shall include references to the return of any other consideration so received (including, if the case so requires, the release of the applicant from any undertaking) or, if it is not reasonably practicable to return the consideration, the payment of money equal to the value of the consideration at the time it was so received, and references to interest shall have effect accordingly.

Pre-emption rights

17.—(1) Subject to the following provisions of this section and sections 18 and 19 below, a company proposing to allot any equity securities—

    (a) shall not allot any of those securities on any terms to any person unless it has made an offer to each person who holds relevant shares or relevant employee shares to allot to him on the same or more favourable terms a proportion of those securities which is as nearly as practicable equal to the proportion in nominal value held by him of the aggregate of relevant shares and relevant employee shares ; and

(b) shall not allot any of those securities to any person unless the period during which any such offer may be accepted has expired or the company has received notice of the acceptance or refusal of every offer so made.

(2) Subsection (3) below applies to any provision of the memorandum or articles of a company which requires the company, when proposing to allot equity securities consisting of relevant shares of any particular class, not to allot those securities on any terms unless it has complied with the condition that it makes such an offer as is described in subsection (1) above to each person who holds relevant shares or relevant employee shares of that class.

(3) If, in accordance with a provision to which this subsection applies—

(a) a company makes an offer to allot any securities to such a holder, and

(b) he or anyone in whose favour he has renounced his right to their allotment accepts the offer,

subsection (1) above shall not apply to the allotment of those securities and the company may allot them accordingly ; but this subsection is without prejudice to the application of subsection (1) above in any other case.

(4) Subsection (1) above shall not apply in relation to a particular allotment of equity securities if the securities are, or are to be, wholly or partly paid up otherwise than in cash, and securities which a company has offered to allot to a holder of relevant shares or relevant employee shares may be allotted to him or anyone in whose favour he has renounced his right to their allotment without contravening subsection (1)(b) above.

(5) Subsection (1) above shall not apply in relation to the allotment of any securities which would apart from a renunciation or assignment of the right to their allotment be held under an employees' share scheme.

(6) An offer which is required by subsection (1) above or by any provision to which subsection (3) above applies to be made to any person shall be made by serving it on him in the manner in which notices are authorised to be given by regulations 131, 132 and 133 of Table A ; but where he is the holder of a share warrant or, if the company had adopted (without modification) regulation 134 of Table A, he would not be entitled to receive

notices of general meetings, the offer may instead be made by causing the offer, or a notice specifying where a copy of the offer can be obtained or inspected, to be published in the Gazette.

(7) Any such offer as is mentioned in subsection (6) above must state a period of not less than 21 days during which the offer may be accepted ; and the offer shall not be withdrawn before the end of that period.

(8) Subsections (6) and (7) above shall not invalidate a provision to which subsection (3) above applies by reason that that provision requires or authorises an offer thereunder to be made in contravention of one or both of those subsections, but, to the extent that the provision requires or authorises such an offer to be so made, it shall be of no effect.

(9) Subsection (1), (6) or (7) above may, in its application in relation to allotments by a private company of equity securities or to such allotments of a particular description, be excluded by a provision contained in the memorandum or articles of that company ; and a requirement or authority contained in the memorandum or articles of a private company shall, if it is inconsistent with any of those subsections, have effect as a provision excluding that subsection, but a provision to which subsection (3) above applies shall not be treated as being inconsistent with subsection (1) above.

(10) Where there is a contravention of subsection (1), (6) or (7) above or of a provision to which subsection (3) above applies, the company, and every officer of the company who knowingly authorised or permitted the contravention, shall be jointly and severally liable to compensate any person to whom an offer should have been made under the subsection or provision contravened for any loss, damage, costs or expenses which that person has sustained or incurred by reason of the contravention ; but no proceedings to recover any such loss, damage, costs or expenses shall be commenced after the expiration of two years from the delivery to the registrar of companies of the return of allotments in question or, where equity securities other than shares are granted, from the date of the grant.

(11) In this section and sections 18 and 19 below—

" equity security ", in relation to a company, means a relevant share in the company (other than a share shown in the memorandum to have been taken by a subscriber thereto or a bonus share) or a right to subscribe for, or to convert any securities into, relevant shares in the company, and references to the allotment of equity securities or of equity securities consisting of relevant shares of a particular class shall include references to the grant of a right to subscribe for, or to convert any securities into, relevant shares in the company or, as the case may be, relevant shares of a particular class, but shall not include references to the allotment of any relevant shares pursuant to such a right;

" relevant employee shares ", in relation to a company, means shares of the company which would be relevant shares in the company but for the fact that they are held under an employees' share scheme ; and

" relevant shares ", in relation to a company, means shares in the company other than—

> (a) shares which as respects dividends and capital carry a right to participate only up to a specified amount in a distribution ; and

> (b) shares held, or to be held, under an employees' share scheme ;

and any reference to a class of shares shall be construed as a reference to shares to which the same rights are attached as to voting and as to participation, both as respects dividends and as respects capital, in a distribution.

(12) This section is without prejudice to any enactment by virtue of which a company is prohibited (whether generally or in specified circumstances) from offering or allotting equity securities to any person ; and, where a company cannot by virtue of any such enactment offer or allot equity securities to a holder of relevant shares or relevant employee shares, this section shall have effect as if the shares held by that holder were not relevant shares or relevant employee shares.

18.—(1) Where the directors of a company are generally authorised for the purposes of section 14 above, they may be given power by the articles or by a special resolution of the company to allot equity securities pursuant to that authority as if— Disapplication of pre-emption rights.

> (a) section 17(1) above did not apply to the allotment ; or

> (b) that subsection applied to the allotment with such modifications as the directors may determine ;

and where the directors make an allotment under this subsection, the said section 17 shall have effect accordingly.

(2) Where the directors of a company are authorised for the purposes of section 14 above (whether generally or otherwise), the company may by special resolution resolve either—

> (a) that section 17(1) above shall not apply to a specified allotment of equity securities to be made pursuant to that authority ; or

(b) that that subsection shall apply to the allotment with such modifications as may be specified in the resolution;

and where such a resolution is passed the said section 17 shall have effect accordingly.

(3) A power conferred by virtue of subsection (1) above or a special resolution under subsection (2) above shall cease to have effect when the authority to which it relates is revoked or would, if not renewed, expire, but if that authority is renewed, the power or, as the case may be, the resolution may also be renewed, for a period not longer than that for which the authority is renewed, by a special resolution of the company.

(4) Notwithstanding that any such power or resolution has expired, the directors may allot equity securities in pursuance of an offer or agreement previously made by the company, if the power or resolution enabled the company to make an offer or agreement which would or might require equity securities to be allotted after it expired.

(5) A special resolution under subsection (2) above, or a special resolution to renew such a resolution, shall not be proposed unless it is recommended by the directors and there has been circulated, with the notice of the meeting at which the resolution is proposed, to the members entitled to have that notice a written statement by the directors setting out—

(a) their reasons for making the recommendation;

(b) the amount to be paid to the company in respect of the equity securities to be allotted; and

(c) the directors' justification of that amount.

(6) A person who knowingly or recklessly authorises or permits the inclusion in a statement circulated under subsection (5) above of any matter which is misleading, false or deceptive in a material particular shall be liable—

(a) on conviction on indictment to imprisonment for a term not exceeding two years or a fine, or both; and

(b) on summary conviction, to imprisonment for a term not exceeding six months or a fine not exceeding the statutory maximum, or both.

Pre-emption rights: transitional provisions.

19.—(1) Sections 17 and 18 above shall not apply—

(a) to any allotment of equity securities made by a company, other than a public company registered as such on its original incorporation, before the date on which the earlier of the following events occurs, that is to say, the holding of the first general meeting of the company after its re-registration or registration as a public company and the end of the transitional period ; or

(b) where subsection (2) below applies, to an allotment of the equity securities which are subject to the requirement mentioned in that subsection.

(2) This subsection applies where any company which is re-registered or registered as a public company is or, but for the provisions of this Act, would be subject at the time of re-registration or, as the case may be, registration to a requirement imposed (whether by the company's memorandum or articles or otherwise) before the relevant time by virtue of which it must, when making an allotment of equity securities, make an offer to allot those securities or some of them in a manner which (otherwise than by virtue of its involving a contravention of section 17(6) or (7) above) is inconsistent with section 17 above.

(3) Any requirement which—

(a) is imposed on a private company before the relevant time otherwise than by the company's memorandum or articles ; and

(b) if contained in the memorandum or articles of the company, would have effect by virtue of section 17(9) above to the exclusion of any provision of that section,

shall have effect, so long as the company remains a private company, as if it were contained in the memorandum or articles of the company.

(4) If at the relevant time a company, other than a public company registered as such on its original incorporation, is subject to a requirement such as is mentioned in section 17(2) above and which was imposed otherwise than by the company's memorandum or articles, the requirement shall be treated for the purposes of that section as if it were contained in the company's memorandum or articles.

(5) In this section " the relevant time " means—

(a) except in a case falling within paragraph (b) below, the end of the transitional period ; and

(b) in the case of a company which is re-registered or registered as a public company in pursuance of an application made before the end of that period, the time at which the application is made.

Payment for share capital

20.—(1) Subject to the following provisions of this Part of this Act, shares allotted by any company and any premium payable on them may be paid up in money or moneys worth (including goodwill and know-how.

Subscription of share capital.

(2) A public company shall not accept at any time in payment up of its shares or any premium on them, an undertaking given by any person that he or another should do work or perform services for the company or any other person.

(3) Where a public company accepts such an undertaking in payment up of its shares or any premium payable on them, the holder of the shares when they or the premium are treated as paid up, in whole or in part, by the undertaking—

(a) shall be liable to pay the company in respect of those shares an amount equal to their nominal value, together with the whole of any premium or, if the case so requires, such proportion of that amount as is treated as paid up by the undertaking ; and

(b) shall be liable to pay interest at the appropriate rate on the amount payable under paragraph (a) above.

(4) Where any person becomes a holder of any shares in respect of which—

(a) there has been a contravention of this section ; and

(b) by virtue of that contravention, another is liable to pay any amount under this section,

that person also shall be liable to pay that amount (jointly and severally with any other person so liable) unless either he is a purchaser for value and, at the time of the purchase, he did not have actual notice of the contravention or he derived title to the shares (directly or indirectly) from a person who became a holder of them after the contravention and was not so liable.

(5) Subsection (1) above shall not prevent a company from allotting bonus shares in the company to its members or from paying up, with sums available for the purpose, any amounts for the time being unpaid on any of its shares (whether on account of the nominal value of the shares or by way of premium).

(6) References in this section to a holder, in relation to any shares in a company, include references to any person who has an unconditional right to be included in the company's register of members in respect of those shares or to have an instrument of transfer of the shares executed in his favour.

Prohibition on allotment of shares at a discount.
1978 c. 30.

21.—(1) Subject to subsection (4) below and without prejudice to any right to allot shares at a discount under section 57 of the 1948 Act which is saved by section 16 of the Interpretation Act 1978, the shares of a company shall not be allotted at a discount.

(2) Where shares are allotted in contravention of subsection (1) above, those shares shall be treated as paid up by the payment to the company of the amount of the nominal value of the shares

less the amount of the discount, but the allottee shall be liable to pay the company the latter amount and shall be liable to pay interest thereon at the appropriate rate.

(3) Subsection (4) of section 20 above shall apply for the purposes of this section as it applies for the purposes of that.

(4) Accordingly, section 57 of the 1948 Act (which authorises shares to be so issued in defined circumstances) shall cease to have effect, but the repeal of that section shall not affect an application for an order sanctioning the issue of shares at a discount which has been made to the court under that section and has not been disposed of before the appointed day, or an order made on or after that day in pursuance of any such application, and—

(a) any such application may be proceeded with and any such order, if not made before that day, may be made as if that section had not been repealed ; and

(b) shares may be allotted at a discount in accordance with any such order (whether made before, on or after that day) accordingly.

22.—(1) Subject to subsection (4) below, a public company Payment shall not allot a share except as paid up at least as to one- for allotted quarter of the nominal value of the share and the whole of shares. any premium on it.

(2) Where a public company allots a share in contravention of subsection (1) above, the share shall be treated as if one-quarter of its nominal value together with the whole of any premium had been received, but the allottee shall be liable to pay the company the minimum amount which should have been received in respect of the share under that subsection less the value of any consideration actually applied in payment up (to any extent) of the share and any premium on it, and interest at the appropriate rate on the amount payable under the foregoing provision.

(3) Subsection (2) above shall not apply in relation to the allotment of a bonus share in contravention of subsection (1) above unless the allottee knew or ought to have known the share was so allotted.

(4) Subsections (1) to (3) above shall not apply to shares allotted in pursuance of an employees' share scheme.

(5) Subsection (4) of section 20 above shall apply for the purposes of this section as it applies for the purposes of that.

23.—(1) A public company shall not allot shares as fully or Payment partly paid up (as to their nominal value or any premium payable of non-cash consideration.

on them) otherwise than in cash if the consideration for the allotment is or includes an undertaking which is to be or may be performed more than five years after the date of the allotment.

(2) Where a public company allots shares in contravention of subsection (1) above, the allottee of the shares shall be liable to pay the company an amount equal to their nominal value, together with the whole of any premium, or, if the case so requires, such proportion of that amount as is treated as paid up by the undertaking and shall be liable to pay interest at the appropriate rate on the amount payable under the foregoing provision.

(3) Where a contract for the allotment of shares does not contravene subsection (1) above, any variation of the contract which has the effect that the contract would have contravened that subsection if the terms of the contract as varied had been its orginal terms shall be void.

(4) Subsection (3) above shall apply to the variation by a public company of the terms of a contract entered into before the company was re-registered as a public company.

(5) Where a public company allots shares for a consideration which consists of or includes (in accordance with subsection (1) above) an undertaking which is to be performed within five years of the allotment but that undertaking is not performed within the period allowed by the contract for the allotment of the shares, the allottee of the shares in question shall be liable to pay the company at the end of that period an amount equal to the nominal value of the shares, together with the whole of any premium, or, if the case so requires, such proportion of that amount as is treated as paid up by the undertaking, together with interest at the appropriate rate on the amount payable under the foregoing provision.

(6) Subsection (4) of section 20 above shall apply in relation to a contravention of this section and to a failure to carry out a term of a contract as mentioned in subsection (5) above as it applies in relation to a contravention of that section.

(7) Any reference in this section to a contract for the allotment of shares includes a reference to an ancillary contract relating to payment in respect of those shares.

24.—(1) Subject to subsection (2) below, a public company shall not allot shares as fully or partly paid up (as to their nominal value or any premium payable on them) otherwise than in cash unless—

    (*a*) the consideration for the allotment has been valued in accordance with the following provisions of this section ;

(b) a report with respect to its value has been made to the company by a person appointed by the company in accordance with those provisions during the six months immediately preceding the allotment of the shares ; and

(c) a copy of the report has been sent to the proposed allottee of the shares.

(2) Subsection (1) above shall not apply to the allotment of shares by a company in connection with—

(a) an offer made by the company to all the holders of the shares in another company to acquire all or some of those shares or to all holders of a particular class of those shares to acquire all or some of the shares of that class ; or

(b) a proposed merger of that company with another company.

(3) In determining for the purposes of subsection (2) above whether an offer is so made by a company (in this subsection referred to as the " offeror company "), shares held by or by a nominee of the offeror company in the other company or held in the other company by or by a nominee of a company which is the offeror company's holding company or its subsidiary or a company which is a subsidiary of its holding company shall be disregarded ; and for those purposes there is a proposed merger of two companies when one of them proposes to acquire all the assets and liabilities of the other in exchange for the issue of shares in that one to shareholders of the other, with or without any cash payment to those shareholders.

(4) The valuation and report required by subsection (1) above shall be made by an independent person, that is to say, a person qualified at the time of the report to be appointed or continue to be auditor of the company, except that where it appears to him to be reasonable for the valuation of the consideration, or a valuation of part of the consideration, to be made, or to accept such a valuation made, by any person who—

(a) appears to him to have the requisite knowledge and experience to value the consideration or that part of the consideration ; and

(b) is not an officer or servant of the company or any other body corporate which is that company's subsidiary or holding company or a subsidiary of that company's holding company or a partner or employee of such an officer or servant ;

he may arrange for or accept such a valuation, together with a report which will enable him to make his own report under that subsection and provide a note in accordance with subsection (7) below.

(5) The independent person's report under subsection (1) above shall state—

   (a) the nominal value of the shares to be wholly or partly paid for by the consideration in question ;

   (b) the amount of any premium payable on those shares ;

   (c) the description of the consideration and, as respects so much of the consideration as he himself has valued, a description of that part of the consideration, the method used to value it and the date of the valuation ;

   (d) the extent to which the nominal value of the shares and any premium are to be treated as paid up—

      (i) by the consideration ;

      (ii) in cash.

(6) Where any consideration is valued under this section by a person other than the independent person, the latter's report under subsection (1) above shall state that fact and shall also—

   (a) state the former's name and what knowledge and experience he has to carry out the valuation ; and

   (b) describe so much of the consideration as was valued by that other person, the method used to value it, and state the date of valuation.

(7) The report of the independent person made under subsection (1) above shall contain or be accompanied by a note by him—

   (a) in the case of a valuation made by another person, that it appeared to the independent person reasonable to arrange for it to be so made or to accept a valuation so made ;

   (b) whoever made the valuation, that the method of valuation was reasonable in all the circumstances ;

   (c) that it appears to the independent person that there has been no material change in the value of the consideration in question since the valuation ; and

   (d) that on the basis of the valuation the value of the consideration, together with any cash by which the nominal value of the shares or any premium payable on them is to be paid up, is not less than so much of the aggregate of the nominal value and the whole of any such premium as is treated as paid up by the consideration and any such cash.

(8) Subsection (9) below applies where a public company allots any share in contravention of subsection (1) above and either—

   (a) the allottee has not received a report under this section ; or

   (b) there has been some other contravention of this section and the allottee knew or ought to have known that it amounted to a contravention.

(9) Where this subsection applies, the allottee shall be liable to pay the company an amount equal to the nominal value of the shares, together with the whole of any premium or, if the case so requires, such proportion of that amount as is treated as paid up by the consideration, and shall be liable to pay interest at the appropriate rate on the amount payable under the foregoing provision.

(10) Subsection (4) of section 20 above shall apply for the purposes of this section as it applies for the purposes of that.

(11) Where the consideration is accepted partly in payment up of the nominal value of the shares and any premium and partly for some other consideration given by the company, the foregoing provisions of this section shall apply as if references to the consideration accepted by the company included references to the proportion of that consideration which is properly attributable to the payment up of that value and any premium ; and

   (a) the independent person shall carry out or arrange for such other valuations as will enable him to determine that proportion ; and

   (b) his report under subsection (1) above shall state what valuations have been made by virtue of this subsection and also the reason for and method and date of any such valuation and any other matters which may be relevant to that determination.

(12) In this section—

   (a) any reference to a company, except where it is or is to be construed as a reference to a public company, includes a reference to any body corporate and any body to which letters patent have been issued under the Chartered Companies Act 1837 ; and   1837 c. 73.

   (b) any reference to an officer or servant shall not include a reference to an auditor.

25.—(1) Any person carrying out a valuation or making a report under section 24 above with respect to any consideration proposed to be accepted or given by a company shall be entitled to require from the officers of the company such information   Experts' reports: supplementary.

and explanation as he thinks necessary to enable him to carry out the valuation or to make the report and provide a note under that section.

(2) A company to which such a report is made as to the value of any consideration for which, or partly for which, it proposes to allot shares shall deliver a copy of the report to the registrar of companies for registration at the same time that it files the return of the allotments of those shares under section 52 of the 1948 Act, and subsection (3) of that section (default) shall apply to a default in complying with this subsection as it applies to a default in complying with that section.

(3) Any person who knowingly or recklessly makes a statement which—

> (*a*) is misleading, false or deceptive in a material particular, and
>
> (*b*) is a statement to which this subsection applies,

shall be guilty of an offence.

(4) Subsection (3) above applies to any statement made (whether orally or in writing) to any person carrying out a valuation or making a report under section 24 above, being a statement which conveys or purports to convey any information or explanation which that person requires, or is entitled to require, under subsection (1) above.

(5) A person guilty of an offence under this section shall be liable—

> (*a*) on conviction on indictment, to imprisonment for a term not exceeding two years or a fine, or both ;
>
> (*b*) on summary conviction, to imprisonment for a term not exceeding six months or a fine not exceeding the statutory maximum, or both.

Experts' reports on non-cash assets acquired from subscribers, etc. **26.**—(1) A public company, other than a company re-registered under section 8 above, shall not, unless the conditions mentioned in subsection (3) below have been complied with, enter into an agreement with a relevant person for the transfer by him during the initial period of one or more non-cash assets to the company or another for a consideration to be given by the company equal in value at the time of the agreement to at least one-tenth of the nominal value of the company's share capital issued at that time.

(2) In this section—

> (*a*) in relation to a company formed as a public company, " relevant person " means any subscriber to the memorandum of the company and " initial period " means

the period of two years beginning with the date on
which the company is issued with a certificate under
section 4 above that it is entitled to do business ;

(*b*) in relation to a company re-registered, or registered in
accordance with section 13 above, as a public company, " relevant person " means any person who was
a member of the company on the date of the re-
registration or registration and " initial period " means
the period of two years beginning with that date ;

and in this subsection the reference to a company re-registered
as a public company includes a reference to a private company
so re-registered which was a public company before it was a
private company.

(3) The conditions referred to in subsection (1) above are
that—

(*a*) the consideration to be received by the company (that
is to say, the asset to be transferred to the company
or the advantage to the company of its transfer to
another person) and any consideration other than
cash to be given by the company have been valued
under the following provisions of this section (without
prejudice to any requirement to value any consideration under section 24 above) ;

(*b*) a report with respect to the consideration to be so
received and given has been made to the company in
accordance with those provisions during the six months
immediately preceding the date of the agreement ;

(*c*) the terms of the agreement have been approved by an
ordinary resolution of the company ; and

(*d*) not later than the giving of the notice of the meeting at
which the resolution is proposed, copies of the resolution and report have been circulated to the members
of the company entitled to receive that notice and, if
the relevant person is not then such a member, to that
person.

(4) Subsection (1) above shall not apply to the following agreements for the transfer of an asset for a consideration to be given
by the company, that is to say—

(*a*) where it is part of the ordinary business of the company
to acquire or arrange for other persons to acquire assets of a particular description, an agreement entered
into by the company in the ordinary course of its
business for the transfer of an asset of that description
to it or such a person, as the case may be ; or

(*b*) an agreement entered into by the company under the
supervision of the court, or an officer authorised by

the court for the purpose, for the transfer of an asset to the company or to another.

(5) Section 24(4) and (6) above shall apply to a valuation and report of any consideration under this section as those subsections apply to a valuation of and report on any consideration under subsection (1) of that section.

(6) The report of the independent person under this section shall—

> (*a*) state the consideration to be received by the company, describing the asset in question, specifying the amount to be received in cash, and the consideration to be given by the company, specifying the amount to be given in cash ;
>
> (*b*) state the method and date of valuation ;
>
> (*c*) contain or be accompanied by a note as to the matters mentioned in section 24(7)(*a*) to (*c*) above ; and
>
> (*d*) contain or be accompanied by a note that on the basis of the valuation the value of the consideration to be received by the company is not less than the value of the consideration to be given by it.

(7) If a public company enters into an agreement with any relevant person in contravention of subsection (1) above and either he has not received a report under this section or there has been some other contravention of this section or section 24(4) or (6) above which he knew or ought to have known amounted to a contravention, then, subject to subsection (8) below—

> (*a*) the company shall be entitled to recover from the relevant person any consideration given by the company under the agreement or an amount equivalent to its value at the time of the agreement ; and
>
> (*b*) the agreement, so far as not carried out, shall be void.

(8) Where a company enters into an agreement in contravention of subsection (1) above and that agreement is or includes an agreement for the allotment of shares in that company, then, whether or not the agreement also contravenes section 24 above—

> (*a*) subsection (7) above shall not apply to the agreement in so far as it is an agreement for the allotment of shares ; and
>
> (*b*) subsection (4) of section 20 and subsection (9) of section 24 above shall apply in relation to the shares as if they had been allotted in contravention of section 24.

27.—(1) Any person carrying out a valuation or making a
report under section 26 above shall be entitled to require from
the officers of the company such information and explanation as
he thinks necessary to enable him to carry out the valuation or
make the report and provide the note required by that section ;
and subsections (3) and (5) of section 25 above shall apply in relation to any such valuation and report as they apply in relation to
a valuation and report under section 24(1) above with the substitution of a reference to this subsection for the reference in
section 25(4) to section 25(1).

(2) A company which has passed a resolution under section
26 above with respect to the transfer of an asset shall, within 15
days of the passing of the resolution, deliver to the registrar of
companies a copy of the resolution together with the report
required by that section and, if it fails to do so, the company
and every officer of the company who is in default shall be liable
on summary conviction to a fine not exceeding one-fifth of the
statutory maximum or, on conviction after continued contravention, a default fine not exceeding one-fiftieth of the statutory
maximum for every day until the resolution is so delivered.

(3) Any reference in section 26 above or this section to
consideration given for the transfer of an asset includes a reference to consideration given partly for its transfer ; but

(a) the value of any consideration partly so given shall be
taken to be the proportion of that consideration
properly attributable to its transfer ;

(b) the independent person shall carry out or arrange for
such valuations of anything else as will enable him to
determine that proportion ; and

(c) his report under that section shall state what valuation
has been made by virtue of this paragraph and also the
reason for and method and date of any such valuation
and any other matters which may be relevant to that
determination.

28.—(1) Where any person is liable to a company under
section 20, 23, 24 or 26 above in relation to payment in respect
of any shares in the company or is liable by virtue of any undertaking given to the company in, or in connection with, payment
for any such shares, the person so liable may make an application to the court under the subsection to be exempted in
whole or in part from that liability.

(2) Where the liability mentioned in subsection (1) above
arises under any of those sections in relation to payment in

respect of any shares the court may, on an application under that subsection, exempt the applicant from that liability only—

    (a) if and to the extent that it appears to the court just and equitable to do so having regard to the following, namely—

        (i) whether the applicant has paid, or is liable to pay, any amount in respect of any other liability arising in relation to those shares under any of those sections or of any liability arising by virtue of any undertaking given in or in connection with payment for those shares ;

        (ii) whether any person other than the applicant has paid or is likely to pay (whether in pursuance of an order of the court or otherwise) any such amount ; and

        (iii) whether the applicant or any other person has performed, in whole or in part, or is likely so to perform any such undertaking or has done or is likely to do any other thing in payment or part payment in respect of those shares ;

    (b) if and to the extent that it appears to the court just and equitable to do so in respect of any interest which he is liable to pay to the company under any of those sections.

(3) Where the liability mentioned in subsection (1) above arises by virtue of an undertaking given to the company in, or in connection with, payment for any shares in the company, the court may, on an application under that subsection, exempt the applicant from that liability only if and to the extent that it appears to the court just and equitable to do so having regard to the following, namely—

    (a) whether the applicant has paid or is liable to pay any amount in respect of any liability arising in relation to those shares under section 20, 23, 24 or 26 above ; and

    (b) whether any person other than the applicant has paid or is likely to pay (whether in pursuance of an order of the court or otherwise) any such amount.

(4) In determining in pursuance of an application under subsection (1) above whether it should exempt the applicant in whole or in part from any liability, the court shall have regard to the following overriding principles, namely—

    (a) that a company which has allotted shares should receive money or money's worth at least equal in value to the aggregate of the nominal value of those shares and the whole of any premium or, if the case so requires, so much of that aggregate as is treated as paid up ; and

(b) subject to paragraph (a) above, that where such a company would, if the court did not grant that exemption, have more than one remedy against a particular person, it should be for the company to decide which remedy it should remain entitled to pursue.

(5) Where a person brings any proceedings against another (" the contributor ") for a contribution in respect of any liability to a company arising under any of sections 20 to 24 and 26 above and it appears to the court that the contributor is liable to make such a contribution, the court, may, if and to the extent that it appears to the court, having regard to the respective culpability in respect of the liability to the company of the contributor and the person bringing the proceedings, that it is just and equitable to do so—

(a) exempt the contributor in whole or in part from his liability to make such a contribution ; or

(b) order the contributor to make a larger contribution than, but for this subsection, he would be liable to make.

(6) Where a person is liable to a company by virtue of section 26(7)(a) above, the court may, on an application under this subsection, exempt that person in whole or in part from that liability if and to the extent that it appears to the court just and equitable to do so having regard to any benefit accruing to the company by virtue of anything done by that person towards the carrying out of the agreement mentioned in that subsection.

29. Any shares taken by a subscriber to the memorandum of a public company in pursuance of an undertaking of his in the memorandum and any premium on the shares shall be paid up in cash.

Special provisions as to issue of shares to subscribers.

30.—(1) Where a company contravenes any of the provisions of sections 20 to 24, 26 and 29 above, the company and any officer of the company who is in default shall be liable on conviction on indictment to a fine and on summary conviction to a fine not exceeding the statutory maximum.

Contravention of ss. 20 to 29 above.

(2) Subject to section 28 above, an undertaking given by any person, in or in connection with payment for shares in a company, to do work or perform services or to do any other thing shall, if it is enforceable by the company apart from this Act,

be so enforceable notwithstanding that there has been a contravention in relation thereto of section 20, 23, or 24 above, and where such an undertaking is given in contravention of section 26 above in respect of the allotment of any shares it shall be so enforceable notwithstanding that contravention.

Application of ss. 20 to 30 in special cases.
31.—(1) Subject to subsection (2) below, sections 20, 22 to 25 and 28 to 30 above shall apply—

   (*a*) to a company which has passed and not revoked a special resolution to be re-registered under section 5 above ;

   (*b*) to a company whose directors have passed and not revoked a resolution to be re-registered under section 8 above ; and

   (*c*) to a joint stock company (within the meaning of section 383 of the 1948 Act) which has passed and not revoked a resolution that the company be a public company ;

as those sections apply to a public company.

(2) Sections 20 and 22 to 24 above shall not apply to the allotment of shares by a company, other than a public company registered as such on its original incorporation, where the contract for their allotment was entered into—

   (*a*) except in a case falling within paragraph (*b*) below, before the end of the transitional period ;

   (*b*) in the case of a company re-registered or registered as a public company in pursuance of a resolution of any description mentioned in subsection (1) above that is passed before the end of that period, before the date on which that resolution is passed.

Class rights

Variation of rights attached to special classes of shares.
32.—(1) This section shall have effect with respect to the variation of the rights attached to any class of shares in a company whose share capital is divided into shares of different classes.

(2) Where the rights are attached to a class of shares in the company otherwise than by the memorandum, and the articles of the company do not contain provision with respect to the variation of the rights, those rights may be varied if, but only if—

   (*a*) the holders of three-quarters in nominal value of the issued shares of that class consent in writing to the variation ; or

(*b*) an extraordinary resolution passed at a separate general
meeting of the holders of that class sanctions the
variation ;

and any requirement (howsoever imposed) in relation to the
variation of those rights is complied with to the extent that it is
not comprised in paragraphs (*a*) and (*b*) above.

(3) Where—
(*a*) the rights are attached to a class of shares in the company by the memorandum or otherwise ;
(*b*) the memorandum or articles contain provision for the
variation of those rights ; and
(*c*) the variation of those rights is connected with the giving,
variation, revocation or renewal of an authority for the
purposes of section 14 above or with a reduction of
the company's share capital under section 66 of the
1948 Act (reduction of share capital),

those rights shall not be varied unless—

(i) the condition mentioned in subsection (2)(*a*) or (*b*) above
is satisfied ; and
(ii) any requirement of the memorandum or articles in
relation to the variation of rights of that class is complied with to the extent that it is not comprised in the
condition in paragraph (i) above.

(4) Where the rights are attached to a class of shares in the
company by the memorandum or otherwise and—
(*a*) where they are so attached by the memorandum, the
articles contain provision with respect to their variation which had been included in the articles at the time
of the company's original incorporation ; or
(*b*) where they are so attached otherwise, the articles contain such provision (whenever first so included) ;

and in either case the variation is not connected as mentioned
in subsection (3)(*c*) above, those rights may only be varied in
accordance with that provision of the articles.

(5) Where the rights are attached to a class of shares in the
company by the memorandum and the memorandum and
articles do not contain provision with respect to the variation
of the rights, those rights may be varied if all the members of
the company agree to the variation.

(6) The provisions of section 133 (length of notice for calling
meetings), section 134 (general provisions as to meetings and
votes) and section 140 (circulation of members' resolutions) of
the 1948 Act and the provisions of the articles relating to general

meetings shall, so far as applicable, apply in relation to any meeting of shareholders required by this section or otherwise to take place in connection with the variation of the rights attached to a class of shares, and shall so apply with the necessary modifications and subject to the following provisions, namely—

> (a) the necessary quorum at any such meeting other than an adjourned meeting shall be two persons holding or representing by proxy at least one-third in nominal value of the issued shares of the class in question and at an adjourned meeting one person holding shares of the class in question or his proxy ;
>
> (b) any holder of shares of the class in question present in person or by proxy may demand a poll.

(7) Any alteration of a provision contained in the articles of a company for the variation of the rights attached to a class of shares or the insertion of any such provision into a company's articles shall itself be treated as a variation of those rights.

(8) Section 72 of the 1948 Act (right of holders of minority of shares of special class to object to variation of rights) shall apply in relation to subsection (2) above as it applies in relation to a provision of the memorandum or articles of a company to the like effect.

(9) In this section and, except where the context otherwise requires, in any provision for the variation of the rights attached to a class of shares contained in a company's memorandum or articles references to the variation of those rights shall include references to their abrogation.

(10) Nothing in subsections (2) to (5) above shall be construed as derogating from the powers of the court under section 11 above or 75 below or any of the following sections of the 1948 Act, that is to say, 5 (alteration of company's objects), 206 (power to compromise with creditors and members) and 208 (provisions for facilitating reconstruction and amalgamation of companies).

(11) This section shall not apply in relation to any variation made by a company, other than a public company registered as such on its original incorporation, before the date on which the earlier of the following events occurs, that is to say, the re-registration or registration of the company as a public company and the end of the transitional period.

33.—(1) Where a company allots shares with rights which PART II are not stated in its memorandum or articles or in any resolution Registration or agreement to which section 143 of the 1948 Act (registration of particulars and copies of certain resolutions and agreements) applies, the of special company shall, unless the shares are in all respects uniform rights. with shares previously allotted, deliver to the registrar of companies within one month from allotting the shares a statement in the prescribed form containing particulars of those rights.

(2) Shares allotted with such rights shall not be treated for the purposes of subsection (1) as different from shares previously allotted by reason only of the fact that the former do not carry the same rights to dividends as the latter during the twelve months immediately following the former's allotment.

(3) Where the rights attached to any shares of a company are varied otherwise than by an amendment of the company's memorandum or articles or by resolution or agreement to which the said section 143 applies, the company shall within one month from the date on which the variation is made deliver to the registrar of companies a statement in the prescribed form containing particulars of the variation.

(4) Where a company (otherwise than by any such amendment, resolution or agreement as is mentioned in subsection (3) above) assigns a name or other designation, or a new name or other designation, to any class of its shares it shall within one month from doing so deliver to the registrar of companies a notice in the prescribed form giving particulars thereof.

(5) Where a company has before the appointed day allotted shares with such rights as are mentioned in subsection (1) above, the company shall within three months from that day deliver to the registrar of companies a statement in the prescribed form containing particulars of those rights.

(6) If a company fails to comply with this section, the company and every officer of the company who is in default shall be liable on summary conviction to a fine not exceeding one-fifth of the statutory maximum or, on conviction after continued contravention, a default fine not exceeding one-fiftieth of the statutory maximum for each day until the statement or notice in question is delivered to the registrar of companies.

Maintenance of capital

34.—(1) Subject to subsection (4) below, where the net assets Obligation of a public company are half or less of the amount of the com- to convene pany's called-up share capital, the directors of the company shall, extraordinary not later than 28 days from the earliest day on which that fact general is known to a director of the company, duly convene an extra- meeting in ordinary general meeting of the company for a date not later serious loss of than 56 days from that day for the purpose of considering capital.

O3

whether any, and if so what, measures should be taken to deal with the situation.

(2) If there is a failure to convene an extraordinary general meeting of a public company as required by subsection (1) above, each of the directors of the company who—

    (*a*) knowingly and wilfully authorises or permits that failure ; or

    (*b*) after the expiry of the period during which that meeting should have been convened, knowingly and wilfully authorises or permits that failure to continue,

shall be liable on conviction on indictment to a fine and on summary conviction to a fine not exceeding the statutory maximum.

(3) Nothing in this section shall be taken as authorising the consideration, at a meeting convened in pursuance of subsection (1) above, of any matter which could not have been considered at that meeting apart from this section.

(4) This section shall not apply where the day mentioned in subsection (1) above is before the appointed day.

Acquisition of a company's shares by the company.

35.—(1) Except as provided by subsection (2) below, no company limited by shares or limited by guarantee and having a share capital shall acquire its own shares (whether by purchase, subscription or otherwise).

(2) A company limited by shares may acquire any of its own fully paid shares otherwise than for valuable consideration and any company may acquire its own shares in a reduction of capital duly made.

(3) If a company purports to act in contravention of this section, the company and every officer of the company who is in default shall be liable—

    (*a*) on conviction on indictment—

        (i) in the case of a company, to a fine ;

        (ii) in the case of an officer, to imprisonment for a term not exceeding two years or a fine, or both ;

    (*b*) on summary conviction—

        (i) in the case of a company, to a fine not exceeding the statutory maximum ;

        (ii) in the case of an officer, to imprisonment for a term not exceeding six months or a fine not exceeding the statutory maximum, or both ;

and the purported acquisition shall be void.

(4) For the purposes of this section and section 37(1)(*b*) below a company does not acquire shares—

(*a*) by redeeming preference shares in pursuance of its articles ;

(*b*) by purchasing shares in pursuance of an order of the court under section 11 above or 75 below or section 5 (alteration of objects) of the 1948 Act ; or

(*c*) by forfeiting shares, or accepting a surrender in lieu, in pursuance of the articles for failure to pay any sum payable in respect of those shares.

36.—(1) Subject to subsections (5) and (6) below, where shares are issued to a nominee of a company mentioned in section 35(1) above or are acquired by a nominee of such a company from a third person as partly paid up, then, for all purposes the shares shall be treated as held by the nominee on his own account and the company shall be regarded as having no beneficial interest in them.

Acquisition of shares in a company by company's nominee.

(2) Subject to subsection (6) below, if a person is called on to pay any amount for the purpose of paying-up, or paying any premium on, any shares in any such company which were issued to him, or which he otherwise acquired, as the nominee of the company and he fails to pay that amount within 21 days from being called on to do so, then—

(*a*) if the shares were issued to him as a subscriber to the memorandum by virtue of an undertaking of his in the memorandum, the other subscribers to the memorandum ; or

(*b*) if the shares were otherwise issued to or acquired by him, the directors of the company at the time of the issue or acquisition,

shall be jointly and severally liable with him to pay that amount.

(3) If in proceedings for the recovery of any such amount from any such subscriber or director under this section it appears to the court that he is or may be liable to pay that amount, but that he has acted honestly and reasonably and that, having regard to all the circumstances of the case, he ought fairly to be excused from liability, the court may relieve him, either wholly or partly, from his liability on such terms as the court thinks fit.

(4) Where any such subscriber or director has reason to apprehend that a claim will or might be made for the recovery of any such amount from him, he may apply to the court for relief and on the application the court shall have the same power to relieve him as it would have had in proceedings for the recovery of that amount.

(5) Subsection (1) above shall not apply to shares acquired otherwise than by subscription by a nominee of a public company in a case falling within section 37(1)(*d*) below.

(6) Subsections (1) and (2) above shall not apply—

(*a*) to shares acquired by a nominee of a company where the company has no beneficial interest in those shares (disregarding any right which the company itself may have as trustee, whether as personal representative or otherwise, to recover its expenses or be remunerated out of the trust property) ; or

(*b*) to shares issued in consequence of an application made before the appointed day or transferred in pursuance of an agreement to acquire them made before that day.

Treatment of shares held by or on behalf of a public company.

37.—(1) Subject to subsections (9) and (12) below, this section applies to a public company—

(*a*) where shares in the company are forfeited, or are surrendered to the company in lieu, in pursuance of the articles for failure to pay any sum payable in respect of those shares ;

(*b*) where shares in the company are acquired by the company and the company has a beneficial interest in those shares ;

(*c*) where the nominee of the company acquires shares in the company from a third person without financial assistance being given directly or indirectly by the company and the company has a beneficial interest in those shares ; or

(*d*) where any person acquires shares in the company with financial assistance given to him directly or indirectly by the company for the purpose of or in connection with the acquisition and the company has a beneficial interest in those shares.

In determining for the purposes of paragraphs (*b*) and (*c*) above whether a company has a beneficial interest in any shares, there shall be disregarded, in any case where the company is a trustee (whether as personal representative or otherwise), any right of the company (as trustee) to recover its expenses or be remunerated out of the trust property.

(2) Unless the shares or any interest of the company in them are previously disposed of, the company must not later than the end of the relevant period from their forfeiture or surrender or, in a case to which subsection (1)(*b*), (*c*) or (*d*) applies, their acquisition—

(*a*) cancel them and diminish the amount of the share capital by the nominal value of the shares ; and (*b*) where the effect of cancelling the shares will be that the nominal value of the company's allotted share capital is brought below the authorised minimum, apply for re-registration as a private company, stating the effect of the cancellation ;

and the directors may take such steps as are requisite to enable the company to carry out its obligations under this subsection without complying with sections 66 and 67 of the 1948 Act (special resolution for, and order confirming reduction of, share capital), including passing a resolution in accordance with subsection (4) below.

(3) The company and, in a case falling within subsection (1)(*c*) or (*d*) above, the company's nominee or, as the case may be, the other shareholder must not exercise any voting rights in respect of the shares and any purported exercise of those rights shall be void.

(4) The resolution authorised by subsection (2) above may alter the company's memorandum so that it no longer states that the company is to be a public company and may make such other alterations in the memorandum as are requisite in the circumstances.

(5) The application for re-registration required by subsection (2)(*b*) above must be in the prescribed form and signed by a director or secretary of the company and must be delivered to the registrar together with a printed copy of the memorandum and articles of the company as altered by the resolution.

(6) If a public company required to apply to be re-registered as a private company under this section fails to do so before the end of the relevant period, section 15 above shall apply to it as if it were a private company such as is mentioned in that section, but, except as aforesaid, the company shall continue to be treated for the purposes of the Companies Acts as a public company until it is so re-registered.

(7) If a company when required to do so by subsection (2) above fails to cancel any shares in accordance with paragraph (*a*) of that subsection or to make an application for re-registration in accordance with paragraph (*b*) of that subsection, the company and every officer of the company who is in default shall be liable on summary conviction to a fine not exceeding one-fifth of the statutory maximum or, on conviction after continued contravention, a default fine not exceeding one-fiftieth of the statutory maximum.

(8) Section 10(3) above shall apply in relation to the re-registration of a company under this section as it applies to the re-registration of a company under that section and subsections (4) and (5) of that section shall apply to the re-registration of a

company in pursuance of an application under this section accordingly, but with the substitution in each case of references to this section for references to that section.

(9) Where, after shares in a private company—

(a) are forfeited in pursuance of the articles of the company or are surrendered to the company in lieu of forfeiture or are otherwise acquired by the company;

(b) are acquired by the nominee of a company in the circumstances mentioned in subsection (1)(c) above; or

(c) are acquired by any person in the circumstances mentioned in subsection (1)(d) above;

the company is re-registered as a public company, the foregoing provisions of this section shall apply to the company as if it had been a public company at the time of the forfeiture, surrender or acquisition and as if for any reference to the relevant period from the forfeiture, surrender or acquisition there were substituted a reference to the relevant period from the re-registration of the company as a public company.

(10) Where a public company or a nominee of a public company acquires shares in the company or an interest in such shares and those shares are or that interest is shown in a balance sheet of the company as an asset, an amount equal to the value of the shares or, as the case may be, the value to the company of its interest in the shares shall be transferred out of profits available for dividend to a reserve fund and shall not be available for distribution.

(11) In this section ' relevant period ', in relation to any shares, means—

(a) in the case of shares forfeited or surrendered to the company in lieu of forfeiture or acquired as mentioned in subsection (1)(b) or (c) above, three years;

(b) in the case of shares acquired as mentioned in subsection (1)(d) above, one year.

(12) Notwithstanding anything in section 8(2) above, a reference in this section to a public company does not include a reference to an old public company; and references in this section to a private company shall be construed accordingly.

Charges taken by public companies on own shares.

38.—(1) A lien or other charge of a public company on its own shares (whether taken expressly or otherwise), except a charge permitted by subsection (2) below, is void.

(2) The following are permitted charges, that is to say—

(a) in the case of every description of company, a charge on its own shares (not being fully paid) for any amount payable in respect of the shares;

(b) in the case of a company whose ordinary business includes the lending of money or consists of the provision of credit or the bailment or (in Scotland) hiring of goods under a hire purchase agreement, or both, a charge of the company on its own shares (whether fully paid or not) which arises in connection with a transaction entered into by the company in the ordinary course of its business;

(c) in the case of a company (other than a company in relation to which paragraph (d) below applies) which is re-registered or is registered under section 13 above as a public company, a charge on its own shares which was in existence immediately before its application for re-registration or, as the case may be, registration;

(d) in the case of any company which after the end of the re-registration period remains or remained an old public company and did not before the end of that period apply to be re-registered under section 8 above as a public company, any charge on its own shares which was in existence immediately before the end of that period.

PART III

RESTRICTIONS ON DISTRIBUTION OF PROFITS AND ASSETS

39.—(1) A company shall not make a distribution (as defined by section 45 below) except out of profits available for the purpose.

(2) For the purposes of this Part of this Act, but subject to section 41(1) below, a company's profits available for distribution are its accumulated, realised profits, so far as not previously utilised by distribution or capitalisation, less its accumulated, realised losses, so far as not previously written off in a reduction or reorganisation of capital duly made.

(3) A company shall not apply an unrealised profit in paying up debentures or any amounts unpaid on any of its issued shares.

(4) For the purposes of subsections (2) and (3) above any provision (within the meaning of Schedule 8 to the 1948 Act), other than one in respect of any diminution in value of a fixed asset appearing on a revaluation of all the fixed assets of the company, shall be treated as a realised loss.

(5) If, on the revaluation of a fixed asset, an unrealised profit is shown to have been made and, on or after the revaluation, a sum is written off or retained for depreciation of that asset over a period, then, an amount equal to the amount by which that

sum exceeds the sum which would have been so written off or retained for depreciation of that asset over that period, if that profit had not been made, shall be treated for the purposes of subsections (2) and (3) above as a realised profit made over that period.

(6) Where there is no record of the original cost of an asset of a company (whether acquired before, on or after the appointed day) or any such record cannot be obtained without unreasonable expense or delay, then, for the purposes of determining whether the company has made a profit or loss in respect of that asset, the cost of the asset shall be taken to be the value ascribed to it in the earliest available record of its value made on or after its acquisition by the company.

(7) Where the directors of a company are, after making all reasonable enquiries, unable to determine whether a particular profit made before the appointed day is realised or unrealised they may treat the profit as realised, and where after making such enquiries they are unable to determine whether a particular loss so made is realised or unrealised, they may treat the loss as unrealised.

(8) In this section " fixed asset " includes any other asset which is not a current asset.

Restriction on distribution of assets.

40.—(1) Subject to section 41 below, a public company may only make a distribution at any time—

    (a) if at that time the amount of its net assets is not less than the aggregate of the company's called-up share capital and its undistributable reserves ; and

    (b) if, and to the extent that, the distribution does not reduce the amount of those assets to less than that aggregate.

(2) For the purposes of this section the undistributable reserves of a company are—

    (a) the share premium account ;

    (b) the capital redemption reserve fund ;

    (c) the amount by which the company's accumulated, unrealised profits, so far as not previously utilised by any capitalisation of a description to which this paragraph applies, exceed its accumulated, unrealised losses, so far as not previously written off in a reduction or reorganisation of capital duly made ; and

    (d) any other reserve which the company is prohibited from distributing by any enactment, other than one contained in this Part of this Act, or by its memorandum or articles.

(3) Subsection (2)(c) above applies to every description of capitalisation except a transfer of any profits of the company to its capital redemption reserve fund on or after the appointed day.

(4) Subsections (4) to (7) of section 39 above shall apply for the purposes of this section as they apply for the purposes of that section.

(5) A public company shall not include any uncalled share capital as an asset in any accounts relevant for the purposes of this section.

41.—(1) Subject to the following provisions of this section, an investment company may also make a distribution at any time out of its accumulated, realised revenue profits, so far as not previously utilised by distribution or capitalisation, less its accumulated revenue losses (whether realised or unrealised), so far as not previously written off in a reduction or reorganisation of capital duly made— Other distributions of investment companies.

> (a) if at that time the amount of its assets is at least equal to one and a half times the aggregate of its liabilities ; and
>
> (b) if, and to the extent that, the distribution does not reduce that amount to less than one and a half times that aggregate.

(2) In subsection (1) above " liabilities " includes any provision (within the meaning of Schedule 8 to the 1948 Act) except to the extent that that provision is taken into account for the purposes of that subsection in calculating the value of any asset of the company in question, and subsection (5) of section 40 above shall apply for those purposes as it applies for the purposes of that section.

(3) In this Part of this Act " investment company " means a public company which has given notice in the prescribed form (which has not been revoked) to the registrar of its intention to carry on business as an investment company (the " requisite notice ") and has since the date of that notice complied with the requirements set out in subsection (4) below.

(4) The requirements referred to in subsection (3) above—

> (a) that the business of the company consists of investing its funds mainly in securities, with the aim of spreading investment risk and giving members of the company the benefit of the results of the management of its funds ;
>
> (b) that none of the company's holdings in companies other than companies which are for the time being investment

companies represents more than 15 per cent. by value of the investing company's investment;

(c) that distribution of the company's capital profits is prohibited by its memorandum or articles of association;

(d) that the company has not retained, otherwise than in compliance with this Part of this Act, in respect of any accounting reference period more than 15 per cent. of the income it derives from securities.

(5) An investment company may not make a distribution by virtue of subsection (1) above unless its shares are listed on a recognised stock exchange and, during the period beginning with the first day of the accounting reference period immediately preceding the accounting reference period in which the proposed distribution is to be made or, where the distribution is proposed to be made during the company's first accounting reference period, the first day of that period and ending with the date of the distribution (whether or not any part of those periods falls before the appointed day), it has not—

(a) distributed any of its capital profits; or

(b) applied any unrealised profits or any capital profits (realised or unrealised) in paying up debentures or any amounts unpaid on any of its issued shares.

(6) An investment company may not make a distribution by virtue of subsection (1) above unless the company gave the requisite notice—

(a) before the beginning of the period referred to in subsection (5) above; or

(b) where that period began before the appointed day, as soon as may be reasonably practicable after the appointed day; or

(c) where the company was incorporated on or after the appointed day, as soon as may be reasonably practicable after the date of its incorporation.

(7) A notice by a company to the registrar under subsection (3) above may be revoked at any time by the company on giving notice in the prescribed form to the registrar that it no longer wishes to be an investment company within the meaning of this section, and, on giving such notice, the company shall cease to be such an investment company.

1970 c. 10.
1972 c. 41.
(8) Section 359(2) and (3) of the Income and Corporation Taxes Act 1970 and section 93(6)(b) of the Finance Act 1972 shall have effect for the purposes of subsection (4)(b) above as those provisions have effect for the purposes of subsection (1)(b) of the said section 359.

(9) The Secretary of State may by regulations made by statutory instrument extend the provisions of this section, with or without modifications, to companies whose principal business consists of investing their funds in securities, land or other assets with the aim of spreading investment risk and giving their members the benefit of the results of the management of the assets.

(10) Regulations made under subsection (9) above—

(a) may make different provision for different classes of companies and may contain such transitional and supplemental provisions as the Secretary of State considers necessary ; and

(b) shall not be made unless a draft of the regulations has been laid before Parliament and approved by a resolution of each House of Parliament.

(11) In determining capital and revenue profits and losses for the purposes of this section an asset which is not a fixed asset or a current asset shall be treated as a fixed asset.

42.—(1) Where an insurance company carries on long term business, any amount properly transferred to the profit and loss account of the company from a surplus in the fund or funds maintained by it in respect of that business and any deficit in that fund or those funds shall be respectively treated for the purposes of this Part of this Act as a realised profit and a realised loss, and, subject to the foregoing, any profit or loss arising in that business shall be left out of account for those purposes.

(2) In subsection (1) above—

(a) the reference to a surplus in any fund or funds of an insurance company is a reference to an excess of the assets representing that fund or those funds over the liabilities of the company attributable to its long term business, as shown by an actuarial investigation ; and

(b) the reference to a deficit in any such fund or funds is a reference to the excess of those liabilities over those assets, as so shown.

(3) In this section—

" actuarial investigation " means an investigation to which section 14 of the Insurance Companies Act 1974 (periodic actuarial investigation of company with long term business) applies or which is made in pursuance of a requirement imposed by section 34 of that Act (actuarial investigation required by the Secretary of State) ;

" insurance company " means an insurance company to which Part II of that Act applies ;

" long term business " has the same meaning as in that Act.

The relevant accounts.

43.—(1) Subject to the following provisions of this section, the question whether a distribution may be made by a company without contravening section 39, 40 or 41 above (the relevant section) and the amount of any distribution which may be so made shall be determined by reference to the relevant items as stated in the relevant accounts, and the relevant section shall be treated as contravened in the case of a distribution unless the requirements of this section about those accounts are complied with in the case of that distribution.

(2) The relevant accounts for any company in the case of any particular distribution are—

(a) except in a case falling within paragraph (b) or (c) below, the last annual accounts that is to say, the accounts prepared under section 1 of the 1976 Act which were laid or filed in respect of the last preceding accounting reference period in respect of which accounts so prepared were laid or filed ;

(b) if that distribution would be found to contravene the relevant section if reference were made only to the last annual accounts, such accounts (interim accounts) as are necessary to enable a proper judgment to be made as to the amounts of any of the relevant items ;

(c) if that distribution is proposed to be declared during the company's first accounting reference period or before any accounts are laid or filed in respect of that period, such accounts (initial accounts) as are necessary as aforesaid.

(3) The following requirements apply where the last annual accounts of a company constitute the only relevant accounts in the case of any distribution, that is to say—

(a) those accounts must have been properly prepared or have been so prepared subject only to matters which are not material for the purpose of determining, by reference to the relevant items as stated in those accounts, whether that distribution would be in contravention of the relevant section ;

(b) the auditors of the company must have made a report under section 14 of the 1967 Act (auditors' report) in respect of those accounts ;

(c) if, by virtue of anything referred to in that report, the report is not an unqualified report, the auditors must also have stated in writing (either at the time the report was made or subsequently) whether, in their opinion, that thing is material for the purpose of determining, by reference to the relevant items as stated in those accounts, whether that distribution would be in contravention of the relevant section ; and

(*d*) a copy of any such statement must have been laid before the company in general meeting or delivered to the registrar of companies according as those accounts have been laid or filed.

(4) A statement under subsection (3)(*c*) above suffices for the purposes of a particular distribution not only if it relates to a distribution which has been proposed but also if it relates to distributions of any description which includes that particular distribution, notwithstanding that at the time of the statement it has not been proposed.

(5) The following requirements apply to interim accounts prepared for a proposed distribution by a public company, that is to say—

(*a*) the accounts must have been properly prepared or have been so prepared subject only to matters which are not material for the purpose of determining, by reference to the relevant items as stated in those accounts, whether that distribution would be in contravention of the relevant section ;

(*b*) a copy of those accounts must have been delivered to the registrar of companies ; and

(*c*) if the accounts are in a language other than English and section 1(7)(*b*) of the 1976 Act (translations) does not apply, a translation into English of the accounts which has been certified in the prescribed manner to be a correct translation must also have been delivered to the registrar.

(6) The following requirements apply to initial accounts prepared for a proposed distribution by a public company, that is to say—

(*a*) those accounts must have been properly prepared or have been so prepared subject only to matters which are not material for the purpose of determining, by reference to the relevant items as stated in those accounts, whether that distribution would be in contravention of the relevant section ;

(*b*) the auditors of the company must have made a report stating whether in their opinion the accounts have been properly prepared ;

(c) if, by virtue of anything referred to in that report, the report is not an unqualified report, the auditors must also have stated in writing whether, in their opinion, that thing is material for the purpose of determining, by reference to the relevant items as stated in those accounts, whether that distribution would be in contravention of the relevant section ;

(d) a copy of those accounts, of the report made under paragraph (b) above and of any such statement must have been delivered to the registrar of companies ; and

(e) if the accounts are, or that report or statement is, in a language other than English and section 1(7)(b) of the 1976 Act (translations) does not apply, a translation into English of the accounts, the report or statement, as the case may be, which has been certified in the prescribed manner to be a correct translation, must also have been delivered to the registrar.

(7) For the purpose of determining by reference to particular accounts whether a proposed distribution may be made by a company, this section shall have effect, in any case where one or more distributions have already been made in pursuance of determinations made by reference to those same accounts, as if the amount of the proposed distribution was increased by the amount of the distributions so made.

(8) In this section—

" properly prepared " means, in relation to any accounts of a company, that the following conditions are satisfied in relation to those accounts, that is to say—

(a) in the case of annual accounts, that they have been properly prepared in accordance with the provisions of the Companies Acts ;

(b) in the case of interim or initial accounts, that they comply with the requirements of section 149 of the 1948 Act (contents and form of accounts) and any balance sheet comprised in those accounts has been signed in accordance with section 155 of that Act (directors to sign balance sheet of company) ; and

(c) in either case, without prejudice to the foregoing, that, except where the company is entitled to avail itself, and has availed itself, of any of the provisions of Part III of Schedule 8 to the 1948 Act (exemptions from requirements as to accounts)—

(i) so much of the accounts as consists of a balance sheet gives a true and fair view of the state of the company's affairs as at the balance sheet date ; and

(ii) so much of those accounts as consists of a profit and loss account gives a true and fair view of the company's profit or loss for the period in respect of which the accounts were prepared.

" relevant item " means any of the following, that is to say profits, losses, assets, liabilities, provisions (within the meaning of Schedule 8 to the 1948 Act), share capital and reserves ;

" reserves " includes undistributable reserves within the meaning of section 40 above ; "

" unqualified report ", in relation to any accounts of a company, means a report, without qualification, to the effect that in the opinion of the person making the report the accounts have been properly prepared ;

and, for the purposes of this section, accounts are laid or filed if subsection (6) or, as the case may be, subsection (7) (where applicable) of section 1 of the 1976 Act has been complied with in relation to those accounts.

(9) For the purpose of paragraph (b) of the definition of " properly prepared " in subsection (8) above, section 149 of, and Schedule 8 to, the 1948 Act shall be deemed to have effect in relation to interim and initial accounts with such modifications as are necessary by reason of the fact that the accounts are prepared otherwise than in respect of an accounting reference period.

44.—(1) Where a distribution, or part of one, made by a company to one of its members is made in contravention of the foregoing provisions of this Part of this Act and, at the time of the distribution, he knows or has reasonable grounds for believing that it is so made, he shall be liable to repay it or that part, as the case may be, to the company or (in the case of a distribution made otherwise than in cash) to pay the company a sum equal to the value of the distribution or part at that time. Consequences of making unlawful distribution.

(2) The provisions of this section are without prejudice to any obligation imposed apart from this section on a member of a company to repay a distribution unlawfully made to him.

45.—(1) Where immediately before the appointed day a company is authorised by any provision of its articles to apply its unrealised profits in paying up in full or in part unissued shares to be allotted to members of the company as fully or partly paid bonus shares, that provision shall, subject to any subsequent alteration of the articles, continue to be construed as authorising those profits to be so applied after the appointed day. Ancillary provisions.

(2) In this Part of this Act " distribution " means every description of distribution of a company's assets to members of the company, whether in cash or otherwise, except distributions made by way of—

    (a) an issue of shares as fully or partly paid bonus shares ;

    (b) the redemption of preference shares out of the proceeds of a fresh issue of shares made for the purposes of the redemption and the payment of any premium on their redemption out of the company's share premium account ;

    (c) the reduction of share capital by extinguishing or reducing the liability of any of the members on any of its shares in respect of share capital not paid up or by paying off paid up share capital ; and

    (d) a distribution of assets to members of the company on its winding up.

(3) In this Part of this Act " capitalisation ", in relation to any profits of a company, means any of the following operations, whether carried out before, on or after the appointed day, that is to say, applying the profits in wholly or partly paying up unissued shares in the company to be allotted to members of the company as fully or partly paid bonus shares or transferring the profits to the capital redemption reserve fund.

(4) In this Part of this Act references to profits and losses of any description are references respectively to profits and losses of that description made at any time, whether before, on or after the appointed day and, except in relation to an investment company, are references respectively to revenue and capital profits and revenue and capital losses.

(5) The provisions of this Part of this Act are without prejudice to any enactment or rule of law or any provision of a company's memorandum or articles restricting the sums out of which, or the cases in which, a distribution may be made.

(6) The provisions of this Part of this Act shall not apply to any distribution made by a company, other than a public company registered as such on its original incorporation, before the date on which the earlier of the following events occurs, that is to say, the re-registration or registration of the company as a public company and the end of the transitional period.

PART IV

DUTIES OF DIRECTORS AND CONFLICTS OF INTERESTS

Duty in relation to employees

Directors to have regard to interests of employees.

46.—(1) The matters to which the directors of a company are to have regard in the performance of their functions shall include the interests of the company's employees in general as well as the interests of its members.

(2) Accordingly, the duty imposed by subsection (1) above on the directors of a company is owed by them to the company (and the company alone) and is enforceable in the same way as any other fiduciary duty owed to a company by its directors.

Particular transactions giving rise to a conflict of interest

47.—(1) Subject to subsection (6) below, a company shall not incorporate in any agreement a term to which this section applies unless the term is first approved by a resolution of the company in general meeting and, in the case of a director of a holding company, by a resolution of that company in general meeting.

Contracts of employment of directors.

(2) This section applies to any term by which a director's employment with the company of which he is the director or, where he is the director of a holding company, his employment within the group is to continue, or may be continued, otherwise than at the instance of the company (whether under the original agreement or under a new agreement entered into in pursuance of the original agreement), for a period exceeding five years during which the employment—

(a) cannot be terminated by the company by notice ; or

(b) can be so terminated only in specified circumstances.

(3) In any case where—

(a) a person is or is to be employed with a company under an agreement which cannot be terminated by the company by notice or can be so terminated only in specified circumstances ; and

(b) more than six months before the expiration of the period for which he is or is to be so employed, the company enters into a further agreement (otherwise than in pursuance of a right conferred by or by virtue of the original agreement on the other party thereto) under which he is to be employed with the company or, where he is a director of a holding company, within the group,

subsection (2) above shall apply as if to the period for which he is to be employed under that further agreement there were added a further period equal to the unexpired period of the original agreement.

(4) A resolution of a company approving a term to which this section applies shall not be passed at a general meeting of the company unless a written memorandum setting out the proposed agreement incorporating the term is available for inspection, by members of the company both—

(a) at the registered office of thecompany for not less than the period of 15 days ending with the date of the meeting ; and

(b) at the meeting itself.

(5) A term incorporated in an agreement in contravention of this section shall to the extent that it contravenes this section be void ; and that agreement and in a case where subsection (3) above applies the original agreement shall be deemed to contain a term entitling the company to terminate it at any time by the giving of reasonable notice.

(6) No approval is required to be given under this section by any body corporate unless it is a company within the meaning of the 1948 Act or registered under Part VIII of that Act or if it is, for the purposes of section 150 of that Act, a wholly owned subsidiary of any body corporate, wherever incorporated.

(7) In this section—

    (a) " employment " includes employment under a contract for services ; and

    (b) " group ", in relation to a director of a holding company, means the group which consists of that company and its subsidiaries.

Substantial property transactions involving directors, etc.

48.—(1) A company shall not enter into an arrangement—

    (a) whereby a director of the company or its holding company or a person connected with such a director is to acquire one or more non-cash assets of the requisite value from the company ; or

    (b) whereby the company acquires one or more non-cash assets of the requisite value from such a director or a person so connected ;

unless the arrangement is first approved by a resolution of the company in general meeting and, if the director or connected person is a director of its holding company or a person connected with such a director, by a resolution in general meeting of the holding company.

(2) For the purposes of this section a non-cash asset is of the requisite value if at the time the arrangement in question is entered into its value is not less than £1,000 but, subject to that, exceeds £50,000 or ten per cent. of the amount of the company's relevant assets, and for those purposes the amount of a company's relevant assets is—

    (a) except in a case falling within paragraph (b) below, the value of its net assets determined by reference to the accounts prepared and laid under section 1 of the 1976 Act in respect of the last preceding accounting reference period in respect of which such accounts were so laid ;

    (b) where no accounts have been prepared and laid under that section before that time, the amount of its called-up share capital.

(3) An arrangement entered into by a company in contravention of this section and any transaction entered into in
pursuance of the arrangement (whether by the company or any
other person) shall be voidable at the instance of the company
unless—

    (a) restitution of any money or any other asset which is
the subject-matter of the arrangement or transaction
is no longer possible or the company or the person
nominated by it has been indemnified in pursuance of
subsection (4)(b) below by any other person for the loss
or damage suffered by it ; or

    (b) any rights acquired bona fide for value and without
actual notice of the contravention by any person who
is not a party to the arrangement or transaction would
be affected by its avoidance ; or

    (c) the arrangement is, within a reasonable period, affirmed
by the company in general meeting and, if it is an
arrangement for the transfer of an asset to or by a
director of its holding company or a person who is
connected with such a director, is so affirmed with
the approval of the holding company given by a resolution in general meeting.

(4) Without prejudice to any liability imposed otherwise than
by this subsection, but subject to subsection (5) below, where an
arrangement is entered into with a company by a director of
the company or its holding company or a person connected with
him in contravention of this section, that director and the person
so connected, and any other director of the company who
authorised the arrangement or any transaction entered into in
pursuance of such an arrangement, shall (whether or not it has
been avoided in pursuance of subsection (3) above) be liable—

    (a) to account to the company for any gain which he had
made directly or indirectly by the arrangement or transaction ; and

    (b) (jointly and severally with any other person liable under
this subsection) to indemnify the company for any loss
or damage resulting from the arrangement or transaction.

(5) Where an arrangement is entered into by a company and
a person connected with a director of the company or its holding
company in contravention of this section, that director shall not
be liable under subsection (4) above if he shows that he took all
reasonable steps to secure the company's compliance with this
section, and, in any case, a person so connected and any such
other director as is mentioned in that subsection shall not
be so liable if he shows that, at the time the arrangement was

entered into, he did not know the relevant circumstances constituting the contravention.

(6) No approval is required to be given under this section by any body corporate unless it is a company within the meaning of the 1948 Act or registered under Part VIII of that Act or, if it is, for the purposes of section 150 of that Act, a wholly-owned subsidiary of any body corporate, wherever incorporated.

Prohibition of loans, etc., to directors and connected persons.

49.—(1) Except as provided by section 50 below—

(*a*) a company shall not—

(i) make a loan to a director of the company or of its holding company ;

(ii) enter into any guarantee or provide any security in connection with a loan made by any person to such a director ; and

(*b*) a relevant company shall not—

(i) make a quasi-loan to a director of the company or of its holding company ;

(ii) make a loan or a quasi-loan to a person connected with such a director ;

(iii) enter into a guarantee or provide any security in connection with a loan or quasi-loan made by any other person for such a director or a person so connected.

(2) Except as provided by that section, a relevant company shall not—

(*a*) enter into a credit transaction as creditor for such a director or a person so connected ;

(*b*) enter into any guarantee or provide any security in connection with a credit transaction made by any other person for such a director or a person so connected.

(3) A company shall not arrange for the assignment to it or the assumption by it of any rights, obligations or liabilities under a transaction which, if it had been entered into by the company, would have contravened subsection (1) or (2) above ; but for the purposes of this Part of this Act the transaction shall be treated as having been entered into on the date of the arrangement.

(4) A company shall not take part in any arrangement whereby—

(*a*) another person enters into a transaction which, if it had been entered into by the company, would have contravened subsection (1), (2) or (3) above ; and

(*b*) that other person, in pursuance of the arrangement, has obtained or is to obtain any benefit from the company or its holding company or a subsidiary of the company or its holding company.

50.—(1) Where a director of a relevant company or of its holding company is associated with a subsidiary of either of those companies, subsection (1)(*b*)(ii) and (iii) of section 49 above shall not by reason only of that fact prohibit the relevant company from—

> (*a*) making a loan or quasi-loan to that subsidiary ; or
>
> (*b*) entering into a guarantee or providing any security in connection with a loan or quasi-loan made by any person to that subsidiary.

Exceptions from s. 49.

(2) Subsection (1)(*b*) of that section shall not prohibit a relevant company (" the creditor ") from making a quasi-loan to one of its directors or to a director of its holding company if—

> (*a*) the quasi-loan contains a term requiring the director or a person on his behalf to reimburse the creditor his expenditure within two months of its being incurred ; and
>
> (*b*) the aggregate of the amount of that quasi-loan and of the amount outstanding under each relevant quasi-loan does not exceed £1,000.

For the purposes of this subsection, a quasi-loan is relevant if it was made to the director by virtue of this subsection by the creditor or by its subsidiary or, where the director is a director of the creditor's holding company, any other subsidiary of that company ; and " amount outstanding " has the same meaning as in section 56(8) below.

(3) Subsection (2) of that section shall not prohibit a company's entering into—

> (*a*) any transaction for any person if the aggregate of the relevant amounts does not exceed £5,000 ; or
>
> (*b*) any transaction for any person if—
>
>> (i) the company enters into the transaction in the ordinary course of its business ; and
>>
>> (ii) the value of the transaction is not greater, and the terms on which it is entered into are no more favourable in respect of the person for whom the transaction is made than that or those which it is reasonable to expect the company to have offered to or in respect of a person of the same financial standing as that person but unconnected with the company.

(4) Subject to the following provisions of this section, each of the following is excepted from the prohibitions in section 49 above, that is to say—

(a) a loan or quasi-loan by a company to its holding company or a company's entering into a guarantee or providing any security in connection with a loan or quasi-loan made by any person to its holding company;

(b) a company's entering into a credit transaction as creditor for its holding company or entering into a guarantee or providing any security in connection with any credit transaction made by any other person for its holding company ;

(c) a company's doing anything to provide any of its directors with funds to meet expenditure incurred or to be incurred by him for the purposes of the company or for the purpose of enabling him properly to perform his duties as an officer of the company or a company's doing anything to enable any of its directors to avoid incurring such expenditure ;

(d) a loan or quasi-loan made by a money-lending company to any person or a money-lending company's entering into a guarantee in connection with any other loan or quasi-loan.

(5) The exception specified in subsection (4)(c) above operates only if one of the following conditions is satisfied, that is to say—

(a) the thing in question is done with prior approval of the company given at a general meeting at which the purpose of the expenditure incurred or to be incurred or which would otherwise be incurred by the director and the amount of the funds to be provided by the company and the extent of the company's liability under any transaction which is or is connected with that thing are disclosed ;

(b) that thing is done on condition that, if the approval of the company is not so given at or before the next following annual general meeting, the loan shall be repaid or any other liability arising under any such transaction discharged within six months from the conclusion of that meeting ;

but that exception does not authorise a relevant company to enter into any transaction if the aggregate of the relevant amounts exceeds £10,000.

(6) The exception specified in subsection (4)(*d*) above operates only if both the following conditions are satisfied, that is to say—

(*a*) the loan or quasi-loan in question is made by the company or it enters into the guarantee in the ordinary course of the company's business ; and

(*b*) the amount of the loan or quasi-loan or the amount guaranteed is not greater, and the terms of the loan, quasi-loan or guarantee are not more favourable, in the case of the person to whom the loan or quasi-loan is made or in respect of whom the guarantee is entered into, than that or those which it is reasonable to expect that company to have offered to or in respect of a person of the same financial standing as that person but unconnected with the company ;

but that exception does not authorise a relevant company which is not a recognised bank to enter into any transaction if the aggregate of the relevant amounts exceeds £50,000.

In determining for the purposes of this subsection the aggregate of the relevant amounts, a company which a director does not control shall be deemed not to be connected with him.

(7) The condition specified in subsection (6)(*b*) above shall not of itself prevent a company from making a loan to one of its directors or a director of its holding company—

(*a*) for the purpose of facilitating the purchase, for use as that director's only or main residence, of the whole or part of any dwelling-house together with any land to be occupied and enjoyed therewith ;

(*b*) for the purpose of improving a dwelling-house or part of a dwelling-house so used or any land occupied and enjoyed therewith ;

(*c*) in substitution for any loan made by any person and falling within paragraph (*a*) or (*b*) above,

if loans of that description are ordinarily made by the company to its employees and on terms no less favourable than those on which the transaction in question is made, and the aggregate of the relevant amounts does not exceed £50,000.

51.—(1) The following provisions of this section shall have effect for the purpose of defining the amounts relevant for determining whether any transaction or arrangement (a " proposed transaction or arrangement ") falls within the exception provided by subsection (3)(*a*) or (4)(*c*) or (*d*) of section 50 above, and for that purpose " the relevant exception " in subsection (2) below means that exception.

Relevant amounts.

(2) The relevant amounts in relation to a proposed transaction or arrangement are—

  (a) the value of the proposed transaction or arrangement ;

  (b) the value of any existing relevant arrangement falling within subsection (3) or (4) of section 49 and entered into by virtue of the relevant exception by the company or by a subsidiary of the company or, where the proposed transaction or arrangement is to be made for a director of its holding company or a person connected with such a director, by a subsidiary of its holding company ;

  (c) the amount outstanding under any other relevant transaction made by virtue of the relevant exception by the company or by a subsidiary of the company or, where the proposed transaction or arrangement is to be made for a director of its holding company or a person connected with such a director, by a subsidiary of its holding company.

(3) For the purposes of this section, a transaction is relevant if it was made—

  (a) for the director for whom the proposed transaction or arrangement is to be made or for any person connected with that director ; or

  (b) where the proposed transaction or arrangement is to be made for a person connected with a director of a company, for that director or any person connected with him ;

and an arrangement is relevant if it relates to a relevant transaction.

(4) For the purposes of this section, a transaction entered into by a company which is (at the time that transaction was entered into) a subsidiary of the company which is to make the proposed transaction or is a subsidiary of that company's holding company, is not a relevant transaction if at the time of the determination referred to in subsection (1) above it no longer is such a subsidiary.

(5) The amount outstanding under any transaction within subsection (2)(c) above is the value of the transaction less any amount by which that value has been reduced.

Civil remedies for breach of s. 49.
52.—(1) Where a company enters into a transaction or arrangement in contravention of section 49 the transaction or arrangement shall be voidable at the instance of the company unless—

  (a) restitution of any money or any other asset which is the subject matter of the arrangement or transaction is no longer possible, or the company has been indemnified in pursuance of subsection (2)(b) below for the loss or damage suffered by it ; or (*b*) any rights acquired bona fide for value and without actual notice of the contravention by any person other than the person for whom the transaction or arrangement was made would be affected by its avoidance.

(2) Without prejudice to any liability imposed otherwise than by this subsection but subject to subsection (3) below, where an arrangement or transaction is made by a company for a director of the company or its holding company or person connected with such a director in contravention of section 49, that director and the person so connected and any other director of the company who authorised the transaction or arrangement shall (whether or not it has been avoided in pursuance of subsection (1) above) be liable—

(*a*) to account to the company for any gain which he has made directly or indirectly by the arrangement or transaction ; and

(*b*) (jointly and severally with any other person liable under this subsection) to indemnify the company for any loss or damage resulting from the arrangement or transaction.

(3) Where an arrangement or transaction is entered into by a company and a person connected with a director of the company or its holding company in contravention of section 49, that director shall not be liable under subsection (2) above if he shows that he took all reasonable steps to secure the company's compliance with that section, and, in any case, a person so connected and any such other director as is mentioned in that subsection shall not be so liable if he shows that, at the time the arrangement or transaction was entered into, he did not know the relevant circumstances constituting the contravention.

53.—(1) A director of a relevant company who authorises or permits the company to enter into a transaction or arrangement knowing or having reasonable cause to believe that the company was thereby contravening section 49 above shall be guilty of an offence.

(2) A relevant company which enters into a transaction or arrangement for one of its directors or for a director of its holding company in contravention of section 49 above shall be guilty of an offence.

(3) A person who procures a relevant company to enter into a transaction or arrangement knowing or having reasonable cause to believe that the company was thereby contravening section 49 above shall be guilty of an offence.

(4) A relevant company shall not be guilty of an offence under subsection (2) of this section if it shows that, at the time the transaction was entered into, it did not know the relevant circumstances.

(5) A person guilty of an offence under this section shall be liable—

    (*a*) on conviction on indictment, to a term of imprisonment not exceeding two years or a fine, or both ; and

    (*b*) on summary conviction to a term of imprisonment not exceeding six months or a fine not exceeding the statutory maximum, or both.

Disclosure of transactions involving directors and others

Substantial contracts, etc., with directors and others to be disclosed in accounts.

54.—(1) Subject to subsections (5) and (6) and to section 58 below, group accounts prepared by a holding company in accordance with the requirements of section 1 of the 1976 Act in respect of a financial year (the " relevant period ") ending on or after the appointed day shall contain the particulars specified in section 55 below of—

    (*a*) any transaction or arrangement of a kind described in section 49 above entered into by the company or by a subsidiary of the company for a person who at any time during the relevant period was a director of the company or was connected with such a director ;

    (*b*) an agreement by the company or by a subsidiary of the company to enter into any such transaction or arrangement for a person who at any time during the relevant period was a director of the company or was connected with such a director ; and

    (*c*) any other transaction or arrangement with the company or with a subsidiary of the company in which a person who at any time during the relevant period was a director of the company had, directly or indirectly, a material interest.

(2) Subject as aforesaid, accounts so prepared by any company other than a holding company in respect of a financial year (the " relevant period ") ending on or after the appointed day shall contain the particulars specified in section 55 below of—

    (*a*) any transaction or arrangement of a kind described in section 49 above entered into by the company for a person who at any time during the relevant period was a director of the company or of its holding company or was connected with such a director ;

    (*b*) an agreement by the company to enter into any such transaction or arrangement for a person who at any time during the relevant period was a director of the company or its holding company or was connected with such a director ; and

(c) any other transaction or arrangement with the company in which a person who at any time during the relevant period was a director of the company or of its holding company had, directly or indirectly, a material interest.

(3) Where by virtue of section 150(2) of the 1948 Act a company does not produce group accounts in relation to any financial year, subsection (1) above shall have effect in relation to the company and that financial year as if the word " group " were omitted.

(4) For the purposes of subsections (1)(c) and (2)(c) above—

(a) a transaction or arrangement between a company and a director of the company or of its holding company or a person connected with such a director shall (if it would not otherwise be so treated) be treated as a transaction, arrangement or agreement in which that director is interested ; and

(b) an interest in such a transaction or arrangement is not material if in the opinion of the majority of the directors (other than that director) of the company which is preparing the accounts in question it is not material (but without prejudice to the question whether or not such an interest is material in any case where those directors have not considered the matter).

(5) Subsections (1) and (2) above do not apply, for the purposes of any accounts prepared by any company which is, or is the holding company of, a recognised bank, in relation to a transaction or arrangement of a kind described in section 49 above, or an agreement to enter into such a transaction or arrangement, to which that recognised bank is a party.

(6) Subsections (1) and (2) above do not apply in relation to the following transactions, arrangements and agreements—

(a) a transaction, arrangement or agreement between one company and another in which a director of the first or of its subsidiary or holding company is interested only by virtue of his being a director of the other ;

(b) a contract of service between a company and one of its directors or a director of its holding company ;

(c) a transaction, arrangement or agreement which was not entered into during the relevant period for the accounts in question or which did not subsist at any time during that period ;

(d) a transaction, arrangement or agreement which was made before the appointed day and which does not subsist on or after that day.

(7) Subsections (1) and (2) above apply whether or not—

(a) the transaction or arrangement was prohibited by section 49 above;

(b) the person for whom it was made was a director of the company or was connected with a director of the company at the time it was made;

(c) in the case of a transaction or arrangement made by a company which at any time during a relevant period is a subsidiary of another company, it was a subsidiary of that other company at the time the transaction or arrangement was made.

55. The particulars of a transaction, arrangement or agreement which are required by section 54 to be included in the annual accounts prepared by a company are particulars of the principal terms of the transaction, arrangement or agreement and (without prejudice to the generality of the foregoing provision)—

(a) a statement of the fact either that the transaction, arrangement or agreement was made or subsisted, as the case may be, during the financial year in respect of which those accounts are made up;

(b) the name of the person for whom it was made, and, where that person is or was connected with a director of the company or of its holding company, the name of that director;

(c) in any case where subsection (1)(c) or (2)(c) of section 54 applies, the name of the director with the material interest and the nature of that interest;

(d) in the case of a loan or an agreement for a loan or an arrangement within section 49(3) or (4) above relating to a loan—

(i) the amount of the liability of the person to whom the loan was or was agreed to be made, in respect of principal and interest, at the beginning and at the end of that period;

(ii) the maximum amount of that liability during that period;

(iii) the amount of any interest which, having fallen due, has not been paid; and

(iv) the amount of any provision (within the meaning of Schedule 8 to the 1948 Act) made in respect of any failure or anticipated failure by the borrower to repay the whole or part of the loan or to pay the whole or part of any interest thereon;

(e) in the case of a guarantee or security or an arrangement within section 49(3) above relating to a guarantee or security—

    (i) the amount for which the company (or its subsidiary) was liable under the guarantee or in respect of the security both at the beginning and at the end of the financial year in question ;

    (ii) the maximum amount for which the company (or its subsidiary) may become so liable ; and

    (iii) any amount paid and any liability incurred by the company (or its subsidiary) for the purpose of fulfilling the guarantee or discharging the security (including any loss incurred by reason of the enforcement of the guarantee or security) ; and

(f) in the case of any other transaction, arrangement or agreement, the value of the transaction or arrangement, or, as the case may be, the value of the transaction or arrangement to which the agreement relates.

56.—(1) This section applies in relation to the following classes of transactions, arrangements and agreements—

(a) loans, guarantees and securities relating to loans, arrangements of a kind described in subsection (3) or (4) of section 49 relating to loans and agreements to enter into any of the foregoing transactions and arrangements ;

(b) quasi-loans, guarantees and securities relating to quasi-loans, arrangements of a kind described in the said subsection (3) or (4) relating to quasi-loans and agreements to enter into any of the foregoing transactions and agreements ;

(c) credit transactions, guarantees and securities relating to credit transactions, arrangements of a kind described in the said subsection (3) or (4) relating to credit transactions and agreements to enter into any of the foregoing transactions and arrangements.

(2) The group accounts of a holding company and the accounts of any other company prepared in accordance with the requirements of section 1 of the 1976 Act in respect of a financial year (the " relevant period ") ending on or after the appointed day, shall contain a statement in relation to transactions, arrangements and agreements made by the company and, in the case of a holding company, by a subsidiary of the company for persons who at any time during the relevant period were officers of the company (but not directors) of the aggregate amounts outstanding at the end of the relevant period under

transactions, arrangements and agreements within paragraphs (*a*), (*b*) and (*c*) respectively of subsection (1) above, and the numbers of officers for whom the transactions, arrangements and agreements falling within each of those paragraphs were made.

(3) Subsection (2) above shall not apply in relation to any transaction, arrangement or agreement made by a recognised bank for any of its officers or for any of the officers of its holding company.

(4) The group accounts of a company which is, or is the holding company of, a recognised bank, and the accounts of any other company which is a recognised bank, prepared in accordance with the requirements of section 1 of the 1976 Act in respect of a financial year (the " relevant period ") ending on or after the appointed day, shall contain a statement in relation to transactions, arrangements and agreements made by the company preparing the accounts, if it is a recognised bank, and (in the case of a holding company) by any of its subsidiaries which is a recognised bank, for persons who at any time during the relevant period were directors of the company or were connected with a director of the company, of the aggregate amounts outstanding at the end of the relevant period under transactions, arrangements and agreements within paragraphs (*a*), (*b*) and (*c*) respectively of subsection (1) above, and the numbers of persons for whom the transactions, arrangements and agreements falling within each of those paragraphs were made.

(5) For the purposes of the application of subsection (4) above in relation to loans and quasi-loans made by a company to persons connected with a person who at any time is a director of the company or of its holding company, a company which a person does not control is not connected with him.

(6) Where by virtue of section 150(2) of the 1948 Act a company does not produce group accounts in relation to any financial year, subsections (2) and (4) above shall have effect in relation to the company and that financial year as if the word " group " were omitted.

(7) Subsections (2) and (4) above do not apply in relation to a transaction, arrangement or agreement which was made before the appointed day and which does not subsist on or after that day.

(8) For the purposes of this section, " amount outstanding " means the amount of the outstanding liabilities of the person for whom the transaction, arrangement or agreement in question was made, or, in the case of a guarantee or security, the amount guaranteed or secured.

PART IV
Further
provisions
relating to
recognised
banks.

57.—(1) Subject to section 58 below, a company which is, or is the holding company of, a recognised bank shall maintain a register containing a copy of every transaction, arrangement or agreement of which particulars would, but for subsection (5) of section 54 above, be required by subsection (1) or (2) of that section to be disclosed in the company's accounts or group accounts for the current financial year and for each of the preceding ten financial years or, if such a transaction or arrangement is not in writing, a written memorandum setting out its terms.

(2) Subject to section 58 below, a company which is, or is the holding company of, a recognised bank shall before its annual general meeting make available, at the registered office of the company for not less than the period of 15 days ending with the date of the meeting, for inspection by members of the company a statement containing the particulars of transactions, arrangements and agreements which the company would, but for subsection (5) of section 54 above, be required by subsection (1) or (2) of that section to disclose in its accounts or group accounts for the last complete financial year preceding that meeting, and such a statement shall also be made available for inspection by the members at the annual general meeting.

(3) It shall be the duty of the auditors of the company to examine any such statement before it is made available to the members of the company in accordance with subsection (2) above and to make a report to the members on that statement ; and the report shall be annexed to the statement before it is made so available.

(4) A report under subsection (3) above shall state whether in the opinion of the auditors the statement contains the particulars required by subsection (2) above and, where their opinion is that it does not, they shall include in the report, so far as they are reasonably able to do so, a statement giving the required particulars.

(5) Subsection (2) above shall not apply in relation to a recognised bank which is for the purposes of section 150 of the 1948 Act the wholly-owned subsidiary of a company incorporated in the United Kingdom.

(6) Where a company fails to comply with subsection (1) or (2) above, every person who at the time of that failure is a director of the company shall be guilty of an offence and liable on conviction on indictment to a fine and on summary conviction to a fine not exceeding the statutory maximum.

(7) It shall be a defence in proceedings against a person for an offence under subsection (6) above for him to prove that he took all reasonable steps for securing compliance with subsection (1) or (2) above, as the case may be.

(8) For the purposes of the application of this section in relation to loans and quasi-loans made by a company to persons connected with a person who at any time is a director of the company or of its holding company, a company which a person does not control is not connected with him.

Transactions, etc., excluded from ss. 54 and 57.

58.—(1) Subsections (1) and (2) of section 54 above do not apply, in relation to the accounts prepared by a company in respect of a relevant period, to transactions of the kind mentioned in subsection (2) below which are made by the company or by a subsidiary of the company for a person who at any time during the relevant period was a director of the company or of its holding company or was connected with such a director, if the aggregate of the values of each transaction, arrangement or agreement so made for that director or any person connected with him, less the amount (if any) by which the liabilities of the person for whom the transaction or arrangement was made has been reduced, did not at any time during the relevant period exceed £5,000.

(2) The said transactions are—

   (*a*) credit transactions ;
   (*b*) guarantees provided or securities entered into in connection with credit transactions ;
   (*c*) arrangements within subsection (3) or (4) of section 49 above relating to credit transactions ;
   (*d*) agreements to enter into credit transactions.

(3) Subsections (1)(*c*) and (2)(*c*) of section 54 above do not apply, in relation to the accounts prepared by a company in respect of a relevant period, to any transaction or arrangement made by the company or by a subsidiary of the company for a person who at any time during the relevant period was a director of the company or of its holding company or was connected with such a director, if the aggregate of the values of each transaction or arrangement within the said subsection (1)(*c*) or (2)(*c*), as the case may be, so made for that director or any person connected with him, less the amount (if any) by which the liabilities of the person for whom the transaction or arrangement was made has been reduced, did not at any time during the relevant period exceed £1,000 or, if more, did not exceed £5,000 or one per cent. of the value of the net assets of the company which is preparing the accounts in question as at the end of the relevant period for those accounts, whichever is the less.

(4) Section 57 above does not apply in relation to transactions or arrangements made or subsisting during a relevant period by a company or by a subsidiary of a company for a person who at any time during that period was a director of the company

or of its holding company or was connected with such a director,
or to any agreement made or subsisting during that period to
enter into such a transaction or arrangement, if the aggregate
of the values of each transaction or arrangement made for that
person and of each agreement for such a transaction or arrangement, less the amount (if any) by which the value of those transactions, arrangements and agreements has been reduced, did not
exceed £1,000 at any time during the relevant period.

59. If in the case of any group or other accounts of a com- Duty of
pany the requirements of sections 54 or 56 above are not com- auditors of
plied with, it shall be the duty of the auditors of the company company in
by whom the accounts are examined to include in their report ss. 54 or 56.
on the balance sheet of the company, so far as they are reasonably able to do so, a statement giving the required particulars.

60.—(1) Any reference in section 199 of the 1948 Act (disclo- Disclosure by
sure by a director of a company of his interest in a contract with directors of
the company) to a contract shall be construed as including a interests in
reference to any transaction or arrangement (whether or not contracts, etc.
constituting a contract) made or entered into on or after the
appointed day.

(2) For the purposes of the said section 199, a transaction or
arrangement of a kind described in section 49 above made by a
company for a director of the company or a person connected
with such a director shall, if it would not otherwise be so treated
(and whether or not prohibited by that section), be treated as a
transaction or arrangement in which that director is interested.

61.—(1) In subsection (1) of section 26 of the 1967 Act Extension
(disclosure of director's service contract with company) the of s. 26 of
following paragraph shall be inserted after paragraph (*b*)— 1967 Act.

" (*c*) in the case of each director who is employed under a
contract of service with a subsidiary of the company, a
copy of that contract or, if it is not in writing, a written
memorandum setting out the terms of that contract ; "

(2) The following subsection shall be inserted after subsection
(3) of that section—

" (3A) Subsection (1) above shall not apply in relation to
a director's contract of service with the company or with a

subsidiary of the company if that contract required him to work wholly or mainly outside the United Kingdom, but the company shall keep a memorandum—

    (*a*) in the case of a contract of service with the company, setting out the name of the director and the provisions of the contract relating to its duration ;

    (*b*) in the case of a contract of service with a subsidiary of the company, setting out the name of the director, the name and place of incorporation of the subsidiary and the provisions of the contract relating to its duration,

at the same place as copies and the memorandums are kept by the company in pursuance of subsection (1) above.".

(3) Each reference in subsections (4), (5) and (7) of that section to subsection (1) shall be construed as including a reference to subsection (3A) of that section ; the reference in subsection (7) of that section to a contract of service with a company shall be construed as including a contract of service with a subsidiary of a company ; and in subsection (8) of that section, paragraph (*a*) shall cease to have effect.

Supplemental

Power to
increase
financial
limits under
Part IV.

62.—(1) The Secretary of State may by order made by statutory instrument substitute for any sum of money specified in this Part of this Act a larger sum specified in the order.

(2) An order under this section shall be subject to annulment in pursuance of a resolution of either House of Parliament.

(3) An order under this section shall not have effect in relation to anything done or not done before the coming into force of the order and, accordingly, proceedings in respect of any liability (whether civil or criminal) incurred before that time may be continued or instituted as if the order had not been made.

Shadow directors.

63.—(1) Subject to subsections (2) and (5) below, a person in accordance with whose directions or instructions the directors of a company are accustomed to act (" a shadow director ") shall be treated for the purposes of this Part of this Act as a director of the company unless the directors are accustomed so to act by reason only that they do so on advice given by him in a professional capacity.

(2) A shadow director shall not be guilty of an offence under section 57(6) above by virtue only of subsection (1) above.

(3) Section 199 of the 1948 Act (disclosure by a director of a company of his interests in a contract, transaction or arrangement with the company) shall apply in relation to a shadow

director of a company as it applies in relation to a director of a company, except that the shadow director shall declare his interest, not at a meeting of the directors, but by a notice in writing to the directors which is either—

(a) a specific notice given before the date of the meeting at which, if he had been a director, the declaration would be required by subsection (2) of that section to be made; or

(b) a notice which under subsection (3) of that section (general notices) falls to be treated as a sufficient declaration of that interest or would fall to be so treated apart from the proviso;

and section 145 of that Act (minutes of proceedings of meetings) shall have effect as if the declaration had been made at the meeting in question and had accordingly formed part of the proceedings at that meeting.

(4) A shadow director of a company shall be treated for the purposes of section 26 of the 1967 Act (directors' service contracts, etc., to be open to inspection by a company's members) as a director of the company.

(5) A body corporate shall not be treated as the director of any of its subsidiary companies by reason only of subsection (1) above.

64.—(1) For the purposes of this Part of this Act, a person is connected with a director of a company if, but only if, he is— *Connected persons.*

(a) that director's spouse, child or step-child; or

(b) except where the context otherwise requires, a body corporate with which the director is associated; or

(c) a person acting in his capacity as the trustee (other than as trustee under an employees' share scheme or a pension scheme) of any trust the beneficiaries of which include the director, his spouse or any of his children or step-children or a body corporate with which he is associated or the terms of which confer a power on the trustees that may be exercised for the benefit of the director, his spouse or any of his children or step-children or any such body corporate; or

(d) a person acting in his capacity as partner of that director or of any person who, by virtue of paragraph (a), (b) or (c) above, is connected with that director,

unless that person is also a director of the company.

(2) In subsection (1) above a reference to the child or step-child of any person includes a reference to any illegitimate child of that person, but does not include a reference to any person who has attained the age of 18 years.

PART IV

(3) For the purposes of this Part of this Act—

(a) a director of a company is associated with a body corporate if, but only if, he and the persons connected with him, together, are interested in shares comprised in the equity share capital of that body corporate of a nominal value equal to at least one-fifth of that share capital or are entitled to exercise or control the exercise of more than one-fifth of the voting power at any general meeting of that body ; and

(b) a director of a company shall be deemed to control a body corporate if, but only if—

(i) he or a person connected with him is interested in any part of the equity share capital of that body or is entitled to exercise or control the exercise of any part of the voting power at any general meeting of that body ; and

(ii) that director, the persons connected with him and the other directors of that company, together, are interested in more than one-half of that share capital or are entitled to exercise or control the exercise of more than one-half of that voting power.

For the purposes of this subsection, a body corporate with which a director is associated and a trustee of a trust the beneficiary of which is or may be such a body corporate shall be regarded as if they were not connected with that director.

(4) The rules set out in section 28 of the 1967 Act (interest in shares) shall have effect for the purposes of subsection (3) above with the substitution of the words " more than one-half " for the words " one-third or more " in subsection (3)(b) of that section ; and in subsection (3) above—

(a) " equity share capital " has the same meaning as in section 154 of the 1948 Act ; and

(b) references to voting power the exercise of which is controlled by a director shall, without prejudice to the other provisions of that subsection, include references to voting power the exercise of which is controlled by a body corporate controlled by that director.

Interpretation
of Part IV.

65.—(1) In this Part of this Act—

" guarantee " includes indemnity, and cognate expressions shall be construed accordingly ;

" money-lending company " means a company the ordinary business of which includes the making of loans or quasi-loans or the giving of guarantees in connection with loans or quasi-loans ;

"recognised bank" means a company which is recognised
as a bank for the purposes of the Banking Act 1979 ;

"relevant company" means any company which—

(a) is not a private company ; or

(b) is a subsidiary of a company which either is itself not a private company or has another subsidiary which is not a private company ; or

(c) has a subsidiary which is not a private company ;

"services" means anything other than goods or land.

(2) For the purposes of this Part of this Act—

(a) a quasi-loan is a transaction under which one party ("the creditor") agrees to pay, or pays otherwise than in pursuance of an agreement, a sum for another ("the borrower"), or agrees to reimburse, or reimburses otherwise than in pursuance of an agreement, expenditure incurred by another party for another ("the borrower")—

(i) on terms that the borrower (or a person on his behalf) will reimburse the creditor ; or

(ii) in circumstances giving rise to a liability on the borrower to reimburse the creditor ;

(b) any reference to the person to whom a quasi-loan is made is a reference to the borrower ; and

(c) the liabilities of a borrower under a quasi-loan include the liabilities of any person who has agreed to reimburse the creditor on behalf of the borrower.

(3) For the purposes of this Part of this Act, a credit transaction is a transaction under which one party ("the creditor"),—

(a) supplies any goods or sells any land under a hire-purchase agreement or conditional sale agreement ;

(b) leases or hires any land or goods in return for periodical payments ;

(c) otherwise disposes of land or supplies goods or services on the understanding that payment (whether in a lump sum or instalments or by way of periodical payments or otherwise) is to be deferred.

(4) For the purposes of this Part of this Act, the value of a transaction or arrangement is—

(a) in the case of a loan, the principal of the loan ;

(b) in the case of a quasi-loan, the amount, or maximum amount, which the person to whom the quasi-loan is made is liable to reimburse the creditor ;

(c) in the case of a transaction or arrangement, other than a loan or quasi-loan or a transaction or arrangement within paragraph (d) or (e) below, the price which it is reasonable to expect could be obtained for the goods, land or services to which the transaction or arrangement relates if they had been supplied at the time the transaction or arrangement is entered into in the ordinary course of business and on the same terms (apart from price) as they have been supplied or are to be supplied under the transaction or arrangement in question ;

(d) in the case of a guarantee or security, the amount guaranteed or secured ;

(e) in the case of an arrangement to which subsection (3) or (4) of section 49 above applies, the value of the transaction to which the arrangement relates less any amount by which the liabilities under the arrangement or transaction of the person for whom the transaction was made have been reduced.

(5) For the purposes of subsection (4) above, the value of a transaction or arrangement which is not capable of being expressed as a specific sum of money (because the amount of any liability arising under the transaction is unascertainable, or for any other reason) shall, whether or not any liability under the transaction has been reduced, be deemed to exceed £50,000.

(6) For the purposes of this Part of this Act, a transaction or arrangement is made for a person if—

(a) in the case of a loan or quasi-loan, it is made to him ;

(b) in the case of a credit transaction, he is the person to whom goods or services are supplied, or land is sold or otherwise disposed of, under the transaction ;

(c) in the case of a guarantee or security, it is entered into or provided in connection with a loan or quasi-loan made to him or a credit transaction made for him ;

(d) in the case of an arrangement within subsection (3) or (4) of section 49 above, the transaction to which the arrangement relates was made for him ; and

(e) in the case of any other transaction or arrangement for the supply or transfer of goods, land or services (or any interest therein), he is the person to whom the goods, land or services (or the interest) are supplied or transferred.

(7) This Part of the Act, except sections 54, 56 and 57, does not apply to arrangements or transactions entered into before the appointed day but, for the purposes of determining whether an arrangement is one to which section 49 (3) or (4) applies, the transaction to which the arrangement relates shall, if it was entered into before the appointed day, be deemed to have been entered into after that day.

(8) For the purposes of this Part of this Act it is immaterial whether the law which (apart from this Act) governs any arrangement or transaction is the law of the United Kingdom, or of a part of the United Kingdom, or not.

66.—(1) Section 190 of the 1948 Act (prohibition on loans to directors) shall cease to have effect.

(2) Section 197 of the 1948 Act (particulars in accounts of loans to officers, etc.) and section 16(1)(*c*) of the 1967 Act (particulars in the directors' report of contracts in which a director has a significant and material interest) shall, except—

> (*a*) in relation to accounts and directors' reports prepared in respect of any financial year ending before the appointed day ; and
>
> (*b*) in relation to accounts and directors' reports prepared in respect of the first financial year ending after the appointed day but only in relation to loans and contracts entered into before the appointed day which do not subsist on or after that day,

cease to have effect.

67.—Section 435 of and Schedule 14 to the 1948 Act (which provide for the application of certain provisions of that Act to unregistered companies) shall have effect as if sections 54 to 58 and 62 to 66 above were provisions of that Act and were included among the provisions of that Act specified in that Schedule which relate to accounts and audit ; and the reference in the last entry in column 3 of that Schedule to provisions applied by virtue of the foregoing entries in that Schedule shall be construed accordingly.

PART IV

Consequential repeals and savings.

Application of ss. 54 to 58 and 62 to 66 to unregistered companies.

PART V

INSIDER DEALING

68.—(1) Subject to subsection (8) below, an individual who is, or at any time in the preceding six months has been, knowingly connected with a company shall not deal on a recognised stock exchange in securities of that company if he has information which—

> (*a*) he holds by virtue of being connected with the company ;

Prohibition on stock exchange deals by insiders, etc.

(*b*) it would be reasonable to expect a person so connected and in the position by virtue of which he is so connected not to disclose except for the proper performance of the functions attaching to that position; and

(*c*) he knows is unpublished price sensitive information in relation to those securities.

(2) Subject to subsections (8) and (10) below, an individual who is, or at any time in the preceding six months has been, knowingly connected with a company shall not deal on a recognised stock exchange in securities of any other company if he has information which—

(*a*) he holds by virtue of being connected with the first company;

(*b*) it would be reasonable to expect a person so connected and in the position by virtue of which he is so connected not to disclose except for the proper performance of the functions attaching to that position;

(*c*) he knows is unpublished price sensitive information in relation to those securities of that other company; and

(*d*) relates to any transaction (actual or contemplated) involving both the first company and that other company or involving one of them and securities of the other or to the fact that any such transaction is no longer contemplated.

(3) Subject to subsections (8) and (10) below, where—

(*a*) any individual has information which he knowingly obtained (directly or indirectly) from another individual who is connected with a particular company, or was at any time in the six months preceding the obtaining of the information so connected and who the former individual knows or has reasonable cause to believe held the information by virtue of being so connected; and

(*b*) the former individual knows or has reasonable cause to believe that, because of the latter's connection and position, it would be reasonable to expect him not to disclose the information except for the proper performance of the functions attaching to that position;

then, the former individual—

(i) shall not himself deal on a recognised stock exchange in securities of that company if he knows that the information is unpublished price sensitive information in relation to those securities; and

(ii) shall not himself deal on a recognised stock exchange in securities of any other company if he knows that the information is unpublished price sensitive information in relation to those securities and it relates to any transaction (actual or contemplated) involving the first company and the other company or involving one of them and securities of the other or to the fact that any such transaction is no longer contemplated.

(4) Subject to subsections (8) and (10) below, where an individual is contemplating, or has contemplated, making, whether with or without another person, a take-over offer for a company in a particular capacity, that individual shall not deal on a recognised stock exchange in securities of that company in another capacity if he knows that information that the offer is contemplated or is no longer contemplated is unpublished price sensitive information in relation to those securities.

(5) Subject to subsections (8) and (10) below, where an individual has knowingly obtained (directly or indirectly), from an individual to whom subsection (4) above applies, information that the offer referred to in subsection (4) is being contemplated or is no longer contemplated, the former individual shall not himself deal on a recognised stock exchange in securities of that company if he knows that the information is unpublished price sensitive information in relation to those securities.

(6) Subject to subsections (8) and (10) below, an individual who is for the time being prohibited by any provision of this section from dealing on a recognised stock exchange in any securities shall not counsel or procure any other person to deal in those securities, knowing or having reasonable cause to believe that that person would deal in them on a recognised stock exchange.

(7) Subject to subsections (8) and (10) below, an individual who is for the time being prohibited as aforesaid from dealing on a recognised stock exchange in any securities by reason of his having any information, shall not communicate that information to any other person if he knows or has reasonable cause to believe that that or some other person will make use of the information for the purpose of dealing, or of counselling or procuring any other person to deal, on a recognised stock exchange in those securities.

(8) The provisions of this section shall not prohibit an individual by reason of his having any information from—

    (a) doing any particular thing otherwise than with a view to the making of a profit or the avoidance of a loss (whether for himself or another person) by the use of that information;

    (b) entering into a transaction in the course of the exercise in good faith of his functions as liquidator, receiver or trustee in bankruptcy; or

    (c) doing any particular thing if the information—

        (i) was obtained by him in the course of a business of a jobber in which he was engaged or employed ; and

        (ii) was of a description which it would be reasonable to expect him to obtain in the ordinary course of that business ;

    and he does that thing in good faith in the course of that business.

(9) In subsection (8) above " jobber " means an individual, partnership or company dealing in securities on a recognised stock exchange and recognised by the Council of the Stock Exchange as carrying on the business of a jobber.

(10) An individual shall not, by reason only of having information relating to any particular transaction, be prohibited—

    (a) by subsection (2), (3)(ii), (4) or (5) above from dealing on a recognised stock exchange in any securities ; or

    (b) by subsection (6) or (7) above from doing any other thing in relation to securities which he is prohibited from dealing in by any of the provisions mentioned in paragraph (a) above ;

if he does that thing in order to facilitate the completion or carrying out of the transaction.

(11) Where a trustee or personal representative, or, where a trustee or personal representative is a body corporate, an individual acting on behalf of that trustee or personal representative, who, apart from subsection (8)(a) above, would be prohibited by this section from dealing, or counselling or procuring any other person to deal, in any securities deals in those securities, or counsels or procures any other person to deal in them, he shall be presumed to have acted as mentioned in that paragraph if he acted on the advice of a person who—

    (a) appeared to him to be an appropriate person from whom to seek such advice ; and

    (b) did not appear to him to be prohibited by this section from dealing in those securities.

Prohibition on abuse of information obtained in official capacity.

69.—(1) This section applies to any information which—

    (a) is held by a Crown servant or former Crown servant by virtue of his position or former position as a Crown servant or is knowingly obtained by an individual (directly or indirectly) from a Crown servant or former Crown servant who he knows or has reasonable cause to believe held the information by virtue of any such position ;

    (*b*) it would be reasonable to expect an individual in the position of the Crown servant or former position of the former Crown servant not to disclose except for the proper performance of the functions attaching to that position ; and

    (*c*) the individual holding it knows is unpublished price sensitive information in relation to securities of a particular company (relevant securities).

(2) This section applies to a Crown servant or former Crown servant holding information to which this section applies and to any individual who knowingly obtained any such information (directly or indirectly) from a Crown servant or former Crown servant who that individual knows or has reasonable cause to believe held the information by virtue of his position or former position as a Crown servant.

(3) An individual to whom this section applies—

    (*a*) shall not deal on a recognised stock exchange in any relevant securities ;

    (*b*) shall not counsel or procure any other person to deal in any such securities, knowing or having reasonable cause to believe that that other person would deal in them on a recognised stock exchange ; and

    (*c*) shall not communicate to any other person the information held or, as the case may be, obtained by him as mentioned in subsection (2) above if he knows or has reasonable cause to believe that that or some other person will make use of that information for the purpose of dealing, or of counselling or procuring any other person to deal, on a recognised stock exchange in any such securities.

(4) Section 68(8) and (11) above shall apply for the purposes of this section as they apply for the purposes of that section.

(5) An individual shall not, by reason only of having information relating to a particular transaction, be prohibited by any provision of this section from doing anything if he does that thing in order to facilitate the completion or carrying out of the transaction.

70.—(1) Subject to section 71 below, sections 68 and 69 above shall apply in relation to— Off-market deals.

    (*a*) dealing otherwise than on a recognised stock exchange in the advertised securities of any company—

        (i) through an off-market dealer who is making a market in those securities, in the knowledge that he is an off-market dealer, that he is making a market in those securities and that the securities are advertised securities ; or

           (ii) as an off-market dealer who is making a market in those securities or as an officer, employee or agent of such a dealer acting in the course of the dealer's business ;

    (*b*) counselling or procuring a person to deal in advertised securities in the knowledge or with reasonable cause to believe that he would deal in them as mentioned in paragraph (*a*) above ;

    (*c*) communicating any information in the knowledge or with reasonable cause to believe that it would be used for such dealing or for such counselling or procuring,

as they apply in relation to dealing in securities on a recognised stock exchange and to counselling or procuring or communicating any information in connection with such dealing.

(2) An individual who, by reason of his having information, is for the time being prohibited by any provision of section 68 or 69 above from dealing in any securities shall not—

    (*a*) counsel or procure any other person to deal in those securities in the knowledge or with reasonable cause to believe that that person would deal in the securities outside Great Britain on any stock exchange other than a recognised stock exchange ; or

    (*b*) communicate that information to any other person in the knowledge or with reasonable cause to believe that that or some other person will make use of the information for the purpose of dealing or of counselling or procuring any other person to deal in the securities outside Great Britain on any stock exchange other than a recognised stock exchange.

Sections 68(8) and (11) and 69(5) shall have effect as if any reference therein to either of those sections included a reference to this subsection.

(3) In this section—

    " advertised securities ", in relation to a particular occurrence, means listed securities or securities in respect of which, not more than six months before that occurrence, information indicating the prices at which persons have dealt or were willing to deal in those securities has been published for the purpose of facilitating deals in those securities ;

" off-market dealer " means a person who—

    (*a*) holds a licence under section 3 of the Prevention of Fraud (Investments) Act 1958 (principals' and representatives' licences for dealers in securities) ; or

    (*b*) is a member of a recognised stock exchange or recognised association of dealers in securities within the meaning of that Act ; or

(c) is an exempted dealer within the meaning of that Act.

(4) For the purposes of this section an off-market dealer shall be taken to deal in advertised securities if he deals in such securities or acts as an intermediary in connection with deals made by other persons in such securities ; and references in this section to such a dealer's officer, employee or agent dealing in such securities shall be construed accordingly.

(5) For those purposes an individual shall be taken to deal through an off-market dealer if the latter is a party to the transaction, is an agent for either party to the transaction or is acting as an intermediary in connection with the transaction.

71.—(1) Section 68 above shall not by virtue of section 70 above prohibit an individual from doing anything in relation to any debenture if—   International bonds.

(a) that thing is done by him in good faith in connection with an international bond issue—

(i) not later than three months after the issue date, or,

(ii) in a case where the international bond issue is not proceeded with, before the date on which it is decided not to proceed with the issue,

and he is an issue manager for that issue or is an officer, employee or agent of an issue manager for that issue ; or

(b) he is or was an issue manager for an international bond issue who is making a market in that debenture, or is an officer, employee or agent of such an issue manager, and that thing is done by him in good faith as a person making a market in that debenture or as an officer, employee or agent of such a person ;

and in either case the unpublished price sensitive information by virtue of which section 68 would but for this section apply in relation to that thing is information which he holds by virtue of his being (or having been) such an issue manager or an officer, employee or agent of such an issue manager, and is information which it would be reasonable to expect him to have obtained as an issue manager, or as such officer, employee or agent.

(2) In subsection (1) above—

" international bond issue " means an issue of debentures of a company (the " issuing company ")—

(a) all of which are offered or to be offered by an off-market dealer to persons (whether principals or agents) whose ordinary business includes the buying or selling of debentures, and (*b*) where the debentures are denominated in sterling, not less than 50 per cent. in nominal value of the debentures are so offered to persons who are neither citizens of the United Kingdom and Colonies nor companies incorporated or otherwise formed under the law of any part of the United Kingdom ;

" issue date " means the date on which the first of those debentures is issued by the issuing company ; and

" issue manager " means—

(*a*) an off-market dealer acting as an agent of the issuing company for the purposes of an international bond issue ; or

(*b*) where the issuing company issues or proposes to issue the debentures to an off-market dealer under an arrangement in pursuance of which he is to sell the debentures to other persons, that off-market dealer.

Contravention of ss. 68 and 69.

72.—(1) An individual who contravenes the provisions of section 68 or 69 above shall be liable—

(*a*) on conviction on indictment to imprisonment for a term not exceeding two years or a fine, or both ; and

(*b*) on summary conviction to imprisonment for a term not exceeding six months or a fine not exceeding the statutory maximum, or both.

(2) Proceedings for an offence under this section shall not be instituted in England and Wales except by the Secretary of State or by, or with the consent of, the Director of Public Prosecutions.

(3) No transaction shall be void or voidable by reason only that it was entered into in contravention of section 68 or 69 above.

Interpretation of Part V.

73.—(1) For the purposes of this Part of this Act, an individual is connected with a company if, but only if,—

(*a*) he is a director of that company or a related company ; or

(*b*) he occupies a position as an officer (other than director) or employee of that company or a related company or a position involving a professional or business relationship between himself (or his employer or a company of which he is a director) and the first company or a related company which in either case may reasonably be expected to give him access to information which, in relation to securities of either company, is unpublished price sensitive information, and which it would

be reasonable to expect a person in his position not to
disclose except for the proper performance of his
functions.

(2) Any reference in this Part of this Act to unpublished
price sensitive information in relation to any securities of any
company is a reference to information which—

   (*a*) relates to specific matters relating or of concern (directly
       or indirectly) to that company, that is to say, is not of
       a general nature relating or of concern to that com-
       pany ; and

   (*b*) is not generally known to those persons who are
       accustomed or would be likely to deal in those
       securities but which would if it were generally known
       to them be likely materially to affect the price of those
       securities.

(3) For the purposes of this Part of this Act a person deals in
securities if (whether as principal or agent) he buys or sells or
agrees to buy or sell any securities ; and references in this Part
of this Act to dealing in securities on a recognised stock
exchange shall include references to dealing in securities through
an investment exchange.

(4) For the purposes of this Part of this Act, an off-market
dealer shall be taken to make a market in any securities if in the
course of his business as an off-market dealer he holds himself
out both to prospective buyers and to prospective sellers of
those securities (other than particular buyers or sellers) as willing
to deal in them otherwise than on a recognised stock exchange.

(5) In this Part of this Act, except where the context otherwise requires—

   " company " means any company, whether a company
       within the meaning of the 1948 Act or not ;

   " Crown servant " means an individual who holds office
       under, or is employed by, the Crown ;

   " debenture " has the same meaning in relation to com-
       panies which were not incorporated under the 1948
       Act as it has in relation to companies which were so
       incorporated ;

   " investment exchange " means an organisation maintain-
       ing a system whereby an offer to deal in securities
       made by a subscriber to the organisation is commu-
       nicated, without his identity being revealed, to other
       subscribers to the organisation, and whereby any
       acceptance of that offer by any of those other sub-
       scribers is recorded and confirmed ;

   " listed securities ", in relation to a company, means any
       securities of the company listed on a recognised stock
       exchange ;

" related company ", in relation to any company, means any body corporate which is that company's subsidiary or holding company, or a subsidiary of that company's holding company ;

" securities " means listed securities and, in the case of a company within the meaning of the 1948 Act or a company registered under Part VIII of that Act or an unregistered company, the following securities (even if they are not listed securities), that is to say, any shares, any debentures or any right to subscribe for, call for or make delivery of a share or debenture ;

" share " has the same meaning in relation to companies which were not incorporated under the 1948 Act as it has in relation to companies which were so incorporated ;

" take-over offer for a company " means an offer made to all the holders (or all the holders other than the person making the offer and his nominees) of the shares in the company to acquire those shares or a specified proportion of them, or to all the holders (or all the holders other than the person making the offer and his nominees) of a particular class of those shares to acquire the shares of that class or a specified proportion of them ; and

" unregistered company " means any body corporate to which the provisions specified in Schedule 14 to the 1948 Act apply by virtue of section 435 of that Act (application of provisions to unregistered companies).

PART VI

MISCELLANEOUS AND GENERAL

Interests of employees and members

Power of company to provide for employees on cessation or transfer of business.

74.—(1) The powers of a company shall, if they would not otherwise do so, be deemed to include power to make the following provision for the benefit of persons employed or formerly employed by the company or any of its subsidiaries, that is to say, provision in connection with the cessation or the transfer to any person of the whole or part of the undertaking of that company or that subsidiary.

(2) The power conferred by subsection (1) above to make any such provision may be exercised notwithstanding that its exercise is not in the best interests of the company.

(3) The power which a company may exercise by virtue only of subsection (1) above shall only be exercised by the company if sanctioned—

    (a) in a case not falling within paragraph (b) or (c) below, by an ordinary resolution of the company ; or

(b) if so authorised by the memorandum or articles, a resolution of the directors ; or

(c) if the memorandum or articles require the exercise of the power to be sanctioned by a resolution of the company of some other description for which more than a simple majority of the members voting is necessary, with the sanction of a resolution of that description ;

and in any case after compliance with any other requirements of the memorandum or articles applicable to its exercise.

(4) On the winding up of a company (whether by the court or a voluntary winding up) the liquidator may, subject in the case of a winding up by the court to section 245(3) of the 1948 Act as applied by subsection (7) below, make any payment which the company has, before the commencement of the winding up, decided to make under subsection (3) above.

(5) The power which a company may exercise by virtue only of subsection (1) above may be exercised by the liquidator after the winding up of the company has commenced if, after the company's liabilities have been fully satisfied and provision has been made for the costs of the winding up, the exercise of that power has been sanctioned by such a resolution of the company as would be required of the company itself by subsection (3) above before that commencement if paragraph (b) of that sub-section were omitted and any other requirement applicable to its exercise by the company has been met.

(6) Any payment which may be made by a company under this section may—

(a) in the case of a payment made before the commence-ment of any winding up of the company, be made out of profits of the company which are available for dividend ; and

(b) in the case of any other payment, be made out of the assets of the company which are available to the members on its winding up.

(7) On a winding up by the court section 245(3) of the 1948 Act (powers of the liquidator to be subject to the control of the court on winding up by the court) shall apply to the exercise by the liquidator of his powers under subsection (4) or (5) above as it applies to the exercise of his powers under that section.

(8) Subsections (4) and (5) above shall have effect notwith-standing anything in any rule of law or in section 302 of the 1948 Act (property of company after satisfaction of liabilities to be distributed among members).

PART VI
Power of
court to
grant relief
against
company
where
members
unfairly
prejudiced.

75.—(1) Any member of a company may apply to the court by petition for an order under this section on the ground that the affairs of the company are being or have been conducted in a manner which is unfairly prejudicial to the interests of some part of the members (including at least himself) or that any actual or proposed act or omission of the company (including an act or omission on its behalf) is or would be so prejudicial.

(2) If in the case of any company—

> (*a*) the Secretary of State has received a report under section 168 of the 1948 Act (inspectors' reports) or exercised his powers under Part III of the 1967 Act or section 36(2) to (6) of the Insurance Companies Act 1974 (inspection of company's books and papers); and

1974 c. 49.

> (*b*) it appears to him that the affairs of the company are being or have been conducted in a manner which is unfairly prejudicial to the interests of some part of the members or that any actual or proposed act or omission of the company (including an act or omission on its behalf) is or would be so prejudicial,

he may himself (in addition to or instead of presenting a petition for the winding-up of the company under section 35(1) of the 1967 Act) apply to the court by petition for an order under this section.

(3) If the court is satisfied that a petition under this section is well founded it may make such order as it thinks fit for giving relief in respect of the matters complained of.

(4) Without prejudice to the generality of subsection (3) above, an order under this section may—

> (*a*) regulate the conduct of the company's affairs in the future ;
>
> (*b*) require the company to refrain from doing or continuing an act complained of by the petitioner or to do an act which the petitioner has complained it has omitted to do ;
>
> (*c*) authorise civil proceedings to be brought in the name and on behalf of the company by such person or persons and on such terms as the court may direct ;
>
> (*d*) provide for the purchase of the shares of any members of the company by other members or by the company itself and, in the case of a purchase by the company itself, the reduction of the company's capital accordingly.

(5) Where an order under this section requires the company not to make any, or any specified, alteration in the memorandum or articles then, notwithstanding anything in the Companies Acts, the company shall not have power without the leave of the court to make any such alteration in breach of that requirement.

(6) Any alteration in the memorandum or articles of the company made by virtue of an order under this section shall be of the same effect as if duly made by resolution of the company and the provisions of the Companies Acts shall apply to the memorandum or articles as so altered accordingly.

(7) An office copy of any order under this section altering, or giving leave to alter, a company's memorandum or articles shall, within 14 days from the making of the order or such longer period as the court may allow, be delivered by the company to the registrar of companies for registration; and if a company makes default in complying with this subsection, the company and every officer of the company who is in default shall be liable on summary conviction to a fine not exceeding one-fifth of the statutory maximum or, on conviction after continued contravention, a default fine not exceeding one-fiftieth of the statutory maximum for every day until that copy is delivered.

(8) In relation to a petition under this section, section 365 of the 1948 Act (general rules for winding up) shall apply as it applies in relation to a winding-up petition.

(9) This section shall apply to a person who is not a member of a company but to whom shares in the company have been transferred or transmitted by operation of law as it applies to a member of the company, and references to a member or members shall be construed accordingly.

(10) In subsections (2) to (9) above " company " means any body corporate which is liable to be wound up under the 1948 Act.

(11) Section 210 of the 1948 Act and section 35(2) of the 1967 Act (which are superseded by this section) shall cease to have effect except in relation to proceedings on a petition presented before the appointed day.

Miscellaneous

76.—(1) A person who is not a public company or (after the end of the transitional period) is an old public company shall be guilty of an offence if he carries on any trade, profession or business under a name which includes, as its last part, the words " public limited company " or their equivalent in Welsh.

Trading under misleading name, etc.

(2) A public company other than an old public company shall be guilty of an offence if, in circumstances in which the fact that it is a public company is likely to be material to any person, it uses a name which may reasonably be expected to give the impression that it is a private company.

(3) Where, within the re-registration period, an old public company applies to be re-registered under section 8 above as a public company, then—

(a) during the twelve months following the re-registration, any provision of section 108(1)(b) or (c) of the 1948 Act (publication of name of company), and

(b) during the three years following the re-registration, section 108(1)(a) of the 1948 Act or any provision of any other Act or subordinate instrument requiring or authorising the name of the company to be shown on any document or other object,

shall apply as if any reference in that provision to the name of the company were a reference to a name which either is its name or was its name before re-registration.

(4) A person guilty of an offence under subsection (1) or (2) above and, if that person is a company, any officer of the company who is in default shall be liable on summary conviction to a fine not exceeding one-fifth of the statutory maximum or, on conviction after continued contravention, a default fine not exceeding one-fiftieth of the statutory maximum.

77. Where the name of a public company includes, as its last part, the equivalent in Welsh of the words " public limited company ", the fact that the company is a public limited company shall be stated in English and in legible characters—

(a) in all prospectuses, bill heads, letter paper, notices and other official publications of the company ; and

(b) in a notice conspicuously displayed in every place in which the company's business is carried on ;

and if this section is contravened the company and every officer of the company who is in default shall be liable on summary conviction to a fine not exceeding one-fifth of the statutory maximum or, on conviction after continued contravention, a default fine not exceeding one-fiftieth of the statutory maximum.

78.—(1) It is hereby declared that a company which by any of the provisions of the Companies Acts is either required or entitled to include in its name, as its last part, any of the words specified in subsection (3) below, may, instead of those words, include in its name, as its last part, the abbreviation so specified as an alternative in relation to those words ; and any reference in those Acts to the name of a company or to the inclusion of any of those words in the name of a company shall include a reference to the name of the company including (in place of any of the words so specified) the appropriate alternative, or to the inclusion of the appropriate alternative, as the case may be.

(2) Any provision of those Acts requiring a company not to include any of those words in its name also requires it not to include in its name the abbreviation specified in subsection (3) below as an alternative in relation to these words.

(3) For the purposes of subsections (1) and (2) above—

(a) the alternative of " limited " is the abbreviation " ltd." ;

(b) the alternative of " public limited company " is the abbreviation " p.l.c." ;

(c) the alternative of " cyfyngedig " is the abbreviation " cyf." ; and

(d) the alternative of " cwmni cyfyngedig cyhoeddus " is the abbreviation " c.c.c.".

(4) For the purposes of this Act—

(a) the equivalent in Welsh of " limited " is " cyfyngedig " ;

(b) the equivalent in Welsh of " company " is " cwmni " ;

(c) the equivalent in Welsh of " and company " is " a'r cwmni " ; and

(d) the alternative of " cwmni cyfygedig cyhoeddus " is " cwmni cyfyngedig cyhoeddus ".

79.—(1) It shall be the duty of the directors of a public company, to take all reasonable steps to secure that the secretary or each joint secretary of the company is a person who appears to them to have the requisite knowledge and experience to discharge the functions of secretary of the company and who—

(a) on the appointed day held the office of secretary or assistant or deputy secretary of the company ; or

(b) for at least three years of the five years immediately preceding his appointment as secretary held the office of secretary of a company other than a private company ; or

(c) is a member of any of the bodies specified in subsection (2) below ; or

(d) is a barrister, advocate or solicitor called or admitted in any part of the United Kingdom ; or

(e) is a person who, by virtue of his holding or having held any other position or his being a member of any other body, appears to the directors to be capable of discharging those functions.

(2) The bodies referred to in subsection (1)(c) above are : —

(a) the Institute of Chartered Accountants in England and Wales ;

(b) the Institute of Chartered Accountants of Scotland ;

(c) the Association of Certified Accountants ;

(d) the Institute of Chartered Accountants in Ireland ;

(e) the Institute of Chartered Secretaries and Administrators ;

(f) the Institute of Cost and Management Accountants ;

(g) the Chartered Institute of Public Finance and Accountancy.

Increase of
penalties and
change of
mode of trial.

80.—(1) Each of the enactments listed in column 1 of Schedule 2 to this Act (being enactments under which penalties may be imposed in respect of the offences or other contraventions which are broadly described or the nature of which is indicated in column 2 of that Schedule) shall have effect as if the penalty which may be imposed under that enactment for the offence in question on a conviction thereof described in column 4 of that Schedule were the penalty shown in column 4 instead of that shown in column 3 of that Schedule as the penalty which may be imposed on any conviction described in column 3 ; and any offence punishable under any such enactment shall be triable on indictment where the penalty shown in column 4 may be imposed on any conviction described in column 3 ; and summarily where the penalty so shown may be imposed on summary conviction.

(2) Where any enactment to which this subsection applies imposes liability to a default fine on conviction of an offence after continued contravention, then, if after a person has been summarily convicted of that offence the original contravention is continued, he shall be liable on a second or subsequent summary conviction of that offence to the fine specified in the enactment for each day on which the contravention is continued instead of to the penalty which may be imposed on the first conviction of that offence.

(3) Subsection (2) above applies to any enactment contained in the Companies Acts and to any enactment applying all the provisions of the 1948 Act or section 440 of that Act or construed as one with that Act.

(4) Section 49(1) of the 1967 Act (offences punishable with a fine to be triable only summarily) shall cease to have effect.

(5) The provisions of this section shall not apply to any offence committed before the appointed day ; and nothing in this section shall authorise the bringing of any proceedings in respect of any such offence on or after that day if, but for this section, the latest time for bringing those proceedings would have been before that day.

Amendment
of s. 454 of
the 1948 Act.

81. In section 454(1) of the 1948 Act (power of Secretary of State to alter or add to requirements of 1948 and 1967 Acts relating to balance sheets and accounts) after the words " group accounts " there shall be inserted the words " and a report of the directors of a company which is required by section 157 of this Act to be attached to the company's balance sheet ".

82. The following provisions of the 1948 Act shall cease to have effect, that is to say—

(a) section 48 (prohibition of allotment in certain cases unless statement in lieu of prospectus is delivered to the registrar);

(b) section 65 (power of company to pay interest out of capital in certain cases);

(c) section 109 (restrictions on commencement of business);

(d) section 130 (statutory meeting and statutory report);

(e) section 181 (restrictions on advertisement of directors); and

(f) section 438 and Schedule 15 (penalty for false statements).

83.—(1) The repeal by the Banking Act 1979 (the "1979 Act") of the Protection of Depositors Act 1963 (the "1963 Act") shall not affect, and shall be deemed never to have affected, the application of the following provisions of the 1963 Act to unexempted companies on and after the commencement of Parts I and III of the 1979 Act, that is to say—

(a) sections 6 to 17; and

(b) so far as relevant to the operation of those sections, sections 5 and 22 to 27.

(2) In this section "unexempted company" means any company within the meaning of the 1963 Act which is not excepted by section 2(1) of the 1979 Act from the prohibition on the acceptance of deposits imposed by section 1 of the latter Act.

General

84.—(1) The following provisions of the 1948 Act, that is to say—

(a) section 428 (enforcement of duty of company to make returns to the registrar);

(b) section 440(2) (officer in default);

(c) section 444 (application of fines); and

(d) section 449 (power to enforce orders);

shall apply in relation to this Act as they apply in relation to that Act.

(2) Subsections (2) to (5) of section 49 of the 1967 Act (summary proceedings) shall apply in relation to this Act as they apply in relation to that Act.

(3) The criminal proceedings mentioned in section 111(1)(a) of the 1967 Act (proceedings for the purpose of which the Secretary of State may disclose information obtained by him

under his powers of inspecting a company's books and papers) shall include criminal proceedings pursuant to or arising out of this Act.

85.—(1) In this Act "the authorised minimum" means £50,000, or such other sum as the Secretary of State may by order made by statutory instrument specify instead.

(2) An order under this section which increases the authorised minimum may—

(a) require any public company having an allotted share capital of which the nominal value is less than the amount specified in the order as the authorised minimum to increase that value to not less than that amount or make an application to be re-registered as a private company ;

(b) make, in connection with any such requirement, provision for any of the matters for which provision is made by any enactment in the Companies Acts relating to a company's registration, re-registration or change of name, to payment for any share comprised in a company's capital and to offers of shares in or debentures of a company to the public, including provision as to the consequences (whether in criminal law or otherwise) of a failure to comply with any requirement of the order ; and

(c) contain such supplemental and transitional provision as the Secretary of State thinks appropriate, make different provision for different cases and, in particular, provide for any provision of the order to come into operation on different days for different purposes.

(3) An order shall not be made under this section unless a draft of the order has been laid before Parliament and approved by a resolution of each House of Parliament.

Application
of this Act
to certain
companies
not formed
under the
1948 Act.
86. Part VII of the 1948 Act (which relates to companies formed or registered under the former Acts there mentioned) and section 394 of that Act (which relates to companies not formed under that Act but registered under it) shall apply for the purpose of the application of the provisions of this Act to such companies as aforesaid as they apply for the purpose of the application thereto of the provisions of that Act.

87.—(1) In this Act, except so far as the context otherwise requires,—

" accounting reference period " has the meaning given by section 2 of the 1976 Act;

" appointed day " has the meaning given by section 90(3) below ;

" the appropriate rate ", in relation to interest, means five per cent. per annum or such other rate as may be specified by order made by the Secretary of State by statutory instrument ;

" balance sheet date " in relation to a balance sheet, means the date as at which the balance sheet was prepared ;

" called-up share capital ", in relation to a company, means so much of its share capital as equals the aggregate amount of the calls made on its shares, whether or not those calls have been paid, together with any share capital paid up without being called and any share capital to be paid on a specified future date under the articles, the terms of allotment of the relevant shares or any other arrangements for payment of those shares, and " uncalled share capital " shall be construed accordingly ;

" the Companies Acts " means the enactments which under section 90(2) below may be cited together as the Companies Acts 1948 to 1980 ;

" conditional sale agreement " has the same meaning as in the Consumer Credit Act 1974 ; 1974 c. 39.

" employees' share scheme " means a scheme for encouraging or facilitating the holding of shares or debentures in a company by or for the benefit of—

(a) the bona fide employees or former employees of the company, the company's subsidiary or holding company or a subsidiary of the company's holding company ; or

(b) the wives, husbands, widows, widowers or children or step-children under the age of 18 of such employees or former employees ;

" hire-purchase agreement " has the same meaning as in the Consumer Credit Act 1974 ; 1974 c. 39.

" the 1948 Act ", " the 1967 Act " and " the 1976 Act " mean the Companies Act 1948, the Companies Act 1967 and the Companies Act 1976 respectively ; 1948 c. 38. 1967 c. 81. 1976 c. 69.

" non-cash asset " means any property or interest in property other than cash (including foreign currency) ;

" old public company " has the meaning given by section 8 above ;

" re-registration period " has the meaning given by section 9 above ;

" the statutory maximum " means—

> (a) in England and Wales the prescribed sum within the meaning of section 28 of the Criminal Law Act 1977 (that is to say, £1,000 or another sum fixed by order under section 61 of that Act to take account of changes in the value of money) ; and

> (b) in Scotland, the prescribed sum within the meaning of section 289B of the Criminal Procedure (Scotland) Act 1975 (that is to say £1,000 or another sum fixed by order under section 289D of that Act for that purpose) ;

" transitional period " means the period of 18 months from the appointed day in question.

(2) In relation to an allotment of shares in a company, the shares shall be taken for the purposes of the Companies Acts to be allotted when a person acquires the unconditional right to be included in the company's register of members in respect of those shares.

(3) For the purposes of the Companies Acts—

> (a) a share in a company shall be taken to have been paid up (as to its nominal value or any premium on it) in cash or allotted for cash if the consideration for the allotment or the payment up is cash received by the company or is a cheque received by the company in good faith which the directors have no reason for suspecting will not be paid or is the release of a liability of the company for a liquidated sum or is an undertaking to pay cash to the company at a future date ; and

> (b) in relation to the allotment or payment up of any shares in a company, references in the Companies Acts, except in section 17 of this Act, to consideration other than cash and to the payment up of shares and premiums on shares otherwise than in cash include references to the payment of, or an undertaking to pay, cash to any person other than the company ;

and for the purposes of determining whether a share is or is to be allotted for cash or paid up in cash, " cash " includes foreign currency.

(4) For the purposes of this Act—

> (a) any reference to a balance sheet or to a profit and loss account shall include a reference to any notes thereon or document annexed thereto giving information which is required by the Companies Acts and is thereby allowed to be so given ;

(b) any reference to the transfer or acquisition of a non-cash asset includes a reference to the creation or extinction of an estate or interest in, or a right over, any property and also a reference to the discharge of any person's liability, other than a liability for a liquidated sum ; and

(c) the net assets of a company are the aggregate of its assets less the aggregate of its liabilities ;

and in paragraph (c) above " liabilities " includes any provision (within the meaning of Schedule 8 to the 1948 Act) except to the extent that that provision is taken into account in calculating the value of any asset of the company.

(5) Expressions used in this Act and the 1948 Act have the same meanings in this Act as they have in that Act.

(6) Any order under this section specifying a rate of interest shall be subject to annulment in pursuance of a resolution of either House of Parliament.

(7) Any reference in the Companies Acts 1948 to 1976 or any Act passed before this Act to an enactment which is amended by this Act shall, unless the context otherwise requires, be construed as referring to that enactment as so amended.

88.—(1) The enactments specified in Schedule 3 to this Act shall have effect subject to the amendments there specified, being minor amendments and amendments consequential on the provisions of this Act.

(2) The enactments mentioned in Schedule 4 to this Act (which include certain spent and unnecessary enactments) are hereby repealed to the extent specified in the third column of that Schedule, but the repeal of any enactment specified in the note to that Schedule shall have effect subject to the saving specified in relation to that enactment in that note.

(3) Nothing in the repeals made by this Act shall affect the operation of any enactment repealed in relation to any offence—

(a) for which a penalty was before the date on which the repeal comes into operation provided by reference to the days during which the offence had continued ; and

(b) which is continuing at, but begun before, that date.

(4) Paragraphs 36 and 37 of Schedule 3 to this Act (which amend Table A and Table C in Schedule 1 to the 1948 Act) and any repeal specified in Schedule 4 to this Act of anything contained in the said Table A shall not affect any company registered before the paragraph or, as the case may be, repeal comes into operation.

PART VI
Corresponding
provision for
Northern
Ireland.
1974 c. 28.

89. An Order in Council under paragraph 1(1)(*b*) of Schedule 1 to the Northern Ireland Act 1974 (legislation for Northern Ireland in the interim period) which contains a statement that it is made only for purposes corresponding to the purposes of this Act—

> (*a*) shall not be subject to paragraph 1(4) and (5) of that Schedule (affirmative resolution of both Houses of Parliament) ; but
>
> (*b*) shall be subject to annulment by a resolution of either House.

Short title,
citation,
commence-
ment and
extent.
1948 c. 38.
1967 c. 81.
1972 c. 67.
1972 c. 68.
1976 c. 47.
1976 c. 60.
1976 c. 69.

90.—(1) This Act may be cited as the Companies Act 1980.

(2) The Companies Act 1948, Parts I and III of the Companies Act 1967, the Companies (Floating Charges and Receivers) (Scotland) Act 1972, section 9 of the European Communities Act 1972, sections 1 to 4 of the Stock Exchange (Completion of Bargains) Act 1976, section 9 of the Insolvency Act 1976, the Companies Act 1976 and this Act may be cited together as the Companies Acts 1948 to 1980.

(3) This Act shall come into operation on such day as may be appointed by the Secretary of State by order made by statutory instrument, and different days may be so appointed for different purposes of this Act or for different purposes of the same provision ; and references in this Act to the appointed day shall be construed accordingly.

(4) Nothing in this Act, except so much of it as applies in relation to companies incorporated outside Great Britain, shall apply to or in relation to companies registered or incorporated in Northern Ireland ; and nothing in this Act shall affect the law in force in Northern Ireland at the passing of this Act, without prejudice to section 89 above.

SCHEDULES

SCHEDULE 1

FORMS OF MEMORANDUM OF ASSOCIATION OF A PUBLIC COMPANY

PART I

A PUBLIC COMPANY LIMITED BY SHARES

1. The name of the company is " The Western Steam Packet, public limited company ".

2. The company is to be a public company.

3. The registered office of the company will be situated in England and Wales.

4. The objects for which the company is established are, " the conveyance of passengers and goods in ships or boats between such places as the company may from time to time determine, and the doing of all such things as are incidental or conducive to the attainment of the above object ".

5. The liability of the members is limited.

6. The share capital of the company is £50,000 divided into 50,000 shares of £1 each.

We, the several persons whose names and addresses are subscribed are desirous of being formed into a company, in pursuance of this memorandum of association, and we respectively agree to take the number of shares in the capital of the company set opposite our respective names.

Names, Addresses and Descriptions of Subscribers			Number of shares taken by each Subscriber
" 1. Thomas Jones	in the county of	merchant	1
2. Andrew Smith	in the county of	merchant	1
Total shares taken ...	...	... ...	2 "

Dated   day of   19 .

Witness to the above signatures

A.B., 13, Hute Street, Clerkenwell, London.

PART II

A PUBLIC COMPANY LIMITED BY GUARANTEE AND HAVING A SHARE CAPITAL

1. The name of the company is " Gwestai Glyndwr, cwmni cyfyngedig cyhoeddus ".

2. The company is to be a public company.

3. The registered office of the company will be situated in Wales.

4. The objects for which the company is established are " the facilitating of travelling in Wales by providing hotels and conveyances by sea and by land for the accommodation of travellers and the doing of all such other things as are incidental or conducive to the attainment of the above object ".

5. The liability of the members is limited.

6. Every member of the company undertakes to contribute to the assets of the company in the event of its being wound up while he is a member, or within one year afterwards, for payment of the debts and liabilities of the company, contracted before he ceases to be a member, and the costs, charges and expenses of winding up the same and for the adjustment of the rights of the contributories amongst themselves, such amount as may be required, not exceeding £20.

7. The share capital of the company shall consist of £50,000 divided into 50,000 shares of £1 each.

We, the several persons whose names and addresses are subscribed, are desirous of being formed into a company, in pursuance of this memorandum of association, and we respectively agree to take the number of shares in the capital of the company set opposite our respective names.

Names, Addresses and Descriptions of Subscribers	Number of shares taken by each Subscriber
" 1. Thomas Jones in the county of merchant	1
2. Andrew Smith in the county of merchant	1
Total shares taken	2 "

Dated   **day** of   19 .

Witness to the above signatures

A.B. 13, Bute Street, Cardiff.

Section 80.

SCHEDULE 2

INCREASE OF PENALTIES AND CHANGE OF MODE OF TRIAL

Enactment (1)	General description of offence or contravention (2)	Old mode of trial and penalty (3)	New mode of trial and penalty (4)
		COMPANIES ACT 1948 (c. 38)	
5(8)	Failing to give the registrar a copy of the memorandum as altered or to give him notice of an application to the court in relation to such an alteration and other documents in connection with the application.	On summary conviction a fine not exceeding £10 for every day during which the default continues.	On summary conviction a fine not exceeding one-fifth of the statutory maximum or, on conviction after continued contravention, a default fine not exceeding one-fiftieth of the statutory maximum.
7(3)	Failing to give notice to the registrar of an increase in members of an unlimited company or a company limited by guarantee.	On summary conviction a fine not exceeding £5 for every day during which the default continues.	On summary conviction a fine not exceeding one-fifth of the statutory maximum or, on conviction after continued contravention, a default fine not exceeding one-fiftieth of the statutory maximum.
18(2)	Company failing to comply with a direction of the Secretary of State to change its name.	On summary conviction a fine not exceeding £5 for every day during which the default continues.	On summary conviction a fine not exceeding one-fifth of the statutory maximum or, on conviction after continued contravention, a default fine not exceeding one-fiftieth of the statutory maximum.
19(7)	Body failing to change its name so as not to include "Chamber of Commerce", on revocation of a licence to include those words.	On summary conviction a fine not exceeding £50 for every day during which the default continues.	(a) On conviction on indictment a fine. (b) On summary conviction a fine not exceeding the statutory maximum or, on conviction after continued contravention, a default fine not exceeding one-tenth of the statutory maximum.

Q 2

Enactment (1)	General description of offence or contravention (2)	Old mode of trial and penalty (3)	New mode of trial and penalty (4)
	COMPANIES ACT 1948 (*contd*)		
24(2) ...	Company, on being required to do so by a member, failing to send a copy of the memorandum or articles or of any Act of Parliament which alters them.	On summary conviction a fine not exceeding £25.	On summary conviction a fine not exceeding one-fifth of the statutory maximum.
25(2) ...	Issuing copies of a memorandum not in accordance with an alteration.	On summary conviction a fine not exceeding £25 for each copy issued.	On summary conviction a fine not exceeding one-fifth of the statutory maximum for each occasion on which copies are issued after the date of the alteration.
38(3) ...	Issuing a form of application for shares in, or debentures of, a company without a prospectus complying with the requirements of section 38.	On summary conviction a fine not exceeding £500.	(*a*) On conviction on indictment a fine. (*b*) On summary conviction a fine not exceeding the statutory maximum.
40(2) ...	Issuing a prospectus including an expert's statement where the expert has not given his written consent to the issue of the prospectus, or where a statement that the expert has given his consent does not appear in the prospectus.	On summary conviction a fine not exceeding £500.	(*a*) On conviction on indictment a fine. (*b*) On summary conviction a fine not exceeding the statutory maximum.
41(4) ...	Issuing a prospectus without due delivery of copy to registrar.	On summary conviction a fine not exceeding £5 for every day until due delivery of the copy to the registrar.	On summary conviction a fine not exceeding one-fifth of the statutory maximum or, on conviction after continued contravention, a default fine not exceeding one-fiftieth of the statutory maximum.

Enactment (1)	General description of offence or contravention (2)	Old mode of trial and penalty (3)	New mode of trial and penalty (4)
	COMPANIES ACT 1948 (*contd*)		
44(1)... ...	Authorising the issue of a prospectus including an untrue statement.	(*a*) On conviction on indictment a term of imprisonment not exceeding 2 years or a fine, or both. (*b*) On summary conviction a term of imprisonment not exceeding 3 months or a fine not exceeding the statutory maximum, or both.	(*a*) On conviction on indictment a term of imprisonment not exceeding 2 years or a fine, or both. (*b*) On summary conviction a term of imprisonment not exceeding 6 months or a fine not exceeding the statutory maximum, or both.
50(3)... ...	Allotting shares or debentures before the third day after the issue of a prospectus.	On summary conviction a fine not exceeding £500.	(*a*) On conviction on indictment a fine. (*b*) On summary conviction a fine not exceeding the statutory maximum.
51(3)... ...	Failing to keep money in a separate bank account where received in pursuance of a prospectus stating that stock exchange listing is to be applied for.	On summary conviction a fine not exceeding £500.	(*a*) On conviction on indictment a fine. (*b*) On summary conviction a fine not exceeding the statutory maximum.
52(3)... ...	Failing to deliver return of allotments, or contracts or particulars of allotment, to the registrar.	On summary conviction a fine not exceeding £50 for every day during which the default continues.	(*a*) On conviction on indictment a fine. (*b*) On summary conviction a fine not exceeding the statutory maximum or, on conviction after continued contravention, a default fine not exceeding one-tenth of the statutory maximum.

COMPANIES ACT 1948 (*contd*)

Enactment (1)	General description of offence or contravention (2)	Old mode of trial and penalty (3)	New mode of trial and penalty (4)
53(5)	Failing to deliver to the registrar the prescribed form disclosing amount or rate of any share commission.	On summary conviction a fine not exceeding £50.	On summary conviction a fine not exceeding one-fifth of the statutory maximum.
54(2)	Company giving financial assistance for the purchase or subscription of its own shares.	On summary conviction a fine not exceeding £100.	(a) On conviction on indictment a term of imprisonment not exceeding 2 years or a fine, or both. (b) On summary conviction a term of imprisonment not exceeding 6 months or a fine not exceeding the statutory maximum, or both.
62(2)	Failing to give notice to the registrar of consolidation of share capital, etc.	On summary conviction a fine not exceeding £5 for every day during which the default continues.	On summary conviction a fine not exceeding one-fifth of the statutory maximum or, on conviction, after continued contravention, a default fine not exceeding one-fiftieth of the statutory maximum.
63(3)	Failing to give proper notice to the registrar of an increase of share capital.	On summary conviction a fine not exceeding £5 for every day during which the default continues.	On summary conviction a fine not exceeding one-fifth of the statutory maximum or, on conviction, after continued contravention, a default fine not exceeding one-fiftieth of the statutory maximum.

Enactment (1)	General description of offence or contravention (2)	Old mode of trial and penalty (3)	New mode of trial and penalty (4)
	COMPANIES ACT 1948 (*contd*)		
71	In relation to a reduction of share capital, concealing the name of a creditor or misrepresenting the nature or amount of a debt, etc.	(*a*) In England and Wales, a term of imprisonment not exceeding 2 years or a fine, or both; (*b*) In Scotland— (i) on conviction on indictment a term of imprisonment or a fine, or both; (ii) on summary conviction a term of imprisonment not exceeding 3 months or a fine not exceeding the statutory maximum, or both.	(*a*) On conviction on indictment a fine. (*b*) On summary conviction a fine not exceeding the statutory maximum.
72(5) ...	Failing to forward to the registrar a copy of an order of the court made on an application to cancel a resolution to vary shareholders' rights.	On summary conviction a fine not exceeding £5 for every day during which the default continues.	On summary conviction a fine not exceeding one-fifth of the statutory maximum or, on conviction after continued contravention, a default fine not exceeding one-fiftieth of the statutory maximum.
78(2) ...	Failing to send notice of refusal to register a transfer of shares or debentures.	On summary conviction a fine not exceeding £5 for every day during which the default continues.	On summary conviction a fine not exceeding one-fifth of the statutory maximum or, on conviction after continued contravention, a default fine not exceeding one-fiftieth of the statutory maximum.

COMPANIES ACT 1948 (*contd*)

Enactment (1)	General description of offence or contravention (2)	Old mode of trial and penalty (3)	New mode of trial and penalty (4)
80(2) ...	Failing within two months of allotment or transfer of any share, debenture or debenture stock to complete and have ready for delivery a share certificate, the debenture or a certificate of debenture stock.	On summary conviction a fine not exceeding £5 for every day during which the default continues.	On summary conviction a fine not exceeding one-fifth of the statutory maximum or, on conviction after continued contravention, a default fine not exceeding one-fiftieth of the statutory maximum.
85(1) ...	Offences of fraud and forgery in connection with share warrants in Scotland.	On conviction on indictment a term of imprisonment or a fine, or both.	(a) On conviction on indictment a term of imprisonment not exceeding 7 years or a fine, or both. (b) On summary conviction a term of imprisonment not exceeding 6 months or a fine not exceeding the statutory maximum, or both.
85(2) ...	Unauthorised making, or using or possessing apparatus for making, share warrants in Scotland.	On conviction on indictment a term of imprisonment not exceeding 14 years or a fine, or both.	(a) On conviction on indictment a term of imprisonment not exceeding 7 years or a fine, or both. (b) On summary conviction a term of imprisonment not exceeding 6 months or a fine not exceeding the statutory maximum, or both.
87(4) ...	Refusing to allow inspection, or refusing or failing to provide or forward a copy, of the register of debentures or of a trust deed securing an issue of debentures.	On summary conviction a fine not exceeding £25 and a fine not exceeding £2 for every day during which the refusal or default continues.	On summary conviction a fine not exceeding one-fifth of the statutory maximum or, on conviction after continued contravention, a default fine not exceeding one-fiftieth of the statutory maximum.

Enactment (1)	General description of offence or contravention (2)	Old mode of trial and penalty (3)	New mode of trial and penalty (4)
	COMPANIES ACT 1948 (contd)		
96(3) ...	Failing to send to the registrar particulars of a registrable charge or of the issue of debentures of a series.	On summary conviction a fine not exceeding £50 for every day during which the default continues.	(a) On conviction on indictment a fine. (b) On summary conviction a fine not exceeding the statutory maximum or, on conviction after continued contravention, a default fine not exceeding one-tenth of the statutory maximum.
97(2) ...	Failing to send to the registrar particulars and a copy of an existing charge over property acquired by a company.	On summary conviction a fine not exceeding £50 for every day during which the default continues.	(a) On conviction on indictment a fine. (b) On summary conviction a fine not exceeding the statutory maximum or, on conviction after continued contravention, a default fine not exceeding one-tenth of the statutory maximum.
99(2) ...	Knowingly and wilfully authorising or permitting delivery of a debenture or a certificate of debenture stock without a copy of a certificate of registration of the charge being endorsed thereon.	On summary conviction a fine not exceeding £100.	On summary conviction a fine not exceeding one-fifth of the statutory maximum.
102(3) ...	Failing to give notice to the registrar of the appointment of a receiver or manager or of his ceasing to act.	On summary conviction a fine not exceeding £5 for every day during which the default continues.	On summary conviction a fine not exceeding one-fifth of the statutory maximum or, on conviction after continued contravention, a default fine not exceeding one-fiftieth of the statutory maximum.

Enactment (1)	General description of offence or contravention (2)	Old mode of trial and penalty (3)	New mode of trial and penalty (4)
	COMPANIES ACT 1948 (*contd*)		
104(2)	Omitting an entry required to be made in the register of charges.	On summary conviction a fine not exceeding £50.	(a) On conviction on indictment a fine. (b) On summary conviction a fine not exceeding the statutory maximum.
105(2)	Refusing to allow inspection by creditors or members of registrable instruments of charge or of the register of charges.	On summary conviction a fine not exceeding £25 and a fine not exceeding £2 for every day during which the refusal continues.	On summary conviction a fine not exceeding one-fifth of the statutory maximum or, on conviction after continued contravention, a default fine not exceeding one-fiftieth of the statutory maximum.
106B(3) ...	In respect of a company registered in Scotland, failing to send to the registrar particulars of a registrable charge or of the issue of debentures of a series.	On summary conviction a fine not exceeding £50 for every day during which the default continues.	(a) On conviction on indictment a fine, (b) On summary conviction a fine not exceeding the statutory maximum or, on conviction after continued contravention, a default fine not exceeding one-tenth of the statutory maximum.
106C(2) ...	Failing to send to the registrar particulars and a copy of an existing charge over property acquired by a company registered in Scotland.	On summary conviction a fine not exceeding £50 for every day during which the default continues.	(a) On conviction on indictment a fine, (b) On summary conviction a fine not exceeding the statutory maximum or, on conviction after continued contravention, a default fine not exceeding one-tenth of the statutory maximum.

Enactment (1)		General description of offence or contravention (2)	Old mode of trial and penalty (3)	New mode of trial and penalty (4)
		COMPANIES ACT 1948 (*contd*)		
106I(2)	...	In respect of a company registered in Scotland, omitting an entry required to be made in the register of charges.	On summary conviction a fine not exceeding £50.	(a) On conviction on indictment a fine. (b) On summary conviction a fine not exceeding the statutory maximum.
106J(2)	...	In respect of a company registered in Scotland, refusing to allow inspection by creditors or members, of registrable instruments of charge or of the register of charges.	On summary conviction a fine not exceeding £25 and a fine not exceeding £2 for every day during which the refusal continues.	On summary conviction a fine not exceeding one-fifth of the statutory maximum or, on conviction after continued contravention, a default fine not exceeding one-fiftieth of the statutory maximum.
108(2)	...	Failing to paint or affix a company's name or keep it painted or affixed in the specified manner.	On summary conviction— (a) in the case of a failure to paint, or affix a company's name, a fine not exceeding £25; (b) in the case of a failure to keep it painted or affixed, a fine not exceeding £5 for every day during which the default continues.	On summary conviction, a fine not exceeding one-fifth of the statutory maximum or, in the case of a failure to keep a company's name painted or affixed, on conviction after continued contravention, a default fine not exceeding one-fiftieth of the statutory maximum.
108(3)	...	Failing to have the name of a company in legible characters on its seal or certain documents.	On summary conviction a fine not exceeding £50.	On summary conviction a fine not exceeding one-fifth of the statutory maximum.

COMPANIES ACT 1948 (*contd*)

Enactment (1)	General description of offence or contravention (2)	Old mode of trial and penalty (3)	New mode of trial and penalty (4)
108(4)	An officer of a company using or authorising the use of a seal not engraved as required by section 108 or issuing or authorising the issue of certain documents in which the name of the company is not mentioned as required by that section.	On summary conviction a fine not exceeding £50.	On summary conviction a fine not exceeding one-fifth of the statutory maximum.
110(4)	Failing to keep a register of members or failing to give notice to the registrar of where the register is kept.	On summary conviction a fine not exceeding £5 for every day during which the default continues.	On summary conviction a fine not exceeding one-fifth of the statutory maximum or, on conviction after continued contravention, a default fine not exceeding one-fiftieth of the statutory maximum.
111(4)	In respect of a company with more than 50 members, failing to keep an index of the names of the members.	On summary conviction a fine not exceeding £5 for every day during which the default continues.	On summary conviction a fine not exceeding one-fifth of the statutory maximum or, on conviction after continued contravention, a default fine not exceeding one-fiftieth of the statutory maximum.
113(3)	Refusing inspection of the register or index of members or not sending a copy of the register when required to do so.	On summary conviction a fine not exceeding £25 and a fine not exceeding £2 for every day during which the refusal or default continues.	On summary conviction a fine not exceeding one-fifth of the statutory maximum.
119(3)	Failing to give notice to the registrar of the situation of the office where any dominion register is kept.	On summary conviction a fine not exceeding £5 for every day during which the default continues.	On summary conviction a fine not exceeding one-fifth of the statutory maximum, or on conviction after continued contravention, a default fine not exceeding one-fiftieth of the statutory maximum.

Enactment (1)	General description of offence or contravention (2)	Old mode of trial and penalty (3)	New mode of trial and penalty (4)
	COMPANIES ACT 1948 (*contd*)		
120(7)	Failing to send to the registered office of a company copies of the entries in the dominion register or to keep a duplicate of the dominion register.	On summary conviction a fine not exceeding £5 for every day during which the default continues.	On summary conviction a fine not exceeding one-fifth of the statutory maximum or, on conviction after continued contravention, a default fine not exceeding one-fiftieth of the statutory maximum.
124(3)	Company having a share capital failing to make an annual return to the registrar.	On summary conviction a fine not exceeding £5 for every day during which the default continues.	On summary conviction a fine not exceeding one-fifth of the statutory maximum or, on conviction after continued contravention, a default fine not exceeding one-fiftieth of the statutory maximum.
125(3)	Company not having a share capital failing to make an annual return to the registrar.	On summary conviction a fine not exceeding £5 for every day during which the default continues.	On summary conviction a fine not exceeding one-fifth of the statutory maximum or, on conviction after continued contravention, a default fine not exceeding one-fiftieth of the statutory maximum.
126(2)	Failing to complete an annual return or to forward it to the registrar forthwith.	On summary conviction a fine not exceeding £5 for every day during which the default continues.	On summary conviction a fine not exceeding one-fifth of the statutory maximum or, on conviction after continued contravention, a default fine not exceeding one-fiftieth of the statutory maximum.

COMPANIES ACT 1948 (*contd*)

Enactment (1)	General description of offence or contravention (2)	Old mode of trial and penalty (3)	New mode of trial and penalty (4)
131(5)	Failing to hold an annual general meeting in accordance with subsection (1), to comply with directions about such a meeting in accordance with subsection (2) or to forward a copy of a resolution to treat a general meeting as the annual general meeting to the registrar in accordance with subsection (4).	On summary conviction— (*a*) in the case of a failure to hold a meeting in accordance with subsection (1) or to comply with directions under subsection (2), a fine not exceeding £50; (*b*) in the case of a failure to forward a copy of such a resolution in accordance with subsection (4) a fine not exceeding £2 for every day during which the default continues.	(*a*) In the case of a failure to hold a meeting in accordance with subsection (1) or to comply with directions under subsection (2)— (i) on conviction on indictment a fine; (ii) on summary conviction a fine not exceeding the statutory maximum. (*b*) In the case of a failure to forward a copy of a resolution in accordance with subsection (4), on summary conviction a fine not exceeding one-fifth of the statutory maximum or, on conviction after continued contravention, a default fine not exceeding one-fiftieth of the statutory maximum.
136(2) ...	Failing to state in a notice calling a meeting of a company that a member entitled to attend and vote may appoint a proxy.	On summary conviction a fine not exceeding £50.	On summary conviction a fine not exceeding one-fifth of the statutory maximum.
136(4) ...	Officer of a company knowingly and wilfully authorising or permitting invitations to appoint proxies to be issued to some only of the members of the company.	On summary conviction a fine not exceeding £100.	On summary conviction a fine not exceeding one-fifth of the statutory maximum.
140(7) ...	Failing to comply with the provisions of section 140 (circulation of members' resolutions, etc.).	On summary conviction a fine not exceeding £500.	(*a*) On conviction on indictment a fine. (*b*) On summary conviction a fine not exceeding the statutory maximum.

Enactment (1)	General description of offence or contravention (2)	Old mode of trial and penalty (3)	New mode of trial and penalty (4)
	COMPANIES ACT 1948 (*contd*)		
143(5)	Failing to send to the registrar a copy of a resolution or agreement to which section 143 applies.	On summary conviction a fine not exceeding £2 for every day during which the default continues.	On summary conviction a fine not exceeding one-fifth of the statutory maximum or, on conviction after continued contravention, a default fine not exceeding one-fiftieth of the statutory maximum.
143(6)	Failing to include a copy of a resolution or agreement to which section 143 applies in every copy of the articles issued, or failing to forward a copy to a member on request.	On summary conviction a fine not exceeding £25 for each copy in respect of which default is made.	On summary conviction a fine not exceeding one-fifth of the statutory maximum for each occasion on which copies are issued or, as the case may be, requested.
145(4)	Failing to keep minutes of general meetings of the company, meetings of directors or meetings of managers.	On summary conviction a fine not exceeding £5 for every day during which the default continues.	On summary conviction a fine not exceeding one-fifth of the statutory maximum or, on conviction after continued contravention, a default fine not exceeding one-fiftieth of the statutory maximum.
146(3)	Refusing to allow inspection of the book containing the minutes of any general meeting or to supply a copy of any such minute requested by a member.	On summary conviction a fine not exceeding £25 and a fine not exceeding £2 for every day during which the refusal or default continues.	On summary conviction a fine not exceeding one-fifth of the statutory maximum.
155(3)	Laying a balance-sheet before the company or delivering it to the registrar or issuing, circulating or publishing it, without its having been signed in accordance with section 155, etc.	On summary conviction a fine not exceeding £50.	On summary conviction a fine not exceeding one-fifth of the statutory maximum.

Enactment (1)	General description of offence or contravention (2)	Old mode of trial and penalty (3)	New mode of trial and penalty (4)
	COMPANIES ACT 1948 (*contd*)		
156(3) ...	Issuing, circulating or publishing a balance-sheet without the required accounts or report being annexed to it.	On summary conviction a fine not exceeding £50.	On summary conviction a fine not exceeding one-fifth of the statutory maximum.
158(3) ...	Failing to send company members and other persons a copy of a balance-sheet, together with other documents, at least 21 days before a general meeting in accordance with sub-section (1), or to comply with a demand for such documents made under subsection (2).	On summary conviction— (a) in the case of a failure to comply with subsection (1), a fine not exceeding £50; (b) in the case of a failure to comply with such a demand, a fine not exceeding £5 for every day during which the default continues.	(a) In the case of a failure to comply with subsection (1)— (i) on conviction on indictment a fine; (ii) on summary conviction, a fine not exceeding the statutory maximum. (b) In the case of a failure to comply with a demand under subsection (2), on summary conviction, a fine not exceeding one-fifth of the statutory maximum or, on conviction after continued contravention, a default fine not exceeding one-fiftieth of the statutory maximum.
173(3) ...	Failing to give information, when required to do so, about interests in shares, etc., or giving false information.	On conviction on indictment, a term of imprisonment not exceeding six months or a fine or both.	(a) On conviction on indictment a term of imprisonment not exceeding 2 years or a fine, or both. (b) On summary conviction a term of imprisonment not exceeding 6 months or a fine not exceeding the statutory maximum, or both.

Enactment (1)	General description of offence or contravention (2)	Old mode of trial and penalty (3)	New mode of trial and penalty (4)
	COMPANIES ACT 1948 (*contd*)		
174(5)	Exercising a right to dispose of, or vote in respect of, shares subject to restrictions imposed by section 174 or failing to give notice in respect of shares subject to such restrictions.	On conviction on indictment, a term of imprisonment not exceeding six months or a fine or both.	(a) On conviction on indictment a fine. (b) On summary conviction a fine not exceeding the statutory maximum.
174(6)	Issuing shares in contravention of a restriction imposed by section 174.	On summary conviction a fine not exceeding £500.	(a) On conviction on indictment a fine. (b) On summary conviction a fine not exceeding the statutory maximum.
182(5)	Acting as a director without holding qualification shares required by the articles.	On summary conviction a fine not exceeding £5 for every day between the expiration of the period within which the shares should have been obtained, or the director ceased to be qualified, and the last day on which it is proved that he acted as a director.	On summary conviction a fine not exceeding one-fifth of the statutory maximum or, on conviction after continued contravention, a default fine not exceeding one-fiftieth of the statutory maximum for every day until the last day on which it is proved that he acted as a director.
186(2)	Failure of a person appointed or proposed to be appointed a director of a public company after retiring age to give notice of his age in accordance with subsection (1); and acting as a director under an appointment which is invalid or has been terminated by reason of age.	On summary conviction a fine not exceeding £5 for every day during which the contravention continues.	On summary conviction a fine not exceeding one-fifth of the statutory maximum or, on conviction after continued contravention, a default fine not exceeding one-fiftieth of the statutory maximum.

COMPANIES ACT 1948 (*contd*)

Enactment (1)	General description of offence or contravention (2)	Old mode of trial and penalty (3)	New mode of trial and penalty (4)
193(2) ...	Failing to take reasonable steps to ensure that particulars of a proposed payment for loss of office are included in, or sent with, any offer made for the shares of the company to which section 193 applies or to include the particulars in or send them with a specified notice.	On summary conviction a fine not exceeding £50.	On summary conviction a fine not exceeding one-fifth of the statutory maximum.
198(4) ...	Failing to disclose to a company matters required to be disclosed for the purposes of provisions in connection with directors' salaries, pensions, etc., and with loans to officers.	On summary conviction a fine not exceeding £50.	On summary conviction a fine not exceeding one-fifth of the statutory maximum.
199(4) ...	Director failing to disclose interest in contract.	On summary conviction a fine not exceeding £100.	(*a*) On conviction on indictment a fine. (*b*) On summary conviction a fine not exceeding the statutory maximum.
200(7) ...	Refusing to allow inspection of the register of directors and secretaries to any member of the company or failing to comply with the requirements of section 200 as to the register.	On summary conviction a fine not exceeding £5 for every day during which the refusal or default continues.	On summary conviction a fine not exceeding one-fifth of the statutory maximum or, on conviction after continued contravention, a default fine not exceeding one-fiftieth of the statutory maximum.
201(3) ...	Failing to state particulars of every director in all trade catalogues, trade circulars, etc.	On summary conviction a fine not exceeding £25.	On summary conviction a fine not exceeding one-fifth of the statutory maximum.

Enactment (1)	General description of offence or contravention (2)	Old mode of trial and penalty (3)	New mode of trial and penalty (4)
	COMPANIES ACT 1948 (*contd*)		
202(3) ...	Failing to state that liability of directors and managers will be unlimited or to notify proposed directors and managers of that fact.	On summary conviction a fine not exceeding £100.	(*a*) On conviction on indictment a fine. (*b*) On summary conviction a fine not exceeding the statutory maximum.
206(4) ...	Failing to annex to every copy of the memorandum of a company a copy of every order sanctioning a compromise or arrangement with creditors or members.	On summary conviction a fine not exceeding £25 for each copy in respect of which default is made.	On summary conviction a fine not exceeding one-fifth of the statutory maximum.
207(4) ...	Failing to comply with requirements as to the information to be provided for a meeting of creditors or members.	On summary conviction a fine not exceeding £500.	(*a*) On conviction on indictment a fine. (*b*) On summary conviction a fine not exceeding the statutory maximum.
207(5) ...	Director or trustee for debenture holders failing to give notice to the company of matters necessary for the purposes of section 207.	On summary conviction a fine not exceeding £50.	On summary conviction a fine not exceeding one-fifth of the statutory maximum.
208(3) ...	Failing to deliver to the registrar an office copy of an order made under section 208 (reconstruction and amalgamation of companies).	On summary conviction a fine not exceeding £5 for every day during which the default continues.	On summary conviction a fine not exceeding one-fifth of the statutory maximum or, on conviction after continued contravention, a default fine not exceeding one-fiftieth of the statutory maximum.

COMPANIES ACT 1948 (*contd*)

Enactment (1)	General description of offence or contravention (2)	Old mode of trial and penalty (3)	New mode of trial and penalty (4)
235(5)	Failing to comply with the requirements of section 235 as to a statement of affairs to be submitted to the official receiver.	On summary conviction a fine not exceeding £10 for every day during which the default continues.	(*a*) On conviction on indictment a fine. (*b*) On summary conviction a fine not exceeding the statutory maximum or, on conviction after continued contravention, a default fine not exceeding one-tenth of the statutory maximum.
274(3)	Failure of liquidator to send registrar copy of order to dissolve a company or to make a minute of its dissolution.	On summary conviction a fine not exceeding £25 for every day during which the liquidator is in default.	On summary conviction a fine not exceeding one-fifth of the statutory maximum or, on conviction after continued contravention, a default fine not exceeding one-fiftieth of the statutory maximum.
279(2)	Failing to give notice in the Gazette of a resolution to wind up voluntarily.	On summary conviction a fine not exceeding £25 for every day during which the default continues.	On summary conviction a fine not exceeding one-fifth of the statutory maximum or, on conviction after continued contravention, a default fine not exceeding one-fiftieth of the statutory maximum.
283(3)	Director making a declaration of solvency without having reasonable grounds for the opinion that a company will be able to pay its debts.	On conviction on indictment, a term of imprisonment not exceeding six months or a fine or both.	(*a*) On conviction on indictment a term of imprisonment not exceeding 2 years or a fine, or both. (*b*) On summary conviction a term of imprisonment not exceeding 6 months or a fine not exceeding the statutory maximum, or both.

COMPANIES ACT 1948 (*contd*)

Enactment (1)	General description of offence or contravention (2)	Old mode of trial and penalty (3)	New mode of trial and penalty (4)
288(2)	Liquidator failing to summon a meeting of creditors in case of insolvency (members' voluntary winding-up).	On summary conviction a fine not exceeding £50.	On summary conviction a fine not exceeding one-fifth of the statutory maximum.
289(2)	Liquidator failing to summon a general meeting of the company at end of each year (members' voluntary winding-up).	On summary conviction a fine not exceeding £25.	On summary conviction a fine not exceeding one-fifth of the statutory maximum.
290(3)	Liquidator failing to send to the registrar a copy of the account of a winding-up and a return of the final general meeting (members' voluntary winding-up).	On summary conviction a fine not exceeding £5 for every day during which the default continues.	On summary conviction a fine not exceeding one-fifth of the statutory maximum or, on conviction after continued contravention, a default fine not exceeding one-fiftieth of the statutory maximum.
290(5)	Failing to deliver to the registrar an office copy of an order deferring the date of dissolution following a members' voluntary winding-up.	On summary conviction a fine not exceeding £5 for every day during which the default continues.	On summary conviction a fine not exceeding one-fifth of the statutory maximum or, on conviction after continued contravention, a default fine not exceeding one-fiftieth of the statutory maximum.
290(6)	Liquidator failing to call the final general meeting of the company (members' voluntary winding-up).	On summary conviction a fine not exceeding £50.	On summary conviction a fine not exceeding one-fifth of the statutory maximum.
293(6)	Default by a company, its directors, etc., in relation to the summoning or advertisement of a meeting of creditors (creditors' voluntary winding-up).	On summary conviction a fine not exceeding £100.	(*a*) On conviction on indictment a fine. (*b*) On summary conviction a fine not exceeding the statutory maximum.

Enactment (1)	General description of offence or contravention (2)	Old mode of trial and penalty (3)	New mode of trial and penalty (4)
	COMPANIES ACT 1948 (*contd*)		
299(2)	Liquidator failing to summon a general meeting of the company and a meeting of creditors at end of each year (creditors' voluntary winding-up).	On summary conviction a fine not exceeding £25.	On summary conviction a fine not exceeding one-fifth of the statutory maximum.
300(3)	Liquidator failing to send to the registrar a copy of the account of a winding-up and a return of the final general meeting and the final meeting of creditors (creditors' voluntary winding-up).	On summary conviction a fine not exceeding £5 for every day during which the default continues.	On summary conviction a fine not exceeding one-fifth of the statutory maximum or, on conviction after continued contravention, a default fine not exceeding one-fiftieth of the statutory maximum.
300(5)	Failing to deliver to the registrar an office copy of an order deferring the date of dissolution following a creditors' voluntary winding-up.	On summary conviction a fine not exceeding £5 for every day during which the default continues.	On summary conviction a fine not exceeding one-fifth of the statutory maximum or, on conviction after continued contravention, a default fine not exceeding one-fiftieth of the statutory maximum.
300(6)	Liquidator failing to call the final general meeting of the company or the final meeting of creditors (creditors' voluntary winding-up).	On summary conviction a fine not exceeding £50.	On summary conviction a fine not exceeding one-fifth of the statutory maximum.
305(2)	Liquidator failing to publish notice of his appointment in the Gazette or to deliver notice of appointment to registrar.	On summary conviction a fine not exceeding £5 for every day during which the default continues.	On summary conviction a fine not exceeding one-fifth of the statutory maximum or, on conviction after continued contravention, a default fine not exceeding one-fiftieth of the statutory maximum.

Enactment (1)	General description of offence or contravention (2)	Old mode of trial and penalty (3)	New mode of trial and penalty (4)
	COMPANIES ACT 1948 (*contd*)		
328(1)	Failure of officer of a company in liquidation or subsequently wound up to disclose or deliver property of, or documents or information relating to, the company to the liquidator, fraudulent conduct by any such officer in relation to the property or affairs of such a company, and other offences by such officers.	In the case of an offence— (*a*) under paragraph (*o*) (pledging, pawning or disposing of unpaid-for property of such a company in year before, or during winding-up)— (i) on conviction on indictment, a term of imprisonment not exceeding 5 years or a fine, or both; (ii) on summary conviction, a term of imprisonment not exceeding 6 months or fine not exceeding the statutory maximum; (*b*) under any other paragraph— (i) on conviction on indictment, a term of imprisonment not exceeding 2 years or a fine, or both; (ii) on summary conviction, a term of imprisonment not exceeding 6 months or a fine not exceeding the statutory maximum.	(*a*) On conviction on indictment a term of imprisonment not exceeding 7 years or a fine, or both. (*b*) On summary conviction a term of imprisonment not exceeding 6 months or a fine not exceeding the statutory maximum, or both.

COMPANIES ACT 1948 (*contd*)

Enactment (1)	General description of offence or contravention (2)	Old mode of trial and penalty (3)	New mode of trial and penalty (4)
329	Officer or contributory of a company being wound up destroying, mutilating, altering or falsifying books, etc., with intent to defraud.	On conviction on indictment a term of imprisonment not exceeding 2 years or a fine, or both.	(a) On conviction on indictment a term of imprisonment not exceeding 7 years or a fine, or both. (b) On summary conviction a term of imprisonment not exceeding 6 months or a fine not exceeding the statutory maximum, or both.
330	Officer of a company subsequently wound up making or causing to be made a gift or transfer of the company's property or concealing or removing any part of the company's property with intent to defraud creditors.	(a) On conviction on indictment a term of imprisonment not exceeding 2 years or a fine, or both. (b) On summary conviction a term of imprisonment not exceeding 6 months or a fine not exceeding the statutory maximum.	(a) On conviction on indictment a term of imprisonment not exceeding 2 years or a fine, or both. (b) On summary conviction a term of imprisonment not exceeding 6 months, or a fine not exceeding the statutory maximum, or both.
332(3) ...	Being a party to the carrying on of a company's business where it is carried on with intent to defraud creditors or for any fraudulent purpose.	On conviction on indictment a term of imprisonment not exceeding 2 years, or a fine, or both.	(a) On conviction on indictment a term of imprisonment not exceeding 7 years or a fine, or both. (b) On summary conviction a term of imprisonment not exceeding 6 months or a fine not exceeding the statutory maximum, or both.
335	Body corporate acting as a liquidator.	On summary conviction a fine not exceeding £100.	(a) On conviction on indictment a fine. (b) On summary conviction a fine not exceeding the statutory maximum.

COMPANIES ACT 1948 (*contd*)

Enactment (1)	General description of offence or contravention (2)	Old mode of trial and penalty (3)	New mode of trial and penalty (4)
336	Giving or agreeing or offering to give a corrupt inducement affecting the appointment of a liquidator.	On summary conviction a fine not exceeding £100.	(a) On conviction on indictment a fine. (b) On summary conviction a fine not exceeding the statutory maximum.
338(2) ...	Failing to state on certain documents that a company is being wound up.	On summary conviction a fine not exceeding £50.	On summary conviction a fine not exceeding one-fifth of the statutory maximum.
341(4) ...	Acting in contravention of any general rules or any direction thereunder made or given for the purpose of preserving books and papers of a company which has been wound up.	On summary conviction a fine not exceeding £100.	On summary conviction a fine not exceeding one-fifth of the statutory maximum.
342(2) ...	Liquidator failing to send to the registrar a statement as to the position of a liquidation which is not concluded within one year of its commencement.	On summary conviction a fine not exceeding £50 for every day during which the default continues.	On summary conviction a fine not exceeding one-fifth of the statutory maximum or, on conviction after continued contravention, a default fine not exceeding one-fiftieth of the statutory maximum.
352(2) ...	Failing to deliver to the registrar a copy of an order declaring the dissolution of a company void.	On summary conviction a fine not exceeding £5 for every day during which the default continues.	On summary conviction a fine not exceeding one-fifth of the statutory maximum or, on conviction after continued contravention, a default fine not exceeding one-fiftieth of the statutory maximum.
366	Body corporate acting as a receiver.	On summary conviction a fine not exceeding £100.	(a) On conviction on indictment a fine. (b) On summary conviction a fine not exceeding the statutory maximum.

Enactment (1)	General description of offence or contravention (2)	Old mode of trial and penalty (3)	New mode of trial and penalty (4)
	COMPANIES ACT 1948 (*contd*)		
370(2)	Not stating on company documents that a receiver or manager has been appointed.	On summary conviction a fine not exceeding £50.	On summary conviction a fine not exceeding one-fifth of the statutory maximum.
372(7)	Receiver making default in complying with provisions as to information where receiver or manager appointed.	On summary conviction a fine not exceeding £5 for every day during which the default continues.	On summary conviction a fine not exceeding one-fifth of the statutory maximum or, on conviction after continued contravention, a default fine not exceeding one-fiftieth of the statutory maximum.
373(5)	Default in relation to provisions as to statement to be submitted to receiver.	On summary conviction a fine not exceeding £10 for every day during which the default continues.	On summary conviction a fine not exceeding one-fifth of the statutory maximum or, on conviction after continued contravention, a default fine not exceeding one-fiftieth of the statutory maximum.
374(2)	Receiver or manager not delivering accounts to registrar.	On summary conviction a fine not exceeding £5 for every day during which the default continues.	On summary conviction a fine not exceeding one-fifth of the statutory maximum or, on conviction after continued contravention, a default fine not exceeding one-fiftieth of the statutory maximum.

Enactment (1)	General description of offence or contravention (2)	Old mode of trial and penalty (3)	New mode of trial and penalty (4)
	COMPANIES ACT 1948 (*contd*)		
414	Failure of an oversea company having a place of business in Great Britain to comply with sections 407 to 413 (documents to be delivered and information to be given to the registrar and other requirements as to the giving of information by such a company).	(a) For an offence which is not a continuing offence, on summary conviction a fine not exceeding £50. (b) For an offence which is a continuing offence, on summary conviction a fine not exceeding £5 for every day during which the default continues.	(a) For an offence which is not a continuing offence, on summary conviction a fine not exceeding one-fifth of the statutory maximum. (b) For an offence which is a continuing offence, on summary conviction a fine not exceeding one-fifth of the statutory maximum or, on conviction after continued contravention, a default fine not exceeding one-fiftieth of the statutory maximum.
421	Being responsible for the issue, circulation or distribution of a prospectus or form of application for shares or debentures of an oversea company in contravention of sections 417 to 420 (contents, issue and registration of prospectuses).	On summary conviction a fine not exceeding £500.	(a) On conviction on indictment a fine. (b) On summary conviction a fine not exceeding the statutory maximum.
426(4)	A person untruthfully stating himself in writing to be a member or creditor of a company for the purpose of inspecting or obtaining documents of a company where a receiver or manager has been appointed.	On summary conviction a fine not exceeding £50.	On summary conviction a fine not exceeding one-fifth of the statutory maximum.

Enactment (1)	General description of offence or contravention (2)	Old mode of trial and penalty (3)	New mode of trial and penalty (4)
	COMPANIES ACT 1948 (*contd*)		
433(4)	Banking and certain other companies not publishing periodical statement.	On summary conviction a fine not exceeding £5 for every day during which the default continues.	On summary conviction a fine not exceeding one-fifth of the statutory maximum or, on conviction after continued contravention, a default fine not exceeding one-fiftieth of the statutory maximum.
436(2) ...	Not taking adequate precautions against falsification, etc., of company records where these are not kept in bound books.	On summary conviction a fine not exceeding £50 and a fine not exceeding £5 for every day during which the default continues.	On summary conviction a fine not exceeding one-fifth of the statutory maximum or, on conviction after continued contravention, a default fine not exceeding one-fiftieth of the statutory maximum.
439	Improperly using the word "limited" in the name or title of a business.	On summary conviction a fine not exceeding £5 for every day on which the name or title is used.	On summary conviction a fine not exceeding one-fifth of the statutory maximum or, on conviction after continued contravention, a default fine not exceeding one-fiftieth of the statutory maximum.
	COMPANIES ACT 1967 (c. 81)		
3(6)	Failure by company, where taking advantage of exemption from requirements in relation to statements in its accounts as to its subsidiaries, to annex required particulars to annual return.	On summary conviction a fine not exceeding £5 for every day during which the default continues.	On summary conviction a fine not exceeding one-fifth of the statutory maximum or, on conviction after continued contravention, a default fine not exceeding one-fiftieth of the statutory maximum.

Enactment (1)	General description of offence or contravention (2)	Old mode of trial and penalty (3)	New mode of trial and penalty (4)
	COMPANIES ACT 1967 (*contd*)		
4(6)	Failure by company, where taking advantage of exemption from requirements in relation to statements in its accounts as to the companies whose shares it holds, to annex required particulars to the annual return.	On summary conviction a fine not exceeding £5 for every day during which the default continues.	On summary conviction a fine not exceeding one-fifth of the statutory maximum or, on conviction after continued contravention, a default fine not exceeding one-fiftieth of the statutory maximum.
11(2)	Director of a company failing to take steps to secure compliance with the requirements of section 11 (statements annexed to accounts to include corresponding amounts for the preceding year).	On summary conviction a term of imprisonment not exceeding 6 months or a fine not exceeding £200.	(*a*) On conviction on indictment a fine. (*b*) On summary conviction a fine not exceeding the statutory maximum.
25(1)	Director dealing in options to buy or sell quoted shares or debentures.	(*a*) On conviction on indictment a term of imprisonment not exceeding 2 years or a fine, or both. (*b*) On summary conviction a term of imprisonment not exceeding 3 months or a fine not exceeding the statutory maximum or both.	(*a*) On conviction on indictment a term of imprisonment not exceeding 2 years or a fine, or both. (*b*) On summary conviction a term of imprisonment not exceeding 6 months or a fine not exceeding the statutory maximum, or both.

COMPANIES ACT 1967 (contd)

Enactment (1)	General description of offence or contravention (2)	Old mode of trial and penalty (3)	New mode of trial and penalty (4)
26(5) ...	Company— (a) failing to keep copy of memorandum of directors' service contracts in accordance with subsection (1); or (b) failing to send notice to the registrar in accordance with subsection (3) of the place where copies of such memorandums are kept; or (c) refusing to allow inspection of copies of such memorandums in accordance with subsection (4).	On summary conviction— (a) in the case of any failure or refusal mentioned in paragraph (a) or (c) of column 2 of this entry, a fine not exceeding £500 and a fine not exceeding £5 for every day during which the default or refusal continues; (b) in the case of any failure mentioned in paragraph (b) of that column, a fine not exceeding £5 for every day during which the default continues.	In each case, on summary conviction a fine not exceeding one-fifth of the statutory maximum, or, on conviction after continued contravention, a default fine not exceeding one-fifth of the statutory maximum.
27(8) ...	Director failing to notify a company of interests in shares or debentures in the company or associated companies, or making a false statement when purporting so to notify the company.	(a) On conviction on indictment a term of imprisonment not exceeding 2 years or a fine, or both. (b) On summary conviction a term of imprisonment not exceeding 3 months or a fine not exceeding the statutory maximum, or both.	(a) On conviction on indictment a term of imprisonment not exceeding 2 years or a fine, or both. (b) On summary conviction a term of imprisonment not exceeding 6 months or a fine not exceeding the statutory maximum, or both.

Enactment (1)	General description of offence or contravention (2)	Old mode of trial and penalty (3)	New mode of trial and penalty (4)
	COMPANIES ACT 1967 (*contd*)		
29(12) ...	Company— (*a*) failing to comply with any of subsections (1) to (4), (which relate to the keeping of a register of directors with interests in securities of companies and the recording of information about those interests); (*b*) refusing to allow the register to be inspected in accordance with subsection (7); (*c*) failing for 14 days to send the registrar notice of the place where the register is kept or of any change in that place in accordance with subsection (8); (*d*) failing to keep an index of the register in accordance with subsection (9); (*e*) failing to send copies of the register to members in accordance with subsection (10); (*f*) failing to produce register and keep it accessible at general meeting in accordance with subsection (11).	On summary conviction— (*a*) in the case of any failure or refusal mentioned in paragraph (*a*), (*b*), (*d*) or (*e*) of column 2 of this entry, a fine not exceeding £500 and a fine not exceeding £5 for every day during which the default or refusal continues; (*b*) in the case of any failure mentioned in paragraph (*c*) of that column, a fine not exceeding £5 for every day during which the default continues; and (*c*) in the case of any failure mentioned in paragraph (*f*) of that column, a fine not exceeding £50.	In each case, on summary conviction, a fine not exceeding one-fifth of the statutory maximum or, except in the case of a failure mentioned in the said paragraph (*f*), on conviction after continued contravention, a default fine not exceeding one-fifth of the statutory maximum.
31(3) ...	Director failing to notify the company that certain members of his family have, or have exercised, options to buy shares or debentures, and making a false statement when purporting so to notify the company.	(*a*) On conviction on indictment a term of imprisonment not exceeding 2 years or a fine, or both. (*b*) On summary conviction a term of imprisonment not exceeding 3 months or a fine not exceeding the statutory maximum, or both.	(*a*) On conviction on indictment a term of imprisonment not exceeding 2 years or a fine, or both. (*b*) On summary conviction a term of imprisonment not exceeding 6 months or a fine not exceeding the statutory maximum, or both.

Enactment (1)	General description of offence or contravention (2)	Old mode of trial and penalty (3)	New mode of trial and penalty (4)
	COMPANIES ACT 1967 (*contd*)		
33(6)	Failing to notify the company of acquisition, changes in amounts of, and disposal of shares in the company, or making a false statement when purporting so to notify the company.	(*a*) On conviction on indictment a term of imprisonment not exceeding 2 years or a fine, or both. (*b*) On summary conviction a term of imprisonment not exceeding 3 months or a fine not exceeding the statutory maximum, or both.	(*a*) On conviction on indictment a term of imprisonment not exceeding 2 years or a fine, or both. (*b*) on summary conviction a term of imprisonment not exceeding 6 months or a fine not exceeding the statutory maximum, or both.
34(8)	Contravention of provisions for securing that information about acquisitions, changes of amounts and disposals of shares in a company are recorded and made available by the company.	On summary conviction, a fine not exceeding £500 and a fine not exceeding £5 for every day during which the contravention continues.	On summary conviction a fine not exceeding one-fifth of the statutory maximum or, on conviction after continued contravention, a default fine not exceeding one-fiftieth of the statutory maximum.
46(4)	Company not complying with a direction of the Secretary of State to abandon misleading name.	On summary conviction a fine not exceeding £5 for every day during which the default continues.	On summary conviction a fine not exceeding one-fifth of the statutory maximum or, on conviction after continued contravention, a default fine not exceeding one-fiftieth of the statutory maximum.
109(4)	Failing to comply with a direction of the Secretary of State to produce books or papers or provide an explanation or make a statement.	On summary conviction a term of imprisonment not exceeding 3 months or a fine not exceeding £200, or both.	(*a*) On conviction on indictment a fine. (*b*) On summary conviction a fine not exceeding the statutory maximum.

Enactment (1)	General description of offence or contravention (2)	Old mode of trial and penalty (3)	New mode of trial and penalty (4)
	COMPANIES ACT 1967 (*contd*)		
110(4)... ...	Obstructing the exercise of a right of entry or search or a right to take possession of books or papers.	On summary conviction a term of imprisonment not exceeding 3 months or a fine not exceeding £200, or both.	(*a*) On conviction on indictment a fine. (*b*) On summary conviction a fine not exceeding the statutory maximum.
111(2)... ...	Wrongful disclosure of information obtained by the exercise of the powers as to the production of documents conferred by the 1967 Act, the Protection of Depositors Act 1963 or the Insurance Companies Act 1974 or by the exercise of the powers of entry and search conferred by any of those Acts.	(*a*) On conviction on indictment a term of imprisonment not exceeding 2 years or a fine, or both. (*b*) On summary conviction a term of imprisonment not exceeding 3 months or a fine not exceeding the statutory maximum, or both.	(*a*) On conviction on indictment a term of imprisonment not exceeding 2 years or a fine, or both. (*b*) On summary conviction a term of imprisonment not exceeding 6 months or a fine not exceeding the statutory maximum, or both.
113	Destroying, mutilating, falsifying, etc., a document affecting or relating to a company, insurance company or other body in contravention of subsection (1) or fraudulently parting with, altering or making an omission in such a document in contravention of subsection (2) or being privy to the parting with the document or to its alteration or to the making of such an omission.	(*a*) On conviction on indictment, a term of imprisonment not exceeding 2 years or a fine or both. (*b*) On summary conviction a term of imprisonment not exceeding 3 months or a fine not exceeding the statutory maximum, or both.	(*a*) On conviction on indictment, a term of imprisonment not exceeding 7 years or a fine, or both. (*b*) On summary conviction, a term of imprisonment not exceeding 6 months or a fine not exceeding the statutory maximum, or both.

Enactment (1)	General description of offence or contravention (2)	Old mode of trial and penalty (3)	New mode of trial and penalty (4)
	COMPANIES ACT 1967 (*contd*)		
114	Making a false statement or explanation in purported compliance with a requirement to make a statement or provide an explanation.	(*a*) On conviction on indictment a term of imprisonment not exceeding 2 years or a fine, or both. (*b*) On summary conviction a term of imprisonment not exceeding 3 months or a fine not exceeding the statutory maximum, or both.	(*a*) On conviction on indictment a term of imprisonment not exceeding 2 years or a fine, or both. (*b*) On summary conviction a term of imprisonment not exceeding 6 months or a fine not exceeding the statutory maximum, or both.
	EUROPEAN COMMUNITIES ACT 1972 (c. 68)		
9(5)	Failing to send to the registrar, a printed copy of an Act or statutory instrument which alters a company's memorandum or articles, or a printed copy of the memorandum or articles as altered by any document.	On summary conviction a fine not exceeding £5 for every day during which the default continues.	On summary conviction a fine not exceeding one-fifth of the statutory maximum or, on conviction after continued contravention, a default fine not exceeding one-fiftieth of the statutory maximum.
9(7)	Failing to mention required particulars in business letters and order forms.	On summary conviction a fine not exceeding £50.	On summary conviction a fine not exceeding one-fifth of the statutory maximum.
	COMPANIES ACT 1976 (c. 69)		
4(1)	Directors failing to comply with the requirements of section 1(6) or (7) to lay annual accounts before the general meeting or to deliver such accounts, if necessary with a translation into English, to the registrar.	On summary conviction a fine not exceeding the aggregate of £400 and £40 for each day which falls— (*a*) after the end of the period allowed for laying and delivering accounts, and	On summary conviction a fine not exceeding the statutory maximum or, on conviction after continued contravention, a default fine not exceeding one-tenth of the statutory maximum.

COMPANIES ACT 1976 (*contd*)

Enactment (1)	General description of offence or contravention (2)	Old mode of trial and penalty (3)	New mode of trial and penalty (4)
		(*b*) before the earliest day by which all the requirements of section 1(6) or 1(7) (as the case may be) have been complied with.	
11(1)... ...	Oversea company failing to comply with the requirements of section 9(2) to deliver annual accounts, if necessary with a translation into English.	On summary conviction a fine not exceeding the aggregate of £400 and £40 for each day which falls— (*a*) after the end of the period allowed for delivering accounts; and (*b*) before the earliest day by which all the requirements of section 9(2) have been complied with.	(*a*) On conviction on indictment a fine. (*b*) On summary conviction a fine not exceeding the statutory maximum or, on conviction after continued contravention, a default fine not exceeding one-tenth of the statutory maximum.
13(6)... ...	Acting as auditor when disqualified from doing so or failing to give notice of vacating office of auditor.	(*a*) On conviction on indictment a fine. (*b*) On summary conviction a fine not exceeding £40 for every day during which the contravention continues.	(*a*) On conviction on indictment a fine. (*b*) On summary conviction a fine not exceeding the statutory maximum or, on conviction after continued contravention, a default fine not exceeding one-tenth of the statutory maximum.

Enactment (1)	General description of offence or contravention (2)	Old mode of trial and penalty (3)	New mode of trial and penalty (4)
	COMPANIES ACT 1976 (*contd*)		
14(7) ...	Failing to notify the Secretary of State that no auditor has been appointed or re-appointed, or failing to notify the registrar that auditor has been removed.	On summary conviction a fine not exceeding £5 for every day during which the default continues.	On summary conviction a fine not exceeding one-fifth of the statutory maximum or, on conviction after continued contravention, a default fine not exceeding one-fiftieth of the statutory maximum.
16(7) ...	Failing to comply with the requirements as to the giving of notices in connection with the resignation of an auditor.	(*a*) On conviction on indictment a fine. (*b*) On summary conviction a fine not exceeding £40 for every day during which the default continues.	(*a*) On conviction on indictment a fine. (*b*) On summary conviction a fine not exceeding the statutory maximum or, on conviction after continued contravention, a default fine not exceeding one-tenth of the statutory maximum.
18 ...	Failure of subsidiary to give its holding company, and failure of holding company to obtain from its subsidiary, information needed for purposes of audit.	On summary conviction a fine not exceeding £200	On summary conviction a fine not exceeding one-fifth of the statutory maximum.
23(4) ...	Not having a registered office or failing to notify the registrar of a change in its situation.	On summary conviction a fine not exceeding £5 for every day during which the default continues.	On summary conviction a fine not exceeding one-fifth of the statutory maximum or, on conviction after continued contravention, a default fine not exceeding one-fiftieth of the statutory maximum.

Enactment (1)	General description of offence or contravention (2)	Old mode of trial and penalty (3)	New mode of trial and penalty (4)
COMPANIES ACT 1976 (*contd*)			
25(3) ...	Failing to notify recognised stock exchange of acquisition, etc., of company's securities by a director.	On summary conviction a fine not exceeding £500 and a fine not exceeding £5 for every day during which the default continues.	On summary conviction a fine not exceeding one-fifth of the statutory maximum or, on conviction after continued contravention, a default fine not exceeding one-fiftieth of the statutory maximum.
30(5) ...	Failure in case of private limited company using Welsh form of name to include in certain documents, etc., a statement in English that the company is a limited company.	On summary conviction a fine not exceeding £50.	On summary conviction a fine not exceeding one-fifth of the statutory maximum.
31(5) ...	An oversea company carrying on business under its corporate name in contravention of a direction by the Secretary of State.	(a) On conviction on indictment a fine. (b) On summary conviction a fine not exceeding £40 for every day during which the contravention continues.	(a) On conviction on indictment a fine. (b) On summary conviction a fine not exceeding the statutory maximum or, on conviction after continued contravention, a default fine not exceeding one-tenth of the statutory maximum.

SCHEDULE 3

MINOR AND CONSEQUENTIAL AMENDMENTS

GENERAL

1. In the Companies Acts 1948 to 1976, a reference to a company registered under any specified enactment shall continue to have effect as a reference to a company registered under that enactment, notwithstanding that it has subsequently been re-registered under this Act.

COMPANIES ACT 1948 (c.38)

2. In sections 1(1), 4 and 10, for the words " this Act " wherever occurring, there shall be substituted the words " the Companies Acts 1948 to 1980 ".

3. Paragraph (*a*) of section 2(1) (memorandum) shall have effect in relation to a public company as if the words from " with " to the end were omitted.

4. In section 5 (alteration of objects), for the proviso to subsection (4), there shall be substituted the following subsections—

" (4A) An order under this section may, if the court thinks fit, provide for the purchase by the company of the shares of any members of the company and for the reduction accordingly of the company's capital and may make such alterations in the memorandum and articles of the company as may be required in consequence of that provision.

(4B) Where an order under this section requires the company not to make any, or any specified, alteration in its memorandum or articles, then, notwithstanding anything in the Companies Acts 1948 to 1980, the company shall not have power without the leave of the court to make any such alteration in breach of that requirement.

(4C) Any alteration in the memorandum or articles of a company made by virtue of an order under this section, other than one made by resolution of the company, shall be of the same effect as if duly made by resolution of the company, and the provisions of the Companies Acts 1948 to 1980 shall apply to the memorandum or articles as so altered accordingly.".

5. No licence under section 19 (power to dispense with " limited ") shall be granted in respect of a public company or an association about to be formed into a public company or have effect in respect of such a company.

6. In section 23 (alteration of memorandum)—

(*a*) in subsection (1) for the words " two hundred and ten of this Act " there shall be substituted the words " 75 of the Companies Act 1980 " ; and

(*b*) in subsection (3) for " (3), (4) " there shall be substituted the words " to (4C) ".

7. For section 31 (members liable for debts where business carried on with less than minimum number of members) there shall be substituted the following section—

"Liability for debts where business carried on without minimum number of members.

31. If a company carries on business without having at least two members and does so for more than six months, a person who, for the whole or any part of the period that it so carries on business after those six months,—

(a) is a member of the company, and

(b) knows that it is carrying on business with only one member,

shall be liable (jointly and severally with the company) for the payment of the debts of the company contracted during the period or, as the case may be, that part of it.".

8. In section 49 (effect of irregular allotment)—

(a) in subsection (1), for the words from " of the two " to " made after the holding of the statutory meeting " there shall be substituted the words " of section 47 of this Act shall be voidable at the instance of the applicant " ; and

(b) in subsection (2), for the word " sections " there shall be substituted the word " section ".

9. In section 53(1)(c)(ii) (disclosure of amount and rate of any commission where shares not offered to public), for the words from " disclosed ", in the first place where it occurs, to " delivered " there shall be substituted the words " disclosed in a statement in the prescribed form signed by every director of the company, or by his agent authorised in writing, and delivered ".

10. In section 54 (prohibition on company providing financial assistance for purchase of own shares, etc.)—

(a) the following paragraph shall be substituted for paragraph (b) of subsection (1)—

" (b) the provision by a company in accordance with an employee share scheme (within the meaning of the Companies Act 1980) of money for the purchase of, or subscription for, fully-paid shares in the company or its holding company by the trustees of the scheme ; " ;

(b) after subsection (1) there shall be inserted the following subsections—

" (1A) The proviso to the foregoing subsection shall authorise a public company to give financial assistance to any person only if the company's net assets are not thereby reduced or, to the extent that those assets are thereby reduced, if the financial assistance is provided out of profits which are available for dividend.

(1B) In this section, " net assets " in relation to any company, means the aggregate of that company's assets

R 4

less the aggregate of its liabilities ; and " liabilities " include any provision (within the meaning of Schedule 8 to this Act) except to the extent that that provision is taken into account in calculating the value of any asset to the company.".

11. In section 55 (construction of references to offering shares or debentures to the public) after subsection (2) there shall be added the following subsections—

" (3) For the purposes of this section an offer of shares in or debentures of a private company or an invitation to subscribe for such shares or debentures shall, if it is of any of the following descriptions—

(*a*) an offer or invitation made to any member of the relevant class ;

(*b*) an offer or invitation to subscribe for shares or debentures to be held under an employees' share scheme ;

(*c*) an offer or invitation falling within paragraph (*a*) or (*b*) above and made on terms which permit the person to whom the offer or invitation is made to renounce his right to the allotment of shares or issue of debentures, but only in favour of a member of a relevant class, or, where there is an employees' share scheme, of a person entitled to hold shares or debentures under the scheme ;

be regarded, unless the contrary is proved, as being a domestic concern of the person or persons making and receiving the offer or invitation.

(4) In this section—

" employees' share scheme " has the same meaning as in the Companies Act 1980 ;

" family " means, in relation to a person, that person's husband or wife, widow or widower and children (including step-children) and their descendants and any trustee (acting in his capacity as such) of a trust the principal beneficiary of which is that person or any of those relatives ; and

" member of a relevant class " means an existing member of the company making the offer or invitation, or an existing employee of that company, or a member of the family of such a member or employee, or an existing debenture holder."

12. In section 56(2) (application of share premium account in paying up bonus shares, etc.) for the word " issued " there shall be substituted the word " allotted ".

13. In section 58(1) (power to issue redeemable preference shares) in proviso (*c*), for the words " the profits of the company " there shall be substituted the words " profits of the company which would otherwise be available for dividend ".

14. In section 58(5) (application of capital redemption reserve in paying up bonus shares) for the word " issued " there shall be substituted the word " allotted ".

15. For the proviso to section 95(8) and to section 106A(7) (particulars to be sent to the registrar of each issue of debentures of a series in England and Wales and in Scotland, respectively) there shall be substituted the following proviso:

" Provided that there shall be sent to the registrar for entry in the register particulars in the prescribed form of the date and amount of each issue of debentures of the series, but any omission to do this shall not affect the validity of any of those debentures.".

16. In section 134(c) (quorum for meetings), for the words from the beginning to " three members " there shall be substituted the words " two members ".

17. In section 143(4) (resolutions to be forwarded to the registrar) after paragraph (e) there shall be inserted the following paragraph: —

" (f) resolutions of the directors of a company passed by virtue of section 8(3)(a) or 37(2) of the Companies Act 1980.".

18. In section 149(6) (accounts not complying with requirements of Act)—
  (a) for the words " this Act " there shall be substituted the words " the Companies Acts 1948 to 1980 " ; and
  (b) for paragraphs (a) and (b) there shall be substituted the following paragraphs: —

  " (a) on conviction on indictment, to a fine ;

  (b) on summary conviction, to a fine not exceeding the statutory maximum (within the meaning of the Companies Act 1980).".

19. In section 149(7)(a) (meaning of balance-sheet), for the words " this Act " there shall be substituted the words " the Companies Acts 1948 to 1980 ".

20. In section 150(3) (group accounts not complying with requirements of Act)—
  (a) after the word " Act " there shall be inserted the words " and with the other requirements of the Companies Acts 1948 to 1980 as to the matters to be stated in group accounts " ; and
  (b) for paragraphs (a) and (b) there shall be substituted the following paragraphs: —

  " (a) on conviction on indictment, to a fine ;

  (b) on summary conviction, to a fine not exceeding the statutory maximum (within the meaning of the Companies Act 1980).".

21. In section 165 (circumstances in which Secretary of State may appoint inspectors to investigate affairs of company)—
  (a) at the beginning there shall be inserted the word " (1) " ;

(*b*) for paragraph (*b*)(i) there shall be substituted the following sub-paragraph:—

" (i) that its affairs are being or have been conducted with intent to defraud its creditors or the creditors of any other person or otherwise for a fraudulent or unlawful purpose or in a manner which is unfairly prejudicial to some part of its members, or that any actual or proposed act or omission of the company (including an act or omission on its behalf) is or would be so prejudicial, or that it was formed for any fraudulent or unlawful purpose ; or " ; and

(*c*) at the end there shall be added the following subsection—

" (2) The power conferred by subsection (1)(*b*) above shall be exercisable with respect to a body corporate notwithstanding that it is in course of being voluntarily wound up ; and the reference in sub-paragraph (i) of that paragraph to the members of a company shall have effect as if it included a reference to any person who is not a member but to whom shares in the company have been transferred or transmitted by operation of law.".

22. In section 183(1) (appointment of directors to be voted on individually), for the words " a company other than a private company " there shall be substituted the words " a public company ".

23. In section 185(8) (companies to which provisions as to retirement of directors under age limit apply), for the words from " if it is not " to " rank as a private company " there shall be substituted the words " if it is a public company or, being a private company, it is a subsidiary of a public company or of a body corporate registered under the law relating to companies for the time being in force in Northern Ireland as a public company ".

24. In section 196(1) (particulars in accounts of directors' salaries, etc.), for the words " laid before it in general meeting " there shall be substituted the words " prepared under section 1 of the Companies Act 1976 ".

25. In section 199(3) (general notice of director's interest in contract made with a specified company or firm) for all the words before the proviso there shall be substituted the following provision—

" For the purposes of this section, a general notice given to the directors of a company by a director to the effect that—

(*a*) he is a member of a specified company or firm and is to be regarded as interested in any contract which may, after the date of the notice, be made with that company or firm ; or

(*b*) he is to be regarded as interested in any contract which may after the date of the notice be made with a specified person who is connected with him (within the meaning of section 64 of the Companies Act 1980) ;

shall be deemed to be a sufficient declaration of interest in relation to any such contract.".

26. In section 205(*b*) (exclusion of prohibition on indemnifying officers of company against liabilities) after the words "this Act" there shall be inserted the words "or section 36 of the Companies Act 1980".

27. In section 222 (grounds for winding up), for paragraph (*b*) there shall be substituted the following paragraphs—

"(*b*) being a public company which was registered as such on its original incorporation, the company has not been issued with a certificate under section 4 of the Companies Act 1980 and more than a year has expired since it was so registered ;

(*bb*) after the end of the transitional period, within the meaning of that Act, the company is an old public company within the meaning of that Act ; ".

28. In section 224(1) (persons who may apply for winding up), for paragraph (*b*) of the proviso there shall be substituted the following paragraph—

"(*b*) if the ground of the petition is that in section 222(*b*) or (*bb*) of this Act, a winding up petition may be presented by the Secretary of State ; and ".

29. In section 382 (companies capable of being registered under Part VIII), in subsection (1)(*a*) and (*b*) for the word "seven" there shall be substituted the word "two", and at the end of that section there shall be added the following subsection—

"(3) Before a company is registered in pursuance of this section, it shall deliver to the registrar—

(*a*) a statement that the registered office of the company is to be situated in England, or in Wales or in Scotland, as the case may be ; and

(*b*) a statement specifying the intended situation of the company's registered office after registration.".

30. In section 384(*c*) (statement of particulars to be delivered to registrar in connection with registration of a joint stock company), sub-paragraph (iii) shall have effect in relation to a company which is intended to be registered as a public company as if the words from "with" to the end were omitted.

31. Section 390 (certificate of registration of companies registered under Part VIII) shall be renumbered as subsection (1) of that section, and after that subsection there shall be added the following subsection : —

"(2) A certificate given under this section in respect of a company shall be conclusive evidence that the requirements of this Part of this Act in respect of registration and of matters precedent and incidental thereto have been complied with.".

32. In section 394 (effect of registration under Part VIII)—

(*a*) in subsection (2) after the words "amount of the guarantee" there shall be inserted the words "and including the

statement under section 382(3)(*a*) of this Act and any
statement under section 384(*c*) of this Act " ;

    (*b*) in subsection (6) for the words from " this Act " to " there-
of " there shall be substituted the words " the Companies
Acts 1948 to 1980 (apart from those of section 75(5) of
the Companies Act 1980) ".

33. In section 451 (annual report by Secretary of State) for the
words " and the Companies Act 1976 " there shall be substituted the
words ", the Companies Act 1976 and the Companies Act 1980 ".

34. In section 454(2) (power to alter Tables and forms), after
paragraph (*b*) there shall be inserted the words " and

    (*c*) alter the forms set out in Schedule 1 to the Companies Act
1980 ; ".

35. In section 455(1) (interpretation), in the definition of " articles ",
for the words " special resolution " there shall be substituted the
words " a resolution of the company ".

36.—(1) In Schedule 1, Part I of Table A (regulations for the
management of a company limited by shares not being a private
company) shall be amended in accordance with the following sub-
paragraphs and shall apply in relation to private companies limited
by shares as it applies in relation to public companies so limited, and
accordingly Part II of that Table shall cease to have effect.

(2) In regulation 53 (quorums), for the words from " three "
onwards there shall be substituted the words " two members present
in person or by proxy shall be a quorum ".

(3) In regulation 58(*b*) (number of members who may demand a
poll) for the word " three " there shall be substituted the word
" two ".

(4) After regulation 73, there shall be inserted the following regulation : —

    " 73A. Subject to the provisions of the Companies Acts 1948
to 1980, a resolution in writing signed by all the members for
the time being entitled to receive notice of and to attend and
vote at general meetings (or being corporations by their duly
authorised representatives) shall be as valid and effective as if
the same had been passed at a general meeting of the company
duly convened and held.".

(5) In regulation 79 (borrowing powers), after the words " thereof
and " there shall be inserted the words ", subject to section 14 of
the Companies Act 1980.".

(6) In regulation 80 (powers and duties of the directors) for the
word " Act ", wherever occurring, there shall be substituted the words
" Companies Acts 1948 to 1980 ".

(7) For regulation 116 there shall be substituted the following
regulation—

    " 116. No dividend or interim dividend shall be paid other-
wise than in accordance with the provisions of Part III of the
Companies Act 1980 which apply to the company.".

(8) In the proviso to regulation 128 (power to apply reserve funds in paying up bonus shares) for the word " issued " there shall be substituted the word " allotted ".

SCH. 3

(9) The following regulation is added after regulation 128:

" 128A. The company in general meeting may on the recommendation of the directors resolve that it is desirable to capitalise any part of the amount for the time being standing to the credit of any of the company's reserve accounts or to the credit of the profit and loss account which is not available for distribution by applying such sum in paying up in full unissued shares to be allotted as fully paid bonus shares to those members of the company who would have been entitled to that sum if it were distributed by way of dividend (and in the same proportions), and the directors shall give effect to such resolution.".

(10) In regulation 129 (duties of directors on resolutions under regulation 128) for the words from the beginning to " have been passed " there shall be substituted the words " Whenever a resolution is passed in pursuance of regulation 128 or 128A above.".

37. In regulations 10 and 15(*b*) of Table C in Schedule 1 (quorum and minimum number of members who may demand a poll at a meeting of a company limited by guarantee), for the word " three " there shall be substituted the word " two ".

38. In Part II of Schedule 6, in the form of the annual return (which was substituted by the Companies (Annual Return) Regulations 1977), in note 14 (which relates to the entries in respect of the directors of a public company or a private company which is a subsidiary of a public company), for the words from " which is not a private company " to " rank as a private company " there shall be substituted the words " which is a public company or, being a private company, is a subsidiary of a public company or of a body corporate registered under the law relating to companies for the time being in force in Northern Ireland as a public company.".

S.I. 1977/1368.

39.—(1) Schedule 8, and accordingly that Schedule as set out in Schedule 2 to the 1967 Act, shall be amended as follows.

(2) In paragraph 11 (miscellaneous requirements as to balance sheet), after sub-paragraph (2) there shall be inserted the following sub-paragraphs:—

" (2A) Where shares in a public company, other than an old public company within the meaning of the Companies Act 1980 (the " 1980 Act ") are acquired by the company by forfeiture or surrender in lieu of forfeiture or in pursuance of section 35(2) of the 1980 Act or are acquired by another person in circumstances where paragraph (*c*) or (*d*) of section 37(1) of the 1980 Act applies or are made subject to a lien or charge taken (whether expressly or otherwise) by the company and permitted by section 38(2)(*a*), (*c*) or (*d*) of the 1980 Act—

(*a*) the number and nominal value of the shares so acquired by the company, acquired by another person in such circumstances and so charge respectively during the financial year ;

(b) the maximum number and nominal value of shares which, having been so acquired by the company, acquired by another person in such circumstances or so charged (whether or not during the financial year) are held at any time by the company or that other person during that year ;

(c) the number and nominal value of the shares so acquired by the company, acquired by another person in such circumstances or so charged (whether or not during that year) which are disposed of by the company or that other person or cancelled by the company during that year ;

(d) where the number and nominal value of the shares of any particular description are stated in pursuance of any of the preceding paragraphs, the percentage of the called-up share capital which shares of that description represent ;

(e) where any of the shares have been so charged, the amount of the charge in each case ;

(f) where any of the shares have been disposed of by the company or the person who acquired them in such circumstances for money or money's worth, the amount or value of the consideration in each case.

(2B) Any distribution made by an investment company within the meaning of Part III of the Companies Act 1980 which reduces the amount of its net assets to less than the aggregate of its called-up share capital and undistributable reserves.

In this sub-paragraph 'net assets' and 'called-up share capital' have the same meanings as in the Companies Act 1980 and 'undistributable reserves' has the same meaning as in section 40 of that Act."

40. In Schedule 14 (provisions applied to unregistered companies), in column 2 of the entry relating to registration of documents, enforcement and other supplemental matters—

(a) for the words " to four hundred and thirty-eight " there shall be substituted the words " 437 " ; and

(b) for the words from " section four hundred and fifty-five " onwards there shall be substituted the words " and section 455 ".

COMPANIES ACT 1967 (C. 81)

41.—(1) In section 3(1), 4(1), and (2), 5(1), 6(1), 7(1) and 8(1), (statements and particulars to be included in company's accounts), for the words " laid before it in general meeting " there shall be substituted the words " prepared under section 1 of the Companies Act 1976 ".

(2) In sections 3(5)(b) and 4(5)(b), for the words " its accounts " there shall be substituted the words " copies of its accounts ".

(3) In section 14(3) (auditors' report)—

(a) in paragraph (a) for the words " principal Act and this Act and " there shall be substituted the words " Companies Acts 1948 to 1980 and, without prejudice to the foregoing," ; and

(b) in paragraph (b) for the words " principal Act and this Act " there shall be substituted the words " Companies Acts 1948 to 1980 ".

42. In section 23(1) (penalties for default in relation to directors' report) for paragraphs (a) and (b) there shall be substituted the following paragraphs : —

" (a) on conviction on indictment, to a fine ;

(b) on summary conviction, to a fine not exceeding the statutory maximum (within the meaning of the Companies Act 1980) ".

43. No public company may apply under section 43 (limited companies may be re-registered as unlimited) to be re-registered under the 1948 Act as an unlimited company.

44. In section 44 (unlimited companies may be re-registered as limited), for subsection (2) there shall be substituted the following subsection—

" (2) The said requirement is that the resolution must state whether the company is to be limited by shares or by guarantee and—

(a) if it is to be limited by shares, must state what the share capital is to be and provide for the making of such alterations in the memorandum as are necessary to bring it, both in substance and in form, into conformity with the requirements of this Act with respect to the memorandum of a company so limited, and such alterations in the articles as are requisite in the circumstances ;

(b) if it is to be limited by guarantee, must provide for the making of such alterations in its memorandum and articles as are necessary to bring them, both in substance and in form, into conformity with the requirements of this Act with respect to the memorandum and articles of a company so limited.".

EUROPEAN COMMUNITIES ACT 1972 (C. 68)

45.—(1) In section 9(3) (documents of which notice must be published by the registrar in the Gazette) after paragraph (d) there shall be inserted the following paragraphs : —

" (da) any written statement delivered in pursuance of section 4(2) of the Companies Act 1980 ;

(db) any report as to the value of a non-cash asset under section 24 or 26 of the Companies Act 1980 ;

(dc) any copy of a resolution of a public company which gives, varies, revokes or renews an authority for the purposes of section 14 of the Companies Act 1980 ;

(dd) any copy of a special resolution of a public company passed under section 18(1), (2) or (3) or the Companies Act 1980 ;

(*de*) any statement or notice delivered by a public company under section 33 of the Companies Act 1980 ;

(*df*) a copy of any resolution or agreement to which section 143 of the Companies Act 1948 applies and which—

(i) states the rights attached to any shares in a public company, other than shares which are, in all respects, uniform (for the purposes of section 33(1) of the Companies Act 1980) with shares previously allotted ;

(ii) varies rights attached to any shares in a public company ; or

(iii) assigns a name or other designation, or a new name or other designation, to any class of shares in a public company ;

(*dg*) any return of allotments of a public company ;

(*dh*) any notification of the redemption of preference shares under section 62 of the Companies Act 1948 by a public company ; ".

(2) In section 9(7) (particulars to be mentioned in company's letters and order forms) for the word " and " at the end of paragraph (*b*) there shall be substituted the following paragraph:—

" (*bb*) in the case of an investment company within the meaning of Part III of the Companies Act 1980, the fact that it is such an investment company ; and ".

Insurance Companies Act 1974 (c. 49)

46. In section 17(1) (audit of accounts) for the words " 1976 " there shall be substituted the words " 1980 ".

Iron and Steel Act 1975 (c. 64)

47. In Schedule 5 (constitution and proceedings of publicly-owned companies), for paragraph 1 there shall be substituted the following paragraph: —

" 1. This Schedule applies to any publicly-owned company that is a private company within the meaning of the Companies Acts 1948 to 1980 (in this Schedule referred to as a relevant company)." ;

and in that Schedule, for the words " publicly-owned company " wherever occurring there shall be substituted the words " relevant company ".

Stock Exchange (Completion of Bargains) Act 1976 (c. 47)

48. In section 3(3) and (4) (computerised records), for the words " 1976 " there shall be substituted the words " 1980 ".

Companies Act 1976 (c. 69)

49. In section 9(1) (accounts of overseas companies), for the words " the Act of 1948 and this Act " there shall be substituted the words " the Companies Acts ".

50. In section 30(2) (power, exercisable by companies registered before the coming into operation of that section and within twelve months of its coming into operation, to provide that the registered

office of the company is to be situated in Wales), the words " registered before the coming into operation of this section " and " within the period of twelve months beginning with the coming into operation of this section " shall be omitted.

51. In section 44(1) (interpretation), in the definition of the Companies Acts, after the words " 1976 " there shall be inserted the words " and the Companies Act 1980 ".

52. In Schedule 1 (prescribed forms), in the entries relating to sections 95(8) and 106A(7) of the 1948 Act, for the words " in both places " there shall be substituted the words " in the first place ".

SCHEDULE 4

REPEALS

Chapter	Short Title	Extent of Repeal
11 & 12 Geo. 6. c. 38.	Companies Act 1948.	In section 1(1), the words from " Any seven " to " private company ". In section 10, in subsection (1) the words " or add to " and in subsection (2) the words " or addition ". In section 13(2), the words " and having perpetual succession and a common seal ". Section 15. Sections 28 to 30. Section 42. In section 47, subsection (3) and in subsection (6) the words " except subsection (3) thereof ". Section 48. In section 55(2), paragraph (*b*) and the word " and " preceding it. Section 57. Section 65. Section 109. Section 128. Section 130. Section 181. In section 182(1), the words from " Without " to " section ". Section 190. Section 197. In section 198, in subsection (1) the words from " and of " to the end, and in subsection (3), paragraph (*a*) and in paragraph (*b*) the words " and the last foregoing section ".'. Section 210.

Chapter	Short title	Extent of repeal
11 & 12 Geo. 6 c. 38—*cont.*	Companies Act 1948—*cont.*	In section 222, in paragraph (*d*), the words " in the case of a private company " and the words from " or " to " seven ". In section 224, in subsection (1), in paragraph (*a*)(i), the words " in the case of a private company " and the words " or, in the case of any other company, below seven"; and subsection (3). Section 225(3). Section 438. Section 440(1). In section 454(2)(*b*) the words " or add to ". In section 455(1), the definitions of " private company ", " statutory meeting " and " statutory report ". In Schedule 1, in Part I of Table A— (*a*) in regulation 4, the words " (unless otherwise provided by the terms of issue of the shares of that class) ", and the second sentence; (*b*) in regulation 11, the words from " and the company " to " to the company "; (*c*) in regulation 54, the words from " and if " onwards; and Part II of Table A; and in Table C, in regulation 11, the words from " and if " onwards. Schedule 3. Schedule 5. In Schedule 6, the forms of the certificate to be given by the director and the secretary of every private company and the further certificate to be given as aforesaid if the number of members of the company exceeds fifty. Schedule 15.
1961 c. 46.	Companies (Floating Charges) (Scotland) Act 1961.	Section 7(*d*).
1967 c. 81.	Companies Act 1967.	Section 14(8)(*b*). Section 16(1)(*c*). Section 26(8)(a). Section 35(2). Section 38.

Chapter	Short title	Extent of repeal
1967 c. 81— *cont.*	Companies Act 1967— *cont.*	In section 43, in subsections (2)(*b*) and 3(*d*) the words " and additions thereto " and in subsection (4)(*b*) the words " and additions " and " or added to ". Section 49(1). In section 56(2), the words from " and in section 149(7) " onwards. In Schedule 4, the entry relating to section 149(6) of the Companies Act 1948.
1976 c. 69.	Companies Act 1976.	Section 21(6). Section 23(7). In section 30(2), the words " registered before the coming into operation of this section " and " within the period of twelve months beginning with the coming into operation of this section ". In Schedule 1, the entries relating to sections 15(2) and 181(1)(*a*) of the 1948 Act. In Schedule 2, the entry relating to section 15(2) of the 1948 Act.
1977 c. 45.	Criminal Law Act 1977.	In section 63(2), the words " Companies Act 1967 ". In Schedule 12 the entry relating to the Companies Act 1967.

NOTE:

  (*a*) The repeal by this Schedule of section 57 of the 1948 Act shall have effect subject to the saving in section 21(4) above;

  (*b*) The repeal by this Schedule of section 197 of the 1948 Act and section 16(1)(*c*) of the 1967 Act shall have effect subject to the saving in section 66(2) above.

  (*c*) The repeal by this Schedule of section 210 of the 1948 Act and section 35(2) of the 1967 Act shall have effect subject to the saving in section 75(11) above;

  (*d*) The repeals made by this Schedule in Table A in Schedule 1 to the 1948 Act are subject to the saving in section 88(4) above;

  (*e*) The repeal by this Schedule of section 49(1) of the 1967 Act (and the consequential repeals made in the Criminal Law Act 1977) shall have effect subject to the saving in section 80(5) above.

Consular Fees Act 1980

1980 CHAPTER 23

An Act to re-enact with amendments so much of the Consular Salaries and Fees Act 1891 as relates to consular fees together with certain enactments amending that Act.   [1st May 1980]

BE IT ENACTED by the Queen's most Excellent Majesty, by and with the advice and consent of the Lords Spiritual and Temporal, and Commons, in this present Parliament assembled, and by the authority of the same, as follows:—

Fees for doing consular and similar acts.

1.—(1) Her Majesty may, by Order in Council, prescribe the fees to be levied by persons authorised by the Secretary of State to exercise consular functions, or functions in the United Kingdom which correspond with consular functions, for doing anything in the exercise of such functions.

1968 c. 18.

(2) "Consular functions" means any of the functions described in Article 5 of the Vienna Convention on Consular Relations set out in Schedule 1 to the Consular Relations Act 1968 but subsection (1) above applies in relation to persons who are not as well as in relation to persons who are consular officers.

(3) All fees prescribed under subsection (1) above shall be levied, accounted for and applied, and may be remitted, in accordance with regulations made by the Secretary of State by statutory instrument with the approval of the Treasury.

(4) Copies of or extracts from the table of fees so prescribed shall be exhibited in every office where such fees are levied.

(5) The following enactments (which are replaced by the foregoing provisions of this section) are hereby repealed, namely—

    (*a*) the Consular Salaries and Fees Act 1891;   1891 c. 36.

    (*b*) section 8 of the Fees (Increase) Act 1923; and   1923 c. 4.

    (*c*) section 13(4) of the Consular Relations Act 1968;   1968 c. 18.

and in section 20 of the Foreign Marriage Act 1892 and section 1892 c. 23. 1(4) of the Marriage with Foreigners Act 1906 (which make 1906 c. 40. consular fees chargeable for things done under those Acts) for the words " Consular Salaries and Fees Act 1891 " there shall be substituted the words " Consular Fees Act 1980 ".

2. This Act may be cited as the Consular Fees Act 1980.   Short title.

Limitation Amendment Act 1980

1980 CHAPTER 24

An Act to amend the law with respect to the limitation of actions and arbitrations and with respect to the liability of a debtor who becomes his creditor's executor by representation or administrator.   [1st May 1980]

BE IT ENACTED by the Queen's most Excellent Majesty, by and with the advice and consent of the Lords Spiritual and Temporal, and Commons, in this present Parliament assembled, and by the authority of the same, as follows:—

Miscellaneous amendments of Limitation Act 1939

1. After section 2 of the Limitation Act 1939 (referred to below in this Act as " the principal Act ") there shall be inserted the following section—

Limitation in case of certain loans.

1939 c. 21.

" Limitation in case of certain loans.

2AA.—(1) Subject to subsection (3) of this section, section 2(1)(*a*) of this Act shall not bar the right of action on a contract of loan to which this section applies.

(2) This section applies to any contract of loan which—

    (*a*) does not provide for repayment of the debt on or before a fixed or determinable date ; and

    (*b*) does not effectively (whether or not it purports to do so) make the obligation to repay the debt conditional on a demand for repayment made by or on behalf of the creditor or on any other matter ;

except where in connection with taking the loan the debtor enters into any collateral obligation to pay the amount of the debt or any part of it (as, for example, by delivering a promissory note as security for the debt) on terms which would exclude the application of this section to the contract of loan if they applied directly to repayment of the debt.

(3) Where a demand in writing for repayment of the debt under a contract of loan to which this section applies is made by or on behalf of the creditor (or, where there are joint creditors, by or on behalf of any one of them) section 2(1)(*a*) of this Act shall thereupon apply as if the cause of action to recover the debt had accrued on the date on which the demand was made.

(4) In this section ' promissory note ' has the same meaning as in the Bills of Exchange Act 1882 ".

Limitation in case of theft.

2. After section 3 of the principal Act (limitation in case of successive conversions and extinction of title of owner of converted goods) there shall be inserted the following section—

"Limitation in case of theft.

3A.—(1) The right of any person from whom a chattel is stolen to bring an action in respect of the theft shall not be subject to the time limits under sections 2(1)(*a*) and 3(1) of this Act, but if his title to the chattel is extinguished under section 3(2) of this Act he may not bring an action in respect of a theft preceding the loss of his title, unless the theft in question preceded the conversion from which time began to run for the purposes of section 3(2).

(2) Subsection (1) above shall apply to any conversion related to the theft of a chattel as it applies to the theft of a chattel ; and, except as provided below, every conversion following the theft of a chattel before the person from whom it is stolen recovers possession of it shall be regarded for the purposes of this section as related to the theft.

If anyone purchases the stolen chattel in good faith neither the purchase nor any conversion following it shall be regarded as related to the theft.

(3) Any cause of action accruing in respect of the theft or any conversion related to the theft of a chattel to any person from whom the chattel is stolen shall be disregarded for the purpose of applying section 3(1) or (2) of this Act to his case.

(4) Where in any action brought in respect of the conversion of a chattel it is proved that the chattel was stolen from the plaintiff or anyone through whom he claims it shall be presumed that any conversion following the theft is related to the theft unless the contrary is shown.

(5) In this section ' theft ' includes—

    (*a*) any conduct outside England and Wales which would be theft if committed in England and Wales ; and

    (*b*) obtaining any chattel (in England and Wales or elsewhere) in the circumstances described in section 15(1) of the Theft Act 1968 (obtaining by deception) or by blackmail within the meaning of section 21 of that Act ;

and references in this section to a chattel being ' stolen ' shall be construed accordingly."

3.—(1) Subsection (1) of section 9 of the principal Act (special rule for accrual of the right of action in respect of the reversion on a tenancy at will) shall cease to have effect. Accrual of right of action in case of certain tenancies.

(2) In subsection (3) of that section (accrual of right of action where rent is received by a person wrongfully claiming to be entitled to the land in reversion), for the words " twenty shillings " there shall be substituted the words " ten pounds a year ".

(3) Subsection (2) above shall not affect the operation of section 9(3) in any case where the lease in question was granted before the commencement of this Act.

(4) For subsection (4) of that section there shall be substituted the following subsection—

    " (4) Subsection (3) of this section shall not apply to any lease granted by the Crown ".

4. The following subsection shall be added at the end of section 10 of the principal Act (right of action not to accrue or continue unless there is adverse possession)— Licence not to be implied by law to defeat adverse possession.

    " (4) For the purpose of determining whether a person occupying any land is in adverse possession of the land it shall not be assumed by implication of law that his occupation is by permission of the person entitled to the land merely by virtue of the fact that his occupation is not inconsistent with the latter's present or future enjoyment of the land.

This provision shall not be taken as prejudicing a finding to the effect that a person's occupation of any land is by implied permission of the person entitled to the land in any case where such a finding is justified on the actual facts of the case."

Relief for
trustee
retaining
trust property
as beneficiary.
5.—(1) After subsection (1) of section 19 of the principal Act (limitation of actions in respect of trust property) there shall be inserted the following subsection—

" (1A) Where a trustee who is also a beneficiary under the trust receives or retains trust property or its proceeds as his share on a distribution of trust property under the trust, his liability in any action brought by virtue of paragraph (b) of the foregoing subsection to recover that property or its proceeds after the expiration of the period of limitation prescribed by this Act for bringing an action to recover trust property shall be limited to the excess over his proper share.

This subsection only applies if the trustee acted honestly and reasonably in making the distribution."

(2) In sections 7(1) and 20 of that Act, for the words " subsection (1) " there shall be substituted the words " subsections (1) and (1A) ".

Effect of
acknowledge-
ment or part
payment.
6.—(1) The following subsection shall be added at the end of section 23 of the principal Act (fresh accrual of action on acknowledgement or part payment)—

" (5) Subject to the proviso to the last foregoing subsection, a current period of limitation may be repeatedly extended under this section by further acknowledgements or payments, but a right of action, once barred by this Act, shall not be revived by any subsequent acknowledgement or payment."

(2) In subsection (4) of that section the words " the last " (which are redundant in view of the provision made by subsection (1) above) shall be omitted.

(3) In section 25 of that Act, the provisos to subsections (5) and (6) (which respectively limit the effect of an acknowledgement or payment made after the expiration of the period of limitation prescribed for the bringing of an action to recover a debt or other liquidated pecuniary claim) shall cease to have effect.

(4) In section 33(a) of that Act (actions already barred) the words from " except " to " Act " shall cease to have effect.

(5) Nothing in this section (or in the corresponding repeals made by this Act) shall affect the operation of the principal Act in relation to any acknowledgement or payment made before the commencement of this Act.

7. For section 26 of the principal Act there shall be substituted the following section—

26.—(1) Subject to subsection (3) of this section, where in the case of any action for which a period of limitation is prescribed by this Act, either—

(a) the action is based upon the fraud of the defendant ; or

(b) any fact relevant to the plaintiff's right of action has been deliberately concealed from him by the defendant ; or

(c) the action is for relief from the consequences of a mistake ;

the period of limitation shall not begin to run until the plaintiff has discovered the fraud, concealment or mistake (as the case may be) or could with reasonable diligence have discovered it.

(2) For the purposes of the last foregoing subsection, deliberate commission of a breach of duty in circumstances in which it is unlikely to be discovered for some time amounts to deliberate concealment of the facts involved in that breach of duty.

(3) Nothing in this section shall enable any action—

(a) to recover, or recover the value of, any property ; or

(b) to enforce any charge against, or set aside any transaction affecting, any property ;

to be brought against the purchaser of the property or any person claiming through him in any case where the property has been purchased for valuable consideration by an innocent third party since the fraud or concealment or (as the case may be) the transaction in which the mistake was made took place.

(4) A purchaser is an innocent third party for the purposes of this section—

(a) in the case of fraud or concealment of any fact relevant to the plaintiff's right of action, if he was not a party to the fraud or (as the case may be) to the concealment of that fact and did not at the time of the purchase know or have reason to believe that the fraud or concealment had taken place ; and (*b*) in the case of mistake, if he did not at the time of the purchase know or have reason to believe that the mistake had been made.

(5) References in this section to the defendant include references to the defendant's agent and to any person through whom the defendant claims and his agent."

Limitation in case of new claims in pending actions: rules of court.

8. For section 28 of the principal Act (provisions as to set-off or counterclaim) there shall be substituted the following section—

"New claims in pending actions: rules of court.

28.—(1) For the purposes of this Act, any new claim made in the course of any action shall be deemed to be a separate action and to have been commenced—

(*a*) in the case of a new claim made in or by way of third party proceedings, on the date on which those proceedings were commenced ; and

(*b*) in any other case, on the same date as the original action.

(2) In this section a new claim means any claim by way of set-off or counterclaim, and any claim involving either—

(*a*) the addition or substitution of a new cause of action ; or

(*b*) the addition or substitution of a new party ; and " third party proceedings " means any proceedings brought in the course of any action by any party to the action against a person not previously a party to the action, other than proceedings brought by joining any such person as defendant to any claim already made in the original action by the party bringing the proceedings.

(3) Except as provided by section 2D of this Act or by rules of court, neither the High Court nor any county court shall allow a new claim within subsection (1)(*b*) of this section, other than an original set-off or counterclaim, to be made in the course of any action after the expiry of any time limit under this Act which would affect a new action to enforce that claim.

For the purposes of this subsection, a claim is an original set-off or an original counterclaim if it is a claim made by way of set-off or (as the case may be) by way of counterclaim by a party who has not previously made any claim in the action.

(4) Rules of court may provide for allowing a new claim to which the last foregoing subsection applies

to be made as there mentioned, but only if the conditions specified in the next following subsection are satisfied, and subject to any further restrictions the rules may impose.

(5) The conditions referred to in the last foregoing subsection are the following—

(*a*) in the case of a claim involving a new cause of action, if the new cause of action arises out of the same facts or substantially the same facts as are already in issue on any claim previously made in the original action ; and

(*b*) in the case of a claim involving a new party, if the addition or substitution of the new party is necessary for the determination of the original action.

(6) The addition or substitution of a new party shall not be regarded for the purposes of subsection (5)(*b*) of this section as necessary for the determination of the original action unless either—

(*a*) the new party is substituted for a party whose name was given in any claim made in the original action in mistake for the new party's name ; or

(*b*) any claim already made in the original action cannot be maintained by or against an existing party unless the new party is joined or substituted as plaintiff or defendant in that action.

(7) Subject to subsection (4) of this section, rules of court may provide for allowing a party to any action to claim relief in a new capacity in respect of a new cause of action notwithstanding that he had no title to make that claim at the date of the commencement of the action.

This subsection shall not be taken as prejudicing the power of rules of court to provide for allowing a party to claim relief in a new capacity without adding or substituting a new cause of action.

(8) Subsections (3) to (7) of this section shall apply in relation to a new claim made in the course of third party proceedings as if those proceedings were the original action, and subject to such other modifications as may be prescribed by rules of court in any case or class of case.

(9) In this section 'rules of court' means rules made under section 99 of the Supreme Court of Judicature (Consolidation) Act 1925 or section 102 of the County Courts Act 1959 (as the case may require).".

Admiralty actions.

9.—(1) Subject to section 32 of the principal Act (saving for other limitation enactments), that Act shall apply to any cause of action within the Admiralty jurisdiction of the High Court as it applies to any other cause of action.

(2) Sections 2(6) and 18(6) of that Act (which respectively exclude the application of section 2(1) to certain causes of action within the Admiralty jurisdiction of the High Court and exclude the application of section 18 to a mortgage or charge on a ship) shall cease to have effect.

Miscellaneous and supplementary

Debtor who becomes creditor's executor by representation or administrator to account for debt to estate.
1925 c. 23.

10. After section 21 of the Administration of Estates Act 1925 (rights and liabilities of administrator) there shall be inserted the following section—

" Debtor who becomes creditor's executor by representation or administrator to account for debt to estate.

21A.—(1) Subject to subsection (2) of this section, where a debtor becomes his deceased creditor's executor by representation or administrator—

> (a) his debt shall thereupon be extinguished; but
>
> (b) he shall be accountable for the amount of the debt as part of the creditor's estate in any case where he would be so accountable if he had been appointed as an executor by the creditor's will.

(2) Subsection (1) of this section does not apply where the debtor's authority to act as executor or administrator is limited to part only of the creditor's estate which does not include the debt ; and a debtor whose debt is extinguished by virtue of paragraph (a) shall not be accountable for its amount by virtue of paragraph (b) of that subsection in any case where the debt was barred by the Limitation Act 1939 before he became the creditor's executor or administrator.

(3) In this section 'debt' includes any liability, and 'debtor' and 'creditor' shall be construed accordingly."

Application to the Crown.

11. Without prejudice to the application of section 30 of the principal Act in relation to any provision inserted in that Act by any of the preceding provisions of this Act, that section shall apply for the purposes of this Act as it applies for the purposes of the principal Act.

12.—(1) Nothing in any provision of this Act shall—   Transitional provisions.

    (*a*) enable any action to be brought which was barred by the principal Act before that provision comes into force; or

    (*b*) affect any action or arbitration commenced before that provision comes into force or the title to any property which is the subject of any such action or arbitration.

(2) Subject to subsection (1) above and sections 3(3) and 6(5) of this Act, the provisions of this Act shall have effect in relation to causes of action accruing and things taking place before, as well as in relation to causes of action accruing and things taking place after, those provisions respectively come into force.

(3) In this section " action " has the same meaning as in the principal Act.

13.—(1) The principal Act shall have effect subject to the amendments specified in Schedule 1 to this Act, being amendments consequential on the provisions of this Act and amendments to facilitate consolidation of the Limitation Acts 1939 to 1975 and this Act.   Amendments and repeals.

(2) The provisions of the principal Act specified in Schedule 2 to this Act are hereby repealed to the extent specified in the third column of that Schedule.

14.—(1) This Act may be cited as the Limitation Amendment Act 1980.   Citation, commencement and extent.

(2) This Act and the Limitation Acts 1939 to 1975 may be cited together as the Limitation Acts 1939 to 1980.

(3) This Act, except section 8, shall come into force at the end of the period of three months beginning with the date on which it is passed; and any reference in any provision of this Act to the commencement of this Act is a reference to the date on which that provision comes into force.

(4) Section 8 of this Act shall come into force on such day as the Lord Chancellor may by order made by statutory instrument appoint, and different days may be appointed for different purposes of that section (including its application in relation to different courts or proceedings).

(5) This Act does not extend to Scotland or to Northern Ireland.

SCHEDULES

SCHEDULE 1

AMENDMENTS

1. Any reference below in this Schedule to a numbered section is a reference to the section of that number in the principal Act.

2. In section 2—

    (*a*) subsection (1)(*b*) shall be omitted ;

    (*b*) in subsection (1)(*d*), the words from " other than " to the end shall be omitted ;

    (*c*) subsection (2) shall be omitted ;

    (*d*) in subsection (4), for the word " twelve " there shall be substituted the word " six " ; and

    (*e*) subsection (5) shall be omitted.

3. In section 2A—

    (*a*) in subsection (4) (*b*), for the words from " (if later " to the end there shall be substituted the words " of knowledge (if later) of the person injured " ;

    (*b*) in subsection (7), for the words from " this " to " plaintiff " there shall be substituted the words " subsection (6) above an injury is significant if the person whose date of knowledge is in question " ; and

    (*c*) in subsection (8), for the words " the said sections " there shall be substituted the words " subsection (6) above ".

4. In section 2B—

    (*a*) in subsection (4), for the words " and section 2A " there shall be substituted the words " (whether passed before or after the passing of this Act), and sections 2 and 2A " ; and

    (*b*) in subsection (5), for the words from " section " to " applies " there shall be substituted the words " sections 22 and 28 of this Act apply ".

5. In section 3—

    (*a*) the words " or wrongful detention " and the words " or detention " shall be omitted wherever they occur in subsection (1) ; and

    (*b*) in subsection (2), the words from " and for " to " aforesaid " shall be omitted.

6. Section 13 shall cease to have effect.

7. In section 17, the words " or dower " shall be omitted.

8. After section 20 there shall be inserted the following section—

"Limitation of actions for an account.   20A. An action for an account shall not be brought after the expiration of any time limit under this Act which is applicable to the claim which is the basis of the duty to account."

9. In section 25—

    (*a*) in subsection (2) after the word " or " in the first place where it occurs there shall be inserted the words " any other person liable for the debt or by " ; and

    (*b*) in subsection (4), for the words " right to " there shall be substituted the words " equity of ".

10. In section 27—

    (*a*) in subsection (1), after the word " actions " there shall be inserted the words " (whether passed before or after the passing of this Act) " ; and

    (*b*) in subsection (5), after the word " arbitration " in the second place where it occurs there shall be inserted the word " agreement ".

11. In the proviso to section 30(1), for the words from " Customs Acts " to "excise " there shall be substituted the words " customs and excise Acts (within the meaning of the Customs and Excise Management Act 1979) ".

12. In section 31(1)—

    (*a*) in the definition of " land " the words from " (except " to " sole) " shall be omitted ; and

    (*b*) in the definition of " rentcharge " the words from " a modus " to " sole or " shall be omitted.

13. In section 31(3) for the words from " but " to " presumed " there shall be substituted the words " a person is of unsound mind if he is a person who, by reason of mental disorder within the meaning of the Mental Health Act 1959, is incapable of managing and administering his property and affairs ; and, without prejudice to the generality of the foregoing provision, a person shall be conclusively presumed for the purposes of that subsection ".

14. In section 31(7)—

    (*a*) paragraph (*a*) shall be omitted ; and

    (*b*) in paragraph (*c*), the word " dower " shall be omitted in both places where it occurs.

15. In section 32 the references to any other enactment shall be construed as references to any other enactment, whether passed before or after the passing of the principal Act (or this Act).

SCHEDULE 2

ENACTMENTS REPEALED

Chapter	Short title	Extent of repeal
2 & 3 Geo. 6. c. 21.	The Limitation Act 1939.	In section 2, subsections (1)(*b*), (2), (5) and (6) and in subsection (1)(*d*) the words from " other than " to the end. In section 3, the words " or wrongful detention " and " or detention " wherever they occur in subsection (1), and in subsection (2) the words from " and for " to " aforesaid ". Section 9(1). Section 13. In section 17, the words " or dower". Section 18(6). In section 22, paragraph (*e*) of the proviso. In section 23(4), the words " the last ". In section 25, the provisos to subsections (5) and (6). In section 31(1), the words from " (except " to " sole) " in the definition of " land " and the words from " a modus " to " sole or " in the definition of " rentcharge ". In section 31(7), paragraph (*a*), and in paragraph (*c*), the word " dower" in both places where it occurs. In section 33(*a*), the words from " except " to " Act ".

Insurance Companies Act 1980

1980 CHAPTER 25

An Act to extend the Insurance Companies Act 1974 to
Northern Ireland, to amend that Act with respect to the
functions of the Industrial Assurance Commissioner,
and for connected purposes.   [1st May 1980]

B E IT ENACTED by the Queen's most Excellent Majesty, by and
with the advice and consent of the Lords Spiritual and
Temporal, and Commons, in this present Parliament
assembled, and by the authority of the same, as follows:—

1. Subject to section 2(1) below—

   (a) the Insurance Companies Act 1974, and

   (b) any other Act to the extent that it amends or extends
that Act,

shall extend to Northern Ireland.

Extension of Insurance Companies Act 1974 to Northern Ireland.
1974 c. 49.

2.—(1) In consequence of section 1 above, the Insurance
Companies Act 1974 shall have effect subject to the amendments
specified in Part I of Schedule 1 to this Act.

(2) The said Act of 1974 shall have effect subject to the other
amendments specified in Part II of the said Schedule 1.

Amendments of the Insurance Companies Act 1974.

3.—(1) The instruments specified in Part I of Schedule 2 to
this Act shall, subject to the modifications thereof specified in
Part II of that Schedule, extend to Northern Ireland.

(2) For the purposes of regulation 6 of the Insurance Companies (Solvency: General Business) Regulations 1977 (which

Extension of certain instruments to Northern Ireland.

1958 c. 45.

1965 c. 2. is extended to Northern Ireland by subsection (1) above) section 4(2) and (3) of the Prevention of Fraud (Investments) Act 1958 and section 14 of the Administration of Justice Act 1965 shall extend to Northern Ireland with the modification that in section 4(2)(*a*) of the said Act of 1958 the reference to the trustee in bankruptcy includes a reference to the assignees in bankruptcy.

S.I. 1978/917. (3) In consequence of subsection (2) above, the Insurance Companies (Deposits) Regulations 1978 shall extend to Northern Ireland.

Consequential amemdments, savings, transitional provisions and repeals.

4.—(1) The enactments specified in Schedule 3 to this Act shall have effect subject to the amendments there specified, being amendments consequential on the provisions of this Act.

(2) The saving and transitional provisions specified in Schedule 4 to this Act shall have effect.

(3) Subject to subsection (2) above, the enactments specified in Schedule 5 to this Act (which include certain spent provisions) are hereby repealed to the extent specified in the third column of that Schedule.

(4) Subject to subsection (2) above, the statutory rules specified in Schedule 6 to this Act are hereby revoked.

Short title, commencement and extent.

5.—(1) This Act may be cited as the Insurance Companies Act 1980.

(2) This Act shall come into operation on such day as the Secretary of State may by order made by statutory instrument appoint.

(3) This Act extends to Northern Ireland.

SCHEDULES

SCHEDULE 1

Section 2.

AMENDMENTS OF THE INSURANCE COMPANIES ACT 1974

PART I

AMENDMENTS OF THAT ACT CONSEQUENTIAL ON ITS EXTENSION TO NORTHERN IRELAND

1. In section 2—

   (*a*) in subsection (1)—

   (i) for " Great Britain " where it first occurs substitute " the United Kingdom " ;

   (ii) in paragraph (*b*), for the words from " 3rd November " onwards substitute—

   " (i) 3rd November 1966 was carrying on in Great Britain, or

   (ii) 21st December 1967 was carrying on in Northern Ireland,

   insurance business (whether of that class or not) " ;

   (iii) in paragraph (*e*) after " 1974) " insert " or, in Northern Ireland, a body which is, or is deemed to be, registered under the Acts relating to trade unions " and for " or association " substitute " , association or body " ;

   (*b*) in subsection (2)—

   (i) for " Great Britain " substitute " the United Kingdom " ;

   (ii) in paragraph (*b*) after " 1896 " insert " or the Friendly Societies Act (Northern Ireland) 1970" and for " that Act " substitute " either of those Acts ".

2. In section 3—

   (*a*) in subsection (1)—

   (i) for " Great Britain " where it first occurs substitute " the United Kingdom " and omit " either " ;

   (ii) after paragraph (*a*) insert—

   " (*aa*) it was carrying on in Northern Ireland insurance business of that class immediately before 21st December 1967 (and was entitled to carry on that business under the Assurance Companies Acts (Northern Ireland) 1909 to 1947) ; or " ;

   (*b*) in subsection (2) for " either paragraph " substitute " paragraph (*a*), (*aa*) or (*b*) " and for the words from " in Great Britain " onwards substitute " insurance business (whether of that class or not)—

   (*a*) in Great Britain, immediately before 3rd November 1966, or

S 3

(*b*) in Northern Ireland, immediately before 21st December 1967 ".

3. In sections 4(1)(*a*), 7(3) and (5) and 8(1) for " Great Britain " wherever it occurs substitute " the United Kingdom ".

4. In section 9—
   (*a*) in subsection (1) for " either paragraph " substitute " paragraph (*a*), (*aa*) or (*b*) " and for " Great Britain " substitute " the United Kingdom " ;
   (*b*) in subsection (2) for " Great Britain " substitute " the United Kingdom ".

5. In section 11(4) for " 27th July 1967 " substitute—
" (*a*) 27th July 1967 in Great Britain, or
   (*b*) 4th April 1968 in Northern Ireland ".

6. In section 12—
   (*a*) in subsection (1) for " Great Britain " where it twice occurs substitute " the United Kingdom " ;
   (*b*) in subsection (3) after " association " where it first occurs insert " or, in Northern Ireland, a body which is, or is deemed to be, registered under the Acts relating to trade unions ".

7. In section 20—
   (*a*) in subsection (1) omit " (other than one registered in Northern Ireland) " and after " registrar " insert " in the case of a society registered in Great Britain or with the registrar in the case of a society registered in Northern Ireland," ;
   (*b*) in subsection (3) after " Act) " insert " and section 97(1) of the Industrial and Provident Societies Act (Northern Ireland) 1969 (which confers similar regulation making powers on the Department of Commerce for Northern Ireland) " and for " that Act " in the second place where it occurs substitute " that Act of 1965 or, as the case may be, by the registrar under that Act of 1969 " ;
   (*c*) in subsection (4) at the end add " and ' registrar ' has the meaning given by section 101(1) of the said Act of 1969 ".

8. In section 21(5) after " companies " insert " or with the registrar of companies in Northern Ireland or with both ".

9. In section 22(3) after " companies " insert " or with the registrar of companies in Northern Ireland or with both ".

10. In section 24(4) omit " and " and after " diligence " insert " and a charge imposed by the Enforcement of Judgments Office in Northern Ireland ".

11. In section 25(3)(*b*) for " and Edinburgh " substitute ", Edinburgh and Belfast ".

12. In section 26(7)—

(*a*) for the definition of " company " and " equity share capital " substitute—

"'company' (except in the expression 'insurance company') includes any body corporate and 'equity share capital' means, in relation to a company, its issued share capital excluding any part thereof which, neither as respects dividends nor as respects capital, carries any right to participate beyond a specified amount in a distribution ; " ;

(*b*) in the definition of " share " at the end add " or the Companies Act (Northern Ireland) 1960 ".

13. In section 28(2)(*a*) after " 1948 " insert " or section 210 or 349 of the Companies Act (Northern Ireland) 1960 ".

14. For section 36(6) substitute—

" (6) In this section 'books or papers' includes accounts, deeds, writings and documents.".

15. In section 40—

(*a*) in subsection (4) for " and Edinburgh " substitute ", Edinburgh and Belfast " ;

(*b*) in subsection (5)—

(i) in paragraph (*a*) at the end add " or on the registrar of companies in Northern Ireland or on both " ;

(ii) in paragraph (*b*), omit " (other than one registered in Northern Ireland) " and at the end add " in the case of a society registered in Great Britain or on the registrar as defined by section 101(1) of the Industrial and Provident Societies Act (Northern Ireland) 1969 in the case of a society registered in Northern Ireland " ;

(*c*) in subsection (6) after " registrar of companies " where it twice occurs insert " or the registrar of companies in Northern Ireland " and after " State " insert " or, in the case of a notice served on the registrar of companies in Northern Ireland, the Department of Commerce for Northern Ireland " ;

(*d*) in subsection (7) after " Act) " insert " and section 97(1) of the said Act of 1969 (which confers similar regulation making powers on the Department of Commerce for Northern Ireland) " and at the end add " or, as the case may be, on the registrar ".

16. In section 41—

(*a*) after subsection (1) insert—

"(1A) The Secretary of State may bring civil proceedings in the name and on behalf of an insurance company to which this Part of this Act applies (whether or not a body corporate) under subsection (1) of section 163 of the

Companies Act (Northern Ireland) 1960 and that subsection shall have effect in relation to such an insurance
company as if the reference to any information or document obtained under the provisions there mentioned included a reference to any information or document
obtained under this Act or any enactment repealed by the
Insurance Companies Act 1980 and any reference to the
Department of Commerce for Northern Ireland were a
reference to the Secretary of State." ;

(*b*) in subsection (2) for " the said section 37(1) " substitute
" section 37(1) of the said Act of 1967 or section 163(1) of
the said Act of 1960 ".

17. In section 42—

    (*a*) in subsection (3)—

        (i) in paragraph (*a*), for " and Edinburgh " substitute
", Edinburgh and Belfast " ;

        (ii) in paragraph (*d*), for " Great Britain " substitute
" the United Kingdom " ;

    (*b*) in subsection (7) after " 1948 " insert " or section 197 or 199
of the Companies Act (Northern Ireland) 1960 " ;

    (*c*) in subsection (8)—

        (i) in paragraph (*a*) for " registered or " substitute
" both registered or both " ;

        (ii) for paragraph (*b*) substitute—

        " (*b*) the High Court of Justice in Northern Ireland
if the transferor company and the transferee
company are both registered or both have their
head offices in Northern Ireland ; and

        (*c*) either the High Court of Justice in England or
the Court of Session if either the transferor
company or the transferee company is registered
or has its head office in Scotland ; and

        (*d*) either the High Court of Justice in England or
the High Court of Justice in Northern Ireland
if either the transferor company or the transferee
company is registered or has its head office in
Northern Ireland ; and

        (*e*) either the Court of Session or the High Court
of Justice in Northern Ireland if the transferor
company or the transferee company is registered
or has its head office in Scotland and the other
such company is registered or has its head
office in Northern Ireland." ;

    (*d*) omit subsection (9) ;

    (*e*) in subsection (10) for " Great Britain " where it twice
occurs substitute " the United Kingdom ".

18. In section 43—

    (*a*) in subsection (3) after " 1946 " insert " and section 75 of the Companies Act (Northern Ireland) 1960 and section 27(4) of the Finance (No. 2) Act (Northern Ireland) 1946 " ;

    (*b*) in subsection (5) at the end add " or the Companies Act (Northern Ireland) 1960 ".

19. In section 44(1) for " Great Britain " substitute " the United Kingdom " and after " 1948 " insert " or sections 210 and 349 of the Companies Act (Northern Ireland) 1960 ".

20. In section 45 after " 1948 " insert " or, as the case may be, the Companies Act (Northern Ireland) 1960 " and after " that Act " insert " of 1948 or, as the case may be, that Act of 1960 ".

21. In section 46—

    (*a*) after subsection (1) insert—

        " (1A) The Secretary of State may present a petition for the winding up, in accordance with the Companies Act (Northern Ireland) 1960, of an insurance company to which this Part of this Act applies, being a company which may be wound up by the court under the provisions of that Act, on the ground—

        (*a*) that the company is unable to pay its debts within the meaning of sections 210 and 211 or section 349 of that Act ;

        (*b*) that the company has failed to satisfy an obligation to which it is or was subject by virtue of this Act or any enactment repealed by the Insurance Companies Act 1980 ; or

        (*c*) that the company, being under an obligation imposed by Article 25 of the Companies (Northern Ireland) Order 1978 with respect to the keeping of accounting records, has failed to satisfy that obligation or to produce records kept in satisfaction of that obligation and that the Secretary of State is unable to ascertain its financial position ;

        and subsection (3) of section 163 of the said Act of 1960 shall have effect in relation to such an insurance company as if any reference to the Department of Commerce for Northern Ireland were a reference to the Secretary of State." ;

    (*b*) in subsection (2) after " subsection (1) " insert " or (1A) " ;

    (*c*) in subsection (3) after " 1948 " insert " or, as the case may be, the said Act of 1960 ".

22. In section 47—

    (*a*) in subsection (5) after " 1948 " insert " or, as the case may be, paragraphs (1) and (2) of Article 73 of the Companies (Northern Ireland) Order 1978 " ;

(*b*) in subsection (6) after " 1948 " insert " or section 299(1) of the Companies Act (Northern Ireland) 1960 ".

23. In section 48—

(*a*) in subsection (4) after " 1948 " insert " or, in the case of a special manager appointed in proceedings in Northern Ireland, subsections (2) and (3) of section 236A of the Companies Act (Northern Ireland) 1960 " and for " that section " substitute " section 263 of the said Act of 1948 or, as the case may be, section 236A of the said Act of 1960 " ;

(*b*) in subsection (7) after " 1948 " insert " or, as the case may be, section 227(1) of the said Act of 1960 ".

24. In section 51—

(*a*) in subsection (1) after " 1948 " insert " or section 317 of the Companies Act (Northern Ireland) 1960 " ;

(*b*) in subsection (2)—

(i) for " the said section 365 " substitute " section 365 of the said Act of 1948 or, as the case may be, section 317 of the said Act of 1960 " ;

(ii) after " 1948 " insert " or, as the case may be, section 287 of the said Act of 1960 ".

25. After section 55 insert—

" Documents deposited in Northern Ireland.   55A. Any insurance company which is required to prepare and deliver accounts under Article 3 or 11 of the Companies (Northern Ireland) Order 1978 shall deposit with the registrar of companies in Northern Ireland one copy of—

(*a*) any document deposited with the Secretary of State under section 18(1), 18(2), 18(6), 34(4) or 43(4) above ;

(*b*) any document supplied by the company to the Secretary of State under section 18(5) above.".

26. In sections 60(2) and 64(2) for " Great Britain " substitute " the United Kingdom "

27. In section 68(2)(*d*) after " companies " insert " or the registrar of companies in Northern Ireland or with both such registrars ".

28. In section 69 after " 1958 " insert " and section 12(1) of the Prevention of Fraud (Investments) Act (Northern Ireland) 1940 " and after " that Act " insert " of 1958 and section 22(1) of that Act of 1940 ".

29. In section 75—
   (*a*) in subsection (1) for " Great Britain " substitute " the United Kingdom " ;
   (*b*) in subsection (2) after " 1976 " insert " and sections 356, 358 to 364 and 373 of the Companies Act (Northern Ireland) 1960 and Articles 11 to 13 of the Companies (Northern Ireland) Order 1978 ", for " Great Britain " where it first occurs substitute " the United Kingdom ", after " Great Britain " where it occurs in the second place insert " or, as the case may be, Northern Ireland " and at the end add " or, as the case may be, companies to which Part X of the said Act of 1960 applies ".

30. In section 76(1) after " 1948 " insert " , under the Companies Act (Northern Ireland) 1960 ".

31. In section 80(3) for the words from the beginning to " this Act " substitute " In a case in which an unincorporated body is charged with an offence under this Act—
   (*a*) in England or Wales, section 33 of the Criminal Justice Act 1925 and Schedule 2 to the Magistrates' Courts Act 1952 (procedure on charge of offence against a corporation),
   (*b*) in Northern Ireland, section 18 of the Criminal Justice Act (Northern Ireland) 1945 and Schedule 5 to the Magistrates' Courts Act (Northern Ireland) 1964 (procedure on charge of offence against a corporation),

shall have effect ".

32. In section 81 for the words from " in England " onwards substitute " be instituted—
   (*a*) in England or Wales, except by or with the consent of the Secretary of State, the Industrial Assurance Commissioner or the Director of Public Prosecutions,
   (*b*) in Northern Ireland, except by or with the consent of the Secretary of State, the Department of Commerce for Northern Ireland or the Director of Public Prosecutions for Northern Ireland ".

33. In section 82—
   (*a*) after subsection (3) insert—
      " (3A) Notwithstanding anything in section 34 of the Magistrates' Courts Act (Northern Ireland) 1964, a complaint relating to an offence under this Act which is triable by a court of summary jurisdiction in Northern Ireland may be so tried if it is made at any time within three years after the commission of the offence and within twelve months after the date on which evidence sufficient, in the opinion of the Director of Public Prosecutions for Northern Ireland, the Secretary of State or the Department of Commerce for Northern Ireland, as the case may

be, to justify the proceedings comes to his or that Department's knowledge." ;

(b) in subsection (4) for the words " Secretary of State " there shall be substituted the words " Director of Public Prosecutions for Northern Ireland, the Secretary of State, the Department of Commerce for Northern Ireland " and after the word " his " there shall be inserted the words ", or that Department's,".

34. In section 83(1) at the end add " or Articles 2(2) and 3(1) of the Industrial Assurance (Northern Ireland) Order 1979 ".

35. In section 85—

(a) in subsection (1)—

(i) in the definition of " body corporate ", for " Great Britain " substitute " the United Kingdom " ;

(ii) in the definition of " court ", at the end add " or, in the case of an insurance company registered or having its head office in Northern Ireland, the High Court of Justice in Northern Ireland " ;

(iii) after the definition of " director " insert—

" ' enactment ' includes an enactment of the Parliament of Northern Ireland and a Measure of the Northern Ireland Assembly ; " ;

(iv) in the definition of " former Companies Acts ", after " 1929 " insert " or the Companies Act (Northern Ireland) 1932 " and after " that Act " insert " of 1929 or, as the case may be, that Act of 1932 " ;

(v) in the definition of " industrial assurance business " at the end add " or Articles 2(2) and 3(1) of the Industrial Assurance (Northern Ireland) Order 1979 " ;

(vi) in the definition of " insolvent ", after " 1948 " insert " or, as the case may be " sections 210 and 211 or section 349 of the Companies Act (Northern Ireland) 1960 " ;

(vii) in the definition of " registered society " for the words from " or any " onwards substitute " or the Industrial and Provident Societies Act (Northern Ireland) 1969 " ;

(viii) in the definition of " registrar of companies ", at the end add " and ' registrar of companies in Northern Ireland ' means the registrar of companies within the meaning of section 399(1) of the Companies Act (Northern Ireland) 1960 " ;

(ix) in the definition of " subsidiary " at the end add " or section 148 of the Companies Act (Northern Ireland) 1960 " ;

(b) in subsection (2) at the end add " or section 14(1) of the Insurance Companies Act (Northern Ireland) 1968 " ;

(*c*) after subsection (4) insert—

" (5) Any reference in this Act to an enactment of the Parliament of Northern Ireland or a Measure of the Northern Ireland Assembly shall include a reference to any enactment re-enacting it with or without modifications.".

36. In section 89—

(*a*) in subsection (2) after " made " insert " under section 365 of the Companies Act 1948 " ;

(*b*) in subsection (6) for " under the said section 30(5) or under " substitute " made under section 365 of the said Act of 1948 by virtue of the said section 30(5) or ".

37. In section 90(3) omit " not ".

PART II

OTHER AMENDMENTS OF THAT ACT

38. In section 72—

(*a*) for subsection (2) substitute—

" (2) Where an insurance company carries on any industrial assurance business, the company shall deposit with the Industrial Assurance Commissioner and the Industrial Assurance Commissioner for Northern Ireland a copy of any document which relates to industrial assurance business and which is deposited with the Secretary of State under section 18(1), (2) and (6) above or which is supplied by the company to the Secretary of State under section 18(5) above." ;

(*b*) in subsection (3) for " which relates to industrial assurance business " substitute " mentioned in subsection (2) above " and at the end add " and the Commissioner for Northern Ireland " ;

(*c*) omit subsections (4), (7) and (8) ;

(*d*) in subsections (5), (6) and (9) after " Commissioner " insert " and the Commissioner for Northern Ireland " ;

(*e*) in subsection (10) for " before 1st January 1924 " substitute " in Great Britain before 1st January 1924 or in Northern Ireland before 1st January 1925 ".

SCHEDULE 2

REGULATIONS EXTENDED TO NORTHERN IRELAND BY SECTION 3

PART I

REGULATIONS EXTENDED

The Assurance Companies Rules 1950 (S.I. 1950/533).

The Insurance Companies (Accounts and Forms) Regulations 1968 (S.I. 1968/1408).

The Industrial Assurance (Companies Forms, etc.) Regulations 1968 (S.I. 1968/1571).

The Insurance Companies (Contents of Advertisements) Regulations 1974 (S.I. 1974/901).

The Insurance Companies (Contents of Advertisements) (Amendment) Regulations 1974 (S.I. 1974/1052).

The Insurance Companies (Linked Properties and Indices) Regulations 1975 (S.I. 1975/929).

The Insurance Companies (Accounts and Forms) (Amendment) Regulations 1975 (S.I. 1975/1996).

The Insurance Companies (Valuation of Assets) Regulations 1976 (S.I. 1976/87).

The Insurance Companies (Intermediaries) Regulations 1976 (S.I. 1976/521).

The Insurance Companies (Accounts and Forms) (Amendment) Regulations 1976 (S.I. 1976/549).

The Insurance Companies (Accounts and Forms) (Amendment) (No. 2) Regulations 1976 (S.I. 1976/869).

The Insurance Companies (Valuation of Assets) (Amendment) Regulations 1976 (S.I. 1976/2039).

The Insurance Companies (Accounts and Forms) (Amendment) (No. 3) Regulations 1976 (S.I. 1976/2040).

The Insurance Companies (Classes of General Business) Regulations 1977 (S.I. 1977/1552).

The Insurance Companies (Solvency: General Business) Regulations 1977 (S.I. 1977/1553).

The Insurance Companies (Authorisation and Accounts: General Business) Regulations 1978 (S.I. 1978/720).

The Insurance Companies (Accounts and Forms) (Amendment) Regulations 1978 (S.I. 1978/721).

The Insurance Companies (Changes of Director, Controller or Manager) Regulations 1978 (S.I. 1978/722).

The Insurance Companies (Notice of Long-Term Policy) Regulations 1978 (S.I. 1978/1304).

The Lloyd's (General Business) Regulations 1979 (S.I. 1979/956).

The Insurance Companies (Valuation of Assets) (Amendment) Regulations 1980 (S.I. 1980/5).

PART II

MODIFICATIONS OF REGULATIONS EXTENDED

The Insurance Companies (Accounts and Forms)   S.I. 1968/1408.
Regulations 1968

1. In regulation 1 of the Insurance Companies (Accounts and Forms) Regulations 1968 for the words " the Insurance Companies Act 1958 as so amended " there shall be substituted the words " Part II of the Insurance Companies Act 1974 " and for the words from " Great Britain " onwards there shall be substituted the words " the United Kingdom no insurance business other than industrial assurance business ".

2. In regulation 2(2) of the said Regulations of 1968 after " 1967 " there shall be inserted the words " or sections 187 and 188 of the Companies Act (Northern Ireland) 1960 and Articles 14 to 20 of the Companies (Northern Ireland) Order 1978 " and after " 1948 " in the second place where it occurs there shall be inserted the words " or, as the case may be, the Companies Act (Northern Ireland) 1960 ".

3. In regulation 18(1) of the said Regulations of 1968—

(a) after the definition of " accounts " there shall be inserted the following definition—

" ' the Act ' means the Insurance Companies Act 1958 as amended by the Companies Act 1967 ; " ;

(b) at the end of the definitions of " authorised unit trust scheme " and " unit trust scheme " there shall be added the words " or the Prevention of Fraud (Investments) Act (Northern Ireland) 1940 " ;

(c) in the definition of " capital redemption contracts " for the words " section 59(6)(c) of the Companies Act 1967 " there shall be substituted the words " section 83(2)(c) of the Insurance Companies Act 1974 " ;

(d) in the definition of " company " for the words from " the Act " onwards there shall be substituted the words " these Regulations apply " ;

(e) in the definition of " equity share capital " for the words from " has " to " 1948 " there shall be substituted the words " , in relation to a company, means its issued share capital excluding any part thereof which, neither as respects dividends nor as respects capital, carries any right to participate beyond a specified amount in a distribution " ;

(f) in the definition of " long-term personal accident contracts " for the words " section 59(6)(b) of the Companies Act 1967 " there shall be substituted the words " section 83(2)(b) of the Insurance Companies Act 1974 " ;

(g) in the definition of " quoted investment " for the words from " has " to " 1948 " there shall be substituted the words " means an investment as respects which there has been granted a quotation or permission to deal on a recognised stock exchange, or on any stock exchange of repute outside the United Kingdom " ;

(*h*) at the end of the definition of " subsidiary " there shall be added the words " or section 148 of the Companies Act (Northern Ireland) 1960 ".

4. In paragraph 5 of Schedule 5 to the said Regulations of 1968 after " 1929 " there shall be inserted the words " or under the Industrial Assurance (Northern Ireland) Order 1979 ".

S.I. 1968/1571.

The Industrial Assurance (Companies Forms, etc.)
Regulations 1968

5. In regulation 1(1) of the Industrial Assurance (Companies Forms, etc.) Regulations 1968 at the end of the definition of " collecting society " there shall be added the words " or Article 2(2) of the Industrial Assurance (Northern Ireland) Order 1979 ".

6. In regulation 5 of the said Regulations of 1968 after the words " that class " there shall be inserted the words " in respect of such business carried on in Great Britain and such a statement in respect of such business carried on in Northern Ireland ".

7. In regulation 7 of the said Regulations of 1968 after " 1923 " there shall be inserted the words " or Schedule 5 to the Industrial Assurance (Northern Ireland) Order 1979 ".

S.I. 1974/901.

The Insurance Companies (Contents of Advertisements)
Regulations 1974

8. In regulation 2 of the Insurance Companies (Contents of Advertisements) Regulations 1974 for the words from " Great Britain " onwards there shall be substituted the words " the United Kingdom ".

9. In regulation 4(2) of the said Regulations of 1974 at the end there shall be added the words " with the addition, in subsection (9) of that section of a reference to a scheme made under section 25 of the Charities Act (Northern Ireland) 1964 and to an authorised unit trust scheme within the meaning of the Prevention of Fraud (Investment) Act (Northern Ireland) 1940 ".

10. In regulation 5 of the said Regulations of 1974 for the words " the Insurance Companies Act 1958 " there shall be substituted the words " Part II of the Insurance Companies Act 1974 ".

S.I. 1974/1052.

The Insurance Companies (Contents of Advertisements)
(Amendment) Regulations 1974

11. In regulation 2 of the Insurance Companies (Contents of Advertisements) (Amendment) Regulations 1974 for the words from " Great Britain " onwards there shall be substituted the words " the United Kingdom otherwise than by virtue of an authorisation to do so by or under section 3 of the Insurance Companies Act 1974 ".

SCH. 2
S.I. 1976/87.

The Insurance Companies (Valuation of Assets) Regulations 1976

12. In regulation 2 of the Insurance Companies (Valuation of Assets) Regulations 1976—

(*a*) in the definition of " approved financial institution "—

    (i) in sub-paragraph (*c*) for the words " Trustee Savings Bank Act 1969 " there shall be substituted the words " Trustee Savings Banks Act 1976 " ;

    (ii) in sub-paragraph (*d*) at the end there shall be added the words " or paragraph 23 of the Sixth Schedule to the Companies Act (Northern Ireland) 1960 " ;

(*b*) in the definition of " equity share capital " for the words from " has " to " 1948 " there shall be substituted the words " , in relation to a company, means its issued share capital excluding any part thereof which, neither as respects dividends nor as respects capital, carries any right to participate beyond a specified amount in a distribution ;

(*c*) in the definition of " holding company " at the end there shall be added the words " or section 148 of the Companies Act (Northern Ireland) 1960 " ;

(*d*) in the definition of " quoted "—

    (i) in sub-paragraph (*a*) at the end there shall be added the words " or the Companies Act (Northern Ireland) 1960 " ;

    (ii) in sub-paragraphs (*b*) and (*c*) for the words " Great Britain " there shall be substituted the words " the United Kingdom ".

S.I. 1976/521.

The Insurance Companies (Intermediaries) Regulations 1976

13. In regulation 3 of the Insurance Companies (Intermediaries) Regulations 1976—

(*a*) in paragraph (1)(*e*) after " 1948 " there shall be inserted the words " or section 144 of the Companies Act (Northern Ireland) 1960 " ;

(*b*) in paragraph (4) after " 1948 " there shall be inserted the words " or section 148 of the Companies Act (Northern Ireland) 1960 ".

14. Regulation 7(1)(*f*) of the said Regulations of 1976 shall be omitted.

S.I. 1977/1552.

The Insurance Companies (Classes of General Business) Regulations 1977

15. In paragraph 7 of Schedule 3 to the Insurance Companies (Classes of General Business) Regulations 1977—

(*a*) in sub-paragraph (*a*) at the end there shall be inserted the words " or sections 77(1)(*a*) and 86 of the Road Traffic Act (Northern Ireland) 1970 " ;

(*b*) in sub-paragraph (*c*) at the end there shall be inserted the words " or Article 5(3)(*b*) of the Employer's Liability (Defective Equipment and Compulsory Insurance) (Northern Ireland) Order 1972 ".

The Insurance Companies (Changes of Director, Controller or Manager) Regulations 1978

16. In the Schedule to the Insurance Companies (Changes of Director, Controller or Manager) Regulations 1978—

(*a*) in Forms A, B and C for the words " Great Britain " wherever they occur there shall be substituted the words " the United Kingdom " ;

(*b*) in item 12 of Form A and item 12 of Form B after " 1948 " there shall be inserted the words " or section 148 of the Companies Act (Northern Ireland) 1960 " ;

(*c*) in item 8 of Form C after " 1948 " in the first place where it occurs there shall be inserted " or section 355 of the Companies Act (Northern Ireland) 1960 " ; after the words " address(es) of " there shall be inserted the word " any " and after " 1948 " in the second place where it occurs there shall be inserted the words " or under Part X of the Companies Act (Northern Ireland) 1960 ".

SCHEDULE 3

CONSEQUENTIAL AMENDMENTS

The Companies Act (Northern Ireland) 1960

1. In section 381(6) of the Companies Act (Northern Ireland) 1960 for " the Insurance Companies (Northern Ireland) Order 1976 " substitute " the Insurance Companies Act 1974 ".

2. In paragraph 24(1) of Schedule 6 to the said Act of 1960 for " Part III of the Insurance Companies (Northern Ireland) Order 1976 " substitute " Part II of the Insurance Companies Act 1974 ".

The Building Societies Act (Northern Ireland) 1967

3. In section 128(1) of the Building Societies Act (Northern Ireland) 1967 for " Part III of the Insurance Companies (Northern Ireland) Order 1976 " substitute " Part II of the Insurance Companies Act 1974 ".

The Children and Young Persons Act (Northern Ireland) 1968

4. In section 7 of the Children and Young Persons Act (Northern Ireland) 1968 for " Insurance Companies Act (Northern Ireland) 1968 " substitute " Insurance Companies Act 1974 ".

The Fire Services Act (Northern Ireland) 1969

Sch. 3
1969 c. 13 (N.I.).

5. In section 24(3) of the Fire Services Act (Northern Ireland) 1969 for " Insurance Companies Act (Northern Ireland) 1968 " substitute " Insurance Companies Act 1974 ".

The Judgments (Enforcement) Act (Northern Ireland) 1969

1969 c. 30 (N.I.).

6. In section 129(1) of the Judgments (Enforcement) Act (Northern Ireland) 1969, in the definition of " life policy " for " section 72(1) of the Insurance Companies Act (Northern Ireland) 1968 " substitute " section 85(1) of the Insurance Companies Act 1974 ".

The Road Traffic Act (Northern Ireland) 1970

1970 c. 2 (N.I.).

7. In section 86 of the Road Traffic Act (Northern Ireland) 1970 for " Insurance Companies Act (Northern Ireland) 1968 " substitute " Insurance Companies Act 1974 ".

The Employer's Liability (Defective Equipment and Compulsory Insurance) (Northern Ireland) Order 1972

S.I. 1972/963 (N.I. 6).

8. In Article 5(3)(*b*) of the Employer's Liability (Defective Equipment and Compulsory Insurance) (Northern Ireland) Order 1972 for " Insurance Companies Act (Northern Ireland) Order 1968 " substitute " Insurance Companies Act 1974 "

The Policyholders Protection Act 1975

1975 c. 75.

9. In section 3(2) of the Policyholders Protection Act 1975 for the words from " Great Britain " onwards substitute " the United Kingdom ".

10. In section 27 of the said Act of 1975 for " section 34 of the Insurance Companies Act (Northern Ireland) 1968 " substitute " Article 109 of the Companies (Northern Ireland) Order 1978 ".

11. In section 29 of the said Act of 1975 after " 1967 " insert " or Article 109 of the Companies (Northern Ireland) Order 1978 ".

The Companies (Northern Ireland) Order 1978

S.I. 1978/1042 (N.I. 12).

12. In Article 108(1) of the Companies (Northern Ireland) Order 1978 for " Article 40 of the Insurance Companies (Northern Ireland) Order 1976 " substitute " section 36 of the Insurance Companies Act 1974 ".

13. In Article 109(1) of the said Order of 1978—

(*a*) for " Article 40 of the Insurance Companies (Northern Ireland) Order 1976 " substitute " section 36 of the Insurance Companies Act 1974 " ;

(*b*) in sub-paragraph (*a*) for " Insurance Companies (Northern Ireland) Order 1976 " substitute " Insurance Companies Act 1974 " ;

(c) for sub-paragraph (c) substitute—

"(c) for the purpose of enabling the Secretary of State to exercise a power conferred on him by the Insurance Companies Act 1974".

14. In Article 110(1) of the said Order of 1978 for "Article 40(1) of the Insurance Companies (Northern Ireland) Order 1976" substitute "section 36(1) of the Insurance Companies Act 1974".

S.I. 1979/1574 (N.I. 13).

The Industrial Assurance (Northern Ireland) Order 1979

15. In Article 3(4) of the said Order of 1979—

(a) for "Order and in particular to Article 6(2) of that Order" substitute "Act 1974 and in particular to section 2(2) of that Act";

(b) for "Northern Ireland" substitute "the United Kingdom";

(c) for "Article 7 of that Order" substitute "section 3 of that Act".

16. In Article 18(1) of the said Order of 1979 for "Insurance Companies Order" substitute "Insurance Companies Act 1974".

17. In Article 32(1)(b) of the said Order of 1979 for "Insurance Companies Order" substitute "Insurance Companies Act 1974".

18. In Article 40 of the said Order of 1979—

(a) for the words from the beginning to "Order" substitute "Sections 42 and 43 of the Insurance Companies Act 1974";

(b) for "Article 83(5)" substitute "section 72(6)".

19. In Article 50(2) of the said Order of 1979 for "Order" substitute "Act 1974".

20. In Schedule 5 to the said Order of 1979—

(a) in paragraph 1 for "Article 2(2) of the Insurance Companies Order" substitute "section 85(1) of the Insurance Companies Act 1974";

(b) in paragraph 6 for "Order" substitute "Act 1974".

Section 4(2).

SCHEDULE 4

SAVING AND TRANSITIONAL PROVISIONS

1. In this Schedule—

"the appointed day" means the day appointed under section 5(2) of this Act for the coming into operation of this Act;

"the Department" means the Department of Commerce for Northern Ireland.

2. Any thing done (including any instrument or document made, issued, confirmed or granted and any decision, authorisation, direction, consent, application, request or thing made, issued, given or 1974 c. 49.   done) under the Insurance Companies Act 1974 or the instruments

specified in section 3(3) of this Act or in Part I of Schedule 2 to this Act shall in so far as it had effect immediately before the appointed day have effect on or after that day in relation to Northern Ireland as if that Act or those instruments extended to Northern Ireland at the time when that thing was done and that thing was done in relation to Northern Ireland as well as Great Britain.

3. Articles 17 to 26 and 66 of the Insurance Companies (Northern Ireland) Order 1976 and regulations made under those Articles or Article 55(5) of that Order (preparation and submission to the Department of accounts and returns and other documents) shall continue to have effect after the appointed day in respect of any financial year ending on or before the day immediately preceding the appointed day and Article 72 of that Order (offences) shall also continue to have effect accordingly.

S.I. 1976/59 (N.I. 3).

4. Where it appears to the Secretary of State that before the appointed day an insurance company has failed to comply with the obligations referred to in sub-paragraph (*b*) of Article 32(1) of the said Order of 1976, the Secretary of State may exercise the powers under paragraph (*b*) of section 28(1) of the said Act of 1974 as if the failure had been a failure to comply with the obligations referred to in that paragraph.

5. Where it appears to the Secretary of State that an insurance company has furnished misleading or inaccurate information to the Department as referred to in sub-paragraph (*c*) of Article 32(1) of the said Order of 1976, the Secretary of State may exercise the powers under paragraph (*c*) of section 28(1) of the said Act of 1974 as if the misleading or inaccurate information furnished had been furnished as referred to in that paragraph.

6. Any requirement imposed by the Department under Articles 33 to 41 of the said Order of 1976 which is in force immediately before the appointed day shall be deemed to have been imposed by the Secretary of State under sections 29 to 37 of the said Act of 1974 and may on or after that day be varied or rescinded by him under section 40 of the said Act of 1974.

7. Any notice issued by the Department under Article 44 or 45 of the said Order of 1976 which is in force immediately before the appointed day shall be deemed to have been issued by the Secretary of State under sections 38 and 39 of the said Act of 1974.

8. Articles 19(2) and 65(2) of the said Order of 1976 (duty to notify changes of appointed actuaries or of directors, controllers or managers) shall continue to have effect after the appointed day in respect of any changes which take place before that day.

9. Articles 67 to 70 of the said Order of 1976 (power to make certain orders and to alter financial year) and orders made under

SCH. 4   those Articles which are in force immediately before the appointed day shall continue to have effect after that day in respect of any financial year ending on or before the day immediately preceding the appointed day.

10. Articles 83 to 87 of the said Order of 1976 and regulations made under those Articles (industrial assurance business, Lloyd's, unregistered companies) shall continue to have effect after the appointed day in respect of the business carried on in, and the returns relating to, any financial year ending on or before the day immediately preceding the appointed day.

11. Any asset valuation regulations made under Article 88 of the said Order of 1976 shall continue to have effect after the appointed day in relation to any valuation required to be made in respect of periods before that day.

12. Articles 89 to 92 of the said Order of 1976 (criminal proceedings) shall apply to proceedings under the said Order whether instituted before, on or after the appointed day.

13. Article 94 of the said Order of 1976 (annual report) shall continue to have effect as long as the Department exercises any functions under the said Order.

14. In so far as any power or duty conferred or imposed under any provision of the said Order of 1976 can be performed under a corresponding provision of the said Act of 1974 after the appointed day, all information obtained or provided under or for the purposes of any provision of the said Order shall be deemed to have been obtained or provided under or for the purposes of that corresponding provision.

15. The repeal of section 44(2) and (3) of, and Schedules 3 and 4 to, the Insurance Companies Act (Northern Ireland) 1968 (which by virtue of Article 96(6) of the said Order of 1976 is not to take effect until the first rules under Article 62(2) of the said Order come into operation) shall not take effect until the first rules made under section 317 of the Companies Act (Northern Ireland) 1960 by virtue of section 51(2) of the said Act of 1974 come into operation.

1968 c. 6 (N.I.).

1960 c. 22 (N.I.).

16. The provisions of the Act of 1974, so far as extended to Northern Ireland in substitution for provisions of the said Order of 1976 relating to winding up, shall not affect any winding up commenced before the date on which the first rules made under section 317 of the Companies Act (Northern Ireland) 1960 by virtue of section 51(2) of the said Act of 1974 come into operation.

17. Without prejudice to section 4(1) of this Act, any enactment or document whatsoever referring to any enactment repealed by this Act shall be construed as referring (or including a reference) to the corresponding enactment in the said Act of 1974.

18. Until Articles 3, 11, 13 and 25 of the Companies (Northern Ireland) Order 1978 come into operation the following provisions of Part I of Schedule 1 to this Act shall have effect subject to the following modifications— Sᴄʜ. 4 S.I. 1978/1042 (N.I. 12).

    (*a*) in paragraph 21(*a*) for the reference to Article 25 of that Order there shall be substituted a reference to sections 141 and 297 of the Companies Act (Northern Ireland) 1960 ;

    (*b*) in paragraph 25 for the reference to Article 3 or 11 of that Order there shall be substituted a reference to section 122, 142 or 359 of that Act ;

    (*c*) in paragraph 29 for the reference to Articles 11 to 13 of that Order there shall be substituted a reference to sections 359 and 363 of that Act.

19. Nothing in this Schedule shall be taken as prejudicing the operation of section 16(1) of the Interpretation Act 1978 (which relates to repeals).   1978 c. 30.

SCHEDULE 5   Section 4(3).

Rᴇᴘᴇᴀʟs

Chapter or Number	Short title	Extent of repeal
13 & 14 Geo. 5. c. 8.	The Industrial Assurance Act 1923.	In section 16, in subsection (1) the words " or company ", the words " or an industrial assurance company " and the words " or the Assurance Companies Act 1909 " and subsection (2).
11 & 12 Geo. 6. c. 39.	The Industrial Assurance and Friendly Societies Act 1948.	In section 13, in subsection (1) the words " and an industrial assurance company " and the words " or company "; in subsection (2) the words " or companies " in both places where they occur and the words " or company "; in subsection (3) the words " or the Assurance Companies Act 1909 " and in subsection (4) the words from " and, in relation to " onwards.
1947 c. 1 (N.I.).	The Assurance Companies Act (Northern Ireland) 1947.	The whole Act so far as unrepealed.
1968 c. 6 (N.I.).	The Insurance Companies Act (Northern Ireland) 1968.	The whole Act so far as unrepealed.
1973 c. 58.	The Insurance Companies (Amendment) Act 1973.	Section 56. Schedules 3 to 5.

SCH. 5

Chapter or Number	Short title	Extent of repeal
1974 c. 49.	The Insurance Companies Act 1974.	In section 2(4) the words from " and the reference " onwards. In section 3(1) the word " either ". In section 20(1) the words " (other than one registered in Northern Ireland) ". In section 24(4) the word " and ". In section 40(5)(*b*) the words " (other than one registered in Northern Ireland) ". Section 42(9). Section 72(4), (7) and (8). In section 90(3) the word " not ".
1974 c. 52.	The Trade Union and Labour Relations Act 1974.	In Schedule 3, paragraph 13.
1975 c. 7.	The Finance Act 1975.	In paragraph 11 of Schedule 5, in sub-paragraph (10A)(*b*) the words from " or Part II of " onwards.
1975 c. 75.	The Policyholders Protection Act 1975.	In section 3(2) the word " or " and paragraph (*b*). Section 22(2). In section 32, in subsection (2) the words " but subject to subsection (3) below " and subsection (3). In Schedule 3, paragraph 5(5).
S.I. 1976/59 (N.I. 3).	The Insurance Companies (Northern Ireland) Order 1976.	The whole Order.
1977 c. 36.	The Finance Act 1977.	In section 50(1) the words " or Part II of the Insurance Companies (Northern Ireland) Order 1976 ".
1977 c. 46.	The Insurance Brokers (Registration) Act 1977.	In section 29(1), in the definition of " authorised insurers " the words " or the Insurance Companies (Northern Ireland) Order 1976 " and in the definition of " insurance business " the words " or Part II of the Insurance Companies (Northern Ireland) Order 1976 ".
S.I. 1978/1042 (N.I. 12).	The Companies (Northern Ireland) Order 1978.	Article 96(2). In Schedule 6, in Part II the entries relating to the Insurance Companies (Northern Ireland) Order 1976.

Chapter or Number	Short title	Extent of repeal
1979 c. 37.	The Banking Act 1979.	In Schedule 1, in paragraph 8 the words from " or Article " to " 1976 " and the words from " or, as " onwards.
S.I. 1979/1574 (N.I. 13).	The Industrial Assurance (Northern Ireland) Order 1979.	In Article 2(2) the definition of " Insurance Companies Order ". In Article 23, in paragraph (1) the words " and an industrial assurance company " and the words " or company " and in paragraph (3), sub-paragraph (*b*). In Schedule 8 the entry relating to the Insurance Companies (Northern Ireland) Order 1976.

SCHEDULE 6

Section 4(4).

REVOCATIONS

Number	Title
S.R. & O. (N.I.) 1969 No. 242.	The Insurance Companies (Accounts and Forms) Regulations (Northern Ireland) 1969.
S.R. & O. (N.I.) 1969 No. 351.	The Industrial Assurance (Companies Forms, etc.) Regulations (Northern Ireland) 1969.
S.R. & O. (N.I.) 1973 No. 507.	The Insurance Companies (Identification of Long Term Assets and Liabilities) Regulations (Northern Ireland) 1973.
S.R. (N.I.) 1974 No. 251.	The Insurance Companies (Contents of Advertisements) Regulations (Northern Ireland) 1974.
S.R. (N.I.) 1976 No. 131.	The Insurance Companies (Linked Properties and Indices) Regulations (Northern Ireland) 1976.
S.R. (N.I.) 1976 No. 156.	The Insurance Companies (Changes of Director, Controller or Manager) Regulations (Northern Ireland) 1976.
S.R. (N.I.) 1976 No. 315.	The Insurance Companies (Intermediaries) Regulations (Northern Ireland) 1976.
S.R. (N.I.) 1977 No. 72.	The Insurance Companies (Valuation of Assets) Regulations (Northern Ireland) 1977.
S.R. (N.I.) 1977 No. 214.	The Insurance Companies (Accounts and Forms) (Amendment) Regulations (Northern Ireland) 1977.

British Aerospace Act 1980

1980 CHAPTER 26

An Act to provide for the vesting of all the property, rights, liabilities and obligations of British Aerospace in a company nominated by the Secretary of State and the subsequent dissolution of British Aerospace; and to make provision with respect to the finances of that company.　　　　　　　　　　　　**▌▌[1st May 1980]**

BE IT ENACTED by the Queen's most Excellent Majesty, by and with the advice and consent of the Lords Spiritual and Temporal, and Commons, in this present Parliament assembled, and by the authority of the same, as follows:—

Vesting of property, etc., of British Aerospace in a company nominated by the Secretary of State

1.—(1) On the appointed day all the property, rights, liabilities and obligations to which British Aerospace was entitled or subject immediately before that day shall (subject to section 2 of this Act and to the following provisions of this section) become by virtue of this section property, rights, liabilities and obligations of a company nominated for the purposes of this section by the Secretary of State (referred to below in this Act as " the successor company ").

Vesting of property, etc., of British Aerospace in a company nominated by the Secretary of State.

(2) The Secretary of State may, after consulting British Aerospace, by order made by statutory instrument nominate for the purposes of this section any company formed and registered under the Companies Act 1948 ; but on the appointed day the company in question must be a company limited by shares which is wholly owned by the Crown.

1948 c. 38.

(3) Any agreement made, transaction effected or other thing done by, to or in relation to British Aerospace which is in force or effective immediately before the appointed day shall have effect on and after that day as if made, effected or done by, to or in relation to the successor company, in all respects as if the successor company were the same person, in law, as British Aerospace ; and accordingly references to British Aerospace—

> (a) in any agreement (whether or not in writing) and in any deed, bond or instrument ;
>
> (b) in any process or other document issued, prepared or employed for the purpose of any proceeding before any court or other tribunal or authority ; and
>
> (c) in any other document whatsoever (other than an enactment) relating to or affecting any property, right, liability or obligation of British Aerospace which vests by virtue of this section in the successor company ;

shall be taken on and after the appointed day as referring to the successor company.

(4) Without prejudice to subsection (3)(b) above, any proceedings on an application made by British Aerospace before the appointed day under section 31(3) of the Act of 1977 may be continued on and after that day by the successor company, and any order made under subsection (9) of that section with respect to any loss resulting to British Aerospace from the transaction to which the application relates shall be made in favour of the successor company.

(5) Any liability of British Aerospace under section 40(4) of the Act of 1977 shall not vest in the successor company by virtue of this section, but the Secretary of State shall be liable to indemnify the Bank of England against any loss suffered by them arising out of, or in connection with, the issue of compensation stock under Part II of that Act in respect of the vesting of any securities in British Aerospace (and any sums required by the Secretary of State for the purpose shall be paid out of moneys provided by Parliament).

(6) Schedule 1 to this Act contains specific provisions with respect to the effect in certain respects of the vesting of the property, rights, liabilities and obligations of British Aerospace in the successor company by virtue of this section ; but nothing in those provisions shall be taken as prejudicing the general effect of the preceding provisions of this section.

(7) References in this Act to property, rights, liabilities and obligations of British Aerospace are references to all such property, rights, liabilities and obligations, whether or not capable of being transferred or assigned by British Aerospace.

(8) It is hereby declared for the avoidance of doubt that—

(*a*) any reference in this Act to property of British Aerospace is a reference to property of British Aerospace whether situated in the United Kingdom or elsewhere ; and

(*b*) any such reference to rights, liabilities or obligations of British Aerospace is a reference to rights to which British Aerospace is entitled, or (as the case may be) liabilities or obligations to which British Aerospace is subject, whether under the law of the United Kingdom or of any part of the United Kingdom or under the law of any country or territory outside the United Kingdom.

2. Subject to paragraphs 2 and 3 of Schedule 2 to this Act, any entitlement of the Secretary of State and any liability of British Aerospace— _{Cancellation of certain Government investment in British Aerospace.}

(*a*) in respect of the commencing capital of British Aerospace ;

(*b*) in respect of the capital amounts outstanding immediately before the appointed day in respect of sums paid to British Aerospace by the Secretary of State under section 16 of the Act of 1977 ; and

(*c*) in respect of the capital amounts outstanding immediately before that day in respect of sums paid to British Aerospace under section 45 of that Act but treated in accordance with the terms and conditions applicable to the payment as if they had been paid under section 16 of that Act ;

shall be extinguished immediately before the appointed day.

3.—(1) As a consequence of the vesting in the successor company by virtue of section 1 of this Act of all the property, rights, liabilities and obligations of British Aerospace, the successor company shall issue— _{Initial Government shareholding in the successor company.}

(*a*) to the Secretary of State ; or

(*b*) to any person entitled to require the issue of the shares in question following their initial allotment to the Secretary of State ;

such shares in the company as the Secretary of State may direct.

(2) Shares required to be issued in pursuance of this section shall be issued or allotted at such time or times and on such terms (as to allotment) as the Secretary of State may direct.

(3) Shares issued in pursuance of this section—

(*a*) shall be of such nominal value as the Secretary of State may direct ; and

(b) shall be issued as fully paid and treated for the purposes of the Companies Acts 1948 to 1980 as if they had been paid up by virtue of the payment to the successor company of their nominal value in cash.

(4) The Secretary of State may not dispose of any shares issued or of any rights to shares initially allotted to him in pursuance of this section, or give any directions for the purposes of this section, without the consent of the Treasury.

(5) Any dividends or other sums received by the Secretary of State in right of or on the disposal of any shares or rights acquired by virtue of this section shall be paid into the Consolidated Fund.

1973 c. 51.

(6) Stamp duty shall not be chargeable under section 47 of the Finance Act 1973 in respect of any increase in the capital of the successor company which is certified by the Treasury as having been effected for the purpose of complying with the requirements of this section.

Financial structure of the successor company and its subsidiaries.

4.—(1) If the aggregate nominal value of the shares in the successor company issued in pursuance of section 3 of this Act is less than the aggregate amount of the former Government investment in British Aerospace, a sum equal to the amount of the difference shall be carried by the successor company to a reserve (" the statutory reserve ").

(2) The statutory reserve may only be applied by the successor company in paying up unissued shares of the company to be allotted to members of the company as fully paid bonus shares.

1980 c. 22.

(3) Notwithstanding subsection (2) above, the statutory reserve shall not count as an undistributable reserve of the successor company for the purposes of section 40(2)(d) of the Companies Act 1980 ; but for the purpose of determining under that section whether the successor company may make a distribution at any time any amount for the time being standing to the credit of the statutory reserve shall be treated for the purposes of section 40(2)(c) as if it were unrealised profits of the company.

(4) For the purposes of any statutory accounts of the successor company the value of any asset and the amount of any liability of British Aerospace vesting in that company on the appointed day (as at the date of vesting) shall be taken to be the value or (as the case may be) the amount assigned to that asset or liability for the purposes of the corresponding statement of accounts prepared by British Aerospace in accordance with section 10(6) of this Act in respect of the last accounting year of British Aerospace ending before the appointed day.

(5) For the purposes of any statutory accounts of the successor company the amount to be included in respect of any item shall be determined as if anything done by British Aerospace (whether by way of acquiring, revaluing or disposing of any asset or incurring, revaluing or discharging any liability, or by carrying

any amount to any provision or reserve, or otherwise) had been done by the successor company.

Accordingly (but without prejudice to the generality of the preceding provision) the amount to be included from time to time in any reserves of the successor company as representing its accumulated realised profits available for distribution shall be determined as if any profits realised and retained by British Aerospace had been realised and retained by the successor company.

(6) References in this section to the former Government investment in British Aerospace are references to the aggregate of the following, that is to say—

(a) the amount included in the closing statement of the accounts of British Aerospace as representing the commencing capital of British Aerospace ; and

(b) the capital amounts mentioned in section 2(b) and (c) of this Act ;

and in this subsection " the closing statement of the accounts of British Aerospace " means the statement of those accounts prepared by British Aerospace as mentioned in subsection (4) above.

(7) References in this section to the statutory accounts of the successor company are references to any accounts prepared by the successor company for the purposes of any provision of the Companies Acts 1948 to 1980 (including group accounts).

5.—(1) The Secretary of State may at any time, with the consent of the Treasury, acquire— Government investment in shares and securities of the successor company.

(a) ordinary voting shares in the successor company ;

(b) securities of the successor company or of any subsidiary of the successor company which are convertible into or carry rights to subscribe for ordinary voting shares in the successor company ; or

(c) rights to subscribe for any such shares.

(2) In subsection (1) above " ordinary voting shares " means shares in the company which—

(a) carry voting rights at general meetings of the company ; and

(b) carry a right to participate in any distribution (whether of dividends or of capital) without limit as to amount (but the right to participate in distributions need not extend to a dividend declared out of profits earned during any period falling wholly or partly before the date of acquisition of the shares).

(3) The Secretary of State may not dispose of any shares or other securities or rights acquired under this section without the consent of the Treasury.

(4) Any expenses incurred by the Secretary of State in consequence of the provisions of this section shall be paid out of moneys provided by Parliament.

(5) Any dividends or other sums received by the Secretary of State in right of, or on the disposal of, any shares or other securities or rights acquired under this section shall be paid into the Consolidated Fund.

Exercise of Secretary of State's functions under sections 3 and 5 through nominees.

6.—(1) The Secretary of State may with the consent of the Treasury appoint such person or persons as he thinks fit to act as his nominees for the purposes of section 3 or 5 of this Act ; and—

   (a) shares in the successor company may be issued under section 3 of this Act to any nominee of the Secretary of State appointed for the purposes of that section, or to any person entitled to require the issue of the shares in question following their initial allotment to any such nominee ; and

   (b) any such nominee appointed for the purposes of section 5 of this Act may acquire shares or other securities or rights in accordance with that section ;

in accordance with directions given from time to time by the Secretary of State with the consent of the Treasury.

(2) Any person holding any shares or other securities or rights as a nominee of the Secretary of State by virtue of subsection (1) above shall hold and deal with them (or any of them) on such terms and in such manner as the Secretary of State may direct with the consent of the Treasury.

Target investment limit for Government shareholding under sections 3 and 5.

7.—(1) As soon as the successor company ceases to be wholly owned by the Crown, the Secretary of State shall by order made by statutory instrument fix a target investment limit in relation to the shares for the time being held in that company by the Secretary of State or his nominees by virtue of any provision of this Act (referred to below in this section as " the Government shareholding ").

(2) The target investment limit shall be expressed as a proportion of the voting rights exercisable at general meetings of the successor company.

(3) The first target investment limit fixed under this section shall be equal to the proportion of those voting rights which is carried by the Government shareholding at the time when the order fixing the limit is made.

(4) The Secretary of State may from time to time by order made by statutory instrument fix a new target investment limit in place of the one previously in force under this section ; but—

   (a) any new limit must be lower than the one it replaces ; and (*b*) an order under this section may only be revoked by an order fixing a new limit.

(5) It shall be the duty of the Secretary of State so to exercise—

(*a*) his powers under section 5 of this Act and his power to dispose of any shares held by him by virtue of any provision of this Act ; and

(*b*) his power to give directions to his nominees ;

as to secure that the Government shareholding does not carry a proportion of the voting rights exercisable at general meetings of the successor company exceeding any target investment limit for the time being in force under this section.

(6) Notwithstanding subsection (5) above, the Secretary of State may take up, or direct any nominee of his to take up, any rights for the time being available to him, or to that nominee, as an existing holder of shares or other securities of the successor company or of any subsidiary of the successor company ; but if as a result the Government shareholding at any time exceeds the target investment limit it shall be the duty of the Secretary of State to comply with subsection (5) as soon after that time as is reasonably practicable.

(7) A statutory instrument containing an order under this section shall be subject to annulment in pursuance of a resolution of either House of Parliament.

8.—(1) Subject to subsection (2) below, if any sum required by any judgment or order to be paid by a company which became a wholly owned subsidiary of the successor company on the appointed day by virtue of section 1 of this Act is not paid by the company concerned within the period of fourteen days beginning on the date on which the judgment or order becomes enforceable, the successor company shall be liable to pay that sum and that judgment or order shall be enforceable against the successor company accordingly. *Liability of the successor company for defaulting subsidiary where cause of action arose before appointed day.*

(2) Subsection (1) above applies only if the cause of action arose before the appointed day.

(3) Where any such sum as is referred to in subsection (1) above is required to be paid in respect of a liability arising under a contract made by the defaulting company, the cause of action shall be regarded, for the purposes of this section, as having arisen at the time when the contract was made.

Liability of
Secretary
of State in
respect of
obligations
vesting in
the successor
company
by virtue of
section 1, etc.
1948 c. 38.

9.—(1) This section applies where—

(a) a resolution has been passed, in accordance with the provisions of the Companies Act 1948, for the voluntary winding up of the successor company, otherwise than merely for the purpose of reconstruction or amalgamation with another company; or

(b) without any such resolution having been passed beforehand, an order has been made for the winding up of the successor company by the court under that Act.

(2) The Secretary of State shall become liable on the commencement of the winding up to discharge any outstanding liability of the successor company in respect of—

(a) any obligation of the successor company which vested in that company by virtue of section 1 of this Act; and

(b) any liability imposed on the successor company by section 8 of this Act.

(3) Any sums required by the Secretary of State for discharging any liability imposed on him by this section shall be paid out of moneys provided by Parliament.

(4) Where the Secretary of State makes a payment to any person in discharge of what appears to him to be a liability imposed on him by this section, he shall thereupon become a creditor of the successor company to the extent of the amount paid, his claim being treated for the purposes of the winding up as a claim in respect of the original liability.

(5) Any sums received by the Secretary of State in respect of any claim made by him by virtue of subsection (4) above in the winding up of the successor company shall be paid into the Consolidated Fund.

(6) The reference in subsection (2) above to the commencement of the winding up is a reference—

(a) in a case within subsection (1)(a) above, to the passing of the resolution; and

(b) in a case within subsection (1)(b) above, to the making of the order.

Dissolution
of British
Aerospace
and
transitional
provisions.

10.—(1) Subject to the following provisions of this section and to the transitional provisions contained in Schedule 2 to this Act, Part I and sections 40(4), 41(4), 44(4), 48, 49, 50 and 53 of the Act of 1977 and paragraphs 3(2) and 9 of Schedule 5 to that Act shall cease to have effect on the appointed day in relation to British Aerospace; and any reference in those provisions or in paragraph 14 of Schedule 6 to the Act of 1977 (in whatever terms expressed) to either or both of the Corporations originally established by section 1 of that Act shall be construed after that day as a reference to the other Corporation so established (that is to say, British Shipbuilders).

(2) Notwithstanding subsection (1) above, British Aerospace shall continue in existence after the appointed day, and section 1(1) to (4) and (6) of the Act of 1977 shall continue to have effect in relation to its constitution and proceedings, until it is dissolved in accordance with subsection (9) below ; and the period of its continued existence after the appointed day is referred to below in this section as " the transitional period ".

(3) It shall be the duty of British Aerospace and of the successor company to take, as and when during the transitional period the successor company considers appropriate, all such steps as may be requisite to secure that the vesting in the successor company by virtue of section 1 of this Act of any foreign property, right, liability or obligation of British Aerospace is effective under the relevant foreign law.

(4) During the transitional period, until the vesting in the successor company by virtue of section 1 of any foreign property, right or obligation of British Aerospace is effective under the relevant foreign law, it shall be the duty of British Aerospace to hold that property or right for the benefit of the successor company and to perform that obligation as it falls to be performed.

(5) Nothing in subsections (3) and (4) above shall be taken as prejudicing the effect under the law of the United Kingdom or of any part of the United Kingdom of the vesting in the successor company by virtue of section 1 of this Act of any property, right, liability or obligation of British Aerospace (including any foreign property, right, liability or obligation).

(6) Notwithstanding subsection (1) above—

(a) it shall be the duty of British Aerospace to prepare statements of accounts in accordance with section 17(1)(b) and (c) of the Act of 1977 in respect of the last accounting year of British Aerospace ending before the appointed day, and that section shall continue to apply during the transitional period in relation to those statements and in relation also to the auditing of accounts kept in accordance with subsection (1)(a) of that section in respect of that accounting year ; and

(b) it shall be the duty of British Aerospace to make a report to the Secretary of State in accordance with section 18 of that Act in respect of that accounting year (but subsection (5) of that section shall not apply to any such report).

(7) British Aerospace shall have all such powers as may be requisite for the performance of its duties under this section; but—

> (a) it shall be the duty of the successor company during the transitional period to act on behalf of British Aerospace (so far as possible) in performing any duty imposed on British Aerospace by subsection (3) or (4) above; and

> (b) any rights, liabilities and obligations acquired or incurred by British Aerospace during that period in the performance of any such duty shall become rights, liabilities and obligations of the successor company after the dissolution of British Aerospace in accordance with subsection (9) below.

(8) Any expenses incurred by British Aerospace in performing any of its duties under this section shall be met by the successor company.

(9) The Secretary of State may, by order made by statutory instrument after consulting British Aerospace and the successor company, dissolve British Aerospace on a day specified in the order, as soon as he is satisfied that nothing further remains to be done by British Aerospace under subsection (3) or (6) above.

(10) References in this section to any foreign property, right, liability or obligation of British Aerospace are references respectively to—

> (a) property of British Aerospace situated in a country or territory outside the United Kingdom; and

> (b) any right to which British Aerospace is entitled or (as the case may be) any liability or obligation to which it is subject under the law of any such country or territory.

Miscellaneous and supplemental

Application of Trustee Investments Act 1961 in relation to investment in the successor company.
1961 c. 62.

11.—(1) For the purpose of applying paragraph 3(b) of Part IV of Schedule 1 to the Trustee Investments Act 1961 (which provides that shares and debentures of a company shall not count as wider-range and narrower-range investments respectively within the meaning of that Act unless the company has paid dividends in each of the five years immediately preceding that in which the investment is made) in relation to investment in shares or debentures of the successor company during the calendar year in which the appointed day falls (" the first investment year ") or during any year following that year, the successor company shall be deemed to have paid a dividend as there mentioned—

> (a) in any year preceding the first investment year which is included in the relevant five years; and

(*b*) in the first investment year, if that year is included in the relevant five years and the successor company does not in fact pay such a dividend in that year.

(2) In subsection (1) above " the relevant five years " means the five years immediately preceding the year in which the investment in question is made or proposed to be made.

12.—(1) Subject to subsection (2) below, the successor com- Corporation pany shall be treated for all purposes of corporation tax and tax and development land tax as if it were the same person as British development Aerospace.

(2) The successor company shall not by virtue of subsection (1) above be regarded as a body falling within section 272(5) of the Income and Corporation Taxes Act 1970 (bodies estab- 1970 c. 10. lished for carrying on industries or undertakings under national ownership or control).

13. Any administrative expenses incurred by the Secretary Adminis- of State in consequence of the provisions of this Act shall be trative paid out of moneys provided by Parliament.

14.—(1) In this Act— Interpretation.

" the Act of 1977 " means the Aircraft and Shipbuilding Industries Act 1977 ; 1977 c. 3.

" appointed day " means such day as the Secretary of State may appoint by order made by statutory instrument after consulting British Aerospace and the Treasury ;

" share " includes stock ;

" subsidiary " has the same meaning as in the Companies 1948 c. 38. Act 1948 ;

" the successor company " has the meaning given by section 1(1) of this Act ; and

" wholly owned subsidiary " has the same meaning as it has for the purposes of section 150 of the Companies Act 1948.

(2) An order under section 1 of this Act nominating any company for the purposes of that section and an order under subsection (1) above appointing a day may be varied or revoked by a subsequent order at any time before any property, rights, liabilities or obligations of British Aerospace vest in any company by virtue of section 1.

(3) A company shall be regarded for the purposes of this Act as wholly owned by the Crown at any time when all the issued shares in the company are held by or on behalf of the Crown.

T 3

Citation,
repeals and
extent.

15.—(1) This Act may be cited as the British Aerospace Act 1980.

(2) Subject to section 10 of and Schedule 2 to this Act, the enactments mentioned in Schedule 3 to this Act are repealed on the appointed day to the extent specified in column 3 of that Schedule.

(3) It is hereby declared that this Act extends to Northern Ireland.

SCHEDULES

SCHEDULE 1

EFFECT OF SECTION 1 IN CERTAIN CASES

Modification of agreements

1. Where immediately before the appointed day there is in force an agreement which—

(a) confers or imposes on British Aerospace any rights, liabilities or obligations which vest in the successor company by virtue of section 1 of this Act ; and

(b) refers (in whatever terms and whether expressly or by implication) to a member or officer of British Aerospace ;

the agreement shall have effect, in relation to anything falling to be done on or after that day, as if for that reference there were substituted a reference to such person as that company may appoint or, in default of appointment, to the officer of that company who corresponds as nearly as may be to the member or officer of British Aerospace in question.

Contracts of employment and pensions

2. It is hereby declared for the avoidance of doubt that—

(a) the effect of section 1 of this Act in relation to any contract of employment with British Aerospace in force immediately before the appointed day is merely to modify the contract (as from that day) by substituting the successor company as the employer (and not to terminate the contract or vary it in any other way) ; and

(b) section 1 is effective to vest the rights, liabilities and obligations of British Aerospace under any agreement or arrangement for the payment of pensions, allowances or gratuities in the successor company along with all other rights, liabilities and obligations of British Aerospace ;

and accordingly for the purposes of any such agreement or arrangement (as it has effect by virtue of section 1(3) in relation to employment with the successor company or with a wholly owned subsidiary of that company) any period of employment with British Aerospace or with any wholly owned subsidiary of British Aerospace which becomes a wholly owned subsidiary of the successor company on the appointed day shall count as employment with the successor company or (as the case may be) with a wholly owned subsidiary of that company.

Regional development grants

3.—(1) Where an asset, or the right to receive an asset, vests in the successor company by virtue of section 1 of this Act, then for the purposes of Part I of the Industry Act 1972—

(a) so much of any expenditure incurred by British Aerospace in providing that asset as is approved capital expenditure (of any description mentioned in section 1(3) of that Act) in respect of which no payment of regional development grant has been made to British Aerospace shall be treated as having been incurred by the successor company and not by British Aerospace ; and

(b) where the asset itself vests in the successor company by virtue of section 1, it shall be treated as a new asset if it would have fallen to be so treated if it had remained vested in British Aerospace.

(2) In this paragraph "regional development grant" means a grant under Part I of the Industry Act 1972 and "approved capital expenditure" has the same meaning as in that Part of that Act.

SCHEDULE 2

TRANSITIONAL PROVISIONS

1.—(1) Subject to the following provisions of this paragraph, subsections (2) to (6) of section 12 of the Act of 1977 (provisions with respect to loans made to British Aerospace or British Shipbuilders by the Secretary of State under section 12(1)) shall continue to apply in relation to any loan made to British Aerospace by the Secretary of State under that section in respect of which any outstanding liability of British Aerospace becomes a liability of the successor company by virtue of section 1 of this Act.

(2) No further directions may be given by the Secretary of State under section 12(2) as it applies in relation to any such loan by virtue of sub-paragraph (1) above, but those applying to any such loan immediately before the appointed day shall apply in relation to payments by the successor company in respect of the loan under section 12(2).

(3) In relation to sums received from the successor company by virtue of this paragraph the reference in section 12(4) to British Aerospace shall be taken as referring to the successor company.

2.—(1) Section 2 of this Act shall not operate to extinguish any liability of British Aerospace under section 15 of the Act of 1977 (commencing capital of each Corporation)—

(a) to repay any part of the principal of its commencing debt which falls due for repayment before the appointed day ; or

(b) to pay interest on its commencing debt in respect of a period falling before that day.

(2) The terms applicable to any such liability immediately before the appointed day by virtue of section 15(4) shall continue to apply to that liability after it becomes a liability of the successor company by virtue of section 1 of this Act, and section 15(5) shall continue to apply to sums received by the Secretary of State from the successor company by virtue of this paragraph.

3. Section 2 of this Act shall not operate to extinguish—

(a) any liability of British Aerospace under section 16 of the Act of 1977 (public dividend capital and public dividends) to make any payment in pursuance of section 16(2) in respect of a period falling before the appointed day ; or

(b) any liability of British Aerospace under section 45 of that SCH. 2
Act (other payments to British Aerospace) to make any
payment in respect of the capital amounts mentioned in
section 2(c) of this Act corresponding to a payment under
section 16(2) and relating to a period falling before the
appointed day ;

and any sums received by the Secretary of State from the successor
company in discharge of any such liability shall be paid into the
Consolidated Fund.

4.—(1) Section 41(5) or (as the case may be) section 44(5) of the
Act of 1977 shall apply to any sums repaid to the Secretary of State
by the successor company in discharge of any liability of British
Aerospace under section 41(4) or section 44(4) which became a
liability of that company on the appointed day.

(2) Section 44(4) (as it has effect by virtue of section 10(1) of this
Act) shall not require the Secretary of State to demand repayment
from British Shipbuilders of the whole of any amounts paid by him
in respect of his expenses under section 44, but he may instead, if
he thinks fit, require repayment of such proportion only of any such
amounts as in his opinion ought to be defrayed by that Corporation.

5.—(1) Any record kept in accordance with arrangements made by
British Aerospace before the appointed day under paragraph 3(2) of
Schedule 5 to the Act of 1977 shall be maintained by the Secretary
of State during such part of the period specified in paragraph 3(1)
as falls after that day ; and paragraph 9 of that Schedule shall apply
to the Secretary of State as it applies to British Shipbuilders.

(2) The reference in paragraph 14 of Schedule 6 to the Act of 1977
to any record kept by British Shipbuilders under Schedule 5 shall
include a reference to any record maintained by the Secretary of
State in accordance with this paragraph.

6. The repeals made by this Act in the House of Commons Disqualification Act 1975 and the Northern Ireland Assembly Dis- 1975 c. 24.
qualification Act 1975, and the corresponding repeal in section 1(10) 1975 c. 25.
of the Act of 1977, shall not take effect until British Aerospace is
dissolved.

SCHEDULE 3

ENACTMENTS REPEALED

Chapter	Short title	Extent of repeal
1975 c. 24.	The House of Commons Disqualification Act 1975.	In Part II of Schedule 1, the entry relating to British Aerospace.
1975 c. 25.	The Northern Ireland Assembly Disqualification Act 1975.	In Part II of Schedule 1, the entry relating to British Aerospace.
1977 c. 3.	The Aircraft and Shipbuilding Industries Act 1977.	In section 1, subsection (1)(*a*), in subsection (7) the words from " British Aerospace " to " to ", and in subsection (10) the words " ' British Aerospace '; and ". Section 2(1). In section 5, subsection (1) and in subsections (4) and (5)(*a*) the words " (1) or ". In section 7, subsection (3) and in subsection (4) the definition of " estimated cost ". In section 11, in subsection (1) the words " (6) and ", subsection (6), in subsection (8) the words " (6) or ", in subsection (9) the words " (6) and " and heads (i), (ii) and (iv) of paragraph (*b*), and in subsection (10) the words " subsection (6) or ". In section 13(4), the words from "to whose" to "relates". In section 14, subsections (1) and (3)(*a*) and (*d*). In section 15(2), in paragraph (*b*)(ii), the words " subsection (1) or ", and paragraph (*c*). Sections 45 and 46. In section 48, in subsection (1) the words " respective ", " British Aerospace and " and " each ", and subsection (2)(*a*). Section 49 (13).

Import of Live Fish (England and Wales) Act 1980

1980 CHAPTER 27

An Act to restrict in England and Wales the import, keeping or release of live fish or shellfish or the live eggs or milt of fish or shellfish of certain species. [15th May 1980]

BE IT ENACTED by the Queen's most Excellent Majesty, by and with the advice and consent of the Lords Spiritual and Temporal, and Commons, in this present Parliament assembled, and by the authority of the same, as follows:—

1.—(1) Without prejudice to section 1(1) of the Diseases of Fish Act 1937 and subject to subsection (2) below, the Minister may by order forbid either absolutely or except under a licence granted under this section, the import into, or the keeping or the release, in any part of England and Wales of live fish, or the live eggs of fish, of a species which is not native to England and Wales and which in the opinion of the Minister might compete with, displace, prey on or harm the habitat of any freshwater fish, shellfish or salmon in England and Wales. *Power to limit the import etc. of fish and fish eggs.* *1937 c. 33.*

(2) Before determining whether or not to make an order under this section, the Minister shall consult the Nature Conservancy Council and any other person with whom the Minister considers that consultation is appropriate.

(3) The Minister may, subject to such conditions as he thinks fit, grant a licence to any person to import or keep live fish, or the live eggs of fish, of a species specified in an order under this section and the Minister may revoke or vary any such licence.

(4) An order under this section may, with the consent of the Treasury, authorise the making of a charge for a licence under this section and shall specify a maximum charge.

(5) The power conferred by this section to make orders shall be exercisable by statutory instrument, which shall be subject to annulment in pursuance of a resolution of either House of Parliament.

Powers of
entry and
inspection.
2.—(1) While an order under section 1 of this Act is in force any officer commissioned by the Commissioners of Customs and Excise, a police constable or a person duly authorised by the Minister may at all reasonable times, on production of his authority if so required, enter and inspect any land occupied by a person holding a licence granted under that section and any other land upon which he has reason to believe that live fish, or the live eggs of fish, of the species specified in the order are being kept or may be found.

(2) In this section " land " includes land covered with water but does not include a dwelling-house.

Offences etc.
3.—(1) Subject to subsection (2) below, any person who—

    (*a*) imports or attempts to import into, or keeps or releases, in any part of England and Wales any live fish, or the live eggs of fish, of a species specified in an order under section 1 of this Act—

        (i) in a case where the order forbids absolutely such import, keeping or release ;

        (ii) without having a valid licence granted under the said section 1 authorising such import or keeping, in a case where the order forbids the import or keeping except under such a licence;

    (*b*) being the holder of a licence granted to him under the said section 1, acts in contravention of or fails to comply with any term of the licence;

    (*c*) obstructs any person from entering or inspecting any land in pursuance of section 2 of this Act;

shall be guilty of an offence under this Act and shall be liable on summary conviction to a fine not exceeding £500.

(2) A person shall not be guilty of an offence under this Act in respect of any act if he does the act for some scientific or research purpose authorised by the Minister.

(3) The Court by whom any person is convicted of an offence under paragraph (*a*) or (*b*) of subsection (1) above shall order any fish or eggs in respect of which the offence was committed to be forfeited and destroyed.

(4) Any person who is empowered to enter land under section 2 of this Act may seize any fish or eggs with respect to which he has reason to believe that an offence under paragraph (*a*) or (*b*) of subsection (1) above has been committed, and may detain them pending the determination of any proceedings to be instituted under the said paragraph (*a*) or (*b*), or until the Minister is satisfied that no such proceedings are likely to be instituted.

4. In this Act—   Interpretation.

" eggs " include milt;

" fish " includes shellfish;

" freshwater fish " means any fish living in fresh water including eels and the fry of eels, but excluding salmon;

" Minister " means

> (*a*) in relation to England, the Minister of Agriculture, Fisheries and Food; and

> (*b*) in relation to Wales, the Secretary of State for Wales;

" salmon " includes all migratory fish of the species Salmo salar and Salmo trutta commonly known as salmon and sea trout respectively;

" shellfish " includes crustaceans and molluscs of any kind and any spat or spawn of shellfish.

5.—(1) This Act may be cited as the Import of Live Fish   Short title (England and Wales) Act 1980.   and extent.

(2) This Act extends to England and Wales only.

Iran
(Temporary Powers) Act 1980

1980 CHAPTER 28

An Act to enable provision to be made in consequence of breaches of international law by Iran in connection with or arising out of the detention of members of the embassy of the United States of America.

[15th May 1980]

BE IT ENACTED by the Queen's most Excellent Majesty, by and with the advice and consent of the Lords Spiritual and Temporal, and Commons, in this present Parliament assembled, and by the authority of the same, as follows:—

Powers with respect to certain contracts relating to or connected with Iran.

1.—(1) Her Majesty may by Order in Council make such provision in relation to contracts in any way relating to or connected with Iran, being either contracts for services or contracts for the sale, supply or transport of goods, as appears to Her to be necessary or expedient in consequence of breaches of international law by Iran in connection with or arising out of the detention of members of the embassy of the United States of America.

(2) An Order in Council under subsection (1)—

(*a*) shall not apply to any contract made before the date on which the Order is made; and

(*b*) shall not apply to any contract with a bank or other financial institution for the provision of banking or other financial services.

(3) Without prejudice to the generality of subsection (1), but subject to subsection (2), an Order in Council under subsection (1) may make such provision for imposing prohibitions, restrictions or obligations in respect of contracts within subsection (1) as appears to Her Majesty to be necessary or expedient as aforesaid.

(4) Any provision made by or under an Order in Council under subsection (1) may apply to acts or omissions outside as well as within the United Kingdom or other country or territory to which the Order extends; but no provision so made shall render a person guilty of an offence in respect of anything done or omitted by him otherwise than within, or within the territorial waters of, the United Kingdom or a country or territory to which this Act extends unless at the time of the act or omission that person is—

> (*a*) a citizen of the United Kingdom and Colonies, a person who is a British subject by virtue of section 2, 13 or 16 of the British Nationality Act 1948 or the British 1948 c. 56. Nationality Act 1965 or a British protected person 1965 c. 34. within the meaning of the said Act of 1948; or
>
> (*b*) a body incorporated or constituted under the law of any part of the United Kingdom or the law of any other country or territory to which this Act extends; or
>
> (*c*) in control of a ship or aircraft registered in the United Kingdom or any other country or territory to which this Act extends.

(5) An Order in Council under this section may make or authorise the making of such incidental, supplemental and consequential provisions as appear to Her Majesty to be expedient for the purposes of the Order.

(6) An Order in Council under this section shall be laid before Parliament after being made and shall expire at the end of the period of twenty-eight days beginning with the day on which it was made unless during that period it is approved by resolution of each House of Parliament.

The expiration of an Order in pursuance of this subsection shall not affect the power to make a new Order; and in calculating the period aforesaid no account shall be taken of any time during which Parliament is dissolved or prorogued or during which both Houses are adjourned for more than four days.

2.—(1) This Act may be cited as the Iran (Temporary Powers) Short title, etc. Act 1980.

(2) This Act shall come into force on 17th May 1980.

(3) Section 1 shall continue in force until such date as Her Majesty may by Order in Council appoint, and shall then expire.

(4) Her Majesty may by Order in Council make such provision in relation to contracts of any description mentioned in section 1(1) as appears to Her to be necessary or expedient in connection with the expiration of section 1; and an Order in Council under this subsection may make or authorise the making of such incidental, supplemental and consequential provisions as appear to Her Majesty to be expedient for the purposes of the Order.

(5) This Act extends to the Channel Islands, the Isle of Man and any colony and (to the extent of Her Majesty's jurisdiction therein) to any foreign country or territory in which for the time being Her Majesty has jurisdiction.

Concessionary Travel For Handicapped Persons (Scotland) Act 1980

1980 CHAPTER 29

An Act to enable local authorities in Scotland to provide concessionary travel schemes for handicapped persons; and for connected purposes. [23rd May 1980]

BE IT ENACTED by the Queen's most Excellent Majesty, by and with the advice and consent of the Lords Spiritual and Temporal, and Commons, in this present Parliament assembled, and by the authority of the same, as follows:—

1.—(1) Without prejudice to the Travel Concessions Acts 1955 and 1964, any local authority operating a public service vehicle undertaking may make arrangements for the granting of travel concessions to handicapped persons travelling on the public service vehicles run by the authority, or on any of those vehicles to which the arrangements relate.

Travel concessions for handicapped persons.
1955 c. 26.
1964 c. 95.

(2) The provisions of subsections (1), (3) and (4) of section 138 of the Transport Act 1968 (arrangements as to travel concessions to be granted by Passenger Transport Executive or by other person) shall apply in relation to handicapped persons as those provisions apply in relation to persons mentioned in subsection (5) of that section.

1968 c. 73.

(3) A local authority may contribute to any cost incurred by any other local authority in granting travel concessions under this Act.

Interpretation.

2.—(1) In section 1 of this Act—

" handicapped persons " means persons who, not being qualified persons within the meaning of the Travel Concessions Acts 1955 and 1964—

1960 c. 61.

    (*a*) suffer from mental disorder within the meaning of the Mental Health (Scotland) Act 1960 ;

    (*b*) are deaf or dumb ; or

    (*c*) are substantially and permanently handicapped by illness, injury, defective hearing, defective sight or congenital deformity or by such other disabilities as may be prescribed by the Secretary of State by regulations ;

" local authority " means a regional or islands council ;

1955 c. 26.

" public service vehicle " has the same meaning as in the Public Service Vehicles (Travel Concessions) Act 1955, and " public service vehicle undertaking " shall be construed accordingly ; and

" travel concession " has the same meaning as in the said Act of 1955.

(2) The power to make regulations under subsection (1)(*c*) above shall be exercisable by statutory instrument which shall be subject to annulment in pursuance of a resolution of either House of Parliament.

Expenses.

3. There shall be defrayed out of money provided by Parliament any increase attributable to this Act in the sums payable out of such moneys under any other Act.

Short title, and extent.

4.—(1) This Act may be cited as the Concessionary Travel For Handicapped Persons (Scotland) Act 1980.

(2) This Act extends to Scotland only.

Social Security Act 1980

1980 CHAPTER 30

An Act to amend the law relating to social security and the
Pensions Appeal Tribunals Act 1943.
[23rd May 1980]

BE IT ENACTED by the Queen's most Excellent Majesty, by and
with the advice and consent of the Lords Spiritual and
Temporal, and Commons, in this present Parliament
assembled, and by the authority of the same, as follows:—

Amendments of certain enactments relating to social security

1.—(1) For the purposes of any review under section 125 of Amendments
the Social Security Act 1975 (under which the Secretary of State relating to
is required in each tax year to review the sums mentioned in up-rating.
subsection (1) of that section and in section 23(1) of the Social 1975 c. 14.
Security Pensions Act 1975 for the purpose of determining 1975 c. 60.
whether they have retained their value in relation to the general
level of earnings or prices obtaining in Great Britain) the Secretary of State shall have regard only to prices except that as respects the sum specified in section 30(1) (excluding paragraphs
(a) and (b)) of the Social Security Act 1975 he shall have regard
only to earnings ; and accordingly in subsection (1) of the said
section 125 for the words " earnings or prices obtaining in Great
Britain " there shall be substituted the words " prices obtaining
in Great Britain except that as respects the sum specified in
section 30(1) (excluding paragraphs (a) and (b)) of this Act
he shall instead have regard to the general level of earnings
obtaining in Great Britain ".

(2) In relation to a draft of an up-rating order which, in consequence of a review under the said section 125 made before the passing of this Act, falls to be prepared after the passing of this Act in pursuance of subsection (3) of that section (which provides for increasing reviewed sums which have not retained their value as mentioned in subsection (1) of that section), the restoration of value mentioned in the said subsection (3) shall be deemed to be a restoration of value by reference to prices except as respects the sum specified as aforesaid.

1975 c. 14.

(3) In section 126(5) of the Social Security Act 1975 (under which a draft order under section 125(3) of that Act to increase a sum must provide for the increase to come into force in certain cases not later than at the end of the period of 12 months beginning with the date on which the provision fixing the current amount of the sum came into force) for the words from " of 12 months " to " came into force " there shall be substituted the words " beginning with the date on which the provision fixing the current amount of that sum came into force and ending with the last day of the month in which the first anniversary of that date falls ".

Other amendments of Social Security Act 1975.

2. The Social Security Act 1975 (hereafter in this Act referred to as " the principal Act ") shall have effect with the amendments specified in Schedule 1 to this Act, and references in that Schedule to sections and Schedules are to sections of and Schedules to that Act.

Amendments of Social Security Pensions Act 1975.
1975 c. 60.

3.—(1) In section 62(1) of the Social Security Pensions Act 1975 (which provides among other things that regulations under section 9(3) of that Act prescribing a maximum for the additional component of a Category A retirement pension are subject to the affirmative resolution procedure) the words " or 9(3) " shall be omitted ; and accordingly a statutory instrument containing regulations under the said section 9(3) is subject to annulment in pursuance of a resolution of either House of Parliament by virtue of section 66(2) of that Act (hereafter in this Act referred to as " the Pensions Act ") and section 167(3) of the principal Act.

(2) At the end of section 11 of the Pensions Act (which excludes certain sums from the rate of a pension mentioned in section 30(1) of the principal Act) there shall be inserted the words " ; but the preceding provisions of this section shall be disregarded for the purposes of section 27(3)(*b*)(ii) of that Act (which provides for a person to be treated as retired by reference to the said section 30(1)) ".

(3) In subsection (3) of section 21 of the Pensions Act (which provides that if on a review under that section of the general

level of earnings the Secretary of State concludes that certain earnings factors have not retained their value during the review period he shall prepare and lay before Parliament the draft of an order increasing the factors so as to make up the fall in their value together with falls made up by earlier orders) for the words from " prepare " to " draft of " there shall be substituted the word " make " ; and accordingly—

(a) the same amendment shall be made in subsection (5) of that section (which provides that where the Secretary of State determines that he is not required to prepare and lay such a draft he shall report to Parliament his reasons for the determination) ; and

(b) a statutory instrument containing an order under the said subsection (3) is subject to annulment as mentioned in subsection (1) of this section.

(4) In section 21(1) of the Social Security (Miscellaneous 1977 c. 5. Provisions) Act 1977 (which provides that, unless the prescribed person otherwise elects, section 35(5) of the Pensions Act shall have effect, in a case where pension rights are preserved under approved arrangements, without taking into account any orders under section 21 of the Pensions Act which were made in the five years ending with the year in which the scheme ceases to be contracted-out and as if relevant earnings factors were increased by 12 per cent. for each of the years there mentioned), for the words from " have effect " onwards there shall be substituted the words " in a case where one or more of the five tax years ending with the tax year in which the scheme ceases to be contracted-out is a relevant year in relation to the earner, have effect, unless the prescribed person otherwise elects in the prescribed manner, subject to the following provisions, that is to say—

(a) any order made under section 21 above in any of those five tax years increasing an earnings factor shall be disregarded (but without prejudice to any increase made by the last order made under that section before the beginning of those five tax years) ; and

(b) any relevant earnings factor derived from contributions in respect of any year (hereafter in this subsection referred to as ' the relevant contributions year ') shall be treated as increased by 12 per cent. compound for each of those five tax years, other than any of those years which—

(i) constitutes or begins before the relevant contributions year, or

(ii) begins after the final relevant year in relation to the earner.".

(5) In section 38(1) of the Pensions Act (which among other things provides that where a person leaves employment which is contracted-out by reference to a scheme, the scheme may provide for his rights to benefits under the scheme to be transferred to another scheme but, except in prescribed cases, only with his consent and to another contracted-out scheme) for the words " to another contracted-out scheme " there shall be substituted the words " if the other scheme is a contracted-out scheme in relation to an employment of his at the time of the transfer ".

(6) In section 41 of the Pensions Act, after subsection (1) (which provides that for an occupational pension scheme, other than a public service scheme, to be contracted-out the Occupational Pensions Board must be satisfied that the scheme's resources are sufficient for meeting claims in respect of guaranteed minimum pensions as mentioned in paragraph (*a*), for paying state scheme premiums as mentioned in paragraph (*b*) and for meeting on winding up the liabilities and expenses mentioned in paragraph (*c*) of that subsection) there shall be inserted the following subsection—

(1A) Regulations may—

    (*a*) provide for subsection (1) above to have effect, in cases specified in the regulations, with the omission of paragraphs (*b*) and (*c*) of that subsection or either of those paragraphs or with the substitution for those paragraphs or either of them of provisions so specified ; and

1977 c. 5.

    (*b*) make such amendments to section 22(9)(*a*) of the Social Security (Miscellaneous Provisions) Act 1977 (which refers to paragraphs (*b*) and (*c*) of subsection (1) above) as the Secretary of State considers appropriate in consequence of regulations made by virtue of paragraph (*a*) of this subsection.

(7) It is hereby declared—

    (*a*) that an approval of arrangements relating to a scheme may be withdrawn in pursuance of section 44(4) of the Pensions Act at any time notwithstanding that the scheme has been wound up ; and

    (*b*) that on the withdrawal of such an approval after the winding up of the scheme a premium becomes payable in pursuance of section 44(2) of that Act ;

and in subsection (10) of section 22 of the Social Security (Miscellaneous Provisions) Act 1977 (which provides for the cancellation of a certificate issued under subsection (9) of that section if the Secretary of State considers that it was issued in consequence of a mistake and provides for the payment of a premium in pursuance of the said section 44(2) on the cancellation of such a certificate) after the word " considers " there shall be inserted the word " (*a*) " and after the word " mistake " there shall be inserted the words " ; or

(*b*) that the person upon whom an obligation to pay benefits in respect of an employment is imposed by the policy of insurance or annuity contract to which such a certificate relates is likely to fail to discharge the obligation,".

(8) For subsection (6) of section 44 of the Pensions Act (which provides that the costs which an accrued rights premium or a pensioner's rights premium is to defray shall, unless the person liable for the premium elects otherwise, be calculated on the basis there mentioned) there shall be substituted the following subsection—

(6) In determining the amount of any state scheme premium payable under this section where one or more of the five tax years ending with the tax year in which the scheme ceases to be contracted-out is a relevant year in relation to the earner, the costs referred to in subsection (5)(*a*) and (*b*) above shall, unless the person liable for the premium elects in the prescribed manner that this subsection shall not apply, be calculated as follows—

(*a*) any order made under section 21 above in any of those five tax years increasing a relevant earnings factor shall be disregarded (but without prejudice to any increase made by the last order made under that section before the beginning of those five tax years) ; and

(*b*) any relevant earnings factor derived from contributions in respect of any year (hereafter in this subsection referred to as " the relevant contributions year ") shall be treated as increased by 12 per cent. compound for each of those five tax years, other than any of those years which—

(i) constitutes or begins before the relevant contributions year, or

(ii) begins after the final relevant year in relation to the earner ;

and in this subsection " relevant year " and " final relevant year " have the same meanings as in section 35 above and references to the earner shall be construed as references to the earner in respect of whom or, as the case may be, in respect of whose widow the premium in question has become payable.

(9) In subsection (3) of section 45 of the Pensions Act (which provides that the costs the difference between which a limited revaluation premium is to defray shall, unless the person liable for the premium elects otherwise, be calculated on the basis there mentioned) for the words from " be calculated " onwards there shall be substituted the words " unless the person liable for the premium elects in the prescribed manner that this subsection shall not apply, be calculated as follows—

    (*a*) any order made under section 21 above increasing an earnings factor and made in any of the five tax years ending with the tax year in which the scheme ceases to be contracted-out shall be disregarded (but without prejudice to any increase made by the last order made under that section before the beginning of those five tax years) ; and

    (*b*) any relevant earnings factor derived from contributions in respect of any year (hereafter in this subsection referred to as ' the relevant contributions year ') shall be treated as increased by 12 per cent. compound for each of those five tax years, other than any of those years which constitutes or begins before the relevant contributions year.".

(10) Without prejudice to their powers apart from this subsection, the Occupational Pensions Board may withhold or cancel by virtue of this subsection a contracting-out certificate in respect of a scheme if they consider that the rules of the scheme are such that persons over particular ages may be prevented from participating in the scheme ; and without prejudice to the effect apart from this subsection of subsections (1) and (2) of section 50 of the Pensions Act (which among other things provide that certain alterations of the rules of certain schemes are not to be made without the consent of the Board), those subsections shall apply to an alteration of the rules of a scheme mentioned in subsection (1) of that section which would make the rules such as aforesaid as those subsections apply to an alteration mentioned in that subsection.

(11) In Schedule 1 to the Pensions Act (into which a paragraph 4A providing for further increases of a retirement pension was inserted by the Social Security Act 1979), after the words " increase under paragraph 4 " in paragraph 2(4) there shall be inserted the words " or 4A ".

1979 c. 18.

(12) In paragraph 6 of Schedule 2 to the Pensions Act—

    (*a*) after paragraph (*b*) of sub-paragraph (3) (under which regulations may provide for treating a premium as actually paid in certain circumstances) there shall be inserted the following paragraph—

> (*bb*) for treating part of a premium payable in prescribed circumstances in respect of a person as actually paid and for modifying Part III of this Act in relation to a case in which such a part is so treated ;

(*b*) at the end of sub-paragraph (3) there shall be inserted the words " and the Secretary of State may accept payments in connection with a case in which a premium or part of it is treated as actually paid and shall pay into the National Insurance Fund any sums received by him by way of such payments." ; and

(*c*) after sub-paragraph (3) there shall be inserted the following sub-paragraph—

> (4) Without prejudice to sub-paragraph (3) above, regulations may provide—
>
> > (*a*) that for the purpose of extinguishing accrued rights to guaranteed minimum pensions and rights to receive such pensions a state scheme premium is to be treated as actually paid on a date determined under the regulations ;
> >
> > (*b*) for disregarding the effect of regulations made by virtue of paragraph (*a*) of this sub-paragraph in a case where the premium in question is not paid on or before the date when it becomes payable or such later date as may be determined under the regulations ; and
> >
> > (*c*) for obtaining repayment of benefits paid by virtue of regulations so made in a case where the effect of the regulations is to be disregarded, and, where the repayment is obtained from assets of the relevant scheme, for reducing the sums payable under the scheme to the beneficiary by the amount of the repayment.

4.—(1) In the definitions of " public service pension scheme " in section 51(3) of the Social Security Act 1973 and section 66(1) of the Pensions Act (which provide among other things that the definition includes any scheme prescribed by such regulations as are there mentioned) after the word " includes " there shall be inserted the words " any occupational pension scheme established, with the concurrence of the Minister for the Civil Service, by or with the approval of another Minister of the Crown and ".

Miscellaneous amendments.
1973 c. 38.

(2) Subsection (3) of section 97 of the Social Security Act 1973 (which provides for orders made by the Secretary of State under that Act to be subject to annulment in pursuance of a resolution of either House of Parliament) shall have effect in relation to orders under section 65 of that Act (under which a public service pension scheme may be modified or wound up by an order made by an authority designated by the Minister for the Civil Service) as if the reference in that subsection to the Secretary of State were a reference to an appropriate authority within the meaning of the said section 65.

1975 c. 16.

(3) In section 6(2) of the Industrial Injuries and Diseases (Old Cases) Act 1975 (which provides that a scheme under section 5 of that Act shall not provide for benefit for or in respect of a person disabled or dying from byssinosis unless he was employed for five years in an occupation prescribed in relation to that disease and shall not provide for benefit for a person so disabled unless the disablement is likely to be permanent) the words from " shall " where it first occurs to " disease, and " shall be omitted and for the words " so disabled " there shall be substituted the words " disabled as a result of the disease of byssinosis ".

1975 c. 61.

(4) Regulations under subsection (1) of section 81 of the principal Act or subsection (5) of section 6 of the Child Benefit Act 1975 (which among other things enable regulations to be made about the manner of paying benefit) may provide that, in relation to payments of benefit under the principal Act, or as the case may be of child benefit, which in pursuance of regulations under the said subsection (1) or (5) have been credited to a bank account or other account under arrangements made with the agreement of the beneficiary, section 119 of the principal Act (which among other things provides for the repayment of over-payments of benefit under that Act and is applied to child benefit by section 8(1) of the other Act) shall have effect with such modifications as are prescribed by the regulations ; but any modifications so prescribed shall not apply in relation to any payment of benefit unless notice of the effect of the modifications was given to the beneficiary in accordance with the regulations before he agreed to the arrangements.

In this subsection " modifications " includes additions, omissions and amendments.

(5) In section 2(3) of the Child Benefit Act 1975 (which among other things enables regulations to provide that a person who ceases in any week to be a child for the purposes of Part I of that Act shall be treated as continuing to be such a child for a prescribed period ending not more than 13 weeks after the end of that week) the words from " ending " to " that week " shall be omitted.

(6) It is hereby declared that in paragraph (*a*) of section 18(1) of the Social Security (Miscellaneous Provisions) Act 1977 (which 1977 c. 5. among other things enables regulations to provide that certain sums shall be deemed for the purposes of the principal Act to be such earnings as are mentioned in that paragraph) the reference to the purposes of the principal Act includes the purposes of the Pensions Act.

5.—(1) Where— Maternity grant.

    (*a*) the date of a woman's confinement is the same as or later than the appointed date ; or

    (*b*) a woman claims a maternity grant by virtue of regulations under section 21(5) of the principal Act in a case where the week which is treated in pursuance of the regulations as that in which she is expected to be confined includes or begins after the appointed date,

the following provisions of the principal Act shall have effect in relation to the confinement or claim with the following amendments, namely—

    (i) in section 12, in subsection (1)(*d*) (under which maternity benefit comprising maternity grant and maternity allowance is a contributory benefit under Chapter I of Part II of that Act) for the words from the beginning to " allowance " there shall be substituted the words " maternity allowance " and in subsection (2) (which specifies the benefits which are short-term benefits for the purposes of that Part) the words " maternity grant " shall be omitted ;

    (ii) in section 13(1) (which relates to contribution conditions) the words " Maternity grant . . . Class 1, 2 or 3 " shall be omitted ;

    (iii) in section 21 (under subsections (1) and (2) of which certain contribution conditions are to be satisfied in order to confer entitlement to a maternity grant) for the words from " and either " onwards in subsection (1) there shall be substituted the words " and satisfies prescribed conditions as to residence and presence in Great Britain " and subsection (2) and in subsection (5) the words from " and may modify the contribution conditions " onwards shall be omitted ;

    (iv) at the end of section 135(2) (which specifies the benefits which are to be paid out of money provided by Parliament instead of from the National Insurance Fund) there shall be inserted the words " (*g*) a maternity grant " ;

    (v) in Schedule 3, paragraphs 2 and 11 (which relate to contribution conditions for a maternity grant) and in paragraph 8(3) the words " a maternity grant " shall be omitted ;

(vi) in the definition of " short-term benefit " in Schedule 20 the words " maternity grant " shall be omitted.

(2) In the preceding subsection " the appointed date " means such date as the Secretary of State may appoint for the purposes of that subsection by order made by statutory instrument ; and subsection (1) of section 23 of the principal Act (which among other things defines the expression " confinement " for the purposes of the Chapter which contains that section) shall have effect as if paragraphs (*a*) and (*b*) of the preceding subsection were provisions of that Chapter.

(3) References in any enactment to maternity benefit under the principal Act shall continue to be references to maternity grant and maternity allowance under that Act.

(4) Nothing in subsection (1) of this section affects the operation of paragraphs 9, 10, 12 and 13 of Schedule 3 to the principal Act (which relate to entitlement to certain benefits by reference to other benefits which include a maternity grant) so far as they relate to a maternity grant to which that subsection does not apply.

Amendments of enactments relating to supplementary benefit and family income supplement

Amendments
of Supple-
mentary
Benefits Act
1976.
1976 c. 71.

6.—(1) The Supplementary Benefits Act 1976 shall have effect with the amendments specified in Part I of Schedule 2 to this Act, and except where the context otherwise requires references in that Part to sections and Schedules are to sections of and Schedules to that Act.

(2) The Supplementary Benefits Commission is hereby abolished.

(3) In accordance with subsection (1) of this section but subject to section 14 of this Act, Parts I to III of the Supplementary Benefits Act 1976, except sections 31, 32, 35 and 36 (which relate to reciprocity and to transitional, consequential and supplemental matters), and Schedules 1 and 5 to that Act are to have effect, after the coming into force of subsection (1) of this section and Part I of Schedule 2 to this Act, as set out in Part II of that Schedule (which reproduces those provisions as amended by Part I of the said Schedule 2 and with consequential adjustments in headings and sidenotes).

(4) Until the coming into force of subsection (1) of this section and Part I of Schedule 2 to this Act, section 34 of the said Act of 1976 (which provides for the interpretation of that

Act) shall have effect as if after subsection (2) of that section there were inserted the following subsection—

(3) In determining for the purposes of this Act whether a person (in this subsection referred to as "the provider") has to provide for, or for the requirements of, another person to or in respect of whom any payments are made otherwise than by the provider, the other person shall not by reason only of the payments or the amount of them be treated as a person who is, or whose requirements are, provided for otherwise than by the provider.

7.—(1) In section 1 of the Family Income Supplements Act 1970 (of which subsection (1) specifies the persons who constitute a family for the purposes of that Act)—

Amendments of Family Income Supplements Act 1970. 1970 c. 55.

(a) for paragraphs (a) and (b) of subsection (1) there shall be substituted the following—

" (a) a man or woman engaged and normally engaged in remunerative full-time work ; and

(b) if the person mentioned in the preceding paragraph is one of a married or unmarried couple, the other member of the couple ; and "

(b) at the end of that subsection there shall be inserted the words " except that persons who include a married or unmarried couple shall not be a family for the purposes of this Act if one of the couple is engaged and normally engaged as aforesaid and the other member of the couple is receiving such payments as may be specified by regulations " ; and

(c) after that subsection there shall be inserted the following subsection—

(1A) It shall be the duty of the Secretary of State to appoint persons to perform the functions conferred by this Act on supplement officers.

(2) For any reference to the Supplementary Benefits Commission in that Act, except section 7(1), there shall be substituted a reference to a supplement officer.

(3) At the end of section 6(1) of that Act (which provides for the determination of certain questions relating to family income supplement) there shall be inserted the words " , and regulations may provide for different aspects of the same question to be dealt with by different supplement officers ".

(4) In section 7(1) of that Act (which provides for an appeal from a determination of the Supplementary Benefits Commission) for the words from " the Supplementary " to " the Commission " there shall be substituted the words " a supplement officer including a refusal ".

(5) In section 10 of that Act (which specifies the matters for which provision may be made by regulations)—

(*a*) after paragraph (*b*) of subsection (2) there shall be inserted the following paragraph—

(*bb*) for determining the circumstances in which persons are to be treated as being or not being members of the same household ;

(*b*) for subsection (3) there shall be substituted the following subsections—

(3) Regulations may also provide—

(*a*) for specified questions to be referred to the Appeal Tribunal or other bodies or persons exercising functions under the Social Security Act 1975, the Child Benefit Act 1975 or the Supplementary Benefits Act 1976 and for the application of provisions of this Act or any of those Acts, with or without modifications, to the questions and to decisions given in consequence of references in pursuance of the regulations ;

(*b*) for such decisions, and any other specified decisions given in pursuance of any of those Acts, to be effective or conclusive for specified purposes of this Act ; and

(*c*) for dealing, by postponement or otherwise, with cases in which questions are referred by virtue of paragraph (*a*) of this sub-section ;

and section 6(1) of this Act shall have effect subject to any regulations made in pursuance of this subsection.

1975 c. 14.

(3A) Subsections (2) and (3) of section 166 of the Social Security Act 1975 (which among other things make provision about the extent of powers to make regulations) shall apply to powers to make regulations conferred by this Act as they apply to powers to make regulations conferred by that Act but as if for references to that Act there were substituted references to this Act.

(6) In section 17(1) of that Act (which defines expressions used in that Act) the following definitions shall be inserted at the appropriate places in alphabetical order—

" married couple " means a man and a woman who are married to each other and are members of the same household ;

" supplement officer " means a person appointed in pursuance of section 1(1A) of this Act ;

" unmarried couple " means a man and a woman who are not married to each other but are living together as husband and wife ;

and the definition of " single woman " shall be omitted.

8.—(1) The Secretary of State may by regulations make such Provisions supplementary to ss. 6 and 7. provision as he considers appropriate for dealing with transitional matters connected with or arising out of the coming into force of any provision of section 6 or 7 of this Act or Schedule 2 or 5 to this Act including in particular, but without prejudice to the generality of the preceding provisions of this subsection,—

(a) provision for modifying any enactment passed before this Act ;

(b) provision for treating anything done under an enactment which is altered or replaced by a provision of the sections or Schedules aforesaid as done under the enactment as so altered or replaced ; and

(c) provision for the payment of supplementary benefit, of an amount specified in or determined in pursuance of the regulations, to a person who, apart from the provision, would by virtue of this Act cease to be entitled to supplementary benefit or become entitled to supplementary benefit of an amount smaller than that to which he would have been entitled apart from this Act ;

and regulations made by virtue of this subsection may be made so as to have effect from a date before that on which they are made but not before the date of the passing of this Act.

(2) An order under section 21(5) of this Act which brings into force a provision of this Act which is mentioned in the preceding subsection—

(a) may contain such transitional provisions, including savings, as the Secretary of State considers appropriate in connection with or arising out of the coming into force of that provision ; and

(b) may, without prejudice to the generality of the preceding paragraph, provide that the provision shall come into force in relation to such cases only as are specified in the order and accordingly that in relation to other cases the law shall remain unaffected by that provision ;

and the Secretary of State may by order made by statutory instrument vary or revoke any provision which by virtue of this subsection is included in another order.

(3) Nothing in either of the preceding subsections shall be construed as derogating from the other of them.

(4) The power to make regulations conferred by subsection (1) of this section shall be exercisable by statutory instrument and a statutory instrument made by virtue of this subsection shall be subject to annulment in pursuance of a resolution of either House of Parliament.

Advisory Committees

The Social Security Advisory Committee.

9.—(1) There shall be a committee, to be known as the Social Security Advisory Committee (and hereafter in this section and in the following section referred to as " the Committee "),—

> (a) to give (whether in pursuance of a reference under this Act or otherwise) advice and assistance to the Secretary of State in connection with the discharge of his functions under the relevant enactments ;
>
> (b) to give (whether in pursuance of a reference under this Act or otherwise) advice and assistance to the Department of Health and Social Services for Northern Ireland (hereafter in this section and in the following section referred to as " the Northern Ireland Department ") in connection with the discharge of its functions under the relevant Northern Ireland enactments ; and
>
> (c) to perform such other duties as may be assigned to the Committee by or under this Act, any of the relevant enactments or relevant Northern Ireland enactments or any other enactment ;

and the National Insurance Advisory Committee is hereby abolished.

(2) Part I of Schedule 3 to this Act shall have effect with respect to the constitution of the Committee and the other matters there mentioned.

(3) The Secretary of State may from time to time refer to the Committee for consideration and advice such questions relating to the operation of any of the relevant enactments as he thinks fit (including questions as to the advisability of amending any of them) ; and the Northern Ireland Department may from time to time refer to the Committee for consideration and advice such questions relating to the operation of any of the relevant Northern Ireland enactments as the Department thinks fit (including questions as to the advisability of amending any of them).

(4) The Secretary of State and the Northern Ireland Department shall furnish the Committee with such information as the Committee may reasonably require for the proper discharge of its functions.

(5) The Secretary of State may by regulations make transitional provision in connection with the abolition of the National Insurance Advisory Committee and the establishment of the Social Security Advisory Committee; and, without prejudice to the generality of the preceding provisions of this subsection, such regulations may contain provision—

> (a) for treating anything done by or in relation to the National Insurance Advisory Committee as having been done by or in relation to the other Committee; and
>
> (b) for repealing section 11(1) of this Act.

The power to make regulations conferred by this subsection shall be exercisable by statutory instrument and a statutory instrument made by virtue of this subsection shall be subject to annulment in pursuance of a resolution of either House of Parliament.

(6) In Part II of Schedule 1 to the House of Commons Disqualification Act 1975 and Part II of Schedule 1 to the Northern Ireland Assembly Disqualification Act 1975 (which list the bodies of which all the members are disqualified under those Acts) there shall be inserted at the appropriate place in alphabetical order the words " The Social Security Advisory Committee ".
1975 c. 24.
1975 c. 25.

(7) In this section and the following section—

> " the relevant enactments " means the Family Income Supplements Act 1970, the Social Security Acts 1975 to 1979, Part I of Schedule 3 to the Social Security (Consequential Provisions) Act 1975, the Child Benefit Act 1975 and the Supplementary Benefits Act 1976; and
1970 c. 55.
1975 c. 18.
1975 c. 61.
1976 c. 71.
>
> " the relevant Northern Ireland enactments " means the Family Income Supplements Act (Northern Ireland) 1971, the Social Security (Northern Ireland) Acts 1975 to 1979, Part I of Schedule 3 to the Social Security (Consequential Provisions) Act 1975, the Child Benefit (Northern Ireland) Order 1975 and the Supplementary Benefits (Northern Ireland) Order 1977;
1971 c. 8 (N.I.).
S.I. 1975/1504 (N.I. 16).
S.I. 1977/2156 (N.I. 27).

but in the preceding provisions of this subsection references to the Social Security Acts 1975 to 1979 and to the Social Security (Northern Ireland) Acts 1975 to 1979 shall be construed as excluding those Acts as they apply to industrial injuries benefit within the meaning respectively of the principal Act and of the Social Security (Northern Ireland) Act 1975 and as excluding respectively Parts III and IV of the Pensions Act and Parts IV and V of the Social Security Pensions (Northern Ireland) Order 1975.
1975 c. 15.
S.I. 1975/1503 (N.I. 15).

10.—(1) Subject to the following subsection, where—

> (*a*) the Secretary of State proposes to make regulations under any of the relevant enactments or under section 123(2) or (3) of the Social Security (Northern Ireland) Act 1975 (which contains provision for modifying that Act in its application to members of Her Majesty's forces) ; or
>
> (*b*) the Northern Ireland Department proposes to make regulations under any of the relevant Northern Ireland enactments,

the Secretary of State or, as the case may be, the Department shall refer the proposals, in the form of draft regulations or otherwise, to the Committee.

(2) The preceding subsection shall not apply to the regulations specified in Part II of Schedule 3 to this Act ; and nothing in that subsection shall require any proposals to be referred to the Committee if—

> (*a*) it appears to the Secretary of State or, as the case may be, the Northern Ireland Department that by reason of the urgency of the matter it is inexpedient so to refer the proposals ; or
>
> (*b*) the Committee has agreed that the proposals should not be referred to it.

(3) The Committee shall consider any proposals referred to it by the Secretary of State or the Northern Ireland Department under this section and shall make to the Secretary of State or, as the case may be, the Department a report containing such recommendations with regard to the subject-matter of the proposals as the Committee thinks appropriate.

(4) If after receiving a report of the Committee the Secretary of State lays before Parliament any regulations or draft regulations which comprise the whole or any part of the subject-matter of the proposals referred to the Committee, he shall lay with the regulations or draft regulations a copy of the Committee's report and a statement showing—

> (*a*) the extent (if any) to which he has, in framing the regulations, given effect to the Committee's recommendations ; and
>
> (*b*) in so far as effect has not been given to them, his reasons why not.

(5) In the case of any regulations laid before Parliament at a time when Parliament is not sitting, the requirements of the preceding subsection shall be satisfied as respects either House of Parliament if a copy of the report and statement there referred to are laid before that House not later than the second day on which the House sits after the laying of the regulations.

(6) If after receiving a report of the Committee the Northern Ireland Department lays before the Northern Ireland Assembly any regulations which comprise the whole or any part of the subject-matter of the proposals referred to the Committee, the Department shall lay with the regulations a copy of the Committee's report and a statement showing—

    (*a*) the extent (if any) to which the Department has, in framing the regulations, given effect to the Committee's recommendations ; and

    (*b*) in so far as effect has not been given to them, the Department's reasons why not.

(7) Where by virtue only of paragraph (*a*) of subsection (2) of this section regulations are made without proposals in respect of the regulations having been referred to the Committee, then, unless the Committee agrees that this subsection shall not apply, the Secretary of State or, as the case may be, the Northern Ireland Department shall, as soon as practicable after making the regulations, refer them to the Committee, which shall consider them and make a report to the Secretary of State or, as the case may be, to the Northern Ireland Department containing such recommendations with regard to the regulations as the Committee thinks appropriate ; and—

    (*a*) a copy of any report made to the Secretary of State in pursuance of this subsection shall be laid by him before each House of Parliament together, if the report contains recommendations, with a statement of the extent (if any) to which the Secretary of State proposes to give effect to the recommendations ;

    (*b*) a copy of any report made to the Northern Ireland Department in pursuance of this subsection shall be laid by the Department before the Northern Ireland Assembly together, if the report contains recommendations, with a statement of the extent (if any) to which the Department proposes to give effect to the recommendations.

(8) Section 41(3) of the Interpretation Act (Northern Ireland) 1954 (which specifies the procedure for laying statutory instruments or statutory documents before the Northern Ireland Assembly) shall apply in relation to any document which by virtue of subsection (6) or (7) of this section is required to be laid before that Assembly as if it were a statutory document within the meaning of that Act.

    1954 c. 33 (N.I.).

(9) In relation to regulations required or authorised to be made by the Secretary of State in conjunction with the Treasury or by the Northern Ireland Department in conjunction with the Department of Finance for Northern Ireland, any reference in

this section to the Secretary of State or the Northern Ireland Department shall be construed as a reference to the authorities making or proposing to make the regulations.

Exclusion of requirements to consult Advisory Committees.

11.—(1) Section 139(1) of the principal Act (which requires the Secretary of State to seek the advice of the National Insurance Advisory Committee on certain proposals to make regulations under that Act) shall, while it remains in force, not apply to—

(*a*) regulations contained in a statutory instrument which states that it contains only provisions in consequence of an order under section 126A of that Act (which provides for the up-rating of certain increments) ; and

(*b*) regulations made during the period of six months beginning with the date of the passing of this Act if the regulations are contained in a statutory instrument which states that it contains only regulations to make provision consequential on the passing of this Act.

(2) Section 141(2) of the principal Act (which requires the Secretary of State to seek the advice of the Industrial Injuries Advisory Council on certain proposals to make regulations under that Act) shall not apply to—

(*a*) regulations contained in a statutory instrument which states that the only provision with respect to industrial injuries benefit or its administration that is made by the regulations is the same or substantially the same as provision made by the instrument with respect to other benefit under Part II of that Act or the administration of such benefit ; and

(*b*) regulations made during the period of six months beginning with the date of the passing of this Act and contained in a statutory instrument which states that it contains only regulations to make provision consequential on the passing of this Act.

Commissioners

Change of title of National Insurance Commissioners.

12. National Insurance Commissioners shall, instead of being so called, be called Social Security Commissioners ; and accordingly—

(*a*) any enactment or instrument passed or made before the coming into force of this section shall have effect, so far as may be necessary in consequence of the change of title made by this section, as if for any reference to a Chief or other National Insurance Commissioner there were substituted respectively a reference to a Chief or other Social Security Commissioner ; and (*b*) documents and forms printed or duplicated for use in connection with functions of National Insurance Commissioners may be used notwithstanding that they contain references to such Commissioners and those references shall be construed as references to Social Security Commissioners.

13.—(1) Subject to subsections (2), (3) and (5) of this section, a Social Security Commissioner appointed after the coming into force of this section shall vacate his office at the end of the completed year of service in which he attains the age of seventy-two. *Tenure of office of Commissioner.*

(2) Where the Lord Chancellor considers it desirable in the public interest to retain a Commissioner in office after the time at which he would be required by the preceding subsection to vacate it, the Lord Chancellor may from time to time authorise the continuance of the Commissioner in office until any date not later than that on which the Commissioner attains the age of seventy-five.

(3) A Social Security Commissioner appointed after the coming into force of this section may be removed from office by the Lord Chancellor on the ground of misbehaviour or incapacity.

(4) Subject to the following subsection, a person who holds office as a Social Security Commissioner shall not practise as a barrister or advocate or act for any remuneration to himself as arbitrator, arbiter or referee or be directly or indirectly concerned in any matter as a conveyancer, notary public or solicitor.

(5) If the Lord Chancellor considers that, in order to facilitate the disposal of the business of Social Security Commissioners, he should make an appointment in pursuance of this subsection, he may appoint a barrister, advocate or solicitor of not less than ten years standing to be a Social Security Commissioner (but to be known as a deputy Commissioner) for such period or on such occasions as the Lord Chancellor thinks fit ; but

(*a*) nothing in subsection (1), (2) or (4) of this section or paragraph 5 or 6 of Schedule 10 to the principal Act (which relate to pensions for Commissioners) shall apply to a person by virtue of his appointment in pursuance of this subsection ; and

(*b*) any reference to a Social Security Commissioner in Part I of Schedule 1 to the House of Commons Disqualification Act 1975 and the Northern Ireland Assembly Disqualification Act 1975 as amended by section 12 of this Act shall be construed as excluding a person appointed in pursuance of this subsection. *1975 c. 24.* *1975 c. 25.*

U 3

(6) When the Lord Chancellor proposes to exercise a power conferred on him by subsection (2), (3) or (5) of this section otherwise than in relation to Northern Ireland, it shall be his duty to consult the Lord Advocate with respect to the proposal.

(7) In relation to a Social Security Commissioner appointed for Northern Ireland after the coming into force of this section—

1975 c. 15.

(a) paragraph 5(1) of Schedule 10 to the Social Security (Northern Ireland) Act 1975 (which provides for retirement) shall not apply ;

(b) in paragraph 6(1)(a) of that Schedule (which relates to pensions on retirement in pursuance of paragraph 5 of that Schedule) for the reference to paragraph 5 there shall be substituted a reference to this section ; and

(c) for the reference in subsection (5) of this section to the paragraph 5 or 6 there mentioned there shall be substituted a reference to paragraph 6 or 7 of that Schedule.

Appeal from Commissioners etc on point of law.

14.—(1) Subject to subsections (2) and (3) of this section, an appeal on a question of law shall lie to the appropriate court from any decision of a Commissioner.

(2) No appeal under this section shall lie from a decision except—

(a) with the leave of the Commissioner who gave the decision or, in a case prescribed by regulations, with the leave of a Commissioner selected in accordance with regulations ; or

(b) if he refuses leave, with the leave of the appropriate court.

(3) An application for leave under this section in respect of a Commissioner's decision may only be made by—

(a) a person who, before the proceedings before the Commissioner were begun, was entitled to appeal to the Commissioner from the decision to which the Commissioner's decision relates ;

(b) any other person who was a party to the proceedings in which the first decision mentioned in the preceding paragraph was given ;

(c) the Secretary of State or the Department of Health and Social Services for Northern Ireland in a case where he or the Department is not entitled to apply for leave by virtue of either of the preceding paragraphs ; and

(d) any other person who is authorised by regulations to apply for leave ;

and regulations may make provision with respect to the manner in which and the time within which applications must be made to a Commissioner for leave under this section and with respect to the procedure for dealing with such applications.

(4) On an application to a Commissioner for leave under this section it shall be the duty of the Commissioner to specify as the appropriate court—

    (a) the Court of Appeal if it appears to him that the relevant place is in England or Wales ;

    (b) the Court of Session if it appears to him that the relevant place is in Scotland ; and

    (c) the Court of Appeal in Northern Ireland if it appears to him that the relevant place is in Northern Ireland,

except that if it appears to him, having regard to the circumstances of the case and in particular to the convenience of the persons who may be parties to the proposed appeal, that he should specify a different court mentioned in paragraphs (a) to (c) of this subsection as the appropriate court it shall be his duty to specify the different court as the appropriate court.

(5) In this section—

    " the appropriate court ", except in subsection (4), means the court specified in pursuance of that subsection ;

    " Commissioner ", except in subsections (7) and (8), has the meanings assigned to it by the principal Act and the Social Security (Northern Ireland) Act 1975 ; and   1975 c. 15.

    " the relevant place ", in relation to an application for leave to appeal from a decision of a Commissioner, means the premises where the authority whose decision was the subject of the Commissioner's decision usually exercises its functions.

(6) Regulations may provide for the preceding provisions of this section to have effect, with such modifications as may be prescribed by the regulations, in relation to a decision of a medical appeal tribunal appointed under the Social Security 1975 c. 15. (Northern Ireland) Act 1975.

(7) In relation to a decision of a Commissioner within the meaning of the principal Act which was given in consequence of a reference under subsection (4) of section 112 of that Act (which enables a medical appeal tribunal to refer a question of law to a Commissioner), subsections (3) and (5) of this section shall have effect with such modifications as may be prescribed by regulations.

(8) The powers to make regulations conferred by this section shall be exercisable—

    (a) so far as they relate to a Commissioner within the meaning of the principal Act, by the Secretary of State by statutory instrument ; and

U 4

(*b*) so far as they relate to a Commissioner within the meaning of the Social Security (Northern Ireland) Act 1975, or a medical appeal tribunal appointed under that Act, by the Department of Health and Social Services for Northern Ireland by statutory rule for the purposes of the Statutory Rules (Northern Ireland) Order 1979 ;

S.I. 1979/1573 (N.I. 12).

and any statutory instrument made by virtue of this subsection shall be subject to annulment in pursuance of a resolution of either House of Parliament and any statutory rule so made shall be subject to negative resolution as defined by section 41(6) of the Interpretation Act (Northern Ireland) 1954 as if it were a statutory instrument within the meaning of that Act.

1954 c. 33 (N.I.).

Leave required for appeal from local tribunal to Commissioner.

15.—(1) No appeal shall lie to a Commissioner within the meaning of the principal Act from a decision which is given after the coming into force of this subsection by a local tribunal appointed under section 97 of that Act and is the unanimous decision of the members of the tribunal except—

(*a*) with the leave of the person who was the chairman of the tribunal when the decision was given or, in a case prescribed by regulations, with the leave of a person appointed to act as chairman of such a local tribunal who is selected in accordance with regulations ; or

(*b*) if he refuses leave, with the leave of such a Commissioner,

and regulations may make provision with respect to the manner in which and the time within which applications must be made for leave under this subsection and with respect to the procedure for dealing with such applications.

(2) The powers to make regulations conferred by the preceding subsection shall be exercisable by the Secretary of State by statutory instrument ; and any statutory instrument made by virtue of this subsection shall be subject to annulment in pursuance of a resolution of either House of Parliament.

(3) Subsection (5) of section 101 of the principal Act (under which, among other things, an appeal to a Commissioner from a decision of a local tribunal must be brought within 3 months beginning with the date when notice of the decision is given to the claimant) shall have effect, in relation to an appeal for which leave is required by virtue of this section, as if for the reference to that date there were substituted a reference to the date when leave under subsection (1) of this section is given for the appeal.

Miscellaneous

16.—(1) Her Majesty may by Order in Council provide for an appeal under any provision of the Pensions Appeal Tribunals Act 1943 (hereafter in this section referred to as " the Act ") in respect of a claim for benefit under any instrument mentioned in the Act to be brought or continued by another person after the death of the claimant ; and—

> Amendments of Pensions Appeal Tribunals Act 1943.
> 1943 c. 39.

> (a) such an Order may make such modifications of the Act as Her Majesty considers appropriate for the purposes of this subsection ; but

> (b) nothing in this subsection shall be construed as prejudicing the generality of the power to make rules which is conferred by paragraph 5 of the Schedule to the Act.

(2) An Order in Council under this section—

> (a) may contain such incidental and supplemental provisions as Her Majesty considers appropriate ; and

> (b) shall be subject to annulment in pursuance of a resolution of either House of Parliament.

(3) In section 5(1) of the Act (which enables a Pensions Appeal Tribunal to uphold an interim assessment by the Minister of a degree of disablement or to assess the disablement at such degree higher or lower than that specified by the Minister as they think proper) for the words from " assess " to " proper " there shall be substituted the words " alter the assessment in one or both of the following ways, namely—

> (a) by increasing or reducing the degree of disablement it specifies ; and

> (b) by reducing the period for which the assessment is to be in force.".

(4) In section 6 of the Act (which relates to the jurisdiction and procedure of a Tribunal) after subsection (2A) there shall be inserted the following subsection—

> (2B) Rules made under the Schedule to this Act may provide that where an appeal under this Act is struck out in pursuance of such rules no further appeal under this Act shall be brought in respect of the matters to which the struck-out appeal related except with leave given in pursuance of such rules.

(5) Section 8(3)(a) of the Act (which is spent) shall be omitted.

(6) For paragraph (b) of paragraph 5(4) of the Schedule to the Act (which requires rules to provide for payments by the Tribunal of certain expenses of an appellant) there shall be substituted the following paragraph—

> (b) sums, in respect of expenses, allowances and fees connected with appeals to the Tribunal, to such persons

and in such circumstances as are specified in the rules and of such amounts as are determined by the Lord Chancellor with the consent of the Minister for the Civil Service ; and

and accordingly in section 14 of the Act (under which the Act has effect, in its application to Northern Ireland, with the substitution of a reference to the Lord Chief Justice for Northern Ireland for any reference to the Lord Chancellor except in paragraph 7A of the Schedule to the Act) for the words " paragraph 7A " there shall be substituted the words " paragraph 5(4)(*b*) ".

Proof of
decisions of
statutory
authorities.

17.—(1) A document bearing a certificate which—

    (*a*) is signed by a person authorised in that behalf by the Secretary of State ; and

    (*b*) states that the document, apart from the certificate, is a record of a decision of a relevant authority,

shall be conclusive evidence of the decision ; and a certificate purporting to be signed as aforesaid shall be deemed to be so signed unless the contrary is proved.

(2) In the preceding subsection " a relevant authority " means each of the following, namely a Commissioner within the meaning of the principal Act, a local tribunal appointed in pursuance of section 97 of that Act, an insurance officer so appointed, a tribunal constituted in accordance with Schedule 4 to the Supplementary Benefits Act 1976, a benefit officer within the meaning of that Act and a supplement officer within the meaning of the Family Income Supplements Act 1970.

1976 c. 71.

1970 c. 55.

Computation
of age in
Scotland.

18.—(1) For the purposes of this Act and the following enactments, namely—

the Family Income Supplements Act 1970 ;

1973 c. 38.

the Social Security Act 1973 ;

the Social Security Acts 1975 to 1979 ;

1975 c. 16.

the Industrial Injuries and Diseases (Old Cases) Act 1975 ;

1975 c. 61.

the Child Benefit Act 1975 ; and

the Supplementary Benefits Act 1976,

the time at which a person attains a particular age expressed in years shall be the commencement of the relevant anniversary of the date of his birth.

(2) This section applies only to Scotland.

General

19.—(1) Any expenses under this Act of a Minister of the Expenses. Crown shall be paid out of money provided by Parliament.

(2) Any increase attributable to this Act in the sums which under any other Act are payable out of money provided by Parliament or into the Consolidated Fund shall be paid out of such money or, as the case may be, into that Fund.

(3) There shall be paid out of the National Insurance Fund into the Consolidated Fund, at such times and in such manner as the Treasury may direct, such sums as the Secretary of State may estimate (in accordance with directions given by the Treasury) to be the amount of any expenses incurred by a Minister of the Crown by virtue of this Act in connection with benefits payable out of the National Insurance Fund, excluding any such expenses which the Treasury direct shall be disregarded for the purposes of this subsection ; and nothing in the preceding subsection prejudices the operation of subsection (5) of section 135 of the principal Act (which contains provisions corresponding to this subsection in connection with certain expenses).

20.—(1) The enactments specified in Schedule 4 to this Act Consequential shall have effect with the amendments specified in that and minor Schedule. amendments of enactments.

(2) An order under section 21(5) of this Act which brings into force a provision of the said Schedule 4 may contain such transitional provisions, including savings, as the Secretary of State considers appropriate in connection with or arising out of the coming into force of that provision ; and the Secretary of State may by order made by statutory instrument vary or revoke any provision which by virtue of this subsection is included in another order.

(3) Section 26 of the Supplementary Benefit Act 1966 (which 1966 c. 20. contained provision corresponding to section 20 of the Supple- 1976 c. 71. mentary Benefits Act 1976 for the recovery of payments in cases of misrepresentation or non-disclosure) shall have effect and be deemed always to have had effect as if the said Act of 1976 had not been passed ; but subsections (2) to (4) of the said section 26 shall not apply to any question to which subsections (2) to (4) of the said section 20 apply by virtue of this Act.

21.—(1) This Act may be cited as the Social Security Act Supplemental. 1980 and this Act and the Social Security Acts 1975 to 1979 may be cited together as the Social Security Acts 1975 to 1980.

(2) In this Act " the principal Act " means the Social Security 1975 c. 14. Act 1975 and " the Pensions Act " means the Social Security 1975 c. 60. Pensions Act 1975.

(3) Subsections (2) and (3) of section 166 of the principal Act (which among other things make provision about the extent of powers to make regulations and orders) shall apply to powers to make regulations and orders conferred by sections 8 and 20(2) of this Act and by subsection (5) of this section as extended by the said sections 8 and 20(2) as they apply to powers to make regulations and orders conferred by that Act but as if for references to that Act there were substituted references to the said sections 8 and 20(2) and the said subsection (5) as so extended.

(4) The enactments and instruments mentioned in the first and second columns of Schedule 5 to this Act are hereby repealed to the extent specified in the third column of that Schedule.

(5) The following provisions of this Act, namely, section 6 (except subsection (4)) and sections 7 to 10, 14 and 15, Part I and paragraphs 10 and 14 of Schedule 1, Schedules 2 to 4 and Part II of Schedule 5, shall come into force on such day as the Secretary of State may appoint by order made by statutory instrument, and different days may be appointed in pursuance of this subsection for different provisions of this Act; and accordingly the other provisions of this Act come into force on the passing of this Act.

(6) The following provisions only of this Act shall extend to Northern Ireland, namely—

sections 9 to 16, except sections 11, 13(6) and 15;

1947 c. 19.
1950 c. 37.

section 20(1) and (2) and Schedule 4 so far as they relate to the Polish Resettlement Act 1947 and the Maintenance Orders Act 1950;

this section;

Schedule 3; and

1943 c. 39.
1970 c. 36.

1975 c. 24.
1975 c. 25.
1976 c. 71.
1977 c. 38.

Schedule 5 so far as it relates to the Pensions Appeal Tribunals Act 1943, the Polish Resettlement Act 1947, the Merchant Shipping Act 1970, section 142(5) of the principal Act, the House of Commons Disqualification Act 1975, the Northern Ireland Assembly Disqualification Act 1975, section 36(2) of the Supplementary Benefits Act 1976 and Part III of Schedule 2 to the Administration of Justice Act 1977.

SCHEDULES

SCHEDULE 1

AMENDMENTS OF SOCIAL SECURITY ACT 1975

PART I

AMENDMENTS RELATING TO SIMILAR TREATMENT FOR MEN AND WOMEN

1.—(1) Subsection (6) of section 41 and subsection (4) of section 65 (under which a married woman residing with her husband is not entitled to an increase in benefit in respect of dependent children by virtue of that section unless her husband is incapable of self-support) shall be amended as follows—

 (a) in the said subsection (6) for the words " incapable of self-support " there shall be substituted the words " not engaged in any one or more employments from which his weekly earnings exceed the amount specified in relation to the benefit or beneficiary in question in Schedule 4, Part IV, column (3) " ;

 (b) in the said subsection (4) for the words " not incapable of self-support " there shall be substituted the words " engaged in any one or more employments from which his weekly earnings exceed the amount specified in relation to the benefit or pension in Schedule 4, Part V, paragraph 11 or, as the case may be, paragraph 12 ".

(2) The said subsections (6) and (4) as amended by the preceding sub-paragraph shall cease to have effect on the coming into force of this sub-paragraph.

2. In sections 44(3)(a) and 47(1)(a) (which provide for increases of specified amounts in a woman's unemployment or sickness benefit, maternity allowance or invalidity pension to be made for periods during which, among other things, her husband is incapable of self-support) for the words " incapable of self-support " there shall be substituted the words " not engaged in any one or more employments from which his weekly earnings exceed the amount so specified ".

3. Paragraph (b) of section 44(3), paragraph (b) of section 47(1) and paragraph (c) of section 66(1) (by virtue of which certain benefits are increased for any period during which the beneficiary has living with him and is maintaining such a relative as is there mentioned) shall cease to have effect ; but a person who, immediately before the date when this paragraph comes into force, was entitled to an increase by virtue of any of those paragraphs, shall continue to be entitled to it for any period not exceeding two years beginning with that date, during which, if the paragraph in question and any regulations having effect by virtue of the paragraph immediately before that date were still in force, he would have been, and would not have ceased to be, entitled to the increase by virtue of that paragraph.

4. Sections 44(3)(*c*), 46(2) and 66(1)(*d*) (which relate to increases of benefit by reference to a female person, not a child, who has the care of a child or children in respect of whom the beneficiary is entitled to child benefit) shall be amended by substituting for the words " female person (not a child) "—

(*a*) in sections 44(3)(*c*) and 66(1)(*d*) the words " person who is neither the spouse of the beneficiary nor a child " ;

(*b*) in section 46(2) the words " person who is neither the spouse of the pensioner nor a child " ;

and in sections 46(4) and 66(6)(*b*) (which refer to the female person mentioned in sections 46(2) and 66(1)(*d*) respectively) for the words from " female person " to " residing " there shall be substituted the words " person there referred to is a female residing ".

5.—(1) Subsection (5) of section 44 and subsection (2) of section 47 (which provide that, in the case of unemployment or sickness benefit or invalidity pensions payable to certain persons over pensionable age, the benefit or pensions shall not be increased under provisions providing for increases in respect of certain periods and shall only be increased by the amounts of the increases which would be made in relevant retirement pensions where the rates of those pensions would be calculated under provisions relating to the partial satisfaction of contribution conditions) shall cease to have effect ; and after section 47 there shall be inserted the following section—

Rate of increase where associated retirement pension is attributable to reduced contributions.

47A. Where a person is entitled to unemployment or sickness benefit by virtue of section 14(2)(*b*) or (*c*) or to an invalidity pension by virtue of section 15(2) of this Act and would have been entitled only by virtue of section 33 to the retirement pension by reference to which the rate of the said benefit or invalidity pension is determined, the amount of any increase of the said benefit or invalidity pension attributable to sections 44 to 47 of this Act shall not be determined in accordance with those sections but shall be determined in accordance with regulations.

(2) Accordingly in section 44(1) for the words " Subject to the provisions of this section " there shall be substituted the words " Subject to section 47A ", in section 44(2) for the words " Subject to the following subsections " there shall be substituted the words " Subject to subsection (4) below and section 47A " and in section 47(1) for the words " Subject to subsection (2) below " there shall be substituted the words " Subject to section 47A ".

6. In section 66(1)(*a*) (which provides for increases of injury benefit and in certain cases of disablement pension for periods during which the pensioner's wife is residing with him or he is contributing to the maintenance of his wife at a specified rate), for the word " wife " in both places there shall be substituted the word " spouse ".

7. In Schedule 20 (which contains a glossary of expressions) the entry relating to the expression " Incapable of self-support " (including both paragraphs in the second column of the entry) shall be

omitted, and after the entry relating to the expression "Pensionable age" there shall be inserted the following—

"Permanently incapable of self-support"	A person is "permanently incapable of self-support" if (but only if) he is incapable of supporting himself by reason of physical or mental infirmity and is likely to remain so incapable for the remainder of his life.

Part II

Other amendments

8. After subsection (4) of section 35 (which among other things provides that an attendance allowance shall not be payable to a person for any period preceding the date on which he makes a claim for it) there shall be inserted the following subsection—

(4A) Notwithstanding anything in the preceding subsection, provision may be made by regulations for an attendance allowance to be paid to a person for a period preceding the date on which he makes a claim for it if such an allowance has previously been paid to or in respect of him.

9. In section 96(2) (which among other things prevents the Secretary of State from reviewing a decision of his on a question within section 93(1) or section 95(1)(*b*) or (*c*) while an appeal is pending on a question of law arising in connection with the decision and provides for an appeal on a question of law raised with a view to a review of such a decision)—

(*a*) for the words "Such a decision" there shall be substituted the words "A decision on a question within section 93(1)"; and

(*b*) for the words from "and section 94" onwards there shall be substituted the words "and, on a review of a decision on a question within section 93(1), any question of law may be referred under subsection (1) of section 94, or where it is not so referred may be the subject of an appeal under subsection (3) of that section, and the other provisions of that section shall apply accordingly".

10. In subsection (4) of section 100 (which provides that an appeal to a local tribunal from a decision of an insurance officer must be brought within 21 days after the date of the decision or within a further time allowed by the chairman of the tribunal) for the words "21 days after the date of the decision" there shall be substituted the words "28 days beginning with the date when the Secretary of State gives to the claimant notice in writing of the decision"; and in subsection (5) of section 101 (which provides that an appeal to a Commissioner from a decision of a local tribunal must be brought within 3 months from the date of the decision or a further period allowed by the Commissioner) for the words "from the date of the decision of the local tribunal or" there shall be substituted the words "beginning with the date when the proper officer of the local tribunal gives to the claimant notice in writing of the decision or within".

11. In section 111 (which among other things provides that an assessment of a single medical practitioner under that section must be by reference to a period not exceeding 6 months and that regulations may make provision with respect to cases in which the practitioner considers that a final assessment can be made by reference to a longer period) for the words " 6 months " in subsections (1) and (3) there shall be substituted the words " 12 months ".

1979 c. 18.

12. For paragraph (*cc*) of subsection (4) of section 119 (which as amended by the Social Security Act 1979 provides that regulations may modify subsections (1) to (2A) of that section in relation to payments in respect of a person which are paid to another person on his behalf) there shall be substituted the following paragraph—

> (*cc*) modifying those subsections in relation to sums by way of benefit which are paid to another person on behalf of the beneficiary ;.

13. In subsection (6) of section 122 (which provides that no order shall be made under that section so as to increase the percentage rate for Class 1 or Class 4 contributions to a percentage more than 0·25 per cent. higher than that specified in section 4(6) or, as the case may be, section 9(2) as for the time being amended by any other Act and, in the case of section 4(6), by an order under section 1(6) of the Social Security (Miscellaneous Provisions) Act 1977), for the words from " so " onwards there shall be substituted the words " so as—

> (*a*) to increase for any tax year the percentage rate for primary or secondary Class 1 contributions to a percentage rate more than 0·25 per cent. higher than the percentage rate applicable for the preceding tax year for the contributions in question ; or

> (*b*) to increase the percentage rate for Class 4 contributions to more than 8·25 per cent.".

14. Section 158 and Schedule 19 (which relate to schemes promoted by representatives of earners and their employers for supplementing certain rights to benefit in respect of industrial injuries and diseases which are conferred on the earners by the principal Act) shall cease to have effect.

15. In section 167(3) (which among other things applies the negative resolution procedure to orders under the principal Act except an order under section 17(3), 30(6), 120 or 122 or an uprating order for the words " or 122 " there shall be substituted the words ", 122 or 126A ".

16. In paragraph 1 of Schedule 1 (which among other things provides for earnings from different employments to be aggregated for the purpose of calculating the amount of any Class 1 contributions in respect of the earnings), after sub-paragraph (1) there shall be inserted the following sub-paragraph—

> (1A) Where earnings in respect of employments which include any contracted-out employment and any employment which is not a contracted-out employment are aggregated under sub-paragraph (1) above and the aggregated earnings are not less than the current lower earnings limit, then, except as may be

provided by regulations, the amount of the Class 1 contribution in respect of the aggregated earnings shall be the aggregate of the amounts obtained—

(*a*) by applying the rates of Class 1 contributions applicable to contracted-out employments—

(i) to the part of the aggregated earnings attributable to any contracted-out employments, or

(ii) if that part exceeds the current upper earnings limit, to so much of that part as does not exceed that limit ; and

(*b*) if that part is less than that limit, by applying the rates of Class 1 contributions applicable to employments which are not contracted-out employments to so much of the remainder of the aggregated earnings as, when added to the part aforesaid, does not exceed that limit ;

and in relation to earners paid otherwise than weekly any reference in the preceding provisions of this sub-paragraph to the lower or upper earnings limit shall be construed as a reference to the prescribed equivalent of that limit.

SCHEDULE 2

AMENDMENTS OF SUPPLEMENTARY BENEFITS ACT 1976

PART I

THE AMENDMENTS

1. In section 1—

(*a*) for paragraphs (*a*) and (*b*) of subsection (1) there shall be substituted the following paragraphs—

(*a*) a supplementary pension if he is one of a married or unmarried couple of whom one is or both are over the age of 65 or if he is not one of such a couple and has attained pensionable age ; and

(*b*) a supplementary allowance in any other case ;

(*b*) at the end of subsection (1) there shall be inserted the words " Paragraph (*a*) of this subsection shall have effect until the prescribed date as if the words from ' is one ' to ' couple and ' were omitted " ;

(*c*) after subsection (1) there shall be inserted the following subsection—

(1A) Regulations may provide for a person's entitlement under subsection (1) above to continue during prescribed periods of the person's temporary absence from Great Britain. ;

(*d*) at the end of subsection (3) there shall be inserted the words " ; and regulations may provide that the requirements which by virtue of this subsection are not included in a person's requirements include or exclude prescribed requirements ".

SCH. 2   2. In section 2—

(*a*) for the words " shall be determined by the Supplementary
Benefits Commission " in subsection (1) there shall be substituted the words " and any other question relating to
supplementary benefit which arises under this Act shall be
determined by a benefit officer except so far as this
Act or regulations provide otherwise ; and regulations may
provide for different aspects of the same question to be
dealt with by different benefit officers." ;

(*b*) after subsection (1) there shall be inserted the following
subsection—

(1A) Regulations may provide for prescribed questions
to be determined otherwise than by benefit officers and,
without prejudice to the generality of the preceding provisions of this subsection,—

(*a*) for prescribed questions to be referred to bodies
or persons exercising functions under the Social
Security Act 1975 and for the application of
provisions of that Act, with or without modifications, to the questions and to decisions given
in consequence of references in pursuance of the
regulations ;

(*b*) for such decisions, and any other prescribed decisions given in pursuance of that Act, to be effective or conclusive for prescribed purposes of
this Act ; and

(*c*) for dealing, by postponement or otherwise, with
cases in which questions are referred by virtue
of paragraph (*a*) of this subsection. ;

(*c*) the words from the second " and " in subsection (2)(*a*) to
the end of the section shall be omitted.

3. In section 3—

(*a*) for the words from the beginning to " person " in subsection (1) there shall be substituted the words " There
shall be payable in prescribed cases, to a person who is
entitled or would if he satisfied prescribed conditions be
entitled to a supplementary pension or allowance, supplementary benefit " ;

(*b*) after the word " payment " in subsection (1) there shall be
inserted the words " of a prescribed amount " ;

(*c*) for the words " the Commission may have regard " in subsection (2) there shall be substituted the words " regard
shall be had, so far as regulations so provide," ; and

(*d*) for the words from " Part III " onwards in subsection (2)
there shall be substituted the words " regulations made in
pursuance of paragraph 1(2)(*b*) of Schedule 1 to this Act "

4. For section 4 there shall be substituted the following section—

Provision for cases of urgent need.

4.—(1) In urgent cases supplementary benefit shall be payable in accordance with this Act as modified by virtue of this section ; and regulations may—

(a) prescribe the cases which are urgent cases for the purposes of this section ;

(b) provide that in relation to such cases any of the provisions of sections 3, 5 to 8 and 10 of this Act and Schedule 1 to this Act shall have effect with prescribed modifications.

(2) Any sums paid to a person by virtue of the preceding subsection, except a sum as to which it has been determined in accordance with regulations that it is not to be recovered in pursuance of this subsection, shall be recoverable from him by the Secretary of State by making deductions from prescribed benefits or in any other manner.

5. In section 5 for the words " The Commission may determine that " there shall be substituted the words " Except in prescribed cases," and for the words from " by regulations " onwards there shall be substituted the words " and is available for employment ; and regulations may make provision as to—

(a) what is and is not to be treated as employment for the purposes of this section ; and

(b) the circumstances in which a person is or is not to be treated for those purposes as available for employment ".

6. For sections 6 and 7 there shall be substituted the following section—

Exclusion from supplementary benefit of certain employed persons and pupils.

6.—(1) A person who is engaged in remunerative full-time work shall not be entitled to supplementary benefit ; and regulations may make provision as to the circumstances in which a person is or is not to be treated for the purposes of this subsection as so engaged.

(2) A person who has not attained the age of 19 and is receiving relevant education shall not be entitled to supplementary benefit except in prescribed circumstances.

(3) Regulations may make provision as to the circumstances in which a person is or is not to be treated for the purposes of the preceding subsection as receiving relevant education ; and in this section " relevant education " means full-time education by attendance at an establishment recognised by the Secretary of State as being, or as comparable to, a college or school.

7. In section 8—

(a) in subsection (1), for the words " the requirement to provide for any other person " there shall be substituted the words " requirements of another person which are to be treated as his by virtue of any other provision of this Act and are not to be disregarded by virtue of this subsection as it applies to the other person " ; and

(b) subsection (3) shall be omitted.

8. In section 9—

    (*a*) in subsection (1), for the words "requirement to provide for " there shall be substituted the words "requirements of " and for the words "section 6 of this Act (exclusion of persons in full-time employment)" there shall be substituted the words "section 6(1) of this Act ";

    (*b*) in subsection (2), for the words from "in accordance " onwards there shall be substituted the words "or another person in accordance with regulations ";

    (*c*) in subsection (3), for the words from the beginning to "work)" there shall be substituted the words "Regulations made by virtue of section 6(1) of this Act providing for a person not to be treated as engaged in remunerative full-time work "; and

    (*d*) subsections (4) to (8) shall be omitted.

9. For section 10 there shall be substituted the following section—

Modification of right to supplementary allowance in certain cases.

10.—(1) Where—

    (*a*) a person is registered for employment in pursuance of section 5 of this Act and is not receiving unemployment benefit under the Social Security Act 1975 ; and

    (*b*) it appears to a benefit officer that the person refuses or neglects to maintain himself or any other person whom for the purposes of this Act he is liable to maintain,

the officer may give him in the prescribed manner a direction in writing requiring him to attend a course of instruction or training which is approved or provided by the Secretary of State and is specified in the direction.

(2) A person to whom such a direction is given may, in accordance with rules made by the Secretary of State, appeal against the direction to the Appeal Tribunal ; and on an appeal in pursuance of this subsection the tribunal shall either confirm or cancel the direction.

(3) A direction under subsection (1) of this section shall not come into force—

    (*a*) until the expiration of the period within which, without any extension of time, an appeal against it may be brought in pursuance of the preceding subsection ; and

    (*b*) if during that period such an appeal is brought, until the appeal is withdrawn or the direction is confirmed by the tribunal.

(4) A person in respect of whom a direction under subsection (1) of this section is in force shall not be entitled to a supplementary allowance while he fails to comply with the direction.

(5) Regulations may make provision with respect to the consequences of the cancellation of a direction which has come into force.

10. In section 11, for subsections (1) and (2) there shall be substituted the following subsection—

(1) Regulations may make provision—

(*a*) for the requirements of any person to be met in prescribed circumstances by the provision of goods or services instead of by making the whole or part of any payment to which he would otherwise be entitled under this Act;

(*b*) for any provision of this Act or regulations under it to be disregarded in connection with the provision of goods or services by virtue of the preceding paragraph;

(*c*) as to the manner of providing goods and services to be provided by virtue of that paragraph. ;

and accordingly subsection (3) of that section shall be subsection (2) of that section.

11. In section 12—

(*a*) for subsection (1) there shall be substituted the following subsections—

(1) Where a prescribed payment which apart from this subsection falls to be made from public funds in the United Kingdom or under the law of any other member State is not made on or before the date which is the prescribed date in relation to the payment, then—

(*a*) in the case of a payment from such public funds, the authority responsible for making it may abate it by the relevant amount; and

(*b*) in the case of any other payment, the Secretary of State shall be entitled to receive the relevant amount out of the payment;

and in this subsection "the relevant amount", in relation to a payment, means the amount which a benefit officer determines has been paid by way of supplementary benefit and would not have been paid if the payment had been made on the date aforesaid.

(1A) Where—

(*a*) a payment by way of prescribed income is made after the date which is the prescribed date in relation to the payment; and

(*b*) a benefit officer determines that an amount which has been paid by way of supplementary benefit would not have been paid if the said payment had been made on the date aforesaid,

the Secretary of State shall be entitled to recover that amount from the person to whom it was paid. ;

(*b*) in subsection (2) for the words from " , or to " to " security benefit ') " in paragraph (*a*) there shall be substituted the words " any prescribed benefit ", for the words from " or of " to " security " in paragraph (*c*) and where they first occur after that paragraph there shall be substituted the words " the prescribed ", for the words " the Commission determine " there shall be substituted the words " a benefit officer determines " and for the words from " equal " onwards there shall be substituted the words " equal to the amount of the prescribed benefit " ;

(*c*) in subsection (3) for the words " the Commission of " there shall be substituted the words " a benefit officer of " and for the words " Commission have " there shall be substituted the words " officer has " ; and

(*d*) for subsection (4) there shall be substituted the following subsections—

(4) Where a benefit officer makes—

(*a*) a determination in pursuance of the preceding provisions of this section in respect of an amount of supplementary benefit ; or

(*b*) a determination altering on review or refusing to review a determination in respect of such an amount which has been made for the purposes of this section by a benefit officer or on appeal,

the relevant person may appeal to the Appeal Tribunal against the determination ; and subsection (3) of section 15 of this Act shall apply to an appeal under this subsection as it applies to an appeal under that section.

(5) In the preceding subsection " the relevant person " means the person who is entitled, apart from subsection (1), (2) or (3) of this section, to the prescribed payment or the prescribed benefit or the rebate or allowance in question or, as the case may be, to whom the amount mentioned in subsection (1A) of this section was paid.

12.—(1) In section 14, in subsection (1) for the words from the beginning to " section," there shall be substituted the words " Regulations may " and for the words " and Part II of Schedule 2 to this Act " there shall be substituted the words " to this Act ; and nothing in any other provision of this Act shall be construed as prejudicing the generality of this subsection ".

(2) Section 14(2) shall be amended as follows—

(*a*) for the words preceding paragraph (*a*) there shall be substituted the words " Regulations may make provision— " ;

(*b*) in paragraph (*a*) after the word " manner " there shall be inserted the words " and within such time " ;

(*c*) for paragraph (*b*) there shall be substituted the following paragraph—

(*b*) for enabling a person to be appointed to exercise, on behalf of a claimant who may be or become unable to act in relation to his claim, any power in relation to it which the claimant is entitled to exercise ;

(*d*) in paragraph (*d*), for the words " the Commission " in both places there shall be substituted the words " a benefit officer " and the words " National Insurance " shall be omitted ;

(*e*) in paragraph (*e*) for the words from " period " to " in the regulations " there shall be substituted the words " prescribed period of not less than twelve months " ;

(*f*) the word " and " at the end of paragraphs (*e*) and (*ee*) shall be omitted ;

(*g*) for paragraph (*f*) there shall be substituted the following paragraphs—

(*f*) as to the day on which entitlement to a supplementary pension or allowance is to begin or end or the amount of a supplementary pension or allowance is to change ;

(*g*) as to the time and manner of paying supplementary benefit and the information and evidence to be furnished in connection with payments of it ;

(*h*) for withholding payments of a supplementary pension or allowance in prescribed circumstances and for subsequently making withheld payments in prescribed circumstances ;

(*i*) as to the circumstances and manner in which payments of supplementary benefit may be made to another person on behalf of the beneficiary for any purpose (which may be to discharge, in whole or in part, an obligation of the beneficiary or any other person):

(*j*) for the payment or distribution of supplementary benefit to or among persons claiming to be entitled to it on the death of any person and for dispensing with strict proof of their title ;

(*k*) for the payment of travelling expenses in connection with claims for supplementary benefit.

(3) Accordingly subsections (3) and (4) of section 14 (which relate to the payment of benefit to a person other than the beneficiary and to travelling expenses in connection with claims for benefit) shall be omitted.

13. In section 15—

(*a*) in subsection (1), for the words from " the Commission or " onwards there shall be substituted the words " a benefit officer (including a determination to refuse to review a determination) with respect to the claim or benefit, except that no appeal shall lie by virtue of this subsection in a case falling within section 10(2), 12(4) or 20(3) of this Act " ;

(*b*) subsection (2) (which is superseded by the amendment in paragraph 2(*b*) of this Schedule) shall be omitted ; and

(*c*) in subsection (3) paragraph (*b*) shall be omitted and for the words " the Commission " in paragraph (*c*) there shall be substituted the words " a benefit officer ".

14. In section 15A the words " National Insurance " in both places and the words from " and includes " onwards in subsection (5) shall be omitted.

15. Section 16 shall be amended as follows—

(*a*) the words " or, in Scotland, on the sequestration of the estate " shall be omitted ; and

(*b*) that section as amended by sub-paragraph (*a*) of this para- graph shall be subsection (1) of that section and after that subsection there shall be inserted the following subsection—

(2) In the application of the preceding subsection to Scotland—

(*a*) the reference to assignment of supplementary benefit shall be read as a reference to its assignation, " assign " being construed accord- ingly ; and

(*b*) the reference to the bankruptcy of a person entitled to supplementary benefit shall be read as a reference to the sequestration of his estate or the appointment on his estate of a judicial factor under section 14 of the Bankruptcy (Scot- land) Act 1913 or section 15 of the Solicitors (Scotland) Act 1958.

16. In section 17—

(*a*) after paragraph (*b*) of subsection (1) there shall be inserted the words " ; and

(*c*) a person shall be liable to maintain another person throughout any period in respect of which the first- mentioned person has, on or after the date of the pass- ing of the Social Security Act 1980 and either alone or jointly with a further person, given an undertaking in writing in pursuance of immigration rules within the meaning of the Immigration Act 1971 to be responsible for the maintenance and accommodation of the other person." ; and

(*b*) after subsection (2) there shall be inserted the following subsection—

(3) A document bearing a certificate which—

(*a*) is signed by a person authorised in that behalf by the Secretary of State ; and

(*b*) states that the document apart from the certi- ficate is, or is a copy of, such an undertaking as is mentioned in subsection (1)(*c*) of this section,

shall be conclusive evidence for the purposes of this Act of the undertaking in question ; and a certificate purporting to be signed as aforesaid shall be deemed to be so signed until the contrary is proved.

17. In section 18—

(*a*) in subsection (1), for the words " relative ') the Commission " there shall be substituted the words " person ') the Secretary of State " and for the words " relative to " there shall be substituted the words " person to " ;

(*b*) in subsection (2) for the word " No " there shall be substituted the words " Except in a case falling within section 17(1)(*c*) of this Act, no " ;

(*c*) in subsections (2) to (4), for the word " relative " and " relative's " there shall be substituted respectively the word " person " and " person's " ;

(*d*) at the end of subsection (3) there shall be inserted the words ", except that in a case falling within section 17(1)(*c*) of this Act that sum shall not include any amount which is not attributable to supplementary benefit (whether paid before or after the making of the order)." ; and

(*e*) subsection (6) shall be omitted.

18. In section 19—

(*a*) for the word " Commission " wherever it occurs, except in subsection (7), there shall be substituted the words " Secretary of State " ;

(*b*) subsection (7) shall be omitted, and

(*c*) in subsection (8) for the figure " (7) " there shall be substituted the figure " (6) ".

19. In section 20—

(*a*) in subsection (2), for the words from " referred to " onwards there shall be substituted the words " determined by a benefit officer " ;

(*b*) for subsection (3) there shall be substituted the following subsection—

(3) A person from whom, in pursuance of a determination of a benefit officer under the preceding subsection, an amount is recoverable under this section may appeal to the Appeal Tribunal against the determination ; and subsection (3) of section 15 of this Act shall apply to an appeal under this subsection as it applies to an appeal under that section. ;

(*c*) in subsection (4) for the words from " benefit under " onwards there shall be substituted the words " prescribed benefits " ; and

(*d*) for subsection (5) there shall be substituted the following subsection—

(5) Subsections (2) and (3) of this section shall apply to any question as to whether any amount or what

amount is recoverable by the Secretary of State under section 45 of the National Assistance Act 1948 or section 26 of the Supplementary Benefit Act 1966 (which contain provisions corresponding to subsection (1) of this section) and subsection (4) of this section shall apply to an amount recoverable under either of those sections—

> (*a*) as if for any reference in those subsections to this section there were substituted references to the said section 45 or 26, as the case may be; and

> (*b*) as respects a question relating to recovery under the said section 45 and an amount recoverable under that section, as if the words " paid by way of supplementary benefit " in subsections (2) and (4) of this section were omitted.

20. In section 21 before the word " liable " there shall be inserted the words " guilty of an offence and ".

21. In section 22 the words " or the Commission " shall be omitted and before the word " liable " there shall be inserted the words " guilty of an offence and ".

22. In section 24—
> (*a*) for the words " to which this section applies " in subsection (1) there shall be substituted the words " of regulations under section 9(2) of this Act " ;
> (*b*) before the word " liable " in subsection (1) there shall be inserted the words " guilty of an offence and " ; and
> (*c*) subsection (2) shall be omitted.

23. In section 25(1), paragraph (*b*) and the word " or " at the end of paragraph (*a*) shall be omitted and before the words " liable on " there shall be inserted the words " guilty of an offence and ".

24. In section 27—
> (*a*) for the words from the beginning to " Act " in subsection (1) there shall be substituted the words " It shall be the duty of the Secretary of State to make arrangements with a view to ensuring that benefit officers and other officers of his concerned with the administration of this Act exercise their functions " ; and
> (*b*) for subsections (2) to (4) there shall be substituted the following subsection—
>> (2) It shall be the duty of the Secretary of State to appoint persons to perform the functions conferred by virtue of this Act on benefit officers.

25. In section 30—
> (*a*) for subsection (1) there shall be substituted the following subsection—
>> (1) The provisions of Schedule 5 to this Act shall have effect with respect to re-establishment courses and re-settlement units. ;

(*b*) in subsection (2) for the words from " in exercise " to " may " there shall be substituted the words " the Secretary of State so directs, payment at such rates as he may " and for the words " a centre " there shall be substituted the words " connection with courses provided or units " ; and

(*c*) subsections (3) and (4) shall be omitted.

26. In section 31—

    (*a*) in subsection (3), for the words from the beginning to " him " there shall be substituted the words " Regulations may provide for such modifications of this Act as appear to the Secretary of State " ; and

    (*b*) in subsection (4), for the words from the beginning to " adjustments " there shall be substituted the words " The power to make regulations conferred by the preceding subsection ".

27. After section 32 there shall be inserted the following section—

Modification of Act for special cases. 32A. Regulations may provide for any provision of this Act except this section to have effect with prescribed modifications—

    (*a*) in cases involving a marriage celebrated under a law which permits polygamy or a marriage during the subsistence of which a party to it is at any time married to more than one person ;

    (*b*) in cases where the Secretary of State considers that without the modifications the provision in question would give rise to an anomaly or an injustice or would produce impractical consequences.

28. In section 33—

    (*a*) in subsection (1A) the words " and regulations " shall be omitted ; and

    (*b*) for subsections (2) and (3) there shall be substituted the following subsections—

    (2) Subsections (2) and (3) of section 166 of the Social Security Act 1975 (which among other things make provision about the extent of powers to make regulations) shall apply to powers to make regulations conferred by this Act as they apply to powers to make regulations conferred by that Act but as if for references to that Act there were substituted references to this Act.

    (3) Regulations of the following kinds, namely—

        (*a*) regulations of which the effect is to increase an amount which is specified in regulations made in pursuance of section 3 of this Act or which, by virtue of regulations made in pursuance of paragraph (*b*) of section 4(1) of this Act, is specified in a provision mentioned in that paragraph ;

        (*b*) regulations made in pursuance of section 32A(*b*) of this Act except regulations made for the purpose only of consolidating regulations which they revoke ;

(c) regulations made in pursuance of paragraph 1 or 2 of Schedule 1 to this Act except regulations made for the purpose only of consolidating regulations which they revoke,

shall not be made unless a draft of the regulations has been laid before Parliament and approved by a resolution of each House and, in the case of regulations falling within paragraph (a) or (c) of this subsection, shall not be made without the consent of the Treasury.

(4) A statutory instrument containing regulations of which a draft is not required by the preceding subsection to be approved as there mentioned or containing rules made under this Act shall be subject to annulment in pursuance of a resolution of either House of Parliament.

(5) Without prejudice to the generality of any power conferred by this Act to make regulations, regulations may provide for a person to exercise a discretion in dealing with any matter.

29. In section 34—
(a) the following definitions shall be inserted at the appropriate places in alphabetical order in subsection (1) of that section—

" benefit officer " means a person appointed in pursuance of section 27(2) of this Act ;

" married couple " means a man and a woman who are married to each other and are members of the same household ;

" modifications " includes additions, omissions and amendments, and related expressions shall be construed accordingly ;

" prescribed " means specified in or determined in accordance with regulations ;

" regulations " means regulations made by the Secretary of State under this Act ;

" unmarried couple " means a man and a woman who are not married to each other but are living together as husband and wife otherwise than in prescribed circumstances ;

(b) in subsection (1) the definitions of " blind " and " the Commission " and " school " shall be omitted and in the definition of " supplementary benefit " the words from " and includes " onwards shall be omitted ; and

(c) after subsection (2) there shall be inserted the following subsection—

(3) Regulations may make provision as to the circumstances in which a person is to be treated for the purposes of any specified provision of this Act—
(a) as being or not being a member of the same household as another person ;
(b) as responsible for another person.

30. For Schedule 1 there shall be substituted the following Schedule—

Sections 2,3, 4,14 and 33.

SCH. 2

SCHEDULE 1

PROVISIONS FOR DETERMINING RIGHT TO BENEFIT AND AMOUNT OF BENEFIT

General

1.—(1) The amount of any supplementary benefit to which a person is entitled shall, subject to the following provisions of this Schedule, be the amount by which his resources fall short of his requirements.

(2) For the purpose of ascertaining that amount—

    (*a*) a person's requirements shall be determined in accordance with paragraph 2 of this Schedule ; and

    (*b*) a person's resources shall be calculated in the prescribed manner ;

and, without prejudice to the generality of paragraph (*b*) of this sub-paragraph, regulations in pursuance of that paragraph may provide for a person to be treated as possessing resources which he does not possess and for disregarding resources which a person does possess.

(3) Regulations may provide that a person whose resources as ascertained in pursuance of paragraph (*b*) of the preceding sub-paragraph or a prescribed part of them exceed or exceeds a prescribed amount shall not be entitled to a supplementary pension or allowance.

Requirements

2.—(1) For the purposes of this Schedule requirements shall be of three categories, namely, normal requirements, additional requirements and housing requirements ; and the items to which each category relates and, subject to sub-paragraph (3) of this paragraph, the weekly amounts for those categories shall be such as may be prescribed.

(2) A person's requirements shall consist of normal requirements together with requirements, if any, of such of the other categories as are applicable in his case.

(3) In the case of a person specified in the first column of the following table his normal requirements shall be taken to be the weekly amount specified in relation to him in the second column of that table ; and in that table—

    " householder " means a person who is not one of a married or unmarried couple but who satisfies prescribed conditions with respect to living accommodation ; and

    " relevant person " means a person whose requirements include those of another person by virtue of sub-paragraph (1) of paragraph 3 of this Schedule.

TABLE

Person	*Weekly amount*
1. A relevant person who— (*a*) is such a person as is mentioned in section 1(1)(*a*) of this Act ; or (*b*) is not such a person as is so mentioned but satisfies prescribed conditions.	The aggregate of the sums for the time being specified in section 6(1)(*a*) of the Social Security Pensions Act 1975 and column (3) of paragraph 6 of Part IV of Schedule 4 to the Social Security Act 1975 (which specify the amounts of the basic component of a Category A retirement pension and the increase of the pension for an adult dependant).
2. A relevant person not falling within paragraph 1 of this table.	The aggregate of the sums for the time being specified in paragraph 1 of Part I of the said Schedule 4 and column (3) of paragraph 1(*a*) of the said Part IV (which specify the amounts of unemployment or sickness benefit and the increase of it for an adult dependant of a beneficiary under pensionable age).
3. A householder who— (*a*) has attained pensionable age ; or (*b*) has not attained pensionable age but satisfies prescribed conditions.	The sum for the time being specified in the said section 6(1)(*a*).
4. A householder not falling within paragraph 3 of this table.	The sum for the time being specified in paragraph 1 of the said Part I.

(4) Regulations may provide that the preceding sub-paragraph shall have effect with prescribed modifications.

(5) Notwithstanding anything in the preceding provisions of this paragraph, regulations may provide for a person to be treated as having no normal requirements in prescribed cases.

Aggregation of requirements and resources

3.—(1) Where two persons are a married or unmarried couple, their requirements and resources shall be aggregated and treated—

(*a*) until the prescribed date, as those of the man ; and

(*b*) on and after that date, as those of such one of them as satisfies prescribed conditions or, where both of them satisfy or neither of them satisfies those conditions, as those of such one of them as they may jointly nominate in accordance with regulations or, in default of such a nomination, as the Secretary of State may determine.

(2) Where a person is responsible for, and is a member of the same household as, another person and they are not a married or unmarried couple, then—

(*a*) if the other person is a child or is excluded from entitlement to supplementary benefit by section 6(2) of this Act ; or

(*b*) if the circumstances are such as are prescribed,

their requirements and resources shall be aggregated and treated as those of the first-mentioned person.

(3) Regulations may provide that, in a case falling within the preceding sub-paragraph, sub-paragraph (1) of this paragraph shall apply in relation to the other person with prescribed modifications.

Exclusion of small payments

4. Where the amount of any supplementary benefit would be less than a prescribed amount, the benefit shall not be payable except in prescribed circumstances.

31. In Schedule 5—

(*a*) for the word " Commission ", wherever it occurs except in paragraphs 1, 2(1) and 3, there shall be substituted the words " Secretary of State " ;

(*b*) in paragraph 1(1) for the words from the beginning to " where " there shall be substituted the words " The Secretary of State may provide courses, to be known as re-establishment courses, at which " and for the words from " attend " to " afforded by the Commission " there shall be substituted the words "be afforded " ;

(*c*) in paragraph 1(2) for the words from " or be " onwards there shall be substituted the words " re-establishment courses either in consequence of a direction under section 10(1) of this Act or otherwise, and the Secretary of State may provide temporary board and lodging for persons attending re-establishment courses." ;

(*d*) in paragraph 2(1) for the words from " Commission to " onwards there shall be substituted the words " Secretary of

State to provide and maintain places, to be known as resettlement units, at which persons without a settled way of life are afforded temporary board and lodging with a view to influencing them to lead a more settled life." ;

(*e*) in paragraph 2(2) for the words "reception centres" there shall be substituted the words "resettlement units" ;

(*f*) in paragraph 2(4) for the word "them" there shall be substituted the word "him" ;

(*g*) paragraph 3 shall be omitted ;

(*h*) in paragraph 4 for the words "maintaining centres" there shall be substituted the words "providing courses or places" and for the words "centres or reception centres are maintained" there shall be substituted the words "courses or resettlement units are provided".

32.—(1) In Schedule 6 paragraphs 6 and 7 (which relate to transitional cases involving a pension under the Old Age Pensions Act 1936 or an assistance grant under the National Assistance Act 1948 or an appeal to a tribunal constituted under Schedule 3 to the Supplementary Benefit Act 1966) shall cease to have effect, but any supplementary benefit payable to a woman instead of to another person by virtue of sub-paragraph (4) of the said paragraph 6 shall continue to be so payable subject to any regulations relating to that sub-paragraph which are made in pursuance of section 8(1) of this Act.

(2) In paragraph 8 of Schedule 6 (which among other things provides for certain proceedings for the recovery of sums which could previously have been taken by the National Assistance Board to be taken by the Supplementary Benefits Commission in some cases and the Secretary of State in others) for paragraphs (*a*) and (*b*) of sub-paragraph (1) there shall be substituted the words "by the Secretary of State", and sub-paragraph (3) shall be omitted.

PART II

PROVISIONS OF THE ACT AS AMENDED

PART I

SUPPLEMENTARY BENEFIT

Right to and amount of supplementary benefit

Right to supple-mentary benefit.

1.—(1) Subject to the provisions of this Act, every person in Great Britain of or over the age of 16 whose resources are insufficient to meet his requirements shall be entitled to benefit as follows—

(*a*) a supplementary pension if he is one of a married or unmarried couple of whom one is or both are over the age of 65 or if he is not one of such a couple and has attained pensionable age ; and (*b*) a supplementary allowance in any other case ; and to such benefit by way of a single payment to meet an exceptional need as may be determined under section 3 of this Act.

Paragraph (*a*) of this subsection shall have effect until the prescribed date as if the words from " is one " to " couple and " were omitted.

(1A) Regulations may provide for a person's entitlement under subsection (1) above to continue during prescribed periods of the person's temporary absence from Great Britain.

(2) Where, under the provisions of this Act, the requirements and resources of any person fall to be aggregated with, and treated as, those of another person, that other person only shall be entitled to supplementary benefit.

(3) The requirements of any person to be taken into account for the purposes of this Act do not include any medical, surgical, optical, aural or dental requirements ; and regulations may provide that the requirements which by virtue of this subsection are not included in a person's requirements include or exclude prescribed requirements.

Determination of right to and amount of supplementary benefit.

2.—(1) Subject to sections 15 and 15A of this Act (appeals), the question whether any person is entitled to supplementary benefit and the amount of any such benefit and any other question relating to supplementary benefit which arises under this Act shall be determined by a benefit officer except so far as this Act or regulations provide otherwise ; and regulations may provide for different aspects of the same question to be dealt with by different benefit officers.

(1A) Regulations may provide for prescribed questions to be determined otherwise than by benefit officers and, without prejudice to the generality of the preceding provisions of this subsection,—

1975 c. 14.

(*a*) for prescribed questions to be referred to bodies or persons exercising functions under the Social Security Act 1975 and for the application of provisions of that Act, with or without modifications, to the questions and to decisions given in consequence of references in pursuance of the regulations ;

(*b*) for such decisions, and any other prescribed decisions given in pursuance of that Act, to be effective or conclusive for prescribed purposes of this Act ; and

(*c*) for dealing, by postponement or otherwise, with cases in which questions are referred by virtue of paragraph (*a*) of this subsection.

(2) Entitlement to, and the amount of, any supplementary benefit shall be determined in accordance with the provisions of this Part of this Act and Schedule 1 to this Act.

SCH. 2

Supplementary benefit to meet exceptional need.

3.—(1) There shall be payable in prescribed cases, to a person who is entitled or would if he satisfied prescribed conditions be entitled to a supplementary pension or allowance, supplementary benefit by way of a single payment of a prescribed amount to meet an exceptional need.

(2) In determining whether supplementary benefit shall be paid under this section, and the amount of any such benefit, regard shall be had, so far as regulations so provide, to any resources which would otherwise fall to be disregarded under regulations made in pursuance of paragraph 1(2)(*b*) of Schedule 1 to this Act.

Provision for cases of urgent need.

4.—(1) In urgent cases supplementary benefit shall be payable in accordance with this Act as modified by virtue of this section ; and regulations may—

(*a*) prescribe the cases which are urgent cases for the purposes of this section ;

(*b*) provide that in relation to such cases any of the provisions of sections 3, 5 to 8 and 10 of this Act and Schedule 1 to this Act shall have effect with prescribed modifications.

(2) Any sums paid to a person by virtue of the preceding subsection, except a sum as to which it has been determined in accordance with regulations that it is not to be recovered in pursuance of this subsection, shall be recoverable from him by the Secretary of State by making deductions from prescribed benefits or in any other manner.

Power to require registration for employment.

5.—Except in prescribed cases the right of any person to a supplementary allowance shall be subject to the condition that he is registered for employment in such manner as may be prescribed and is available for employment ; and regulations may make provision as to—

(*a*) what is and is not to be treated as employment for the purposes of this section ; and

(*b*) the circumstances in which a person is or is not to be treated for those purposes as available for employment.

Exclusion from supplementary benefit of certain employed persons and pupils.

6.—(1) A person who is engaged in remunerative full-time work shall not be entitled to supplementary benefit ; and regulations may make provision as to the circumstances in which a person is or is not to be treated for the purposes of this subsection as so engaged.

(2) A person who has not attained the age of 19 and is receiving relevant education shall not be entitled to supplementary benefit except in prescribed circumstances.

(3) Regulations may make provision as to the circumstances in which a person is or is not to be treated for the purposes of the preceding subsection as receiving relevant education ; and in this section " relevant education " means full-time education by attendance at an establishment recognised by the Secretary of State as being, or as comparable to, a college or school.

SCH. 2

Persons affected by trade disputes.

8.—(1) Subject to subsection (2) below, where a person—

> (*a*) is, by reason of a stoppage of work which is due to a trade dispute at his place of employment, without employment for any period during the stoppage ; and
>
> (*b*) has not during that stoppage become bona fide employed elsewhere in the occupation which he usually follows, or become regularly engaged in some other occupation,

his requirements for that period shall be disregarded for the purposes of supplementary benefit except so far as those requirements include requirements of another person which are to be treated as his by virtue of any other provision of this Act and are not to be disregarded by virtue of this subsection as it applies to the other person.

(2) Subsection (1) above does not apply in the case of a person who proves that he is not participating in or directly interested in the trade dispute which caused the stoppage of work.

. . . .

Recovery of supplementary benefit paid after return to full-time employment following trade dispute.

9.—(1) Where a person—

> (*a*) has, by reason of a stoppage of work which was due to a trade dispute at his place of employment, been without employment for any period during the stoppage ; and
>
> (*b*) is a person whose requirements for that period (except so far as those requirements included the requirements of any other person) fall to be disregarded for the purposes of supplementary benefit by virtue of section 8 of this Act (persons affected by trade disputes) ; and
>
> (*c*) becomes engaged in remunerative full-time work again in consequence of the ending of the stoppage ;

section 6(1) of this Act shall not apply in his case until the expiration of the period of fifteen days from the beginning of the engagement mentioned in paragraph (*c*) above ; but subsection (2) below shall have effect in such a case.

(2) Any sum paid to a person on an award of supplementary benefit made to him during the period of fifteen days specified in subsection (1) above by virtue of that subsection shall be recoverable from him or another person in accordance with regulations.

(3) Regulations made by virtue of section 6(1) of this Act providing for a person not to be treated as engaged in remunerative full-time work shall not apply to a person to whom subsection (1) above applies as regards the engagement mentioned in paragraph (*c*) of that subsection.

. . . .

X 2

Modification of right to supplementary allowance in certain cases.
1975 c. 14.

10.—(1) Where—

(*a*) a person is registered for employment in pursuance of section 5 of this Act and is not receiving unemployment benefit under the Social Security Act 1975 ; and

(*b*) it appears to a benefit officer that the person refuses or neglects to maintain himself or any other person whom for the purposes of this Act he is liable to maintain,

the officer may give him in the prescribed manner a direction in writing requiring him to attend a course of instruction or training which is approved or provided by the Secretary of State and is specified in the direction.

(2) A person to whom such a direction is given may, in accordance with rules made by the Secretary of State, appeal against the direction to the Appeal Tribunal ; and on an appeal in pursuance of this subsection the tribunal shall either confirm or cancel the direction.

(3) A direction under subsection (1) of this section shall not come into force—

(*a*) until the expiration of the period within which, without any extension of time, an appeal against it may be brought in pursuance of the preceding subsection ; and

(*b*) if during that period such an appeal is brought, until the appeal is withdrawn or the direction is confirmed by the tribunal.

(4) A person in respect of whom a direction under subsection (1) of this section is in force shall not be entitled to a supplementary allowance while he fails to comply with the direction.

(5) Regulations may make provision with respect to the consequences of the cancellation of a direction which has come into force.

Supplementary benefit in kind.

11.—(1) Regulations may make provision—

(*a*) for the requirements of any person to be met in prescribed circumstances by the provision of goods or services instead of by making the whole or part of any payment to which he would otherwise be entitled under this Act ;

(*b*) for any provision of this Act or regulations under it to be disregarded in connection with the provision of goods or services by virtue of the preceding paragraph ;

(*c*) as to the manner of providing goods and services to be provided by virtue of that paragraph.

SCH. 2

(2) In relation to any goods or services provided in pursuance of this section, references in this Act to the amount of supplementary benefit shall be taken to refer to the value of the goods or services.

Supplementary provisions

Prevention of duplication of payments.

12.—(1) Where a prescribed payment which apart from this subsection falls to be made from public funds in the United Kingdom or under the law of any other member State is not made on or before the date which is the prescribed date in relation to the payment, then—

(*a*) in the case of a payment from such public funds, the authority responsible for making it may abate it by the relevant amount ; and

(*b*) in the case of any other payment, the Secretary of State shall be entitled to receive the relevant amount out of the payment ;

and in this subsection " the relevant amount ", in relation to a payment, means the amount which a benefit officer determines has been paid by way of supplementary benefit and would not have been paid if the payment had been made on the date aforesaid.

(1A) Where—

(*a*) a payment by way of prescribed income is made after the date which is the prescribed date in relation to the payment ; and

(*b*) a benefit officer determines that an amount which has been paid by way of supplementary benefit would not have been paid if the said payment had been made on the date aforesaid,

the Secretary of State shall be entitled to recover that amount from the person to whom it was paid.

(2) Where for any period—

(*a*) a person (in this subsection referred to as A) is entitled to any prescribed benefit in respect of another person (in this subsection referred to as B) ; and

(*b*) B's requirements have been taken into account in determining the amount of any supplementary benefit payable for that period to B or some other person (other than A) ; and

(*c*) the amount of the supplementary benefit so payable has been determined on the basis that A has not made payments for the maintenance of B at a rate equal to or exceeding the amount of the prescribed benefit ;

the amount of the prescribed benefit may, at the discretion of the authority administering it, be abated by the amount

X 3

by which the amounts paid under this Act exceed what a benefit officer determines they would have been had A, at the time the amount of the supplementary benefit was determined, been making payments for the maintenance of B at a rate equal to the amount of the prescribed benefit.

(3) Where, in determining the amount of any supplementary benefit, the requirements of any person have been taken into account for the whole or part of a period in respect of which there might be afforded or granted to him—

(a) a rate rebate under a scheme under section 11 or 12 of the Local Government Act 1974 or, in Scotland, the standard scheme prescribed under section 112 of the Local Government (Scotland) Act 1973 (including that scheme as varied under section 114 of that Act) ; or

1974 c. 7.

1973 c. 65.

(b) a rebate or allowance under Part II of the Housing Finance Act 1972 or, in Scotland, Part II of the Housing (Financial Provisions) (Scotland) Act 1972 ;

1972 c. 47.
1972 c. 46.

and before the whole or part of the rebate or allowance has been afforded or granted, the authority administering the rebate or allowance, as the case may be, are notified by a benefit officer of the amount by which the amounts paid under this Act exceed what the officer has determined they would have been had the rebate or allowance been afforded or granted before the amount of the supplementary benefit was determined, the amount of the rebate or allowance to be afforded or granted shall be reduced by the amount so notified.

(4) Where a benefit officer makes—

(a) a determination in pursuance of the preceding provisions of this section in respect of an amount of supplementary benefit ; or

(b) a determination altering on review or refusing to review a determination in respect of such an amount which has been made for the purposes of this section by a benefit officer or on appeal,

the relevant person may appeal to the Appeal Tribunal against the determination ; and subsection (3) of section 15 of this Act shall apply to an appeal under this subsection as it applies to an appeal under that section.

(5) In the preceding subsection " the relevant person " means the person who is entitled, apart from subsection (1), (2) or (3) of this section, to the prescribed payment or the prescribed benefit or the rebate or allowance in question or, as the case may be, to whom the amount mentioned in subsection (1A) of this section was paid.

Payment of supplementary benefits.

13. Any sums payable under this Act by way of supplementary benefit shall be paid by the Secretary of State out of moneys provided by Parliament.

Administration of supplementary benefits.

14.—(1) Regulations may make provision for carrying into effect this Part of this Act and Schedule 1 to this Act ; and nothing in any other provision of this Act shall be construed as prejudicing the generality of this subsection.

(2) Regulations may make provision—

(*a*) for requiring claims for supplementary benefit to be made in such manner and within such time as may be specified in the regulations ;

(*b*) for enabling a person to be appointed to exercise, on behalf of a claimant who may be or become unable to act in relation to his claim, any power in relation to it which the claimant is entitled to exercise ;

(*c*) for prescribing the evidence which is to be provided in support of claims for supplementary benefit ;

(*d*) for requiring or enabling a benefit officer, in such circumstances as may be specified in the regulations, to review any determination with respect to supplementary benefit, whether the determination is made by a benefit officer or by the Appeal Tribunal or by a Commissioner or Tribunal of Commissioners by virtue of rules under section 15A of this Act ;

(*e*) for extinguishing the right to payment of any sum by way of supplementary benefit if payment is not obtained within a prescribed period of not less than twelve months from the date on which the right is to be treated under the regulations as having arisen ;

(*ee*) for suspending the payment of supplementary benefit pending the determination of questions ;

(*f*) as to the day on which entitlement to a supplementary pension or allowance is to begin or end or the amount of a supplementary pension or allowance is to change ;

(*g*) as to the time and manner of paying supplementary benefit and the information and evidence to be furnished in connection with payments of it ;

(*h*) for withholding payments of a supplementary pension or allowance in prescribed circumstances and for subsequently making withheld payments in prescribed circumstances ;

X 4

(*i*) as to the circumstances and manner in which payments of supplementary benefit may be made to another person on behalf of the beneficiary for any purpose (which may be to discharge, in whole or in part, an obligation of the beneficiary or any other person) ;

(*j*) for the payment or distribution of supplementary benefit to or among persons claiming to be entitled to it on the death of any person and for dispensing with strict proof of their title ;

(*k*) for the payment of travelling expenses in connection with claims for supplementary benefit.

. . . .

Appeals.

15.—(1) A person claiming, or in receipt of, supplementary benefit may appeal to the Appeal Tribunal against any determination of a benefit officer (including a determination to refuse to review a determination) with respect to the claim or benefit, except that no appeal shall lie by virtue of this subsection in a case falling within section 10(2), 12(4) or 20(3) of this Act ;

. . . .

(3) On an appeal under this section the Appeal Tribunal may—

(*a*) confirm the determination appealed against ; or

. . . .

(*c*) substitute for any determination appealed against any determination which a benefit officer could have made.

(4) Subject to section 15A of this Act, any determination of an Appeal Tribunal shall be final ; but nothing in this section shall make any finding of fact or other determination embodied in or necessary to a decision, or on which it is based, conclusive for the purpose of any further decision.

Appeals from Appeal Tribunal.

15A.—(1) The Secretary of State may by rules make provision for any party to proceedings before an Appeal Tribunal (whether under this or any other Act) to appeal to a Commissioner against a decision of the tribunal.

(2) Rules under this section may, in particular, make provision—

(*a*) as to the cases and circumstances in which, and the conditions subject to which, appeals may be made, including provision either generally or in relation to specified classes of case for appeals—

(i) to be confined to points of law ;

(ii) to be made only with leave;

SCH. 2

(*b*) as to the manner in which, and the time within which, appeals are to be brought and (where appropriate) applications are to be made for leave to appeal ;

(*c*) as to the procedure to be followed on appeals ;

(*d*) as to the payment by the Secretary of State to persons attending proceedings before a Commissioner of travelling and other allowances (including compensation for loss of remunerative time).

(3) The power to make provision as to procedure under subsection (2)(*c*) above includes power to make provision as to the representation of one person in any proceedings by another person.

(4) Rules under this section may provide for a Commissioner hearing an appeal—

(*a*) to give any decision which might have been given by the tribunal ;

(*b*) to refer the case to another tribunal, with directions ;

(*c*) to dispose of the appeal in such other manner as may be specified ;

and in any case where directions are given to a tribunal in accordance with rules under this section the tribunal shall proceed accordingly.

(5) In this section " Commissioner " has the same meaning as in the Social Security Act 1975.

1975 c. 14.

Supplementary benefits to be inalienable.

16.—(1) Every assignment of, or charge on, any supplementary benefit, and every agreement to assign or charge any such benefit, shall be void ; and, on the bankruptcy . . . of a person entitled to any supplementary benefit, no rights in respect of the benefit shall pass to any trustee or other person acting on behalf of his creditors.

(2) In the application of the preceding subsection to Scotland—

(*a*) the reference to assignment of supplementary benefit shall be read as a reference to its assignation, " assign " being construed accordingly ; and

(*b*) the reference to the bankruptcy of a person entitled to supplementary benefit shall be read as a reference to the sequestration of his estate or the appointment on his estate of a judicial factor under section 14 of the Bankruptcy (Scotland) Act 1913 or section 15 of the Solicitors (Scotland) Act 1958.

1913 c. 20.
1958 c. 28.

PART II

LIABILITY TO MAINTAIN, RECOVERY OF EXPENDITURE AND OFFENCES

Liability to maintain

Liability to
maintain.

17.—(1) For the purposes of this Act—

(*a*) a man shall be liable to maintain his wife and his children ; and

(*b*) a woman shall be liable to maintain her husband and her children ; and

(*c*) a person shall be liable to maintain another person throughout any period in respect of which the first-mentioned person has, on or after the date of the passing of the Social Security Act 1980 and either alone or jointly with a further person, given an undertaking in writing in pursuance of immigration rules within the meaning of the Immigration Act 1971 to be responsible for the maintenance and accommodation of the other person.

1971 c. 77.

(2) In subsection (1) above—

(*a*) the reference to a man's children includes a reference to children of whom he has been adjudged to be the putative father or, in Scotland, to children his paternity of whom has been admitted or otherwise established ; and

(*b*) the reference to a woman's children includes a reference to her illegitimate children.

(3) A document bearing a certificate which—

(*a*) is signed by a person authorised in that behalf by the Secretary of State ; and

(*b*) states that the document apart from the certificate is, or is a copy of, such an undertaking as is mentioned in subsection (1)(*c*) of this section,

shall be conclusive evidence for the purposes of this Act of the undertaking in question ; and a certificate purporting to be signed as aforesaid shall be deemed to be so signed until the contrary is proved.

Recovery of expenditure

Recovery of
expenditure
on supple-
mentary
benefits from
persons liable
for main-
tenance.

18.—(1) Where supplementary benefit is paid or claimed to meet requirements which are, or include, those of a person whom another person is, for the purposes of this Act, liable to maintain (in this section referred to respectively as " the dependant " and " the liable person ") the Secretary of State may make a complaint against the liable person to a magistrates' court for an order under this section.

(2) Except in a case falling within section 17(1)(c) of this Act, no complaint under subsection (1) above shall be made where the dependant is an illegitimate child and the liable person is his father.

(3) On the hearing of a complaint under subsection (1) above the court shall have regard to all the circumstances and, in particular, to the resources of the liable person, and may order him to pay such sum, weekly or otherwise, as it may consider appropriate, except that in a case falling within section 17(1)(c) of this Act that sum shall not include any amount which is not attributable to supplementary benefit (whether paid before or after the making of the order).

(4) In determining whether to order any payments to be made in respect of supplementary benefit for any period before the complaint was made, or the amount of any such payments, the court shall disregard any amount by which the liable person's resources exceed the resources which were his during that period.

(5) Any payments ordered to be made under this section shall be made—

    (a) to the Secretary of State in so far as they are attributable to any supplementary benefit (whether paid before or after the making of the order);

    (b) to the person claiming supplementary benefit or (if different) the dependant; or

    (c) to such other person as appears to the court expedient in the interests of the dependant.

. . . .

(7) An order under this section shall be enforceable as an affiliation order.

(8) In the application of this section to Scotland, subsections (2) and (7) shall be omitted, and for the references to a complaint and to a magistrates' court there shall be substituted respectively references to an application and to the sheriff.

Affiliation orders.

19.—(1) The provisions of this section apply in any case in which supplementary benefit is paid to meet requirements which include those of an illegitimate child.

(2) If no affiliation order is in force the Secretary of State may, within three years from the time when any payment by way of supplementary benefit was made, make application to a justice of the peace acting for the petty sessions area in which the mother of the child resides for a summons to be served under section 1 of the Affiliation Proceedings Act 1957.

1957 c. 55.

(3) In any proceedings on an application under sub-section (2) above the court shall hear such evidence as the Secretary of State may produce, and shall in all other respects, subject to the provisions of subsection (4) below, proceed as on an application made by the mother under section 1 of the said Act of 1957.

(4) An affiliation order—

(*a*) made on an application made by the Secretary of State under subsection (2) above ; or

(*b*) made on an application made by the Secretary of State in proceedings brought by the mother of the child under section 1 of the said Act of 1957,

may be made so as to provide that the payments, or a part of the payments, to be made under the order shall, instead of being made to the mother or a person having custody of the child, be made to the Secretary of State or to such other person as the court may direct.

(5) Any affiliation order, whether made before or after the commencement of this Act, may, on the application of the Secretary of State, be varied so as to provide for the making of payments, or part thereof, as mentioned in subsection (4) above ; and an application by the Secretary of State under this subsection may be made—

(*a*) notwithstanding that the mother has died and no person has been appointed to have the cus-tody of the child ; and

(*b*) where the child is not in the care of the mother and she is not contributing to his maintenance, without making her a party to the proceedings.

(6) Any affiliation order which provides for the making of payments, or part thereof, as mentioned in subsection (4) above may, on the application of the mother of the child, be varied so as to provide that the payments shall be made to the mother or a person having the custody of the child.

.   .   .   .

(8) In the application of this section to Scotland, the following provisions shall have effect in substitution for subsections (2) to (6) above—

(*a*) the Secretary of State shall have the like right as the mother to raise an action of affiliation and aliment concluding for payment of aliment for the child ;

(*b*) where in any action of affiliation and aliment in respect of the child, whether at the instance of the Secretary of State under the foregoing para-graph or at the instance of the mother, the sheriff grants or has granted decree against any person for payment of aliment for the child, the sheriff may at the time of granting the decree or at any subsequent time on the application of the Secretary of State, order that the sums due under the decree or any part thereof shall, instead of being paid to the mother of the child, be paid to the Secretary of State or to such other person as the sheriff may direct ;

(c) if such an order is made in favour of the Secretary of State, the Secretary of State, or, if it is made in favour of another person, that person, shall have the like right to enforce the decree (so far as relating to the said sums) by diligence, including the right to take proceedings under the Civil Imprisonment (Scotland) Act 1882, as if the decree were a decree in favour of the Secretary of State or other person.

1882 c. 42.

Recovery in cases of misrepresentation or non-disclosure.

20.—(1) If, whether fraudulently or otherwise, any person misrepresents, or fails to disclose, any material fact, and in consequence of the misrepresentation or failure—

(a) the Secretary of State incurs any expenditure under this Act ; or

(b) any sum recoverable under this Act by or on behalf of the Secretary of State is not recovered,

the Secretary of State shall be entitled to recover the amount thereof from that person.

(2) If, whether in connection with any legal proceedings or otherwise, any question arises whether any amount paid by way of supplementary benefit is recoverable by the Secretary of State under this section, or as to the amount so recoverable, the question shall be determined by a benefit officer.

(3) A person from whom, in pursuance of a determination of a benefit officer under the preceding subsection, an amount is recoverable under this section may appeal to the Appeal Tribunal against the determination ; and subsection (3) of section 15 of this Act shall apply to an appeal under this subsection as it applies to an appeal under that section.

(4) Where any amount paid by way of supplementary benefit is recoverable under this section, it may, without prejudice to any other method of recovery, be recovered by deduction from prescribed benefits.

(5) Subsections (2) and (3) of this section shall apply to any question as to whether any amount or what amount is recoverable by the Secretary of State under section 45 of the National Assistance Act 1948 or section 26 of the Supplementary Benefit Act 1966 (which contain provisions corresponding to subsection (1) of this section) and subsection (4) of this section shall apply to an amount

1948 c. 29.
1966 c. 20.

recoverable by the Secretary of State under either of those sections—

    (*a*) as if for any reference in those subsections to this section there were substituted references to the said section 45 or 26, as the case may be ; and

    (*b*) as respects a question relating to recovery under the said section 45 and an amount recoverable under that section, as if the words " paid by way of supplementary benefit " in subsections (2) and (4) of this section were omitted.

Offences

False statements.

21. If any person, for the purpose of obtaining supple- mentary benefit or any other payment under this Act for himself or another person or for any other purpose connected with this Act—

    (*a*) makes any statement or representation which he knows to be false ; or

    (*b*) produces or furnishes, or causes or knowingly allows to be produced or furnished, any docu- ment or information which he knows to be false in a material particular,

he shall be guilty of an offence and liable on summary conviction to a fine not exceeding £400 or to imprison- ment for a term not exceeding three months or to both.

Imperson- ation of officers.

22. If any person, with intent to deceive, falsely repre- sents himself to be a person authorised by the Secretary of State for Social Services to act in any capacity (whether under this Act or otherwise) he shall be guilty of an offence and liable on summary conviction to a fine not exceeding £400.

Illegal possession of documents.

23.—(1) If any person—

    (*a*) as a pledge or a security for a debt ; or

    (*b*) with a view to obtaining payment from the person entitled to it of a debt due either to himself or to any other person ;

receives, detains or has in his possession any document issued by or on behalf of the Secretary of State for Social Services in connection with any benefit, pension or allowance (whether payable under this Act or otherwise) he shall be guilty of an offence.

(2) If any person has such a document in his possession without lawful authority or excuse (the proof whereof shall lie on him) he shall be guilty of an offence.

(3) A person guilty of an offence under this section shall be liable on summary conviction to imprisonment for a term not exceeding three months or to a fine not exceeding £400 or to both.

Failure to notify.

24.—(1) If any person fails to comply with a provision of regulations under section 9(2) of this Act requiring him to give notice of any matter to the Secretary of State, he shall be guilty of an offence and liable on summary conviction to a fine not exceeding £100.

SCH. 2

.　.　.　.　.

Failure to maintain.

25.—(1) If any person persistently refuses or neglects to maintain himself or any person whom for the purposes of this Act he is liable to maintain and in consequence of his refusal or neglect supplementary benefit is awarded to meet requirements which are, or include, his or those of such a person he shall be guilty of an offence and liable on summary conviction to imprisonment for a term not exceeding three months or to a fine not exceeding £400 or to both.

(2) For the purposes of this section a person shall not be taken to refuse or neglect to maintain himself or any other person by reason only of anything done or omitted in furtherance of a trade dispute.

Legal proceedings

Legal proceedings.

26.—(1) Any person authorised by the Secretary of State in that behalf may conduct any proceedings under this Act before a magistrates' court although not a barrister or solicitor.

(2) Without prejudice to any other method of recovery, any sum due under this Act to the Secretary of State, other than a sum due under an order enforceable as an affiliation order, shall be recoverable summarily as a civil debt.

(3) Notwithstanding anything in any Act—

    (*a*) proceedings under this Act for the recovery of a sum recoverable summarily as a civil debt may be begun at any time within three years after the sum became due ;

    (*b*) proceedings for an offence under this Act may be begun at any time within the period of three months from the date on which evidence, sufficient in the opinion of the Secretary of State to justify a prosecution for the offence, comes to his knowledge, or within the period of twelve months from the commission of the offence, whichever period last expires.

(4) For the purposes of subsection (3) above, a certificate purporting to be signed by, or on behalf of, the Secretary of State as to the date on which such evidence as is mentioned in paragraph (*b*) of that subsection came to his knowledge shall be conclusive evidence of that date.

(5) In any proceedings for an offence under this Act the wife or husband of the accused shall be competent to give evidence, whether for or against the accused, but shall not be compellable either to give evidence or, in giving evidence, to disclose any communication made to her or to him by the accused during the marriage.

(6) In the application of this section to Scotland, the following provisions shall have effect in substitution for subsections (1) to (4) above—

(a) proceedings for an offence under this Act may, notwithstanding anything in section 331 of the Criminal Procedure (Scotland) Act 1975, be commenced at any time within the period of three months from the date on which evidence sufficient in the opinion of the appropriate authority to justify proceedings comes to his knowledge, or within the period of twelve months from the commission of the offence, whichever period last expires ;

1975 c. 21.

(b) for the purposes of this subsection—

> (i) " the appropriate authority " means the Secretary of State or, in the case of proceedings which are not preceded by a report of the facts made by the Secretary of State to the Lord Advocate, means the Lord Advocate ;
>
> (ii) a certificate of the appropriate authority as to the date on which such evidence as is mentioned above comes to his knowledge shall be conclusive evidence ; and
>
> (iii) subsection (3) of section 331 of the said Act of 1975 (date of commencement of proceedings) shall have effect as it has effect for the purposes of that section.

Part III

Administration, General and Supplemental

Administration

Duties of Secretary of State.

27.—(1) It shall be the duty of the Secretary of State to make arrangements with a view to ensuring that benefit officers and other officers of his concerned with the administration of this Act exercise their functions in such manner as shall best promote the welfare of persons affected by the exercise of those functions.

(2) It shall be the duty of the Secretary of State to appoint persons to perform the functions conferred by virtue of this Act on benefit officers.

The Appeal
Tribunal.

28. The Appeal Tribunal for the purposes of this Act shall be such of the tribunals constituted in accordance with Schedule 4 to this Act as, under that Schedule, has jurisdiction in the case in question.

Re-
establish-
ment
courses and
resettlement
units.

30.—(1) The provisions of Schedule 5 to this Act shall have effect with respect to re-establishment courses and resettlement units.

(2) If the Secretary of State so directs, payment at such rates as he may determine shall be made by persons for whom temporary board and lodging are provided in connection with courses provided or units maintained under that Schedule.

• • • • • • •

Modifi-
cation of
Act for
special cases.

32A. Regulations may provide for any provision of this Act except this section to have effect with prescribed modifications—

> (a) in cases involving a marriage celebrated under a law which permits polygamy or a marriage during the subsistence of which a party to it is at any time married to more than one person ;
>
> (b) in cases where the Secretary of State considers that without the modifications the provision in question would give rise to an anomaly or an injustice or would produce impractical consequences.

Rules and
regulations.

33.—(1) Powers conferred by this Act to make rules or regulations are exercisable by statutory instrument.

(1A) Rules under this Act may make different provision for different classes of case and otherwise for different circumstances.

1975 c. 14.

(2) Subsections (2) and (3) of section 166 of the Social Security Act 1975 (which among other things make provision about the extent of powers to make regulations) shall apply to powers to make regulations conferred by this Act as they apply to powers to make regulations conferred by that Act but as if for references to that Act there were substituted references to this Act.

(3) Regulations of the following kinds, namely—

> (a) regulations of which the effect is to increase an amount which is specified in regulations made in pursuance of section 3 of this Act or which, by virtue of regulations made in pursuance of paragraph (b) of section 4(1) of this Act, is specified in a provision mentioned in that paragraph ;
>
> (b) regulations made in pursuance of section 32A(b) of this Act except regulations made for the purpose only of consolidating regulations which they revoke ;

SCH. 2

(*c*) regulations made in pursuance of paragraph 1 or 2 of Schedule 1 to this Act except regulations made for the purpose only of consolidating regulations which they revoke,

shall not be made unless a draft of the regulations has been laid before Parliament and approved by a resolution of each House and, in the case of regulations falling within paragraph (*a*) or (*c*) of this subsection, shall not be made without the consent of the Treasury.

(4) A statutory instrument containing regulations of which a draft is not required by the preceding subsection to be approved as there mentioned or containing rules made under this Act shall be subject to annulment in pursuance of a resolution of either House of Parliament.

(5) Without prejudice to the generality of any power conferred by this Act to make regulations, regulations may provide for a person to exercise a discretion in dealing with any matter.

Interpre-
tation.

34.—(1) In this Act—

" the Appeal Tribunal " means the tribunal which has jurisdiction in accordance with section 28 of this Act ;

" benefit officer " means a person appointed in pursuance of section 27(2) of this Act ;

.   .   .   .

" child " means a person under the age of 16 ;

.   .   .   .

" enactment " includes an enactment of the Parliament of Northern Ireland and a provision of a Measure of the Northern Ireland Assembly ;

" married couple " means a man and a woman who are married to each other and are members of the same household ;

" modifications " includes additions, omissions and amendments, and related expressions shall be construed accordingly ;

" pensionable age " means, in the case of a man, the age of 65, and, in the case of a woman, the age of 60 ;

1975 c. 14.

" place of employment " has the same meaning as in section 19 of the Social Security Act 1975 ;

" prescribed " means specified in or determined in accordance with regulations ;

" regulations " means regulations made by the Secretary of State under this Act ;

.   .   .   .

"supplementary benefit" means any benefit under this Act ;

"trade dispute" has the same meaning as in section 19 of the Social Security Act 1975 ;

"unmarried couple" means a man and a woman who are not married to each other but are living together as husband and wife otherwise than in prescribed circumstances ;

"voluntary organisation" means a body, other than a public or local authority, the activities of which are carried on otherwise than for profit.

(2) Except where the context otherwise requires, any reference in this Act to any enactment is a reference to that enactment as amended or extended by or under any other enactment, including this Act.

(3) Regulations may make provision as to the circumstances in which a person is to be treated for the purposes of any specified provision of this Act—

(a) as being or not being a member of the same household as another person ;

(b) as responsible for another person.

Sections 2, 3, 4, 14 and 33.

SCHEDULE 1

PROVISION FOR DETERMINING RIGHT TO BENEFIT AND AMOUNT OF BENEFIT

General

1.—(1) The amount of any supplementary benefit to which a person is entitled shall, subject to the following provisions of this Schedule, be the amount by which his resources fall short of his requirements.

(2) For the purpose of ascertaining that amount—

(a) a person's requirements shall be determined in accordance with paragraph 2 of this Schedule ; and

(b) a person's resources shall be calculated in the prescribed manner ;

and without prejudice to the generality of paragraph (b) of this sub-paragraph, regulations in pursuance of that paragraph may provide for a person to be treated as possessing resources which he does not possess and for disregarding resources which a person does possess.

(3) Regulations may provide that a person whose resources as ascertained in pursuance of paragraph (b) of the preceding sub-paragraph or a prescribed part of them exceed or exceeds a prescribed amount shall not be entitled to a supplementary pension or allowance.

Requirements

2.—(1) For the purposes of this Schedule requirements shall be of three categories, namely, normal requirements, additional requirements and housing requirements; and the items to which each category relates and, subject to sub-paragraph (3) of this paragraph, the weekly amounts for those categories shall be such as may be prescribed.

(2) A person's requirements shall consist of normal requirements together with requirements, if any, of such of the other categories as are applicable in his case.

(3) In the case of a person specified in the first column of the following table his normal requirements shall be taken to be the weekly amount specified in relation to him in the second column of that table; and in that table—

> " householder " means a person who is not one of a married or unmarried couple but who satisfies prescribed conditions with respect to living accommodation; and

> " relevant person " means a person whose requirements include those of another person by virtue of sub-paragraph (1) of paragraph 3 of this Schedule.

TABLE

Person	Weekly amount
1. A relevant person who—	The aggregate of the sums for the time being specified in section 6(1)(a) of the Social Security Pensions Act 1975 and column (3) of paragraph 6 of Part IV of Schedule 4 to the Social Security Act 1975 (which specify the amounts of the basic component of a Category A retirement pension and the increase of the pension for an adult dependant).
(a) is such a person as is mentioned in section 1(1)(a) of this Act; or	
(b) is not such a person as is so mentioned but satisfies prescribed conditions.	
2. A relevant person not falling within paragraph 1 of this table.	The aggregate of the sums for the time being specified in paragraph 1 of Part I of the said Schedule 4 and column (3) of paragraph 1(a) of the said Part IV (which specify the amounts of

1975 c. 60.

1975 c. 14.

	unemployment or sickness benefit and the increase of it for an adult dependant of a beneficiary under pensionable age).
3. A householder who— (*a*) has attained pensionable age ; or (*b*) has not attained pensionable age but satisfies prescribed conditions.	The sum for the time being specified in the said section 6(1)(*a*).
4. A householder not falling within paragraph 3 of this table.	The sum for the time being specified in paragraph 1 of the said Part I.

(4) Regulations may provide that the preceding sub-paragraph shall have effect with prescribed modifications.

(5) Notwithstanding anything in the preceding provisions of this paragraph, regulations may provide for a person to be treated as having no normal requirements in prescribed cases.

Aggregation of requirements and resources

3.—(1) Where two persons are a married or unmarried couple, their requirements and resources shall be aggregated and treated—

(*a*) until the prescribed date, as those of the man ; and

(*b*) on and after that date, as those of such one of them as satisfies prescribed conditions or, where both of them satisfy or neither of them satisfies those conditions, as those of such one of them as they may jointly nominate in accordance with regulations or, in default of such a nomination, as the Secretary of State may determine.

(2) Where a person is responsible for, and is a member of the same household as, another person and they are not a married or unmarried couple, then—

(*a*) if the other person is a child or is excluded from entitlement to supplementary benefit by section 6(2) of this Act ; or

(*b*) if the circumstances are such as are prescribed,

their requirements and resources shall be aggregated and treated as those of the first-mentioned person.

(3) Regulations may provide that, in a case falling within the preceding sub-paragraph, sub-paragraph (1) of this paragraph shall apply in relation to the other person with prescribed modifications.

Exclusion of small payments

4. Where the amount of any supplementary benefit would be less than a prescrbed amount, the benefit shall not be payable except in prescribed circumstances.

Section 30.

SCHEDULE 5

RE-ESTABLISHMENT COURSES AND RESETTLEMENT UNITS

Re-establishment courses

1.—(1) The Secretary of State may provide courses, to be known as re-establishment courses, at which persons who are in need of re-establishment through lack of regular occupation or lack of instruction or training may be afforded the occupation, instruction or training required to fit them for entry into, or return to, regular employment.

(2) Persons mentioned in sub-paragraph (1) above may attend re-establishment courses either in consequence of a direction under section 10(1) of this Act or otherwise, and the Secretary of State may provide temporary board and lodging for persons attending re-establishment courses.

Resettlement units

2.—(1) It shall be the duty of the Secretary of State to provide and maintain places, to be known as re-settlement units, at which persons without a settled way of life are afforded temporary board and lodging with a view to influencing them to lead a more settled life.

(2) The Secretary of State may require the councils of counties, other than metropolitan counties, and of metropolitan districts, regions, island areas and London boroughs and the Common Council of the City of London to exercise, on behalf of the Secretary of State and in accordance with any directions given by the Secretary of State, the functions of providing and maintaining resettlement units.

(3) A council may recover from the Secretary of State any expenditure incurred by them under this paragraph with the approval of the Secretary of State, given either as respects that expenditure or generally as respects expenditure up to a specified amount.

(4) Before giving directions under sub-paragraph (2) above the Secretary of State shall consult with such local authorities, or associations of local authorities, as appear to him to be concerned.   SCH. 2

. . . . -

Contributions for courses and places provided by voluntary organisations

4. The Secretary of State may make contributions to the funds of any voluntary organisation providing courses or places for purposes similar to the purposes for which re-establishment courses or resettlement units are provided by the Secretary of State.

SCHEDULE 3

Sections 9 and 10.

SOCIAL SECURITY ADVISORY COMMITTEE

PART I

CONSTITUTION ETC OF COMMITTEE

1. The Committee shall consist of a chairman appointed by the Secretary of State and not less than 8 nor more than 11 other members so appointed.

2. Subject to paragraph 4 of this Schedule, the chairman and other members of the Committee shall hold office for such period of not more than 5 nor less than 3 years as the Secretary of State may determine ; but any member—

(a) shall be eligible for reappointment from time to time on or after the expiration of his term of office ;

(b) may by notice in writing to the Secretary of State resign office at any time, while remaining eligible for reappointment.

3.—(1) Of the members of the Committee (other than the chairman) there shall be appointed—

(a) one after consultation with organisations representative of employers ;

(b) one after consultation with organisations representative of workers ; and

(c) one after consultation with the Head of the Department of Health and Social Services for Northern Ireland ;

and the Committee shall include at least one person with experience of work among, and of the needs of, the chronically sick and disabled.

(2) In selecting a person with such experience as aforesaid regard shall be had to the desirability of having a chronically sick or disabled person.

4. The Secretary of State may remove a member of the Committee on the ground of incapacity or misbehaviour.

5. The Secretary of State shall appoint a secretary to the Committee and may appoint such other officers and such servants to the Committee, and there shall be paid to them by the Secretary of State such salaries and allowances, as the Secretary of State may with the consent of the Minister for the Civil Service determine.

6. The expenses of the Committee to such an amount as may be approved by the Minister for the Civil Service shall be paid by the Secretary of State.

7. There may be paid as part of the expenses of the Committee—

  (a) to all or any of the members of the Committee, such salaries or other remuneration and travelling and other allowances ; and

  (b) to persons attending its meetings at the request of the Committee, such travelling and other allowances (including compensation for loss of remunerative time),

as the Secretary of State may with the consent of the Minister for the Civil Service determine.

8.—(1) The Secretary of State may pay or make provision for paying, to or in respect of any member of the Committee, such sums by way of pensions, superannuation allowances and gratuities as the Secretary of State may determine with the consent of the Minister for the Civil Service.

(2) Where a person ceases to be a member of the Committee otherwise than on the expiry of his term of office and it appears to the Secretary of State that there are special circumstances which make it right for the person to receive compensation the Secretary of State may make to him a payment of such amount as the Secretary of State may determine with the consent of the Minister for the Civil Service.

9. The Committee may act notwithstanding any vacancy among the members.

10. The Committee may make rules for regulating its procedure (including the quorum of the Committee).

PART II

REGULATIONS NOT REQUIRING PRIOR SUBMISSION
TO COMMITTEE

Family Income Supplement

1970 c. 55.   11. Regulations under section 2(1) or 3(1) of the Family Income
1971 c. 8 (N.I.).   Supplements Act 1970 or the Family Income Supplements Act (Northern Ireland) 1971 (under which amounts may be prescribed for the purposes of determining the amount of family income supplement payable to any person).

Social Security Sch. 3

12.—(1) Regulations relating only to industrial injuries benefit within the meaning of the principal Act or the Social Security 1975 c. 15. (Northern Ireland) Act 1975.

(2) Regulations contained in a statutory instrument which states that it contains only provisions in consequence of an order under section 120, 122 or 126A of the principal Act (which provide for the re-rating of contributions and the up-rating of certain increments) or an up-rating order within the meaning of that Act or contained in a statutory rule which states that it contains only provisions in consequence of an order under section 120 of the said Act of 1975 (which provides for re-rating and up-rating in Northern Ireland).

(3) Regulations contained in a statutory instrument or rule which states that the regulations relate only to matters which in accordance with the principal Act, the said Act of 1975 or any enactment directed to be construed as one with either of those Acts, have been referred to the Attendance Allowance Board or the Attendance Allowance Board for Northern Ireland.

Social Security Pensions

13.—(1) Regulations under section 1 of the Pensions Act or Article 3 of the Social Security Pensions (Northern Ireland) Order S.I. 1975/1503 1975 (which provide for the fixing of the upper and lower earnings (N.I. 15). limits) or regulations contained in a statutory instrument or rule which states that it contains only regulations to make provision consequential on regulations under that section or, as the case may be, that Article.

(2) Regulations made only for the purposes of Part III or IV of that Act or Part IV or V of that Order (which relate to contracting-out and occupational pensions).

Child Benefit

14.—(1) Regulations under section 5 of the Child Benefit Act 1975 c. 61. 1975 or Article 7 of the Child Benefit (Northern Ireland) Order 1975 S.I. 1975/1504 (under which the rate of child benefit may be prescribed). (N.I. 16).

(2) Regulations under section 17 of that Act or Article 19 of that Order (under which social security benefits may be varied following an increase of the rate of child benefit).

Supplementary Benefits

15. Regulations of which the effect is to increase any amount which is—

  (a) specified in regulations made for the purposes of section 3 of the Supplementary Benefits Act 1976 (which relates to 1976 c. 71. cases of exceptional need) ; or

  (b) specified in any provision mentioned in section 4 of that Act (which provides for the modification for urgent cases of

Sch. 3

sections 3, 5 to 8 and 10 of that Act and Schedule 1 to that Act) by virtue of regulations made in pursuance of the said section 4 ; or

(c) specified in regulations made by virtue of paragraph 1(2)(b) or (3) or 2(1) of Schedule 1 to that Act (which relate to resources and requirements) ; or

(d) specified in paragraph 2(3) of that Schedule (which relates to the requirements of couples and householders) by virtue of regulations made in pursuance of paragraph 2(4) of that Schedule,

and corresponding regulations applying to Northern Ireland.

National Insurance Surcharge

1976 c. 85.

1975 c. 15.

16. Regulations contained in a statutory instrument or rule which states that it contains only provisions in consequence of the National Insurance Surcharge Act 1976 or of that Act and either an order under section 120 or 122 of the principal Act or an order under section 120 of the Social Security (Northern Ireland) Act 1975.

Miscellaneous

1970 c. 55.
1971 c. 8 (N.I.).
1975 c. 61.
S.I. 1975/1504
(N.I. 16).
1976 c. 71.
S.I. 1977/2156.
(N.I. 27).

17. Regulations made within a period of six months beginning with the date of the passing of this Act under the Family Income Supplements Act 1970, the Family Income Supplements Act (Northern Ireland) 1971, the Child Benefit Act 1975, the Child Benefit (Northern Ireland) Order 1975, the Supplementary Benefits Act 1976 or the Supplementary Benefits (Northern Ireland) Order 1977.

18. Regulations not falling within paragraph 17 of this Schedule which are made during the period of six months beginning with the passing of this Act and contained in a statutory instrument or rule which states that it contains only regulations to make provision consequential on the passing of this Act.

1971 c. 62.

19. Regulations in so far as they consist only of procedural rules for a tribunal in respect of which consultation with the Council on Tribunals is required by section 10(1) of the Tribunals and Inquiries Act 1971.

20. Regulations made for the purpose only of consolidating other regulations revoked thereby.

21. Regulations making in relation to Northern Ireland only provision corresponding to provision contained in regulations made by the Secretary of State in relation to Great Britain.

Section 20.

SCHEDULE 4

CONSEQUENTIAL AND MINOR AMENDMENTS OF ENACTMENTS

1947 c. 19.

Polish Resettlement Act 1947

1.—(1) Section 3 of the Polish Resettlement Act 1947 and Part II of the Schedule to that Act (which among other things authorise the Supplementary Benefits Commission to provide accommodation and

goods and services for former members of certain Polish forces)   SCH. 4
shall be amended as follows—

    (*a*) for references to the Supplementary Benefits Commission, wherever they occur except in section 3(5), there shall be substituted references to the Secretary of State ;

    (*b*) in section 3(2) the words " by making payments to persons for whom accommodation is provided " shall be omitted and for the word " another " there shall be substituted the words " the other ".

    (*c*) subsections (4), (5), (10) and (10A) of section 3 (which among other things provide for the making and observance of rules about conduct in accommodation and that the Commission's functions under that section are exercised on behalf of the Secretary of State) shall be omitted ;

    (*d*) in paragraph 3 of that Schedule the words from " (including " to " repealed) " (which relate to the recovery of certain charges from a step-father) shall be omitted ; and

    (*e*) in paragraph 4 of that Schedule the proviso (which provides for an appeal about the amounts of certain charges) shall be omitted.

(2) In sections 4(1), 6(1) and 7(1) of that Act (which contain references to persons for whom there is power to provide accommodation under section 3 of that Act) for the words from " for whom " to " power " there shall be substituted the words " for whom the Secretary of State has power " ; and for subsection (3) of section 12 of that Act (which modifies references to such persons in the application of the Act to Northern Ireland) there shall be substituted the following subsection—

    (3) References in sections 4 to 7 of this Act to persons of any description for whom the Secretary of State has power to provide accommodation under section 3 of this Act shall include references to persons in Northern Ireland of any description for whom he would have power so to provide if those persons were in Great Britain.

The National Assistance Act 1948   1948 c. 29.

2.—(1) In section 22 of the National Assistance Act 1948, in subsection (5) (which provides that in assessing a person's ability to pay for certain accommodation a local authority shall have regard to Part III of Schedule 1 to the Supplementary Benefits Act 1976) for the words from " Part III " onwards there shall be substituted the words " regulations made by the Secretary of State for the purposes of this subsection ", and subsection (9) (under which payments of benefit may be diverted to a local authority to discharge a liability in respect of accommodation provided by the authority) shall cease to have effect.

(2) Section 27 of that Act (under which among other things questions as to the circumstances of a person applying for accommodation under the Act may be referred to the Supplementary Benefits Commission) shall cease to have effect.

SCH. 4

(3) In paragraph 8(3)(*b*) of Schedule 6 to that Act (which refers to a centre to be maintained for the like purposes as a reception centre maintained by the Supplementary Benefits Commission) for the words from " a centre " to " the centre " there shall be substituted the words " a place for the like purposes as a resettlement unit maintained by the Secretary of State, and that place ".

1950 c. 37.

The Maintenance Orders Act 1950

3. In section 8(1) of the Maintenance Orders Act 1950 (which relates to jurisdiction in certain actions of affiliation and aliment in Scotland) for the words from " or at the instance " to " local authority " there shall be substituted the words " or at the instance of the Secretary of State or of a local authority ".

1967 c. 43.

The Legal Aid (Scotland) Act 1967

4.—(1) Section 4(5) of the Legal Aid (Scotland) Act 1967 (which provides, in relation to legal aid, for computing resources by reference to the rules set out in certain paragraphs of Schedule 1 to the Supplementary Benefits Act 1976) shall cease to have effect.

(2) In section 4(6) of that Act (which among other things provides for the income and capital of a person and the maximum amount of his contribution to the legal aid fund to be determined by the Supplementary Benefits Commission) for the words from " determined " onwards there shall be substituted the words " determined in accordance with regulations ; and regulations for the purposes of this subsection may make different provision for different cases or classes of cases.".

1968 c. 49.

The Social Work (Scotland) Act 1968

5.—(1) In section 87(3) of the Social Work (Scotland) Act 1968 (under which accommodation provided under that Act is regarded as provided under Part III of the National Assistance Act 1948) for the words " sections 22(2) to (9) " there shall be substituted the words " sections 22(2) to (8) ".

(2) Section 87(6) of that Act (under which among other things questions as to the circumstances of a person applying for accommodation under that Act may be referred to the Supplementary Benefits Commission) shall cease to have effect.

1970 c. 42.

The Local Authority Social Services Act 1970

6. In Schedule 1 to the Local Authority Social Services Act 1970 (which lists the functions of a local authority assigned to its Social Services Committee), in column 2 of the entry relating to Schedule 5 to the Supplementary Benefits Act 1976, for the words " reception centres " there shall be substituted the words " resettlement units ".

1972 c. 46.

The Housing (Financial Provisions) (Scotland) Act 1972

7. In section 16A(4) of the Housing (Financial Provisions) (Scotland) Act 1972 (which relates to a housing authority and the Supplementary Benefits Commission providing each other with information

for purposes connected with supplementary benefits), for the words
" Supplementary Benefits Commission " in both places where they
occur there shall be substituted the words " Secretary of State " and
for the words " the Commission " there shall be substituted the
words " the Secretary of State ".

The Employment and Training Act 1973

8. In section 12(2)(*b*) of the Employment and Training Act 1973
(which refers to the Supplementary Benefits Commission), for the
words " the Supplementary Benefits Commission " there shall be
substituted the words " a benefit officer within the meaning of the
Supplementary Benefits Act 1976 " and for the words " latter Commission " there shall be substituted the word " officer ".

The Legal Aid Act 1974

9.—(1) Section 11(6) of the Legal Aid Act 1974 (which provides,
in relation to legal aid, for computing resources by reference to the
rules set out in certain paragraphs of Schedule 1 to the Supplementary Benefits Act 1976) shall cease to have effect.

(2) In section 11(7) of that Act (which among other things provides
for the income and capital of a person and the maximum amount
of his contribution to the legal aid fund to be determined by the
Supplementary Benefits Commission) for the words from " determined " onwards there shall be substituted the words " determined in
accordance with regulations ; and regulations for the purposes of
this subsection may make different provision for different cases or
classes of cases.".

(3) In section 33(1) of that Act (which relates to enquiries into
persons' means) for the words " Supplementary Benefits Commission " there shall be substituted the words " Secretary of State
to arrange for an officer of his ", for the words " the Commission "
there shall be substituted the words " the Secretary of State " and
before the word " report " there shall be inserted the words " arrange
for the officer to ".

The Child Benefit Act 1975

10. In section 21(6) of the Child Benefit Act 1975 (which refers
to sections 139(1) and 141(2) of the principal Act) for the words
from the beginning to " that Act " there shall be substituted the
words " Section 141(2) of the Social Security Act 1975 ".

The Sex Discrimination Act 1975

11. In section 35(1)(*a*) of the Sex Discrimination Act 1975 (which
refers to a reception centre provided by the Supplementary Benefits
Commission) for the words " reception centre provided by the Supplementary Benefits Commission " there shall be substituted the words
" resettlement unit provided under Schedule 5 to the Supplementary
Benefits Act 1976 ".

The Social Security (Miscellaneous Provisions) Act 1977

12. In subsection (13) of section 22 of the Social Security (Miscellaneous Provisions) Act 1977 (which refers to section 44(6) of the Pensions Act as amended by a subsection repealed by this Act) for the words " the said section 44(6) as amended by the preceding subsection " there shall be substituted the words " section 44(6) of the Pensions Act ".

The Employment Protection (Consolidation) Act 1978

13.—(1) In section 132(3) of the Employment Protection (Consolidation) Act 1978 (which among other things refers to section 15(2) to (4) of the Supplementary Benefits Act 1976)—

    (*a*) for the words " the Supplementary Benefits Commission " and " the Commission " in paragraphs (*b*) and (*e*) there shall be substituted the words " a benefit officer within the meaning of the Supplementary Benefits Act 1976 " ; and

    (*b*) for the words " 15(2) to (4) of that Act (appeals) " in paragraph (*e*) there shall be substituted the words " 15(3) and (4) and regulations under section 2(1A) of that Act ".

(2) For paragraph (*b*) of section 132(4) of that Act (which provides that certain provisions of the Supplementary Benefits Act 1976 relating to the recovery of benefit shall not apply to supplementary benefit recouped by virtue of that section) there shall be substituted the following paragraph—

    (*b*) no sum shall be recoverable under the Supplementary Benefits Act 1976, and no abatement, payment or reduction shall be made under section 12(1), (2) or (3) of that Act, by reference to the supplementary benefit recouped.

The Pensioners' Payments and Social Security Act 1979

14. In section 2(7) of the Pensioners' Payments and Social Security Act 1979 (under which an unmarried couple are to be treated as spouses for the purposes of section 1 of that Act if among other things the man is entitled to a supplementary pension) for the words " the man " there shall be substituted the words " one of them ".

SCHEDULE 5

Enactments and instruments repealed

Part I

Enactments and instruments repealed on passing of Act

Chapter	Short title	Extent of repeal
6 & 7 Geo. 6. c. 39.	The Pensions Appeal Tribunals Act 1943.	Section 8(3)(*a*). Paragraph 7A of the Schedule.
1975 c. 14.	The Social Security Act 1975.	In section 125(2) the words from " and shall have regard either " onwards.
1975 c. 16.	The Industrial Injuries and Diseases (Old Cases) Act 1975.	In section 6, in subsection (2) the words from " shall " where it first occurs to " disease, and ", and subsection (5).
1975 c. 60.	The Social Security Pensions Act 1975.	Section 21(6). In section 23, in subsection (1) the words " (4) and " and subsection (4). In section 62(1)(*b*) the words " or 9(3) ". Paragraph 49 of Schedule 4.
1975 c. 61.	The Child Benefit Act 1975.	In section 2(3) the words from " ending " to " that week ".
1977 c. 5.	The Social Security (Miscellaneous Provisions) Act 1977.	Section 1(7)(*a*). Section 7(2) and (4). Section 11(2). Section 22(12).
1977 c. 38.	The Administration of Justice Act 1977.	Part III of Schedule 2.
1979 c. 18.	The Social Security Act 1979.	Paragraph 9(*b*)(ii) of Schedule 3.

Number	Title	Extent of repeal
S.I. 1966 No. 164.	The Pneumoconiosis, Byssinosis and Miscellaneous Diseases Benefit Scheme 1966.	Article 2(2)(iii).
S.I. 1977 No. 1104.	The Pneumoconiosis, Byssinosis and Miscellaneous Diseases Benefit (Amendment) (No. 3) Scheme 1977.	The whole scheme.

Part II

Enactments Repealed on Appointed Day

Chapter	Short title	Extent of repeal
10 & 11 Geo. 6. c. 19.	The Polish Resettlement Act 1947.	In section 3, in subsection (2) the words " by making payments to persons for whom accommodation is provided " and subsections (4), (5), (10) and (10A). In the Schedule, the words from " (including " to " repealed) " in paragraph 3, the proviso in paragraph 4 and the words from " whether " to " the tribunal " in paragraph 6.
11 & 12 Geo. 6. c. 29.	The National Assistance Act 1948.	Sections 22(9) and 27.
1967 c. 43.	The Legal Aid (Scotland) Act 1967.	Section 4(5).
1968 c. 49.	The Social Work (Scotland) Act 1968.	Section 87(6).
1970 c. 36.	The Merchant Shipping Act 1970.	In section 17(10) the words " Secretary of State or the ", the words " Secretary of State or " in the second place where they occur and the words "the Supplementary Benefits Commission or, as the case may be,".
1970 c. 55.	The Family Income Supplements Act 1970.	In section 7(2) the words from " (or, if " to " the refusal) ". In section 10(2)(*h*) the words " National Insurance ". In section 17(1) the definition of " single woman ".
1972 c. 46.	The Housing (Financial Provisions) (Scotland) Act 1972.	In paragraph 18(2) of Schedule 3, the words " and the Supplementary Benefits Commission ".
1972 c. 47.	The Housing Finance Act 1972.	In paragraph 17(2) of Schedule 4 the words " and the Supplementary Benefits Commission ".
1974 c. 4.	The Legal Aid Act 1974.	Section 11(6).
1975 c. 14.	The Social Security Act 1975.	Section 41(6). In section 44, subsection (3)(*b*) and subsections (5) and (6). In section 47 the words from the last " or " in subsection (1)(*a*) onwards. Section 65(4). In section 66, subsection (1)(*b*) and (*c*) and subsection (8). Sections 138 and 139.

Chapter	Short title	Extent of repeal
1975 c. 14— *cont.*	The Social Security Act 1975—*cont.*	In section 142(5) the words from "section 139" to "and". Section 158. In section 166(4) the words from "except" to "scheme)". In section 168(4) the figures "139". In Part IV of Schedule 4 the words from "Where unemployment" onwards. Schedule 15. Schedule 19. In Schedule 20 the entry relating to the expression "Incapable of self-support" (including both paragraphs in the second column of the entry).
1975 c. 18.	The Social Security (Consequential Provisions) Act 1975.	In Schedule 3, in paragraph 11(2), the words "139(1)", the words "reference to N.I.A.C. and" and the words from "except" onwards.
1975 c. 24.	The House of Commons Disqualification Act 1975.	In Part II of Schedule 1 the words "The National Insurance Advisory Committee" and "The Supplementary Benefits Commission".
1975 c. 25.	The Northern Ireland Assembly Disqualification Act 1975.	In Part II of Schedule 1 the words "The National Insurance Advisory Committee" and "The Supplementary Benefits Commission".
1975 c. 60.	The Social Security Pensions Act 1975.	Sections 22(6) and 61(1).
1975 c. 61.	The Child Benefit Act 1975.	In Schedule 4, paragraph 36.
1976 c. 71.	The Supplementary Benefits Act 1976.	In section 2, the words from the second "and" in subsection (2)(*a*) to the end of the section. Section 8(3). In section 9, subsections (4) to (8). In section 14, in subsection (2) the words "National Insurance" in paragraph (*d*) and the word "and" at the end of paragraphs (*e*) and (*ee*), and subsections (3) and (4). In section 15, subsections (2) and (3)(*b*). In section 15A the words "National Insurance" in both places and the words from "and includes" onwards in subsection (5).

Chapter	Short title	Extent of repeal
1976 c. 71— *cont.*	The Supplementary Benefits Act 1976—*cont.*	In section 16 the words " or, in Scotland, on the sequestration of the estate ". Sections 18(6) and 19(7). In section 22 the words " or the Commission ". Section 24(2). In section 25(1), paragraph (b) and the word " or " at the end of paragraph (a). Section 30(3) and (4). In section 32(1) the words " or adapting ". In section 33(1A) the words " and regulations ". In section 34(1) the definitions of " blind ", " the Commission " and " school " and in the definition of " supplementary benefit " the words from " and includes " onwards. In section 36(2) the words " 27 (including Schedule 3) " and the words " ' the Commission' and ". Schedules 2 and 3. In Schedule 5, paragraph 3. In Schedule 6, paragraphs 3, 6, 7 and 8(3). In Schedule 7, paragraphs 1(a), 2, 3(b) and (c) and 34.
1976 c. 85.	The National Insurance Surcharge Act 1976.	Section 1(4).
1977 c. 5.	The Social Security (Miscellaneous Provisions) Act 1977.	Section 8(3). In section 14, subsections (1) to (4) and (7) to (10). Section 15. In section 24(4) the words " 139(1) and " and the words " the National Insurance Advisory Committee or ".
1978 c. 44.	The Employment Protection (Consolidation) Act 1978.	In Schedule 16, paragraph 19(2).
1979 c. 18.	The Social Security Act 1979.	Sections 4(3), 15(2) and 17. Paragraphs 28 and 30(a) of Schedule 3.
1979 c. 26.	The Legal Aid Act 1979.	Paragraphs 2 and 14 of Schedule 1.
1980 c. 9.	The Reserve Forces Act 1980.	In Schedule 9, paragraph 16.

Port of London (Financial Assistance) Act 1980

1980 CHAPTER 31

An Act to provide financial assistance for and in connection with measures taken by the Port of London Authority to restore the profitability of their undertaking by reducing the number of persons employed by them.
[30th June 1980]

BE IT ENACTED by the Queen's most Excellent Majesty, by and with the advice and consent of the Lords Spiritual and Temporal, and Commons, in this present Parliament assembled, and by the authority of the same, as follows:—

1.—(1) The Minister of Transport may, with the consent of the Treasury, give financial assistance to the Port of London Authority—

> (a) for measures taken by the Authority to reduce the number of persons employed by them, being measures taken with a view to restoring the profitability of their undertaking; and

> (b) for the carrying on of their undertaking while such measures are being taken.

Financial assistance for and in connection with measures taken by Port of London Authority.

(2) Assistance under subsection (1) above may be given by way of a grant or loan or in the form of a guarantee; and in giving assistance under that subsection the Minister may impose such conditions as he thinks fit, including conditions requiring a grant to be repaid in specified circumstances.

(3) The Secretary of State may, with the consent of the Treasury and on such conditions as he thinks fit, reimburse the

National Dock Labour Board for any payments made by them
to dock workers who become entitled to compensation from the
Board in consequence of measures for which financial assistance
is provided under subsection (1)(*a*) above.

(4) The aggregate at any time of—

    (*a*) grants made under subsection (1) above and not repaid;

    (*b*) outstanding loans made under that subsection;

    (*c*) amounts in respect of which guarantees under that
    subsection are in force; and

    (*d*) payments made by the Secretary of State under sub-
    section (3) above,

shall not exceed £70 million.

(5) Any grant, loan, guarantee or payment made or given
by any Minister of the Crown before the passing of this Act for
the purposes specified in subsection (1) or (3) above shall be
taken into account for the purposes of subsection (4) above as
if it were a grant, loan, guarantee or payment made or given
under subsection (1) or (3); and in this subsection the reference
to a guarantee given by a Minister of the Crown includes a
reference to any undertaking given by any such Minister for the
purpose of facilitating borrowing by the Authority from a third
party.

(6) Any sums required by the Minister of Transport or the
Secretary of State for making payments under this section shall
be defrayed out of moneys provided by Parliament; and any
sums received by them by virtue of this section shall be paid
into the Consolidated Fund.

Short title.

    2. This Act may be cited as the Port of London (Financial
Assistance) Act 1980.

Licensed Premises (Exclusion of Certain Persons) Act 1980

1980 CHAPTER 32

An Act to empower the courts to make orders excluding certain categories of convicted persons from licensed premises. [30th June 1980]

B E IT ENACTED by the Queen's most Excellent Majesty, by and with the advice and consent of the Lords Spiritual and Temporal, and Commons, in this present Parliament assembled, and by the authority of the same, as follows:—

1.—(1) Where a court by or before which a person is convicted of an offence committed on licensed premises is satisfied that in committing that offence he resorted to violence or offered or threatened to resort to violence, the court may, subject to subsection (2) below, make an order (in this Act referred to as an " exclusion order ") prohibiting him from entering those premises or any other specified premises, without the express consent of the licensee of the premises or his servant or agent.

Exclusion orders.

(2) An exclusion order may be made either—

    (*a*) in addition to any sentence which is imposed in respect of the offence of which the person is convicted; or

    (*b*) where the offence was committed in England or Wales, notwithstanding the provisions of sections 2, 7 and 13 of the Powers of Criminal Courts Act 1973 (cases in which probation orders and absolute and conditional discharges may be made, and their effect), in addition to a probation order or an order discharging him absolutely or conditionally; or

1973 c. 62.

Y 3

(*c*) where the offence was committed in Scotland, notwithstanding the provisions of sections 182, 183, 191,
383, 384 and 392 of the Criminal Procedure (Scotland)
Act 1975 (cases in which probation orders and absolute
discharges may be made, and their effect), in addition
to a probation order or an order discharging him
absolutely;

1975 c. 21.

but not otherwise.

(3) An exclusion order shall have effect for such period, not
less than three months or more than two years, as is specified
in the order, unless it is terminated under section 2(2) below.

Penalty for
non-
compliance
with
exclusion
order.

2.—(1) A person who enters any premises in breach of an
exclusion order shall be guilty of an offence and shall be liable
on summary conviction or, in Scotland, on conviction in a court
of summary jurisdiction to a fine not exceeding £200 or to
imprisonment for a term not exceeding one month or both.

(2) The court by which a person is convicted of an offence
under subsection (1) above shall consider whether or not the
exclusion order should continue in force, and may, if it thinks
fit, by order terminate the exclusion order or vary it by deleting
the name of any specified premises, but an exclusion order
shall not otherwise be affected by a person's conviction for such
an offence.

Power to
expel
person from
licensed
premises.

3. Without prejudice to any other right to expel a person
from premises, the licensee of licensed premises or his servant
or agent may expel from those premises any person who has
entered or whom he reasonably suspects of having entered the
premises in breach of an exclusion order; and a constable shall
on the demand of the licensee or his servant or agent help to
expel from licensed premises any person whom the constable
reasonably suspects of having entered in breach of an exclusion
order.

Supplemental.

4.—(1) In this Act—
"licensed premises", in relation to England and Wales, means
premises in respect of which there is in force a justices'
on-licence (within the meaning of section 1 of the
Licensing Act 1964) and, in relation to Scotland, means
premises in respect of which a licence under the Licensing
(Scotland) Act 1976, other than an off-sales licence or
a licence under Part III of that Act (licences for seamen's
canteens), is in force; and

1964 c. 26.
1976 c. 66.

"licensee" in relation to any licensed premises means the
holder of the licence granted in respect of those premises;
and

" specified premises ", in relation to an exclusion order,
means any licensed premises which the court may
specify by name and address in the order.

(2) In the application of section 1 above to Scotland, the
reference in subsection (1) of that section to a person's being
convicted of an offence shall, in relation to proceedings in a
court of summary jurisdiction in which the court, without
proceeding to conviction, discharges him absolutely under
section 383 of the Criminal Procedure (Scotland) Act 1975 or 1975 c. 21.
makes a probation order under section 384 of that Act, shall
be construed as a reference to the court's being satisfied that he
committed the offence.

(3) Where a court makes an exclusion order or an order
terminating or varying an exclusion order, the clerk of the court,
or the appropriate officer of the Crown Court, as the case may be,
shall send a copy of the order to the licensee of the premises to
which the order relates.

5.—(1) This Act shall be cited as the Licensed Premises Short title,
(Exclusion of Certain Persons) Act 1980 and this Act, in its citation
application to Scotland, and the Licensing (Scotland) Act 1976 and extent.
may be cited together as the Licensing (Scotland) Acts 1976 to
1980.

(2) This Act shall not extend to Northern Ireland.

Y 4

Industry Act 1980

1980 CHAPTER 33

An Act to make further provision in relation to the National Enterprise Board, the Scottish Development Agency, the Welsh Development Agency and the English Industrial Estates Corporation; to authorise the Secretary of State to acquire securities of, make loans to and provide guarantees for companies in which he acquires shares from the National Enterprise Board; to amend the Industry Act 1972 and the Industry Act 1975; to authorise the provision by the Secretary of State of an advisory service; to remove the requirement for a register of the financial interests of members of British Shipbuilders; and for connected purposes.

[30th June 1980]

BE IT ENACTED by the Queen's most Excellent Majesty, by and with the advice and consent of the Lords Spiritual and Temporal, and Commons, in this present Parliament assembled, and by the authority of the same, as follows:—

The National Enterprise Board and the Scottish and Welsh Development Agencies

1.—(1) In section 2(2) of the Industry Act 1975—

    (a) in paragraph (b) the words " reorganisation or " and paragraphs (c) and (d) shall cease to have effect ; and

    (b) after paragraph (e) there shall be added—

        " (f) promoting the private ownership of interests in industrial undertakings by the disposal of securities and other property held by the Board or any of their subsidiaries."

Functions of the Board and Agencies.
1975 c. 68.

1975 c. 69.   (2) In section 2 of the Scottish Development Agency Act
1975—

    (*a*) in subsection (1), in paragraph (*a*), at the end there
shall be added the words ", including in that connection the provision, maintenance or safeguarding of
employment " ;

    (*b*) in subsection (2), after paragraph (*i*) there shall be
added—

        " (*j*) promoting the private ownership of interests
in industrial undertakings by the disposal of securities and other property held by the Agency or any of
their subsidiaries." ; and

    (*c*) subsection (1)(*b*), in subsection (2)(*c*) the word "re-
organisation ", and subsection (2)(*f*) shall cease to have
effect.

1975 c. 70.   (3) In section 1 of the Welsh Development Agency Act
1975—

    (*a*) in subsection (2), in paragraph (*a*), at the end there shall
be added the words ", and in that connection to pro-
vide, maintain or safeguard employment " ;

    (*b*) in subsection (3), after paragraph (*i*) there shall be
added—

        " (*j*) to promote the private ownership of interests
in industrial undertakings by the disposal of securities and other property held by the Agency or any
of their subsidiaries." ;

    (*c*) subsection (2)(*c*), in subsection (3)(*d*) the word
" reorganisation ", and subsection (3)(*e*) shall cease to
have effect ; and

    (*d*) in subsection (11) the words from " in connection " to
" above " shall cease to have effect.

Transfer of
property to
Secretary of
State.

    2.—(1) Without prejudice to any power otherwise conferred
on them and notwithstanding anything in any other enactment,
the National Enterprise Board, the Scottish Development
Agency and the Welsh Development Agency may transfer securities or other property held by them, and may procure the transfer of securities or other property held by any of their subsidiaries, to the Secretary of State or to a nominee of his ;
and the power of the Secretary of State to give directions—

    (*a*) to the National Enterprise Board under section 7 of
1975 c. 68.   the Industry Act 1975,

    (*b*) to the Scottish Development Agency under section 4
of the Scottish Development Agency Act 1975, and

    (*c*) to the Welsh Development Agency under section 1(9)
of the Welsh Development Agency Act 1975,

shall extend to the giving of directions as to the making and terms of a transfer.

(2) Stamp duty shall not be chargeable on any instrument which is certified to the Commissioners of Inland Revenue by the Secretary of State as having been made or executed for the purpose of the transfer of property to him or a nominee of his from, or from any subsidiary of, the National Enterprise Board, the Scottish Development Agency or the Welsh Development Agency.

(3) There may be defrayed out of money provided by Parliament any expenditure incurred by the Secretary of State in respect of the acquisition of property by him or a nominee of his from, or from a subsidiary of, the National Enterprise Board, the Scottish Development Agency or the Welsh Development Agency ; and any sums received by him on the disposal of property so acquired shall be paid into the Consolidated Fund.

(4) In this section " subsidiary " means a subsidiary as defined by section 154 of the Companies Act 1948 or section 148 of the Companies Act (Northern Ireland) 1960.

1948 c. 38.
1960 c. 22.
(N.I.).

3.—(1) This section applies to a company if the National Enterprise Board has at any time transferred to the Secretary of State a controlling interest in the company and the Secretary of State has not since that time ceased to hold such an interest in it.

Finance for companies transferred to Secretary of State.

(2) Subject to subsection (3) below and section 5 of this Act, the Secretary of State may with the approval of the Treasury—

(a) acquire securities of a company to which this section applies,

(b) make loans to such a company on such conditions and at such rates of interest as he may with that approval determine, and

(c) guarantee obligations (arising out of loans or otherwise) incurred by such a company.

(3) The Secretary of State shall not determine a rate of interest in respect of a loan under subsection (2)(b) above which is lower than the lowest rate for the time being determined by the Treasury under section 5 of the National Loans Act 1968 in respect of comparable loans out of the National Loans Fund.

1968 c. 13.

(4) Not later than six months after the end of any financial year in which this section has applied to one or more companies the Secretary of State shall prepare and lay before each House of Parliament a report on the exercise during that year of his powers under subsection (2) above ; and the report shall specify

in relation to each company which at the end of that year is a company to which this section applies—

> (a) particulars of the securities of the company held by the Secretary of State at the end of that year,
>
> (b) the amount then outstanding, otherwise than by way of interest, in respect of any loans to the company made under paragraph (b) of subsection (2) above,
>
> (c) particulars of guarantees then subsisting which were given under paragraph (c) of that subsection in respect of obligations incurred by the company, and
>
> (d) any sums paid to meet guarantees so given, to the extent that they have not by then been repaid.

(5) As soon as practicable after the holding of any general meeting of a company to which this section applies, the Secretary of State shall lay before each House of Parliament a copy of any accounts which, in accordance with any requirement of the Companies Acts 1948 to 1980, are laid before the company at that meeting, and of any documents which are annexed or attached to any such accounts.

(6) Any expenditure incurred by the Secretary of State under subsection (2) above may be defrayed out of money provided by Parliament; and any sums received by him by virtue of this section (including sums received on the disposal of securities acquired by virtue of this section) shall be paid into the Consolidated Fund.

(7) In this section and in section 5 of this Act—

1948 c. 38.
1960 c. 22
(N.I.).

> " company " means a company within the meaning of the Companies Act 1948 or the Companies Act (Northern Ireland) 1960,
>
> " controlling interest " means, in relation to a company, shares carrying in the aggregate more than half the voting rights exercisable at general meetings of the company,
>
> " shares " includes stock,
>
> " subsidiary " means a subsidiary as defined by section 154 of the said Act of 1948 or section 148 of the said Act of 1960,

and references to the transfer of securities to or the holding or acquisition of securities by the Secretary of State include references to the transfer of securities to or the holding or acquisition of securities by any nominee of his.

Public
dividend
capital.
1975 c. 68.

4.—(1) In paragraph 5 of Schedule 2 to the Industry Act 1975, after sub-paragraph (3) there shall be inserted—

> " (3A) The Board may with the agreement of the Secretary of State, and shall if the Secretary of State with the

approval of the Treasury requires them to do so, make payments to the Secretary of State in reduction of the public dividend capital of the Board ; and any sums received by the Secretary of State in pursuance of this sub-paragraph shall be paid into the Consolidated Fund."

(2) In paragraph 1 of Schedule 2 to the Scottish Development Agency Act 1975, after sub-paragraph (3) there shall be inserted— 1975 c. 69.

" (3A) The Agency may with the agreement of the Secretary of State, and shall if the Secretary of State with the approval of the Treasury requires them to do so, make payments to the Secretary of State in reduction of the public dividend capital of the Agency ; and any sums received by the Secretary of State in pursuance of this sub-paragraph shall be paid into the Consolidated Fund."

(3) In paragraph 1 of Schedule 3 to the Welsh Development Agency Act 1975, after sub-paragraph (3) there shall be inserted— 1975 c. 70.

" (3A) The Agency may with the agreement of the Secretary of State, and shall if the Secretary of State with the approval of the Treasury requires them to do so, make payments to the Secretary of State in reduction of the public dividend capital of the Agency ; and any sums received by the Secretary of State in pursuance of this sub-paragraph shall be paid into the Consolidated Fund."

5.—(1) In section 8(2) of the Industry Act 1975, section 13(3) of the Scottish Development Agency Act 1975 and section 18(3) of the Welsh Development Agency Act 1975 (which set limits on the amounts outstanding in respect of certain borrowings and other liabilities of the National Enterprise Board and the Scottish and Welsh Development Agencies and their subsidiaries, but enable the Secretary of State to raise the limits) the words from " but " to the end shall cease to have effect. Financial limits. 1975 c. 68.

(2) After section 8(2) of the Industry Act 1975, there shall be inserted—

" (2A) The Secretary of State may by order provide for the limit specified in subsection (2) above to be reduced or further reduced to such amount not less than £750 million as may be specified in the order.

(2B) Notwithstanding section 38(2) below, an order under subsection (2A) above may not be revoked or varied by a later order except in connection with the making of a further reduction in the limit specified in subsection (2) above.

(2C) No order shall be made under subsection (2A) above unless a draft of it has been approved by resolution of the House of Commons."

(3) Subject to subsection (4) below, the Secretary of State shall by order specify an amount as the financial limit for the purposes of section 3 of this Act, and may by order increase or further increase the amount so specified.

1975 c. 68.

(4) The aggregate of the amounts for the time being specified under subsection (3) above and in section 8(2) of the Industry Act 1975 shall not exceed £3,000 million.

(5) The power to make orders under subsection (3) above shall be exercisable by statutory instrument, and no such order shall be made unless a draft of it has been laid before and approved by resolution of the House of Commons.

(6) Subject to subsection (7) below, the aggregate of—

   (a) any sums paid by the Secretary of State under this Act in respect of the acquisition of shares in any company which before or immediately after the acquisition was a company to which section 3 of this Act applied,

   (b) the amounts outstanding, otherwise than by way of interest, in respect of the general external borrowing of companies to which that section applies, and

   (c) any sums paid by the Secretary of State to meet guarantees given under subsection (2)(c) of that section, to the extent that they have not been repaid,

shall not exceed the amount which is for the time being the financial limit for the purposes of that section.

(7) The sums paid by the Secretary of State under this Act in respect of the acquisition from the National Enterprise Board of shares in any company shall be treated for the purposes of subsection (6) above as reduced by an amount equal to so much of the debt of the Board assumed under paragraph 6(1) of Schedule 2 to the Industry Act 1975 on their acquisition of securities of the company as was, immediately before section 3 of this Act applied to the company, treated by virtue of paragraph 5(2) of that Schedule as part of the Board's public dividend capital.

(8) For the purposes of subsection (6)(b) above, the general external borrowing of a company is the aggregate of—

   (a) sums borrowed by the company otherwise than from any subsidiary of the company, and

   (b) sums borrowed by such a subsidiary otherwise than from the company or another such subsidiary.

Restrictions on powers to acquire shares. **6.**—(1) In section 10(1)(b) of the Industry Act 1975 (which restricts the acquisition of share capital by the Board and their subsidiaries where the value of the consideration, together with that for share capital previously acquired, would exceed

£10,000,000) for the words "previously acquired, would exceed £10,000,000" there shall be substituted the words "already held by the Board or any of their subsidiaries, would exceed £5,000,000".

(2) In section 14(1)(*b*) of the Scottish Development Agency Act 1975 (which makes similar provision in relation to the Scottish Development Agency, but with a limit of £2,000,000) for the words "previously acquired, would exceed £2,000,000" there shall be substituted the words "already held by the Agency or any of their subsidiaries, would exceed £1,000,000".   1975 c. 69.

(3) In section 20(1)(*b*) of the Welsh Development Agency Act 1975 (which makes similar provision in relation to the Welsh Development Agency, with a limit of £2,000,000) for the words "previously acquired, would exceed £2 million" there shall be substituted the words "already held by the Agency or any of their subsidiaries, would exceed £1,000,000".   1975 c. 70.

(4) Section 10(3) of the Industry Act 1975, section 14(3) of the Scottish Development Agency Act 1975 and section 20(3) of the Welsh Development Agency Act 1975 (savings for powers to form bodies corporate) shall cease to have effect.   1975 c. 68.

7.—(1) In section 1 of the Industry Act 1975—   Members and chief executive of the Board.

    (*a*) in subsection (2) (membership of the National Enterprise Board) for the word "sixteen" there shall be substituted the word "twelve"; and

    (*b*) subsection (8) (register of members' financial interests) shall cease to have effect.

(2) In Part III of Schedule 1 to the House of Commons Disqualification Act 1975 and in Part III of Schedule 1 to the Northern Ireland Assembly Disqualification Act 1975 there shall be inserted, at the appropriate place in alphabetical order—   1975 c. 24.   1975 c. 25.

    " Chief executive of the National Enterprise Board.".

8.—(1) The Secretary of State shall not after the commencement of this Act give any direction under section 3 of the Industry Act 1975 (exercise by the National Enterprise Board of powers to give selective financial assistance under the Industry Act 1972) other than a direction varying or revoking an earlier direction.   Selective financial assistance under the Industry Act 1972.   1972 c. 63.

(2) Section 5 of the Scottish Development Agency Act 1975 and section 12 of the Welsh Development Agency Act 1975 (which make corresponding provision in relation to the Scottish and Welsh Development Agencies) shall cease to have effect.

Overseas aid.
1975 c. 68.
1975 c. 69.
1975 c. 70.

9. Section 4 of the Industry Act 1975, section 18 of the Scottish Development Agency Act 1975 and section 3 of the Welsh Development Agency Act 1975 shall cease to have effect.

The English Industrial Estates Corporation

Functions
and status
of the
Corporation.

10.—(1) The English Industrial Estates Corporation may, in accordance with directions given under subsection (3) below,—

(a) provide, facilitate the provision of, and manage sites and premises in England for occupation by industrial or commercial undertakings,

(b) provide, and facilitate the provision of, means of access, services and other facilities required in connection with sites and premises in England occupied or to be occupied by such undertakings, and

(c) dispose for any purpose of land and other property held by the Corporation.

(2) Subject to directions given under subsection (3) below, the Corporation may do anything, whether in England or elsewhere, which is calculated to facilitate or is conducive or incidental to the discharge of their functions, and in particular, without prejudice to the generality of the preceding provisions of this subsection, may—

(a) act alone or with other persons, either in partnership or otherwise,

(b) acquire land, plant, machinery and equipment and other property,

(c) form, or acquire interests in, bodies corporate, and

(d) make loans and guarantee obligations (arising out of loans or otherwise) incurred by other persons.

(3) The Secretary of State may give the Corporation general or specific directions and the Corporation shall comply with any such directions.

(4) After the commencement of this Act—

(a) the Corporation shall not be regarded as the servant or agent of the Crown or as enjoying any status, immunity or privilege of the Crown, or as exempt from any tax, duty, rate, levy or other charge whatsoever, whether general or local, and

(b) the property of the Corporation shall not be regarded as the property of, or property held on behalf of, the Crown.

(5) Planning permission shall be deemed to have been granted under section 29 of the Town and Country Planning Act 1971 1971 c. 78. in respect of any development initiated by the Corporation before the end of March 1981.

(6) In this section references to the provision of premises include references to the carrying out of any works, and the provision of any plant, machinery or equipment, on or for the purposes of any premises ; and references to an industrial or commercial undertaking include references to any activity providing employment.

(7) Subsections (1) to (3) of section 11 of the Local Employ- 1972 c. 5. ment Act 1972 (which are superseded by this section) shall cease to have effect.

11.—(1) Any land which, immediately before the commence- Transfer of ment of this Act, is vested in a Minister of the Crown subject land to the to a lease to the English Industrial Estates Corporation shall by Corporation. virtue of this Act vest in the Corporation, subject to all rights, liabilities and obligations relating to it (except those arising out of the lease).

(2) The power to acquire land conferred on the Secretary of State by section 5 of the Local Employment Act 1972 (provision of sites and premises) shall include power to acquire land with a view to transferring it to the English Industrial Estates Corporation.

12. In section 10(2) of the Local Employment Act 1972 (which Members provides that the English Industrial Estates Corporation shall of the consist of a chairman and four other members appointed by the Corporation. Secretary of State) for the words from " four " to " and the members " there shall be substituted the words " such number of other members as the Secretary of State thinks fit ; and the members shall be appointed by the Secretary of State and ".

13.—(1) The English Industrial Estates Corporation may, in Power for the accordance with directions under section 10(3) of this Act Corporation to given with the approval of the Treasury, borrow in any currency borrow. from the Commission of the European Communities or from the European Investment Bank, but subject to subsection (2) below.

(2) The aggregate amount outstanding in respect of the principal of sums borrowed under this section shall not exceed £30 million or such greater sum not exceeding £50 million as the Secretary of State may with the approval of the Treasury by order specify.

(3) The power to make orders under this section shall be exercisable by statutory instrument, and no such order shall be made unless a draft of it has been laid before and approved by resolution of the House of Commons.

(4) In section 11(8) of the Local Employment Act 1972 (receipts of Corporation, with certain exceptions, to be paid over to Secretary of State) after paragraph (*a*) there shall be inserted—

> " (*aa*) receipts consisting of sums borrowed under section 13 of the Industry Act 1980 ; and ".

14.—(1) The Treasury may guarantee, in such manner and on such conditions as they think fit, the repayment of the principal of, and the payment of interest on, any sums borrowed under section 13 of this Act.

(2) Immediately after a guarantee is given under this section, the Treasury shall lay a statement of the guarantee before each House of Parliament ; and where any sum is issued for fulfilling a guarantee so given the Treasury shall, as soon as possible after the end of each financial year (beginning with that in which the sum is issued and ending with that in which all liability in respect of the principal of the sum and in respect of interest thereon is finally discharged) lay before each House of Parliament a statement relating to that sum.

(3) Any sums required by the Treasury for fulfilling a guarantee under this section shall be charged on and issued out of the Consolidated Fund.

(4) If any sums are issued in fulfilment of a guarantee given under this section, the Corporation shall make to the Treasury, at such times and in such manner as the Treasury may from time to time direct, payments of such amounts as the Treasury may so direct in or towards repayment of the sums so issued and payments of interest at such rate as the Treasury may so direct on what is outstanding for the time being in respect of sums so issued.

(5) Any sums received under subsection (4) above by the Treasury shall be paid into the Consolidated Fund.

15. In subsection (9) of section 11 of the Local Employment Act 1972 (certain expenses of the English Industrial Estates Corporation incurred under that section to be defrayed by the Secretary of State) after the word " section " there shall be inserted the words " or under the Industry Act 1980 ".

Grants and other financial assistance for industry

16.—(1) For the Table in section 1 of the Industry Act 1972 (which sets out the expenditure towards which, and the rates at which, grants may be made under that section) there shall be substituted—

Regional
development
grants.
1972 c. 63.

TABLE

Expenditure incurred in	Prescribed percentage
1. Providing a building as part of, or providing works on, qualifying premises in a development area … … …	If the qualifying premises are in a special development area: 22 per cent. If not: 15 per cent.
2. Providing new machinery or plant for use in qualifying premises in a development area …	If the qualifying premises are in a special development area: 22 per cent. If not: 15 per cent.

(2) The Regional Development Grants (Variation of Prescribed Percentages) Order 1979 (which is superseded by subsection (1) above) is hereby revoked.

S.I. 1979/975.

(3) Subsections (1) and (2) above shall not have effect in relation to—

(*a*) expenditure incurred in providing an asset, other than mining works, as part of, or on or for use in, qualifying premises if—

 (i) the asset is provided before 1st August 1980, or

 (ii) the expenditure was defrayed before 18th July 1979 ;

(*b*) expenditure incurred in providing a building as part of, or providing works on, qualifying premises in a derelict land clearance area, if the construction of the building or the carrying out of the works was begun before 22nd March 1974 ;

(*c*) expenditure incurred in providing mining works if—

 (i) the works were provided before 1st April 1977, or

 (ii) the expenditure was defrayed before 6th August 1976 ;

(d) expenditure incurred in providing new machinery or plant for use in activities which are within Order XX of the Standard Industrial Classification (construction industry) if the machinery or plant was provided before 1st April 1977.

1972 c. 63.

(4) Where, apart from this subsection, the amount of a grant under Part I of the Industry Act 1972 towards expenditure falling within subsection (5) below would be less than 20 per cent. of the expenditure, the amount shall instead be 20 per cent. of the expenditure.

(5) The expenditure falling within this subsection is expenditure incurred—

S.I. 1979/837.

(a) in providing an asset as part of, or on or for use in, qualifying premises in a relevant special development area in such circumstances that, by reason of Article 5(1) and (4)(d) or Article 5A(2) and (5)(b) of the Assisted Areas Order 1979, any grant under Part I of the Industry Act 1972 towards the expenditure is to be made at the rate appropriate to a development area which is not a special development area, or

(b) in providing a building or works at any time as part of or on qualifying premises in a relevant development area in such circumstances that, by reason of Article 5(2) and (4)(d) of that order, no grant may be made under Part I of that Act towards any expenditure incurred in providing machinery or plant at that time for use in those premises.

(6) In subsection (5) above—

S.I. 1977/683.
S.I. 1979/1642.

(a) " relevant special development area " means an area which became a special development area on the coming into operation of the Assisted Areas Order 1977, the Assisted Areas Order 1979 or the Assisted Areas (Amendment) Order 1979, and

S.I. 1977/706.

(b) " relevant development area " means an area which became a development area on the coming into operation of the Assisted Areas Order 1977, the Assisted Areas (No. 2) Order 1977 or the Assisted Areas Order 1979.

(7) Expressions used in this section and in Part I of the Industry Act 1972 have the same meanings in this section as in that Act.

Assistance under Part II of the Industry Act 1972.

17.—(1) For subsection (4) of section 7 of the Industry Act 1972 there shall be substituted—

" (4) Financial assistance shall not be given under this section in the way described in subsection (3)(a) above unless the Secretary of State is satisfied that it cannot, or cannot appropriately, be so given in any other way, and the Secretary of State, in giving financial assistance in the way so described, shall not acquire any shares or stock in a company without the consent of that company."

(2) In section 8(1) of that Act, after paragraph (b) there shall be added—

" and

(c) the financial assistance cannot, or cannot appropriately, be so provided otherwise than by the Secretary of State."

(3) For subsection (3) of section 8 of that Act there shall be substituted—

" (3) Financial assistance shall not be given under this section in the way described in subsection (3)(a) of the last preceding section unless the Secretary of State is satisfied that it cannot, or cannot appropriately, be so given in any other way, and the Secretary of State, in giving financial assistance in the way so described, shall not acquire any shares or stock in a company without the consent of that company ".

(4) The provisions of Schedule 1 to this Act (which relate to the limits on the financial assistance that may be given by the Secretary of State under section 8 of that Act) shall have effect.

Miscellaneous and general

18.—(1) The Secretary of State may make provision for the giving of advice (whether free of charge or otherwise) to persons carrying on or proposing to carry on a business.

Advice for businesses.

(2) Any expenditure incurred by the Secretary of State by virtue of this section may be defrayed out of money provided by Parliament.

(3) Not later than six months after the end of any financial year in which this power is used the Secretary of State shall prepare and lay before Parliament a report on the exercise during the year of his powers under this section.

19. Sections 21 (planning agreements) and 28 to 34 (disclosure of information by companies) of the Industry Act 1975 shall cease to have effect.

Planning agreements and disclosure of information.
1975 c. 68.

British
Shipbuilders:
members'
interests.
1977 c. 3.

20. Sections 1 (9) and 18(5) of the Aircraft and Shipbuilding Industries Act 1977 (register of members' financial interests to be kept by Secretary of State) shall cease to have effect in respect of British Shipbuilders.

Repeals and
transitional
provisions.

21.—(1) The enactments mentioned in Schedule 2 to this Act are hereby repealed to the extent specified in column 3 of that Schedule.

1975 c. 68.
1975 c. 69.
1975 c. 70.

(2) Notwithstanding the repeal by this Act of any provision of section 2(2) of the Industry Act 1975, section 2(2) of the Scottish Development Agency Act 1975 or section 1(3) of the Welsh Development Agency Act 1975, the National Enterprise Board, the Scottish Development Agency and the Welsh Development Agency may continue to hold property held by them, and to carry on activities in which they are engaged, at the commencement of this Act.

Short title
and extent.

22.—(1) This Act may be cited as the Industry Act 1980.

(2) The provisions of this Act so far as they relate to the Scottish Development Agency extend to Scotland only.

(3) Subject to subsection (2) above, the provisions of this Act except—

> (a) sections 10 to 16, and
>
> (b) any other provision so far as it relates to the Welsh Development Agency,

extend to Northern Ireland.

SCHEDULES

SCHEDULE 1

LIMITS ON FINANCIAL ASSISTANCE UNDER INDUSTRY ACT 1972
SECTION 8

1. Part II of the Industry Act 1972 shall be amended as follows. 1972 c. 63.

2. In subsection (6) of section 8—

(a) after the word " section " in paragraph (a) there shall be inserted the words ", other than sums paid in respect of foreign currency guarantees," ;

(b) after the word " guaranteed " in paragraph (b) there shall be inserted the words " and of any liability under a foreign currency guarantee " ;

(c) after the words " guarantee under this section " there shall be inserted the words " (other than a foreign currency guarantee) ".

3. After subsection (7) of that section there shall be inserted—

" (7A) Subject to section 8A of this Act, the aggregate of—

(a) the liabilities of the Secretary of State under foreign currency guarantees (exclusive of any liability in respect of interest on a principal sum guaranteed by him under this section) and

(b) any sums paid by the Secretary of State in respect of foreign currency guarantees,

less any sums received by the Secretary of State by way of repayment of principal sums paid to meet foreign currency guarantees, shall not at any time exceed the limit specified in subsection (7B) below.

(7B) The said limit shall be 1,000 million special drawing rights, but the Secretary of State may, on not more than four occasions, by order made with the consent of the Treasury increase or further increase that limit by an amount specified in the order, being an amount not exceeding 500 million special drawing rights.

An order under this subsection shall be contained in a statutory instrument, and such an order shall not be made unless a draft of the order has been approved by a resolution of the Commons House of Parliament."

4. In subsection (8) of that section after the word " project " there shall be inserted the words " , excluding sums paid or to be paid in respect of foreign currency guarantees,".

5. After subsection (8) of that section there shall be inserted—

" (9) In this section—

' foreign currency ' means any currency other than sterling, including special drawing rights ;

'foreign currency guarantee' means a guarantee given under this section by the Secretary of State under which his liability is measured in a foreign currency, whether or not it is to be discharged in a foreign currency, and for this purpose—

(a) a liability measured in sterling but expressed to be subject to a limit in a foreign currency shall be taken to be measured in foreign currency, and

(b) a liability measured in foreign currency but expressed to be subject to a limit in sterling shall be taken to be measured in sterling ;

'guarantee' includes any form of insurance."

6. After section 8 there shall be inserted—

"Limit on foreign currency liabilities: supplementary provisions.   8A.—(1) The amount to be taken into account under section 8(7A) of this Act at any time in respect of a liability of the Secretary of State shall, if the amount of the liability is not expressed in special drawing rights, be the equivalent at that time in special drawing rights of the amount of the liability.

(2) The equivalent in special drawing rights of the amount of a liability shall be determined by the Secretary of State—

(a) by reference to the day on which the guarantee is given, and

(b) by reference to the last day of each quarter at the end of which the guarantee remains in force,

and shall be so determined having regard to what appears to him to be the appropriate rate of exchange.

(3) A determination made under subsection (2)(a) above shall take effect as from the day by reference to which it is made and (unless it ceases to be required at an earlier date) shall remain in force until the end of the quarter in which the guarantee is given.

(4) A determination made by reference to the last day of the quarter under subsection (2)(b) above shall take effect as from the end of that quarter and (unless it ceases to be required at an earlier date) shall remain in force throughout the next succeeding quarter.

(5) The amount to be taken into account under section 8(7A) of this Act in respect of a sum paid or received by the Secretary of State otherwise than in special drawing rights shall be an amount determined by him, by reference to the day of payment or receipt and having regard to what appears to him to be the appropriate rate of exchange, as being the equivalent in special drawing rights of that sum.

(6) The limit imposed by section 8(7A) of this Act may be exceeded if the excess is attributable only to, or to a combination of,—

 (*a*) a quarterly revaluation ;

 (*b*) the Secretary of State's liability under a guarantee given in pursuance of a previous undertaking of his, so far as the amount to be taken into account for the purposes of the limit in respect of the liability exceeds what it would have been if determined by reference to the day on which the undertaking was given ;

 (*c*) a payment made by the Secretary of State under a guarantee, so far as the amount to be taken into account for the purposes of the limit in respect of the payment exceeds what it would have been if determined by reference to the day on which the guarantee was given.

(7) In this section—

' guarantee ' has the same meaning as in section 8 of this Act ;

' quarter ' means a quarter ending with 31st March, 30th June, 30th September or 31st December in any year ;

' quarterly revaluation ' means a determination made under subsection (2)(*b*) above."

SCHEDULE 2
REPEALS

Chapter	Short title	Extent of Repeal
1972 c. 5.	The Local Employment Act 1972.	In section 11— subsections (1) to (3); in subsection (4), the words from " but " to " Secretary of State "; subsections (6), (7) and (10)(*a*). In section 13— in subsection (1), the words from " or vested " to " 1960 "; in subsection (2), the words from " or vested " to " 1960 " and the words " or vested in ". In Schedule 2, paragraph 2.
1972 c. 63.	The Industry Act 1972.	In section 3(2)(*a*), the words from " or vary the " to " this Act ". In section 9, the subsection (5) inserted by paragraph 3 of Schedule 4 to the Scottish Development Agency Act 1975. Section 13(6). In section 16(1)(*a*), the words from " and section 5 " to " Agency Act 1975 ".
1975 c. 68.	The Industry Act 1975.	Section 1(8). In section 2(2), in paragraph (*b*) the words " reorganisation or ", and paragraphs (*c*) and (*d*). Section 4. In section 8, in subsection (2) the words from " but " to the end, and subsection (3). Section 10(3). Section 21. In section 22, the words from " and " to the end. Sections 28 to 34. In section 37(1), the definitions of " the Ministers " and " planning agreement ". In section 39(5), paragraph (*b*) and the word " and " immediately preceding it, and the words from " and the latter Act " to the end. In Schedule 2, paragraph 8(3). In Schedule 4, paragraphs 1(*a*), 2(*a*), 2(*b*)(i), 3 and 4, and Part II. In Schedule 5, paragraph 9. Schedule 6.

Chapter	Short title	Extent of Repeal

1975 c. 69.	The Scottish Development Agency Act 1975.	Section 2(1)(*b*).
		In section 2(2)—
		  in paragraph (*c*) the word "reorganisation";
		  paragraph (*f*);
		  at the end of paragraph (*h*), the word "and".
		Section 5.
		In section 13—
		  in subsection (2)(*d*), the words from "otherwise" to "Act";
		  in subsection (3), the words from "but" to the end;
		  subsection (4);
		  in subsection (5)(*a*), sub-paragraph (iii) and the word "or" immediately preceding it.
		Section 14(3).
		In section 17, the words from "with" to the end.
		Section 18.
		In section 20(5), the words "section 5 of this Act and".
		In Schedule 2—
		  in paragraph 3(1), the words from "other than" to "Act";
		  in paragraph 7(2), paragraph (*b*) and the word "or" immediately preceding it;
		  paragraph 7(5).
		In Schedule 4, paragraphs 3 and 4.

1975 c. 70.	The Welsh Development Agency Act 1975.	Section 1(2)(*c*).
		In section 1(3)—
		  in paragraph (*d*) the word "reorganisation";
		  paragraph (*e*);
		  at the end of paragraph (*h*), the word "and".
		In section 1(11), the words from "in connection" to "above".
		Section 3.
		Section 12.
		In section 18—
		  in subsection (2)(*d*), the words "otherwise than under section 12 above";
		  in subsection (3), the words from "but" to the end;
		  subsection (4);
		  in subsection (5)(*a*), sub-paragraph (iii) and the word "or" immediately preceding it.

Sch. 2

Chapter	Short title	Extent of Repeal
1975 c. 70— *cont.*	The Welsh Development Agency Act 1975—*cont.*	In section 19, in subsection (3) the words " Subject to sub-section (4) below ", and sub-section (4). Section 20(3). In Schedule 3— in paragraph 2(*a*), the words from " without " to " above "; paragraph 3(4); in paragraph 7(2), paragraph (*b*) and the word " or " immediately preceding it; paragraph 7(5); in paragraph 9(3), the words from " which was " to " but ".

Transport Act 1980

1980 CHAPTER 34

An Act to amend the law relating to public service vehicles;
to make provision for and in connection with the
transfer of the undertaking of the National Freight
Corporation to a company; to provide for the making
of payments by the Minister of Transport in aid of
certain railway and other pension schemes; to amend
Part VI of the Road Traffic Act 1972 as regards car-
sharing arrangements; to make amendments about
articulated vehicles; to prohibit the display of certain
roof-signs on vehicles other than taxis; to abolish the
Freight Integration Council and the Railways and
Coastal Shipping Committee; to repeal certain provisions about special authorisations for the use of large
goods vehicles and about charges on independent
tramways, trolley vehicles and the like; and for
connected purposes.   [30th June 1980]

B E IT ENACTED by the Queen's most Excellent Majesty, by and
with the advice and consent of the Lords Spiritual and
Temporal, and Commons, in this present Parliament
assembled, and by the authority of the same, as follows:—

PART I

PUBLIC SERVICE VEHICLES

Preliminary

1.—(1) The purposes for which this Part is enacted include— Preliminary.

(a) redefining and reclassifying public service vehicles;

(b) abolishing road service licences for express carriages as
redefined;

PART I

(c) making it easier for applicants to obtain road service licences, and restricting the power to attach thereto conditions as to fares ;

(d) providing for the designation of areas as trial areas in which road service licences are not required for stage carriage services ;

(e) making new provision for securing the fitness of public service vehicles ;

(f) substituting a system of public service vehicle operators' licences for the system of public service vehicle licences ; and

(g) providing an appeal against a refusal by the London Transport Executive to enter into an agreement with a person other than the Executive for the provision of a London bus service ;

and accordingly the provisions mentioned in subsection (2) (which, except so far as they are re-enacted with or without alteration in this Part, are no longer required) shall cease to have effect.

(2) Those provisions are—

1960 c. 16.

(a) in the Road Traffic Act 1960—

    (i) sections 117 and 118 and Schedule 12 (classification of public service vehicles) ;

    (ii) sections 127, 129 and 132 to 133A (licensing and fitness of public service vehicles) ; and

    (iii) sections 134 to 140 (road service licences) ;

1968 c. 73.

(b) section 30 of the Transport Act 1968 (permits for certain bus services in lieu of road service licences).

(3) This Part and the 1960 Act shall be construed and have effect as if this Part (except so far as it textually amends any enactment) were contained in Part III of that Act ; and section 44 of this Act shall apply for the interpretation of the said Part III as well as for the interpretation of this Part.

(4) Without prejudice to subsection (3), any reference to, or to Part III of, the 1960 Act in any statutory provision not contained in this Part or the 1960 Act shall, unless the context otherwise requires, be construed as including a reference to this Part.

Definition and classification of public service vehicles

Definition of " public service vehicle ".

2.—(1) Subject to the provisions of this section, in this Part " public service vehicle " means a motor vehicle (other than a tramcar) which—

(a) being a vehicle adapted to carry more than eight passengers, is used for carrying passengers for hire or reward ; or (*b*) being a vehicle not so adapted, is used for carrying passengers for hire or reward at separate fares in the course of a business of carrying passengers.

(2) For the purposes of subsection (1) a vehicle " is used " as mentioned in paragraph (*a*) or (*b*) of that subsection if it is being so used or if it has been used as mentioned in that paragraph and that use has not been permanently discontinued.

(3) A vehicle carrying passengers at separate fares in the course of a business of carrying passengers, but doing so in circumstances in which the conditions set out in Part I, II or III of Schedule 1 are fulfilled, shall be treated as not being a public service vehicle unless it is adapted to carry more than eight passengers.

(4) For the purposes of this section a journey made by a vehicle in the course of which one or more passengers are carried at separate fares shall not be treated as made in the course of a business of carrying passengers if—

(*a*) the fare or aggregate of the fares paid in respect of the journey does not exceed the amount of the running costs of the vehicle for the journey; and

(*b*) the arrangements for the payment of fares by the passenger or passengers so carried were made before the journey began;

and for the purposes of paragraph (*a*) the running costs of a vehicle for a journey shall be taken to include an appropriate amount in respect of depreciation and general wear.

(5) For the purposes of this section, section 3 and Schedule 1—

(*a*) a vehicle is to be treated as carrying passengers for hire or reward if payment is made for, or for matters which include, the carrying of passengers, irrespective of the person to whom the payment is made and, in the case of a transaction effected by or on behalf of a member of any association of persons (whether incorporated or not) on the one hand and the association or another member thereof on the other hand, notwithstanding any rule of law as to such transactions;

(*b*) a payment made for the carrying of a passenger shall be treated as a fare notwithstanding that it is made in consideration of other matters in addition to the journey and irrespective of the person by or to whom it is made;

(*c*) a payment shall be treated as made for the carrying of a passenger if made in consideration of a person's being given a right to be carried, whether for one or more journeys and whether or not the right is exercised.

(6) Where a fare is paid for the carriage of a passenger on a journey by air, no part of that fare shall be treated for the purposes of subsection (5) as paid in consideration of the carriage of the passenger by road by reason of the fact that, in case of mechanical failure, bad weather or other circumstances outside the operator's control, part of that journey may be made by road.

Classification of public service vehicles as stage, express or contract carriages.

3.—(1) For the purpose of this Part—

(a) a " stage carriage " is a public service vehicle being used in the operation of a local service ;

(b) an " express carriage " is a public service vehicle being used in the operation of an express service ; and

(c) a " contract carriage " is a public service vehicle being used to carry passengers otherwise than at separate fares ;

and references in this Part to use as a stage, express or contract carriage shall be construed accordingly.

(2) In this section—

(a) " local service " means a service for the carriage of passengers by road at separate fares, not being an express service ;

(b) " express service " means a service for the carriage of passengers by road at separate fares, being a service as regards which the conditions specified in subsection (3) are satisfied.

(3) The conditions referred to in subsection (2)(b) are—

(a) except in the case of an emergency, either of the following requirements as to length of journey is satisfied in respect of every passenger using the service, namely—

(i) the place where he is set down is 30 miles or more, measured in a straight line, from the place where he was taken up ; or

(ii) some point on the route between those places is 30 miles or more, measured in a straight line, from either of those places ; and

(b) either—

(i) the service is an excursion or tour ; or

(ii) the prescribed particulars of the service (including the route and the timetable) and of every change of any prescribed kind made in the service have, not later than the prescribed time for doing so, been notified in the prescribed manner to the traffic commissioners in whose area the place specified in the notification as the beginning of the route is situated.

(4) Where, in the case of any service for the carriage of passengers by road at separate fares, the condition specified in subsection (3)(*a*) is satisfied as regards any part of the service taken in isolation, but not as regards the service as a whole—

(*a*) that part of the service shall be treated for the purposes of subsections (2)(*b*) and (3) as a separate service (and will accordingly be an express service if the condition specified in subsection (3)(*b*) is satisfied as regards it) ; and

(*b*) any part of the service which is not an express service by virtue of the preceding paragraph shall be treated for the purposes of this section as a separate local service.

(5) A public service vehicle carrying passengers at separate fares shall be treated as a contract carriage, and not as a stage carriage or an express carriage, when used in circumstances in which the conditions set out in Part II or III of Schedule 1 are fulfilled.

Road service licences

4.—(1) Subject to section 13 and to the provisions of section 23 of the Transport (London) Act 1969 as to London bus services, a stage carriage service shall not be provided except under a road service licence granted in accordance with the following provisions of this Part.

(2) The authority having power to grant a road service licence in respect of a stage carriage service is the traffic commissioners for any traffic area in which the service is proposed to be provided, not being an area in which passengers will be neither taken up nor set down in the course of the service ; and a road service licence authorises the holder to provide the service specified in the licence in the area of the traffic commissioners by whom it was granted and in any other traffic area in which passengers are neither taken up nor set down in the course of the service.

(3) Where a stage carriage service is proposed to be provided on a route running through more than one traffic area, a separate road service licence is required for each traffic area in which passengers will be either taken up or set down in the course of the service.

(4) Subject to subsection (5) and section 9(2), a road service licence granted by the traffic commissioners for any traffic area

shall be of no effect at any time at which the holder does not also hold a PSV operator's licence granted by the commissioners for that or any other traffic area, not being a licence which is at that time of no effect by reason of its suspension.

(5) Subsection (4) does not apply—

> (a) to a road service licence held by a local education authority or, in Scotland, an education authority;

> (b) to a road service licence granted in respect of a community bus service within the meaning of section 5 of the Transport Act 1978.

1978 c. 55.

(6) If a stage carriage service is provided in contravention of subsection (1), the operator of the service shall be liable on summary conviction to a fine not exceeding £200.

(7) If a condition attached under section 6 or 7 to a road service licence is contravened, the holder of the licence shall be liable on summary conviction to a fine not exceeding £200.

(8) A road service licence is required for a stage carriage service notwithstanding that the provision of such a service is authorised under Part V of the Road Traffic Act 1930 or by a special Act or an order having the force of an Act.

1930 c. 43.

Grant of road service licences.

5.—(1) An application for a road service licence shall be made in such form as the traffic commissioners may require, and an applicant shall give the commissioners such information as they may reasonably require for disposing of the application.

(2) Where an application for the grant of a road service licence is made, the traffic commissioners—

> (a) shall grant the licence unless they are satisfied that to do so would be against the interests of the public; and

> (b) if they grant the licence, shall do so in accordance with the application except to the extent that they are satisfied that to do so would be against the interests of the public.

(3) In considering under subsection (2) whether the grant of a licence would be against the interests of the public, or the extent to which the grant of a licence in accordance with the application would be against those interests, the traffic commissioners shall in particular have regard to—

> (a) the transport requirements of the area as a whole (including so much as is relevant not only of the commissioners' own traffic area but also of adjoining traffic areas) and of particular communities in the area;

(b) any transport policies or plans which have been made
   by the local authorities concerned and have been drawn
   to the commissioners' attention by those authorities;
   and

(c) any objections or other representations made to the
   commissioners in the prescribed manner which in
   their opinion are relevant.

(4) In subsection (3) " the local authorities concerned "
means—

   (a) in Greater London, the Greater London Council;

   (b) elsewhere in England and Wales, county councils; and

   (c) in Scotland, regional and islands councils.

(5) The traffic commissioners, on granting a road service
licence, shall send notice thereof, including particulars of the
services to be provided thereunder, to the chief officer of police
of every police district in which any such service is to be provided and to each of the following councils in whose area any
such service is to be provided, that is to say—

   (a) the Greater London Council, any London borough
      council and the Common Council of the City of
      London;

   (b) any county council or district council in England or
      Wales; and

   (c) any regional, islands or district council in Scotland.

6.—(1) Subject to subsection (2) and to any regulations, traffic
commissioners granting a road service licence may attach to the
licence such conditions as they think fit having regard to the
interests of the public, and in particular to the matters mentioned in section 5(3)(a) to (c), and may in particular attach
thereto such conditions as they think fit (having regard as aforesaid) for securing—

Attachment to
road service
licences of
conditions
as to matters
other than
fares.

   (a) that suitable routes are used in providing any service
      which may be provided under the licence;

   (b) that copies of the timetable and fare-table are carried
      and are available for inspection in vehicles used on any
      such service;

   (c) that passengers are not taken up or are not set down
      except at specified points, or are not taken up or are not
      set down between specified points,

and generally for securing the safety and convenience of the
public, including persons who are disabled.

(2) No such condition as to fares as is mentioned in section 7(1) shall be attached under this section to a road service licence.

(3) The traffic commissioners by whom a road service licence was granted may at any time while it is in force vary the licence by—

(a) altering, in such manner as they think fit having regard to the interests of the public, any condition attached to the licence ; or

(b) removing any condition attached to the licence, if they think fit having regard to those interests ; or

(c) attaching to the licence any such condition or additional condition as they think fit having regard to those interests.

(4) Where the holder of such a licence makes an application to the traffic commissioners requesting them to exercise their powers under subsection (3), the commissioners shall exercise those powers in accordance with the application except to the extent that they are satisfied that to do so would be against the interests of the public.

(5) Compliance with any condition attached to a road service licence under this section may be temporarily dispensed with by the traffic commissioners by whom the licence was granted if they are satisfied—

(a) that compliance with the condition would be unduly onerous by reason of circumstances not foreseen when the condition was attached or, if the condition has been altered, when it was last altered ; and

(b) that such a dispensation would not be against the interests of the public.

Attachment to road service licences of conditions as to fares.

7.—(1) Subject to subsection (3) and any regulations, traffic commissioners may (whether at the time when the licence is granted or at any time thereafter, and whether or not in response to any particulars received by them under this Part) attach to a road service licence granted by them conditions or additional conditions as to the fares, or the minimum or maximum fares, which may be charged for services provided under the licence.

(2) Subject to subsection (3), the traffic commissioners by whom a road service licence was granted may at any time while it is in force vary the licence by—

(a) altering in such manner as they think fit any condition as to fares attached under subsection (1) to the licence ; or (*b*) removing any condition as to fares so attached to the licence.

(3) The traffic commissioners shall not exercise their powers under subsection (1) or their powers of alteration under subsection (2) in any particular case unless satisfied that the proposed exercise of those powers in that case is essential in the interests of the public—

(*a*) to protect the public from unreasonable use by the holder of the licence of his position as such ; or

(*b*) to regulate the terms of competition between stage carriage services on any route or routes.

(4) Where the holder of a road service licence makes an application to the traffic commissioners requesting them to exercise their powers (whether of alteration or removal) under subsection (2), the commissioners—

(*a*) shall remove all the conditions attached under subsection (1) to the licence except to the extent that they are satisfied that it is essential in the interests of the public to maintain them, with or without alteration, for one or both of the purposes mentioned in paragraphs (*a*) and (*b*) of subsection (3) ; and

(*b*) shall not exercise their powers of alteration under subsection (2) unless satisfied that the proposed exercise of those powers is consistent with their reasons for not removing all the conditions attached under subsection (1) to the licence.

(5) Compliance with any condition attached to a road service licence under subsection (1) may be temporarily dispensed with by the traffic commissioners by whom the licence was granted if they are satisfied—

(*a*) that compliance with the condition would be unduly onerous by reason of circumstances not foreseen when the condition was attached or, if the condition has been altered, when it was last altered ; and

(*b*) that such a dispensation would not be against the interests of the public.

(6) Where it is proposed to make any change in the fares charged for any service provided under a road service licence, it shall be the duty of the holder of the licence to supply to the traffic commissioners, not later than the prescribed time before the date of the proposed change, the prescribed particulars of the proposed change.

(7) A person who fails to supply within the prescribed time any particulars which he is required to supply under subsection (6) shall be liable on summary conviction to a fine not exceeding £200.

(8) A person who in purporting to comply with subsection (6) supplies any particulars which he knows to be false or does not believe to be true shall be liable on summary conviction to a fine not exceeding £500.

Grant of road service licences for services on routes not otherwise served.

8.—(1) If, in the case of any application for a road service licence, the traffic commissioners are satisfied that there are no other transport facilities available to meet the reasonable needs of the route on which the service which the applicant proposes to provide under the licence would operate—

> (a) the commissioners shall grant the applicant a road service licence in respect of that route, and shall do so in accordance with the application except to the extent that they are satisfied that to do so would be against the interests of the public ; and

> (b) in relation to the application and to the licence granted on it, sections 5 and 6 shall have effect as if section 5(2) to (4) and, in section 6(1), the words " and in particular to the matters mentioned in section 5(3)(a) to (c) " were omitted.

(2) Every road service licence granted in pursuance of this section shall include a statement that it is so granted.

(3) No appeal shall lie under section 28 from a decision of the traffic commissioners to refuse to grant a road service licence in pursuance of this section.

Grant of road service licences for certain excursions or tours.

9.—(1) If, in the case of any application for a road service licence, the traffic commissioners are satisfied that the service which the applicant proposes to provide under the licence (" the proposed service ") would be an excursion or tour and are also satisfied either—

> (a) that the proposed service would not compete directly with—

>> (i) any other road service for which a road service licence has been granted, not being an excursion or tour, or

>> (ii) any London bus service within the meaning of section 23 of the Transport (London) Act 1969, or

>> (iii) any service being provided by means of one or more tramcars ; or

> (b) that the proposed service would operate only to enable passengers to attend special events,

the commissioners shall grant the applicant a road service licence in accordance with the application and, in relation to the application and to the licence granted on it, sections 5(2) to (4), 6 and 7 shall not apply.

(2) Section 4(4) does not prevent a road service licence granted in pursuance of this section from having effect for the purposes of the provision of a service by means of a vehicle whose operator holds a PSV operator's licence granted by the traffic commissioners for any traffic area, not being a licence which is for the time being of no effect by reason of its suspension.

(3) Every road service licence granted in pursuance of this section shall include a statement that it is so granted.

(4) No appeal shall lie under section 28 from a decision of the traffic commissioners to refuse to grant a road service licence in pursuance of this section.

10.—(1) Subject to subsection (2), a road service licence may be revoked or suspended by the traffic commissioners who granted the licence on the ground that there has been a contravention of any condition attached to it.

(2) The traffic commissioners shall not revoke or suspend a road service licence unless, owing to the frequency of the breach of conditions, or to the breach having been committed intentionally, or to the danger to the public involved in the breach, the commissioners are satisfied that the licence should be revoked or suspended.

(3) On revoking or suspending a road service licence the traffic commissioners shall send notice thereof—

    (*a*) to the chief officer of police of every police district in which the service to which the licence relates was provided ; and

    (*b*) to each of the councils mentioned in section 5(5)(*a*) to (*c*) in whose area that service was provided.

(4) A road service licence suspended under this section shall during the time of suspension be of no effect.

11.—(1) Regulations shall specify the dates in the year on which road service licences are to expire.

(2) Subject to subsection (3), a road service licence shall, unless previously revoked, continue in force up to and including that one of the dates so specified which occurs next before the expiration of five years from the date on which the licence is expressed to take effect unless at the time of the granting of the licence the traffic commissioners for special reasons determine that it shall continue in force only up to and including an earlier date (being one of those so specified), in which case it shall, unless previously revoked, continue in force only up to and including that date.

(3) If, on the date on which a road service licence is due to expire, proceedings are pending before the traffic commissioners on an application for the grant of a new licence in substitution for it, the existing licence shall continue in force until the application is disposed of, but without prejudice to the exercise in the meantime of the powers conferred by section 10.

(4) Nothing in this section shall prevent—

> (*a*) the grant of a road service licence in respect of a service limited to one or more particular periods or occasions ; or
>
> (*b*) the attachment to a road service licence of a condition that the service shall be so limited.

Trial areas

Designation of trial areas.

12.—(1) For the purposes of this Part a trial area is any area in Great Britain (outside Greater London) for the time being designated in accordance with the following provisions of this section as an area in which road service licences are not required for stage carriage services.

(2) The Minister may, if he thinks fit, make an order (in this section referred to as a " designation order ") so designating any area consisting of the whole or part of the area of a local authority, but shall not make such an order in respect of any area except on an application made to him by the local authority concerned.

(3) An application for a designation order shall specify the area which the local authority concerned wishes to be designated by the order ; and the area designated by such an order as originally made—

> (*a*) shall not include any area outside the area specified in the application on which the order is made ; and
>
> (*b*) shall not consist of less than the whole of the area so specified unless the reduction is made with the consent of the local authority concerned.

(4) Subject to subsection (5), the Minister may by order vary or revoke a designation order but shall not do so except on an application made to him by the local authority concerned ; and the Minister—

> (*a*) on an application for an order varying a designation order, may at his discretion refuse the application or make the order applied for either with or without modifications ; and
>
> (*b*) on an application for an order revoking a designation order may at his discretion refuse the application or make the order applied for.

(5) A designation order—

(a) shall not be revoked before the end of the period specified in the order, as originally made, as the minimum period for which the order is to be in force, being a period of not less than two and not more than five years beginning with the day on which it comes into force ;

(b) shall not before the end of that period be varied so as to exclude from the area designated by it any part of the area originally so designated ; and

(c) shall at no time be varied so as to include in the area designated by it any area outside the area originally so designated.

(6) The preceding provisions of this section have effect subject to the provisions of Schedule 2 (which relate to the making of applications for, and the variation and revocation of, designation orders).

(7) Any order under this section shall be made by statutory instrument subject to annulment in pursuance of a resolution of either House of Parliament.

(8) In this section and Schedule 2—

" designation order " has the meaning given by subsection (2) (but does not include an order under this section altering the area designated by a designation order) ;

" local authority " means, for England and Wales, a county council and, for Scotland, a regional or islands council ;

" the local authority concerned ", in relation to any area designated or proposed to be designated under this section, means the local authority whose area is or contains that area.

13.—(1) A road service licence is not required for the provision of a stage carriage service within a trial area.

(2) Where a stage carriage service operates partly within one or more trial areas and partly not within a trial area—

(a) a road service licence is not required in respect of so much of the service as operates not within a trial area but within a traffic area in which (except in any trial area) passengers are neither taken up nor set down in the course of the service ; and

(b) any conditions attached to a road service licence under which any part of that service is provided shall not apply in relation to so much of the service as operates within any trial area.

(3) So much of subsection (3) of section 1 of the Road Traffic Regulation Act 1967 as provides that no prohibition or restriction on waiting imposed by a traffic regulation order under that section shall apply to a stage carriage shall not operate within a trial area.

Duty to
publish
particulars of
stage carriage
services in
trial areas.

14.—(1) This section applies to any stage carriage service which operates wholly within a trial area; but where a stage carriage service operates only partly within a trial area, so much of it as operates within that area shall for the purposes of this section be treated as a separate service to which this section applies.

(2) Before—

> (a) starting to provide a new service to which this section applies; or
>
> (b) making, otherwise than temporarily, any changes in a service to which this section applies; or
>
> (c) discontinuing a service to which this section applies,

the operator of the service shall—

> > (i) give to the local authority concerned, and to every district council in whose area passengers will be or are taken up or set down in the course of the service in question (including, in a case within paragraph (b), the service as proposed to be changed), a notice giving the prescribed information about the new service, the changes or the discontinuance, as the case may be; and
> >
> > (ii) publish in a local newspaper circulating in the locality served or to be served by the service a notice giving the prescribed information about the new service, the changes or the discontinuance, as the case may be.

(3) Subject to subsection (4), any notice required by subsection (2) shall be given or published not later than the prescribed time before the operator does as mentioned in subsection (2)(a), (b) or (c), as the case may be.

(4) Where the operator of a service to which this section applies does as mentioned in subsection (2)(a), (b) or (c) in consequence of unforeseen circumstances making it impracticable for him to give or, as the case may be, publish in accordance with subsection (3) a notice required by subsection (2), subsection (3) shall not apply to that notice, but instead the notice in question shall be given or, as the case may be, published (with any necessary modifications) as soon as is practicable.

(5) If, at the time when any area becomes a trial area, there is being provided under a road service licence a stage carriage service which operates wholly or partly within that area, that service shall for the purposes of subsection (1) be treated as one which operates wholly or, as the case may be, partly within a trial area.

(6) A person who fails to give or publish as required by this section any notice which this section requires him to give or publish shall be liable on summary conviction to a fine not exceeding £200.

(7) Where more than one person falls to be regarded as the operator of a service to which this section applies, the requirements of this section are complied with if the requisite notices are given and published by any of those persons.

(8) In this section—

" the local authority concerned " has the meaning given by section 12(8) ;

" operator " includes a prospective operator.

15.—(1) Subject to subsection (3) the duties of public passenger transport operators under the provisions mentioned in subsection (2), being duties to co-operate with and afford information to one another, shall not apply in relation to a service so far as it is provided within a trial area.

Relaxation in trial areas of operators' duties to co-operate and exchange information. 1968 c. 73.

(2) The provisions referred to in subsection (1) are—

(a) section 24(2) and (3) of the Transport Act 1968 (services in passenger transport areas) ;

(b) section 1(1)(c) of the Transport Act 1978 (services in England and Wales outside passenger transport areas) ; and

1978 c. 65.

(c) section 151(1)(b) of the Local Government (Scotland) Act 1973 (services in Scotland outside passenger transport areas).

1973 c. 65.

(3) Subsection (1) shall not affect the duties of public passenger transport operators to co-operate with or afford information to—

(a) a Passenger Transport Executive ;

(b) a county council ; or

(c) a regional or islands council,

for the purpose of the discharge by any such Executive or council of its function of co-ordinating passenger transport services.

(4) In this section " public passenger transport operators " means persons providing public passenger transport services within the meaning of section 1(2) of the Transport Act 1978.

PART I
Powers of,
and facilities
for, inspection
of public
service
vehicles.

Fitness of public service vehicles

16.—(1) A certifying officer or public service vehicle examiner, on production if so required of his authority—

(*a*) may at any time inspect any public service vehicle, and for that purpose—

(i) may enter the vehicle ; and

(ii) may detain the vehicle during such time as is required for the inspection ;

(*b*) may at any time which is reasonable having regard to the circumstances of the case enter any premises on which he has reason to believe that there is a public service vehicle.

(2) A person who intentionally obstructs a certifying officer or public service vehicle examiner acting in the exercise of his powers under subsection (1) shall be liable on summary conviction to a fine not exceeding £200.

(3) The Minister may—

(*a*) provide and maintain stations where inspections of public service vehicles for the purposes of this Part may be carried out ;

(*b*) designate premises as stations where such inspections may be carried out ; and

(*c*) provide and maintain apparatus for the carrying out of such inspections ;

and in this Part " official PSV testing station " means a station provided, or any premises for the time being designated, under this subsection.

Certificate of
initial fitness
(or equivalent)
required for
use of public
service
vehicle.

17.—(1) A public service vehicle adapted to carry more than eight passengers shall not be used on a road unless—

(*a*) a certifying officer has issued a certificate (in this section referred to as a " certificate of initial fitness ") that the prescribed conditions as to fitness are fulfilled in respect of the vehicle ; or

(*b*) a certificate under section 130 of the 1960 Act (type approval) was in force immediately before this section came into force or has since been issued in respect of the vehicle ; or

(*c*) there has been issued in respect of the vehicle a certificate under section 47 of the Road Traffic Act 1972 (type approval) of a kind which by virtue of regulations is to be treated as the equivalent of a certificate of initial fitness.

(2) For the purposes of this Part and Part III of the 1960 Act a certificate of fitness issued in respect of a vehicle under section

129 of that Act which is in force immediately before the date on which this section comes into force shall have effect on and after that date as if it were a certificate of initial fitness issued in respect of the vehicle on that date.

(3) If a vehicle is used in contravention of subsection (1), the operator of the vehicle shall be liable on summary conviction to a fine not exceeding £500.

18.—(1) If on any inspection of a public service vehicle it appears to a certifying officer or public service vehicle examiner that owing to any defects therein the vehicle is, or is likely to become, unfit for service, he may prohibit the driving of the vehicle on a road either—

   (*a*) absolutely ; or

   (*b*) for one or more specified purposes ; or

   (*c*) except for one or more specified purposes.

Power to prohibit driving of unfit public service vehicles.

(2) A prohibition under subsection (1) may be imposed with a direction making it irremovable unless and until the vehicle has been inspected at an official PSV testing station.

(3) Where a certifying officer or examiner prohibits the driving of a vehicle under subsection (1), he shall forthwith give notice in writing of the prohibition to the person in charge of the vehicle at the time of the inspection—

   (*a*) specifying the defects which occasioned the prohibition ;

   (*b*) stating whether the prohibition is on all driving of the vehicle or driving it for one or more specified purposes or driving it except for one or more specified purposes (and, where applicable, specifying the purpose or purposes in question) ; and

   (*c*) stating whether the prohibition is to come into force immediately or at the end of a specified period.

(4) If the person to whom written notice of a prohibition is given under subsection (3) as being the person in charge of the vehicle at the time of the inspection is not—

   (*a*) the operator of the vehicle ; or

   (*b*) if there is no operator at that time, the owner of the vehicle,

the officer or examiner shall as soon as practicable take steps to bring the contents of the notice to the attention of the said operator or owner.

(5) If, in the opinion of the certfying officer or examiner concerned, the defects in the vehicle in question are such that driving it, or driving it for any purpose prohibited by the notice given to the person in charge of it, would involve danger to the

PART I
driver or to passengers or other members of the public, the prohibition under subsection (1) with respect to the vehicle shall come into force as soon as that notice has been given.

(6) In any other case a prohibition under subsection (1) shall come into force at such time not later than ten days from the date of the inspection as seems appropriate to the certifying officer or examiner having regard to all the circumstances.

(7) Where a notice has been given under subsection (3), any certifying officer or public service vehicle examiner may—

(a) grant an exemption in writing for the use of the vehicle in such manner, subject to such conditions and for such purpose or purposes as may be specified in the exemption ;

(b) by endorsement on the notice vary its terms and, in particular—

(i) alter the time at which the prohibition is to come into force, or suspend it if it has come into force ; or

(ii) cancel a direction under subsection (2) with which the prohibition was imposed.

(8) Subject to any subsisting direction under subsection (2), a prohibition under subsection (1) with respect to any vehicle may be removed by any certifying officer or public service vehicle examiner if he is satisfied that the vehicle is fit for service ; and a person aggrieved by the refusal of a public service vehicle examiner to remove a prohibition may make an application to the traffic commissioners for any area to have the vehicle inspected by a certifying officer and, where such an application is made, the certifying officer to whom the matter is referred by the commissioners shall, if he considers that the vehicle is fit for service, remove the prohibition.

(9) Except in such cases as may be prescribed, a person who—

(a) knowingly drives a vehicle in contravention of a prohibition under subsection (1) ; or

(b) causes or permits a vehicle to be driven in contravention of such a prohibition,

shall be liable on summary conviction to a fine not exceeding £1,000.

Public service vehicle operators' licences

PSV operators' licences.
19.—(1) A vehicle shall not be used on a road as a stage, express or contract carriage except under a PSV operator's licence granted in accordance with the following provisions of this Part.

(2) The authority having power to grant a PSV operator's licence is the traffic commissioners for any traffic area in which, if the licence is granted, there will be one or more operating

centres of vehicles used under the licence ; and, subject to the provisions of this Part, a PSV operator's licence authorises the holder to use anywhere in Great Britain vehicles which have their operating centre in the area of the traffic commissioners by whom the licence was granted.

(3) A person may hold two or more PSV operators' licences each granted by the traffic commissioners for different areas, but shall not at the same time hold more than one such licence granted by the commissioners for the same area.

(4) An application for a PSV operator's licence shall be made in such form as the traffic commissioners may require, and an applicant shall give the commissioners such information as they may reasonably require for disposing of the application.

(5) If a vehicle is used in contravention of subsection (1) the operator of the vehicle shall be liable on summary conviction to a fine not exceeding £500.

20.—(1) A PSV operator's licence may be either a standard licence or a restricted licence.

Classification of licences.

(2) A standard licence authorises the use of any description of public service vehicle and may authorise use either—

    (*a*) on both national and international operations ; or

    (*b*) on national operations only.

(3) A restricted licence authorises the use (whether on national or international operations) of—

    (*a*) public service vehicles not adapted to carry more than eight passengers ; and

    (*b*) public service vehicles not adapted to carry more than sixteen passengers when used—

        (i) otherwise than in the course of a business of carrying passengers ; or

        (ii) by a person whose main occupation is not the operation of public service vehicles adapted to carry more than eight passengers.

(4) For the purposes of subsection (3)(*b*)(i), a vehicle used for carrying passengers by a local or public authority shall not be regarded as used in the course of a business of carrying passengers unless it is used by the public service vehicle undertaking of that authority.

21.—(1) An application for a standard licence shall not be granted unless the traffic commissioners are satisfied that the applicant meets the following requirements, namely—

Grant and duration of licences.

    (*a*) the requirement to be of good repute ;

    (*b*) the requirement to be of appropriate financial standing ; and (*c*) the requirement as to professional competence;

and an application for a restricted licence shall not be granted unless the traffic commissioners are satisfied that the applicant meets the requirements to be of good repute and of appropriate financial standing.

(2) The provisions of Schedule 3 shall have effect for supplementing the provisions of subsection (1), and for modifying the operation of that subsection in the case of persons engaged in road passenger transport before 1st January 1978.

(3) Notwithstanding that it appears to the traffic commissioners on an application for a standard or restricted licence that the requirements mentioned in subsection (1) are met, the application shall not be granted unless the commissioners are further satisfied—

> (*a*) that there will be adequate facilities or arrangements for maintaining in a fit and serviceable condition the vehicles proposed to be used under the licence; and
>
> (*b*) that there will be adequate arrangements for securing compliance with the requirements of the law relating to the driving and operation of those vehicles.

(4) If on an application for a PSV operator's licence the traffic commissioners determine that the relevant requirements mentioned in subsection (1) and the further requirements mentioned in subsection (3) are satisfied they shall, subject to the following provisions of this section and to section 22, grant the licence in accordance with the application.

(5) There shall be specified in every PSV operator's licence the date on which the licence is to come into force and the date with which it is to expire; and, subject to subsection (6), the last-mentioned date shall be such as will make the duration of the licence such period not exceeding five years as the traffic commissioners on granting the licence consider appropriate in the circumstances.

(6) Traffic commissioners on granting a PSV operator's licence may direct that the duration of the licence shall be such period not exceeding five years as is in the opinion of the commissioners desirable in order to arrange a reasonably convenient programme of work for the commissioners.

(7) If, immediately before a PSV operator's licence is due to expire, proceedings are pending before the traffic commissioners on an application by the holder of that licence for the grant to him of a new licence in substitution for it, the existing licence shall continue in force until the application is disposed of, but without prejudice to the exercise in the meantime of the powers conferred by section 23.

(8) Where an application is made to the traffic commissioners by the holder of a PSV operator's licence for the grant to him of a new licence to take effect on the expiry of the existing licence and the traffic commissioners decide not to grant the new licence, they may direct that the existing licence continue in force for such period as appears to them reasonably required to enable the business carried on under the licence to be transferred to another person duly licensed to carry it on.

22.—(1) Traffic commissioners on granting a PSV operator's licence shall attach to it one or more conditions specifying the maximum number of vehicles (being vehicles having their operating centre in the area of those commissioners) which the holder of the licence may at any one time use under the licence.

(2) Conditions attached under subsection (1) to a PSV operator's licence may specify different maximum numbers for different descriptions of vehicle.

(3) Traffic commissioners may (whether at the time when the licence is granted or at any time thereafter) attach to a PSV operator's licence granted by them such conditions or additional conditions as they think fit for restricting or regulating the use of vehicles under the licence, being conditions of any prescribed description.

(4) Without prejudice to the generality of the power to prescribe descriptions of conditions for the purposes of subsection (3), the descriptions which may be so prescribed include conditions for regulating the places at which vehicles being used under a PSV operator's licence may stop to take up or set down passengers.

(5) The traffic commissioners by whom a PSV operator's licence was granted may at any time while it is in force vary the licence by—

> (a) altering in such manner as they think fit any condition attached under subsection (3) to the licence ; or
>
> (b) removing any condition so attached to the licence.

(6) On the application of the holder of a PSV operator's licence, the traffic commissioners by whom the licence was granted may at any time while it is in force—

> (a) vary the conditions attached under subsection (1) to the licence ; or
>
> (b) exercise their powers (whether of alteration or removal) under subsection (5) ;

and a person making an application under this subsection shall give to the traffic commissioners such information as they may reasonably require for the discharge of their duties in relation to the application.

(7) If a condition attached to a PSV operator's licence is contravened, the holder of the licence shall be liable on summary conviction to a fine not exceeding £200.

(8) Compliance with any condition attached to a PSV operator's licence under this section may be temporarily dispensed with by the traffic commissioners by whom the licence was granted if they are satisfied that compliance with the condition would be unduly onerous by reason of circumstances not foreseen when the condition was attached or, if the condition has been altered, when it was last altered.

(9) It is hereby declared that the conditions attached under subsection (1) to a PSV operator's licence granted by the traffic commissioners for any area do not affect the use by the holder of the licence of a vehicle—

> (*a*) under a PSV operator's licence granted to him by the traffic commissioners for another area ; or
>
> (*b*) in circumstances such that another person falls to be treated as the operator of the vehicle (for example, by virtue of regulations under section 44(2)(*a*)).

Revocation, suspension, etc. of licences.

23.—(1) The traffic commissioners by whom a standard licence was granted shall revoke the licence if it appears to them at any time that the holder no longer satisfies the requirement to be of good repute, the requirement to be of appropriate financial standing or the requirement as to professional competence.

(2) Without prejudice to subsection (1), the traffic commissioners by whom a PSV operator's licence was granted may, on any of the grounds specified in subsection (3), at any time—

> (*a*) revoke the licence ;
>
> (*b*) suspend the licence for such period as the commissioners direct (during which time it shall be of no effect) ;
>
> (*c*) curtail the period of validity of the licence ;
>
> (*d*) vary any condition attached under subsection (1) of section 22 to the licence, or attach to the licence (whether in addition to or in place of any existing condition so attached to it) any such condition as is mentioned in that subsection.

(3) The grounds for action under subsection (2) are—

> (*a*) that the holder of the licence made or procured to be made for the purposes of his application for the licence, or for the purposes of an application for a variation of the licence, a statement of fact which (whether to his knowledge or not) was false, or a statement of intention or expectation which has not been fulfilled ;
>
> (*b*) that there has been a contravention of any condition attached to the licence ;

(c) that a prohibition under section 18 has been imposed with respect to a vehicle owned or operated by the holder of the licence, or that the holder of the licence has been convicted of an offence under subsection (9) of that section ;

(d) in the case of a restricted licence, that the holder no longer satisfies the requirement to be of good repute or the requirement to be of appropriate financial standing ;

(e) that there has been since the licence was granted or varied a material change in any of the circumstances of the holder of the licence which were relevant to the grant or variation of his licence.

(4) Traffic commissioners shall not take any action under subsection (1) or (2) in respect of any licence without first holding a public sitting if the holder of the licence requests them to do so.

(5) Where traffic commissioners decide to revoke a licence under this section, they may direct that the revocation shall not take effect for such period as appears to them reasonably required to enable the business carried on under the licence to be transferred to another person duly licensed to carry it on.

(6) The provisions of Schedule 3 shall apply for the purposes of subsections (1) and (3)(d) as they apply for the purposes of section 21(1).

24.—(1) Where a vehicle is being used in circumstances such that a PSV operator's licence is required, there shall be fixed and exhibited on the vehicle in the prescribed manner an operator's disc issued under this section showing particulars of the operator of the vehicle and of the PSV operator's licence under which the vehicle is being used.

Duty to exhibit operator's disc.

(2) Traffic commissioners on granting a PSV operator's licence shall supply the person to whom the licence is granted with a number of operator's discs equal to the maximum number of vehicles which he may use under the licence in accordance with the condition or conditions attached to the licence under section 22(1) ; and if that maximum number is later increased on the variation of one or more of those conditions, the traffic commissioners on making the variation shall supply him with further operator's discs accordingly.

(3) Regulations may make provision—

(a) as to the form of operator's discs and the particulars to be shown on them ;

(b) with respect to the custody and production of operator's discs ;

(c) for the issue of new operator's discs in place of those lost, destroyed, or defaced ;

(d) for the return of operator's discs on the revocation or expiration of a PSV operator's licence or in the event of a variation of one or more conditions attached to a licence under section 22(1) having the effect of reducing the maximum number of vehicles which may be used under the licence.

(4) If a vehicle is used in contravention of subsection (1), the operator of the vehicle shall be liable on summary conviction to a fine not exceeding £200.

Duty to inform traffic commissioners of relevant convictions, etc.

25.—(1) A person who has applied for a PSV operator's licence shall forthwith notify the traffic commissioners to whom the application was made if, in the interval between the making of the application and the date on which it is disposed of, a relevant conviction occurs of the applicant, or any employee or agent of his, or of any person proposed to be engaged as transport manager whose repute and competence are relied on in connection with the application.

(2) It shall be the duty of the holder of a PSV operator's licence to give notice in writing to the traffic commissioners by whom the licence was granted of—

(a) any relevant conviction of the holder ; and

(b) any relevant conviction of any officer, employee or agent of the holder for an offence committed in the course of the holder's road passenger transport business,

and to do so within 28 days of the conviction in the case of a conviction of the holder or his transport manager and within 28 days of the conviction coming to the holder's knowledge in any other case.

(3) It shall be the duty of the holder of a PSV operator's licence within 28 days of the occurrence of—

(a) the bankruptcy or liquidation of the holder, or the sequestration of his estate or the appointment of a receiver, manager or trustee of his road passenger transport business ; or

(b) any change in the identity of the transport manager of the holder's road passenger transport business,

to give notice in writing of that event to the traffic commissioners by whom the licence was granted.

(4) Traffic commissioners on granting or varying a PSV operator's licence, or at any time thereafter, may require the holder of the licence to inform them forthwith or within a time specified by them of any material change specified by them in any of his circumstances which were relevant to the grant or variation of the licence.

(5) A person who fails to comply with subsection (1), (2) or (3) or with any requirement under subsection (4) shall be liable on summary conviction to a fine not exceeding £200.

26.—(1) It shall be the duty of the holder of a PSV operator's licence, on the happening to any public service vehicle owned by him of any failure or damage of a nature calculated to affect the safety of occupants of the public service vehicle or of persons using the road, to report the matter as soon as is practicable to the traffic commissioners who granted the licence.

(2) It shall be the duty of the holder of a PSV operator's licence, on any alteration otherwise than by replacement of parts being made in the structure or fixed equipment of any public service vehicle owned by him, to give notice of the alteration as soon as is practicable to the traffic commissioners who granted the licence.

(3) The traffic commissioners by whom a PSV operator's licence was granted may—

> (a) require the holder of the licence to supply them forthwith or within a specified time with such information as they may reasonably require about the public service vehicles owned by him and normally kept at an operating centre within the area of those commissioners, and to keep up to date information supplied by him under this paragraph ; or

> (b) require the holder or former holder of the licence to supply them forthwith or within a specified time with such information as they may reasonably require about the public service vehicles owned by him at any material time specified by them which were at that time normally kept at an operating centre within the area of those commissioners.

In this subsection " material time " means a time when the PSV operator's licence in question was in force.

(4) A person who fails to comply with the provisions of subsection (1) or (2) or with any requirement under subsection (3) shall be liable on summary conviction to a fine not exceeding £200.

(5) A person who in purporting to comply with any requirement under subsection (3) supplies any information which he knows to be false or does not believe to be true shall be liable on summary conviction to a fine not exceeding £500.

(6) Where a certifying officer or public service vehicle examiner imposes or removes a prohibition on the driving of a public service vehicle, he shall forthwith give notice of that fact to the traffic commissioners who granted the PSV operator's licence under which the vehicle was last used before the prohibition was imposed.

27.—(1) A person who wishes to do either of the following things in another member State or in Northern Ireland, namely to carry on a road passenger transport business or to be the transport manager of such a business, may apply—

   (a) if he holds a standard licence, to the traffic commissioners by whom that licence was granted or, if he holds more than one, by whom the last such licence was granted ;

   (b) in any other case, to the traffic commissioners for any traffic area,

for a certificate as to his repute and professional competence and, where relevant, his financial standing.

(2) A person applying for a certificate under subsection (1) shall give to the traffic commissioners such information as they may reasonably require for the discharge of their duties in relation to the application.

(3) The traffic commissioners to whom an application under subsection (1) is made shall certify such matters relating to the applicant as—

   (a) they are satisfied they may properly certify, and

   (b) appear to them to be of assistance to the applicant in satisfying the requirements of the law of the other member State in which he wishes to carry on business or to work or, as the case may be, the requirements of the law of Northern Ireland.

Supplementary provisions relating to licences

28.—(1) A person who has applied for the grant of a licence under this Part may appeal to the Minister against any decision of the traffic commissioners—

   (a) to refuse to grant the licence in accordance with the application ; or

   (b) to attach any condition to the licence otherwise than in accordance with the application.

(2) Where a person who has applied for a new licence under this Part in substitution for a licence held by him and in force at the date of his application appeals to the Minister under subsection (1) against any such decision of the traffic commissioners as is mentioned in paragraph (a) or (b) of that subsection, the existing licence shall continue in force until the appeal is disposed of, but without prejudice to the exercise in the meantime of the powers conferred by section 10 or 23.

(3) The holder of a licence granted under this Part may appeal to the Minister against any decision of the traffic commissioners—

   (a) to refuse an application by the holder for the variation or removal of any condition attached to the licence ;

(*b*) to vary any such condition, or to attach any new condition to the licence, otherwise than on an application by the holder ; or

(*c*) to revoke or suspend the licence or to curtail its period of validity.

(4) Traffic commissioners making any such decision with respect to a licence as is mentioned in paragraph (*b*) or (*c*) of subsection (3) may, if the holder of the licence so requests, direct that their decision shall not have effect until the expiration of the period within which an appeal against it may be made to the Minister under that subsection and, if such an appeal is made, until the appeal is disposed of ; and if they refuse to give such a direction, the holder of the licence may apply to the Minister for such a direction, and the Minister shall give his decision on the application within 14 days.

(5) A person who has applied for the grant of a licence under this Part, or for the variation or removal of any conditions attached to such a licence, shall, if the traffic commissioners to whom the application was made fail to come to a decision on the application within a reasonable time, have the same right to appeal to the Minister as if the commissioners had decided to refuse the application.

(6) A person applying for—

(*a*) a certificate of initial fitness ; or

(*b*) a certificate under section 130 of the 1960 Act (type approval),

may appeal to the Minister against the refusal of a certifying officer to issue such a certificate.

(7) A person other than the applicant for, or holder of, a road service licence may, if he has standing in the matter in accordance with subsection (8), appeal to the Minister against any decision of the traffic commissioners with respect to—

(*a*) the grant, revocation or suspension of a road service licence ; or

(*b*) the attachment of any condition to the road service licence or the variation or removal of any condition attached to such a licence.

(8) The persons having standing to appeal under subsection (7) against a decision of the traffic commissioners with respect to a road service licence are—

(*a*) any local authority in whose area the service, or any part of the service, is being or is to be provided under the licence ; and

(*b*) any person providing transport facilities along or near the route, or part of the route, of the service which is being or is to be provided under the licence, being an authority or person who has made objections or other representations to the traffic commissioners in the course of the proceedings resulting in that decision.

In this subsection " local authority " means—

(i) in relation to England and Wales, any local authority within the meaning of the Local Government Act 1972 ;

(ii) in relation to Scotland, a regional, islands or district council.

(9) An appeal under this section must be made within the prescribed time and in the prescribed manner, and provision may be made by regulations as to the procedure to be followed in connection with appeals under this section.

(10) On the determination of an appeal under this section, the Minister may confirm, vary or reverse the decision appealed against, and may give such directions as he thinks fit to the traffic commissioners or, as the case may be, to the certifying officer for giving effect to his decision ; and it shall be the duty of the traffic commissioners or certifying officer to comply with any such directions.

Further appeals on points of law.
29.—(1) An appeal lies at the instance of any of the persons mentioned in subsection (2) on any point of law arising from a decision of the Minister on an appeal from a decision of the traffic commissioners for any area—

(*a*) to the High Court where the proceedings before the traffic commissioners were in England or Wales ; and

(*b*) to the Court of Session where the proceedings before the traffic commissioners were in Scotland.

(2) The persons who may appeal against any such decision of the Minister are—

(*a*) the person who appealed to the Minister ;

(*b*) any person who had a right to appeal to the Minister against the relevant decision of the traffic commissioners but did not exercise that right ; and

(*c*) the traffic commissioners whose decision was appealed against.

(3) If on an appeal under this section the High Court or Court of Session is of opinion that the decision appealed against was erroneous in point of law, it shall remit the matter to the Minister with the opinion of the court for rehearing and determination by him.

(4) No appeal to the Court of Appeal may be brought from a decision of the High Court under this section except with the leave of the High Court or the Court of Appeal.

(5) An appeal shall lie, with the leave of the Court of Session or the House of Lords, from any decision of the Court of Session under this section ; and such leave may be given on such terms as to costs, expenses or otherwise as the Court of Session or the House of Lords determine.

30.—(1) Provision may be made by regulations for modifying the provisions of this Part, and any other statutory provisions relating to public service vehicles, in their application to the operation of vehicles and the provision of services by persons in partnership.

(2) A road service licence or PSV operator's licence shall not be granted to an unincorporated body as such or to more than one person jointly except in cases permitted by regulations under this section.

31.—(1) A road service licence or PSV operator's licence is not assignable or, subject to the following provisions of this section, transmissible on death or in any other way.

(2) A road service licence or PSV operator's licence held by an individual terminates if he—

(a) dies ; or

(b) is adjudged bankrupt or, in Scotland, has his estate sequestrated ; or

(c) becomes a patient within the meaning of Part VIII of the Mental Health Act 1959 or, in Scotland, becomes incapable of managing his own affairs.

(3) In relation to a road service licence or PSV operator's licence held by an individual or by a company regulations may specify other events relating to the licence-holder on the occurrence of which the licence is to terminate.

(4) The traffic commissioners by whom a road service licence or PSV operator's licence was granted may—

(a) direct that the termination of the licence by subsection (2), or under subsection (3), be deferred for a period not exceeding 12 months or, if it appears to the commissioners that there are special circumstances, 18 months ; and

(b) authorise the business of the licence-holder to be carried on under the licence by some other person during the period of deferment, subject to such conditions as the commissioners may impose.

Other matters

32.—(1) Subject to subsection (2), a local education authority may—

(a) use a school bus, when it is being used to provide free school transport, to carry as fare-paying passengers persons other than those for whom the free school transport is provided ; and

(b) use a school bus belonging to the authority, when it is not being used to provide free school transport, to provide a local bus service ;

and the following provisions, that is to say section 144 of the 1960 Act (public service vehicle drivers' licences) and sections 16, 17, 18 and 19(1) of this Act, shall not apply to a school bus belonging to a local education authority in the course of its use by the authority in accordance with this subsection.

(2) Subsection (1) does not affect the duties of a local education authority in relation to the provision of free school transport or authorise a local education authority to make any charge for the carriage of a pupil on a journey which he is required to make in the course of his education at a school maintained by such an authority.

(3) In this section—

1944 c. 31.
" free school transport " means transport provided by a local education authority in pursuance of arrangements under section 55(1) of the Education Act 1944 for the purpose of facilitating the attendance of pupils at a place of education ;

" local bus service " means a stage carriage service other than a service as regards which the condition specified in section 3(3)(a) is satisfied ;

" school bus ", in relation to a local education authority, means a motor vehicle which is used by that authority to provide free school transport.

(4) In the application of this section to Scotland—

(a) for the references to a local education authority there shall be substituted references to an education authority ;

(b) in subsection (2) for " maintained by " there shall be substituted " under the management of " ; and

(c) in subsection (3) for the definition of " free school transport " there shall be substituted—

1962 c. 47.
" " free school transport " means transport between a pupil's home and place of education provided in pursuance of arrangements under subsection (1)(a) of section 51 of the Education (Scotland) Act 1962 (pupils for whom such transport facilities are necessary) or in pursuance of subsection (2) of that section (other pupils allowed to use vacant seats free of charge) ".

1953 c. 33.
(5) The repeal by this Act of section 12 of the Education (Miscellaneous Provisions) Act 1953 and section 118(4) of the

1960 Act shall not affect the operation of those provisions in relation to any consent given under the said section 12 which is in force immediately before that repeal takes effect

33.—(1) In subsection (1) of section 1 of the Minibus Act 1977 (exemption of certain vehicles from requirements applicable to public service vehicles) for " vehicle which is adapted to carry more than seven but not more than sixteen passengers " there shall be substituted " small passenger-carrying vehicle ", and after that subsection there shall be inserted the following sub-section—

" (1A) If a large passenger-carrying vehicle is used for carrying passengers for hire or reward, then, if and so long as the conditions set out in paragraphs (*a*) to (*c*) of sub-section (1) above are satisfied, the following provisions shall not apply to the driving or use of the vehicle, namely—

> (*a*) section 144 of the Road Traffic Act 1960 (public service vehicle drivers' licences) ;

> (*b*) section 23(2) of the Transport (London) Act 1969 and section 4 of the Transport Act 1980 (licensing of stage carriage services) ; and

> (*c*) section 19(1) of the Transport Act 1980 (PSV operators' licences).".

(2) In section 1(2) of that Act (persons authorised to grant permits)—

> (*a*) at the beginning of paragraph (*a*) (powers of traffic commissioners) there shall be inserted " in the case of small passenger-carrying vehicles," ; and

> (*b*) at the beginning of paragraph (*b*) (power of designated bodies) there shall be inserted " in the case of small or large passenger-carrying vehicles,".

(3) After section 1(3) of that Act (designation orders) there shall be inserted the following subsection—

" (3A) Different provision may be made by orders under subsection (3) above in relation to large passenger-carrying vehicles from that made in relation to small passenger-carrying vehicles." ;

and a designation order made under the said section 1(3) before the commencement of this section shall not apply in relation to large passenger-carrying vehicles.

(4) In section 3(1) of that Act (power to make regulations), in paragraph (*e*) (power to prescribe conditions of fitness) for " vehicles " there shall be substituted " small passenger-carrying vehicles ".

(5) After section 3(1) of that Act there shall be inserted the following subsection—

" (1A) Regulations made by virtue of any of paragraphs (*a*) to (*d*) of subsection (1) above may make different provision in relation to large passenger-carrying vehicles from that made in relation to small passenger-carrying vehicles.".

(6) In section 3(2) of that Act (consequences of breach of regulations) for " Section 1(1) " substitute " Subsection (1) or, as the case may be, subsection (1A) of section 1 ".

(7) In section 4(2) of that Act (interpretation) after paragraph (*b*) there shall be inserted the following paragraph—

" (*bb*) " small passenger-carrying vehicle " means a vehicle which is adapted to carry more than eight but not more than sixteen passengers, and " large passenger-carrying vehicle " means a vehicle which is adapted to carry more than sixteen passengers ; ".

Obligatory test certificates for passenger-carrying vehicles.

1972 c. 20.

34. In section 44 of the Road Traffic Act 1972 (obligatory test certificates), in subsection (4) (excluded classes of vehicles) the following words (which relate to the exclusion of large public service vehicles) shall be omitted—

(*a*) the words from " to public service vehicles " to " passengers or " ; and

(*b*) the words from " but shall apply " onwards.

Amendment of Transport (London) Act 1969.

1969 c. 35.

35. After section 23 of the Transport (London) Act 1969 (restrictions on provision of London bus services otherwise than by the London Transport Executive and their subsidiaries) there shall be inserted :—

" Right of appeal where Executive refuse to make or vary an agreement authorising a London bus service.

23A.—(1) Where a person other than the Executive or a subsidiary of theirs seeks—

(*a*) an agreement with the Executive under subsection (2) of section 23 of this Act to enable him to provide a London bus service ; or

(*b*) an agreement with the Executive to vary the terms of an agreement under that subsection (whenever made) which for the time being subsists between himself and the Executive,

then, if the Executive refuse to enter into the agreement sought or fail to enter into it within a reasonable period, that person may appeal to the Minister on the ground of the refusal or failure.

(2) A person appealing under this section shall give notice of the appeal—

(*a*) to the Council ;

(*b*) to the commissioner or commissioners of police concerned ; and

(*c*) to any of the councils of the London boroughs or the Common Council within whose area it is proposed to provide a service under the agreement sought by the appellant ;

and the Minister shall not proceed with the appeal unless he is satisfied that such notice has been given.

(3) In determining an appeal under this section the Minister shall take into account—

(*a*) any representations made by the Council ; and

(*b*) any representations with respect to relevant road traffic matters made by any of the persons notified as mentioned in paragraph (*b*) or (*c*) of subsection (2) of this section.

(4) An appeal under this section must be made within the prescribed time and in the prescribed manner ; and provision may be made by regulations as to the procedure to be followed in connection with appeals under this section.

(5) On such an appeal the Minister may make such order, if any, as he thinks fit requiring the Executive to enter into an agreement with the appellant on such terms as may be specified in the order ; and it shall be the duty of the Executive to comply with any such order.

(6) For the purposes of any reference in this or any other Act to an agreement under subsection (2) of section 23 of this Act any agreement entered into or varied by the Executive in compliance with an order under subsection (5) above shall be taken to be such an agreement.

(7) In this section—

" commissioner of police " and " London bus service " have the same meaning as in section 23 of this Act ;

" prescribed " means prescribed by regulations made by the Minister ;

" relevant road traffic matters ", in relation to an appeal, means the following matters relating to the service proposed to be provided under the agreement sought by the appellant—

(*a*) the route of the service and its terminal points ;

(*b*) the points at which passengers may or may not be taken up or set down ;

(*c*) the places at which, and streets by the use of which, vehicles used for the service may turn at a terminal point.

Further appeals on points of law.

23B.—(1) An appeal lies to the High Court at the instance of any of the persons mentioned in subsection (2) of this section on any point of law arising from a decision of the Minister on an appeal under section 23A of this Act.

(2) The persons who may appeal against any such decision of the Minister are—

(*a*) the person who appealed to the Minister ;

(*b*) any person required to be notified of that appeal under subsection (2) of section 23A of this Act ; and

(*c*) the Executive.

(3) If on an appeal under this section the High Court is of opinion that the decision appealed against was erroneous in point of law, it shall remit the matter to the Minister with the opinion of the court for rehearing and determination by him.

(4) No appeal to the Court of Appeal may be brought from a decision of the High Court under this section except with the leave of the High Court or the Court of Appeal.".

Abolition of licensing of conductors of public service vehicles.

36. Subsection (1) of section 144 of the 1960 Act (drivers' and conductors' licences) shall cease to have effect so far as it requires a person acting as conductor of a public service vehicle on a road to be licensed for the purpose under that section or prohibits the employment for that purpose of a person not so licensed.

Reduction of minimum age for drivers of public service vehicles.

37.—(1) In subsection (3) of section 144 of the 1960 Act (PSV drivers' licences: minimum age and other conditions) for the words from " unless ", in the first place where it occurs, to the end of the subsection there shall be substituted " unless he fulfils such conditions as may be prescribed ".

1972 c. 20.

(2) Subsection (1) of section 96 of the Road Traffic Act 1972 (minimum ages at which licences may be held for different classes of vehicles) shall have effect as if in the Table in that subsection, in item 6, the age of 18 were substituted for the age of 21 in relation to a large passenger vehicle where—

(*a*) the driver is not engaged in the carriage of passengers and either holds a PSV driver's licence or is acting under the supervision of a person who holds a PSV driver's licence ; or

(b) the driver holds a PSV driver's licence and is engaged in the carriage of passengers—

    (i) on a regular service over a route which does not exceed 50 kilometres ; or

    (ii) on a national transport operation when the vehicle used is constructed and equipped to carry not more than 15 persons including the driver,

and in either case the operator of the vehicle holds a PSV operator's licence granted by the traffic commissioners for any area, not being a licence which is of no effect by reason of its suspension.

(3) In subsection (2)—

" large passenger vehicle " means a motor vehicle which is constructed solely to carry passengers and their effects and is adapted to carry more than nine persons inclusive of the driver ;

" PSV driver's licence " means a licence to drive a public service vehicle granted under section 144 of the 1960 Act.

(4) The provisions of subsections (2) and (3) may be amended or repealed by regulations under section 96(2) of the Road Traffic Act 1972.

1972 c. 20.

38. For section 159(1) of the 1960 Act (fees for grant or issue of licences) there shall be substituted—

Fees for grant of licences, etc.

" (1) Such fees, payable at such times, and whether in one sum or by instalments, as may be prescribed shall be charged—

(a) by the traffic commissioners for each traffic area in respect of—

    (i) applications for, and the grant of, road service licences and PSV operators' licences ;

    (ii) applications for, and the issue of, certificates of initial fitness under section 17 of the Transport Act 1980 ;

    (iii) the issue of operators' discs under section 24 of that Act ;

    (iv) applications for, and the issue of, certificates under section 27 of that Act as to repute, professional competence or financial standing ; and

    (v) applications for, and the issue of, documents required in relation to public service vehicles registered in Great Britain while making journeys to or from places outside Great Britain or in relation to public service vehicles registered outside Great Britain ;

(b) by the traffic commissioners for each traffic area and by the commissioner of police for the metropolis in respect of—

    (i) applications for, and the issue of, licences to drive public service vehicles ; and

    (ii) the provision by the traffic commissioners or the said commissioner of police of facilities for a person to undergo a test of his competence as a driver in connection with an application by him for a licence to drive a public service vehicle, being a test which he is by virtue of regulations required to undergo in that connection.

(1A) The traffic commissioners or the said commissioner may, if any fee or instalment of a fee due in respect thereof has not been paid, decline to proceed with—

(a) any such application as is mentioned in subsection (1) above,

(b) the grant of any licence or issue of any certificate, disc or other document referred to in that subsection, or

(c) the provision of any such facilities as are mentioned in paragraph (b)(ii) of that subsection,

until the fee or instalment in question has been paid.".

Arrangements for appointment of traffic commissioners.

39. In section 121 of the 1960 Act (appointment etc. of traffic commissioners), for subsections (4) and (5) (appointments, and constitution of panels of nominees for appointment) there shall be substituted—

" (4) Of the three commissioners—

(a) one shall be such person as the Minister thinks fit to appoint to be chairman of the commissioners ;

(b) one shall be appointed by the Minister from a panel of persons nominated by such of the following councils, namely in England and Wales county councils and the Greater London Council and in Scotland regional or islands councils, as are councils whose area is wholly or partly comprised in the traffic area ; and

(c) the third shall be appointed by the Minister from a panel of persons nominated by such of the following councils, namely in England and Wales district councils, London borough councils and the Common Council of the City of London and in Scotland district councils, as are councils whose area is wholly or partly comprised in the traffic area.

(5) Provision shall be made by regulations as to the arrangements for constituting the panels mentioned in subsection (4) above.".

PART I

40. In the case of an offence against any provision of the 1960 Act specified in column 1 of Schedule 4 (of which the general nature is indicated in column 2) the maximum punishment is increased from that now in force (which is indicated in column 3) to that specified in column 4; and for that purpose the provisions of that Act specified in column 1 shall have effect subject to the amendments specified in column 5.

Increase of penalties.

41.—(1) Where an offence under this Part or Part III of the 1960 Act committed by a company is proved to have been committed with the consent or connivance of, or to be attributable to any neglect on the part of, any director, manager, secretary or other similar officer of the company, or any person who was purporting to act in any such capacity, he, as well as the company, shall be guilty of that offence and be liable to be proceeded against and punished accordingly.

Offences by bodies corporate.

(2) Where the affairs of a company are managed by its members, subsection (1) shall apply in relation to the acts and defaults of a member in connection with his functions of management as if he were a director of the company.

42.—(1) It shall be a defence for a person charged with an offence under any of the provisions mentioned in subsection (2) to prove that there was a reasonable excuse for the act or omission in respect of which he is charged.

Defences available to persons charged with certain offences.

(2) The provisions referred to in subsection (1) are—

(a) sections 7(7), 14(6), 25(5) and 26(4);

(b) in the 1960 Act—

(i) so much of section 144(8) as relates to contravention of section 144(1)(a);

(ii) sections 146(2) and (3), 147(2) and 148(2);

(iii) so much of section 232(3) as relates to failure to comply with the requirement of section 232 (2) (b); and

(iv) section 239.

(3) It shall be a defence for a person charged with an offence under any of the provisions mentioned in subsection (4) to prove

Part I
2 A

PART I

that he took all reasonable precautions and exercised all due diligence to avoid the commission of any offence under that provision.

(4) The provisions referred to in subsection (3) are—

(*a*) sections 4(6) and (7), 17(3), 18(9)(*b*), 19(5) 22(7) and 24(4) ;

(*b*) in the 1960 Act—

(i) so much of section 144(8) as relates to contravention of section 144(1)(*b*) ; and

(ii) sections 148(2) and 157(2).

Amendments of other Acts.

43.—(1) The provisions of the 1960 Act mentioned in Part I of Schedule 5, and the enactments specified in Part II of that Schedule, shall have effect subject to the amendments there specified, being minor amendments and amendments consequential on the provisions of this Part.

(2) Where the running of public service vehicles is restricted or prohibited by any provision contained in—

(*a*) a local Act (including an Act confirming a provisional order) passed before the commencement of this subsection ; or

(*b*) an instrument made before the commencement of this subsection under any such local Act,

the Minister may, on the application of any person affected by the restriction or prohibition, by order made by statutory instrument modify or revoke the restriction or prohibition.

Interpretation of Part I.
1960 c. 16.

44.—(1) In this Part, unless the context otherwise requires—

" the 1960 Act " means the Road Traffic Act 1960 ;

" company " means a body corporate ;

" contract carriage " has the meaning given by section 3 ;

" contravention ", in relation to any condition or provision, includes a failure to comply with the condition or provision, and " contravene " shall be construed accordingly ;

" director ", in relation to a company, includes any person who occupies the position of a director, by whatever name called ;

" excursion or tour " means a stage or express carriage service on which the passengers travel together on a journey, with or without breaks, from one or more places to one or more other places and back ;

" express carriage " has the meaning given by section 3, and " express carriage service " means a service provided by means of one or more express carriages ;

" international operation " means a passenger transport operation starting or terminating in the United Kingdom and involving an international journey by the vehicle concerned, whether or not any driver leaves or enters the United Kingdom with that vehicle ;

" national operation " means a passenger transport operation wholly within the United Kingdom ;

" official PSV testing station " has the meaning given by section 16(3) ;

" operating centre ", in relation to a vehicle, means the base or centre at which the vehicle is normally kept ;

" operator " has the meaning given by subsections (2) and (3) ;

" owner ", in relation to a vehicle which is the subject of an agreement for hire, hire-purchase, conditional sale or loan, means the person in possession of the vehicle under that agreement, and references to owning a vehicle shall be construed accordingly ;

" PSV operator's licence " means a PSV operator's licence granted under the provisions of this Part ;

" public service vehicle " has the meaning given by section 2 ;

" relevant conviction " means a conviction (other than a spent conviction) of any offence prescribed for the purposes of this Part, or of an offence under the law of Northern Ireland, or of a country or territory outside the United Kingdom, corresponding to an offence so prescribed ;

" restricted licence " means such a PSV operator's licence as is mentioned in section 20(3) ;

" road service licence " means a road service licence granted under the provisions of this Part ;

" stage carriage " has the meaning given by section 3, and " stage carriage service " means a service provided by means of one or more stage carriages ;

" standard licence " means a PSV operator's licence which is not a restricted licence ;

" transport manager ", in relation to a business, means an individual who, either alone or jointly with one or more other persons, has continuous and effective responsibility for the management of the road passenger transport operations of the business ;

" trial area " has the meaning given by section 12(1).

(2) For the purposes of this Part—

    (*a*) regulations may make provision as to the person who is to be regarded as the operator of a vehicle which is made available by one holder of a PSV operator's licence to another under a hiring arrangement; and

(b) where regulations under paragraph (a) do not apply, the operator of a vehicle is—

(i) the driver, if he owns the vehicle; and

(ii) in any other case, the person for whom the driver works (whether under a contract of employment or any other description of contract personally to do work).

(3) For the purposes of this Part the operator of a stage or express carriage service is the person, or each of the persons, providing the service; and for those purposes the operator of a vehicle being used as a stage or express carriage shall be taken to be providing the service thereby provided unless he proves that the service is or forms part of a service provided not by himself but by one or more other persons.

(4) Any reference in this Part to a Community instrument or to a particular provision of such an instrument—

(a) is a reference to that instrument or provision as amended from time to time, and

(b) if that instrument or provision is replaced, with or without modification, shall be construed as a reference to the instrument or provision replacing it.

PART II

TRANSFER OF UNDERTAKING OF NATIONAL FREIGHT CORPORATION

Transfer of undertaking of National Freight Corporation to a company limited by shares

Transfer of undertaking of National Freight Corporation.

45.—(1) On the appointed day the whole of the undertaking of the National Freight Corporation (in this Part referred to as " the Corporation ") shall, subject to subsection (4), be transferred by virtue of this section and without further assurance to a company formed for the purposes of this section and nominated under subsection (5) (in this Part referred to as " the successor company ").

(2) In this Part " the appointed day " means such day as the Minister, with the consent of the Treasury, may appoint for the purposes of this section by order made by statutory instrument.

(3) References in this Part to the undertaking of the Corporation are references to all the property, rights, liabilities and obligations of the Corporation, whether or not of such a nature that they could be assigned by the Corporation.

(4) Any entitlement of the Minister and any liability of the Corporation in respect of—

(a) the commencing capital debt of the Corporation; and

(*b*) outstanding loans to the Corporation from the Minister, shall be extinguished immediately before the appointed day.

(5) The Minister may by order made by statutory instrument nominate for the purposes of this section a company formed and registered under the Companies Act 1948 which on the 1948 c. 38. appointed day satisfies the following requirements, that is to say—

(*a*) it is a company limited by shares ; and

(*b*) all the issued shares of the company are held by the Minister or by nominees for him.

(6) This section shall have effect subject to the provisions of Schedule 6, being supplementary provisions with respect to the transfer by virtue of this section of the undertaking of the Corporation to the successor company ; but nothing in those provisions shall be taken as prejudicing the general effect of subsection (1).

46.—(1) In consideration of the transfer of the undertaking of Initial the Corporation to the successor company by virtue of section government 45, the successor company shall issue to the Minister or, if the holding in Minister so directs, to nominees for him such securities of the company. company as the Minister may direct.

(2) Any shares issued in pursuance of subsection (1)—

(*a*) shall be of such nominal value as the Minister may direct ; and

(*b*) shall be credited as fully paid up.

(3) The Minister shall not give any directions for the purposes of this section without the consent of the Treasury.

(4) Securities of the successor company held by the Minister or by nominees for him shall not be disposed of except with the consent of the Treasury and in such manner and on such terms as the Treasury may direct.

(5) Subject to section 49(5), any dividends or other sums received by the Minister, or by nominees for him, in right of, on the disposal of, or otherwise in connection with, any securities of the successor company shall be paid into the Consolidated Fund.

(6) Stamp duty shall not be chargeable under section 47 of the Finance Act 1973 in respect of any increase in the capital of the 1973 c. 51. successor company which is certified by the Treasury as having been—

(*a*) effected for the purpose of complying with the requirements of this section ; or

(*b*) where any convertible securities were issued in pursuance of this section, effected in consequence of the exercise of the conversion rights attached to those securities.

47.—(1) An amount corresponding to any reserves of the Corporation immediately before the appointed day which represent accumulated profits shall be treated by the successor company as reserves of that company applicable for the same purposes as the corresponding reserves of the Corporation.

(2) Nothing in section 56 of the Companies Act 1948 (which requires premiums received on the issue of shares to be transferred to a share premium account) shall affect the operation of subsection (1).

(3) The successor company shall treat the reserves of any company in which the Corporation held shares which were available for distribution immediately before the appointed day as if they had arisen immediately after the appointed day.

(4) Where any dividend is paid to the successor company in respect of shares transferred to the company by virtue of section 45, that dividend shall be available for distribution as profits of the successor company notwithstanding that it is paid out of profits of the company paying the dividend attributable to a period falling wholly or partly before the appointed day.

(5) In ascertaining for the purposes of section 56 of the Companies Act 1948 what amount (if any) falls to be treated as a premium received on the issue of any shares in pursuance of section 46, the amount of the net assets transferred by virtue of section 45 shall be taken to be reduced by an amount corresponding to the amount of any reserve within subsection (1).

Dissolution
and final
accounts of
National
Freight
Corporation.

48.—(1) The Corporation shall cease to exist on the appointed day.

(2) The successor company shall prepare a statement of the Corporation's accounts for the period from the end of that dealt with in the last annual statement of accounts published by the Corporation down to the appointed day (in the following provisions of this section referred to as " the final period ").

(3) The statement shall be in such form and contain such particulars, compiled in such manner, as the Minister may direct with the approval of the Treasury.

(4) The successor company shall arrange for the accounts of the Corporation for the final period to be audited by auditors appointed by the Minister ; and a person shall not be qualified to be so appointed unless he is a member of, or is a Scottish firm in which all the partners are members of, one or more bodies of accountants established in the United Kingdom and for the time being recognised by the Secretary of State for the purposes of section 161(1)(a) of the Companies Act 1948.

(5) As soon as the accounts for the final period have been audited, the successor company shall send to the Minister a copy

of the statement of accounts for that period together with a copy of the auditors' report on that statement; and the Minister shall lay a copy of the statement and report before each House of Parliament.

Funding of certain pension obligations

49.—(1) If it appears to the Minister, having determined that all or any of the securities of the successor company held by him or by nominees for him should be offered for sale, that on the date on which those securities are to be so offered the relevant pension obligations will not be completely funded, he may, with the consent of the Treasury, undertake to make to the persons administering the relevant pension schemes such payments towards the funding of those obligations as he may specify in the undertaking.

(2) An undertaking under subsection (1)—

    (*a*) shall specify the aggregate amount of the payments which the Minister proposes to make in pursuance of the undertaking; and

    (*b*) shall be conditional on the amount received by the Minister in consideration for the disposal of the securities being not less than that amount.

(3) If the Minister gives an undertaking under subsection (1) but the condition mentioned in subsection (2) is not fulfilled, he may nevertheless, with the consent of the Treasury, make to the persons administering the relevant pension schemes such payments towards the funding of the relevant pension obligations as he thinks fit.

(4) If no undertaking is given under subsection (1) but it appears to the Minister that, on the date on which all or any of the securities of the successor company held by him or by nominees for him are offered for sale, the relevant pension obligations are not completely funded, he may, with the consent of the Treasury, make to the persons administering the relevant pension schemes such payments towards the funding of those obligations as he thinks fit.

(5) The aggregate amount of any payments made under subsection (3) or (4) shall not exceed the amount received in consideration for the disposal of the securities of the successor company; and the sums required for making any such payments or any payments in pursuance of an undertaking under subsection (1) shall be paid out of that amount.

(6) In this section—

    " the relevant pension obligations " has the meaning given by section 50;

    " the relevant pension schemes " means the National Freight Corporation (Salaried Staff) Pension Fund, the National

Freight Corporation (Wages Grades) Pension Fund and the N.F.C. (1978) Pension Fund ;

and for the purposes of this section the N.F.C. (1978) Pension Fund shall be taken to comprise the pension schemes specified or described in the Schedule to the Central Trust deed within S.I. 1978/1290. the meaning of the National Freight Corporation (Central Trust) Order 1978.

Meaning of "the relevant pension obligations".   **50.**—(1) In section 49 " the relevant pension obligations " means, subject to subsection (2)—

(a) any obligations of the successor company or a relevant subsidiary which were owed on 1st April 1975 (" the operative date ") in connection with any of the relevant pension schemes ; and

(b) where any such obligation is one to pay or secure the payment of pensions, any obligation of the successor company or a relevant subsidiary arising after the operative date to pay or secure the payment of increases of those pensions ; and

(c) any obligation of the successor company or a relevant subsidiary arising after the operative date to pay or secure the payment of increases payable under any of the relevant pension schemes, being increases of pensions payable under any other pension scheme established before that date (whether one of the relevant pension schemes or not) ; and

1962 c. 46.   (d) any obligation of the successor company or a relevant subsidiary which results from an amendment made to any of the relevant pension schemes by virtue of section 74 of the Transport Act 1962 after the operative date and before 1st January 1980.

(2) The definition in subsection (1) does not include—

(a) any obligation which, in relation to one of the relevant pension schemes, is a relevant pension obligation for the purposes of Part III ;

(b) any obligation to pay or secure the payment of increases of pensions in excess of increases payable on official 1971 c. 56.   pensions under the Pensions (Increase) Act 1971 and 1975 c. 60.   section 59 of the Social Security Pensions Act 1975 ;

(c) any obligation to pay contributions in respect of current periods of employment of a member of a scheme ;

(d) any obligation to pay expenses incurred in connection with a scheme which is specifically imposed on the body by which it is owed ;

(e) any obligation owed by a body in their capacity as the trustees of a scheme or the persons administering a scheme ; and

(f) any obligation in respect of which the body by which it is owed have a right to be indemnified by any other body.

(3) In this section—

" pension ", in relation to any of the relevant pension schemes, has the same meaning as in Part III ;

" the relevant pension schemes " has the same meaning as in section 49 ;

" relevant subsidiary " means any subsidiary of the successor company other than National Carriers Limited and any subsidiary of National Carriers Limited ;

" sudbsidiary " has the same meaning as in the Transport Act 1962. 1962 c. 46.

(4) For the purposes of this section—

(a) any increase in an obligation which results from an amendment made to a scheme after the operative date shall be treated as a separate obligation ; and

(b) where at any time, whether before or after the operative date, any pensions or increases payable under any of the relevant pension schemes are or have been paid by any person, that person shall be treated as being or having been under an obligation at that time to make those payments.

Supplementary

51.—(1) In this Part—   Interpretation of Part II and consequential amendments.

" the appointed day " has the meaning given by section 45(2) ;

" the Corporation " has the meaning given by section 45(1) ;

" securities " of the successor company includes shares, debentures, debenture stock, bonds and other securities of the company, whether or not constituting a charge on the assets of the company ;

" shares " includes stock ;

" the successor company " has the meaning given by section 45(1) ;

and references to the undertaking of the Corporation shall be construed in accordance with section 45(3).

(2) The enactments mentioned in Schedule 7 shall have effect subject to the amendments there specified, being amendments consequential on the provisions of this Part.

Payments by
Minister in
respect of
B.R. and
N.F.C.
pension
schemes.

PART III
RAILWAY ETC. PENSIONS

52.—(1) Subject to the provisions of this section and section 58, the Minister shall, in relation to each B.R. or N.F.C. pension scheme and for each financial year, make to the persons administering the scheme payments equal in aggregate to the product of—

(a) the proportion determined under section 54(1) as the proportion of the relevant pension obligations which has not been funded ;

(b) the proportion determined in relation to that year under section 55(1) as the proportion of the pensions, increases and expenses payable under or incurred in connection with the scheme which corresponds to those obligations ; and

(c) the aggregate amount of the pensions, increases and expenses payable under or incurred in connection with the scheme for that year.

(2) Where in the case of any such scheme the funding of the relevant pension obligations has, by virtue of subsection (3) of section 54, been left out of account in making a determination under subsection (1) of that section, the aggregate amount of the payments made under subsection (1) to the persons administering the scheme shall be reduced for each financial year—

(a) by the amount of any income accruing to the scheme for that year which may be applied towards the payment of such of the pensions, increases and expenses payable under or incurred in connection with the scheme as correspond to the obligations ; and

(b) in the case of the first financial year, by an amount equal to the value of the assets by which the obligations are funded.

(3) Where, for any financial year, the aggregate amount of the payments made under subsection (1) to the persons administering any such scheme requires adjustment by reason of—

(a) any variation between the proportion finally determined under section 55(1) in relation to that year and the proportion previously so determined ; or

(b) any unforeseen increase or reduction in the aggregate amount of the pensions, increases and expenses payable under or incurred in connection with the scheme for that year,

that adjustment shall be made by increasing or, as the case may require, reducing the aggregate amount of the payments made under subsection (1) for the following financial year.

(4) Payments under subsection (1) shall be made, so far as practicable, not later than the day on which the pensions,

increases and expenses to which they relate fall to be paid or incurred.

(5) The making of any payment under subsection (1) shall be subject to compliance with such conditions as to the keeping of records, the issue of certificates and the auditing of accounts as the Minister may with the approval of the Treasury determine.

(6) Any sums required for making payments under subsection (1) shall be paid out of money provided by Parliament.

53.—(1) In this Part " the relevant pension obligations ", in relation to a B.R. pension scheme, means subject to subsection (3)— Meaning of " the relevant pension obligations ".

(a) any obligations of the Board which were owed on 1st January 1975 (" the operative date ") in connection with the scheme ; and

(b) where any such obligation is one to pay or secure the payment of pensions, any obligation of the Board arising after the operative date to pay or secure the payment of increases of or sums representing accrued rights in respect of those pensions ; and

(c) any obligation of the Board arising after the operative date to pay or secure the payment of increases payable under the scheme, being increases of pensions payable under any other pension scheme established before that date (whether a B.R. pension scheme or not).

(2) In this Part " the relevant pension obligations ", in relation to an N.F.C. pension scheme, means subject to subsection (3)—

(a) any obligations of the successor company or a relevant subsidiary which were owed on 1st April 1975 (" the operative date ") in connection with the scheme ; and

(b) where any such obligation is one to pay or secure the payment of pensions, any obligation of the successor company or a relevant subsidiary arising after the operative date to pay or secure the payment of increases of or sums representing accrued rights in respect of those pensions ; and

(c) any obligation of the successor company or a relevant subsidiary arising after the operative date to pay or secure the payment of increases payable under the scheme, being increases of pensions payable under any other pension scheme established before that date (whether an N.F.C. pension scheme or not) ; and

(d) any obligation of the successor company or a relevant subsidiary which results from an amendment made to the scheme by virtue of section 74 of the Transport Act 1962 after the operative date and before 1st January 1980, 1962 c. 46.

PART III

being (in each case) obligations which relate to employees or former employees of a relevant subsidiary or employees or former employees of the successor company or the Corporation who are or were employed as directors or managers of a relevant subsidiary.

(3) The definitions in subsections (1) and (2) do not include—

1971 c. 56.
1975 c. 60.

(a) any obligation to pay or secure the payment of increases of pensions in excess of increases payable on official pensions under the Pensions (Increase) Act 1971 and section 59 of the Social Security Pensions Act 1975;

(b) any obligation to pay contributions in respect of current periods of employment of a member of a scheme;

(c) any obligation to pay expenses incurred in connection with the management of a scheme which is specifically imposed on the body by which it is owed;

(d) any obligation owed by a body in their capacity as the trustees of a scheme or the persons administering a scheme; and

(e) subject to subsection (4), any obligation in respect of which the body by which it is owed have a right to be indemnified by any other body.

(4) Subsection (3)(e) does not apply—

(a) in the case of an obligation owed by the Board, where the Board has a right to be indemnified by the successor company;

(b) in the case of an obligation owed by the successor company, where the successor company has a right to be indemnified by a relevant subsidiary;

(c) in the case of an obligation owed by the successor company, where the successor company has a right to be indemnified by the Board and the obligation relates to employees or former employees of Freightliners Limited or employees or former employees of the successor company or the Corporation who are or were employed as directors or managers of Freightliners Limited;

(d) in the case of an obligation owed by a relevant subsidiary, where that subsidiary has a right to be indemnified by the successor company or by another relevant subsidiary; and

(e) in the case of an obligation owed by Freightliners Limited, where Freightliners Limited has a right to be indemnified by the Board.

(5) In this section "relevant subsidiary" means National Carriers Limited, Freightliners Limited and any subsidiary of National Carriers Limited.

(6) For the purposes of this section—

(a) any increase in an obligation which results from an amendment made to a scheme after the operative date shall be treated as a separate obligation ; and

(b) where at any time, whether before or after the operative date, any pensions or increases payable under a B.R. or N.F.C. pension scheme are or have been paid by any person, that person shall be treated as being or as having been under an obligation at that time to make those payments.

54.—(1) The Minister shall, in relation to each B.R. or N.F.C. pension scheme—

(a) determine, as soon as practicable after the passing of this Act, what proportion of the relevant pension obligations has not been funded ; and

(b) after consulting with the persons administering the scheme and the Board or, as the case may be, the successor company, confirm or vary that determination, before the end of the first financial year, by a further determination of that proportion contained in an order.

Unfunded proportion of relevant pension obligations.

(2) Where at the time when a determination under subsection (1) falls to be made any class of the relevant pension obligations appear to be completely funded, that class of obligations and their funding may, if the Minister thinks fit, be left out of account in making that determination.

(3) Where at the time when a determination under subsection (1) falls to be made the assets by which the relevant pension obligations are funded appear to be insufficient to meet such of the pensions, increases and expenses payable under or incurred in connection with the scheme for the first financial year as correspond to those obligations, that funding may, if the Minister thinks fit, be left out of account in making that determination.

(4) An order under subsection (1)—

(a) shall be made by statutory instrument which shall be subject to annulment in pursuance of a resolution of the Commons House of Parliament ; and

(b) may be varied or revoked by a subsequent order made before the end of the first financial year.

(5) References in subsection (1) to a determination or further determination made by the Minister shall include references to a determination or further determination made by the actuary to the scheme and approved by the Minister.

55.—(1) The Minister shall, in relation to each B.R. or N.F.C. pension scheme and for each financial year—

(a) determine, before the beginning of the year or, in the case of the first financial year, as soon as practicable

Proportion of pensions etc. which corresponds to relevant pension obligations.

after the passing of this Act, what proportion of the pensions, increases and expenses payable under or incurred in connection with the scheme corresponds to the relevant pension obligations; and

(b) confirm or vary that determination, from time to time during the year and as soon as practicable after the end of the year, by a further determination of that proportion.

(2) Where in the case of any such scheme any class of the relevant pension obligations and their funding have, by virtue of subsection (2) of section 54, been left out of account in making a determination under subsection (1) of that section, that class of obligations shall not be regarded as relevant pension obligations for the purposes of any determination under subsection (1).

(3) References in subsection (1) to a determination or further determination made by the Minister shall include references to a determination or further determination made by the actuary or auditor to the scheme and approved by the Minister.

Reduction of payments in respect of certain supplementation schemes.

56.—(1) This section applies where, in relation to a B.R. or N.F.C. pension scheme (" the supplementation scheme "), the relevant pension obligations include obligations arising after the passing of this Act to pay or secure the payment of increases of pensions payable under any other pension scheme, being a scheme established by the Board or the Corporation (" the basic scheme ").

(2) If the actuary to the basic scheme certifies that the assets of that scheme exceed its liabilities, then, in relation to the supplementation scheme, any obligation arising after the date of the actuary's certificate to pay or secure the payment of any increases of pensions payable under the basic scheme or, if less, the relevant proportion of any such increases shall not be regarded as a relevant pension obligation for the purposes of any determination under section 55(1).

(3) In subsection (2) " the relevant proportion ", in relation to any increases, means, subject to subsection (4), the proportion (if any) certified by the actuary to the basic scheme to be the proportion of those increases which, if payable under that scheme, could be funded by 75 per cent. of the amount by which the assets of that scheme exceed its liabilities.

(4) Where any obligation arising after the date of a certificate under subsection (3) is an obligation to pay or secure the payment of a proportion only of any increases to which the certi-

ficate relates, then, in relation to that obligation, the relevant proportion for the purposes of subsection (2) shall be given by the formula—

$$\frac{A+B-1}{A}$$

where A is the first mentioned proportion and B is the proportion certified by the actuary.

(5) The Minister may direct the persons administering the basic scheme—

(a) to arrange for the actuary to the scheme to certify whether or not the assets of the scheme exceed its liabilities ; and

(b) to send a copy of the actuary's certificate to the Minister ;

but no direction shall be given under this subsection within the period of three years beginning with the giving by the actuary of such a certificate.

(6) References in this section to the assets and liabilities of the basic scheme are references to the assets and liabilities of that scheme so far as it relates to the payment of pensions increases of which are or are likely to become payable under the supplementation scheme.

57. Where the whole or any part of a person's accrued pension rights under a B.R. or N.F.C. pension scheme are transferred to any other pension scheme, being a scheme established by the Board or the successor company or any subsidiary of either of those bodies, the Minister may direct that for the purposes of—

(a) any determination of the aggregate amount of the pensions, increases and expenses payable under or incurred in connection with the first-mentioned scheme ; and

(b) any determination under section 55(1) in relation to that scheme,

it shall be assumed that the said rights had not been transferred and that the payment of any sum representing those rights had not been made.

Exclusion of payments in respect of certain transfer values.

58.—(1) In consequence of the foregoing provisions of this Part—

(a) the debts owed by the Board by virtue of sections 5 and 6 of the Railways Act 1974 (funding of the relevant pension obligations of the Board) ; and

(b) the debts owed by the Corporation by virtue of sections 19 and 20 of the Transport Act 1978 (funding of the

Consequential cancellation of debts owed by Board and Corporation.

1974 c. 48.

1978 c. 55.

relevant pension obligations of the Corporation),
are hereby cancelled and those sections are hereby repealed.

(2) Any payments in respect of the principal of or interest on
any such debt—

    (a) which are made on or after 1st April 1980 and before
the passing of this Act to the persons administering a
scheme to which this subsection applies ; and

    (b) in respect of which the Minister reimburses the Board
or, as the case may be, the Corporation,

shall be deemed to be payments made to those persons in
advance under section 52(1), and any money which is deemed
to be money so paid, and any investments representing any such
money, shall be left out of account in making any determination
under section 54(1).

(3) Subsection (2) applies to any B.R. or N.F.C. pension
scheme other than one in the case of which the relevant pension
obligations have been completely funded.

(4) The Minister may discharge his liability to make any payment under section 52(1) to the persons administering a scheme
to which subsection (2) applies by appropriating to that payment
so much of any money which is deemed to be money paid to
those persons in advance under section 52(1) as, with the appropriate interest thereon, is equal to the amount of that payment.

(5) Any money which is deemed to be money paid in advance
under section 52(1) shall carry interest for the period beginning
with the date on which it was paid to the persons administering
the scheme and ending with the date on which it is appropriated
by the Minister at such rate as the Minister may with the
consent of the Treasury determine.

Supplemental
provisions.

59.—(1) The making of any payment under section 52(1) to
the persons administering any B.R. or N.F.C. pension scheme
shall not discharge any relevant pension obligation so far as it is
an obligation to pay pensions or increases of pensions under the
scheme or is an obligation to secure the payment of those
pensions or increases.

(2) If the persons administering any such scheme or any other
pension scheme established by the Board or the Corporation
have no power to amend the scheme apart from this subsection,
they may amend it by instrument in writing for the purpose of—

    (a) enabling them to pay increases of any pensions payable
under the scheme ; or

    (b) bringing the scheme into conformity with any provision
of this Part ;

and the power of amending any such scheme apart from this sub-section may for either purpose be exercised without regard to any limitations on the exercise of the power and without compliance with any procedural provisions applicable to its exercise.

60.—(1) In this Part— Interpretation of Part III.

" the Board " means the British Railways Board ;

" B.R. pension scheme " means any section of the British Railways Superannuation Fund specified in Schedule 8 or any other pension scheme so specified ;

" the Corporation " means the National Freight Corporation ;

" first financial year ", in relation to a B.R. or N.F.C. pension scheme, means such period as—

    (*a*) begins on 1st April 1980 ; and

    (*b*) ends with the last day of an accounting year of the scheme,

and is a period of not less than twelve months and less than two years, and " financial year ", in relation to any such scheme, means that period and each successive accounting year of the scheme ;

" N.F.C. pension scheme " means the National Freight Corporation (Salaried Staff) Pension Fund, the National Freight Corporation (Wages Grades) Pension Fund or the N.F.C. (1978) Pension Fund ;

" pension ", in relation to a B.R. or N.F.C. pension scheme, means any pension, whether contributory or not, payable under the scheme to or in respect of any person and includes—

    (*a*) a gratuity or lump sum so payable ;

    (*b*) a return of contributions to the scheme, with or without interest thereon or any other addition thereto ;

    (*c*) any sum payable under the scheme on or in respect of the death of any person ; and

    (*d*) any sum payable under the scheme in respect of any person and representing the whole or any part of his accrued pension rights under the scheme ;

" the relevant pension obligations " has the meaning given by section 53 ;

" subsidiary " has the same meaning as in the Transport 1962 c. 46 Act 1962 ;

" the successor company " has the same meaning as in Part II.

(2) For the purposes of this Part—

    (*a*) the B.R. (1974) Pension Fund shall be taken to comprise the pension schemes specified or described in the

PART III
S.I. 1974/2001.

Schedule to the Central Trust deed within the meaning of the British Railways (Central Trust) Order 1974 ; and

S.I. 1978/1290.

(b) the N.F.C. (1978) Pension Fund shall be taken to comprise the pension schemes specified or described in the Schedule to the Central Trust deed within the meaning of the National Freight Corporation (Central Trust) Order 1978.

S.I. 1962/2758.

(3) References in this Part to any pension scheme established by the Board include references to any scheme in relation to which the rights, liabilities and functions of the British Transport Commission were transferred to the Board by the British Transport Reorganisation (Pensions of Employees) (No. 3) Order 1962.

(4) In relation to any time before the day appointed by the Minister for the purposes of Part II, references in this Part to the successor company shall be construed as references to the Corporation.

PART IV

MISCELLANEOUS AND GENERAL

Insurance
or security
in respect of
private use of
vehicle to
cover use
under
car-sharing
arrangements.
1972 c. 20.

61. At the end of section 148 of the Road Traffic Act 1972 (avoidance of certain exceptions to policies or securities, etc.) there shall be added the following subsections—

" (5) To the extent that a policy or security issued or given for the purposes of this Part of this Act—

(a) restricts, as the case may be, the insurance of the persons insured by the policy or the operation of the security to use of the vehicle for specified purposes (for example, social, domestic and pleasure purposes) of a non-commercial character ; or

(b) excludes from, as the case may be, that insurance or the operation of the security—

(i) use of the vehicle for hire or reward ; or

(ii) business or commercial use of the vehicle ; or

(iii) use of the vehicle for specified purposes of a business or commercial character,

then, for the purposes of that policy or security so far as it relates to such liabilities as are required to be covered by a policy under section 145 of this Act, the use of a vehicle on a journey in the course of which one or more passengers are carried at separate fares shall, if the conditions specified in subsection (6) below are satisfied, be treated as falling within that restriction or as not falling within that exclusion, as the case may be.

(6) The conditions referred to in subsection (5) above PART IV
are—

(a) the vehicle is not adapted to carry more than eight
passengers and is not a motor cycle ;

(b) the fare or aggregate of the fares paid in respect of
the journey does not exceed the amount of the
running costs of the vehicle for the journey (which
for the purposes of this paragraph shall be taken
to include an appropriate amount in respect of
depreciation and general wear) ; and

(c) the arrangements for the payment of fares by the
passenger or passengers carried at separate fares
were made before the journey began.

(7) Subsections (5) and (6) above apply however the
restrictions or exclusions described in subsection (5) are
framed or worded ; and in those subsections " fare " and
" separate fares " have the same meaning as in section 2(4)
of the Transport Act 1980.".

62.—(1) In subsection (8) of section 92 of the Finance Act Grants
1965 (grants towards duty charged on bus fuel), for the definition towards duty
of " bus service " there shall be substituted— charged on
bus fuel, and
" " bus service " means a stage carriage service within the new bus
meaning of Part I of the Transport Act 1980 which grants.
is available to the general public and is neither an 1965 c. 25.
excursion or tour within the meaning of that Part nor
a service as regards which the condition specified in
section 3(3)(a) of that Act (long journeys only) is
satisfied ; ".

(2) In section 32 of the Transport Act 1968 (new bus grants)— 1968 c. 73.

(a) in subsection (1), for the words " wholly or mainly as a
stage carriage " there shall be substituted the words
" wholly or mainly in the operation of bus services " ;
and

(b) in subsection (2), after paragraph (c) there shall be
inserted—

" (d) " bus service " has the same meaning as in
section 92 of the Finance Act 1965 ".

63. For section 191 of the Road Traffic Act 1972 (certain Articulated
articulated vehicles to be treated for the purposes of that Act as vehicles.
a motor vehicle with a trailer attached) there shall be 1972 c. 20.
substituted—

" 191.—(1) Unless it falls within subsection (2) below,
a vehicle so constructed that it can be divided into two
parts both of which are vehicles and one of which is a motor

vehicle shall (when not so divided) be treated for the purposes of the enactments mentioned in subsection (3) below as that motor vehicle with the other part attached as a trailer.

(2) A passenger vehicle so constructed that—

    (*a*) it can be divided into two parts, both of which are vehicles and one of which is a motor vehicle, but cannot be so divided without the use of facilities normally available only at a workshop ; and

    (*b*) passengers carried by it when not so divided can at all times pass from either part to the other,

shall (when not so divided) be treated for the purposes of the enactments mentioned in subsection (3) below as a single motor vehicle.

1960 c. 16.
1967 c. 76.

(3) The enactments referred to in subsections (1) and (2) above are the Road Traffic Act 1960, the Road Traffic Regulation Act 1967, this Act and Part I of the Transport Act 1980.

(4) In this section " passenger vehicle " means a vehicle constructed or adapted for use solely or principally for the carriage of passengers.".

Roof-signs on vehicles other than taxis.

64.—(1) There shall not, in any part of England and Wales outside the metropolitan police district and the City of London, be displayed on or above the roof of any vehicle which is used for carrying passengers for hire or reward but which is not a taxi—

    (*a*) any sign which consists of or includes the word " taxi " or " cab ", whether in the singular or plural, or " hire ", or any word of similar meaning or appearance to any of those words, whether alone or as part of another word ; or

    (*b*) any sign, notice, mark, illumination or other feature which may suggest that the vehicle is a taxi.

(2) Any person who knowingly—

    (*a*) drives a vehicle in respect of which subsection (1) is contravened ; or

    (*b*) causes or permits that subsection to be contravened in respect of any vehicle,

shall be liable on summary conviction to a fine not exceeding £200.

1847 c. 89.
1869 c. 115.
1892 c. 55.

(3) In this section " taxi " means a vehicle licensed under section 37 of the Town Police Clauses Act 1847, section 6 of the Metropolitan Carriage Act 1869, section 270 of the Burgh Police (Scotland) Act 1892 or any similar local enactment.

65. The provisions of section 2 of, and Schedule 1 to, the Transport Charges &c. (Miscellaneous Provisions) Act 1954 (which relate to charges on independent tramways, trolley vehicles and railways of the nature of a tramway), including those provisions as extended or applied by or under any other Act (including a local or private Act), shall cease to have effect.

PART IV
Repeal of s. 2
of 1954 c. 64.

66.—(1) The Freight Integration Council established under section 6 of the Transport Act 1968 is hereby abolished.

(2) The provisions of Part V of the Transport Act 1968 relating to special authorisations for the use of large goods vehicles (which have not been brought into force) are hereby repealed, and accordingly—

    (a) in section 82(1)(b) of that Act, for " either of those sections " there shall be substituted " that section " ; and

    (b) in section 91(1)(a) of that Act, for " sections 69 and 79 " there shall be substituted " section 69 ".

Abolition
of Freight
Integration
Council and
repeal of
certain
provisions
about special
authorisations
for use of
large goods
vehicles.
1968 c. 73.

67. The Railways and Coastal Shipping Committee established under section 150 of the Transport Act 1968 is hereby abolished.

Abolition of
Railways and
Coastal
Shipping
Committee.

68. There shall be paid out of money provided by Parliament—

    (a) any administrative expenses incurred by any government department in consequence of the provisions of this Act ; and

    (b) any increase attributable to this Act in the sums payable out of money so provided under any other Act.

Expenses.

69. The enactments mentioned in Schedule 9 (which include spent enactments) are hereby repealed to the extent specified in the third column of that Schedule.

Repeals.

70.—(1) This Act may be cited as the Transport Act 1980.

(2) In this Act—

    " the Minister " means the Minister of Transport ;

    " modification " includes addition, omission and alteration, and related expressions shall be construed accordingly ;

    " statutory provision " means a provision contained in an Act or in subordinate legislation within the meaning of the Interpretation Act 1978.

Citation, etc.

1978 c. 30.

PART IV   (3) The following provisions of this Act, namely—

(a) Part II, except section 51(2) and Schedule 7 ;

(b) Part III ;

(c) sections 66 to 68 and this section ;

(d) Part II of Schedule 9 (and section 69 so far as it relates to that Part),

shall come into force on the passing of this Act.

(4) The following provisions of this Act, namely—

(a) section 51(2) and Schedule 7 ; and

(b) Part III of Schedule 9 (and section 69 so far as it relates to that Part),

shall come into force on the appointed day within the meaning of Part II of this Act.

(5) Subject to subsections (3) and (4), this Act shall come into force on such day as the Minister may by order made by statutory instrument appoint, and different days may be appointed under this subsection for different purposes.

(6) An order under subsection (5) may contain such transitional provisions and savings (whether or not involving the modification of any statutory provision) as appear to the Minister necessary or expedient in connection with the provisions thereby brought (wholly or partly) into force.

(7) The following provisions of this Act do not extend to Northern Ireland, namely,—

(a) Part I (which includes Schedules 1 to 5) ;

(b) sections 61 to 65 and 66(2) ; and

(c) Parts I and IV of Schedule 9 (and section 69 so far as it relates to those Parts).

SCHEDULES

SCHEDULE 1

Sections 2 and 3.

PUBLIC SERVICE VEHICLES: CONDITIONS AFFECTING STATUS OR CLASSIFICATION

PART I

SHARING OF TAXIS AND HIRE-CARS

1. The making of the agreement for the payment of separate fares must not have been initiated by the driver or by the owner of the vehicle, by any person who has made the vehicle available under any arrangement, or by any person who receives any remuneration in respect of the arrangements for the journey.

2.—(1) The journey must be made without previous advertisement to the public of facilities for its being made by passengers to be carried at separate fares, except where the local authorities concerned have approved the arrangements under which the journey is made as designed to meet the social and welfare needs of one or more communities, and their approvals remain in force.

(2) In relation to a journey the local authorities concerned for the purposes of this paragraph are those in whose area any part of the journey is to be made; and in this sub-paragraph " local authority " means—

(a) in relation to England and Wales, the Greater London Council or a county council;

(b) in relation to Scotland, a regional or islands council.

3. The journey must not be made in conjunction with, or in extension of, a service provided under a road service licence if the vehicle is owned by, or made available under any arrangement with, the holder of the licence or any person who receives any remuneration in respect of the service provided under it or in respect of arrangements for that service.

PART II

PARTIES OF OVERSEAS VISITORS

4. Each of the passengers making the journey must have been outside Great Britain at the time of concluding his arrangements to make the journey.

PART III

ALTERNATIVE CONDITIONS AFFECTING STATUS OR CLASSIFICATION

5. Arrangements for the bringing together of all the passengers for the purpose of making the journey must have been made otherwise than by, or by a person acting on behalf of—

(a) the holder of the operator's licence under which the vehicle is to be used, if such a licence is in force,

SCH. 1

(*b*) the driver or the owner of the vehicle or any person who has made the vehicle available under any arrangement, if no such licence is in force,

and otherwise than by any person who receives any remuneration in respect of the arrangements.

6. The journey must be made without previous advertisement to the public of the arrangements therefor.

7. All the passengers must, in the case of a journey to a particular destination, be carried to, or to the vicinity of, that destination, or, in the case of a tour, be carried for the greater part of the journey.

8. No differentiation of fares for the journey on the basis of distance or of time must be made.

PART IV

SUPPLEMENTARY

9. For the purposes of paragraphs 2 and 6 no account shall be taken of any such advertisement as follows, that is to say—

(*a*) a notice displayed or announcement made—

(i) at or in any place of worship for the information of persons attending that place of worship;

(ii) at or in any place of work for the information of persons who work there; or

(iii) by any club or other voluntary association at or in any premises occupied or used by the club or association;

(*b*) a notice or announcement contained in any periodical published for the information of, and circulating wholly or mainly among—

(i) persons who attend or might reasonably be expected to attend a particular place of worship or a place of worship in a particular place; or

(ii) persons who work at a particular place of work or at any of two or more particular places of work; or

(iii) the members of a club or other voluntary association.

Section 12.

SCHEDULE 2

ORDERS DESIGNATING TRIAL AREAS

Applications for designation orders

1.—(1) Not less than 21 days before making an application to the Minister for a designation order in respect of any area the local authority concerned shall publish in one or more relevant newspapers a notice describing the area in question and stating their intention to apply for a designation order in respect of it and the date on which they propose to make the application.

(2) For the purposes of any notice under this paragraph a "relevant newspaper" is any local newspaper which the local authority concerned may consider appropriate.

2.—(1) Before making such an application the local authority concerned shall also notify—

(a) every local authority (if any) whose area adjoins the area specified in the application ;

(b) every district council whose area is wholly or partly comprised in, or adjoins, the area so specified ;

(c) any person who is already providing a stage carriage service in the area so specified ; and

(d) such organisations as appear to the local authority concerned appropriate as representing persons providing or employed in the provision of public passenger transport services in the area so specified.

(2) In this paragraph " public passenger transport services " has the meaning given by section 1(2) of the Transport Act 1978. 1978 c. 55.

3. Every application for a designation order shall be accompanied by the original or a copy of any representations in writing (by whoever made) which relate to the application and were received by the local authority concerned before the date on which the application is made ; and before making a designation order the Minister shall consider any such representations.

Variation or revocation of designation orders

4. Before making an application to the Minister for an order under section 12(4) varying or revoking a designation order the local authority concerned—

(a) shall notify—

(i) every local authority (if any) whose area adjoins the trial area in question ;

(ii) every district council whose area adjoins the trial area ;

(iii) any person who is for the time being providing a stage carriage service in the trial area ; and

(iv) such organisations as appear to the local authority concerned appropriate as representing persons providing or employed in the provision of public passenger transport services (within the meaning of paragraph 2) in the trial area ; and

(b) shall consult with every district council whose area is wholly or partly comprised in the trial area.

5. Paragraph 3 shall apply in relation to an application for, and the making of, an order under section 12(4) as it applies in relation to an application for, and the making of, a designation order.

6.—(1) Subject to sub-paragraph (2), an order under section 12 which revokes or varies a designation order may contain such transitional provisions as the Minister thinks fit.

(2) An order under section 12(4) which revokes a designation order or varies it so as to exclude from the area designated by it any part of that area shall contain such transitional provisions as the Minister thinks fit for securing that any person who has, throughout the relevant period ending with the date of the order, provided a stage carriage service which he will be unable to continue to provide after the time when the revocation or variation takes effect unless granted a road service licence in respect of it, can obtain as of right a road service licence that will enable him to continue to provide that service for as long as the licence remains in force after that time.

(3) In sub-paragraph (2) " the relevant period ", in relation to an order under section 12(4), means such period of not less than three months as may be specified in the order.

SCHEDULE 3

SUPPLEMENTARY PROVISIONS AS TO QUALIFICATIONS FOR PSV OPERATOR'S LICENCE

Good repute

1.—(1) In determining whether an individual is of good repute, traffic commissioners shall have regard to all the relevant evidence and in particular to—

    (*a*) relevant convictions of his and of his employees and agents ; and

    (*b*) such other information as the commissioners may have as to his previous conduct, in whatever capacity, in relation to the operation of vehicles of any description in the course of a business.

(2) In determining whether a company is of good repute, traffic commissioners shall have regard to all the relevant evidence and in particular to—

    (*a*) relevant convictions of the company and its officers, employees and agents ;

    (*b*) such other information as the commissioners may have as to the previous conduct of—

        (i) the company's officers, employees and agents in relation to the operation of vehicles of any description in the course of any business carried on by the company ; and

        (ii) each of the company's directors, in whatever capacity, in relation to the operation of vehicles of any description in the course of any other business.

Appropriate financial standing

2. Being of appropriate financial standing in relation to an applicant for, or holder of, a PSV operator's licence consists in having available sufficient financial resources to ensure the establishment and

proper administration of the business carried on, or proposed to be carried on, under the licence.

Professional competence

3. References in this Part of this Act to professional competence are to the professional competence of an individual ; and a company satisfies the requirement as to professional competence if, and so long as, it has a transport manager of its road passenger transport business who is of good repute and professionally competent.

4. Where an individual is not himself professionally competent, the requirement as to professional competence shall be regarded as satisfied in relation to him if, and so long as, he has a transport manager of his road passenger transport business who is of good repute and professionally competent.

5. Where the holder of a PSV operator's licence relies on a transport manager to satisfy the requirement as to professional competence and that manager—

    (*a*) dies or ceases by reason of physical disability or mental disorder to be capable of discharging his duties as transport manager ;

    (*b*) ceases to work for the business ; or

    (*c*) ceases to be of good repute,

the holder shall nevertheless not be treated as failing to satisfy that requirement until the expiry of such period as in the opinion of the relevant traffic commissioners is reasonably required for the appointment of a new transport manager.

6. Subject to paragraph 10, an individual shall be regarded as professionally competent for the purposes of this Part of this Act if, and only if,—

    (*a*) he is the holder of a certificate issued by an approved body to the effect that he possesses the requisite skills ; or

    (*b*) he is the holder of any other certificate of competence, diploma or other qualification recognised for the purposes of this paragraph by the Minister.

7. In paragraph 6 " approved body " means—

    (*a*) a body approved by the Minister for the purposes of that paragraph ; or

    (*b*) a body approved by the Department of the Environment for Northern Ireland for the purposes of section 46A(5)(*c*) of the Transport Act (Northern Ireland) 1967 ; or 1967 c. 37 (N.I.).

    (*c*) a body or authority designated by another member State for the purposes of Article 2(4) of Council Directive (EEC) 74/562 of 12th November 1974 on admission to the occupation of road passenger transport operator in national and international transport operations ;

and " the requisite skills " means skills in the subjects listed in Part A of the Annex to that Directive and, in the case of a licence to cover international operations, also skills in the subjects listed in Part B of that Annex.

Persons engaged in road passenger transport before 1st January 1978

8.—(1) Paragraphs 9 and 10 apply only to persons applying for, and to holders of, standard licences, and accordingly in those paragraphs " a licence " means a standard licence.

(2) For the purposes of those paragraphs, a person was authorised to engage in the occupation of road passenger transport operator at any time if, and only if, at that time—

  (a) he was the holder, or one of the joint holders, of a public service vehicle licence under section 127 of the Road Traffic Act 1960, or the corresponding provision of the law of Northern Ireland, relating to a vehicle adapted to carry more than eight passengers ; or

  (b) he was by virtue of a permit under Regulation 20 of the Public Service Vehicles (Licences and Certificates) Regulations 1952, or the corresponding provision of the law of Northern Ireland, deemed to be the holder or one of the joint holders of such a licence ; or

  (c) he was so authorised under the law of another member State ; or

  (d) he was the transport manager of a person within paragraph (a), (b) or (c).

9.—(1) An individual or company authorised to engage in the occupation of road passenger transport operator at any time before 1st January 1978 shall be deemed until the contrary is proved to satisfy the requirements to be of good repute and appropriate financial standing and, if so authorised before 1st January 1975, also to satisfy the requirement as to professional competence.

(2) An applicant for a PSV operator's licence, or for the variation of such a licence, shall not be obliged to furnish to the traffic commissioners in support of his application information relating to a requirement which is deemed to be satisfied by virtue of sub-paragraph (1) unless it appears to the commissioners that there are grounds for thinking that the requirement is not in fact satisfied.

10. For the purpose of this Part of this Act, an individual shall be regarded as professionally competent if he was authorised to engage in the occupation of road passenger transport operator before 1st January 1978, and was so authorised—

  (a) for a period of, or for periods amounting in the aggregate to, two years during the period 1st January 1975 to 31st December 1979 ; or

  (b) at any time in the period 1st January 1970 to 31st December 1974.

Section 40.

SCHEDULE 4

Increase of Penalties in the 1960 Act

Provision creating offence	General nature of offence	Existing maximum punishment	New maximum punishment	Amendment
Section 144	Unlicensed person driving public service vehicle, or employment of such a person.	£100	£500	In section 144(8) for "£100" substitute "£500".
Section 146(2)	Contravention of regulations as to conduct of persons licensed to act as drivers of public service vehicles.	£20	£50	In section 146(2) for "£20" substitute "£50".
Section 146(3)	Failure to produce driver's licence for purpose of endorsement.	£100	£200	In section 146(3) for "£100" substitute "£200".
Section 147(2)	Contravention of regulations as to conduct of passengers in public service vehicles.	£100	£200	In section 147(2) for "£100" substitute "£200".
Section 157(2)	Failure by person carrying on the business of operating public service vehicles to keep accounts and records and to make financial and statistical returns.	£100	£200	In section 157(2) for "£100" substitute "£200".
Section 235	Making of false statements.	£200	£500	In section 235(3) for "£200" substitute "£500".
Section 249(2)	Failure to comply with an order requiring evidence to be given or documents to be produced at an inquiry.	£25	£200	In section 249(2) for the words from "to a fine" onwards substitute "to a fine not exceeding £200".

SCHEDULE 5

Minor and Consequential Amendments Relating to Public Service Vehicles

Part I

Amendments of Road Traffic Act 1960 (c.16)

1.—(1) Section 128 (certifying officers and public service vehicle examiners) shall be amended as follows.

(2) In subsection (1) (appointment and duties of certifying officers) before " fitness ", where last occurring, insert " initial ".

(3) In subsection (2) (appointment of public service vehicle examiners), for " shall appoint " substitute " may, with the approval of the Minister for the Civil Service, appoint ".

(4) For subsection (3) substitute—

" (3) A certifying officer or public service vehicle examiner shall, in exercising any of the functions of such an officer or examiner, act under the general directions of the Minister."

2. In section 130 (approval of type vehicles), in subsection (3) (withdrawal of approval), for the words from " and " onwards substitute " and thereafter no certificate that any other vehicle conforms to the type vehicle shall be issued ; but as regards any such certificate previously issued, the withdrawal of the approval shall not affect the operation of that certificate for the purposes of section 17 of the Transport Act 1980 (certificates of initial fitness or their equivalents).".

3.—(1) Section 131 (certificates of fitness for experimental vehicles) shall be amended as follows.

(2) For subsection (1) (and the side-note), substitute—

" Modification of s. 17 of Transport Act 1980 in relation to experimental vehicles.   131.—(1) Where it appears to the Minister expedient to do so for the purpose of the making of tests or trials of a vehicle or its equipment, he may by order made in respect of that vehicle for the purposes of section 17 of the Transport Act 1980 dispense with such of the prescribed conditions as to fitness referred to in subsection (1)(a) of that section as are specified in the order.

(1A) While such an order is in force in respect of a vehicle, the said section 17 shall have effect in relation to the vehicle as if the prescribed conditions as to fitness referred to in subsection (1)(a) of that section did not include such of those conditions as are dispensed with by the order.".

(3) For subsections (4) and (5) substitute—

" (4) Where an order under this section in respect of a vehicle is revoked or otherwise ceases to have effect, any certificate of initial fitness issued under section 17 of the Transport Act 1980 in respect of the vehicle while the order was in force shall, for the purpose of that section as regards any use of the vehicle after the order has ceased to have effect, be deemed never to have been issued.".

4. In section 144 (drivers' licences)—

(*a*) in subsection (3), for " either such " substitute " such a " ;

(*b*) in subsection (6) (duration of licences), for " three years " substitute " five years " ; and

(*c*) after subsection (8) insert—

" (9) Notwithstanding section 2(1) of the Transport Act 1980, in this section and sections 145 to 148 of this Act " public service vehicle " shall be construed as meaning a stage, express or contract carriage.".

5.—(1) Section 146 (regulation of conduct of drivers and conductors) shall be amended as follows.

(2) For subsection (1) (power to make regulations as to conduct of drivers or conductors of public service vehicles) substitute—

" (1) Regulations may make provision for regulating the conduct, when acting as such, of—

(*a*) persons licensed to act as drivers of public service vehicles ; and

(*b*) conductors of such vehicles.".

(3) In subsection (2) (penalty for contravention of regulations), after the words " £20, and " insert ", in the case of an offence by a person acting as driver,".

6.—(1) Section 146 (regulation of conduct of drivers and conductors) and section 147 (regulation of conduct of passengers) shall apply in relation to inspectors as they apply in relation to conductors.

(2) In sub-paragraph (1) " inspector ", in relation to a public service vehicle, means a person authorised to act as such by the holder of the PSV operator's licence under which the vehicle is being used.

(3) In section 147(1)(*d*) the words " or other person authorised by the licensee of the vehicle " shall be omitted.

7. Section 149 (power of Minister to modify restrictions on use of roads by public service vehicles) shall cease to have effect.

8. In section 152 (wages and conditions of employment of persons employed in connection with public service vehicles), for any reference to, or to the holder of, a public service vehicle licence or to the holder of a road service licence there shall be substituted a reference to, or to the holder of, a PSV operator's licence.

9.—(1) Section 153 (procedure of traffic commissioners) shall be amended as follows.

(2) Omit subsection (2) (requirement to hold public sittings for certain purposes).

(3) In subsection (3), for " of an application " substitute " of an opposed application for the grant of a road service licence ", and after " where " insert " such ".

(4) In subsection (4) (power of commissioners to delegate functions to one of their members), for " requiring to be discharged at a

public sitting " substitute " of hearing and determining opposed applications for the grant of road service licences ".

(5) After subsection (4) insert—

" (5) So much of subsection (3) above as requires not less than two commissioners to be present at the hearing of an opposed application for the grant of a road service licence shall not apply—

(*a*) to so much of the hearing of any such application as is devoted to determining whether the commissioners are satisfied as mentioned in section 8(1) or 9(1) of the Transport Act 1980 (grant of road service licences for services on routes not otherwise served, or for certain excursions or tours) ; or

(*b*) to the remainder of the hearing of any such application in the case of which the commissioners have determined that they are so satisfied.

(6) In this section ' opposed application ' means an application with respect to which an objection has been made and not withdrawn, being an objection to which the traffic commissioners are obliged to have regard by virtue of section 5(3)(*c*) of the Transport Act 1980."

10. In section 158 (power to regulate procedure on applications for licences etc.), in paragraph (*a*)—

(*a*) for " public service vehicle licences " substitute " PSV operators' licences " ; and

(*b*) after " road service licences ", in the second place where it occurs, insert " or PSV operators' licences ".

11. In section 160(1) (regulations for purposes of Part III)—

(*a*) in paragraphs (*b*) and (*g*), before " fitness " insert " initial " ;

(*b*) in paragraph (*cc*) for " section 5(6) " substitute " section 5(2) " ;

(*c*) for paragraphs (*k*) to (*n*) substitute—

" (*k*) for providing that this Part of this Act, or any provision thereof, shall have effect in relation to—

(i) public service vehicles registered in Great Britain, while making journeys to or from places outside Great Britain ; and

(ii) public service vehicles registered outside Great Britain,

with such additions, omissions, alterations or other modifications (whether conditional or not) as may be prescribed ;"; and

(*d*) for " and different regulations may be made " substitute " and regulations under this section may make different provision for different circumstances, and may in particular make different provision ".

12. The documents to which section 233 (forgery and misuse of documents, etc.) applies shall include—

(*a*) a certificate of initial fitness under section 17 of this Act ;

(*b*) an operator's disc under section 24 of this Act ;

(c) a certificate under section 27 of this Act as to the repute, financial standing or professional competence of any person ;

(d) a certificate under section 130 of the 1960 Act that a vehicle conforms to a type vehicle ; and

(e) a document evidencing the appointment of a person as a certifying officer or public service vehicle examiner ;

and in section 235 (false statements to obtain licence, etc.) the reference to obtaining the grant of a licence shall include a reference to obtaining the issue of such a certificate or disc.

13. In section 248 (power to hold inquiries) after " the London Government Act 1963 " insert " or section 23A of the Transport (London) Act 1969 ".

14. In section 257(1) (general interpretation), for the words from " and the expressions " onwards substitute " and any expression used in this Part of this Act which is defined for the purposes of Part III of this Act or Part I of the Transport Act 1980 has the same meaning in this Part of this Act as in those Parts.".

15. In section 260(2) (consultation before regulations are made), for " or they think " substitute " thinks ".

PART II

OTHER AMENDMENTS

LOCAL GOVERNMENT (MISCELLANEOUS PROVISIONS) ACT 1953 (c. 26)

In section 4 (power of local authority to provide bus shelters), in subsection (4) (definitions), for the words from " and the references " onwards substitute " and " public service vehicle " has the meaning which it would have in Part I of the Transport Act 1980 if in section 2(1) of that Act the words " (other than a tramcar) " were omitted.".

LOCAL GOVERNMENT (OMNIBUS SHELTERS AND QUEUE BARRIERS) (SCOTLAND) ACT 1958 (c. 50)

In section 7(1) (interpretation), after the definition of " local authority " insert—

" " public service vehicle " has the meaning which it would have in Part I of the Transport Act 1980 if in section 2(1) of that Act the words " (other than a tramcar) " were omitted.".

TRANSPORT ACT 1962 (c. 46)

In section 4(5) (by virtue of which the Railways Board are not authorised to carry passengers by road in certain hackney carriages adapted to carry less than eight passengers), for " eight " substitute " nine ".

FINANCE ACT 1965 (c. 25)

In section 92 (grants towards duty charged on bus fuel), in the definition of " operator " in subsection (8), after paragraph (c) insert—

" (d) if and to the extent that the service operates within a trial area (within the meaning of Part I of the Transport Act 1980), the person by whom the service is provided ; ".

ROAD TRAFFIC REGULATION ACT 1967 (c. 76)

1. So much of subsection (3) of section 1 as prevents a prohibition or restriction on waiting imposed by a traffic regulation order under that section from applying to an express carriage shall cease to have effect.

2. In sections 6(8) and 9(8), for the words from " section 135(8) " to " 1960 " substitute " section 28 of the Transport Act 1980 ".

3. In section 104(1) (interpretation), for the words from " shall be construed " onwards substitute " have the same meaning as in Part I of the Transport Act 1980 ".

4.—(1) Schedule 5 (speed limits for vehicles of certain classes) shall be amended as follows.

(2) In paragraph 1—

    (a) for " 7 passengers ", wherever occurring, substitute " 8 passengers " ;

    (b) in sub-paragraphs (1) and (5), for the words from " in respect " to " force " substitute " while being used under a PSV operator's licence " ; and

    (c) in sub-paragraph (2), for the words from " and " onwards substitute " while being used otherwise than under a PSV operator's licence ".

(3) In paragraph 26, after the definition of " maximum gross weight " insert—

" PSV operator's licence " means a PSV operator's licence granted under Part I of the Transport Act 1980 ; ".

(4) This paragraph does not affect the power to vary Schedule 5 by regulations under section 78.

TRANSPORT ACT 1968 (c. 73)

In section 159(1) (interpretation)—

    (a) for the definition of " excursion or tour " substitute—

        " " excursion or tour " means a stage or express carriage service on which the passengers travel together on a journey, with or without breaks, from one or more places to one or more other places and back ; " ; and

    (b) for the definition of " bus service " substitute—

        " "bus service " means a stage carriage service within the meaning of Part I of the Transport Act 1980 which is neither—

            (a) an excursion or tour ; nor

(*b*) a service as regards which the condition specified in section 3(3)(*a*) of the Transport Act 1980 (long journeys only) is satisfied ; ".

TRANSPORT (LONDON) ACT 1969 (c. 35)

1. In section 23(7) (regulation of London bus services : interpretation) after the definition of " road service licence " insert—

" " service of express carriages" means an express carriage service within the meaning of Part I of the Transport Act 1980 or a stage carriage service within the meaning of that Part as to which the condition in section 3(3)(*a*) of that Act (long journeys only) is satisfied.".

2. In section 24(4)(*c*), for " sections 135(8) and 163(1) " substitute " section 163(1) ".

ROAD TRAFFIC ACT 1972 (c. 20)

In section 44(4) (test certificates: exemption for certain public service vehicles), for " eight " substitute " nine ".

ROAD TRAFFIC (FOREIGN VEHICLES) ACT 1972 (c. 27)

1. In section 4(2)(*b*) (circumstances in which drivers of foreign public service vehicles may be required to produce certain documents)—

(*a*) for " section 127(1) of the Road Traffic Act 1960 " substitute section 19(1) of the Transport Act 1980 " ; and

(*b*) for " brought into Great Britain to carry persons staying there temporarily " substitute " registered outside Great Britain ".

2. In section 7 (interpretation), in the definition of " public service vehicle " for " sections 117 and 118 " substitute " Part III ".

3. In Schedule 1 (enactments conferring functions on examiners), for " Section 128(3) of the Road Traffic Act 1960 " substitute " Section 16(1) of the Transport Act 1980 ".

ROAD TRAFFIC ACT 1974 (c. 50)

An order under section 24(4) of the Road Traffic Act 1974 appointing a day for the coming into operation of the repeal by that Act of section 130 of the 1960 Act may include provision, to take effect on that day, for the repeal of sections 17(1)(*b*) and 28(6)(*b*) of, and paragraphs 2 and 12(*d*) of Part I of Schedule 5 to, this Act.

LOCAL GOVERNMENT (MISCELLANEOUS PROVISIONS) ACT 1976 (c. 57)

1. In section 63(3)(*b*) (hackney carriage stands not to be appointed so as to impede use of authorised stopping places by public service vehicles), for the words from " granted " to " 1968 " substitute " or PSV operator's licence granted under Part I of the Transport Act 1980 ".

2. In section 80(1) (interpretation of Part II)—

(*a*) in the definition of " private hire vehicle ", for " fewer than eight passengers " substitute " fewer than nine passengers " ; and

(*b*) in the definition of " public service vehicle ", for " section 117 " substitute " Part III ".

2 B 2

ENERGY ACT 1976 (c. 76)

In Schedule 1 (permissible relaxations of road traffic and transport law), in paragraph 1(1)—

(a) for " use, or cause or permit the use of," substitute " provide any stage carriage service or use " ;

(b) in paragraph (a), for " permit " substitute " certificate " ;

(c) at the end of paragraph (b) insert " ; and

(c) notwithstanding that any conditions attached to any licence under Part I of the Transport Act 1980 are not complied with ; and

(d) without being obliged to comply with the requirements of section 14 of that Act (duty to publish particulars of stage carriage services in trial areas).".

PASSENGER VEHICLES (EXPERIMENTAL AREAS) ACT 1977 (c. 21)

1. In section 2(8) (authorised vehicle in experimental area not to be regarded as a public service vehicle) at the beginning insert " Subject to subsection (8A) below," and after that subsection insert—

" (8A) Nothing in subsection (8) above shall affect the operation of section 14 of the Transport Act 1980 (duty to publish particulars of stage carriage services in trial areas).".

2. In section 2(9)—

(a) in the definition of " commercial vehicle ", for " not more than five passengers " substitute " not more than eight passengers " ; and

(b) for " section 118(3) of the Road Traffic Act 1960 " substitute " section 2(5) of the Transport Act 1980 ".

3. In the Schedule, in paragraph 14—

(a) after " notice ", in both places where it occurs, insert " or announcement " ; and

(b) for " section 118(3) of the Road Traffic Act 1960 " substitute " paragraph 9 of Schedule 1 to the Transport Act 1980 ".

MINIBUS ACT 1977 (c. 25)

In section 4(2)(c) for the words from " as if " onwards substitute " in accordance with section 2(5) of the Transport Act 1980 ".

TRANSPORT ACT 1978 (c. 55)

1. In section 1(5) (power of non-metropolitan counties to make grants) for paragraph (b) substitute—

" (b) to persons providing facilities for sharing motor vehicles not adapted to carry more than eight passengers with a view to meeting the social and welfare needs of one or more communities.".

2. For subsections (1) to (9) of section 5 (community bus services) substitute the following subsections—

" (1) Where on an application in that behalf the traffic commissioners for any traffic area grant a road service licence under Part I of the Transport Act 1980 in respect of a community bus service—

(*a*) the licence shall state that it is granted in respect of such a service ;

(*b*) the conditions specified in subsection (2) below shall be attached to the licence ; and

(*c*) such provision as is mentioned in subsection (3) below may be included in the licence with respect to the use of the community bus otherwise than in the operation of the community bus service.

(2) The conditions to be attached in every case to a road service licence granted in respect of a community bus service are—

(*a*) that any vehicle used in the course of the service is adapted to carry more than eight but not more than sixteen passengers ;

(*b*) that the driver of any vehicle being used in the course of the service—

(i) is a volunteer ; and

(ii) if not the holder of a public service vehicle driver's licence, fulfils any prescribed conditions for drivers of community buses ;

(*c*) that any vehicle used in the course of the service fulfils the prescribed conditions of fitness for use as a community bus ; and

(*d*) that there is displayed on any vehicle being used in the course of the service such disc or other document issued by the traffic commissioners as may be prescribed for a vehicle used as a community bus ;

and the powers conferred by section 6(3) and (5) of the Transport Act 1980 to alter, remove or dispense from compliance with conditions attached to a road service licence shall not apply to conditions attached under this subsection.

(3) Traffic commissioners on granting a road service licence in respect of a community bus service may, if they are satisfied that in all the circumstances it is reasonable to do so with a view to providing financial support for that service, include in the licence provision authorising the use of the community bus as a contract carriage or as an express carriage (or both), subject to such restrictions (if any) as the commissioners think fit to impose ; and where such provision is included in a licence, the conditions attached under subsection (2) to the licence shall apply to the use of the community bus as a contract carriage or express carriage as they apply to the use of a vehicle in the course of the community bus service.

(4) None of the following provisions, that is to say—

(*a*) section 144 of the Road Traffic Act 1960 (public service vehicle drivers' licences) ;

1960 c. 16.

2 B 3

    (*b*) section 17 of the Transport Act 1980 (certificate of initial fitness, or equivalent, required for use of public service vehicle) ;

    (*c*) section 18 of that Act (power to prohibit driving of unfit public service vehicle) ; and

    (*d*) section 19(1) of that Act (PSV operator's licence required for use of vehicle as stage, express or contract carriage),

shall apply to the driving or use of a vehicle in the course of a community bus service or in the course of its use as a contract carriage or express carriage in accordance with any such provision as is mentioned in subsection (3) above.

(5) Where a community bus service is provided in whole or in part in Greater London, that service or part shall not be regarded as a London bus service within section 23 of the Transport (London) Act 1969 (under which the agreement or consent of the London Transport Executive is required instead of a road service licence) ; but where the traffic commissioners for the Metropolitan Traffic Area propose—

    (*a*) to grant a road service licence in respect of such a service ; or

    (*b*) to vary the conditions attached to such a licence,

they shall consult the London Transport Executive about the proposal.

(6) Subsection (7) of section 4 of the Transport Act 1980 (penalty for breach of condition attached to a road service licence) shall apply in relation to a condition so attached under subsection (2) above as it applies in relation to a condition so attached under section 6 of that Act.

(7) Regulations may provide that, in relation to any community bus service provided in whole or in part within a trial area, the preceding provisions of this section shall have effect with such additions, omissions, alterations or other modifications as may be prescribed.

(8) In this section—

    " community bus service " means a stage carriage service provided—

        (*a*) by a body of persons (whether corporate or unincorporate) concerned for the social and welfare needs of one or more communities ; and

        (*b*) without a view to profit, either on the part of those persons or of anyone else ;

    and in relation to such a service " the community bus " means any vehicle used on a regular basis in the course of the service ;

    " volunteer ", in reference to the driver of a vehicle on any journey, means that he is not paid for driving the vehicle on that journey, disregarding—

        (*a*) any payment of reasonable expenses incurred by him in making himself available to drive ; and

(b) any payment representing earnings lost as a result of making himself available to drive in exceptional circumstances ;

and section 1(3) and (4) of the Transport Act 1980 (construction as one, etc) shall have effect as if references in those subsections to Part I of that Act included a reference to this section.".

3. Section 6 shall be omitted.

4. In section 7(3) (vehicles excluded from regulation as private hire vehicles)—

(a) for the words " section 118 of the 1960 Act " there shall be substituted the words " section 2(3) of the Transport Act 1980 " ;

(b) for the words " no more than 7 passengers " there shall be substituted the words " no more than 8 passengers " ; and

(c) for the words " 8 to 16 seaters " substitute " 9 to 16 seaters ".

SCHEDULE 6

Supplementary Provisions with Respect to Transfer under Section 45

Legal remedies and pending proceedings

1.—(1) Where any right, liability or obligation is transferred to the successor company by virtue of section 45 that company and all other persons shall, on and after the appointed day, have the same rights, powers and remedies (and, in particular, the same rights as to the taking or resisting of legal proceedings) for ascertaining, perfecting or enforcing that right, liability or obligation as they would have had if it had at all times been a right, liability or obligation of that company.

(2) Any legal proceedings by or against the Corporation which relate to any property, right, liability or obligation transferred to the successor company by virtue of section 45 and are pending on the appointed day, may be continued on and after that day by or against that company.

(3) Any reference in sub-paragraph (1) or (2) to legal proceedings shall be construed as including a reference to any application to an authority, and any reference to the taking or resisting of legal proceedings shall be construed accordingly.

Powers of other bodies

2. The transfer to the successor company by virtue of section 45 of the property, rights, liabilities and obligations of the Corporation shall have effect notwithstanding any statutory or other restriction on the powers of any other body affected by the transfer.

Modification of agreements

3. Where immediately before the appointed day there is in force an agreement which confers or imposes on the Corporation any

rights, liabilities or obligations which are transferred to the successor company by virtue of section 45, that agreement shall have effect on and after that day as if—

(a) the successor company had been a party to the agreement; and

(b) for any reference (in whatever terms and whether expressly or by implication) to the Corporation there were substituted, in relation to anything falling to be done on or after that day, a reference to the successor company; and

(c) for any reference (in whatever terms and whether expressly or by implication) to an officer or employee of the Corporation, not being a party to the agreement and beneficially interested therein, there were substituted, in relation to anything falling to be done on or after that day, a reference to such person as the successor company may appoint or, in default of appointment, to the officer or employee of that company who corresponds as nearly as may be to the officer or employee of the Corporation.

Loss of office by members of Corporation

4.—(1) Subject to sub-paragraph (2), no right, liability or obligation under any agreement for the rendering by any person of services to the Corporation as a member of the Corporation shall be transferred by virtue of section 45.

(2) Sub-paragraph (1) does not apply to any liability for remuneration or allowances payable in respect of any period before the appointed day.

(3) If it appears to the Minister that a person who was a member of the Corporation immediately before the appointed day should receive compensation for loss of office, he may, subject to sub-paragraph (4), require the successor company to pay that person such sum as the Minister, with the approval of the Minister for the Civil Service, may determine.

(4) No such requirement as is mentioned in sub-paragraph (3) shall be made after the expiration of the period of three months beginning with the appointed day.

Compensation payments arising from earlier reorganisations

5. The obligations of the Corporation transferred by virtue of section 45 include any obligations of the Corporation to make payments under regulations made under section 135 of the Transport Act 1968 or section 2(4) of the Transport Holding Company Act 1972 (compensation for loss of employment, etc. in consequence of reorganisations under those Acts).

1968 c. 73.
1972 c. 14.

Pensions of former members of the Corporation

6. The obligations of the Corporation transferred by virtue of section 45 include any obligation of the Corporation to comply with a determination of the Minister under paragraph 8(1) of Schedule

1 to the Transport Act 1962 relating to the pension (within the meaning of that Act) payable to or in respect of a former member of the Corporation.

SCH. 6
1962 c. 46.

Pension schemes

7.—(1) Subject to sub-paragraph (2), the provisions of section 74 of the Transport Act 1962 (Minister's powers to make provision about pensions in the nationalised transport industry) shall have effect on and after the appointed day as if—

(a) the expression " Board " included the successor company ; and

(b) the references in subsection (1)(a)(ii) of that section to the Commission included references to the Corporation ; and

(c) the reference in subsection (2)(a) of that section to a pension scheme in which employees of the Commission, or a subsidiary of the Commission, participated before the date there mentioned included a reference to a pension scheme in which employees of, or of a subsidiary of, the Corporation participated before the appointed day.

(2) Except on the application of the successor company, no order shall be made under the said section 74 on or after the appointed day which has the effect of placing the successor company or a subsidiary of the successor company in any worse position ; but for this purpose the successor company or a subsidiary shall not be regarded as being placed in a worse position because an order provides that any changes in a pension scheme are not to be effected without the consent of the Minister.

(3) An order such as is mentioned in sub-paragraph (2) which is made without the application of the successor company shall not be invalid because in fact it does not have the effect of securing that the successor company and its subsidiaries are not placed in any worse position, but except in so far as the successor company approves the effect of the order the Minister shall as soon as may be make the necessary amending order.

(4) Subject to sub-paragraph (6), any order under the said section 74 and any regulations to which paragraph 17 of Schedule 7 to the Transport Act 1962 applies (which continues in force certain earlier pension provisions) which—

(a) are in force immediately before the appointed day ; and

(b) relate to the Corporation, its employees or its pensions schemes,

shall continue in force, subject to any provision made by virtue of sub-paragraph (1), and as respects anything falling to be done on or after the appointed day shall have effect as if for any reference (however worded and whether express or implied) to the Corporation there were substituted a reference to the successor company.

(5) A person who on the appointed day—

(a) ceases to be employed by the Corporation and becomes employed by the successor company ; or

(b) is employed by a company which immediately before the appointed day was a subsidiary of the Corporation but on that day becomes a subsidiary of the successor company,

shall not thereby cease to be eligible to participate in any pension scheme in which he was a participant immediately before the appointed day.

(6) Subject to sub-paragraph (5), a person who on or after the appointed day leaves or enters the employment of the group consisting of the successor company and its subsidiaries (in this sub-paragraph referred to as " the NFC group ") shall not be eligible by virtue of any provision of an order under the said section 74 made before that day—

    (a) to participate in any of the Corporation's pension schemes by reason of any employment outside the NFC group; or

    (b) to participate in a pension scheme other than one of the Corporation's pension schemes by reason of his employment within the NFC group.

(7) In this paragraph—

    (a) " participant ", in relation to a pension scheme, means—

        (i) in relation to a scheme under which benefits are or will be receivable as of right, a person who has pension rights under the scheme (whether he has contributed or not) ; and

        (ii) in relation to a scheme under which benefits are not or will not be receivable as of right, a person who (whether he is referred to in the scheme as a member, as a contributor or otherwise) has contributed under the scheme and has pension rights thereunder ;

    and " participate " and " eligible to participate " shall be construed accordingly ;

    (b) " pension ", " pension rights " and " pension scheme " have the same meaning as in section 74 of the Transport Act 1962 ; and

    (c) references to the Corporation's pension schemes are to schemes established by the Corporation or in relation to which the rights, liabilities and functions of the Transport Holding Company were transferred to the Corporation by the British Transport (Pensions of Employees) (No. 1) Order 1968.

1962 c. 46.

S.I. 1968/2011.

Grants in respect of certain capital expenditure

8.—(1) The obligations of the Corporation transferred by virtue of section 45 include any obligation to comply with terms and conditions attached to a grant made under section 18 of the Transport Act 1978 (grants in respect of capital expenditure by National Carriers Limited or its subsidiaries).

1978 c. 55.

(2) For the reference in that section to the Corporation there shall be substituted, as from the appointed day, a reference to the successor company.

(3) In considering the exercise of his powers under that section in favour of the successor company, the Minister shall take into account any capital expenditure within that section not previously taken into account, including expenditure incurred before the appointed day; and the financial limits set by subsection (2) of that section shall apply in relation to such an exercise of the Minister's powers as if grants made to the Corporation at any time before the appointed day had been made to the successor company at that time.

Reimbursement for certain travel concessions

9.—(1) The obligations of the Corporation transferred by virtue of section 45 include any obligation to comply with terms attached to a payment made under section 21 of the Transport Act 1978 (reimbursement of amounts paid in connection with travel concessions enjoyed by certain employees and others).

1978 c. 55.

(2) For the references in that section to the Corporation there shall be substituted, as from the appointed day, references to the successor company.

(3) In considering the exercise of his powers under that section in favour of the successor company, the Minister shall take into account any amounts paid as mentioned in that section and not previously taken into account, including amounts paid by the Corporation and amounts paid in respect of concessionary travel enjoyed before the appointed day.

Rating

10.—(1) The obligations of the Corporation transferred by virtue of section 45 include any obligation of the Corporation under subsection (2) of section 162 of the Transport Act 1968 to make a payment to the British Railways Board in respect of any period of occupation before the appointed day by the Corporation or a subsidiary of premises which by virtue of subsection (1) of that section are to be treated for rating purposes as occupied by the Board.

1968 c. 73.

(2) If any dispute between the Board and the Corporation as to the amount so payable stands referred to the Minister immediately before the appointed day, it shall be dealt with thereafter as if the successor company had at all times been a party to the reference.

(3) Any dispute arising on or after the appointed day between the Board and the successor company as to the amount due under the said subsection (2) shall be referred to the Minister for determination, and his determination shall be final.

SCHEDULE 7

Section 51.

Amendments Consequential on Part II

TRANSPORT ACT 1968 (c.73)

1. In section 7 substitute the words " the Board "—

    (a) in subsection (1)(a) for the words from " the authority " to the end;

(b) in subsection (3) for the words " the authority or authorities making it " ; and

(c) in subsection (4) for the words " the authority or authorities by whom the scheme was prepared ".

2. In section 8(1) (b) for " either of those authorities " substitute " the Railways Board ".

3. In section 29(6) for the words from " subsection (2) of the said section " to the end substitute " subsection (1)(b) of the said section 7 or, as the case may be, to an order under subsection (1)(b) of the said section 8 making any such provision as is mentioned in the said section 7(1)(b), but as if for the reference in subsection (6)(a) of the said section 8 to the Railways Board there were substituted a reference to the Scottish Group and the Railways Board ".

4. In section 45(5) for " the authority to whom the directions are given " substitute " the Board ".

5. In paragraph 4 of Schedule 16 for the words from " subsection (1) " to " of that section " substitute " subsection (2) of section 67 of the Act of 1962 ".

6. In paragraph 5 of Schedule 16—

(a) in sub-paragraph (2), for " either of the authorities to whom this section applies " substitute " the Scottish Group " and for " authority " in both places where it occurs substitute " Group " ;

(b) in sub-paragraph (3), for " the authority or subsidiary in question " substitute " the Scottish Group or, as the case may be, the subsidiary in question " ;

(c) in sub-paragraph (4), for " either or both of the authorities to whom this paragraph applies " substitute " the Scottish Group " and for the words from " authority " to " each of those authorities " substitute " Group ".

SCHEDULE 8

B.R. PENSION SCHEMES

British Railways Superannuation Fund:
New Section
GWR Section
LMSR Section
LNER Section so far as relating to persons admitted to the London and North Eastern Railway Superannuation Fund before 1st June 1957
LNER Section so far as not so relating
RCS Section
SR Section
British Railways (Wages Grades) Pension Fund
British Transport Police Force Superannuation Fund
B.R. (1974) Pension Fund
Great Eastern Railway New Pension Fund and New Pension (Supplemental) Fund Trust Account

Great Northern Railway Superannuation Fund

Great Western Railway Inspectors and Foremen's Special Pension Fund

Great Western Railway Pension Society

Great Western Railway Salaried Staff Supplemental Pension Fund

Great Western Railway Supplemental Pensions Reserve Fund

Great Western Railway Widows and Orphans' Benevolent Fund

Lancashire and Yorkshire Railway Pension Fund Society

London, Brighton and South Coast Railway Pension Fund

London Midland and Scottish Railway (L.N.W.) Insurance Society

London Midland and Scottish Railway (L.N.W.) Provident and Pensions Society

London Midland and Scottish Railway (L.N.W.) Supplementary Pension Fund and Locomotive Foremen's Pension Fund

London Midland and Scottish Railway Midland Friendly Society

London Midland and Scottish Railway (North Staffordshire Section) Friendly Society

North British Railway Insurance Society

North Eastern and Great Eastern Superannuation Societies and Pensions Funds Joint Trust Account

Southern Railway (South Eastern & Chatham Section) Enginemen & Motormen's Pension Fund Society

Thomas Bantock & Co. Superannuation Fund.

SCH. 8

SCHEDULE 9

REPEALS

PART I

PUBLIC SERVICE VEHICLES

Section 69.

Chapter	Short title	Extent of repeal
1 & 2 Eliz. 2. c. 33.	Education (Miscellaneous Provisions) Act 1953.	Section 12.
2 & 3 Eliz. 2. c. 64.	Transport Charges &c. (Miscellaneous Provisions) Act 1954.	Section 2. Schedule 1.
3 & 4 Eliz. 2. c. 26.	Public Service Vehicles (Travel Concessions) Act 1955.	In section 1(7), the words " and two ".
6 & 7 Eliz. 2. c. 50.	Local Government (Omnibus Shelters and Queue Barriers) (Scotland) Act 1958.	In section 7(1), the words from " and the references " onwards.
8 & 9 Eliz. 2. c. 16.	Road Traffic Act 1960.	Sections 117 and 118. In section 119(3)(*a*), the words " or backed ". Section 127.

Chapter	Short title	Extent of repeal
8 & 9 Eliz. 2. c. 16—*contd.*	Road Traffic Act 1960—*contd.*	In section 128(2), the words from " In the application " onwards. Section 129. In section 130, in subsection (2), the words from " and such " onwards. Sections 132 to 140. Section 143. In section 144, the words " or act as conductor of ", wherever occurring, and, in subsection (3), the words from " and for " to " eighteen ". In section 145(1), the words " or act as conductor of ". In section 147(1)(*d*) the words " or other person authorised by the licensee of the vehicle ". Section 149. Section 153(2). In section 154, the words " or act as conductor of ". In section 155, the words " or act as conductor of ". In section 156(1), the words " or backed ". In section 158, the words " or act as conductor of ". In section 160— (*a*) in subsection (1), the words " or the Twelfth Schedule thereto "; (*b*) in subsection (1)(*f*), the words " and conductors "; (*c*) in subsection (2), the words " and the Twelfth Schedule thereto ". In section 163(1), the words " or act as conductor of." Section 234. Section 240. In section 247(2), the words from " or (in a case " onwards. In section 257(1), the definitions of " owner " and " road service licence ". Section 258. Schedule 12. In Schedule 17, the entries relating to the Local Government (Miscellaneous Provisions) Act 1953 and the Local Government (Omnibus Shelters and Queue Barriers) (Scotland) Act 1958.

Chapter	Short title	Extent of repeal
10 & 11 Eliz. 2. c. 46.	Transport Act 1962.	In Schedule 2, in Part I, the entries relating to section 12 of the Education (Miscellaneous Provisions) Act 1953 and section 135 of the 1960 Act.
1963 c. 33.	London Government Act 1963.	In section 9(6)(*b*), the words from " except " to " 1960 ". Section 14(6)(*d*). In Schedule 5, in Part I, paragraph 25.
1965 c. 25.	Finance Act 1965.	In section 92(8), the definition of " road service licence ".
1967 c. 76.	Road Traffic Regulation Act 1967.	In section 1(3), the words " or express carriage ". In Schedule 6, the amendment of section 135(2) of the 1960 Act.
1968 c. 73.	Transport Act 1968.	Section 21(1). Section 30. Section 35(1), (2) and (3)(*a*). In section 138, in subsection (1)(*a*) the words from " subject " to " granted or backed ", and in subsection (3)(*a*) the words " subject as mentioned in subsection (1)(*a*) of this section ". Section 145(1). In section 159(1), in the definition of " road service licence " the words from " and except " onwards.
1969 c. 35.	Transport (London) Act 1969.	In section 23(6), the words from " except " to " that section ". In section 23(7), in the definition of " road service licence " the words from "and includes " onwards. In section 24(2), the words " or act as conductor of ". Section 24(3). Section 24(4)(*b*) and (*d*). In Schedule 3, in paragraph 8, in the subsection substituted in section 92 of the Finance Act 1965, the definition of " road service licence "; and paragraph 11.
1971 c. 62.	Tribunals and Inquiries Act 1971.	Section 13(5). In section 13(6)(*a*) the words from " or to a decision " to " traffic commissioners ". In Schedule 1, in paragraph 30(*a*), the words from " and " onwards.

Chapter	Short title	Extent of repeal
1972 c. 20.	Road Traffic Act 1972.	In section 44(4)— (a) the words from " to public service vehicles " to " passengers or "; (b) the words from " but shall apply " to " 1978 "; (c) the words from " if no " to the end.
1972 c. 68.	European Communities Act 1972.	In Schedule 4, paragraph 10.
1972 c. 70.	Local Government Act 1972.	Section 186(3).
1973 c. 65.	Local Government (Scotland) Act 1973.	In Schedule 18, paragraphs 26 and 30 to 35.
1974 c. 50.	Road Traffic Act 1974.	In Schedule 2, paragraphs 1 and 3 to 5. In Schedule 5, all the entries in Part I except those relating to sections 148(2) and 239 of the 1960 Act. In Schedule 6, paragraph 1 and, in paragraph 2, the words " or act as conductor of ". In Schedule 7, the entry relating to section 131(1)(b) of the 1960 Act.
1976 c. 76.	Energy Act 1976.	In Schedule 1, in paragraph 2, the words " or act as conductor of " in both places where they occur.
1978 c. 55.	Transport Act 1978.	Section 5(10). Section 6. Section 7(1) and (2). Section 8. Schedule 1. Schedule 2, except paragraph 5.

PART II
REPEALS TAKING EFFECT ON PASSING OF THIS ACT

Chapter	Title	Extent of repeal
1960 c. 16.	Road Traffic Act 1960.	In section 232(1)(b), the words " or 71 ".
1968 c. 73.	Transport Act 1968.	Section 6. In section 7(5), the words " or under section 6(1) of this Act ". In section 8(6)(a), sub-paragraph (iv). In section 45(6)(a), the words " or under section 6(1) of this Act ".

Chapter	Title	Extent of repeal
1968 c. 73 —*cont.*	Transport Act 1968— *cont.*	In section 71— (*a*) subsections (1) to (5); (*b*) in subsection (6), the words " this section and "; (*c*) subsection (7); (*d*) in subsection (8) the definition of " pallet "; (*e*) subsections (9) and (10). Sections 72 to 80. In section 81(3), the words from " (or, if " to " last vehicle) ". In section 82— (*a*) in subsection (1), the words " record or other ", " 76 or ", " record or other " and " record or "; (*b*) in subsection (2), the words " records or " and " record or ". In section 83, the words " record or other ", " 76 or " and " record or ". In section 84— (*a*) in paragraph (*a*), the words " a special authorisation "; (*b*) in paragraph (*b*), the words " or authorisation "; (*c*) in paragraph (*c*), the words " or special authorisation "; (*d*) in paragraph (*d*), the words " a special authorisation "; (*e*) in paragraph (*f*), the words " or authorisation ". Section 85(1)(*b*). In section 86, the words " and a special authorisation " and " or special authorisation ". In section 87, subsection (2) and in subsection (3) the words " or 79 ". In section 89(1), the words " and special authorisations ". In section 91— (*a*) in subsection (1)(*a*), the words " and special authorisations "; (*b*) in subsection (1)(*b*), the words " and special authorisations ", " or authorisations " and " or authorisations "; (*c*) in subsection (1)(*c*), the words from " or as vehicles " to the end;

Chapter	Title	Extent of repeal
1968 c. 73 —*cont.*	Transport Act 1968— *cont.*	(*d*) in subsection (1)(*d*), the words " and special authorisations ", " or authorisations " and " or 79 "; (*e*) in subsection (1)(*e*), the words " or special authorisation "; (*f*) in subsection (2), the words " or as vehicles used under a special authorisation " and " or special authorisation "; (*g*) subsection (4)(*b*). In section 92(6), the words " or authorisation " in both places where they occur. In section 94, subsections (4) to (6) and in subsection (8) the words from " but if " to the end. Section 150. In section 162(2), the words from " who may " to " their recommendations ". In Schedule 10, in Part I— (*a*) in the amendment of section 233(1)(*a*) of the Road Traffic Act 1960, the words " or authorisation "; (*b*) in the amendment of section 233(1)(*c*) of that Act, the words from " and that paragraph " to the end; (*c*) in the amendment of section 235(1) of that Act the words " or authorisation "; (*d*) in the amendment of section 263(1) of that Act, the words from " and the references " to the end. In Schedule 10, in Part II, in the amendment of section 232(1) (*b*) of the Road Traffic Act 1960, the words " or 71 ".
1969 c. 48.	Post Office Act 1969.	In Schedule 4, paragraph 88.
1974 c. 48.	Railways Act 1974.	Sections 5 to 7.
1975 c. 24.	House of Commons Disqualification Act 1975.	In Schedule 1, in Part II, the entry relating to the Freight Integration Council.
1975 c. 25.	Northern Ireland Assembly Disqualification Act 1975.	In Schedule 1, in Part II, the entry relating to the Freight Integration Council.
1978 c. 55.	Transport Act 1978.	Sections 19 and 20.

PART III

REPEALS TAKING EFFECT ON APPOINTED DAY UNDER PART II OF THIS ACT

Chapter	Title	Extent of repeal
1938 c. 44.	Road Haulage Wages Act 1938.	In section 4(2), the words " the National Freight Corporation,".
1964 c. 40.	Harbours Act 1964.	In section 57(1), in the definition of " the Boards ", the words " the National Freight Corporation " and " Corporation or ".
1966 c. 27.	Building Control Act 1966.	In the Schedule, the entry relating to the National Freight Corporation.
1966 c. 34.	Industrial Development Act 1966.	In Schedule 2, the entry relating to the National Freight Corporation.
1968 c. 73.	Transport Act 1968.	Sections 1 to 5. In section 7— (a) in subsection (1), the words from " or the Freight Corporation " to " acting jointly " and in paragraph (b) the words " the Corporation " and " or Corporation "; (b) subsection (2); (c) in subsection (3), the words " subsection (1) or (2) of "; (d) in subsection (4), in paragraph (a) the words " or the Freight Corporation " and " respective " and paragraph (b); (e) in subsection (5), the words " or subsection (2) "; (f) in subsection (6), the words " or subsection (2) "; (g) in subsection (7), the words from " and in the application " to the end. In section 8— (a) in subsection (1), paragraph (a) and in paragraph (b) the words " or paragraph (b) of subsection (4) "; (b) subsection (2); (c) in subsection (3), the words " subsection (1) or (2) of "; (d) in subsection (4), the words " subsection (1) of " and the words from " and in the case " to " of this section;

Chapter	Title	Extent of repeal
1968 c. 73— *cont.*	Transport Act 1968— *cont.*	(*e*) in subsection (5), the words from " and in the application " to the end; (*f*) in subsection (6), the words from the beginning to " Corporation; and " and in paragraph (*a*), sub-paragraph (i), in sub-paragraph (ii) the words from " in the case " to " of this section " and sub-paragraph (iii). In section 44— (*a*) in subsection (1)(*a*)(iii), the words " 3(1) or " and the words " the Freight Corporation or "; (*b*) in subsection (1)(*b*)(iii), the words " the Freight Corporation or "; (*c*) in the concluding words of subsection (1)(*b*), the reference to section 3(1). In section 45— (*a*) in subsection (1), paragraph (*b*), the word " and " immediately preceding that paragraph and the words " or, as the case may be, the Corporation "; (*b*) in subsection (2), the words " or, as the case may be, the Corporation " in both places where they occur; (*c*) in subsection (3), the words " or the Freight Corporation "; (*d*) in subsection (5), the Words " or the Freight Corporation or each of them " and " respective "; (*e*) in subsection (6), the words " or the Freight Corporation ". In section 52(2), the words " and the Freight Corporation ", " or the Corporation " and " or Corporation ". In section 55— (*a*) in subsection (1)(*b*), the words " the Freight Corporation and " and the words " of that Corporation or "; (*b*) in subsection (1)(ii), the words " but including a reference to the Freight Corporation ";

Chapter	Title	Extent of repeal
1968 c. 73 —*cont.*	Transport Act 1968— *cont.*	(*c*) in subsection (1)(iii), the words " or the Freight Corporation ", (*d*) subsection (1)(iv); (*e*) in subsection (4) the words " or with the Freight Corporation " and the words " or Corporation " in both places where they occur. In section 121, in subsection (1) the words from "and sections 116 and 117 " to the end and in subsection (2)(*a*) the words " the Freight Corporation or the subsidiaries of that Corporation ". In section 125(4), the words " and to the Freight Corporation ". In section 134(3)(*b*), the reference to section 2(1)(*g*)(ii) and (*m*). In section 156(1), the words " the Freight Corporation ", " or Corporation ", " Corporation or ", " the Minister or, in the case of the Scottish Group ", and " the Minister or, as the case may be,". In section 159(1),the definition of " the Freight Corporation " and in the definition of " the new authorities " the words " the Freight Corporation ". In section 160(3), paragraph (*a*) and in paragraph (*b*) the reference to section 4(1). In section 162— (*a*) in subsection (1), paragraph (*b*) and the word " or " immediately preceding it, the words " or (*b*) " and the words from " or, as the case may be ", to " that Corporation "; (*b*) subsection (2); (*c*) in subsection (3), the words " or the Freight Corporation " and the words " or that Corporation "; (*d*) in subsection (4), the words " or (*b*) " and the words " of the Freight Corporation or ".

Chapter	Short title	Extent of repeal
1968 c. 73 —*cont.*	Transport Act 1968— *cont.*	In Schedule 1, paragraph 1 and in paragraph 5 the words from " and, in the case " to the end. In Schedule 2, in paragraph 3(*a*), the words " 5(3)(*a*) or ". Schedule 3. In Schedule 4, in paragraph 5 the words from " by or on behalf " to " Freight Corporation, or " and in paragraph 6 the words " the Freight Corporation ". In Schedule 10, in Part I, in the second amendment to section 4(2) of the Road Haulage Wages Act 1938, the words " the National Freight Corporation,". In Schedule 16— (*a*) paragraphs 1 and 2; (*b*) in paragraph 4, in sub-paragraph (1) the words " the Corporation and ", sub-paragraph (2) and in sub-paragraph (5) the words " the Freight Corporation " and " Corporation "; (*c*) in paragraph 5, sub-paragraph (1); (*d*) in paragraph 7(1), the words " to the Freight Corporation and " and " of the Freight Corporation or "; (*e*) in paragraph 8, in sub-paragraph (1)(*d*)(i), the words " the National Freight Corporation " and " Corporation or " and in sub-paragraph (2) the words "the Freight Corporation"; (*f*) in paragraph 9, the words " The National Freight Corporation "; (*g*) in paragraph 10, the words " The National Freight Corporation ".
1974 c. 8.	Statutory Corporations (Financial Provisions) Act 1974.	In Schedule 2, in the first column of the entry amending section 19(2) of the Transport Act 1962, the reference to the National Freight Corporation.
1975 c. 24.	House of Commons Disqualification Act 1975.	In Schedule 1, in Part II, the entry relating to the National Freight Corporation.

Chapter	Title	Extent of repeal
1975 c. 25.	Northern Ireland Assembly Disqualification Act 1975.	In Schedule 1, in Part II, the entry relating to the National Freight Corporation.
1977 c. 20.	Transport (Financial Provisions) Act 1977.	Section 2.
1978 c. 55.	Transport Act 1978.	Section 17.

PART IV

OTHER REPEALS

Chapter	Title	Extent of repeal
1967 c. 76.	Road Traffic Regulation Act 1967.	Section 100.

Sea Fish Industry Act 1980

1980 CHAPTER 35

An Act to enable the White Fish Authority to impose a levy in respect of white fish and white fish products trans-shipped within British fishery limits.

[30th June 1980]

BE IT ENACTED by the Queen's most Excellent Majesty, by and with the advice and consent of the Lords Spiritual and Temporal, and Commons, in this present Parliament assembled, and by the authority of the same, as follows:—

Levies on trans-shipments of white fish, etc.

1970 c. 11.

1.—(1) In subsection (1)(a) of section 17 of the Sea Fish Industry Act 1970 (power of White Fish Authority to impose levies in respect of white fish and white fish products landed in the United Kingdom) after the words " Great Britain " there are inserted the words " or trans-shipped within British fishery limits " and after the words " so landed " in each place where they occur there are inserted the words " or trans-shipped ".

(2) The following subsection is inserted after subsection (2) of that section—

" (2A) The Authority may not impose a general levy—

    (a) more than once in respect of the same fish or fish products; or

    (b) in respect of the products of any fish in respect of which such a levy is imposed.".

Citation and extent.

2.—(1) This Act may be cited as the Sea Fish Industry Act 1980.

(2) It is hereby declared that this Act extends to Northern Ireland.

New Towns Act 1980

1980 CHAPTER 36

An Act to increase the limit imposed by section 43 of the New Towns Act 1965 on the amounts which may be borrowed by development corporations and the Commission for the New Towns.   [30th June 1980]

BE IT ENACTED by the Queen's Most Excellent Majesty by and with the advice and consent of the Lords Spiritual and Temporal, and Commons, in this present Parliament assembled, and by the authority of the same, as follows:—

1. In section 43 of the New Towns Act 1965 (limit on borrowing by development corporations and Commission for New Towns) for " £2,750 million or such greater sum not exceeding £3,250 million " there shall be substituted " £3,625 million or such greater sum not exceeding £4,000 million ".

Increase of limit on borrowing.
1965 c. 59.

2.—(1) This Act may be cited as the New Towns Act 1980.

(2) This Act does not extend to Northern Ireland.

Citation and extent.

Gas Act 1980

1980 CHAPTER 37

An Act to provide that the supply of gas to any premises at an annual rate in excess of 25,000 therms shall be subject to the special agreement of the British Gas Corporation and that charges for therms supplied to any premises in excess of 25,000 therms a year may be fixed by the Corporation under section 25(3) of the Gas Act 1972 without regard to the requirements of section 24(1) or 25(5) of that Act.   [30th June 1980]

BE IT ENACTED by the Queen's most Excellent Majesty, by and with the advice and consent of the Lords Spiritual and Temporal, and Commons, in this present Parliament assembled, and by the authority of the same, as follows:—

Supply of gas to any premises in excess of 25,000 therms a year to be subject to special agreement of British Gas Corporation or liable to special rates of charge.

1972 c. 60.

1.—(1) The general obligation of the British Gas Corporation under paragraph 2 of Schedule 4 to the Gas Act 1972 to supply gas on demand shall not extend to requiring the Corporation to supply gas to any premises in any period of twelve months beginning after the passing of this Act in excess of 25,000 therms.

(2) Section 25(5) of that Act shall not apply in relation to tariffs fixed by the Corporation under subsection (3) of that section with respect to the prices to be charged for therms supplied to any premises in excess of 25,000 therms in any such period of twelve months; and nothing in section 24(1) of that Act shall be construed as affecting the power of the Corporation to fix such tariffs as they think fit with respect to the prices to be charged for therms so supplied.

(3) The power of the Corporation under section 25(6) of that Act to enter into a special agreement with any consumer which provides for a minimum supply of gas to any premises in excess of 25,000 therms in any such period of twelve months shall not be subject to the proviso to that subsection (which restricts the Corporation's power to enter into a special agreement to cases where the tariffs in force are not appropriate owing to special circumstances).

(4) Section 13 of the Energy Act 1976 (which is superseded by 1976 c. 76. this section) shall cease to have effect.

2.—(1) This Act may be cited as the Gas Act 1980.

(2) This Act does not extend to Northern Ireland.

Citation and extent.

Coroners Act 1980

1980 CHAPTER 38

An Act to abolish the obligation of coroners under the law
of England and Wales to view the bodies on which they
hold inquests; to make fresh provision for inquests
to be held in districts other than that in which the
body lies; to confer new powers for the exhumation
of bodies; and for connected purposes.

[17th July 1980]

BE IT ENACTED by the Queen's most Excellent Majesty, by and
with the advice and consent of the Lords Spiritual and
Temporal, and Commons, in this present Parliament
assembled, and by the authority of the same, as follows:—

Abolition of
requirement
for a coroner
holding an
inquest to
view the body.

1. It shall not be obligatory for a coroner holding an inquest
on a body to view the body and—

    (*a*) the validity of an inquest shall not be questioned in any
court on the ground that the coroner did not view the
body;

    (*b*) the enactments specified in Schedule 1 and Schedule 2 to
this Act (which relate to the view of the body by the
coroner and jury) are amended or repealed as provided
in those Schedules; and

    (*c*) no body shall be ordered by a coroner to be exhumed
except under section 4 of this Act.

Power to hold
inquests in
areas other
than that in
which the
body lies.

2.—(1) If it appears to a coroner that an inquest ought to be
held on a body lying within his area but it is expedient that the
inquest should be held by some other coroner he may request
that coroner to assume jurisdiction to hold the inquest and if that

coroner agrees he, and not the coroner within whose area the body is lying, shall have jurisdiction to hold the inquest.

(2) If the coroner who has been requested to assume jurisdiction declines to assume it the coroner who has made the request may apply to the Secretary of State for a direction designating the coroner who is to hold the inquest.

(3) On the making of an application under subsection (2) above the Secretary of State shall determine by which coroner (whether one of the two mentioned in that subsection or another) the inquest should in all the circumstances be held and shall direct him to assume jurisdiction or, as the case may be, to exercise his jurisdiction to hold the inquest; and where a direction is given under this subsection directing a coroner to assume jurisdiction he, and not the coroner within whose area the body is lying, shall have jurisdiction to hold the inquest and shall hold it accordingly.

(4) Where jurisdiction to hold an inquest is assumed under this section it shall not be necessary to remove the body into the area of the coroner who is to hold the inquest.

(5) Any request made or agreement given, any application for a direction and any direction under any of the preceding provisions of this section shall be made or given in writing.

(6) Notice of the making of an application by one coroner under subsection (2) above shall be given to the other coroner and notice of the direction given pursuant to it shall be given, in a case where the direction is given to the coroner who has made or the coroner who had notice of the application, to the other coroner and, in a case where the direction is given to some other coroner, to the coroner who made and the coroner who had notice of the application.

3.—(1) On the assumption by a coroner of jurisdiction to hold Provisions an inquest under section 2 above that coroner shall also assume, supplementary in relation to the body and the inquest, all the powers and duties to s. 2. which would belong to him if the body were lying within his area (including the power to order its exhumation under section 4 below) and may exercise those powers notwithstanding that the body remains outside his area or, having been removed into it, is removed out of it by virtue of any order of his for its examination or burial.

(2) On the assumption of the powers and duties referred to in subsection (1) above by the coroner who assumes jurisdiction to hold the inquest the coroner within whose area the body is lying shall cease to have any powers or duties in relation to the body

or the inquest notwithstanding that the body remains within his area or comes to be buried there.

(3) It shall be for the coroner who assumes, and not for the coroner who ceases to have, jurisdiction to hold an inquest under section 2 above to pay any fees or other expenses incurred in the course of his duties by the latter coroner before he ceased to have jurisdiction and such fees and expenses shall be accounted for and repaid accordingly.

1887 c. 71.

(4) At the beginning of section 7(1) of the Coroners Act 1887 (jurisdiction of a coroner dependent on the presence of the body in his area) there shall be inserted the words " Unless he has assumed jurisdiction under section 2 of the Coroners Act 1980 ".

1926 c. 59.

(5) Sections 16 and 17 of the Coroners (Amendment) Act 1926 (which are superseded by section 2 above and this section) are hereby repealed.

Power of coroner to order exhumation of bodies.

4.—(1) A coroner may order the exhumation of the body of a person buried within the area within which he has jurisdiction where it appears to him that it is necessary for the body to be examined—

    (*a*) for the purpose of his holding an inquest touching that person's death or discharging any other function of his in relation to the body or the death; or

    (*b*) for the purposes of any criminal proceedings which have been instituted or are contemplated in respect of the death of that person or of some other person who came by his death in circumstances connected with the death of the person whose body is needed for examination.

(2) The power of a coroner under this section shall be exercisable by warrant under his hand.

Citation, construction and extent.

5.—(1) This Act may be cited as the Coroners Act 1980 and shall be construed as one with the Coroners Acts 1887 to 1954 and those Acts and this Act may be cited together as the Coroners Acts 1887 to 1980.

(2) This Act extends to England and Wales only except that the repeal in section 30(2)(*a*) of the Merchant Shipping Act 1979 extends also to Northern Ireland.

SCHEDULES

SCHEDULE 1   Section 1.

CONSEQUENTIAL AMENDMENTS

The Coroners Act 1887

1. In section 3(2) of the Coroners Act 1887, for the words " on 1887 c. 71. the body ", there shall be substituted the words " touching the death ".

2. In section 29(4) of the said Act of 1887, for the word " body " in the second place where it occurs, there shall be substituted the word " person ".

The Coroners (Amendment) Act 1926

3. In section 13(1) of the Coroners (Amendment) Act 1926, for the 1926 c. 59. words " on the body ", there shall be substituted the words " into the death of that person ".

4. In section 18 of the said Act of 1926, for the words from " held otherwise " to " lying ", there shall be substituted the words " one into the death of a person whose body does not lie ".

5. In section 20(8) of the said Act of 1926, for the words " upon the body ", there shall be substituted the words " touching the death ".

6. In section 21(1) of the said Act of 1926, for the words " upon the body ", there shall be substituted the words " touching the death ".

7. In section 24(3) of the said Act of 1926, for the word " thereon ", there shall be substituted the words " touching the death of the person whose body it is ".

SCHEDULE 2

REPEALS

Chapter	Short title	Extent of repeal
50 & 51 Vict. c. 71.	The Coroners Act 1887.	In section 3(3), the words from " of the person " to " held ". Section 6(3).
16 & 17 Geo. 5. c. 59.	The Coroners (Amendment) Act 1926.	Section 14. In section 15(2), the words from " except " to the end. Sections 16 and 17. In section 20(6), the words from " except " to the end.
1 & 2 Eliz. 2. c. 20.	The Births and Deaths Registration Act 1953.	In section 16(3), in the proviso, the words " on the body or ". In section 17(3), in the proviso, the words " on the body or ". In section 19(1), in the proviso, the words " on the body or ". In section 22(2) and (3), the words " on the body or ". In section 23(1), the words " on any dead body or ". In section 29(4), the words " a dead body upon which or ".
1979 c. 39.	The Merchant Shipping Act 1979.	In section 30(2)(a), the words " on a dead body or ".

Social Security (No. 2) Act 1980

1980 CHAPTER 39

An Act to amend the law relating to social security for the purpose of reducing or abolishing certain benefits and of relaxing or abolishing certain duties to increase sums.

[17th July 1980]

BE IT ENACTED by the Queen's most Excellent Majesty, by and with the advice and consent of the Lords Spiritual and Temporal, and Commons, in this present Parliament assembled, and by the authority of the same, as follows:—

1.—(1) Where in consequence of a review under section 125 of the Social Security Act 1975 (hereafter in this Act referred to as " the principal Act ") in the tax year 1979–1980 the Secretary of State is required by subsection (3) of that section to prepare and lay before Parliament the draft of an order increasing a specified sum, the increase provided by the draft in respect of the sum may be less, by up to 5 per cent. of the sum, than the increase required by that subsection in respect of the sum.

Reduction of compulsory up-rating of certain benefits.
1975 c. 14.

(2) In the preceding subsection " a specified sum " means—

(a) a sum specified in any of the following provisions of Schedule 4 to the principal Act, namely—

  (i) paragraphs 1 and 4 of Part I (which specify the weekly rates of unemployment benefit, sickness benefit and maternity allowance),

  (ii) column (3) of paragraphs 1, 2 and 3 of Part IV (which specify the increases for adult dependants of unemployment benefit, sickness benefit, invalidity pension and maternity allowance),

2 C

(iii) paragraphs 1, 4, 5, 11 and 12 of Part V (which specify the weekly rates of injury benefit, unemployability supplement of disablement pension, an increase of that supplement and the increases for adult dependants of injury benefit and disablement pension);

(b) any sum specified in paragraph 3 of Part I of the said Schedule 4 (which specifies the weekly rates of invalidity allowance) except so far as the sum is relevant for the purpose of section 28(7) of the principal Act (which provides for an increase of a retirement pension in certain cases to be of the same amount as the weekly rate of an invalidity allowance);

1975 c. 60.

(c) the sum mentioned in section 23(1)(a) of the Social Security Pensions Act 1975 so far as the sum is relevant for the purpose of calculating under section 14(6) of the principal Act the rate of unemployment or sickness benefit and of calculating under section 14, 15 or 16 of the said Act of 1975 or section 15(4) of the principal Act the rate of an invalidity pension;

and " tax year " has the same meaning as in the principal Act.

(3) An order under section 124 of the principal Act which increases a sum specified in paragraph 3 of Part I of the said Schedule 4 or the sum mentioned in the said section 23(1)(a) may provide—

(a) in relation to a sum so specified, for an increase of it for the purpose referred to in paragraph (b) of the preceding subsection and for a different increase of it for other purposes;

(b) in relation to the sum so mentioned, for an increase of it for the purpose referred to in paragraph (c) of the preceding subsection and for a different increase of it for other purposes;

and sections 125 and 126 of the principal Act (which among other things provide for reviews and increases of the amounts of certain benefits) shall have effect in relation to a sum so specified and the sum so mentioned as if the requirement to review it which is imposed by subsection (1) of the said section 125 were a requirement to review it as it applies for the purpose referred to in paragraph (b) or (c) of the preceding subsection and to review it separately as it applies for other purposes.

(4) The Secretary of State may by order provide that subsection (1) of this section shall have effect—

(a) with the addition after the words " 1979–1980 " of the words " or 1980–1981 ";

(b) if he has made an order in pursuance of the preceding paragraph, with the substitution for the words " or 1980–1981 " of the words ", 1980–1981 or 1981–1982 ";

(c) if he has not made an order in pursuance of either of the preceding paragraphs, with the addition after the words " 1979–1980 " of the words " or 1981–1982 ";

but no order shall be made by virtue of this subsection unless a draft of the order has been laid before Parliament and approved by a resolution of each House of Parliament.

(5) Section 126(4) of the principal Act (which among other things provides for rounding down an increase under section 125(3) of that Act) shall apply to an increase in pursuance of subsection (1) of this section as it applies to an increase in pursuance of the said section 125(3) but shall be disregarded in determining for the purposes of subsection (1) of this section and increase required by the said section 125(3); and nothing in this section shall be construed as prejudicing section 166(2) of that Act (which among other things relates to the extent of powers to make orders under that Act).

2.—(1) In section 125(1) of the principal Act, paragraph (c) (under which the sum which certain Category A or B retirement pensioners may earn without abating their pensions is included among the sums which must be reviewed under the said section 125(1) in each tax year) shall be omitted.

(2) In relation to a draft of an up-rating order which, in consequence of a review under section 125 of the principal Act made before the passing of this Act, falls to be prepared after the passing of this Act in pursuance of subsection (3) of that section, subsection (1)(c) of that section shall be disregarded.

Abolition of compulsory up-rating of amount certain pensioners may earn without abating pensions.

3.—(1) For paragraph (d) of subsection (1) of section 17 of the principal Act (which provides that for the purposes mentioned in that subsection any two days of interruption of employment within a period of 6 consecutive days shall be treated as a period of interruption of employment and any two such periods not separated by 13 weeks shall be treated as one period of interruption of employment) there shall be substituted the following paragraph—

Alteration of period of interruption of employment and of periods relating to invalidity allowance and unemployability supplement.

" (d) the following periods, namely—

(i) any two days of unemployment, whether consecutive or not, within a period of 6 consecutive days,

(ii) any four or more consecutive days of incapacity for work,

shall be treated as a period of interruption of employment, and any two such periods not separated by a period of more than 8 weeks (' week ' for this purpose meaning any period of 7 days) shall be treated as one period of interruption of employment; ".

(2) Accordingly in section 56(6) of the principal Act (which among other things provides for section 17(1) of that Act to have effect for the purposes of injury benefit as it has effect for the purposes of unemployment benefit or sickness benefit) the words " unemployment benefit or " shall be omitted.

(3) In section 28(7) of the principal Act (under which a Category A retirement pension is to be increased if among other things the pensioner was entitled to invalidity allowance in respect of any day in the 13 weeks preceding the day on which he attains pensionable age) and in subsection (4) of section 59 of that Act (which among other things provides that for the purposes of that subsection a break of more than 13 weeks in entitlement to unemployability supplement means that the periods before and after the break are different periods, and a break of 13 weeks or less is to be disregarded), for the words " 13 weeks " wherever they occur there shall be substituted the words " 8 weeks ".

(4) The Secretary of State may by regulations provide for any provision amended by subsection (1) or (3) of this section to have effect as if for the reference to 8 weeks there were substituted a reference to a larger number of weeks specified in the regulations.

Reduction and abolition of earnings-related supplement and addition.

4.—(1) In Schedule 6 to the principal Act, in paragraph 3(1)(*a*)(ii) (under which the weekly rate of earnings-related supplement of unemployment benefit, sickness benefit and a maternity allowance and the earnings-related addition to a widow's allowance are calculated by reference to 15 per cent. of the earnings there mentioned) for the words " 15 per cent." there shall be substituted the words " 10 per cent.".

(2) Except as provided in pursuance of section 7(2) of this Act, no earnings-related supplement of unemployment benefit, sickness benefit or a maternity allowance and no earnings-related addition to a widow's allowance shall be payable under the principal Act in respect of any period which is after the coming into force of this subsection.

Abatement of unemployment benefit on account of payments of occupational pension.

5.—(1) If payments by way of occupational pension which in the aggregate exceed the maximum sum are made for any week to a person who has attained the age of 60, the rate of any unemployment benefit under the principal Act to which apart from this section he is entitled for that week shall be reduced by 10 pence for each 10 pence of the excess; and in this subsection " the maximum sum " means such sum not less than £35 as is prescribed.

(2) Regulations may provide—

    (*a*) for such sums as are specified in or determined under the regulations to be disregarded for the purposes of this section;

    (*b*) for securing that no reduction in pursuance of the preceding subsection is made in the unemployment benefit for any day before the day which in pursuance of the regulations is treated as that on which relevant payments by way of occupational pension begin;

    (*c*) for this section to apply, in cases where—

        (i) a lump sum is paid to a person in connection with a former employment of his or arrangements are made for a lump sum to be so paid; or

        (ii) benefits of any description are made available to a person in connection with a former employment of his or arrangements are made for them to be made so available; or

        (iii) payments by way of occupational pension to a person are assigned, reduced or postponed or are made otherwise than weekly,

    as if there were made to the person such weekly payments by way of occupational pension as are specified in or determined under the regulations;

    (*d*) for the method of determining whether payments by way of occupational pension are made to a person for any week and the amount of any such payments which are so made;

    (*e*) for sections 14(7), 17(1) and 18(1) of the principal Act (which relate respectively to earnings-related supplement of unemployment benefit, the days for which unemployment benefit is payable and the duration of unemployment benefit) to have effect, in relation to a person whose rate of unemployment benefit is reduced by virtue of this section, with such modifications as are prescribed.

(3) In this section—

    " employer " means—

        (*a*) in relation to an employment under a contract of service, the employer under the contract;

        (*b*) in relation to an employment in an office with emoluments, the person responsible for paying the emoluments;

    " employment " means an employment under a contract of service or in an office with emoluments;

    " modifications " includes additions, omissions and amendments;

" payments by way of occupational pension " means, in relation to a person, periodical payments which, in connection with the coming to an end of an employment of his, fall to be made to him and to be so made out of money provided wholly or partly by the employer or under arrangements made by the employer or out of money provided under an enactment or instrument having the force of law in any part of the United Kingdom or elsewhere and such other payments as are prescribed;

" prescribed " means prescribed by regulations; and

" regulations " means regulations made by the Secretary of State;

and the reference in subsection (1) of this section to unemployment benefit includes any earnings-related supplement of the benefit and any increase of the benefit on account of dependants.

(4) Regulations prescribing payments for the purposes of the definition of " payments by way of occupational pension " in the preceding subsection shall not be made unless a draft of the regulations has been laid before Parliament and approved by a resolution of each House of Parliament.

1980 c. 30.   (5) Section 10 of the Social Security Act 1980 (which among other things requires the Secretary of State to refer to the Social Security Advisory Committee certain proposals to make regulations) shall apply to proposals to make regulations in pursuance of subsection (2) of this section and such regulations as are mentioned in the preceding subsection, other than regulations which are made during the period of 6 months beginning with the date of the passing of this Act, as it applies to such proposals of the Secretary of State as are mentioned in subsection (1) of that section.

(6) For the purposes of this section as it applies to Scotland, the time at which a person attains the age of 60 shall be the commencement of the sixtieth anniversary of the date of his birth.

Supplementary benefit in cases affected by trade disputes.
1976 c. 71.

6.—(1) Where in consequence of a stoppage of work which is due to a trade dispute the requirements of a person for any period are, by virtue of section 8 of the Supplementary Benefits Act 1976 (which relates to cases affected by trade disputes), to be disregarded to any extent for the purposes of supplementary benefit, then, except so far as regulations provide otherwise—

(*a*) there shall not be disregarded for the purposes of that Act—

(i) any relevant payments of his for that period or any part of it, and

(ii) without prejudice to the generality of the preceding sub-paragraph, any amount which becomes or would on an application duly made become available to him in that period by way of repayment of income tax deducted from his emoluments in pursuance of section 204 of the Income and Cor- 1970 c. 10. poration Taxes Act 1970 (pay as you earn);

(b) any payment by way of a supplementary pension or allowance for that period or any part of it which apart from this paragraph would be made to him, or to any other person whose resources are to be aggregated with his in pursuance of the said Act of 1976, shall not be made if the weekly rate of the payment is £12 or less and, if it is more than £12, shall be at a weekly rate equal to the difference; and

(c) no payments in pursuance of section 4 of the said Act of 1976 (which relates to urgent cases) shall be made, in respect of requirements relating to that period, to him or to any other person whose resources are to be aggregated with his in pursuance of that Act.

(2) If an order under section 124 of the principal Act (which enables the Secretary of State to increase the sums mentioned in that section and section 23 of the Social Security Pensions Act 1975 c. 60. 1975) specifies in pursuance of subsection (2) of the said section 23 a percentage by which certain sums are to be increased, then, subject to the following subsection and to the operation of this subsection by reference to any later order under the said section 124,—

(a) paragraph (b) of the preceding subsection shall have effect, from the time when the first-mentioned order comes into force, with the substitution for the references to the specified sum of references to a sum arrived at by—

(i) increasing the specified sum by that percentage of it, and

(ii) if that sum as so increased is not a multiple of 50p, disregarding the remainder if it is 25p and, if it is not, rounding it up or down to the nearest 50p; and

(b) it shall be the duty of the Secretary of State to make an order stating the sum which by reference to the first-mentioned order is arrived at in pursuance of the preceding paragraph.

(3) Regulations may provide—

(a) that the preceding subsection shall not apply in relation to a particular order under the said section 124; and (*b*) that paragraph (*b*) of subsection (1) of this section shall have effect with the substitution for the references to the specified sum of references to a sum prescribed by the regulations;

and the preceding subsection shall not apply in relation to a percentage if that percentage of the specified sum is 25p or less.

No regulations shall be made by virtue of this subsection unless a draft of the regulations has been laid before Parliament and approved by a resolution of each House of Parliament.

(4) In this section—

" regulations " means regulations made by the Secretary of State;

" relevant payments " means, in relation to a person and a period, payments which the person receives or is entitled to obtain by reason of his being without employment for that period;

" the specified sum " means £12 or, if by virtue of subsection (2) or (3) of this section another sum is for the time being mentioned in the places in subsection (1)(*b*) of this section as originally enacted where £12 was mentioned, that other sum; and

" trade dispute " has the same meaning as in the principal Act;

1976 c. 71.

and for the purposes of subsection (1) of this section any modification of section 8 of the Supplementary Benefits Act 1976 which has effect by virtue of any other provision of that Act shall be disregarded.

1980 c. 30.

(5) Section 2 of the Supplementary Benefits Act 1976 (which among other things relates to the determination of any question as to entitlement to and the amount of supplementary benefit and any other question relating to supplementary benefit which arises under that Act) shall have effect, after the preceding provisions of this section and section 6(1) of the Social Security Act 1980 (which amends the said section 2) have come into force, with the addition after the words " under this Act " in subsection (1) of the said section 2 of the words " or section 6 of the Social Security (No. 2) Act 1980 ".

(6) If provisions of this section come into force before the date when the said section 6(1) comes into force, regulations may provide for the said Act of 1976 to have effect until that date with such modifications, if any, as the Secretary of State considers appropriate in consequence of the coming into force of those provisions; and in this subsection " modifications " includes additions, omissions and amendments.

7.—(1) Section 19(3) of the Social Security Act 1980 (which Supplemental. provides for sums in respect of expenses under that Act which 1980 c. 30. are connected with benefits payable out of the National Insurance Fund to be paid from that Fund into the Consolidated Fund) shall have effect as if the references to expenses incurred by virtue of that Act included administrative expenses of the Secretary of State which are attributable to this Act.

(2) The Secretary of State may by regulations make such provision as he considers appropriate for dealing with transitional matters connected with or arising out of the coming into force of any provision of this Act including in particular, but without prejudice to the generality of the preceding provisions of this subsection—

(*a*) provision for disregarding the effect of subsection (1) or (3) of section 3 of this Act in relation to periods which include the day on which that subsection comes into force;

(*b*) provision for disregarding the effect of subsection (1) of section 4 of this Act in relation to any period after that subsection comes into force;

(*c*) provision for the payment in respect of any period after subsection (2) of section 4 of this Act comes into force of such a supplement or addition as is mentioned in that subsection.

(3) Subsections (1) to (3) of section 166 of the principal Act (which among other things make provision about the extent of powers to make orders and regulations) shall apply to any power to make an order or regulations conferred by the preceding provisions of this Act as they apply to any power to make an order or regulations conferred by that Act but as if for references to that Act there were substituted references to those provisions.

(4) A statutory instrument containing regulations made by virtue of this Act, other than an instrument containing only such regulations as are mentioned in section 5(4) or regulations made by virtue of section 6(3) of this Act, shall be subject to annulment in pursuance of a resolution of either House of Parliament.

(5) An Order in Council under paragraph 1 of Schedule 1 to the Northern Ireland Act 1974 (which among other things 1974 c. 28. provides for legislation for Northern Ireland in the interim period) may be made without regard to sub-paragraph (4) of that paragraph (which among other things provides for the affirmative resolution procedure for certain Orders) if the Order contains a statement that its effect is confined to making for Northern Ireland provision corresponding to provisions of this Act; and such an Order shall not be subject to sub-paragraph

(5) of that paragraph (which relates to the approval by Parliament of Orders which have not been approved under the affirmative resolution procedure) but shall be subject to annulment in pursuance of a resolution of either House of Parliament.

(6) The enactments mentioned in the first and second columns of the Schedule to this Act are hereby repealed to the extent specified in the third column of that Schedule.

1977 c. 5.

(7) In section 22(6)(*a*) of the Social Security (Miscellaneous Provisions) Act 1977 (which refers to certain payments which are analogous to the earnings-related supplement mentioned in section 14(7) of the principal Act) after the words " principal Act " there shall be inserted the words " when it was in force ".

Citation, commencement and extent.

8.—(1) This Act may be cited as the Social Security (No. 2) Act 1980 and shall be included among the Acts which may be cited together as the Social Security Acts 1975 to 1980.

(2) The following provisions of this Act, namely sections 3 to 6 and 7(7) and the Schedule so far as it relates to the principal Act except sections 125 and 126 of that Act, shall come into force on such day as the Secretary of State may appoint by order made by statutory instrument, and different days may be appointed in pursuance of this subsection for different provisions of this Act; and accordingly the other provisions of this Act come into force on the passing of this Act.

(3) This Act, except section 7(5) and this section so far as it relates to section 7(5), does not extend to Northern Ireland.

SCHEDULE

ENACTMENTS REPEALED

Chapter	Short title	Extent of repeal
1975 c. 14.	The Social Security Act 1975.	In section 12(1) the words "earnings-related supplement, and" wherever they occur and the words "earnings-related addition, and". In section 13, subsection (2)(*b*), in subsection (3) the words from "and for" onwards and in subsection (4) the words from "but not" onwards. Section 14(7). In section 17(3) the words from "for the purposes" to "Act and" and the words "for all other purposes of this Part of this Act". Sections 22(4) and 24(3). In section 56(6) the words "unemployment benefit or". In section 79(4), paragraphs (*a*) and (*c*) and the words from "to cause" to "supplement or". In section 92(2) the words "earnings-related supplement, under section 14(7) or 22(4)". Section 124(1)(*b*). In section 125, in subsection (1) paragraph (*c*) and the words from "except" onwards, and in subsection (2) the words "earnings and". In section 126(4) the words "in the case of a sum specified in a provision mentioned in section 125(1)(*a*) or (*b*)". Schedule 6.
1977 c. 5.	The Social Security (Miscellaneous Provisions) Act 1977.	Section 7.
1980 c. 30.	The Social Security Act 1980.	In section 1, in subsection (1) the words from "except" where it first occurs to "to earnings" and the words from "except" in the second place where it occurs onwards, and in subsection (2) the words from "except" onwards.

Licensing (Amendment) Act 1980

1980 CHAPTER 40

An Act to amend the Licensing Act 1964 in relation to special hours certificates and the extension of existing on-licences to additional types of liquor.

[17th July 1980]

BE IT ENACTED by the Queen's most Excellent Majesty, by and with the advice and consent of the Lords Spiritual and Temporal, and Commons, in this present Parliament assembled, and by the authority of the same, as follows:—

Amendment of provisions for upgrading of on-licences.
1964 c. 26.

1.—(1) In subsection (1) of section 37 of the Licensing Act 1964 after " a justices' on-licence " where those words first appear there shall be inserted " to which this section applies " and for the same words where they appear for the second time there shall be substituted " such a licence ".

(2) At the end of the said section 37 there shall be added the following new subsection:

" (3) This section applies to any justices' on-licence granted by way of renewal from time to time of a licence in force on or before 3rd August 1961, no account being taken of any transfer or removal."

(3) This section shall not have effect in relation to any application made under the said section 37 before the end of the period of one month beginning with the day on which this Act is passed.

2. At the end of subsection (2) of section 76 of the Licensing Act 1964 there shall be inserted:

" ; and

 (c) in any premises or part for which a certificate is in force subject to a condition imposed in pursuance of section 81A of this Act, the permitted hours on any day to which the condition relates shall not extend beyond the time specified in the condition.".

Special hours certificates: amendment of provisions as to permitted hours.

1964 c. 26.

3. After section 81 of the Licensing Act 1964 there shall be inserted:

Special hours certificates: amendment of supplementary provisions.

" Special hours certificates: condition restricting hours.

 81A.—(1) If, on an application for a special hours certificate or for revocation of a special hours certificate for any premises or part of any premises (other than premises situated as mentioned in section 76(3) of this Act), the licensing justices or, as the case may be, the magistrates' court, are of opinion—

  (a) that the bona fide user of the premises for the purpose of providing music and dancing is or is likely to be applicable to a period ending earlier than the second period mentioned in section 76(2) of this Act, or

  (b) that in order to avoid or reduce any disturbance of or annoyance to residents in the neighbourhood of the premises or the occurrence of disorderly conduct in the premises it is desirable for the permitted hours to end earlier than the second period so mentioned,

they may, in the case of an application for a certificate, grant it subject to the condition mentioned in subsection (3) of this section, and in the case of an application for revocation, instead of revoking the certificate, impose such a condition.

 (2) At any time while a special hours certificate for any premises or part of any premises (other than premises situated as mentioned in section 76(3) of this Act) is in force, the chief officer of police may apply to the licensing justices or, if it was granted under section 78 of this Act, to the magistrates' court, for the imposition of the condition mentioned in subsection (3) of this section on either of the grounds set out in subsection (1) of this section, and if the licensing justices or the magistrates' court are satisfied that the ground of the application is made out they may impose the condition.

(3) The condition referred to in the preceding provisions of this section is that the permitted hours shall not on any weekday, or any specified weekday, extend beyond such time earlier than 2 o'clock in the morning but not earlier than midnight as may be specified.

Special hours certificates: appeals.

81B.—(1) Subject to subsection (2) of this section, any person aggrieved by a decision of licensing justices or a magistrates' court—

> (*a*) to revoke or not to revoke a special hours certificate on an application under subsection (2) or (4) of section 81 of this Act,

> (*b*) to impose or not to impose a condition under subsection (1) of section 81A of this Act on an application for the grant of a special hours certificate or to impose a condition under that subsection on an application for the revocation of such a certificate, or

> (*c*) to impose or not to impose a condition on an application under section 81A(2) of this Act,

may appeal to the Crown Court against that decision.

(2) Only the chief officer of police may appeal against a decision not to revoke a certificate as mentioned in paragraph (*a*) of subsection (1) of this section or not to impose a condition as mentioned in paragraph (*c*) of that subsection; and a person may appeal against a decision not to impose a condition under section 81A(1) of this Act only if he has appeared before the licensing justices or magistrates' court and made representations that the condition be imposed.

(3) A person other than the appellant shall be a party to an appeal under this section if, and only if, he has appeared before the licensing justices or magistrates' court and made representations on the application to which the decision appealed against relates.

(4) Licensing justices shall have the same power to make an order for the payment of costs on the abandonment of an appeal under this section as a magistrates' court has by virtue of section 85 of the Magistrates' Courts Act 1952 on the abandonment of an appeal to which that section relates."

4.—(1) This Act may be cited as the Licensing (Amendment) Act 1980.

Short title, commencement and extent.

(2) Sections 2 and 3 of this Act shall not come into force until such day as the Secretary of State may appoint by order made by statutory instrument.

(3) This Act does not extend to Scotland or Northern Ireland.

Films Act 1980

1980 CHAPTER 41

An Act to amend the enactments relating to the financing and exhibition of films.   [17th July 1980]

BE IT ENACTED by the Queen's most Excellent Majesty, by and with the advice and consent of the Lords Spiritual and Temporal, and Commons, in this present Parliament assembled, and by the authority of the same, as follows:—

The National Film Finance Corporation

1.—(1) In section 1(1) of the Films Act 1970 (which authorises the making of certain loans by the National Film Finance Corporation at any time before the end of 1980)—

> (a) paragraph (b) and the word " or " immediately preceding it ; and

> (b) the words from " but " to the end ;

shall cease to have effect ; and the following subsection shall be inserted after that subsection—

> " (1A) The National Film Finance Corporation may, at any time before the end of the year 1985, make loans or otherwise give financial assistance, for the purpose of enabling rights to be acquired or work to be undertaken with a view to the production of films, to any persons who, in the judgment of the Corporation, will be able (with such assistance) to acquire those rights or to carry that work to a satisfactory conclusion.

Extended functions of National Film Finance Corporation.

1970 c. 26.

1949 c. 20.
Section 2 of the Cinematograph Film Production (Special Loans) Act 1949 shall not apply to loans made under this subsection ".

(2) In section 1(1), and also in subsections (2) and (4) of that section (which respectively authorise the Corporation to agree to make loans and to acquire copyright in films, up to the end of 1980), for the words " 1980 " there shall in each case be substituted the words " 1985 ".

1957 c. 21.
(3) In section 12(1) of the Cinematograph Films Act 1957 (which provides for the transfer of the Corporation's assets and liabilities and the cesser of their functions in certain circumstances before the end of 1980), for the words " before the end of the year 1980 " there shall be substituted the words " before the end of the year 1985 ".

(4) In paragraph 8(1) of the Schedule to the Cinematograph Film Production (Special Loans) Act 1949 (which provides for the dissolution of the Corporation at any time after the end of 1980 or on their functions ceasing to be exercisable by virtue of section 12 of the Cinematograph Films Act 1957), for the words " after the end of the year 1980 " there shall be substituted the words " after the end of the year 1985 ".

Finances of National Film Finance Corporation.

2.—(1) Section 4 of the Cinematograph Film Production (Special Loans) Act 1949 (which authorises Government lending to the National Film Finance Corporation during the period up to the end of 1980) shall cease to have effect.

(2) Any liability of the Corporation to repay the principal and any interest outstanding immediately before the commencement date in respect of any advances made under section 4(1) is hereby extinguished.

(3) For the purpose of enabling the Corporation to perform their functions the Secretary of State shall make a grant of £1 million to the Corporation out of money provided by Parliament on the day next following the commencement date.

(4) The Corporation shall have power, with the consent of the Secretary of State and the Treasury, to borrow such sums as the Corporation may require for performing their functions; but the aggregate amount of the principal outstanding in respect of sums borrowed under this subsection shall not at any time exceed £5 million.

(5) For the purpose mentioned in subsection (3) above, it shall be the duty of the British Film Fund Agency to pay to the Corporation, in respect of each levy period wholly or partly

included in the period of five years beginning with the commencement date—

    (a) the appropriate sum ; or

    (b) twenty per cent. of the amount received by the Agency in respect of that period, or (as the case may be) in respect of the part of that period so included, as proceeds of the levy on exhibitors imposed under section 2 of the Cinematograph Films Act 1957 ;   1957 c. 21.

whichever is the greater.

(6) In subsection (5)(a) above " the appropriate sum " means the sum of £1·5 million or, where part only of the levy period in question is included in the period of five years mentioned in that subsection, the proportion of that sum which corresponds to the proportion of the levy period so included.

(7) Sums on account of the amount due under subsection (5) above from the Agency to the Corporation in respect of any levy period may be paid from time to time during and after that period in accordance with arrangements agreed between the Secretary of State and the Agency, notwithstanding that the amount so due has not yet been finally ascertained.

(8) It shall be the duty of the Agency to make any payments in respect of any amount due to the Corporation under subsection (5) above in preference to any other payments they are authorised or required to make in accordance with section 1 of the Cinematograph Films Act 1957.

(9) In this section " the commencement date " means the date on which this section comes into force ; and references to a levy period are references to any period in respect of which a levy is imposed in accordance with regulations made under section 2 of the Cinematograph Films Act 1957.

(10) Paragraph (e) of section 1(1) of the Cinematograph Films Act 1957 (which is superseded by subsections (5) to (8) above) shall cease to have effect, and section 1(5) of that Act (which, as amended by section 1(2) of the Cinematograph Films Act 1975 c. 73. 1975, refers to that paragraph) shall have effect as originally enacted by section 6(2) of the Films Act 1970.   1970 c. 26.

3. In section 1(2) of the Cinematograph Film Production (Special Loans) Act 1949 (which provides that the National Film Finance Corporation shall consist of a chairman, a managing director and not less than three nor more than five other members) for the word " five " there shall be substituted the word " six ".   Constitution of National Film Finance Corporation. 1949 c. 20.

Extension of period of levy under Cinematograph Films Act 1957

Extension of period of levy under Cinematograph Films Act 1957.

1957 c. 21.

4.—(1) In section 2 of the Cinematograph Films Act 1957 (which provides for the imposition of a levy on exhibitors in respect of each of twenty-three successive periods of fifty-two weeks)—

(*a*) in subsection (1) for the words from " a levy " to the end of the subsection there shall be substituted the words " a levy in respect of—

(*a*) the period of fifty-two weeks beginning on 23rd September 1979 ; and

(*b*) each of five successive periods following that period, of which the first shall be a period of fifty-six weeks beginning on 21st September 1980 and each of the remaining four shall be a period of fifty-two weeks " ; and

(*b*) in subsection (3), paragraph (*a*) shall be omitted and in paragraph (*b*), for the words from " so yielded " to " first ' there shall be substituted the words " yielded by way of levy in respect of each period in respect of which it is imposed ".

(2) The first of the five successive periods mentioned in section 2(1)(*b*) of that Act (as amended by subsection (1) above) shall be a financial year of the British Film Fund Agency, notwithstanding that it is longer than a year.

Amendments of Films Act 1960

Extension of period of quota.

1960 c. 57.

5. In section 1 of the Films Act 1960 (which obliges exhibitors to include British or Community films among those shown but would, by virtue of subsection (6), expire at the end of the year 1980), for the words " 1980 " in subsection (6) there shall be substituted the words " 1985 ".

Amendment of quota requirements.

6. After section 3 of the Films Act 1960 there shall be inserted the following section—

" Exhibitions in more than one cinema in the same building.

3A.—(1) This section applies where an exhibitor carries on business as an exhibitor at more than one cinema in the same building, and references below in this section to the associated cinemas are references to all cinemas within that building at which that exhibitor carries on business.

(2) Subsection (2) of section 1 of this Act shall apply as if the associated cinemas were a single cinema, but aggregating as respects any year—

      (*a*) exhibitions in all the associated cinemas of
films registered as quota films; and

      (*b*) the number of days on which films registered as long films are exhibited in any
of those cinemas;

for the purpose of determining whether the prescribed percentage mentioned in subsection (2) has
been reached in that year.

    (3) Subsection (3) of section 1 shall apply as if the
associated cinemas were a single cinema, but the
total showing time of the films of any description
there mentioned exhibited by the exhibitor at that
cinema during any year shall be taken for the
purposes of that subsection to be the aggregate of
the total showing time of the films of that description exhibited by the exhibitor at any of the
associated cinemas during that year."

7.—(1) The Secretary of State may by order made by statutory
instrument suspend the operation of Part I and sections 30 and
31 of the Films Act 1960 (referred to below in this section as
" the quota requirements ").

    (2) Without prejudice to the making of a further order under
subsection (1) above, the Secretary of State may by order so
made revoke any previous order under that subsection.

    (3) Before making any order under this section the Secretary
of State shall consult the Cinematograph Films Council.

    (4) No order shall be made under this section unless a draft
of the order has been laid before Parliament and approved by
a resolution of each House of Parliament.

    (5) Any suspension of the quota requirements under this
section shall not affect the operation of any other provision of
the Films Act 1960 which is expressed to have effect by reference
to the operation of section 1 of that Act.

Power of Secretary of State to suspend quota requirements.
1960 c. 57.

8. The requirements with respect to what description of
persons must be directly engaged in the making of a film for
the film in question to qualify for registration as a British film
under section 17 of the Films Act 1960 shall be modified by
inserting the words " or of any country that is a member State "
after the words " of the Republic of Ireland " wherever those
words occur—

Amendment of requirements for registration as a British film.

      (*a*) in section 17(2)(*c*) (which requires a certain proportion
of the labour costs to be referable to labour of British
subjects or citizens of the Republic of Ireland or

persons ordinarily resident in a Commonwealth country or the Republic of Ireland) ; and

(*b*) in section 22(2) of that Act (which defines the required proportion).

Supplementary

9.—(1) This Act may be cited as the Films Act 1980 ; and—

(*a*) this Act and the Cinematograph Film Production (Special Loans) Acts 1949 to 1970 may be cited together as the Cinematograph Film Production (Special Loans) Acts 1949 to 1980 ;

(*b*) this Act and the Cinematograph Films Acts 1957 to 1970 may be cited together as the Cinematograph Films Acts 1957 to 1980 ; and

(*c*) this Act and the Films Acts 1960 to 1979 may be cited together as the Films Acts 1960 to 1980.

(2) Section 8 of this Act shall come into force on such day as the Secretary of State may by order made by statutory instrument appoint ; and the remaining provisions of this Act shall come into force on the Sunday next following the day on which it is passed.

(3) The enactments mentioned in the Schedule to this Act are hereby repealed to the extent specified in column 3 of the Schedule.

(4) This Act does not extend to Northern Ireland.

SCHEDULE

ENACTMENTS REPEALED

Chapter	Short Title	Extent of Repeal
12 & 13 Geo. 6 c. 20.	The Cinematograph Film Production (Special Loans) Act 1949.	Sections 4 and 8. In the Schedule, paragraph 8(2)(a).
15 & 16 Geo. 6 & 1 Eliz. 2 c. 20.	The Cinematograph Film Production (Special Loans) Act 1952.	The whole Act.
2 & 3 Eliz. 2 c. 15.	The Cinematograph Film Production (Special Loans) Act 1954.	Section 2(2) and (3).
5 & 6 Eliz. 2. c. 21.	The Cinematograph Films Act 1957.	Section 1(1)(e) and the word " and " immediately preceding it. Section 2(3)(a).
1966 c. 48.	The Films Act 1966.	In section 2, subsections (1) and (2)(a).
1968 c. 13.	The National Loans Act 1968.	Section 10(4).
1970 c. 26.	The Films Act 1970.	In section 1(1), paragraph (b) and the word " or " immediately preceding it, and the words from " but " to the end. Section 1(7). Sections 2, 4 and 9.
1975 c. 73.	The Cinematograph Films Act 1975.	The whole Act.

Employment Act 1980

1980 CHAPTER 42

An Act to provide for payments out of public funds towards trade unions' expenditure in respect of ballots, for the use of employers' premises in connection with ballots, and for the issue by the Secretary of State of Codes of Practice for the improvement of industrial relations; to make provision in respect of exclusion or expulsion from trade unions and otherwise to amend the law relating to workers, employers, trade unions and employers' associations; to repeal section 1A of the Trade Union and Labour Relations Act 1974; and for connected purposes. [1st August 1980]

BE IT ENACTED by the Queen's most Excellent Majesty, by and with the advice and consent of the Lords Spiritual and Temporal, and Commons, in this present Parliament assembled, and by the authority of the same, as follows:—

Trade union ballots and Codes of Practice

1.—(1) The Secretary of State may by regulations make a scheme (below called "the scheme") providing for payments by the Certification Officer towards expenditure incurred by independent trade unions in respect of such ballots to which this section applies as may be prescribed by the scheme.

(2) This section applies to a ballot if the purpose of the question to be voted upon (or if there is more than one such question, the purpose of any of them) falls within the purposes mentioned in subsection (3) below.

Payments in respect of secret ballots.

(3) The purposes referred to in subsection (2) above are—

   (*a*) obtaining a decision or ascertaining the views of members of a trade union as to the calling or ending of a strike or other industrial action ;

   (*b*) carrying out an election provided for by the rules of a trade union ;

   (*c*) electing a worker who is a member of a trade union to be a representative of other members also employed by his employer ;

   (*d*) amending the rules of a trade union ;

1964 c. 24.   (*e*) obtaining a decision in accordance with the Trade Union (Amalgamations, etc.) Act 1964 on a resolution to approve an instrument of amalgamation or transfer ;

and such other purposes as the Secretary of State may by order specify.

(4) The scheme may include provision for payments to be made towards expenditure incurred by an independent trade union in respect of arrangements to hold a ballot which is not proceeded with but which, if it had been held, would have been a ballot to which this section applies.

(5) The circumstances in which and the conditions subject to which payments may be made under the scheme, and the amounts of the payments, shall be such as may be prescribed by or determined in accordance with the scheme ; and the scheme shall include provision for restricting the cases in which payments are made to cases in which the ballot is so conducted as to secure, so far as reasonably practicable, that those voting may do so in secret.

(6) The Secretary of State shall out of money provided by Parliament pay to the Certification Officer such sums as he may require for making payments under the scheme.

(7) Any power to make regulations or orders under this section shall be exercisable by statutory instrument ; and—

   (*a*) a statutory instrument containing regulations under this section shall be subject to annulment in pursuance of a resolution of either House of Parliament ;

   (*b*) no order shall be made under this section unless a draft of it has been laid before and approved by resolution of each House of Parliament.

(8) Expressions used in this section and in the 1974 Act have the same meanings in this section as in that Act.

Secret ballots on employer's premises.   **2.**—(1) Subject to subsection (3) below, where an independent trade union proposes that a relevant ballot be held and requests an employer to permit premises of his to be used for the purpose of giving workers employed by him who are members of the union a convenient opportunity of voting, the employer shall, so far as reasonably practicable, comply with the request.

(2) A ballot is a relevant ballot for the purposes of this section if—

    (a) as respects the purpose of the question (or one of the questions) to be voted upon, the ballot satisfies the requirements of a scheme under section 1 of this Act, and

    (b) the proposals for the conduct of the ballot are such as to secure, so far as reasonably practicable, that those voting may do so in secret.

(3) Subsection (1) above shall not apply where, at the time the request is made,—

    (a) the union is not recognised by the employer to any extent for the purpose of collective bargaining, or

    (b) the number of workers employed by the employer, added to the number employed by any associated employer, does not exceed twenty.

(4) A trade union may present a complaint to an industrial tribunal that it has made a request in accordance with subsection (1) above and that it was reasonably practicable for the employer to comply with it, but that he has failed to do so.

(5) An industrial tribunal shall not entertain a complaint under this section unless it is presented to the tribunal before the end of the period of three months beginning with the date of the failure, or within such further period as the tribunal considers reasonable in a case where it is satisfied that it was not reasonably practicable for the complaint to be presented before the end of the period of three months.

(6) Where a tribunal finds that a complaint under this section is well-founded, the tribunal shall make a declaration to that effect, and may make an award of compensation to be paid by the employer to the union which shall be of such amount as the tribunal considers just and equitable in all the circumstances having regard to the employer's default in failing to comply with the request and to any expenses incurred by the union in consequence of the failure.

(7) An appeal shall lie to the Employment Appeal Tribunal on a question of law arising from any decision of, or arising in proceedings before, an industrial tribunal under this section.

(8) The remedy of a trade union for a failure to comply with a request made in accordance with subsection (1) above shall be by way of a complaint under this section and not otherwise.

(9) Expressions used in this section and in the 1974 Act have the same meanings in this section as in that Act.

Issue by
Secretary of
State of Codes
of Practice.

3.—(1) The Secretary of State may issue Codes of Practice containing such practical guidance as he thinks fit for the purpose of promoting the improvement of industrial relations.

(2) The Secretary of State shall after consultation with the Advisory, Conciliation and Arbitration Service (whether carried out before or after the passing of this Act) prepare and publish a draft of any Code of Practice that he proposes to issue under this section.

(3) The Secretary of State shall consider any representations made to him about a draft prepared under subsection (2) above and may modify the draft accordingly.

(4) If the Secretary of State determines to proceed with the draft he shall lay it before both Houses of Parliament and, if it is approved by resolution of each House, shall issue the Code in the form of the draft.

(5) A Code of Practice issued under this section shall come into operation on such day as the Secretary of State may by order appoint ; and an order under this subsection—

> (*a*) may contain such transitional provisions or savings as appear to the Secretary of State to be necessary or expedient ;
>
> (*b*) shall be made by statutory instrument, which shall be subject to annulment in pursuance of a resolution of either House of Parliament.

(6) The Secretary of State may from time to time revise the whole or any part of a Code of Practice issued under this section and issue that revised Code, and subsections (2) to (5) above shall apply to such a revised Code as they apply to the first issue of a Code.

(7) If the Secretary of State is of the opinion that the provisions of a Code of Practice to be issued under this section will supersede the whole or part of a Code previously issued by him under this section or by the Advisory, Conciliation and Arbitration Service under section 6 of the 1975 Act or having effect by virtue of paragraph 4 of Schedule 17 to that Act, he shall in the new Code state that on the day on which the new Code comes into operation in pursuance of an order under subsection (5) above the old Code or a specified part of it shall cease to have effect (subject to any transitional provisions or savings made by the order).

(8) A failure on the part of any person to observe any provision of a Code of Practice issued under this section shall not

of itself render him liable to any proceedings; but in any proceedings before a court or industrial tribunal or the Central Arbitration Committee—

>   (*a*) any such Code shall be admissible in evidence, and
>
>   (*b*) any provision of the Code which appears to the court, tribunal or Committee to be relevant to any question arising in the proceedings shall be taken into account in determining that question.

Exclusion from trade union membership

4.—(1) This section applies to employment by an employer with respect to which it is the practice, in accordance with a union membership agreement, for the employee to belong to a specified trade union or one of a number of specified trade unions.

Unreasonable exclusion or expulsion from trade union.

(2) Every person who is, or is seeking to be, in employment to which this section applies shall have the right—

>   (*a*) not to have an application for membership of a specified trade union unreasonably refused;
>
>   (*b*) not to be unreasonably expelled from a specified trade union.

(3) The rights conferred by subsection (2) above are in addition to and not in substitution for any right which exists apart from that subsection; and, without prejudice to any remedy for infringement of any such other right, the remedies for infringement of a right conferred by that subsection shall be those provided by the following provisions of this section and section 5 below.

(4) A complaint may be presented to an industrial tribunal against a trade union by a person that an application by him for membership of the union has been unreasonably refused, or that he has been unreasonably expelled from the union, in contravention of subsection (2) above.

(5) On a complaint under this section, the question whether a trade union has acted reasonably or unreasonably shall be determined in accordance with equity and the substantial merits of the case, and in particular a union shall not be regarded as having acted reasonably only because it has acted in accordance with the requirements of its rules or unreasonably only because it has acted in contravention of them.

(6) A tribunal shall not entertain a complaint under this section unless it is presented to the tribunal before the end of the period of six months beginning with the date of the refusal or expulsion, as the case may be, or within such further period as the tribunal considers reasonable in a case where it

is satisfied that it was not reasonably practicable for the complaint to be presented before the end of the period of six months.

(7) Where a tribunal finds that a complaint under this section is well-founded, the tribunal shall make a declaration to that effect.

(8) An appeal shall lie to the Employment Appeal Tribunal on any question of law or fact arising from any decision of, or arising in any proceedings before, an industrial tribunal under this section.

(9) For the purposes of this section and section 5 below—

> (a) if an application for membership of a trade union has been neither granted nor rejected before the end of the period within which it might reasonably have been expected to be granted if it was to be granted, the application shall be treated as having been refused on the last day of that period, and

> (b) if under the rules of a trade union any person ceases to be a member of the union on the happening of an event specified in the rules, he shall be treated as having been expelled from the union.

(10) Any expression used in any provision of this section or section 5 below and in the 1974 Act has the same meaning in that provision as it has in that Act, except that any reference in such a provision to a trade union includes a reference to a branch or section of a trade union.

(11) Any provision in an agreement shall be void in so far as it purports to exclude or limit the operation of, or to preclude any person from presenting a complaint or making an application under, this section or section 5 below ; but this subsection shall not apply to an agreement to refrain from instituting or continuing proceedings where a conciliation officer has taken action in accordance with section 133(2) or (3) of the 1978 Act.

Compensation.   **5.**—(1) A person who has made a complaint against a trade union under section 4 above which has been declared to be well-founded may make an application in accordance with subsection (2) below for an award of compensation to be paid to him by the union.

(2) If at the time when the application under this section is made the applicant has been admitted or re-admitted to membership of the union against which he made the complaint, the application shall be to an industrial tribunal ; and if at that time he has not been so admitted or re-admitted, the application shall be to the Employment Appeal Tribunal.

(3) An industrial tribunal or the Employment Appeal Tribunal shall not entertain an application for compensation under this section if it is made before the end of the period of four weeks beginning with the date of the declaration under section 4 above or after the end of the period of six months beginning with that date.

(4) Subject to the following provisions of this section, the amount of compensation awarded on an application under this section—

  (a) in the case of an application to an industrial tribunal, shall be such as the tribunal considers appropriate for the purpose of compensating the applicant for the loss sustained by him in consequence of the refusal or expulsion which was the subject of his complaint, and

  (b) in the case of an application to the Employment Appeal Tribunal, shall be such as the Appeal Tribunal considers just and equitable in all the circumstances.

(5) In determining the amount of compensation to be awarded under this section, the industrial tribunal or the Employment Appeal Tribunal shall apply the same rule concerning the duty of a person to mitigate his loss as applies to damages recoverable under the common law of England and Wales or of Scotland, as the case may be.

(6) Where the industrial tribunal or the Employment Appeal Tribunal finds that the refusal or expulsion which was the subject of the applicant's complaint was to any extent caused or contributed to by any action of the applicant, it shall reduce the amount of the compensation by such proportion as it considers just and equitable having regard to that finding.

(7) The amount of compensation awarded on an application to an industrial tribunal under this section shall not exceed the aggregate of—

  (a) an amount equal to thirty times the limit for the time being imposed by paragraph 8(1)(b) of Schedule 14 to the 1978 Act (maximum amount of a week's pay for purpose of calculating basic award in unfair dismissal cases), and

  (b) an amount equal to the limit for the time being imposed by section 75 of that Act (maximum compensatory award in such cases).

(8) The amount of compensation awarded on an application to the Employment Appeal Tribunal under this section shall not exceed the aggregate of—

  (a) the amount referred to in paragraph (a) of subsection (7) above, and

  (b) the amount referred to in paragraph (b) of that subsection, and

(c) an amount equal to fifty-two times the limit for the time being imposed by paragraph 8(1)(*a*) of Schedule 14 to the 1978 Act (maximum amount of a week's pay for purpose of calculating additional award of compensation in unfair dismissal cases).

(9) An appeal shall lie to the Employment Appeal Tribunal on a question of law arising from any decision of, or arising in proceedings before, an industrial tribunal under this section.

Unfair dismissal

Determination of fairness of dismissal.

6. In section 57(3) of the 1978 Act (determination of question of fairness to depend on whether employer can satisfy tribunal that he acted reasonably) for the words from " the employer can " to the end there shall be substituted the words " in the circumstances (including the size and administrative resources of the employer's undertaking) the employer acted reasonably or unreasonably in treating it as a sufficient reason for dismissing the employee ; and that question shall be determined in accordance with equity and the substantial merits of the case ".

Dismissal relating to trade union membership.

7.—(1) In subsection (3) of section 58 of the 1978 Act (dismissal of employee for non-membership of a union to be fair where there is a union membership agreement unless he objects to membership on grounds of religious belief) for the words from " unless " to the end there shall be substituted the words " but subject to subsections (3A) to (3C) ".

(2) After subsection (3) of that section there shall be inserted—

" (3A) The dismissal of an employee in the circumstances set out in subsection (3) shall be regarded as unfair if he genuinely objects on grounds of conscience or other deeply-held personal conviction to being a member of any trade union whatsoever or of a particular trade union.

(3B) The dismissal of an employee by an employer in the circumstances set out in subsection (3) shall be regarded as unfair if the employee—

(*a*) has been among those employees of the employer who belong to the class to which the union membership agreement relates since before the agreement had the effect of requiring them to be or become members of a trade union, and

(*b*) has not at any time while the agreement had that effect been a member of a trade union in accordance with the agreement.

(3C) Where a union membership agreement takes effect after the commencement of section 7 of the Employment Act 1980 in relation to the employees of any class of an employer, and an employee of that class is dismissed by the employer in the circumstances set out in subsection (3), the dismissal shall be regarded as unfair if—

> (*a*) the agreement has not been approved in relation to those employees in accordance with section 58A, or
>
> (*b*) it has been so approved through a ballot in which the dismissed employee was entitled to vote, but he has not at any time since the day on which the ballot was held been a member of a trade union in accordance with the agreement.

(3D) Where the employer of any employees changes in such circumstances that the employees' period of continuous employment is not broken, this section and section 58A shall have effect as if any reference to the employees of any class of the later employer included a reference to the employees of that class of the former employer.

(3E) In determining for the purposes of subsection (3B) and of section 58A(2) whether a person belongs to a class of employees, any restriction of the class by reference to membership (or objection to membership) of a trade union shall be disregarded."

(3) After that section there shall be inserted—

" Ballots as to union membership agreements.   **58A.**—(1) A union membership agreement shall be taken for the purposes of section 58(3C) to have been approved in relation to the employees of any class of an employer if a ballot has been held on the question whether the agreement should apply in relation to them and not less than 80 per cent. of those entitled to vote in the ballot voted in favour of the agreement's application.

(2) The persons entitled to vote in a ballot under this section in relation to the application of a union membership agreement to the employees of any class of an employer shall be all those employees who belong to that class, and are in the employment of the employer, on the day on which the ballot is held.

(3) A ballot under this section shall be so conducted as to secure that, so far as reasonably practicable, all those entitled to vote have an opportunity of voting, and of doing so in secret."

8.—(1) After section 64 of the 1978 Act there shall be inserted—   Exclusions of rights.

" Extended qualifying period where no more than twenty employees.   **64A.**—(1) Subject to subsection (2), section 54 does not apply to the dismissal of an employee from any employment if—

> (*a*) the period (ending with the effective date of termination) during which the employee was

continuously employed did not exceed two years ; and

(*b*) at no time during that period did the number of employees employed by the employer for the time being of the dismissed employee, added to the number employed by any associated employer, exceed twenty.

(2) Subsection (1) shall not apply to the dismissal of an employee by reason of any such requirement or recommendation as is referred to in section 19(1), or if it is shown that the reason (or, if more than one, the principal reason) for the dismissal was an inadmissible reason."

(2) In section 142(1) of the 1978 Act (which provides that section 54 does not apply in relation to a contract for a fixed term of two years or more) for the words " two years " there shall be substituted the words " one year ".

Basic award.   **9.**—(1) Section 73 of the 1978 Act (calculation of basic award for unfair dismissal) shall be amended as follows.

(2) In subsection (1) (provisions to which calculation of basic award is subject)—

(*a*) after paragraph (*b*) there shall be inserted—

" (*ba*) subsection (7A) (which provides for the amount of the award to be reduced where the employee has unreasonably refused an offer of reinstatement) ;

(*bb*) subsection (7B) (which provides for the amount of the award to be reduced because of the employee's conduct) ; " ; and

(*b*) paragraph (*c*) shall cease to have effect.

(3) In subsection (3) (calculation by reference to number of years of employment) for paragraphs (*b*) and (*c*) there shall be substituted—

" (*b*) one week's pay for each year of employment not falling within paragraph (*a*) which consists wholly of weeks in which the employee was not below the age of twenty-two ; and

(*c*) half a week's pay for each such year of employment not falling within either of paragraphs (*a*) and (*b*).".

(4) After subsection (7) there shall be inserted—

" (7A) Where the tribunal finds that the complainant has unreasonably refused an offer by the employer which if accepted would have the effect of reinstating the complainant in his employment in all respects as if he had not been dismissed, the tribunal shall reduce or further reduce the amount of the basic award to such extent as it considers just and equitable having regard to that finding.

(7B) Where the tribunal considers that any conduct of the complainant before the dismissal (or, where the dismissal was with notice, before the notice was given), other than conduct taken into account by virtue of subsection (7), was such that it would be just and equitable to reduce or further reduce the amount of the basic award to any extent, the tribunal shall reduce or further reduce that amount accordingly.".

(5) Subsection (8) (minimum basic award of two weeks' pay) shall cease to have effect.

10. After section 76 of the 1978 Act there shall be inserted— Contribution in respect of compensation.

" Contribution in respect of compensation. **76A.**—(1) If in proceedings before an industrial tribunal on a complaint against an employer under section 67 the employer claims—

 (*a*) that he was induced to dismiss the complainant by pressure which a trade union or other person exercised on him by calling, organising, procuring or financing a strike or other industrial action, or by threatening to do so, and

 (*b*) that the pressure was exercised because the complainant was not a member of any trade union or of a particular trade union,

the employer may before the hearing of the complaint require the person who he claims exercised the pressure to be joined, or in Scotland sisted, as a party to the proceedings.

(2) Where any person has been joined, or in Scotland sisted, as a party to proceedings before an industrial tribunal by virtue of subsection (1), and the tribunal—

 (*a*) makes an award of compensation under section 68(2) or 71(2)(*a*) or (*b*), but

 (*b*) finds that the claim of the employer (as specified in subsection (1)) is well-founded,

the tribunal may make an order requiring that person to pay to the employer a contribution in respect of that compensation.

(3) The amount of any contribution ordered to be paid under this section in respect of any compensation shall be such as the tribunal considers to be just

2 D 2

and equitable in the circumstances, and may constitute a complete indemnity.

76B.—(1) If in proceedings before an industrial tribunal on a complaint against an employer under section 67 the employer claims that—

(a) he and another person (in this section and in section 76C called " the contractor ") were parties to a contract requiring that work done by employees of his for the purposes of the contract should be done only by employees who were members of trade unions or of a particular trade union,

(b) the complainant could not, consistently with that requirement, be employed on that work,

(c) the employer had requested the contractor to consent to the employment of the complainant on that work notwithstanding that requirement,

(d) the contractor had withheld his consent,

(e) apart from the work to which that requirement (or any similar requirement under other contracts to which the employer was a party) related, the employer had no work available which was suitable for the complainant to do, and

(f) the employer would not have dismissed the complainant but for that requirement,

then, subject to subsection (2), the employer may before the hearing of the complaint require the contractor to be joined, or in Scotland sisted, as a party to the proceedings.

(2) An employer may not by virtue of this section require more than one person to be joined, or in Scotland sisted, in proceedings in respect of any complaint.

(3) Where a person has been joined, or in Scotland sisted, as a party to proceedings before an industrial tribunal by virtue of subsection (1), and the tribunal—

(a) makes an award of compensation under section 68(2) or 71(2)(a) or (b), but

(b) finds that the claim of the employer (as specified in subsection (1)) is well-founded, the tribunal shall order that person to pay to the employer an amount equal to the amount of that compensation.

Contribu-
tion in
respect of
indemnity
under s. 76B.

76C.—(1) If in the proceedings referred to in section 76B the contractor claims that he was induced to withhold the consent referred to in sub-section (1) of that section by pressure which a trade union or other person exercised on him by calling, organising, procuring or financing a strike or other industrial action, or by threatening to do so, the contractor may before the hearing of the complaint require the person who he claims exercised the pressure to be joined, or in Scotland sisted, as a party to the proceedings.

(2) Where any person has been joined, or in Scotland sisted, as a party to proceedings before an industrial tribunal by virtue of subsection (1), and the tribunal—

(a) makes an order under section 76B, but

(b) finds that the claim of the contractor (as specified in subsection (1)) is well-founded,

the tribunal may make an order requiring that person to pay to the contractor a contribution in respect of the contractor's liability to the employer by virtue of the order under section 76B.

(3) The amount of any contribution ordered to be paid under this section in respect of any such liability shall be such as the tribunal considers to be just and equitable in the circumstances, and may constitute a complete indemnity."

Maternity

11.—(1) In subsection (3) of section 33 of the 1978 Act (which specifies conditions to which the rights to maternity pay and to return to work are subject) for paragraph (c) (information to employer) there shall be substituted— Notices to employer.

" (c) in the case of the right to maternity pay, she informs her employer, in writing if he so requests, at least twenty-one days before her absence begins or, if that is not reasonably practicable, as soon as reasonably practicable, that she will be (or is) absent from work wholly or partly because of pregnancy or confinement; and

(d) in the case of the right to return, she informs her employer in writing at least twenty-one days before her absence begins or, if that is not reasonably practicable, as soon as reasonably practicable,—

(i) that she will be (or is) absent from work wholly or partly because of pregnancy or confinement,

(ii) that she intends to return to work with her employer, and

(iii) of the expected week of confinement or, if the confinement has occurred, the date of confinement."

(2) After that subsection there shall be inserted—

" (3A) Where not earlier than forty-nine days after the beginning of the expected week of confinement (or the date of confinement) notified under subsection (3)(*d*) an employee is requested in accordance with subsection (3B) by her employer or a successor of his to give him written confirmation that she intends to return to work, she shall not be entitled to the right to return unless she gives that confirmation within fourteen days of receiving the request or, if that is not reasonably practicable, as soon as reasonably practicable.

(3B) A request under subsection (3A) shall be made in writing and shall be accompanied by a written statement of the effect of that subsection.".

(3) In section 47 of the 1978 Act, in subsection (1) (employee to exercise her right to return to work by notifying the employer at least seven days in advance)—

(*a*) for the word " notifying " there shall be substituted the words " giving written notice to ", and

(*b*) for the word " seven " there shall be substituted the word " twenty-one " ;

and in subsections (6) and (7) for the word " fourteen " there shall be substituted the word " twenty-eight ".

Right to return.

12. After section 56 of the 1978 Act there shall be inserted—

"Exclusion of s.56 in certain cases.   **56A.**—(1) Section 56 shall not apply in relation to an employee if—

(*a*) immediately before her absence began the number of employees employed by her employer, added to the number employed by any associated employer of his, did not exceed five, and

(*b*) it is not reasonably practicable for the employer (who may be the same employer or a successor of his) to permit her to return to work in accordance with section

45(1), or for him or an associated employer to offer her employment under a contract of employment satisfying the conditions specified in subsection (3).

(2) Section 56 shall not apply in relation to an employee if—

(*a*) it is not reasonably practicable for a reason other than redundancy for the employer (who may be the same employer or a successor of his) to permit her to return to work in accordance with section 45(1), and

(*b*) he or an associated employer offers her employment under a contract of employment satisfying the conditions specified in subsection (3), and

(*c*) she accepts or unreasonably refuses that offer.

(3) The conditions referred to in subsections (1) and (2) are—

(*a*) that the work to be done under the contract is of a kind which is both suitable in relation to the employee and appropriate for her to do in the circumstances; and

(*b*) that the provisions of the contract as to the capacity and place in which she is to be employed and as to the other terms and conditions of her employment are not substantially less favourable to her than if she had returned to work in accordance with section 45(1).

(4) Where on a complaint of unfair dismissal any question arises as to whether the operation of section 56 is excluded by subsection (1) or (2), it shall be for the employer to show that the provisions of that subsection were satisfied in relation to the complainant."

13. After section 31 of the 1978 Act there shall be inserted— Time off for ante-natal care.

" Time off for ante-natal care.

   31A.—(1) An employee who is pregnant and who has, on the advice of a registered medical practitioner, registered midwife or registered health visitor, made an appointment to attend at any place for the purpose of receiving ante-natal care shall, subject to the following provisions of this section, have the right not to be unreasonably refused time off during her working hours to enable her to keep the appointment.

(2) Subject to subsection (3), an employer shall not be required by virtue of this section to permit an employee to take time off to keep an appointment unless, if he requests her to do so, she produces for his inspection—

    (*a*) a certificate from a registered medical practitioner, registered midwife or registered health visitor stating that the employee is pregnant, and

    (*b*) an appointment card or some other document showing that the appointment has been made.

(3) Subsection (2) shall not apply where the employee's appointment is the first appointment during her pregnancy for which she seeks permission to take time off in accordance with subsection (1).

(4) An employee who is permitted to take time off during her working hours in accordance with subsection (1) shall be entitled to be paid remuneration by her employer for the period of absence at the appropriate hourly rate.

(5) The appropriate hourly rate in relation to an employee shall be the amount of one week's pay divided by—

    (*a*) the number of normal working hours in a week for that employee when employed under the contract of employment in force on the day when the time off is taken ; or

    (*b*) where the number of such normal working hours differs from week to week or over a longer period, the average number of such hours calculated by dividing by twelve the total number of the employee's normal working hours during the period of twelve weeks ending with the last complete week before the day on which the time off is taken ; or

    (*c*) in a case falling within paragraph (*b*) but where the employee has not been employed for a sufficient period to enable the calculation to be made under that paragraph, a number which fairly represents the number of normal working hours in a week having regard to such of the following considerations as are appropriate in the circumstances, that is to say,—

    (i) the average number of normal working hours in a week which the employee could expect in accordance with the terms of her contract;

    (ii) the average number of such hours of other employees engaged in relevant comparable employment with the same employer.

(6) An employee may present a complaint to an industrial tribunal that her employer has unreasonably refused her time off as required by this section or that he has failed to pay her the whole or part of any amount to which she is entitled under subsection (4).

(7) An industrial tribunal shall not entertain a complaint under subsection (6) unless it is presented within the period of three months beginning with the day of the appointment concerned, or within such further period as the tribunal considers reasonable in a case where it is satisfied that it was not reasonably practicable for the complaint to be presented within the period of three months.

(8) Where on a complaint under subsection (6) the tribunal finds the complaint well-founded it shall make a declaration to that effect; and—

(*a*) if the complaint is that the employer has unreasonably refused the employee time off, the tribunal shall order the employer to pay to the employee an amount equal to the remuneration to which she would have been entitled under subsection (4) if the time off had not been refused; and

(*b*) if the complaint is that the employer has failed to pay the employee the whole or part of any amount to which she is entitled under subsection (4), the tribunal shall order the employer to pay to the employee the amount which it finds due to her.

(9) Subject to subsection (10), a right to any amount under subsection (4) shall not affect any right of an employee in relation to remuneration under her contract of employment (in this section referred to as " contractual remuneration ").

(10) Any contractual remuneration paid to an employee in respect of a period of time off under this section shall go towards discharging any liability of the employer to pay remuneration under subsection (4) in respect of that period, and conversely any payment of remuneration under subsection (4) in respect of a period shall go towards discharging any liability of the employer to pay contractual remuneration in respect of that period.

1979 c. 36.

(11) Until the coming into operation of section 10 of the Nurses, Midwives and Health Visitors Act 1979, this section shall have effect as if for any reference to a registered midwife or registered health visitor there were substituted a reference to a certified midwife."

Other rights of employees

Guarantee payments.

14.—(1) In section 15(2) of the 1978 Act (which restricts entitlement to five days in any one of the periods of three months beginning on 1st February, 1st May, 1st August and 1st November) for the words from " any " to the end there shall be substituted the words " any period of three months ".

(2) This section shall not have effect in relation to workless days (within the meaning of section 12 of that Act) falling before the commencement of this section except so far as they are relevant in determining entitlement to guarantee payments in respect of days falling after that time.

Action short of dismissal relating to trade union membership and activities.

15.—(1) In subsection (1)(c) of section 23 of the 1978 Act (right of employee not to have action taken by his employer to compel him to belong to a union which is not independent) the words " which is not independent " shall cease to have effect.

(2) After subsection (2) of that section there shall be inserted—

" (2A) Where it is the practice, in accordance with a union membership agreement, for the employees of any class of an employer to belong to a specified independent trade union, or to one of a number of specified independent trade unions, then—

(a) subject to subsection (2B), the right conferred on employees of that class by virtue of subsection (1)(b) in relation to a union's activities shall extend to activities on the employer's premises only if the union is a specified union ; and

(b) employees of that class shall not have the right conferred by virtue of subsection (1)(c) except in respect of action which, if it amounted to dismissal from employment to which section 54 applies, would be regarded as unfair by reason of section 58(3A), (3B) or (3C).

(2B) A union membership agreement which takes effect after the commencement of section 7 of the Employment Act 1980 in relation to the employees of any class of an employer shall be disregarded for the purposes of the application of subsection (2A)(*a*) to employees of that class of the employer unless the agreement has, for the purposes of section 58(3C), been approved in relation to them in accordance with section 58A."

(3) Subsections (3), (4), (5)(*a*) and (6) of section 23 and subsection (1)(*b*) of section 25 of the 1978 Act shall cease to have effect.

(4) After section 26 of the 1978 Act there shall be inserted—

" Contribution in respect of compensation on certain complaints under s. 24.

26A.—(1) Where—

    (*a*) a complaint is presented to an industrial tribunal under section 24 on the ground that action has been taken against the complainant by his employer for the purpose of compelling him to be or become a member of a trade union, and

    (*b*) the employer claims in proceedings before the tribunal that he was induced to take the action by pressure which a trade union or other person exercised on him by calling, organising, procuring or financing a strike or other industrial action, or by threatening to do so,

the employer may before the hearing of the complaint require the person who he claims exercised the pressure to be joined, or in Scotland sisted, as a party to the proceedings.

(2) Where any person has been joined, or in Scotland sisted, as a party to proceedings before an industrial tribunal by virtue of subsection (1), and the tribunal—

    (*a*) makes an award of compensation in favour of the complainant, but

    (*b*) finds that the claim of the employer (as specified in subsection (1)) is well-founded,

the tribunal may make an order requiring that person to pay to the employer a contribution in respect of that compensation.

(3) The amount of any contribution ordered to be paid under this section in respect of any compensation shall be such as the tribunal considers to be just

and equitable in the circumstances, and may constitute a complete indemnity."

Restrictions on legal liability

Picketing.   **16.**—(1) For section 15 of the 1974 Act there shall be substituted—

"Peaceful picketing.   **15.**—(1) It shall be lawful for a person in contemplation or furtherance of a trade dispute to attend—

(a) at or near his own place of work, or

(b) if he is an official of a trade union, at or near the place of work of a member of that union whom he is accompanying and whom he represents,

for the purpose only of peacefully obtaining or communicating information, or peacefully persuading any person to work or abstain from working.

(2) If a person works or normally works—

(a) otherwise than at any one place, or

(b) at a place the location of which is such that attendance there for a purpose mentioned in subsection (1) above is impracticable,

his place of work for the purposes of that subsection shall be any premises of his employer from which he works or from which his work is administered.

(3) In the case of a worker who is not in employment and whose last employment was terminated in connection with a trade dispute, subsection (1) above shall in relation to that dispute have effect as if any reference to his place of work were a reference to his former place of work.

(4) A person who is an official of a trade union by virtue only of having been elected or appointed to be a representative of some of the members of the union shall be regarded for the purposes of subsection (1) above as representing only those members; but otherwise an official of a trade union shall be regarded for those purposes as representing all its members."

(2) Nothing in section 13 of the 1974 Act shall prevent an act done in the course of picketing from being actionable in tort unless it is done in the course of attendance declared lawful by section 15 of that Act.

(3) In subsection (2) above "tort" has as respects Scotland the same meaning as in the 1974 Act.

17.—(1) Nothing in section 13 of the 1974 Act shall prevent an act from being actionable in tort on a ground specified in subsection (1)(*a*) or (*b*) of that section in any case where—

    (*a*) the contract concerned is not a contract of employment, and

    (*b*) one of the facts relied upon for the purpose of establishing liability is that there has been secondary action which is not action satisfying the requirements of subsection (3), (4) or (5) below.

(2) For the purposes of this section there is secondary action in relation to a trade dispute when, and only when, a person—

    (*a*) induces another to break a contract of employment or interferes or induces another to interfere with its performance, or

    (*b*) threatens that a contract of employment under which he or another is employed will be broken or its performance interfered with, or that he will induce another to break a contract of employment or to interfere with its performance,

if the employer under the contract of employment is not a party to the trade dispute.

(3) Secondary action satisfies the requirements of this subsection if—

    (*a*) the purpose or principal purpose of the secondary action was directly to prevent or disrupt the supply during the dispute of goods or services between an employer who is a party to the dispute and the employer under the contract of employment to which the secondary action relates : and

    (*b*) the secondary action (together with any corresponding action relating to other contracts of employment with the same employer) was likely to achieve that purpose.

(4) Secondary action satisfies the requirements of this subsection if—

    (*a*) the purpose or principal purpose of the secondary action was directly to prevent or disrupt the supply during the dispute of goods or services between any person and an associated employer of an employer who is a party to the dispute ; and

    (*b*) the goods or services are in substitution for goods or services which but for the dispute would have fallen to be supplied to or by the employer who is a party to the dispute ; and

(c) the employer under the contract of employment to which the secondary action relates is either the said associated employer or the other party to the supply referred to in paragraph (a) above ; and

(d) the secondary action (together with any corresponding action relating to other contracts of employment with the same employer) was likely to achieve the purpose referred to in paragraph (a) above.

(5) Secondary action satisfies the requirements of this subsection if it is done in the course of attendance declared lawful by section 15 of the 1974 Act—

(a) by a worker employed (or, in the case of a worker not in employment, last employed) by a party to the dispute, or

(b) by a trade union official whose attendance is lawful by virtue of subsection (1)(b) of that section.

(6) In subsections (3)(a) and (4)(a) above—

(a) references to the supply of goods or services between two persons are references to the supply of goods or services by one to the other in pursuance of a contract between them subsisting at the time of the secondary action, and

(b) references to directly preventing or disrupting the supply are references to preventing or disrupting it otherwise than by means of preventing or disrupting the supply of goods or services by or to any other person.

(7) Expressions used in this section and in the 1974 Act have the same meanings in this section as in that Act ; and for the purposes of this section an employer who is a member of an employers' association which is a party to a trade dispute shall by virtue of his membership be regarded as a party to the dispute if he is represented in the dispute by the association, but not otherwise.

(8) Subsection (3) of section 13 of the 1974 Act shall cease to have effect.

Acts to compel trade union membership. **18.**—(1) Nothing in section 13 of the 1974 Act shall prevent an act to which this section applies from being actionable in tort on a ground specified in subsection (1)(a) or (b) of section 13 in any case where—

(a) the contract concerned is a contract of employment, or

(b) the contract concerned is not a contract of employment but one of the facts relied upon for the purpose of establishing liability is that any person has—

(i) induced another to break a contract of employment or interfered or induced another to interfere with its performance, or

(ii) threatened that a contract of employment under which he or another is employed will be broken or its performance interfered with, or that he will induce another to break a contract of employment or to interfere with its performance.

(2) This section applies to an act done for the purpose of compelling workers to become members of a particular trade union or of one of two or more particular trade unions, if none of those workers works for the same employer or at the same place as the employee working under the contract of employment referred to in subsection (1) above.

(3) Expressions used in this section and in the 1974 Act have the same meanings in this section as in that Act.

Miscellaneous and general

19. The following enactments shall cease to have effect, that is to say— Enactments ceasing to have effect.

(a) section 1A of the 1974 Act (charter on freedom of the press) ;

(b) sections 11 to 16 of the 1975 Act (procedure for dealing with issues relating to recognition of trade unions) ; and

(c) section 98 of and Schedule 11 to the 1975 Act (extension of terms and conditions of employment) and the Road Haulage Wages Act 1938 (fixing of statutory remuneration). 1938 c. 44.

20.—(1) In this Act— Interpretation, minor and consequential amendments] and repeals.

" the 1974 Act " means the Trade Union and Labour Relations Act 1974 ;

" the 1975 Act " means the Employment Protection Act 1975 ; 1974 c. 52.

" the 1978 Act " means the Employment Protection (Consolidation) Act 1978. 1975 c. 71. 1978 c. 44.

(2) Schedule 1 to this Act (which makes minor and consequential amendments) shall have effect.

(3) The enactments mentioned in Schedule 2 to this Act are hereby repealed to the extent specified in the third column of that Schedule.

21.—(1) This Act may be cited as the Employment Act 1980. Short title commencement and extent.

(2) Sections 2, 4 to 19 and 20(2) and (3) of this Act, and Schedules 1 and 2, shall not come into operation until such day as the Secretary of State may appoint by order made by statutory instrument, and different days may be so appointed for different purposes.

(3) An order under this section may contain such transitional and supplementary provisions as appear to the Secretary of State to be necessary or expedient.

(4) Paragraph 7 of Schedule 1 to this Act shall extend to Northern Ireland, but otherwise this Act shall not extend there.

SCHEDULES

SCHEDULE 1

Minor and Consequential Amendments

The Post Office Act 1969

1. In section 81(1) of the Post Office Act 1969 (exclusion of road 1969 c. 48. haulage workers employed by Post Office from the workers in relation to whom wages councils may operate) the words from the beginning to "the Road Haulage Wages Act 1938 ; and " shall cease to have effect.

The Trade Union and Labour Relations Act 1974

2. In Schedule 1 to the 1974 Act, paragraph 32(2)(*a*) shall cease to have effect.

3. In Schedule 2 to the 1974 Act, in paragraph 32(1) (periodical re-examination of members' superannuation schemes) at the beginning there shall be inserted the words " Subject to paragraph 33A below " and after paragraph 33 there shall be inserted—

" 33A. The Certification Officer, on the application of a trade union or employers' association, may exempt any members' superannuation scheme which it maintains from the requirements of paragraph 32 above if he is satisfied that, by reason of the small number of members to which the scheme is applicable or for any other special reasons, it is unnecessary for the scheme to be examined in accordance with those requirements.

33B. The Certification Officer may at any time revoke any exemption granted under paragraph 33A above if it appears to him that the circumstances by reason of which the exemption was granted have ceased to exist ; and for the purposes of paragraph 32 above the relevant date next following the revocation shall be such date as the Certification Officer may direct."

The Employment Protection Act 1975

4. In section 6 of the 1975 Act, after subsection (10) there shall be inserted—

" (10A) If the Service is of the opinion that the provisions of a Code of Practice to be issued under this section will supersede the whole or part of a Code previously issued by it under this section or by the Secretary of State under section 3 of the Employment Act 1980, it shall in the new Code state that on the day on which the new Code comes into effect in pursuance of an order under subsection (5) or (8) above the old Code or a specified part of it shall cease to have effect (subject to any transitional provisions or savings made by the order)."

5. In section 121(1) of the 1975 Act, for the words " 98 to " there shall be substituted the words " 99 to ".

6. In section 126(1) of the 1975 Act, in the definition of " recognition ", for the words from " has " to " above " there shall

SCH. 1   be substituted the words " in relation to a trade union, means the recognition of the union by an employer, or two or more associated employers, to any extent, for the purpose of collective bargaining ".

7. In section 127(1) of the 1975 Act, after paragraph (*f*) there shall be inserted—

" (*ff*) the Employment Act 1980 ; and ".

The Employment Protection (Consolidation) Act 1978

8. In section 15(5) of the 1978 Act, for the words " relevant periods " there shall be substituted the words " length of the period ".

9. In section 32(1) of the 1978 Act, for " 31 " there shall be substituted " 31A ".

10. In section 55(5) of the 1978 Act, after " 64(1)(*a*) " there shall be inserted " 64A ".

11. In section 56 of the 1978 Act, after the word " then " there shall be inserted the words " subject to section 56A ".

12. In section 58(5) of the 1978 Act, for the words " subsection (1) or (3) " there shall be substituted the words " subsection (1), (3A), (3B) or (3C) ".

13. In section 66 of the 1978 Act (revocation of exclusion orders under section 65)—

(*a*) subsection (1) shall cease to have effect ; and

(*b*) in subsection (2) for the words from " on " to " satisfied " there shall be substituted the words " at any time when an order under section 65 is in force in respect of a dismissal procedures agreement the Secretary of State is satisfied, whether on an application by any of the parties to the agreement or otherwise,".

14. In section 71(3)(*a*) of the 1978 Act, for the words " section 58(1) or (3) " there shall be substituted the words " section 58(1), (3A), (3B) or (3C) ".

15. In section 121(2)(*c*) of the 1978 Act, for the words " or 31(3) " there shall be substituted the words " 31(3) or 31A(4) ".

16. In section 128(4) of the 1978 Act, after the word " references " there shall be inserted the word " applications ".

17. In section 133(1) of the 1978 Act, in paragraph (*a*) after " 31 " there shall be inserted " 31A ", and after paragraph (*c*) there shall be inserted—

" or

(*d*) arising out of a contravention, or alleged contravention, of section 4 of the Employment Act 1980 ".

18. In section 134 of the 1978 Act, for subsection (3) there shall be substituted—

" (3) Where—

(*a*) a person claims that action has been taken in respect of which a complaint could be presented by him under section 67, and (*b*) before any complaint relating to that action has been so presented, a request is made to a conciliation officer (whether by that person or by the employer) to make his services available to them,

the conciliation officer shall act in accordance with subsections (1) and (2) above as if a complaint had been presented."

19. In section 136(5) of the 1978 Act, after the words " subsection (1) " there shall be inserted the words " or under section 2, 4 or 5 of the Employment Act 1980 ".

20. In section 140 of the 1978 Act (restrictions on contracting out of 1978 Act) subsection (2)(*b*) shall cease to have effect.

21. In section 149 of the 1978 Act—

(*a*) in subsection (1)(*c*), after " 64(1) " there shall be inserted " 64A(1) " ;

(*b*) in subsection (2), after " 58 " there shall be inserted " 58A ".

22. In section 154 of the 1978 Act (orders, rules and regulations)—

(*a*) in subsection (1) the words "or an order under section 65 or 66 " shall cease to have effect ; and

(*b*) in subsection (4) for the words from " section 96 " to the end there shall be substituted the words " section 65, 66 or 96 ".

23. In the subsection set out in paragraph 2(1) of Schedule 2 to the 1978 Act, for the words from " the employer can " to the end there shall be substituted the words " in the circumstances (including the size and administrative resources of the employer's undertaking) the employer would have been acting reasonably or unreasonably in treating it as a sufficient reason for dismissing the employee if she had not been absent from work ; and that question shall be determined in accordance with equity and the substantial merits of the case ".

24. In paragraphs 2(4) and 6(3) of Schedule 2 to the 1978 Act, for " 58(3) " there shall be substituted " 58(3) to (3E), 58A ".

25. In paragraph 5 of Schedule 3 to the 1978 Act, for the words " or 31 " there shall be substituted the words " 31 or 31A ".

26. In paragraph 1(2)(*a*) of Schedule 9 to the 1978 Act, after the word " question " there shall be inserted the word " application ".

27. In paragraph 7 of Schedule 9 to the 1978 Act, for sub-paragraph (2) there shall be substituted—

" (2) Any order for the payment of any sum made by an industrial tribunal in Scotland (or any copy of such an order certified by the Secretary of the Tribunals) may be enforced in like manner as an extract registered decree arbitral bearing a warrant for execution issued by the Sheriff Court of any Sheriffdom in Scotland."

28. In paragraph 18 of Schedule 11 to the 1978 Act, after sub-paragraph (*a*) there shall be inserted—

" (*aa*) with respect to the manner in which an application to the Appeal Tribunal under section 5 of the Employment Act 1980 may be made ; "

and after sub-paragraph (*c*) there shall be inserted—

" (*d*) for the registration and proof of any award made on an application to the Appeal Tribunal under section 5 of the Employment Act 1980.".

29. After paragraph 21 of Schedule 11 to the 1978 Act there shall be inserted—

" 21A.—(1) Any sum payable in England and Wales in pursuance of an award of the Appeal Tribunal under section 5 of the Employment Act 1980 which has been registered in accordance with the rules shall, if a county court so orders, be recoverable by execution issued from the county court or otherwise as if it were payable under an order of that court.

(2) Any order by the Appeal Tribunal for the payment in Scotland of any sum in pursuance of such an award (or any copy of such an order certified by the Secretary of the Tribunals) may be enforced in like manner as an extract registered decree arbitral bearing a warrant for execution issued by the Sheriff Court of any Sheriffdom in Scotland."

30. In paragraph 23(1) of Schedule 11 to the 1978 Act, for the words from " section 14 " to " those provisions " there shall be substituted the words " sections 31 and 32 of the Powers of Criminal Courts Act 1973 (powers of Crown Court in relation to fines and forfeited recognisances) shall have effect as if ".

31. In paragraph 10 of Schedule 13 to the 1978 Act, for the words " section 47 " there shall be substituted the words " section 45(1) or in pursuance of an offer made in the circumstances described in section 56A(2) ".

32. In paragraph 11 of Schedule 13 to the 1978 Act, after " 64(1)(*a*) " there shall be inserted " 64A(1) ".

33. In paragraph 7(1) of Schedule 14 to the 1978 Act, after paragraph (*c*) there shall be inserted—

" (*cc*) where the calculation is for the purposes of section 31A the day of the appointment concerned ; ".

SCHEDULE 2
REPEALS

Chapter	Short title	Extent of repeal
1 & 2 Geo. 6. c. 44.	The Road Haulage Wages Act 1938.	The whole Act.
12, 13 & 14 Geo. 6. c. 7.	The Wages Councils Act 1948.	In section 1(1)(*c*), the words from " Parts II and III " to the end, and Schedule 1.
1968 c. 73.	The Transport Act 1968.	Section 69(4)(*d*). So much of Schedules 10 and 11 as amends the Road Haulage Wages Act 1938.
1969 c. 35.	The Transport (London) Act 1969.	In Schedule 3, paragraph 1(2)(*a*).
1969 c. 48.	The Post Office Act 1969.	In section 81, in subsection (1), the words from the beginning to " the Road Haulage Wages Act 1938; and ", and subsection (2).
1972 c. 68.	The European Communities Act 1972.	In paragraph 9(4) of Schedule 4, the words from the beginning to " 1938 " and the words from " after " to " Part VI; and ".
1974 c. 52.	The Trade Union and Labour Relations Act 1974.	Section 1A. Section 13(3). In Schedule 1, in paragraph 32(1) the words from " Except " to " below ", and paragraph 32(2). In Schedule 3, paragraph 4.
1975 c. 18.	The Social Security (Consequential Provisions) Act 1975.	In Schedule 2, paragraph 4.
1975 c. 60.	The Social Security Pensions Act 1975.	Section 31(9).
1975 c. 71.	The Employment Protection Act 1975.	Sections 11 to 16. In section 17(2), paragraph (*b*) and the word " or " immediately preceding it. In section 21(5), paragraph (*b*) and the word " or " immediately preceding it. Section 98. Section 106(1). In section 118(2)(*d*), the words " 16(7)(*b*) or (*c*) or ", the words from " or paragraph " to " this Act ", the words " 16 or " and the words from " or, as " to the end. In section 121(1), the reference to section 16. In section 127(1)(*g*), the words " in paragraphs (*a*) to (*f*) ". Schedule 11. In Part IV of Schedule 16, paragraphs 4 and 17. In Schedule 17, paragraph 13

Chapter	Short title	Extent of repeal
1976 c. 3.	The Road Traffic (Drivers' Ages and Hours of Work) Act 1976.	In section 2(3), the words from " the following " to " 1938 " and the word " and ".
1976 c. 7.	The Trade Union and Labour Relations (Amendment) Act 1976.	Section 2.
1976 c. 79.	The Dock Work Regulation Act 1976.	In section 15(1), in the definition of " recognised ", the words from " and a union " to the end.
1977 c. 3.	The Aircraft and Shipbuilding Industries Act 1977.	In section 56(1), in the definition of " relevant trade union ", the words from " or as " to the end.
1978 c. 36.	The House of Commons (Administration) Act 1978.	In Schedule 1, in paragraph 5(6), the words " Part IV of ".
1978 c. 44.	The Employment Protection (Consolidation) Act 1978.	In section 23, in subsection (1)(*c*), the words " which is not independent ", and subsections (3) to (6). In section 25(1), paragraph (*b*) and the word " and " immediately preceding it. In section 32(1)(*a*), the words " not only " and the words from " but " to " 1975 ". In section 33(3), the word " and " at the end of paragraph (*b*). Section 58(4). Section 66(1). Section 73(1)(*c*) and (8). Section 97. In section 135(1), the words from " for the purpose " to the end. Section 140(2)(*b*). In section 154(1), the words " or an order under section 65 or 66 ". In Schedule 6, in paragraph 12(2)(*b*), sub-paragraph (ii) and the word " or " immediately preceding it.
1979 c. 12.	The Wages Councils Act 1979.	In Schedule 6, paragraph 1.

Magistrates' Courts Act 1980

1980 CHAPTER 43

An Act to consolidate certain enactments relating to the jurisdiction of, and the practice and procedure before, magistrates' courts and the functions of justices' clerks, and to matters connected therewith, with amendments to give effect to recommendations of the Law Commission.   [1st August 1980]

B E IT ENACTED by the Queen's most Excellent Majesty, by and with the advice and consent of the Lords Spiritual and Temporal, and Commons, in this present Parliament assembled, and by the authority of the same, as follows:—

PART I

CRIMINAL JURISDICTION AND PROCEDURE

Jurisdiction to issue process and deal with charges

1.—(1) Upon an information being laid before a justice of the peace for an area to which this section applies that any person has, or is suspected of having, committed an offence, the justice may, in any of the events mentioned in subsection (2) below, but subject to subsections (3) to (5) below,— *Issue of summons to accused or warrant for his arrest.*

    (*a*) issue a summons directed to that person requiring him to appear before a magistrates' court for the area to answer to the information, or

    (*b*) issue a warrant to arrest that person and bring him before a magistrates' court for the area or such magistrates' court as is provided in subsection (5) below.

(2) A justice of the peace for an area to which this section applies may issue a summons or warrant under this section—

   (a) if the offence was committed or is suspected to have been committed within the area, or

   (b) if it appears to the justice necessary or expedient, with a view to the better administration of justice, that the person charged should be tried jointly with, or in the same place as, some other person who is charged with an offence, and who is in custody, or is being or is to be proceeded against, within the area, or

   (c) if the person charged resides or is, or is believed to reside or be, within the area, or

   (d) if under any enactment a magistrates' court for the area has jurisdiction to try the offence, or

   (e) if the offence was committed outside England and Wales and, where it is an offence exclusively punishable on summary conviction, if a magistrates' court for the area would have jurisdiction to try the offence if the offender were before it.

(3) No warrant shall be issued under this section unless the information is in writing and substantiated on oath.

(4) No warrant shall be issued under this section for the arrest of any person who has attained the age of 17 unless—

   (a) the offence to which the warrant relates is an indictable offence or is punishable with imprisonment, or

   (b) the person's address is not sufficiently established for a summons to be served on him.

(5) Where the offence charged is not an indictable offence—

   (a) no summons shall be issued by virtue only of paragraph (c) of subsection (2) above, and

   (b) any warrant issued by virtue only of that paragraph shall require the person charged to be brought before a magistrates' court having jurisdiction to try the offence.

(6) Where the offence charged is an indictable offence, a warrant under this section may be issued at any time notwithstanding that a summons has previously been issued.

(7) A justice of the peace may issue a summons or warrant under this section upon an information being laid before him notwithstanding any enactment requiring the information to be laid before two or more justices.

(8) The areas to which this section applies are any county, any London commission area and the City of London.

2.—(1) A magistrates' court for a county, a London commission area or the City of London shall have jurisdiction to try all summary offences committed within the county, the London commission area or the City (as the case may be).

(2) Where a person charged with a summary offence appears or is brought before a magistrates' court in answer to a summons issued under paragraph (*b*) of section 1(2) above, or under a warrant issued under that paragraph, the court shall have jurisdiction to try the offence.

(3) A magistrates' court for a county, a London commission area or the City of London shall have jurisdiction as examining justices over any offence committed by a person who appears or is brought before the court, whether or not the offence was committed within the county, the London commission area or the City (as the case may be).

(4) Subject to sections 18 to 22 below and any other enactment (wherever contained) relating to the mode of trial of offences triable either way, a magistrates' court shall have jurisdiction to try summarily an offence triable either way in any case in which under subsection (3) above it would have jurisdiction as examining justices.

(5) A magistrates' court shall, in the exercise of its powers under section 24 below, have jurisdiction to try summarily an indictable offence in any case in which under subsection (3) above it would have jurisdiction as examining justices.

(6) A magistrates' court for any area by which a person is tried for an offence shall have jurisdiction to try him for any summary offence for which he could be tried by a magistrates' court for any other area.

(7) Nothing in this section shall affect any jurisdiction over offences conferred on a magistrates' court by any enactment not contained in this Act.

3.—(1) Where an offence has been committed on the boundary between two or more areas to which this section applies, or within 500 yards of such a boundary, or in any harbour, river, arm of the sea or other water lying between two or more such areas, the offence may be treated for the purposes of the preceding provisions of this Act as having been committed in any of those areas.

(2) An offence begun in one area to which this section applies and completed in another may be treated for the purposes of the preceding provisions of this Act as having been wholly committed in either.

(3) Where an offence has been committed on any person, or on or in respect of any property, in or on a vehicle or vessel engaged on any journey or voyage through two or more areas to which this section applies, the offence may be treated for the purposes of the preceding provisions of this Act as having been committed in any of those areas ; and where the side or any part of a road or any water along which the vehicle or vessel passed in the course of the journey or voyage forms the boundary between two or more areas to which this section applies, the offence may be treated for the purposes of the preceding provisions of this Act as having been committed in any of those areas.

(4) The areas to which this section applies are any county, any London commission area and the City of London.

Committal proceedings

General nature of committal proceedings.

4.—(1) The functions of examining justices may be discharged by a single justice.

(2) Examining justices shall sit in open court except where any enactment contains an express provision to the contrary and except where it appears to them as respects the whole or any part of committal proceedings that the ends of justice would not be served by their sitting in open court.

(3) Subject to subsection (4) below and section 102 below, evidence given before examining justices shall be given in the presence of the accused, and the defence shall be at liberty to put questions to any witness at the inquiry.

(4) Examining justices may allow evidence to be given before them in the absence of the accused if—

> (*a*) they consider that by reason of his disorderly conduct before them it is not practicable for the evidence to be given in his presence, or
>
> (*b*) he cannot be present for reasons of health but is represented by counsel or a solicitor and has consented to the evidence being given in his absence.

Adjournment of inquiry.

5.—(1) A magistrates' court may, before beginning to inquire into an offence as examining justices, or at any time during the inquiry, adjourn the hearing, and if it does so shall remand the accused.

(2) The court shall when adjourning fix the time and place at which the hearing is to be resumed ; and the time fixed shall be that at which the accused is required to appear or be brought before the court in pursuance of the remand.

6.—(1) Subject to the provisions of this and any other Act PART I relating to the summary trial of indictable offences, if a magis- Discharge or trates' court inquiring into an offence as examining justices is committal of opinion, on consideration of the evidence and of any state- for trial. ment of the accused, that there is sufficient evidence to put the accused on trial by jury for any indictable offence, the court shall commit him for trial ; and, if it is not of that opinion, it shall, if he is in custody for no other cause than the offence under inquiry, discharge him.

(2) A magistrates' court inquiring into an offence as examining justices may, if satisfied that all the evidence before the court (whether for the prosecution or the defence) consists of written statements tendered to the court under section 102 below, with or without exhibits, commit the accused for trial for the offence without consideration of the contents of those statements, unless—

> (a) the accused or one of the accused is not represented by counsel or a solicitor ;
>
> (b) counsel or a solicitor for the accused or one of the accused, as the case may be, has requested the court to consider a submission that the statements disclose insufficient evidence to put that accused on trial by jury for the offence ;

and subsection (1) above shall not apply to a committal for trial under this subsection.

(3) Subject to section 4 of the Bail Act 1976 and section 41 1976 c. 63. below, the court may commit a person for trial—

> (a) in custody, that is to say, by committing him to custody there to be safely kept until delivered in due course of law, or
>
> (b) on bail in accordance with the Bail Act 1976, that is to say, by directing him to appear before the Crown Court for trial ;

and where his release on bail is conditional on his providing one or more surety or sureties and, in accordance with section 8(3) of the Bail Act 1976, the court fixes the amount in which the surety is to be bound with a view to his entering into his recognizance subsequently in accordance with subsections (4) and (5) or (6) of that section the court shall in the meantime commit the accused to custody in accordance with paragraph (a) of this subsection.

(4) Where the court has committed a person to custody in accordance with paragraph (a) of subsection (3) above, then, if that person is in custody for no other cause, the court may, at any time before his first appearance before the Crown Court,

PART I
1976 c. 63.
grant him bail in accordance with the Bail Act 1976 subject to a duty to appear before the Crown Court for trial.

(5) Where a magistrates' court acting as examining justices commits any person for trial or determines to discharge him, the clerk of the court shall, on the day on which the committal proceedings are concluded or the next day, cause to be displayed in a part of the court house to which the public have access a notice—

(*a*) in either case giving that person's name, address, and age (if known) ;

(*b*) in a case where the court so commits him, stating the charge or charges on which he is committed and the court to which he is committed ;

(*c*) in a case where the court determines to discharge him, describing the offence charged and stating that it has so determined ;

1976 c. 82.
but this subsection shall have effect subject to sections 4 and 6 of the Sexual Offences (Amendment) Act 1976 (anonymity of complainant and accused in rape etc. cases).

(6) A notice displayed in pursuance of subsection (5) above shall not contain the name or address of any person under the age of 17 unless the justices in question have stated that in their opinion he would be mentioned in the notice apart from the preceding provisions of this subsection and should be mentioned in it for the purpose of avoiding injustice to him.

Place of trial on indictment.
7. A magistrates' court committing a person for trial shall specify the place at which he is to be tried, and in selecting that place shall have regard to—

(*a*) the convenience of the defence, the prosecution and the witnesses,

(*b*) the expediting of the trial, and

(*c*) any direction given by or on behalf of the Lord Chief Justice with the concurrence of the Lord Chancellor
1971 c. 23.
under section 4(5) of the Courts Act 1971.

Restrictions on reports of committal proceedings.
8.—(1) Except as provided by subsections (2), (3) and (8) below, it shall not be lawful to publish in Great Britain a written report, or to broadcast in Great Britain a report, of any committal proceedings in England and Wales containing any matter other than that permitted by subsection (4) below.

(2) A magistrates' court shall, on an application for the purpose made with reference to any committal proceedings by the accused or one of the accused, as the case may be, order that

subsection (1) above shall not apply to reports of those proceedings.

(3) It shall not be unlawful under this section to publish or broadcast a report of committal proceedings containing any matter other than that permitted by subsection (4) below—

(*a*) where the magistrates' court determines not to commit the accused, or determines to commit none of the accused, for trial, after it so determines ;

(*b*) where the court commits the accused or any of the accused for trial, after the conclusion of his trial or, as the case may be, the trial of the last to be tried ;

and where at any time during the inquiry the court proceeds to try summarily the case of one or more of the accused under section 25(3) or (7) below, while committing the other accused or one or more of the other accused for trial, it shall not be unlawful under this section to publish or broadcast as part of a report of the summary trial, after the court determines to proceed as aforesaid, a report of so much of the committal proceedings containing any such matter as takes place before the determination.

(4) The following matters may be contained in a report of committal proceedings published or broadcast without an order under subsection (2) above before the time authorised by subsection (3) above, that is to say—

(*a*) the identity of the court and the names of the examining justices ;

(*b*) the names, addresses and occupations of the parties and witnesses and the ages of the accused and witnesses;

(*c*) the offence or offences, or a summary of them, with which the accused is or are charged ;

(*d*) the names of counsel and solicitors engaged in the proceedings ;

(*e*) any decision of the court to commit the accused or any of the accused for trial, and any decision of the court on the disposal of the case of any accused not committed ;

(*f*) where the court commits the accused or any of the accused for trial, the charge or charges, or a summary of them, on which he is committed and the court to which he is committed ;

(*g*) where the committal proceedings are adjourned, the date and place to which they are adjourned ;

> (*h*) any arrangements as to bail on committal or adjournment;
>
> (*i*) whether legal aid was granted to the accused or any of the accused.

(5) If a report is published or broadcast in contravention of this section, the following persons, that is to say—

> (*a*) in the case of a publication of a written report as part of a newspaper or periodical, any proprietor, editor or publisher of the newspaper or periodical;
>
> (*b*) in the case of a publication of a written report otherwise than as part of a newspaper or periodical, the person who publishes it;
>
> (*c*) in the case of a broadcast of a report, any body corporate which transmits or provides the programme in which the report is broadcast and any person having functions in relation to the programme corresponding to those of the editor of a newspaper or periodical,

shall be liable on summary conviction to a fine not exceeding £500.

(6) Proceedings for an offence under this section shall not, in England and Wales, be instituted otherwise than by or with the consent of the Attorney-General.

(7) Subsection (1) above shall be in addition to, and not in derogation from, the provisions of any other enactment with respect to the publication of reports and proceedings of magistrates' and other courts.

(8) For the purposes of this section committal proceedings shall, in relation to an information charging an indictable offence, be deemed to include any proceedings in the magistrates' court before the court proceeds to inquire into the information as examining justices; but where a magistrates' court which has begun to try an information summarily discontinues the summary trial in pursuance of section 25(2) or (6) below and proceeds to inquire into the information as examining justices, that circumstance shall not make it unlawful under this section for a report of any proceedings on the information which was published or broadcast before the court determined to proceed as aforesaid to have been so published or broadcast.

(9) Any report in a newspaper, and any broadcast report, of committal proceedings in a case where publication is permitted by virtue only of subsection (3) above, published as soon as practicable after it is so permitted, shall be treated for the purposes of section 3 of the Law of Libel Amendment Act 1888 (privilege of contemporaneous newspaper reports of court proceedings) and section 9(2) of the Defamation Act 1952 (extension

of the said section 3 to broadcasting) as having been published or broadcast contemporaneously with the committal proceedings.

(10) In this section—

"broadcast" means broadcast by wireless telegraphy sounds or visual images intended for general reception ;

"publish", in relation to a report, means publish the report, either by itself or as part of a newspaper or periodical, for distribution to the public.

Summary trial of information

9.—(1) On the summary trial of an information, the court Procedure shall, if the accused appears, state to him the substance of the on trial. information and ask him whether he pleads guilty or not guilty.

(2) The court, after hearing the evidence and the parties, shall convict the accused or dismiss the information.

(3) If the accused pleads guilty, the court may convict him without hearing evidence.

10.—(1) A magistrates' court may at any time, whether before Adjournment or after beginning to try an information, adjourn the trial, and of trial. may do so, notwithstanding anything in this Act, when composed of a single justice.

(2) The court may when adjourning either fix the time and place at which the trial is to be resumed, or, unless it remands the accused, leave the time and place to be determined later by the court ; but the trial shall not be resumed at that time and place unless the court is satisfied that the parties have had adequate notice thereof.

(3) A magistrates' court may, for the purpose of enabling inquiries to be made or of determining the most suitable method of dealing with the case, exercise its power to adjourn after convicting the accused and before sentencing him or otherwise dealing with him ; but, if it does so, the adjournment shall not be for more than 4 weeks at a time unless the court remands the accused in custody and, where it so remands him, the adjournment shall not be for more than 3 weeks at a time.

(4) On adjourning the trial of an information the court may remand the accused and, where the accused has attained the age of 17, shall do so if the offence is triable either way and—

(a) on the occasion on which the accused first appeared, or was brought, before the court to answer to the information he was in custody or, having been released on bail, surrendered to the custody of the court ; or

PART I
        (b) the accused has been remanded at any time in the course of proceedings on the information ;

and, where the court remands the accused, the time fixed for the resumption of the trial shall be that at which he is required to appear or be brought before the court in pursuance of the remand.

Non-appearance of accused: general provisions.

11.—(1) Subject to the provisions of this Act, where at the time and place appointed for the trial or adjourned trial of an information the prosecutor appears but the accused does not, the court may proceed in his absence.

(2) Where a summons has been issued, the court shall not begin to try the information in the absence of the accused unless either it is proved to the satisfaction of the court, on oath or in such other manner as may be prescribed, that the summons was served on the accused within what appears to the court to be a reasonable time before the trial or adjourned trial or the accused has appeared on a previous occasion to answer to the information.

1973 c. 62.

(3) A magistrates' court shall not in a person's absence sentence him to imprisonment or detention in a detention centre or make an order under section 23 of the Powers of Criminal Courts Act 1973 that a suspended sentence passed on him shall take effect.

(4) A magistrates' court shall not in a person's absence impose any disqualification on him, except on resumption of the hearing after an adjournment under section 10(3) above ; and where a trial is adjourned in pursuance of this subsection the notice required by section 10(2) above shall include notice of the reason for the adjournment.

Non-appearance of accused: plea of guilty.

12.—(1) Subject to subsection (7) below, this section shall apply where a summons has been issued requiring a person to appear before a magistrates' court, other than a juvenile court, to answer to an information for a summary offence, not being an offence for which the accused is liable to be sentenced to be imprisoned for a term exceeding 3 months, and the clerk of the court is notified by or on behalf of the prosecutor that the following documents have been served upon the accused with the summons, that is to say—

        (a) a notice containing such statement of the effect of this section as may be prescribed ; and

        (b) a concise statement in the prescribed form of such facts relating to the charge as will be placed before the court by or on behalf of the prosecutor if the accused pleads guilty without appearing before the court.

(2) Subject to subsections (3) to (5) below, where the clerk of the court receives a notification in writing purporting to be given by the accused or by a solicitor acting on his behalf that the accused desires to plead guilty without appearing before the court, the clerk of the court shall inform the prosecutor of the receipt of the notification and if at the time and place appointed for the trial or adjourned trial of the information the accused does not appear and it is proved to the satisfaction of the court, on oath or in such other manner as may be prescribed, that the notice and statement of facts referred to in subsection (1) above have been served upon the accused with the summons, then—

(a) subject to section 11(3) and (4) above, the court may proceed to hear and dispose of the case in the absence of the accused, whether or not the prosecutor is also absent, in like manner as if both parties had appeared and the accused had pleaded guilty ; or

(b) if the court decides not to proceed as aforesaid, the court shall adjourn or further adjourn the trial for the purpose of dealing with the information as if the notification aforesaid had not been given.

(3) If at any time before the hearing the clerk of the court receives an intimation in writing purporting to be given by or on behalf of the accused that he wishes to withdraw the notification aforesaid, the clerk of the court shall inform the prosecutor thereof and the court shall deal with the information as if this section had not been passed.

(4) Before accepting the plea of guilty and convicting the accused in his absence under subsection (2) above, the court shall cause the notification and statement of facts aforesaid, including any submission received with the notification which the accused wishes to be brought to the attention of the court with a view to mitigation of sentence, to be read out before the court.

(5) If the court proceeds under subsection (2) above to hear and dispose of the case in the absence of the accused, the court shall not permit any statement to be made by or on behalf of the prosecutor with respect to any facts relating to the offence charged other than the statement of facts aforesaid except on a resumption of the trial after an adjournment under section 10(3) above.

(6) In relation to an adjournment by reason of the requirements of paragraph (b) of subsection (2) above or to an adjournment on the occasion of the accused's conviction in his absence under that subsection, the notice required by section 10(2) above shall include notice of the reason for the adjournment.

(7) The Secretary of State may by order made by statutory instrument provide that this section shall not apply in relation to such offences (in addition to an offence for which the accused is liable to be sentenced to be imprisoned for a term exceeding 3 months) as may be specified in the order, and any order under this subsection—

> (a) may vary or revoke any previous order thereunder ; and
>
> (b) shall not be made unless a draft thereof has been approved by resolution of each House of Parliament.

(8) Any such notice or statement as is mentioned in subsection (1) above may be served in Scotland with a summons which is so served under the Summary Jurisdiction (Process) Act 1881.

13.—(1) Subject to the provisions of this section, where the court, instead of proceeding in the absence of the accused, adjourns or further adjourns the trial, the court may, if the information has been substantiated on oath, issue a warrant for his arrest.

(2) Where a summons has been issued, the court shall not issue a warrant under this section unless either it is proved to the satisfaction of the court, on oath or in such other manner as may be prescribed, that the summons was served on the accused within what appears to the court to be a reasonable time before the trial or adjourned trial or the accused has appeared on a previous occasion to answer to the information.

(3) A warrant for the arrest of any person who has attained the age of 17 shall not be issued under this section unless—

> (a) the offence to which the warrant relates is punishable with imprisonment ; or
>
> (b) the court, having convicted the accused, proposes to impose a disqualification on him.

(4) This section shall not apply to an adjournment by reason of the requirements of paragraph (b) of subsection (2) of section 12 above or to an adjournment on the occasion of the accused's conviction in his absence under that subsection.

(5) Where the court adjourns the trial—

> (a) after having, either on that or on a previous occasion, received any evidence or convicted the accused without hearing evidence on his pleading guilty under section 9(3) above ; or
>
> (b) after having on a previous occasion convicted the accused without hearing evidence on his pleading guilty under section 12(2) above,

the court shall not issue a warrant under this section unless it thinks it undesirable, by reason of the gravity of the offence, to continue the trial in the absence of the accused.

14.—(1) Where a summons has been issued under section 1 above and a magistrates' court has begun to try the information to which the summons relates, then, if—

    (*a*) the accused, at any time during or after the trial, makes a statutory declaration that he did not know of the summons or the proceedings until a date specified in the declaration, being a date after the court has begun to try the information ; and

    (*b*) within 21 days of that date the declaration is served on the clerk to the justices,

without prejudice to the validity of the information, the summons and all subsequent proceedings shall be void.

(2) For the purposes of subsection (1) above a statutory declaration shall be deemed to be duly served on the clerk to the justices if it is delivered to him, or left at his office, or is sent in a registered letter or by the recorded delivery service addressed to him at his office.

(3) If on the application of the accused it appears to a magistrates' court (which for this purpose may be composed of a single justice) that it was not reasonable to expect the accused to serve such a statutory declaration as is mentioned in subsection (1) above within the period allowed by that subsection, the court may accept service of such a declaration by the accused after that period has expired ; and a statutory declaration accepted under this subsection shall be deemed to have been served as required by that subsection.

(4) Where any proceedings have become void by virtue of subsection (1) above, the information shall not be tried again by any of the same justices.

15.—(1) Where at the time and place appointed for the trial or adjourned trial of an information the accused appears or is brought before the court and the prosecutor does not appear, the court may dismiss the information or, if evidence has been received on a previous occasion, proceed in the absence of the prosecutor.

(2) Where, instead of dismissing the information or proceeding in the absence of the prosecutor, the court adjourns the trial, it shall not remand the accused in custody unless he has been brought from custody or cannot be remanded on bail by reason of his failure to find sureties.

16. Subject to section 11(3) and (4) and to section 12 above, where at the time and place appointed for the trial or adjourned trial of an information neither the prosecutor nor the accused appears, the court may dismiss the information or, if evidence has been received on a previous occasion, proceed in their

2 E 2

PART I
Certain offences triable either way.

Offences triable on indictment or summarily

17.—(1) The offences listed in Schedule 1 to this Act shall be triable either way.

(2) Subsection (1) above is without prejudice to any other enactment by virtue of which any offence is triable either way.

Initial procedure on information against adult for offence triable either way.

18.—(1) Sections 19 to 23 below shall have effect where a person who has attained the age of 17 appears or is brought before a magistrates' court on an information charging him with an offence triable either way.

(2) Without prejudice to section 11(1) above, everything that the court is required to do under sections 19 to 22 below must be done before any evidence is called and, subject to subsection (3) below and section 23 below, with the accused present in court.

(3) The court may proceed in the absence of the accused in accordance with such of the provisions of sections 19 to 22 below as are applicable in the circumstances if the court considers that by reason of his disorderly conduct before the court it is not practicable for the proceedings to be conducted in his presence ; and subsections (3) to (5) of section 23 below, so far as applicable, shall have effect in relation to proceedings conducted in the absence of the accused by virtue of this subsection (references in those subsections to the person representing the accused being for this purpose read as references to the person, if any, representing him).

(4) A magistrates' court proceeding under sections 19 to 23 below may adjourn the proceedings at any time, and on doing so on any occasion when the accused is present may remand the accused, and shall remand him if—

    (a) on the occasion on which he first appeared, or was brought, before the court to answer to the information he was in custody or, having been released on bail, surrendered to the custody of the court ; or

    (b) he has been remanded at any time in the course of proceedings on the information ;

and where the court remands the accused, the time fixed for the resumption of the proceedings shall be that at which he is required to appear or be brought before the court in pursuance of the remand.

(5) The functions of a magistrates' court under sections 19 to 23 below may be discharged by a single justice, but the foregoing provision shall not be taken to authorise the summary trial of an information by a magistrates' court composed of less than two justices.

19.—(1) The court shall consider whether, having regard to the matters mentioned in subsection (3) below and any representations made by the prosecutor or the accused, the offence appears to the court more suitable for summary trial or for trial on indictment.

(2) Before so considering, the court—

　(*a*) shall cause the charge to be written down, if this has not already been done, and read to the accused ; and

　(*b*) shall afford first the prosecutor and then the accused an opportunity to make representations as to which mode of trial would be more suitable.

(3) The matters to which the court is to have regard under subsection (1) above are the nature of the case ; whether the circumstances make the offence one of serious character ; whether the punishment which a magistrates' court would have power to inflict for it would be adequate ; and any other circumstances which appear to the court to make it more suitable for the offence to be tried in one way rather than the other.

(4) If the prosecution is being carried on by the Attorney General, the Solicitor General or the Director of Public Prosecutions and he applies for the offence to be tried on indictment, the preceding provisions of this section and sections 20 and 21 below shall not apply, and the court shall proceed to inquire into the information as examining justices.

20.—(1) If, where the court has considered as required by section 19(1) above, it appears to the court that the offence is more suitable for summary trial, the following provisions of this section shall apply (unless excluded by section 23 below).

(2) The court shall explain to the accused in ordinary language—

　(*a*) that it appears to the court more suitable for him to be tried summarily for the offence, and that he can either consent to be so tried or, if he wishes, be tried by a jury ; and

　(*b*) that if he is tried summarily and is convicted by the court, he may be committed for sentence to the Crown Court under section 38 below if the convicting court, on obtaining information about his character and antecedents, is of opinion that they are such that greater punishment should be inflicted than the convicting court has power to inflict for the offence.

(3) After explaining to the accused as provided by subsection (2) above the court shall ask him whether he consents to be tried summarily or wishes to be tried by a jury, and—

(a) if he consents to be tried summarily, shall proceed to the summary trial of the information ;

(b) if he does not so consent, shall proceed to inquire into the information as examining justices.

Procedure where trial on indictment appears more suitable.

21. If, where the court has considered as required by section 19(1) above, it appears to the court that the offence is more suitable for trial on indictment, the court shall tell the accused that the court has decided that it is more suitable for him to be tried for the offence by a jury, and shall proceed to inquire into the information as examining justices.

Certain offences triable either way to be tried summarily if value involved is small.

22.—(1) If the offence charged by the information is one of those mentioned in the first column of Schedule 2 to this Act (in this section referred to as " scheduled offences ") then, subject to subsection (7) below, the court shall, before proceeding in accordance with section 19 above, consider whether, having regard to any representations made by the prosecutor or the accused, the value involved (as defined in subsection (10) below) appears to the court to exceed the relevant sum.

For the purposes of this section the relevant sum is £200.

(2) If, where subsection (1) above applies, it appears to the court clear that, for the offence charged, the value involved does not exceed the relevant sum, the court shall proceed as if the offence were triable only summarily, and sections 19 to 21 above shall not apply.

(3) If, where subsection (1) above applies, it appears to the court clear that, for the offence charged, the value involved exceeds the relevant sum, the court shall thereupon proceed in accordance with section 19 above in the ordinary way without further regard to the provisions of this section.

(4) If, where subsection (1) above applies, it appears to the court for any reason not clear whether, for the offence charged, the value involved does or does not exceed the relevant sum, the provisions of subsections (5) and (6) below shall apply.

(5) The court shall cause the charge to be written down, if this has not already been done, and read to the accused, and shall explain to him in ordinary language—

(a) that he can, if he wishes, consent to be tried summarily for the offence and that if he consents to be so tried, he will definitely be tried in that way ; and

(*b*) that if he is tried summarily and is convicted by the
court, his liability to imprisonment or a fine will be
limited as provided in section 33 below.

(6) After explaining to the accused as provided by subsection
(5) above the court shall ask him whether he consents to be tried
summarily and—

(*a*) if he so consents, shall proceed in accordance with subsection (2) above as if that subsection applied ;

(*b*) if he does not so consent, shall proceed in accordance
with subsection (3) above as if that subsection applied.

(7) Subsection (1) above shall not apply where the offence
charged—

(*a*) is one of two or more offences with which the accused
is charged on the same occasion and which appear to
the court to constitute or form part of a series of two
or more offences of the same or a similar character ; or

(*b*) consists in the incitement to commit two or more
scheduled offences.

(8) Where a person is convicted by a magistrates' court of a
scheduled offence, it shall not be open to him to appeal to the
Crown Court against the conviction on the ground that the
convicting court's decision as to the value involved was mistaken.

(9) If, where subsection (1) above applies, the offence charged
is one with which the accused is charged jointly with a person
who has not attained the age of 17, the reference in that subsection to any representations made by the accused shall be read
as including any representations made by the person under 17.

(10) In this section " the value involved ", in relation to any
scheduled offence, means the value indicated in the second
column of Schedule 2 to this Act, measured as indicated in the
third column of that Schedule ; and in that Schedule " the
material time " means the time of the alleged offence.

23.—(1) Where—   Power of
court, with
(*a*) the accused is represented by counsel or a solicitor who   consent of
in his absence signifies to the court the accused's con-   legally
sent to the proceedings for determining how he is to   represented
be tried for the offence being conducted in his absence ;   accused, to
and   proceed in
his absence.
(*b*) the court is satisfied that there is good reason for proceeding in the absence of the accused,

the following provisions of this section shall apply.

(2) Subject to the following provisions of this section, the
court may proceed in the absence of the accused in accordance

2 E 4

with such of the provisions of sections 19 to 22 above as are applicable in the circumstances.

(3) If, in a case where subsection (1) of section 22 above applies, it appears to the court as mentioned in subsection (4) of that section, subsections (5) and (6) of that section shall not apply and the court—

    (*a*) if the accused's consent to be tried summarily has been or is signified by the person representing him, shall proceed in accordance with subsection (2) of that section as if that subsection applied ; or

    (*b*) if that consent has not been and is not so signified, shall proceed in accordance with subsection (3) of that section as if that subsection applied.

(4) If, where the court has considered as required by section 19(1) above, it appears to the court that the offence is more suitable for summary trial then—

    (*a*) if the accused's consent to be tried summarily has been or is signified by the person representing him, section 20 above shall not apply, and the court shall proceed to the summary trial of the information ; or

    (*b*) if that consent has not been and is not so signified, section 20 above shall not apply and the court shall proceed to inquire into the information as examining justices and may adjourn the hearing without remanding the accused.

(5) If, where the court has considered as required by section 19(1) above, it appears to the court that the offence is more suitable for trial on indictment, section 21 above shall not apply, and the court shall proceed to inquire into the information as examining justices and may adjourn the hearing without remanding the accused.

Summary trial of information against child or young persons for indictable offence.
1933 c. 12.

24.—(1) Where a person under the age of 17 appears or is brought before a magistrates' court on an information charging him with an indictable offence other than homicide, he shall be tried summarily unless—

    (*a*) he has attained the age of 14 and the offence is such as is mentioned in subsection (2) of section 53 of the Children and Young Persons Act 1933 (under which young persons convicted on indictment of certain grave crimes may be sentenced to be detained for long periods) and the court considers that if he is found guilty of the offence it ought to be possible to sentence him in pursuance of that subsection ; or

   (*b*) he is charged jointly with a person who has attained
        the age of 17 and the court consider it necessary in
        the interests of justice to commit them both for trial;
and accordingly in a case falling within paragraph (*a*) or (*b*) of
this subsection the court shall commit the accused for trial if
either it is of opinion that there is sufficient evidence to put him
on trial or it has power under section 6(2) above so to commit
him without consideration of the evidence.

   (2) Where, in a case falling within subsection (1)(*b*) above,
a magistrates' court commits a person under the age of 17 for
trial for an offence with which he is charged jointly with a person
who has attained that age, the court may also commit him for
trial for any other indictable offence with which he is charged
at the same time (whether jointly with the person who has
attained that age or not) if that other offence arises out of
circumstances which are the same as or connected with those
giving rise to the first-mentioned offence.

   (3) If on trying a person summarily in pursuance of subsection (1) above the court finds him guilty, it may impose a
fine of an amount not exceeding £200 or may exercise the same
powers as it could have exercised if he had been found guilty
of an offence for which, but for section 19(1) of the Powers of 1973 c. 62.
Criminal Courts Act 1973, it could have sentenced him to
imprisonment for a term not exceeding 3 months.

   (4) In relation to a person under the age of 14 subsection (3)
above shall have effect as if for the words " £200 " there were
substituted the words " £50 "; but this subsection shall cease to
have effect on the coming into force of section 4 of the Children 1969 c. 54.
and Young Persons Act 1969 (which prohibits criminal proceedings against children).

   25.—(1) Subsections (2) to (4) below shall have effect where Power to
a person who has attained the age of 17 appears or is brought change from
before a magistrates' court on an information charging him with summary trial
an offence triable either way. to committal
                                                              proceedings,
   (2) Where the court has (otherwise than in pursuance of and vice versa.
section 22(2) above) begun to try the information summarily, the
court may, at any time before the conclusion of the evidence
for the prosecution, discontinue the summary trial and proceed
to inquire into the information as examining justices and, on
doing so, may adjourn the hearing without remanding the
accused.

   (3) Where the court has begun to inquire into the information
as examining justices, then, if at any time during the inquiry it
appears to the court, having regard to any representations made
in the presence of the accused by the prosecutor, or made by the

accused, and to the nature of the case, that the offence is after all more suitable for summary trial, the court may, after doing as provided in subsection (4) below, ask the accused whether he consents to be tried summarily and, if he so consents, may proceed to try the information summarily ; but if the prosecution is being carried on by the Attorney General, the Solicitor General or the Director of Public Prosecutions, the court shall not act under this subsection without his consent.

(4) Before asking the accused under subsection (3) above whether he consents to be tried summarily, the court shall in ordinary language—

> (*a*) explain to him that it appears to the court more suitable for him to be tried summarily for the offence, but that this can only be done if he consents to be so tried ; and

> (*b*) unless it has already done so, explain to him, as provided in section 20(2)(*b*) above, about the court's power to commit to the Crown Court for sentence.

(5) Where a person under the age of 17 appears or is brought before a magistrates' court on an information charging him with an indictable offence other than homicide, and the court—

> (*a*) has begun to try the information summarily on the footing that the case does not fall within paragraph (*a*) or (*b*) of section 24(1) above and must therefore be tried summarily, as required by the said section 24(1) ; or

> (*b*) has begun to inquire into the case as examining justices on the footing that the case does so fall,

subsection (6) or (7) below, as the case may be, shall have effect.

(6) If, in a case falling within subsection (5)(*a*) above, it appears to the court at any time before the conclusion of the evidence for the prosecution that the case is after all one which under the said section 24(1) ought not to be tried summarily, the court may discontinue the summary trial and proceed to inquire into the information as examining justices and, on doing so, may adjourn the hearing without remanding the accused.

(7) If, in a case falling within subsection (5)(*b*) above, it appears to the court at any time during the inquiry that the case is after all one which under the said section 24(1) ought to be tried summarily, the court may proceed to try the information summarily.

Power to issue summons to accused in certain circumstances. **26.**—(1) Where—

> (*a*) in the circumstances mentioned in section 23(1)(*a*) above the court is not satisfied that there is good reason for proceeding in the absence of the accused ; or

(*b*) subsection (4)(*b*) or (5) of section 23 or subsection (2) or (6) of section 25 above applies, and the court adjourns the hearing in pursuance of that subsection without remanding the accused,

the justice or any of the justices of which the court is composed may issue a summons directed to the accused requiring his presence before the court.

(2) If the accused is not present at the time and place appointed—

(*a*) in a case within subsection (1)(*a*) above, for the proceedings under section 19(1) or 22(1) above, as the case may be ; or

(*b*) in a case within subsection (1)(*b*) above, for the resumption of the hearing,

the court may issue a warrant for his arrest.

27. Where on the summary trial of an information for an offence triable either way the court dismisses the information, the dismissal shall have the same effect as an acquittal on indictment.

Effect of dismissal of information for offence triable either way.

28. Where under section 25(3) or (7) above a magistrates' court, having begun to inquire into an information as examining justices, proceeds to try the information summarily, then, subject to sections 102(9) and 103(3) below, any evidence already given before the court shall be deemed to have been given in and for the purposes of the summary trial.

Using in summary trial evidence given in committal proceedings.

Power to remit person under 17 for trial to juvenile court

29.—(1) Where—

(*a*) a person under the age of 17 (" the juvenile ") appears or is brought before a magistrates' court other than a juvenile court on an information jointly charging him and one or more other persons with an offence ; and

(*b*) that other person, or any of those other persons, has attained that age,

Power of magistrates' court to remit a person under 17 for trial to a juvenile court in certain circumstances.

subsection (2) below shall have effect notwithstanding proviso (*a*) in section 46(1) of the Children and Young Persons Act 1933 (which would otherwise require the charge against the juvenile to be heard by a magistrates' court other than a juvenile court).

1933 c. 12.

In the following provisions of this section " the older accused " means such one or more of the accused as have attained the age of 17.

(2) If—

    (*a*) the court proceeds to the summary trial of the information in the case of both or all of the accused, and the older accused or each of the older accused pleads guilty ; or

    (*b*) the court—

        (i) in the case of the older accused or each of the older accused, proceeds to inquire into the information as examining justices and either commits him for trial or discharges him ; and

        (ii) in the case of the juvenile, proceeds to the summary trial of the information,

then, if in either situation the juvenile pleads not guilty, the court may before any evidence is called in his case remit him for trial to a juvenile court acting for the same place as the remitting court or for the place where he habitually resides.

(3) A person remitted to a juvenile court under subsection (2) above shall be brought before and tried by a juvenile court accordingly.

(4) Where a person is so remitted to a juvenile court—

    (*a*) he shall have no right of appeal against the order of remission ; and

    (*b*) the remitting court may give such directions as appear to be necessary with respect to his custody or for his release on bail until he can be brought before the juvenile court.

(5) The preceding provisions of this section shall apply in relation to a corporation as if it were an individual who has attained the age of 17.

Remand for medical examination

Remand for medical examination.   **30.**—(1) If, on the trial by a magistrates' court of an offence punishable on summary conviction with imprisonment, the court is satisfied that the accused did the act or made the omission charged but is of opinion that an inquiry ought to be made into his physical or mental condition before the method of dealing with him is determined, the court shall adjourn the case to enable a medical examination and report to be made and shall remand him ; but the adjournment shall not be for more than 3 weeks at a time where the court remands him in custody nor for more than 4 weeks at a time where it remands him on bail.

(2) Where on an adjournment under subsection (1) above the accused is remanded on bail, the court shall impose conditions under paragraph (*d*) of section 3(6) of the Bail Act 1976 and the requirements imposed as conditions under that paragraph shall be or shall include requirements that the accused—

> (*a*) undergo medical examination by a duly qualified medical practitioner or, where the inquiry is into his mental condition and the court so directs, two such practitioners ; and

> (*b*) for that purpose attend such an institution or place, or on such practitioner, as the court directs and, where the inquiry is into his mental condition, comply with any other directions which may be given to him for that purpose by any person specified by the court or by a person of any class so specified.

(3) The Costs in Criminal Cases Act 1973 shall apply to a duly qualified medical practitioner who makes a report otherwise than in writing for the purposes of this section as it applies to a person called to give evidence, and shall so apply notwithstanding that the proceedings for the purposes of which the report is made are not proceedings to which section 1 of that Act applies.

Powers in respect of offenders

31.—(1) Without prejudice to section 133 below, a magistrates' court shall not have power to impose imprisonment for more than 6 months in respect of any one offence.

(2) Unless expressly excluded, subsection (1) above shall apply even if the offence in question is one for which a person would otherwise be liable on summary conviction to imprisonment for more than 6 months.

(3) Any power of a magistrates' court to impose a term of imprisonment for non-payment of a fine, or for want of sufficient distress to satisfy a fine, shall not be limited by virtue of subsection (1) above.

(4) In subsection (3) above "fine" includes a pecuniary penalty but does not include a pecuniary forfeiture or pecuniary compensation.

32.—(1) On summary conviction of any of the offences triable either way listed in Schedule 1 to this Act a person shall be liable to imprisonment for a term not exceeding 6 months or to a fine not exceeding the prescribed sum or both, except that—

> (*a*) a magistrates' court shall not have power to impose imprisonment for an offence so listed if the Crown

Court would not have that power in the case of an adult convicted of it on indictment ;

(b) on summary conviction of an offence consisting in the incitement to commit an offence triable either way a person shall not be liable to any greater penalty than he would be liable to on summary conviction of the last-mentioned offence : and

(c) on summary conviction of attempting to commit an offence triable either way a person shall not be liable to any greater penalty than he would be liable to on summary conviction of the completed offence.

(2) For any offence triable either way which is not listed in Schedule 1 to this Act, being an offence under a relevant enactment, the maximum fine which may be imposed on summary conviction shall by virtue of this subsection be the prescribed sum unless the offence is one for which by virtue of an enactment other than this subsection a larger fine may be imposed on summary conviction.

(3) Where, by virtue of any relevant enactment, a person summarily convicted of an offence triable either way would, apart from this section, be liable to a maximum fine of one amount in the case of a first conviction and of a different amount in the case of a second or subsequent conviction, subsection (2) above shall apply irrespective of whether the conviction is a first, second or subsequent one.

(4) Subsection (2) above shall not affect so much of any enactment as (in whatever words) makes a person liable on summary conviction to a fine not exceeding a specified amount for each day on which a continuing offence is continued after conviction or the occurrence of any other specified event.

(5) Subsection (2) above shall not apply on summary conviction of any of the following offences : —

1971 c. 38.

(a) offences under section 5(2) of the Misuse of Drugs Act 1971 (having possession of a controlled drug) where the controlled drug in relation to which the offence was committed was a Class B or Class C drug ;

(b) offences under the following provisions of that Act, where the controlled drug in relation to which the offence was committed was a Class C drug, namely—

(i) section 4(2) (production, or being concerned in the production, of a controlled drug) ;

(ii) section 4(3) (supplying or offering a controlled drug or being concerned in the doing of either activity by another) ;

(iii) section 5(3) (having possession of a controlled drug with intent to supply it to another) ;

(iv) section 8 (being the occupier, or concerned in the management, of premises and permitting or suffering certain activities to take place there) ;

(v) section 12(6) (contravention of direction prohibiting practitioner etc. from possessing, supplying etc. controlled drugs) ; or

(vi) section 13(3) (contravention of direction prohibiting practitioner etc. from prescribing, supplying etc. controlled drugs).

(6) Where, as regards any offence triable either way, there is under any enactment (however framed or worded) a power by subordinate instrument to restrict the amount of the fine which on summary conviction can be imposed in respect of that offence—

(a) subsection (2) above shall not affect that power or override any restriction imposed in the exercise of that power ; and

(b) the amount to which that fine may be restricted in the exercise of that power shall be any amount less than the maximum fine which could be imposed on summary conviction in respect of the offence apart from any restriction so imposed.

(7) Where there is under any relevant enactment (however framed or worded) a power by subordinate instrument to impose penal provisions, being a power which allows the creation of offences triable either way—

(a) the maximum fine which may in the exercise of that power be authorised on summary conviction in respect of an offence triable either way shall by virtue of this subsection be the prescribed sum unless some larger maximum fine can be authorised on summary conviction in respect of such an offence by virtue of an enactment other than this subsection ; and

(b) subsection (2) above shall not override any restriction imposed in the exercise of that power on the amount of the fine which on summary conviction can be imposed in respect of an offence triable either way created in the exercise of the power.

(8) In subsection (5) above "controlled drug", "Class B drug" and "Class C drug" have the same meaning as in the Misuse of Drugs Act 1971.

1971 c. 38.

(9) In this section—

" fine " includes a pecuniary penalty but does not include a pecuniary forfeiture or pecuniary compensation;

" the prescribed sum " means £1,000 or such sum as is for the time being substituted in this definition by an order in force under section 143(1) below ;

1977 c. 45.

" relevant enactment " means an enactment contained in the Criminal Law Act 1977 or in any Act passed before, or in the same Session as, that Act.

Maximum penalties on summary conviction in pursuance of section 22.

33.—(1) Where in pursuance of subsection (2) of section 22 above a magistrates' court proceeds to the summary trial of an information, then, if the accused is summarily convicted of the offence—

(a) the court shall not have power to impose on him in respect of that offence imprisonment for more than 3 months or a fine greater than £500 ; and

(b) section 38 below shall not apply as regards that offence.

(2) In subsection (1) above " fine " includes a pecuniary penalty but does not include a pecuniary forfeiture or pecuniary compensation.

Mitigation of penalties, etc.

34.—(1) Where under any enactment whether passed before or after the commencement of this Act a magistrates' court has power to sentence an offender to imprisonment for a period specified by the enactment, or to a fine of an amount specified by the enactment, then, except where an Act passed after 31st December 1879 expressly provides to the contrary, the court may sentence him to imprisonment for less than that period or, as the case may be, to a fine of less than that amount.

(2) Where under any such enactment an offender sentenced on summary conviction to imprisonment or a fine is required to enter into a recognizance with or without sureties to keep the peace or observe any other condition, the court convicting him may dispense with or modify the requirement.

(3) Where under any such enactment a magistrates' court has power to sentence an offender to imprisonment or other detention but not to a fine, then, except where an Act passed after 31st December 1879 expressly provides to the contrary, the court may, instead of sentencing him to imprisonment or other detention, impose a fine which—

(a) for an offence triable either way, shall not exceed the prescribed sum within the meaning of section 32 above ; and (*b*) for a summary offence, shall—

    (i) not exceed £200 ; and

    (ii) not be of such an amount as would subject the offender, in default of payment of the fine, to a longer term of imprisonment or detention than the term to which he is liable on conviction of the offence.

35. In fixing the amount of a fine, a magistrates' court shall take into consideration among other things the means of the person on whom the fine is imposed so far as they appear or are known to the court.

Fixing amount of fine.

36.—(1) Where a person under 17 years of age is found guilty by a magistrates' court of an offence for which, apart from this section, the court would have power to impose a fine of an amount exceeding £200, the amount of any fine imposed by the court shall not exceed £200.

Restriction on fines in respect of young persons.

(2) In relation to a person under the age of 14 subsection (1) above shall have effect as if for the words " £200 ", in both the places where they occur, there were substituted the words " £50 " ; but this subsection shall cease to have effect on the coming into force of section 4 of the Children and Young Persons Act 1969 (which prohibits criminal proceedings against children).

1969 c. 54.

37.—(1) Where a person is convicted by a magistrates' court of an offence punishable on summary conviction with imprisonment, then, if on the day of the conviction he is not less than 15 but under 21 years old and is a person who under section 1(2) and (4) of the Criminal Justice Act 1961 may be committed for a sentence of borstal training, the court may commit him in custody or on bail to the Crown Court for sentence in accordance with the provisions of section 20 of the Criminal Justice Act 1948.

Committal to Crown Court with a view to borstal sentence.
1961 c. 39.
1948 c. 58.

(2) A person committed in custody under subsection (1) above shall be committed—

    (*a*) if the court has been notified by the Secretary of State that a remand centre is available for the reception, from that court, of persons of the class or description of the person committed, to a remand centre ;

    (*b*) if the court has not been so notified, to a prison.

PART I
Committal for
sentence on
summary trial
of offence
triable either
way.

1967 c. 80.

1973 c. 62.

38. Where on the summary trial of an offence triable either way (not being an offence as regards which this section is excluded by section 33 above) a person who is not less than 17 years old is convicted of the offence, then, if on obtaining information about his character and antecedents the court is of opinion that they are such that greater punishment should be inflicted for the offence than the court has power to inflict, the court may, in accordance with section 56 of the Criminal Justice Act 1967, commit him in custody or on bail to the Crown Court for sentence in accordance with the provisions of section 42 of the Powers of Criminal Courts Act 1973.

Cases where
magistrates'
court may
remit offender
to another
such court for
sentence.

39.—(1) Where a person who has attained the age of 17 (" the offender ") has been convicted by a magistrates' court (" the convicting court ") of an offence to which this section applies (" the instant offence ") and—

    (a) it appears to the convicting court that some other magistrates' court (" the other court ") has convicted him of another such offence in respect of which the other court has neither passed sentence on him nor committed him to the Crown Court for sentence nor dealt with him in any other way ; and

    (b) the other court consents to his being remitted under this section to the other court,

the convicting court may remit him to the other court to be dealt with in respect of the instant offence by the other court instead of by the convicting court.

(2) The offender, if remitted under this section, shall have no right of appeal against the order of remission.

(3) Where the convicting court remits the offender to the other court under this section, it shall adjourn the trial of the information charging him with the instant offence, and—

    (a) section 128 below and all other enactments (whenever passed) relating to remand or the granting of bail in criminal proceedings shall have effect in relation to the convicting court's power or duty to remand the offender on that adjournment as if any reference to the court to or before which the person remanded is to be brought or appear after remand were a reference to the court to which he is being remitted ; and

    (b) subject to subsection (4) below, the other court may deal with the case in any way in which it would have power to deal with it (including, where applicable, the remission of the offender under this section to another magistrates' court in respect of the instant offence)

if all proceedings relating to that offence which took PART I
place before the convicting court had taken place
before the other court.

(4) Nothing in this section shall preclude the convicting court
from making any order which it has power to make under
section 28 of the Theft Act 1968 (orders for restitution) by virtue 1968 c. 60.
of the offender's conviction of the instant offence.

(5) Where the convicting court has remitted the offender under
this section to the other court, the other court may remit him
back to the convicting court; and the provisions of subsection
(3) above (so far as applicable) shall apply with the necessary
modifications in relation to any remission under this subsection.

(6) This section applies to—

(*a*) any offence punishable with imprisonment; and

(*b*) any offence in respect of which the convicting court has
a power or duty to order the offender to be disqualified
under section 93 of the Road Traffic Act 1972 (dis- 1972 c. 20.
qualification for certain motoring offences);

and in this section " conviction " includes a finding under section
30(1) above that the person in question did the act or made the
omission charged, and " convicted " shall be construed accordingly.

40.—(1) The compensation to be paid under a compensation Restriction on
order made by a magistrates' court in respect of any offence of amount
which the court has convicted the offender shall not exceed payable under
£1,000; and the compensation or total compensation to be paid compensation
under a compensation order or compensation orders made by a magistrates'
magistrates' court in respect of any offence or offences taken court.
into consideration in determining sentence shall not exceed the
difference (if any) between the amount or total amount which
under the preceding provisions of this subsection is the maximum
for the offence or offences of which the offender has been convicted and the amount or total amounts (if any) which are in
fact ordered to be paid in respect of that offence or those offences.

(2) In subsection (1) above " compensation order " has the
meaning assigned to it by section 35(1) of the Powers of Criminal 1973 c. 62.
Courts Act 1973.

Miscellaneous

41. A person charged with treason shall not be granted bail Restriction on
except by order of a judge of the High Court or the Secretary of grant of bail
State. in treason.

PART I
Restriction on
justices sitting
after dealing
with bail.

42.—(1) A justice of the peace shall not take part in trying the issue of an accused's guilt on the summary trial of an information if in the course of the same proceedings the justice has been informed, for the purpose of determining whether the accused shall be granted bail, that he has one or more previous convictions.

(2) For the purposes of this section any committal proceedings from which the proceedings on the summary trial arose shall be treated as part of the trial.

Bail on arrest
without
warrant.

43.—(1) On a person's being taken into custody for an offence without a warrant, a police officer not below the rank of inspector, or the police officer in charge of the police station to which the person is brought, may, and, if it will not be practicable to bring him before a magistrates' court within 24 hours after his being taken into custody, shall, inquire into the case and, unless the offence appears to the officer to be a serious one, grant him bail

1976 c. 63.

in accordance with the Bail Act 1976 subject to a duty to appear before a magistrates' court at such time and place as the officer appoints.

(2) Where a person has been granted bail under subsection (1) above, the magistrates' court before which he is to appear may appoint a later time as the time at which he is to appear and may enlarge the recognizances of any sureties for him to that time.

(3) Where, on a person's being taken into custody for an offence without a warrant, it appears to any such officer as aforesaid that the inquiry into the case cannot be completed forthwith, he may grant him bail in accordance with the Bail Act 1976 subject to a duty to appear at such a police station and at such a time as the officer appoints unless he previously receives a notice in writing from the officer in charge of that police station that his attendance is not required ; and the recognizance of any surety for that person may be enforced as if it were conditioned for the appearance of that person before a magistrates' court for the petty sessions area in which the police station named in the recognizance is situated.

(4) Where a person is taken into custody for an offence without a warrant and is retained in custody, he shall be brought before a magistrates' court as soon as practicable.

Aiders and
abettors.

44.—(1) A person who aids, abets, counsels or procures the commission by another person of a summary offence shall be guilty of the like offence and may be tried (whether or not he is charged as a principal) either by a court having jurisdiction to try that other person or by a court having by virtue of his own offence jurisdiction to try him.

(2) Any offence consisting in aiding, abetting, counselling or   Part I procuring the commission of an offence triable either way (other than an offence listed in Schedule 1 to this Act) shall by virtue of this subsection be triable either way.

45.—(1) Any offence consisting in the incitement to commit a   Incitement. summary offence shall be triable only summarily.

(2) Subsection (1) above is without prejudice to any other enactment by virtue of which any offence is triable only summarily.

(3) On conviction of an offence consisting in the incitement to commit a summary offence a person shall be liable to the same penalties as he would be liable to on conviction of the last-mentioned offence.

46. The provisions of Schedule 3 to this Act shall have effect   Corporations. where a corporation is charged with an offence before a magistrates' court.

47. Where any enactment requires, expressly or by implica-   Service of tion, that a summons in respect of an offence shall be issued or   summons out served within a specified period after the commission of the   of time after offence, and service of the summons may under the rules be   prove service effected by post, then, if under the rules service of the summons   by post. is not treated as proved, but it is shown that a letter containing the summons was posted at such time as to enable it to be delivered in the ordinary course of post within that period, a second summons may be issued on the same information; and the enactment shall have effect, in relation to that summons, as if the specified period were a period running from the return day of the original summons.

48. Where a summons or warrant has been issued requiring   Return of any person to appear or be brought before a magistrates' court   property taken to answer to an information, or where any person has been   from accused. arrested without a warrant for an offence, and property has been taken from him after the issue of the summons or warrant or, as the case may be, on or after his arrest without a warrant, the police shall report the taking of the property, with particulars of the property, to the magistrates' court which deals with the case; and, if the court, being of opinion that the whole or any part of the property can be returned to the accused consistently with the interests of justice and the safe custody of the accused, so directs, the property, or such part of it as the court directs, shall be returned to the accused or to such other person as he may require.

49.—(1) Where any person not less than 14 years old—

    (*a*) who has been taken into custody is charged with an offence before a magistrates' court ; or

    (*b*) appears before a magistrates' court in answer to a summons for an offence punishable with imprisonment,

the court may, if it thinks fit, on the application of a police officer not below the rank of inspector, order the finger-prints of that person to be taken by a constable.

(2) Finger-prints taken in pursuance of an order under this section shall be taken either at the place where the court is sitting or, if the person to whom the order relates is remanded in custody, at any place to which he is committed ; and a constable may use such reasonable force as may be necessary for that purpose.

(3) The provisions of this section shall be in addition to those of any other enactment under which finger-prints may be taken.

(4) Where the finger-prints of any person have been taken in pursuance of an order under this section, then, if he is acquitted, or the examining justices determine not to commit him for trial, or if the information against him is dismissed, the finger-prints and all copies and records of them shall be destroyed.

(5) In this section " finger-prints " includes palm-prints.

Construction
of references
to complaint
in enactments
dealing with
offences.

50. In any enactment conferring power on a magistrates' court to deal with an offence, or to issue a summons or warrant against a person suspected of an offence, on the complaint of any person, for references to a complaint there shall be substituted references to an information.

PART II

CIVIL JURISDICTION AND PROCEDURE

Jurisdiction to issue summons and deal with complaints

51. Subject to the provisions of this Act, where a complaint is made to a justice of the peace acting for any petty sessions area upon which a magistrates' court acting for that area has power to make an order against any person, the justice may issue a summons directed to that person requiring him to appear before a magistrates' court acting for that area to answer to the complaint.

52. Where no express provision is made by any Act or the rules specifying what magistrates' courts shall have jurisdiction to hear a complaint, a magistrates' court shall have such jurisdiction if the complaint relates to anything done within the commission area for which the court is appointed or anything left undone that ought to have been done there, or ought to have been done either there or elsewhere, or relates to any other matter arising within that area.

In this section " commission area " has the same meaning as in the Justices of the Peace Act 1979.

Hearing of complaint

53.—(1) On the hearing of a complaint, the court shall, if the defendant appears, state to him the substance of the complaint.

(2) The court, after hearing the evidence and the parties, shall make the order for which the complaint is made or dismiss the complaint.

(3) Where a complaint is for an order for the payment of a sum recoverable summarily as a civil debt, or for the variation of the rate of any periodical payments ordered by a magistrates' court to be made, or for such other matter as may be prescribed, the court may make the order with the consent of the defendant without hearing evidence.

54.—(1) A magistrates' court may at any time, whether before or after beginning to hear a complaint, adjourn the hearing, and may do so, notwithstanding anything in this Act, when composed of a single justice.

(2) The court may when adjourning either fix the time and place at which the hearing is to be resumed or, unless it remands the defendant under section 55 below, leave the time and place to be determined later by the court ; but the hearing shall not be resumed at that time and place unless the court is satisfied that the parties have had adequate notice thereof.

55.—(1) Where at the time and place appointed for the hearing or adjourned hearing of a complaint the complainant appears but the defendant does not, the court may, subject to subsection (3) below, proceed in his absence.

(2) Where the court, instead of proceeding in the absence of the defendant, adjourns, or further adjourns, the hearing, the court may, if the complaint has been substantiated on oath, and subject to the following provisions of this section, issue a warrant for his arrest.

(3) The court shall not begin to hear the complaint in the absence of the defendant or issue a warrant under this section unless either it is proved to the satisfaction of the court, on oath or in such other manner as may be prescribed, that the summons was served on him within what appears to the court to be a

reasonable time before the hearing or adjourned hearing or the defendant has appeared on a previous occasion to answer to the complaint.

(4) Where the defendant fails to appear at an adjourned hearing, the court shall not issue a warrant under this section unless it is satisfied that he has had adequate notice of the time and place of the adjourned hearing.

(5) Where the defendant is arrested under a warrant issued under this section, the court may, on any subsequent adjournment of the hearing, but subject to the provisions of subsection (6) below, remand him.

(6) The court shall not issue a warrant or remand a defendant under this section or further remand him by virtue of section 128(3) below after he has given evidence in the proceedings.

(7) Where the court remands the defendant, the time fixed for the resumption of the hearing shall be that at which he is required to appear or be brought before the court in pursuance of the remand.

(8) A warrant under this section shall not be issued in any proceedings for the recovery or enforcement of a sum recoverable summarily as a civil debt or in proceedings in any matter of bastardy.

Non-
appearance of
complainant.
56. Where at the time and place appointed for the hearing or adjourned hearing of a complaint the defendant appears but the complainant does not, the court may dismiss the complaint or, if evidence has been received on a previous occasion, proceed in the absence of the complainant.

Non-
appearance of
both parties.
57. Where at the time and place appointed for the hearing or adjourned hearing of a complaint neither the complainant nor the defendant appears, the court may dismiss the complaint.

Civil debt

Money
recoverable
summarily as
civil debt.
58.—(1) A magistrates' court shall have power to make an order on complaint for the payment of any money recoverable summarily as a civil debt.

(2) Any sum payment of which may be ordered by a magistrates' court shall be recoverable summarily as a civil debt except—

(a) a sum recoverable on complaint for an affiliation order or order enforceable as an affiliation order ; or

(b) a sum that may be adjudged to be paid by a summary conviction or by an order enforceable as if it were a summary conviction.

Orders for periodical payment

59.—(1) Where a magistrates' court orders money to be paid periodically by one person to another, the court may order that the payment shall be made to the clerk of the court or the clerk of any other magistrates' court.

Periodical payment through justices' clerk.

(2) Where the order is an affiliation order, an order under the Guardianship of Minors Acts 1971 and 1973 or an order under Part I of the Domestic Proceedings and Magistrates' Courts Act 1978, the court shall, unless upon representations expressly made in that behalf by the applicant for the order it is satisfied that it is undesirable to do so, exercise its power under subsection (1) above.

1978 c. 22.

(3) Where periodical payments under an order of any court are required to be paid to or through the clerk of a magistrates' court and any sums payable under the order are in arrear, the clerk shall, if the person for whose benefit the payment should have been made so requests in writing, and unless it appears to the clerk that it is unreasonable in the circumstances to do so, proceed in his own name for the recovery of those sums ; but the said person shall have the same liability for all the costs properly incurred in or about the proceedings as if the proceedings had been taken by him.

(4) Nothing in this section shall affect any right of a person to proceed in his own name for the recovery of sums payable on his behalf under an order of any court.

60. Where a magistrates' court has made an order for the periodical payment of money, the court may, by order on complaint, revoke, revive or vary the order.

Revocation, variation, etc., of orders for periodical payment.

The power to vary an order by virtue of this section shall include power to suspend the operation of any provision of that order temporarily and to revive the operation of any provision so suspended.

61.—(1) The power to make rules conferred by section 144 below shall, without prejudice to the generality of subsection (1) of that section, include power to make provision—

Periodical payments payable by one person under more than one order.

    (a) for enabling a person to make one complaint for the recovery of payments required to be made to him by another person under more than one periodical payments order ; and

    (b) for apportioning between two or more periodical payments orders, in such manner as may be prescribed by the rules, any sum paid to a clerk to a magistrates' court on any date by the person liable to make payments under the orders which is less than the total

PART II

sum required to be paid on that date to that clerk by that person in respect of those orders (being orders one of which requires payments to be made for the benefit of a child to the person with whom the child has his home and one or more of which requires payments to be made to that person either for his own benefit or for the benefit of another child who has his home with him).

(2) In this section—

" child " means a person who has not attained the age of 18 ;

" periodical payments order " means an order made by a magistrates' court, or registered in a magistrates' court under Part II of the Maintenance Orders Act 1950 or Part I of the Maintenance Orders Act 1958, which requires the making of periodical payments,

1950 c. 37.
1958 c. 39.

and any payments required under a periodical payments order to be made to a child shall for the purposes of subsection (1) above be treated as if they were required to be made to the person with whom the child has his home.

Payments to children

Provisions as to payments required to be made to a child, etc.

62.—(1) Where—

(a) periodical payments are required to be made, or a lump sum is required to be paid, to a child under an order made by a magistrates' court, or

(b) periodical payments are required to be made to a child under an order which is registered in a magistrates' court,

any sum required under the order to be paid to the child may be paid to the person with whom the child has his home, and that person—

(i) may proceed in his own name for the variation, revival or revocation of the order, and

(ii) may either proceed in his own name for the recovery of any sum required to be paid under the order or request the clerk to the magistrates' court, under subsection (3) of section 59 above, to proceed for the recovery of that sum.

(2) Where a child has a right under any enactment to apply for the revival of an order made by a magistrates' court which provided for the making of periodical payments to or for the benefit of the child, the person with whom the child has his home may proceed in his own name for the revival of that order.

(3) Where any person by whom periodical payments are required to be paid to a child under an order made by or registered in a magistrates' court makes a complaint for the variation or revocation of that order, the person with whom the child has his home may answer the complaint in his own name.

(4) Nothing in subsections (1) and (2) above shall affect any right of a child to proceed in his own name for the variation, revival or revocation of an order or for the recovery of any sum payable thereunder.

(5) In this section references to the person with whom a child has his home shall be construed in accordance with Part IV of the Children Act 1975, except that, in the case of any child in the 1975 c. 72. care of a local authority, the local authority shall be treated for the purposes of this section as the person with whom the child has his home.

(6) In this section any reference to an order registered in a magistrates' court is a reference to an order registered in a magistrates' court under Part II of the Maintenance Orders Act 1950 c. 37. 1950 or Part I of the Maintenance Orders Act 1958. 1958 c. 39.

(7) In this section " child " means a person who has not attained the age of 18.

Orders other than for payment of money

63.—(1) Where under any Act passed after 31st December Orders other 1879 a magistrates' court has power to require the doing of any- than for thing other than the payment of money, or to prohibit the doing payment of of anything, any order of the court for the purpose of exercising money. that power may contain such provisions for the manner in which anything is to be done, for the time within which anything is to be done, or during which anything is not to be done, and generally for giving effect to the order, as the court thinks fit.

(2) The court may by order made on complaint suspend or rescind any such order as aforesaid.

(3) Where any person disobeys an order of a magistrates' court made under an Act passed after 31st December 1879 to do anything other than the payment of money or to abstain from doing anything the court may—

(a) order him to pay a sum not exceeding £50 for every day during which he is in default or a sum not exceeding £1,000 ; or

(b) commit him to custody until he has remedied his default or for a period not exceeding 2 months ;

but a person who is ordered to pay a sum for every day during which he is in default or who is committed to custody until he has remedied his default shall not by virtue of this section be ordered to pay more than £1,000 or be committed for more than 2 months in all for doing or abstaining from doing the same thing contrary to the order (without prejudice to the operation of this section in relation to any subsequent default).

(4) Any sum ordered to be paid under subsection (3) above shall for the purposes of this Act be treated as adjudged to be paid by a conviction of a magistrates' court.

(5) The preceding provisions of this section shall not apply to any order for the enforcement of which provision is made by any other enactment.

Costs

64.—(1) On the hearing of a complaint, a magistrates' court shall have power in its discretion to make such order as to costs—

    (*a*) on making the order for which the complaint is made, to be paid by the defendant to the complainant;

    (*b*) on dismissing the complaint, to be paid by the complainant to the defendant,

as it thinks just and reasonable; but if the complaint is for an order for the periodical payment of money, or for the revocation, revival or variation of such an order, or for the enforcement of such an order, the court may, whatever adjudication it makes, order either party to pay the whole or any part of the other's costs.

(2) The amount of any sum ordered to be paid under subsection (1) above shall be specified in the order, or order of dismissal, as the case may be.

(3) Subject to subsection (4) below, costs ordered to be paid under this section shall be enforceable as a civil debt.

(4) Any costs awarded on a complaint for an affiliation order or order enforceable as an affiliation order, or for the enforcement, variation, revocation, discharge or revival of such an order, against the person liable to make payments under the order shall be enforceable as a sum ordered to be paid by an affiliation order.

(5) The preceding provisions of this section shall have effect subject to any other Act enabling a magistrates' court to order a successful party to pay the other party's costs.

Domestic proceedings

65.—(1) In this Act " domestic proceedings " means proceedings under any of the following enactments, that is to say—

    (*a*) the Maintenance Orders (Facilities for Enforcement) Act 1920;

(*b*) section 43 or section 44 of the National Assistance Act 1948 ;

PART II
1948 c. 29.

(*c*) section 3 of the Marriage Act 1949 ;

1949 c. 76.

(*d*) the Affiliation Proceedings Act 1957 ;

1957 c. 55.

(*e*) the Guardianship of Minors Acts 1971 and 1973 ;

(*f*) Part I of the Maintenance Orders (Reciprocal Enforce- 1972 c. 18.
ment) Act 1972 ;

(*g*) Part II of the Children Act 1975 ;

1975 c. 72.

(*h*) the Adoption Act 1976, except proceedings under 1976 c. 36.
section 34 of that Act ;

(*i*) section 18 or section 19 of the Supplementary Benefits 1976 c. 71.
Act 1976 ;

(*j*) Part I of the Domestic Proceedings and Magistrates' 1978 c. 22.
Courts Act 1978 ;

(*k*) section 47, 49 or 50 of the Child Care Act 1980 ;

1980 c. 5.

(*l*) section 60 of this Act ;

except that, subject to subsection (2) below, it does not include—

(i) proceedings for the enforcement of any order made, confirmed or registered under any of those enactments ;

(ii) proceedings for the variation of any provision for the periodical payment of money contained in an order made, confirmed or registered under any of those enactments ; or

(iii) proceedings on an information in respect of the commission of an offence under any of those enactments.

(2) The court before which there fall to be heard any of the following proceedings, that is to say—

(*a*) proceedings (whether under this Act or any other enactment) for the enforcement of any order made, confirmed or registered under any of the enactments specified in paragraphs (*a*) to (*k*) of subsection (1) above ;

(*b*) proceedings (whether under this Act or any other enactment) for the variation of any provision for the making of periodical payments contained in an order made, confirmed or registered under any of those enactments ;

(*c*) proceedings for an attachment of earnings order to secure maintenance payments within the meaning of the Attachment of Earnings Act 1971 or for the discharge 1971 c. 32.
or variation of such an order ; or

(*d*) proceedings for the enforcement of a maintenance order which is registered in a magistrates' court under Part II of the Maintenance Orders Act 1950 or Part I of 1950 c. 37.

the Maintenance Orders Act 1958 or for the variation of the rate of payments specified by such an order,

may if it thinks fit order that those proceedings and any other proceedings being heard therewith shall, notwithstanding anything in subsection (1) above, be treated as domestic proceedings for the purposes of this Act.

(3) Where the same parties are parties—

    (*a*) to proceedings which are domestic proceedings by virtue of subsection (1) above, and

    (*b*) to proceedings which the court has power to treat as domestic proceedings by virtue of subsection (2) above,

and the proceedings are heard together by a magistrates' court, the whole of those proceedings shall be treated as domestic proceedings for the purposes of this Act.

(4) No appeal shall lie from the making of, or refusal to make, an order under subsection (2) above.

(5) Until the Adoption Act 1976 comes into force subsection (1) above shall have effect as if for paragraph (*h*) thereof there were substituted the following paragraph—

    " (*h*) the Adoption Act 1958, the Adoption Act 1960 or Part I of the Children Act 1975, except proceedings under section 42 or 43 of the Adoption Act 1958."

(6) Until the Child Care Act 1980 comes into force subsection (1) above shall have effect as if for paragraph (*k*) thereof there were substituted the following paragraph—

    " (*k*) section 87 or section 88 of the Children and Young Persons Act 1933 or section 26 of the Children Act 1948."

Composition of magistrates' courts for domestic proceedings: general.

66.—(1) Subject to the provisions of this section, a magistrates' court when hearing domestic procedings shall be composed of not more than 3 justices of the peace, including, so far as practicable, both a man and a woman.

(2) Subsection (1) above shall not apply to a magistrates' court for an inner London petty sessions area, and, notwithstanding anything in section 67 below, for the purpose of exercising jurisdiction to hear domestic proceedings such a court shall be composed of—

    (*a*) a metropolitan stipendiary magistrate as chairman and one or 2 lay justices who are members of the domestic court panel for that area ; or

    (*b*) 2 or 3 lay justices who are members of that panel ;

or, if it is not practicable for such a court to be so composed, the court shall for that purpose be composed of a metropolitan stipendiary magistrate sitting alone.

(3) Where in pursuance of subsection (2) above a magistrates' court includes lay justices it shall, so far as practicable, include both a man and a woman.

(4) In the preceding provisions of this section " lay justices " means justices of the peace for the inner London area who are not metropolitan stipendiary magistrates.

(5) In this section " inner London petty sessions area " means the City of London or any petty sessional division of the inner London area.

67.—(1) Magistrates' courts constituted in accordance with the provisions of this section and sitting for the purpose of hearing domestic proceedings shall be known as domestic courts. Domestic courts and panels.

(2) A justice shall not be qualified to sit as a member of a domestic court unless he is a member of a domestic court panel, that is to say a panel of justices specially appointed to deal with domestic proceedings.

(3) Without prejudice to the generality of the power to make rules under section 144 below relating to the procedure and practice to be followed in magistrates' courts, provision may be made by such rules with respect to any of the following matters, that is to say—

(a) the formation and revision of domestic court panels and the eligibility of justices to be members of such panels ;

(b) the appointment of persons as chairmen of domestic courts ; and

(c) the composition of domestic courts.

(4) Any provision made by rules by virtue of subsection (3) above for the formation of domestic court panels shall include provision for the formation of at least one domestic court panel for each commission area, but provision shall not be made by the rules for the formation of more than one domestic court panel for any petty sessions area.

In this subsection " commission area " has the same meaning as in the Justices of the Peace Act 1979. 1979 c. 55.

(5) Rules made by virtue of subsection (3) above may confer powers on the Lord Chancellor with respect to any of the matters specified in the rules and may, in particular, provide for the appointment of domestic court panels by him and for the removal from a domestic court panel of any justice who, in his opinion, is unsuitable to serve on a domestic court.

(6) Rules made by virtue of subsection (3) above may make different provision in relation to different areas for which domestic court panels are formed ; and in the application of this section to the counties of Greater Manchester, Merseyside and Lancashire for any reference in subsection (5) above to the Lord Chancellor there shall be substituted a reference to the Chancellor of the Duchy of Lancaster.

(7) A stipendiary magistrate who is a member of a domestic court panel may, notwithstanding anything in section 66(1) above, hear and determine domestic proceedings when sitting alone.

(8) Nothing in this section shall require the formation of a domestic court panel for the City of London.

Combined
domestic
court panels.

68.—(1) Where the Secretary of State considers—

> (a) that a combined domestic court panel should be formed for 2 or more petty sessions areas, or

> (b) that any combined domestic court panel which has been so formed should be dissolved,

he may direct the magistrates' courts committee for the area concerned to review the functioning of domestic courts in their area and on completion of the review to submit a report to the Secretary of State.

(2) Where the Secretary of State gives a direction under subsection (1) above, then—

> (a) after consideration of any report submitted to him under that subsection, or

> (b) if the committee fail to comply with the direction within 6 months from the giving thereof, after the expiration of that period of 6 months,

the Secretary of State may, if he thinks fit, make an order for the formation of a combined domestic court panel for the petty sessions areas concerned or, as the case may be, for the dissolution of the combined domestic court panel concerned.

(3) Where the Secretary of State proposes to make an order under subsection (2) above, he shall send a copy of the proposed order to the magistrates' courts committee for any area the whole or part of which is concerned and to any domestic court panel which is concerned.

(4) Where a copy of the proposed order is required to be sent under subsection (3) above to any committee or panel, the Secretary of State shall, before making an order, consider any representations made to him by the committee or panel within one month from the time the copy of the proposed order was sent.

(5) An order of the Secretary of State under subsection (2) above shall be made by statutory instrument and may be revoked or varied by a subsequent order thereunder.

(6) Any order made under subsection (2) above may contain supplementary, incidental and consequential provisions.

(7) In the application of this section to the inner London area any reference to the magistrates' courts committee shall be treated as a reference to the committee of magistrates.

69.—(1) The business of magistrates' courts shall, so far as is consistent with the due dispatch of business, be arranged in such manner as may be requisite for separating the hearing and determination of domestic proceedings from other business.

Sittings of magistrates' courts for domestic proceedings.

(2) In the case of domestic proceedings in a magistrates' court other than proceedings under the Adoption Act 1976, no person shall be present during the hearing and determination by the court of the proceedings except—

1976 c. 36.

> (*a*) officers of the court ;
> (*b*) parties to the case before the court, their solicitors and counsel, witnesses and other persons directly concerned in the case ;
> (*c*) representatives of newspapers or news agencies ;
> (*d*) any other person whom the court may in its discretion permit to be present, so, however, that permission shall not be withheld from a person who appears to the court to have adequate grounds for attendance.

(3) In relation to any domestic proceedings under the Adoption Act 1976, subsection (2) above shall apply with the omission of paragraphs (*c*) and (*d*).

(4) When hearing domestic proceedings, a magistrates' court may, if it thinks it necessary in the interest of the administration of justice or of public decency, direct that any persons, not being officers of the court or parties to the case, the parties' solicitors or counsel, or other persons directly concerned in the case, be excluded during the taking of any indecent evidence.

(5) The powers conferred on a magistrates' court by this section shall be in addition and without prejudice to any other powers of the court to hear proceedings in camera.

(6) Nothing in this section shall affect the exercise by a magistrates' court of the power to direct that witnesses shall be excluded until they are called for examination.

(7) Until the coming into operation of the Adoption Act 1976 this section shall have effect as if for any reference to

PART II
1958 c. 5
(7 & 8 Eliz. 2).
1960 c. 59.
1975 c. 72.

that Act there were substituted a reference to the Adoption Act 1958, the Adoption Act 1960 and Part I of the Children Act 1975.

Jurisdiction of magistrates' courts in inner London for domestic proceedings.

70.—(1) A relevant court for an inner London petty sessions area shall, in addition to hearing proceedings which (apart from subsection (2) below) may be heard by a relevant court for that area, have jurisdiction to hear proceedings which could be heard before a relevant court for any other such area, but shall not exercise the jurisdiction conferred by this subsection except in such cases or classes of case as may be determined by the committee of magistrates.

(2) A magistrates' court for an inner London petty sessions area shall not hear any domestic proceedings if the committee of magistrates so determine.

(3) In this section—

" relevant court " means a magistrates' court when composed for the purpose of exercising jurisdiction to hear domestic proceedings ;

" inner London petty sessions area " means the City of London or any petty sessional division of the inner London area.

Newspaper reports of domestic proceedings.
1976 c. 36.

71.—(1) In the case of domestic proceedings in a magistrates' court (other than proceedings under the Adoption Act 1976) it shall not be lawful for the proprietor, editor or publisher of a newspaper or periodical to print or publish, or cause or procure to be printed or published, in it any particulars of the proceedings other than the following, that is to say—

(*a*) the names, addresses and occupations of the parties and witnesses ;

(*b*) the grounds of the application, and a concise statement of the charges, defences and counter-charges in support of which evidence has been given ;

(*c*) submissions on any point of law arising in the course of the proceedings and the decision of the court on the submissions ;

(*d*) the decision of the court, and any observations made by the court in giving it.

(2) In the case of domestic proceedings in a magistrates' court under the Adoption Act 1976, subsection (1) above shall apply with the omission of paragraphs (*a*) and (*b*) and the reference in that subsection to the particulars of the proceedings

shall, in relation to any child concerned in the proceedings,
include—

(a) the name, address or school of the child,

(b) any picture as being, or including, a picture of the child, and

(c) any other particulars calculated to lead to the identification of the child.

(3) Any person acting in contravention of this section shall be liable on summary conviction to a fine not exceeding £500.

(4) No prosecution for an offence under this section shall be begun without the consent of the Attorney General.

(5) Nothing in this section shall prohibit the printing or publishing of any matter in a newspaper or periodical of a technical character bona fide intended for circulation among members of the legal or medical professions.

(6) Until the coming into operation of the Adoption Act 1976 this section shall have effect as if for any reference to that Act there were substituted a reference to the Adoption Act 1958, the Adoption Act 1960 and Part I of the Children Act 1975.
 1976 c. 36.
 1958 c. 5
 (7 & 8 Eliz. 2).
 1960 c. 59.
 1975 c. 72.

72.—(1) Where in any domestic proceedings in which an order may be made for the payment of money by any person, or in any proceedings for the enforcement or variation of any such order, a magistrates' court has requested a probation officer to investigate the means of the parties to the proceedings, the court may direct the probation officer to report the result of his investigation to the court in accordance with the provisions of this section; but in the case of any such domestic proceedings no direction to report to the court shall be given to a probation officer under this subsection until the court has determined all issues arising in the proceedings other than the amount to be directed to be paid by such an order.
 Report by probation officer on means of parties.

(2) Where the court directs a probation officer under this section to report to the court the result of any such investigation as aforesaid, the court may require him—

(a) to furnish to the court a statement in writing about his investigation; or

(b) to make an oral statement to the court about his investigation.

(3) Where the court requires a probation officer to furnish a statement in writing under subsection (2) above—

(a) a copy of the statement shall be given to each party to the proceedings or to his counsel or solicitor at the hearing; and

2 F 2

(*b*) the court may, if it thinks fit, require that the statement, or such part of the statement as the court may specify, shall be read aloud at the hearing.

(4) The court may and, if requested to do so at the hearing by a party to the proceedings or his counsel or solicitor shall, require the probation officer to give evidence about his investigation, and if the officer gives such evidence, any party to the proceedings may give or call evidence with respect to any matter referred to either in the statement or in the evidence given by the officer.

(5) Any statement made by a probation officer in a statement furnished or made by him under subsection (2) above, or any evidence which he is required to give under subsection (4) above, may be received by the court as evidence, notwithstanding anything to the contrary in any enactment or rule of law relating to the admissibility of evidence.

Examination of witnesses by court.

73. Where in any domestic proceedings, or in any proceedings for the enforcement or variation of an order made in domestic proceedings, it appears to a magistrates' court that any party to the proceedings who is not legally represented is unable effectively to examine or cross-examine a witness, the court shall ascertain from that party what are the matters about which the witness may be able to depose or on which the witness ought to be cross-examined, as the case may be, and shall put, or cause to be put, to the witness such questions in the interests of that party as may appear to the court to be proper.

Reasons for decisions in domestic proceedings.

74.—(1) The power to make rules conferred by section 144 below shall, without prejudice to the generality of subsection (1) of that section, include power to make provision for the recording by a magistrates' court, in such manner as may be prescribed by the rules, of reasons for a decision made in such domestic proceedings or class of domestic proceedings as may be so prescribed, and for making available a copy of any record made in accordance with those rules of the reasons for a decision of a magistrates' court to any person who requests a copy thereof for the purposes of an appeal against that decision or for the purpose of deciding whether or not to appeal against that decision.

(2) A copy of any record made by virtue of this section of the reasons for a decision of a magistrates' court shall, if certified by such officer of the court as may be prescribed, be admissible as evidence of those reasons.

PART III

SATISFACTION AND ENFORCEMENT

General provisions

75.—(1) A magistrates' court by whose conviction or order a sum is adjudged to be paid may, instead of requiring immediate payment, allow time for payment, or order payment by instalments.

Power to dispense with immediate payment.

(2) Where a magistrates' court has allowed time for payment, the court may, on application by or on behalf of the person liable to make the payment, allow further time or order payment by instalments.

(3) Where a court has ordered payment by instalments and default is made in the payment of any one instalment, proceedings may be taken as if the default had been made in the payment of all the instalments then unpaid.

76.—(1) Subject to the following provisions of this Part of this Act, and to section 132 below and section 19 of the Powers of Criminal Courts Act 1973, where default is made in paying a sum adjudged to be paid by a conviction or order of a magistrates' court, the court may issue a warrant of distress for the purpose of levying the sum or issue a warrant committing the defaulter to prison.

Enforcement of sums adjudged to be paid.
1973 c. 62.

(2) A warrant of commitment may be issued as aforesaid either—

    (*a*) where it appears on the return to a warrant of distress that the money and goods of the defaulter are insufficient to satisfy the sum with the costs and charges of levying the sum ; or

    (*b*) instead of a warrant of distress.

(3) The period for which a person may be committed to prison under such a warrant as aforesaid shall not, subject to the provisions of any enactment passed after 31st December 1879, exceed the period applicable to the case under Schedule 4 to this Act.

77.—(1) Where a magistrates' court has power to issue a warrant of distress under this Part of this Act, it may, if it thinks it expedient to do so, postpone the issue of the warrant until such time and on such conditions, if any, as the court thinks just.

Postponement of issue of warrant.

(2) Where a magistrates' court has power to issue a warrant of commitment under this Part of this Act, it may, if it thinks

it expedient to do so, fix a term of imprisonment and postpone the issue of the warrant until such time and on such conditions, if any, as the court thinks just.

Defect in
distress
warrant and
irregularity in
its execution.

78.—(1) A warrant of distress issued for the purpose of levying a sum adjudged to be paid by the conviction or order of a magistrates' court shall not, if it states that the sum has been so adjudged to be paid, be held void by reason of any defect in the warrant.

(2) A person acting under a warrant of distress shall not be deemed to be a trespasser from the beginning by reason only of any irregularity in the execution of the warrant.

(3) Nothing in this section shall prejudice the claim of any person for special damages in respect of any loss caused by a defect in the warrant or irregularity in its execution.

(4) If any person removes any goods marked in accordance with the rules as articles impounded in the execution of a warrant of distress, or defaces or removes any such mark, he shall be liable on summary conviction to a fine not exceeding £25.

(5) If any person charged with the execution of a warrant of distress wilfully retains from the proceeds of a sale of the goods on which distress is levied, or otherwise exacts, any greater costs and charges than those properly payable, or makes any improper charge, he shall be liable on summary conviction to a fine not exceeding £25.

Release from
custody and
reduction of
detention on
payment.

79.—(1) Where imprisonment or other detention has been imposed on any person by the order of a magistrates' court in default of payment of any sum adjudged to be paid by the conviction or order of a magistrates' court or for want of sufficient distress to satisfy such a sum, then, on the payment of the sum, together with the costs and charges, if any, of the commitment and distress, the order shall cease to have effect; and if the person has been committed to custody he shall be released unless he is in custody for some other cause.

(2) Where, after a period of imprisonment or other detention has been imposed on any person in default of payment of any sum adjudged to be paid by the conviction or order of a magistrates' court or for want of sufficient distress to satisfy such a sum, payment is made in accordance with the rules of part of the sum, the period of detention shall be reduced by such number of days as bears to the total number of days in that period less one day the same proportion as the amount so paid bears to so much of the said sum, and the costs and charges of any distress levied to satisfy that sum, as was due at the time the period of detention was imposed.

(3) In calculating the reduction required under subsection (2) PART III above any fraction of a day shall be left out of account.

80.—(1) Where a magistrates' court has adjudged a person to Application pay a sum by a conviction or has ordered the enforcement of a of money sum due from a person under an affiliation order or an order found on enforceable as an affiliation order, the court may order him to satisfy sum be searched. adjudged.

(2) Any money found on the arrest of a person adjudged to pay such a sum as aforesaid, or on a search as aforesaid, or on his being taken to a prison or other place of detention in default of payment of such a sum or for want of sufficient distress to satisfy such a sum, may, unless the court otherwise directs, be applied towards payment of the said sum ; and the balance, if any, shall be returned to him.

(3) A magistrates' court shall not allow the application as aforesaid of any money found on a person if it is satisfied that the money does not belong to him or that the loss of the money would be more injurious to his family than would be his detention.

Sums adjudged to be paid by a conviction

81.—(1) Where a magistrates' court would, but for the statu- Enforcement tory restrictions upon the imprisonment of young offenders, of fines have power to commit to prison a person under the age of 17 for imposed on young a default consisting in failure to pay, or want of sufficient dis- offenders. tress to satisfy, a sum adjudged to be paid by a conviction, the court may, subject to the following provisions of this section, make—

> (a) an order requiring the defaulter's parent or guardian to enter into a recognizance to ensure that the defaulter pays so much of that sum as remains unpaid ; or
>
> (b) an order directing so much of that sum as remains unpaid to be paid by the defaulter's parent or guardian instead of by the defaulter.

(2) An order under subsection (1) above shall not be made in respect of a defaulter—

> (a) in pursuance of paragraph (a) of that subsection, unless the parent or guardian in question consents ;
>
> (b) in pursuance of paragraph (b) of that subsection, unless the court is satisfied in all the circumstances that it is reasonable to make the order.

(3) None of the following orders, namely—

(*a*) an order under section 19(1) of the Criminal Justice Act 1948 for attendance at an attendance centre ; or

(*b*) any order under subsection (1) above,

shall be made by a magistrates' court in consequence of a default of a person under the age of 17 years consisting in failure to pay, or want of sufficient distress to satisfy, a sum adjudged to be paid by a conviction unless the court has since the conviction inquired into the defaulter's means in his presence on at least one occasion.

(4) An order under subsection (1) above shall not be made by a magistrates' court unless the court is satisfied that the defaulter has, or has had since the date on which the sum in question was adjudged to be paid, the means to pay the sum or any instalment of it on which he has defaulted, and refuses or neglects or, as the case may be, has refused or neglected, to pay it.

(5) An order under subsection (1) above may be made in pursuance of paragraph (*b*) of that subsection against a parent or guardian who, having been required to attend, has failed to do so ; but, save as aforesaid, an order under that subsection shall not be made in pursuance of that paragraph without giving the parent or guardian an opportunity of being heard.

(6) A parent or guardian may appeal to the Crown Court against an order under subsection (1) above made in pursuance of paragraph (*b*) of that subsection.

(7) Any sum ordered under subsection (1)(*b*) above to be paid by a parent or guardian may be recovered from him in like manner as if the order had been made on the conviction of the parent or guardian of an offence.

(8) In this section—

" guardian ", in relation to a person under the age of 17, means a person appointed, according to law, to be his guardian by deed or will, or by order of a court of competent jurisdiction ;

" the statutory restrictions upon the imprisonment of young offenders " has the meaning given by section 39(1) of the Criminal Justice Act 1961 ;

" sum adjudged to be paid by a conviction " means any fine, costs, compensation or other sum adjudged to be paid by an order made on a finding of guilt, including an order made under section 35 of the Powers of Criminal Courts Act 1973 (compensation orders) as applied by section 3(6) of the Children and Young Persons Act 1969.

82.—(1) A magistrates' court shall not on the occasion of
convicting an offender of an offence issue a warrant of commitment for a default in paying any sum adjudged to be paid by
the conviction unless—

PART III
Restriction
on power to
impose
imprisonment
for default.

    (*a*) in the case of an offence punishable with imprisonment,
he appears to the court to have sufficient means to pay
the sum forthwith ;

    (*b*) it appears to the court that he is unlikely to remain
long enough at a place of abode in the United Kingdom to enable payment of the sum to be enforced
by other methods ; or

    (*c*) on the occasion of that conviction the court sentences
him to immediate imprisonment or detention in a
detention centre for that or another offence or he is
already serving a term of imprisonment or detention
in a detention centre.

(2) A magistrates' court shall not in advance of the issue of
a warrant of commitment fix a term of imprisonment which is
to be served by an offender in the event of a default in paying a
sum adjudged to be paid by a conviction, except where it has
power to issue a warrant of commitment forthwith, but post-
pones issuing the warrant under section 77(2) above.

(3) Where on the occasion of the offender's conviction a magistrates' court does not issue a warrant of commitment for a
default in paying any such sum as aforesaid or fix a term of
imprisonment under the said section 77(2) which is to be served
by him in the event of any such default, it shall not thereafter
issue a warrant of commitment for any such default or for want
of sufficient distress to satisfy such a sum unless—

    (*a*) he is already serving a term of imprisonment or detention
in a detention centre ; or

    (*b*) the court has since the conviction inquired into his means
in his presence on at least one occasion.

(4) Where a magistrates' court is required by subsection (3)
above to inquire into a person's means, the court may not on the
occasion of the inquiry or at any time thereafter issue a warrant
of commitment for a default in paying any such sum unless—

    (*a*) in the case of an offence punishable with imprisonment,
the offender appears to the court to have sufficient
means to pay the sum forthwith ; or

    (*b*) the court—

        (i) is satisfied that the default is due to the
offender's wilful refusal or culpable neglect ; and

(ii) has considered or tried all other methods of enforcing payment of the sum and it appears to the court that they are inappropriate or unsuccessful.

(5) After the occasion of an offender's conviction by a magistrates' court, the court shall not, unless—

(a) the court has previously fixed a term of imprisonment under section 77(2) above which is to be served by the offender in the event of a default in paying a sum adjudged to be paid by the conviction ; or

(b) the offender is serving a term of imprisonment or detention in a detention centre,

issue a warrant of commitment for a default in paying the sum or fix such a term except at a hearing at which the offender is present.

(6) Where a magistrates' court issues a warrant of commitment on the ground that one of the conditions mentioned in subsection (1) or (4) above is satisfied, it shall state that fact, specifying the ground, in the warrant.

Process for securing attendance of offender for purposes of section 82.

83.—(1) A magistrates' court may, for the purpose of enabling inquiry to be made under section 82 above or for securing the attendance of an offender at a hearing required to be held by subsection (5) of that section—

(a) issue a summons requiring the offender to appear before the court at the time and place appointed in the summons ; or

(b) issue a warrant to arrest him and bring him before the court.

(2) On the failure of the offender to appear before the court in answer to a summons under this section the court may issue a warrant to arrest him and bring him before the court.

(3) A warrant issued under this section may be executed in like manner, and the like proceedings may be taken with a view to its execution, in any part of the United Kingdom, as if it had been issued under section 13 above.

(4) Notwithstanding anything in section 125 below, a warrant under this section shall cease to have effect when the sum in respect of which the warrant is issued is paid to the police officer holding the warrant.

Power to require statement of means.

84.—(1) A magistrates' court may, either before or on inquiring into a person's means under section 82 above, and a justice of the peace acting for the same petty sessions area as that court may before any such inquiry, order him to furnish to the court within a period specified in the order such a statement of his means as the court may require.

(2) A person who fails to comply with an order under subsection (1) above shall be liable on summary conviction to a fine not exceeding £50.

(3) If a person in furnishing any statement in pursuance of an order under subsection (1) above makes a statement which he knows to be false in a material particular or recklessly furnishes a statement which is false in a material particular, or knowingly fails to disclose any material fact, he shall be liable on summary conviction to imprisonment for a term not exceeding 4 months or a fine not exceeding £100 or both.

(4) Proceedings in respect of an offence under subsection (3) above may, notwithstanding anything in section 127(1) below, be commenced at any time within 2 years from the date of the commission of the offence or within 6 months from its first discovery by the prosecutor, whichever period expires the earlier.

85.—(1) Where a fine has been imposed on conviction of an offender by a magistrates' court, the court may, on inquiring into his means or at a hearing under section 82(5) above, remit the whole or any part of the fine if the court thinks it just to do so having regard to any change in his circumstances since the conviction, and where the court remits the whole or part of the fine after a term of imprisonment has been fixed, it shall also reduce the term by an amount which bears the same proportion to the whole term as the amount remitted bears to the whole fine or, as the case may be, shall remit the whole term. *Power to remit fine.*

In calculating the reduction in a term of imprisonment required by this subsection any fraction of a day shall be left out of account.

(2) Notwithstanding the definition of " fine " in section 150(1) below, references in this section to a fine do not include any other sum adjudged to be paid on conviction, whether as a pecuniary penalty, forfeiture, compensation or otherwise.

86.—(1) Where under section 75(1) above a magistrates' court allows time for payment of a sum adjudged to be paid by a conviction of the court (" the adjudged sum "), the court may on that or any subsequent occasion fix a day on which, if any part of that sum remains unpaid on that day, the offender must appear in person before the court for either or both of the following purposes, namely— *Power of magistrates' court to fix day for appearance of offender at means inquiry etc.*

    (*a*) to enable an inquiry into his means to be made under section 82 above ;

(*b*) to enable a hearing required by subsection (5) of the said section 82 to be held.

(2) Except as provided in subsection (3) below, the power to fix a day under this section shall be exercisable only in the presence of the offender.

(3) Where a day has been fixed under this section, the court may fix a later day in substitution for the day previously fixed, and may do so—

(*a*) when composed of a single justice ; and

(*b*) whether the offender is present or not.

(4) Subject to subsection (5) below, if on the day fixed under this section—

(*a*) any part of the adjudged sum remains unpaid ; and

(*b*) the offender fails to appear in person before the court,

the court may issue a warrant to arrest him and bring him before the court ; and subsections (3) and (4) of section 83 above shall apply in relation to a warrant issued under this section.

(5) Where under subsection (3) above a later day has in the absence of the offender been fixed in substitution for a day previously fixed under this section, the court shall not issue a warrant under this section unless it is proved to the satisfaction of the court, on oath or in such other manner as may be prescribed, that notice in writing of the substituted day was served on the offender not less than what appears to the court to be a reasonable time before that day.

Enforcement of payment of fines by High Court and county court.

87.—(1) Subject to the provisions of subsection (2) below, payment of a sum adjudged to be paid by a conviction of a magistrates' court may be enforced by the High Court or a county court (otherwise than by issue of a writ of fieri facias or other process against goods or by imprisonment or attachment of earnings) as if the sum were due to the clerk of the magistrates' court in pursuance of a judgment or order of the High Court or county court, as the case may be.

(2) Subsection (1) above shall not be construed as authorising the enforcement by a county court of payment of a fine exceeding the limit for the time being in force under section 40 of the County Courts Act 1959 on the amount of any penalty recoverable by statute in a county court.

1959 c. 22.

(3) The clerk of the magistrates' court shall not take proceedings by virtue of subsection (1) above to recover any sum adjudged to be paid by a conviction of the court from any person unless authorised to do so by the court after an inquiry under section 82 above into that person's means.

(4) Any expenses incurred by the clerk of a magistrates' court in recovering any such sum shall be treated for the purposes of Part VI of the Justices of the Peace Act 1979 as expenses of the magistrates' courts committee.

88.—(1) Where any person is adjudged to pay a sum by a Supervision summary conviction and the convicting court does not commit pending him to prison forthwith in default of payment, the court may, payment. either on the occasion of the conviction or on a subsequent occasion, order him to be placed under the supervision of such person as the court may from time to time appoint.

(2) An order placing a person under supervision in respect of any sum shall remain in force so long as he remains liable to pay the sum or any part of it unless the order ceases to have effect or is discharged under subsection (3) below.

(3) An order under this section shall cease to have effect on the making of a transfer of fine order under section 89 below with respect to the sum adjudged to be paid and may be discharged by the court that made it, without prejudice in either case to the making of a new order.

(4) Where a person under 21 years old has been adjudged to pay a sum by a summary conviction and the convicting court does not commit him to prison forthwith in default of payment, the court shall not commit him to prison in default of payment of the sum, or for want of sufficient distress to satisfy the sum, unless he has been placed under supervision in respect of the sum or the court is satisfied that it is undesirable or impracticable to place him under supervision.

(5) Where a court, being satisfied as aforesaid, commits a person under 21 years old to prison without an order under this section having been made, the court shall state the grounds on which it is so satisfied in the warrant of commitment.

(6) Where an order placing a person under supervision with respect to a sum is in force, a magistrates' court shall not commit him to prison in default of payment of the sum, or for want of sufficient distress to satisfy the sum, unless the court has before committing him taken such steps as may be reasonably practicable to obtain from the person appointed for his supervision an oral or written report on the offender's conduct and means and has considered any report so obtained, in addition, in a case where an inquiry is required by section 82 above, to that inquiry.

89.—(1) Where a magistrates' court has, or is treated by any Transfer of enactment as having, adjudged a person by a conviction to fine order. pay a sum and it appears to the court that the person is residing in any petty sessions area other than that for which the court acted, the court may make a transfer of fine order, that is to say, an order making payment enforceable in the petty sessions area in which it appears to the court that he is residing; and that area shall be specified in the order.

(2) As from the date on which a transfer of fine order is made with respect to any sum, all functions under this Part of this Act relating to that sum which, if no such order had been made, would have been exercisable by the court which made the order, or the clerk of that court, shall be exercisable by a court acting for the petty sessions area specified in the order, or the clerk of that court, as the case may be, and not otherwise.

(3) Where it appears to a court by which functions in relation to any sum are for the time being exercisable by virtue of a transfer of fine order that the person liable to pay the sum is residing in a petty sessions area other than that for which the court is acting, the court may make a further transfer of fine order with respect to that sum.

(4) In this section and sections 90 and 91 below, references to this Part of this Act do not include references to section 81(1) above.

Transfer of fines to Scotland or Northern Ireland.
90.—(1) Where a magistrates' court has, or is treated by any enactment as having, adjudged a person by a conviction to pay a sum, and it appears to the court that he is residing—

    (a) within the jurisdiction of a court of summary jurisdiction in Scotland, or

    (b) in any petty sessions district in Northern Ireland,

the court may order that payment of the sum shall be enforceable by that court of summary jurisdiction or, as the case may be, in that petty sessions district.

(2) An order under this section shall specify the court of summary jurisdiction by which or petty sessions district in which payment of the sum in question is to be enforceable; and if—

    (a) that sum is more than £100 or is a fine originally imposed by the Crown Court or the sheriff court, and

    (b) payment is to be enforceable in Scotland,

the court to be so specified shall be the sheriff court.

(3) Where an order is made under this section with respect to any sum, any functions under this Part of this Act relating to that sum which, if no such order had been made, would have been exercisable by the court which made the order or by the clerk of that court shall cease to be so exercisable.

91.—(1) Where a transfer of fine order under section 403 of the Criminal Procedure (Scotland) Act 1975 or section 104A of the Magistrates' Courts Act (Northern Ireland) 1964 provides that payment of a sum shall be enforceable in a specified petty sessions area in England and Wales, a magistrates' court acting for that area, and the clerk of that court, shall, subject to the provisions of this section, have all the like functions under this Part of this Act in respect of the sum (including power to make an order under section 89 or section 90 above) as if the sum were a sum adjudged to be paid by a conviction of that court and as if any order made under the said Act of 1975 or, as the case may be, 1964 in respect of the sum before the making of the transfer of fine order had been made by that court.

PART III

Transfer of fines from Scotland or Northern Ireland.

1975 c. 21.

1964 c. 21 (N.I.).

(2) For the purpose of determining the period of imprisonment which may be imposed under this Act in default of payment of a fine originally imposed by a court in Scotland, Schedule 4 to this Act shall have effect as if for the Table set out in paragraph 1 there were substituted the Table set out in section 407 of the Criminal Procedure (Scotland) Act 1975.

(3) Where a transfer of fine order under section 403 of the Criminal Procedure (Scotland) Act 1975 or section 104A of the Magistrates' Courts Act (Northern Ireland) 1964 provides for the enforcement in a petty sessions area in England and Wales of a fine originally imposed by the Crown Court, a magistrates' court acting for that area shall have all the like functions under this Part of this Act, exercisable subject to the like restrictions, as if it were the magistrates' court by which payment of the fine fell to be enforced by virtue of section 32(1) of the Powers of Criminal Courts Act 1973, and as if any order made under the said Act of 1975 or, as the case may be, 1964 in respect of the fine before the making of the transfer of fine order had been made by that court.

1973 c. 62.

Sums adjudged to be paid by an order

92.—(1) A magistrates' court shall not exercise its power under section 76 above to issue a warrant to commit to prison a person who makes default in paying a sum adjudged to be paid by an order of such a court except where the default is under—

Restriction on power to impose imprisonment for default.

    (*a*) a magistrates' court maintenance order ;

    (*b*) an order under section 32 of the Legal Aid Act 1974 (contribution by legally assisted person to cost of his defence in a criminal case) ; or

1974 c. 4.

    (*c*) an order for the payment of any of the taxes, contributions, premiums or liabilities specified in Schedule 4 to the Administration of Justice Act 1970.

1970 c. 31.

(2) This section does not affect the power of a magistrates' court to issue such a warrant as aforesaid in the case of default

in paying a sum adjudged to be paid by a conviction, or treated (by any enactment relating to the collection or enforcement of fines, costs, compensation or forfeited recognizances) as so adjudged to be paid.

(3) In this section—

" magistrates' court maintenance order " means a maintenance order enforceable by a magistrates' court ;

1970 c. 31. " maintenance order " means any order specified in Schedule 8 to the Administration of Justice Act 1970 and includes such an order which has been discharged, if any arrears are recoverable thereunder.

Complaint for arrears. **93.**—(1) Where default is made in paying a sum ordered to be paid by an affiliation order or order enforceable as an affiliation order, the court shall not enforce payment of the sum under section 76 above except by an order made on complaint.

(2) A complaint under this section shall be made not earlier than the fifteenth day after the making of the order for the enforcement of which it is made ; but subject to this such a complaint may be made at any time notwithstanding anything in this or any other Act.

(3) In relation to complaints under this section, section 55 above shall not apply and section 56 above shall have effect as if the words " if evidence has been received on a previous occasion " were omitted.

(4) Where at the time and place appointed for the hearing or adjourned hearing of a complaint under this section the complainant appears but the defendant does not, the court may proceed in his absence ; but the court shall not begin to hear the complaint in the absence of the defendant unless either it is proved to the satisfaction of the court, on oath or in such other manner as may be prescribed, that the summons was served on him within what appears to the court to be a reasonable time before the hearing or adjourned hearing or the defendant has appeared on a previous occasion to answer the complaint.

(5) If a complaint under this section is substantiated on oath, any justice of the peace acting for the same petty sessions area as a court having jurisdiction to hear the complaint may issue a warrant for the defendant's arrest, whether or not a summons has been previously issued.

(6) A magistrates' court shall not impose imprisonment in respect of a default to which a complaint under this section relates unless the court has inquired in the presence of the defendant whether the default was due to the defendant's wilful refusal or culpable neglect, and shall not impose imprisonment

as aforesaid if it is of opinion that the default was not so due ;
and, without prejudice to the preceding provisions of this subsection, a magistrates' court shall not impose imprisonment as
aforesaid—

   (*a*) in a case in which the court has power to make an
         attachment of earnings order unless the court is of
         opinion that it is inappropriate to make such an order ;
   (*b*) in any case, in the absence of the defendant.

(7) Notwithstanding anything in section 76(3) above, the
period for which a defendant may be committed to prison under
a warrant of commitment issued in pursuance of a complaint
under this section shall not exceed 6 weeks.

(8) The imprisonment or other detention of a defendant under
a warrant of commitment issued as aforesaid shall not operate
to discharge the defendant from his liability to pay the sum in
respect of which the warrant was issued.

94. Where a person is committed to custody under this Part Effect of
of this Act for failure to pay a sum due under an affiliation order committal
or order enforceable as an affiliation order, then, unless the on arrears.
court that commits him otherwise directs, no arrears shall accrue
under the order while he is in custody.

95. On the hearing of a complaint for the enforcement, Power to
revocation, revival, variation or discharge of an affiliation order remit arrears.
or an order enforceable as an affiliation order, the court may
remit the whole or any part of the sum due under the order.

96.—(1) A magistrates' court shall not commit any person to Civil debt:
prison or other detention in default of payment of a sum en- complaint for
forceable as a civil debt or for want of sufficient distress to non-payment.
satisfy such a sum except by an order made on complaint and on
proof to the satisfaction of the court that that person has, or has
had since the date on which the sum was adjudged to be paid,
the means to pay the sum or any instalment of it on which he
has defaulted, and refuses or neglects or, as the case may be, has
refused or neglected to pay it.

(2) A complaint under this section may be made at any time
notwithstanding anything in this or any other Act.

(3) Where on any such complaint the defendant is committed
to custody, such costs incurred by the complainant in proceedings
for the enforcement of the sum as the court may direct shall be
included in the sum on payment of which the defendant may be
released from custody.

PART IV

WITNESSES AND EVIDENCE

Procuring attendance of witness

Summons to
witness and
warrant for
his arrest.
97.—(1) Where a justice of the peace for any county, any London commission area or the City of London is satisfied that any person in England or Wales is likely to be able to give material evidence, or produce any document or thing likely to be material evidence, at an inquiry into an indictable offence by a magistrates' court for that county, that London commission area or the City (as the case may be) or at the summary trial of an information or hearing of a complaint by such a court and that that person will not voluntarily attend as a witness or will not voluntarily produce the document or thing, the justice shall issue a summons directed to that person requiring him to attend before the court at the time and place appointed in the summons to give evidence or to produce the document or thing.

(2) If a justice of the peace is satisfied by evidence on oath of the matters mentioned in subsection (1) above, and also that it is probable that a summons under that subsection would not procure the attendance of the person in question, the justice may instead of issuing a summons issue a warrant to arrest that person and bring him before such a court as aforesaid at a time and place specified in the warrant; but a warrant shall not be issued under this subsection where the attendance is required for the hearing of a complaint.

(3) On the failure of any person to attend before a magistrates' court in answer to a summons under this section, if—

   (a) the court is satisfied by evidence on oath that he is likely to be able to give material evidence or produce any document or thing likely to be material evidence in the proceedings; and

   (b) it is proved on oath, or in such other manner as may be prescribed, that he has been duly served with the summons, and that a reasonable sum has been paid or tendered to him for costs and expenses; and

   (c) it appears to the court that there is no just excuse for the failure,

the court may issue a warrant to arrest him and bring him before the court at a time and place specified in the warrant.

(4) If any person attending or brought before a magistrates' court refuses without just excuse to be sworn or give evidence, or to produce any document or thing, the court may commit him to custody until the expiration of such period not exceeding 7 days as may be specified in the warrant or until he sooner gives evidence or produces the document or thing.

Evidence generally

98. Subject to the provisions of any enactment or rule of law Evidence on authorising the reception of unsworn evidence, evidence given oath. before a magistrates' court shall be given on oath.

99. Where a magistrates' court has ordered one person to pay Proof of to another any sum of money, and proceedings are taken before non-payment that or any other magistrates' court to enforce payment of that of sum sum, then— adjudged.

(*a*) if the person to whom the sum is ordered to be paid is a clerk of a magistrates' court, a certificate purporting to be signed by the clerk that the sum has not been paid to him ; and

(*b*) in any other case a document purporting to be a statutory declaration by the person to whom the sum is ordered to be paid that the sum has not been paid to him,

shall be admissible as evidence that the sum has not been paid to him, unless the court requires the clerk or other person to be called as a witness.

100. A statement in writing to the effect that wages of any Statement amount have been paid to a person during any period, purport- of wages to ing to be signed by or on behalf of his employer, shall be evi- be evidence. dence of the facts therein stated in any proceedings taken before a magistrates' court—

(*a*) for enforcing payment by the person to whom the wages are stated to have been paid of a sum adjudged to be paid by a summary conviction or order ; or

(*b*) on any application made by or against that person for the making of an order in any matter of bastardy or an order enforceable as an affiliation order, or for the variation, revocation, discharge or revival of such an order.

101. Where the defendant to an information or complaint Onus of relies for his defence on any exception, exemption, proviso, proving excuse or qualification, whether or not it accompanies the des- exceptions, cription of the offence or matter of complaint in the enactment etc. creating the offence or on which the complaint is founded, the burden of proving the exception, exemption, proviso, excuse or qualification shall be on him ; and this notwithstanding that the information or complaint contains an allegation negativing the exception, exemption, proviso, excuse or qualification.

Written
statements
before
examining
justices.

Evidence in criminal cases

102.—(1) In committal proceedings a written statement by any person shall, if the conditions mentioned in subsection (2) below are satisfied, be admissible as evidence to the like extent as oral evidence to the like effect by that person.

(2) The said conditions are—

(*a*) the statement purports to be signed by the person who made it ;

(*b*) the statement contains a declaration by that person to the effect that it is true to the best of his knowledge and belief and that he made the statement knowing that, if it were tendered in evidence, he would be liable to prosecution if he wilfully stated in it anything which he knew to be false or did not believe to be true ;

(*c*) before the statement is tendered in evidence, a copy of the statement is given, by or on behalf of the party proposing to tender it, to each of the other parties to the proceedings ; and

(*d*) none of the other parties, before the statement is tendered in evidence at the committal proceedings, objects to the statement being so tendered under this section.

(3) The following provisions shall also have effect in relation to any written statement tendered in evidence under this section, that is to say—

(*a*) if the statement is made by a person under 21 years old, it shall give his age ;

(*b*) it is not practicable for examining justices to take the be read to him before he signs it and shall be accompanied by a declaration by the person who so read the statement to the effect that it was so read ; and

(*c*) if it refers to any other document as an exhibit, the copy given to any other party to the proceedings under subsection (2)(*c*) above shall be accompanied by a copy of that document or by such information as may be necessary in order to enable the party to whom it is given to inspect that document or a copy thereof.

(4) Notwithstanding that a written statement made by any person may be admissible in committal proceedings by virtue of this section, the court before which the proceedings are held may, of its own motion or on the application of any party to the proceedings, require that person to attend before the court and give evidence.

(5) So much of any statement as is admitted in evidence by virtue of this section shall, unless the court commits the accused

for trial by virtue of section 6(2) above or the court otherwise directs, be read aloud at the hearing, and where the court so directs an account shall be given orally of so much of any statement as is not read aloud.

(6) Any document or object referred to as an exhibit and identified in a written statement tendered in evidence under this section shall be treated as if it had been produced as an exhibit and identified in court by the maker of the statement.

(7) Subsection (3) of section 13 of the Criminal Justice Act 1925 c. 86. 1925 (reading of deposition as evidence at the trial) shall apply to any written statement tendered in evidence in committal proceedings under this section as it applies to a deposition taken in such proceedings, but in its application to any such statement that subsection shall have effect as if paragraph (*b*) thereof were omitted.

(8) In section 2(2) of the Administration of Justice (Miscel- 1933 c. 36. laneous Provisions) Act 1933 (procedure for preferring bills of indictment) the reference in proviso (i) to facts disclosed in any deposition taken before a justice in the presence of the accused shall be construed as including a reference to facts disclosed in any such written statement as aforesaid.

(9) Section 28 above shall not apply to any such statement as aforesaid.

(10) A person whose written statement is tendered in evidence in committal proceedings under this section shall be treated for the purposes of section 1 of the Criminal Procedure 1965 c. 69. (Attendance of Witnesses) Act 1965 (witness orders) as a witness who has been examined by the court.

103.—(1) In any proceedings before a magistrates' court Evidence of inquiring into a sexual offence as examining justices— children in committal
  (*a*) a child shall not be called as a witness for the prosecu- proceedings tion ; but for sexual
  (*b*) any statement made in writing by or taken in writing offences. from the child shall be admissible in evidence of any matter of which his oral testimony would be admissible, except in a case where the application of this subsection is excluded under subsection (2) below.

(2) Subsection (1) above shall not apply—
  (*a*) where at or before the time when such a statement is tendered in evidence the defence objects to the application of that subsection ; or
  (*b*) where the prosecution requires the attendance of the child for the purpose of establishing the identity of any person ; or

    (c) where the court is satisfied that it has not been possible to obtain from the child a statement that may be given in evidence under this section ; or

    (d) where the inquiry into the offence takes place after the court has discontinued to try it summarily and the child has given evidence in the summary trial.

(3) Section 28 above shall not apply to any statement admitted in pursuance of subsection (1) above.

1933 c. 12.
1956 c. 69.
1960 c. 33.
1978 c. 37.

(4) In this section " child " has the same meaning as in the Children and Young Persons Act 1933 and " sexual offence " means any offence under the Sexual Offences Act 1956 or the Indecency with Children Act 1960 or section 1(1)(a) of the Protection of Children Act 1978, or any attempt to commit such an offence.

Proof of previous convictions.

104. Where a person is convicted of a summary offence by a magistrates' court, other than a juvenile court, and—

    (a) it is proved to the satisfaction of the court, on oath or in such other manner as may be prescribed, that not less than 7 days previously a notice was served on the accused in the prescribed form and manner specifying any alleged previous conviction of the accused of a summary offence proposed to be brought to the notice of the court in the event of his conviction of the offence charged ; and

    (b) the accused is not present in person before the court,

the court may take account of any such previous conviction so specified as if the accused had appeared and admitted it.

Deposition of person dangerously ill.

105.—(1) Where a person appears to a justice of the peace to be able and willing to give material information relating to an indictable offence or to any person accused of an indictable offence, and—

    (a) the justice is satisfied, on a representation made by a duly qualified medical practitioner, that the person able and willing to make the statement is dangerously ill and unlikely to recover ; and

    (b) it is not practicable for examining justices to take the evidence of the sick person in accordance with the provisions of this Act and the rules,

the justice may take in writing the deposition of the sick person on oath.

(2) A deposition taken under this section may be given in evidence before examining justices inquiring into an information against the offender or in respect of the offence to which the

deposition relates, but subject to the same conditions as apply, under section 6 of the Criminal Law Amendment Act 1867, to its being given in evidence upon the trial of the offender or offence.

PART IV
1867 c. 35.

Offences

106.—(1) If any person in a written statement tendered in evidence in criminal proceedings by virtue of section 102 above wilfully makes a statement material in those proceedings which he knows to be false or does not believe to be true, he shall be liable on conviction on indictment to imprisonment for a term not exceeding 2 years or a fine or both.

False written statements tendered in evidence.

(2) The Perjury Act 1911 shall have effect as if this section were contained in that Act.

1911 c. 6.

107. If, in any solemn declaration, certificate or other writing made or given for the purpose of its being used in pursuance of the rules as evidence of the service of any document or the handwriting or seal of any person, a person makes a statement that he knows to be false in a material particular, or recklessly makes any statement that is false in a material particular, he shall be liable on summary conviction to imprisonment for a term not exceeding 6 months or a fine not exceeding £100 or both.

False statements in declaration proving service, etc.

PART V

APPEAL AND CASE STATED

Appeal

108.—(1) A person convicted by a magistrates' court may appeal to the Crown Court—

Right of appeal to the Crown Court.

(a) if he pleaded guilty, against his sentence ;

(b) if he did not, against the conviction or sentence.

(2) A person sentenced by a magistrates' court for an offence in respect of which a probation order or an order for conditional discharge has been previously made may appeal to the Crown Court against the sentence.

(3) In this section " sentence " includes any order made on conviction by a magistrates' court, not being—

(a) a probation order or an order for conditional discharge ;

(b) an order for the payment of costs ;

(c) an order under section 2 of the Protection of Animals Act 1911 (which enables a court to order the destruction of an animal) ; or

1911 c. 27.

(d) an order made in pursuance of any enactment under which the court has no discretion as to the making of the order or its terms.

109.—(1) Where notice to abandon an appeal has been duly given by the appellant—

> (*a*) the court against whose decision the appeal was brought may issue process for enforcing that decision, subject to anything already suffered or done under it by the appellant ; and
>
> (*b*) the said court may, on the application of the other party to the appeal, order the appellant to pay to that party such costs as appear to the court to be just and reasonable in respect of expenses properly incurred by that party in connection with the appeal before notice of the abandonment was given to that party.

(2) In this section " appeal " means an appeal from a magistrates' court to the Crown Court, and the reference to a notice to abandon an appeal is a reference to a notice shown to the satisfaction of the magistrates' court to have been given in accordance with Crown Court rules.

110. After the determination by the Crown Court of an appeal from a magistrates' court the decision appealed against as confirmed or varied by the Crown Court, or any decision of the Crown Court substituted for the decision appealed against, may, without prejudice to the powers of the Crown Court to enforce the decision, be enforced—

> (*a*) by the issue by the court by which the decision appealed against was given of any process that it could have issued if it had decided the case as the Crown Court decided it ;
>
> (*b*) so far as the nature of any process already issued to enforce the decision appealed against permits, by that process ;

and the decision of the Crown Court shall have effect as if it had been made by the magistrates' court against whose decision the appeal is brought.

Case stated

111.—(1) Any person who was a party to any proceeding before a magistrates' court or is aggrieved by the conviction, order, determination or other proceeding of the court may question the proceeding on the ground that it is wrong in law or is in excess of jurisdiction by applying to the justices composing the court to state a case for the opinion of the High Court on the question of law or jurisdiction involved ; but a person shall not make an application under this section in respect of a decision against which he has a right of appeal to the High Court or which by virtue of any enactment passed after 31st December 1879 is final.

(2) An application under subsection (1) above shall be made within 21 days after the day on which the decision of the magistrates' court was given.

(3) For the purpose of subsection (2) above, the day on which the decision of the magistrates' court is given shall, where the court has adjourned the trial of an information after conviction, be the day on which the court sentences or otherwise deals with the offender.

(4) On the making of an application under this section in respect of a decision any right of the applicant to appeal against the decision to the Crown Court shall cease.

(5) If the justices are of opinion that an application under this section is frivolous, they may refuse to state a case, and, if the applicant so requires, shall give him a certificate stating that the application has been refused ; but the justices shall not refuse to state a case if the application is made by or under the direction of the Attorney General.

(6) Where justices refuse to state a case, the High Court may, on the application of the person who applied for the case to be stated, make an order of mandamus requiring the justices to state a case.

112. Any conviction, order, determination or other proceeding of a magistrates' court varied by the High Court on an appeal by case stated, and any judgment or order of the High Court on such an appeal, may be enforced as if it were a decision of the magistrates' court from which the appeal was brought. Effect of decision of High Court on case stated by magistrates' court.

Supplemental provisions as to appeal and case stated

113.—(1) Where a person has given notice of appeal to the Crown Court against the decision of a magistrates' court or has applied to a magistrates' court to state a case for the opinion of the High Court, then, if he is in custody, the magistrates' court may grant him bail. Bail on appeal or case stated.

(2) If a person is granted bail under subsection (1) above, the time and place at which he is to appear (except in the event of the determination in respect of which the case is stated being reversed by the High Court) shall be—

(*a*) if he has given notice of appeal, the Crown Court at the time appointed for the hearing of the appeal ;

(*b*) if he has applied for the statement of a case, the magistrates' court at such time within 10 days after the judgment of the High Court has been given as may be specified by the magistrates' court ;

and any recognizance that may be taken from him or from any surety for him shall be conditioned accordingly.

Part V

(3) Subsection (1) above shall not apply where the accused has been committed to the Crown Court for sentence under section 37 or 38 above.

1948 c. 58.

(4) Section 37(6) of the Criminal Justice Act 1948 (which relates to the currency of a sentence while a person is released on bail by the High Court) shall apply to a person released on bail by a magistrates' court under this section pending the hearing of a case stated as it applies to a person released on bail by the High Court under section 22 of the Criminal Justice Act 1967.

1967 c. 80.

Recognizances and fees on case stated.

114. Justices to whom application has been made to state a case for the opinion of the High Court on any proceeding of a magistrates' court shall not be required to state the case until the applicant has entered into a recognizance, with or without sureties, before the magistrates' court, conditioned to prosecute the appeal without delay and to submit to the judgment of the High Court and pay such costs as that Court may award; and (except in any criminal matter) the clerk of a magistrates' court shall not be required to deliver the case to the applicant until the applicant has paid him the fees payable for the case and for the recognizances.

Part VI

Recognizances

Recognizances to keep the peace or be of good behaviour

Binding over to keep the peace or be of good behaviour.

115.—(1) The power of a magistrates' court on the complaint of any person to adjudge any other person to enter into a recognizance, with or without sureties, to keep the peace or to be of good behaviour towards the complainant shall be exercised by order on complaint.

(2) Where a complaint is made under this section, the power of the court to remand the defendant under subsection (5) of section 55 above shall not be subject to the restrictions imposed by subsection (6) of that section.

(3) If any person ordered by a magistrates' court under subsection (1) above to enter into a recognizance, with or without sureties, to keep the peace or to be of good behaviour fails to comply with the order, the court may commit him to custody for a period not exceeding 6 months or until he sooner complies with the order.

116.—(1) On complaint being made to a justice of the peace for any area to which this section applies by a surety to a recognizance to keep the peace or to be of good behaviour entered into before a magistrates' court that the person bound by the recognizance as principal has been, or is about to be, guilty of conduct constituting a breach of the conditions of the recognizance, the justice may, if the complaint alleges that the principal is, or is believed to be, in that area, or if the recognizance was entered into before a magistrates' court for that area, issue a warrant to arrest the principal and bring him before a magistrates' court for that area or a summons requiring the principal to appear before such a court; but the justice shall not issue a warrant unless the complaint is in writing and substantiated on oath.

PART VI

Discharge of recognizance to keep the peace or be of good behaviour on complaint of surety.

(2) The magistrates' court before which the principal appears or is brought in pursuance of such a summons or warrant as aforesaid may, unless it adjudges the recognizance to be forfeited, order the recognizance to be discharged and order the principal to enter into a new recognizance, with or without sureties, to keep the peace or to be of good behaviour.

(3) The areas to which this section applies are any county, any London commission area and the City of London.

Other provisions

117.—(1) A justice of the peace on issuing a warrant for the arrest of any person may grant him bail by endorsing the warrant for bail, that is to say, by endorsing the warrant with a direction in accordance with subsection (2) below.

Warrant endorsed for bail.

(2) A direction for bail endorsed on a warrant under subsection (1) above shall—

(a) in the case of bail in criminal proceedings, state that the person arrested is to be released on bail subject to a duty to appear before such magistrates' court and at such time as may be specified in the endorsement;

(b) in the case of bail otherwise than in criminal proceedings, state that the person arrested is to be released on bail on his entering into such a recognizance (with or without sureties) conditioned for his appearance before a magistrates' court as may be specified in the endorsement;

and the endorsement shall fix the amounts in which any sureties and, in a case falling within paragraph (b) above, that person is or are to be bound.

(3) Where a warrant has been endorsed for bail under subsection (1) above, then, on the person referred to in the warrant being taken to a police station on arrest under the warrant, the officer in charge of the police station shall (subject to his approving any surety tendered in compliance with the endorsement) release him from custody as directed in the endorsement.

Varying or dispensing with requirement as to sureties.

118.—(1) Subject to subsection (2) below, where a magistrates' court has committed a person to custody in default of finding sureties, the court may, on application by or on behalf of the person committed, and after hearing fresh evidence, reduce the amount in which it is proposed that any surety should be bound or dispense with any of the sureties or otherwise deal with the case as it thinks just.

(2) Subsection (1) above does not apply in relation to a person granted bail in criminal proceedings.

Postponement of taking recognizance.

119.—(1) Where a magistrates' court has power to take any recognizance, the court may, instead of taking it, fix the amount in which the principal and his sureties, if any, are to be bound ; and thereafter the recognizance may be taken by any such person as may be prescribed.

(2) Where, in pursuance of this section, a recognizance is entered into otherwise than before the court that fixed the amount of it, the same consequences shall follow as if it had been entered into before that court ; and references in this or any other Act to the court before which a recognizance was entered into shall be construed accordingly.

(3) Nothing in this section shall enable a magistrates' court to alter the amount of a recognizance fixed by the High Court.

Forfeiture of recognizance.

120.—(1) Where a recognizance to keep the peace or to be of good behaviour has been entered into before a magistrates' court or any recognizance is conditioned for the appearance of a person before a magistrates' court or for his doing any other thing connected with a proceeding before a magistrates' court, and the recognizance appears to the court to be forfeited, the court may, subject to subsection (2) below, declare the recognizance to be forfeited and adjudge the persons bound thereby, whether as principal or sureties, or any of them, to pay the sum in which they are respectively bound.

(2) Where a recognizance is conditioned to keep the peace or to be of good behaviour, the court shall not declare it forfeited except by order made on complaint.

(3) **The** court which declares the recognizance to be forfeited may, instead of adjudging any person to pay the whole sum in which he is bound, adjudge him to pay part only of the sum or remit the sum.

(4) Payment of any sum adjudged to be paid under this section, including any costs awarded against the defendant, may be enforced, and any such sum shall be applied, as if it were a fine and as if the adjudication were a summary conviction of an offence not punishable with imprisonment and so much of section 85(1) above as empowers a court to remit fines shall not apply to the sum but so much thereof as relates to remission after a term of imprisonment has been imposed shall so apply; but at any time before the issue of a warrant of commitment to enforce payment of the sum, or before the sale of goods under a warrant of distress to satisfy the sum, the court may remit the whole or any part of the sum either absolutely or on such conditions as the court thinks just.

(5) A recognizance such as is mentioned in this section shall not be enforced otherwise than in accordance with this section, and accordingly shall not be transmitted to the Crown Court nor shall its forfeiture be certified to that Court.

PART VII

MISCELLANEOUS AND SUPPLEMENTARY

Constitution and place of sitting of magistrates' courts

121.—(1) A magistrates' court shall not try an information Constitution summarily or hear a complaint except when composed of at and place of least 2 justices unless the trial or hearing is one that by virtue sitting of of any enactment may take place before a single justice. court.

(2) A magistrates' court shall not hold an inquiry into the means of an offender for the purposes of section 82 above except when composed of at least 2 justices.

(3) A magistrates' court shall not—

    (a) try summarily an information for an indictable offence or hear a complaint except when sitting in a petty-sessional court-house;

    (b) try an information for a summary offence or hold an inquiry into the means of an offender for the purposes of section 82 above, or impose imprisonment, except when sitting in a petty-sessional court-house or an occasional court-house.

(4) Subject to the provisions of any enactment to the contrary, where a magistrates' court is required by this section to sit in a petty-sessional or occasional court-house, it shall sit in open court.

(5) A magistrates' court composed of a single justice, or sitting in an occasional court-house, shall not impose imprisonment for a period exceeding 14 days or order a person to pay more than £1.

(6) Subject to the provisions of subsection (7) below, the justices composing the court before which any proceedings take place shall be present during the whole of the proceedings; but, if during the course of the proceedings any justice absents himself, he shall cease to act further therein and, if the remaining justices are enough to satisfy the requirements of the preceding provisions of this section, the proceedings may continue before a court composed of those justices.

(7) Where the trial of an information is adjourned after the accused has been convicted and before he is sentenced or otherwise dealt with, the court which sentences or deals with him need not be composed of the same justices as that which convicted him; but, where among the justices composing the court which sentences or deals with an offender there are any who were not sitting when he was convicted, the court which sentences or deals with the offender shall before doing so make such inquiry into the facts and circumstances of the case as will enable the justices who were not sitting when the offender was convicted to be fully acquainted with those facts and circumstances.

(8) This section shall have effect subject to the provisions of this Act relating to domestic proceedings.

Appearance by counsel or solicitor

Appearance by counsel or solicitor.

122.—(1) A party to any proceedings before a magistrates' court may be represented by counsel or solicitor.

(2) Subject to subsection (3) below, an absent party so represented shall be deemed not to be absent.

(3) Appearance of a party by counsel or solicitor shall not satisfy any provision of any enactment or any condition of a recognizance expressly requiring his presence.

Process

Defect in process.

123.—(1) No objection shall be allowed to any information or complaint, or to any summons or warrant to procure the presence of the defendant, for any defect in it in substance or in form, or for any variance between it and the evidence adduced on behalf of the prosecutor or complainant at the hearing of the information or complaint.

(2) If it appears to a magistrates' court that any variance between a summons or warrant and the evidence adduced on behalf of the prosecutor or complainant is such that the defendant

has been misled by the variance, the court shall, on the applica- tion of the defendant, adjourn the hearing.

124. A warrant or summons issued by a justice of the peace Process valid shall not cease to have effect by reason of his death or his notwith- ceasing to be a justice. standing death, etc., of justice.

125.—(1) A warrant of arrest issued by a justice of the peace Warrants. shall remain in force until it is executed or withdrawn.

(2) A warrant of arrest, warrant of commitment, warrant of distress or search warrant issued by a justice of the peace may be executed anywhere in England and Wales by any person to whom it is directed or by any constable acting within his police area.

This subsection does not apply to a warrant of commitment or a warrant of distress issued under Part VI of the General 1967 c. 9. Rate Act 1967.

(3) A warrant to arrest a person charged with an offence may be executed by a constable notwithstanding that it is not in his possession at the time ; but the warrant shall, on the demand of the person arrested, be shown to him as soon as practicable.

126. Sections 12 to 14 of the Indictable Offences Act 1848 Execution of (which relate, among other things, to the execution in Scotland, certain Northern Ireland, the Isle of Man and the Channel Islands of warrants warrants of arrest for the offences referred to in those sections) outside shall, so far as applicable, apply to— England and Wales.

(a) warrants of arrest issued under section 1 above for 1848 c. 42. offences other than those referred to in the said sections 12 to 14 ;

(b) warrants of arrest issued under section 13 above ;

(c) warrants of arrest issued under section 97 above other than warrants issued in bastardy proceedings to arrest a witness ; and

(d) warrants of commitment issued under this Act.

Limitation of time

127.—(1) Except as otherwise expressly provided by any Limitation enactment and subject to subsection (2) below, a magistrates' of time. court shall not try an information or hear a complaint unless the information was laid, or the complaint made, within 6 months from the time when the offence was committed, or the matter of complaint arose.

(2) Nothing in—

(a) subsection (1) above ; or

(b) subject to subsection (4) below, any other enactment (however framed or worded) which, as regards any offence to which it applies, would but for this section impose a time-limit on the power of a magistrates' court to try an information summarily or impose a limitation on the time for taking summary proceedings,

shall apply in relation to any indictable offence.

(3) Without prejudice to the generality of paragraph (b) of subsection (2) above, that paragraph includes enactments which impose a time-limit that applies only in certain circumstances (for example, where the proceedings are not instituted by or with the consent of the Director of Public Prosecutions or some other specified authority).

(4) Where, as regards any indictable offence, there is imposed by any enactment (however framed or worded, and whether falling within subsection (2) (b) above or not) a limitation on the time for taking proceedings on indictment for that offence no summary proceedings for that offence shall be taken after the latest time for taking proceedings on indictment.

Remand

Remand in custody or on bail.
1976 c. 63.

128.—(1) Where a magistrates' court has power to remand any person, then, subject to section 4 of the Bail Act 1976 and to any other enactment modifying that power, the court may—

(a) remand him in custody, that is to say, commit him to custody to be brought before the court at the end of the period of remand or at such earlier time as the court may require ; or

(b) where it is inquiring into or trying an offence alleged to have been committed by that person or has convicted him of an offence, remand him on bail in accordance with the Bail Act 1976, that is to say, by directing him to appear as provided in subsection (4) below ; or

(c) except in a case falling within paragraph (b) above, remand him on bail by taking from him a recognizance (with or without sureties) conditioned as provided in that subsection ;

and may, in a case falling within paragraph (c) above, instead of taking recognizances in accordance with that paragraph, fix the amount of the recognizances with a view to their being taken subsequently in accordance with section 119 above.

(2) Where the court fixes the amount of a recognizance under subsection (1) above or section 8(3) of the Bail Act 1976 with a view to its being taken subsequently the court shall in the meantime commit the person so remanded to custody in accordance with paragraph (*a*) of the said subsection (1).

(3) Where a person is brought before the court after remand, the court may further remand him.

(4) Where a person is remanded on bail under subsection (1) above the court may, where it remands him on bail in accordance with the Bail Act 1976 direct him to appear or, in any other case, direct that his recognizance be conditioned for his appearance—

(*a*) before that court at the end of the period of remand; or

(*b*) at every time and place to which during the course of the proceedings the hearing may be from time to time adjourned;

and, where it remands him on bail conditionally on his providing a surety during an inquiry into an offence alleged to have been committed by him, may direct that the recognizance of the surety be conditioned to secure that the person so bailed appears—

(*c*) at every time and place to which during the course of the proceedings the hearing may be from time to time adjourned and also before the Crown Court in the event of the person so bailed being committed for trial there.

(5) Where a person is directed to appear or a recognizance is conditioned for a person's appearance in accordance with paragraph (*b*) or (*c*) of subsection (4) above, the fixing at any time of the time for him next to appear shall be deemed to be a remand; but nothing in this subsection or subsection (4) above shall deprive the court of power at any subsequent hearing to remand him afresh.

(6) Subject to the provisions of section 129 below, a magistrates' court shall not remand a person for a period exceeding 8 clear days, except that—

(*a*) if the court remands him on bail, it may remand him for a longer period if he and the other party consent;

(*b*) where the court adjourns a trial under section 10(3) or 30 above, the court may remand him for the period of the adjournment;

(c) where a person is charged with an offence triable either way, then, if it falls to the court to try the case summarily but the court is not at the time so constituted, and sitting in such a place, as will enable it to proceed with the trial, the court may remand him until the next occasion on which it will be practicable for the court to be so constituted, and to sit in such a place, as aforesaid, notwithstanding that the remand is for a period exceeding 8 clear days.

(7) A magistrates' court having power to remand a person in custody may, if the remand is for a period not exceeding 3 clear days, commit him to the custody of a constable.

129.—(1) If a magistrates' court is satisfied that any person who has been remanded is unable by reason of illness or accident to appear or be brought before the court at the expiration of the period for which he was remanded, the court may, in his absence, remand him for a further time; and section 128(6) above shall not apply.

(2) Notwithstanding anything in section 128(1) above, the power of a court under subsection (1) above to remand a person on bail for a further time—

(a) where he was granted bail in criminal proceedings, includes power to enlarge the recognizance of any surety for him to a later time;

(b) where he was granted bail otherwise than in criminal proceedings, may be exercised by enlarging his recognizance and those of any sureties for him to a later time.

(3) Where a person remanded on bail is bound to appear before a magistrates' court at any time and the court has no power to remand him under subsection (1) above, the court may in his absence—

(a) where he was granted bail in criminal proceedings, appoint a later time as the time at which he is to appear and enlarge the recognizances of any sureties for him to that time;

(b) where he was granted bail otherwise than in criminal proceedings, enlarge his recognizance and those of any sureties for him to a later time;

and the appointment of the time or the enlargement of his recognizance shall be deemed to be a further remand.

(4) Where a magistrates' court commits a person for trial on bail and the recognizance of any surety for him has been conditioned in accordance with paragraph (a) of subsection (4) of section 128 above the court may, in the absence of the surety,

enlarge his recognizance so that he is bound to secure that the person so committed for trial appears also before the Crown Court.

PART VII

130.—(1) A magistrates' court adjourning a case under section 5, 10(1) or 18(4) above, and remanding the accused in custody, may, if he has attained the age of 17, order that he be brought up for any subsequent remands before an alternate magistrates' court nearer to the prison where he is to be confined while on remand.

Transfer of remand hearings.

(2) The order shall require the accused to be brought before the alternate court at the end of the period of remand or at such earlier time as the alternate court may require.

(3) While the order is in force, the alternate court shall, to the exclusion of the court which made the order, have all the powers in relation to further remand (whether in custody or on bail) and the grant of legal aid which that court would have had but for the order.

(4) The alternate court may, on remanding the accused in custody, require him to be brought before the court which made the order at the end of the period of remand or at such earlier time as that court may require ; and, if the alternate court does so, or the accused is released on bail, the order under subsection (1) above shall cease to be in force.

(5) Schedule 5 to this Act shall have effect to supplement this section.

131.—(1) When a magistrates' court remands an accused person in custody and he is already detained under a custodial sentence, the period for which he is remanded may be up to 28 clear days.

Remand of accused already in custody.

(2) But the court shall inquire as to the expected date of his release from that detention ; and if it appears that it will be before 28 clear days have expired, he shall not be remanded in custody for more than 8 clear days or (if longer) a period ending with that date.

(3) So long as he is detained under a custodial sentence, an application for him to be further remanded in custody may be made and determined without his appearance in court, provided that he is represented by counsel or a solicitor who signifies the accused's consent to the application being heard in his absence.

Restrictions on imprisonment

132. A magistrates' court shall not impose imprisonment for less than 5 days.

Minimum term.

2 G 2

PART VII
Consecutive
terms of
imprisonment.
133.—(1) A magistrates' court imposing imprisonment on any person may order that the term of imprisonment shall commence on the expiration of any other term of imprisonment imposed by that or any other court ; but where a magistrates' court imposes two or more terms of imprisonment to run consecutively the aggregate of such terms shall not, subject to the provisions of this section, exceed 6 months.

(2) If two or more of the terms imposed by the court are imposed in respect of an offence triable either way which was tried summarily otherwise than in pursuance of section 22(2) above, the aggregate of the terms so imposed and any other terms imposed by the court may exceed 6 months but shall not, subject to the following provisions of this section, exceed 12 months.

(3) The limitations imposed by the preceding subsections shall not operate to reduce the aggregate of the terms that the court may impose in respect of any offences below the term which the court has power to impose in respect of any one of those offences.

(4) Where a person has been sentenced by a magistrates' court to imprisonment and a fine for the same offence, a period of imprisonment imposed for non-payment of the fine, or for want of sufficient distress to satisfy the fine, shall not be subject to the limitations imposed by the preceding subsections.

(5) For the purposes of this section a term of imprisonment shall be deemed to be imposed in respect of an offence if it is imposed as a sentence or in default of payment of a sum adjudged to be paid by the conviction or for want of sufficient distress to satisfy such a sum.

Detention for short periods

Detention in
police cells,
etc.
134.—(1) A magistrates' court having power to impose imprisonment on any person may instead of doing so order him to be detained for any period not exceeding 4 days in a place certified by the Secretary of State to be suitable for the purpose.

(2) The Secretary of State may certify under this section any police cells, bridewell or similar place provided by him and, on the application of any other police authority, any such place provided by that authority.

(3) A woman or girl shall not be detained in any such place except under the supervision of women.

1978 c. 30.
Section 6(*b*) of the Interpretation Act 1978 (feminine includes masculine) does not apply for the purposes of this subsection.

(4) The Secretary of State may make regulations for the inspection of places certified by him under this section, for the treatment of persons detained in them and generally for the purpose of carrying this section into effect.

(5) Any expenses incurred in the maintenance of persons detained under this section shall be defrayed out of moneys provided by Parliament.

(6) In this section " maintenance " has the same meaning in relation to a person detained under this section as it has under section 53 of the Prison Act 1952 in relation to a prisoner.

1952 c. 52.

(7) Subsection (2) above shall, in its application to the City of London, have effect as if for the references therein to the police authority there were substituted references to the Commissioner of Police for the City of London.

135.—(1) A magistrates' court that has power to commit to prison a person convicted of an offence, or would have that power but for section 82 or 88 above, may order him to be detained within the precincts of the court-house or at any police station until such hour, not later than 8 o'clock in the evening of the day on which the order is made, as the court may direct, and, if it does so, shall not, where it has power to commit him to prison, exercise that power.

Detention of offender for one day in court-house or police station.

(2) A court shall not make such an order under this section as will deprive the offender of a reasonable opportunity of returning to his abode on the day of the order.

136.—(1) A magistrates' court that has power to commit to prison a person in default of payment of a sum adjudged to be paid by a summary conviction, or would have that power but for section 82 or 88 above, may issue a warrant for his detention in a police station, and, if it does so, shall not, where it has power to commit him to prison, exercise that power.

Committal to custody overnight at police station for non-payment of sum adjudged by conviction.

(2) A warrant under this section, unless the sum adjudged to be paid by the conviction is sooner paid,—

(a) shall authorise any police constable to arrest the defaulter and take him to a police station, and

(b) shall require the officer in charge of the station to detain him there until 8 o'clock in the morning of the day following that on which he is arrested, or, if he is arrested between midnight and 8 o'clock in the morning, until 8 o'clock in the morning of the day on which he is arrested.

PART VII   (3) Notwithstanding subsection (2)(*b*) above, the officer may release the defaulter at any time within 4 hours before 8 o'clock in the morning if the officer thinks it expedient to do so in order to enable him to go to his work or for any other reason appearing to the officer to be sufficient.

Fees, fines, forfeitures, etc.

Fees.   **137.**—(1) Subject to the provisions of this section, the court fees set out in Part I of Schedule 6 to this Act, and no others, shall be chargeable by clerks of magistrates' courts ; and any enactment providing for the payment of any fees for the payment of which provision is made in the said Part I shall have effect accordingly.

(2) No fee shall be chargeable by a clerk of a magistrates' court in respect of any matter specified in Part II of the said Schedule.

(3) Nothing in this section shall affect the fees chargeable in respect of the matters specified in Part III of the said Schedule.

(4) The Secretary of State may from time to time by order make such variations in Part I of the said Schedule as may seem to him proper.

(5) The power to make an order under subsection (4) above shall be exercisable by statutory instrument ; and a draft of any such statutory instrument shall be laid before Parliament.

(6) This section shall apply to magistrates' courts held by metropolitan stipendiary magistrates as it applies to other magistrates' courts.

Remission of   **138.** A magistrates' court may on the ground of poverty or
fees.   for other reasonable cause remit in whole or in part any fee payable in proceedings before the court.

Disposal of   **139.** A clerk of a magistrates' court shall apply moneys
sums adjudged   received by him on account of a sum adjudged to be paid by a
to be paid by   summary conviction as follows—
conviction.

(*a*) in the first place in payment of any compensation adjudged by the conviction to be paid to any person ;

(*b*) in the second place in payment of any costs so adjudged to be paid to the prosecutor ; and

(*c*) the balance to the fund to which, or the person to whom,
1979 c. 55.   he is required to pay the sum by section 61 of the Justices of the Peace Act 1979 or any other enactment relating to the sum.

140. Subject to any enactment relating to customs or excise, PART VII anything other than money forfeited on a conviction by a magis- Disposal of trates' court or the forfeiture of which may be enforced by a non-pecuniary magistrates' court shall be sold or otherwise disposed of in such forfeitures. manner as the court may direct; and the proceeds shall be applied as if they were a fine imposed under the enactment on which the proceedings for the forfeiture are founded.

Clerks to justices

141.—(1) Any reference in this Act to a clerk of any magis- Clerks to trates' court shall be construed as a reference to the clerk to the justices. justices for the petty sessions area for which the court is acting, or was acting at the relevant time.

(2) Where there is more than one clerk to the justices for any petty sessions area, anything that this Act requires or authorises to be done by or to the clerk to the justices shall or may be done by or to any of the clerks or by or to such of the clerks as the magistrates' courts committee having power over the appointment of clerks to justices for that area generally or in any particular case or cases may direct.

(3) Subsections (1) and (2) above shall apply to the justices' clerks for the inner London area as if the reference in subsection (2) to the magistrates' courts committee were a reference to the committee of magistrates.

Power to rectify mistakes etc.

142.—(1) Subject to subsection (4) below, a magistrates' court Power of may vary or rescind a sentence or other order imposed or made magistrates' by it when dealing with an offender; and it is hereby declared court to re-open cases that this power extends to replacing a sentence or order which to rectify for any reason appears to be invalid by another which the court mistakes etc. has power to impose or make.

(2) Where a person is found guilty by a magistrates' court in a case in which he has pleaded not guilty or the court has proceeded in his absence under section 11(1) above, and it subsequently appears to the court that it would be in the interests of justice that the case should be heard again by different justices, the court may, subject to subsection (4) below, so direct.

(3) Where a court gives a direction under subsection (2) above—

(a) the finding of guilty and any sentence or other order imposed or made in consequence thereof shall be of no effect; and

(b) section 10(4) above shall apply as if the trial of the person in question had been adjourned.

2 G 4

(4) The powers conferred by subsections (1) and (2) above shall be exercisable only within the period of 28 days beginning with the day on which the sentence or order was imposed or made or the person was found guilty, as the case may be, and only—

    (*a*) by a court constituted in the same manner as the court by which the sentence or order was imposed or made or, as the case may be, by which the person in question was found guilty, or

    (*b*) where that court comprised 3 or more justices of the peace, by a court which consists of or comprises a majority of those justices.

(5) Where a sentence or order is varied under subsection (1) above, the sentence or other order, as so varied, shall take effect from the beginning of the day on which it was originally imposed or made, unless the court otherwise directs.

Power to alter sums specified in certain provisions

Power to alter sums specified in certain provisions.

143.—(1) If it appears to the Secretary of State that there has been a change in the value of money since the last occasion when the sum or sums specified in a provision mentioned in subsection (2) below were fixed, he may by order substitute for the sum or sums for the time being specified in that provision such other sum or sums as appear to him justified by the change.

(2) The said provisions are—

    (*a*) section 22(1) above ;

    (*b*) the definition of " the prescribed sum " in section 32(9) above ;

    (*c*) paragraph (*a*) of section 33(1) above ;

    (*d*) section 40(1) above ;

    (*e*) the Table in paragraph 1 of Schedule 4 to this Act.

(3) A sum specified in a provision mentioned in subsection (2) above (a " relevant provision ") may have been fixed as mentioned in subsection (1) above—

1977 c. 45.

    (*a*) by the coming into force of a provision of the Criminal Law Act 1977 (being a provision re-enacted in the relevant provision concerned or a provision amending a provision of another Act so re-enacted), or

    (*b*) by an order made under subsection (1) above in respect of the relevant provision concerned.

(4) Where it appears to the Secretary of State that the difference between a sum to which subsection (5) below applies and the prescribed sum (within the meaning of section 32 above) has

been or would be altered or eliminated by an order made or proposed to be made under subsection (1) above, he may by order amend the enactment specifying the first-mentioned sum so as to substitute for that sum such other sum as appears to him to be justified by a change in the value of money appearing to him to have taken place between—

(*a*) the last occasion on which the sum in question was fixed ; and

(*b*) the making of the order or proposed order under subsection (1) above.

(5) This subsection applies to any sum specified in any enactment contained in any Act passed before, or in the same Session as, the Criminal Law Act 1977 as—   1977 c. 45.

(*a*) the maximum fine which may be imposed on summary conviction of an offence triable either way ; or

(*b*) the maximum fine which, in the exercise of any power by subordinate instrument to impose penal provisions, may be authorised on summary conviction in respect of an offence triable either way.

(6) An order under subsection (1) or (4) above—

(*a*) shall be made by statutory instrument subject to annulment in pursuance of a resolution of either House of Parliament and may be revoked by a subsequent order thereunder ; and

(*b*) shall not affect the punishment for an offence committed before that order comes into force.

Rules

144.—(1) The Lord Chancellor may appoint a rule committee Rule for magistrates' courts, and may on the advice of or after con- committee and sultation with the rule committee make rules for regulating and rules of prescribing the procedure and practice to be followed in magi- procedure. strates' courts and by justices' clerks.

(2) The rule committee shall consist of the Lord Chief Justice, the President of the Family Division of the High Court, the chief metropolitan stipendiary magistrate and such number of other persons appointed by the Lord Chancellor as he may determine.

(3) Among the members of the committee appointed by the Lord Chancellor there shall be at least one justices' clerk, one practising barrister and one practising solicitor of the Supreme Court.

(4) The power to make rules conferred by this section shall be exercisable by statutory instrument which shall be subject to annulment by resolution of either House of Parliament.

(5) In this section the expression " justices' clerk " means a clerk to the justices for a petty sessions area.

Rules:
supplementary
provisions.

145.—(1) The power to make rules conferred by section 144 above shall, without prejudice to the generality of subsection (1) of that section, include power to make provision—

(a) as to the practice and procedure of justices in exercising functions preliminary or incidental to proceedings before a magistrates' court ;

(b) as to the service and execution of process issued by or for the purposes of a magistrates' court, including the service and execution in England and Wales of process issued in other parts of the United Kingdom ;

(c) as to the keeping of records of proceedings before magistrates' courts and the manner in which things done in the course of, or as preliminary or incidental to, any such proceedings, or any proceedings on appeal from a magistrates' court to the Crown Court, may be proved in any legal proceedings ;

(d) as to the extent to which a justices' clerk may engage in practice as a solicitor or barrister ;

(e) as to the functions of officers of the Crown Court for the purposes of securing the attendance at a trial on indictment of persons in respect of whom conditional witness orders, or orders treated as conditional witness orders, have been made under section 1 of the Criminal Procedure (Attendance of Witnesses) Act 1965 ;

1965 c. 69.

(f) as to the furnishing by any person having custody of the depositions of copies thereof, and of copies of the information if it is in writing, to a person committed for trial ;

(g) as to what magistrates' court shall have jurisdiction to hear any complaint ;

(h) as to the matters additional to those specified in section 53 above on complaint for which a magistrates' court shall have power to make an order with the consent of the defendant without hearing evidence ;

(i) as to any other matters as to which immediately before the coming into force of section 15 of the Justices of the Peace Act 1949 provision was or could have been made by virtue of the enactments and parts of enactments repealed by Part II of Schedule 7 to the said Act of 1949.

1949 c. 101.

(2) Where any Act expressly confers jurisdiction on any magistrates' court to hear a complaint, rules made under sub-section (1)(*g*) above shall not take away that jurisdiction, but may extend it to any other magistrates' court.

(3) Any Act passed before 16th December 1949, in so far as that Act relates to matters about which rules may be made under section 144 above, shall have effect subject to any rules so made and may be amended or repealed by the rules accordingly; but nothing in the said section shall authorise the rules to reduce the number of justices required for any purpose by any Act.

(4) No provision included in rules under section 144 above which dispenses with the need to prove that a summons issued under section 1 above and served in accordance with the rules has come to the knowledge of the accused shall apply to a summons for an indictable offence.

(5) Any rules, directions, forms or other instrument having effect immediately before this subsection comes into force as if contained in rules made under section 15 of the Justices of the 1949 c. 101. Peace Act 1949 by virtue of section 15(8) of that Act (rules etc. which previously had effect under the enactments repealed by Part II of Schedule 7 to that Act) shall have effect as if contained in rules made under section 144 above.

Rules about juvenile courts

146.—(1) Without prejudice to the generality of the power Rules relating to make rules under section 144 above relating to the procedure to juvenile and practice to be followed by magistrates' courts, provision court panels may be made by such rules with respect to any of the following composition matters, namely,— of juvenile court.

    (*a*) the formation and revision of juvenile court panels, that is to say, panels of justices specially qualified to deal with juvenile cases and the eligibility of justices to be members of such panels;

    (*b*) the appointment of persons as chairmen of juvenile courts; and

    (*c*) the composition of juvenile courts.

(2) Rules making any such provisions as are referred to in subsection (1) above may confer powers on the Lord Chancellor with respect to any of the matters specified in the rules and may, in particular, provide for the appointment of juvenile court panels by him and for the removal from a juvenile court panel of any justice who, in his opinion, is unsuitable to serve on a juvenile court.

(3) Rules made by virtue of this section may make different provision in relation to different areas for which juvenile court panels are formed ; and in the application of this section to the county palatine of Lancaster, for any reference in subsection (2) above to the Lord Chancellor there shall be substituted a reference to the Chancellor of the Duchy.

(4) Nothing in this section or in any rules made under section 144 above shall affect—

(a) the areas for which juvenile court panels are formed and juvenile courts are constituted ;

1963 c. 37.

(b) the provisions of Part I of Schedule 2 to the Children and Young Persons Act 1963 (and, as it has effect by virtue of section 17(1) of that Act, Part I of Schedule

1933 c. 12.

2 to the Children and Young Persons Act 1933) with respect to the making of recommendations and orders relating to the formation of combined juvenile court panels ; or

(c) the provisions of paragraph 14 of that Schedule relating to the divisions of the metropolitan area for which juvenile courts sit ;

but rules under section 144 above may repeal, either generally or with respect to any part of the metropolitan area, any provision contained in paragraphs 15 to 18 of that Schedule (which contain provisions applicable in the metropolitan area with respect to certain of the matters referred to in subsection (1) above) and in subsections (2) and (3) of section 12 of the

1964 c. 42.

Administration of Justice Act 1964 (which amend those paragraphs).

(5) In this section " the metropolitan area " means the inner London area and the City of London.

Occasional court-houses

Occasional court-house.

147.—(1) The justices acting for a petty sessions area may appoint as an occasional court-house any place that is not a petty-sessional court-house.

(2) A place appointed as an occasional court-house after 31st May 1953 shall not be used as such unless public notice has been given that it has been appointed.

(3) There may be more than one occasional court-house for each petty sessions area ; and an occasional court-house may be outside the petty sessions area for which it is appointed, and if so shall be deemed to be in that area for the purpose of the jurisdiction of the justices acting for that area.

Interpretation   PART VII

148.—(1) In this Act the expression " magistrates' court " " Magistrates' means any justice or justices of the peace acting under any court ". enactment or by virtue of his or their commission or under the common law.

(2) Except where the contrary is expressed, anything authorised or required by this Act to be done by, to or before the magistrates' court by, to or before which any other thing was done, or is to be done, may be done by, to or before any magistrates' court acting for the same petty sessions area as that court.

149. For the purposes of this Act the Isles of Scilly form part Isles of Scilly. of the county of Cornwall.

150.—(1) In this Act, unless the context otherwise requires, Interpretation the following expressions have the meaning hereby assigned to of other terms. them, that is to say—

" Act " includes local Act ;

" affiliation order " has the same meaning as in the 1957 c. 55. Affiliation Proceedings Act 1957 ;

" bail in criminal proceedings " has the same meaning as in the Bail Act 1976 ;   1976 c. 63.

" commit to custody " means commit to prison or, where any enactment authorises or requires committal to some other place of detention instead of committal to prison, to that other place ;

" committal proceedings " means proceedings before a magistrates' court acting as examining justices ;

" domestic proceedings " has the meaning assigned to it by section 65 above ;

" enactment " includes an enactment contained in a local Act or in any order, regulation or other instrument having effect by virtue of an Act ;

" fine ", except for the purposes of any enactment imposing a limit on the amount of any fine, includes any pecuniary penalty or pecuniary forfeiture or pecuniary compensation payable under a conviction ;

" impose imprisonment " means pass a sentence of imprisonment or fix a term of imprisonment for failure to pay any sum of money, or for want of sufficient distress to satisfy any sum of money, or for failure to do or abstain from doing anything required to be done or left undone ;

" London commission area " has the same meaning as in the Justices of the Peace Act 1979 ;

" petty-sessional court-house " means any of the following, that is to say—

(a) a court-house or place at which justices are accustomed to assemble for holding special or petty sessions or for the time being appointed as a substitute for such a court-house or place (including, where justices are accustomed to assemble for either special or petty sessions at more than one court-house or place in a petty sessional division, any such court-house or place) ;

(b) a court-house or place at which a stipendiary magistrate is authorised by law to do alone any act authorised to be done by more than one justice of the peace ;

" petty sessions area " means any of the following areas, that is to say, a non-metropolitan county which is not divided into petty sessional divisions, a petty sessional division of a non-metropolitan county, a metropolitan district which is not divided into petty sessional divisions, a petty sessional division of a metropolitan district, a London commission area which is not divided into petty sessional divisions, a petty sessional division of a London commission area and the City of London ;

" prescribed " means prescribed by the rules ;

" the register " means the register of proceedings before a magistrates' court required by the rules to be kept by the clerk of the court ;

" the rules " means rules made under section 144 above ;

" sentence " does not include a committal in default of payment of any sum of money, or for want of sufficient distress to satisfy any sum of money, or for failure to do or abstain from doing anything required to be done or left undone ;

" sum enforceable as a civil debt " means—

(a) any sum recoverable summarily as a civil debt which is adjudged to be paid by the order of a magistrates' court ;

(b) any other sum expressed by this or any other Act to be so enforceable ;

" transfer of fine order " has the meaning assigned to it by section 89 above.

(2) Except where the contrary is expressed or implied, any- PART VII
thing required or authorised by this Act to be done by justices
may, where two or more justices are present, be done by one of
them on behalf of the others.

(3) Any reference in this Act to a sum adjudged to be paid
by a conviction or order of a magistrates' court shall be construed as including a reference to any costs, damages or compensation adjudged to be paid by the conviction or order of which
the amount is ascertained by the conviction or order ; but this
subsection does not prejudice the definition of " sum adjudged
to be paid by a conviction " contained in subsection (8) of section 81 above for the purposes of that section.

(4) Where the age of any person at any time is material for
the purposes of any provision of this Act regulating the powers
of a magistrates' court, his age at the material time shall be
deemed to be or to have been that which appears to the court
after considering any available evidence to be or to have been
his age at that time.

(5) Except where the context otherwise requires, any reference
in this Act to an offence shall be construed as including a
reference to an alleged offence ; and any reference in this Act
to an offence committed, completed or begun anywhere shall
be construed as including a reference to an offence alleged to
have been committed, completed or begun there.

(6) References in this Act to an offence punishable with
imprisonment or punishable on summary conviction with
imprisonment shall be construed without regard to any prohibition or restriction imposed by or under this or any other Act
on imprisonment of young offenders.

(7) The provisions of this Act authorising a magistrates' court
on conviction of an offender to pass a sentence or make an
order instead of dealing with him in any other way shall not
be construed as taking away any power to order him to pay
costs, damages or compensation.

Miscellaneous

151.—(1) Justices may state a case under this Act when Application
called upon to issue a warrant of distress for any rate other than of Act to
a rate within the meaning of the General Rate Act 1967. distress
for rates.

(2) Sections 79(2) and 100 above shall apply to proceedings 1967 c. 9.
for the non-payment of any rate to which subsection (1) above
applies as they apply to proceedings for the non-payment of
a sum adjudged to be paid by a magistrates' court.

PART VII

(3) Except as provided in the preceding provisions of this section, the power of justices to issue a warrant of distress for a rate, the form and execution of such a warrant and the committal of persons for want of sufficient distress to satisfy a rate shall not be subject to the provisions of this Act.

Saving for juvenile courts.

152. The provisions of this Act relating to the constitution, place of sitting and procedure of magistrates' courts shall, in their application to juvenile courts, have effect subject to any provision contained in the rules or any enactment regulating the constitution, place of sitting or procedure of juvenile courts.

Magistrates' court may sit on Sundays and public holidays.

153. It is hereby declared that a magistrates' court may sit on any day of the year, and in particular (if the court thinks fit) on Christmas Day, Good Friday or any Sunday.

Repeals, short title, etc.

Consequential amendments, transitional provisions, repeals, etc.

154.—(1) Subject to subsection (2) below, the enactments mentioned in Schedule 7 to this Act shall have effect subject to the amendments specified in that Schedule, being amendments consequential on the provisions of this Act.

(2) The transitional provisions and savings in Schedule 8 to this Act shall have effect.

(3) Subject to subsection (2) above, the enactments specified in Schedule 9 to this Act (which include enactments which were spent before the passing of this Act) are hereby repealed to the extent specified in the third column of that Schedule.

1978 c. 30.

(4) Nothing in this Act shall be taken as prejudicing the operation of sections 16 and 17 of the Interpretation Act 1978 (which relate to the effect of repeals).

Short title, extent and commencement.

155.—(1) This Act may be cited as the Magistrates' Courts Act 1980.

(2) The following provisions of this Act extend to Scotland—

(*a*) sections 8 (except subsection (9)), 12(8), 83(3), 90 and 91 and this section ; and

(*b*) section 154 and Schedules 7, 8 and 9 so far as they relate to any enactment extending to Scotland.

(3) The following provisions of this Act extend to Northern Ireland—

(*a*) sections 83(3), 90 and 91 and this section ; and

(*b*) section 154 and Schedules 7, 8 and 9 so far as they relate to an enactment extending to Northern Ireland.

(4) The provisions of section 126 above have the same extent as the sections of the Indictable Offences Act 1848 to which they refer.

(5) The provisions of section 32(7) and (9) above, in their operation in relation to the provision that may be made under subsection (2) of section 2 of the European Communities Act 1972, extend to all places to which the said section 2 extends (except Scotland).

(6) Except as stated in subsections (2) to (5) above, and except so far as relates to the interpretation or commencement of the provisions mentioned in those subsections, this Act extends to England and Wales only.

(7) This Act shall come into force on such date as the Secretary of State may appoint by order made by statutory instrument.

SCHEDULES

SCHEDULE 1

Section 17.

OFFENCES TRIABLE EITHER WAY BY VIRTUE OF SECTION 17

1. Offences at common law of public nuisance.

1751 c. 36.
2. Offences under section 8 of the Disorderly Houses Act 1751 (appearing to be keeper of bawdy house etc.).

1835 c. 62.
3. Offences consisting in contravention of section 13 of the Statutory Declarations Act 1835 (administration by a person of an oath etc. touching matters in which he has no jurisdiction).

1861 c. 97.
4. Offences under section 36 of the Malicious Damage Act 1861 (obstructing engines or carriages on railways).

1861 c. 100.
5. Offences under the following provisions of the Offences against the Person Act 1861—

  (*a*) section 16 (threats to kill) ;

  (*b*) section 20 (inflicting bodily injury, with or without a weapon) ;

  (*c*) section 26 (not providing apprentices or servants with food etc.) ;

  (*d*) section 27 (abandoning or exposing child) ;

  (*e*) section 34 (doing or omitting to do anything so as to endanger railway passengers) ;

  (*f*) section 36 (assaulting a clergyman at a place of worship etc.) ;

  (*g*) section 38 (assault with intent to resist apprehension) ;

  (*h*) section 47 (assault occasioning bodily harm—common assault) ;

  (*i*) section 57 (bigamy) ;

  (*j*) section 60 (concealing the birth of a child).

1868 c. 110.
6. Offences under section 20 of the Telegraph Act 1868 (disclosing or intercepting messages).

1869 c. 62.
7. Offences under section 13 of the Debtors Act 1869 (transactions intended to defraud creditors).

1875 c. 25.
8. Offences under section 5 of the Public Stores Act 1875 (obliteration of marks with intent to conceal).

1882 c. 37.
9. Offences under section 12 of the Corn Returns Act 1882 (false returns).

1882 c. 56.
10. Offences under section 22 of the Electric Lighting Act 1882 (injuring works with intent to cut off electricity supply).

11. Offences under section 3 of the Submarine Telegraph Act 1885 (damaging submarine cables). SCH. 1
1885 c. 49.

12. Offences under section 13 of the Stamp Duties Management Act 1891 (offences in relation to dies and stamps). 1891 c. 38.

13. Offences under section 8(2) of the Cremation Act 1902 (making false representations etc. with a view to procuring the burning of any human remains). 1902 c. 8.

14. All offences under the Perjury Act 1911 except offences under— 1911 c. 6.
   (*a*) section 1 (perjury in judicial proceedings) ;
   (*b*) section 3 (false statements etc. with reference to marriage) ;
   (*c*) section 4 (false statements etc. as to births or deaths).

15. The following offences under the Forgery Act 1913— 1913 c. 27.
   (*a*) offences under paragraph (*a*) of section 2(2) (forgery of valuable security etc.) in relation to—
       (i) any document being an accountable receipt, release, or discharge, or any receipt or other instrument evidencing the payment of money, or the delivery of any chattel personal ; or
       (ii) any document being an authority or request for the payment of money or for the delivery or transfer of goods and chattels, where the amount of money or the value of the goods or chattels does not exceed £1,000 ;
   (*b*) offences under section 4 (forgery of documents in general) ; and
   (*c*) offences under paragraph (*a*) of section 7 (demanding property on forged documents), where the amount of the money or the value of the property in respect of which the offence is committed does not exceed £1,000.

16. Offences under section 17 of the Deeds of Arrangement Act 1914 (trustee making preferential payments). 1914 c. 47.

17. Offences under section 3(4) of the Checkweighing in Various Industries Act 1919 (false statements). 1919 c. 51.

18. Offences under section 8(2) of the Census Act 1920 (disclosing census information). 1920 c. 41.

19. Offences under section 36 of the Criminal Justice Act 1925 (forgery of passports etc.). 1925 c. 86.

20. Offences under section 11 of the Agricultural Credits Act 1928 (frauds by farmers). 1928 c. 43.

21. Offences under the following provisions of the Coinage Offences Act 1936— 1936 c. 16.
   (*a*) section 4(1) (defacing coins) ;
   (*b*) section 5(1) (uttering counterfeit coin) ;

(*c*) section 5(2) (uttering counterfeit gold or silver coin) ;

(*d*) section 5(3) (possession of counterfeit gold or silver coin) ;

(*e*) section 5(4) (possession of counterfeit copper coin) ;

(*f*) section 5(6) (uttering coins etc. as gold or silver coins) ;

(*g*) section 7 (importing and exporting counterfeit coin) ;

(*h*) section 8 (making, possessing or selling medals resembling gold or silver coin).

1953 c. 36.

22. Offences under the following provisions of the Post Office Act 1953—

(*a*) section 53 (unlawfully taking away or opening mail bag) ;

(*b*) section 55 (fraudulent retention of mail bag or postal packet) ;

(*c*) section 57 (stealing, embezzlement, destruction etc. by officer of Post Office of postal packet) ;

(*d*) section 58 (opening or delaying of postal packets by officers of the Post Office).

1956 c. 69.

23. Offences under the following provisions of the Sexual Offences Act 1956—

(*a*) section 6 (unlawful sexual intercourse with a girl under 16) ;

(*b*) section 13 (indecency between men) ;

(*c*) section 26 (permitting a girl under 16 to use premises for sexual intercourse).

1964 c. 87.

24. Offences under section 3(1) of the Shipping Contracts and Commercial Documents Act 1964 (offences), so far as it relates to the contravention of any directions given under that Act before 20th March 1980.

1967 c. 29.

25. Offences under section 24B(7) of the Housing Subsidies Act 1967 (failure to notify lender that residence condition not fulfilled or ceased to be fulfilled).

1967 c. 58.

26. The following offences under the Criminal Law Act 1967—

(*a*) offences under section 4(1) (assisting offenders) ; and

(*b*) offences under section 5(1) (concealing arrestable offences and giving false information),

where the offence to which they relate is triable either way.

1967 c. 60.

27. Offences under section 4(1) of the Sexual Offences Act 1967 (procuring others to commit homosexual acts).

1968 c. 60.

28. All indictable offences under the Theft Act 1968 except:—

(*a*) robbery, aggravated burglary, blackmail and assault with intent to rob ;

(*b*) burglary comprising the commission of, or an intention to commit, an offence which is triable only on indictment ;

(*c*) burglary in a dwelling if any person in the dwelling was subjected to violence or the threat of violence.

29. Offences under the following provisions of the Criminal Damage Act 1971—

> section 1(1) (destroying or damaging property) ;
>
> section 1(1) and (3) (arson) ;
>
> section 2 (threats to destroy or damage property) ;
>
> section 3 (possessing anything with intent to destroy or damage property).

30. Offences in relation to stamps issued for the purpose of national insurance under the provisions of any enactments as applied to those stamps.

31. Uttering any forged document the forgery of which is an offence listed in this Schedule.

32. Committing an indecent assault upon a person whether male or female.

33. Aiding, abetting, counselling or procuring the commission of any offence listed in the preceding paragraphs of this Schedule except paragraph 26.

34. Attempting to commit an offence triable either way except an offence mentioned in paragraph 26 or 33 above.

35. Any offence consisting in the incitement to commit an offence triable either way except an offence mentioned in paragraph 33 or 34 above.

Section 22.

SCHEDULE 2

OFFENCES FOR WHICH THE VALUE INVOLVED IS RELEVANT TO THE MODE OF TRIAL

Offence	Value involved	How measured

1. Offences under section 1 of the Criminal Damage Act 1971* (destroying or damaging property), excluding any offence committed by destroying or damaging property by fire.	As regards property alleged to have been destroyed, its value.
	
	As regards property alleged to have been damaged, the value of the alleged damage.
		What the property would probably have cost to buy in the open market at the material time.
		
		(a) If immediately after the material time the damage was capable of repair—
		  (i) what would probably then have been the market price for the repair of the damage, or
		  (ii) what the property alleged to have been damaged would probably have cost to buy in the open market at the material time, whichever is the less; or
		(b) if immediately after the material time the damage was beyond repair, what the said property would probably have cost to buy in the open market at the material time.

2. The following offences, namely—
  (a) aiding, abetting, counselling or procuring the commission of any offence mentioned in paragraph 1 above;
  (b) attempting to commit any offence so mentioned; and
  (c) inciting another to commit any offence so mentioned.
	The value indicated in paragraph 1 above for the offence alleged to have been aided, abetted, counselled or procured, or attempted or incited.	As for the corresponding entry in paragraph 1 above.

* 1971 c. 48.

SCHEDULE 3

CORPORATIONS

1.—(1) A magistrates' court may commit a corporation for trial by an order in writing empowering the prosecutor to prefer a bill of indictment in respect of the offence named in the order.

(2) An order under this paragraph shall not prohibit the inclusion in the bill of indictment of counts that under section 2 of the Administration of Justice (Miscellaneous Provisions) Act 1933 may 1933 c. 36. be included in the bill in substitution for, or in addition to, counts charging the offence named in the order.

2. A representative may on behalf of a corporation—

   (*a*) make a statement before examining justices in answer to the charge ;

   (*b*) consent to the corporation being tried summarily ;

   (*c*) enter a plea of guilty or not guilty on the trial by a magistrates' court of an information.

3.—(1) Where a representative appears, any requirement of this Act that anything shall be done in the presence of the accused, or shall be read or said to the accused, shall be construed as a requirement that that thing shall be done in the presence of the representative or read or said to the representative.

(2) Where a representative does not appear, any such requirement, and any requirement that the consent of the accused shall be obtained for summary trial, shall not apply.

4.—(1) Notification or intimation for the purposes of subsections (2) and (3) of section 12 above may be given on behalf of a corporation by a director or the secretary of the corporation ; and those subsections shall apply in relation to a notification or intimation purporting to be so given as they apply to a notification or intimation purporting to be given by an individual accused.

(2) In this paragraph " director ", in relation to a corporation which is established by or under any enactment for the purpose of carrying on under national ownership any industry or part of an industry or undertaking and whose affairs are managed by the members thereof, means a member of that corporation.

5. The provisions of this Act relating to committal to the Crown Court for sentence shall not apply to a corporation.

6. Subject to the preceding provisions of this Schedule, the provisions of this Act relating to the inquiry into, and trial of, indictable offences shall apply to a corporation as they apply to an adult.

7. Where a corporation and an individual who has attained the age of 17 are jointly charged before a magistrates' court with an offence triable either way, the court shall not try either of the accused summarily unless each of them consents to be so tried.

8. Subsection (6) of section 33 of the Criminal Justice Act 1925 shall apply to a representative for the purposes of this Schedule as it applies to a representative for the purposes of that section.

SCHEDULE 4

MAXIMUM PERIODS OF IMPRISONMENT IN DEFAULT OF PAYMENT

1. Subject to the following provisions of this Schedule, the periods set out in the second column of the following Table shall be the maximum periods applicable respectively to the amounts set out opposite thereto, being amounts due at the time the imprisonment is imposed.

TABLE

An amount not exceeding £25	7 days
An amount exceeding £25 but not exceeding £50 ...	14 days
An amount exceeding £50 but not exceeding £200 ...	30 days
An amount exceeding £200 but not exceeding £500 ...	60 days
An amount exceeding £500 but not exceeding £1,000	90 days
An amount exceeding £1,000 but not exceeding £2,500	6 months
An amount exceeding £2,500 but not exceeding £5,000	9 months
An amount exceeding £5,000	12 months

2.—(1) Where the amount due at the time imprisonment is imposed is so much of a sum adjudged to be paid by a summary conviction as remains due after part payment, then, subject to sub-paragraph (2) below, the maximum period applicable to the amount shall be the period applicable to the whole sum reduced by such number of days as bears to the total number of days therein the same proportion as the part paid bears to the whole sum.

(2) In calculating the reduction required under sub-paragraph (1) above any fraction of a day shall be left out of account and the maximum period shall not be reduced to less than 5 days.

3. The maximum period applicable to a sum of any amount enforceable as a civil debt shall be 6 weeks.

SCHEDULE 5

TRANSFER OF REMAND HEARINGS

1. A court which, on adjourning a case, makes an order under section 130(1) of this Act is not required at that time to fix the time and place at which the case is to be resumed but shall do so as soon as practicable after the order ceases to be in force.

2. Where an order under subsection (1) of section 130 of this Act is made in the course of proceedings which, for the purposes of section 8 of this Act, are committal proceedings, proceedings relating to the accused before the alternate court are also committal proceedings for those purposes.

3. A court making an order under subsection (1) of section 130 SCH. 5 of this Act or remanding the accused under subsection (4) shall at once notify the court before which the accused is to be brought as to the terms of the order or remand.

4. A person to whom an order under section 130(1) of this Act applies shall, if released on bail, be bailed to appear before the court which made the order.

5. Section 130 of this Act and this Schedule have effect notwithstanding anything in sections 5, 10 or 18(4) of this Act.

SCHEDULE 6

Section 137.

FEES

PART I

FEES TO BE TAKEN BY CLERKS TO JUSTICES

	£
APPOINTMENT:—	
Of any constable (other than special)	0·05
Of special constables, if less than 28, for each person, to include notice, oath, and certificate	0·05
If more than 28 are appointed on one occasion, for attending to summons, swearing in, and making out appointments, and the business thereof, for each day	2·10
ATTENDANCE:—	
On a justice, to view deserted premises in order to affix notice or to give possession thereof, or to view a highway, bridge or nuisance ...	0·33
If required to go more than one mile from the place of holding petty sessions, for each mile after the first (one way) ...	0·05
CASE FOR THE OPINION OF HIGH COURT (s. 111 of this Act):—	
Drawing case and copy, when the case does not exceed 5 folios of 90 words	0·50
For every additional folio beyond 5	0·05
Taking recognizance as required by s. 114 of this Act ...	0·25
Every enlargement or renewal thereof	0·13
For certificate of refusal of case ...	0·10
CERTIFICATE:—	
Every certificate not otherwise charged ...	0·10
CIVIL DEBT (not including rates):—	
Summons and copy	0·07
Complaint ...	0·05
Order and copy	0·15
Oath (each witness)	0·05
Summons on complaint for commitment and copy, including hearing ...	0·15
Warrant of distress ...	0·10
Commitment. (*See* **Warrant.**)	

SCH. 6   £

COMPLAINT:—

Every complaint not otherwise charged ...   .   0·05

COPY:—

Of any document, per folio of 72 words ...   .   0·02

DUPLICATE:—

For the duplicate of any document   ...   .   { One-half the original fee.

EXHIBIT:—

Each document annexed to or referred to in any affidavit or declaration and marked   ...   .   0·05

HEARING:—

When no order is made   ...   .   0·05

LICENCES:—

For every licence, consent, or authority not otherwise provided for, to include registration when necessary   0·25

LIST:—

Every list not otherwise provided for which it is the duty of the clerk to the justices to make or transmit   ...   0·13

NOTICE:—

Every notice not otherwise provided for ...   .   0·05

OATH:—

Every oath, affirmation, or solemn declaration not otherwise charged   ...   .   0·05

(See note at end of table.)

ORDER:—

Order, certificate, or record of proceedings in case of deserted premises, or relating to a highway, bridge, or nuisance ...   .   0·25

Order as to the removal of a person of unsound mind ...   0·25

Every order or minute thereof not otherwise charged ...   0·15

1978 c. 22.   Order as to the affiliation of a bastard or under Part I of the Domestic Proceedings and Magistrates' Courts Act 1978 ...   .   0.10

Variation, revocation, or revival of order   ...   ...   0·05

RATE:—

Enforcement of any rate, to include complaint, summons, and all other proceedings for which separate fees are not provided hereunder ...   .   0·10

Order   ...   .   0·10

Warrant of distress ...   .   0·10

Commitment   ...   .   0·10

If more than one rate is included in the summons, for each rate after the first   ...   .   0·03

£

When the form of warrant specified as C(2) in Schedule 12 to the General Rate Act 1967, or a form to the like effect, is used, for each name inserted in the particulars over and above eight   ...   .   0·01

Summons:—

Every summons   ...   .   0·05
Every copy ...   .   0·03
Backing summons for service from outside jurisdiction   0·05

Warrant:—

Every warrant of distress when not otherwise provided for ...   .   0·10
To commit after order in which the order is set forth ...   0·10
Every other warrant   ...   .   0·05
Return to warrant or endorsing warrant, including oath   0·05
Backing warrant for execution from outside jurisdiction   0·05

Note—Nothing herein contained shall be construed as authorising the demand of any fee for any oath, affirmation, or declaration to obtain pay, pension, or allowance from government or friendly society, or charitable fund, or for any declaration relating to lost duplicates of articles pledged where the amount advanced on such articles does not exceed £1, or in any other case where an Act of Parliament directs that no fee shall be taken.

Part II

Matters in respect of which no Fees are Chargeable

1. Any summons, warrant, notice or order issued, given or made under sections 83(1) or (2), 88, 89 or 136 of this Act, or section 104 of the General Rate Act 1967, or under any rule made for the purposes of those provisions.

2. Any criminal matter, but this paragraph shall not prevent the charging of a fee for supplying, for use in connection with a matter which is not a criminal matter, a copy of a document prepared for use in connection with a criminal matter.

Part III

Matters to which Part I does not Apply

1. Billiard licences under section 10 of the Gaming Act 1845.

2. The registration of music and dancing licences under section 51 of the Public Health Acts Amendment Act 1890.

3. Licences under the Cinematograph Act 1909.

4. Appeals from pilotage authority under section 28 of the Pilotage Act 1913.

5. Matters in respect of which fees are authorised to be charged by section 29 of the Licensing Act 1964.

Section 154.

SCHEDULE 7

CONSEQUENTIAL AMENDMENTS

Summary Jurisdiction Act 1857 (20 & 21 Vict. c. 43)

1. In sections 6 and 10 of the Summary Jurisdiction Act 1857 for " the Magistrates' Courts Act 1952 " (wherever the words occur) substitute " the Magistrates' Courts Act 1980 ".

Criminal Law Amendment Act 1867 (30 & 31 Vict. c. 35)

2. In section 6 of the Criminal Law Amendment Act 1867 for " section forty-one of the Magistrates' Courts Act 1952 " substitute " section 105 of the Magistrates' Courts Act 1980 " and for " section fifteen of the Justices of the Peace Act 1949 " substitute " section 144 of that Act ".

Gun Barrel Proof Act 1868 (c. cxiii)

3. In section 4 of the Gun Barrel Proof Act 1868, in the definition of " statutory maximum ", for " section 28 of the Criminal Law Act 1977 " substitute " section 32 of the Magistrates' Courts Act 1980 ".

Criminal Justice Act 1925 (15 & 16 Geo. 5 c. 86)

4. In section 12(4) of the Criminal Justice Act 1925 for " section fifteen of the Justices of the Peace Act 1949 " substitute " section 144 of the Magistrates' Courts Act 1980 ".

5. In section 33(4) of the Criminal Justice Act 1925 for the words following " may be made by rules " in the second place where those words occur substitute " under section 144 of the Magistrates' Courts Act 1980 ".

Children and Young Persons Act 1933 (23 & 24 Geo. 5 c. 12)

6. In section 46(1A) of the Children and Young Persons Act 1933 for " section 1 of the Magistrates' Courts Act 1957 " substitute " section 12 of the Magistrates' Courts Act 1980 ".

Criminal Justice Act 1948 (11 & 12 Geo. 6 c. 58)

7. In section 27(3) of the Criminal Justice Act 1948 for " section 105(5) of the Magistrates' Courts Act 1952 " substitute " section 128(7) of the Magistrates' Courts Act 1980 ".

Maintenance Orders Act 1950 (14 Geo. 6 c. 37)

8. In section 25(1) of the Maintenance Orders Act 1950 for " section fifteen of the Justices of the Peace Act 1949 " substitute " section 144 of the Magistrates' Courts Act 1980 ".

Rag Flock and Other Filling Materials Act 1951 (14 & 15 Geo. 6 c. 63)

9. In section 20 of the Rag Flock and Other Filling Materials Act 1951 for " section one hundred and fifteen of the Magistrates' Courts Act 1952 " substitute " section 140 of the Magistrates' Courts Act 1980.".

Pharmacy Act 1954 (2 & 3 Eliz. 2 c. 61)

10. In section 21 of the Pharmacy Act 1954 for " the Magistrates' Courts Act 1952 " substitute " the Magistrates' Courts Act 1980 ".

Mines and Quarries Act 1954 (2 & 3 Eliz. 2 c. 70)

11. In section 153(*a*) of the Mines and Quarries Act 1954 for " section thirty-five of the Magistrates' Courts Act 1952 " substitute " section 44 of the Magistrates' Courts Act 1980 ".

Army Act 1955 (3 & 4 Eliz. 2 c. 18)

12. In sections 187(4) and 215(9) of the Army Act 1955 for " the Magistrates' Courts Act 1952 " substitute, in each case, " the Magistrates' Courts Act 1980 ".

Air Force Act 1955 (3 & 4 Eliz. 2 c. 19)

13. In sections 187(4) and 215(9) of the Air Force Act 1955 for " the Magistrates' Courts Act 1952 " substitute, in each case, " the Magistrates' Courts Act 1980 ".

Food and Drugs Act 1955 (4 & 5 Eliz. 2 c. 16)

14. In section 108(1) of the Food and Drugs Act 1955 for " the Magistrates' Courts Act 1952 " (where the words first occur) substitute " the Magistrates' Courts Act 1980 " and for " section one hundred and four of the Magistrates' Courts Act 1952 " substitute "section 127(1) of the Magistrates' Courts Act 1980 ".

15. In section 117(1) of the Food and Drugs Act 1955 for " the Magistrates' Courts Act 1952 " substitute " the Magistrates' Courts Act 1980 ".

Magistrates' Courts (Appeals from Binding Over Orders) Act 1956
(4 & 5 Eliz. 2 c. 44)

16. In section 1(1) of the Magistrates' Courts (Appeals from Binding Over Orders) Act 1956 for " the Magistrates' Courts Act 1952 " substitute " the Magistrates' Courts Act 1980 ".

Sexual Offences Act 1956 (4 & 5 Eliz. 2 c.69)

17. In section 37(7) of the Sexual Offences Act 1956—

   (*a*) in paragraph (*a*) for " section 6 of the Children and Young Persons Act 1969 " substitute " section 24 of the Magistrates' Courts Act 1980 " ;

   (*b*) in paragraph (*b*) for " subsection (5) of section ninety-eight of the Magistrates' Courts Act 1952 " substitute " subsection (5) of section 121 of the Magistrates' Courts Act 1980 ".

18. In Part II of Schedule 2 to the Sexual Offences Act 1956, in paragraphs 17 and 18—

   (*a*) in sub-paragraph (ii) in the second column of each paragraph, for " section 16(2) of the Criminal Law Act 1977 " substitute " section 17(1) of the Magistrates' Courts Act 1980 " ;

   (*b*) in the third column of each paragraph, for " section 28(1) of that Act " substitute " section 32(1) of that Act ".

             Dentists Act 1957 (5 & 6 Eliz. 2 c.28)

19. In section 34(3) of the Dentists Act 1957 for "section one hundred and four of the Magistrates' Courts Act 1952" substitute "section 127(1) of the Magistrates' Courts Act 1980"

Affiliation Proceedings Act 1957 (5 & 6 Eliz. 2 c.55)

20. In section 5(5) of the Affiliation Proceedings Act 1957 for "section fifty-two of the Magistrates' Courts Act 1952" substitute "section 59 of the Magistrates' Courts Act 1980".

21. In section 6A of the Affiliation Proceedings Act 1957—

(*a*) in subsection (1) for "section 53 of the Magistrates' Courts Act 1952" substitute "section 60 of the Magistrates' Courts Act 1980";

(*b*) in subsection (2) for "the said section 53" substitute "the said section 60";

(*c*) in subsection (5) for "section 63 of the Magistrates' Courts Act 1952" substitute "section 75 of the Magistrates' Courts Act 1980"

Housing Act 1957 (5 & 6 Eliz. 2 c. 56)

22. In section 191(5) of the Housing Act 1957 for "subsection (3) of section one hundred and twenty-two of the Magistrates' Courts Act 1952" substitute "subsection (3) of section 145 of the Magistrates' Courts Act 1980"

Maintenance Orders Act 1958 (6 & 7 Eliz. 2 c.39)

23. In section 18 of the Maintenance Orders Act 1958—

(*a*) in subsection (1) for "subsection (2) of section sixty-five of the Magistrates' Courts Act 1952" substitute "subsection (2) of section 77 of the Magistrates' Courts Act 1980";

(*b*) in subsection (6) for "section sixty-seven of the Magistrates' Courts Act 1952" substitute "section 79 of the Magistrates' Courts Act 1980".

24. In section 21(1) of the Maintenance Orders Act 1958 for "the Magistrates' Courts Act 1952" substitute "the Magistrates' Courts Act 1980" and for "subsection (2) of section one hundred and twenty-four thereof" substitute "subsection (2) of section 148 thereof".

Adoption Act 1958 (7 Eliz. 2 c. 5)

25. In section 9(2) and (4) of the Adoption Act 1958 for "section fifteen of the Justices of the Peace Act 1949" substitute "section 144 of the Magistrates' Courts Act 1980".

26. In section 48 of the Adoption Act 1958 for "the Magistrates' Courts Act 1952" substitute "the Magistrates' Courts Act 1980".

Manœuvres Act 1958 (7 & 8 Eliz. 2 c.7)

27. In section 9 of the Manoeuvres Act 1958 for " the Magistrates' Courts Act 1952 " substitute " the Magistrates' Courts Act 1980 ".

County Courts Act 1959 (7 & 8 Eliz. 2 c. 22)

28. In section 179(*b*) of the County Courts Act 1959 for " the Magistrates' Courts Act 1952 " substitute " the Magistrates' Courts Act 1980 (disregarding section 81(1) of that Act) ".

Highways Act 1959 (7 & 8 Eliz.2 c.25)

29. In section 295(1) of the Highways Act 1959, in the definition of " petty sessions area ", for " the Magistrates' Courts Act 1952 " substitute " the Magistrates' Courts Act 1980 ".

Street Offences Act 1959 (7 & 8 Eliz.2 c.57)

30. In section 2(2) of the Street Offences Act 1959 for " section fifteen of the Justices of the Peace Act 1949 " substitute " section 144 of the Magistrates' Courts Act 1980 " and for " sections forty-seven to forty-nine of the Magistrates' Courts Act 1952 " substitute " sections 55 to 57 of that Act ".

Mental Health Act 1959 (7 & 8 Eliz. 2 c. 72)

31. In section 67(4) of the Mental Health Act 1959 for " section twenty-nine of the Magistrates' Courts Act 1952 " substitute " section 38 of the Magistrates' Courts Act 1980 ".

32. In section 72(6)(*b*) of the Mental Health Act 1959 for " subsection (3) of section ninety-one of the Magistrates' Courts Act 1952 " substitute " subsection (3) of section 115 of the Magistrates' Courts Act 1980 ".

33. In section 73(2)(*b*) of the Mental Health Act 1959 for " section twenty-eight or section twenty-nine of the Magistrates' Courts Act 1952 " substitute " section 37 or section 38 of the Magistrates' Courts Act 1980 ".

34. In section 77(3) of the Mental Health Act 1959 for " section one hundred and five of the Magistrates' Courts Act 1952 " substitute " section 128 of the Magistrates' Courts Act 1980 ".

Road Traffic Act 1960 (8 & 9 Eliz. 2 c.16)

35. In section 257(1) of the Road Traffic Act 1960, in the definitions of " magistrates' court " and "petty sessions area ", for " the Magistrates' Courts Act 1952 " substitute " the Magistrates' Courts Act 1980 ".

Administration of Justice Act 1960 (8 & 9 Eliz.2 c.65)

36. In section 13(5) of the Administration of Justice Act 1960, in paragraph (*c*) for " subsection (3) of section fifty-four of the Magistrates' Courts Act 1952 " substitute " subsection (3) of section 63 of the Magistrates' Courts Act 1980 ", and in the words following paragraph (*c*) for " the Magistrates' Courts Act 1952 " substitute " the Magistrates' Courts Act 1980 ".

Factories Act 1961 (9 & 10 Eliz.2 c.34)

37. In section 176(1) of the Factories Act 1961, in the definition of " magistrates' court ", for " the Magistrates' Courts Act 1952 " substitute " the Magistrates' Courts Act 1980 ".

Criminal Justice Act 1961 (9 & 10 Eliz. 2 c. 39)

38. In section 1(4) of the Criminal Justice Act 1961 for " section twenty-eight of the Magistrates' Courts Act 1952 " substitute " section 37 of the Magistrates' Courts Act 1980 ".

39. In section 3(4) of the Criminal Justice Act 1961 for " section one hundred and eight of the Magistrates' Courts Act 1952 " substitute " section 133 of the Magistrates' Courts Act 1980 ".

40. In section 4(4) of the Criminal Justice Act 1961 for " subsection (3) of section fourteen of the Magistrates' Courts Act 1952 " substitute " subsection (3) of section 10 of the Magistrates' Courts Act 1980 ".

41. In section 5(5) of the Criminal Justice Act 1961 for " Part III of the Magistrates' Courts Act 1952 " substitute " Part III of the Magistrates' Courts Act 1980 ".

42. In section 12(4) of the Criminal Justice Act 1961 for " subsection (3) of section fourteen of the Magistrates' Courts Act 1952 " substitute " subsection (3) of section 10 of the Magistrates' Courts Act 1980 ".

Plant Varieties and Seeds Act 1964 (c.14)

43. In section 23(2) of the Plant Varieties and Seeds Act 1964 for " section 104 of the Magistrates' Courts Act 1952 " substitute " section 127(1) of the Magistrates' Courts Act 1980 ".

44. In section 28 of the Plant Varieties and Seeds Act 1964—

    (*a*) in subsection (1) for " section 104 of the Magistrates' Courts Act 1952 " substitute " section 127(1) of the Magistrates' Courts Act 1980 " ;

    (*b*) in subsection (2) for " the said section 104 " substitute " the said section 127(1) ".

Licensing Act 1964 (c.26)

45. In section 22(4) of the Licensing Act 1964 for " section 85(2) of the Magistrates' Courts Act 1952 " substitute " section 109(1) of the Magistrates' Courts Act 1980 ".

46. In section 28(2) of the Licensing Act 1964 for " Section 118(2) of the Magistrates' Courts Act 1952 " substitute " Section 141(2) of the Magistrates' Courts Act 1980 ".

47. In section 48(3) of the Licensing Act 1964 for " section 104 of the Magistrates' Courts Act 1952 " substitute " section 127(1) of the Magistrates' Courts Act 1980 ".

48. In section 192(2) of the Licensing Act 1964 for " section 3 of the Magistrates' Courts Act 1952 " substitute " section 3 of the Magistrates' Courts Act 1980 ".

49. In Schedule 2 to the Licensing Act 1964, in paragraph 9, for " Subsections (1), (3) and (4) of section 77 of the Magistrates' Courts Act 1952 " substitute " Subsections (1), (3) and (4) of section 97 of the Magistrates' Courts Act 1980 ".

50. In Schedule 6 to the Licensing Act 1964—

   (a) in paragraph 16(2), for " subsections (1) and (3) of section 77 and section 98 of the Magistrates' Courts Act 1952 " substitute " subsections (1) and (3) of section 97 and section 121 of the Magistrates' Courts Act 1980 " ;

   (b) in paragraph 18, for the words from " section 15 of the Justices of the Peace Act 1949 " to the end substitute " section 144 of the Magistrates' Courts Act 1980, shall have effect subject to any rules so made and to any rules made under section 15 of the Justices of the Peace Act 1949 (which was re-enacted in the said section 144) after 3rd August 1961 ".

Administration of Justice Act 1964 (c.42)

51. In section 38(1) of the Administration of Justice Act 1964 for " section 28 or 29 of the Magistrates' Courts Act 1952 " substitute " section 37 or 38 of the Magistrates' Courts Act 1980 ".

Magistrates' Courts Act (Northern Ireland) 1964 (c.21 (N.I.))

52. In section 104B of the Magistrates' Courts Act (Northern Ireland) 1964—

   (a) in subsection (1) for " section 72A of the Magistrates' Courts Act 1952 " substitute " section 90 of the Magistrates' Courts Act 1980 " and for " the said Act of 1952 " substitute " the said Act of 1980 " ;

   (b) in subsection (2) for " section 72A of the Magistrates' Courts Act 1952 " substitute " section 90 of the Magistrates' Courts Act 1980 ".

Finance Act 1965 (c.25)

53. In section 92(7) of the Finance Act 1965 for " Section 104 of the Magistrates' Courts Act 1952 " substitute " Section 127(1) of the Magistrates' Courts Act 1980 ".

Gas Act 1965 (c.36)

54. In section 21(4) of the Gas Act 1965 for " section 35 of the Magistrates' Courts Act 1952 " substitute " section 44 of the Magistrates' Courts Act 1980 ".

Backing of Warrants (Republic of Ireland) Act 1965 (c.45)

55. In the Schedule to the Backing of Warrants (Republic of Ireland) Act 1965, in the proviso to paragraph 2, for " the Magistrates' Courts Act 1952 " (in both places) substitute " the Magistrates' Courts Act 1980 ".

Criminal Procedure (Attendance of Witnesses) Act 1965 (c.69)

56. In section 8 of the Criminal Procedure (Attendance of Witnesses) Act 1965 for " section 77 of the Magistrates' Courts Act 1952 " substitute " section 97 of the Magistrates' Courts Act 1980 ".

General Rate Act 1967 (c.9)

57. In section 97(3) of the General Rate Act 1967 for " section 15 of the Justices of the Peace Act 1949 " substitute " section 144 of the Magistrates' Courts Act 1980 ".

58. In section 98 of the General Rate Act 1967 for " the Magistrates' Courts Act 1952 " substitute " the Magistrates' Courts Act 1980 ".

59. In section 104(2) of the General Rate Act 1967 for "section 15 of the Magistrates' Courts Act 1952 " substitute " section 13 of the Magistrates' Courts Act 1980 ".

60. In section 107(1) of the General Rate Act 1967 for " section 122(3) of the Magistrates' Courts Act 1952 " substitute " section 145(3) of the Magistrates' Courts Act 1980 ".

Criminal Law Act 1967 (c.58)

61. In section 2(1) of the Criminal Law Act 1967 for " section 29 of the Criminal Law Act 1977 " substitute " section 33 of the Magistrates' Courts Act 1980 ", for " subsection (2) of section 23 of the said Act of 1977 " substitute " subsection (2) of section 22 of the said Act of 1980 " and for " the said section 23 " substitute " the said section 22 ".

Wireless Telegraphy Act 1967 (c.72)

62. In section 11(4) of the Wireless Telegraphy Act 1967 for " section 115 of the Magistrates' Courts Act 1952 " substitute " section 140 of the Magistrates' Courts Act 1980 ".

Criminal Justice Act 1967 (c.80)

63. In section 7 of the Criminal Justice Act 1967 for " section 2 of this Act " substitute " section 102 of the Magistrates' Courts Act 1980 ".

64. In section 11(3) of the Criminal Justice Act 1967 for " section 15 of the Justices of the Peace Act 1949 " substitute " section 144 of the Magistrates' Courts Act 1980 ".

65. In section 32(3)(*b*) of the Criminal Justice Act 1967 for " section 26 of the Magistrates' Courts Act 1952 " substitute " section 30 of the Magistrates' Courts Act 1980 ".

66. In section 36(2) of the Criminal Justice Act 1967 for " the Magistrates' Courts Act 1952 " substitute " the Magistrates' Courts Act 1980 ".

67. In section 56 of the Criminal Justice Act 1967—

(*a*) in subsection (2) for " sections 28 and 29 of the Magistrates' Courts Act 1952 " substitute " sections 37 and 38 of the Magistrates' Courts Act 1980 " ;

(*b*) in subsection (6) for " section 28 of the Magistrates' Courts Act 1952 " substitute " section 37 of the Magistrates' Courts Act 1980 ".

68. In section 62(7) of the Criminal Justice Act 1967 for " section 29 of the Magistrates' Courts Act 1952 " substitute " section 38 of the Magistrates' Courts Act 1980 ".

69. In section 90(2) and (4) of the Criminal Justice Act 1967 for " section 104 of the Magistrates' Courts Act 1952 " substitute, in each case, " section 127(1) of the Magistrates' Courts Act 1980 ".

Companies Act 1967 (c.81)

70. In section 49(3) of the Companies Act 1967 for " section 104 of the Magistrates' Courts Act 1952 " substitute " section 127(1) of the Magistrates' Courts Act 1980 ".

Criminal Appeal Act 1968 (c.19)

71. In section 1 of the Criminal Appeal Act 1968—

(*a*) in subsection (1) insert at the beginning " Subject to subsection (3) below " ;

(*b*) insert after subsection (2)—

" (3) Where a person is convicted before the Crown Court of a scheduled offence it shall not be open to him to appeal to the Court of Appeal against the conviction on the ground that the decision of the court which committed him for trial as to the value involved was mistaken.

(4) In subsection (3) above " scheduled offence " and " the value involved " have the same meanings as they have in section 22 of the Magistrates' Courts Act 1980 (certain offences against property to be tried summarily if value of property or damage is small).".

Firearms Act 1968 (c.27)

72. In section 51(4) of the Firearms Act 1968 for " section 104 of the Magistrates' Courts Act 1952 " substitute " section 127(1) of the Magistrates' Courts Act 1980 ".

73. In Part II of Schedule 6 to the Firearms Act 1968, in paragraph 3—

(*a*) in sub-paragraph (1) for " Schedule 3 to the Criminal Law Act 1977 " substitute " Schedule 1 to the Magistrates' Courts Act 1980 " ;

(*b*) in sub-paragraph (2) for " sections 19 to 24 of the said Act of 1977 " substitute " sections 18 to 23 of the said Act of 1980 " ;

(*c*) in sub-paragraph (3) for "the said sections 19 to 24" substitute "the said sections 18 to 23" and for "section 25(3) and (4) of the said Act of 1977" substitute "section 25(3) and (4) of the said Act of 1980".

Trade Descriptions Act 1968 (c.29)

74. In sections 19(2) and 40(1)(*a*) of the Trade Descriptions Act 1968 for "section 104 of the Magistrates' Courts Act 1952" substitute "section 127(1) of the Magistrates' Courts Act 1980".

Civil Evidence Act 1968 (c.64)

75. In section 8(6) of the Civil Evidence Act 1968 for "section 15 of the Justices of the Peace Act 1949" substitute "section 144 of the Magistrates' Courts Act 1980".

Medicines Act 1968 (c.67)

76. In section 125(1) of the Medicines Act 1968 for "section 104 of the Magistrates' Courts Act 1952" substitute "section 127(1) of the Magistrates' Courts Act 1980".

Sea Fisheries Act 1968 (c.77)

77. In section 12(3) of the Sea Fisheries Act 1968 for "Sections 65(1) and 66 of the Magistrates' Courts Act 1952" substitute "Sections 77(1) and 78 of the Magistrates' Courts Act 1980".

Children and Young Persons Act 1969 (c. 54)

78. In section 2 of the Children and Young Persons Act 1969—

(*a*) in subsection (4) for "subsections (3) and (4) of section 47 of the Magistrates' Courts Act 1952" substitute "subsections (3) and (4) of section 55 of the Magistrates' Courts Act 1980";

(*b*) in subsection (6) for "Section 77 of the Magistrates' Courts Act 1952" substitute "Section 97 of the Magistrates' Courts Act 1980";

(*c*) in subsection (13) for "section 96 of the Magistrates' Courts Act 1952" substitute "section 120 of the Magistrates' Courts Act 1980".

79. In section 7(1) of the Children and Young Persons Act 1969 for "section 28(1) of the Magistrates' Courts Act 1952" substitute "section 37(1) of the Magistrates' Courts Act 1980".

80. In section 8(3) of the Children and Young Persons Act 1969 for "Subsections (2) and (4) of section 40 of the Magistrates' Courts Act 1952" substitute "Subsections (2) and (4) of section 49 of the Magistrates' Courts Act 1980".

81. In section 16(2) of the Children and Young Persons Act 1969 for "subsections (3) and (4) of section 47 of the Magistrates' Courts Act 1952" substitute "subsections (3) and (4) of section 55 of the Magistrates' Courts Act 1980".

82. In section 18(2) of the Children and Young Persons Act 1969 for " section 15 of the Justices of the Peace Act 1949 " substitute " section 144 of the Magistrates' Courts Act 1980 ".

83. In section 23 of the Children and Young Persons Act 1969—

    (*a*) in subsection (4) for " section 28 of the Magistrates' Courts Act 1952 " substitute " section 37 of the Magistrates' Courts Act 1980 " ;

    (*b*) in subsction (5) for " section 105(5) of the said Act of 1952 " substitute " section 128(7) of the said Act of 1980 ".

84. In section 31(6) of the Children and Young Persons Act 1969 for " the Magistrates' Courts Act 1952" substitute " the Magistrates' Courts Act 1980 ".

85. In section 70(1) of the Children and Young Persons Act 1969, in the definition of " petty sessions area ", for " the Magistrates' Courts Act 1952 " substitute " the Magistrates' Courts Act 1980 ".

86. In Schedule 4 to the Children and Young Persons Act 1969, in paragraph 5(1), for " section 28(1) of the Magistrates' Courts Act 1952 " substitute " section 37(1) of the Magistrates' Courts Act 1980 ".

87. In Schedule 5 to the Children and Young Persons Act 1969, in paragraph 55, for " sections 2 and 9 of the Criminal Justice Act 1967 " substitute " section 9 of the Criminal Justice Act 1967 and section 102 of the Magistrates' Courts Act 1980 ".

Administration of Justice Act 1970 (*c.* 31)

88. In section 41(8) of the Administration of Justice Act 1970 for " section 64 of the Magistrates' Courts Act 1952 " substitute " section 76 of the Magistrates' Courts Act 1980 " and for " paragraph 2 of Schedule 3 to that Act " substitute " paragraph 2 of Schedule 4 to that Act ".

89. In Schedule 1 to the Administration of Justice Act 1970 for " section 54(3) of the Magistrates' Courts Act 1952 " substitute " section 63(3) of the Magistrates' Courts Act 1980 ".

Merchant Shipping Act 1970 (*c.* 36)

90. In section 56(2) and (7) of the Merchant Shipping Act 1970 for " subsections (1), (3) and (4) of section 77 of the Magistrates' Courts Act 1952 " substitute, in each place, " subsections (1), (3) and (4) of section 97 of the Magistrates' Courts Act 1980 ".

Guardianship of Minors Act 1971 (*c.* 3)

91. In section 13(1) of the Guardianship of Minors Act 1971 for " section 54(3) of the Magistrates' Courts Act 1952 " substitute " section 63(3) of the Magistrates' Courts Act 1980 ".

92. In section 16(5) of the Guardianship of Minors Act 1971—

  (*a*) for " section 15 of the Justices of the Peace Act 1949 " substitute " section 144 of the Magistrates' Courts Act 1980 " ;

  (*b*) for " section 55(1) of the Magistrates' Courts Act 1952 " substitute " section 64(1) of the Magistrates' Courts Act 1980 ".

Vehicles (Excise) Act 1971 (*c.*10)

93. In section 34 of the Vehicles (Excise) Act 1971—

  (*a*) for " section 1(2) of the Magistrates' Courts Act 1957 " substitute " section 12(2) of the Magistrates' Courts Act 1980 " ;

  (*b*) for " section 15 of the Justices of the Peace Act 1949 " substitute " section 144 of the Magistrates' Courts Act 1980 " ;

  (*c*) for " the said section 1(2) " substitute " the said section 12(2) ".

Courts Act 1971 (*c.*23)

94. In section 7(2) of the Courts Act 1971 for " subsection (1) above " substitute " section 7 of the Magistrates' Courts Act 1980 ".

95. In section 13 of the Courts Act 1971—

  (*a*) in subsection (5)(*e*) for " sections 94 and 95 of the Magistrates' Courts Act 1952 " substitute " sections 118 and 119 of the Magistrates' Courts Act 1980 " ;

  (*b*) in subsection (8) for " the Magistrates' Courts Act 1952 " substitute " the Magistrates' Courts Act 1980 ".

96. In section 52(5) of the Courts Act 1971 for " section 55 of the Magistrates' Courts Act 1952 " substitute " section 64 of the Magistrates' Courts Act 1980 ".

Attachment of Earnings Act 1971 (*c.*32)

97. In section 3 of the Attachment of Earnings Act 1971—

  (*a*) in subsection (1)(*c*) for " section 52(1) of the Magistrates' Courts Act 1952 " substitute " section 59(1) of the Magistrates' Courts Act 1980 " ;

  (*b*) in subsection (4) for " section 64 of the Magistrates' Courts Act 1952 " substitute " section 76 of the Magistrates' Courts Act 1980 " and for " section 64 of the said Act of 1952 " substitute " section 76 of the said Act of 1980 ".

98. In section 8(3) of the Attachment of Earnings Act 1971 for " section 65(2) of the Magistrates' Courts Act 1952 " substitute " section 77(2) of the Magistrates' Courts Act 1980 ".

99. In section 17(3)(*e*) of the Attachment of Earnings Act 1971 for " Part III of the Magistrates' Courts Act 1952 " substitute " Part III of the Magistrates' Courts Act 1980 ".

100. In section 19 of the Attachment of Earnings Act 1971—
   (*a*) in subsection (4) for " section 43 of the Magistrates' Courts Act 1952 " substitute " section 51 of the Magistrates' Courts Act 1980 " ;
   (*b*) in subsection (5) for " section 104 of the Magistrates' Courts Act 1952 " substitute " section 127(1) of the Magistrates' Courts Act 1980 ".

101. In section 25 of the Attachment of Earnings Act 1971—
   (*a*) in subsection (1), in the definition of " rules of court ", for " section 15 of the Justices of the Peace Act 1949 " substitute " section 144 of the Magistrates' Courts Act 1980 " ; and
   (*b*) in subsection (6) for " Part III of the Magistrates' Courts Act 1952 " substitute " Part III of the Magistrates' Courts Act 1980 ".

Misuse of Drugs Act 1971 (*c.*38)

102. In section 25(4) of the Misuse of Drugs Act 1971 for " section 104 of the Magistrates' Courts Act 1952 " substitute " section 127(1) of the Magistrates' Courts Act 1980 ".

Fire Precautions Act 1971 (*c.*40)

103. In section 26(1) of the Fire Precautions Act 1971 for " the Magistrates' Courts Act 1952 " substitute " the Magistrates' Courts Act 1980 ".

Immigration Act 1971 (*c.*77)

104. In section 6(2) of the Immigration Act 1971 for " section 14(3) of the Magistrates' Courts Act 1952 " substitute " section 10(3) of the Magistrates' Courts Act 1980 ".

Maintenance Orders (Reciprocal Enforcement) Act 1972 (*c.*18)

105. In section 14(3) and (6) of the Maintenance Orders (Reciprocal Enforcement) Act 1972 for " section 77(1), (3) and (4) of the Magistrates' Courts Act 1952 " substitute, in each case, " section 97(1), (3) and (4) of the Magistrates' Courts Act 1980 ".

106. In section 18(1) of the Maintenance Orders (Reciprocal Enforcement) Act 1972 for " section 15 of the Justices of the Peace Act 1949 " substitute " section 144 of the Magistrates' Courts Act 1980 ".

107. In section 21(1) of the Maintenance Orders (Reciprocal Enforcement) Act 1972, in the definition of " prescribed ", for " section 15 of the Justices of the Peace Act 1949 " substitute " section 144 of the Magistrates' Courts Act 1980 ".

108. In section 27 of the Maintenance Orders (Reciprocal Enforcement) Act 1972—
   (*a*) in subsection (9) for " section 52 of the Magistrates' Courts Act 1952 " substitute " section 59 of the Magistrates' Courts Act 1980 " ;
   (*b*) in subsection (10) for " section 15 of the Justices of the Peace Act 1949 " substitute " section 144 of the Magistrates' Courts Act 1980 ".

109. In section 38(4) and (6) of the Maintenance Orders (Reciprocal Enforcement) Act 1972 for " section 77(1), (3) and (4) of the Magistrates' Courts Act 1952 " substitute, in each case, " section 97(1), (3) and (4) of the Magistrates' Courts Act 1980 ".

110. In section 41 of the Maintenance Orders (Reciprocal Enforcement) Act 1972—

(*a*) in subsections (1), (2A) and (2B) for " section 53 of the Magistrates' Courts Act 1952 " substitute, in each case, " section 60 of the Magistrates' Courts Act 1980 " ;

(*b*) in subsection (2A) for " section 15 of the Justices of the Peace Act 1949 " substitute " section 144 of the Magistrates' Courts Act 1980 " ;

(*c*) in subsection (2B) for " section 47(3) of the Magistrates' Courts Act 1952 " substitute " section 55(3) of the Magistrates' Courts Act 1980 ".

Road Traffic Act 1972 (*c.*20)

111. In section 104(2) of the Road Traffic Act 1972 for " section 1(2) of the Magistrates' Courts Act 1957 " substitute " section 12(2) of the Magistrates' Courts Act 1980 ".

112. In Part I of Schedule 4 to the Road Traffic Act 1972, in column 4 of the entries relating to section 2 and section 99(*b*), for " section 28 of the Criminal Law Act 1977 " substitute, in each case, " section 32 of the Magistrates' Courts Act 1980 ".

Civil Evidence Act 1972 (*c.*30)

113. In section 2(8) of the Civil Evidence Act 1972 for " section 15 of the Justices of the Peace Act 1949 " substitute " section 144 of the Magistrates' Courts Act 1980 ".

Criminal Justice Act 1972 (*c.*71)

114. In section 46 of the Criminal Justice Act 1972—

(*a*) in subsection (1) for the words from " Sections 2 " to " those sections) " substitute " Section 102 of the Magistrates' Courts Act 1980 and section 9 of the Criminal Justice Act 1967 (which respectively allow written statements to be used as evidence in committal proceedings and in other criminal proceedings) and section 106 of the said Act of 1980 and section 89 of the said Act of 1967 (which punish the making of false statements which are tendered in evidence under the said section 102 or 9, as the case may be) " ;

(*b*) in subsection (2) for " The said section 2 " substitute " The said section 102 ".

115. In section 49(1) of the Criminal Justice Act 1972 for " Part III of the Magistrates' Courts Act 1952 " substitute " Part III of the Magistrates' Courts Act 1980 ".

Guardianship Act 1973 (*c.*29)

116. In section 3(4) of the Guardianship Act 1973 for " section 15 of the Justices of the Peace Act 1949 " substitute " section 144 of the Magistrates' Courts Act 1980 ".

117. In section 6(4) of the Guardianship Act 1973 for " section 46(2) of the Magistrates' Courts Act 1952 " substitute " section 54(2) of the Magistrates' Courts Act 1980 ".

Fair Trading Act 1973 (*c.*41)

118. In section 129(2) and (4) of the Fair Trading Act 1973 for " section 104 of the Magistrates' Courts Act 1952 " substitute " section 127(1) of the Magistrates' Courts Act 1980 ".

Powers of Criminal Courts Act 1973 (*c.*62)

119. In section 1(6) of the Powers of Criminal Courts Act 1973 for " section 14(1) of the Magistrates' Courts Act 1952 " substitute " section 10(1) of the Magistrates' Courts Act 1980 ", for " section 15 of that Act " substitute " sections 11(1) and 13(1), (2) and (5) of that Act ", and for " applies " substitute " apply ".

120. In section 32 of the Powers of Criminal Courts Act 1973—

   (*a*) in subsection (2) for " section 67(2) of the Magistrates' Courts Act 1952 " substitute " section 79(2) of the Magistrates' Courts Act 1980 ", for " section 44(10) of the Criminal Justice Act 1967 " substitute " section 85(1) of that Act " and for " Schedule 3 to the Magistrates' Courts Act 1952 " substitute " Schedule 4 to that Act " ;

   (*b*) in subsection (4) for " section 44(10) of the Criminal Justice Act 1967 or section 96 of the Magistrates' Courts Act 1952 " substitute " section 85(1) or 120 of the Magistrates' Courts Act 1980 " and for " and section 44(10) " substitute " and section 85(1) ".

121. In section 42 of the Powers of Criminal Courts Act 1973 for " section 29 of the Magistrates' Courts Act 1952 " substitute " section 38 of the Magistrates' Courts Act 1980 ".

122. In section 44(1) of the Powers of Criminal Courts Act 1973 for " section 29 of the Magistrates' Courts Act 1952 " substitute " section 38 of the Magistrates' Courts Act 1980 ".

123. In section 57(1) of the Powers of Criminal Courts Act 1973, in the definition of " the register ", for " section 15 of the Justices of the Peace Act 1949 " substitute " section 144 of the Magistrates' Courts Act 1980 ".

Slaughterhouses Act 1974 (c.3)

124. In section 6(2) of the Slaughterhouses Act 1974 for " the Magistrates' Courts Act 1952 " substitute " the Magistrates' Courts Act 1980 ".

125. In sections 38(6) and 43(3) of the Slaughterhouses Act 1974 for " section 35 of the Magistrates' Courts Act 1952 " substitute, in each case, " section 44 of the Magistrates' Courts Act 1980 ".

Legal Aid Act 1974 (c.4)

126. In section 23(2) of the Legal Aid Act 1974 for " the Magistrates' Courts Act 1952 " substitute " the Magistrates' Courts Act 1980 ".

127. In section 30(11) of the Legal Aid Act 1974 for " section 91 of the Magistrates' Courts Act 1952 " substitute " section 115 of the Magistrates' Courts Act 1980 ".

128. In section 40(1) of the Legal Aid Act 1974 for " section 28 or 29 of the Magistrates' Courts Act 1952 " substitute " section 37 or 38 of the Magistrates' Courts Act 1980 ".

129. In Schedule 3 to the Legal Aid Act 1974—

(*a*) in paragraph 2 for " section 63 of the Magistrates' Courts Act 1952 " substitute " section 75 of the Magistrates' Courts Act 1980 " ;

(*b*) in paragraph 3 for " Sections 74 (complaint for arrears), 75 (effect of committal on arrears) and 76 (power to remit arrears) of the Magistrates' Courts Act 1952 " substitute " Sections 93 (complaint for arrears), 94 (effect of committal on arrears) and 95 (power to remit arrears) of the Magistrates' Courts Act 1980 " ;

(*c*) in paragraph 4 for " section 55 of the Magistrates' Courts Act 1952 " substitute " section 64 of the Magistrates' Courts Act 1980 " ;

(*d*) in paragraph 6 for " Section 68 of the Magistrates' Courts Act 1952 " substitute " Section 80 of the Magistrates' Courts Act 1980 ".

Control of Pollution Act 1974 (c.40)

130. In section 87(3) of the Control of Pollution Act 1974 for " section 104 of the Magistrates' Courts Act 1952 " substitute " section 127(1) of the Magistrates' Courts Act 1980 ".

Friendly Societies Act 1974 (c.46)

131. In section 102 of the Friendly Societies Act 1974 for " the Magistrates' Courts Act 1952 " substitute " the Magistrates' Courts Act 1980 ".

Solicitors Act 1974 (c.47)

132. In sections 26, 42(2) and 44(4) of the Solicitors Act 1974 for " the Magistrates' Courts Act 1952 " substitute, in each case, " the Magistrates' Courts Act 1980 ".

Insurance Companies Act 1974 (c.49)

133. In section 82(2) of the Insurance Companies Act 1974 for " section 104 of the Magistrates' Courts Act 1952 " substitute " section 127(1) of the Magistrates' Courts Act 1980 ".

Rehabilitation of Offenders Act 1974 (c.53)

134. In section 6(6)(*a*) of the Rehabilitation of Offenders Act 1974 for " section 23 of the Criminal Law Act 1977 " substitute " section 22 of the Magistrates' Courts Act 1980 ".

Social Security Act 1975 (c.14)

135. In section 152(1) of the Social Security Act 1975—

(*a*) for " section 1(2) of the Magistrates' Courts Act 1957 " substitute " section 12(2) of the Magistrates' Courts Act 1980 " ;

(*b*) for " section 15 of the Justices of the Peace Act 1949 " substitute " section 144 of the Magistrates' Courts Act 1980 ".

Criminal Procedure (Scotland) Act 1975 (c.21)

136. In section 397(1) of the Criminal Procedure (Scotland) Act 1975 for " section 72A of the Magistrates' Courts Act 1952 " substitute " section 90 of the Magistrates' Courts Act 1980 ".

137. In section 403 of the Criminal Procedure (Scotland) Act 1975—

(*a*) in subsection (4) for " section 72A of the Magistrates' Courts Act 1952 " substitute " section 90 of the Magistrates' Courts Act 1980 ", for " the said Act of 1952 " (in the first place where the words occur) substitute " the said Act of 1980 " and for " the Table set out in paragraph 1 of Schedule 3 to the said Act of 1952 " substitute " the Table set out in paragraph 1 of Schedule 4 to the said Act of 1980 " ;

(*b*) in subsecton (6) for " section 72A of the Magistrates' Courts Act 1952 " substitute " section 90 of the Magistrates' Courts Act 1980 ".

Children Act 1975 (c.72)

138. In section 46(4) of the Children Act 1975 for " section 55(1) of the Magistrates' Courts Act 1952 " substitute " section 64(1) of the Magistrates' Courts Act 1980 ".

Prevention of Terrorism (Temporary Provisions) Act 1976 (c.8)

139. In section 12(3) of the Prevention of Terrorism (Temporary Provisions) Act 1976 for " Section 38 of the Magistrates' Courts Act 1952 " substitute " Section 43 of the Magistrates' Courts Act 1980 ".

Restrictive Trade Practices Act 1976 (c.34)

140. In sections 39(2) and 41(5) and (7) of the Restrictive Trade Practices Act 1976 for " section 104 of the Magistrates' Courts Act 1952 " substitute, in each case, " section 127(1) of the Magistrates' Courts Act 1980 ".

Adoption Act 1976 (c.36)

141. In section 66(2) of the Adoption Act 1976 for " section 15 of the Justices of the Peace Act 1949 " substitute " section 144 of the Magistrates' Courts Act 1980 ".

142. In section 72(1) of the Adoption Act 1976, in the definition of " rules ", for " section 15 of the Justices of the Peace Act 1949 " substitute " section 144 of the Magistrates' Courts Act 1980 ".

Bail Act 1976 (c.63)

143. In section 2(1)(c) of the Bail Act 1976 for " section 26(1) of the Magistrates' Courts Act 1952 " substitute " section 30(1) of the Magistrates' Courts Act 1980 ".

144. In section 3(9) of the Bail Act 1976 for " subsection (3) of section 26 of the Magistrates' Courts Act 1952 " substitute " subsection (2) of section 30 of the Magistrates' Courts Act 1980 ".

145. In section 4(7) of the Bail Act 1976 for " section 8 of the Magistrates' Courts Act 1952 " substitute " section 41 of the Magistrates' Courts Act 1980 ".

146. In Part I of Schedule 1 to the Bail Act 1976, in paragraph 8(3), for " section 26(3) of the Magistrates' Courts Act 1952 " substitute " section 30(2) of the Magistrates' Courts Act 1980 " and for " the said section 26(3) " substitute " the said section 30(2) ".

Land Drainage Act 1976 (c.70)

147. In section 19(2) of the Land Drainage Act 1976 for " the Magistrates' Courts Act 1952 " substitute " the Magistrates' Courts Act 1980 ".

Sexual Offences (Amendment) Act 1976 (c.82)

148. In section 3(3) of the Sexual Offences (Amendment) Act 1976 for " section 6(1) of the Children and Young Persons Act 1969 " substitute " section 24(1) of the Magistrates' Courts Act 1980 ".

Criminal Law Act 1977 (c.45)

149. In section 28(8) of the Criminal Law Act 1977 for " Schedule 3 to this Act " substitute " Schedule 1 to the Magistrates' Courts Act 1980 ".

150. In section 38(1) of the Criminal Law Act 1977 for " subsection (4) of section 102 of the Magistrates' Courts Act 1952 " substitute " subsection (3) of section 125 of the Magistrates' Courts Act 1980 ".

151. In section 48(1) of the Criminal Law Act 1977 for " section 15 of the Justices of the Peace Act 1949 " substitute " section 144 of the Magistrates' Courts Act 1980 ".

152. In section 64(2) of the Criminal Law Act 1977 for " section 23 above " substitute " section 22 of the Magistrates' Courts Act 1980 (cases where value involved is small) ".

153. In section 65(2) of the Criminal Law Act 1977 for " 14 " substitute " 15 " and for " Magistrates' Courts Act 1952 " substitute " Magistrates' Courts Act 1980 ".

154. In paragraph 1 of Schedule 5 to the Criminal Law Act 1977—

(*a*) in subparagraph (1)(*b*), for " subparagraph (2)(*b*) below " substitute " subparagraph (1A) below " ;

(*b*) after subparagraph (1) insert—

" (1A) The offences mentioned in subparagraph (1)(*b*) above are offences under the following provisions of the Misuse of Drugs Act 1971, where the controlled drug in relation to which the offence was committed was a Class C drug, namely—

(i) section 4(2) (production, or being concerned in the production, of a controlled drug) ;

(ii) section 4(3) (supplying or offering a controlled drug or being concerned in the doing of either activity by another) ;

(iii) section 5(3) (having possession of a controlled drug with intent to supply it to another) ;

(iv) section 8 (being the occupier, or concerned in the management, of premises and permitting or suffering certain activities to take place there) ;

(v) section 12(6) (contravention of direction prohibiting practitioner etc. from possessing, supplying etc. controlled drugs) ; or

(vi) section 13(3) (contravention of direction prohibiting practitioner etc. from prescribing, supplying etc. controlled drugs).".

155. In paragraph 1 of Schedule 14 to the Criminal Law Act 1977 for " 14 to 26, 34 and 35 " substitute " 15 and 17 ".

Civil Aviation Act 1978 (c.8)

156. In section 2(7)(*a*) of the Civil Aviation Act 1978 for " section 28 of the Criminal Law Act 1977 " substitute " section 32 of the Magistrates' Courts Act 1980 " and for " section 61 of that Act " substitute " section 143 of that Act ".

Domestic Proceedings and Magistrates' Courts Act 1978 (c.22)

157. In section 8(8) of the Domestic Proceedings and Magistrates' Courts Act 1978 for " the proviso to section 60(1) of the Magistrates' Courts Act 1952 " substitute " section 72(1) of the Magistrates' Courts Act 1980 ".

158. In section 12(8) of the Domestic Proceedings and Magistrates' Courts Act 1978 for " section 46(2) of the Magistrates' Courts Act 1952 " substitute " section 54(2) of the Magistrates' Courts Act 1980 ".

159. In section 16(8) of the Domestic Proceedings and Magistrates' Courts Act 1978 for " Part II of the Magistrates' Courts Act 1952 " substitute " Part II of the Magistrates' Courts Act 1980 ".

160. In section 22 of the Domestic Proceedings and Magistrates' Courts Act 1978 for " section 63 of the Magistrates' Courts Act 1952 " substitute " section 75 of the Magistrates' Courts Act 1980 ".

161. In section 23 of the Domestic Proceedings and Magistrates' Courts Act 1978—

(*a*) in subsection (1) for " section 55(1) of the Magistrates' Courts Act 1952 " substitute " section 64(1) of the Magistrates' Courts Act 1980 " ;

(*b*) in subsection (2) for " section 53 of the Magistrates' Courts Act 1952 " substitute " section 60 of the Magistrates' Courts Act 1980 " and for " section 54(2) of that Act " substitute " section 63(2) of that Act ".

162. In section 24(3) of the Domestic Proceedings and Magistrates' Courts Act 1978 for " section 47(3) of the Magistrates' Courts Act 1952 " substitute " section 55(3) of the Magistrates' Courts Act 1980 ".

163. In section 30(1) of the Domestic Proceedings and Magistrates' Courts Act 1978 for " section 11 of the Administration of Justice Act 1964 " substitute " section 70 of the Magistrates' Courts Act 1980 ".

164. In section 32(2) of the Domestic Proceedings and Magistrates' Courts Act 1978 for " section 52 of the Magistrates' Courts Act 1952 " substitute " section 59 of the Magistrates' Courts Act 1980 " and for " the said section 52 " substitute " the said section 59 ".

165. In section 33 of the Domestic Proceedings and Magistrates' Courts Act 1978 for " section 54(3) of the Magistrates' Courts Act 1952 " substitute " section 63(3) of the Magistrates' Courts Act 1980 ".

166. In section 47(2) of the Domestic Proceedings and Magistrates' Courts Act 1978 for " section 53 of the Magistrates' Courts Act 1952 " substitute " section 60 of the Magistrates' Courts Act 1980 " and for " section 54(2) of that Act " substitute " section 63(2) of that Act ".

167. In section 88(1) of the Domestic Proceedings and Magistrates' Courts Act 1978 for " section 56 of the Magistrates' Courts Act 1952 " substitute " section 65 of the Magistrates' Courts Act 1980 " and for " section 15 of the Justices of the Peace Act 1949 " substitute " section 144 of the Magistrates' Courts Act 1980 ".

Nuclear Safeguards and Electricity (Finance) Act 1978 (c. 25)

168. In section 2(6) of the Nuclear Safeguards and Electricity (Finance) Act 1978 for " section 28 of the Criminal Law Act 1977 " substitute " section 32 of the Magistrates' Courts Act 1980 " and for " the provisions of the Criminal Law Act 1977 " substitute " the provisions of the Magistrates' Courts Act 1980 ".

Interpretation Act 1978 (c. 30)

169. In Schedule 1 to the Interpretation Act 1978—
    (a) in paragraph (a) of the definition of " committed for trial " for " section 7 of the Magistrates' Courts Act 1952 " substitute " section 6 of the Magistrates' Courts Act 1980 " ;
    (b) in paragraph (a) of the definition of " magistrates' court " for " section 124 of the Magistrates' Courts Act 1952 " substitute " section 148 of the Magistrates' Courts Act 1980 " ;
    (c) in the entry about expressions relating to offences for " section 23 of the Criminal Law Act 1977 " substitute " section 22 of the Magistrates' Courts Act 1980 ".

Theft Act 1978 (c. 31)

170. In section 4(3)(b) of the Theft Act 1978 for " section 28 of the Criminal Law Act 1977 " substitute " section 32 of the Magistrates' Courts Act 1980 ".

Protection of Children Act 1978 (c. 37)

171. In section 6(3)(b) of the Protection of Children Act 1978 for " section 28 of the Criminal Law Act 1977 " substitute " section 32 of the Magistrates' Courts Act 1980 ".

Consumer Safety Act 1978 (c. 38)

172. In section 9(4) of the Consumer Safety Act 1978, in the definition of " the statutory maximum ", for " section 28 of the Criminal Law Act 1977 " substitute " section 32 of the Magistrates' Courts Act 1980 ".

173. In section 11(g) of the Consumer Safety Act 1978 for " the Criminal Law Act 1977 " substitute " the Magistrates' Courts Act 1980 ".

Employment Protection (Consolidation) Act 1978 (c. 44)

174. In section 104(10)(a) of the Employment Protection (Consolidation) Act 1978 for " section 28 of the Criminal Law Act 1977 " substitute " section 32 of the Magistrates' Courts Act 1980 " and for " section 61 of that Act " substitute " section 143 of that Act ".

175. In section 107(5)(a) of the Employment Protection (Consolidation) Act 1978 for " section 28 of the Criminal Law Act 1977 " substitute " section 32 of the Magistrates' Courts Act 1980 " and for " section 61 of that Act " substitute " section 143 of that Act ".

Customs and Excise Management Act 1979 (c. 2)

176. In section 147(2) of the Customs and Excise Management Act 1979 for " section 25(3) of the Criminal Law Act 1977 " substitute " section 25(3) of the Magistrates' Courts Act 1980 "

177. In section 151 of the Customs and Excise Management Act 1979 for "section 114 of the Magistrates' Courts Act 1952" substitute "section 139 of the Magistrates' Courts Act 1980".

178. In section 171(2)(*a*) of the Customs and Excise Management Act 1979 for "section 28 of the Criminal Law Act 1977 (£1,000 or other sum substituted by order under section 61(1) of that Act)" substitute "section 32 of the Magistrates' Courts Act 1980 (£1,000 or other sum substituted by order under section 143(1) of that Act)".

Customs and Excise Duties (General Reliefs) Act 1979 (c. 3)

179. In section 15(3)(*a*) of the Customs and Excise Duties (General Reliefs) Act 1979 for "section 28 of the Criminal Law Act 1977 (£1,000 or other sum substituted by order under section 61(1) of that Act)" substitute "section 32 of the Magistrates' Courts Act 1980 (£1,000 or other sum substituted by order under section 143(1) of that Act)".

Alcoholic Liquor Duties Act 1979 (c. 4)

180. In section 4(1) of the Alcoholic Liquor Duties Act 1979, in the definition of "the prescribed sum", for "section 28 of the Criminal Law Act 1977 (£1,000 or other sum substituted by order under section 61(1) of that Act)" substitute "section 32 of the Magistrates' Courts Act 1980 (£1,000 or other sum substituted by order under section 143(1) of that Act)".

Hydrocarbon Oil Duties Act 1979 (c. 5)

181. In section 27(1) of the Hydrocarbon Oil Duties Act 1979, in the definition of "the prescribed sum", for "section 28 of the Criminal Law Act 1977 (£1,000 or other sum substituted by order under section 61(1) of that Act)" substitute "section 32 of the Magistrates' Courts Act 1980 (£1,000 or other sum substituted by order under section 143(1) of that Act)".

Agricultural Statistics Act 1979 (c. 13)

182. In section 6(1) of the Agricultural Statistics Act 1979, in the definition of "the prescribed sum", for "section 28 of the Criminal Law Act 1977 (£1,000 or other sum substituted by order under section 61(1) of that Act)" substitute "section 32 of the Magistrates' Courts Act 1980 (£1,000 or other sum substituted by order under section 143(1) of that Act)".

Credit Unions Act 1979 (c. 34)

183. In section 31(1) of the Credit Unions Act 1979, in the definition of "statutory maximum", for "section 28 of the Criminal Law Act 1977" substitute "section 32 of the Magistrates' Courts Act 1980".

Banking Act 1979 (c. 37)

184. In section 50(1) of the Banking Act 1979, in the definition of "statutory maximum", for "section 28 of the Criminal Law Act 1977" substitute "section 32 of the Magistrates' Courts Act 1980" and for "the provisions of the Criminal Law Act 1977" substitute "the provisions of the Magistrates' Courts Act 1980".

Estate Agents Act 1979 (c. 38)

185. In section 33(1) of the Estate Agents Act 1979, in the definition of " the statutory maximum ", for " section 28 of the Criminal Law Act 1977 " substitute " section 32 of the Magistrates' Courts Act 1980 " and for " the provisions of the Criminal Law Act 1977 " substitute " the provisions of the Magistrates' Courts Act 1980 ".

Merchant Shipping Act 1979 (c. 39)

186. In section 42(4) of the Merchant Shipping Act 1979 for " Section 18 of the Criminal Law Act 1977 " substitute " Section 127(2) to (4) of the Magistrates' Courts Act 1980 ".

187. In section 43(5) of the Merchant Shipping Act 1979 for " subsection (1) of section 61 of the Criminal Law Act 1977 " substitute " subsection (1) of section 143 of the Magistrates' Courts Act 1980 " and for " section 28 of that Act " substitute " section 32 of that Act ".

Weights and Measures Act 1979 (c. 45)

188. In section 12(3) of the Weights and Measures Act 1979 for " section 28 of the Criminal Law Act 1977 " substitute " section 32 of the Magistrates' Courts Act 1980 ".

189. In paragraph 8 of Schedule 6 to the Weights and Measures Act 1979 for " the Criminal Law Act 1977 " substitute " the Magistrates' Courts Act 1980 ".

Ancient Monuments and Archaeological Areas Act 1979 (c. 46)

190. In section 61(1) of the Ancient Monuments and Archaeological Areas Act 1979, in the definition of " the statutory maximum ", for " section 28 of the Criminal Law Act 1977 (that is to say, £1,000 or another sum fixed by order under section 61 of that Act " substitute " section 32 of the Magistrates' Courts Act 1980 (that is to say, £1,000 or another sum fixed by order under section 143 of that Act ".

Justices of the Peace Act 1979 (c. 55)

191. In section 16 of the Justices of the Peace Act 1979—

(*a*) in subsection (1) for " the Magistrates' Courts Act 1952 " substitute " the Magistrates' Courts Act 1980 " ;

(*b*) in subsection (5) for " section 56 of the Magistrates' Courts Act 1952 " substitute " section 65 of the Magistrates' Courts Act 1980 ".

192. In section 18(4) of the Justices of the Peace Act 1979 for " section 15 of the Justices of the Peace Act 1949 " substitute " section 144 of the Magistrates' Courts Act 1980 ".

193. In section 27(8) of the Justices of the Peace Act 1979 for " section 15 of the Justices of the Peace Act 1949 " substitute " section 144 of the Magistrates' Courts Act 1980 ".

SCH. 7   194. In section 28(1) of the Justices of the Peace Act 1979 for
" section 15 of the Justices of the Peace Act 1949 " substitute " section
144 of the Magistrates' Courts Act 1980 ".

195. In section 29(3) of the Justices of the Peace Act 1979 for
" section 52 of the Magistrates' Courts Act 1952 " substitute " section
59 of the Magistrates' Courts Act 1980 " and for " section 53A of
that Act " substitute " section 62 of that Act ".

196. In section 30(2) of the Justices of the Peace Act 1979 for
" section 15 of the Justices of the Peace Act 1949 " substitute " section
144 of the Magistrates' Courts Act 1980 ".

197. In section 61(1) of the Justices of the Peace Act 1979 for
" paragraphs (*a*) and (*b*) of section 114(1) of the Magistrates' Courts
Act 1952 " substitute " paragraphs (*a*) and (*b*) of section 139 of the
Magistrates' Courts Act 1980 ".

Isle of Man Act 1979 (c.58)

198. In section 5 of the Isle of Man Act 1979—

(*a*) in subsection (2)(*a*) for " section 77 of the Magistrates' Courts
Act 1952 " substitute " section 97 of the Magistrates'
Courts Act 1980 " ;

(*b*) in subsection (3)(*a*) for " sections 2 and 9 of the Criminal
Justice Act 1967 " substitute " section 9 of the Criminal
Justice Act 1967 and section 102 of the Magistrates' Courts
Act 1980 " and for " section 2 " substitute " section 102 ".

Child Care Act 1980 (c.5)

199. In section 48(1) of the Child Care Act 1980 for " section 53
of the Magistrates' Courts Act 1952 " substitute " section 60 of the
Magistrates' Courts Act 1980 ".

200. In section 49(4)(*a*) of the Child Care Act 1980 for " section 53
of the Magistrates' Courts Act 1952 " substitute " section 60 of the
Magistrates' Courts Act 1980 ".

Foster Children Act 1980 (c.6)

201. In section 16(4) of the Foster Children Act 1980 for " section
104 of the Magistrates' Courts Act 1952 " substitute " section 127(1)
of the Magistrates' Courts Act 1980 ".

Residential Homes Act 1980 (*c.* 7)

202. In section 4(2) of the Residential Homes Act 1980 for " the
Magistrates' Courts Act 1952 " substitute " the Magistrates' Courts
Act 1980 ".

Reserve Forces Act 1980 (*c.* 9)

203. In section 144(2)(*a*) of the Reserve Forces Act 1980 for " section 28 of the Criminal Law Act 1977 " substitute " section 32 of the
Magistrates' Courts Act 1980 ".

204. In paragraph 2(4) of Schedule 5 to the Reserve Forces Act 1980 for " the Magistrates' Courts Act 1952 " substitute " the Magistrates' Courts Act 1980 ".

Protection of Trading Interests Act 1980 (*c.* 11)

205. In section 3(5) of the Protection of Trading Interests Act 1980 for " section 28 of the Criminal Law Act 1977 " substitute " section 32 of the Magistrates' Courts Act 1980 " and for " the said Act of 1977 " substitute " the said Act of 1980 ".

Competition Act 1980 (*c.* 21)

206. In section 19(7) of the Competition Act 1980 for " section 28 of the Criminal Law Act 1977 " substitute " section 32 of the Magistrates' Courts Act 1980 " and for " the provisions of the Criminal Law Act 1977 " substitute " the provisions of the Magistrates' Courts Act 1980 ".

Companies Act 1980 (*c.*22)

207. In section 87(1) of the Companies Act 1980, in the definition of " the statutory maximum ", for " section 28 of the Criminal Law Act 1977 " substitute " section 32 of the Magistrates' Courts Act 1980 " and for " section 61 of that Act " substitute " section 143 of that Act.".

SCHEDULE 8

TRANSITIONAL PROVISIONS AND SAVINGS

Interpretation

1. In this Schedule references to the old enactments are to enactments repealed or amended by this Act and references to the appointed day are to the day on which this Act comes into force.

Proceedings commenced before appointed day

2.—(1) Where proceedings were commenced before the appointed day, the old enactments relating to the proceedings continue to apply and nothing in this Act affects those enactments.

(2) Without prejudice to the generality of sub-paragraph (1) above, the old enactments relating to proceedings which continue in force by virtue of it include any provision of those enactments which creates an offence, which relates to civil or criminal procedure, which relates to the punishment for an offence, or which relates to enforcing, appealing against, questioning, varying or rescinding anything ordered or done in the proceedings.

Offences committed before appointed day

3.—(1) This paragraph applies where proceedings are commenced under this Act in relation to an offence committed before the appointed day.

(2) Nothing in this Act renders a person liable to punishment by way of fine or imprisonment for the offence which differs from the punishment to which he would have been liable if this Act had not been passed and proceedings for the offence had been commenced under the old enactments.

(3) Nothing in this Act renders a person liable to pay compensation under a compensation order in respect of the offence which differs from the compensation he would have been liable to pay if this Act had not been passed and proceedings for the offence had been commenced under the old enactments.

(4) The provisions of this Act corresponding to the old enactments relating to punishment and compensation are to be construed accordingly.

Other matters : general

4. Paragraphs 5 and 6 below have effect subject to paragraphs 2 and 3 above.

5. Without prejudice to any express amendment made by this Act, a reference in an enactment or other document, whether express or implied, to an enactment repealed by this Act shall, unless the context otherwise requires, be construed as, or as including, a reference to this Act or to the corresponding provision of this Act.

6. Where a period of time specified in an enactment repealed by this Act is current at the commencement of this Act, this Act shall have effect as if the corresponding provision of it had been in force when that period began to run.

Saving for transitionals in orders

7.—(1) This paragraph applies where any provision of an old enactment—

(a) was brought into force by order which made transitional provision in connection with the provision brought into force, or

(b) fell to be brought into force by order which could have made transitional provision in connection with the provision brought into force, if this Act had not been passed.

(2) In that case, an order under section 155(7) of this Act may make corresponding transitional provision in connection with any provision of this Act corresponding to that of the old enactment.

Savings of amendments

8. Notwithstanding the repeal by this Act of the Magistrates' Courts Act 1952, the amendments made in other enactments ("the amended enactments") by that Act shall, to the extent that they had effect immediately before the coming into force of this Act, continue to have effect subject to any amendment of any of the amended enactments by this Act.

Savings for Local Government Act 1972

9. The provisions of this Act shall have effect without prejudice to the exercise of any power conferred by section 67 of the Local Government Act 1972 (consequential and transitional arrangements relating to Part IV), section 252 of that Act (general power to adapt Acts and instruments) or section 254 of that Act (consequential

and supplementary provision) ; and any such power which, if this
Act had not been passed, would have been exercisable in relation
to an enactment repealed by this Act shall be exercisable in the
like manner and to the like extent in relation to the corresponding
provision (if any) of this Act.

SCH. 8

Scottish saving

10.—(1) This paragraph applies to Schedule 7B to the Criminal
Procedure (Scotland) Act 1975, which was inserted by paragraph 12
of Schedule 11 to the Criminal Law Act 1977 and takes the same
form as Schedule 5 to that Act (subject to certain modifications
specified in that paragraph).

1975 c. 21.
1977 c. 45.

(2) Schedule 7B is not affected by—

   (*a*) the repeal by Schedule 9 to this Act of paragraph 1(2)(*a*)
        and (*b*) of Schedule 5 ;

   (*b*) the amendments made to paragraph 1 of Schedule 5 by
        Schedule 7 to this Act.

SCHEDULE 9

REPEALS

Chapter	Short title	Extent of repeal
12, 13 & 14 Geo. 6. c. 101.	Justices of the Peace Act 1949.	Section 15(1), (2), (3), (7), (8) and (9).
15 & 16 Geo. 6 & 1 Eliz. 2. c. 55.	Magistrates' Courts Act 1952.	The whole Act.
5 & 6 Eliz. 2. c. 29.	Magistrates' Courts Act 1957.	The whole Act.
6 & 7 Eliz. 2. c. 39.	Maintenance Orders Act 1958.	Section 16. Section 20(6).
7 & 8 Eliz. 2. c. 72.	Mental Health Act 1959.	In Schedule 7, in Part I, the entry relating to the Magistrates' Courts Act 1952.
7 & 8 Eliz. 2. c. 73.	Legitimacy Act 1959.	Section 5(2).
9 & 10 Eliz. 2. c. 39.	Criminal Justice Act 1961.	In section 1(5) the words " and subsections (2) and (3) of section twenty-eight of the Magistrates' Courts Act 1952 ". Section 8(3). In section 41(4), the words " section twenty-eight of the Magistrates' Courts Act 1952 ". In Schedule 4, the entries relating to sections 28 and 126 of the Magistrates' Courts Act 1952. In Schedule 6, the text of the Magistrates' Courts Act 1952, section 28.
1963 c. 37.	Children and Young Persons Act 1963.	Section 27.
1964 c. 42.	Administration of Justice Act 1964.	Section 11. In Schedule 3, paragraphs 20(2) and 22(3) and (5).
1965 c. 69.	Criminal Procedure (Attendance of Witnesses) Act 1965.	In Schedule 2, in Part I, the entry relating to the Magistrates' Courts Act 1952.
1967 c. 80.	Criminal Justice Act 1967.	Sections 1 to 6. Section 19. In section 20, the words " or section 28 or 29 of the Magistrates' Courts Act 1952 (committal for sentence) ". Section 24. Section 26. Sections 28 to 30. In section 33, the words from the beginning to " that section and ".

Chapter	Short title	Extent of repeal
1967 c. 80—*cont.*	Criminal Justice Act 1967 —*cont.*	In section 36(1), the definitions of " broadcast " and " publish ". Sections 44, 44A and 45. In section 50, the words from the beginning to " Part of that Act ". Section 56(4). In section 89(1), the words " 2 or ". In section 90(1) the words " an order under section 44(8) or ". Section 94. In section 106(2)(*b*), the figure " 3 ". In Schedule 6, paragraphs 9 to 13 and 17 to 20.
1968 c. 69.	Justices of the Peace Act 1968.	In Schedule 3, paragraph 8.
1969 c. 54.	Children and Young Persons Act 1969.	Section 6. Section 10(3). Section 61. In Schedule 4, paragraph 4.
1970 c. 31.	Administration of Justice Act 1970.	Section 12. In section 28(1), the definitions of " the Act of 1952 " and " magistrates' court maintenance order ". Section 30(1) and (2) as respects section 12. Section 41(6). Section 42. Section 50. In section 51, subsection (1), and in subsection (3) the definition of " the Act of 1952 ".
1971 c. 23.	Courts Act 1971.	Section 7(1). In Schedule 8, paragraph 34, in paragraph 48(*b*) in the words " 56(4)(6) " the word " (4) ", and paragraph 52. In Schedule 9, in Part I, the entry relating to the Magistrates' Courts Act 1952.
1972 c. 18.	Maintenance Orders (Reciprocal Enforcement) Act 1972.	Section 22(2)(*b*).
1972 c. 70.	Local Government Act 1972.	In Schedule 27, paragraph 16.
1972 c. 71.	Criminal Justice Act 1972.	Section 41. Sections 44 and 45. Section 50. In Schedule 5, the entries relating to the Magistrates' Courts Act 1952 and the entry relating to section 6(1) of the Children and Young Persons Act 1969.

Chapter	Short title	Extent of repeal
1973 c. 14.	Costs in Criminal Cases Act 1973.	In Schedule 1, paragraph 1.
1973 c. 29.	Guardianship Act 1973.	Section 9(2)(*b*).
1973 c. 38.	Social Security Act 1973.	In Schedule 27, in paragraph 85, the words " and 12(2)(*b*) " and " (in each place) ".
1973 c. 62.	Powers of Criminal Courts Act 1973.	Section 35(5). In Schedule 5, paragraphs 4, 5, 7, 16 and 34.
1974 c. 4.	Legal Aid Act 1974.	In Schedule 4, paragraph 3.
1975 c. 21.	Criminal Procedure (Scotland) Act 1975.	Section 326(2). In section 463(1)(*b*), the words " 326(2) ".
1976 c. 63.	Bail Act 1976.	In Schedule 2, paragraphs 14 to 29 and 35.
1977 c. 45.	Criminal Law Act 1977.	Section 14. In section 15, in subsection (1), paragraph (*b*) and the word " and " immediately preceding it, and, in subsection (3), paragraph (*a*). Section 16. Sections 18 to 27. In section 28, subsections (1) to (7) and in subsection (8) the words from " and subsection (2) above " to the end. Section 29. Section 30(4). Section 32(2). Sections 34 and 35. In section 36, subsections (2) to (8) and in subsection (9) the definitions of " guardian " and " the statutory restrictions upon the imprisonment of young offenders ". Sections 41 and 42. Section 45. In section 58, subsections (1), (4) and (6). Sections 59 to 61. In section 63(2), in the entry relating to section 65(4) and Schedule 12 so far as they relate to the Criminal Justice Act 1967, the words " 3 and ". In section 65(10)(*e*) the words from " and the provisions " to " all such places (except Scotland) ". Schedule 2. Schedule 3. Schedule 4. In Schedule 5, paragraph 1(2)(*a*) and (*b*). In Schedule 7, paragraph 1. Schedule 8.

Chapter	Short title	Extent of repeal
1977 c. 45— *cont.*	Criminal Law Act 1977 —*cont.*	In Schedule 12, the entries relating to the Magistrates' Courts Act 1952, the entries relating to sections 3, 24, 44(5) and 44A of the Criminal Justice Act 1967, and paragraphs 2 and 3 of the entries relating to the Criminal Justice Act 1972. In Schedule 14, paragraph 2, in paragraph 3(1) the words " or 2 ", paragraph 4, and in paragraph 5 the words " (other than section 29 or any provision mentioned in paragraph 4 above) ".
1978 c. 22.	Domestic Proceedings and Magistrates' Courts Act 1978.	Sections 75 to 85. In Schedule 1, in paragraph 5 the words " or in any of sections 79 to 82 ", paragraph 6 and paragraph 7. In Schedule 2, paragraphs 15 and 21.
1978 c. 37.	Protection of Children Act 1978.	Section 2(2).
1979 c. 55.	Justices of the Peace Act 1979.	In Schedule 2, paragraphs 7 to 9 and paragraph 14.
1980 c. 5.	Child Care Act 1980.	In Schedule 5, paragraph 5.
1980 c. 11.	Protection of Trading Interests Act 1980.	In section 8(5), the words from " together with " to the end.

INDEX

TO THE

PUBLIC GENERAL ACTS

AND

GENERAL SYNOD MEASURES 1980

A

C

PART I

POWERS AND DUTIES OF LOCAL AUTHORITIES IN RELATION
TO THE WELFARE AND CARE OF CHILDREN

General duty of local authorities to promote welfare of children

D

E

F

PART III

INCOME TAX, CORPORATION TAX AND CAPITAL GAINS TAX

CHAPTER I

GENERAL

CHAPTER II

CAPITAL ALLOWANCES

Machinery and plant

Foster children for purposes of the Act

Duties of local authorities

Notification of fostering to local authorities

Disqualification for fostering

Control by local authorities of fostering

Proceedings

G

H

X 3

HOUSE OF LORDS. *See also* PARLIAMENT.

PART I

PUBLIC SECTOR TENANTS

CHAPTER I

THE RIGHT TO BUY

Chapter II

Security of Tenure and Rights of Secure Tenants

Secure tenancies

Terms of a secure tenancy

Housing management

Application to existing tenancies

Application to licences

Housing associations

I

IMPORT OF LIVE FISH (ENGLAND AND WALES) ACT: c. 27 ... I, p. 587

IMPRISONMENT (TEMPORARY PROVISIONS) ACT: c. 57 ... ... III, p. 1909

PART I

TEMPORARY PROVISIONS

PART II

OTHER PROVISIONS

L

M

PART III

SATISFACTION AND ENFORCEMENT

General provisions

PART IV

WITNESSESS AND EVIDENCE

Procuring attendance of witness

PART V

APPEAL AND CASE STATED

Appeal

N

O

P

Orders, regulations etc, subject to annulment in pursuance of a resolution of
the House of Commons under—

Resolution of each House of Parliament required for approval of Orders,
regulations etc. under—

R

PART VII

ULSTER DEFENCE REGIMENT

Membership of Ulster Defence Regiment

*Military status of members of
Ulster Defence Regiment*

Offences

PART VIII

MISCELLANEOUS AND SUPPLEMENTAL

*Reinstatement in civil employment, and protection
of other civil interests*

Charitable property on disbanding of units

Further powers as to orders and regulations

Other provisions as to orders, schemes and regulations

Other supplemental provisions

S

W

St